THE SCOUTING REPORT: 1983

THE SCOUTING REPORT: 1983

An in-depth analysis of the strengths and weaknesses of every active major league baseball player

by
Jerry Coleman
Ernie Harwell
Ralph Kiner
Tim McCarver
Ned Martin
and
Brooks Robinson

1817

HARPER & ROW, PUBLISHERS, New York
Cambridge, Philadelphia, San Francisco,
London, Mexico City, São Paulo, Sydney

The player photographs that appear in THE SCOUTING REPORT were furnished individually by the twenty-six teams that comprise Major League Baseball. Their cooperation is gratefully acknowledged: Baltimore Orioles, Boston Red Sox, California Angels, Chicago White Sox, Cleveland Indians, Detroit Tigers, Kansas City Royals, Milwaukee Brewers, Minnesota Twins, New York Yankees, Oakland A's, Seattle Mariners, Texas Rangers, Toronto Blue Jays, Atlanta Braves, Chicago Cubs, Cincinnati Reds, Houston Astros, Los Angeles Dodgers, Montreal Expos, New York Mets, Philadelphia Phillies, Pittsburgh Pirates, St. Louis Cardinals, San Diego Padres and the San Francisco Giants.

EDITORIAL STAFF

Phil Collier
Charlie Feeney
Tom Flaherty
Bob Gallas
Paul Hagan
John Hillyer
Greg Hoard

Rick Hummel
Marvin Karp
Neil MacCarl
Mike McKenzie
Marty Noble
Terry Pluto
Tracy Ringolsby

Anson Schloat
Harry Shattuck
Bob Silbernagel
Kit Steir
John Strege
Gordon Verrell
Charlie Walters

Marybeth Sullivan
Managing Editor

THE SCOUTING REPORT: 1983

Published simultaneously in Canada by Fitzhenry & Whiteside Limited, Toronto.

FIRST EDITION
Designer: Marybeth Sullivan

Library of Congress Cataloging in Publication Data
Main entry under title:

THE SCOUTING REPORT: 1983.

(Harper colophon books; CN/1027)
Includes index.
1. Baseball--United States--Records. 2. Baseball players--United States. I. Coleman, Jerry.
GV877.S39 1983 796.357'092'2 82-48225
ISBN 0-06-091027-5 (pbk.)

83 84 85 86 87 10 9 8 7 6 5 4 3 2 1

CONTENTS

INTRODUCTION

For the first time, carefully constructed and fully developed scouting reports of every major league baseball player are available to the fan. During the 1982 season, six well-known and respected baseball broadcasters (four of them former major league players) spent countless hours compiling their opinions and evaluations of the strengths, weaknesses and potential of each player in the league. Their evaluations were made based on their own season-long observations and extremely extensive experience in major league baseball.

In the American League, we called upon Ernie Harwell of Detroit, Ned Martin of Boston, and Brooks Robinson of Baltimore. The National League reports were developed by Jerry Coleman of San Diego, Ralph Kiner of the New York Mets, and Tim McCarver, formerly of Philadelphia, and now with the Mets.

The result of their efforts, THE SCOUTING REPORT, is a baseball fan's delight. Any interested fan can now examine what professional baseball people really expect from each player and what major league ballclubs hold confidential. Furthermore, seasoned fans now have the opportunity to test their own judgments against these professionals who make their living reporting the national pastime.

Each broadcaster recorded his evaluations in a standard format on a comprehensive skills-evaluation form which was developed under the consultation of a professional major league advance scout. These reports were then compiled to offer a clear and detailed analysis of every player's abilities in the field, at the plate and on the basepaths.

It is important to point out that scouting reports, as any major league ballclub knows, represent the best opinion possible. A scouting report is a professional evaluation whose accuracy cannot be judged by a single player's performance in one specific situation on a given day. Scouting reports indicate a player's overall strengths, weaknesses, habits and tendencies. Unlike the one-dimensional scheme of statistics, these reports will enable the fan to become familiar with a completely different method of comparison.

THE SCOUTING REPORT will introduce you to the human element of each player's approach to the game. The twenty-six teams that comprise Major League Baseball are themselves made up of twenty-five individuals. Each player is different--each pitcher has his own special assortment of pitches and a unique way of mixing them up and delivering them to the plate. Each hitter looks for pitches in his favorite spot in the strike zone, and is vulnerable to certain types of pitches and velocities. In the field, some players have trouble with balls hit to the left, others to the right, and still others have difficulty in accurately hitting their target. In reading THE SCOUTING REPORT, both the knowledgeable fan and the neophyte will be exposed to never before released reports--information that will undoubtedly offer a new understanding of the complex decisions and intricacies of the game of baseball.

A word about the format . . .

THE SCOUTING REPORT is divided into first, the fourteen teams of the American League, followed by the twelve teams of the National League. The player reports appear alphabetically with each team. With the unpredictable nature of trades and free-agency, numerous player trades will have occurred since THE SCOUTING REPORT went to press. The Player Index which begins on page 665 will enable you to locate these players. Some team members who have experienced relatively little playing time are not located alphabetically within their club, but rather appear within the last few pages of their team's section.

The player's name appears in the upper right corner of each page followed by his position (OF-outfielder, INF-infielder, C-catcher, RHP-righthanded pitcher, LHP-lefthanded pitcher), and uniform number. The third line displays a two-letter code with one of the following combinations: RR, RL, LL, LR, SR or SL. The first letter indicates from which side of the plate he hits, right (R), left (L), or switch (S). The second letter indicates whether he throws with his right (R) or left (L) hand. The fourth line reports the length of the player's Major League Service (these were rounded off to the closest number of seasons). The final line indicates the player's date and place of birth.

A "strike zone chart" appears on the hitters' reports and indicates with a shaded area the player's "power spot" in the strike zone, that is, the place where the hitter wants to see the ball pitched against both left and righthanded pitching. It also shows the location on the field where the player is most likely to hit the ball.

Each team is introduced by a description of the quirks, idiosyncrasies, dimensions, and playing characteristics of the team's home park. In the American League, this information was furnished by Brooks Robinson, who spent twenty-three years getting to know most of these fields quite well. In the National League, Tim McCarver provided the insights on the parks he spent twenty-one years looking at from the catcher's position.

Have fun this summer watching Major League Baseball. We hope that THE SCOUTING REPORT will make each and every game even better for you.

Acknowledgements

THE SCOUTING REPORT is an unusual project that was slowly pieced together by a group of unusually talented people. For lessons in the art of scouting, we would like to thank Loren Babe, Frank Malzone, and Tony Pacheco. For his foresight, Buddy Skydell. For their hard work, attention to detail and their magical fingers, grateful appreciation goes to Sandy Kahn, Maureen Lundgren, Andrea Schneider, and Nessa Sternfeld. For their belief in the merits of the project and their dedication to bringing a massive task such as this to major league baseball fans, Jerry Coleman, Ernie Harwell, Ralph Kiner, Ned Martin, Tim McCarver, and Brooks Robinson.

THE AMERICAN LEAGUE

ERNIE HARWELL

Ernie Harwell has been the voice of the Detroit Tigers since 1960, and has been broadcasting major league baseball games since 1949. He has covered games for the New York Giants, Brooklyn Dodgers and Baltimore Orioles.

In 1981, Mr. Harwell received the prestigious Ford C. Frick Award which is presented annually to members of the broadcasting profession who have made a significant contribution to the game of baseball. With this award he was granted automatic induction into the Baseball Hall of Fame in Cooperstown, New York.

In 1965, Mr. Harwell donated his own personal collection of sports information to the Detroit Public Library. This enormous donation included thousands of photographs of baseball players, issues of THE SPORTING LIFE from 1884-1917, baseball guides dating into the 1860s, hundreds of issues of SPORT Magazine, and 90,000 clippings of sports writings that Mr. Harwell had cataloged over a long period of time.

Mr. Harwell is a diversified talent, having written song lyrics for a number of musical pieces throughout the years. His most recent work is a poetic recitation entitled, "The Game for All America," which he performs on Terry Cashman's album, "Talkin' Baseball."

Since 1976, Mr. Harwell had broadcast the play-by-play action of the American League Championship series on the worldwide CBS radio network. Prior to that, he broadcast the World Series in 1963 and 1968 on the NBC radio network.

NED MARTIN

Ned Martin, one of the most popular broadcasters in the New England area, is entering his 22nd year of radio and television play-by-play for the Boston Red Sox. Mr. Martin graduated from Duke University and served in the Marine Corps in World War II before starting his career by announcing minor league games. He joined Curt Gowdy on the Red Sox network in 1961 and has been a favorite with Red Sox fans ever since.

In the fall of 1979, Mr. Martin traveled to Japan to telecast the games between the Major League All Stars and the top professional Japanese teams. From 1976-79, he broadcast the American League Championship Series on the CBS worldwide radio network.

His sportscasting talents extend beyond football and include announcing for international ski jumping and professional ski racing, as well as Yale, Dartmouth, Boston Patriots and the Sun Bowl football games. Such varied experience led him to be named the top Massachusetts TV-Radio Sports Personality three times.

BROOKS ROBINSON

Brooks Robinson's major league playing career spanned an incredible 23 seasons--every one of them as a Baltimore Oriole. His retirement from playing after the 1977 season ended one of the most glorious careers in the history of the game. There is virtually no award that Mr. Robinson did not win. He played in 18 consecutive All Star Games from 1960 through 1974 and was voted the All Star Games Most Valuable Player in 1966. In 1964, he was voted the MVP of the American League and in 1970, received the MVP Award for the World Series. He won 16 straight Gold Gloves for his outstanding playing at third base from 1960 through 1975.

Brooks Robinson was voted into the Hall of Fame in Cooperstown, New York in 1983. He is one of the few players to be so honored in his first year of eligibility.

Mr. Robinson was inducted into the Baltimore Orioles' Hall of Fame in 1977, and on the Orioles' Opening Day in 1978, his uniform and his No. 5 were officially retired.

Now entering his sixth year as a color broadcaster for the Baltimore Orioles, Mr. Robinson is also Executive Vice-President and Director of Personal Management Associates, a Baltimore firm which provides athletes with advice and assistance in areas of professional, personal and financial management. Further, he is actively involved as a Special Assistant for the Crown Petroleum Company.

THE NATIONAL LEAGUE

JERRY COLEMAN

Jerry Coleman is the Director of Broadcasting for the San Diego Padres and served as the manager of the Padres in 1980. For the past six years, he has handled the play-by-play for the worldwide CBS radio network broadcasts of the National League Championship Series and is entering his eleventh season as the radio and television voice of the Padres. Mr. Coleman had previously worked in broadcasting both in Los Angeles and New York where he covered the Yankees for seven years.

He is a veteran major league player of nine seasons with the New York Yankees, and in 1949, led all of the American League second basemen in fielding and received the Associated Press "Rookie of the Year" Award as well. The following year, in 1950, he was a member of the American League All Star team and won the World Series Most Valuable Player Award.

RALPH KINER

Ralph Kiner begins his 22nd season as a member of the New York Mets broadcasting team in 1983. He has been broadcasting for the Mets since their first season in 1962 and is the host of the popular "Kiner's Korner" television program seen following Met's games.

Ralph Kiner had a ten year career in the major leagues and has been dubbed, "The Home Run King." He was inducted into baseball's Hall of Fame in 1975 and is one of only two players who have hit more than 50 home runs in two major league seasons (Willie Mays is the other).

Mr. Kiner hit 51 homers in 1947 and 54 in 1949, both while playing for the Pittsburgh Pirates. In 1949, he also knocked in 127 runs to lead the league in RBIs and had a batting average of .310. He belted a total of 369 home runs throughout his career.

After a chronic sciatic problem ended his playing days in 1955, Mr. Kiner served as a general manager of the San Diego Padres while they were in the Pacific Coast League and was a broadcaster with the Chicago White Sox before joining the Mets in 1962.

TIM McCARVER

Tim McCarver is the only catcher in modern baseball history to play in four decades, a tremendous accomplishment when you consider the enormous physical requirements of baseball's toughest position.

He broke into the major leagues with the St. Louis Cardinals in 1959 and also played for the Philadelphia Phillies, Montreal Expos and the Boston Red Sox. During his days with the Cardinals, Mr. McCarver played in three World Series and two All Star games. He has a .311 lifetime World Series average and was three-for-three for a 1.000 average in his All Star appearances.

While playing for Philadelphia, Mr. McCarver developed a special rapport with his longtime friend, Steve Carlton, and the two became a potent duo whenever it was Carlton's turn to pitch.

He retired from playing following the 1979 season, and began a new career in 1980 doing play-by-play broadcasting with the Philadelphia Phillies. Mr. McCarver remained with Philadelphia until the 1983 season, when he joined THE SCOUTING REPORT's Ralph Kiner and the broadcasting team of the New York Mets.

During his 19 years as a player, Mr. McCarver compiled a .272 lifetime batting average. He hit 97 career home runs and struck out just 422 times in 5,529 at bats.

Since 1981, Mr. McCarver has been the co-host of HBO's popular "Race for the Pennant," a weekly broadcast highlighting baseball's divisional races and featuring interviews with top players and managers.

Mr. McCarver was honored by his home town of Memphis, Tennessee in 1978 when a Double A League ballpark was named "Tim McCarver Stadium" in his honor.

THE AMERICAN LEAGUE

MEMORIAL STADIUM
Baltimore Orioles

Seating Capacity: 53,862
Playing Surface: Natural Grass

Dimensions
Left Field Pole: 309 ft.
Left-Center Field: 378 ft.
Center Field: 405 ft.
Right-Center Field: 378 ft.
Right Field Pole: 309 ft.
Height of Outfield Walls:
Left Field: 14 ft.
Center Field: 7 ft.
Right Field: 14 ft.

The home of the Baltimore Orioles is one of the better ballparks for pitchers to perform in, despite a left field and right field fence that are only 309 feet from home plate. Obviously, a pull hitter can benefit from the short distances, but only a pull hitter. Outfielders tend to give hitters each foul line, and "bunch" in the gaps in left and right-center, cutting down on extra base hits.

Wind is rarely a factor in this ballpark, but when it is, it tends to favor left-handed batters because it will blow towards right field. The stadium is not a "pretty" stadium, despite a lovely view of suburban homes over the center field fence. The seats are fairly drab, and the huge oval-shaped upper tier does not offer a good view of the field in general. The grass in the infield, however, is among the best in the league, and is generally cut short. The only trouble infielders have with ground balls are those which seem to hit the edge of the grass where it meets the infield dirt. Those balls, and it seems to happen quite a bit in Memorial Stadium, take odd hops.

The original park was built in 1953, but has undergone several major alterations. The center field fence, once 450 feet from home plate, is now 405 feet away, and foul territory near the first and third base lines has been snipped away because of the addition of box seats in 1961.

When the Orioles play day games, particularly on days with a glaring sun and a high sky, the batters are at a disadvantage because the ball, when released by the pitcher, comes out of the background of the white houses nestled on a hill over the center field fence.

Fans do not know who is warming up in either bullpen because both are hidden by a canvas support draped around the fences from left-center (the O's bullpen) to right-center (the visiting bullpen). A message board in left-center, however, keeps fans advised of the bullpen activities.

No lefthanded batter has ever hit a fair ball out of the stadium, but Frank Robinson, a righty, accomplished that feat when he cleared the auxiliary fence, bullpen and the entire left field seating section by blasting one of Luis Tiant's pitches out of the stadium 15 years ago. Many batters have also lost potential home runs over the center field fence because it is only seven feet tall and fairly simple for an agile center fielder to time his leap and pluck possible homers from clearing the wall.

AL BUMBRY
OF, No. 1
LR, 5'8", 175 lbs.
ML Svc: 10 years
Born: 4-21-47 in Fredricksburg, VA

1982 STATISTICS

AVG	G	AB	R	H	2B	3B	HR	RBI	BB	SO	SB
.262	150	562	77	147	20	4	5	40	44	77	10

CAREER STATISTICS

AVG	G	AB	R	H	2B	3B	HR	RBI	BB	SO	SB
.285	1185	4236	662	1206	191	47	47	337	408	633	231

HITTING:

Al Bumbry is a low ball hitter who has the ability to spray the ball to all fields. He looks for pitches on the outside of the plate to poke into the alleys, but has a tendency to chase the high outside fastball.

Since Bumbry has more difficulty batting against southpaws than right-handers, he is often platooned. When he does play, Bumbry usually bats in the leadoff spot to take advantage of his speed. Surprisingly, Al rarely bunts for a base hit. He has a good eye and generally makes contact.

Pitchers in the league throw Bumbry a lot of inside fastballs and sliders. He can be fooled with a good change-up, but continues to go after the high fastball. Blyleven of Cleveland has had better than average lifetime success against Al, and in 1981 the entire Red Sox staff performed exceptionally well against him. On the other hand, Bumbry feasted on Brewer pitching, and also seems to do very well against Rick Waits of the Indians.

BASERUNNING:

Excellent speed to first. Al beats out a fair share of infield grounders each season. He is one of the few Orioles that rival pitchers have to worry about on the basepaths, and will often go head first in an effort to beat the tag. Bumbry may have lost a step during the 1982 season but he is still rated an above average to excellent baserunner.

FIELDING:

Bumbry's arm is rated average to below average in both strength and accuracy. Opposing runners take advantage of this and will try for the extra base on balls hit to center.

VS. RHP

VS. LHP

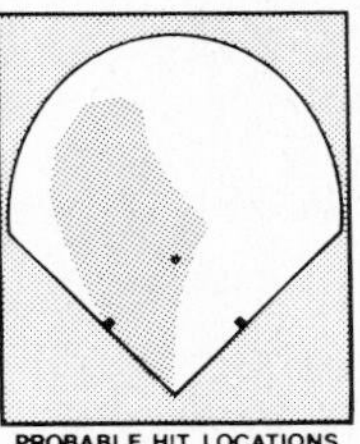
PROBABLE HIT LOCATIONS

Bumbry's speed is his greatest asset in the field and enables him to cover more than his share of territory. He is considered more effective coming in than going back on the ball and tends to play deeper in the outfield because of that.

OVERALL:

Martin: "Al is a heads-up player who had been effectively platooned by Weaver although he could start for some teams in the league. A good team player."

Robinson: "Bumbry has lost a step in the field and on the bases this year but he still gives you a good job in center field."

Harwell: "A solid leadoff batter. He is the type of guy who can really ignite an offense."

TERRY CROWLEY
INF, No. 10
LL, 6'0", 182 lbs.
ML Svc: 11 years
Born: 2-16-47 in
Staten Island, NY

1982 STATISTICS

AVG	G	AB	R	H	2B	3B	HR	RBI	BB	SO	SB
.237	65	93	8	22	2	0	3	17	21	9	0

CAREER STATISTICS

AVG	G	AB	R	H	2B	3B	HR	RBI	BB	SO	SB
.252	815	1474	172	371	62	1	42	226	213	177	3

VS. RHP

VS. LHP

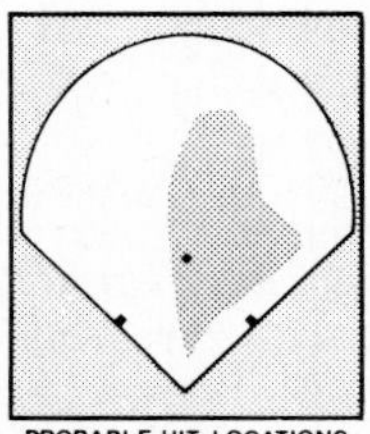
PROBABLE HIT LOCATIONS

HITTING:

Terry Crowley is a no-nonsense lefthanded pull hitter. He is used exclusively against righthanded pitchers and consistently hits fastballs on the inside half of the plate. He has enough power to reach the alleys and is considered better than average in clutch situations.

Opposing pitchers throw a lot of breaking balls to Crowley. He also has a bit of trouble with the straight change. However, over the years, Crowley has learned to be a patient hitter. He's willing to accept a walk if he doesn't get a good pitch to hit. Among the top ten in career pinch-hits, Crowley should go over the 100 mark in the near future.

BASERUNNING:

Crowley has average to below average speed. He seldom gets a chance on the basepaths; if he gets on base late in a game, it would be best to send in a pinch-runner.

FIELDING:

On occasion Crowley has filled in for a game or two at first base. He has good hands and has performed adequately when called upon.

OVERALL:

Crowley has done the job over the years for the Orioles. With the exceptional year that John Lowenstein had last season, Crowley saw little duty last season. At this stage of his career, there is little chance of improving his situation.

Harwell: "Excellent pinch-hitter, especially productive with men on base."

Martin: "Outstanding record as a pinch-hitter. Made a living in that role under Weaver in Baltimore."

Robinson: "Terry has gotten more out of his ability than most players. He's stayed in the majors a long time--strictly with his bat."

RICH DAUER
INF, No. 25
RR, 6'0", 180 lbs.
ML Svc: 6 years
Born: 7-27-52 in
San Bernardino, CA

1982 STATISTICS

AVG	G	AB	R	H	2B	3B	HR	RBI	BB	SO	SB
.280	158	558	75	156	24	2	8	57	50	34	0

CAREER STATISTICS

AVG	G	AB	R	H	2B	3B	HR	RBI	BB	SO	SB
.265	788	2765	345	733	141	3	34	293	206	160	4

VS. RHP

VS. LHP

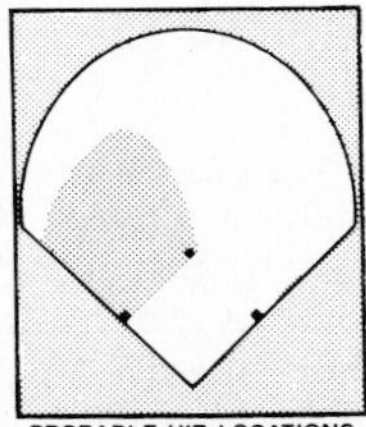
PROBABLE HIT LOCATIONS

HITTING:

Dauer is primarily a contact hitter. Year after year, he is among the league leaders in the least number of strike-outs per times at bat. His ability to get the bat on the ball makes him an excellent hit-and-run batter and Dauer is considered most productive in the No. 2 spot in the batting order.

He handles righthanded pitchers just about as well as lefthanders and has enough power to jump on the high fastball regardless of who throws it. In parks with short left field dimensions, like Fenway and Memorial Stadium in Baltimore, Dauer can hurt you with the long ball.

Pitchers like Lansford of Oakland who have exceptional control can give Dauer trouble. Sometimes he tries to pull the outside pitch instead of going to right, and this leads to harmless ground-outs. Pitchers often feed him curves and sliders away, but if they hang one or groove an inside fastball, Dauer can pop it.

BASERUNNING:

Dauer has below average speed and is no threat to steal a base. Bothered by leg problems last year, he's considered a very conservative baserunner. He will seldom take an extra base and because of his lack of speed he's an easy target for double plays.

FIELDING:

Dauer is most valuable as a second baseman, but he can also fill in adequately at third and has even seen some action at first. He has an average to above average arm and goes equally well to his right and left at second base.

He lacks exceptional range at second base but he has quick hands and can turn the double play effectively. At third, he protects the line well but is only considered average in his ability to field bunts.

Dauer won't hurt you in the field. He is a steady big league infielder who knows what to do with the ball.

OVERALL:

Robinson: "This is a guy who grows on you . . . nothing flashy and generally underrated. Most managers I speak to always have high praise for Rich."

Martin: "Fine steady player. He makes the hit-and-run play work for the Orioles and is generally regarded as a tough out."

Harwell: "An all-around winning type ballplayer. Good in the clutch and reliable in the field."

STORM DAVIS
RHP, No. 62
RR, 6'4", 207 lbs.
ML Svc: 1 year
Born: 12-26-61 in Dallas, TX

PITCHING:

At twenty years of age, Storm Davis was the youngest pitcher in the American League in 1982. Weaver used him in long relief, as a spot starter, and occasionally as a short reliever. Along with Tom Stoddard, he's the hardest thrower on the Orioles with a fastball clocked at over 90 MPH. He has a big overhand motion and relies almost entirely on his crackling fastball. Davis' fastball, however, often lacks movement, and when he begins to lose velocity in the 5th or 6th inning, he can be hit hard. He improved his curveball during the season, but is still in the process of learning to throw a major league slider and change.

Davis is still learning the hitters in the league and needs work to be able to attack their weak spots consistently. When he's behind in the count, he relies on his fastball, but late in the season he began to surprise hitters with a sharp curve in tight spots.

In the tough pennant race last year, Davis handled the pressure exceptionally well for someone his age. With additional experience, he should only improve.

FIELDING:

An average fielder, Davis is still in the learning process. He covers first adequately on balls hit to the right side and shows promise fielding bunts.

OVERALL:

Davis has the physical tools and mental poise to become a consistent winner in the majors. He throws hard but has to develop one or two other pitches. Inexperience and some wildness should be corrected this season.

Robinson: "Storm looks like he's going to be a good one. His poise and presence on the mound are fantastic when you consider how young he is."

Martin: "Davis needs work but he certainly can be a good major league pitcher. He can already intimidate hitters with his heater."

Harwell: "A great young prospect with outstanding natural ability."

1982 STATISTICS

W	L	ERA	G	GS	CG	IP	H	R	ER	BB	SO	SV
8	4	3.49	29	8	1	100	96	40	39	28	67	0

CAREER STATISTICS

W	L	ERA	G	GS	CG	IP	H	R	ER	BB	SO	SV
8	4	3.49	29	8	1	100	96	40	39	28	67	0

RICK DEMPSEY
C, No. 24
RR, 6'0", 184 lbs.
ML Svc: 10 years
Born: 9-13-49 in
Fayetteville, TN

1982 STATISTICS

AVG	G	AB	R	H	2B	3B	HR	RBI	BB	SO	SB
.256	125	344	35	88	15	1	5	36	46	37	0

CAREER STATISTICS

AVG	G	AB	R	H	2B	3B	HR	RBI	BB	SO	SB
.241	928	2583	272	623	122	9	38	233	291	298	14

VS. RHP

VS. LHP

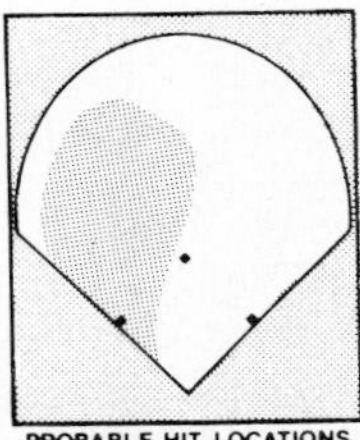
PROBABLE HIT LOCATIONS

HITTING:

Rick Dempsey struggles as a hitter. Pitchers take advantage of his tendency to pull every pitch, and this makes him a prime target for breaking balls away and hard stuff on the outside corner of the plate. Dempsey also has trouble with off-speed pitches and is rated as just average in his ability to handle curves and sliders.

Because he struggles so at the plate, he's a risk in hit-and-run situations. Rick is only an average bunter. He lacks the power to reach the alleys and seems to do best in small ballparks like the ones in Boston and Minnesota. Dempsey can hit a pitcher's mistake. A hanging curve or a lagging fastball will generally be jerked into left or left-center. At this stage of his career, Dempsey is often platooned against righthanded pitching.

BASERUNNING:

Rick is an alert baserunner and can be counted on not to make any foolish or reckless plays on the basepaths. He has average speed to first and will try hard to break up the double play at second. He seldom ventures too far off the bag at first and will only steal two or three bases a year.

FIELDING:

Dempsey's value to the Orioles is obviously in his ability to handle pitchers and to field his position. Rick is a premier catcher and the Oriole staff trusts his judgment and relies on him to call a smart game. Rick has come a long way in the past few years and is now rated well above average in his knowledge of opposing batters' strengths and weaknesses.

His arm is rated as outstanding. Strength, accuracy, and his knowledge of baserunners make him one of the toughest catchers in the American League to try to steal against.

He fields his position with the best and is rated between above average and excellent in fielding bunts and blocking errant pitches.

OVERALL:

Dempsey is a stalwart behind the plate and his effectiveness there compensates for his weak bat.

Robinson: "I would have to say Dempsey has the strongest arm I've seen in 25 years of pro ball. Rick tries harder than anyone else to improve his skills, and his all-out effort makes him a well deserved favorite of the Oriole fans."

Harwell: "Outstanding defensive catcher with one of the finest arms in the game. A leader among the Orioles because of his effort and hustle."

MIKE FLANAGAN
LHP, No. 46
LL, 6'0", 195 lbs.
ML Svc: 7 years
Born: 12-16-51 in Manchester, NH

PITCHING:

Mike Flanagan has a good fastball that hovers around 88 MPH, and a sharp curve that is generally considered the best in the American League. Add an above average straight change that he saves for big situations and you have one of the premier lefthanded pitchers in the game.

Righthanded hitters have to be careful of Flanagan's slider because it rides in on them. He'll also throw a lot of hard inside fastballs to righties. As difficult as he is on righthanded batters, Mike is even rougher on lefties. Look for lefties to swing at a lot of first pitches when Flanagan is on the mound. Lefties hate to get behind in the count against Mike; when he gets two strikes on a hitter, he will drop down into a sidearm delivery. When he delivers a curve off this motion, most lefty hitters head straight to the dugout.

Flanagan is aggressive on the mound. He knows opposing hitters and when he has good control of his curve and fastball, he can be exceptionally tough to beat. During his career he has had outstanding success against Oakland, Toronto, and Minnesota.

FIELDING:

A greatly improved pick-off move to first base helps him keep opposing runners close. Flanagan is rated average to above average as a fielder. His poise on the mound and his ability to control the flow of a game are other key assets.

OVERALL:

Flanagan has outstanding stuff. When he has control and can stay healthy all season, he should be a regular twenty-game winner.

Martin: "Flanagan, a former Cy Young winner, is a real jewel. He's a tough competitor, with excellent stuff. In a word, he's a winner."

Robinson: "Outstanding poise on the mound. Goes about his business like the pro he is. A top flight pitcher."

Harwell: "One of the American League's best lefthhanders. A solid starter with one of the best curveballs in the game today."

1982 STATISTICS

W	L	ERA	G	GS	CG	IP	H	R	ER	BB	SO	SV
15	11	3.97	36	35	11	236	233	110	104	76	103	0

CAREER STATISTICS

W	L	ERA	G	GS	CG	IP	H	R	ER	BB	SO	SV
100	70	3.81	230	214	78	1480	1462	666	627	450	872	1

HITTING:

Dan Ford uses an extremely closed stance and waits for the low, outside fastball. His stance and batting style make him an opposite field hitter. He has the power to reach the right-center field alley and is clearly more effective against lefthanded pitching.

Dan had a disappointing year and certainly failed to fulfill his potential. Most pitchers have had success over-powering him with fastballs up and in. Southpaws have had luck with hard inside sliders and have gotten Ford to chase the bad breaking ball.

A streak hitter, Ford has the ability to carry a team when he's hot. He's strong against off-speed pitches and strikes on the outside portion of the plate. Unfortunately, inconsistency during the 1982 season has limited his value to the Orioles.

BASERUNNING:

Average speed, mental mistakes, and so-so hustle characterize Ford as a baserunner. He seldom steals, is only fair trying to break up the double play, and seldom goes for the extra base.

FIELDING:

Ford has a stronger than average arm but is erratic with it. In a pressure situation, opposing teams are willing to gamble against him. He is only rated as average in the field and often plays as if he were unsure of himself. He's weak going back on the ball, doesn't get an exceptional jump, and has only fair range.

DAN FORD
OF, No. 15
RR, 6'1", 185 lbs.
ML Svc: 8 years
Born: 5-19-52 in
Los Angeles, CA

1982 STATISTICS

AVG	G	AB	R	H	2B	3B	HR	RBI	BB	SO	SB
.235	123	421	46	99	21	3	10	43	23	71	5

CAREER STATISTICS

AVG	G	AB	R	H	2B	3B	HR	RBI	BB	SO	SB
.271	997	3590	524	974	178	34	110	505	260	637	61

VS. RHP

VS. LHP

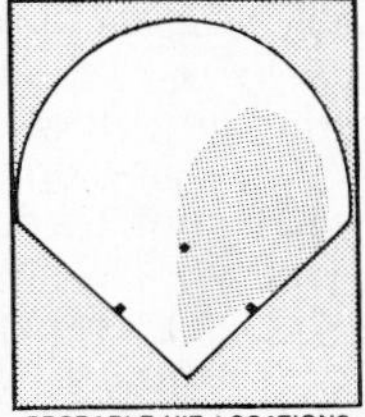
PROBABLE HIT LOCATIONS

OVERALL:

Ford's bat is his chief asset, though he was not as productive as the Orioles had hoped when they traded for him with California. However, he does have a reputation as a streak hitter and he could explode next season.

Robinson: "Ford needs to hit to help a team. He's a streak hitter and a team just has to wait and hope that he gets hot for them."

Harwell: "A dangerous hitter when he's hot, but too inconsistent."

Martin: "Enigmatic. Too given to inconsistency and moods. Can hit with power and drive in runs but will probably be traded."

ROSS GRIMSLEY
LHP, No. 48
LL, 6'3", 200 lbs.
ML Svc: 10 years
Born: 1-7-50 in
Topeka, KS

PITCHING:

Grimsley is a ten year pro who has spent time in both leagues. His chief value to a team is his versatility. He's been used as a spot starter, in long relief, short relief and as a mop-up man.

Ross is a smart veteran who's getting by without a big league fastball. He pitches at two speeds--slow and slower. He relies on soft curves and change-ups about 90% of the time. When he is behind in the count, he'll usually resort to a curve or a slider. When he gets ahead in the count or needs a groundout, Grimsley is known to throw a spitball.

On the mound he hides the ball well and goes through a lot of Gaylord Perry-like gyrations to divert attention when he loads the wet one. He has good poise and seldom gets rattled. When he resorts to the fastball, he can be hit hard. At this stage of his career, he has better luck against lefties than righties. Primarily a control pitcher, Grimsley's best days as a major league pitcher are behind him.

FIELDING:

Grimsley has a better than average move to first base, fields bunts well, and is rated an average fielder at his position.

OVERALL:

Grimsley usually appeared in games the Orioles have already lost. He lacks the big league fastball and when hitters figure out his rhythm, he can be hit hard. On occasion, he can help a staff get through a crunch of mid-season doubleheaders. He knows the tricks of the trade and gets by on guts and guile.

Martin: "Grimsley's been around. He's a cute, smart pitcher who's getting by on his experience. He'll help you over the season-long haul."

Robinson: "Grimsley is a real pro. He did the job the Orioles want him to do, and he does it without complaining. He doesn't get rattled on the mound; his versatility and experience are his chief assets."

1982 STATISTICS

W	L	ERA	G	GS	CG	IP	H	R	ER	BB	SO	SV
1	2	5.25	21	0	0	60	65	35	35	22	18	0

CAREER STATISTICS

W	L	ERA	G	GS	CG	IP	H	R	ER	BB	SO	SV
124	99	3.81	345	295	79	2039	2105	947	863	559	750	3

JOHN LOWENSTEIN
OF, No. 38
LR, 6'1", 180 lbs.
ML Svc: 12 years
Born: 1-27-47 in
Wolf Point, MT

1982 STATISTICS

AVG	G	AB	R	H	2B	3B	HR	RBI	BB	SO	SB
.320	122	322	69	103	15	2	24	66	54	59	7

CAREER STATISTICS

AVG	G	AB	R	H	2B	3B	HR	RBI	BB	SO	SB
.254	1129	2870	424	728	111	16	93	351	362	484	125

VS. RHP

VS. LHP

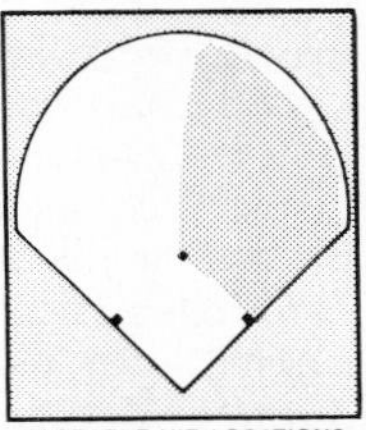
PROBABLE HIT LOCATIONS

HITTING:

John Lowenstein was the most pleasant surprise of the 1982 Oriole season. Twenty plus home runs had him challenging Eddie Murray for team leadership. Lowenstein is a lefthanded power hitter who likes to pull anything that's fast and over the plate. Weaver platooned him most of the time, and he rarely hit against lefthanders.

He has a deserved reputation as a clutch performer, and hits especially well with men in scoring position. His concentration at the plate seems to improve in situations when the game is on the line. He seldom bunts and is only rated as average when called on in hit-and-run situations.

Lowenstein has trouble with off-speed pitches and is only mediocre when facing a tough curveball pitcher. If he guesses right on a fastball, however, you're in trouble. He reaches the alley in right-center regularly. He has had his best success at home in Memorial Park with the short (309') right field line.

BASERUNNING:

Lowenstein has better than average speed and gets out of the batter's box quickly. He may be the best base-stealer on the Orioles. He takes a good lead off of first and works hard to distract opposing pitchers. He's smart and fast, and knows which outfielders he can safely challenge. He hurt his ankle last season and may have lost a step, but he's still dangerous and opposing teams are leery of him.

FIELDING:

John is rated as only an average defensive outfielder. His arm is not one of the strongest in the league nor is it especially accurate. Although he lacks outstanding range, Lowenstein goes all out in the field and has injured himself several times by crashing into outfield fences. He's a smart fielder, catches what he can reach, and seldom makes an error.

OVERALL:

Martin: "John is a blithe spirit around the clubhouse and helps his team stay loose. He's durable and can be counted on to come up with a big hit in a clutch situation."

Robinson: "John is a role player. He does his job as a designated hitter, pinch-hitter, and part-time outfielder. He does the job as well or better than anyone in the American League."

Harwell: "Lowenstein is a solid, productive platoon player. He can beat you with his baserunning as well as his bat."

DENNIS MARTINEZ
RHP, No. 30
RR, 6'1", 185 lbs.
ML Svc: 6 years
Born: 5-14-55 in
Granada, NIC

PITCHING:

Dennis Martinez is a righthanded power pitcher with a fastball that can be overpowering at 90 MPH. Dennis also has an above average slider which he frequently uses as his "out" pitch. Last season, he worked on perfecting a change-up and when he remembers to use it, the pitch can be devastating.

When Martinez gets in a groove, he's equally tough on both righthanders and lefties. He studies hitters and will try to pitch to their weaknesses. He relies on his fastball when he falls behind in the count, but when he's ahead of a hitter, he can be murder with his hard slider. He has better than average control, a great arm, and three excellent pitches.

Dennis gets in trouble when he loses his composure. Errors, a bad call by an umpire, or a couple of base hits can break his concentration. When runners get on base, Martinez will slow down and lose his rhythm. The slower he works the more trouble he seems to get into. Another problem with Dennis is that sometimes he tries to show every pitch he has to every hitter. Unfortunately, this often confuses him more than his rivals.

FIELDING:

Dennis is rated as above average in fielding ability. He generally is among the leaders in put-outs, assists and chances accepted. He is quick to come off the mound and his agility in fielding bunts is a definite asset. He has an average to above average move to first base.

OVERALL:

Most of Dennis' problems can be traced to a lack of composure and concentration. When he doesn't allow himself to be psyched out either by his opponents or by circumstances, he can be tough to beat. His mechanics are among the best in the league and he should only improve with experience.

Robinson: "Dennis has such great stuff--maybe we all expected too much too soon from him. He's a definite asset already and he can only get better."

Harwell: "A solid starter on the Oriole staff. He has excellent command of three pitches. I think he's developed the best change of pace in the American League."

Martin: "If you can find his rhythm, he'll challenge you and beat you. Outstanding stuff."

1982 STATISTICS

W	L	ERA	G	GS	CG	IP	H	R	ER	BB	SO	SV
16	12	4.21	40	39	10	252	263	123	118	87	111	0

CAREER STATISTICS

W	L	ERA	G	GS	CG	IP	H	R	ER	BB	SO	SV
82	57	3.75	216	167	60	1294	1255	595	539	436	640	5

TIPPY MARTINEZ
LHP, No. 23
LL, 5'10", 175 lbs.
ML Svc: 7 years
Born: 5-31-50 in LaJunta, CO

PITCHING:

Martinez provides the lefthanded arm in Baltimore's short relief arsenal. He is primarily a curveball pitcher, but when Tippy finds the groove, his breaking ball can be almost unhittable. He uses an overhand motion and his curve breaks down and hard making it especially tough on lefthanded hitters. He has a fastball that's been clocked at about 87 MPH and uses it primarily to set a hitter up for the breaking pitch. He only has a so-so change-up and it's a pitch he rarely throws. Control is a major problem for Martinez. When he can't find a groove, he gets in trouble quickly.

The hard curve makes him most effective against lefthanded hitters. Another plus for Martinez is that he rarely gives up the home run ball. Even when he's in trouble, he manages to keep his pitches down--a valuable trait for a short reliever who only sees action when a game is close and on the line.

Martinez is developing more and more poise on the mound but still tends to challenge hitters with his curve rather than adjusting his pitches to a batter's weakness. His record is best against Oakland, Toronto, and Seattle. The Yankees, Brewers, and Tigers have all had better than average success against him.

FIELDING:

For a lefthander, Tippy has a relatively weak move to first and opposing runners are often able to get an extra step or two on his motion. As a fielder, Martinez is only rated as average.

OVERALL:

Martinez is only used when the game is on the line. He has an excellent curveball and a better than average fastball, but he can have trouble controlling both pitches. When he's good, he's very good. He keeps the ball down and keeps you in the game. His major fault is his inconsistency. He has to improve his command of his pitches.

Robinson: "Tippy can be awesome. He probably throws the hardest curve in the American League, but he's yet to put it together over an entire season."

Martin: "Tippy keeps improving. He's used to critical situations and keeps his head. He's a good lefthanded relief pitcher."

Harwell: "He has great stuff but his lack of control keeps him from being an outstanding pitcher."

1982 STATISTICS

W	L	ERA	G	GS	CG	IP	H	R	ER	BB	SO	SV
8	8	3.41	76	0	0	95	81	39	36	37	78	16

CAREER STATISTICS

W	L	ERA	G	GS	CG	IP	H	R	ER	BB	SO	SV
39	25	3.16	360	2	0	552	472	218	194	284	418	72

SCOTT McGREGOR
LHP, No. 16
SL, 6'1", 190 lbs.
ML Svc: 6 years
Born: 1-18-54 in Inglewood, CA

PITCHING:

Scott McGregor is a thinking man's pitcher. Not gifted with an overpowering fastball, McGregor relies on pinpoint control to win games. Scott calls on a three-pitch arsenal when he's on the mound. He has a good curve, an excellent straight change, and a less than intimidating fastball. He's a successful starter in the rotation because he knows when and where to throw each of these pitches.

McGregor rarely falls behind in the count, but when he does, he's more apt to show the batter something off-speed rather than his fastball. He's tough mentally and won't give in to a hitter. Not only does he mix his pitches exceptionally well, but he can also rear back in a tight spot and put a little extra on the fastball, maybe pushing the velocity from 83-84 MPH to 86-87 MPH. That's often enough to throw a hitter off stride in a pressure situation.

Scott's lack of stamina over a long, grueling season may limit his statistical success. The only other problem is that like most control pitchers, McGregor gives up the long ball. He has to work hard to keep all his pitches down. McGregor has had extremely good success during his career against the Angels, Twins, and Rangers.

FIELDING:

Scott has a bit of a herky-jerky motion and seems to stop midway through his windup. This keeps opposing baserunners close to first. He's a cat off the mound and is rated an excellent fielder.

OVERALL:

An essential pitcher in the Oriole starting rotation. If he avoids the gopher ball and keeps his control, he'll always be tough to beat.

Robinson: "An outstanding athlete. He outhit George Brett when they played baseball together in high school. He has excellent concentration and knows how to pitch within himself."

Martin: "One of the game's smartest pitchers. Is able to win without a blazing fastball. He's super at keeping hitters off stride."

Harwell: "One of the best at setting up opposing hitters. He has outstanding command of all his pitches."

1982 STATISTICS

W	L	ERA	G	GS	CG	IP	H	R	ER	BB	SO	SV
14	12	4.61	37	37	7	226	238	126	116	52	84	0

CAREER STATISTICS

W	L	ERA	G	GS	CG	IP	H	R	ER	BB	SO	SV
78	50	3.68	191	157	48	1175	1177	522	480	255	521	5

EDDIE MURRAY
INF, No. 33
SR, 6'2", 200 lbs.
ML Svc: 6 years
Born: 2-14-56 in Los Angeles, CA

1982 STATISTICS

AVG	G	AB	R	H	2B	3B	HR	RBI	BB	SO	SB
.316	151	550	87	174	30	1	32	110	70	82	7

CAREER STATISTICS

AVG	G	AB	R	H	2B	3B	HR	RBI	BB	SO	SB
.295	888	3376	500	997	178	12	165	586	353	474	32

VS. RHP

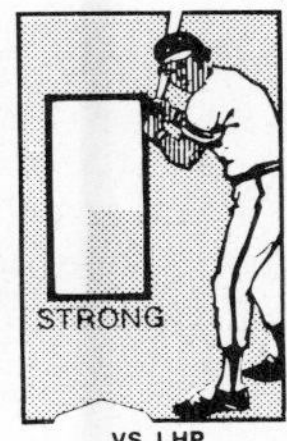

VS. LHP

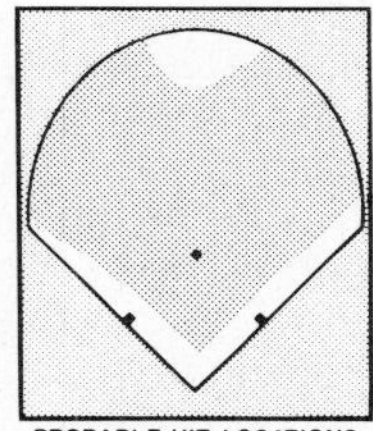
PROBABLE HIT LOCATIONS

HITTING:

Murray is a switch-hitting power hitter who hits equally well against both righthanded and lefthanded pitching. At the plate he seems to spring out of his crouched stance and leap at the ball. He feasts on low fastballs and has the strength to hit between 25 and 30 home runs every year. He can power the ball to both alleys and is rated as an excellent hitter in clutch situations. Year after year, Murray is among the league leaders in homers and RBIs.

Most pitchers feed him a steady diet of off-speed breaking balls. He rarely gets to see a fastball in or near the strike zone. With his power and consistency at the plate, he is always a legitimate MVP candidate. He has had exceptional success against Stanley of Boston, Vuckovich of the Brewers, Matlack of the Rangers, and Langford of the A's.

BASERUNNING:

Murray has better than average speed and a reputation as an aggressive baserunner. He'll slide hard to break up the double play and has average ability as a basestealer. He can be careless on the bases, however, and occasionally makes a costly mistake by taking unnecessary chances.

FIELDING:

At first base, he is rated above average to excellent in arm strength, accuracy, and fielder's range. He excels at making the 3-6-3 double play and is agile and aggressive protecting against the bunt.

OVERALL:

Murray does it all for the Orioles. He improves each year as a hitter and he's already one of the best in baseball. He's solid in the field and a genuine team leader.

Robinson: "A team leader with tremendous potential. He's improved every year he's been in the majors. A top-notch natural hitter and an excellent first baseman."

Harwell: "One of the best in baseball. He's both consistent and dependable . . . an all around star."

Martin: "If he played in New York, he'd be enshrined by now."

HITTING:

Joe Nolan was new to the American League last season. After hitting over .300 for two seasons in the National League, he had trouble adjusting. Primarily a high fastball hitter who likes the ball inside, Nolan has been frustrated by a steady diet of off-speed curves down and away. Joe has the power to reach the alley in right-center and is at his best when he's challenged by hard throwers like Guidry and Gossage of the Yankees.

Nolan has been platooned with Dempsey and doesn't get much opportunity to hit against southpaws. In the beginning of the 1982 season, he was a disappointment, especially with men on base, but improved as he got more chances to play. He has the potential to hit around .275 and the power to hit home runs. He just seems to need more playing time and the confidence that comes with it.

BASERUNNING:

Nolan is no threat on the basepaths. He's slow out of the box and never wanders more than a few feet from the base at first. His lack of speed makes him a cautious baserunner, and rival pitchers can safely ignore him on the basepaths.

FIELDING:

Nolan is an adequate fill-in for Dempsey. He is still learning the hitters in his new league but he already calls a smart game. His arm, though not as strong as Dempsey's, is rated above average. His throws to second are quick and accurate. He manages to get in front of almost everything when he's behind the plate, but is only average in his ability to field bunts.

JOE NOLAN
C, No. 17
LR, 6'0", 190 lbs.
ML Svc: 6 years
Born: 5-12-51 in St. Louis, MO

1982 STATISTICS

AVG	G	AB	R	H	2B	3B	HR	RBI	BB	SO	SB
.233	77	219	24	51	7	1	6	35	16	35	1

CAREER STATISTICS

AVG	G	AB	R	H	2B	3B	HR	RBI	BB	SO	SB
.263	482	1170	128	308	52	8	21	139	131	137	7

VS. RHP

VS. LHP

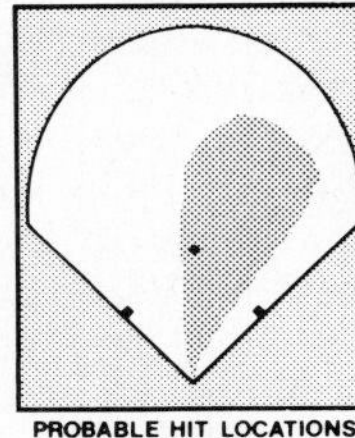

PROBABLE HIT LOCATIONS

OVERALL:

A powerful lefthanded hitter who can do the job behind the plate. He's not flashy but is an excellent No. 2 catcher and a worthwhile addition to the Oriole roster.

Robinson: "Joe is a fairly consistent player. He's been going through a learning process since coming to the American League. I saw a big improvement with his bat as the season went on."

Martin: "Joe is a good back up catcher. He won't embarrass you if you let him play for a week or two at a time. He'll get his hits."

PITCHING:

Jim Palmer has been a consistent winner for the Orioles for over a decade. He combines power, control, and a crafty veteran's knowledge of his opponents' strengths and weaknesses. He still relies on his 88 MPH fastball as his primary "out" pitch. He throws the curve and slider irregularly--usually to confuse batters.

When he's behind in the count, he generally comes in with a fastball, and he has the control necessary to nip the corners with the pitch. Sometimes when the count is 3-1 or 2-0 and the batter is thinking fastball, Palmer will cross him up with the slider, another of his excellent pitches. Palmer disdains the brushback, and hitters tend to dig in against him. As a result, he gives up a fair share of home runs.

Jim's assorted aches and pains whether real or imagined, and his outspoken opinions, kept Earl Weaver on the brink of exasperation. Weaver, however, understood that Palmer is a consummate professional and a fierce competitor. Jim has excellent control and knows the opposition. He may have lost some of the zip off his fastball last season, but he's still one of the best pitchers in baseball.

JIM PALMER
RHP, No. 22
RR, 6'3", 194 lbs.
ML Svc: 16 years
Born: 10-15-45 in
New York, NY

FIELDING:

Palmer has an above average move to first and this compensates for the high leg kick he uses in his regular motion to the plate. He is rated as outstanding at fielding his own position and will often orchestrate his other fielders from the mound. Palmer is an excellent athlete and has been known to glare down at a teammate who boots one Palmer thought should have been handled.

OVERALL:

He's the ace of the Oriole staff.

Martin: "A future Hall of Famer. Year in and year out, one of the best in the game."

Robinson: "Terrific presence on the mound. One of the best in the game."

Harwell: "Hall of Fame candidate."

1982 STATISTICS

W	L	ERA	G	GS	CG	IP	H	R	ER	BB	SO	SV
15	5	3.13	36	32	8	227	195	85	79	63	103	1

CAREER STATISTICS

W	L	ERA	G	GS	CG	IP	H	R	ER	BB	SO	SV
263	145	2.80	539	505	211	3853	3241	1334	1199	1275	2174	3

CAL RIPKEN, JR.
INF, No. 8
RR, 6'4", 200 lbs.
ML Svc: 1 year plus
Born: 8-24-60 in
Havre de Grace, MD

1982 STATISTICS

AVG	G	AB	R	H	2B	3B	HR	RBI	BB	SO	SB
.264	160	598	90	158	32	5	28	93	46	95	3

CAREER STATISTICS

AVG	G	AB	R	H	2B	3B	HR	RBI	BB	SO	SB
.256	183	637	91	163	32	5	28	93	47	103	3

VS. RHP

VS. LHP

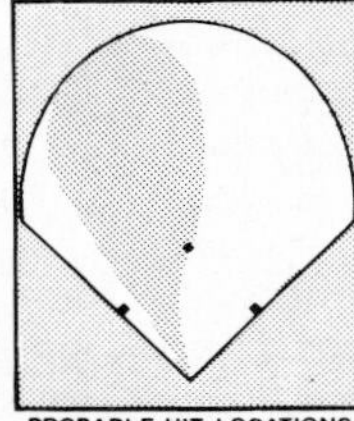
PROBABLE HIT LOCATIONS

HITTING:

Ripken got off to a confused start in 1982, and was totally ineffective against big league pitching. After the first twenty or so games, however, he began to develop as a major league hitter. By the close of the season he had proved that he could handle lefthanders and righthanders equally well. He has better than average power and strokes the ball consistently to left and left-center.

He's a real bright spot on the Oriole roster and is gradually developing a reputation as a clutch hitter and as someone who has the ability and the discipline to hit behind runners and move them up a base. Better than average bat control adds to his value in hit-and-run situations.

Ripken still has some trouble with change of speed pitches. He is also vulnerable to fastballs and curves on the outside corner, especially from righties. Cal knows what he's doing as a hitter. He studies opposing pitchers and has the eye and the patience to wait for his pitch. He has demonstrated some very fine hitting potential, and is rated above average.

BASERUNNING:

Ripken has above average speed to first base and is aggressive enough to be effective in breaking up potential double plays. If he sees an opportunity, he'll take the extra base but will only try to steal a dozen or so bases a season.

FIELDING:

Ripken is also a definite asset in the field. After impressing everyone as an excellent third baseman at the begining of the season, Weaver was forced to use him to plug the hole at shortstop. Cal has an outstanding arm for either position and better than average range.

At third, he showed that he could field the bunt as well as protect the line. At short, he can still be tentative turning the double play and may lack that step of quickness that separates the great ones from the good.

Ripken was the 1982 Rookie of the Year in the American League.

OVERALL:

Robinson: "Ripken is going to be a great one. He has a fantastic attitude and has always risen to the top of every league he's played in. I believe that he'll do the same in the majors."

Harwell: "I like him better at third than at shortstop but at either position I think he'll be one of the brightest American League stars of the future."

Martin: "One of the 'can't miss' players in the league. He has all the right instincts. I think he'll be a franchise type player if he isn't one already."

GARY ROENICKE

OF, No. 35
RR, 6'3", 200 lbs.
ML Svc: 4 years
Born: 12-5-54 in Covina, CA

1982 STATISTICS

AVG	G	AB	R	H	2B	3B	HR	RBI	BB	SO	SB
.270	137	393	58	106	25	1	21	74	70	73	6

CAREER STATISTICS

AVG	G	AB	R	H	2B	3B	HR	RBI	BB	SO	SB
.258	529	1433	203	369	76	3	64	206	207	246	10

VS. RHP

VS. LHP

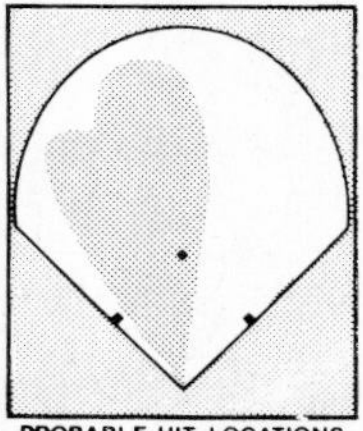
PROBABLE HIT LOCATIONS

HITTING:

Roenicke is a righthanded power hitter. He's strictly a pull hitter, and has a tendency to try and overpower a pitch regardless of its location. When he does connect, he hits line drives and can consistently drive the ball to the left-center alleyway. He's murder on fastballs but only average on curves and sliders.

Gary developed a new stance last season. He dropped his hands down and back and no longer bails out against the high inside pitch--a habit he seems to have picked up while recovering from being hit in the face by former Philadelphia pitcher, Lerrin LaGrow in 1980. In contrast, he now tends to swing at anything inside. Some pitchers try to jam him and then throw him breaking balls. Others prefer to work the outside corner with fastballs and off-speed curves.

Roenicke is considered a streak hitter. When he's hot, he's above average in clutch situations, driving in runs and advancing men on base. When he cools off, his effectiveness diminishes noticeably.

BASERUNNING:

Roenicke has above average speed, slides hard breaking up the double play, and has better than average base-stealing ability. He's smart and aggressive on the basepaths, and will take an extra base whenever possible. He has good instincts, seldom makes mistakes, and plays rough.

FIELDING:

Gary played all three outfield positions for the Orioles, but is best in left. He has a strong and accurate throwing arm and better than average range going after fly balls. He knows opposing hitters, gets a good jump on the ball, and has the necessary speed to make all the plays. Roenicke may be the best defensive outfielder on the Orioles.

OVERALL:

Roenicke had been platooned with Lowenstein in left much of last season. Most observers feel that he could play regularly. He's been hampered by injuries and inconsistent hitting. If he ever solves these two problems, he'd be hard to keep out of a daily lineup.

Harwell: "Gary is a dangerous power hitter who will kill a pitcher's mistakes. I'd like to see him play every day."

Robinson: "Roenicke is a very fine outfielder at all three outfield spots. He's had awesome streaks as a hitter and just lacks consistency."

LENN SAKATA
INF, No. 12
RR, 5'9", 160 lbs.
ML Svc: 4 years
Born: 6-8-53 in
Honolulu, HI

1982 STATISTICS

AVG	G	AB	R	H	2B	3B	HR	RBI	BB	SO	SB
.259	136	343	40	89	18	1	6	31	30	39	7

CAREER STATISTICS

AVG	G	AB	R	H	2B	3B	HR	RBI	BB	SO	SB
.226	327	822	93	186	33	3	14	71	64	101	15

VS. RHP

VS. LHP

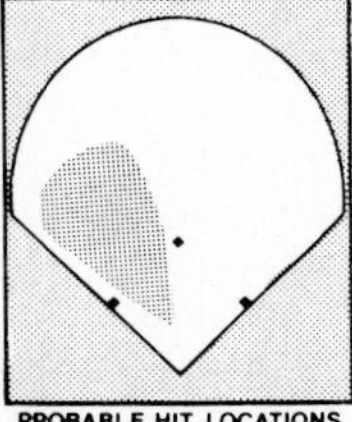
PROBABLE HIT LOCATIONS

HITTING:

Sakata is a low .200 type hitter. He does better against righthanded pitchers but his tendency to pull every pitch makes him especially vulnerable to anything over the outside half of the plate. He's frequently fooled by sliders and off-speed pitches and has a habit of fishing for the breaking ball away.

Lenn has solid upper body strength and good power for someone only 5'9". He gets a surprising number of line drive base hits. He is at best, however, an average hitter who can be handled by a good pitcher.

Sakata doesn't strike out often and this makes him effective in hit-and-run situations. Lenn also tends to be a streaky hitter especially against certain teams, having had good success against Brewer pitching, but done poorly against the White Sox. Overall rating, average to below average.

BASERUNNING:

Sakata is faster than average especially from home to first. He's conservative on the basepaths and will seldom steal more than a dozen bases a season. He generally slides feet first and although he doesn't make mistakes on the basepaths, he seldom worries the opposition with his speed.

FIELDING:

Lenn played both second base and shortstop in Baltimore's unsettled 1982 infield. It's generally agreed that he's more effective at the keystone sack than at short. At second, his arm is above average. He goes equally well to his left and right and has good range. Sakata is rated as excellent in his ability to turn the double play as a second baseman.

OVERALL:

Sakata's weak bat forced Weaver to play Ripkin out of position at short last year. His value is as a utility player who can fill in without hurting the club at both short and second.

Robinson: "I think Sakata gets the most out of his ability and makes the double play as a second baseman as well as anyone in the league."

Harwell: "An excellent back up player . . . his versatility is a real plus for the Orioles."

Martin: "Good to have on your club. Can fill a couple of gaps when a regular is injured or needs a rest."

KEN SINGLETON
OF, No. 29
SR, 6'4", 212 lbs.
ML Svc: 12 years
Born: 6-10-47 in
Mt. Vernon, NY

1982 STATISTICS

AVG	G	AB	R	H	2B	3B	HR	RBI	BB	SO	SB
.251	156	561	71	141	27	2	14	77	86	93	0

CAREER STATISTICS

AVG	G	AB	R	H	2B	3B	HR	RBI	BB	SO	SB
.287	1820	6319	905	1811	289	21	222	945	1126	1103	21

VS. RHP

VS. LHP

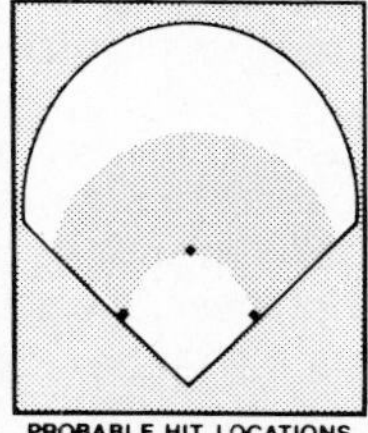
PROBABLE HIT LOCATIONS

HITTING:

Ken Singleton is a very valuable hitter for the Orioles. He's a natural lefty and far more productive from that side. The feeling around the league is that Singleton can be handled by lefthanded pitchers who can keep their pitches high and away from the plate. Righthanded hurlers have more trouble with him. Ken is seldom fooled by off-speed pitches and will jump on any curves or sliders that don't break sharply.

Batting mostly as a lefthander, Singleton is a consistent line drive hitter and has the power to drive the ball to the alley. He is especially valuable as a clutch hitter and is most dangerous with men in scoring position.

Ken is rarely called upon to bunt. He has an excellent batting eye and this makes him a consistent leader in drawing walks. However, he is really a power hitter and relishes coming up in clutch situations. The Seattle Kingdome has been his most productive park to hit in away from home. The Red Sox, White Sox, and Royals are other teams that seem to bring out the best in Kenny.

BASERUNNING:

Singleton is not a threat on the basepaths. He has little speed and seldom if ever attempts to steal. He's conservative in going from first to third and relies on his head more than his legs when he's on the basepaths.

FIELDING:

Shoulder surgery in 1978 limits Singleton's effectiveness as an outfielder. He has only an average arm both in strength and accuracy. His lack of speed coupled with an inability to get a good jump on the ball have reduced his playing time as a fielder.

OVERALL:

Singleton is a leader on the Orioles. He's a proven clutch performer and an important RBI man on the club.

Robinson: "A valuable guy on the Oriole team. He's a clutch performer at the plate and a consistent leader in the clubhouse."

Martin: "Kenny hits with power and has a high on-base percentage. His dependability in the clutch makes him a quality leader on the team."

SAMMY STEWART
RHP, No. 53
RR, 6'3", 208 lbs.
ML Svc: 4 years
Born: 10-28-54 in Asheville, NC

PITCHING:

Stewart is the Orioles' long man out of the bullpen. Primarily a power pitcher with a fastball clocked at just below 90 MPH, he mixes the hard one with a sharp breaking slider. While he may show a change-up to a batter, Stewart is basically a two-pitch pitcher. He's also a smart pitcher and will try to adjust to a particular batter's weakness. He has better success against righties, but he's not afraid to challenge a lefthander.

A lack of control is the chief complaint against Stewart. When his control lapses, he gets into trouble. The trouble only gets worse when Sammy tries to blow his fastball by instead of placing it.

Although Stewart is highly valued as a reliever, he's grown restless in that capacity and is anxious to get a shot at the starting rotation. In the past, however, he's usually proved ineffective as a starter.

FIELDING:

Stewart has an unorthodox move to second which keeps runners off balance, as well as a better than average move to first. He fields bunts quickly and is rated above average as a fielder.

OVERALL:

Sammy fills a vital role for the Orioles. Whether or not he can continue to accept that role and be as effective as he has been in the past is the most important question about his future with this club.

Harwell: "Stewart has good command of his pitches. He should be winning more."

Robinson: "Long relief might be his bag. Right now I think that's where he can most help the club."

Martin: "Sammy exudes confidence on the mound. He's a fast worker and has a durable arm. He's underrated because he works out of the pen in long relief, but I think he's extremely valuable."

1982 STATISTICS

W	L	ERA	G	GS	CG	IP	H	R	ER	BB	SO	SV
10	9	4.14	39	12	1	139	140	68	64	62	69	5

CAREER STATISTICS

W	L	ERA	G	GS	CG	IP	H	R	ER	BB	SO	SV
30	30	3.43	134	23	4	499	438	204	190	253	286	13

TIM STODDARD
RHP, No. 49
RR, 6'7", 250 lbs.
ML Svc: 4 years
Born: 1-24-53 in
East Chicago, IN

NOTE: In September 1982, Tim Stoddard was operated on to repair a torn ligament in his right knee, damaged in a fall at Yankee Stadium. The following report is based on his 1982 pre-surgery form.

PITCHING:

Stoddard is the righthanded component of Baltimore's short relief staff. Tim is an imposing 6'7", 250 pounder who can intimidate batters with his better than 90 MPH fastball. When he has control and command of his slider, he is especially tough against righthanded hitters.

Tim seldom throws a curve or a change-up. Instead of trying to pitch to spots dictated by a hitter's weakness, he tries to overpower opponents with his speed. He is aggressive on the mound and is not afraid to send his hummer under a batter's chin to move him off the plate.

Stoddard seemed to have lost some of his poise on the mound last year. He had problems with his control and it caused a lack of self-confidence. The Rangers, Red Sox and White Sox have all hit Stoddard hard in the past. On the other hand, he's had his best success against the Royals, Yankees and Athletics.

FIELDING:

Stoddard has only an average move to first base. His tremendous size works against him as a fielder, and he is rated average in fielding bunts and covering his position.

OVERALL:

Before his injury, Stoddard was Baltimore's main weapon against righthanded hitters. He relied almost entirely on a fastball and a hard slider to get by opposing hitters. Control problems seem to have undermined his confidence and that can be a critical shortcoming in a late inning relief pitcher.

Martin: "Tim is an imposing figure on the mound. He challenges rival hitters but seemed to take second seat to Tippy Martinez in 1982."

Harwell: "A solid short reliever. He can work on consecutive days without coming up empty."

Robinson: "When he's in the groove, he can be overpowering but he has to improve his control. Short relievers have to throw strikes."

1982 STATISTICS

W	L	ERA	G	GS	CG	IP	H	R	ER	BB	SO	SV
3	4	4.02	50	0	0	56	53	26	25	29	42	12

CAREER STATISTICS

W	L	ERA	G	GS	CG	IP	H	R	ER	BB	SO	SV
15	11	3.13	183	0	0	256	231	99	89	112	199	48

BENNY AYALA
OF, No. 27
RR, 6'1", 195 lbs.
ML Svc: 5 years
Born: 2-7-51 in
Yauco, PR

HITTING, BASERUNNING, FIELDING:

Ayala is strictly a righthanded power hitter. He likes to go after the high fastball and handles the pitch best when it's on the inside half of the plate. He has above average power and tends to pull everything to left field. He's strong enough to reach the alley and is used mostly as a pinch-hitter or a DH.

Ayala has trouble with off-speed pitches and good curves. Most pitchers avoid the high hard one and the slider when working against Ayala.

He is considered an above average as a clutch-hitter and is used as a late inning pinch-hitter against lefties. He swings too hard to be effective at the plate in hit-and-run situations and is rarely called upon to bunt.

Ayala does not run well. He is slow by major league standards, never steals, and is seldom in a position to break up the double play.

Benny has had little opportunity to play the field. When the rest of the Orioles play catch, Benny plays hit.

OVERALL:

In the late innings he has the potential to decide the outcome of a ballgame with a single swing of the bat, and can come through a dozen or so times a season.

Robinson: "Ayala is a role player and is happy about it. When the game is in the balance, you like to see Benny with a bat in his hands."

BOB BONNER
INF, No. 2
RR, 6'0", 185 lbs.
ML Svc: 1 year plus
Born: 8-12-56 in
Uvalde, TX

HITTING, BASERUNNING, FIELDING:

The Orioles looked to Bonner to solve their shortstop problems early last year. His lack of hitting overwhelmed his defensive skills and he was forced into the role of a utility infielder. Bonner is a pull hitter who has real problems with any pitch on the outside part of the plate. Consequently, he sees a lot of curves and sliders away. His tendency to try and pull everything leads to a lot of harmless ground balls. Until he learns to go to right and develops his hitting skills, Bonner will find it difficult to stay in the majors.

Bonner is considered an average baserunner. He's quick out of the box but doesn't have the natural speed to leg out many infield hits. He's careful on the bases and doesn't make many mistakes or force any errors.

Bonner is a better than average infielder. His throws from short are strong and accurate. He has good range and moves well both to his left and right. He has quick hands and is agile when he's the middleman in the 4-6-3 double play. Fielding is a definite plus for Bonner and he is often used for defensive purposes late in a game.

OVERALL:

Bob is still young enough to improve his hitting and stay in the majors. He is trying to develop as a switch-hitter and this could be a big help to him. He has a good glove and can be used at second and third as well as short.

JIM DWYER
OF, No. 28
LL, 5'10", 175 lbs.
ML Svc: 8 years
Born: 1-3-50 in
Evergreen, IL

HITTING, BASERUNNING, FIELDING:

Dwyer is used primarily as a left-handed pinch-hitter and occasionally as a designated hitter. He rarely, if ever sees action against lefthanded pitching. Jim has better than average power and prefers the ball on the inside half of the plate. He pulls the ball most of the time and handles the bat better against fastball pitchers than against those who throw a lot of curves and off-speed stuff.

Dwyer is considered a good clutch performer and handles the pressure of hitting in tight situations better than most. He generally makes contact and is better than average in hit-and-run situations.

Dwyer is not particularly fast on the bases, but he tries hard. He will dive head first into the bag to beat a throw, and will come in high and hard to break up the double play.

He logs little time in the field. In an emergency, he can play at first as well as in the outfield.

OVERALL:

Jim is a good lefthanded hitter who won't freeze in the clutch. He can hit a fastball or a hanging curve out of the park, but he can be made to look bad with breaking balls and changes of pace.

Martin: "A good hitter off the bench who can be used as a pinch-hitter or designated hitter. He has an excellent attitude."

FLOYD RAYFORD
INF, No. 9
RR, 5'10", 195 lbs.
ML Svc: 1 year plus
Born: 7-27-57 in
Memphis, TN

HITTING, BASERUNNING, FIELDING:

Rayford didn't get many opportunities to play during the 1982 season, and when he did, he filled in as a utility infielder and third string catcher. At the plate Rayford is a line drive hitter. When he gets his pitch, he can spray the ball to all fields and has the power to occasionally reach the alleys. Opposing pitchers have success feeding Floyd a steady diet of breaking balls. Rayford also has difficulty handling off-speed junk on the outside corner.

Floyd has average to below average speed and runs the bases tentatively. He doesn't make many mistakes, but seldom takes any chances.

As a utility infielder, Rayford shows limited range and only an average arm. His strongest suit last season was his willingness and ability to fill in at a variety of positions.

OVERALL:

Floyd's value is in his potential for the future. In the meantime, his attitude and willingness to work hard and stay in shape have helped earn him a spot on a big league roster.

Robinson: "Floyd can play some third base and has the ability to come off the bench after a long stay and play well. Every team in the majors needs a guy like Floyd. He's a hard worker, accepts his role for what it is, and is ready when you need him."

FENWAY PARK
Boston Red Sox

Seating Capacity: 33,536
Playing Surface: Natural Grass

Dimensions
Left Field Pole: 315 ft.
Left-Center Field: 379 ft.
Center Field: 390 ft.
Deep-Center Field: 420 ft.
Right-Center Field: 380 ft.
Right Field Pole: 302 ft.
Height of Outfield Walls:
Left Field: 37 ft. (aka The Wall, and The Green Monster)
Center Field: 17 ft.
Right Field Wall: 3-5 ft.

Although Fenway Park does not have the mystique of Yankee Stadium, it comes very close to rivalling "The House that Ruth Built" when it comes to tradition and sheer electricity. The very fact that it has nooks, crannies, the famed "Green Monster" in left field, and absolutely no place in it or on it that can be considered symmetrical makes it a marvel to behold.

It is 315 feet down the line, where The Monster meets the upper deck and extends to center field. The Wall is 37 feet high, and above it is a screen which catches many balls. Those balls which clear The Wall, however, are homers. The Wall and the screen run straight from the foul pole to the edge of the bleachers in center field. Where The Wall ends, the distance is approximately 390 feet.

The bleacher wall is 17 feet high, but as the seating area heads towards right-center field (where both bullpens are back-to-back and in full view of bleacherites), it drops off. Balls hit towards the bullpen area must carry from the right of a 420-foot cove in dead center to a distance of 380 feet, and must clear a five-foot high bullpen fence. Many outfielders are easily able to get back on long high smashes and merely lean over the wall to rob a batter of a homer.

Lefthanded pitchers rarely win in this park, because one mistake usually winds up in the screen. But, in reality, the park is tailor-made for lefthanded hitters, despite the distance in right-center and right. A lefty can flick his bat and hit The Wall for a double or a triple, and has all the area in right-center to shoot for. Jimmy Foxx led the American League in hitting in 1938 as did Carney Lansford in the strike-shortened 1981 season (both were righties). In between, however, thirteen lefthanded Red Sox hitters managed thirteen batting titles. Champions included Ted Williams, Billy Goodman, Pete Runnels, Carl Yastrzemski and Fred Lynn.

Wind does play a part at Fenway. In any given three-game series, the wind can whip in from left the first day, switch to blowing out the next, and return to blowing in on the third day. The "sun field" is right field, particularly in September and October, and Lou Piniella of the New York Yankees, playing in right field in the classic playoff game of 1978, may have saved the pennant for New York when he fought off the sun to catch Lynn's long smash with two on, and to stop Jerry Remy's single in the ninth inning, keeping Rick Burleson at second base.

Despite the pitfalls, the axiom remains: No lead is ever safe at Fenway Park.

PITCHING:

Luis Aponte was used in both short and long relief for Sox manager Ralph Houk last season. Aponte combined an awkward pitching motion, an excellent sinking fastball and a good slider to post a 2-2 record in his first full major league season.

Aponte lacks overwhelming stuff and his fastball seldom exceeds 85 MPH. However, everything he throws moves quite a bit and hitters had trouble with him especially their first time around. When he falls behind in the count, he will throw either his fastball which sinks or his slider which is considered his second best pitch. During the past season, Aponte also developed a third pitch which is referred to as a forkball by some and a spitter by others. Aponte has good poise on the mound and doesn't seem to get rattled by a bad call or an untimely error. He still has to learn to pitch to a batter's weakness and the Red Sox are hoping that he will develop better control of his pitches. Nevertheless, he served an important role as a utility pitcher on the Boston staff.

FIELDING:

Aponte has an above average pick-off move, and this manages to keep opposing runners from getting too long a lead. He won't hurt himself in the field and is rated average to above average in fielding bunts.

LUIS APONTE
RHP, No. 45
RR, 6'0", 165 lbs.
ML Svc: 1 year plus
Born: 7-14-54 in
Lel Tigre, VEN

OVERALL:

Aponte was effective in his utility role for the Sox. He saw most of his action when it was too early to bring in Clear and too late to bring in Stanley. If his motion and good sinker can keep batters off balance the second and third time around, Aponte should be able to earn a permanent spot on the Boston staff.

Martin: "Luis was not spectacular but he was effective. He'll never be a strikeout pitcher like Clear but his ball moves and it's difficult for hitters to pick up."

Harwell: "Luis is most effective when he manages to keep the ball down."

Robinson: "Aponte is a good guy to have on your staff. He can pitch in any situation, either as a starter or a reliever--long or short."

1982 STATISTICS

W	L	ERA	G	GS	CG	IP	H	R	ER	BB	SO	SV
2	2	3.18	40	0	0	85	78	31	30	25	44	3

CAREER STATISTICS

W	L	ERA	G	GS	CG	IP	H	R	ER	BB	SO	SV
3	2	2.67	51	0	0	108	95	33	32	30	56	4

TONY ARMAS
OF, No. 20
RR, 6'1", 182 lbs.
ML Svc: 6 years
Born: 7-12-53 in
Anzoatequi, VEN

1982 STATISTICS

AVG	G	AB	R	H	2B	3B	HR	RBI	BB	SO	SB
.233	138	536	58	125	19	2	28	89	33	128	2

CAREER STATISTICS

AVG	G	AB	R	H	2B	3B	HR	RBI	BB	SO	SB
.250	698	2490	268	624	84	19	111	375	127	601	15

VS. RHP

VS. LHP

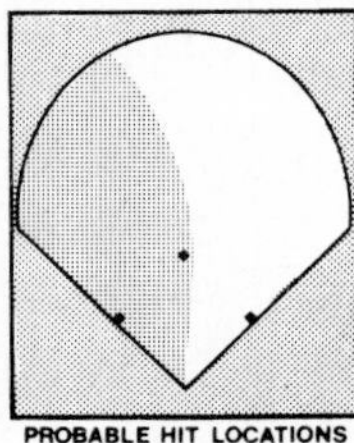
PROBABLE HIT LOCATIONS

HITTING:

Tony Armas is a power hitter, pure and simple. Give him a high fastball and he'll park it in the nickel seats, usually in the direction of left field or left-center.

Armas has trouble with breaking balls thrown away by righthanders. Lefties might be advised to jam him inside or give him sinkers away. Pitchers who get ahead of him on the count might try throwing a pitch up and out of the strike zone and get Armas to fish for it. He, like most power hitters, strikes out a lot. Line drives are his specialty and he has better success against lefthanders than righthanders. He can pull and he can hit the alleys.

It is said of Armas that he can get as hot as any hitter who ever lived or can be as cold. He is definitely a streak hitter. He can handle a curve if it is up in the strike zone. He is an above average clutch hitter and is a good RBI man. He doesn't walk often because he comes up swinging. He is not the best at hitting behind the runner. He is a good ideal cleanup hitter.

BASERUNNING:

Armas does not steal bases, but probably could if asked to do so. He has good speed, is a smart runner and pitchers don't ignore him when he reaches base. He slides feet first and can break up a double play.

FIELDING:

As a right fielder, Armas is as good as there is in the game today. His arm is excellent and his throws are almost always accurate. While in Oakland, Armas liked to play shallow because he is superb at going back on the ball. He can also charge balls hit in front of him. His range from left to right deserves top billing. Defense is definitely the strong point of Armas' game.

OVERALL:

Robinson: "If Armas hits, the team should win. He is a good all around player with tremendous power."

Martin: "Armas is a good player who provides the long ball in the middle of the lineup. Yes, he does live up to his potential. His strong arm and defense make him a constant right field. He does his job, often spectacularly, but without fanfare."

Harwell: "A good long ball threat with an excellent arm in the outfield."

DOUG BIRD
RHP, No. 47
RR, 6'4", 189 lbs.
ML Svc: 9 years
Born: 3-5-50 in
Carona, CA

PITCHING:

Bird was out of his element in 1982, and no one knew it better than Bird and the Cubs who, out of necessity, had to use him as a fifth starter. He is most effective in relief, either long or short. In a three year stretch with four teams, including Triple A Columbus, Bird won 18 straight games, mostly in relief.

The book on Bird--effective until he has the batter in a two-strike hole, then--duck! Batters wait him out, looking for a mistake. He gave up a team high of 26 home runs, mostly on careless mistakes.

Although he is 32 years old, Bird still has an 88 MPH fastball, a better-than-average slider and a palmball that he probably should use more often. It's effective against lefthanded hitters. He may be too true with his slider, but nothing gets him in more trouble than his "slurve," a combination slider/curve that used to draw the wrath of Whitey Herzog when the two of them were with Kansas City.

FIELDING:

For a veteran, Bird is like a beginner defensively. His move to first is weak, and he is average at fielding bunts and in fielding his position. He needs improvement, but after nine years in the majors, he is unlikely to change.

OVERALL:

Kiner: "Pitching in Wrigley Field with its short alleys and wind often blowing out was a hindrance for him. Bird is best suited for bigger parks and in relief with his 88 MPH fastball."

McCarver: "A short relief man turned starter is unusual. Usually he doesn't have the stamina, but Doug made the adjustment. When I caught him, I couldn't understand why he didn't use his palmball more often."

Coleman: "Bird is just an average pitcher who uses his brain more than his abilities."

1982 STATISTICS

W	L	ERA	G	GS	CG	IP	H	R	ER	BB	SO	SV
9	14	5.14	35	33	2	191	230	119	109	30	71	0

CAREER STATISTICS

W	L	ERA	G	GS	CG	IP	H	R	ER	BB	SO	SV
72	56	3.84	405	94	8	1145	1182	538	488	280	647	59

WADE BOGGS
INF, No. 26
LR, 6'2", 185 lbs.
ML Svc: 1 year
Born: 6-15-58 in
Omaha, NE

1982 STATISTICS

AVG	G	AB	R	H	2B	3B	HR	RBI	BB	SO	SB
.349	104	338	51	118	14	1	5	44	35	21	1

CAREER STATISTICS

AVG	G	AB	R	H	2B	3B	HR	RBI	BB	SO	SB
.349	104	338	51	118	14	1	5	44	35	21	1

VS. RHP

VS. LHP

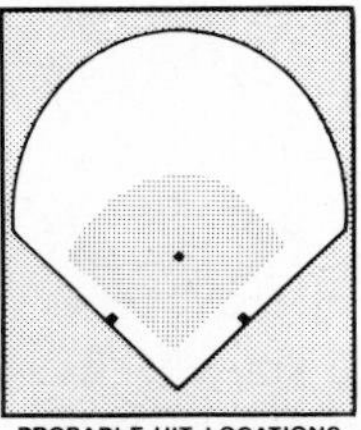
PROBABLE HIT LOCATIONS

HITTING:

Wade Boggs was perhaps the biggest and most pleasant surprise on the Sox roster in 1982. He got his chance after Lansford was hurt and his hot bat kept him in the lineup for the rest of the season. Boggs is primarily a contact hitter. He waits exceptionally well on the ball, and has the discipline and bat control necessary to go with the pitch. He has the power to reach the alleys, but his true strength lies in his ability to slap the ball all over the field.

Opposing pitchers tried everything during his rookie season, but his .349 average attests to their lack of success. He did have some problems with good breaking pitches, but was smart enough to lay off them until he fell behind in the count. His consistency with the bat makes him exceptionally reliable in hit-and-run situations and with men in scoring position. He has a good batting eye and a veteran's patience at the plate. He has the tools to be a regular .300 hitter for many years to come.

BASERUNNING:

Boggs is fairly quick down the first base line but he ran the bases rather timidly in his rookie year. He didn't stretch any base hits, steal many bases, or take any chances. That kind of conservative baserunning may change as he develops more confidence in his ability to play major league ball.

FIELDING:

With Wade's red hot bat, the Red Sox were forced to find a place for him to play every day. They tried him both at third and later at first. He seemed much more comfortable at first. He was aggressive in the field, and when he got to play regularly, seemed to improve on a daily basis. His range at first base was above average, and he was surprisingly effective going back after flies in the short right field foul territory.

OVERALL:

Boggs had a remarkable rookie season at the plate. His defensive play at first base was adequate but clearly improved as the season went on. Boggs has excellent potential to be a Red Sox regular for many years.

Robinson: "Wade has a great attitude and a good bat. These qualities should keep him in the big leagues for a long time."

Martin: "Best looking rookie hitter for the Red Sox to come along in a while. Wade is a smart, natural hitter who should become the starting first baseman from now on."

MARK CLEAR
RHP, No. 25
RR, 6'4", 200 lbs.
ML Svc: 4 years
Born: 5-27-56 in
Los Angeles, CA

PITCHING:

Clear is the "stopper" in Ralph Houk's bullpen. The team's number one relief man, Mark relies on a better than 90 MPH fastball and a wicked curve to get his team out of tight spots. Opposing hitters don't worry about Clear pitching to their weak spots. When Mark gets the call in the bullpen, everyone in the park knows that he's going to challenge batters with his fastball. If he gets ahead in the count, they then have to look out for one of the best curves in the majors. When you combine all that natural ability with Mark's quiet, easygoing personality, you have all but one of the ingredients necessary for a top-notch short relief man.

The missing ingredient is control. Clear has had serious control problems throughout his career, and the second half of last season was just the most recent example. In a close game, there's always the possibility that Mark will put more people on base with walks than he gets out with strikeouts. Unfortunately for Mark and for the Red Sox, his lack of control has the potential to offset all the advantages--a superior fastball, an outrageous curve, and the perfect disposition for a major league relief pitcher.

FIELDING:

Clear is probably the worst fielding pitcher on the Red Sox staff. He is slow and often off balance when fielding bunts, has troubles covering first, and seems to lose his concentration after he throws the ball. Mark needs to improve in all the defensive aspects of the game.

OVERALL:

Mark has excellent presence on the mound. His fastball and curve can intimidate rival batters, but his control problems worry even his own teammates. Clear remains one of the better short relievers in baseball, but he has to develop more consistency and control.

Harwell: "Mark's outstanding curve makes him one of the prime strikeout relievers in the league."

Robinson: "Clear is what you like in a relief pitcher. He can get you a strikeout or two and save the game. One of the league's best relievers."

Martin: "Mark is a quiet and professional pitcher and individual. He keeps in excellent shape. He can strike hitters out and that makes him a valuable addition to any club."

1982 STATISTICS

W	L	ERA	G	GS	CG	IP	H	R	ER	BB	SO	SV
14	9	3.00	55	0	0	105	92	39	35	61	109	14

CAREER STATISTICS

W	L	ERA	G	GS	CG	IP	H	R	ER	BB	SO	SV
44	28	3.47	199	0	0	397	330	174	153	245	394	46

DENNIS ECKERSLEY
RHP, No. 43
RR, 6'2", 190 lbs.
ML Svc: 8 years
Born: 10-3-54 in
Oakland, CA

PITCHING:

Dennis Eckersley is the ace of the Red Sox staff, but has just managed to struggle through the past three seasons. His 13-13 showing in 1982, coming on the heels of a 9-8 mark in 1981 and a 12-14 record in 1980, was a big disappointment. If Boston is to improve in the tough American League East, Eckersley has to be the man to lead them.

Dennis pitches without a windup, and his delivery often drops down from three-quarters to sidearm, making him especially tough on opposing right-handed hitters. Chronic back problems and recurring spasms in the biceps of his throwing arm have taken a little off Dennis' fastball. He can still throw it in the high 80 MPH range, and with his above average control, the fastball remains his out pitch. Eckersley also throws an excellent slider that breaks from six to eight inches. When he has control of these two pitches, he generally uses his curve as a waste pitch and often shelves his change-up completely. This is unfortunate because it makes him a two-pitch pitcher, and hitters can afford to sit back and wait for the fastball. This may explain the high number of homers Eckersley gives up.

Dennis has the reputation of being a combative pitcher, and he's not afraid to crowd a hitter with a brushback pitch. He has confidence in his pitches and will challenge any hitter in the league.

FIELDING:

Eckersley seldom helps or hurts himself in the field. His move to first is only adequate, and good baserunners will take advantage of his big kick and slow release. He's a step slow in reacting to bunts, and is not exceptionally quick off the mound either to field them or to cover first on grounders to the right side.

OVERALL:

Eckersley has the talent to help the Red Sox move up in the standings. However, injuries, a tendency to give up the gopher ball, combined with a lack of offensive support have made him a .500 pitcher.

Martin: "The Sox didn't score runs for Dennis this season. Dennis is a top competitor and Boston needs a big year from him to improve their place in the standings."

Robinson: "Dennis is still the best pitcher the Sox have to keep them in the game for seven or more innings."

Harwell: "I think Dennis is a much improved pitcher since he started to go inside on hitters. That plus his delivery makes him real tough on righthanded hitters."

1982 STATISTICS

W	L	ERA	G	GS	CG	IP	H	R	ER	BB	SO	SV
13	13	3.73	33	33	11	224	228	101	93	43	127	0

CAREER STATISTICS

W	L	ERA	G	GS	CG	IP	H	R	ER	BB	SO	SV
111	85	3.44	257	241	87	1724	1584	715	658	474	1182	3

DWIGHT EVANS
OF, No. 24
RR, 6'3", 205 lbs.
ML Svc: 10 years
Born: 11-3-51 in
Santa Monica, CA

1982 STATISTICS

AVG	G	AB	R	H	2B	3B	HR	RBI	BB	SO	SB
.292	162	609	122	178	37	7	32	98	112	125	3

CAREER STATISTICS

AVG	G	AB	R	H	2B	3B	HR	RBI	BB	SO	SB
.269	1334	4415	691	1188	243	42	182	612	612	855	45

VS. RHP

VS. LHP

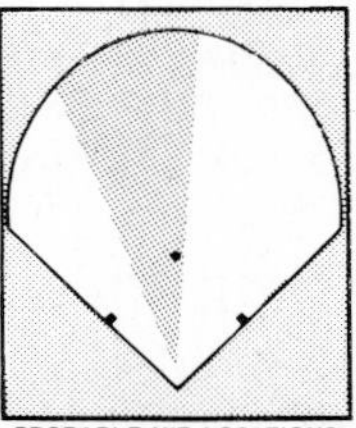
PROBABLE HIT LOCATIONS

HITTING:

In 1982, Dwight Evans had a season most players only dream about. He led the Sox in hits, home runs, triples, doubles, runs scored, and runs batted in. During the past two years, Evans has become one of the most productive hitters in the game. He hits with power and has the ability to go to right field with an outside pitch. He's awesome in the clutch and seems to bear down just a little more intensely with men in scoring position. He's also become more disciplined at the plate and chases far fewer bad balls. He has an excellent batting eye and led the Sox in drawing walks last season.

Most pitchers try to change speeds on Evans, and have had their best success against him with curves down and away. He jumps on anything high and inside and has recently begun to have better than average success against sinkers and sliders. He's been a consistent power hitter the past two seasons and can drive the ball to either alley. At the plate Evans can do it all.

BASERUNNING:

Evans gets out of the box quickly, and has better than average speed to first base. He is an aggressive baserunner and although he seldom attempts to steal, he'll run hard to break up a double play or to try and score from second on a single. He's smart on the bases and opposing pitchers and rival outfielders can't afford to ignore him.

FIELDING:

Evans is quite simply the best defensive right fielder in the American League. He has a gun for an arm and is devastatingly accurate with it. He lacks blazing speed, but positions himself perfectly to compensate. He tends to play closer to the foul line in Fenway than other right fielders, but covers the gap in right-center as well as anyone. He intimidates runners with his arm and plays the ball off the wall as if he had a magnet in his glove.

OVERALL:

Evans is a complete ballplayer, excellent at the plate and outstanding in the field.

Martin: "A revelation at the plate the past two seasons. Sure he strikes out, but he also walks a lot, gets on base, and leads the team in home runs and RBIs. He also intimidates runners with his arm in the outfield."

Robinson: "Dwight used to have a different stance every two times at bat. Now he's found a groove, aims up the middle, and makes things happen whenever he swings the bat."

Harwell: "Evans is a great outfielder with a top notch arm. He's durable and has made himself a much better hitter the past two seasons."

RICH GEDMAN
C, No. 10
LR, 6'0", 210 lbs.
ML Svc: 2 years
Born: 9-26-59 in Worcester, MA

1982 STATISTICS

AVG	G	AB	R	H	2B	3B	HR	RBI	BB	SO	SB
.249	92	289	30	72	17	2	4	26	10	37	0

CAREER STATISTICS

AVG	G	AB	R	H	2B	3B	HR	RBI	BB	SO	SB
.263	163	518	54	136	32	2	9	53	19	73	0

VS. RHP

VS. LHP

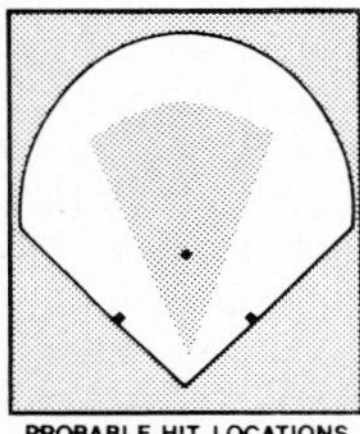
PROBABLE HIT LOCATIONS

HITTING:

Gedman represents the lefthanded hitting side of Houk's catching tandem. Rich is a stronger hitter than Allenson, but catching is a relatively new position for him and he's still in the learning process. In his rookie year in 1981, Rich demonstrated that he could handle major league fastballs. In 1982, opposing pitchers shelved their fastballs and served Gedman a lot of curves and other off-speed pitches.

Rich has better than average power and can reach the alleys when he connects. He is still overanxious at the plate, however, and apt to swing at bad pitches. Righthanders usually throw him a lot of curves down and away, and fastballs up and out of the strike zone. The few times he went up against lefties he saw a lot of curves on the outside half of the plate. The Sox are confident that Gedman will improve as a hitter. He needs more patience and has to be careful not to try to pull everything to right, especially with the friendly left field wall in Fenway. If he can do that and learn to handle a major league curve, Boston will be overjoyed.

BASERUNNING:

Gedman is slow out of the box and doesn't build up much speed going down the line. He doesn't get to second in time to break up the double play and is not considered any kind of threat on the bases.

FIELDING:

Gedman's troubles at the plate seemed to ruin his concentration when he was working behind it as a catcher. He has a strong arm, but his accuracy is rated only adequate. The Red Sox pitching staff doesn't keep opposing runners particularly close at first, so many teams were willing to challenge Gedman's arm. He also had troubles behind the plate handling errant pitches, and ended the season among the leaders in errors and passed balls. He needs more work and experience to improve as a catcher, and still has a lot to learn about opposing hitters. However, if his own hitting improves, the Sox will probably give him the time and opportunities he needs.

OVERALL:

Gedman has a chance to develop into a better than average hitter. If he continues to show improvement, the Sox can afford to live with his defensive lapses until he gains the experience necessary to eliminate them.

Robinson: "Rich seems to be growing as a player. He's only 23 years old, and he's learning a new position. I think he'll develop into an outstanding hitter."

Martin: "Gedman is strong and gutsy. He has power to all fields but tried to pull the ball too much in 1982. He should come along as a good hitter when he learns the strike zone and begins to handle the curveball."

BRUCE HURST
LHP, No. 47
LL, 6'3", 185 lbs.
ML Svc: 1 year plus
Born: 3-24-58 in
St. George, UT

PITCHING:

Bruce Hurst failed to pitch up to expectations last season. Houk was counting on him to bolster the left side of his starting rotation, but his 3-7 record and 5.77 ERA clearly indicate that something went wrong.

Hurst relies on his fastball, but he lacks the velocity necessary to keep hitters honest. He also throws curves, sliders, and change-ups but none of these pitches is outstanding for him. Part of his ineffectiveness is due to his inability to locate and then pitch to a batter's weakness. Too often, he appears to lack confidence in his pitches and he seems to throw randomly rather than with a purpose. All of this coupled with spotty control made the past season a long and painful one for Hurst.

When he did pitch effectively, he had his best success with his curve which was delivered off a fairly high leg kick and came sweeping across the outside of the plate. He has the potential to be tough on lefthanded hitters, but needs work and the poise and confidence that should come with it.

FIELDING:

Bruce has a southpaw's natural advantage on his move to first, and he manages to hold most runners fairly close. He's only rated average as a fielder and has shown no remarkable strengths or weaknesses either in handling bunts or in getting in place to cover the bag.

OVERALL:

The feeling is that Hurst has the potential to develop into a major league pitcher. The question is how much longer should the Red Sox have to wait. He seems to have all the necessary physical tools but he still lacks the confidence, poise, and experience necessary to be a winner.

Harwell: "Hurst is limited because he only has an average fastball and this forces him to over-use his breaking stuff."

Robinson: "Bruce is another guy the Sox keep waiting for to make the grade. He's done well enough in the minors but he still has to prove he can win in the bigs."

Martin: "Bruce has all the physical tools and ability to win, but he seems to be his own worst enemy. He has to learn to override trouble."

1982 STATISTICS

W	L	ERA	G	GS	CG	IP	H	R	ER	BB	SO	SV
3	7	5.77	28	19	0	117	161	87	75	40	53	0

CAREER STATISTICS

W	L	ERA	G	GS	CG	IP	H	R	ER	BB	SO	SV
7	9	6.16	45	31	0	171	223	131	117	68	80	0

HITTING:

In 1982, Jeff Newman's bat took a holiday. It remains questionable if it will return to work this year. Newman has power, but his home run production has dropped steadily since 1979. Pitches he used to rope, now go for grounders, and some of them are weak at that.

Newman will pull the ball against lefthanded pitchers, but hits straightaway against righthanders. Since the lifetime .226 hitter produced a meek .199 average last year, Newman apparently didn't hit much of anything. Righthanders handle him best with curves and sliders, while lefthanders have success with sinkers. Newman can hit a change-up, and fastballs up and over the plate are his specialty.

He squares himself at the plate, giving the appearance of a closed, upright stance. His ability to hit in almost any situation is average, including in the clutch, behind the runner, with men in scoring position and in the hit-and-run. He is not a particularly good bunter, and does not draw an exceptional number of walks. Seventh or eighth in the batting order is about where he belongs.

BASERUNNING:

With seven career steals, Newman cannot be considered a major threat on the bases. He is relatively slow afoot and his basestealing needs work. However, he is a smart baserunner, although conservative because of his lack of speed. He can break up a double play with his feet first slide. His work on the bases is considered the weakest part of his game.

FIELDING:

Newman has been a catcher first, but can also play at first base. His

JEFF NEWMAN
C, No. 5
RR, 6'2", 215 lbs.
ML Svc: 7 years
Born: 9-11-48 in
Fort Worth, TX

1982 STATISTICS

AVG	G	AB	R	H	2B	3B	HR	RBI	BB	SO	SB
.199	72	251	19	50	11	0	6	30	14	49	0

CAREER STATISTICS

AVG	G	AB	R	H	2B	3B	HR	RBI	BB	SO	SB
.226	652	1928	173	436	79	4	59	223	101	322	7

VS. RHP

VS. LHP

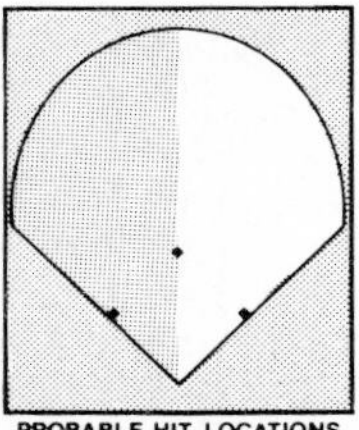
PROBABLE HIT LOCATIONS

knowledge of hitters is above average, and more often than not he calls the shots behind the plate. His arm strength and release point are average. He experienced some soreness in his arm last season. He is accurate, and he is considered good at bunts and holding runners. Newman does not spend much time trying to unsettle hitters.

OVERALL:

Robinson: "What you have seen of Newman is his best. He can play several positions for you. He is a veteran player with a good arm who can help you by catching or at first, but he's not going to hit much."

Martin: "He's handy to have as a DH or as a replacement catcher or first baseman. He didn't do much last year."

REID NICHOLS
OF, No. 51
RR, 5'11", 165 lbs.
ML Svc: 2 years
Born: 8-5-58 in
Ocala, FL

1982 STATISTICS

AVG	G	AB	R	H	2B	3B	HR	RBI	BB	SO	SB
.302	92	245	35	74	16	1	7	33	14	28	5

CAREER STATISTICS

AVG	G	AB	R	H	2B	3B	HR	RBI	BB	SO	SB
.277	143	329	53	91	16	3	7	39	19	42	5

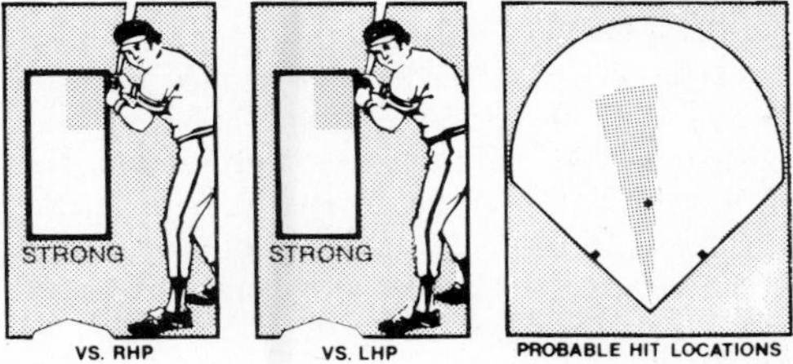

HITTING:

Nichols was another one of Boston's biggest and most pleasant surprises last season. He was platooned in center field with Rick Miller and was used primarily against lefthanded pitching. He played in less than 100 games but made the most of his chances, hit over .300, and showed lots of promise for the future.

Nichols has a quick bat and handles the high inside fastball very well. He has more trouble with curveballs, especially those low and away. He's still in the process of learning the pitchers in the league and has been inconsistent in his ability to handle change-ups, sliders, and sinkers.

Nichols showed some power, and on occasion proved he had the strength to drill the ball down the left-center field alley. However, he still shows signs of impatience at the plate and too often swings at the pitcher's pitch rather than waiting for something he could handle better. The Sox are confident that Nichols is a comer and that he will be a regular outfielder for them in the future.

BASERUNNING:

Nichols has outstanding speed. He gets out of the box quickly and will get a fair share of leg hits during a full season. He's aggressive going into second and willing to try for an extra base when he spots an outfielder just going through the motions. He has the speed and quickness to steal bases in the majors, but may never get the chance with Boston's deliberate style of play.

FIELDING:

Nichols has an excellent arm in terms of both strength and accuracy. He tends to play a little deep in center because he's better coming in than going out on the ball. His arm however, is strong enough to compensate for his deeper position. His speed and quickness give him better than average range, but he's still learning opposing hitters and needs to get a better jump on the ball if he is to truly excel in center field.

OVERALL:

Nichols has proved he can hit against lefthanders. If he can also swing effectively against righthanders, the Red Sox must find a spot for him in the everyday lineup. He's fast, has an exceptionally strong arm, and a good attitude.

Robinson: "The Red Sox still don't know how good this kid really is. He improves every day and I think he's almost ready to break into their regular lineup."

Martin: "Reid is young and fast, has a quick bat, and is a fine defensive outfielder. He's very poised for a youngster and has a great attitude."

Harwell: "I think Nichols is an excellent, young, all around player."

BOB OJEDA
LHP, No. 19
LL, 6'1", 185 lbs.
ML Svc: 1 year plus
Born: 12-17-57 in
Los Angeles, CA

PITCHING:

Bob Ojeda was yet another disappointment on the Red Sox staff last season. After an encouraging debut in 1981, Ojeda tailed off to a 4-6 record in 1982. Houk used him as a starter but Ojeda seemed to lose rather than gain confidence as the season went on. To be effective, Ojeda has to be able to hit his spots. He lacks the speed to overpower anyone and his curves simply don't break that sharply. Instead of one intimidating pitch, Ojeda has to rely on finesse, pinpoint accuracy, and an occasional change of pace.

He uses a herky-jerky motion and has better success against lefties than righties. When he gets behind in the count, he lacks confidence in everything but his fastball. Opposing batters with a 3-0 or a 3-1 count can just sit back and wait for the fastball. Bob needs to develop his slider or curve to the point where he'll feel comfortable throwing it in a pressure situation. That and improved concentration on the mound are two important things for Sox fans to look for if Ojeda is to have a successful career at Fenway.

FIELDING:

Bob has an adequate move to first and opposing baserunners don't get a good jump on his motion. He gets to first quickly on balls hit to the right side but is rated only average at fielding his position and handling bunts.

OVERALL:

Ojeda is the latest in a long line of southpaws who have had trouble pitching for the Red Sox. Houk was very impressed with his 1981 performance, but called his work last season a major disappointment. Ojeda needs to improve his control, develop a second pitch, and regain his confidence if he is to help this club in the future.

Martin: "Bob seemed to have lost the idea where to locate his pitches in 1982. When he had control problems, he also seemed to lose his poise on the mound."

Robinson: "Ojeda doesn't have overpowering speed so he has to consistently hit the right spots or he can get in trouble quickly."

1982 STATISTICS

W	L	ERA	G	GS	CG	IP	H	R	ER	BB	SO	SV
4	6	5.63	22	14	0	78	95	53	49	29	52	0

CAREER STATISTICS

W	L	ERA	G	GS	CG	IP	H	R	ER	BB	SO	SV
11	9	4.87	39	31	2	170	189	98	92	68	92	0

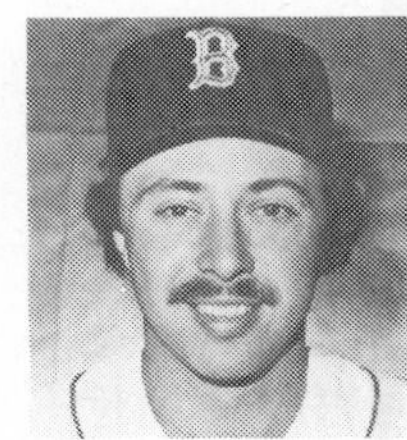

JERRY REMY
INF, No. 2
LR, 5'9", 165 lbs.
ML Svc: 8 years
Born: 11-8-52 in
Fall River, MA

1982 STATISTICS

AVG	G	AB	R	H	2B	3B	HR	RBI	BB	SO	SB
.280	155	636	89	178	22	3	0	47	55	77	16

CAREER STATISTICS

AVG	G	AB	R	H	2B	3B	HR	RBI	BB	SO	SB
.276	978	3759	524	1037	123	32	7	278	309	358	193

VS. RHP

VS. LHP

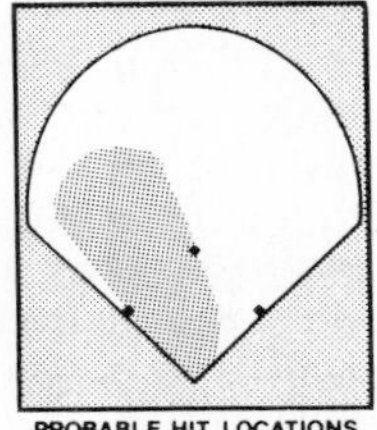
PROBABLE HIT LOCATIONS

HITTING:

Jerry Remy is an opposite field hitter who prefers the ball low and on the inside half of the plate. He lacks the power to reach the alleys and collects most of his hits on line drives to left and choppers through the infield. He consistently makes contact with the ball and is rated better than average in hit-and-run situations.

Remy has trouble handling fastball pitchers who can consistently throw the high hard one inside for strikes. Other pitchers try to knock him off the plate and then feed him a diet of slow curves away. Lefthanders, particularly those with good curveballs, are also tough on Remy. He handles the straight change fairly well and is adept at hitting down on sliders and sinkers and legging out base hits.

He is one of the better bunters in the game. Remy will try to bunt for a base hit at least once every game or two. He drag bunts, push bunts, and last season even experimented bunting to short. When opposing third basemen cheat too much, Remy excels at slapping the ball by them. With his speed and ability to get the bat on the ball he's a first class leadoff man for the Sox.

BASERUNNING:

Jerry is probably the fastest man on the Red Sox team. He is quick out of the box and exceptionally fast down the first base line. He generally leads the Sox in stolen bases but Boston's style of play frequently calls for him to wait for the big hit rather than gamble on the bases. Nevertheless, he is quick, smart, and fast on the basepaths and rival pitchers have to be wary of him.

FIELDING:

Remy is an adequate defensive second baseman. He has an average to above average arm and fairly good range. He goes to his left and his right equally well and is reliable turning the double play. He seldom makes that remarkable game-turning play in the field but he is dependable and plays his position without making costly mistakes.

OVERALL:

Remy is a valuable hitter in the Red Sox offensive machine. He knows how to get on base for the power hitters behind him, is a quick and intelligent baserunner, and doesn't hurt his team in the field.

Robinson: "When Jerry is healthy, he's a good overall player both offensively and defensively."

Harwell: "Jerry is a fine team man with all around ability. Injuries have plagued his career."

Martin: "Remy is a fine leadoff hitter and offensive player. He's also good and steady in the field."

HITTING:

Rice is one of the most feared power hitters in the American League. He has the strength to hit the ball out of the park even in the deepest right and left center field alleys. He's rated above average to excellent in clutch situations and with men in scoring position. Seldom called to hit-and-run and never asked to bunt, Rice is a key RBI man for Boston.

Rice can be handcuffed by a good fastball up and in, and he still gets fooled by curves down and away. Once a pitcher throws the ball in the strike zone, however, Rice is awesome. His long swing makes him devastating against sliders and anything else that he can extend his arms to hit. He's still inclined to be impatient at the plate and his chief flaw as a hitter is that he's not selective enough. When he waits for his pitch, there's no one more devastating in the league.

BASERUNNING:

Rice gets out of the box and off to first with average speed, but he lacks the quickness to make opposing teams nervous. He may steal two or three bases a season, and will run hard to break up the double play at second. Otherwise his baserunning is cautious and conservative.

FIELDING:

Rice has improved dramatically as a defensive ballplayer over the past two or three seasons. His arm is strong and accurate and his speed going after fly balls is better than most people expect. He's better coming in on balls than going back, and has learned to play the ball off The Wall in left almost as well as Yaz used to play it.

JIM RICE
OF, No. 14
RR, 6'2", 205 lbs.
ML Svc: 9 years
Born: 3-8-53 in
Anderson, SC

1982 STATISTICS

AVG	G	AB	R	H	2B	3B	HR	RBI	BB	SO	SB
.309	145	573	86	177	24	5	24	97	55	98	0

CAREER STATISTICS

AVG	G	AB	R	H	2B	3B	HR	RBI	BB	SO	SB
.305	1179	4680	733	1429	213	61	237	828	355	861	49

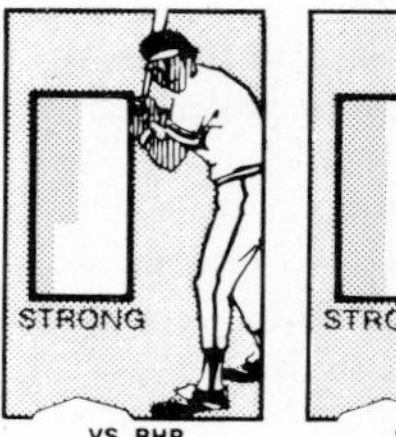

VS. RHP

VS. LHP

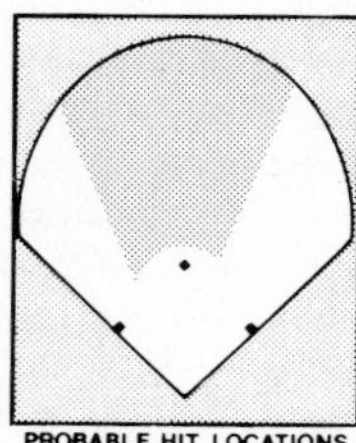
PROBABLE HIT LOCATIONS

OVERALL:

One of the premier power hitters in the American League, he still hits over .300 for average. He keeps improving defensively and has become a legitimate and perennial All Star.

Robinson: "Jim is as good as anyone in the league when it comes to offense."

Martin: "Jim is durable and will play hurt, taped, or strapped without complaining. He's still impatient at the plate but, nevertheless, he's one of the most feared hitters in the league."

Harwell: "One of the American League's strongest men. An excellent power hitter who's always a long ball threat."

BOB STANLEY
RHP, No. 46
RR, 6'4", 205 lbs.
ML Svc: 6 years
Born: 11-10-54 in Portland, ME

PITCHING:

Many experts think that Bob Stanley was the most effective pitcher on the Red Sox staff during the past season. He came out of the bullpen in long as well as short relief situations and did both jobs as well as any pitcher in the league.

Stanley relies almost entirely on his sinker. When it drops, the bottom seems to fall out of the ball and hitters are lucky to get a piece of it. When they do make contact, they hit a lot of ground balls. This makes Stanley especially effective with men on base and less than two outs. He prefers to work in parks with grass infields which help slow down ground balls as opposed to artificial turf on which grounders have a way of skipping through for singles.

In the past few seasons, Stanley has developed a palmball which he uses against lefthanded hitters, especially when he gets ahead of them in the count. He doesn't throw a curve or slider but his ability to keep his sinker down is enough to guarantee his success as a reliever. He has great poise on the mound and has begun to throw tight in an effort to move hitters off the plate. Stanley is durable, thrives on work, and has had exceptional success during his career against Oakland and Seattle.

FIELDING:

Stanley takes a long time to deliver the ball to the plate and good baserunners will take advantage of that. He forces a lot of ground balls and fields his position adequately. He's not exceptionally quick off the mound, but he has an accurate arm and knows what to do with the ball when he gets it.

OVERALL:

1982 was an excellent season for Stanley. He shut teams down in his long relief roles and frequently forced the big double play in his short relief stints. The addition of the off-speed palmball to complement his devastating sinker makes him a top man on the Red Sox staff.

Martin: "Bob was the best overall pitcher on the staff in 1982. If a long or middle reliever ever had a chance for MVP, he'd get my vote."

Harwell: "Stanley is a versatile pitcher with an excellent sinking fastball."

Robinson: "Stanley got a lot of work because of Boston's season-long problems with their starters. He thrived on it and did an excellent job."

1982 STATISTICS

W	L	ERA	G	GS	CG	IP	H	R	ER	BB	SO	SV
12	7	3.10	48	0	0	168	161	60	58	50	83	14

CAREER STATISTICS

W	L	ERA	G	GS	CG	IP	H	R	ER	BB	SO	SV
71	44	3.50	268	64	17	952	1025	415	370	261	320	42

HITTING:

Stapleton is a high ball hitter who can spray the ball all over the field. He has a good batting eye and hits equally well against left and righthanded pitching. He has enough strength to drive the ball into the alleys, but his chief asset as a hitter is his uncanny ability to hit behind the baserunner. He rarely strikes out and is unselfish in his willingness to move runners up a base. He's a manager's delight in hit-and-run situations because he's the best in the league at waiting until the last instant and then poking the ball through the hole left by either the shortstop or second baseman.

Dave has trouble with off-speed pitches, especially slow curves. Curves and sliders low and away also give him problems. However, he feasts on fastballs and hanging curves and has improved his hitting against pitchers who specialize in sinkers and sliders.

He's a consistent and versatile ballplayer who knows how to handle his bat. Although his average fell off in 1982, he still impressed followers with his keen batting eye and exceptionally smart and unselfish attitude at the plate.

BASERUNNING:

Dave lacks exceptional speed and doesn't get an outstanding jump out of the box. He doesn't get a good lead off first and is very conservative on the basepaths. He seldom steals, will not usually try for an extra base, and isn't fast or quick enough to break up double plays. On the other hand, he doesn't take any foolish chances and is considered a smart baserunner.

FIELDING:

Stapleton's chief asset in the field is his versatility. He's played all four infield positions for the Sox and doesn't hurt them defensively at any of them. He has better than average range as an infielder and his arm, though not exceptionally strong, is very accurate. He can turn the double play from either side of second but handles bunts better from third than first. He's not outstanding at any one position but he can play all four at the major league level.

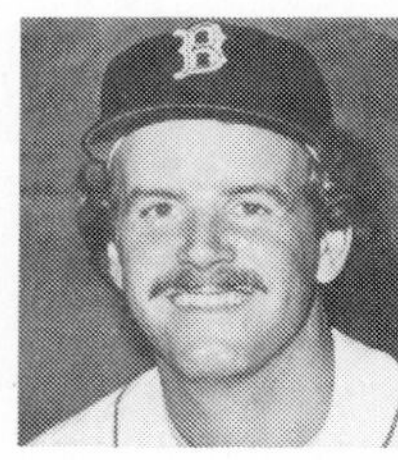

DAVE STAPLETON
INF, No. 11
RR, 6'1", 170 lbs.
ML Svc: 2 years
Born: 1-6-54 in Fairhope, AL

1982 STATISTICS

AVG	G	AB	R	H	2B	3B	HR	RBI	BB	SO	SB
.264	150	538	66	142	28	1	14	65	31	40	2

CAREER STATISTICS

AVG	G	AB	R	H	2B	3B	HR	RBI	BB	SO	SB
.288	349	1342	172	387	78	7	31	152	65	94	5

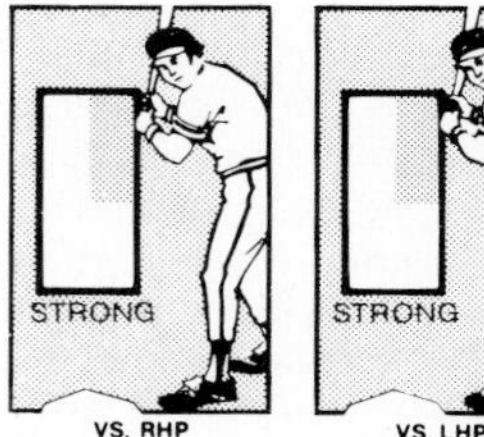

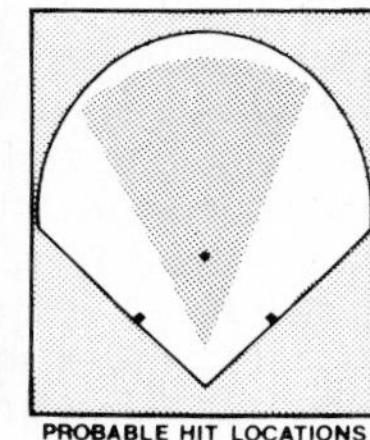

OVERALL:

An extremely versatile and dependable athlete in the field. He hits well and knows what he's doing with the bat. A genuine asset to the Red Sox.

Martin: "Dave is a sound hitter who's most effective when he goes with the pitch. When he tries to pull everything, he cuts down on his value to the club."

Robinson: "You have to find a spot in the lineup for Dave because he can help you in so many ways. He gets the utmost out of his abilities."

Harwell: "Stapleton is a versatile performer who should improve with experience."

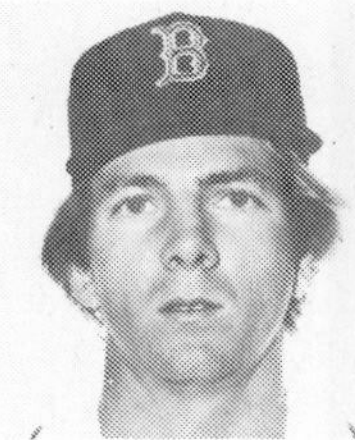

JOHN TUDOR
LHP, No. 30
LL, 6'0", 185 lbs.
ML Svc: 3 years
Born: 2-2-54 in Schenectady, NY

PITCHING:

John Tudor was manager Ralph Houk's pet project in the spring of 1982. Houk was determined to help mold him into a consistent major league starting pitcher. After a hot April, a dreary mid-season, and a good August, the jury is still out on Tudor. He has a strong arm and his fastball has been clocked close to the 90 MPH mark. That's the good news. His curve and change-up are just average, and his knuckleball is not good enough to be a consistent out pitch. Tudor also seemed to give up on his slider mid way though the season and is now regarded strictly as a fastball pitcher.

He wins as often as he does because he's developed excellent control of his fastball, and has learned to hit the inside corner of the plate against righties as well as lefties. This, and Tudor's reputation for being aggressive on the mound, keeps hitters from digging in and getting comfortable at the plate. Tudor's fastball also moves a lot and this helps keep hitters off balance. However, if John is going to have a truly successful major league career, he's going to have to develop better control of his breaking pitches.

FIELDING:

Tudor has an excellent move to first base, and picked off eleven runners during the past season. He's fairly agile fielding bunts and moves well to cover first on anything hit to the right side. John is rated average to above average as a fielder.

OVERALL:

1983 should be the year of decision for John Tudor. He seemed to find his confidence during the past season, and now knows that he can pitch in the majors. With an improved breaking ball, he might develop into a consistent winner, something Red Sox fans have been waiting a long time for.

Martin: "Tudor has a good arm and a live fastball. He turned it around in 1982, and looked aggressive and confident on the mound."

Harwell: "John has a great arm and a good future. He needs to work on his breaking pitches."

Robinson: "I like Tudor, but he's no longer a spring chicken. He has to develop consistency. He's been hot and cold for too much of his career."

1982 STATISTICS

W	L	ERA	G	GS	CG	IP	H	R	ER	BB	SO	SV
13	10	3.63	32	30	6	195	215	90	79	59	146	0

CAREER STATISTICS

W	L	ERA	G	GS	CG	IP	H	R	ER	BB	SO	SV
26	20	3.88	72	60	14	394	409	192	170	127	246	1

HITTING:

Carl Yastrzemski has an illustrious past which includes the MVP award and a bright future which undoubtably holds a place in the Hall of Fame. However, in the more immediate future, Yaz will probably be confined to limited duty as a DH or pinch-hitter against right-handed pitching.

At age 43, Yaz is still able to get around on the fastball, and still strong enough to drive the ball up the alley or over the right field wall. He prefers low, inside pitches but still manages to make contact wherever the ball is pitched. Pitchers like Tommy John who throw a lot of off-speed curves have become the most difficult for Carl to handle. Other pitchers have fair success against him with sliders in on the hands and fastballs up and away.

Yastrzemski is still rated above average in clutch situations, and he obviously relishes coming to the plate with men in scoring position. He's always had a superior batting eye and over the years has acquired the discipline to lay off bad pitches.

OVERALL:

1983 will be Yaz's final year, and he will see limited, if any, action defensively. He runs the bases carefully and at his age rival pitchers don't have to worry him taking too long a lead. Yaz will end his career as a hitter, and the fans who come out to see him at Fenway will still get their money's worth.

CARL YASTRZEMSKI
INF, No. 8
LR, 5'11", 185 lbs.
ML Svc: 22 years
Born: 8-22-39 in Southampton, NY

1982 STATISTICS

AVG	G	AB	R	H	2B	3B	HR	RBI	BB	SO	SB
.275	131	459	53	126	22	1	16	72	59	50	0

CAREER STATISTICS

AVG	G	AB	R	H	2B	3B	HR	RBI	BB	SO	SB
.286	3189	11608	1778	3318	622	59	442	1788	1791	1364	168

VS. RHP

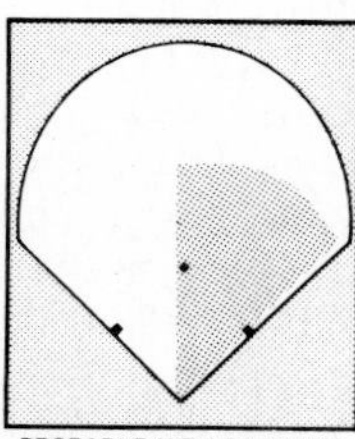
PROBABLE HIT LOCATIONS

Harwell: "A future Hall of Famer --a great clutch hitter, team player, and leader."

Martin: "Will do it one more time in 1983, probably as a DH against right-handed pitching. A sure Hall of Famer when it's all over."

Robinson: "He works hard to stay in shape. He's also a true inspiration to the other men on the team."

GARY ALLENSON
C, No. 39
RR, 5'11", 185 lbs.
ML Svc: 4 years
Born: 2-4-55 in Culver City, CA

HITTING, BASERUNNING, FIELDING:

Allenson is more valuable to the team catching the ball than hitting it. Lacks the power to consistently drive the ball up the alley or even to take advantage of the short left field wall in Fenway. Pitchers feed Allenson a steady diet of curves on the outside half of the plate. He has a lot of trouble adjusting to change-ups and hard sliders. He can manage to surprise rival clubs by knocking in an important run. Whether he just concentrates harder in tough situations, or if opposing pitchers simply get careless is hard to determine.

Allenson is slow getting to first and smart enough to know it. He'll never steal a base and he won't distract rival pitchers. Will be pinch-run for.

He is familiar with opposing batters and is confident of his ability to call a smart game. The pitching staff respects Allenson, and he handles their strengths, weaknesses, and quirks exceptionally well. Arm is rated average to above average in terms of strength as well as accuracy. Works hard to block bad pitches and handles bunts in front of the plate quickly and effectively.

OVERALL:

Allenson is a platoon or back up catcher. Doubtful that he could ever become a full-time starter with his weak bat.

Martin: "Gary is a gutsy, plug-away catcher who has handled all the disparaging comparisons with Fisk very well. He does the best with his ability and that's enough to help the Sox."

Robinson: "Gary gives the Sox a good job behind the plate. When he hits, it's an unexpected bonus."

GLENN HOFFMAN
INF, No. 18
RR, 6'2", 180 lbs.
ML Svc: 3 years
Born: 7-7-58 in Orange, CA

HITTING, BASERUNNING, FIELDING:

Hoffman has yet to prove that he can hit consistently against major league pitching. Glenn has trouble with anything on the inside half of the plate. A good fastball ties him up and he can be overpowered by most of the right-handed pitchers in the league. The major league curveball still seems to be a mystery to Hoffman, and he can also be fooled with change-ups and good sinkers. Has tried a vigorous off-season conditioning program but fails to show any improvement.

Hoffman is rated average in speed, and is cautious to a fault, seldom worries opposing pitchers, and almost never tries to stretch a hit or go for an extra base.

Hoffman moved from third base to shortstop. His arm is exceptionally strong--in fact it's rated as one of the best in the league--and he throws with outstanding accuracy. His range at short is also top-rate. Hoffman may be a step better going to his right, hangs in well against hard sliding runners, and turns the double play effectively.

OVERALL:

Hoffman has to hit better if he's going to stay in the majors. An excellent defensive shortstop who, thanks to his outstanding arm, can also make the spectacular play.

Robinson: "Glenn is sure to improve as a hitter. He's a smart kid, he works hard, and has a great attitude. I don't think he's as bad at bat as he seemed last year."

Martin: "Glenn is a quality defensive shortstop. He has to improve his hitting and I think he will."

RICK MILLER
OF, No. 3
LL, 6'0", 185 lbs.
ML Svc: 11 years
Born: 4-19-48 in
Grand Rapids, MI

HITTING, BASERUNNING, FIELDING:

Miller only bats regularly against righthanded pitching. He is primarily an opposite field hitter. He lacks the power to hit the ball up the alleys, but can start late inning rallies and keep them alive.

Miller has trouble getting around on fastballs that are thrown up and in. Righthanded pitchers give him a lot of curves and hard sliders. It's a mistake to throw Miller an off-speed pitch. Never a feared hitter in the league, Rick saw less action last season, and his average droppped almost 30 points.

Miller is frisky on the bases. Runs hard to break up the double play, and works to distract a pitcher. Doesn't try to steal as often as he once did, and is not as aggressive as in the past.

Miller gets an outstanding jump on the ball. Knows where to play hitters, making his range appear greater than it really is. Gets the ball off quickly, but his arm isn't actually that strong. Accuracy is above average. Miller seldom makes an error, and gets his hands on almost everything.

OVERALL:

Rick covers the ground in center field and gets his share of big hits for the Red Sox. He will probably be platooned again next year.

Robinson: "Miller is a platoon player who does a good job in center field. I think he's still underrated as a player."

Harwell: "Rick is a fine outfielder with excellent range."

Martin: "Rick is a quiet pro who does his job well. He provides excellent defense and is a pleasure to watch in center."

JULIO VALDEZ
INF, No. 12
SR, 6'2", 160 lbs.
ML Svc: 1 year plus
Born: 7-3-56 in
San Cristobal, DR

HITTING, BASERUNNING, FIELDING:

Valdez is a switch-hitter who does better hitting lefthanded than right, but with only twenty at-bats that's hardly conclusive. Valdez has never been impressive with his bat either with the Red Sox or in the minor leagues. He can hit an average fastball but he can also be overpowered. Major league curves, change-ups, and sliders still seem to puzzle him. It doesn't look as if he'll ever get a chance to play regularly with Boston.

Valdez has above average speed and this will make pitchers aware when, and if, he's on base.

His fielding is what brought Valdez to the majors. He has excellent range at short and an above average arm. However, his throws to first can be erratic. Julio has the ability to make unbelievable plays in the hole or in back of the bag, but he's also displayed a tendency to make an error on a routine ground ball.

OVERALL:

It's hard to evaluate Valdez's potential as a big league infielder. His hitting has always been suspect and his ability to make the big play defensively has to be measured against his inconsistency.

Robinson: "Valdez can come off the bench and give you three or four days of steady play. He's still an untested player. The future will have to tell."

Martin: "Julio could possibly be a good shortstop for some other team. I don't think he'll get enough opportunity to prove himself with the Red Sox."

ANAHEIM STADIUM
California Angels

Seating Capacity: 65,158
Playing Surface: Natural Grass

Dimensions
Left Field Pole: 333 ft.
Left-Center Field: 386 ft.
Center Field: 404 ft.
Right-Center Field: 386 ft.
Right Field Pole: 333 ft.
Height of Outfield Wall: 8 ft.

The dimensions and working facilities at the home park of the California Angels seem to suggest that the same designer who worked on Royals Stadium was also in Anaheim. That's true, because Cedric Tallis, current vice president of the New York Yankees, was the mastermind behind the erection of both Anaheim and Royals Stadium. Unlike Royals Stadium, however, the Angels play on natural (Hybrid Bermuda) grass. The dimensions are symmetrical and very similar to the home of the Kansas City Royals.

The park was originally (like Royals Stadium) built with the seats in a horseshoe fashion. Center field was open, but in 1979, new construction (to add seats for the NFL Los Angeles Rams) closed the center field opening. Although viewing is a pleasure from anywhere in the park, the enclosure in center has caused complaints from many hitters, who claim they cannot pick up the ball when it is released from the pitcher's hand.

The infield dirt is reddish and comprised of hard clay. It is an extremely fast infield and, coupled with low-cropped grass in the infield, allows ground balls to elude infielders. When the ball is traveling well, righthanders can easily hit homers to the opposite field and lefties can do the same. The park has shown that a power hitter like Reggie Jackson can hit the ball to any field and add another homer to his growing total.

In the day time, balls travel much further . . . and faster . . . than they do at nighttime. The Angels schedule many of their games for a six o'clock starting time. It was then, at twilight, that the ball is extremely difficult to pick up, and it was usually on those days the Angels pencilled in Nolan Ryan to start. Ryan, of course, has since departed to the Houston Astros, so American League batters do not have to worry about his 100 MPH fastball buzzing past them as dusk approaches.

JUAN BENIQUEZ
OF, No. 12
RR, 5'11", 175 lbs.
ML Svc: 11 years
Born: 5-13-50 in
San Sebastian, DR

1982 STATISTICS

AVG	G	AB	R	H	2B	3B	HR	RBI	BB	SO	SB
.265	112	196	25	52	11	2	3	24	15	21	3

CAREER STATISTICS

AVG	G	AB	R	H	2B	3B	HR	RBI	BB	SO	SB
.257	930	2915	375	750	126	24	45	270	218	339	24

HITTING:

Your basic pull hitter, Juan Beniquez is a platoon player who can be useful against lefthanded pitchers. Righthanders have made him a below average hitter, fooling him with the breaking stuff away. Beniquez can also be struck out with a good, low fastball on the inside part of the plate.

Although he does not handle off-speed pitches well, he can hurt pitchers who try and slip a fastball up past him. He hits line drives, mostly against lefties. Against righties, he'll hit the ball on the ground, especially if a pitcher has a sinker.

With Gene Mauch as manager, Beniquez also was effective with the hit-and-run and became a fine bunter. He has some speed, and can be a very effective player when used properly, although he tends toward streakiness. Some feel he has not played up to his full potential.

BASERUNNING:

There is nothing special about Beniquez as a runner. Even though he has some speed, he is not a serious threat to steal. He is also unsure of himself on the basepaths, and at times, will run too conservatively.

FIELDING:

Fielding is Beniquez' strongest department. He can go get the ball, coming in or running back, and gets a good jump. He has an above average arm, and is a good defensive player for late innings to protect a lead.

OVERALL:

Robinson: "Juan gave California a good year, playing in and out of the lineup. Has been a valuable player . . . (as a platoon man). I think that is his best bet at this stage of his career."

BOB BOONE
C, No. 8
RR, 6'2", 202 lbs.
ML Svc: 10 years
Born: 11-19-47 in San Diego, CA

1982 STATISTICS

AVG	G	AB	R	H	2B	3B	HR	RBI	BB	SO	SB
.256	143	472	42	121	17	0	7	58	39	34	0

CAREER STATISTICS

AVG	G	AB	R	H	2B	3B	HR	RBI	BB	SO	SB
.260	1268	4162	391	1081	189	21	72	514	404	345	23

VS. RHP

VS. LHP

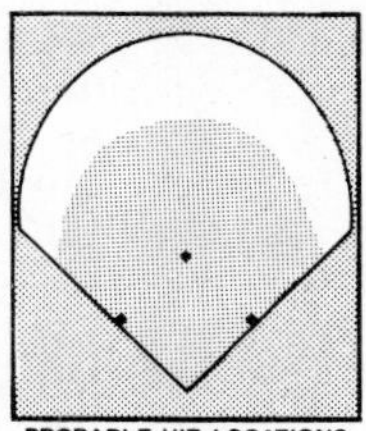
PROBABLE HIT LOCATIONS

HITTING:

Bob Boone is extremely effective at what his former Manager Gene Mauch calls "Little Ball." He has superb bat control and is a reliable bunter in sacrifice and squeeze situations. He is also capable of executing the hit-and-run and in scoring runners from third on sacrifice flies. In other words, he is an intelligent hitter. He is also strong in clutch situations, and helps make the bottom of the Angels' batting order formidable.

Boone is vulnerable to breaking pitches, particularly down and away. He likes fastballs up and over the plate, and shows occasional power with such pitches. He is more effective against lefthanded pitchers, but has become adept at handling righthanded pitchers as well. He has learned to spray the ball to all fields. Overall, he is not the hitter he was in his younger days, but he is now a smarter hitter. He is among the game's most intelligent players.

BASERUNNING:

Boone's speed is slow, which prevents doing anything creative while he's on base. He is simply no threat to steal, or to take an extra base on a base hit. His one baserunning asset is that he's smart. He knows his liabilities and is not about to abuse them.

FIELDING:

His intelligence and ability make him among baseball's best catchers. Boone is of particular value to the Angels in that he handles their pitching staff so competently. He learned the American League hitters in an amazingly short amount of time. He is able to utilize a pitcher's strength, allowing them to pitch at levels equal to or above their ability.

Boone's arm is extremely accurate; his release is as quick as there is. He is most valuable to the Angels defensively.

OVERALL:

Robinson: "Bob Boone is a study in consistency. His ability to handle the staff is his biggest plus, as well as calling a great game."

Harwell: "He's a great catcher."

Martin: "One of the league's most intelligent catchers."

NOTE: In April 1982, Rick Burleson suffered a torn rotator cuff and missed the entire 1982 season. The following report is based on his pre-injury form.

RICK BURLESON
INF, No. 7
RR, 5'10", 160 lbs.
ML Svc: 8 years
Born: 4-29-51 in Lynwood, CA

1982 STATISTICS

AVG	G	AB	R	H	2B	3B	HR	RBI	BB	SO	SB
.156	11	45	4	7	1	0	0	2	6	3	0

CAREER STATISTICS

AVG	G	AB	R	H	2B	3B	HR	RBI	BB	SO	SB
.275	1151	4539	571	1247	221	22	43	395	358	401	71

VS. RHP

VS. LHP

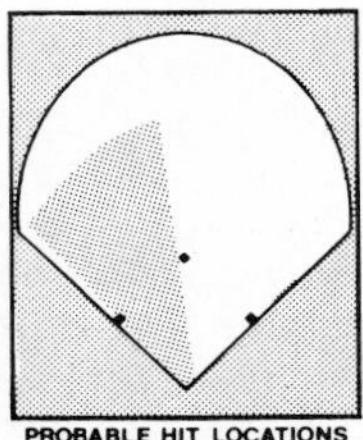
PROBABLE HIT LOCATIONS

HITTING:

Rick Burleson is one of those hitters who makes sure he gets the fullest possible measure out of each at-bat. He stands from a slight crouch, slightly closed stance, and has the ability to pull an inside fastball if the situation calls for it, or "inside-out" his swing and hit that very same pitch to the opposite field. He is much more dangerous with men on base, particularly with a runner on first, because, more so than any infielder in the league with the exception of MVP Robin Yount of the Brewers, Burleson can hit-and-run and hit behind the runner.

When he was with the Red Sox, Burleson had the reputation of actually bearing down too much as a hitter. When facing the Yankees, he invariably tried to win so much that he was affected both at the plate and in the field by the intensity of his desire to win and do well. With the Angels, before the rotator cuff injury, he seemed more at ease at the plate. He did not try to do too much, and had excellent success with the Angels and their powerful three-four-five and six hitters.

BASERUNNING:

He is the type of player you do not mind having on base in the later innings of a close game. He has speed and guts, and will go all-out to break up a double play or get the extra base. He is not afraid to knock over any infielder or catcher if he thinks he can take an extra base or score an important run.

FIELDING:

Burleson will commit several errors that make fans and players shake their heads--but when the money is on the line, he will make plays that only the premier shortstops could even try. Although he is a bit faster than Bucky Dent of Texas, Burleson, like Dent, knows how to position himself at short, and will frequently take away a base hit by playing in the right spot. He turns over the double play as well as any shortstop in the league, and is not afraid of contact around the bag.

OVERALL:

Burleson's arm was one of his greatest assets as a shortstop, and it remains to be seen if he can overcome the shoulder injury. If the rotator cuff does not heal sufficiently, Burleson may have to be moved to second or possibly third. With top-quality, time-tested players like Bobby Grich and Doug DeCinces at those spots, Burleson may not have any move to make. His entire future as an All Star shortstop depends on his recovery.

ROD CAREW
INF, No. 29
LR, 6'0", 182 lbs.
ML Svc: 16 years
Born: 10-1-45 in
Gatun, Pan. CZ

1982 STATISTICS

AVG	G	AB	R	H	2B	3B	HR	RBI	BB	SO	SB
.319	138	523	88	167	25	5	3	44	67	49	10

CAREER STATISTICS

AVG	G	AB	R	H	2B	3B	HR	RBI	BB	SO	SB
.331	2120	8071	1247	2672	396	106	85	91	857	894	338

VS. RHP

VS. LHP

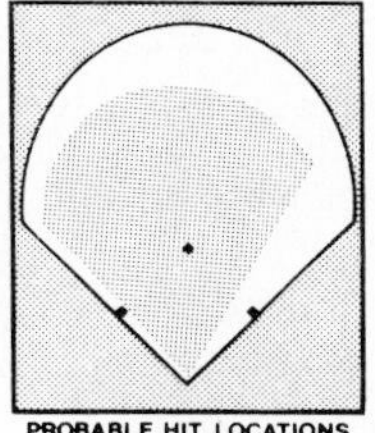
PROBABLE HIT LOCATIONS

HITTING:

How do you pitch to a career .330 hitter? With men in scoring position is the best way to pitch to Rod Carew, who remains an incredible hitter with the bases empty, and yet something else in clutch situations.

Carew employs a crouched open stance from which he can spray the ball to all fields. If there is a "best way" to pitch him, perhaps it is inside, for he is not a strong pull hitter. Even then, he has the ability to fight off an inside pitch and loop it to the opposite field.

He is strictly a line drive singles hitter. Occasionally, he will drive the ball up an alley or hit a home run. The defense should play him slightly toward left field.

There likely isn't a pitcher alive who can retire Carew consistently. Perhaps the best way to get him out is with a lefthanded junk pitcher who has superb control. Even then . . .

An added dimension to Carew's offense is his bunting ability. He may be the best in baseball. The manner in which he bunts makes it nearly impossible to tell that he's bunting until the pitch has reached home plate.

BASERUNNING:

He is no longer the basestealing threat he once was, though he is not an automatic out when he does run. He is an extremely smart baserunner who will turn a single into a double should an outfielder hesitate.

His speed is still above average, and the pitchers must beware of his presence. He is not much of a threat to break up a double play, however.

FIELDING:

Carew simply refuses to keep a ground ball or line drive in front of him. If it is hit at him, he will try to sidestep it, then backhand it. He will not dive for a ball and his range is limited, even for a first baseman. He has difficulty in catching a throw from another infielder unless it is directly to him. He will not stretch for a throw. His arm is average, at best, but his accuracy is efficient enough. Fielding is not his strong point.

OVERALL:

Martin: "One of the game's best pure hitters, as his record attests. He's hard to defense in the infield. But he tends to be a selfish hitter."

Harwell: "A real magician with the bat."

Robinson: "You can't get him out the same way twice in a row."

BOBBY CLARK
OF, No. 32
RR, 6'0", 190 lbs.
ML Svc: 2 years
Born: 6-13-55 in Sacramento, CA

1982 STATISTICS

AVG	G	AB	R	H	2B	3B	HR	RBI	BB	SO	SB
.211	102	90	11	19	1	0	2	8	0	29	1

CAREER STATISTICS

AVG	G	AB	R	H	2B	3B	HR	RBI	BB	SO	SB
.237	233	493	57	117	15	4	12	55	23	100	2

VS. RHP

VS. LHP

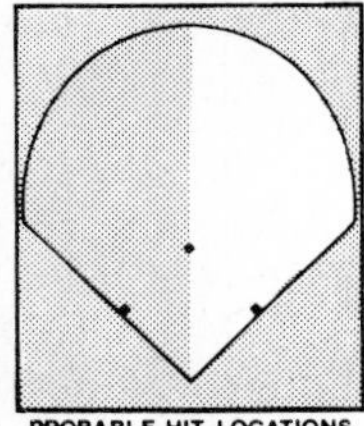
PROBABLE HIT LOCATIONS

HITTING:

The verdict on Bobby Clark offensively remains in doubt. He has never had an opportunity to play every day in the major leagues, though those around him say he has the ability to hit 20 or more home runs. Teammate Reggie Jackson said Clark has one of the top five pure home run swings in the American League.

Clark employs an upright, squared stance, and stands fairly deep in the batter's box. He is a high ball hitter who is most effective with high fastballs over the plate. Like most power hitters, the best way to pitch to him is to throw him breaking balls down and away. He will have some problems with inside pitches, too. He can also be struck out by changing speeds, primarily due to his lack of experience.

Clark has the ability to hit for power, but has not been given an opportunity to show what he can do in the clutch.

BASERUNNING:

Clark has better than average speed and is an aggressive player, thus making him strong at breaking up double plays. He is not a strong threat to steal bases, but does not make many mistakes in running the basepaths. His running is mediocre, neither a strength nor a weakness.

FIELDING:

Clark may be one of the best outfielders in baseball, though he hasn't had much of an opportunity to show it. He has a strong throwing arm, and is quite accurate; runners should think twice about testing his arm. He gets a superb jump on the ball, and is not averse to diving for a ball. His hands are sure. He can charge a ball or go back on a ball with equal ability. Unquestionably, fielding is his strength.

OVERALL:

Martin: "He is a good defensive outfielder. He has some hitting potential because of his power."

Harwell: "A good young player with a bright future."

Robinson: "He has demonstrated that he can hit, hit with power, run and throw, but so far it hasn't been good enough. The only way he can improve is to play regularly. And he is getting to the point in his career where it is vital he does."

DOUG CORBETT
RHP, No. 23
RR, 6'1", 192 lbs.
ML Svc: 3 years
Born: 11-4-52 in Sarasota, FL

PITCHING:

At one time, Doug Corbett was among the premier relief pitchers in the American League. But that was with the Minnesota Twins, a non-contender at the time. With a contending team, he still must prove himself.

He is, and only can be, a short reliever. He throws almost sidearm, and his best pitch is a sinkerball. When it works, it enables him to get either a strikeout or a ground ball, both of which are vital to the success of a short relief pitcher. When his sinker is working, it is equally effective against both righthanded and lefthanded hitters.

Corbett's problem is consistency. Oftentimes, he will throw two hellacious sinkers, then hang the third one. He also has a problem with control. If the umpire is not giving him the low strike, he tends to come up too high with it and it is hit hard.

His ability in the clutch was once respected, but that has changed in the course of a dismal 1982 season.

FIELDING:

He has an average move to first, made so by the fact he throws everything sidearm. Corbett can field bunts well, for his follow-through puts him in a position ready to field. Basically, though, he is an average fielder.

OVERALL:

Martin: "He has the mental makeup of the short reliever. He also has the ability to come back to his 1981 form and be a prime reliever."

Robinson: "It was a long year for Corbett in 1982. His pitches were not doing the same thing that they did in the past."

Harwell: "His sinker makes him a strong reliever and he has a good command of his pitches."

1982 STATISTICS

W	L	ERA	G	GS	CG	IP	H	R	ER	BB	SO	SV
1	9	5.13	43	0	0	79	73	45	45	35	52	11

CAREER STATISTICS

W	L	ERA	G	GS	CG	IP	H	R	ER	BB	SO	SV
11	21	2.97	170	0	0	303	255	105	100	111	201	51

JOHN CURTIS
LHP, No. 51
LL, 6'2", 185 lbs.
ML Svc: 11 years
Born: 3-9-48 in
Newton, MA

PITCHING:

John Curtis has spent the majority of his career as a starting pitcher, but also has been employed in long relief by managers who cannot understand his inconsistency. An overhand pitcher with an erect delivery, Curtis has an average big league fastball clocked at 84-86 MPH, an average curve and a below average change-up. He throws an occasional slider.

When he has control of his best two pitches, the curveball and fastball, Curtis is capable of shutting out even the best of teams. When he is unable to throw his curve for strikes, or on days when it doesn't break normally, he has trouble lasting more than a few innings.

Curtis knows how to pitch but must spot his pitches to be effective. He gives up long home runs when he is unable to keep the ball low in the strike zone and get batters to hit the ball on the ground. His fastball tails away from righthanded hitters and it is a pitch he can use to jam lefthanders when he's on his stick. Although he walks too many batters, his biggest problem is getting behind in the count and having to come over the middle of the plate.

Curtis is only slightly more effective against lefthanders than righthanders, and has problems in small ballparks such as Wrigley Field because he gives up a lot of long fly balls. He'll throw the breaking ball when he's behind in the count, providing he's having a day when he can throw it for a strike. Curtis has had back and shoulder problems that have contributed to his inconsistency.

FIELDING, HITTING, BASERUNNING:

Curtis is an average fielder who needs to improve his move to first to keep baserunners from taking so many liberties. He is an average major league bunter who greatly improved his hitting in 1982, winning two games with his bat. He struck out 40% of the time, but averaged .500 when he made contact. Curtis is a below average baserunner lacking speed to go from first to third on most singles, and is no threat to steal.

OVERALL:

Intelligent and conscientious, Curtis must overcome physical problems and acquire more consistent control, but is aided by the fact that there is a shortage of experienced lefthanded pitchers in the majors and by changing leagues.

Coleman: "Curtis does not have a strong body and lacks endurance. He could be coming to the end of his career."

McCarver: "He has good stuff but is erratic with his control. He falls behind in the count too often."

Kiner: "Probably at the end of his career."

1982 STATISTICS

W	L	ERA	G	GS	CG	IP	H	R	ER	BB	SO	SV
8	6	4.10	26	18	1	116	121	62	53	46	54	0

CAREER STATISTICS

W	L	ERA	G	GS	CG	IP	H	R	ER	BB	SO	SV
87	92	3.95	376	196	42	1510	1560	742	662	615	761	4

HITTING:

Doug DeCinces has proven that he can be one of the game's dangerous hitters. He stands upright with a closed stance, and pitchers will pay if they make a mistake and send him a pitch from the waist up. Although he prefers fastballs, he can also handle the curve if it's up. DeCinces should be pitched away with breaking stuff, but can sometimes be caught leaning; thus, a hard fastball down and in will work, too.

DeCinces is a line drive hitter with power. When playing for Baltimore, he had bouts of streakiness, but was more consistent in 1982 for California. He still retains some of that streakiness, however, but Doug is a power hitter who can go on a tear with the long ball.

He bears down with runners in scoring position, but because of the lingering suspicions of his inconsistent bat, DeCinces cannot always be counted on to advance or move the baserunners along. The 1983 season should be more telling.

BASERUNNING:

DeCinces has average speed but can be aggressive. He will surprise a pitcher who ignores him, and does a decent job of breaking up a double play.

FIELDING:

In a word, DeCinces' fielding is outstanding. He makes all the routine plays and can be spectacular, too. Whether he goes to his left or with his backhand, DeCinces is an excellent clutch defensive fielder. He is perhaps finally getting the credit he deserves playing in California, rather than in Baltimore where he was compared often with Brooks Robinson.

DOUG DeCINCES
INF, No. 11
RR, 6'2", 194 lbs.
ML Svc: 10 years
Born: 8-29-50 in
Burbank, CA

1982 STATISTICS

AVG	G	AB	R	H	2B	3B	HR	RBI	BB	SO	SB
.301	153	575	94	173	42	5	30	97	66	80	7

CAREER STATISTICS

AVG	G	AB	R	H	2B	3B	HR	RBI	BB	SO	SB
.261	1011	3491	467	911	203	19	137	494	364	536	47

VS. RHP

VS. LHP

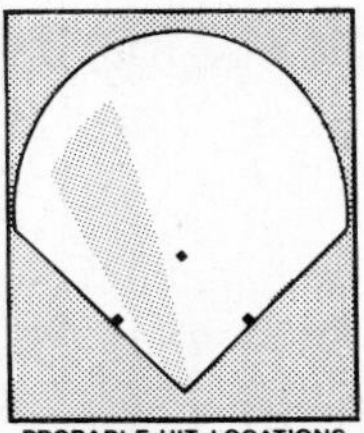
PROBABLE HIT LOCATIONS

OVERALL:

Martin: "A solid all around player. He hits with power and drives people in. Doug has become a fine defensive third baseman, tremedously improved over the last three years."

BRIAN DOWNING
C, No. 5
RR, 5'10", 200 lbs.
ML Svc: 9 years
Born: 10-9-50 in
Los Angeles, CA

1982 STATISTICS

AVG	G	AB	R	H	2B	3B	HR	RBI	BB	SO	SB
.281	158	623	109	175	37	2	28	84	86	58	2

CAREER STATISTICS

AVG	G	AB	R	H	2B	3B	HR	RBI	BB	SO	SB
.267	1015	3226	416	861	142	9	84	410	484	449	30

VS. RHP

VS. LHP

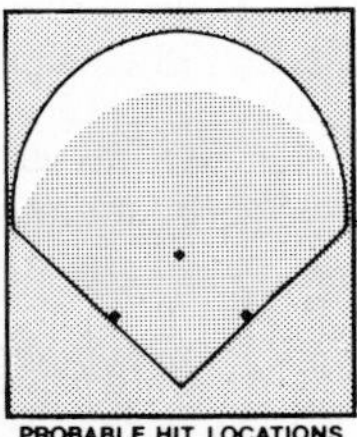
PROBABLE HIT LOCATIONS

HITTING:

Brian Downing has made himself physically into a superb hitter, one who can hit for power as well as average. He uses a wide open stance which enables him to see pitches better. But when he strides into a pitch, he is square to the plate, slightly crouched. He can utilize most of the field. Pitch him away and he will go to right field. Pitch him in and he will pull the ball to left field. He is particularly effective in clutch situations.

Downing is strong enough to hit either a mistake or a good pitch out of the park. His weaknesses would be in hitting a curveball-away from a right-handed pitcher, and a good hard slider inside from a lefthander.

He became the Angels' leadoff hitter and adjusted amazingly well. Realizing that he was not a threat to steal second, he concentrated on driving the ball more, looking for the extra base hit. He is an aggressive hitter, but one with a keen eye, too. He often walks.

Downing is remarkably consistent. Before he slumps too far, he corrects whatever it was he is doing wrong. He is a strong hitter.

BASERUNNING:

Downing is an aggressive baserunner, who always runs hard. He is strong in taking a fielder out on a potential double play. His speed is average at best, but he will always run out grounders, and his strength makes him a threat to overpower a catcher on a play at the plate.

FIELDING:

Once he accepted the fact that he no longer was a catcher and that he would be a left fielder, Downing worked extremely hard at his new position. So hard, in fact, that he made himself into an extremely valuable outfielder, one who did not commit an error in 158 games in left field in 1982. He plays the position aggressively; he is willing to crash into fences or dive for fly balls in an effort to make a catch. He rarely makes a mistake, and almost never throws to the wrong base.

His range is average, limited by his lack of speed. His arm is below average, the result of chronic arm problems. But he makes up for his liabilities with his intelligence.

OVERALL:

Robinson: "An outstanding job as a leadoff man. A strong righthanded hitter. Anytime your leadoff hitter has 20 or more home runs, you know you have a team that can hit. He went to left field reluctantly, but has made himself into a good one."

Martin: "He is a good aggressive, hustling player, who has extra base power and knocks in runs."

JOE FERGUSON
C, No. 13
RR, 6'2", 190 lbs.
ML Svc: 13 years
Born: 9-19-46 in
San Francisco, CA

1982 STATISTICS

AVG	G	AB	R	H	2B	3B	HR	RBI	BB	SO	SB
.226	36	84	10	19	2	0	3	8	12	19	0

CAREER STATISTICS

AVG	G	AB	R	H	2B	3B	HR	RBI	BB	SO	SB
.241	1001	2974	404	717	121	11	122	443	567	599	22

VS. RHP

VS. LHP

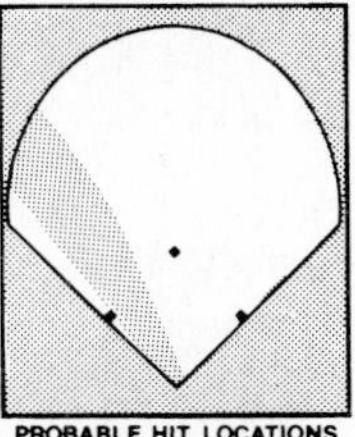
PROBABLE HIT LOCATIONS

HITTING:

Despite the fact that Joe Ferguson has a lot of holes in his swing, a pitcher still cannot make a mistake pitching to him. A pull hitter, he not only has trouble with breaking pitches, off-speed, he also has occasional difficulty handling the fastball down and away. He can hurt you with power on a fastball up and over the plate.

Ferguson also is a very unaggressive hitter. He can draw walks, but is quite often caught on called third strikes. He is constantly looking for that one fastball in his zone and seldom gets it. When he was playing regularly, Ferguson tended toward being a streak hitter.

BASERUNNIG:

When he was a Los Angeles Dodger, some players joked about the "Joe Ferguson School of Baserunning." He has better speed than he has generally been given credit for, but lacks good baserunning instincts.

FIELDING:

As a catcher, Ferguson studies opposing batters and calls most of the games. He presents a good target. His arm strength is above average, though his quickness, release point and accuracy are mediocre. Ferguson is on an off-season weight program to improve in these areas. He does an adequate job of blocking balls in the dirt, but is so-so when it comes to taking throws from the outfield and blocking the plate. For his size, he is a fair athlete who also can play in the outfield.

OVERALL:

Martin: "Valuable as a back up and trade bait."

TIM FOLI
INF, No. 20
RR, 6'0", 175 lbs.
ML Svc: 12 years
Born: 12-8-50 in
Culver City, CA

1982 STATISTICS

AVG	G	AB	R	H	2B	3B	HR	RBI	BB	SO	SB
.252	150	480	46	121	14	2	3	56	14	22	2

CAREER STATISTICS

AVG	G	AB	R	H	2B	3B	HR	RBI	BB	SO	SB
.251	1528	5517	538	1384	220	20	23	454	254	363	79

VS. RHP

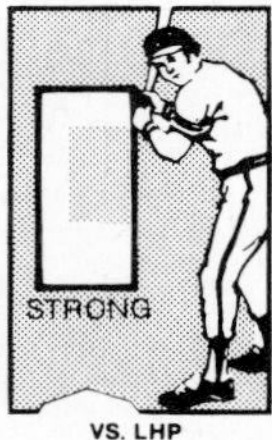

VS. LHP

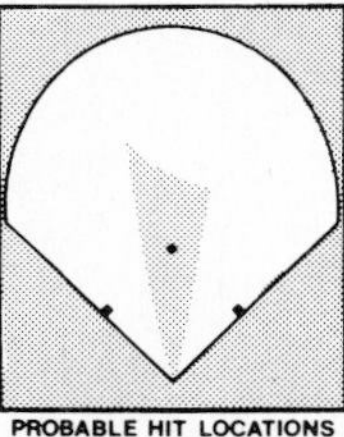
PROBABLE HIT LOCATIONS

HITTING:

Tim Foli is a straightaway hitter, and the defense can play this man shallow. But he is also a situational hitter who is one of the best at moving the runners along. He will take a semi-crouched stance occasionally, which enables him to hit the pitch he likes the best, the high fastball. Foli can be had by a good slider. He can generally be pitched away, but with a runner on first and the right side open, he should be pitched down and in.

Foli is a very tough strikeout and chokes up on the bat. He is one of the league's best bunters, but is unlikely to beat out many of them because of his average speed. He will occasionally try to fake bunt and slap the ball past the infielders.

Foli seems to be an ideal No. 2 hitter, but in the California lineup, with so many big RBI hitters at the top of the order, he was most effective in the No. 8 spot.

BASERUNNING:

Foli's baserunning is similar to his all around play: heady. He has average speed and is aggressive when breaking up a double play.

FIELDING:

In Pittsburgh, Foli lost much of his range on the artificial surface. But on the California grass, he is one of the league's most solid shortstops.

Originally obtained as a utility player, Foli proved to be one of the Angels' most valuable players when shortstop Rick Burleson went down early with a torn rotator cuff injury. He has shown above average range at times, and his power of concentration is excellent. Foli seldom muffed the routine plays. He combines with Bobby Grich for a strong double play combination.

OVERALL:

Robinson: "Tim is an old fashioned player. He comes to the park to win the game any way he can. He has done the job at shortstop, and that is what he has had to do. He certainly gets the most out of his ability."

KEN FORSCH
RHP, No. 43
RR, 6'4", 215 lbs.
ML Svc: 12 years
Born: 9-8-46 in Sacramento, CA

PITCHING:

Look for breaking balls from this guy. Ken Forsch throws a sinker, slider, curve and an occasional palmball. He needs to have control, and when he does have it, he is a good bet to win. He knows a batter's weaknesses and will consistently try to pitch to them from his three-quarter delivery.

He is particularly productive against a righthanded-hitting lineup. Forsch's sinker runs in on righties. His sinker can be devastating when it's on. Against lefthanders, he will throw a cut fastball that breaks two or three inches. His slider is sharp. Normally, Forsch has outstanding control.

He experienced an off-year in 1982. Some attribute it to his age, but most consider that excuse a cop-out because, it is a fastball pitcher, not a breaking ball pitcher, who is most susceptible to the ravages of time. He is not a strikeout pitcher, either. His problems come when he is not hitting spots, and then his sinker and slider will hang. When this happens, Forsch allows more than his share of home runs.

FIELDING:

There is nothing special about Forsch as a fielder, but he does not hurt himself in the field. He is usually ready to field his position because he knows he'll get a lot of ground balls. He has an average move to first base.

OVERALL:

Martin: "Forsch is steady and dependable. He has the ability to complete his game. He probably has more trouble on artificial turf because of his sinker. He is a class pitcher who works a steady, rhythmic game."

Harwell: "A solid sinker, slider pitcher with fine control."

Robinson: "He has a lot of confidence out there. I thought he would do better with the California defense. Forsch changes speeds well, but has to hit the right spot to get by."

1982 STATISTICS

W	L	ERA	G	GS	CG	IP	H	R	ER	BB	SO	SV
13	11	3.87	37	35	12	228	225	108	98	57	73	0

CAREER STATISTICS

W	L	ERA	G	GS	CG	IP	H	R	ER	BB	SO	SV
102	99	3.24	478	208	58	1873	1807	749	675	512	943	50

DAVE GOLTZ
RHP, No. 38
RR, 6'4", 215 lbs.
ML Svc: 11 years
Born: 6-23-49 in Pelican Rapids, MN

PITCHING:

Although he did give the Angels some good innings in relief, Dave Goltz is primarily a starter. After two worthless (at least, on the field) years with the Dodgers, he came back to the American League and was effective with a pitch that he had previously junked, the knucklecurve.

Goltz throws overhand to three-quarters. He has good movement on the ball when he's on, and his sinker must be going well in order for him to win. He also has a slider, which he uses often. The slider is his best pitch against righthanders.

Goltz' control is spotty. When he gets behind in the count, he comes in with his fastball, and it's not a good enough pitch to throw consistently. He does not brush batters back as often as he should. Goltz is enthusiastic about his job and has a "give me the ball" attitude.

If he regains some of the confidence he lost last year, he could become a 15-game winner once again.

FIELDING:

Goltz lacks general athletic ability, but fields his position adequately because he never loses control of himself. He is not afraid to charge the ball and field bunts. He has a good move to first, and throws there often. He is always accurate, even when hurried, displaying his good poise on the mound. He has improved tremendously at holding runners close to the bag.

OVERALL:

Robinson: "He should be a better pitcher than he is. He hasn't lost that much off of any pitch since his big years with Minnesota, but more than anything, however, I think he lost his confidence."

Martin: "I think Dave is still capable of being a decent pitcher. He needed this year to readjust to the American Leage. He's not worth all that money, but then again, who is?"

1982 STATISTICS

W	L	ERA	G	GS	CG	IP	H	R	ER	BB	SO	SV
8	5	4.08	28	7	1	86	82	43	39	32	49	3

CAREER STATISTICS

W	L	ERA	G	GS	CG	IP	H	R	ER	BB	SO	SV
113	102	3.61	336	257	83	1972	2017	898	790	609	1076	8

BOBBY GRICH
INF, No. 4
RR, 6'2", 190 lbs.
ML Svc: 12 years
Born: 1-15-49 in Muskegon, MI

HITTING:

Bobby Grich is classified as a pull hitter, but with his closed stance, he has excellent power to both alleys and can hit the ball out to any field. When he's having troubles, it's usually with the breaking ball. The up and in fastball and down and away breaking stuff give you the best chance of getting him out. He also can be fooled with an occasional change-up.

When Grich gets ahead on the count, he'll look for the fastball. If he does not get what he's looking for, he will take the pitch and has a good eye. He doesn't hesitate to walk.

Although he had a down year in 1982, he is the type of player who often bounces back with a superlative one right on its heels. Grich is an excellent competitor and a good clutch player with a tremendous amount of pride.

Grich is still in his peak years, unless he proves differently with another sub-par season. His back, which was operated on a couple of years ago, is always a concern.

1982 STATISTICS

AVG	G	AB	R	H	2B	3B	HR	RBI	BB	SO	SB
.261	145	506	74	132	28	5	19	65	82	109	3

CAREER STATISTICS

AVG	G	AB	R	H	2B	3B	HR	RBI	BB	SO	SB
.267	744	5348	792	1427	253	43	168	661	834	1015	96

VS. RHP

VS. LHP

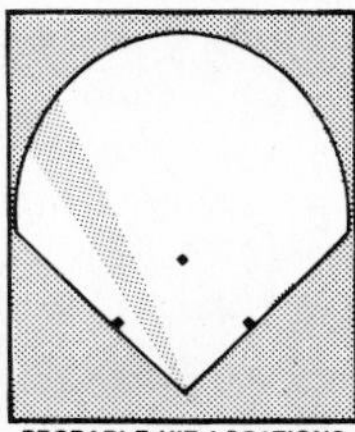
PROBABLE HIT LOCATIONS

BASERUNNING:

Considering that there are a lot of second basemen in the league who can run, Grich gets lower grades in terms of speed and basestealing. He is an intelligent runner, however, capable of taking the extra base if an outfielder ignores him.

FIELDING:

A former Gold Glove winner, Grich remains one of the best in the field. He has above average range and, despite his back problems, plays with reckless abandon. He possesses a strong arm and throws overhand. Although he looks awkward when turning the double play, he is excellent, on target, and fearless.

OVERALL:

Robinson: "Grich is a very good player who does a lot of things for you. He did not have quite the year he did during last two, but is still one of the best. He is tough and comes to play."

ANDY HASSLER
LHP, No. 41
LL, 6'5", 220 lbs.
ML Svc: 9 years
Born: 10-18-51 in Texas City, TX

PITCHING:

Hassler can be used in either short or long relief, and can be equally effective in either role. He is at his best, however, in a short relief role, usually pitching to one or two batters as long as they are lefthanders. When one out is needed and the batter is lefthanded, Hassler usually is the man to go to.

He is a large man who can be called a power pitcher. He possesses a good fastball, but his hard slider, delivered from three-quarters, is his most effective. His fastball is his out pitch.

Unquestionably, Hassler is a more effective pitcher against lefthanders. His size and the angle with which he delivers his pitches prevents lefthanded hitters from digging in against him.

He is strong in pressure situations for he has the ability to consistently keep the ball down. His weakness is his control. If it is off, he will issue walks in key situations.

FIELDING:

The best that can be said of Hassler's fielding is that it is mediocre. His move to first is only average despite the fact he is lefthanded.

OVERALL:

Martin: "Hassler is very durable, with strong enough stuff to be effective as a short reliever. He had great potential, but has not realized it."

Robinson: "He has gone from a mediocre starter to an outstanding reliever."

1982 STATISTICS

W	L	ERA	G	GS	CG	IP	H	R	ER	BB	SO	SV
2	1	2.78	54	0	0	71	58	24	22	40	38	4

CAREER STATISTICS

W	L	ERA	G	GS	CG	IP	H	R	ER	BB	SO	SV
43	65	3.78	332	112	26	1074	1070	532	451	497	604	25

REGGIE JACKSON
OF, No. 44
LL, 6'0", 208 lbs.
ML Svc: 15 years
Born: 5-18-46 in Wyncote, PA

1982 STATISTICS

AVG	G	AB	R	H	2B	3B	HR	RBI	BB	SO	SB
.275	153	530	92	146	17	1	39	101	85	156	4

CAREER STATISTICS

AVG	G	AB	R	H	2B	3B	HR	RBI	BB	SO	SB
.272	2171	7727	1270	2099	379	43	464	1386	1066	1966	216

VS. RHP

VS. LHP

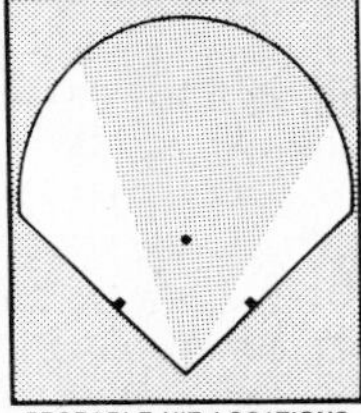
PROBABLE HIT LOCATIONS

HITTING:

Contrary to what many people might believe, Reggie Jackson's power is to straightaway center field. The majority of his home runs are hit to center and left-center fields. When playing in New York, he attempted to pull more pitches to take advantage of the short right field fence. At Anaheim Stadium, he has reverted back to hitting straightaway.

Jackson still seldom gets cheated on a swing. As a result, he continues to strike out frequently. He has shown few signs of slowing down with increasing age. He remains among baseball's best power and clutch hitters. He has some problems with lefthanded pitchers' breaking balls, and does not often make contact on a good high fastball. However, do not make any mistakes; he can hit one a long way.

He is an excellent low ball hitter, and his ability to hit to all fields makes location difficult. A pitcher ordinarily must fool him to get him out.

Jackson primarily is a streak hitter, one of the few players in baseball who can carry a team when he's hot. Despite his reputation as strictly a power hitter, he is also an extremely smart hitter. If a single will suffice, and a pitcher is throwing him breaking balls down and away, he will settle for a line drive single to left.

BASERUNNING:

Age has slowed him somewhat, but he always runs as hard as he can. Former California manager Mauch often said that Jackson had beaten out the highest number of infield singles on the club, through hustle more than speed. He is an aggressive baserunner, sometimes overly so. He is not a good slider.

FIELDING:

Jackson's arm is above average in strength, below average in accuracy. He has become very tentative in right field, apparently in an effort to prevent his looking bad. He has particular problems with balls hit over his head or into the right field corner. He is at an age where he will benefit himself and his team by being used more as a designated hitter.

OVERALL:

Martin: "He has terrifying power and the ability to deliver it in clutch situations. He makes things happen."

Robinson: "A unique personality and one who thrives on challenges. He is as good a player as there is when a game is on the line."

TOMMY JOHN
RHP, No. 25
RR, 6'3", 203 lbs.
ML Svc: 20 years
Born: 5-5-43 in
Terre Haute, IN

PITCHING:

The very fact that Tommy John is one of only eight pitchers to win 20 games in both the American and National Leagues attests to his success against any type of hitter, in any type of ballpark and in any type of weather. In addition to "any time, any place, any where," John can also pitch on artificial surface or natural grass, but obviously is more effective on grass.

It has been suggested that John "doctors" the baseball, causing it to sink unnaturally, but until caught, John must be considered baseball's premier sinkerball pitcher.

He works extremely rapidly while on the mound, and throws from a three-quarters motion. Against certain left-handers, like Carl Yastrzemski, Cecil Cooper and George Brett, John will drop to sidearm and throw a big breaking curve, something he does not use against righthanded hitters. When facing righties, John throws sinker, sinker, sinker, whether he is ahead or behind in the count. At times, John is actually more comfortable when behind in the count, particularly if he does use his very mediocre fastball. If a batter looks for a fastball, he will see one--John's fastball drops sharply as it approaches the hitting zone. He relies on a good infield defense, because at least two-thirds of his outs are on ground balls.

Because of his age and experience, when Tommy is pitching in bigger parks, he is not afraid to throw a sinker, curve or fastball out over the plate. Batters may tee off on a pitch above the knees, but they usually hit 400-foot fly balls to center field. John rarely uses his curve against righties, and has no slider to speak of. Instead of sinking, his fastball, when turned over, may break slightly in on righthanded hitters.

FIELDING:

John is slow coming of the mound on bunts, but does handle hard shots through the box better than most pitchers. He keeps runers close to their respective bases, either with frequent tosses or fake throws. John has been around for a long time, and with runners on base, he knows exactly where to throw to when he fields a grounder.

OVERALL:

Martin: "Tommy John is purely a professional pitcher. He came back from impossible elbow surgery to pitch and win. He should surely win 250-260 games. If a hitter tries to pull him, you'll have four ground ball outs. He is a class pitcher and person. He's got guts."

Robinson: "John is John. As they say in the business, he is a soft collar. (0-for-four)"

1982 STATISTICS

W	L	ERA	G	GS	CG	IP	H	R	ER	BB	SO	SV
14	12	3.69	37	33	10	221	239	102	91	39	68	0

CAREER STATISTICS

W	L	ERA	G	GS	CG	IP	H	R	ER	BB	SO	SV
237	171	3.05	580	535	145	3707	3563	1472	1256	996	1918	4

HITTING:

Mick Kelleher is one of the lightest-hitting players in baseball. He has no power--he has yet to hit a home run in the major leagues. He is not even much of a threat to get a base hit, as his pathetic career batting average will attest.

He uses a closed stance and crouches somewhat at the plate. If he has a strength, he can hit high pitches better than low pitches. He is a spray hitter, one who is more effective against lefthanded pitchers than righthanders. He can be struck out on most any pitch, but curveballs down and away will elude him nearly every time.

Kelleher is primarily a singles hitter and he almost never reaches the alleys. Hitting, obviously, is not his strength.

BASERUNNING:

Throughout his career, he has not had ample opportunity to display his baserunning skills. He possesses average speed, and in no way is a threat to steal a base. He is a cautious and intelligent runner.

FIELDING:

It is this aspect of Kelleher's game which enables him to remain in the major leagues. He is a foremost utility infielder, one capable of playing second base, shortstop or third base.

He is best at shortstop. He possesses soft, reliable hands and can field grounders with anyone in baseball. His range is limited, but he makes up for it by getting a strong jump. He is equally adept at fielding grounders to his left or right, and he is strong at turning the double play.

MICK KELLEHER
INF, No. 2
RR, 5'9", 170 lbs.
ML Svc: 10 years
Born: 7-25-47 in Seattle, WA

1982 STATISTICS

AVG	G	AB	R	H	2B	3B	HR	RBI	BB	SO	SB
.160	36	50	9	8	1	0	0	1	5	5	1

CAREER STATISTICS

AVG	G	AB	R	H	2B	3B	HR	RBI	BB	SO	SB
.213	622	1081	108	230	32	6	0	65	74	133	9

VS. RHP

VS. LHP

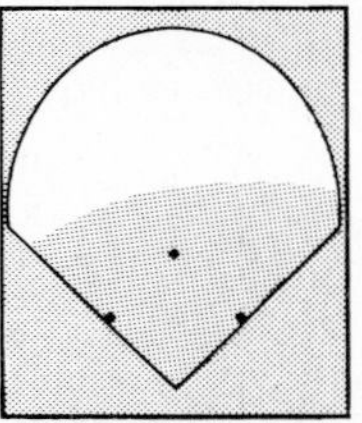
PROBABLE HIT LOCATIONS

Only his arm is a liability. He has had arm problems in the past and his throws to first are not very strong. However, he does have a super quick release. His defense is the strongest part of his game.

OVERALL:

Harwell: "He is a fine defensive player, but is quite limited on offense."

Robinson: "He fits the bill as a utility infielder. He's average in every department, but every team needs a player like this and he's happy to do the job."

BRUCE KISON
RHP, No.24
RR, 6'4", 180 lbs.
ML Svc: 12 years
Born: 2-18-50 in
Pasco, WA

PITCHING:

Bruce Kison has done some relieving, but his arm problems would indicate that he is best suited as a starter. He throws sidearm and three-quarters, and his irregular motion bothers some hitters.

He used to be a power pitcher, but since his arm surgery in 1980, Kison has gone more and more to the breaking ball. Still, he has the ability to pop a fastball, which runs in on righthanded hitters most of the time. He can get lefthanded hitters out, too, when he's changing speeds. Kison is a tough competitor and is not afraid at all to brush batters back.

Kison is at his best in pressure situations and has had uncanny success in September. He has guts and wants the ball all the time. Even when his curveball is lacking, which it often is, Kison is always in control and gets by on his nature as a competitor. He does not work more than 200 innings a year, however.

FIELDING:

Kison is quick and has a good move to first base. He has good mound savvy and will not beat himself. He is an average fielding pitcher, but is very intense.

OVERALL:

Martin: "Kison is a No. 3 or No. 4 type starter and is flexible enough to be used in relief. He is a little cute to hit at."

Robinson: "Kison was in and out of the rotation all year and, consequently, was very inconsistent. He is still recovering from arm problems, but look for him to do better in 1983. He seems to pitch better in the second half."

1982 STATISTICS

W	L	ERA	G	GS	CG	IP	H	R	ER	BB	SO	SV
10	5	3.17	33	16	3	142	120	54	50	44	86	1

CAREER STATISTICS

W	L	ERA	G	GS	CG	IP	H	R	ER	BB	SO	SV
95	75	3.53	312	49	200	1525	1395	695	598	559	868	7

FRED LYNN
OF, No. 19
LL, 6'1", 190 lbs.
ML Svc: 8 years
Born: 2-3-52 in Chicago, IL

1982 STATISTICS

AVG	G	AB	R	H	2B	3B	HR	RBI	BB	SO	SB
.299	138	472	89	141	38	1	21	86	58	72	1

CAREER STATISTICS

AVG	G	AB	R	H	2B	3B	HR	RBI	BB	SO	SB
.301	1042	3790	640	1141	263	31	150	638	478	508	45

VS. RHP

VS. LHP

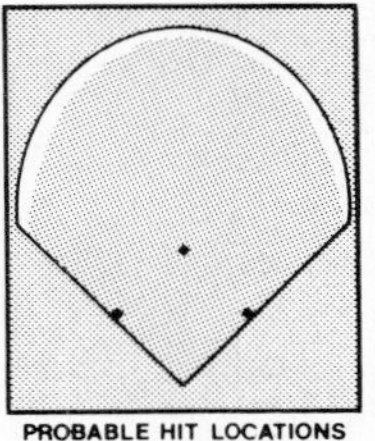
PROBABLE HIT LOCATIONS

HITTING:

Fred Lynn is the quintessence of versatility as a hitter. He can hit for power and hit for average. He can homer down the left field line as well as the right field line. Pitch him away and he'll hit to left. Pitch him in and he'll pull the ball.

Lynn uses a slightly closed stance, and crouches a bit. When he is swinging the bat well, it doesn't matter where the pitches are thrown--inside, outside, high or low, he can handle them. If he has a weakness, it is with a breaking ball delivered by a lefthanded pitcher. Sometimes he can be fooled by them and swings while leaning away from the plate, taking away his power, and usually, the chance for a hit.

It is best to pitch Lynn away, for although he can homer to left field, his power is in pulling the ball. It is better to serve up a single than a home run.

His swing is such that when his bat meets the ball, he is in perfect position, the kind that every hitter strives for. Lynn is a better than average clutch hitter, and one who can drive in runs in bunches when he's hot.

BASERUNNING:

Lynn has average to above average speed, but is not often a threat to steal a base. He is a conservative baserunner, but will not shy away from breaking up a double play. His baserunning ability might be considered the weakest aspect of his game.

FIELDING:

He is a former Gold Glove outfielder, who remains one of the game's best center fielders. He gets a remarkably quick jump on fly balls, which makes him appear faster than he really is. When he can get his glove on the ball, he seldom drops it. He plays the position aggressively, too, sometimes too much so, causing injury. Nevertheless, he is willing to dive or run into fences in pursuit of a fly ball.

His arm is above average, his accuracy strong. Given half a chance, he has the ability to cut down runners at home plate. He has equal ability in going back or coming in on fly balls.

OVERALL:

Martin: "A superior athlete, although injuries prevent him from being a superstar every year. He is one of the game's premier players, though somewhat injury prone. He can beat you with his bat or glove."

Harwell: "He is one of the most complete players in the league."

STEVE RENKO
RHP, No. 45
RR, 6'6", 240 lbs.
ML Svc: 13 years
Born: 12-10-44 in Kansas City, KS

PITCHING:

Steve Renko's former manager Gene Mauch liked to say that Renko "hired out for work," meaning that he would do anything asked of him and would work especially hard to be successful. He has been used as both a starter and a long reliever and has shown proficiency at both. He is the type of starter that you cannot expect to pitch nine innings. Rather, Renko will usually give six or seven strong innings, then turn the game over to a reliever.

Despite his size, Renko is not a power pitcher. His fastball is average, maybe slightly above, but it is its location that makes it effective. He must move the fastball around and keep hitters off balance. He has a decent curveball, too. His control is his strength; his durability his weakness. Nonetheless, Renko is a pitcher who has utilized his abilities to the utmost.

FIELDING:

Renko is an average fielder, but has been criticized for taking too long to deliver the ball to the plate, a weakness in most pitchers his size. He must work hard at keeping runners close to the base.

OVERALL:

Harwell: "Renko is a well travelled pitcher, but one with a good competitive attitude."

Robinson: "He is a big hard thrower who gives you his best every time out."

Martin: "Renko is a good hard worker, a gamer. Give him the ball every fifth day and he'll do the job. He has class. He is more than just a journeyman."

1982 STATISTICS

W	L	ERA	G	GS	CG	IP	H	R	ER	BB	SO	SV
11	6	4.44	31	23	4	156	163	78	77	51	81	0

CAREER STATISTICS

W	L	ERA	G	GS	CG	IP	H	R	ER	BB	SO	SV
128	135	3.98	426	348	56	2372	2294	1170	1049	974	1401	5

LUIS SANCHEZ
RHP, No. 40
RR, 6'2", 210 lbs.
ML Svc: 1 year plus
Born: 8-24-53 in Cariaco, VEN

PITCHING:

Luis Sanchez is an enigma. Anyone who has seen him throw appreciates the strong live arm. However, he is a streak pitcher, one who must have confidence in order to pitch well. If he thinks something is going wrong, he'll usually be unsuccessful.

The Angels use Sanchez primarily as a short reliever. He has a strong lively fastball that is most effective when he keeps it in the right place. Despite a history of arm problems, he must be considered a power pitcher with a fastball ranging in the upper 80s. It sets up his breaking pitches quite well.

When Sanchez gets into a jam or behind in the count, he relies basically on his fastball. Due to his lack of experience, he tends to get flustered in clutch situations and he loses control of his pitches.

With experience, added confidence and more time in a foreign country, this Venezuelan-bred righthander could become a force to be reckoned with.

FIELDING:

His fielding at this point is below average. Ground balls hit through the middle are seldom caught, except by accident. Sanchez seems to get flustered at a ball hit back at him.

OVERALL:

Martin: "He has the ability to get strikeouts when needed. He is an effective short reliever who can also pitch long relief if necessary."

Robinson: "Sanchez is an average pitcher with better than average stuff. The best bet on him is bringing him out of the bullpen."

1982 STATISTICS

W	L	ERA	G	GS	CG	IP	H	R	ER	BB	SO	SV
7	4	3.21	46	0	0	92	89	36	33	34	58	5

CAREER STATISTICS

W	L	ERA	G	GS	CG	IP	H	R	ER	BB	SO	SV
7	6	3.14	63	0	0	126	128	52	44	45	71	7

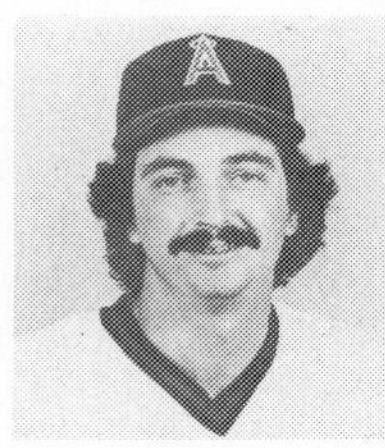

ROB WILFONG
INF, No. 7
LR, 6'1", 185 lbs.
ML Svc: 6 years
Born: 9-1-53 in
Pasadena, CA

1982 STATISTICS

AVG	G	AB	R	H	2B	3B	HR	RBI	BB	SO	SB
.208	80	183	24	38	5	2	1	16	14	30	4

CAREER STATISTICS

AVG	G	AB	R	H	2B	3B	HR	RBI	BB	SO	SB
.261	609	1693	227	442	63	17	23	163	142	241	45

VS. RHP

VS. LHP

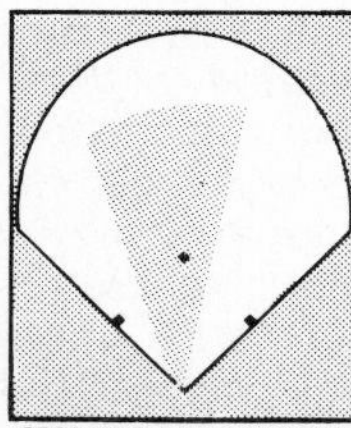
PROBABLE HIT LOCATIONS

HITTING:

Rob Wilfong is not going to win many games with a late-inning home run, but he can be, as pitchers say, a pest. A straightaway hitter, he feeds on low pitches. He has trouble with a hard fastball, up and in. He has trouble with breaking ball southpaws.

In spite of this, Wilfong can hit off-speed pitches with relative success. He handles the bat well, and hits line drives when he's hot, but is generally not one given to streaks. He keeps himself in the game by taking a base on balls or bunting for a hit.

He played infrequently with the Angels in 1982 because there is a very capable second baseman, Bobby Grich, in front of him. If Grich's bad back ever gives, Wilfong would be an adequate replacement. The management still remembers his 1979 season in Minnesota when he batted .313.

BASERUNNING:

Wilfong is as good as any baserunner on the team. He has average speed with outstanding instincts. Pitchers cannot ignore him. He also will take the extra base. His smart baserunning makes him a good choice as a pinch-runner.

FIELDING:

The jury is still out on Wilfong as an all around second baseman. He does have fine quickness, but is generally rated as average in the field. He does have his fans, however, and some baseball people feel that Wilfong is a better fielder than he has been given credit for. A plus is his concentration--he has few mental lapses. He can also play the outfield.

OVERALL:

Martin: "Rob is a good to average middle infielder. He can hit in the .260's and bunts well. He is an underrated team player."

Robinson: "Wilfong is a good back up player with the Angels. He provides you with a good reserve at bat and in the field."

MIKE WITT
RHP, No. 39
RR, 6'7", 185 lbs.
ML Svc: 2 years
Born: 7-20-60 in Fullerton, CA

PITCHING:

Mike Witt is a starting pitcher who is also used in spot relief. He throws overhand and has a herky-jerky delivery with a big kick. Witt is young and obviously still learning--he has not yet figured how to tame his control. Considering his age, this is not actually too big a problem.

Witt has an excellent fastball and a good hard curveball. He gets into trouble when he uses curve too much. Mike's fastball is good, and he should have more confidence in it. When he devlops a major league change-up, his fastball will begin to look even better. He throws a hard curve.

When Witt pitches well enough to get by the early innings, he can usually be effective until the seventh or eighth inning. As he matures more, both mentally and physically, he should be a complete-game pitcher. It often takes a pitcher a few years in the league to get to know the hitters' strengths and weaknesses, but Witt has shown the abiltiy to catch on quickly.

FIELDING:

Witt is an average fielder but can be better if he wants to work at it. He should concentrate on his ability to field bunts which is, at this point, a weakness of his. A tall, lanky pitcher, he was a standout athlete in high school. He had excellent basketball ability and good hands.

OVERALL:

Robinson: "Stardom for Witt is just around the corner. He is a pitcher to watch in 1983. He has made it in a hurry and will get better."

Harwell: "This young pitcher has great potential and is a hard thrower. He is also one of baseball's tallest pitchers."

Martin: "Fine pitcher with a world of potential. I really think he has good enough stuff to be a big winner."

1982 STATISTICS

W	L	ERA	G	GS	CG	IP	H	R	ER	BB	SO	SV
8	6	3.51	33	26	5	179	177	77	70	47	85	0

CAREER STATISTICS

W	L	ERA	G	GS	CG	IP	H	R	ER	BB	SO	SV
16	15	3.42	55	47	12	308	300	137	117	94	160	0

PITCHING:

At one point a few years ago, Geoff Zahn was out of baseball. He had only average stuff which he threw at below average speed. But perseverance won out, and Zahn became one of the most effective pitchers in the American League.

This lefthander is a starter who, despite his slight frame, is durable and capable of pitching well over 200 innings a year. What he has done with less-than-impressive stuff, is consistently put it in places where hitters find it difficult to hit. He has a below average fastball and an above average breaking ball which he can spot on the corners and at the knees. But the pitch that may have changed Zahn's career is a hard slider that he throws on the fists to lefthanded hitters. Basically, it catches them by surprise.

Zahn is extremely effective at pitching to hitters' weaknesses because of his uncanny control. When he is ineffective, it is usually when his control is off ever-so-slightly. Because of his mediocre stuff, he must have pinpoint control to win games.

GEOFF ZAHN
LHP, No. 38
LL, 6'1", 175 lbs.
ML Svc: 8 years
Born: 12-19-46 in Baltimore, MD

FIELDING:

Zahn is an average fielder with a slightly better than average move to first base.

OVERALL:

Robinson: "I think this is one pitcher who undoubtedly is getting the most out of his ability. He's been in double figures in wins for six straight years. He seems to be a more relaxed pitcher now. He does not worry about what happened in his previous outings."

1982 STATISTICS

W	L	ERA	G	GS	CG	IP	H	R	ER	BB	SO	SV
18	8	3.73	34	34	12	229	225	100	95	65	81	0

CAREER STATISTICS

W	L	ERA	G	GS	CG	IP	H	R	ER	BB	SO	SV
87	86	3.88	240	208	58	1409	1522	702	608	413	549	1

RON JACKSON
INF, No. 15
RR, 6'0", 200 lbs.
ML Svc: 8 years
Born: 5-9-53 in
Birmingham, AL

HITTING, BASERUNNING, FIELDING:

Hitting is the strength of Ron Jackson's game. He has consistently proven that he is a quality major league hitter. He is a straightaway hitter, and will pull the ball for power if the pitcher throws him inside. He primarily is a line drive hitter, with no apparent weakness. Jackson has the ability to be a successful pinch-hitter, a quality not found in many players.

His bulk is deceiving--on the surface he would appear to be a slow runner, but Jackson possesses average speed, though he is not a threat to steal.

FIELDING:

Jackson is not a good fielder. He can play either third base or first base, but does not excel at either position. He is just adequate.

OVERALL:

Jackson is a quality utility player and one who is best in a designated hitter role.

MICKEY MAHLER
LHP, No. 22
SL, 6'3", 190 lbs.
ML Svc: 3 years
Born: 7-30-52 in
Montgomery, AL

PITCHING:

If Mickey Mahler is to pitch regularly in the big leagues, it will probably be as a long reliever. He has been a starter for most of his minor league career. He delivers the ball overhand and his best pitch is a fastball which he can throw in the mid to high 80s. He also has a better than average curveball, which complements his fastball extremely well.

Mahler's problem, like with most ineffective pitchers, has been control. Most everyone agrees that his arm is above average, yet he continually has problems with consistency. When he does control his pitches, he is not an easy pitcher to hit, particularly for lefthanders.

FIELDING:

Mahler is an average fielder. His move to first is slightly above average only because he is a lefthanded pitcher.

OVERALL:

Robinson: "Mahler has been up and down in his career. If there is one team he should be able to help, it has to be the California Angels. Look for him to make the staff."

COMISKEY PARK
Chicago White Sox

Seating Capacity: 44,492
Playing Surface: Natural Grass

Dimensions
Left Field Pole: 341 ft.
Left-Center Field: 374 ft.
Center Field: 401 ft.
Right-Center Field: 374 ft.
Right Field Pole: 341 ft.
Height of Outfield Walls:
Left Field: 9 ft. 10 in.
Center Field: 11 ft.
Right Field: 9 ft. 10 in.

Comiskey Park is the grand old lady of major league ballparks. There are none older. Unfortunately, it shows its age. But, like Fenway Park and Tiger Stadium, it holds a sense of history and adds a special flavor that the fairly new, almost antiseptic ball parks, do not.

It has not been an easy park to hit homers in. During the off-season of 1982-83, home plate was moved up eight feet, creating more foul territory behind the catcher, and less area in the outfield. It is now 341 feet to left and right, 374 feet in the alleys in left and right-center, and 401 feet to straightaway center. The fence is 9 feet 10 inches, except in center where an 11 foot fence stands beneath the new Diamond Vision scoreboard.

Ballplayers claim there is something strange about Comiskey Park. There may have been no rain for a week, but the grass is usually wet. Brooks Robinson says flatly, "It is the only park I know in the American League where you think it must have rained before each game, especially in the outfield where it is always soggy. I've been coming to this park for 25 years and that has never changed."

It is almost a square park with the stands in left and right meeting in the center field section that houses the scoreboard.

Despite the fact that home runs do not come easily, the park is a good one to hit in because of the gaps in the alleys, and the tremendous amount of ground a centerfielder must cover. The only time hitters seem to enjoy the game of long ball in Comiskey is when the wind is blowing out, but for some reason, the wind almost always blows in, or from left to right. Some batters have claimed they have hit the hardest balls they have ever hit, but never reach the 352-foot sign in left or right.

The dugouts are unique. They are small and cramped, and the top is almost all cement. In the heat of a game, many a player or manager has jumped up and cracked his head on the low dugout roof.

The mound does not cause any problems, but the infield is not conducive to ordinary hops. Balls tend to take bad hops more often than not in Comiskey. The grass is natural, a bit thick, and almost always moist. It is not a good working park for sportswriters, who must angle through the stands to get to the locker rooms, which are hundreds of feet apart. Fans still tend to gather in the runways after games, and frequently mill around before police force them to leave the park.

BILL ALMON
INF, No. 34
RR, 6'3", 190 lbs.
ML Svc: 6 years
Born: 11-21-52 in Providence, RI

1982 STATISTICS

AVG	G	AB	R	H	2B	3B	HR	RBI	BB	SO	SB
.256	111	308	40	79	10	4	4	26	25	49	10

CAREER STATISTICS

AVG	G	AB	R	H	2B	3B	HR	RBI	BB	SO	SB
.258	709	2128	245	550	68	22	12	155	150	396	75

VS. RHP

VS. LHP

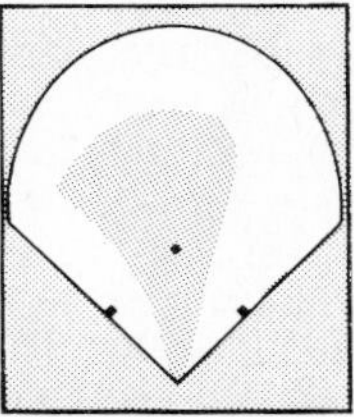
PROBABLE HIT LOCATIONS

HITTING:

Bill Almon's bat has turned major league during the past two seasons, but his glove cost him his starting job in 1982. He doesn't hit many home runs, but hits the ball hard. He gets line drives on the ground, which makes him even better on artificial turf. Almon's key asset as a hitter is his ability to hit behind the runner. He is good on the hit-and-run, and bunts well, often landing a base hit. Fairly consistent at the plate, Almon keeps his average up with occasional hot streaks. He is an especially good hitter in April and May.

More effective against lefthanded pitching, Almon has trouble with breaking pitches, especially sliders, from righthanders. He loves to hit the high fastball. Righthanders should pitch him up and in. Almon isn't nearly as selective against lefties and will go after both the high and low pitch. Lefthanders should pitch him tight. He can be fooled with breaking balls down, but hits the change well.

Almon hit very well over the past two seasons from the No. 9 spot. Since he runs the bases well, he can also hit first or second but does better down in the lineup. He has a near .400 career average against Boston. Overall rating, above average.

BASERUNNING:

Almon has good speed out of the box and down to first. He is a smart runner who doesn't worry a pitcher, but keeps his attention. Gets a good jump, and can steal 20-25 bases a year playing regularly. Not a very aggressive slider, but still rates above average to excellent overall.

FIELDING:

This has been Almon's Achilles heel. He has good ability to get to balls to his left and right, but has the most trouble with balls hit right at him. He committed 17 errors in 103 games in 1981, then lost his starting shortstop job at mid-season in 1982, finishing with 26 errors in 111 games. Almon can play second and third, but shortstop is his best position. He has a strong and fairly accurate arm, but is erratic with the glove. Overall rating, below average.

OVERALL:

Robinson: "Led all American League shortstops in hitting with a .301 average in 1981. Before that though, he was known as a weak bat."

Martin: "Came out of nowhere in 1981 for a fine, all around year, but almost went back there last season. He can run and occasionally hit."

Harwell: "Poor defensive player in a key position."

HITTING:

Harold Baines enjoyed his best big league season last year, establishing himself as one of the better and more complete young players in the game.

Baines was platooned for his first two seasons, facing only righthanded pitchers. But last season, he played every day and surprisingly, hit left-handed pitchers better than righthanders. Baines hits from a closed, upright stance and usually stands low in the box. He is a pull hitter and loves the low fastball. His biggest problem is his overanxiousness--he rarely walks and often swings at the first pitch. He has concentrated on becoming more selective at the plate which was obvious last season, though he still has more work to do. A poor bunter, Baines rarely is called upon to sacrifice.

Ron Guidry and Scott McGregor make Baines struggle at the plate, but Gaines hit Jim Palmer hard and often. Righthanded pitchers generally try and get Baines to chase high fastballs out of the strike zone when he is behind in the count. Lefthanders throw Baines a lot of breaking balls--and he will chase them when he is behind. He has good power to the opposite field, but almost always pulls the ball or reaches the gaps. Detroit and Toronto's right field walls suit Baines' ever-increasing power, but he also hits well in Chicago's cavernous Comiskey Park. Overall rating, above average.

BASERUNNING:

Baines has good speed, but does not steal many bases. He does not get a good jump and is too cautious, but goes from first to third well. This part of his game needs the most work.

FIELDING:

One of the stronger and more accurate arms in the league, Baines has very good natural instincts and gets to a lot of balls. He is better coming in, rather than going back on fly balls. Rarely misses the cutoff man, and his arm has stopped many runners from going from first to third on a single to right. Baines is one of the game's better right fielders, but has the speed and arm to play center.

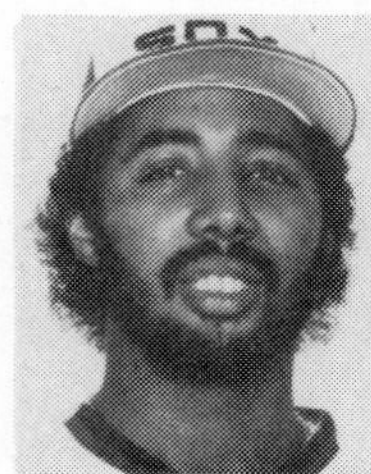

HAROLD BAINES
OF, No. 3
LL, 6'2", 175 lbs.
ML Svc: 3 years
Born: 3-15-59 in Easton, MD

1982 STATISTICS

AVG	G	AB	R	H	2B	3B	HR	RBI	BB	SO	SB
.271	161	608	88	165	29	8	25	105	49	95	10

CAREER STATISTICS

AVG	G	AB	R	H	2B	3B	HR	RBI	BB	SO	SB
.271	384	1379	185	370	63	21	48	195	80	201	18

VS. RHP

VS. LHP

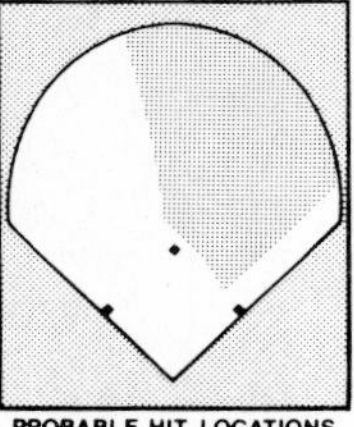
PROBABLE HIT LOCATIONS

OVERALL:

Robinson: "Should be hitting for a better average than he is, but I think that he will do better in 1983. He was more consistent last season than ever before. He is going to be a very good player for a long time."

Martin: "A complete player . . . he hits with power and can run, field, and throw. Baines is one of the league's better young players."

PITCHING:

Floyd Bannister is young, lefthanded, and has a perfect delivery. He has a 90 MPH fastball, and an above average breaking pitch. As if that's not enough, he also has an excellent change-up, and good control. At one time he had some problems with righthanded hitters, but came up with a cut fastball that is quite effective against them.

So far, however, Bannister hasn't gotten the type of results that have been anticipated. He lacks confidence in his own ability, although no one else does. He had been frustrated in Seattle by a mental block about pitching in the Kingdome, even though his career record is better in the Dome than out. The demands that he faced in Seattle as the No. 1 starter also contributed to the pressure he felt there.

He doubts himself when he doesn't have total command, but has such a solid arsenal of pitches that he is capable of keeping his team in a game even on a bad day. Some feel strongly that he would blossom with a contending club where he is not the only player in the limelight every day.

While Bannister had a variety of major injuries last year, he never failed to make it to the mound for his 35 scheduled starts, and averaged more than seven innings an outing.

His control may be too good. Hitters are able to stay in against him because they know he's going to be in the proximity of the plate. Bannister doesn't have that inner force that will allow him to knock a hitter down and keep him honest.

FLOYD BANNISTER
LHP, No. 19
LL, 6'1", 195 lbs.
ML Svc: 6 years
Born: 6-10-55 in
Pierre, SD

FIELDING:

His move to first isn't the best in the league, but it is still above average. He's another outstanding athlete whose athletic abilities are obvious in his fielding. He can take ground balls up the middle and bunts very well.

OVERALL:

Bannister figures to keep on improving. What he needs is confidence, and with Carlton Fisk catching him, he may find it in Chicago. He'll never be held back by a lack of effort. He keeps himself in excellent physical condition, working-out year round, and has never had a serious arm problem. His smooth motion leaves the impression that he will be able to pitch for quite a long time. He does seem to be upset by fielding mistakes made behind him, occasionally becoming visible on the field in his dismay.

Martin: "A franchise type of pitcher, the type of pitcher who can keep a team out of a long losing streak."

Robinson: "In Seattle he learned to pitch without many runs. He is becoming consistent, and should do well in Chicago."

1982 STATISTICS

W	L	ERA	G	GS	CG	IP	H	R	ER	BB	SO	SV
12	13	3.43	35	35	5	247	225	112	94	77	209	0

CAREER STATISTICS

W	L	ERA	G	GS	CG	IP	H	R	ER	BB	SO	SV
51	68	3.90	170	156	30	1021	996	491	443	381	770	0

RICHARD BARNES
LHP, No. 52
RL, 6'4", 186 lbs.
ML Svc: 1 year
Born: 7-11-59 in
Palm Beach, CA

PITCHING:

Barnes was used mainly as a reliever in brief trials with the White Sox last season, but his future lies mainly as a starter. He is lean and tall with a distinctive pause at the top of his three-quarter delivery. His size lures many into thinking he's a power pitcher, but actually Barnes relies more on finesse than speed.

His fastball is in the 84-87 MPH range, and he'll use it 60% of the time. He has a big breaking slider he'll use it 40% of the time.

Barnes doesn't have a curve and rarely throws a straight change, which is rated as average. When he gets behind in the count, he can be a surprise because he'll usually go to his breaking ball. He's more effective against lefthanded hitters.

He will rarely brush a hitter back or go inside. But his tendency to be wild will keep hitters from digging in. He will not challenge hitters, either, and needs more experience to be effective in the big leagues.

FIELDING:

Barnes has an above average move to first and handles his position well. He is quick off the mound and fields bunts well. Overall effectiveness at fielding his position is rated at above average.

OVERALL:

Barnes may be fading as a prospect. He challenged for a spot on the roster in spring training but then had a mediocre year in Triple A. He has not put together a super season anywhere yet, but has progressed through the Sox system on his potential alone. Still is very young, and it is very doubtful the Sox will give up on him yet. He must pitch inside more and challenge hitters. Too timid.

Robinson: "He has a chance to become a starter next year if the Sox make some changes on their pitching staff. Good poise on the mound for a pitcher so young. Control and inexperience are his biggest weaknesses right now."

Martin: "Throws hard enough to get strikeouts. Average rating but should get better. Added plus is that he's a lefthander, always in short supply."

1982 STATISTICS

W	L	ERA	G	GS	CG	IP	H	R	ER	BB	SO	SV
0	2	4.76	6	2	0	17	21	15	9	4	6	1

CAREER STATISTICS

W	L	ERA	G	GS	CG	IP	H	R	ER	BB	SO	SV
0	2	4.76	6	2	0	17	21	15	9	4	6	1

SALOME BAROJAS
RHP, No. 30
RR, 5'11", 175 lbs.
ML Svc: 1 year
Born: 6-16-57 in
Corova, MX

PITCHING:

The White Sox found Barojas pitching in Mexico during the 1981 players' strike and surprisingly, he made the team in spring training last year. Even more surprisingly, he had 11 saves in his first 18 appearances through the end of May. But then he fell victim to overwork and a bit of a confidence problem before a late-season surge gave him 21 saves, a club record for a rookie pitcher.

Barojas is primarily a sinker-slider pitcher who doesn't worry much about pitching to a hitter's weakness. He throws the same, regardless. Most of the time in 1982 he had no idea who was at the plate.

He generally throws three-quarter, but occasionally can drop down a little. He is strictly a short reliever who relies on his control and the breaking pitch, though his fastball is in the 85 MPH range. He has an average curve but rarely uses it. His sinker-slider is average to a little above average. He seldom, if ever, throws a straight change.

With his sinker, it doesn't matter if Barojas is facing a lefthanded or righthanded hitter. He has equal success against both. When behind in the count, Barojas goes with his sinker. He does not throw a spitball or a screwball, like so many other pitchers who have graduated from the Mexican League. He did show excellent poise for a rookie, probably because he came to the majors with six years in the Mexican League under his belt.

Barojas pitched well in Yankee Stadium and Fenway Park last season, but struggled in Minnesota and Anaheim. Part of his early advantage was being new to the league. Later in the season, the hitters began to make him bring the ball up in the strike zone and stopped swinging at balls just below the zone.

FIELDING:

Barojas' time spent in the Mexican Leagues is evident. He is a slightly above average fielder and has been well schooled in the basics. His move to first is average to slightly above average. The same applies to his ability to field bunts and his position overall.

OVERALL:

Barojas doesn't have overpowering stuff and gives up almost a hit an inning, but he keeps the ball down and gives up few home runs, which makes him especially effective in parks like Yankee Stadium and Comiskey Park in Chicago. More effective when used an inning or less. Overall rating as a relief pitcher, average to above average.

Martin: "A find during the strike of 1981 and a savior to the White Sox bullpen. He was one of the reasons they contended all year."

Robinson: "Remains to be seen if he can keep up the pace in 1983. Had a great start in 1982, but slowed after that."

1982 STATISTICS

W	L	ERA	G	GS	CG	IP	H	R	ER	BB	SO	SV
6	6	3.54	61	0	0	106	96	43	42	46	56	21

CAREER STATISTICS

W	L	ERA	G	GS	CG	IP	H	R	ER	BB	SO	SV
6	6	3.54	61	0	0	106	96	43	42	46	56	21

TONY BERNAZARD
INF, No. 14
SR, 5'9", 160 lbs.
ML Svc: 3 years
Born: 8-24-56 in
Caguas, PR

1982 STATISTICS

AVG	G	AB	R	H	2B	3B	HR	RBI	BB	SO	SB
.256	137	540	90	138	25	9	11	56	67	88	11

CAREER STATISTICS

AVG	G	AB	R	H	2B	3B	HR	RBI	BB	SO	SB
.259	347	1147	180	297	48	14	23	116	153	207	25

VS. RHP

VS. LHP

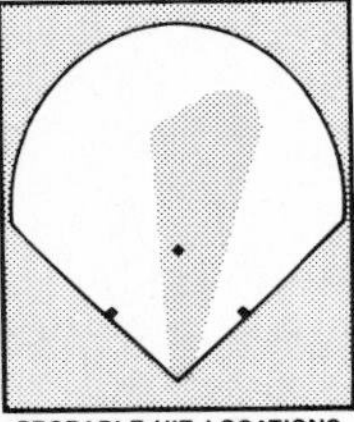
PROBABLE HIT LOCATIONS

HITTING:

Tony Bernazard is a straightaway, line drive hitter with developing power, most of it coming when he bats lefthanded. A switch-hitter, Bernazard hits for about the same average from either side of the plate, but rarely gets the long ball righthanded. Batting, throw him breaking balls and off-speed pitches. Stay away with everything if you can. He likes the fastball in and can turn on it. He is a good contact hitter and can hit behind the runner. Throw him fastballs away.

He is a hungry and steady No. 2 hitter in the lineup, but strikes out too often. He is more patient from the right side and more likely to coax a walk. Bernazard does not hit well in Chicago, but knows how to use Comiskey Park's spacious left- and right-center field gaps, getting seven of his nine triples at home that way last season. He is more prone to go deep on the road, where he got nine of his eleven home runs in 1982.

Bernazard hits a lot of hard ground balls which makes him better on artificial surfaces. He is an above average to excellent bunter, and also executes very well on the hit-and-run. His hitting is very consistent, and overall, average to above average.

BASERUNNING:

Bernazard was 11 for 11 in stolen bases last season, but he is actually a tentative runner, and not a threat to steal with any regularity. He does not slide hard, and is only average at breaking up the double play. He has above average quickness, and if he would become more aggressive on the basepaths, he could become above average. At this point however, he is rated average.

FIELDING:

There is nothing tentative about Bernazard's play at second base. His arm strength, range and throwing accuracy are all rated above average to excellent. His move to both his left and right are also rated excellent. He releases the ball quickly on the pivot, is fearless when a runner is barrelling into second. Among the best at turning the double play.

OVERALL:

Robinson: "Tony is a good little hitter who can handle the bat. He is the steadiest infielder Chicago had last season, and will get better."

Martin: "This guy is durable. Though he strikes out quite a bit, he gets on base and scores runs. He has generally been underrated in the field."

BRITT BURNS
LHP, No. 40
RL, 6'5", 218 lbs.
ML Svc: 4 years
Born: 6-8-59 in Houston, TX

PITCHING:

It's easy for fans to tell when Britt Burns is on his game. When everything in his motion is right, he has a hard time keeping his hat on. The problem is so bad that he needs hairpins to keep his hat on, but when he's right he's constantly adjusting his hat. He also is one of the slowest working pitchers in the major leagues. His games almost always run close to three hours.

Burns is big, strong and throws hard overhand. He is strictly a starter and, until hampered by a shoulder problem, was among the league leaders in several categories last season. He was 13-4 on Aug. 10 with a 3.37 ERA, then suffered a strained shoulder tendon. He tried to come back several times but was ineffective. The injury is not believed to need anything other than a winter of rest to be completely healed.

He is a power pitcher who has an above average ability to pitch to a batter's weakness. His fastball approaches 90 MPH, and he uses it most of the time. He'll mix in a curve that needs a lot of improvement and a big slider that rates above average. He rarely uses the straight change, which also needs a lot of work. When behind in the count, it's Burns' strength against the hitter's strength. No need guessing what's coming; it will be the fastball.

Burns will seldom brush a hitter back, though he did it more in 1982 than ever before. Very poised on the mound, but he's still learning hitters and can be beaten on a mistake in a tight spot. His weaknesses include his control, which sometimes is spotty.

Texas, Oakland and Milwaukee all have good parks for Burns to pitch in, and he usually does well there. Because of those parks' size, he can challenge hitters more without getting burned by a home run. He does well whenever he pitches against the Rangers, but struggles against the Tigers and Indians.

FIELDING:

Burns rushed through the Sox farm system so quickly that he never learned how to field his position. He is not very mobile. As a boy he grew so fast, he had to have pins surgically inserted in both hips to stabilize the bones. That, too, hindered his mobility. His move to first, effectiveness in fielding bunts and overall effectiveness in fielding his position all need improvement. He falls off the mound after delivering the ball and is ripe for a good bunter.

OVERALL:

Very well poised for such a young pitcher. He's better when he works more quickly, but still struggles to pick up the pace. Overall, he rates above average to excellent. A better off-speed pitch would help.

Robinson: "He has a chance to be the best in the league. Definitely has the potential to be a 20-game winner."

Martin: "Has unlimited potential. Pitches in a pitcher's park and has the stuff and now the confidence to be outstanding."

1982 STATISTICS

W	L	ERA	G	GS	CG	IP	H	R	ER	BB	SO	SV
13	5	4.04	28	28	5	169	168	89	76	67	116	0

CAREER STATISTICS

W	L	ERA	G	GS	CG	IP	H	R	ER	BB	SO	SV
38	26	3.29	94	85	21	577	544	241	211	183	362	0

RICH DOTSON
RHP, No. 49
RR, 6'0", 196 lbs.
ML Svc: 3 years
Born: 1-10-59 in Cincinnati, OH

PITCHING:

Richard Dotson grew up being a big fan of Tom Seaver, so much so that he has imitated some of Seaver's delivery and pitching mannerisms.

Like Seaver, Dotson comes straight overhand and has a very fluid delivery. He uses his legs well, taking a long stride. His stride was so long at times his right knee would hit the ground at the end of his delivery.

He is a starter--period. A power pitcher with a great change-up, Dotson's fastball is in the 87-90 MPH range. He relies mainly on the two pitches, and changing speeds a lot. Occasional tendinitis in his shoulder often prevents him from working on his curveball during spring training. As a result, he is hesitant to use the curve during the season and the pitch needs work. Last season he dropped his slider altogether.

Dotson's change is among the best in the league, but he'll throw the fastball when he's behind in the count. He's equally effective against righthanders and lefthanders because he moves hitters off the plate a lot, especially with two strikes and no balls.

Dotson struggled the first half of 1982, going 3-11. But he then won eight straight with an ERA of 1.50 during that span. The White Sox worked closely with Dotson on getting him to get meaner on the mound and pitch inside more. He will use the brushback more now.

Dotson's greatest strength is his work ethic. He's a hard worker willing to pay the price. His fastball is live and his great command of the change makes his fastball that much faster. He has good poise and presence on the mound, but doesn't always cope well in pressure situations. Improvement is needed there.

He doesn't always pitch that well against Baltimore, but he nevertheless beats the Orioles regularly. He struggles against Seattle and California.

Fans can tell easily when it's Dotson's turn to pitch. He never shaves the day before or the day he pitches, so if you see five o'clock shadow, Dotson's starting.

FIELDING:

Dotson's move to first is rated above average. It is quick. He is quick off the mound and fields bunts well. Overall effectiveness in fielding his position is rated above average.

OVERALL:

Dotson still hasn't licked all his growing pains, and the confidence problem that bothered him early in 1982 could return in 1983. A good start would help. His hits-to-innings-pitched ratio isn't good, and the home run gets him in trouble. He led the team in gopher balls last season with 19.

Robinson: "Much better pitcher than his record indicates. Control is average, four to six strikeouts a game."

Martin: "Tremendous potential. Still very young and just learning how to pitch."

1982 STATISTICS

W	L	ERA	G	GS	CG	IP	H	R	ER	BB	SO	SV
11	15	3.84	34	31	3	196	219	97	84	73	109	0

CAREER STATISTICS

W	L	ERA	G	GS	CG	IP	H	R	ER	BB	SO	SV
34	33	4.54	96	92	17	559	577	282	247	215	304	0

HITTING:

Fisk is a pull hitter who has learned there is life without The Green Monster (Fenway Park's left field wall), and continues to produce offensively. He is a low ball, line drive hitter. Righthanders must keep the ball in at his bat. Stay away from the middle of the plate. Lefthanders generally pitch him down and away, then jam him once in a while. He is a little bit of a guess hitter, and can handle the change and curve, especially if he guesses right and is looking for it.

He is a good clutch hitter even though he hit just .235 with runners in scoring position last year. He reaches the alleys quite often, and hits well behind the runner. Fisk used to be among the league leaders in getting hit by pitches, but has backed off the plate since being in Chicago.

BASERUNNING:

Fisk runs well for a big man, and is a very smart baserunner. He is good at taking the extra base, or advancing on a fly ball. The White Sox picked the spots for him to steal, and he had a career-high of 17 stolen bases last season, while being caught just twice. He always slides feet first, and is good at breaking up the double play, but is prone to occasional lapses on the basepaths.

FIELDING:

Regarded as one of the better handlers of pitchers in the game, Fisk is all business in the field. He is a tough, hard-nosed competitor who just thrives on pressure. His arm strength and release point are rated excellent. In 1982, he threw out just 29 of 100 basestealers. This low figure, however might be attributed, in part, to the young Chicago pitching staff which does not hold runners close.

CARLTON FISK
C, No. 72
RR, 6'2", 220 lbs.
ML Svc: 11 years
Born: 12-26-47 in
Bellows Falls, VT

1982 STATISTICS

AVG	G	AB	R	H	2B	3B	HR	RBI	BB	SO	SB
.267	135	476	66	127	17	3	14	65	46	60	17

CAREER STATISTICS

AVG	G	AB	R	H	2B	3B	HR	RBI	BB	SO	SB
.281	1309	4674	737	1313	236	36	183	678	473	685	91

VS. RHP

VS. LHP

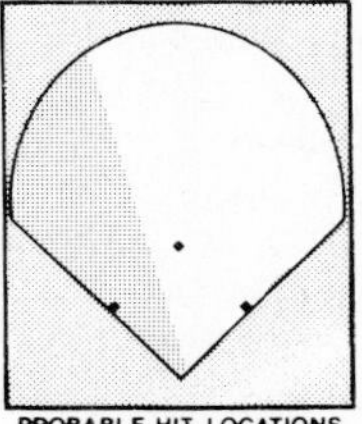
PROBABLE HIT LOCATIONS

Fisk is an aggressive catcher who will fire to any base. He inspires confidence in pitchers, but has been criticized for setting too slow of a pace. He pounces on bunts and balls hit in front of the plate every bit as well as he did 10 years ago. Very durable, plays hurt, and blocks the plate with unfliching resolve. Overall, an excellent catcher.

OVERALL:

Robinson: "A superb handler of pitchers who is valuable to his team in many ways. He can hit anywhere from third through seventh in the batting order."

Martin: "Year in and year out, he is one of the league's best. Runs the ball game and is especially good at handling young pitchers. A tough, competitive hitter."

PITCHING:

Fans who follow the Phillies will notice a resemblance between left-hander Kevin Hickey and Tug McGraw. Hickey patterns himself after the Phils' lefty reliever from the start of his delivery to the finish. He even has the glove slap against his thigh, which he uses after getting a key out.

A youngster who grew up less than a mile from Chicago's Comiskey Park, Hickey also has one other idiosyncrasy: He sprints full speed toward the dugout after getting the final out of an inning.

Hickey can pitch long and short relief, though his function in two seasons with the White Sox was middle man who comes on to get a lefthanded batter or two, or who pitches one time through the order at most. He is strictly a power pitcher and his fastball has gotten faster in the past two years. He throws in the 88 to 90 MPH range, and comes three-quarter.

He has a good slider that is quick and short, breaking no more than six to eight inches. Rarely uses an average curve and rarely goes to the straight change, which still needs a lot of work. When he's behind in the count, look for the fastball.

Hickey is a good pressure pitcher and thrives in Yankee Stadium. He has had inordinate amounts of success against the Yankees and still gets Reggie Jackson out consistently, despite the change in uniforms. Has a good, live rubber arm though the innings caught up with him late in the 1982 season.

KEVIN HICKEY
LHP, No. 45
LL, 6'1", 170 lbs.
ML Svc: 2 years
Born: 2-25-57 in Chicago, IL

FIELDING:

Hickey is a remarkable natural athlete who didn't play baseball in high school or college. The Sox signed him in 1978 from a crowd of several hundred that showed up for an open tryout at Comiskey Park. He won a Gold Glove in the minor leagues in 1980.

His move to first is above average, but he is rated excellent at fielding the bunt and overall effectiveness in fielding his position. Very quick reflexes.

OVERALL:

Is learning in the major leagues and getting stronger and quicker in the process. Accepts his role well and is a tough competitor who doesn't scare. An off-speed pitch would help him tremendously.

Martin: "A young reliever who could go a long way in the White Sox' scheme of things. Doesn't give up many home runs."

Robinson: "The Sox seem to be gaining more and more confidence in him and are using him more often in pressure situations."

1982 STATISTICS

W	L	ERA	G	GS	CG	IP	H	R	ER	BB	SO	SV
4	4	3.00	60	0	0	78	73	32	26	30	38	6

CAREER STATISTICS

W	L	ERA	G	GS	CG	IP	H	R	ER	BB	SO	SV
4	6	3.98	101	0	0	122	111	54	44	48	55	9

LaMARR HOYT
RHP, No. 31
RR, 6'1", 222 lbs.
ML Svc: 3 years
Born: 1-1-59 in Columbia, SC

PITCHING:

Hoyt can do it all--start, long or short relief, or swing back and forth between starting and the bullpen. He won 19 games last season mainly as a starter, but could end up as a short reliever again this season if he is needed.

He was 9-0 with a 1.45 ERA late in May of last season, then began to struggle. After that great start, he was 19-15 at the end of the season.

Hoyt is burly, battles a weight problem and has incredibly small hands for a pitcher. But he is a tough customer on the mound. Mean is actually more like it. If he isn't sporting a bushy beard, he doesn't shave on the days he pitches. He'll do anything to make himself look meaner. Hitters know it. Hoyt pitches in and isn't afraid to dust a hitter off if he starts digging in.

He uses his fastball in the 85-87 MPH range most of the time. The pitch doesn't have extraordinary velocity, but does have a lot of movement. It's rated a little above average because of that. To go with the fastball, he mixes in a curve and slider. He changes speeds on the curve. The slider is down and quick. He will also use a straight change a lot.

When he is behind in the count, Hoyt usually goes to his breaking ball. Righthanded hitters usually have more problems against Hoyt because he drops his arm down in his motion and the ball is hard to pick up for a righthanded hitter. Hoyt has great poise on the mound and has a very durable arm. He never misses a turn and challenges hitters. The toll of innings did catch up with him late last season though, and he battled a tired arm in September.

Hoyt has good success pitching in Fenway Park because he pitches inside well to a predominately righthanded club. He has always pitched well in Oakland and Anaheim, but he hates to pitch in Cleveland.

FIELDING:

Hoyt has a good move to first, but his size hinders his movement around the mound and he is not a good fielder. He doesn't field bunts very well, and needs a lot of improvement in that area. He needs to improve in all defensive areas.

OVERALL:

Hoyt has a great disposition for a pitcher. He works hard, doesn't scare on the mound, and isn't afraid to challenge hitters. He pays the price for his guts, giving up 17 home runs last year. But he is a good man to have on a staff because he can pitch so many different ways. All he needs now is better command of his pitches.

Robinson: "If it means anything, he looks mean. Has a chance to be a 20 game winner, but his real value is his versatility."

Martin: "Seems like a good, solid pitcher, even in an up and down season."

1982 STATISTICS

W	L	ERA	G	GS	CG	IP	H	R	ER	BB	SO	SV
19	15	3.53	39	32	14	239	248	104	94	48	124	0

CAREER STATISTICS

W	L	ERA	G	GS	CG	IP	H	R	ER	BB	SO	SV
37	21	3.78	108	46	17	445	453	210	187	117	239	10

JIM KERN
RHP, No. 32
RR, 6'5", 185 lbs.
ML Svc: 9 years
Born: 3-15-49 in Gladwin County, MI

PITCHING:

Kern is hard to miss when he is anywhere near the mound. Tall and lean, he wears an Abe Lincoln-type beard.

But what really sets Kern apart is his fastball, which is in the 92-plus MPH range. He uses the fastball 75% of the time, but even the best fastball is better when a pitcher has other pitches to show. Kern doesn't, and that's his problem.

Kern uses a slider about 20% of the time. It is an average pitch, but he needs to become more consistent with it so that he can show the hitters that he has something else other than a fastball. He seldom uses the curve, which doesn't have very good rotation. Lack of controlling the pitch really hurts him.

When Kern is wild, he's usually wild and high. The word is that Kern can only pitch in short relief because he can't sustain the velocity. In a late-season start for the Sox last year, he went five innings without losing his velocity, but whether he could do it over an entire season, though, is another question.

Kern's wildness gets him in trouble as a short reliever. The Sox are pondering making him a middle reliever to get the best use out of him. He almost always pitches better when he starts an inning, rather than trying to get out of somebody else's mess. He is also a better pitcher when he stays ahead of the count.

Righthanded batters struggle more than lefthanders against Kern. They are just plain intimidated by his power, and maybe a little by his lack of control. Kern seldom uses an intentional brushback, and he really doesn't have to. Nobody digs in against him--not with his kind of fastball.

Kern is still a zany and colorful character who is good at keeping a ballclub loose. If anything, he seems to lack the killer instinct he had in 1979 when he had his best year, and was possibly the best reliever in the majors. If he gets his toughness back, the White Sox made a steal by getting him for three minor leaguers last season.

FIELDING:

Outwardly, Kern appears carefree, but he is all business on the mound. He looks awkward, but is a good athlete. His move to first is average. He is also rated average at fielding bunts and in his overall effectiveness at fielding his position.

OVERALL

McCarver: "Big league hitters, if allowed to wail away on a fastball will eventually catch up to the heat. A pitcher has to have a pitch to throw off a hitter's timing. Jim would be more effective with an off-speed pitch, though relievers can get away without it more because they usually face the lineup only once."

Coleman: "Still has a great arm. Some of his confidence seems to have erroded, though."

1982 STATISTICS

W	L	ERA	G	GS	CG	IP	H	R	ER	BB	SO	SV
5	6	3.46	63	1	0	104	81	43	40	60	66	4

CAREER STATISTICS

W	L	ERA	G	GS	CG	IP	H	R	ER	BB	SO	SV
51	54	3.01	380	14	1	736	595	279	246	403	625	88

JERRY KOOSMAN
LHP, No. 36
RL, 6'2", 225 lbs.
ML Svc: 15 years
Born: 12-23-43 in Appleton, MN

PITCHING:

The White Sox found some added life in Koosman's arm late in the season, and he was one of the prime reasons the team stayed in contention.

Koosman always was a power pitcher, coming straight overhand and occasionally three-quarter. He still has a good, live fastball of between 87-90 MPH, but he doesn't sustain that velocity for more than five innings. He is becoming a control pitcher, relying on the breaking ball more and more.

His curve is sharp but he often struggles to control it. He has to be able to spot it well to be effective. Very seldom throws his slider, which is average. Last season he added a screwball to his repertoire and will throw it occasionally to righthanded hitters. But when he's behind in the count, look for the fastball.

Lefthanders had better success against Koosman than righthanders last season, though he actually pitches better facing a righthander. His curve overmatches most lefthanders, but the control problem hurts. Lefties hit nearly .300 against him last season.

Fans can look for several things from Koosman. First, he quietly added an occasional spitter last year, and on a night when he doesn't have the good fastball he'll wet a few up. Secondly, Koosman has no fear of using the brushback and will run batters off the plate if they dig in. Third, watch for the cadence in his delivery: his delivery is done to a four-count and a certain movement always comes on the same count.

Koosman pitches inside so well that he does well in the small parks, like Seattle and Boston. Hitters in the small parks usually look for the ball away because everyone's a home run threat, so Koosman jams hitters and surprises them.

FIELDING:

Koosman's move to first is not that good for a lefthander. He has slowed in fielding bunts and does not handle ground balls or balls hit right back to him well at all. Overall fielding is average.

OVERALL:

Koosman is an unlikely candidate to make it as a rotation starter through an entire season. The Sox probably will spot him early, but he will take a little longer now to get in shape and go strong early in the season. Attempts at using him in relief did not work out.

Robinson: "Koosman's mere presence can help the young Sox staff. The Sox have gotten a lot of good mileage out of him."

Martin: "Over the years he has gone from the Blazer to the Cutie. His experience will get the edge somehow."

1982 STATISTICS

W	L	ERA	G	GS	CG	IP	H	R	ER	BB	SO	SV
11	7	3.84	42	19	3	173	194	81	74	38	88	3

CAREER STATISTICS

W	L	ERA	G	GS	CG	IP	H	R	ER	BB	SO	SV
191	183	3.27	520	451	132	3336	3116	1361	1211	1051	2269	15

DENNIS LAMP
RHP, No. 53
RR, 6'3", 210 lbs.
ML Svc: 5 years
Born: 9-23-52 in
Los Angeles, CA

PITCHING:

Lamp is the can-do man of the White Sox. He can start, pitch short or long relief, or can go back and forth between spot starting and long relief.

He is picky on the mound. Everything has to be picture perfect before he starts his windup. It's almost as if he's posing for a picture as he checks his thick, black moustache, shirtsleeves, the positioning of his arms and how his feet are set. When everything is perfect, he delivers.

Lamp pitches three-quarter and primarily relies on his sinker. When it's really on, he'll get 20 or more outs via the ground ball. He doesn't concern himself too much with the hitters, just concentrates on keeping his sinker down in the strike zone.

Since he relies so heavily on ground balls, Lamp is better on parks with natural grass, rather than artificial turf. Lamp throws between 85 and 87 MPH. He has a good slider that he'll throw once in a while. He throws it down and away to righthanded hitters and throws the sinker down and in to righthanders. He has a good curve but won't use it at all. Same goes for his change.

Lamp dabbled with a spitter last year and will wet one up, occasionally. But when he's behind, it's sinker, sinker, sinker.

Lamp is very tough against righthanders. He keeps everything away, and if a hitter tries to pull, he ends up hitting a ground ball out. Then Lamp will come in and jam a hitter.

His strength is an ability to keep the sinker in on the knees. His weakness is his reluctance to go with his other pitches more.

FIELDING:

Lamp's fielding needs a lot of work. His move to first is weak, and hitters like to bunt on him. He doesn't field the bunt well at all, nor does he field his position well. Doesn't react well on balls hit up through the middle and very often will forget to cover first base.

OVERALL:

Valuable because of his versatility. Filled dual role as starter and reliever at various times last season. A clubhouse humorist who can keep a team loose. Far from overpowering, but a lot of poise.

Robinson: "The White Sox lost a little confidence in him when he struggled at times last year. But he can help a pitching staff in many ways."

Martin: "A good pick-up by the Sox in a 1981 deal with their crosstown rivals, the Cubs."

1982 STATISTICS

W	L	ERA	G	GS	CG	IP	H	R	ER	BB	SO	SV
11	8	3.99	44	27	3	189	206	96	84	59	78	5

CAREER STATISTICS

W	L	ERA	G	GS	CG	IP	H	R	ER	BB	SO	SV
46	55	3.85	198	145	20	973	1055	473	416	294	403	5

RUDY LAW
OF, No. 11
LL, 6'1", 165 lbs.
ML Svc: 3 years
Born: 10-7-56 in Waco, TX

1982 STATISTICS

AVG	G	AB	R	H	2B	3B	HR	RBI	BB	SO	SB
.318	121	336	55	107	15	8	3	32	23	41	36

CAREER STATISTICS

AVG	G	AB	R	H	2B	3B	HR	RBI	BB	SO	SB
.287	250	736	112	211	20	12	4	56	47	70	79

VS. RHP

VS. LHP

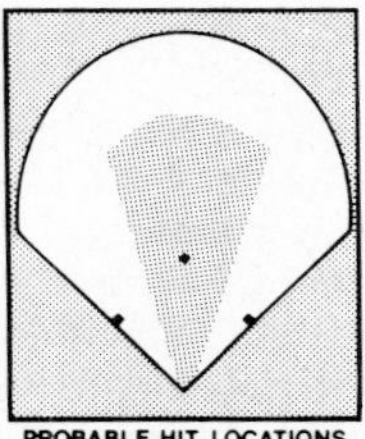
PROBABLE HIT LOCATIONS

HITTING:

Law is a contact hitter who goes up the middle and likes to slap the ball to the opposite field. He is always looking for something over the outer half of the plate and likes the low pitch. Pitch him inside and throw him sliders on his hands. Law's speed helps him leg out a lot of ground balls on the infield. He will chase pitches out of the strike zone and struggles to hit the change-up.

He doesn't walk much for a leadoff man, but he bunts well and will bunt for the base hit quite often. Good hitter on turf and was a consistent .300 hitter since taking over as a starter midway through the 1982 season. Law can handle lefthanders who have average stuff and speed, but against the likes of a Guidry, he just doesn't have a clue. He struck out every six times at bat against lefthanders, but only every nine times at bat against righthanders. Law is an overall above average hitter.

BASERUNNING:

Law is a "disrupter" on base, a definite distraction to any pitcher because of his excellent speed. But as a big league baserunner, he needs to work on his breaks and basic mechanics. He was on his own with the Sox and could steal at his own discretion . . . and was thrown out 10 times in 36 attempts. Excellent speed from the plate to first and from first to third. Not a very aggressive slider, and will have to improve in order to become a first-class base stealer.

FIELDING:

This is the weakest part of Law's game, mostly because he has a below average arm. He gets to a lot of balls because of his speed, but has trouble with balls hit right at him and over his head. This weakness is only compounded when he plays his usual shallow center field. He would probably perform better in left field, a position he prefers to center.

OVERALL:

Robinson: "Law has done a good job for Chicago in a lot of little ways, but it remains to be seen if he can do it on an everyday basis."

Martin: "I don't think that he is playing up to his full potential just yet. He has a chance to become a fair player; a good prospect, but not as brilliant as everyone thought when he first came up."

VANCE LAW
INF, No. 5
RR, 6'2", 185 lbs.
ML Svc: 3 years
Born: 10-1-56 in Boise, ID

1982 STATISTICS

AVG	G	AB	R	H	2B	3B	HR	RBI	BB	SO	SB
.281	114	359	40	101	20	1	5	54	26	46	4

CAREER STATISTICS

AVG	G	AB	R	H	2B	3B	HR	RBI	BB	SO	SB
.254	169	500	52	127	22	4	5	60	31	68	7

HITTING:

Law became the Sox' starting shortstop midway through the 1982 season, and proved to have a consistent and steadily improving bat.

He tries to pull everything, but is learning to go the opposite way. Throw him fastballs and breaking balls down and away. He likes pitches that are down and in or up and away. He will chase the high fastball.

Law still has trouble handling the curve, and is shaky against a good slider pitcher, but he can handle the change-up. He turned into one of the better clutch hitters on the White Sox, but still must learn the strike zone better. A singles and doubles hitter, Law does not show any power. He appears to fare equally well against righthanders or lefthanders, but righthanders have the edge because he fights the curveball. He has a good RBI ratio--54 in just 359 at-bats.

Law murdered California pitching, going 8-for-22 and .364 on the road with seven RBI's against the Angels. Law is best hitting in the bottom of the batting order.. Overall rating, average.

BASERUNNING:

Law has just average speed to first, if that. Not an aggressive slider, he needs to work on getting a better lead off first. He tends to be overly conservative on the basepaths, and is prone to an occasional baserunning blunder.

FIELDING:

His arm is Law's best defensive asset. Above average throwing. He did not get to a lot of balls he should have when he started playing regularly and made a significant number of errors, but improved in the final six weeks of the season. Getting to know the hitters has helped his positioning, and thus his fielding. Law can also play either at second or third base. Could remain a regular shortstop this season.

OVERALL:

Robinson: "An average fielder overall, and probably always will be, but gave the Sox a day in and day out good job at shortstop."

Martin: "Law made some spectacular plays, but some pretty bad ones, too."

RON LeFLORE
OF, No. 8
RR, 6'0", 200 lbs.
ML Svc: 8 years
Born: 6-16-52 in Detroit, MI

1982 STATISTICS

AVG	G	AB	R	H	2B	3B	HR	RBI	BB	SO	SB
.287	91	334	58	96	15	4	4	25	22	91	28

CAREER STATISTICS

AVG	G	AB	R	H	2B	3B	HR	RBI	BB	SO	SB
.288	1099	4458	731	1283	172	66	59	353	363	888	455

VS. RHP

VS. LHP

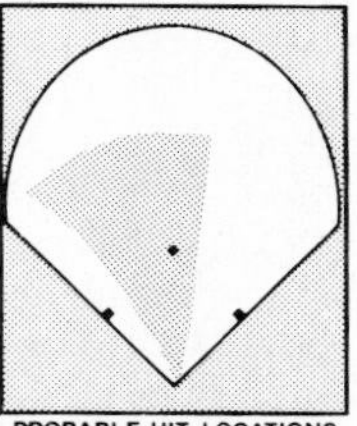
PROBABLE HIT LOCATIONS

HITTING:

Usually a pull hitter, Le Flore likes the high fastball out over the plate, and on the outer half. Pitch him inside. Give him fastballs on the fists. Righthanders should just curve him to death.

Le Flore has opened up his previously closed stance, and is hitting the ball more up the middle now because of it. He remains, however, a free swinger, a little too much so for a leadoff man. He struck out 91 times in only 334 at-bats last season, averaging a whiff every four times up. He doesn't draw many walks either at leadoff, taking down just 22.

He is much more likely to strike out against righthanders. Rates below average in hitting behind the runner, and hit just .203 with runners in scoring position last season. A poor bunter, he is rarely called upon to sacrifice.

Le Flore always hits poorly in Texas, and tends to be a streaky hitter. He will get off to a good start; hits well in the beginning of the season, and then levels off. Overall rating, below average.

BASERUNNING:

Le Flore has lost a step, but still is a competent baserunner who can make a pitcher nervous. He is very aggressive in running the bases, slides hard, and is good at breaking up the double play. Has good speed down to first and runs hard, but does not steal as much as he used to. In a half-season last year, he swiped 28 bases but was caught 14 times. He usually likes to see a pitcher's move to first when he's on base before he tries to steal.

FIELDING:

Le Flore's move back to center field in 1982 was a bust. His weak throwing arm was even more of a liability in center, and he had numerous defensive problems. He committed 12 errors in 91 games. Has the most trouble with balls hit right at him and over his head. Much better at coming in on the ball. He would most likely do better in left field, having handled it adequately in 1981.

OVERALL:

Robinson: "Has lost a few steps, but can do some things for you--hit and steal a base."

Martin: "Usually hits well. Erratic, but his speed still gets him hits. I feel that he is still a competent player, though outside problems have hurt his relationships with several managers. Tends to brood and complain."

GREG LUZINSKI
DH, No. 19
RR, 6'1", 225 lbs.
ML Svc: 11 years
Born: 11-22-51 in Chicago, IL

1982 STATISTICS

AVG	G	AB	R	H	2B	3B	HR	RBI	BB	SO	SB
.292	159	583	87	170	37	1	18	102	89	120	1

CAREER STATISTICS

AVG	G	AB	R	H	2B	3B	HR	RBI	BB	SO	SB
.281	1552	5591	760	1569	305	23	262	975	719	1298	30

HITTING:

Hitting is what Luzinski does best. In fact, it is all he does. He is strictly a designated hitter, and has not played in the field since he left the Phillies for the White Sox in 1980.

He is a killer--he eats up mistakes from opposing pitchers. Both lefthanders and righthanders try to throw him fastballs in on his hands. Change speeds if ahead in the count, even bounce the breaking ball. Luzinski loves the low fastball, but has a short stride and a compact swing that enables him to wait well on breaking pitches. Inside breaking pitches can tie him up. Pitchers who can set him up usually have the best success. Tommy John gave him fits last season. Luzinski has done very well against Toronto for the past two seasons, but had a tough time against Kansas City in 1982.

He is a consistent hitter against both left and righthanders. He walks a lot, but strikes out a lot too. He is a gap hitter, and often reaches the alleys.

Luzinski's hitting style may be changing under the tutelage of the Sox' hitting instructor, Charley Lau. Some adjustments at the plate gave him more base hits up the middle last season, but The Bull's power suffered. He hit just 18 home runs, even though he kept his RBI production high. Even in 1981's strike-shortened season, he hit 21 homers, and his career average is nearly 27 per season.

Luzinski blamed his power shortage on the wide expanses of his home park, but the statistics really don't back him up. He hit .325 at home, and .262 on the road.

Overall rating, above average to excellent.

BASERUNNING:

Luzinski has thick, heavily-muscled legs and absolutely no speed to first. He does not like to run and he does not run well, though he is a very smart baserunner. He knows his physical capabilities, and can stretch a single into an occasional double if he thinks he can make it.

OVERALL:

Martin: "He is a strong, power hitter who hits home runs and knocks them in. With his strength, he can wait on a pitch, or if fooled, he still can muscle it into the outfield."

Harwell: "Super strong, and a good RBI man. I say bat him fourth, then sit back and watch."

SPARKY LYLE
LHP, No. 28
LL, 6'1", 182 lbs.
ML Svc: 16 years
Born: 7-22-44 in DuBois, PA

PITCHING:

You can't miss Sparky. He's the guy with the best handlebar moustache in baseball. He's as natural a short reliever as anyone who's ever put on a pitching toe.

Lyle throws straight overhand and thrives on pressure. He loves to come in with the game on the line. He needs a lot of work to be effective, but he didn't get it with Philadelphia or the White Sox last season. His rustiness, and maybe his age, showed.

His game plan is simple: Slider, slider, slider. That's all he throws and all he needs to throw when things are on the line. His slider used to be even better, but still rates above average when Sparky has it working right. His fastball is about 83-85 MPH, and he'll use it about 25% of the time. The rest of the time look for the slider. He throws it until the opposition starts hitting it.

He's more effective pitching against lefthanded hitters, especially those who try and pull him. His greatest strength is his mental toughness and experience. He doesn't scare, but wildness was a problem in 1982.

If you miss his moustache, Lyle also has another constant trademark--a large chew of tobacco in his mouth. He doesn't take himself seriously and is a good guy to have around the clubhouse to keep things loose when the going gets tough. Loves cheeseburgers, as much his staple as the slider.

FIELDING:

Age has slowed Sparky somewhat and he doesn't move like he did, but he still is an average fielder. Makes up for what he's lost in quickness with experience and anticipation. Average move to first.

OVERALL:

Still wants to pitch, but was unable to convince the Phillies or White Sox last season that his career wasn't over.

McCarver: "Most dominant left-handed reliever in his--or anybody else's--time. Was counted out to make the Phillies roster last season but showed his competitiveness and came through. Wildness probably was caused by lack of work. Revered by his teammates."

Coleman: "Was one of the top three relievers in the game a couple years back, but his better days are behind him."

1982 STATISTICS

W	L	ERA	G	GS	CG	IP	H	R	ER	BB	SO	SV
3	3	4.68	45	0	0	48	61	27	25	19	18	3

CAREER STATISTICS

W	L	ERA	G	GS	CG	IP	H	R	ER	BB	SO	SV
99	76	2.88	944	0	0	1390	1292	519	445	481	873	238

TOM PACIORE K
OF/INF, No. 44
RR, 6'4", 210 lbs.
ML Svc: 11 years
Born: 11-2-46 in Detroit, MI

1982 STATISTICS

AVG	G	AB	R	H	2B	3B	HR	RBI	BB	SO	SB
.312	104	382	49	119	27	4	11	55	24	53	3

CAREER STATISTICS

AVG	G	AB	R	H	2B	3B	HR	RBI	BB	SO	SB
.283	959	2827	343	799	164	24	65	357	177	478	39

VS. RHP

VS. LHP

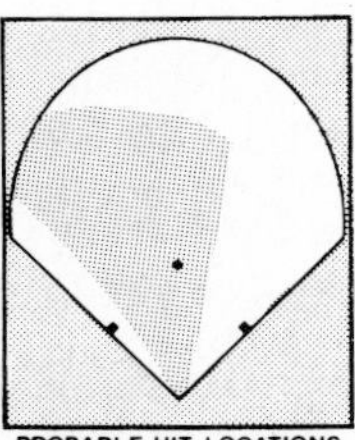
PROBABLE HIT LOCATIONS

HITTING:

Paciorek bats out of a slightly open crouched stance, standing in the center to low in the box. A part-time player throughout most of his career, he blossomed at the plate in Seattle in 1981 and has been a consistent .300 hitter the past two seasons.

Paciorek is a line drive hitter, and likes the ball down in the strike zone. Righthanders get him out with hard breaking pitches and fastballs up and in. Lefthanders should keep the ball away and change speeds often. Paciorek hits a lot of ground balls and usually is a good hitter on turf.

Though he is a pull hitter, Paciorek is a smart, hungry hitter who uses all of the field and reaches the alleys often. His average never dropped below .300 last season but he does tend to hit in streaks, and can be particularly dangerous in the middle of one.

Paciorek is rated average to above average in the clutch and hitting behind the runners, but hit just .275 with runners in scoring position last year. He hit poorly in Chicago's Comiskey Park (.281, 0 HR, 17 RBI in 178 AB) but more than made up for it on the road (.338, 11 HR, 38 RBI in 204 AB). He hit .300 against righthanders, .336 against lefties. Does not bunt well. Overall rating, average to above average.

BASERUNNING:

He has average speed to first and is no threat to steal. A smart runner but conservative on the basepaths.

FIELDING:

Paciorek converted from the outfield to first base last season and still has a lot to learn. Average to below average going to his right and left. Poor going after balls hit down the line. Not very good at digging throws out of the dirt, either.

OVERALL:

Robinson: "Spent a long time as a back up. Was released twice but now is on top of his game as a hitter. Got to give him credit. Best when he has a bat in his hand."

Harwell: "A solid, major league hitter."

AURELIO RODRIGUEZ
INF, No. 20
RR, 5'11", 180 lbs.
ML Svc: 16 years
Born: 12-28-47 in Sonora, MX

1982 STATISTICS

AVG	G	AB	R	H	2B	3B	HR	RBI	BB	SO	SB
.241	118	257	24	62	15	1	3	31	11	35	0

CAREER STATISTICS

AVG	G	AB	R	H	2B	3B	HR	RBI	BB	SO	SB
.239	1950	6524	611	1558	286	46	123	645	324	926	35

HITTING:

Rodriguez hits from a closed, upright stance and stands low in the batter's box. He is a high fastball hitter, so keep everything down and away. A pull hitter, Rodriguez has trouble with breaking balls, although he made some strides toward improving in that area in 1982. It's best to change speeds and to throw him off-speed pitches.

Although his value to a team is a superb glove, Rodriguez hit .328 with runners in scoring position last season, playing the second half as a regular. He is a better hitter when playing regularly, and raised his average from the .150's to .241 when he won a starting role.

Rodriguez' pull-hitting style makes him even more dangerous in Boston, Minnesota and Toronto. Rodriguez does not walk much, but does not strike out much, either. Does not hit very well behind the runner or on the hit-and-run. Occasionally reaches the alleys, and is best when hitting seventh or eighth in the lineup.

Jim Palmer and Bob Stanley give Rodriguez trouble, but he hits lob-throwing Dave LaRoche of New York quite well. Generally, he is a much more effective hitter against lefthanders. Overall rating, average.

BASERUNNING:

His speed to first and stealing are both rated average to below average. Rodriguez is not a particularly good baserunner, will not steal, and is not good at breaking up the double play. He is very conservative on the basepaths.

FIELDING:

A previous Gold Glove winner, age has neither slowed nor tarnished Rodriguez' glove at third base. His defense can still help a team. His arm, throwing accuracy and range are all rated excellent. His move to both his left and right are also good and quick, rated well above average to excellent. Rodriguez made just nine errors in 118 games in 1982. He is especially good at guarding the line and coming in on bunts or slow-choppers.

OVERALL:

Robinson: "One of the best throwing arms I have ever seen. He is doing very well for his age and helped the Sox a lot last season. If he hits just a little, it's a plus."

Martin: "His value now is as a back up third baseman. He can play well for short stretches, and still has a good arm."

MIKE SQUIRES
INF, No. 25
LL, 5'11", 190 lbs.
ML Svc: 5 years
Born: 3-5-52 in Kalamazoo, MI

1982 STATISTICS

AVG	G	AB	R	H	2B	3B	HR	RBI	BB	SO	SB
.267	116	195	33	52	9	3	1	21	14	13	3

CAREER STATISTICS

AVG	G	AB	R	H	2B	3B	HR	RBI	BB	SO	SB
.269	530	1345	180	362	48	9	5	124	114	90	40

VS. RHP

VS. LHP

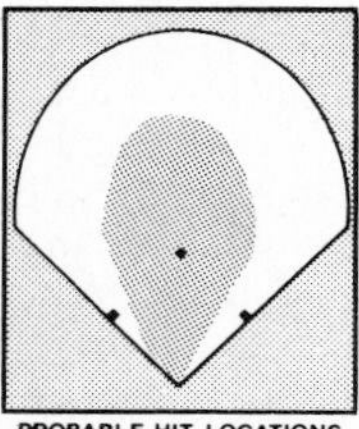
PROBABLE HIT LOCATIONS

HITTING:

Squires is a valuable player to have around, although he does not hit with any real power. Squires stands in with a fairly upright, slightly closed stance. He is a low ball hitter who likes the ball out over the outer half of the plate, but righthanders can get him out by throwing sliders inside. Keep everything else away. Lefthanders should give him fastballs, up. He hits the curve well and can handle the sinker and change-up.

He does not walk much but bunts well. He is a good contact hitter who can fill the No. 2 spot in the batting order but is much better hitting seventh or lower. Squires is much more effective against righthanded pitching (.293 in 157 at-bats last season) than lefthanders (.158 in 38 at-bats). Generally a line drive hitter, Squires hits a lot of ground balls up the middle against righthanders and a lot of fly balls to left-center against lefties.

BASERUNNING:

He is average to above average in speed to first and is a smart baserunner. But Squires is more than conservative on the bases. He can steal a base but is not enough of a threat to distract a pitcher. Good at breaking up the double play, Squires occasionally slides head first, but usually feet first.

FIELDING:

This is Squires' forte. He earned a Gold Glove as a first baseman in 1981, the only season he was used as a regular. Generally regarded as among the best fielding first baseman in baseball, his range and throwing accuracy are rated as above average to excellent though he has only an average arm. He is rated above average to excellent in going both to his left or right. He guards the line well and has a knack for making the big play in the clutch. Picks up the rest of the infield defense with above average ability to scoop throws in the dirt. Had just three errors in 116 games in 1982.

OVERALL:

Probably best off the bench as a defensive replacement or platooned against righthanded pitching. Will hit .260 to .270 and is a superb team man.

Harwell: "Best fielder at his position in the American League."

Robinson: "A good player to have on a team. Being a defensive replacement is about all he can do since he has very little power at the plate."

Martin: "Excellent first baseman with a contact bat but should be platooned. Hard to strike out against righthanders."

STEVE TROUT
LHP, No. 33
LL, 6'4", 189 lbs.
ML Svc: 5 years
Born: 7-20-57 in Detroit, MI

PITCHING:

They call him "Rainbow," and on 90-degree days he wears two sweatshirts when he's pitching. On 40-degree days, he pitches in his shirtsleeves.

Trout's free-spirited ways buried him in White Sox manager Tony LaRussa's doghouse last year. The final straw apparently was when the lefthander threw a breaking ball on a pitchout in a game in Texas. Catcher's interference was called, the runner reached base and the Rangers went on to a big inning and a win. Trout did not pitch much after that last mid-August start, and did not pitch at all in September.

Unfulfilled promise is a tag that is following Trout now, but he still has a golden left arm. He's primarily a power pitcher who throws from a three-quarter delivery. Trout is strictly a starter. As a reliever, he's flopped a couple of times.

Trout probably was the hardest thrower, save for Jim Kern, on the Sox staff last year with a fastball in the 90 MPH range. His biggest problem is control. He constantly struggles to put the ball where he wants to. His curve needs work, and he uses it infrequently. But he has a good slider, down and quick. He also throws a good straight change, but rarely goes to it. He should use it more often.

When behind in the count, Trout goes to his strength, the fastball. Lefthanders hit Trout better than righthanders last season. He doesn't like to pitch in, and it costs him. He has been working on a spitball, and does not respond well to pressure situations.

Trout has always pitched well in Yankee Stadium and in Baltimore. He struggles in Fenway and in Anaheim.

FIELDING:

He has an above average move to first, and runners have a hard time stealing on Trout because he has a quick move to the plate, too. Very quick. Above average quickness. Rated above average in fielding bunts and overall effectiveness in fielding his position.

OVERALL:

A lot has been said about Trout's promise, but if it doesn't happen this year, it probably never will. Critics say he is reluctant to put in the work and pay the price for success.

Robinson: "Needs experience on how to be a complete pitcher and how to gain cunning. Has the stuff to win 20. There are differing opinions on what is best for Trout--a swift kick, gentle nudge or tender loving care."

Martin: "Started out looking like he'd be better. Inconsistent, but still so very young."

1982 STATISTICS

W	L	ERA	G	GS	CG	IP	H	R	ER	BB	SO	SV
6	9	4.26	25	19	2	120	130	76	57	50	62	0

CAREER STATISTICS

W	L	ERA	G	GS	CG	IP	H	R	ER	BB	SO	SV
37	40	3.82	115	78	19	622	665	318	264	207	292	4

MARV FOLEY
C, No. 16
LR, 6'0", 185 lbs.
ML Svc: 4 years
Born: 8-29-53 in Stanford, KY

HITTING, BASERUNNING, FIELDING:

Foley backs up Carlton Fisk and Marc Hill. Pitchers generally get him out with a steady diet of breaking balls. He has trouble with slow stuff and sliders. A pull hitter, Foley has shown flashes of power in earlier major league trials.

He has a big swing, but doesn't strike out much. Usually makes contact, enhancing his value as a pinch-hitter. Not called on to bunt much, and does not draw walks often. He is a more effective hitter against righthanders.

Foley is very slow out of the box and down to first. No threat to steal at all, and is a poor baserunner overall.

Chicago pitchers have the utmost confidence in the fingers he puts down. Arm problems made Foley's throwing suspect, but he appeared to be throwing better last season. He is a hard-nosed, strong competitor who made the 1982 Chicago club on sheer hustle and desire. Despite his slowness afoot, Foley moves well behind the plate, fields the bunt well, and does not shy away from a confrontation when blocking the plate. Does not hesitate to snap throw to any base with runners on.

OVERALL:

Robinson: "Pure hitter who can come off of the bench and sting the ball. His best bet to stay in the big leagues is to continue doing just what he has been doing."

JERRY HAIRSTON
OF, No. 17
SR, 5'10", 180 lbs.
ML Svc: 5 years
Born: 2-16-52 in Birmingham, AL

HITTING, BASERUNNING, FIELDING:

Hairston's main role in 1982 was as a pinch-hitter, and he led the club with nine RBIs and two home runs in 45 at-bats off the bench.

Hairston is much more effective from the left side of the plate against righthanded pitching. Usually a straightaway hitter, but he can pull the ball. Good with men on base in the clutch. He likes to hit fastballs as a righthanded hitter, and both high and low fastballs from the left side. Pitchers get him out by changing speeds and giving him a lot of slow breaking balls. Will jump on a pitcher's "mistake". Overall rating above average.

No threat on the bases whatsoever and will not steal a base.

Hairston makes up for his lack of speed with good instincts. He can play all three outfield positions, and gets a very good jump on fly balls. Arm strength and accuracy are average.

OVERALL:

Hairston's value to any club would be his ability to come off the bench and deliver at the plate consistently as a pinch-hitter.

Robinson: "A good guy to come off the bench and hit. Very aggressive at the plate. He comes out swinging and had some big hits off the bench for the White Sox last year."

Martin: "Good to have around if a team can afford to carry a pinch-hitter only."

MARC HILL
C, No. 7
RR, 6'3", 215 lbs.
ML Svc: 7 years
Born: 2-18-52 in
Elsberry, MO

HITTING, BASERUNNING, FIELDING:

Hill's playing time is usually limited to Sunday afternoon games following Saturday night games so that Fisk can have a day off. He is a pull hitter who likes fastballs up in the strike zone. Jam him with fastballs on his hands or low and inside. Righthanders get him out with fastballs down and away, and with a lot of breaking pitches. Lefthanders come in with the slider. He hits pitches out over the plate very well, and likes to extend his arms. His weakness is the breaking pitch and off-speed stuff.

He is much more effective against lefthanders and plays best on a platoon basis. He has little value as a pinch-hitter, and is rarely called upon to do that.

Hill is big, strong, and very slow. He has no speed whatsoever, whether it is down the line to first or on the bases. He is very conservative, will not take the extra base, and is easy to double up.

OVERALL:

Robinson: "Cannot play every day but can help you when you spot him around and play him against particular pitchers."

Martin: "A low average hitter and part-time player. His good years as a catcher with the Giants are behind him. He could also play first or third in a pinch."

CLEVELAND STADIUM
Cleveland Indians

Seating Capacity: 76,685
Playing Surface: Natural Grass

Dimensions
Left Field Pole: 320 ft.
Left-Center Field: 377 ft.
Center Field: 400 ft.
Right-Center Field: 385 ft.
Right Field Pole: 320 ft.
Height of Outfield Walls:
Left Field: 9 ft.
Center Field: 8 ft.
Right Field: 9 ft.

This stadium was always known as Municipal Stadium, but its name has been changed to Cleveland Stadium. You can call it by any name you want, but several things about it will never change. It is almost always cold, drab and extremely windy; it is the largest stadium in baseball and can seat more than 76,000 people; its dirt and natural grass, particularly in September and October, are always chewed up because the Cleveland Browns play there; the mound is the worst in the American League, and many opposing pitchers claim the loose dirt makes it difficult to plant their front foot into. Several pitchers, including Rich Gossage and Dave Righetti of the New York Yankees, have suffered slight shoulder injuries after pitching in the Stadium; and depending on the type of team that Indians' President Gabe Paul fields, the dimensions of the fences seem to change.

At one time when the Cleveland Indians had powerful teams (in the late 1940s and early 1950s), it was virtually impossible to hit a homer in the stadium because of the unbelievable distances to the left and center field fences. In 1948, Joe DiMaggio hit three homers in one game in the stadium, and the feat was hailed as virtually miraculous. Today, the fences have been moved in and an auxiliary fence has also been added making it 320 feet down each line, 377 to left-center, 385 to right-center, and 400 to straightaway-center.

The problem that batters face, however, is the wind that whips off Lake Erie directly behind the ballpark. It is brutally cold in Cleveland in April and May and with the exception of certain short periods of temperate weather in the summer, retains the cold in August, September and October as well.

Because the Indians have had mediocre teams for the past 15 years, attendance has dwindled and a crowd of 20,000 will look like a mere crowded elevator because of the tremendous amount of empty seats. An advantage to power pitchers becomes greater in here, however, because when the Indians play day games and the sun is shining, that very same sun seems magnified, possibly because of the clouds that hover over the Lake. Fastballs are almost impossible to hit on sunny days. Rain always presents a problem because the field seems to hold excess moisture and players have trouble running through the grass in either the infield or outfield.

Cleveland Stadium is a neutral park favoring neither the hitter nor the pitcher. The stadium is situated on Lake Erie and is affected more by the elements than any other park in the American League. It just depends on which way the wind is blowing as to who has the advantage.

At this time, the park slightly favors the righthanded hitter but that seems to change every couple of years as the distances are constantly changed.

BUD ANDERSON
RHP, No. 51
RR, 6'3", 210 lbs.
ML Svc: 1 year
Born: 5-27-56 in Rockville Ctr, NY

PITCHING:

Bud Anderson is an interesting pitcher, a righthander who did everything--start, long relief and short relief--in his rookie year. He throws straight overhand, a former Rutgers football player who gets by with sheer power. He does not worry about the weaknesses of the hitters or picking spots for his pitches. The Indians hope he will gain more finesse with experience.

Anderson runs into trouble when he loses his control. It is hard to tell when these lapses occur. One inning he is throwing well and the next he is in deep trouble because he can't throw a strike. He has a fastball that has been consistently clocked in the high 80s. More importantly, the ball moves.

In addition to his fastball, he has a sharp slider that can be effective. But he is not consistent with it, sometimes throwing it in the dirt. He does not have a curveball or change-up worth discussing.

He has done everything for the Indians, but he seems best suited for starting or long relief. He does not rattle in pressure situations. But he needs another pitch to set up his fastball and slider. A change-up or slow curve would do the trick.

FIELDING:

A big guy, Anderson does not move very well when it comes to fielding bunts or slow rollers in front of the plate. Nor are his reactions very quick, meaning he fails to glove some hard-hit balls up the middle that other pitchers may handle. Some teams have hurt him by bunting on him.

His move to first base is just fair, and he does not have a very quick delivery to home plate. In other words, he is a typical young pitcher with a lot of raw talent who needs to refine his game.

OVERALL:

Anderson is an average pitcher who can be outstanding on certain days. He needs to be more consistent with his control, improve his move to first and add another pitch.

Robinson: "Anderson has pitched all over, but I like him best in long relief or as a starter. He is a hard thrower, not afraid to challenge hitters. He is the only pitcher I'd seen in 1982 who blew the Orioles away for four innings with nothing more than a fastball. I have only seen a fastball and a slider from him and it's tough to get by with two pitches. Anderson is a pitcher you have to watch. I think he might be one of the surprises in the American League this year. The more I see of him, the more I like him."

1982 STATISTICS

W	L	ERA	G	GS	CG	IP	H	R	ER	BB	SO	SV
3	4	3.35	25	5	1	80	84	37	30	30	44	0

CAREER STATISTICS

W	L	ERA	G	GS	CG	IP	H	R	ER	BB	SO	SV
3	4	3.35	25	5	1	80	84	37	30	30	44	0

CHRIS BANDO
C, No. 23
SR, 6'0", 195 lbs.
ML Svc: 2 years
Born: 2-4-56 in
Cleveland, OH

1982 STATISTICS

AVG	G	AB	R	H	2B	3B	HR	RBI	BB	SO	SB
.212	66	184	13	39	6	1	3	16	24	30	0

CAREER STATISTICS

AVG	G	AB	R	H	2B	3B	HR	RBI	BB	SO	SB
.212	87	231	16	49	9	1	3	22	26	32	0

VS. RHP

VS. LHP

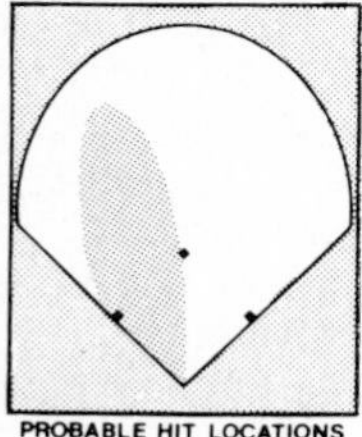
PROBABLE HIT LOCATIONS

HITTING:

A switch-hitter, Bando was a disappointment at the plate for Cleveland in 1982. He won the Class AA Southern League batting title in 1980 and hit over .300 at Class AAA in 1981.

With the Indians, he never produced at bat. He hit barely over .100 with runners in scoring position. He took a lot of pitches and was often called out on strikes. He usually batted righthanded as he platooned with Ron Hassey.

Bando has a slightly open stance. He stands deep in the box with a bit of a crouch. Righthanded, he is a low ball hitter. He prefers to pull everything and looks for the fastball. Batting left, he handles high pitches very well. From both sides of the plate, he has trouble with breaking balls outside. He does not like slow stuff. His ability to bunt, draw walks and hit behind the runner is all below average.

BASERUNNING:

Bando is a below average runner. He slides feet first. He does not steal bases or run well from home to first.

FIELDING:

Bando has the makings of an excellent defensive catcher. He has a great arm with above average accuracy and release point. Because of his inexperience, he does not handle pitchers as well as he will in the future. He gives a good target and blocks most pitches in the dirt.

OVERALL:

Despite his rookie year problems, the Indians are high on Bando. He has all the ingredients of a starting big league catcher. Hitting is the big question mark.

Robinson: "1983 holds the key to Bando's future. He has had enough games in the majors to find out if he can exert himself to become the player everyone thinks he can. He has a long way to go. Switch-hitting is a big plus for him."

Martin: "A young hustling and aggressive player. Like his brother, Sal, Chris has a temper."

Harwell: "A coming star. He will be a solid catcher."

ALAN BANNISTER
INF/OF, No. 7
RR, 5'11", 175 lbs.
ML Svc: 9 years
Born: 9-3-51 in
Buena Park, CA

HITTING:

Bannister makes very good contact and is a straightaway hitter. Many of his hits are of the "cheap" variety--bloopers, grounders through the infield, and soft liners just beyond the reach of the infielders. Yet, he gets these types of hits year after year. A lot of his hits may not look impressive, but they are line drives in the box score.

Early in the count, Bannister looks for the fastball and tries to pull it. He does not get many extra base hits. But when they do occur, they usually come off a fastball on the first or second pitch. He will try to pull the ball until he has two strikes. Then, he becomes an entirely different kind of hitter, one who tries to hit the ball to right field.

He likes the ball inside, so it would be best to start him out with a breaking ball away. In clutch situations, he is average at best, and will drive in less than 50 runs a season. He is a good hit-and-run man, a decent bunter but he has some trouble with the change-up. Often, he starts the season with a low batting average and doesn't begin to hit until June.

BASERUNNING:

Bannister has above average speed and intelligence. He has the ability to steal a base, but will only do it when the need is apparent. He doesn't run just for the sake of padding his stolen base statistics. He slides feet first and seldom is thrown out. In his last two years with Cleveland, Bannister has been successful on 75% of his stolen base attempts.

FIELDING:

Bannister is a player without a position. He has done everything for the Indians but pitch and catch. He has been used primarily at second base and left field. His best spot is the outfield, because he has the speed to run down balls in the alleys. His throwing arm leaves something to be desired.

At second base, he has a weak double play pivot and not much range. He is nothing more than a reserve at shortstop or third.

1982 STATISTICS

AVG	G	AB	R	H	2B	3B	HR	RBI	BB	SO	SB
.267	101	348	40	93	16	1	4	41	42	42	18

CAREER STATISTICS

AVG	G	AB	R	H	2B	3B	HR	RBI	BB	SO	SB
.270	742	2376	340	642	110	22	11	228	224	419	91

VS. RHP

VS. LHP

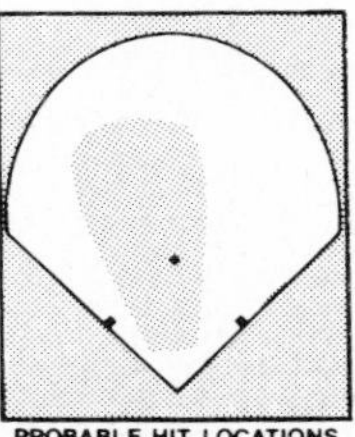
PROBABLE HIT LOCATIONS

OVERALL:

Robinson: "Bannister is a good offensive player who did not perform as well in 1982 as in his two previous seasons with Cleveland. He can bunt, steal, and get some hits for you. Finding a position for him has been a problem."

Harwell: "Bannister is a good major leaguer, especially on offense. His baserunning is outstanding."

LEN BARKER
RHP, No. 39
RR, 6'4", 215 lbs.
ML Svc: 6 years
Born: 7-7-55 in
Ft. Knox, KY

PITCHING:

Len Barker has seemed to be on the edge of greatness for three years now, but an outstanding rating has eluded him. A bone spur in his right elbow has trimmed a 95 MPH fastball to one in the high 80 s. He seems to struggle in the last few innings, and after he pitches, his elbow swells quite a bit.

He has the classic motion for a power pitcher, throwing straight overhand with a strong push-off from the mound. When right, he can be among the most intimidating pitchers in the American League. He has to watch his weight carefully, and is a much better pitcher at 220 pounds than at 235-240. He is best suited as a starter and pitches better in a five-man rotation than a four-man setup.

In addition to his fastball, Barker uses his curve quite often. He throws it so hard that it often is confused with a slider. He does not have a change-up that he uses with any consistency. When in a pressure situation, the hitter usually can count on seeing a fastball early in the count. When he has two strikes, Barker likes to go for the whiff with his sharp curve. In 1980 and 1981, he led the league in strikeouts.

FIELDING:

A big guy, he does not move very well when it comes to handling slow rollers or bunts in front of the plate. His reactions are not very good when it comes to handling shots hit back at him. His big, slow windup often carries him far to the first base side of the pitcher's mound, leaving the middle wide open.

Another weakness is his inability to hold runners on base. In 1980, more bases were stolen against Barker than any other pitcher in the American League. He has a very high and slow leg-kick, which gives runners a great jump from first base. In 1982, he worked on shortening his kick with runners on base. He can do it at times, but feels it hurts his velocity. As a result, he will return to the higher kick and slower motion in pressure situations.

Certain teams have literally run him out of games, especially the Kansas City Royals. To his credit, Barker does not seem to get upset when bases are stolen against him.

OVERALL:

Barker is an above average pitcher with the ability to be outstanding. As he has proven, on certain days he can be virtually unhittable. But he needs to improve his control and fielding skills.

Harwell: "Barker is an over-powering pitcher, but he often gets behind in the count. He is very easy to steal on."

Martin: "People keep waiting for Barker to be sensational. He could be much better in years to come if his arm is okay."

1982 STATISTICS

W	L	ERA	G	GS	CG	IP	H	R	ER	BB	SO	SV
15	11	3.90	33	33	10	244	211	117	106	88	187	0

CAREER STATISTICS

W	L	ERA	G	GS	CG	IP	H	R	ER	BB	SO	SV
54	42	4.10	166	115	30	895	850	445	408	355	685	5

BERT BLYLEVEN
RHP, No. 28
RR, 6'3", 208 lbs.
ML Svc: 13 years
Born: 4-6-51 in Zeist, Holland

PITCHING:

The Indians were expecting big things from Blyleven in 1982, but in late April last year, he injured his right elbow and was out for the season. This put a damper on Cleveland's season, as Blyleven was considered the heart of the pitching staff. Blyleven's operation was a serious one.

What happened to Blyleven was that a muscle in his right elbow literally fell off the bone. The surgery reattached the muscle to the bone. No one is sure how far, or even if, Blyleven will be able to come back.

When healthy, Blyleven had the best and hardest curve in the majors. It is a pitch that is extremely demanding on the arm, especially the elbow. His fastball also was in the 90 MPH range with a good hop. It is impossible to predict if his reconstructed elbow will be able to withstand the strain that Blyleven's curve makes on his arm.

Before joining the Indians, Blyleven pitched for a dozen years in the majors and never had any arm trouble. In his first year with Cleveland, he averaged eight innings per start, but first complained of elbow trouble in September of 1981. Many believe he originally hurt his arm when he pitched nine innings the first game after the two-month baseball strike in 1981.

With the Indians, Blyleven appeared to be coming into his own. Many felt he should have been a consistent 20-game winner, but he was a pitcher who valued strikeouts over victories. In Cleveland, he used his change-up more and was a better pitcher, even though his strikeout total fell.

FIELDING:

Blyleven is a good athlete. He fields his position very well. He does a good job getting off the mound to handle bunts and balls tapped in front of the plate. He has good reactions that help him to spear balls hit hard up the middle.

When it comes to holding runners on first base, Blyleven is only average. He does not ignore the runners, but he won't make a lot of throws to first base. Since he is a power pitcher, the catcher usually has a decent chance to throw out a stealing baserunner.

OVERALL:

When healthy, Blyleven is one of the premier pitchers in the American League. Unsually, you can count on him to go 7-8 innings and hold the opposition under four runs. He is a great competitor who can get the big strikeout for you.

But his arm injury has placed a big cloud over his career. No one is sure if he can come back in 1983. His future will depend upon the condition of his arm.

1982 STATISTICS

W	L	ERA	G	GS	CG	IP	H	R	ER	BB	SO	SV
2	2	4.87	4	4	0	20	16	14	11	11	19	0

CAREER STATISTICS

W	L	ERA	G	GS	CG	IP	H	R	ER	BB	SO	SV
169	150	2.97	411	405	159	3020	2715	1117	995	821	2376	0

TOM BRENNAN
RHP, No. 45
RR, 6'1", 180 lbs.
ML Svc: 1 year plus
Born: 10-30-52 in Chicago, IL

PITCHING:

Brennan has one of the strangest windups in the major leagues. With no one on base, he literally stops in the middle of his motion and stands there on one leg for a moment before continuing his delivery to home plate. He throws sidearm. The Indians use him in long relief, which is his best role.

Brennan is not blessed with overwhelming ability. His fastball is below average, in the low 80s. He does not have a trick pitch, and relies primarily on his fastball and slider. He tries to get his fastball to sink and likes to pitch inside. His assets are his poise and great control. He seldom drops behind in the count and tries to pitch to the weakness of the hitter.

If Brennan does not hit his spot when he gets the ball up in the strike zone, he is very prone to giving up the long ball. He is far more effective against righthanded hitters. When facing lefties, he tends to throw more overhand.

Early in his career, Brennan was a power pitcher who threw straight over the top. But his lack of success and control troubles in the minors caused him to develop his odd delivery.

FIELDING:

One of Brennan's best attributes is his willingness to work. He is a fine fielder, quick off the mound to handle bunts and slow rollers. Despite his windup, he ends up in a fine position to handle shots hit back at him. In sum, he is a good gloveman and obviously got that way by working at it.

Brennan also does a good job holding runners on base. His fine control means the catcher is likely to receive a good pitch to handle, making it easier for him to throw out stealing base runners.

OVERALL:

At best, Brennan is an average pitcher. He could use another pitch to go with his fastball and slider. He is best suited for being the No. 9 or 10 man on a pitching staff.

Robinson: "Brennan has to have everything going for him to be successful. He has great control with two average pitches."

Martin: "Brennan has banged around the minors for 8-9 years and still hasn't cemented a major league job."

Harwell: "Brennan gets by with his unorthodox delivery."

1982 STATISTICS

W	L	ERA	G	GS	CG	IP	H	R	ER	BB	SO	SV
4	2	4.27	30	4	0	92	112	51	44	10	46	2

CAREER STATISTICS

W	L	ERA	G	GS	CG	IP	H	R	ER	BB	SO	SV
6	4	3.92	37	10	1	140	161	71	61	24	61	2

MIGUEL DILONE
OF, No. 27
SR, 6'0", 160 lbs.
ML Svc: 9 years
Born: 11-1-54 in Santiago, DR

1982 STATISTICS

AVG	G	AB	R	H	2B	3B	HR	RBI	BB	SO	SB
.235	104	379	50	89	12	3	3	25	25	36	33

CAREER STATISTICS

AVG	G	AB	R	H	2B	3B	HR	RBI	BB	SO	SB
.272	591	1630	251	444	56	19	5	105	105	155	215

VS. RHP

VS. LHP

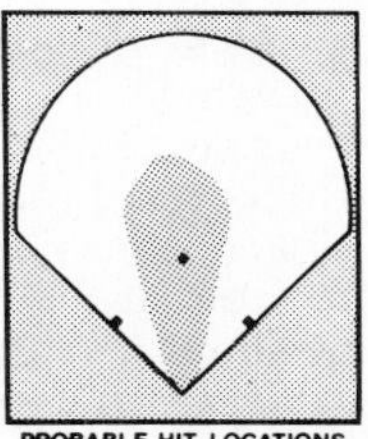
PROBABLE HIT LOCATIONS

HITTING:

1982 was a year to forget for Dilone. He hit three homers early in the year, and though he did not hit another one for the rest of the year, he suddenly thought he was a power hitter. He is a small guy, and was swinging for the fences. This state of mind accounted for the dramatic drop in Dilone's batting average.

When Dilone is right, he hits the ball on the ground and gets a lot of leg hits. This is especially true when he hits from the left side. He has the ability to bunt the ball for a hit, and has been known to bunt the ball to the shortstop. As a righthanded hitter, Dilone does not bunt very well and tends to hit far too many fly balls. When he hits the ball in the air, it usually is an out since he isn't strong enough to reach the fences.

Dilone needs more discipline at the plate. He draws few walks. He likes the ball low in the strike zone. He will swing at high pitches and usually pops them up. He needs to bunt more, especially from the right side of the plate.

BASERUNNING:

He led the Indians in stolen bases in 1982, even though he did not play all the time. Dilone gets a pretty good lead, but his lack of concentration often leads to his being picked off.

Dilone is not a bright baserunner. He has upset his teammates by streaking to third base with two outs and a lefthanded hitter at bat. This strategy usually did not work out well for Cleveland or Dilone.

FIELDING:

Dilone is a below average outfielder with a very poor throwing arm. He does not judge the ball very well. He can run and has the ability to make leaping catches in front of the fence.

The Indians originally obtained Dilone to serve as a back up centerfielder. He did not play very well in center, or later in left. He has real trouble hitting the cutoff man.

OVERALL:

Dilone began the 1982 season as Cleveland's starting leftfielder, but he lost the job. Dilone sometimes pouts and clashed with Manager Dave Garcia, a very easygoing individual. His moods sometimes get in the way of his performance.

If Dilone is to return to his 1980 form, he needs to swing down on the ball and concentrate on hitting grounders. He also must bunt more. Most of all, he must forget about hitting home runs.

JUAN EICHELBERGER
RHP, No. 13
RR, 6'3", 205 lbs.
ML Svc: 3 years plus
Born: 10-21-53 in
St. Louis, MO

PITCHING:

Generally regarded as a starting pitcher, Eichelberger developed some delivery and control problems in 1982 and was moved to relief. He was trying to feel his way through by experimenting with an overhand and three-quarter delivery.

Always a power pitcher, Eichelberger's strong suit is throwing hard. He does not try to pick spots and pitch to a batter's weaknesses. If Eichelberger could throw to spots without sacrificing his velocity, he would be a dominating performer. His fastball is hard, but again, there seems to be the problem of control.

He has a tendency to throw his curveball in the dirt. The slider is average, but often goes wild and away. He has a weak change-up, and tries a sinker occasionally. It's often difficult to tell if he is throwing a brushback pitch or just one that went wild.

Overall rating, needs improvement.

FIELDING, HITTING, BASERUNNING:

Eichelberger is a fine athlete who fields his position fairly well. He has an above average move to first, but takes a long time to deliver the ball home, which takes some effectiveness away from his good move. He also tends to throw the ball away on pick-off attempts, and balks quite a bit.

His hitting needs a lot of work. His teammates cannot understand how such a good athlete could be such a poor hitter. He is an easy strike out, and in 1981 was one shy of a National League record by striking out 14 consecutive times. Bunts adequately.

Eichelberger's athletic prowess does appear on the basepaths and he has good speed.

OVERALL:

Overall, Eichelberger is an average to above average pitcher. On a given day he can be a world beater, and has the potential to be an outstanding pitcher if his control problems are corrected.

Coleman: "Eichelberger should be a better pitcher than he is. He just makes too many mistakes."

McCarver: "If Juan throws strikes early in the count, his chances of winning go up dramatically, but if he falls behind as he often does, hitters will wait for his fastball and often get it. Pitching is location and movement--velocity is important but often overrated and misunderstood."

1982 STATISTICS

W	L	ERA	G	GS	CG	IP	H	R	ER	BB	SO	SV
7	14	4.20	31	24	8	177	171	98	83	72	74	0

CAREER STATISTICS

W	L	ERA	G	GS	CG	IP	H	R	ER	BB	SO	SV
20	25	3.86	77	64	12	431	399	213	185	214	212	0

MIKE FISCHLIN
INF, No. 22
RR, 6'1", 165 lbs.
ML Svc: 4 years
Born: 9-13-55 in Sacramento, CA

1982 STATISTICS

AVG	G	AB	R	H	2B	3B	HR	RBI	BB	SO	SB
.268	112	276	34	74	12	1	0	21	34	36	9

CAREER STATISTICS

AVG	G	AB	R	H	2B	3B	HR	RBI	BB	SO	SB
.230	192	421	40	97	14	1	0	26	41	54	13

VS. RHP

VS. LHP

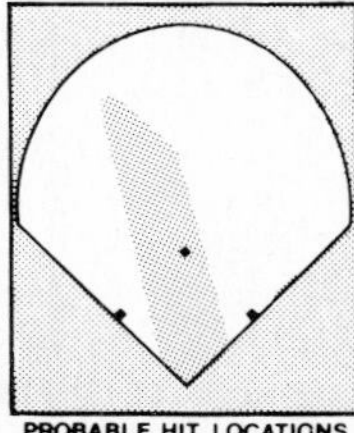
PROBABLE HIT LOCATIONS

HITTING:

Fischlin bounced around the Yankee and Houston farm systems before he came to Cleveland and got a shot at a regular shortstop job in the majors. He began the season as a utility infielder, but he took over for Jerry Dybzinski in June and won the job for the rest of the season. He was the most pleasant surprise of Cleveland's 1982 season.

He has changed his batting stance dramatically. He used to stand straight up and swing for the fences while holding the bat down at the end. That created a lot of 275' fly ball outs. Now, Fischlin hits out of an extreme crouch, holding the bat so low that the barrel actually touches the ground as he awaits the pitch. As a result, he also hits a lot of line drives and grounders. He is getting more hits to right field than ever before.

Fischlin has definitely improved with the bat. He likes high and inside fastballs, but he can hit some low pitches. He has almost no power and is basically a straightaway hitter. When he does get a hit, it usually is a single.

BASERUNNING:

Fischlin has above average speed and has stolen over 30 bases in some minor league seasons. He can steal a base in the right situation and does a good job going from first to third on a single to right. He is a decent bunter, and will get some hits in that fashion.

FIELDING:

The best part of Fischlin's play at shortstop is his aggressiveness. He charges almost every ball and has reliable hands. He has a neat way of catching ground balls on the run and throwing all in one motion. This makes his average arm seem better than it really is. He gets rid of the ball quickly on the double play.

OVERALL:

Fischlin is a self-made player who is getting the optimum out of his talent. He hustles, makes the routine plays and is a pesky hitter, even if he lacks power.

Robinson: "Fischlin is a real surprise for Cleveland and he has played better than anyone ever expected. He is a decent hitter and a steady shortstop."

Martin: "He won the shortstop job in June 1982 with a great series against the Red Sox. He is a pretty steady player, but not an ideal everyday shortstop."

ED GLYNN
LHP, No. 48
RL, 6'2", 180 lbs.
ML Svc: 4 years
Born: 6-3-53 in
Flushing, NY

PITCHING:

Glynn has always had the kind of arm you look for in a lefthanded relief pitcher. He has knocked around for over ten years and the Indians are his third organization. For the first time, he seems to be having some consistent success.

The first thing you notice about Glynn is his high leg kick and jerky motion. That has to help him against hitters as his delivery is very distracting. For most of his career, he has been a relief pitcher. The Indians have used him both in long and short relief. He throws straight over the top, although he will drop down sidearm once in a great while against certain lefthanded hitters. His fastball has been clocked in the middle to high 80s.

Glynn has a very hard slider, which is his best pitch. He tries to catch the outside corner with it against righthanded batters and he gets it to break straight down. The slider makes him especially effective against lefthanded hitters, but he can handle almost anyone when he is throwing well.

What has prevented Glynn from achieving more is lack of control. He has a tendency to fall behind in the count and become rattled. He is very prone to throwing his slider in the dirt and this has led to an abnormal amount of wild pitches. Nevertheless, his slider makes him a pitcher who can be very effective if used in the right spots. Against him, hitters tend to swing at a lot of pitches that are out of the strike zone.

FIELDING:

After he delivers the ball, Glynn's motion carries him far to the third base side of the mound. This leaves the middle wide open and makes it very difficult for him to recover and get to first base in time to cover the bag on a ground ball to the right side of the infield.

Even though he is a lefthanded pitcher, Glynn has lapses of concentration and does not always hold on baserunners the way he should. Furthermore, there is nothing special about his move to first base. Interestingly, he always pitches from the stretch position, even checking runners at first. He does this if there are runners on first or not. He feels pitching exclusively from the stretch aids his control.

OVERALL:

Glynn can be a useful lefthanded reliever. He seems to be maturing, and like many lefthanders, is developing later in his career. The slider and the way he controls it will be what will make or break him. He needs work on his fielding control.

Robinson: "Glynn is pitching better than any time in his undistinguished career. He has graduated from just getting lefthanded hitters out to pitching more innings. At times, his slider is unhittable."

Martin: "He has never come up to expectations. Still, he is valuable as a lefthanded reliever to complement a bullpen."

1982 STATISTICS

W	L	ERA	G	GS	CG	IP	H	R	ER	BB	SO	SV
5	2	4.17	47	0	0	49	43	27	23	30	54	4

CAREER STATISTICS

W	L	ERA	G	GS	CG	IP	H	R	ER	BB	SO	SV
12	15	4.05	161	8	1	249	234	124	112	141	169	12

HITTING:

Hargrove is a maddening hitter to pitch to. He takes forever between each pitch, stepping out of the box, tugging on his helmet, pulling on his batting glove and grabbing at his uniform. He has been appropriately called "the human rain delay."

His forte is getting on base. In fact, he has the best on base percentage of any active player. Perhaps the agonizing amount of time he takes between pitches causes him to draw more walks as pitchers are irritated by his routine.

Hargrove is a low ball hitter and likes pitches out over the plate. No matter who is pitching to him, Hargrove should be given nothing but inside pitches. He is above average in the clutch and handles the change-up very well. The harder you throw to Hargrove, the better chance you have of getting him out. He really hits the off-speed stuff. He hits very well against Boston, New York and Detroit.

He is an extremely disciplined hitter and draws close to 100 walks a season. He hits righthanders about as well as lefties. He is primarily a singles hitter who usually doesn't hit more than ten homers a year.

The best way to get Hargrove out is to get ahead of him in the count. He is probably best suited for leading off, although the Indians usually hit him No. 3 or No. 5 in the lineup.

BASERUNNING:

Through no fault of his own, Hargrove is a below average baserunner. He simply lacks speed. That is why some managers do not like him as a leadoff hitter, despite his great on base percentage. He hits into a lot of double plays and can't steal bases. This is the weakest part of his game.

MIKE HARGROVE
INF, No. 21
LL, 6'0", 195 lbs.
ML Svc: 10 years
Born: 10-26-49 in
Perryton, TX

1982 STATISTICS

AVG	G	AB	R	H	2B	3B	HR	RBI	BB	SO	SB
.281	160	591	67	166	26	1	4	65	101	60	2

CAREER STATISTICS

AVG	G	AB	R	H	2B	3B	HR	RBI	BB	SO	SB
.294	1292	4459	651	1311	217	21	74	558	795	445	23

VS. RHP

VS. LHP

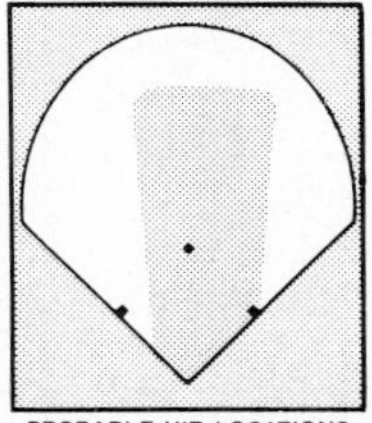
PROBABLE HIT LOCATIONS

FIELDING:

Hargrove is an above average first baseman. If he reaches a ball, he usually catches it. His arm is fair, but accurate. He usually makes fine throws to second base on force plays. He handles throws in the dirt very smoothly.

OVERALL:

Robinson: "Hargrove is a good player who has his limitations. Getting on base is the name of the game for him. He gives you a good all around performance."

Harwell: "A solid hitter with a good eye. He walks a lot."

TOBY HARRAH
INF, No. 11
RR, 6'0", 180 lbs.
ML Svc: 12 years
Born: 10-26-48 in Sissonville, WV

1982 STATISTICS

AVG	G	AB	R	H	2B	3B	HR	RBI	BB	SO	SB
.304	162	602	100	183	29	4	25	78	84	52	17

CAREER STATISTICS

AVG	G	AB	R	H	2B	3B	HR	RBI	BB	SO	SB
.268	1708	5938	893	1589	239	32	169	754	879	678	206

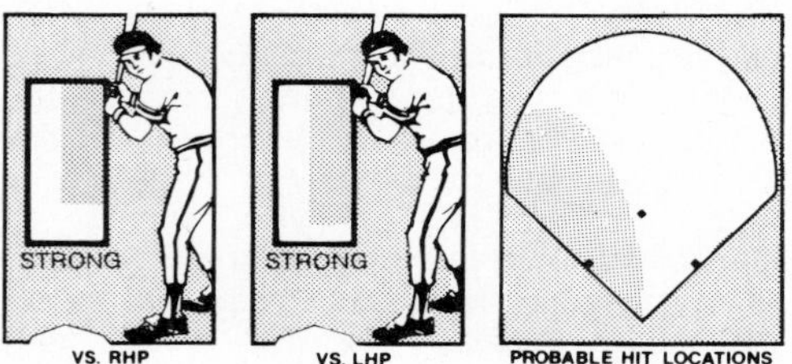

HITTING:

Harrah is a multi-faceted hitter who had his best offensive season in 1982. Since the 1981 baseball strike, Harrah has been a .315 hitter.

There is very little he cannot do with the bat. He loves inside pitches, especially fastballs. He jumps on them and pulls them down the left field line. He looks for a fastball up and early in the count.

In addition to having excellent power, he has tremendous bat control. With two strikes, he likes to hit the ball to right field and he does it very well. The best way to pitch to Harrah is by giving him a lot of breaking balls and change-ups. Make sure to keep everything outside.

Harrah is one of the best in getting on base. In addition to hitting for a high average, he draws a lot of walks. He also led the Indians in being hit by pitches. He is not afraid to take a ball inside and let it bounce off him so he can jog to first base. Harrah's bunting ability means a third baseman has to play him in close.

BASERUNNING:

Not blessed with great speed, Harrah nonetheless manages to steal 15-20 bases a year. He is a highly intelligent baserunner, who knows how to get a good lead and jump.

He has led the Indians in runs scored during his four years with them. He knows how to take an extra base and seldom is thrown out. He is a fine slider and breaks up a lot of double plays.

FIELDING:

A shortstop for most of his career, Harrah has played third since joining the Indians. His range is only average, but he has dependable hands and an accurate arm. While not sensational, his defense is more than adequate.

OVERALL:

Harrah is a very durable player. He has not missed a game in three years. An intelligent veteran, he seldom makes a mistake on the field.

Robinson: "Harrah had a big year with the bat. He can do a lot of things for a team--hit, run, steal bases, draw walks. Just a good all around player who has been awesome since the second half of 1981."

RON HASSEY
C, No. 9
LR, 6'2", 195 lbs.
ML Svc: 5 years
Born: 2-27-53 in
Tucson, AZ

HITTING:

Hassey is a low ball hitter who has trouble with inside pitches. He is a big and strong lefthanded hitter who can pull a pitch that is low and away. He has an uppercut swing, yet he hits few home runs.

In 1979, Hassey was a .280 hitter. He followed that up with a .318 batting average in 1980. Since then, he has not been nearly as successful at the plate. Pitchers have learned to go inside on him and he has failed to adjust.

With the Indians, Hassey has been platooned. His batting average against lefthanded pitchers is respectable, but he has far more power vs. righties. He handles the change-up pretty well, so long as it is out over the plate.

Overall, Hassey probably is a better hitter than he showed in 1982.

BASERUNNING:

Like most catchers, Hassey will never be confused with Rickey Henderson. He is slow getting down the first base line. His sliding ability is average. A couple of times a year he is thrown out trying to stretch a double into a triple.

FIELDING:

Hassey usually calls his own game. He has an average knowledge of the opposing batters' strengths and weaknesses. He likes to call a lot of fastballs, especially with runners on base.

When it comes to throwing, Hassey's arm strength and accuracy are above average. He is not very quick in getting rid of the ball. There is nothing special about the way he blocks home plate or handles balls in the dirt. He is an average defensive catcher.

1982 STATISTICS

AVG	G	AB	R	H	2B	3B	HR	RBI	BB	SO	SB
.251	113	323	33	81	18	0	5	34	53	30	3

CAREER STATISTICS

AVG	G	AB	R	H	2B	3B	HR	RBI	BB	SO	SB
.273	404	1200	109	328	54	4	20	165	143	118	6

VS. RHP

VS. LHP

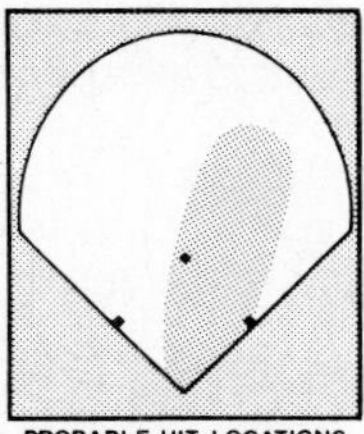
PROBABLE HIT LOCATIONS

OVERALL:

After hitting under .200 in the first half, Hassey was a .300 hitter after the 1982 All Star break. He lacks consistency and experience in the field and at bat.

Robinson: "1982 was a struggle for Hassey. If he is going to help, it has to be with the bat. Since his big year in 1980, it has all been downhill. Best bet is to be platooned with Chris Bando."

Harwell: "Value to his team is Hassey's hitting."

Martin: "Hassey has never come on as expected. He has some power and is fair to good defensively."

RICK MANNING
OF, No. 20
LR, 6'1", 180 lbs.
ML Svc: 8 years
Born: 9-2-54 in
Niagara Falls, NY

1982 STATISTICS

AVG	G	AB	R	H	2B	3B	HR	RBI	BB	SO	SB
.270	152	562	71	152	18	2	8	44	54	60	12

CAREER STATISTICS

AVG	G	AB	R	H	2B	3B	HR	RBI	BB	SO	SB
.263	1013	3803	480	999	136	29	35	326	356	465	135

VS. RHP

VS. LHP

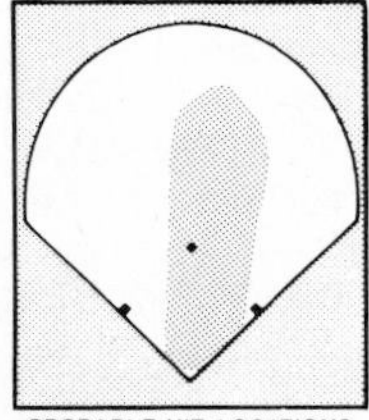
PROBABLE HIT LOCATIONS

HITTING:

At 28, Manning seems to be living up to that early promise as a hitter. He is one of Cleveland's most consistent hitters. He is a dead high ball hitter, especially high fastballs. Righthanders should throw him fastballs down and inside and breaking pitches away. He fares better against righthanded pitching, although he has played against everyone with the Indians.

Manning has below average power and usually hits grounders and line drives. He has good speed and should bunt more. When he does bunt, it is down the third base line. His speed also means he can beat out some infield hits, although he sometimes fails to run out ground balls.

A lefthanded pitcher should keep the ball away from Manning and stick mostly to breaking pitches. He has a tough time with the change-up. He will hit a high curveball, but has serious trouble with it if it is low in the strike zone. Manning's batting average would rise if he learned to bunt and hit grounders to the left side of the infield. He needs to capitalize on his speed.

BASERUNNING:

Manning has the legs to be one of the league's top basestealers, but does not run as often as he should. When he first came up, he was an aggressive and daring baserunner. In late 1982, he became more conservative, although he will steal a base when the situation demands it.

When he runs, he gets from home to first very quickly. Sometimes, he jogs to first on routine grounders or fly balls.

FIELDING:

In center, he uses his speed to the fullest, running down balls in the alleys that most players would never reach. He plays very shallow, meaning he takes away a lot of potential bloop hits over second base. But it also means he will be occasionally burned on a long fly to center.

Manning's arm is only average, but he is very accurate.

OVERALL:

Robinson: "Manning put together a good year in 1982. There has been a lot said about his potential, but I think he played in 1982 as well as he can. He might be the best center fielder in the league, an outstanding all around defensive player."

Harwell: "A defensive star."

Martin: "A fine, often spectacular outfielder who gets a good jump. His speed helps him as a hitter. When he hustles, he is fine. When diffident, he's ordinary."

BAKE McBRIDE
OF, No. 26
LR, 6'2", 184 lbs.
ML Svc: 10 years
Born: 2-3-49 in
Fulton, MO

1982 STATISTICS

AVG	G	AB	R	H	2B	3B	HR	RBI	BB	SO	SB
.365	27	85	8	31	3	3	0	13	2	12	2

CAREER STATISTICS

AVG	G	AB	R	H	2B	3B	HR	RBI	BB	SO	SB
.300	1001	3623	527	1086	159	54	62	412	239	431	175

VS. RHP

VS. LHP

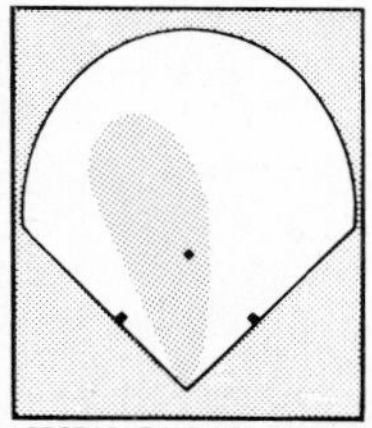
PROBABLE HIT LOCATIONS

HITTING:

McBride's 1982 season was marred by an infection of both eyes called conjunctivitis, and it kept him out of action from late May until the end of the year. As of this writing, it is not known if this condition will have further effect on his 1983 status.

McBride uses the smallest bat in the majors, a 32" model. He has an extremely closed batting stance with a slight crouch.

The Indians used McBride as their No. 5 hitter and he was very effective in that spot. After McBride was injured, Cleveland tried 11 other players in McBride's old spot in the lineup. None approached McBride's success.

While not a power hitter, McBride is basically a straightaway hitter and gets sharp line drives and his share of doubles. He is a tough player in the clutch and was one of the best players in the 1980 World Series for the Phillies. He likes the ball inside, and usually tries to get a fastball to hit. Despite knee problems in recent years, McBride still runs well from home plate to first base. He does not bunt well or very often, however.

McBride is probably most effective against righthanded pitchers, although his fine bat control means he is not an automatic out against lefties. Most seasons, he is a .300 hitter.

Even if his eye problems subside, McBride's knees will probably limit him to 400 at-bats a season.

FIELDING:

A veteran, McBride plays a solid right field. He is very good when it comes to catching balls in the right-center field gap. He is weak on balls hit down the right field line.

McBride has a fair throwing arm and usually hits the cutoff man. He is an average rightfielder who is not likely to make the kind of big mistake that will hurt you.

BASERUNNING:

Before his knee problems, McBride was one of the fastest men in the game. He still runs pretty well, but he does not like to steal. He worries about reinjuring his legs.

In a clutch situation, McBride can steal a base. He knows how to get a good lead and jump off a pitcher. He is a smart runner, not likely to get picked off.

OVERALL:

Robinson: "For all practical purposes, McBride was out all season. He has some tools, but he also has a lot of good years behind him. 1980 was his best year and I don't know if he can come back in 1983."

BILL NAHORODNY
C, No. 15
RR, 6'2", 195 lbs.
ML Svc: 7 years
Born: 8-31-53 in Hamtramck, MI

HITTING:

Nahorodny loves high pitches, especially fastballs that are out over the plate. That is the pitch he looks for early in the count. He has some real problems with breaking stuff and change-ups.

A guy who loves to play, Nahorodny is from the old school. He is one of the first to arrive at the park each day. His hustle and positive attitude are assets to any clubhouse. He is a part-time player who understands and accepts his role very well.

There are certain pitchers Nahorodny can handle. Most of them are lefthanded and throw pretty hard. His main job should be to hit against southpaws. He has some power and has been successful as a pinch-hitter.

He played very little for Cleveland, but had a good at-bat/RBI ratio. A handy player to have on the bench.

BASERUNNING:

Even though Nahorodny hustles, he has virtually no speed. His sliding ability is below average.

Used exclusively as a catcher with the Indians, Nahorodny has played the outfield and third base in the majors. Catching is his best position.

Nahorodny has a weak arm, so it is not wise to play him against fast teams like Kansas City and Oakland. He calls a pretty good game and does a lot of preparation to put together an effective game plan. He does a nice job of blocking pitches in the dirt.

1982 STATISTICS

AVG	G	AB	R	H	2B	3B	HR	RBI	BB	SO	SB
.223	39	94	6	21	5	1	4	18	2	9	0

CAREER STATISTICS

AVG	G	AB	R	H	2B	3B	HR	RBI	BB	SO	SB
.241	294	818	72	197	41	3	24	106	54	111	1

VS. RHP

VS. LHP

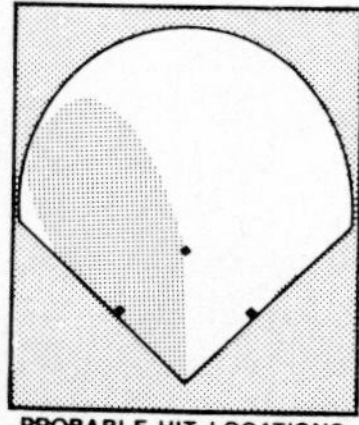
PROBABLE HIT LOCATIONS

OVERALL:

Cleveland is Nahorodny's fourth major league team. The Indians were pleased with his play in 1982 and consider him an effective No. 3 catcher.

Robinson: "He is a fair hitter who can hurt you if you throw into his zone. He has a lot of holes in his swing. I don't think he can help a team on an everyday basis. Spot him around and play him against certain pitchers. Good insurance."

JACK PERCONTE
INF, No. 16
LR, 5'10", 160 lbs.
ML Svc: 1 year plus
Born: 8-31-54 in Joliet, IL

1982 STATISTICS

AVG	G	AB	R	H	2B	3B	HR	RBI	BB	SO	SB
.237	93	219	27	52	4	4	0	15	22	25	9

CAREER STATISTICS

AVG	G	AB	R	H	2B	3B	HR	RBI	BB	SO	SB
.237	115	245	31	58	4	5	0	18	26	28	13

VS. RHP

VS. LHP

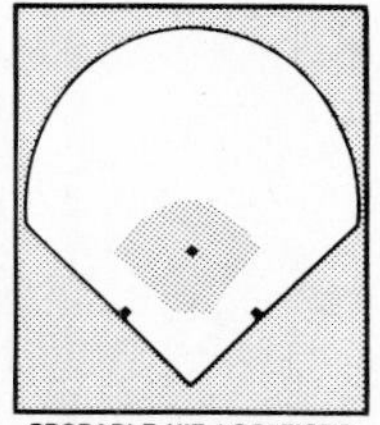
PROBABLE HIT LOCATIONS

HITTING:

Perconte began the 1982 season as the Indians' starting second baseman. By the end of the year, he was on the end of the bench, limited to pinch-running duties.

He has a slightly open stance and is up in the box. He likes high fastballs and looks for them. To get him out, keep the ball low and away. He has pretty good bat control and can hit the change-up. He has virtually no power and seldom hits anything more than a single. He is a good bunter and will bunt down either base line. He also is a good man in a hit-and-run situation. Perconte is far more effective against righthanded pitchers, although he started the season playing against everybody. He has a tendency to up-percut and that creates a lot of soft fly balls. It is doubtful that he will hit big league pitching well enough to be a full-time player.

BASERUNNING:

Perconte stole about 30 bases a year in the minors. He only has slightly above average speed, but he is an intelligent player. He gets a good jump and picks the right pitches to run on. If he hit and fielded well enough to be a regular, he might steal 25 bases a year in the big leagues.

A very good hustler, Perconte runs pretty well from home to first and will get some leg hits.

FIELDING:

More than anything else, it was his glove that earned Perconte a spot on the Cleveland bench. He had serious problems trying to make a double play. A small player, his pivot was slow and he often was taken out by the sliding baserunner.

His range is below average, although he catches most balls that he reaches. His arm is weak and that is another reason the pivot is a difficult play for him.

OVERALL:

At best, Perconte may make a utility infielder in the majors. His only position is second base. He is only a fair hitter with little power.

Robinson: "Perconte has some tools and speed, but he barely is an average big league player. Making the double play gives him trouble. A utility player at best."

HITTING:

Broderick Perkins crouches slightly in a closed stance, deep in the batter's box, and had the National League's highest pinch-hitting average in 1982 because of his ability to make sharp contact and hit the ball where it is pitched. He has a level swing and hits mostly sharp ground balls and short line drives.

Perkins can pull breaking pitches and mediocre fastballs from righthanded pitchers, but is prone to hit to the opposite field against lefthanders, particularly those who throw hard. Although he seldom strikes out, he rarely draws a base on balls. He occasionally reaches the alleys in left-center or right-center, and fielders tend to shade him at least slightly toward left field.

Perkins hits better against righthanders, but hangs in well against lefthanders, too. He is considered primarily a high fastball hitter, but has problems with fastballs in on his hands. He hits off-speed pitches pretty well because he is patient at the plate and has little tendency to try and overswing. Because he makes contact, he should be better than he is at hitting behind the runner. He is average at bunting and hitting in the clutch. He is a fairly consistent hitter, but tends to hit better the first half of the season than later on.

BASERUNNING:

Perkins has average to slightly below average speed, does not collect many leg hits, and is a below average basestealing threat. He is conservative on the bases and is not regarded as a smart baserunner.

FIELDING:

Perkins is fairly adept at digging low throws out of the dirt at first base. However, he is slightly below average in arm strength and accuracy and his range in the field leaves something to be desired. He is willing to dive for ground balls in the hole, but his tools limit his capacity for defensive improvement.

BRODERICK PERKINS
INF, No. 15
LL, 5'10", 180 lbs.
ML Svc: 3 years
Born: 11-23-54 in
Pittsburg, CA

1982 STATISTICS

AVG	G	AB	R	H	2B	3B	HR	RBI	BB	SO	SB
.271	125	347	32	94	10	4	2	34	26	20	2

CAREER STATISTICS

AVG	G	AB	R	H	2B	3B	HR	RBI	BB	SO	SB
.275	379	1007	99	277	51	8	8	129	64	87	8

VS. RHP

VS. LHP

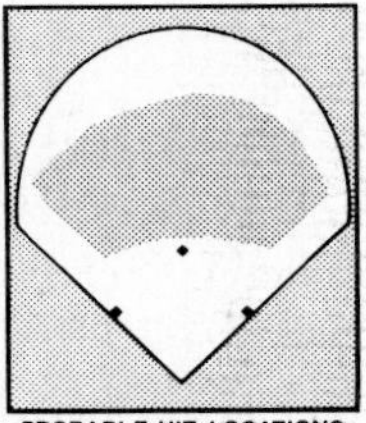
PROBABLE HIT LOCATIONS

OVERALL:

Lacking power, speed and great defensive ability, Perkins' major league future may be limited to his ability to make consistent contact as a pinch-hitter.

Coleman: "Perkins lacks concentration and has not improved much in three years. Must bat near the bottom of the lineup."

Kiner: "Hits for average, but lacks speed and power. He must improve to stay in the majors."

McCarver: "He is a good contact hitter best suited for a ballpark with big dimensions in the outfield."

LARY SORENSEN
RHP, No. 38
RR, 6'2", 200 lbs.
ML Svc: 6 years
Born: 10-4-55 in Detroit, MI

PITCHING:

Sorensen has been an average to above average starter in the majors for five seasons. He had some fine years with Milwaukee, but the Brewers helped him out by scoring a lot of runs. The righthander throws three-quarters overhand and relies on his intelligence and control. He is very good at pitching to the batter's weakness.

Sorensen's fastball is average, in the 85 MPH range. He uses a slider quite often and will throw a change-up just enough to let the hitters know he has one. He does not show much of a curve. When he is right, Sorensen has his fastball sinking and seldom throws a pitch more than a few inches above the knees. His slider makes him more effective against righthanded hitters.

Most of the time, Sorensen gives up a lot of hits. When he is right, they are grounders through the infield. He needs a solid defense behind him, especially one that can turn a double play. In 1982, he was hurt by Cleveland's unsettled and unreliable infield situation. Just as Sorensen cannot afford to make many mistakes with his control, his fielders must make the plays behind him.

When Sorensen does get the ball high in the strike zone, he is prone to giving up a lot of home runs and doubles. He has good poise and is a big, strong pitcher who does not fatigue in the late innings. When he is right, he makes pitching look easy. He takes little time between pitches. For a guy with an unremarkable fastball, you would think Sorensen would have a much better change-up. He doesn't and that is an area which needs improvement.

FIELDING:

Sorensen has a very good move to first base, especially for a righthander. He often throws to first base when a speedy runner is on. This is a great aid to the catcher, as it keeps the runner leaning toward the bag. Also, Sorensen's throws to first are usually strong and accurate. He seldom balks.

Since he is a big guy who sometimes is overweight, he is not especially good at fielding his position. If he reaches a ball, he will make a good throw. Sometimes, he does not make the plays on bunts or slow rollers that he should. He has the tendency to throw his bare, pitching hand out at balls hit up the middle. That is a good way to break a finger.

OVERALL:

Sorensen is a winning pitcher with a successful team. He needs a club that will make the plays behind him and get him 4-5 runs a game. He is an average pitcher, best used as a fourth or fifth starter. He is not the kind of guy who will win you a 1-0 or 2-1 game.

Harwell: "Sorensen must have pinpoint control to be effective."

Martin: "He is a .500 pitcher who knows how to pitch. Not overpowering."

1982 STATISTICS

W	L	ERA	G	GS	CG	IP	H	R	ER	BB	SO	SV
10	15	5.61	32	30	6	189	251	130	118	55	62	0

CAREER STATISTICS

W	L	ERA	G	GS	CG	IP	H	R	ER	BB	SO	SV
69	68	3.97	184	172	59	1182	1316	576	522	254	366	2

DAN SPILLNER
RHP, N0. 37
RR, 6'1", 190 lbs.
ML Svc: 9 years
Born: 11-27-51 in
Casper, WY

PITCHING:

In four years with the Indians, Spillner has done everything--start, long relief and short relief. He has had relative success in each area and won 15 games as a starter in 1980. But in 1982, Cleveland put him in the bullpen and that is his best role.

He is a strong righthander with an above average fastball (86-88 MPH) and a solid slider. The most impressive parts of his game are his poise and his ability to pitch to a hitter's weakness. Since he does not have overwhelming stuff, he must be able to put his fastball and slider in the right spots. Most of the time, he was able to do that coming out of the bullpen.

Spillner throws straight over the top and has the ability to warm up very quickly. That is a great asset in the bullpen. He has been in the majors for eight years and has never had a sore arm. He does not rattle when the situation is tight or when his teammates make errors behind him. He uses his curveball as an off-speed pitch, but doesn't throw it very often. Because he once was a starter, Spillner can come out of the bullpen and throw 4-5 innings. When he gets behind in the count, you can be pretty sure you will see a fastball. Since his fastball moves very well and he has good control, it does not matter if he is pitching to lefthanded or righthanded hitters. He can handle them all very well.

FIELDING:

Spillner is an above average fielder who seldom makes an error in judgement. When the ball is hit to him, he usually knows where to throw it without hesitating. His cool demeanor means he is very good in bunt situations. He is not one to panic when the ball is bunted in front of the plate and he rushes in to grab it. He will make a good strong throw to the right base.

His move to first base is a little above average. He does a pretty good job of watching baserunners and keeping them close. He seldom balks or throws the ball away on pick-off attempts.

OVERALL:

Spillner is probably pitching as well as he can. He would be a great addition to any staff because of his versatility. He is experienced in every facet of pitching, although he does seem best suited for short relief.

Robinson: "Spillner continues to live in undeserved obscurity. He is one of the league's top relievers. He had an outstanding year in 1982 in every department."

Martin: "One of the best relievers around. He can come out of the bullpen and throw hard. He takes charge of the game very well and challenges hitters."

1982 STATISTICS

W	L	ERA	G	GS	CG	IP	H	R	ER	BB	SO	SV
12	10	2.49	65	0	0	133	117	44	37	45	90	21

CAREER STATISTICS

W	L	ERA	G	GS	CG	IP	H	R	ER	BB	SO	SV
68	72	4.15	408	112	19	1209	1264	632	558	498	740	39

RICK SUTCLIFFE
RHP, No. 44
LR, 6'6", 215 lbs.
ML Svc: 5 years
Born: 6-21-56 in
Independence, MO

PITCHING:

Sutcliffe was the biggest surprise of the Indians' 1982 season. Very little was expected of him when Cleveland got him from the Dodgers. He had won only five games in two years and clashed with Los Angeles manager Tommy Lasorda. He started the year in the bullpen with Cleveland but soon pitched his way into the starting rotation. Starting is his best role.

At 6'6", Sutcliffe is an intimidating presence on the mound. He throws three-quarter and pushes off the mound very hard. His motion is rather odd because he is a straight-up pitcher. In other words, he barely bends his back during his delivery.

He is primarily a power pitcher, relying on a fastball, slider and curve. His fastball is in the 88 MPH range and it moves. Before this season, he never had a slider and now owns one of the best around. He often uses it as his strikeout pitch. He throws his curves at different speeds and they have a big break. He does have a change-up, but he rarely uses it.

Sutcliffe is a hard worker with super poise. Little that happens in the game seems to bother him. He is very determined and concentrates on throwing to the hitter's weaknesses. He won't give in to the hitter and likes to throw his slider with a full count. The slider makes him especially tough on righthanded batters.

Once he moved into the starting rotation, Cleveland won 75% of the games he started. He also averaged about eight innings a start, meaning he is a pitcher you can rely on.

FIELDING:

Sutcliffe likes to throw to first base a lot. His move is nothing special, but he pays a lot of attention to baserunners. Overall, he does a decent job of keeping them close.

As a fielder, Sutcliffe is average. Since he is so big, he does not have a lot of mobility, especially when it comes to reaching balls in front of the plate. He does a good job of covering first base on balls hit to the right side of the infield.

OVERALL:

A National League Rookie of the Year in 1979, Sutcliffe had his best season ever in 1982. The slider has made him one of the better starters in the American League. He gets in trouble when he tries to be too fine causing him to start walking hitters.

Robinson: "Sutcliffe has pitched well from the moment he got a chance to start with Cleveland. He developed a new slider which was a great help to him. He is very aggressive on the mound and goes right after the hitters."

Martin: "Sutcliffe has been impressive in his first time around the American League."

1982 STATISTICS

W	L	ERA	G	GS	CG	IP	H	R	ER	BB	SO	SV
14	8	2.96	34	27	6	216	174	81	71	98	142	1

CAREER STATISTICS

W	L	ERA	G	GS	CG	IP	H	R	ER	BB	SO	SV
36	29	3.66	132	74	12	622	558	282	253	272	337	6

ANDRE THORNTON
INF, No. 29
RR, 6'2", 205 lbs.
ML Svc: 9 years
Born: 8-13-49 in Tuskegee, AL

HITTING:

Thornton missed two years because of various injuries--two knee operations, a broken hand and a broken thumb--but came back with the best season of his career. He is a low ball hitter and likes the ball inside. He is a very dangerous hitter, capable of hitting a home run at any time.

While he plays against all types of pitching, Thornton is a better hitter against lefthanders. In 1982, he became more selective at the plate. He walked more than ever before and dramatically cut his strikeouts.

In the past, Thornton tried to pull everything and often refused to swing at pitches on the outside corner. Now, he is rapping those outside pitches up the middle for singles.

To keep Thornton in check, a pitcher should give him a steady diet of breaking balls and change-ups on the outside corner. If you must give him a fastball, be sure to jam him with it.

BASERUNNING:

Thornton never had much speed and he is even slower after his two knee operations. If a pitcher completely ignores him, Thornton can get a good jump and steal a base. He slides feet first and is very good at breaking up a double play at second base.

FIELDING:

Primarily a designated hitter for Cleveland, Thornton can also play first base. He is an adequate fielder with good hands and limited range. In the past, he has experienced some shoulder troubles that have hindered his throwing.

1982 STATISTICS

AVG	G	AB	R	H	2B	3B	HR	RBI	BB	SO	SB
.273	161	589	90	161	26	1	32	116	109	81	6

CAREER STATISTICS

AVG	G	AB	R	H	2B	3B	HR	RBI	BB	SO	SB
.255	989	3249	517	829	162	21	164	160	578	533	30

VS. RHP

VS. LHP

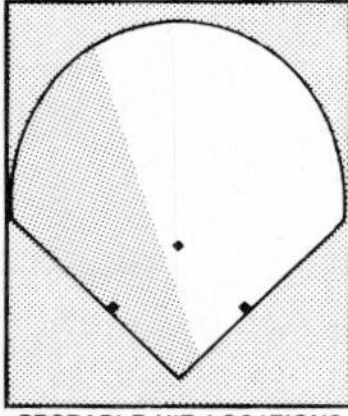
PROBABLE HIT LOCATIONS

OVERALL:

Thornton was hampered by a weak Cleveland lineup. He led the league in intentional walks. The Indians used 12 different players to hit behind him in the fifth spot of the batting order. None of them did the job.

Robinson: "Thornton was awesome in 1982. If he had had someone to hit behind him, he would have led the American League in RBIs. DH is his best spot."

Martin: "One of the game's classiest people. He has a lot of character. He is a deep threat every time he steps up to bat and he'll provide runs in a hurry."

MANNY TRILLO
INF, No. 9
RR, 6'1", 164 lbs.
ML Svc: 8 years
Born: 12-25-50 in Caritito, VEN

1982 STATISTICS

AVG	G	AB	R	H	2B	3B	HR	RBI	BB	SO	SB
.271	149	549	52	149	24	1	0	39	33	53	8

CAREER STATISTICS

AVG	G	AB	R	H	2B	3B	HR	RBI	BB	SO	SB
.265	1156	4088	401	1083	158	29	41	406	305	480	51

VS. RHP

VS. LHP

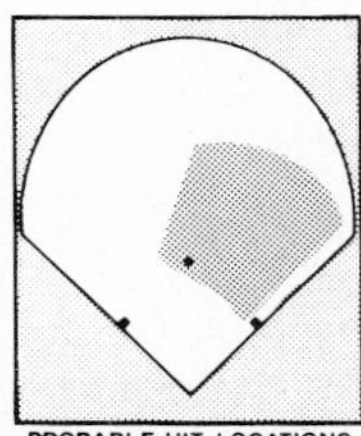
PROBABLE HIT LOCATIONS

HITTING:

Trillo loves to hit anything up above the belt. Against righthanded pitching, he hits to right field with consistency. He tries to pull the ball a bit more against lefthanders. Trillo is not a power hitter, but can reach the alleys and especially to right-center. He is a line drive hitter often going straightaway and toward the opposite field.

Pitchers must keep the ball down. He will hit mistakes up or anything high. He has trouble with curveballs and is vulnerable to sinkers.

Trillo handles the bat well and is effective in executing the hit-and-run. He is an average to above average clutch hitter with men in scoring position. He has an excellent bunt, but because he loves high pitches so much, he does not draw walks as well as he should. He is consistent, and, overall, his hitting is a strong part of his game.

BASERUNNING:

Trillo has average speed and a conservative style on the basepaths. He gets caught as often as he steals, and does not cause pitchers and catchers to become overly concerned. His tall and slim build and lack of good speed prevent him from being a dangerous force in breaking up the double play. Overall, his baserunning is average and the weakest part of his game.

FIELDING:

Trillo's arm strength and accuracy are excellent. His arm is a natural; he was originally signed by the Phillies farm system as a rocket-armed young catcher when he was just 17, but has played his entire Major League career at second base. His style is to field the ball off to the side more often than in front of him, claiming a more precise view of the ball. It works; his fielding range is excellent.

Trillo fields the ball to his right a bit better than to his left but rarely lets anything by either side. Trillo is an agile and graceful fielder. Overall rating, excellent.

OVERALL:

McCarver: "Manny is a ballet artist around second base--short hops never seem to bother him. He is a smooth, and I mean smooth, second baseman."

Coleman: "Trillo is steady as a rock on defense. He is a good situation player on offense; the two combine beautifully to make him the most complete second baseman in the National League."

GEORGE VUKOVICH
OF, No. 29
LR, 6'0", 198 lbs.
ML Svc: 2 years
Born: 6-24-56 in Chicago, IL

1982 STATISTICS

AVG	G	AB	R	H	2B	3B	HR	RBI	BB	SO	SB
.272	123	335	41	91	18	2	6	42	32	47	2

CAREER STATISTICS

AVG	G	AB	R	H	2B	3B	HR	RBI	BB	SO	SB
.272	221	419	52	114	19	3	7	54	39	56	3

VS. RHP

VS. LHP

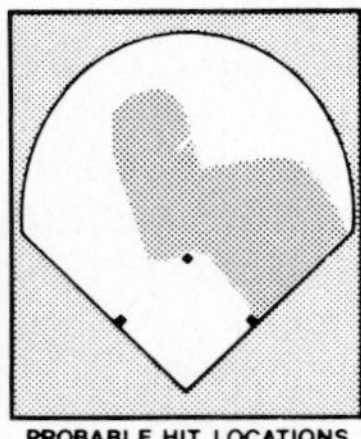
PROBABLE HIT LOCATIONS

HITTING:

Vukovich is a promising young hitter whose primary effectiveness is as a platoon player against righthanded pitching. He is a low ball hitter but has considerable trouble with off-speed pitching. He is sometimes overly aggressive at the plate, and needs to relax. He tends to lunge at the ball, and must learn to wait on pitches if he is to have a future as an everyday player.

Against righthanders, he can be especially deadly with first-ball fastballs down and in. He is a pull hitter who also has good strength to left-center. Lefthanders can jam him with anything inside. He loves the fastball and is always geared up for it, perhaps contributing to his difficulty with off-speed stuff. Has further trouble with curveballs, but can handle the sinker better than the slider.

Vukovich is showing decent pinch-hitting abilities and is rated average in clutch hitting, and in drawing walks. He has an average to below average bunt. Overall, Vukovich seems to fall in and out of his stride, and though his hitting is the strongest part of his game, difficulty with off-speed pitching is a weakness that gives him an average rating.

BASERUNNING:

Vukovich has average speed, and while he is aggressive and smart, he doesn't run well enough to be considered a basestealing threat or to race into second to break up the double play.

FIELDING:

Vukovich is as aggressive in the field as he is at the plate, and will run through a brick wall to catch a ball. His arm strength is above average, but accuracy has been erratic at times. He comes in well on the ball, is agile and charges the ball well, and can make a decent throw to home. He plays a good solid right field and has the potential to become an above average outfielder.

OVERALL:

McCarver: "George is strong and could be a good Major League hitter if he learns to handle the off-speed stuff consistently. Average on defense but he has made some spectacular plays in the outfield with his aggressive style."

Coleman: "Vukovich shows some strong pinch-hitting potential and is a great first-ball fastball hitter who doesn't lose his cool with men in scoring position."

RICK WAITS
LHP, No. 36
SL, 6'3", 195 lbs.
ML Svc: 8 years
Born: 5-15-52 in Atlanta, GA

PITCHING:

Waits' 1982 season was marred by a knee injury that required off-season surgery. Waits had ligament trouble in his left knee and it seemed to bother his follow-through. Nevertheless, he pitched most of the year and had his worst season ever, going 2-13.

Waits is much better than a 2-13 pitcher. At least, he should be. He throws overhand and has an average fastball. Sometimes it doesn't move and he has the frightening tendency of throwing it right down the middle. Hence, he has given up a lot of home runs.

In addition to his fastball, Waits uses his curve quite a bit. Early in his career, he made his reputation as a curveball pitcher. He had a fine one, breaking sharp and straight down. He has lost a little off it the last few years. He also has a change-up, a slider, and a screwball. Part of the reason Waits' curve isn't what it used to be may be due to his constant experimenting with new pitches. He needs to get his change-up over more often to be effective. His breaking pitches make him tougher on lefthanded batters.

One of Waits' major problems is his poise and lack of confidence in himself. He underestimates his fastball and seems to have trouble making the big pitch in the clutch situations. He has won a lot of games against the Boston Red Sox, and is one of the few lefties who is very successful in Fenway Park. Waits has real trouble against the Tigers. He needs to believe he can win and keep his fastball away from the heart of the plate.

FIELDING:

Waits is an average fielder who ends up in good position to handle balls hit back at him after he delivers the pitch. He does a decent job of covering first base.

Usually, Waits keeps baserunners somewhat close to first, although he has lapses of concentration when he seems to forget there is anyone on base.

OVERALL:

He should be a better pitcher than he has shown. He needs to regain his great curveball. Having his knee problem taken care of should help.

Robinson: "The 1982 season was not a good one for Waits. There is no way he should have this kind of year, not with the arm he has. He needs to be more positive about himself and his job. He needs to challenge hitters and make better pitches."

Martin: "The knee injury helped wreck Waits. He is much better than 2-13 and could come back a winner."

1982 STATISTICS

W	L	ERA	G	GS	CG	IP	H	R	ER	BB	SO	SV
2	13	5.40	25	21	2	115	128	74	69	57	44	0

CAREER STATISTICS

W	L	ERA	G	GS	CG	IP	H	R	ER	BB	SO	SV
74	83	4.18	228	187	47	1256	1301	639	584	507	553	4

CARMELO CASTILLO
OF, No. 52
RR, 6'1", 185 lbs.
ML Svc: 1 year
Born: 6-8-58 in
de Macoris, DR

HITTING, BASERUNNING, FIELDING:

Castillo has a lot of raw ability, but clearly lacks experience.

The Indians used Castillo almost exclusively against lefthanded pitchers. He is a low ball hitter who likes pitches on the outside part of the plate. His inexperience is very apparent when he tries to hit the breaking ball or a change-up. He usually is off stride and clearly fooled. When he does connect, he usually hits the ball to left-center. He seems to be a strong young player, but he has not shown much power in the majors.

Castillo has great speed from home to first base and he gets a lot of infield hits. He also can bunt for a hit.

On the bases, he fails to get lengthy leads and does not steal as many bases as he should. He slides feet first and it takes him a long time to make his slide into the bag. Nevertheless, he is an aggressive baserunner with a lot of raw speed, and this is the strongest part of his game.

The Indians used Castillo mostly in left field, and he was very timid. He has a tendency to shy away from walls, which means he sometimes fails to catch balls he should. He has a cannon of an arm, clearly the strongest on the Indians. His throwing is not always accurate, and sometimes, he fails to hit the cutoff man.

OVERALL:

Robinson: "Castillo has a lot of tools and can do several things. He is probably overmatched with the bat at this stage of his career. But look for him to make himself noticed in a couple of years."

ROD CRAIG
OF, No. 56
SR, 6'1", 195 lbs.
ML Svc: 1 year
Born: 1-12-58 in
Los Angeles, CA

HITTING, BASERUNNING, FIELDING:

In 1982, Craig was the surprise of the Indians' spring training. He showed some power, especially from the right side of the plate. He made better contact from the left side, but seldom hit the ball very hard. He has above average speed, but does not use it well. He is not a good bunter.

Craig is a fastball hitter who likes the ball outside. He has big trouble with breaking pitches and change-ups. Fastballs on the inside part of the plate are also a problem for him. Overall, an ineffective pinch-hitter.

While Craig can run, he is not very astute on the bases. He does not get a very big lead and is not aggressive. He slides feet first and the Indians have used him as a pinch-runner.

Craig has the speed to be a fine outfielder, but he does not judge fly balls very well. His best position is left field. His throwing arm is weak and he has some problems hitting the cutoff man.

OVERALL:

So far, Craig has proven to be a marginal major leaguer at best. He is very inexperienced at bat, in the field and on the bases. He would need more power to be a regular player in the majors.

Robinson: "Craig is inexperienced and needs to get a full year of Class AAA under his belt. He doesn't have much power. He has some tools, but he needs to refine them."

JERRY DYBZINSKI
INF, No. 10
RR, 6'2", 180 lbs.
ML Svc: 3 years
Born: 7-7-55 in
Cleveland, OH

HITTING, BASERUNNING, FIELDING:

Dybzinski turned out to be one of the Indians' bigger disappointments. He will never be known for hitting. He did bat over .300 with runners in scoring position, but the Indians would be very happy if he could turn into a consistent .250 hitter. He has a closed stance and holds the bat high, slightly back and above his head. Has a very big swing, and does not hit the ball to right field very well. He likes to look for a fastball. If he guesses right, he can rip it down the third base line for a double.

Dybzinski seems prone to streaks. He lacks confidence in himself, and needs to learn to hit the ball to right field. This will especially help him to handle the breaking ball. Since he has little power, there is no reason for him to try and pull everything.

He has above average speed and stole over 25 bases in the minors. He is a smart baserunner who gets a respectable lead off first base. He also motors pretty well from home to first, although he does not like to bunt.

Dybzinski has a tendency to sort of windup before he throws, giving the baserunner that extra step.

He has fine range and can make the spectacular play. With the exception of a slow release, Dybzinski has everything you look for in a shortstop--soft hands, a cannon arm and covers a lot of ground.

Confidence is a problem for Dybzinski in the field. If he blows an easy play, he often broods about it and that leads to more errors.

OVERALL:

He will never be an outstanding hitter, but he has the speed and the knack of driving in runs that can make him productive.

TIGER STADIUM
Detroit Tigers

Seating Capacity: 52,806
Playing Surface: Natural Grass

Dimensions
Left Field Pole: 340 ft.
Left-Center Field: 365 ft.
Center Field: 440 ft.
Right-Center Field: 370 ft.
Right Field Pole: 325 ft.
Height of Outfield Wall: 9 ft.

Tiger Stadium is the second oldest park in the league. If a player hits the ball to center field (440 feet away), it is invariably a long out. Hit it anyplace else, and it is invariably a homer. With the exception of rainy days when the air is heavy, balls carry extremely well in the home of the Detroit Tigers probably because the ballpark is completely protected by three tiers. When the wind does blow--and it almost always blows out--lefties and righties have a field day at the Stadium.

In an effort to stop homers, or at least to get as many outs as possible and prevent extra at-bats, Tiger manager Sparky Anderson has ordered the infield grass to be allowed to grow high. It is a veritable wheat field and opposing hitters claim it takes a rocket to propel a grounder through the virtual swamp.

Another aid to hitters is the lack of foul territory behind home plate and behind the first and third base foul lines. Foul balls which would be easy outs in most American League parks, wind up in the seats giving a hitter an extra swing or two per game.

It is 340 feet down the line in left and a nine-foot wall (part screen) is all that a batter must clear to have himself a homer. Instead of bulging out, however, like Yankee Stadium, Tiger Stadium offers righty batters a clear shot at homers by staying only at 365 feet in left-center, the power alley for most hitters. It is when the stands start to veer in center that the distance becomes 440 feet. But that extends for no more than 50 yards, and in right-center--the power alley for lefties--the fence is only 370 feet away. As the stands swing toward the right field foul pole, the distance shrivels to 325 feet.

It has been estimated that 95% of batters in the league, be they lefty or righty, would prefer to hit in either Tiger Stadium or Fenway Park because of the proximity of the fences, the wind blowing out and the lack of foul territory.

The bullpens are in full view of the fans with the visitors' in right field in foul territory, and the Tigers' in a similar spot along the left field line.

Babe Ruth was credited as being the first player to clear the tall third deck in right field, but in recent years several players have accomplished that feat, and in 1971, Reggie Jackson hit a light tower atop the right-center field roof in the All Star game.

TOM BROOKENS
INF, No. 16
RR, 5'10", 170 lbs.
ML Svc: 4 years
Born: 8-10-53 in Chambersburg, PA

1982 STATISTICS

AVG	G	AB	R	H	2B	3B	HR	RBI	BB	SO	SB
.231	140	398	40	92	15	3	9	58	27	63	5

CAREER STATISTICS

AVG	G	AB	R	H	2B	3B	HR	RBI	BB	SO	SB
.254	422	1336	146	340	55	15	27	170	84	217	33

VS. RHP

VS. LHP

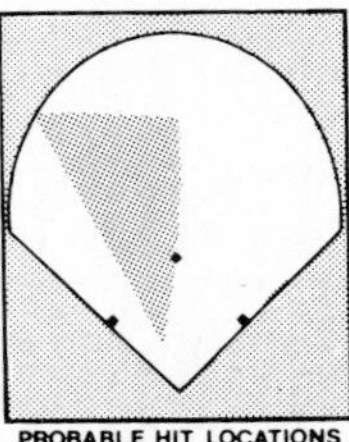
PROBABLE HIT LOCATIONS

HITTING:

Tom Brookens is a dead low ball hitter who is trying to hit more to all fields. This change in style may be hurting him at the plate.

Pitchers still stay outside when pitching to Brookens, who tried to pull everything at one time. Stay up with the fastball and throw him bad breaking balls down. He'll occasionally nibble. But don't throw him any breaking balls up. If Brookens hurts you, it will be on a low fastball or a hanging breaking pitch. Remember, in a spot where a base hit will drive in a key run, Brookens is likely to go to the opposite field rather than pull the ball. Otherwise, pitchers have been getting him out with the same pitches they did when he hit with more power.

Brookens doesn't handle the change too well. The sinker-slider gives him trouble. Chicago's Dennis Lamp's sinker had Brookens baffled last season. He didn't have a clue.

An average clutch hitter, Brookens rates above average on the hit-and-run. He also is an above average bunter, though he did not bunt very much in 1982. Only 27 of his 92 hits last season were for extra bases. He doesn't walk much.

Brookens hit well against Boston and Minnesota last season, driving in four runs in a game against the Twins July 15.

BASERUNNING:

Brookens has average speed to first and is average when it comes to breaking up the double play. He's a smart runner but not a real threat to steal. He stole just five bases last season and was caught stealing nine times. He generally is conservative as a baserunner.

FIELDING:

Brookens' arm strength is average, but his throwing accuracy rates below average and needs improvement. His range, likewise, is below par. When fielding ground balls, he's a little bit better going to his left but no better than average. Going to his right he rates below average. He turns the double play adequately but does not consistently make the big defensive play in the clutch. To be effective both in the field and at bat he has to play regularly.

OVERALL:

Robinson: "Brookens gives you an average job in every area. He is steady but not very flashy. He's the best the Tigers have at third base, though."

Martin: "Steady enough at third base but has filled in at second base, too. Doesn't hit enough to play every day. Versatility is his value."

ENOS CABELL
INF, No. 21
RR, 6'5", 185 lbs.
ML Svc: 10 years
Born: 10-8-49 in
Fort Riley, KS

1982 STATISTICS

AVG	G	AB	R	H	2B	3B	HR	RBI	BB	SO	SB
.261	125	464	45	121	17	3	2	37	15	48	15

CAREER STATISTICS

AVG	G	AB	R	H	2B	3B	HR	RBI	BB	SO	SB
.272	1216	4512	572	1228	193	47	43	444	178	541	207

VS. RHP

VS. LHP

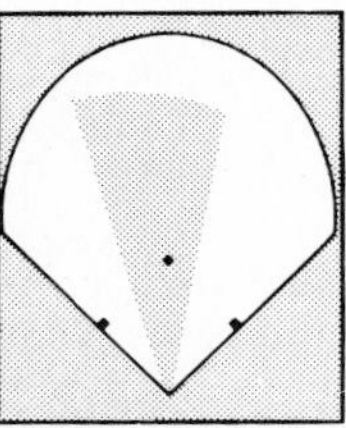
PROBABLE HIT LOCATIONS

HITTING:

Enos Cabell hit the first two home runs of the season for Detroit last year, then didn't hit another one all season. He batted .369 in April, including a 13 game hitting streak, and had a 10+ game hitting streak in May. His hitting tailed off quite a bit after that.

Cabell was a high ball hitter in the National League, but since his return to the American League in 1982, began to hit low fastballs. He doesn't have much power. He bats from a closed, upright stance and stands low in the box.

Pitchers go after Cabell with fastballs down and a lot of breaking pitches. The curve, change and sinker-slider all give Cabell trouble.

A line-drive hitter, Cabell usually hits straightaway and reaches the alleys occasionally. He is rated average at hitting in the clutch but has good bat control and rated above average in hitting behind the runner and in the hit-and-run.

Cabell likes to jump on the first pitch and swings at almost anything he can reach. Dennis Leonard gives Cabell lots of trouble, and Cabell struggles to hit in Royals Stadium and in Toronto. He does well in Yankee Stadium.

He's a streaky hitter, probably most effective hitting down in the order, sixth or seventh.

BASERUNNING:

Cabell's speed to first is average to slightly above. He's not a dangerous threat to steal, but pitchers can't forget he's there. A smart runner, Cabell is good at breaking up the double play. He'll always slide feet first and is considered conservative on the basepaths.

FIELDING:

Cabell has played all over the infield, but first base probably is his best spot. His versatility is a plus, however. His arm strength is average but his accuracy is slightly better than that. Fielding is perhaps the weakest part of Cabell's game, but he rates average, overall, at fielding his position.

OVERALL:

Robinson: "Very versatile player who can play first, third or the outfield. Has given Detroit what they were looking for."

Harwell: "Good team man and very versatile. I think he's more effective hitting second or third."

Martin: "Good National League hitter. Hits line drives and has decent speed. First base is his best position."

KIRK GIBSON
OF, No. 23
LL, 6'3", 210 lbs.
ML Svc: 3 years
Born: 5-28-57 in
Pontiac, MI

1982 STATISTICS

AVG	G	AB	R	H	2B	3B	HR	RBI	BB	SO	SB
.278	69	266	34	74	16	2	8	35	25	41	9

CAREER STATISTICS

AVG	G	AB	R	H	2B	3B	HR	RBI	BB	SO	SB
.291	215	769	111	224	32	6	27	95	31	70	121

VS. RHP

VS. LHP

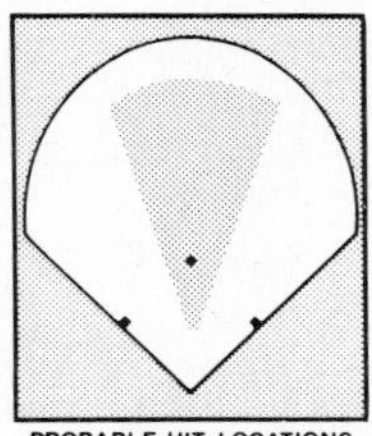
PROBABLE HIT LOCATIONS

HITTING:

Hard and in, or with plenty of junk. That's the way to pitch to Kirk Gibson and get him out. A high ball hitter, Gibson hits out of a slightly closed, upright stance and usually stands in the center of the batter's box. He likes the ball up and out over the plate. He tries to pull almost all the time and hits a lot of fly balls. Any kind of off-speed junk will give Gibson trouble as well as an exceptionally good fastball. Otherwise, Gibson jumps on fastballs. Keep the curve down. He has a better chance of hitting it if it's up.

Injuries have been a big problem to Gibson thus far, limiting him to 69 games last season. A sore left knee, a strained calf muscle, a stomach ailment, and a strained wrist put him on the disabled list for the rest of the season in mid-July.

Gibson is an excellent bunter and the talent is enhanced by his great speed. He still needs to cut down on his strikeouts and improve as a hitter with men in scoring position and on the hit-and-run. He can hit home runs in the cozy parks like Tiger Stadium and use the alleys in big parks. He's a consistent hitter.

BASERUNNING:

Baserunning may be the strongest part of Gibson's game because of his great speed. He gets down to first as fast as anyone in the American League. Also rates among the best, along with Don Baylor, at breaking up the double play. He could steal 50 bases a year if he played in 150 games. He is still learning how to steal, but he is a very smart runner who makes a pitcher nervous.

FIELDING:

Gibson gets to balls nobody else can, but then his problems start. His arm strength and throwing accuracy rate below average. He literally can outrun a fly ball, but he can't run it home. Better coming in on a fly ball, rather than going back.

OVERALL:

Robinson: "I talk about him in glowing terms, though I find it hard to do since he has never played a full year in the big leagues. Still, he has the potential to be awesome. Only time will tell."

Martin: "His manager, Sparky Anderson, has tabbed him as 'the next Mickey Mantle.' Not quite. Has all the tools but has a lot to learn about playing the game. Has to get playing time to reach a certain superiority, but injuries have been a problem. His attitude also is rather poor."

Harwell: "Great potential that has been slowed primarily because of his bad wrist."

HITTING:

Herndon hits from a parallel stance. He stands upright and low in the box. Pitch him inside. He likes the ball out over the plate so he can extend his arms.

He's a low ball hitter. Pitchers get him with fastballs in on his fists and curveballs away. He turns on fastballs out over the plate. Herndon is a pull hitter who frequently hits into the gaps, too. He had a consistent year as a hitter in 1982 but also went through some hot streaks at the plate. He's only so-so at handling breaking pitches.

He adapted very well to the American League after nearly six seasons in the National League. His hitting style is well suited to Tiger Stadium and he had his best ever major league season in 1982. Herndon learned how to use Detroit's cozy confines to hit 23 home runs, compared to 23 combined in six previous seasons in San Francisco. He tied a major league record with four home runs in four consecutive at-bats, his last at-bat against Minnesota on May 16, and then in his first three against Oakland the next day. He hit well against the Twins, driving in five runs in one game.

Oakland pitchers cringed every time Herndon stepped to the plate. He punished A's pitching in 1982, going 19-for-49, a .367 average with six home runs and 18 runs batted in. Consistency was the key for Herndon last season. He had a 17-game hitting streak and two nine-game streaks but never went more than three games without a hit.

Rates above average with runners in scoring position. Does not walk much, just 38 times in 614 at-bats last season.

BASERUNNING:

Above average speed to first. Herndon is an average basestealer; he took just 12 and was caught on 9 others last year. He rates above average in breaking up the double play. He is a smart aggressive runner but not overly so.

LARRY HERNDON
OF, No. 31
RR, 6'3", 190 lbs.
ML Svc: 7 years
Born: 11-3-53 in
Sunflower, MS

1982 STATISTICS

AVG	G	AB	R	H	2B	3B	HR	RBI	BB	SO	SB
.292	157	614	92	179	21	13	23	88	38	92	12

CAREER STATISTICS

AVG	G	AB	R	H	2B	3B	HR	RBI	BB	SO	SB
.273	851	2743	339	748	97	52	47	274	169	444	72

VS. RHP

VS. LHP

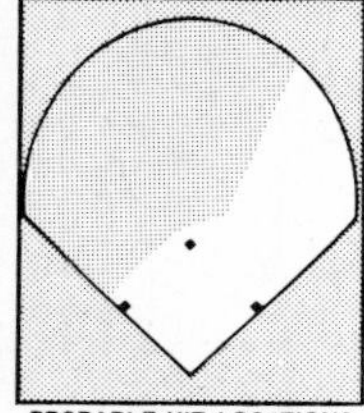
PROBABLE HIT LOCATIONS

FIELDING:

Herndon is not an exceptional outfielder but is fairly solid in left field. He has an above average arm and above average throwing accuracy. His throw to the plate is average to slightly above as is his range in the outfield. He is a little better coming in on a ball than going back.

OVERALL:

Herndon appears to have found a home in Detroit where his abilities are enhanced by the size of the ballpark.

Martin: "A do-it-all player in 1982. Added early offense and left field defense to the Tigers. Has speed, arm and hits with power."

Harwell: "A good, steady player, offensively and defensively. An excellent team player."

MIKE IVIE
INF, No. 15
RR, 6'4", 215 lbs.
ML Svc: 9 years
Born: 8-8-52 in
Atlanta, GA

1982 STATISTICS

AVG	G	AB	R	H	2B	3B	HR	RBI	BB	SO	SB
.232	80	259	35	60	12	1	14	38	24	51	0

CAREER STATISTICS

AVG	G	AB	R	H	2B	3B	HR	RBI	BB	SO	SB
.270	838	2646	305	713	129	17	81	404	211	398	22

VS. RHP

VS. LHP

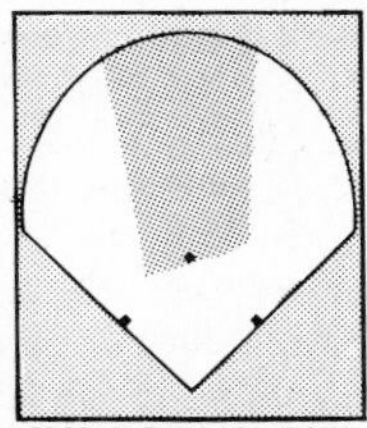
PROBABLE HIT LOCATIONS

HITTING:

Mike Ivie is a low ball hitter who likes the ball out over the plate. Pitch him up and in. He has a big swing and pitchers throw him a steady diet of breaking balls and change speeds often. Ivie is a fastball hitter and doesn't handle anything else that well.

He hits from a slightly open stance and stands upright and low in the batter's box. He's big and strong but is more of a straightaway hitter. When he hits, he gets a bunch of hits up the middle.

Ivie rates average as a clutch hitter but needs improvement when it comes to hitting behind the runner. His big swing doesn't give him very much bat control. He strikes out a lot, 51 times in 259 at-bats last season. He does not bunt much, and needs work in this area.

Ivie didn't hit for much of an average last season, but did hit with power having 14 home runs. Nearly half of his 60 hits were for extra bases.

BASERUNNING:

Ivie doesn't have any speed and isn't daring at all on the bases. His speed to first is poor and he does not slide well enough to break up the double play. At the plate, Ivie might make a pitcher beware, but that changes once he gets on base. He's a very conservative runner who can be doubled up easily.

FIELDING:

Ivie is much more valuable to a team when he stays out of the field. He appeared strictly as a DH in 1982, but when he does play, his arm strength and throwing accuracy at first are rated average. He does not move to his right or left very well.

OVERALL:

Ivie provided the Tigers with a power infusion last year but he should do more to offset his limited skills in other areas. His value seems to be limited strictly to that of being a platoon DH, playing against selected lefthanded pitchers.

Robinson: "Strong, righthanded hitter who gave Detroit a lift, home run wise. Might be better in 1983 after spending a year in the American League. It was an adjustment year."

Martin: "Creates a lot of his own problems, a lot of them in his head, thereby holding back what should have been a good hitting talent. A full swinger with power. Strikes out too much."

RICK LEACH
INF, No. 7
LL, 6'0", 195 lbs.
ML Svc: 2 years
Born: 5-4-57 in
Ann Arbor, MI

1982 STATISTICS

AVG	G	AB	R	H	2B	3B	HR	RBI	BB	SO	SB
.239	82	218	23	52	7	2	3	12	21	29	4

CAREER STATISTICS

AVG	G	AB	R	H	2B	3B	HR	RBI	BB	SO	SB
.226	136	301	32	68	10	3	4	23	37	44	4

VS. RHP

VS. LHP

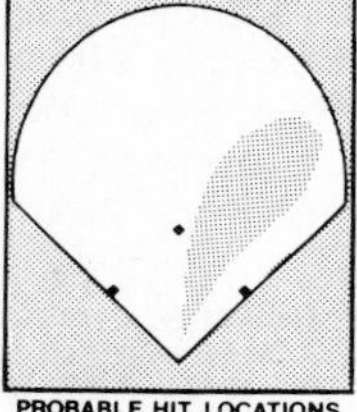
PROBABLE HIT LOCATIONS

HITTING:

Statistically, Rick Leach is a better hitter against righthanded pitching. But he concentrates so much trying to battle a lefty, he just may be a better hitter against lefthanders.

Leach hits from an upright stance, low in the box and square to the plate. Basically a pull hitter, he'll go to the opposite field with two strikes. Pitchers get him out on breaking balls but take note: Leach hits the breaking ball better when he's ahead in the count. If the pitcher gets ahead, Leach is more of a fastball hitter. Primarily a high ball hitter, Leach likes the fastball up and in, so stay away with everything. He has more trouble with finesse pitchers and those with overpowering fastballs.

He can hit the ball into the gap and may be well suited for the turf parks, where the ball will take off and roll. He doesn't have much power and usually hits line drives or grounders. He rates average to slightly above as a clutch hitter, but otherwise is average in hitting behind the runner and hitting with runners in scoring position. He's also an average bunter. Struck out 29 times in just 218 at-bats last season, little more than the 21 times he walked. He needs to improve that ratio.

BASERUNNING:

Leach's speed to first is below average. Likewise, his basestealing ability needs to get better. Stole just four times in 1982 but never was caught. Rates above average at breaking up the double play. He doesn't make a pitcher worry but is a smart, aggressive baserunner. Baserunning, however, probably is the weakest part of his game.

FIELDING:

First base seems to be the best position for Leach. He doesn't have the range or the arm for the outfield, where he also played occasionally. At first base, Leach rates average in all categories, from arm strength and accuracy to fielding to his left and right. He can field the bunt and will make the clutch plays.

OVERALL:

Robinson: "Overall, I think he is a borderline big league player who is best playing first and hitting down in the lineup, spot playing against certain pitchers. He has to hit to help."

Martin: "An 'iffy' year in 1982 for Leach, playing in just 82 games. He is a good athlete and should hit, eventually."

HITTING:

Lemon tries to take some of the pitcher's turf away, and to get him out, the pitcher has to try and take it back. He leans out over the plate and usually leads the league in getting hit by pitchers. But be careful backing him off the plate, because Lemon loves the inside pitch. Back him off, but back him way off. Miss that and Lemon will turn on the inside pitch.

A straightaway hitter, Lemon bats from a closed, semi-crouch and will move around in the batter's box, depending on the pitcher. But he'll usually try to stand low in the box. He likes as much time as he can to get a look at the fastball, but he may cheat up against a breaking ball pitcher.

Keep the ball down against Lemon; he likes it up. He struggles against the slow curve and change, but keep both down. He hits the slider pretty well. Lemon has hit everywhere in the lineup, but he's probably better hitting fifth or sixth. He has been a leadoff man, too, but his baserunning isn't good enough to leadoff regularly.

He is rated average in hitting in the clutch and behind the runner, and is a good bunter. He is a late starter and finishes hard. Last year he brought his average up from the .230s by hitting .304 in the second half, finishing at .266.

BASERUNNING:

Lemon occasionally takes his chances on the bases and it usually gets him in trouble. He does not have good judgment, and is too aggressive. He has excellent speed to first, and will often slide head first, especially into first base trying to beat out infield hits. When he was with the White Sox the team tried unsuccessfully to break him of the habit.

FIELDING:

Lemon's arm strength is rated above average, but he is not consistent in hitting the cutoff man. He will

CHET LEMON
OF, No. 34
RR, 6'0", 190 lbs.
ML Svc: 7 years
Born: 2-12-55 in Jackson, MS

1982 STATISTICS

AVG	G	AB	R	H	2B	3B	HR	RBI	BB	SO	SB
.266	125	436	75	116	20	1	9	52	56	69	1

CAREER STATISTICS

AVG	G	AB	R	H	2B	3B	HR	RBI	BB	SO	SB
.285	809	3230	478	920	198	30	82	400	337	446	46

VS. RHP

VS. LHP

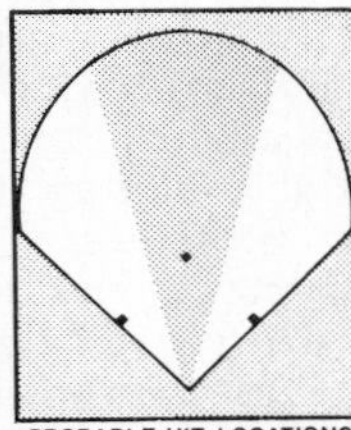
PROBABLE HIT LOCATIONS

sometimes try a long rainbow throw home which looks good, but isn't very effective and will allow other runners on base to advance. His speed gives him tremendous range. He is more effective coming in and he usually plays deep, which means some balls drop in for hits that might be caught.

OVERALL:

Lemon is multi-talented but tends to brood and is easily bruised. It sometimes affects his play. His talents are many but some deficiencies could be improved.

Robinson: "Did not play up to his potential last year. Most effective playing center field and leading off. Has a lot of ability and has been a good player. I thought he would do better in Detroit than he did."

Martin: "A solid ballplayer who had trouble adjusting when traded. Much improved the second half last year. Has plenty of time to move back into the company of the league's best outfielders."

JACK MORRIS
RHP, No. 47
RR, 6'3", 190 lbs.
ML Svc: 5 years
Born: 5-16-56 in
St. Paul, MN

PITCHING:

Jack Morris is a power pitcher to the first degree with a live fastball in the 90+ MPH. But he also has one of the best sliders in the league and a very good change. Add to that the addition of a forkball last season and the hitters will have some trouble.

He pitches overhand and strictly is a starter, which gives him an opportunity to use all of his pitches. He'll use the fastball a lot and the slider as his second pitch, and then mix in the change.

Morris struggled at times in 1982, but still led the Tigers in wins, becoming only the second pitcher in the club's history to lead the team in wins in 4 different seasons. He seems a step short of the necessary consistency and maturity to become a big winner. But he is overpowering at times and that helps him get out of a lot of trouble.

Morris really beat up the last-place teams in 1982, going 4-0 against the Twins, and 3-0 against the Blue Jays. Like most hard-throwers, he was better when it was light, not dark, last season, going 6-2 in day games and 11-14 at night.

He pitches poorly in Fenway but likes Tiger Stadium, where he was 9-6 in 1982, and also does well in Baltimore. The Orioles selected him as the toughest pitcher they faced in 1982, though he was 0-2 against them. No wonder. Morris struck out 10 Orioles in one game. But the Yankees and Red Sox always give him trouble.

FIELDING:

Morris is an outstanding fielder, one of the best at his position. He is very quick and a very good athlete. His move to first base is rated average, but at fielding bunts and overall effectiveness at fielding his position, he rates excellent.

OVERALL:

Had an off-year with a four-plus ERA last season, but still won 17 games. Overwhelming, but not consistently so.

Martin: "Has a tendency to throw the home run ball, but still potentially a big winner. Has quite an arsenal of pitches."

Robinson: "Had some mechanical problems in his delivery. It looked like he was overstriding and slinging the ball instead of throwing it. Should be better in 1983 and I have a feeling he will."

1982 STATISTICS

W	L	ERA	G	GS	CG	IP	H	R	ER	BB	SO	SV
17	16	4.06	37	37	17	266	247	131	120	96	135	0

CAREER STATISTICS

W	L	ERA	G	GS	CG	IP	H	R	ER	BB	SO	SV
68	51	3.76	160	138	53	1064	976	478	445	392	529	0

LARRY PASHNICK
RHP, No. 22
RR, 6'2", 195 lbs.
ML Svc: 1 year
Born: 4-25-56 in
Lincoln Park, MI

PITCHING:

So far, Larry Pashnick's claim to fame is the fact that he was the 999th player to wear a Tiger uniform. But he did show some promise in his rookie season last year, and could be Detroit's fourth starter this year if he can work out some problems.

Pashnick throws somewhere in between overhand and three-quarter, has very good control but his velocity is poor, about 83 MPH. Besides his fastball, Pashnick throws an above average slider that sinks. He has an above average change, and a palmball he'll turn over for his third pitch. Pashnick has a curve as well, but it is not very good and he rarely shows it.

Pashnick's problem comes when he tires. His sinker-slider straightens out and he gets the ball up, which results in a lot of home runs. When his breaking stuff does straighten out, he just doesn't have enough power in his fastball to blow it by the hitters.

He was used about half and half when it came to starting and relieving last season, but starting is probably his niche. The statistics don't agree, however. Pashnick was 3-4 with a 4.17 ERA in 13 starts last season, but was 1-0 with 3.43 ERA in 15 relief appearances.

He gets lefthanders and righthanders out with equal success, although his sinker gives him an added edge against lefthanders.

His greatest asset is his control and his palmball-change, but he still throws too many home runs and could use some experience. His sinker and control give him an advantage in Tiger Stadium.

FIELDING:

Rate Pashnick's move to first as average to above average. When fielding bunts, he is just average. Overall, he fields his position competently.

OVERALL:

Pashnick showed more potential in spring training than he showed during the entire 1982 season, but experience will help. He was 1-3 in the first half of 1982 but 3-1 after the All Star break.

Robinson: "Could be the Tigers' fourth starter this year. He is gaining the experience he needs. Larry is an outstanding competitor with a good variety of pitches and good control."

Martin: "From what I saw, he needs work. But for his rookie season he did not perform that badly."

1982 STATISTICS

W	L	ERA	G	GS	CG	IP	H	R	ER	BB	SO	SV
4	4	4.01	28	13	1	94	110	46	42	25	19	0

CAREER STATISTICS

W	L	ERA	G	GS	CG	IP	H	R	ER	BB	SO	SV
4	4	4.01	28	13	1	94	110	46	42	25	19	0

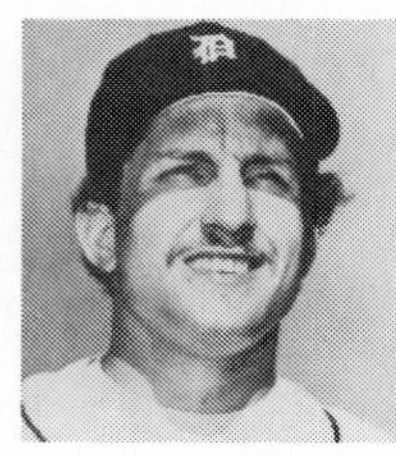

LANCE PARRISH
C, No. 13
RR, 6'3", 210 lbs.
ML Svc: 5 years
Born: 6-15-56 in
Clairton, PA

1982 STATISTICS

AVG	G	AB	R	H	2B	3B	HR	RBI	BB	SO	SB
.284	133	486	75	138	19	2	32	87	40	99	3

CAREER STATISTICS

AVG	G	AB	R	H	2B	3B	HR	RBI	BB	SO	SB
.266	613	2214	305	589	110	16	102	328	170	448	17

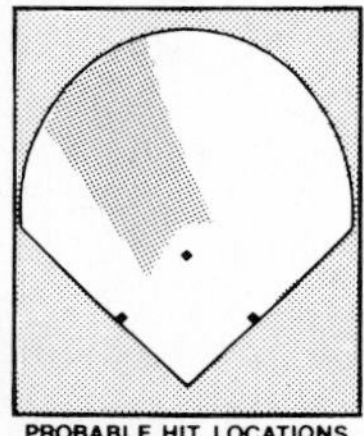

HITTING:

Detroit manager Sparky Anderson said Parrish "improved more in one year than any other player I've had." Parrish hit 32 home runs, drove in 87 runs and had a .529 slugging percentage in 1982.

Parrish is an alleys hitter who likes the ball up and over the plate. Throw him breaking balls down and away and run the fastball in on him. He'll hit a lot of fly balls, expecially to left center, and is about equally successful against left and righthanded pitching.

He is an average hitter in the clutch, but needs improvement when it comes to hitting behind the runner. He is becoming a more disciplined hitter and isn't chasing as many bad pitches as he used to.

Pitchers have some success throwing him a lot of off-speed stuff, but he'll hit a good curve, especially if it's up. He does not handle the sinker well. Dennis Lamp and LaMarr Hoyt of the White Sox gave him fits last season.

Parrish is well suited to hit in Tiger Stadium but did not hit well in bigger Comiskey Park in Chicago. Minnesota pitchers wanted to hide every time Parrish stepped to the plate. He hit seven home runs against Twins' pitching last season.

BASERUNNING:

Parrish rates barely average in speed to first, and he needs work on his basestealing. He does slide well and can break up a double play. He does not make a pitcher beware and is a very conservative, though fairly smart, runner.

FIELDING:

Parrish took over calling pitches in 1982, a job that previously went to pitching coach Roger Craig. Parrish rates average to slightly above in knowledge of opposing batters' strengths and weaknesses.

When it comes to his arm, Parish rates excellent in arm strength and release point to above average in accuracy. He is improving at blocking balls in the dirt and is average in fielding the bunt. But he is excellent at holding runners on and rates above average, overall, as an effective catcher.

OVERALL:

Robinson: "Finally showing a real ability to drive in runs and has become more assertive overall. Might be the best in the American League. Can become anything he wants in this game."

Martin: "Anderson says Parrish is the best catcher in baseball--period. I wouldn't go that far, at least now, but I wouldn't go against it happening soon."

Harwell: "An All Star catcher with great strength and a top-notch hitter."

DAN PETRY
RHP, No. 46
RR, 6'4", 200 lbs.
ML Svc: 3 years
Born: 11-13-58 in Palo Alto, CA

PITCHING:

Petry is a power pitcher, straight overhand and one of the best in the American League. He looks the part on almost every pitch he throws. He works from a no-windup delivery but still labors and looks like he could hurt his arm on every pitch. His fastball is hard, about 90 MPH, and has a lot of movement.

He also has an excellent slider that breaks quick and short. It's one of the better sliders in the league. He has a curve but doesn't show it much. When he first started pitching, the curve was perhaps his best pitch. He rarely uses the straight change, which needs work.

Petry is more effective pitching to righthanders because his fastball runs in on the hitter. Then he will throw the hard slider, away. He's good under pressure and occasionally will use the brushback.

One of Petry's real strengths as a pitcher is his ability to keep the ball down most of the time. But his control is spotty at times, and he often tries to overthrow the ball. He sometimes loses his concentration and that gets him in trouble.

Because he keeps the ball down, Petry can do well in a park like Tiger Stadium. Last season he did well against the White Sox and Twins, but struggled against the Yankees and Brewers. Good poise for a young pitcher.

FIELDING:

Nothing extraordinary about Petry's fielding. He does have an above average move to first that is very quick. Otherwise, he is very average at fielding bunts and rates average in overall effectiveness in fielding his position.

OVERALL:

Came on strong in 1982 and rates above average to excellent overall. If he can gain some consistency, control wise, his potential is unlimited.

Robinson: "Has taken over as the ace of the Detroit staff. He is a hard thrower with a great slider, and pitched very well all year. Petry has been getting better in each of the last three seasons."

Martin: "Superior stuff. Still growing in the big leagues. He has the potential to be outstanding for years if his back doesn't kick up too much."

Harwell: "Great young pitcher who's still improving. Dan will be among the top five in the league."

1982 STATISTICS

W	L	ERA	G	GS	CG	IP	H	R	ER	BB	SO	SV
15	9	3.22	35	35	8	246	220	98	88	100	132	0

CAREER STATISTICS

W	L	ERA	G	GS	CG	IP	H	R	ER	BB	SO	SV
41	32	3.46	100	97	21	650	481	279	250	273	342	0

DAVE ROZEMA
RHP, No. 19
RR, 6'4", 200 lbs.
ML Svc: 6 years
Born: 8-5-56 in
Grand Rapids, MI

PITCHING:

Most of Rozema's 1982 season was lost due to knee surgery. He's been used as a starter and reliever during his career and has an above average ability to pitch accurately and consistently to a batter's weakness.

Rozema throws from an unusual three-quarter delivery that makes it seem like he's going to throw his shoulder out of joint on each pitch. But his control is impeccable.

His fastball is in the 80 MPH range and will sink and run in on righthanded hitters. It also has good movement. He'll use the slider for his second pitch and the curveball for his third. Both are rated average to slightly above.

Rozema also has an outstanding straight change that he uses a lot. When he's behind in the count, hitters look for Rozema to throw a breaking pitch.

He is especially effective against righthanded hitters and occasionally will drop down and pitch sidearm to a righthander, making it even tougher for a hitter to pick up the ball.

Rozema's greatest assets are his stuff and a great change. But he seldom brushes a hitter back and continuously nibbles at the plate, almost as if he's afraid to throw a strike.

Rozema usually pitches well against the A's in Oakland, but the tables are turned when the A's come to Detroit. He also does not pitch well in Fenway.

He is also a nervous type when he pitches and will pace the mound continually.

FIELDING:

Rozema is big and awkward and not terribly coordinated. His move to first is average, but overall, his fielding rates average to slightly below.

OVERALL:

Rozema's command of four pitches and his control can take him a long way if he can come back from the knee operation. Was the best Tiger pitcher in spring training last year before he hurt his knee.

Robinson: "Looks like he was on his way back to his 1977 form (15-7, 3.09 ERA). Is more aggressive now and is going after hitters. His knee still is a question."

1982 STATISTICS

W	L	ERA	G	GS	CG	IP	H	R	ER	BB	SO	SV
3	0	1.63	8	2	0	27	17	5	5	7	15	1

CAREER STATISTICS

W	L	ERA	G	GS	CG	IP	H	R	ER	BB	SO	SV
39	37	3.33	150	96	35	800	796	337	296	186	292	9

DAVE RUCKER
LHP, No. 49
LL, 6'1", 190 lbs.
ML Svc: 1 year plus
Born: 9-1-57 in
San Bernardino, CA

PITCHING:

Rucker has an ordinary fastball, velocity wise, but it is a nasty pitch to hit because it moves so much and Rucker doesn't always have good control of it. The ball sinks, and hitters get a lot of ground balls off him, which is good when you pitch half of the time in cozy Tiger Stadium.

He basically is a one-pitch pitcher, relying on his fastball, but he has been working on a curve to go with his slider. If he ever perfects a second pitch, Rucker will be much tougher to hit against. He also is fooling around with a forkball, but when he's behind in the count, look for the fastball.

Rucker, a lefthander, often defies the percentages by pitching more effectively against righthanders than lefties. His fastball runs away from righthanders and is tough to hit. To lefthanders, the ball runs in and he often starts it out too far. By the time the pitch gets to the hitter, it is right out over the middle of the plate.

His strengths include the movement on his fastball and his ability to pitch every day, if necessary. But his performance in pressure situations could be improved. And until he perfects a second pitch, hitters know he's coming in with the fastball when he gets behind in the count.

FIELDING:

Rucker drives the first baseman crazy because his throws to first base move just as much as his fastball, and the fielder isn't always sure where it's going. His pick-off move also moves like his fastball. Rucker is very quick but overall his fielding needs improvement.

OVERALL:

Rucker is very well suited to pitch in Detroit because he gets the batter to hit ground balls that slow down on Tiger Stadium's high infield grass. A second pitch could turn him from second rate to first class.

Martin: "Interesting to watch. Has a chance to become a starter despite his relief record."

Harwell: "Still a prospect, but needs more big league experience."

Robinson: "Did a good job in Triple A. The next step is up."

1982 STATISTICS

W	L	ERA	G	GS	CG	IP	H	R	ER	BB	SO	SV
5	6	3.38	27	4	1	64	62	26	24	23	31	5

CAREER STATISTICS

W	L	ERA	G	GS	CG	IP	H	R	ER	BB	SO	SV
5	6	3.57	29	4	1	68	65	30	27	24	33	0

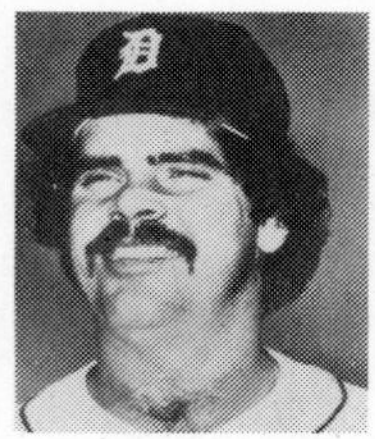

KEVIN SAUCIER
LHP, No. 31
RL, 6'1", 195 lbs.
ML Svc: 4 years
Born: 8-9-56 in
Pensacola, FL

PITCHING:

Patience is the key to hitting Saucier. He will be wild all over the place then come in and make a perfect pitch on the black. Patient hitters will get him, but free swingers can't touch him.

Saucier pitched both as a starter and in short relief in 1982. He throws from a three-quarter, herky-jerky motion that can be disturbing to the hitters. His fastball is relatively slow at 84 MPH, but is alive and moves well which makes up for what it lacks in velocity.

His second best pitch is the curve, but control is a problem here, too. He throws a big, sweeping curve but just doesn't get it over consistently. He has an average slider for his third pitch and rarely uses the straight change. It's not much of a pitch. When he's behind, hitters look for the fastball.

Saucier's motion makes him especially tough on lefthanders. And he is mean. Players say Saucier would knock his mother down. In the absence of his mother, he knocks down anyone who dares to dig in at the plate.

His strength is his ability to get lefthanded hitters out, which makes him valuable as a reliever. But he doesn't have good command and control of his pitches, which can get him in trouble in a hurry in relief.

When he does win a game he shows it, shaking hands and slapping the back of any teammate in sight.

Saucier does very well against Milwaukee but has trouble whenever Boston or Texas come to town.

FIELDING:

Saucier is very awkward as a fielder and his move to first needs improvement. He rates average at fielding bunts at his position but is very slow.

OVERALL:

Saucier has a lot of confidence and it shows, but inconsistency has dogged his entire career. Overall, he rates slightly below average.

Robinson: "Struggled early in 1982 and was sent to the minors. His best bet to return to the big leagues is in short relief because he gets lefthanders out so well."

Martin: "Saucier really should be a better pitcher then he is."

1982 STATISTICS

W	L	ERA	G	GS	CG	IP	H	R	ER	BB	SO	SV
3	1	3.12	31	1	0	40	35	15	14	29	23	4

CAREER STATISTICS

W	L	ERA	G	GS	CG	IP	H	R	ER	BB	SO	SV
15	11	3.33	139	3	0	203	183	82	75	104	93	18

DAVE TOBIK
RHP, No. 45
RR, 6'1", 190 lbs.
ML Svc: 3 years
Born: 3-2-53 in
Euclid, OH

PITCHING:

Tobik found a new weapon, the forkball, in 1982 and made great strides as a pitcher. A short reliever, Tobik pitches straight overhand from a slow and deliberate motion and goes to the back of his cap after almost every pitch. Before he picked up the forkball, Tobik used the fastball almost exclusively and mixed in a curve that perhaps was too slow. He rarely used the slider.

Just the news that Tobik had added the forkball was enough to give him an edge against hitters, who had to look for it. It will be interesting in 1983 to see what happens now that hitters have had time to adjust to the new pitch. A lot of hitters were swinging at forkballs out of the strike zone in 1982.

The forkball should help Tobik pitch in Tiger Stadium because a lot of hitters had been waiting for his fastball then taking him deep. Now they have to look for something else.

Tobik can throw hard but he rarely will brush a hitter back. His ability to pitch in pressure situations rates above average. He did very well against Minnesota last season but poorly against Boston.

FIELDING:

Tobik has a good, quick move to first. Rate it slightly above average. Otherwise, he is an average fielder when it comes to fielding bunts and handling his postion overall.

OVERALL:

Not all of Tobik's statistics last year were terrific, but the forkball could help him turn things around this season. Could be a good reliever.

Robinson: "Surprise of the year for the Tigers. The forkball saved his career."

Martin: "Throws well coming out of pen but inconsistent at times. Walks get him in trouble."

1982 STATISTICS

W	L	ERA	G	GS	CG	IP	H	R	ER	BB	SO	SV
4	9	3.56	51	1	0	98	86	45	39	38	63	9

CAREER STATISTICS

W	L	ERA	G	GS	CG	IP	H	R	ER	BB	SO	SV
10	16	3.66	137	2	0	300	265	132	122	120	188	4

ALAN TRAMMELL
INF, No. 3
RR, 6'0", 170 lbs.
ML Svc: 5 years
Born: 2-21-58 in
Garden Grove, CA

1982 STATISTICS

AVG	G	AB	R	H	2B	3B	HR	RBI	BB	SO	SB
.258	157	489	66	126	34	3	9	57	52	47	19

CAREER STATISTICS

AVG	G	AB	R	H	2B	3B	HR	RBI	BB	SO	SB
.272	708	2392	348	650	95	21	28	237	262	264	61

VS. RHP

VS. LHP

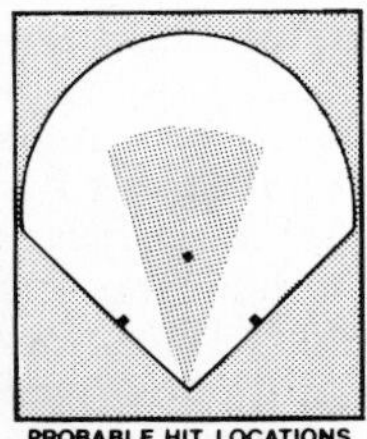
PROBABLE HIT LOCATIONS

HITTING:

Alan Trammell regrouped at the plate after hitting .206 the first half of last season. He batted .309 after the All Star break and tied a career high of nine home runs.

He hits from a closed, crouched stance and usually stands in the center of the box. A good low ball hitter, Trammell should be pitched up and inside and with breaking balls, away. Some teams had even more success by pitching him up and over the plate, getting him to hit a lot of lazy fly balls.

Pitchers try to get Trammell with bad breaking pitches, which he'll swing at, then bust him with a good fastball. He really likes to hit the low fastball on the inside half of the plate. Does not handle the change, curve or slider especially well. The key is to pitch him slowly and set him up. He's an impatient hitter, expecially with men in scoring position. Sometimes this impatience gets him to swing at bad pitches.

A line drive hitter, Trammell will hit a lot of balls to right field, so shade him that way defensively. His impatience as a hitter hurts him in the clutch and with runners in scoring position, but he does have good bat control and rates above average in his ability to hit behind the runner and on the hit-and-run. He's also an above average bunter.

BASERUNNING:

Trammell is a heady baserunner with average speed down the line to first. He's good at breaking up the double play. Although he stole 19 bases last season, it was a career high for him, and he is not really a threat to a pitcher. He'll occasionally flash a little daring on the bases, but generally is fairly conservative as a runner.

FIELDING:

If they make a training film on playing shortstop, Trammell, with all due respect to Robin Yount, could be the film's star. His fielding mechanics are flawless, from the way he gets down to field a ground ball to the way he moves left and right. He's also very sure-handed and was second in fielding among shortstops last season with a .978 fielding percentage.

Rate Trammell's arm strength and throwing accuracy as excellent and his range above average. He rates above average in fielding balls to his left and right. He's also excellent in turning the double play. Fielding is the strongest part of his game.

OVERALL:

Martin: "A fine young player with room to get better as a hitter. Very steady at short with an extremely accurate arm."

Robinson: "Defense is his greatest value to the team. Hitting has been a problem, but he's done everything else. A good player."

JERRY UJDUR
RHP, No. 28
RR, 6'1", 195 lbs.
ML Svc: 1 year plus
Born: 3-5-57 in
Duluth, MN

PITCHING:

Ujdur (pronounced YOU-jer) pitches from a very deliberate and slow three-quarter motion. His control rates above average for a young pitcher and he keeps the ball down, which means he throws a lot of ground ball outs.

He relies on two pitches, the fastball, which is in the 85-88 MPH range, and the slider, which probably is his most effective pitch. But the slider is also the pitch he's most likely to make a mistake with, hence a lot of his sliders end up deposited in the outfield seats as home runs.

This righthander's curve is a downer and a good one. He uses it primarily to get lefthanded hitters out. He uses the palmball for his change. It's just average, and he only shows it to plant the seed in a hitter's mind that he has a palmball. It also makes his other pitches look better.

Ujdur usually will go to his fastball when he's behind in the count and is equally effective against righthanders and lefthanders. He'll seldom brush a hitter back but has good poise under pressure for a rookie.

His sinking fastball and his slider are his greatest strengths, but he doesn't have overpowering speed and has a tendency to sulk on the mound. That causes him to occasionally lose concentration.

Usually a sinkerball pitcher gets even more movement on the ball when he's tired, but Ujder is the exception. He's a good six-inning pitcher but then his slider hangs and his fastball straightens out. That spells trouble.

FIELDING:

Rate Ujdur's move to first as above average. He is a very good athlete and very quick. His quickness is evident fielding bunts and his position overall. Overall, he rates above average at fielding his position.

OVERALL:

A lot of promise here because of Ujder's control and poise at such a tender age. Overall, he rates average but experience could send that rating higher.

Robinson: "Look for him to be more impressive in 1983. He pitched some big games for Detroit last season. Doesn't have overpowering stuff but has good control and goes right after the hitters."

Martin: "So far, only a .500 pitcher but not a bad bet to be better in 1983 with a year of experience under his belt. Was the Tigers' best starter over a month last season."

1982 STATISTICS

W	L	ERA	G	GS	CG	IP	H	R	ER	BB	SO	SV
10	10	3.69	25	25	7	178	150	76	73	69	86	0

CAREER STATISTICS

W	L	ERA	G	GS	CG	IP	H	R	ER	BB	SO	SV
11	10	4.27	38	31	7	213	205	108	101	84	99	0

PAT UNDERWOOD
LHP, No. 40
LL, 6'0", 180 lbs.
ML Svc: 3 years
Born: 2-9-57 in
Kokomo, IN

PITCHING:

Pat Underwood was 3-7 in 12 starts last year and ended up spending a good portion of the year in the bullpen. He did have two complete games but overall he had a disappointing year.

Underwood pitches overhand but short-arms the ball and keeps his arm close to his body. He has pretty good stuff but nothing outstanding. In short, he doesn't have an "out" pitch yet.

Underwood uses his curveball better than any of his pitches. As a result, he's more effective pitching to lefthanders than to righthanders. He also throws a straight change but doesn't use it much in relief.

He has good control but needs to become more aggressive. He often tries to throw the ball too hard and ends up getting the ball up. He's better when he doesn't try to throw hard because he gets better movement on his pitches and keeps the ball down more consistently.

Underwood had a very good strikeouts-to-walks ratio: striking out 43 while walking 22. But he gave up 17 home runs in just 99 innings of work. His poise and presence on the mound need work.

FIELDING:

Underwood's move to first needs work as well. It is a dead giveaway and good baserunners always know when Underwood's going to throw over. There's no deception at all. On the mound Underwood is slow and awkward fielding bunts. Overall, he needs improvement in fielding his position.

OVERALL:

Time should solve Underwood's problems, but it had better happen soon. He's shown good control but has to get some consistency.

Robinson: "Should be a better pitcher at this stage of his career. He has to become more aggressive and go after hitters more. I think he tries to pitch too fine instead of saying, 'OK, get ready. Here it comes.' "

Martin: "He still has potential and can come into a game early and keep you in it. But his tendency to give up the home run ball and his inconsistency are drawbacks. Still he could fill a role as a middle reliever."

1982 STATISTICS

W	L	ERA	G	GS	CG	IP	H	R	ER	BB	SO	SV
4	8	4.73	33	12	2	99	108	66	52	22	43	3

CAREER STATISTICS

W	L	ERA	G	GS	CG	IP	H	R	ER	BB	SO	SV
13	18	4.28	109	34	3	334	355	181	159	86	186	8

HITTING:

Lou Whitaker is a definite high ball hitter and pitchers, especially left-handers, stay down and away with everything. His weakness is the off-speed pitch. He likes to hit the ball to the opposite field and some teams had success against him last season by pitching him that way, out and over the plate. They were fairly successful pitching to Whitaker's strength, getting a lot of fly ball outs to left field.

He's definitely an opposite field hitter with little power to left. But he did try to pull the ball more last season and found some surprising power. Finally realized he has to pull more to keep the outfielders playing him honest.

A streaky, line drive hitter, Whitaker hits righthanders a little better than lefthanders. He reaches the alleys occasionally (career high eight triples last season) and rates above average in hitting behind the runner and on the hit-and-run. He's an average bunter.

Whitaker will hit a curve if it's up, but doesn't handle the slider too well. He did adjust well last year to the leadoff spot, hitting .309 from early July through the end of the season.

Tiger Stadium is well suited for Whitaker as a hitter, and he is showing increasing power as shown by his 15 home runs, three times as many as he hit in any previous season. In fact, Whitaker had just 12 career home runs going into 1982. He led off a game with a home run four times.

BASERUNNING:

Whitaker has above average speed to first but his sliding ability is so poor it's a drawback. He seems to have a fear of sliding and often slides late. As a result, he's not much of a threat to steal a base. Pitchers have to be aware of him on base, but Whitaker is a little below average, aggressive wise, as a baserunner. He did steal home once in 1982.

LOU WHITAKER
INF, No. 1
LR, 5'11", 160 lbs.
ML Svc: 5 years
Born: 5-12-57 in New York, NY

1982 STATISTICS

AVG	G	AB	R	H	2B	3B	HR	RBI	BB	SO	SB
.286	152	560	76	160	22	8	15	65	48	58	11

CAREER STATISTICS

AVG	G	AB	R	H	2B	3B	HR	RBI	BB	SO	SB
.271	683	2311	343	626	82	28	27	248	304	316	53

VS. RHP

VS. LHP

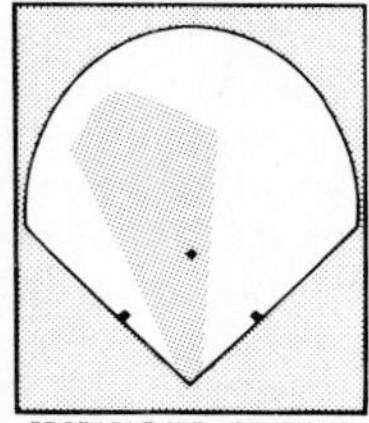
PROBABLE HIT LOCATIONS

FIELDING:

This is Whitaker's strongest asset. He led all second basemen with a .988 fielding percentage last season and rates above average in virtually every fielding category, from arm strength, accuracy and range, to ability to turn the double play and ability to make clutch defensive plays.

OVERALL:

Robinson: "His attitude was much better and 15 home runs was unbelievable. Finally accepted the leadoff spot, which I think is his best spot in the batting order. Very durable with a great eye at the plate."

Martin: "Good, solid player who can spark his team. Has improved all along in the field."

Harwell: "His power is increasing. A solid second baseman and hitter."

MILT WILCOX
RHP, No. 39
RR, 6'2", 215 lbs.
ML Svc: 11 years
Born: 4-20-50 in Honolulu, HI

PITCHING:

Wilcox made some changes in 1982. A severely dislocated index finger suffered during the off-season left the digit permanently bent. But it also helped Wilcox' forkball. It hurt his curve, but Wilcox doesn't use it much, anyway.

Wilcox' forkball breaks sharply down, so much so that many hitters think he's throwing the spitball. The truth may lie somewhere in between. Wilcox knows the spitter and may be throwing both the forkball and spitter.

He has a good fastball, about 87 MPH, but the pitch isn't as effective as it could be because it doesn't have much movement. A starter, Wilcox throws three-quarter and uses the fastball about 60% of the time. He tries to keep the fastball down and throws his curve overhand as his second pitch.

Wilcox discarded his slider in 1982, saying it got him into too much trouble. He rarely uses the straight change, which is average but works well for him. When he's behind in the count, look for the fastball.

A real strength is Wilcox' aggressiveness on the mound. He'll frequently brushback hitters. Just ask George Brett, who went after Wilcox after a brushback attempt. Wilcox' ability in pressure situations is rated average to above average.

His control is better now and he can get his three main pitches over the plate consistently. But he tends to cave in when things go badly, so get him early. The longer he goes in a game, the more confidence he has and the tougher he gets.

Wilcox does well in Tiger Stadium and Oakland, but struggles in Boston and Baltimore. He also does well against Toronto and Seattle.

FIELDING:

Wilcox' move to first is above average. It's quick and effective. He is average at fielding bunts and rates average overall when it comes to fielding his position.

OVERALL:

Wilcox is a great competitor on the mound, which is a real plus, but he needs to learn how to hang in there when things start going badly.

Robinson: "He has a lot of confidence and won't hesitate to run you out of the box a few times. His two new pitches, the forkball and overhand curve, really have helped."

Harwell: "Injuries have hampered his career, but he is a great competitor. Makes good use of his talent."

Martin: "Good No. 3 or No. 4 starter. Nothing flashy, just a solid, slightly over .500 pitcher."

1982 STATISTICS

W	L	ERA	G	GS	CG	IP	H	R	ER	BB	SO	SV
12	10	3.62	29	29	9	193	187	91	78	85	112	0

CAREER STATISTICS

W	L	ERA	G	GS	CG	IP	H	R	ER	BB	SO	SV
90	84	4.04	314	206	64	1539	1519	763	690	588	871	5

GLENN WILSON
OF, No. 12
RR, 6'1", 190 lbs.
ML Svc: 1 year
Born: 12-22-58 in Baytown, TX

1982 STATISTICS

AVG	G	AB	R	H	2B	3B	HR	RBI	BB	SO	SB
.292	84	322	39	94	15	1	12	34	15	51	2

CAREER STATISTICS

AVG	G	AB	R	H	2B	3B	HR	RBI	BB	SO	SB
.292	84	322	39	94	15	1	12	34	15	51	2

VS. RHP

VS. LHP

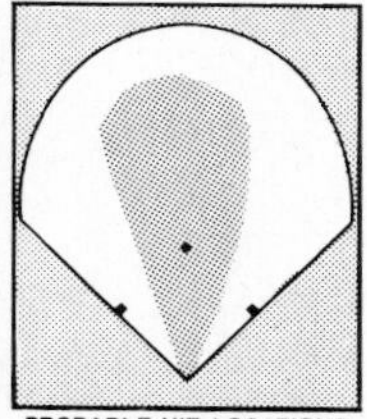
PROBABLE HIT LOCATIONS

HITTING:

Nobody can say that Glenn Wilson doesn't play all-out. The Tiger rookie collapsed late in the season from what was diagnosed as acute muscle strain. He tried to come back and play the final days of the season but wasn't ready. His batting average dropped from .307 to .292 but did not mar what otherwise was a brilliant rookie performance.

Wilson is a high ball hitter. He hits line drives and has 20 home run potential. He has good power to the opposite field, too.

Pitchers throw him a steady diet of breaking pitches, down in the strike zone. He doesn't do too badly against the change, but still can't hit the curve or slider consistently. Don't throw him any fastballs, up. He'll turn on them. Tiger Stadium's dimensions make it possible for Wilson to homer to right or left.

Wilson bats from a barely-closed stance. He stands upright, low in the box. Basically, he's a straightaway hitter who occasionally will reach the alleys. He's still learning and needs to improve as a clutch hitter and batting with men in scoring position. Does not walk much, just 15 times in 322 at-bats.

Wilson hit well in August last season, including a 10-game and 19-game hitting streak. Also had eight home runs in the month, hitting .385 (47-for-122).

BASERUNNING:

Wilson is average to above in speed to first, but needs to work on his sliding. He's an average to above baserunner but does not break up the double play well. He makes a pitcher nervous and is a fairly smart, very aggressive runner.

FIELDING:

Wilson's bat wasn't the only thing that made him a quick favorite of Detroit fans. He can make the dazzling play in the outfield. His arm and throwing accuracy are excellent. His throw to the plate is average but very solid. His range in the outfield rates slightly above average. He's very sound, fundamentally, on defense. Goes back on fly balls just as well as he comes in.

OVERALL:

Robinson: "Good, young player who has a bright future. If he won't be playing every day in Detroit in 1983, though, he should be playing every day in Triple A ball. Good No. 2 hitter and center fielder. Has all the tools, and I look for him to crack the starting lineup in 1983."

Martin: "Took over center field like he'd been out there for years. There has to be room for him in Detroit's plans for 1983."

Harwell: "An up and coming young star who will get even better with the bat."

BILL FAHEY
C, No. 17
LR, 6'0", 195 lbs.
ML Svc: 8 years
Born: 6-14-50 in
Detroit, MI

HITTING, BASERUNNING, FIELDING:

With Parrish starting and Wockenfuss having a career year as a back up, Fahey saw little playing time and few plate appearances. He is a high fastball hitter who tries to pull everything. Lefthanders throw him breaking pitches. Righthanders throw fastballs in on his hands and keep everything else down and away. He usually makes contact, but does not walk much.

Fahey is more effective against righthanded pitchers. Does not bunt well and hits a 50-50 mix of line drives and ground balls. Because he likes to pull, he's suited to hit in Tiger Stadium, though he did not have a home run last year.

Fahey is very slow to first and does not steal. Very conservative as a runner.

Fahey nailed Oakland's Rickey Henderson when he tried to swipe his record-breaking 119th stolen base against the Tigers. He rates average to above average in knowledge of opposing hitters' strengths and weaknesses. Arm strength and release point are average. His accuracy is a little better than average. He works quietly behind the plate, and is above average at handling pitchers. Overall, he rates slightly above average as a receiver. Tiger manager Sparky Anderson rates Fahey as the best managerial prospect on the club.

OVERALL:

Robinson: "Strictly a back up or spot catcher, he handles pitchers very well. Detroit is a good place for him to play since he tries to pull so much."

LYNN JONES
OF, No. 35
RR, 5'9", 165 lbs.
ML Svc: 4 years
Born: 1-1-53 in
Meadville, PA

HITTING, BASERUNNING, FIELDING:

Lynn Jones has learned he can stay in the big leagues doing just what he's doing, playing occasionally against lefthanded pitchers only. He has a knee problem and has lost some speed, but still handles himself well at bat and in the field. A high ball hitter, Jones should be pitched inside and down. He tries to pull everything and likes the ball out over the plate.

Pitchers usually get Jones on breaking pitches and fastballs which they spot over the inside half of the plate. Jones hits the change very well and fastballs up and over the plate. He has a better chance of hitting the curve if it's up. Doesn't handle the sinker or slider well, but he murdered Chicago's Dennis Lamp, primarily a sinkerballer, in 1982. He also was a very tough out for the Orioles.

He can hit behind the runner and execute on the hit and run. He doesn't strike out or walk much. Rate him an average bunter and clutch hitter.

His knee problem has taken the spring from Jones' step. He won't steal when he gets on. Average speed to first and in breaking up the double play. He's a smart runner, and despite his reluctance to steal, pitchers usually keep at least one eye on him.

Jones is a pretty fair outfielder with above average arm strength, and throwing accuracy. His throw home and range are average. He's a little bit better coming in for a fly ball, rather than going back.

OVERALL:

Martin: "A fourth or fifth outfielder who couldn't crack the starting three in Detroit. Might have a better chance somewhere else."

JERRY TURNER
OF, No. 20
LL, 5'9", 180 lbs.
ML Svc: 10 years
Born: 1-17-54 in
Texarkana, AR

HITTING, BASERUNNING, FIELDING:

Jerry Turner can come off the bench and deliver. He is a straightaway hitter who will hit a lot of line drives and likes fastballs up. Pitchers go after him with fastballs down and away and with a lot of breaking pitches. He does not handle the curve or slider well.

The Tigers use Turner primarily as a lefthanded designated hitter. He rates average in the clutch, in hitting behind the runner and in his ability to draw walks. He hits with only occasionally power for a DH, and is more suited to bat seventh or lower in the batting order. Turner's bunting ability could use some work, but overall he rates as an average hitter in the .250 range.

Turner's speed to first is good, rated above average as is his ability to break up the double play. He'll make a pitcher beware but is an average basestealer. He always slides feet first and is conservative.

Turner's arm strength and accuracy are average at best. He is much better coming in on a fly ball, rather than going back. Turner's throw to home is rated average as is his range in the outfield.

OVERALL:

Average, average, average. Everything Turner does seems to rate about average, but he filled a need in Detroit coming off the bench, and players who can come off the bench and deliver have some value.

Robinson: "Living up to his major league potential in a part-time role. You have to have a player like this around."

JOHN WOCKENFUSS
C/INF, No. 14
RR, 6'0", 190 lbs.
ML Svc: 8 years
Born: 2-27-49 in
Welch, WV

HITTING, BASERUNNING, FIELDING:

John Wockenfuss has a very distinctive hitting stance, as closed as any hitter in the league. He is a low ball hitter who enjoyed his best major league season at the plate last year, finishing with a flourish.

Pitchers throw him the fastball up and in. He is a pull hitter and more effective against lefthanded pitching. Keep everything else away and throw him lots of curves. He goes in there swinging hard and hits many fly balls.

Wockenfuss has good bat control, and rates excellent in the hit-and-run, though he's only average at hitting behind the runner and in the clutch. His bunting needs improvement. He is a fair pinch-hitter.

Wockenfuss isn't a very good baserunner. He has poor speed to first, does not break up the double play and does not steal.

Primarily a designated hitter, Wockenfuss can go behind the plate, though his skills there are very limited. Arm strength, release point and throwing accuracy are average to below average. He does not block balls well nor does he field the bunt well. He is an average handler of pitchers.

OVERALL:

Martin: "Good offense though not particularly defensive anywhere on defense."

Harwell: "Very good bat control makes him an excellent hit-and-run man."

ROYALS STADIUM
Kansas City Royals

Seating Capacity: 40,628
Playing Surface: Artificial (Tartan Turf)

Dimensions
Left Field Pole: 330 ft.
Left-Center Field: 385 ft.
Center Field: 410 ft.
Right-Center Field: 385 ft.
Right Field Pole: 330 ft.
Height of Outfield Wall: 12 ft.

In the hit musical, "South Pacific," they told us there was nothing like a dame; in "Oklahoma," we were reminded that everything was up-to-date in Kansas City. Somewhere between the two lies Royals Stadium. The stadium is eminently fair for both pitcher and hitter. It also affords a bucolic view of green grass beyond the outfield fences, coupled with a dazzling water display.

The 40,628 seats are wrapped around the stadium from left to right field with small sections extending beyond either foul pole. Where the seats end, the bullpens begin. Both bullpens run perpendicularly from the field toward the back of the stadium, and to their right and left, respectively, there is grass that slopes upward toward the back wall.

The pasture-like area is split in dead center field by an upright scoreboard that holds more information than a computer bank. In right-center field, water falls endlessly into a unseen tank and is re-circulated. At given times, it spouts upwards in a marvelous display.

The Kansas City Royals have a decided advantage in the stadium because the management has built the team to fit the contours of the artificial surface of the park. Groundballs rocket through the infield, and line drives scoot between the outfielders. Balls that are hit down the right field line, if not cut off before they reach the wall, tend to hug the wall and lock themselves along its base, often leading to triples or inside-the-park homers if the opposing centerfielder does not hustle over to help the right fielder.

The turf is not as springy as the Metrodome in Minnesota, but Royal players, after realizing that a bloop will fall for a base hit, invariably keep running and usually stretch an ordinary single into a double because the ball usually does take a much higher first bounce than on the grass.

The stadium is nestled into a small valley and wind is rarely a factor. There is one problem with this stadium, and it is largely geographical. The TartanTurf holds heat, and in the hot Missouri summers, the temperature on the field can reach 105-110° daily.

WILLIE AIKENS
INF, No. 24
LR, 6'2", 220 lbs.
ML Svc: 4 years
Born: 10-14-54 in Seneca, SC

1982 STATISTICS

AVG	G	AB	R	H	2B	3B	HR	RBI	BB	SO	SB
.281	134	466	50	131	29	1	17	74	45	70	0

CAREER STATISTICS

AVG	G	AB	R	H	2B	3B	HR	RBI	BB	SO	SB
.273	544	1828	418	499	91	1	75	312	242	307	3

VS. RHP

VS. LHP

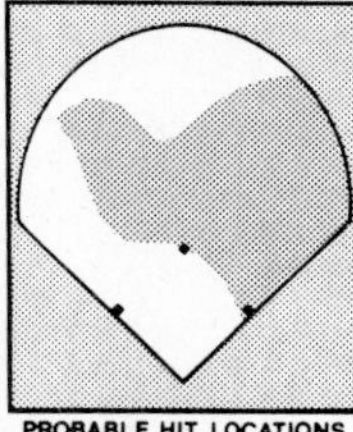
PROBABLE HIT LOCATIONS

HITTING:

Power Plus. Willie Aikens, a mammoth man, uses an oddly dainty stance--feet close together, right foot cocked on to his toes, and knock-kneed. He is deep in the box, parallel to the plate, and he uses a mighty swing on any strike. He will kill low pitches especially in, and he'll go for anything inside and handle it.

He hits deep flies, off into left center because his big swing is late, and hits screaming line drives to the right side. It is the breaking stuff set up by the fastball he's looking for that gives him fits, especially during slumps. Aikens is streaky. He hates change-ups.

He has to hit for double and home run power and produce 80 RBIs or more to be effective because he is slow and average afield. Curves and sliders handcuff him, but watch out if they hang: murder. Critics think he should be platooned against righthanded pitching.

BASERUNNING:

A scout once suggested that Aikens should be walked in dangerous situations regardless of the outs or men on base so he would clog the bases. He is cumbersome afoot, partly because of his size, partly because he is leg-heavy, and partly because he has a bad knee. He will run and slide hard, however.

FIELDING:

Aikens works very long and hard to improve and resents the frequent criticism he draws, but it is warranted. He doesn't get charged with many errors, but the plays he doesn't make are the ones that give him below average marks. He has limited range and he is weak in scooping throws from the dirt. He throws sidearm, not strong.

OVERALL:

When his bat is hot, Aikens is the missing link in the Royals' offense built on speed and all-field hitting; he is the game-breaking slugger. When he is cold at bat, however, he becomes almost a total liability because of severe limitations. Some critics even suggest he be platooned according to ballparks, not pitching, sitting out more games at home. Aikens gets frustrated by big ball parks and this works against him in those 81 games he must play at Royal Stadium. Mental knots tie him up when he has power droughts.

Robinson: "Willie has a tendency to get down on himself. He is certainly capable of bouncing back and has proved he can hit."

Martin: "It's hard to fathom him. He hits in bunches. He must bone up on the strike zone and make more contact."

MIKE ARMSTRONG
RHP, No. 31
RR, 6'3", 193 lbs.
ML Svc: 1 year plus
Born: 3-7-54 in
Glen Cove, NY

PITCHING:

A middle relief specialist, Mike Armstrong was the Royals' biggest discovery of 1982. He is a sidearm fastball pitcher with strikeout power in his 85-87 MPH heat.

He challenges batters with the mixture of both his speed and the sinking, or "moving-in" effect of his sidewinding style. His poor control and lack of an idea on the batters' strengths and weaknesses were problems for him last season.

With just an average slider, Armstrong needs to develop a curve or other third pitch. He seldom changes speeds, throwing hard stuff 95% of the time.

Armstrong is especially tough on righthanders, but lefties found that they could wait on him and often get ahead in the count. He gave up three grand slams in tight situations. Rated average when the pressure is on, he regained confidence and poise late in the season after hitting a lag.

His main asset is durability, and he can work three and four innings two or three times a week. He filled the void made by the trade of Renie Martin and came from virtually nowhere (a minor league trade for a player named later) to do it.

FIELDING:

Because his sidearm delivery carries him away from first base and leaves him off-balance in his follow-through, Armstrong must improve his methods of holding runners and fielding bunts.

OVERALL:

Armstrong is invaluable to the Royals. He is counted on to get them to "Quiz Time"--the eighth and ninth innings when Dan Quisenberry can come in and shut the door. Before Armstrong, Quisenberry's effectiveness was diminished by too many sixth and seventh inning appearances.

Armstrong is a late bloomer, a 28 year old rookie. He is one of those players who had been crying out for an opportunity but was in the wrong place at the wrong time, languishing in the San Diego system. He was overpowering in streaks last year, defying the average rating on him.

Harwell: "Good chance to be a good reliever because of his strikeout potential."

Robinson: "He was happy to be in the big leagues and to be used a lot, and he responded as a real plus. Look for him to get a lot of work this year."

1982 STATISTICS

W	L	ERA	G	GS	CG	IP	H	R	ER	BB	SO	SV
5	5	3.20	52	0	0	112	88	45	40	43	75	6

CAREER STATISTICS

W	L	ERA	G	GS	CG	IP	H	R	ER	BB	SO	SV
5	7	3.72	73	0	0	138	118	64	57	63	98	0

BUD BLACK
LHP, No. 40
LL, 6'1", 180 lbs.
ML Svc: 1 year
Born: 6-30-57 in
San Mateo, CA

PITCHING:

Bud Black is a spotstarter, and a long relief southpaw with a picture-smooth delivery remindful of Guidry. He comes three-quarter overhand with a power mix of a fastball (85-87 MPH) and sinking curve.

His strength is the use of four pitches--also a slider and breaking change--with good control. His obvious weakness is inexperience.

Black relies heavily on his catcher's knowledge of batters, and showed good poise in his rookie season. He appeared especially more at ease after a brief interlude in the minor leagues. The additional work got the rust off, and winning bolstered his confidence.

The strange thing about Black is that he is a power pitcher without any overpowering stuff. If movement is lacking on a given day in his pitches, he'll get tattooed. Batters will sit on his breaking stuff and look for the average fastball he uses 60% of the time.

His father was a professional hockey player, so Black knows the world of professional athletics and isn't awed by it. The management likes his composure, and his ability appears to be above average.

FIELDING:

Black's concentration was disrupted frequently last year by balk calls--he was charged with six. In the minor leagues, he was reputed as having one of the best pick-off moves anywhere, but the major league umpires didn't buy it. Both Black and his coach, Cloyd Boyer, are frustrated further because umpires haven't yet pinpointed what he needs to correct: they have only said it is deceptive and doesn't look legal.

Otherwise, Black gets high marks for fielding his position on bunts and holding runners.

OVERALL:

Black is in a tough situation. He's probably good enough to make the big league club, but not ready yet to assume a regular job in the rotation. He also appears to be more tailored for starting than instant snuffouts.

Time holds most of the answers on Black's abilities. More work in the minor leagues would benefit him more than sitting around the big league bullpen. Layoffs wore on him last year. Troubles arose from his lack of rhythm, throwing him a tad off in the control so essential to his being sneaky fast. Also, batters would wait for the mistakes that go with greenness.

Martin: "Will get better when he gets the chance to pitch more."

Harwell: "With experience can become a solid pitcher."

1982 STATISTICS

W	L	ERA	G	GS	CG	IP	H	R	ER	BB	SO	SV
4	6	4.58	22	14	0	88	92	48	45	34	40	0

CAREER STATISTICS

W	L	ERA	G	GS	CG	IP	H	R	ER	BB	SO	SV
4	6	4.55	24	0	0	89	94	48	45	37	40	0

PITCHING:

Vida Blue has been a standard-setter, clearly visible in his classic, fluid overhand delivery and in his fastball. Exclusively a starter, he has adapted in recent years to not going for the strikeout in every situation.

He still remains a power pitcher and was timed as high as 94 MPH last season. He sprinkles in his curve and off-speed pitches just 10% of the time. Time has brought him wisdom in battling a batter's weaknesses.

Blue's fastball rises, but he consistently pitches high anyway, making him susceptible to bases on balls and home run troubles. He forces a lot of fly outs.

His reputation is one of fierce competitiveness and extraordinary athletic prowess. He thrives on pressure situations and is full of pride. He yields no quarter to the batter and will establish territorial rights on the plate.

Yet Blue suffered inconsistency in his return to the American League last year. Much of it is attributable to not starting the season in good physical condition and was compounded by a pair of injuries that laid him off for a total of six weeks.

As age creeps up on him, he will have to work even harder. Blue also appeared to have concentration problems in early innings; he frequently got into trouble in the first two innings. Overall, he is still rated as one of the premier pitchers in baseball, but time is starting to test him and that is an altogether different kind of opponent than a man trying to stick his fabled fastball.

VIDA BLUE
LHP, No. 33
SL, 6'0", 192 lbs.
ML Svc: 14 years
Born: 7-28-49 in
Mansfield, LA

P.S. Notice the dirty left pantleg where Blue constantly wipes sweat, and it mixes with a tar substance he uses for grip. That and his exceptionally fast working style are his trademarks.

FIELDING:

Blue made several pick-offs at first base last year. Runners don't dare him. His good athletic instincts make him a heads-up fielder, making up for some loss of mobility with his age and paunch.

OVERALL:

Scouts still rave about Blue's abilities which may have carried him to the threshold of the Hall of Fame, but he can't be rated above average based on his inconsistency in 1982. If he had been "vintage" Blue in September as he was in August, the Royals would have been in the playoffs instead of a gasp short.

Harwell: "He could pitch for any major league club."

Martin: "He was worth the trade for young prospects."

1982 STATISTICS

W	L	ERA	G	GS	CG	IP	H	R	ER	BB	SO	SV
13	12	3.78	31	31	6	181	163	80	76	80	103	0

CAREER STATISTICS

W	L	ERA	G	GS	CG	IP	H	R	ER	BB	SO	SV
191	138	3.13	422	411	141	2971	2591	1160	1034	993	1919	2

GEORGE BRETT
INF, No. 5
LR, 6'0", 200 lbs.
ML Svc: 9 years
Born: 5-15-53 in Glendale, WV

1982 STATISTICS

AVG	G	AB	R	H	2B	3B	HR	RBI	BB	SO	SB
.301	144	552	101	166	32	9	21	82	71	51	6

CAREER STATISTICS

AVG	G	AB	R	H	2B	3B	HR	RBI	BB	SO	SB
.316	1235	4843	762	1532	303	98	125	703	417	319	131

VS. RHP

VS. LHP

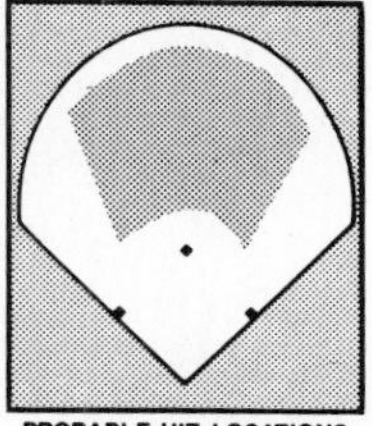
PROBABLE HIT LOCATIONS

HITTING:

When George Brett's rhythm is good, it is almost impossible to keep him from hitting the ball hard to any field. He springs from a semi-crouch closed stance deep in the box and well off the plate. He handles all pitches well, righties or lefties. But he is so intent on staying back for a last split-second uncoiling that pitchers often have success with him by using an annoying array of off-speed breaking pitches, especially tricky lefthanders like Tommy John and Mike Flanagan.

Brett hits mostly straightaway and finds the power alleys frequently, using the big parks to his advantage. He gets a lot of triples for a non-speedster and usually will be among the league leaders in doubles. He has 20-25 home run potential as well. He is one of the game's best clutch hitters, though he was not as prolific as usual in RBIs in 1982. Brett's ability to spray the ball makes him a dangerous hit-and-run threat, and he is patient enough to draw a high number of walks.

His versatility as a hitter is reflected in conflicting reports on how to pitch him. Some teams like to stay very deep inside, while others try to stay away at all times. After April, Brett has always been a consistent hitter throughout the entire schedule; the "400 chase" of 1980 will long be remembered. He is one of the premier hitters in baseball; an ideal third man in any order who will hit, bat them in, and score.

BASERUNNING:

Brett is heavy-legged and not fast, but he loves to run the bases and is as aggressive as anybody in the game. Sometimes, however, he is too aggressive for his own good; he has sustained several injuries on hard slides. He says breaking up a double play is his favorite play. He doesn't steal often, but uses an uncanny instinct in taking the extra base, stretching singles to doubles, or moving from first to third. Pitchers don't like to see him on base.

FIELDING:

Brett is a strong-armed third baseman with good range to either side, but experiences lapses of erratic throwing. He has admitted to concentration problems, once citing his waving goodbye to friends in the stands as leading to an error, for example. He is sharp on double plays and bunts down the line. He is assigned to call the defensive setup on anticipated bunt plays. Defense is the weakest part of his game, though he is still a highly rated third baseman.

OVERALL:

Martin: "George is one of the relatively few you'd pay to see. He is a throwback to the Pepper Martin style, but with more ability."

Robinson: "There is nothing he cannot do. Brett is a better third baseman than he thinks he is."

BILL CASTRO
RHP, No. 39
RR, 6'0", 175 lbs.
ML Svc: 9 years
Born: 12-13-53 in Santiago, DR

PITCHING:

The first footnote on Bill Castro is his "funny" pitch. Officially it is a forkball. It breaks like it's falling off a table. Umpires are very often asked to check baseballs Castro has thrown.

With just average stuff otherwise, like an 82-84 MPH fastball, Castro relies on cunning and his sinker to avoid trouble. He is a good double play pitcher who is both versatile and durable. With an easy three-quarters overhand motion, he has avoided arm strain although used as a spot starter, short and long reliever. He sometimes has to work on little rest and can go for long periods without game work. Few pitchers would adapt well to that irregularity.

Control is Castro's saving grace. When he doesn't have it, watch out. He loves to tease batters by going just outside the strike zone. The way to get to him is with patience, getting him behind in the count, then into the strike zone with inability to power his way back. He knows the pressure of game-making relief situations, and he has been around the league enough times not to have knocking knees.

Because of his sinker, he is effective against hitters from both sides of the plate. Castro's breaking pitch is a slider, but with a wider break than normal. He has trouble in cozy parks, like Fenway, Tiger Stadium, and the domes. He must finesse the hitters and use the groundout.

Probably his most effective role is in middle relief, because he warms up quickly. He was sharp, however, in a rare starting role last year necessitated by staff injuries.

FIELDING:

Nothing to distinguish Castro here. Average all around.

OVERALL:

Royals regard Castro as a "find." He was cut adrift by three teams last year without getting any work. He has savvy, and with regular work, he develops consistency. His career record reflects average accomplishments, but he has flashes of success.

Robinson: "He knows how to pitch, and doesn't mind pitching any place, any time."

Martin: "Good flexible pitcher with the smarts and nastiness required of a reliever. Call his 'funny' pitch a spitter."

Oddity: Castro drew salary from four teams last year--Royals, Angels, A's, Yankees. "That's a strength," quips Martin.

1982 STATISTICS

W	L	ERA	G	GS	CG	IP	H	R	ER	BB	SO	SV
3	2	3.45	21	4	0	75	72	34	29	20	37	1

CAREER STATISTICS

W	L	ERA	G	GS	CG	IP	H	R	ER	BB	SO	SV
29	26	3.07	285	9	0	504	513	211	172	133	186	45

ONIX CONCEPCION
INF, No. 2
RR, 5'6", 160 lbs.
ML Svc: 2 years
Born: 10-5-58 in Dorado, PR

1982 STATISTICS

AVG	G	AB	R	H	2B	3B	HR	RBI	BB	SO	SB
.234	74	205	17	48	9	1	0	15	5	18	2

CAREER STATISTICS

AVG	G	AB	R	H	2B	3B	HR	RBI	BB	SO	SB
.227	88	220	18	50	9	0	0	17	5	19	2

VS. RHP

VS. LHP

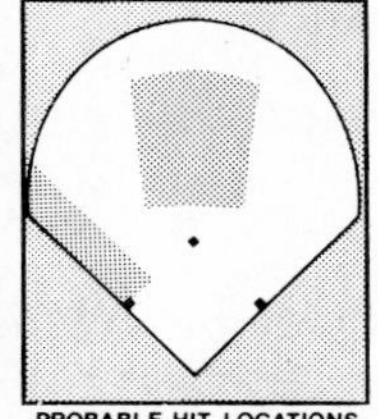
PROBABLE HIT LOCATIONS

HITTING:

Onix Concepcion is small, but powerful. He drives a fastball up, and picks at it down. He hits for power more than a little guy should, but just one look at his arms and upper torso tells you why. This man is built, and can both pull and hit straightaway.

In the minor leagues--and he's seen plenty of them, seven years at age 24, plus winter ball--he has done it all offensively: power, consistency, produce runs. He hasn't had that opportunity in the major leagues yet, so a big question mark sits over his head.

Last year when U. L. Washington was sidelined with injury, Concepcion's bat kept him in the lineup even after Washington healed. But pitchers found they could set Concepcion up with breaking stuff away. He also doesn't walk as much as he could with his patience and a small strike zone.

He is a better than average bunter and makes leg hits. He crouches only slightly, stands closed on the plate. One wonders how he might benefit from an exaggerated crouch, like Rickey Henderson's.

Overall, he must be rated a mystery as a hitter at the big league level. Winter ball: No questions. Minor leagues: No questions. Major leagues: wait and see.

BASERUNNING:

This is where Concepcion will fit in beautifully if he makes it with the Royals. He has above average speed and was a big basestealer in Class AAA. He was used as a pinch-runner numerous times in 1982, capable of keeping a defense edgy for some kind of movement. He is aggressive, too, with the daring of youth unspent. He slides straight in, and hard.

FIELDING:

Overall, fielding will rate as a strong point in Concepcion's game, although he needs to develop more range if he remains a shortstop. He possesses a gun for an arm, and a true one at that. He made a lot of rookie errors and has to develop the know-how of double play action, but then the Royals are spoiled in that department. Concepcion will be a better prospect at third base if his bat warrants the move.

OVERALL:

Concepcion is caught in a bind. The Royals view him as a big leaguer, ready for a fulltime spot in the lineup--but not theirs while Washington is on hand. But they weren't willing to trade him because he is valuable insurance against injury, and other teams bargained for him on the basis of him being a utility backup of unproved quality.

Harwell: "He is a definite comer."

Robinson: "He has a lot of tools and should become a regular someday. He can play almost every position and that might be his best bet."

CESAR GERONIMO
OF, NO. 23
LL, 6'2", 175 lbs.
ML Svc: 13 years
Born: 3-11-48 in
El Seibo, DR

1982 STATISTICS

AVG	G	AB	R	H	2B	3B	HR	RBI	BB	SO	SB
.269	53	119	14	32	6	3	4	23	8	16	2

CAREER STATISTICS

AVG	G	AB	R	H	2B	3B	HR	RBI	BB	SO	SB
.260	1484	3693	458	959	157	50	51	388	352	733	82

VS. RHP

VS. LHP

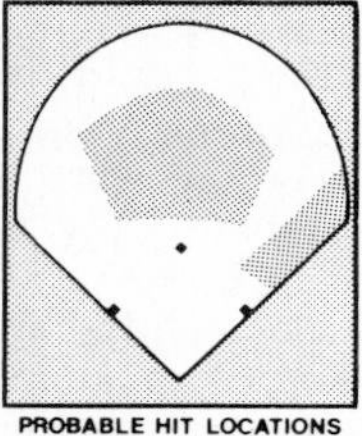
PROBABLE HIT LOCATIONS

HITTING:

Cesar Geronimo seems to be a smarter hitter and a tougher out now than he was in his heyday in the National League. In his two seasons with the Royals while being regarded as primarily filling a defensive role, he has shown a remarkable tendency to produce a lot of RBIs per number of hits.

Standing straight up in the middle of the box, his lead foot opened unusually wide toward first, Geronimo wags the bat and gives a slap-hit appearance. He hits a lot of fly balls and line drives, displaying surprising power at times either pulling or in the gaps. He plays almost solely against righthanded pitching.

Pitchers consistently cross him up with jam stuff, particularly on breaking balls or off-speed offings. Hitting is not what Geronimo built his All Star reputation on with the Reds' powerhouses, and it is still not his forte.

However, like teammate Greg Pryor, he has not been a threat in a pinch role. He hits most consistently when he is in the lineup for more than the cold pinch at-bat. When he is in the regular lineup, pitchers can't pitch through him.

BASERUNNING:

For several years now, Geronimo has not been a basestealing threat. But he will get some leg hits with his above average speed, and he will keep things flowing on the basepaths. He'll fudge the extra leadoff step if a pitcher ignores him as no threat.

FIELDING:

Herein lies Geronimo's special value to the Royals. In Royals Stadium, the club cannot afford weaknesses in the outfield. When someone goes down, there is no appreciable difference defensively with Geronimo in any field. He combines good speed with savvy to get to many balls that might appear to be in for extra bases. He is especially adept at over-the-shoulder work to his right or left while heading for the walls.

He also has a strong and accurate arm, and is too far along in an illustrious career to be throwing to the wrong man or base. Geronimo is a comfort and definite plus to the Royals.

OVERALL:

One of Geronimo's greatest assets is his demeanor. He has not accepted the notion that he is in his twilight years, therefore he stays ever ready and aggressive, yet he fills a secondary role with quiet reserve. His teammates' highest compliment is that he never complains about anything.

Martin: "His best years are behind him, but he fills a necessary role."

Robinson: "He fills the bill anywhere in the outfield."

LARRY GURA
LHP, No. 32
LL, 6'1", 185 lbs.
ML Svc: 9 years
Born: 11-26-47 in Joliet, IL

PITCHING:

Mr. Consistency, Larry Gura, is a Michelangelo--brushstroking corners of the plate, moving spots constantly and keeping batters off-balance with probably the most varied array of breaking pitches in the league.

Gura's nickname is "Slider," but actually, he throws the curve more often and with three to five different speeds from game to game. He uses the variable speed breaking balls to establish an 85 MPH fastball that surprises hitters. He lulls them with a deliberate three-quarters motion that appears to have nothing behind it but a slight leg kick.

Gura is especially tough on left-handed batters and power hitting teams. He keeps batters honest, backing them off the plate and setting up his outside stuff.

Gura ran into a rash of home runs last year and his ERA was higher than normal. He seldom admits to mistake pitches, preferring to give credit to hitters or luck. He seems to get in trouble when his control is off or when he is trying to paint too fine a line. Righthanders can rough him up if they are patient.

His strengths are his uncommon control of all pitches, and his devotedness to fitness. He follows a strict diet, and participates in karate to aid quickness and conditioning.

To get to him, teams must take advantage of his walks, which aren't many, or the rare days when his rhythm is off. Look for a slow game when Gura works.

FIELDING:

Gura's pet peeve is not having a Gold Glove on display as testimony to his three seasons of errorless performance. He prides himself on saving hits and runs and is one of the disappearing breed that even works on it in his spare time. He has an excellent move to first, great reactions (thanks, karate) and fine instincts. He is one of the league's best afield, year in and year out.

OVERALL:

The only American League pitcher with a better winning percentage since Gura became a starter in 1978 is Ron Guidry.

Gura has become a Yankee-killer and relishes beating the team that traded him for next to nothing. He also loves to beat the manager who did it, Billy Martin, and until last year had never lost to Toronto. Oddly enough, he has trouble with the lesser lights, Minnesota, Texas, and in Fenway Park.

Martin: "Proven winner without frills. He goes out, does a job, and wins."

Robinson: "A battler who does everything a winning pitcher has to, including helping himself defensively. He's getting everything out of his ability."

1982 STATISTICS

W	L	ERA	G	GS	CG	IP	H	R	ER	BB	SO	SV
18	12	4.03	37	37	8	248	251	124	111	64	98	0

CAREER STATISTICS

W	L	ERA	G	GS	CG	IP	H	R	ER	BB	SO	SV
103	67	3.40	330	201	63	1653	1584	712	624	447	667	13

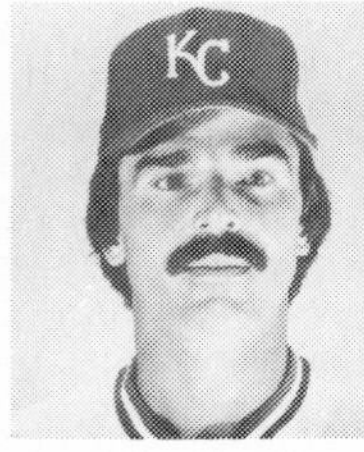

DON HOOD
LHP, No. 17
LL, 6'2", 180 lbs.
ML Svc: 9 years
Born: 10-16-49 in Florence, SC

PITCHING:

Mostly a long relief pitcher, or occasionally called to get out a left-handed batter in a pinch, Don Hood was most effective last year in the clutch when he was called in to spot start. He won all three of his starts.

His fastball is average, 83-85 MPH, as is his assortment of breaking pitches, curves and sliders. He'll break them off when behind in the count. He throws three-quarters overhand with an exaggerated high kick that makes his average pitches hard to pick up.

Until last year, all of the statistics and scouting reports on him were average or below citing him as a ho-hum performer who yo-yoed between somebody's big league club and the minor leagues. But he was productive in his tough role, the intermittent performer, for the Royals. Credit three C's for his strengths--cunning, calm and confidence.

Lack of control led to the few trouble spots he experienced in 1982. Walks got him into holes. Patience was the byword in hitting Hood.

He was good under pressure for the first time in his stormy career, and his poise was notable. Lefthanders don't like to see him. He was given to temperamental outbursts in the past when things didn't go well.

FIELDING:

Nothing noteworthy about his move, although he is lefty. In every category, his fielding marks are average. He is experienced, and therefore not a pushover on bunts or running situations. He is a very slow worker.

OVERALL:

Hood has been around the block, always as a borderline case. He attributes an attitudinal change to a "new life" in baseball, saying he has a lot to prove both to himself and to others. He adapted well to a versatile role and pitched well after long layoffs.

Robinson: "Looking at a 4-0 record and 2.42 ERA, I've always thought he could be better than his past record reflected. He has a good idea of how to pitch."

1982 STATISTICS

W	L	ERA	G	GS	CG	IP	H	R	ER	BB	SO	SV
4	0	3.51	30	3	0	66	71	31	26	22	31	1

CAREER STATISTICS

W	L	ERA	G	GS	CG	IP	H	R	ER	BB	SO	SV
32	32	3.87	270	72	6	799	792	392	345	350	357	6

DENNIS LEONARD
RHP, No. 22
RR, 6'1', 190 lbs.
ML Svc: 8 years
Born: 5-8-51 in
Brooklyn, NY

PITCHING:

Dennis Leonard has won more games than any righthander in baseball since 1975 (130), and more than anybody except Steve Carlton. Leonard has done it with overhand power, although his strikeout figures--long among the league leaders--have slackened over the last couple of years.

He goes with his 88-90 MPH fastball most of the time. However, since 1980, he has gradually developed confidence in a straight change that makes his zip more effective. Batters no longer can sit on the hard one in the strike zone, because Leonard will now throw a change-up or go with a slider when behind in the count. His slider is actually a cut fastball.

Leonard has good control, but is not a spot pitcher. Thus, his control works against him in terms of home runs allowed. He stays around the strike zone consistently, but gives up a lot of dingers and it reflects in an ERA that is high for such a big winner. As he works through his peak years, he will probably have to learn more finesse and pitch to spots.

Those who know him say that his main strength is confidence and poise when the game gets tight. He has an envied ability to put today behind him, regardless of the results, and look ahead to tomorrow. Bad outings don't stay with him or color his temperament.

A mysterious flaw in Leonard's career pattern is his chronically slow starts. His record in April and May is so-so, and from July on, it is sensational. He has had uncanny success against the Angels (14-2), and has been hard on Texas, Detroit and Chicago.

He is tough on hitters from either side of the plate, but lefthanders can have a field day if his fastball is flat because he doesn't get unusual movement on it even on the best of days.

FIELDING:

He has a quick, above average move to first base. His rapid delivery coupled with the fact that he works fast makes Leonard a tough pitcher to get a running game worked up against.

OVERALL:

A big question in 1983 and thereafter is whether an outsized middle finger on his pitching hand will directly affect Leonard's grip or delivery. He broke both the middle and index fingers when he put his hand in front of his face and stopped a line drive by Buddy Bell of Texas last May. The injury cost him 11 weeks. He was 5-3 on either side of the injury, but did not appear as true to form afterward.

As steady as Seattle rain, Leonard's only losing record is against the Yankees.

Robinson: "A tough competitor, Leonard is a proven winner. He has all the tools and know-how to come back a 20-game winner."

1982 STATISTICS

W	L	ERA	G	GS	CG	IP	H	R	ER	BB	SO	SV
10	6	5.10	21	21	2	130	145	82	74	46	58	0

CAREER STATISTICS

W	L	ERA	G	GS	CG	IP	H	R	ER	BB	SO	SV
130	90	3.63	267	262	97	1929	1860	873	777	552	1177	1

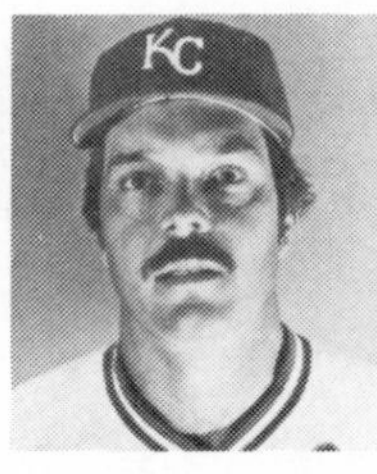

JERRY MARTIN
OF, No. 25
RR, 6'3", 195 lbs.
ML Svc: 8 years
Born: 5-11-49 in Columbia, SC

1982 STATISTICS

AVG	G	AB	R	H	2B	3B	HR	RBI	BB	SO	SB
.266	147	519	52	138	22	1	15	65	38	138	1

CAREER STATISTICS

AVG	G	AB	R	H	2B	3B	HR	RBI	BB	SO	SB
.253	954	2517	327	638	127	17	80	327	200	538	37

VS. RHP

VS. LHP

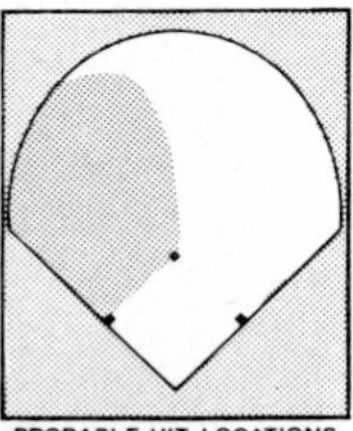
PROBABLE HIT LOCATIONS

HITTING:

Jerry Martin didn't adapt to the curveballing American League very well after several years in the National League. He set a club strikeout record with 137, and was easily fooled by breaking pitches. His strike zone was not tight.

With a wide, closed stance and free swinging tendencies, he is a constant power threat. He pulls fiercely, sometimes hitting awesome fly balls. Some of his foul balls that land on rooftops are legend around Kansas City. He will kill a change-up.

Martin gets a lot of check marks in the "needs improvement" category. Especially, he could be a more productive hitter, given his power, if he could be more patient, more selective, and protect the opposite way with two strikes.

The big curve is poison to Martin. He is a streaky hitter and his power comes in bursts. Batting sixth and seventh in the order, he is always a threat to yank one out, and also, he can be a rally-killer. Until last year, Martin was a platoon player, treacherous to left-handed pitchers, and the Royals tried to switch him out against righties the latter part of the season.

BASERUNNING:

Martin doesn't take full advantage of his aggressiveness and better than average speed. He runs hard, slides hard, but is too conservative in the theft department. He'll get a gleam in his eye while on the lead end of a possible double play.

FIELDING:

Martin stabilized the Royals' outfield last year. Manager Dick Howser said that it was a plus "having three centerfielders at once." Martin had played in center for other teams, but almost exclusively in right for the Royals.

He has good range, especially going back and to his left. Martin is a wall-banger which endears him to foul line fans. His running ability and good sense make him a good competitive outfielder who gives no quarter to a baserunner, although his arm is average.

OVERALL:

Teammates like his all-out style. There's nothing casual about the way Martin attacks the game. He can be even more valuable if platooned with an equally good fielder who can hit left-handed.

Robinson: "He made the transition of leagues in good fashion and is playing about as good as he is able to. At bat, he has holes, but can hurt you if you don't get the pitch into those holes."

Martin: "He has the ability to fill in for any outfielder, and he can get some big hits for you."

HAL McRAE
OF, No. 11
RR, 5'11", 180 lbs.
ML Svc: 13 years
Born: 7-10-46 in
Avon Park, FL

1982 STATISTICS

AVG	G	AB	R	H	2B	3B	HR	RBI	BB	SO	SB
.308	159	613	91	189	46	8	27	133	55	61	4

CAREER STATISTICS

AVG	G	AB	R	H	2B	3B	HR	RBI	BB	SO	SB
.289	1579	5682	758	1640	394	56	154	857	497	579	107

VS. RHP

VS. LHP

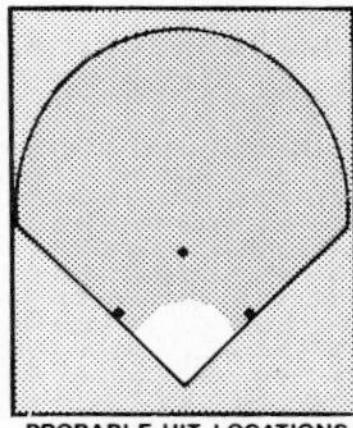
PROBABLE HIT LOCATIONS

HITTING:

Last season, Hal McRae was perhaps the most versatile hitter in the American League--high in average, power, and leading the way in RBIs. He used the whole field better than anybody. He hit home runs that struck the left and right field foul poles, and every direction in between. He reaches both alleys with long fly balls.

His stance is normally closed, feet together, far back in the box, and he leans into every pitch. But McRae shifts in the box according to the way he's being pitched or the way he's guessing. Crafty, he knows how to turn on inside pitches for pulling power, or how to lay back and wait and punch to the right side. If the pitch is high, he kills it; if it's low, he chops it. To get him consistently, precise pitches, down and tight are the best bets.

McRae never bunts, walks an average amount, and is a good contact hitter with runners on base. He is a tough two-strike hitter. Don't hang curves on him or bye-bye! The change-up is an ornery pitch for McRae, but he is rarely fooled twice the same way. He constantly is guessing with the pitcher. Most observers believe he will make an excellent hitting instructor. McRae is tough on small parks, and he has a tendency toward hot, late season streaks.

BASERUNNING:

Age has robbed him of speed, but not his daring. McRae's trademark is taking the extra base, especially second on alley or shallow singles. He breaks up the double play better than anybody, except maybe Brett.

He goes in belly down with stretching hips, and he body slides when breaking up a play. The "Mac Rule" is named for him--adopted to prevent runners from leaving the basepaths to take out the double play pivot.

FIELDING:

McRae originally was an outfielder in the National League, but he has played only a handful of games in the field during the last several years. Shoulder surgery left him unable to throw well enough to play every day. When he plays--which was one game a month last year--he doesn't embarrass anybody, but he does nothing out of the ordinary.

OVERALL:

The big question about McRae is whether he can continue the pace he set last year. He has become the definitive designated hitter, the model by which other teams set standards. In eleven years of working at that position, he has developed methods of staying ready and he has an even keel temperament suited to the role.

Martin: "A fine destructive hitter, aggressive but selective."

Robinson: "He gets my highest rating. He was a definite MVP candidate. There is just no place to pitch him."

HITTING:

Amos Otis is a cagey and dangerous hitter. Always a consistent RBI man, he was among the league leaders last year in game-winners. Many of his game-winning RBIs came just after the opposition had intentionally walked the previous batter. Otis is a guess hitter and has a penchant for striking out, but he is as good as they come at hitting mistakes on breaking pitches. He is especially deadly on weak sliders.

Pitchers should bring tight heat between the hands and knees, then curve him to death away. He stands upright, closed and a mile off the plate. He stands so deep that he draws complaints about being out of the box. Otis has a lot of trouble against the Ryan, Gossage, Barker type of "ultraheat."

Otis loves the first pitch and looks to pull with power whenever possible. He will record healthy numbers in doubles and home runs each season. He uses the whole field well, especially on artificial turf.

An Otis trademark is his stalling tactics. He takes forever to stand in, steps out repeatedly and gripes pitchers with his incessant requests to check the ball. Overall, Otis is one of the most productive time-proven hitters, though he is given to streakiness. He's a strong hitter in the middle of the lineup.

BASERUNNING:

He is slowing slightly with age, but Otis is still sly, and a nemesis on base. He ranks No. 1 among active players with more than 300 stolen bases in percentage of success. He loves to boast that he can steal without sliding because he knows pitchers' moves so well, and he makes good his claim more often than not. He once led the league in steals, and though he won't pile up high numbers anymore, he is always a threat. Otis has an even further value to the club in teaching the team's younger speedsters.

AMOS OTIS
OF, No. 26
RR, 5'11", 166 lbs.
ML Svc: 14 years
Born: 4-26-47 in Mobile, AL

1982 STATISTICS

AVG	G	AB	R	H	2B	3B	HR	RBI	BB	SO	SB
.286	125	475	73	136	25	3	11	88	37	65	9

CAREER STATISTICS

AVG	G	AB	R	H	2B	3B	HR	RBI	BB	SO	SB
.279	2187	6846	1051	1911	354	63	189	956	723	930	336

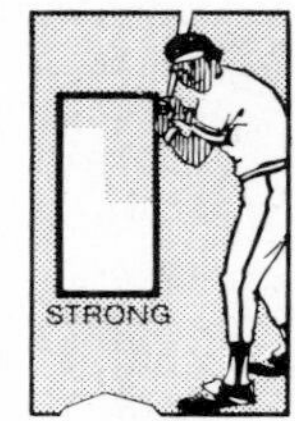

VS. RHP

VS. LHP

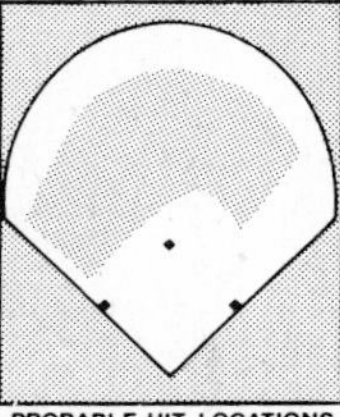
PROBABLE HIT LOCATIONS

FIELDING:

Otis plays a wise and clean centerfield. He is known for his throwing accuracy, always to the right base, never missing the cutoff man. He plays an unusually deep center field, relying on the quick Willie Wilson in left field, and on his own detailed knowledge of each hitter and the characteristics of each park. Many hits drop in front of him, but few go over or past him. He is one of the pioneers of the one-handed catch.

OVERALL:

Martin: "Otis is a fine all around player with good tools who might have been even better . . . an enigmatic personality, somewhat of a hot dog, but with a lot of solid years and finally playing to his potential."

Robinson: "An all around performer that KC looks to for a lot of things. He seems happier than ever, and it shows in his play."

HITTING:

Greg Pryor was productive at the plate for the Royals last year when he was in the lineup as an injury replacement. His background reflects that his average has been 10-15 points better when he is playing regularly.

He has an upright stance, closed, and mid-box. Pitchers are warned not to make mistakes high in the strike zone on him. He has trouble with breaking stuff, low and away, especially when playing intermittently. He has occasional home run power, and is a good doubles hitter with a penchant for soft line drives in the alleys.

Pryor rates no higher than average in any hitting category except that he is a good contact man, and can keep the ball in play. He is not an automatic out. The artificial turf at Royals Stadium works to his advantage because he hits a lot of grounders that pop through for base hits.

BASERUNNING:

Pryor was used as a pinch-runner frequently, not because of his speed, but mainly to keep from using two players in a late-game change. He is a heady runner, no cause for alarm for an opponent wary of the Royals' running style, but he is not a plodder who jams the paths, either.

FIELDING:

Without high marks in the critical fielding areas, his glove is still Pryor's greatest asset for the Royals because he is so versatile. He is equally at home at third, second or short, and has also filled in at first base and in the outfield.

Experience has taught him positioning, and that makes up some for his lack of range. He turns double plays well from all positions. At one time in 1979, he appeared to be the White Sox' shortstop of the future, and last year

GREG PRYOR
INF, No. 4
RR, 6'0", 175 lbs.
ML Svc: 5 years
Born: 10-2-49 in Marietta, OH

1982 STATISTICS

AVG	G	AB	R	H	2B	3B	HR	RBI	BB	SO	SB
.270	73	152	23	41	10	1	2	12	10	20	2

CAREER STATISTICS

AVG	G	AB	R	H	2B	3B	HR	RBI	BB	SO	SB
.260	472	1272	148	331	63	8	8	97	74	123	10

VS. RHP

VS. LHP

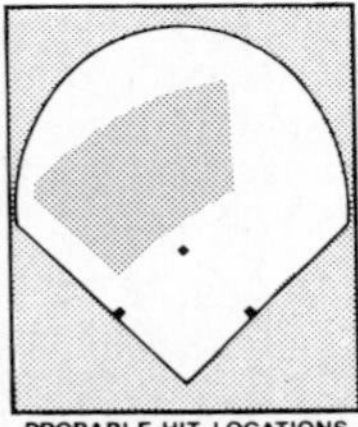
PROBABLE HIT LOCATIONS

he almost became the Royals' shortstop by default: U. L. Washington and Onix Concepcion were injured and Pryor had a hot bat. But he, too, came up with an injury and never cracked the full time lineup.

OVERALL:

Pryor fills all roles with average marks, yet he is above average in value because of his versatility and because he has no real weak points. He plays an integral role with the Royals, who obtained him late in spring training last year for just that--a capable back up without a drastic fall-off in ability.

Martin: "Pryor is a journeyman who is capable of making a big play and is fair at every position."

Robinson: "Pryor will stay around the big leagues a long time as a utility player. Those kind are valuable."

JAMIE QUIRK
C, No. 9
LR, 6'4", 200 lbs.
ML Svc: 8 years
Born: 10-22-54 in Whittier,CA

1982 STATISTICS

AVG	G	AB	R	H	2B	3B	HR	RBI	BB	SO	SB
.231	36	78	8	18	3	0	1	5	3	15	0

CAREER STATISTICS

AVG	G	AB	R	H	2B	3B	HR	RBI	BB	SO	SB
.248	383	823	69	204	43	2	12	82	38	149	3

VS. RHP

VS. LHP

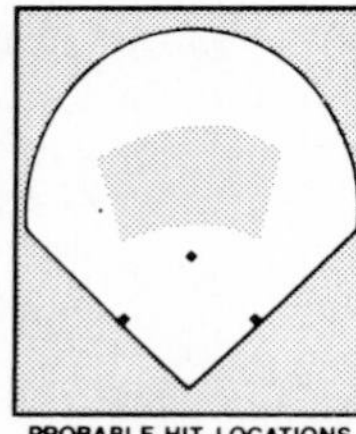
PROBABLE HIT LOCATIONS

HITTING:

Jamie Quirk is a streaky hitter, probably attributable largely to his lack of playing time. He stands erect, squared to the plate and back in the box. He is a line drive hitter to the alleys. He lacks significant power, which is surprising given his good size and strength.

As a back up utility player, Quirk faces righthanded pitching almost exclusively. He can make good contact when "cold," and usually puts the ball in play somewhere. He has trouble with breaking pitches, especially when pitchers keep them away from him.

Quirk's outstanding athletic ability has kept him around a long time. He is workmanlike at bat, but the lack of opportunity to establish continuity in rhythm has hurt his average. He is part of an overall club deficiency in pinch-hitting. He will sting pitchers who try to blow him away high, especially in. Quirk's hitting needs improvement, and he probably hasn't fulfilled his potential because of his permanent seat on the bench. He was drafted by several clubs in free agent re-entry, mainly because he is a rare commodity, that is a lefthanded batter who catches.

BASERUNNING:

Ouch. Quirk is slow. Average righthanders can even beat him to first, though he runs the bases hard and smart like the football player he once was.

Definitely not a threat to steal, he is one of the few conservative elements in the Royals' offensive style. He is not as cumbersome on base as teammate Willie Aikens, however, because Quirk has good basepath instincts.

FIELDING:

Versatile--Quirk also fills in at first, third and in the outfield. He has a strong arm, and though he is a relative newcomer to the catching position, his athletic savvy has helped him develop quickly into a competent backstop.

He blocks pitches and the plate aggressively and works hard at calling a smart game. He doesn't scare opponents into standing still on base, but they don't run rampant when he's in there either.

OVERALL:

Quirk's value for years has been rooted in his readiness and adaptability to a subliminal role at a time in his career when he is antsy to play everyday. He is a clubhouse spirit, and keeps teammates especially loose in the bullpen.

Robinson: "He has realized the way to stay around is to diversify."

PITCHING:

Dan Quisenberry is a unique entity. He has moved quickly to the top of his specialty, short relief, with a rare under-armed delivery and a velocity that is almost laughable. He seldom breaks 80 MPH on a radar gun.

His fastball is actually a vicious sinker, and is all the more wicked because of his uncanny control. Most short men come in and fire away at a zone. Quisenberry goes to spots with unwavering confidence. He believes that every ball will wind up a double play grounder, and darned if most don't.

Trouble beckons for Quisenberry when he gets above the thighs with his pitches. Batters, especially lefthanders, can slap him to the opposite field if they have the grit to wait for a slappable pitch. He probably is tougher on lefthanders because of the down and away movement on his sinker.

Quisenberry is not a one-pitch reliever. He also has an effective slider and last year, he added an unpredictable knuckleball that he will send to lefthanders. Still, he will go to the sinker 90% of the time, especially with a game on the line.

Outstanding assets for his role include his personality makeup, which is remarkably even-keeled. He seldom gives up home runs and draws 85% ground balls. He likes to work tired. When he is too strong, he has a tendency to try to be too powerful and loses sinking action.

His delivery makes the ball tough to pick up the first time around, and most often there is only one time around. He is most effective when used in the eighth and ninth innings, up to three days in a row and five in a week.

DAN QUISENBERRY
RHP, No. 29
RR, 6'2", 180 lbs.
ML Svc: 4 years
Born: 2-7-54 in
Santa Monica, CA

FIELDING:

Because his motion carries him toward third base and into an awkward follow-through, Quisenberry has perfected a quick move to first and a fast delivery. He has no trouble getting to bunts. He has picked off six runners from first base with a runner at third by making a fake move to third and freezing the runner at first.

OVERALL:

Robinson: "He's the kind of pitcher you run up there to hit against because of the way he looks, and then walk back to the dugout because of the way he pitches. He has the short memory--good outing or bad--that a reliever needs."

Martin: "A crowd-pleaser with his delivery and animation on the mound. (Quisenberry is forever stretching and going through gyrations to loosen up between pitches.) But he has demonstrated it is not just for show. He's a laid-back Californian with a sense of humor."

1982 STATISTICS

W	L	ERA	G	GS	CG	IP	H	R	ER	BB	SO	SV
9	7	2.57	72	0	0	136	126	43	39	12	46	35

CAREER STATISTICS

W	L	ERA	G	GS	CG	IP	H	R	ER	BB	SO	SV
25	20	2.68	219	0	0	366	356	122	109	61	116	91

PAUL SPLITTORFF
LHP, No. 34
LL, 6'3", 210 lbs.
ML Svc: 12 years
Born: 10-8-46 in Evansville, IN

PITCHING:

Paul Splittorff has been a regular starter for most of his twelve seasons, but has been occasionally groomed for long relief during the last two. Durable and in possession of all club records that reflect longevity--games, starts, innings pitched, wins--he has become a six-to-seven inning guy who seldom lets his club out of winning range.

With a creamy three-quarter overhand delivery and a high leg kick that gives lefthanded batters fits, Splittorff relies most often on his fastball. That might be a mistake for one in the 83-85 MPH range.

He is crafty at setting up hitters with an assortment of breaking pitches, and goes to his fastball about 60-65% of the time. He is especially slick at using ballparks to whatever advantage they might offer--the turf at Royals Stadium, the space from center to left at Yankee Stadium, the right of center at Fenway Park and Tiger Stadium, et al. He hates the domes: "No place to hide," he says.

Splittorff is an "artist"--splashing the corners, varying in and out. He's in trouble if his control is off. He knows how to go for a double play or the strikeout if needed. At times, however, he tries to reach back for the strikeout a little too often.

With his veteran's poise, he pitches very well out of jams and never shows emotion under pressure. He has had much trouble with the Yankees in recent years. Consistency is his strong point, based on the wisdom of his years.

FIELDING:

Splittorff has one of the better moves to first base, always getting his share of pick-offs. Teams can't run well on him. His mobility in fielding has been reduced over the last few years by chronic back problems, and he must take extra precautions to keep opponents from bunting him crazy.

OVERALL:

Since 1979, people have been trying to put Splittorff out to pasture, or at least to the bullpen. Every spring, though, a job or two comes open and guess who steps into the breach. Though he hasn't piled up big numbers in the last few seasons, a hidden stat of "games won" and "games with a chance to win" when Splittorff pitched is very impressive--about 80%.

Martin: "He is accomplished and always seems to keep his team in a game."

Robinson: "Kansas City has been trying to get someone to take Splittorff's place the last few years, but something always happens and he is there to save their life. He saved them early last year when injuries depleted the starting rotation. He gives great effort every time out and knows how to pitch."

1982 STATISTICS

W	L	ERA	G	GS	CG	IP	H	R	ER	BB	SO	SV
10	10	4.28	29	28	0	162	166	83	77	57	74	0

CAREER STATISTICS

W	L	ERA	G	GS	CG	IP	H	R	ER	BB	SO	SV
152	132	3.77	390	362	84	2371	2438	1136	995	718	992	1

HITTING:

U. L. Washington is a switch-hitter with good power from the right side, surprising for a little man. He has strong arms and wrists. Pitchers like to jam him, run him off the plate, then fool him with breaking stuff away. He especially has trouble batting lefthanded; righthanded, he's a genuinely tough out.

He operates from a closed, upright (almost stiff) stance. His hits go mostly to left field from either side, and he reaches the alleys just moderately well. His speed gives him a high number of leg hits, particularly from his lefthanded choppers.

The slider, he admits, keeps him from considering abandoning the left side. He hits well behind runners, and is a good bunter. In the past, his hitting has been marked by inconsistency, but last year, after a return from an injury from mid-summer on, he was never in a prolonged slump. He shouldn't slump, given his speed and switch-hitting attributes. Washington is ideal for the ninth spot in the "second leadoff" concept allowed by the DH and the Royals' speed-oriented offense. His bat control also fits in well batting second.

BASERUNNING:

Washington is a definite basestealing threat, and should improve his numbers, if he hits. He has the potential to steal 50-60 bases a year. Excellent speed coupled with good base savvy makes him a nuisance to pitchers. He likes to dance off base, leading and teasing. He slides hard and feet first, with the uniqueness of having his arms high above his head.

FIELDING:

Washington has exceptional range to both his right and left, and can play a deeper short because of it. An added advantage in Royals Stadium and other artificial surface stadiums.

U.L. WASHINGTON
INF, No. 30
SR, 5'11", 175 lbs.
ML Svc: 6 years
Born: 10-27-53 in Otaka, OK

1982 STATISTICS

AVG	G	AB	R	H	2B	3B	HR	RBI	BB	SO	SB
.286	119	437	64	125	19	3	10	60	38	48	23

CAREER STATISTICS

AVG	G	AB	R	H	2B	3B	HR	RBI	BB	SO	SB
.263	550	1742	224	458	69	22	20	177	167	237	212

VS. RHP

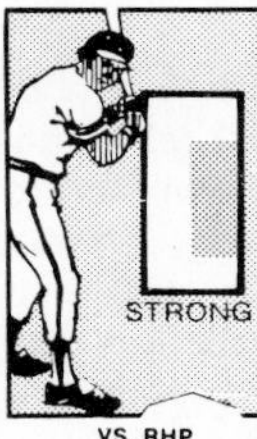

VS. RHP

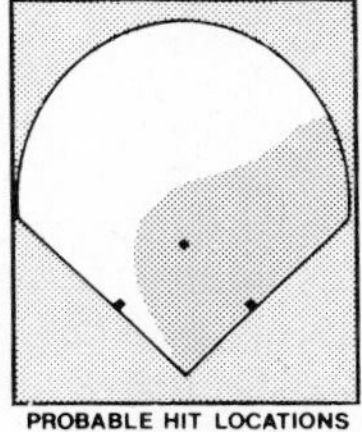
PROBABLE HIT LOCATIONS

His arm is not much above average, but is plenty good enough. He and Frank White have been rated by some to be the best double play combination in the league. Washington makes too many errors and gets frustrated when credited with an error on a wide ranging play that other shortstops might not make.

OVERALL:

Washington is the only player in the major leagues who plays constantly with a toothpick in his mouth. The one year he didn't, he had terrible statistics and then he went back to it. He also practices karate to improve his quickness, agility and durability.

Robinson: "He does everything you want a shortstop to do. Kansas City cannot afford to lose this guy. He has a lot of tools."

Martin: "Washington is a solid shortstop who can turn a standout play. Speed and defense are his strong points."

HITTING:

John Wathan is a "slap" hitter. He is known by his teammates as "Duke", and the right field line is known as "Dukieland." Unlike most righthanded batters who love pitches that are high and hard, Wathan relishes the low fastball and will poke it into the corner. He'll swing inside-out from the wide open stance he switched to in 1982 and go to the opposite field 80% of the time.

He stands straight-legged, slightly leaning over the plate from the middle of the batter's box. He has a tendency to get "sawed off" with tight pitches, and jamming him is the most effective way to get him out. He hits ground balls almost exclusively, making him the club's best hit-and-run batter.

Wathan is very effective against lefthanded pitching and was a .300-plus hitter as a platoon first baseman. Righthanders give him trouble with breaking pitches.

As an everyday player for the last two years, Wathan's average tended to fade as the season wore on. With his bat-handling prowess, Wathan is a good No. 2 hitter, but also is effective as No. 8 or 9 in the DH league with its emphasis on team speed and "double leadoffs." Wathan is a consistent singles hitter. Despite his leading the league in grounding into double plays with 28 last season, he remains a slightly better than average hitter who figures actively in the Royals' offense.

BASERUNNING:

Wathan set a major league record last year for stolen bases by a catcher (36), even nipping several after missing July with a broken left foot. He has perfected a pet "on-the-go" lead off of first base. Faster than he looks, aggressive and smart on the bases, Wathan often scores. He is the best runner among the league's catchers.

JOHN WATHAN
C, No. 12
RR, 6'2", 205 lbs.
ML Svc: 7 years
Born: 10-4-49 in
Cedar Rapids, IA

1982 STATISTICS

AVG	G	AB	R	H	2B	3B	HR	RBI	BB	SO	SB
.270	121	448	79	121	11	3	3	51	48	46	36

CAREER STATISTICS

AVG	G	AB	R	H	2B	3B	HR	RBI	BB	SO	SB
.276	575	1752	228	484	57	20	16	210	134	160	70

VS. RHP

VS. LHP

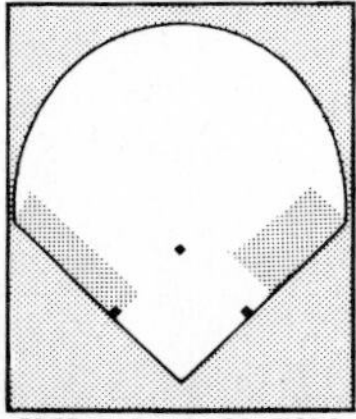
PROBABLE HIT LOCATIONS

FIELDING:

Wathan has silenced his critics. Whispers around the league said that the Royals couldn't survive with him catching every day. In 1982, he strengthened his arm and quickened his release with changes in his footwork. The improved mechanics brought him renewed confidence and respectable results in holding and gunning down baserunners. Pitchers always have had confidence in Wathan's heady manner of calling a game and booking opposing hitters.

OVERALL:

Robinson: "Wathan is getting everything out of his ability and is shirking the tag of only being a back-up player."

FRANK WHITE
INF, No. 20
RR, 5'11", 170 lbs.
ML Svc: 10 years
Born: 9-4-50 in
Greenville, MS

HITTING:

With a wide closed stance and bent low, Frank White attacks high pitches for consistent line drives and he pulls with good power. He has the potential to hit 10-12 home runs each season. But the curve gives him fits and left-handed pitchers can jam him effectively. He is, however, very consistent against lefties.

White reaches the alleys well and racks up a lot of doubles. He exercises good bat control, making him a hit-and-run threat, although he has strikeout tendencies. Pitches on the outside, whether hard or breaking, are the toughest for him to handle. He is an excellent bunter.

White improved his hitting to all-time peaks in almost every category last year, and he has always said he thinks he could be more effective in the second spot in the order, rather than in the sixth through ninth spots where the Royals have him.

1982 STATISTICS

AVG	G	AB	R	H	2B	3B	HR	RBI	BB	SO	SB
.298	145	524	71	156	45	6	11	56	16	65	10

CAREER STATISTICS

AVG	G	AB	R	H	2B	3B	HR	RBI	BB	SO	SB
.258	1394	3943	495	1016	195	38	59	407	182	501	134

VS. RHP

VS. LHP

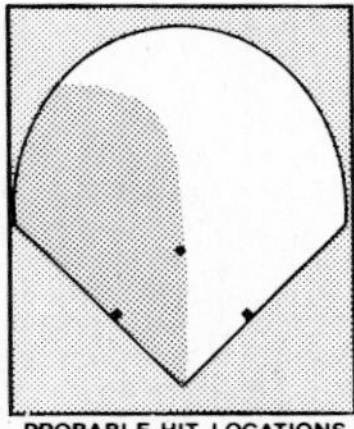
PROBABLE HIT LOCATIONS

BASERUNNING:

White is a stolen base threat, he is aggressive and smart on the paths. He loves working with the green light, which he didn't have for a couple of years, and it disgruntled him. He has outstanding legs and good speed.

FIELDING:

White has no peer at his position. He's a cut above even the outstanding ones. Defense is exhausting to White because he serves as a "field general," constantly communicating with infielders and outfielders on positioning, situations, etc. He is especially helpful to the first baseman, shortstop, center and right fielders.

His arm is strong, and his range makes people blink. He plays artificial turf like no other, positioning beyond the dirt. A patented play of his is the leap to spear a line drive. He knows all the tricks on double plays--the runner's and his own.

White relishes having it said of him that he saves as many runs a year as a heavy hitter bats in. He has made his mark and his money with his glove.

OVERALL:

Because of the raves about his fielding, White is underrated as a complete player. He is one of the finest athletes in the league.

Robinson: "An outstanding player who can do a lot of things for you. He is overshadowed by Brett and Wilson."

Martin: "Just a plain terrific second baseman, a picture to watch in the field. As an underrated hitter, he has outdone his potential as a big leaguer."

WILLIE WILSON
OF, No. 6
SR, 6'3", 190 lbs.
ML Svc: 6 years
Born: 7-9-55 in Montgomery, AL

1982 STATISTICS

AVG	G	AB	R	H	2B	3B	HR	RBI	BB	SO	SB
.332	136	585	87	194	19	15	3	46	26	81	37

CAREER STATISTICS

AVG	G	AB	R	H	2B	3B	HR	RBI	BB	SO	SB
.312	705	2555	440	797	85	52	13	193	117	339	287

VS. RHP

VS. LHP

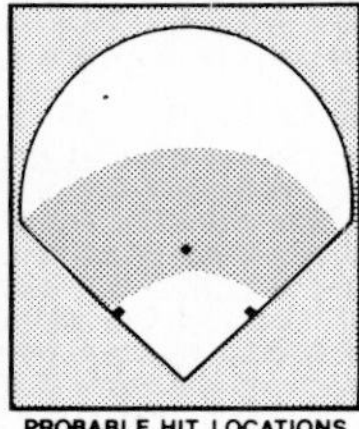
PROBABLE HIT LOCATIONS

HITTING:

Willie Wilson, the reigning American League batting champion, is a versatile and adaptive switch-hitter. Right-handed, Wilson tends to pull, and he is powerful. He crowds the plate with a narrow, parallel stance and leans forward, making him a prime target for brushbacks. Lefthanded, he is a chop and leg hitter. He hunches more in his stance lefthanded, and places his feet closer together and chokes up more on the bat.

The book on Wilson is simple--jam him then go away. Inside pitches frustrate him and make him angry. He handles high stuff and especially left-handed, he gets wood on breaking pitches. He is a slightly more efficient hitter lefthanded (though a natural righty), because he sees twice as much righthanded pitching and because he takes more advantage of his speed.

Wilson's flaws include that he is an impatient hitter that doesn't walk much, cutting his value as a leadoff man. Although not a good bunter, Wilson has not experienced a prolonged slump in four full years because of his speed. He seldom goes more than two games without a hit.

BASERUNNING:

Wilson is a blur going from home to first, first to third, or touching them all on his frequent inside-the-park home runs. But he has yet to develop the fine touches that make a great basestealer. He is tentative in stealing and tends to be streaky. When he is hot he goes; when he gets caught a couple of times he stays for days on end. He will go head first on slides into triples and sometimes on steals, but usually he uses a straight-in slide with a quick stand up.

FIELDING:

Although he has one Gold Glove Award, 1980, he needs improvement in left field, most especially in throwing. Wilson has overcome a tendency to throw to the wrong spot, but still he often overthrows the cutoff in weak and errant throws to home. The big plus is the life he has added to center-fielder Amos Otis's career because Wilson can outrun the ball in all directions. He tends to be wall-shy going to his right.

OVERALL:

Wilson's biggest enemy is Wilson. He has a bad reputation around the league as a mouthy guy on the bench, too often harassing opponents unnecessarily. He is known as a hot dog. He says he is concentrating on better self-control, and he should only get better.

Harwell: "He intimidates with his speed; he is KC's offensive trigger."

Robinson: "He might be the most exciting player in the American League. He can turn nothing into something. He puts the offensive machine into gear. He has blossomed all around."

DENNIS WERTH
INF, No. 16
RR, 6'1", 200 lbs.
ML Svc: 2 years
Born: 12-29-52 in
Lincoln, IL

HITTING, BASERUNNING, FIELDING:

Werth's strong point is he can draw a walk about a third of the time. His value as a hitter is with his on-base ability, getting his club a one-move substitution, that is, he can pinch-hit and field any one of several positions well enough.

Squared to the plate in a closed, upright stance Werth has been a spotty high pitch hitter with pulling tendency. He is big, strong, and occasionally flashes power, but has too many holes to have made a mark so far. Breaking pitches hog-tie him.

The Royals used him frequently as a pinch-runner. He doesn't have above average speed, but he is heady and aggressive. He is not a threat to steal.

Werth can play catcher, a plus for any team when a third one is needed. His best spot is first base which is where the Royals used him in late inning replacement. Werth is nifty with the glove, positions himself intelligently and has an adequate throwing ability.

OVERALL:

Werth is the type player to find himself a job with about any team because of his versatility. He adapts well to the reserve role, and is popular with teammates. They love him because he is accomplished at stringing and breaking in ball clubs.

Robinson: "Nobody knows if he can play or not. His bat is his best tool, but so far he has not exhibited it."

COUNTY STADIUM
Milwaukee Brewers

Seating Capacity: 53,192
Playing Surface: Natural Grass

Dimensions
Left Field Pole: 315 ft.
Left-Center Field: 392 ft.
Center Field: 402 ft.
Right-Center Field: 392 ft.
Right Field Pole: 315 ft.
Height of Outfield Wall: 10 ft.

The home of the American League champion Milwaukee Brewers has usually been cited as a homer haven, but the term in a slight misnomer because the Brewers have legitimate sluggers who can hit homers in any park including the Grand Canyon.

The dimensions seem to favor sluggers like Gorman Thomas and Ben Oglivie, both of whom have led or tied the league in homers during the last five years. Thomas, a righty pull hitter with exceptional power to left-center, deals with a left field foul line that is 315 feet away. Oglivie, a lefty pull hitter, has virtually the same dimensions to aim for. It is 315 feet down the line in right, 362 feet to right and 392 feet to right-center. The stands are not high in left field and offer little protection against winds blowing in. Despite the slugging Brewer crew and despite the seemingly easy targets in the power alleys, both the Brewers and their opponents hit more homers on the road than they did in County Stadium in 1982.

The natural grass surface seems to be a bit faster than those in Yankee Stadium, Fenway Park and Tiger Stadium. That would be due to the fact that hitters like Paul Molitor, Robin Yount, Cecil Cooper and Ted Simmons have a tendency to hit hard grounders and low liners. Low cut grass on which balls travel faster is obviously a benefit to these hitters.

The infield dirt has, in the past, been considered of poor quality, leading to bad hops. Added maintenance work has made the infield smoother and has helped the defensive play of Cooper at first, Jim Gantner at second, Yount at short and Molitor at third.

County Stadium's climatic conditions are similar to Cleveland Stadium, particularly in September and October. Bright sunny days present an added problem to the hitters. Fastball pitchers such as Len Barker of Cleveland and Dave Righetti of the New York Yankees simply throw strike after strike past Brewer hitters, who must squint into the sun.

The fence that traverses the entire outfield is a 10 foot fence, and does not vary an inch around the field. Agile outfielders can, and have, climbed the fence to rob hitters of potential home runs. Like Yankee Stadium, this park has very little foul territory down the right and left field foul lines, and outfielders must be wary of charging towards the line on balls hit close to the line.

Despite comments to the contrary, this park is definitely a pitcher's park. There has been marked improvement in the care of the infield and that makes Yount, Molitor and company feel much better as infielders. Of course that only lasts until the Green Bay Packers start playing football there in the end of August.

DWIGHT BERNARD
RHP, No. 47
RR, 6'2", 180 lbs.
ML Svc: 3 years
Born: 5-31-52 in
Mt. Vernon, IL

PITCHING:

After spending most of his career in the minor leagues, Bernard finally got a chance with the Brewers in 1982 at the age of 30. He was used mainly as a short reliever in the late innings, usually giving way to Rollie Fingers in the eighth or ninth. He was often used to face just one or two righthanded hitters.

Bernard is basically a sinker/slider pitcher who throws from a three-quarter overhand delivery. He will throw his fastball or sinker most of the time, an average sinker that will clock around 83 MPH. His second pitch is an average curveball. He will also throw a lot of sliders, which are actually more like cut fastballs and break three to four inches. He seldom throws a change-up, and if he is behind in the count, look for the sinker.

He is not an overpowering pitcher, and his stuff is just average--he qualifies as a borderline pitcher. He can be used effectively to get a hitter or two out or to pitch one or two innings with a guy like Fingers available to finish up.

FIELDING:

Bernard's move to first is only average, but he has a quick delivery to the plate, which makes it a little more difficult to steal on him. Fields his position adequately.

OVERALL:

Not a great pitcher by any means, but capable of helping a team in certain areas. He is not a candidate to be a No. 1 man out of the bullpen.

Martin: "Bernard is about the best reliever that the Brewers have behind Fingers and Slaton. He seems to have matured--finally."

Robinson: "He is really just another guy to fill out your pitching roster."

1982 STATISTICS

W	L	ERA	G	GS	CG	IP	H	R	ER	BB	SO	SV
3	1	3.76	47	0	0	79	78	39	33	27	45	6

CAREER STATISTICS

W	L	ERA	G	GS	CG	IP	H	R	ER	BB	SO	SV
4	8	4.14	115	2	0	176	196	93	81	86	92	6

MARK BROUHARD
OF, No. 29
RR, 6'1", 210 lbs.
ML Svc: 3 years
Born: 5-22-56 in Burbank, CA

1982 STATISTICS

AVG	G	AB	R	H	2B	3B	HR	RBI	BB	SO	SB
.269	40	108	16	29	4	1	4	10	9	17	0

CAREER STATISTICS

AVG	G	AB	R	H	2B	3B	HR	RBI	BB	SO	SB
.260	145	419	52	109	16	4	11	46	23	82	2

VS. RHP

VS. LHP

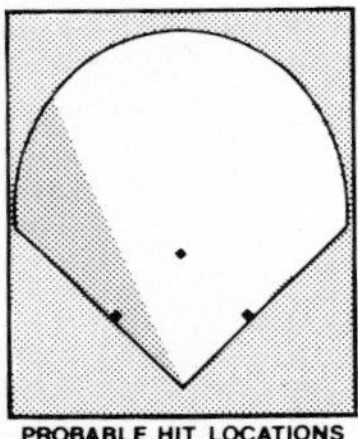
PROBABLE HIT LOCATIONS

HITTING:

Brouhard is a big, strong player who had some big years in the minor leagues but has played sparingly in the majors. He is a line drive hitter who tries to pull everything. He hits lefthanders better than righthanders, partly because he has seen more of them. He uses a closed upright stance in the middle of the batter's box.

He like high fastballs and has trouble with breaking balls or change-ups. He is not a disciplined hitter, and you can set him up inside and then throw breaking balls away. Brouhard has shown some great power, and might be a hitter to reckon with in the future.

BASERUNNING:

He has only average speed to first and on the bases. Doesn't steal and not likely to bother a pitcher too much.

FIELDING:

Defensively, he is average all the way. Brouhard has a tendency to make easy plays look hard, although he is an aggressive player and will make an occasional outstanding defensive play. His arm is average, and you can run on him.

OVERALL:

Brouhard has a chance to be a good big league home run hitter. Milwaukee has too many good players, and he didn't get much playing time while Milwaukee was fighting for the pennant last year.

Robinson: "If he is going to do it, 1983 will be the true test, because he will be 27 years old. He might not get a chance with Milwaukee."

Martin: "Still problematical. He has shown home run power in the minors, but has yet to show it up here in the big leagues."

MIKE CALDWELL
LHP, No. 48
RL, 6'0", 185 lbs.
ML Svc: 11 years
Born: 1-22-49 in Tarboro, NC

PITCHING:

Caldwell is a sinker, slider pitcher who has to keep the ball low to be effective. When he has good control, he can be extremely tough. He throws from a three-quarter delivery, dropping to almost sidearm at times.

His fastball is above average, not because of its speed--only in the low 80s--but because he turns the ball over and it sinks. His second pitch is a slider that breaks about four or five inches. His third pitch is an average curveball and he also throws a change-up. He has often been accused of throwing a spitball and apparently does something to doctor the ball. Although umpires frequently check the ball when he is pitching, no doctoring has ever been found. He's clever. He also isn't afraid to move a hitter off the plate.

Caldwell has had outstanding success in the past and although he hasn't pitched as well as he did in 1978-79, he is a consistent winning pitcher. He gets a lot of ground balls when he is on, and even though a lot of them go through for hits, he doesn't give up many runs. He has excellent control and doesn't walk many. He has given up a lot of home runs in the last three years, which is unusual for a sinkerball pitcher, but when he is tired, he starts to get the ball up. Does not strike out many.

He knows the hitters, and mixes his pitches very well. He has the assortment of pitches to be tough on either the right or lefthanders.

FIELDING:

Caldwell's move to first is only average for a lefthander. You can steal on him. He is an excellent fielding pitcher who makes very few errors. Average at fielding a bunt, but won't throw the ball away.

OVERALL:

Caldwell finished strong last season. He's still a good pitcher but not as good as he was about four years ago.

Martin: "A tough, professional pitcher who keeps the edge. Has a good assortment of pitches and is mean. Looks good to hit at until you go to the plate--gives you a comfortable 0 for 4."

Robinson: "Caldwell is trying to get it back together after several subpar years. Should be a winner."

Harwell: "A valuable veteran. He's a great competitor and a savvy pitcher."

1982 STATISTICS

W	L	ERA	G	GS	CG	IP	H	R	ER	BB	SO	SV
17	13	3.91	35	34	12	258	269	119	112	58	75	0

CAREER STATISTICS

W	L	ERA	G	GS	CG	IP	H	R	ER	BB	SO	SV
119	106	3.68	417	256	84	2053	2152	981	840	525	847	18

CECIL COOPER
INF, No. 15
LL, 6'2", 190 lbs.
ML Svc: 12 years
Born: 12-20-49 in Brenham, TX

1982 STATISTICS

AVG	G	AB	R	H	2B	3B	HR	RBI	BB	SO	SB
.313	155	654	104	205	38	3	32	121	32	53	2

CAREER STATISTICS

AVG	G	AB	R	H	2B	3B	HR	RBI	BB	SO	SB
.308	1237	4662	690	1436	274	32	166	722	296	574	67

VS. RHP

VS. LHP

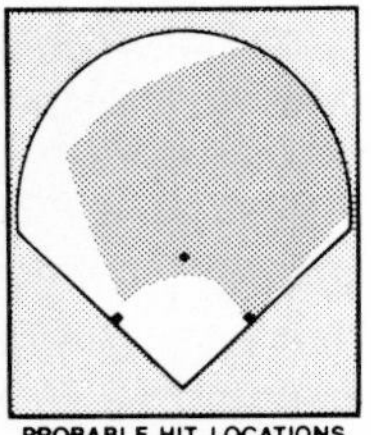
PROBABLE HIT LOCATIONS

HITTING

Cooper is a pure hitter, one of the game's best. He uses a crouching, open stance, similar to Rod Carew, and hits a lot like Carew as well.

There is no real way to defense him because he hits to all parts of the field. He may tend to pull the ball more and hit for more power against righthanders, but still is a threat to hit to the opposite field. Against lefthanders, he slaps the ball to left more frequently. He hits righthanders a little better, but hits both right and lefthanders well. Cooper is tough to strike out.

An extremely hard-throwing left-hander will have the most success against Cooper. Try to pitch him fastballs down and away. Righthanders can start him out with a slider. Hits off-speed pitches very well. Cooper waits better than most hitters before swinging. With two strikes, stay away from him with hard stuff--keep everything you throw him down and away.

His average will suffer a bit when he starts trying to hit home runs, but he will still end up as one of the leading hitters in the league. Probably a better hitter with men on base or in scoring position. Cooper doesn't hit-and-run a lot, but with the Brewers' offense, he doesn't have to.

BASERUNNING:

Not a threat to steal very often, but has good speed and cannot be ignored. Cooper is basically a conservative runner whose ability on the bases is only an average part of his game.

FIELDING:

Cooper has made himself a good first baseman. He is a good target at first base and makes the stretch very well. Moves to his right better than to his left. Fields the bunt very well, and is good at starting or ending a double play. His arm is not strong, but a strong arm is not that important at first.

OVERALL:

Cooper ranks among the best hitters in the game. Since becoming an everyday player at Milwaukee, he has maintained a level of excellence that is finally being recognized.

Martin: "Always a pure hitter. Since going into the crouch a few years ago, he has become a terrorizing hitter. Cooper is just a complete ballplayer."

Robinson: "Cooper is the American League's best-kept secret."

JAMIE EASTERLY
LHP, No. 28
LL, 5'10", 180 lbs.
ML Svc: 5 years
Born: 2-17-53 in Houston, TX

PITCHING:

Easterly missed a lot of the 1982 season because of a knee injury and was ineffective when he returned to active duty last September. Mostly, he had control problems. A lefthander who throws hard for a little guy, he has been used mostly to get a lefthanded hitter or two out before Fingers enters a game. Fenway Park has been a burying ground for a lot of lefthanders, and Easterly has had his biggest problems pitching there.

He throws with a three-quarter delivery, sometimes dropping a little lower, although he doesn't quite drop down far enough to be classified as a sidearm pitcher.

He throws a fastball most of the time. It can be clocked at around 87 MPH, and Easterly is what is known as "sneaky fast." He throws an average slider as his second pitch, and uses a curve as his third pitch. His curveball is average. If he is behind in the count, look for his fastball. He will throw a change-up only occasionally, and doesn't brush too many hitters back.

Easterly can handle himself in pressure situations, but his control is not always good. He walks as many hitters as he strikes out. You might be better off taking a pitch against him.

FIELDING:

Easterly's move to first is only average, but being lefthanded gives him the advantage with runners on first. He fields his position adequately.

OVERALL:

He did a good job of holding a game until Fingers got the call last season. He is the type of pitcher that is handy to have around to get one or two lefthanded hitters out. On days when he has no control problems, he is able to do this effectively.

Robinson: "He runs hot and cold, but has been a pleasant surprise for the Brewers. It has taken him a long time to learn how to pitch. He has the same stuff he always had, but has finally learned where to throw it."

Martin: "A journeyman lefthanded reliever . . . he should have been better as the southpaw counterpart to Fingers."

1982 STATISTICS

W	L	ERA	G	GS	CG	IP	H	R	ER	BB	SO	SV
0	2	4.70	28	0	0	30	39	19	16	15	16	2

CAREER STATISTICS

W	L	ERA	G	GS	CG	IP	H	R	ER	BB	SO	SV
11	25	5.04	163	28	0	323	351	205	181	182	174	8

ROLLIE FINGERS
RHP, No. 34
RR, 6'4", 200 lbs.
ML Svc: 14 years
Born: 8-25-46 in
Steubenville, OH

PITCHING:

Fingers has been one of the best, if not the best, relief pitchers of all time. He's still as good as any of them, although he had a lot of arm problems near the end of last season and may be reaching the stage of his career where age will take its toll.

Fingers throws basically three-quarters overhand, although he will come in sidearm on occasion. He has excellent presence on the mound, and the fact that he is a very smart pitcher who knows the hitters and their weaknesses may be his biggest asset, although he has almost everything going for him. He has excellent control and great confidence in himself. Despite his age, he still throws an excellent fastball which is his bread and butter pitch. It isn't his only pitch, however. He also has an excellent curve and an excellent slider and will throw just about any pitch at any time. He still mixes his pitches when he is behind. He has been throwing a screwball the last three years with excellent results. He uses this pitch a lot against lefthanders.

His fastball sinks, and he keeps all of his pitches at the knees. Left-handers or righthanders don't make much difference against this veteran. His sinker tails away from lefthanders, and his slider breaks in on the hands of lefties. The slider is tough away from righthanders.

FIELDING:

Fingers' move to first is very good. He keeps baserunners honest. He has put on a little weight in his later years and now is just average at fielding his position. He can have problems with balls hit back to the mound.

OVERALL:

Fingers is still one of the best relief pithcers in the game. He's ice-cold on the mound when he comes into a game. Has always had the stuff to beat you and gets smarter and smarter as he gets older. Serious arm troubles, however, may have put his career in jeopardy.

Harwell: "He's the league's No. 1 fireman. He has a great variety of pitches plus savvy and poise."

Robinson: "He can still get you out the way he wants to. Good stuff."

Martin: "Baseball's best reliever ever because he has done it consistently well for 14 years--for good teams and bad ones. Perfect mental makeup for a reliever."

1982 STATISTICS

W	L	ERA	G	GS	CG	IP	H	R	ER	BB	SO	SV
5	6	2.60	50	0	0	79	63	23	23	20	71	29

CAREER STATISTICS

W	L	ERA	G	GS	CG	IP	H	R	ER	BB	SO	SV
112	110	2.86	864	37	4	1599	1377	559	508	460	1235	301

JIM GANTNER
INF, No. 17
LR, 5'11", 175 lbs.
ML Svc: 5 years
Born: 1-5-54 in Eden, WI

1982 STATISTICS

AVG	G	AB	R	H	2B	3B	HR	RBI	BB	SO	SB
.295	132	447	48	132	17	2	4	43	26	36	6

CAREER STATISTICS

AVG	G	AB	R	H	2B	3B	HR	RBI	BB	SO	SB
.278	524	1635	183	454	65	9	14	155	114	137	28

VS. RHP

VS. LHP

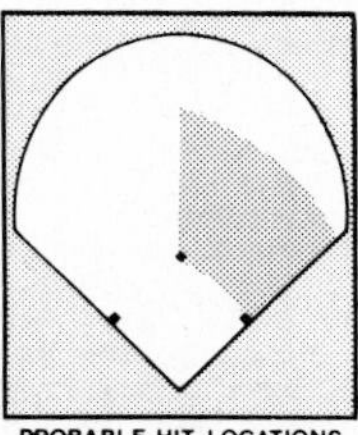
PROBABLE HIT LOCATIONS

HITTING:

Jim Gantner is a line drive hitter who can hurt you on pitches up and over the plate. He's not a power hitter but likes to pull the ball, although he can hit to all fields. He should be played straightaway. Gantner hits from an upright, closed stance, deep in the box.

Gantner had his overall best year at the plate in 1982, and is a better hitter against righthanders. Both right-handers and lefthanders should keep the ball down and on the outside of the plate. Lefthanders can set him up inside, then throw a low, outside breaking ball. He will have trouble with a good breaking ball but can hurt you on a sinker or slider. Gantner jumps on a high fastball, but can be fooled on a change-up.

He is a very aggressive hitter for a little guy and a good clutch hitter. He can bunt and hit and run.

He consistently gets his base hits, and is a good eighth or ninth hitter.

BASERUNNING:

Gantner has good speed but is no big threat to steal, especially on a strong hitting team like the Brewers. He is a smart baserunner but conservative. Picks his spots and will steal when it isn't expected. He doesn't put a lot of pressure on the pitcher when he's on base, but you can't ignore him, either.

FIELDING:

Originally a third baseman, Gantner adapted easily to second base when he made the switch from utility player to regular in 1981. Has a good arm and can go to either side equally well. He will make the clutch defensive play, but his biggest strength is his ability to turn the double play. A tough little guy, he isn't intimidated by a hard slide into second base while making the double play.

OVERALL:

Probably the most underrated player on the team, Gantner is an asset to the Brewers both offensively and defensively.

Robinson: "Gantner is a good hitter who has fit in just right in Milwaukee. Best double play man in the league."

Martin: "He's often overlooked, but he's in the midst of everything. A solid, aggressive player both ways. Under-rated but gets the job done. Gutty."

Harwell: "Gantner is a good, steady team player."

MOOSE HAAS
RHP, No. 30
RR, 6'0", 170 lbs.
ML Svc: 6 years
Born: 4-22-56 in Baltimore, MD

PITCHING:

Haas is a power pitcher with a fastball in the high 80s. He also has a very good curve and an average slider. His fastball has good movement on it, and he also will throw a split-finger fastball occasionally. This pitch has more movement than his regular fastball. His third pitch is a slider, which he does not throw that often, and he will occasionally throw a change-up. The change is almost a waste pitch for him.

Haas' delivery is almost straight overhand, and his pitching motion is almost textbook perfect. He is the closest thing the Brewers have to a strikeout pitcher, and he occasionally has control problems.

Although Haas has good stuff, he has not been a consistent pitcher since an elbow injury early in his major league career. He seems to have one very bad inning almost every game. He is a good pitcher, but has a tendency to get a little excited. He has the reputation that if you stay close, you can get to him. He has had good success against Toronto and Chicago, but has had trouble with Boston.

FIELDING:

Haas has a good, quick move to first base and throws over there a lot. He fields his position well.

OVERALL:

Haas has good command of his pitches and has all the tools to be a big winner in the major leagues. He hasn't had the success that was expected of him, but is still young enough to improve. His inconsistency has held him back so far.

Robinson: "Haas should have have a better record because he is a good pitcher and on the best team in the league."

Martin: "He could be better, but he's still young enough to be better than a .500 pitcher in the big leagues."

1982 STATISTICS

W	L	ERA	G	GS	CG	IP	H	R	ER	BB	SO	SV
11	8	4.47	32	27	3	193	232	101	96	39	104	1

CAREER STATISTICS

W	L	ERA	G	GS	CG	IP	H	R	ER	BB	SO	SV
61	57	4.19	162	150	38	1013	462	512	472	298	563	2

ROY HOWELL
INF, No. 13
LR, 6'1", 195 lbs.
ML Svc: 8 years
Born: 12-18-53 in Lompoc, CA

1982 STATISTICS

AVG	G	AB	R	H	2B	3B	HR	RBI	BB	SO	SB
.260	98	300	31	78	11	2	4	38	21	39	0

CAREER STATISTICS

AVG	G	AB	R	H	2B	3B	HR	RBI	BB	SO	SB
.262	975	3433	387	899	169	24	72	412	295	614	8

VS. RHP

VS. LHP

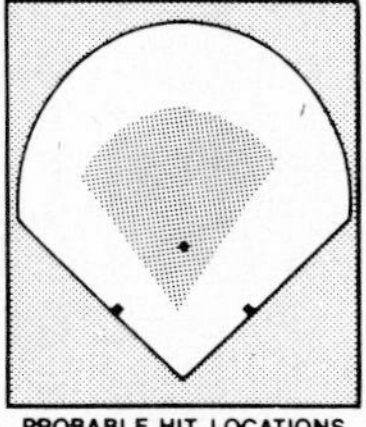
PROBABLE HIT LOCATIONS

HITTING:

Howell has been used almost exclusively against righthanded pitchers for the last couple of years, but had been a good RBI man when he was with Toronto and played against right or lefthanders. He is a line drive hitter with fair power. He uses the entire field and should be played straightaway.

Howell hits from an upright closed stance low in the box. He is basically a low ball hitter. Righthanded pitchers should keep everything on the inside half of the plate and can change speeds against him. Lefthanders should keep the fastball in on his fists. He can hit a righthander's breaking ball but will have trouble against a lefty.

He is a fairly consistent hitter but is not the best clutch hitter in the Brewer lineup. His hitting suffers if he doesn't play for long periods.

BASERUNNING:

Howell has average speed and has stolen only one base in five full years. He is, however, aggressive and is always thinking when he is on base. He will do something unusual at times and has dived over an infielder to successfully avoid a tag. Normally slides head first.

FIELDING:

Howell has been used almost entirely as a designated hitter by the Brewers although he came up as a third baseman. He has poor range, and was an average third baseman who could come up with spectacular plays on rare occasions. Howell lacks good hands, and his arm is too weak for a third baseman.

OVERALL:

Howell is a good role player who can help a team with his bat. He is a consistent hitter against righthanded pitching.

Robinson: "Howell can be a designated hitter, pinch-hit or play third base against righthanded pitching. At this stage of his career with Milwaukee, I don't see him doing much more."

Martin: "Howell hits the ball hard. He can fill in at third base well enough but is primarily a role player."

PETE LADD
RHP, No. 27
RR, 6'3", 240 lbs.
ML Svc: 1 year plus
Born: 7-17-56 in
Portland, ME

PITCHING:

Pete Ladd is a hard-throwing relief pitcher who still has to prove that he can be a major leaguer. He has the potential to be a good short relief man.

He is a strikeout pitcher who usually throws just two pitches--a fastball and a slider. He has been working on a change-up, which he will need if he is going to be successful. His fastball is quite a bit above average. When he first came up with the Brewers, he threw a sinking-type of fastball which he threw high in the strike zone hoping for a strikeout. However, Ladd is now throwing one that rises, and the change in it has made him a better pitcher and harder to hit. His change-up is still below average, but his slider is good. He likes to throw everything high.

Since he is used in relief, Ladd pitches almost exclusively from the stretch. He will pitch from a windup only when he hasn't pitched for a while and is having control problems. Unlike most hard throwers, Ladd short-arms the ball but still gets good velocity. Home runs have hurt him with the Brewers.

FIELDING:

Ladd is a big man but gets off the mound well enough to be a respectable fielder. He has a decent move to first and keeps the runners close.

OVERALL:

Because he is a hard thrower, he could develop into a good short relief pitcher. He needs to work on his change-up to make his fastball more effective. When he first came up, the hitters could just key in on his fastball or slider.

1982 STATISTICS

W	L	ERA	G	GS	CG	IP	H	R	ER	BB	SO	SV
1	3	4.00	16	0	0	18	16	8	8	6	12	3

CAREER STATISTICS

W	L	ERA	G	GS	CG	IP	H	R	ER	BB	SO	SV
11	15	3.60	26	0	0	30	24	13	12	14	18	0

BOB McCLURE
LHP, No. 10
SL, 5'11", 170 lbs.
ML Svc: 6 years
Born: 4-29-53 in Oakland, CA

PITCHING:

McClure, who had been a so-so relief pitcher all of his major league career, was moved into the starting rotation in 1982 and did a good job. He had missed most of the 1981 season with a rotator cuff injury.

McClure is a lefthander who isn't very big and could be described as sneaky fast. His fastball is his best pitch, and sometimes he doesn't use it as much as he should. He also has an above average curveball and an above average slider. When he is behind in the count, he often throws his breaking ball which is a big sweeping curve.

He throws sidearm a lot and his motion is very deliberate, turning his back on the plate before throwing. Because of the delivery and thrownig sidearm, he can be tough on lefthanders. Because of his experience as a relief pitcher, he can handle pressure situations very well. He throws hard and has good control. The only question about the change from a reliever to a starter is the toll it will take on his arm. He isn't used to throwing that many pitches. The home run ball has hurt him.

FIELDING:

McClure's move to first base is the best there is. At times he even picks off his first baseman, the move is so deceptive. He is also frequently called for balks because umpires cannot agree on whether his move is legal or not. McClure fields his position very well and gets off the mound quickly to field bunts.

OVERALL:

After having just moderate success in four years as a relief pitcher, McClure seems to have found his niche as a starter. Not likely to be a big winner, but he has the tools to be a consistent 15-16 game winner.

Robinson: "McClure may have found his niche as a starter. He tried it last year and it turned out to be a lost opportunity when he injured his shoulder."

Martin: "He came back from rotator cuff injury to be a solid lefthanded starter."

Harwell: "Watch his move to first. It's outstanding."

1982 STATISTICS

W	L	ERA	G	GS	CG	IP	H	R	ER	BB	SO	SV
12	7	4.22	34	26	5	172	160	90	81	74	99	0

CAREER STATISTICS

W	L	ERA	G	GS	CG	IP	H	R	ER	BB	SO	SV
27	24	3.55	258	31	7	477	427	215	188	225	211	30

PAUL MOLITOR
INF, No. 4
RR, 6'0", 175 lbs.
ML Svc: 5 years
Born: 8-22-56 in St. Paul, MN

1982 STATISTICS

AVG	G	AB	R	H	2B	3B	HR	RBI	BB	SO	SB
.302	160	666	136	201	26	8	19	71	69	93	41

CAREER STATISTICS

AVG	G	AB	R	H	2B	3B	HR	RBI	BB	SO	SB
.297	600	2472	423	735	119	30	45	234	209	272	148

VS. RHP

VS. LHP

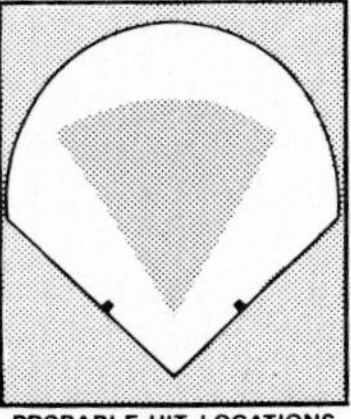
PROBABLE HIT LOCATIONS

HITTING:

Molitor is a leadoff hitter who can do a lot of things for a team. He rates as one of the best bunters in the game and can be expected to try to bunt for a base hit just about once every game. A tough out, and a player who makes things happen. He teams with Robin Yount as one of baseball's best one-two combinations.

Basically a straightaway hitter, he has some power to left and has good bat control with men on base. He hangs over the plate, and pitchers should try to get in on him. Move him away from the plate, then try breaking stuff away. Not a patient hitter and often swings at the first pitch. Doesn't walk a lot for a leadoff hitter. With his good speed, he can beat out a lot of infield hits.

Molitor hits well against right-handers or lefthanders and will jump on a fastball up and over the plate. Only so-so against a change-up, and can be fooled on a good breaking ball if he isn't looking for it. He's a smart hitter, however, and will be thinking right along with the pitcher and catcher. Has great instincts and is always a threat to go for the extra base. Overall rating, above average.

BASERUNNING:

Molitor has probably the best base-running instincts on the team. He gets a good jump and can fly. A very aggressive runner, Molitor is a high-percentage basestealer. Usually steals only when there is a good chance that he will be successful. Always a threat to go from first to third, sometimes on an infield out. When he's on first, you can't ignore him.

FIELDING:

Originally a shortstop, Molitor played second base his first three seasons as a Brewer. After an attempt at playing center field in 1981, he was moved to third base last season. He is going through a learning process at the position, and is a very average third baseman right now. A good athlete who should improve at third in the next couple years if he gets to stay there. Has a strong arm, but tended to make a lot of throwing errors. Only average at fielding bunts.

OVERALL:

An exciting player who can beat you in a lot of ways. The man who makes the Brewer offense go, Molitor is a key player for the team. Was hampered by injuries in 1980 and 1981.

Robinson: "He has a very aggressive attitude and can do everything a player is supposed to do--hit, hit with power, run, field and throw."

Harwell: "Top-star quality."

Martin: "A young veteran with five solid seasons in the majors, Molitor has every tool to make him great. It's up to him how far he can go."

DON MONEY
INF, No. 7
RR, 6'1", 190 lbs.
ML Svc: 14 years
Born: 6-7-47 in
Washington, DC

1982 STATISTICS

AVG	G	AB	R	H	2B	3B	HR	RBI	BB	SO	SB
.284	96	275	40	78	14	3	16	55	32	38	0

CAREER STATISTICS

AVG	G	AB	R	H	2B	3B	HR	RBI	BB	SO	SB
.289	1677	5561	793	1606	297	36	175	721	589	849	80

VS. RHP

VS. LHP

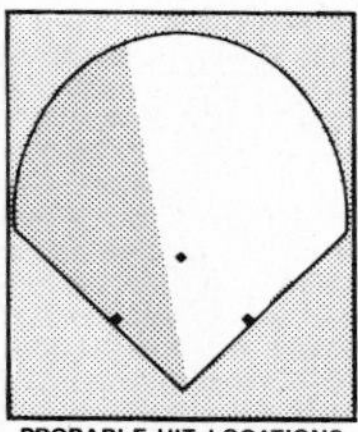
PROBABLE HIT LOCATIONS

HITTING:

Money has been a good hitter throughout his career, although he is now used mostly as a designated hitter against lefthanded pitchers. He still has some punch for the long ball. He can DH, pinch-hit and play some third base, although his playing time in the infield was limited last year. He can be a dangerous hitter coming off the bench. Closed, upright stance, deep in the box.

Almost a straight pull hitter, a pitcher should throw him breaking balls down and on the outside half of the plate. He can handle almost any pitch if it's on the inside half of the plate high in the strike zone. Start him with a breaking ball for a strike since he is a first ball, fastball hitter. Keep everything down and outside. Out pitch should be a breaking ball if possible.

Although used mostly against left-handers, Money still can hit right-handers almost as well. A good clutch hitter, but not much of a threat to take an extra base after being slowed by numerous injuries the last few years. Good bunter for sacrifice situations, but cannot beat out a bunt for a base hit.

BASERUNNING:

Because of age and injuries, Money is no threat to steal, but he is still a smart baserunner. He will go from first to third in the right situation. Baserunning is now the weakest part of his game.

FIELDING:

Once a high-percentage infielder and one of the better third basemen around, Money now plays only rarely in the infield. His range was never outstanding, and is now even more limited because of injuries. Has a good arm and good hands. Will fill in adequately at first and third. Also can play some at second base, but lack of range really hurts him there. His glove is not much of a factor anymore. Used mostly for his bat.

OVERALL:

Money has seen his better days as a big league player. Cannot play everyday, but can still be a dangerous hitter and a tough out.

Martin: "He has served well. A two-way player through the 1970's with Philadelphia and Milwaukee. With injuries and age is now mostly a DH and pinch-hitter, but can fill in as a strong pull hitter with home run power. A gamer."

Robinson: "He has been slowed by injuries the last few years, but spot him and you will get the best out of him."

HITTING:

Moore's average dropped in 1982, the first season he had an opportunity to play regularly, although he had averaged around .300 for several years as a part-time player. A good contact hitter in the lower part of the order, Moore is basically a straightaway hitter who hits line drives and a lot of ground balls through the middle of the infield. He used to try to pull everything but now goes more for base hits instead of home runs. He will hit an occasional home run but does not have a lot of power.

Moore hits from a semi-crouch in the center of the box and is basically a low ball hitter against either right-handers or lefthanders. Righthanders can work him with fastballs in at about the belt and breaking balls on the outside half of the plate. Lefthanders should keep everything away. Hits the fastball but will have trouble with breaking balls and can be fooled with a change-up.

Although he is normally a high-average hitter, Moore is not an exceptionally good hitter with runners in scoring position. Will move runners from first to third but has trouble driving them in.

Overall, he is an above average hitter but not a big RBI man. He fits in well in the bottom part of a strong offensive lineup.

BASERUNNING:

Moore has only average speed and is not a threat to steal. He doesn't take many chances on the basepaths, and isn't liable to affect a pitcher's concentration when he's on first.

FIELDING:

A second-string catcher for his entire career, Moore moved to the outfield last season and played as if he had been there all of his life. In past experiments in the outfield, Moore had been shaky, but he obviously worked hard at his new position and adjusted very well.

CHARLIE MOORE
OF, No. 22
RR, 5'11", 180 lbs.
ML Svc: 9 years
Born: 6-21-53 in Birmingham, AL

1982 STATISTICS

AVG	G	AB	R	H	2B	3B	HR	RBI	BB	SO	SB
.254	133	456	53	116	22	4	6	45	29	49	2

CAREER STATISTICS

AVG	G	AB	R	H	2B	3B	HR	RBI	BB	SO	SB
.264	877	2625	304	693	118	28	28	265	220	299	31

VS. RHP

VS. LHP

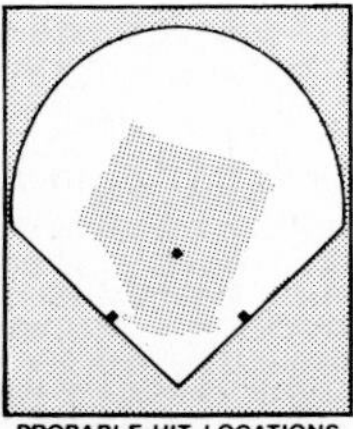
PROBABLE HIT LOCATIONS

He has only average range, but has a strong, accurate arm. He charges the ball like an infielder and comes up throwing. Teams probably will be a little more reluctant to run on him in the future.

He did a very good job in his first season in right field and undoubtedly will improve as he becomes more accustomed to the position.

OVERALL:

An everyday player for the first time in his career, Moore surprised everybody by making a bigger contribution defensively than he did offensively. Should hit better than he did in 1982.

Martin: "Moore is useful to a team because of his catcher-outfielder flexibility. Makes contact at the plate."

Robinson: "He has been trying to dispel the notion that he is a part-time player. Played more than ever in 1982. He's a tough player and gets everything out of his ability."

BEN OGLIVIE
OF, No. 24
LL, 6'2", 170 lbs.
ML Svc: 11 years
Born: 2-11-49 in Colon, PAN

HITTING:

Once considered a platoon player, Oglivie became an everyday player when Larry Hisle was injured in 1979 and showed that he could hit lefthanders as well as righthanders. Almost a straight pull hitter, Oglivie swings hard at everything and hits almost nothing but line drives. He has a lot of power and always hits the ball hard.

Oglivie hits with a closed stance low in the box and hangs over the inside of the plate. Because of this, he can have problems with a good high fastball. He is basically a low ball hitter and can hit pitches almost in the dirt over the fence. He also hits high breaking balls very well. It's probably best to pitch him inside and high with a fastball, then keep a breaking ball on the outside half of the plate and low. He is a big swinger who will jump off the ground to hit one. He will chase a ball up and out of the strike zone with two strikes on him.

He is a very good clutch hitter and almost always drives in around 100 runs a season. Despite low average in 1982, he is a good hitter who still got a lot of big hits.

1982 STATISTICS

AVG	G	AB	R	H	2B	3B	HR	RBI	BB	SO	SB
.244	159	602	92	147	22	1	34	102	70	81	3

CAREER STATISTICS

AVG	G	AB	R	H	2B	3B	HR	RBI	BB	SO	SB
.271	1294	4354	615	1182	205	25	195	661	389	648	82

VS. RHP

VS. LHP

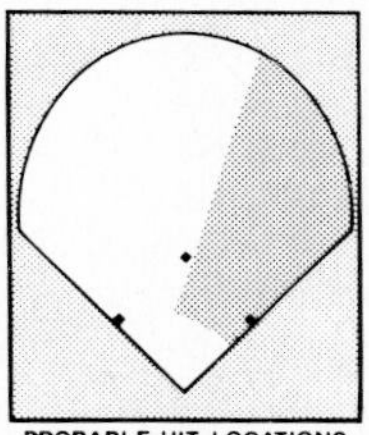
PROBABLE HIT LOCATIONS

BASERUNNING:

Oglivie has very good speed and is a difficult hitter to double up. He is capable of stealing but is not considered a real good baserunner. Does not slide well.

FIELDING:

Oglivie is a much better leftfielder than he is given credit for. He has improved a lot in the last few years since he has gotten to play regularly. He is very good at cutting off balls that are headed for the gap or the corner and keeping a hitter from an extra base. He has a strong arm that is usually accurate but can be erratic at times. He sometimes has problems with balls hit in front of him and is more likely to make an error on one getting past him than on any other play.

OVERALL:

Oglivie has been a consistent RBI man and home run hitter. He is always dangerous.

Harwell: "When he's on a streak, he can be devastating."

Robinson: "He shed the utility player label several years ago and has done well. He's a good player on offense and defense."

Martin: "A charging aggressive hitter, his bat's never still. A quiet player and very intelligent. He was underrated for a long time."

HITTING:

Simmons is a switch-hitter who hits a little better against righthanders, but is a good hitter against either. He is a pull hitter who hits with power from either side. He did not hit for a high average in his first season with Milwaukee but still drove in a lot of runs. His average went up considerably in 1982 although it was still below his previous National League average where he was a very good hitter.

He normally hits from an upright stance, but he went into a crouch for a time last season. His hitting improved considerably from this stance, but he later went back to the upright stance.

Against righthanders he's basically a low ball hitter. Keep the fastball up above the belt, and go in and out. Against lefthanders, he's a high ball hitter. Lefthanders should keep the fastball down and don't throw breaking balls for a strike.

Although he hasn't hit for as high an average in the American League, he can rise to the occasion and deliver an important hit. He hits well in clutch situations and is a good hit-and-run man. A pitcher would be wise to stay away from having to throw a fastball to Simmons in a pressure situation.

BASERUNNING:

Simmons is a smart baserunner but very, very slow. There is little chance of him stealing. Baserunning is, by far, the weakest part of his game.

FIELDING:

After a year in the league, Simmons knows the hitters very well and calls a good game. He has a lot of experience behind the plate, and pitchers like throwing to him. His arm is not real strong and a lot of teams will run on him. He has a quick release, and at times will throw out a high ratio of runners. At other times however, everybody can run on him. Simmons is too inconsistent with his throwing, and should work to improve. He is a big man and does not move well behind the plate. A lot of pitches get past him because of his slow movements.

TED SIMMONS
C, No. 23
SR, 6'0", 200 lbs.
ML Svc: 13 years
Born: 8-9-49 in Highland Park, MI

1982 STATISTICS

AVG	G	AB	R	H	2B	3B	HR	RBI	BB	SO	SB
.269	137	539	73	145	28	0	23	97	32	40	0

CAREER STATISTICS

AVG	G	AB	R	H	2B	3B	HR	RBI	BB	SO	SB
.291	1801	6644	854	1931	373	40	209	1087	679	525	11

VS. RHP

VS. LHP

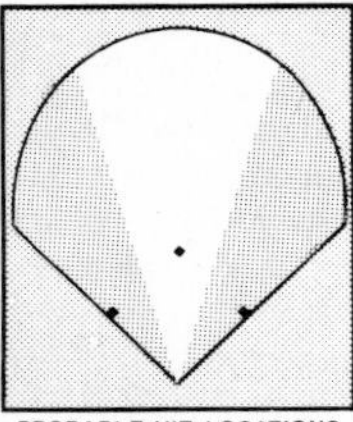
PROBABLE HIT LOCATIONS

OVERALL:

Simmons is an intelligent player and has always been a good hitter. After a bad first year in the American League, his hitting improved and should continue to do so. He's a team leader. A good performer in an RBI spot in the lineup.

Robinson: "He has a great attitude and goes about his business. He has lived up to his prior billing as an outstanding player."

Harwell: "A good team man. Tough in clutch. A winner."

Martin: "Simmons has been a steady performer over the years. An excellent switch-hitter."

JIM SLATON
RHP, No. 41
RR, 6'0", 185 lbs.
ML Svc: 11 years
Born: 6-19-50 in
Long Beach, CA

PITCHING:

A starter throughout his career, Slaton was moved to the bullpen in 1982 and was a very valuable member of the Brewer pitching staff. He did a good job in long and short relief and also as a spot starter.

A righthander who throws between three-quarter overhand and straight over the top, Slaton is basically a power pitcher although he doesn't throw as hard as he used to. He pitches well to a hitter's weaknesses and has excellent control. Gives up a lot of hits per inning, however, and sometimes has problems with his temper.

His main pitch is his fastball which is in the upper 80s range. He throws his curve a lot and it is a good pitch for him because he can use it anytime and throw it for a strike. His slider also is a little above average. If he is behind in the count, he normally will come in with a fastball, but he has good breaking stuff and can be as effective against lefthanders as righthanders when his curve is working well.

He had a rotator cuff problem in 1980 and pitched very little that season, but now appears to have recovered completely.

FIELDING:

Slaton has a good quick move to first base and a runner can't wander too far off the bag when he's pitching. He fields his position better than most pitchers.

OVERALL:

Slaton is a valuable pitcher who can be used as either a starter or a reliever. He adjusted very well to his new bullpen role last season.

Martin: "A good combative pitcher who can be used in a number of ways. He started as a thrower but became a pitcher."

Harwell: "He's a smart pitcher who is very effective when used correctly."

Robinson: "He returned from rotator cuff problems and looked like he was throwing just as good as ever. He's a real bulldog on the mound and does not give in easily. Goes right after the hitter no matter what the count is. He takes a lot of pressure off Fingers."

1982 STATISTICS

W	L	ERA	G	GS	CG	IP	H	R	ER	BB	SO	SV
10	6	3.29	39	7	0	117	117	48	43	41	59	6

CAREER STATISTICS

W	L	ERA	G	GS	CG	IP	H	R	ER	BB	SO	SV
120	126	3.87	353	302	80	2146	2176	1031	922	789	983	6

DON SUTTON
RHP, No. 20
RR, 6'1", 190 lbs.
ML Svc: 17 years
Born: 4-2-45 in
Clio, AL

PITCHING:

Sutton will find some way to beat you. He's a pitcher with extreme confidence and the record to justify it. His only real weakness is probably his age. He's no longer a nine inning pitcher and tends to tire after five or six innings. When he does, his ball comes up too high in the strike zone and can be hit.

Sutton is a control pitcher who comes straight over the top. He consistently pitches accurately to a hitter's weakness and can pitch effectively to either right or lefthanders.

His primary pitch is his fastball, which he throws around 88-90 MPH. He throws it about 50% of the time, usually high in the strike zone. If he has a good fastball, he will rely on it when he's behind a hitter. He also has a good curve that has excellent rotation and goes down in the strike zone well. His slider is not a quality pitch, but it gives him some diversion from his fastball. He seldom throws a change-up but will change speeds on pitches. Against lefthanders, he can be expected to throw a screwball. It's an average one, but lefthanders almost always swing at it out of the strike zone.

He has been accused of cutting the ball and makes good use of the publicity to keep hitters thinking about it. Whether it's there or not, the pitch is a good psychological weapon.

Sutton will throw any pitch any time, so don't try to guess with him. His value as a starter can never be underestimated, even at this late stage of his career.

FIELDING:

Sutton has an above average move to first and often quick-pitches with men on base. Above average at fielding his position.

OVERALL:

He is one of the best and has supreme confidence in his ability. He'll find a way to beat you.

McCarver: "Don Sutton paints corners like Monet painted impressions. His talent in getting people out lies in his knowledge of hitting in general. Refuses to give in."

Coleman: "He's an excellent six inning pitcher. He will very rarely give you a bad outing."

1982 STATISTICS

W	L	ERA	G	GS	CG	IP	H	R	ER	BB	SO	SV
17	9	3.07	34	34	6	249	473	96	85	64	175	0

CAREER STATISTICS

W	L	ERA	G	GS	CG	IP	H	R	ER	BB	SO	SV
258	193	3.06	591	574	168	4136	3805	1553	1404	1059	2931	5

HITTING:

Thomas is one of the leading power hitters in the American League, and maybe the most dangerous hitter in the Brewers' lineup. He can be pitched to, but make a mistake in pitching to him, and it will land in the seats. Although he hits in streaks, he is a dangerous hitter with runners on base or in scoring position. He does not have very good speed, but runs hard on every ground ball.

Thomas uses an upright, closed stance low in the box. He almost always pulls the ball. He likes a low fastball and will cream a hanging curve. If you throw him a fastball, throw it way in. It is best to work him with slow breaking balls, the slower the better. Also has trouble with change-ups, but don't throw him one with two strikes. He has cut down on strikeouts by cutting down on his swing with two strikes, spreads out more and tries to protect the plate. Draws a lot of walks and still has a high strikeout ratio. Will try to go to the opposite field when the situation is right.

He no longer tries to pull everything out of the park, having realized that home runs are the result of a good swing, not a hard one. He is getting to be a smarter hitter every year. Pitchers used to be able to throw him fastballs up and out of the strike zone, but he doesn't chase them as much as he used to. He can carry a club for a week or more when he is hot.

BASERUNNING:

Not much of a threat to steal, although he will try a delayed steal at times. Not a lot of speed, but is an aggressive baserunner. He will slide hard to break up a double play or bowl over a catcher in an attempt to score.

FIELDING:

Thomas may be one of the most underrated center fielders in the league.

GORMAN THOMAS
OF, No. 20
RR, 6'3", 200 lbs.
ML Svc: 7 years
Born: 12-12-50 in
Charleston, SC

1982 STATISTICS

AVG	G	AB	R	H	2B	3B	HR	RBI	BB	SO	SB
.245	158	567	96	139	29	1	39	112	84	143	3

CAREER STATISTICS

AVG	G	AB	R	H	2B	3B	HR	RBI	BB	SO	SB
.235	1012	3235	482	759	162	10	197	577	447	933	34

VS. RHP

VS. LHP

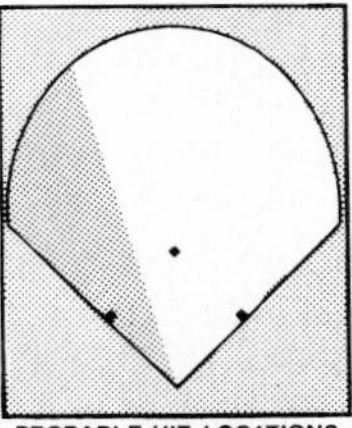
PROBABLE HIT LOCATIONS

Not real fast, but plays the hitters well and gets a good jump on the ball. His arm is above average, and very accurate. His range is very good despite his lack of speed.

OVERALL:

Thomas is an excellent offensive and defensive player who plays hard all of the time. Hits 30 or more home runs and drives in over 100 runs almost every year.

Robinson: "When you see Thomas play, you will see him either strike out, hit a home run or crash into a fence catching a ball. He is a player who has improved in a lot of areas."

Martin: "Thomas is an enthusiastic player whose all around play is infectious."

Harwell: "Thomas is one of the best power hitters and a better fielder than many of his critics believe."

PETE VUCKOVICH
RHP, No. 50
RR, 6'4", 220 lbs.
ML Svc: 7 years
Born: 10-27-52 in Johnstown, PA

PITCHING:

Since returning to the American League, Vuckovich has had the best winning percentage of any pitcher in the majors. He's dogged and aggressive. He throws a lot of pitches, but gets himself out of jams.

Vuckovich is not a hard thrower, but he's a very smart pitcher. Everything he does on the mound, from crossing his eyes at a hitter to shaking his head violently, is for a purpose. He changes speeds on all of his pitches and throws each of them from different angles. He will throw his fastball more than any other pitch. His second pitch is his curve, which breaks down, and third is a big breaking slider. Also throws a change-up, but not as often as the other pitches. He has been accused of throwing a spitball at times, although it isn't a big pitch in his repertoire. His herky-jerky delivery is difficult for righthanders, but he is tough against righthanders or lefthanders when he is on. His biggest weakness is the number of walks he gives up. Puts a lot of runners on base, but not that many of them score.

Stay loose. He isn't averse to knocking a hitter down.

FIELDING:

Vuckovich has a good quick move to both first and second. Runners should be careful when he's pitching. He is an average fielder who handles a bunt fairly well.

OVERALL:

Vuckovich is a good pitcher with a lot of poise. He knows he can get hitters out and goes after them. He moves the ball around a lot and is very unpredictable. He's a winning pitcher, and has been throughout his career. Vuckovich was the 1982 recipient of the Cy Young Award.

Martin: "Vuckovich is durable and can throw all day. He's an aggressive, come-at-you-incessantly pitcher who beats you. Not often prettily, but pretty good."

Robinson: "He's a real battler who gets the most out of his ability. Keeps the hitters off stride and moves the ball around."

Harwell: "He's a money pitcher, a hard competitor with good natural ability. Dependable."

1982 STATISTICS

W	L	ERA	G	GS	CG	IP	H	R	ER	BB	SO	SV
18	6	3.34	30	30	9	223	234	96	83	102	105	0

CAREER STATISTICS

W	L	ERA	G	GS	CG	IP	H	R	ER	BB	SO	SV
85	53	3.51	255	155	122	1294	1272	564	504	474	805	10

NED YOST
C, No. 5
RR, 6'1", 185 lbs.
ML Svc: 2 years
Born: 8-19-55 in Eureka, CA

1982 STATISTICS

AVG	G	AB	R	H	2B	3B	HR	RBI	BB	SO	SB
.276	40	98	13	27	6	3	1	8	7	20	3

CAREER STATISTICS

AVG	G	AB	R	H	2B	3B	HR	RBI	BB	SO	SB
.244	74	156	17	38	6	3	4	11	10	32	3

VS. RHP

VS. LHP

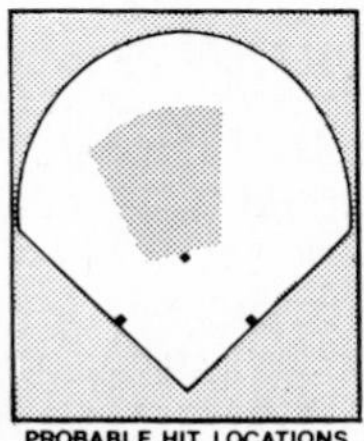
PROBABLE HIT LOCATIONS

HITTING:

Yost plays behind Ted Simmons and so he doesn't get much playing time. He is in the major leagues because of his defensive ability, not his hitting.

Yost hits from an upright stance, slightly open, in the center of the batter's box. He is basically a high ball hitter who hits grounders and line drives. He doesn't have much power and has never hit for a high average, even in the minor leagues. Keep good stuff on the ball and you can get him out. He is not a good clutch hitter and has trouble hitting behind a runner in a hit-and-run situation.

He can handle a fastball on the inside half of the plate but will have trouble with a good breaking ball or a change-up. Has a tendency to swing at bad pitches. Pitchers can throw him a lot of breaking balls, but be careful with a fastball on the inside half of the plate.

BASERUNNING:

Yost has only average speed and isn't much of a threat on the basepaths. A conservative baserunner, pitchers don't have to be too concerned about him.

FIELDING:

Yost has the potential to be a very good defensive catcher but his weak hitting may keep him from playing enough to develop defensively. He has a very, very strong arm but still doesn't throw out as many runners as he should, often because of off-target throws or not getting the ball away fast enough. He handles pitches well and calls his own game. He has a good knowledge of opposing hitters. Yost is built more like an infielder than a catcher and is very agile behind the plate. He is very good at blocking pitches in the dirt.

OVERALL:

Defensive ability got Yost to the major leagues and his hitting probably will limit him to duty as a spot player.

Robinson: "His hitting will have to improve to play more."

Martin: "Strictly a back up catcher. Decent in that role."

Harwell: "Defense is the strongest part of his game."

ROBIN YOUNT
INF, No. 19
RR, 6'0", 170 lbs.
ML Svc: 9 years
Born: 9-16-55 in Danville, IL

1982 STATISTICS

AVG	G	AB	R	H	2B	3B	HR	RBI	BB	SO	SB
.331	156	635	129	210	46	12	29	114	54	63	14

CAREER STATISTICS

AVG	G	AB	R	H	2B	3B	HR	RBI	BB	SO	SB
.281	1240	4847	678	1363	254	55	96	553	285	526	116

VS. RHP

VS. LHP

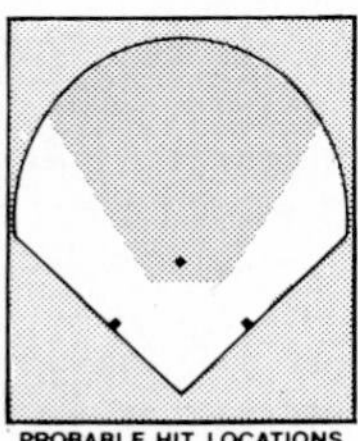
PROBABLE HIT LOCATIONS

HITTING:

Robin Yount put everything together in 1982, and had the greatest season of his career. Look for him to get better. Only 27 years old, he already is a veteran of nine full seasons in the major leagues. He has matured into one of the best players in the game.

Hitting from a semi-crouch, low in the box, Yount hits a lot of line drives and hits them deep. He has power as a straight pull hitter, but also hits very well to right-center. He will hit 20 to 30 home runs and drive in 100 runs, despite batting second.

The best way to pitch Yount--if there is a best way--probably is to run him off the plate and go back to the outside half of the plate. Work him with fastballs, eventually out of the strike zone. He will hit anything up and can handle a good change-up or curve.

Yount has always been a consistent hitter and is getting even better. He is a tough out in clutch situations and teams up with Paul Molitor to give the Brewers an outstanding one-two combination. Having Molitor, who is a threat to steal, on first base quite often helps Yount as a hitter. He can hit behind the runner as well as anybody, and is a good bunter.

BASERUNNING:

An aggressive runner with good speed from home to first or on the basepaths, Yount is a constant threat to steal and pitchers should be wary even though he does not run that often. He is good at breaking up a double play, and will often go for the extra base. You can never take him for granted.

FIELDING:

Yount is the best shortstop in the American League, and may be the best in baseball. His defensive ability is often overlooked because of his hitting, but he is one of the best. His arm, range and ability to go left or right are all rated excellent. He is excellent on the double play and will make the clutch play when needed. Only his throwing accuracy is rated less than excellent, but it has improved a lot in the last few seasons. He used to be somewhat erratic.

OVERALL:

Yount is a good, young veteran who can do everything. He is an outstanding hitter, an outstanding shortstop and a team leader.

Robinson: "Yount can steal, bunt, hit, field, and hit the home run. He's my kind of player."

Harwell: "Robin is a great all around performer. He is an outstanding team player, experienced but still young."

JERRY AUGUSTINE
LHP, No. 46
LL, 6'0", 185 lbs.
ML Svc: 7 years
Born: 7-24-52 in Kewaunee, WI

PITCHING, FIELDING:

A former starter, Augustine has pitched out of the bullpen for the last four years. At first, the Brewers tried to use him in short relief. Has been used mostly as a mop-up pitcher or to get a lefthanded hitter out in the last couple of years.

Augustine is a lefthander who throws fairly hard, but most of his pitches are average or a little below. He relies on the fastball and will throw it when he is behind. His curveball is his second pitch, and he also throws a slider quite frequently. Doesn't change speeds very often. His control is spotty with all of his pitches.

His biggest plus is that he can pitch almost every day, but he has been inconsistent throughout his career. His won-lost percentage has been under .500 throughout his time in the big leagues, and won't improve much. Bases-on-balls and the long ball have hurt him.

His move to first is average, and he is an average fielder.

OVERALL:

A journeyman pitcher who isn't likely to be anything more than a role pitcher. He will do most of his pitching after a game is already out of hand.

Robinson: "He has gone downhill in the last few years, mainly because he has been inconsistent."

Martin: "A disappointment in 1982 after some good years as a starter and reliever for Milwaukee."

MARSHALL EDWARDS
OF, No. 16
LL, 5'6", 157 lbs.
ML Svc: 2 years
Born: 8-27-52 in Los Angeles, CA

HITTING, BASERUNNING, FIELDING:

Edwards finally made the major leagues at the age of 29 after a long minor league career because of his speed and defensive ability. He is a weak hitter who will be limited to part-time duty because of it.

A lefthander who hits from a crouch, he doesn't stride into the ball but almost jumps at it. He stands close to the plate, tries to pull everything, and would be better off going to the opposite field more often. Lefthanders can get him out with breaking balls low and away. Righthanders should throw him hard stuff in on the fists. Edwards has very little power, but his exceptional speed will allow him to beat out a lot of bunts and infield hits.

Edwards is a very good basestealer and usually runs on his own. He gets a good jump and is a high percentage basestealer. If he played regularly, he would be a threat to steal 30 or more bases a season. He is very difficult to double up, and is often used as a pinch-runner.

Edwards misjudges a lot of balls, but his speed helps him make up for his mistakes and he can overcome them. He has had to make diving catches on balls that should have been routine fly balls. He has a strong arm but is sometimes erratic.

OVERALL:

His future is limited to part-time duty as a pinch-runner or as a late-innings defensive player.

ROB PICCIOLO
INF, No. 8
RR, 6'2", 185 lbs.
ML Svc: 6 years
Born: 2-4-53 in
Santa Monica, CA

HITTING, BASERUNNING, FIELDING:

Picciolo's hitting has limited him to a part-time role throughout his career. He will not get much better. Most of his hits will be ground balls through the infield. A spray hitter, Picciolo has little power, and will seldom hit into the alleys.

Right or lefthanders should keep the ball out of the center of the plate and down. Stay away from him and have your best stuff, and you can get him out. Picciolo hits lefthanders better than righthanders, and is not a selective hitter and very seldom walks. He will swing at a lot of questionable pitches. He is a better than average bunter.

Picciolo is only an average baserunner. His speed to first is only average, and he is not a threat to steal. He is a smart runner who will take an extra base in the right situation, but is not very aggressive.

Milwaukee got him for his glove, and he is able to play all over. A shortstop by trade, that is still his best position. He has above average range and a strong, accurate arm. He will make the clutch play for you in the infield.

OVERALL:

Robinson: "He is a very good shortstop, and can help a team like Milwaukee by spot playing. They don't need his bat, just his glove."

Martin: "He is a good man for this type of club. He can step in and do the job defensively."

ED ROMERO
INF, No. 11
RR, 5'11", 175 lbs.
ML Svc: 2 years
Born: 12-9-57 in
Santurce, PR

HITTING, BASERUNNING, FIELDING:

Romero is a utility player. He is not considered much of a threat at the plate. He did hit well last season, however, filling for the injured Jim Gantner.

Romero normally hits line drives and ground balls. He has very little power, and seldom hits into the alleys. His best pitch to hit is the high fastball. Throw him breaking balls, and keep the fastballs down and away. He does not handle change-ups very well. Romero is a good bunter, and will be used in a sacrifice situation, but will usually be pinch-hit for in a clutch situation late in the game.

He has only average speed and is not a threat to steal. Only average at breaking up a double play, and is classified as a smart baserunner. Not the type that a pitcher will have to watch closely.

Romero's ability as an infielder is the strongest part of his game. He has good range and an accurate arm, although not an especially strong one. He moves to his left and right equally well.

Romero can play third, second or short, although he has been used mainly as a second baseman. Originally a shortstop, adjusted to the pivot at second base very well, and is above average at turning the double play.

OVERALL:

Robinson: "He does not look like he will be able to handle big league pitching. He fits the Milwaukee club well as a utility player."

Martin and Harwell: "Romero can fill in more than adequately on defense at second or short."

HUBERT H. HUMPHREY METRODOME
Minnesota Twins

Seating Capacity: 54,711
Playing Surface: Artificial (Super-Turf)

Dimensions
Left Field Pole: 343 ft.
Left-Center Field: 385 ft.
Center Field: 408 ft.
Right-Center Field: 367 ft.
Right Field Pole: 327 ft.
Height of Outfield Wall: 7 ft.

The Minnesota Vikings of the National Football League wanted an indoor stadium, and they got one--the new Hubert H. Humphrey Metrodome. Unfortunately, baseball's Minnesota Twins have to play 81 home games in that very same stadium. It appears that the stadium was built exclusively for football. Virtually every exit ramp, air vent, dugout and both locker rooms are geared for the ease of the football players.

The HHH Metrodome has an inflated, balloon-type of overhead structure as a roof, and the tremendous amount of air pressure needed to keep the dome inflated leads to an entrance that is difficult enough just to enter. Only one door at a time can be opened because of the wind resistance. In addition, there are thirty-six air vents located high atop the third tier, and those vents actually blow out currents toward all parts of the outfield. Any batter who hits a decent fastball can blast a homer to any part of the Dome.

Unquestionably, the Dome is a pitcher's nightmare, and because the artificial surface is so bouncy, high pops that fall will bounce almost 30 feet in the air, allowing a runner to stretch a simple pop fly single into a double or triple with incredible ease.

Unless the air vents stop pumping air towards the outfield, young hitters like Tom Brunansky and Kent Hrbek will EASILY hit 40 homers a year if they stay with the Twins. Hrbek broke his bat (splintered it, as a matter of fact) and wound up hitting a homer into the top tier, over 420 feet away in deep right field.

Day games are brutal for infielders and outfielders because the ball seems to blend in with the grey coloring of the dome's roof. Ordinary fly balls become an adventure here. A pop fly over the shortstop's head will invariably bounce over the left fielder's head and lead to either an inside-the-park home run or extra bases. Roy Smalley, a former member of the Twins and now with the Yankees, frequently had to retrieve balls near the left-center field fence . . . and Smalley was playing shortstop at the time.

The outfield distances as they actually read are, in reality, quite deceptive. There were only three or four games all year that did not see either the Twins or the oppositon hit a homer. As Smalley said, "It's perfect--it has a tent on top, and that makes it a true circus."

PAUL BORIS
RHP, No. 50
RR, 6'2", 200 lbs.
ML Svc: 1 year
Born: 12-13-55 in Irvington, NJ

PITCHING:

Paul Boris, a righthander who throws with a three-quarter delivery, has always been a relief pitcher. He can be used short or long relief. His 23 appearances last season were all in relief. His ability to pitch accurately and consistently to the batter's weakness is rated average.

He is more a fastball pitcher than anything else, but throws a forkball that he calls his "out" pitch. He uses it as an off-speed pitch.

Boris' fastball averages 87 MPH which is slightly above average. His curveball needs improvement. He does not throw a slider and his straight change-up needs work. When behind in the count, Boris most likely will go to his fastball. He has similar effectiveness against both righthanded hitters and lefthanders.

Boris does not throw a brushback pitch, and is at best, average in pressure situations. Perhaps his greatest strength is that he is young. He is inexperienced but will improve. He could use more velocity. He has had an impressive career in the minor leagues.

FIELDING:

Boris is an above average fielder although his move to first base is rated mediocre. He is above average at fielding bunts and is conscientious about being a defensive player.

OVERALL:

Boris, as with many of his teammates, has youth on his side. He has time to improve.

Robinson: "He is a good prospect with some very good minor league statistics. Look for more work from him in 1983 as a reliever."

Harwell: "He has fair presence on the mound; is average overall."

1982 STATISTICS

W	L	ERA	G	GS	CG	IP	H	R	ER	BB	SO	SV
1	2	3.99	23	0	0	49	46	24	22	19	30	0

CAREER STATISTICS

W	L	ERA	G	GS	CG	IP	H	R	ER	BB	SO	SV
1	2	3.99	23	0	0	49	46	24	22	19	30	0

TOM BRUNANSKY
OF, No. 24
RR, 6'4", 205 lbs.
ML Svc: 1 year plus
Born: 8-20-60 in
West Covina, CA

1982 STATISTICS

AVG	G	AB	R	H	2B	3B	HR	RBI	BB	SO	SB
.272	127	463	77	126	30	1	20	46	71	101	1

CAREER STATISTICS

AVG	G	AB	R	H	2B	3B	HR	RBI	BB	SO	SB
.264	138	496	84	131	30	1	23	52	79	111	2

VS. RHP

VS. LHP

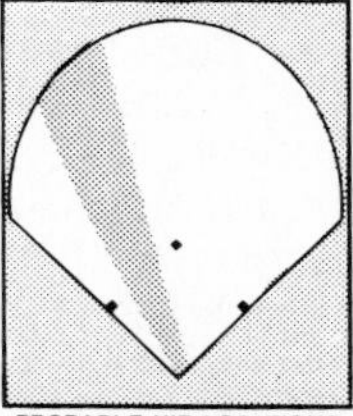
PROBABLE HIT LOCATIONS

HITTING:

Brunansky is among the most highly regarded young players in baseball. He is big and strong and should hit home runs in lage amounts playing in the Metrodome.

His stance is squared to the plate, upright and back in the box. He is a high ball hitter who tends to swing often at the first pitch. He is a much better fastball hitter than breaking ball hitter who should be pitched outside; pitch him fastballs inside, however, and he can lose them in places far, far away from home plate. He hits towering home runs, sometimes as high as they go far.

Pitchers should throw him down and away with everything. Brunansky's primary power is to left-center field. He slams hanging breaking pitches. He also strikes out a lot. Brunansky will hit in critical situations. He had eight game-winning RBIs for a club that won only 60 games. He also is an above average bunter for a big man. He is a streak hitter and is rated average in other hitting categories. He hit well in Fenway Park and the Metrodome seems built for him considering the "carry" of the ball to left field there.

Brunansky has displayed difficulty with sinkers and sliders. With experience, however, his potential appears unlimited. Hitting is the strongest part of his game, but he is loaded with all around potential. All scouts are high on him; once he learns to make more regular contact, he could become one of the game's leading sluggers.

BASERUNNING:

Brunansky has average speed and is regarded as only average on the basepaths, a conservative runner who could stand to improve in this department. He should not be considered a threat to steal--on his three 1982 attempts, he was caught twice. He slides feet first.

FIELDING:

He has a strong throwing arm and throws fairly accurately. His range is also above average. Last season, he was considered one of the top rookies in baseball. He is best at coming in on balls hit to him and is not afraid to attempt the daring catch. His best position might be right field. He should hit third in the lineup.

OVERALL:

Harwell: "Brunansky is a bright, young player on the way up."

Martin: "The Twins did excellently in getting him in a trade with California. Being young, he has enormous potential as a power hitter and strong throwing outfielder. He eventually could be one of the league's best in hitting and production."

BOBBY CASTILLO
RHP, No. 22
RR, 5'10", 170 lbs.
ML Svc: 4 years
Born: 4-18-55 in Los Angeles, CA

PITCHING:

Bobby Castillo was the club's winningest pitcher last season with a 13-11 record, earning a starting spot by taking advantage of an opportunity when others faltered. He started the season in the bullpen, but has proven that he can win as a starter. He has an overhand delivery. His fastball, with a velocity of 86 MPH is his best pitch, and he throws it most of the time. His control is average.

Castillo's curveball is his second most often used pitch. It is only average; breaks down rather than around. He does not throw a slider or a change-up.

Castillo's strikeout pitch is the screwball, which he taught to the Dodgers' Fernando Valenzuela. His screwball may be among the best in the league. It sinks quickly. But when Castillo gets behind in the count, he is most likely to throw the fastball. He seldom throws the brushback pitch. He must keep his stuff low to be effective.

Castillo gets the most of his abilities. His greatest strength is that he knows how to pitch. He is a fighter and a competitor. He is durable and can be a 200-inning pitcher if healthy. He has a solid presence on the mound. A weakness is that his control could be sharper; he has a tendency to fall behind the hitters. Castillo was a nice surprise for the Twins.

FIELDING:

Castillo is considered an above average fielder. He is quick off the mound, and also fields bunts well. He has a quick move to first base.

OVERALL:

Rated an average pitcher overall, Castillo has enough stuff to win because he keeps fighting, and keeps coming at you.

Robinson: "He has made the transition from reliever to starter well. He pitched well for the Twins all year and there is no reason why he won't get better as the Twins do."

Martin: "A hard thrower, he was successful in his first year in the American League, and with a losing team."

1982 STATISTICS

W	L	ERA	G	GS	CG	IP	H	R	ER	BB	SO	SV
13	11	3.66	40	25	6	218	194	96	89	85	124	0

CAREER STATISTICS

W	L	ERA	G	GS	CG	IP	H	R	ER	BB	SO	SV
25	25	3.55	178	27	0	436	380	187	172	202	281	18

JOHN CASTINO
INF, No. 2
RR, 5'11", 169 lbs.
ML Svc: 4 years
Born: 10-23-54 in
Evanston, IL

1982 STATISTICS

AVG	G	AB	R	H	2B	3B	HR	RBI	BB	SO	SB
.241	117	410	48	99	12	6	6	37	36	51	2

CAREER STATISTICS

AVG	G	AB	R	H	2B	3B	HR	RBI	BB	SO	SB
.276	516	1730	205	478	55	30	30	189	110	242	18

VS. RHP

VS. LHP

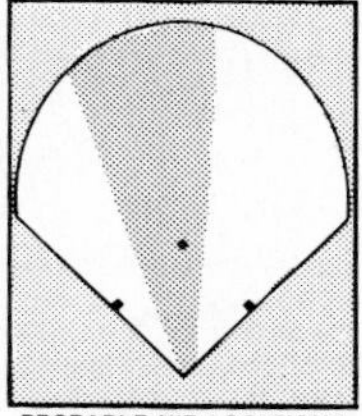
PROBABLE HIT LOCATIONS

HITTING:

An off-season back operation hindered John Castino's 1982 output, but he is expected to be fully recovered for this season. He is a high ball hitter, and should be pitched low and outside by both left and righthanders. A slider by righthanders has proven to be effective against him. He has also shown that he is susceptible to the change-up.

Castino is primarily a line drive, straightaway hitter with occasional power to the alleys. He has the ability to hit in the clutch, although he didn't do so very often in 1982. He has excellent bat control, and with two strikes, can hit well to the opposite field. He is above average at hitting with men in scoring position; the same for the hit-and-run. He also has an above average bunting ability.

Castino is a fierce competitor. He has difficulty with pitchers who mix their pitches well, like lefty Jerry Koosman of the White Sox. He has not hit well in Detroit's Tiger Stadium, but does do well in Chicago's Comiskey Park and in Yankee Stadium. Until his back operation, he was very consistent with his bat.

BASERUNNING:

Castino has above average speed to first, and can be counted on to run hard and aggressively into second to break up the double play. He is average as a basestealer, and doesn't try to steal too many bases. He is a smart runner, and will take what is allowed.

FIELDING:

He was moved to second base last season after an outstanding season as a third baseman. He has an average arm, but is sometimes erratic. He has above average range at second. When he was playing third base, he demonstrated exceptional reflexes and hands. He will make the sensational type of play, and adapted well to his new role at second. Despite his back injury, he can turn the double play very well, and is not afraid of contact with sliding baserunners. He will make the clutch defensive play.

OVERALL:

Robinson: "John is a player who can play better than he has been. It might take a year for him to recover from his back operation, but he has a history of hitting when it counts."

Harwell: "His leadership provides the Twins not only with quality direction, but with an admirable player who has overcome his injuries."

Martin: "I think that Castino converted nicely from third to second base last season. He seems to have come back quickly from surgery, and can still sting the ball at the plate."

RON DAVIS
RHP, No. 39
RR, 6'4", 205 lbs.
ML Svc: 3 years
Born: 8-6-55 in Houston, TX

PITCHING:

Davis is regarded among the best relievers in baseball. Of Minnesota's 32 saves, he had 22. He is most effective in short relief. After pitching in Yankee Stadium, he was not enamored at having to pitch in the Metrodome with its relatively close right field fence, artificial turf, and its tendency for hit balls to carry well.

Davis' delivery is below three-quarters, almost sidearm. He knows hitters' weaknesses and goes after them with above average stuff. He is a power pitcher who throws a 90+ MPH fastball, the best on the club. His best and most often used pitch is his fastball, which from the side makes him extremely effective against righthanded hitters. It is the pitch that has earned him considerable major league success.

Davis doesn't throw many breaking balls, but throws the slider more than his curveball, which he only seldom uses. He will come at the hitter with a fastball-slider combination 99% of the time. Occasionally, he'll mix in a change-up, but a change-up from him is doing the batter a favor.

Davis throws two types of fastballs--one that sinks quickly and away from lefthanders, and another one that he throws with his fingers across the seams, making the ball ride up and in to righthanders. He has a two-to-one strikeout-to-walk ratio. He can also get the big strikeout when it is needed. He pitches best in parks with natural grass, allowing his sinker to work and his infielders more time to make plays.

He will occasionally brush a hitter back. He is very strong in critical situations and loves to challenge hitters. He had an adjustment to make in coming to Minnesota and becoming the primary short relief man. He improved immensely after a terrible start, and is expected to have an outstanding season this year.

FIELDING:

Davis has a quick move to first base. He has a pitcher's savvy, and seems to be thinking what a baserunner thinks in tight situations. He is alert and absolutely cannot be taken for granted by runners. He is an above average fielder who fields bunts well. Defensively, Davis is usually totally in the game; has good ideas about positioning his fielders for different hitters. His concentration is above average.

OVERALL:

Robinson: "Davis will be better this season. In New York, he got the 'holds,' and Goose Gossage got the 'saves.' It is a big difference when you become THE guy in short relief. It took most of last year for him to get it together."

Harwell: "He is a good reliever, but I don't think as effective without the backing of Goose Gossage."

Martin: "He is the kind of bullpen stud every team needs. A strikeout pitcher who can also get the ground ball. He is intimidating, but sometimes erratic."

1982 STATISTICS

W	L	ERA	G	GS	CG	IP	H	R	ER	BB	SO	SV
3	9	4.42	63	0	0	106	106	53	52	47	89	22

CAREER STATISTICS

W	L	ERA	G	GS	CG	IP	H	R	ER	BB	SO	SV
30	19	3.32	207	0	0	397	361	158	147	135	280	44

DAVE ENGLE
OF, No. 20
RR, 6'3", 210
ML Svc: 2 years
Born: 11-30-56 in
San Diego, CA

1982 STATISTICS

AVG	G	AB	R	H	2B	3B	HR	RBI	BB	SO	SB
.226	58	186	20	42	7	2	4	16	10	22	0

CAREER STATISTICS

AVG	G	AB	R	H	2B	3B	HR	RBI	BB	SO	SB
.244	140	434	49	106	21	6	9	48	23	59	0

VS. RHP

VS. LHP

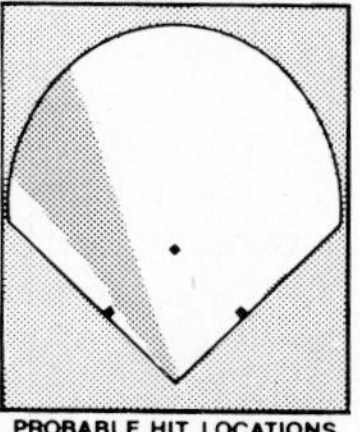
PROBABLE HIT LOCATIONS

HITTING:

The Twins are still waiting for Engle to produce to the potential they feel he has. Engle hits out of a slightly open stance, stands upright and in the center of the batter's box. He is a high ball hitter and hits the fastball better than other pitches. Successful pitchers have pitched him away because he has a tendency to try too hard to pull the ball. He hits the belt-high inside fastball well but does not hit change-ups, breaking balls or sinkers. Engle is primarily a line drive hitter, but possesses some home run power. He hits lefthanders best and can drive the ball to the power alleys.

He rates average in ability to hit in the clutch, to hit behind the runner, to hit with men in scoring position, in drawing walks, in being able to hit-and-run and in bunting ability. He is a streak hitter who does not walk much.

Engle should have begun to show improvement with the bat last season, but instead was sent to the minor leagues after a disappointing start. He returned to the big leagues, hit well for a short period but finished mediocre, as was his overall season. He is rated merely an average hitter. His RBI production was disappointing.

BASERUNNING:

Engle is considered conservative on the basepaths and only average in other baserunning departments. He seldom steals; baserunning is the weakest part of his game. He slides feet first.

FIELDING:

Engle left immediately for the Florida Instructional League following the major league season in an effort to learn the catching position, where the Twins have realized they need help after trading Butch Wynegar to New York early last year. As an outfielder, Engle had difficulty seeing the ball in the Metrodome and was a disappointment in right field although he was credited with only one error. He had difficulty judging fly balls in the Metrodome. He is best at catching balls he has to come in on. Overall, though, he is rated only average.

OVERALL:

Robinson: "He should be a better player this year."

Harwell: "He is improving and could be solid in a year or so."

Martin: "He is still lacking in major league experience; would like to see him hit with more power."

LENNY FAEDO
INF, No. 8
RR, 6'0", 170 lbs.
ML Svc: 1 year plus
Born: 5-13-60 in Tampa, FL

1982 STATISTICS

AVG	G	AB	R	H	2B	3B	HR	RBI	BB	SO	SB
.243	90	255	16	62	8	0	3	22	16	22	1

CAREER STATISTICS

AVG	G	AB	R	H	2B	3B	HR	RBI	BB	SO	SB
.237	107	304	20	72	9	1	3	28	17	27	1

VS. RHP   VS. LHP

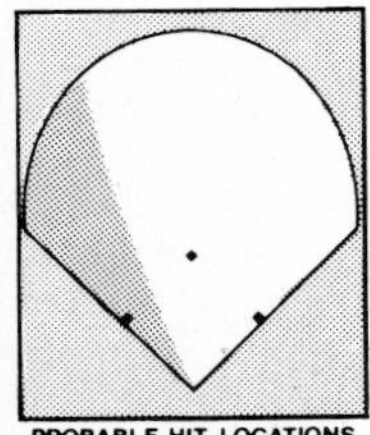

PROBABLE HIT LOCATIONS

HITTING:

Clearly a high ball hitter, Len Faedo bats out of a closed, semi-crouched stance and stands in the center of the box. He bats consistently near the end of the batting order. He seldom hits balls away from him. He is a fastball hitter who surprised some observers late in the season with several key home runs. He only shows this kind of hitting power infrequently, and shouldn't hurt the opponents if pitched properly. He can occasionally drive the ball to the power alleys. Faedo is an opportunist and will take advantage of a pitcher's mistakes, but he will have difficulty hitting the true quality pitchers.

He is a pull hitter who tries too hard to pull, especially for someone who is a singles hitter. He will be more consistent when he realizes that he is only a singles hitter--will always be one--and stop trying for the fences. He can put the bat on the ball fairly well, and will not strike out much.

Pitchers should throw him breaking stuff low and away. Faedo is more effective against lefthanded pitching. He is mostly a ground ball hitter, and categorized as average at that. He has great difficulty against hard, slider-throwing righthanders like Detroit's Dan Petry and Jack Morris. Overall, he is a below average hitter.

BASERUNNING:

Faedo's speed to first is average to above average, but in other areas of running he is strictly average. He is considered a smart runner, but does not present a basestealing threat for pitchers. His lack of speed has prohibited him from taking the extra base on hits into the alleys. He did not hit a triple all season last year.

FIELDING:

Faedo is an exceptional, slick fielder. Obviously, fielding is the reason that he is in the big leagues. He has a strong, accurate throwing arm and has above average range. He is adept at fielding balls to his left as well as to his right. Faedo also possesses quick hands and reflexes. His only apparent fielding flaw is that he occasionally misplays balls that otherwise seem routine.

OVERALL:

Robinson: "If he could hit better, he would certainly play more. He gets overpowered by pitches more than anything else, but is a good shortstop and young enough to improve."

TERRY FELTON
RHP, No. 37
RR, 6'2", 185 lbs.
ML Svc: 1 year plus
Born: 10-29-57 in
Texarkana, TX

PITCHING:

Terry Felton has as strong an arm as any on the young Twins staff. But he did not win in 13 decisions last season and, combined with an 0-3 record in 1981, the youngster owns the record for the most consecutive losses at the start of a major league career. He is befuddled by this unwanted record.

Felton started six games last season, but this righthander is thought of best as a long relief-spotstarter type. He has pitched in just about every situation. He throws overhand, but needs improvement in his consistency with his control. When he releases his fastball the right way, it explodes in on righthanders, and away from lefties. Felton's problem is that he has had difficulty finding consistency with the release of the ball. He has demonstrated that he can have awesome stuff at times. In a spring training game last year against the Red Sox, he had slugger Jim Rice back on his heels with three straight sliders, proving to scouts that the potential is there. The problem now is locating it.

Primarily a fastball pitcher, Felton uses his curveball as his second pitch, and a slider as his third. He also throws a change-up, but aside from the fastball, his pitches require improvement. He has shown, however, that these pitches at times can be better than average; his problem seems to be the ability to throw them regularly.

He needs improvement pitching in pressure situations. Felton is a strikeout pitcher who needs better control. When he gets the ball over the plate, he gets the hitters out. His arm is good and strong.

FIELDING:

Felton has a quick move to first--he works hard at fielding his position. He is, however, average at fielding bunts, and in his overall effectiveness as a fielder.

OVERALL:

The Twins are far from giving up on Felton despite his puzzling inability to win. It is only a matter of time before he wins, and if he becomes more consistent with his pitches, he could begin a winning streak instead of continuing a losing one.

Robinson: "What can you say about a guy who has lost 16 in a row? He has to get better if his control improves. He has outstanding stuff, and there is just no way that he is as bad as his 1982 record indicates. Don't give up on him yet."

Martin: "A good fastball and breaking pitch---but no wins. Thankfully, youth is on his side."

1982 STATISTICS

W	L	ERA	G	GS	CG	IP	H	R	ER	BB	SO	SV
0	13	4.99	48	6	0	117	99	71	65	76	92	3

CAREER STATISTICS

W	L	ERA	G	GS	CG	IP	H	R	ER	BB	SO	SV
0	16	5.54	55	10	0	138	123	95	85	87	108	3

GARY GAETTI
INF, No. 12
RR, 6'0", 180 lbs.
ML Svc: 1 year plus
Born: 8-19-58 in
Maitland, FL

1982 STATISTICS

AVG	G	AB	R	H	2B	3B	HR	RBI	BB	SO	SB
.230	145	508	59	117	25	4	25	84	37	107	0

CAREER STATISTICS

AVG	G	AB	R	H	2B	3B	HR	RBI	BB	SO	SB
.289	154	534	63	122	25	4	27	87	37	113	0

VS. RHP

VS. LHP

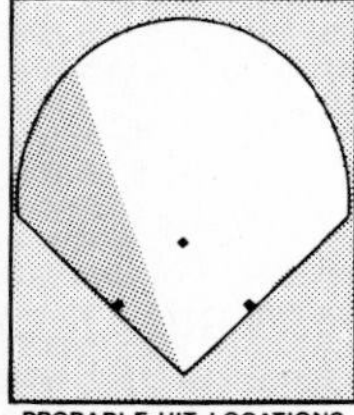
PROBABLE HIT LOCATIONS

HITTING:

Of Gary Gaetti's 117 hits last season, nearly half were for extra bases. He tied for the club lead in game-winning RBIs with 10, but also led in strikeouts with 107. Gaetti is squared to the plate, with an upright stance, and stands low in the box. He is a pull hitter with exceptional power against righthanders who throw him high fastballs. The same holds true for lefties who pitch him fastballs from the belt on up.

Righthanders should pitch Gaetti inside, lefthanders away. He has been a streak hitter. He is a line drive, home run type of hitter. He hits against both right and lefthanders well, and will take either one's mistakes a long way.

Gaetti has not proven to be a good clutch hitter, yet, and is only average at hitting behind the runner. He is also average with men in scoring position, and in drawing walks. Further, he is an average bunter and hit-and-run man.

Pitchers should pitch him breaking balls and off-speed stuff. He is not a good change-up hitter. He will strike out a lot because he is a free swinger, but he will also hit a lot of home runs. He gears himself up to hit the fastball, and has not hit for average. Power clearly is his strength. The Metrodome, where the ball seems to carry well, is particularly suited for him, as is Fenway Park in Boston.

BASERUNNING:

In general, Gaetti is an average baserunner. Pitchers should be cautious with him however, because he will steal if they forget that he is there. He is smart and aggressive. He is a feet first slider, and slides hard. Baserunning, because of his lack of speed, not desire, is an average part of his game.

FIELDING:

Gaetti's throwing accuracy has to improve. He has an average to strong arm, and average range. His movement at third base is mediocre, the same as his ability to turn the double play, to field bunts, and to make the clutch defensive plays. His strongest ability as a fielder is his determination not to let balls get by him. He will take line shots off the chest if he has to. He is a tough fielder, but overall, average.

OVERALL:

Robinson: "He is a strong kid who should be around for a while. Gary seems to be a very anxious hitter who has to learn to be a little more selective in RBI situations. He is best at third base, and hitting sixth or seventh."

Martin: "Might be most effective batting fifth. He has excellent power at the plate, but needs to cut down on his strikeouts. He will knock in a lot of runs, and is a fair fielder."

MICKEY HATCHER
OF, No. 9
RR, 6'2", 195 lbs.
ML Svc: 3 years
Born: 3-15-55 in Newbury, OH

1982 STATISTICS

AVG	G	AB	R	H	2B	3B	HR	RBI	BB	SO	SB
.249	84	277	23	69	13	2	3	26	8	27	0

CAREER STATISTICS

AVG	G	AB	R	H	2B	3B	HR	RBI	BB	SO	SB
.252	273	831	72	209	42	5	8	73	32	80	4

VS. RHP

VS. LHP

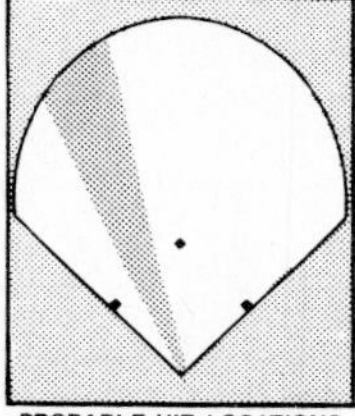
PROBABLE HIT LOCATIONS

HITTING:

Hatcher, a promising prospect when the Twins acquired him two seasons ago, has not played to that promise. He is a high ball hitter against both left and righthanded pitching. Against righthanders, he should be pitched inside on the fists, and against southpaws, on the outside. He tends to hit the ball to left field against righties and is more of a straightaway hitter against lefties.

Hatcher is a line drive and ground ball hitter, and he has displayed occasional power to the alleys, but not the kind that might be expected from someone his size. He rates average in the clutch, and in hitting behind the runner. He needs to improve his ability with men in scoring position.

Hatcher needs to become more selective with pitches. He is an average hit-and-run batter, and an average bunter. He is weak at hitting breaking balls, and does not handle the change-up well. He has difficulty with good curveballs, sinkers and sliders. Hitting is supposed to be the best part of his game, but he is actually a mediocre hitter, and not expected to improve much.

BASERUNNING:

Running the bases is the weakest part of Hatcher's game. He was caught stealing both times that he tried it last season. Though he has above average speed to first, he is only average in his ability to break up a double play. Needs improvement in his basestealing techniques, and should choose better times to run. He uses a feet first slide, but will go head first when necessary.

FIELDING:

Hatcher's throwing arm and accuracy are rated above average. His range is average, and he is best at fielding balls right in front of him. He is an adequate outfielder, but with the Twins, he has little opportunity for experience there. He made only one error last season despite playing extremely aggressively in the outfield. He is not afraid of walls or fences, and has suffered injuries as a result. Mostly, however, his average fielding keeps him as a designated hitter.

OVERALL:

Robinson: "I think he is playing about as good as he can. He is an average player with no position to speak of. He might be best as a righthanded DH batting around second in the lineup."

Martin: "His aggressiveness is eye-catching, but can't always be confused with pure talent. He is a hustler and a bit of a 'flake,' although an engaging one."

BRAD HAVENS
LHP, No. 27
LL, 6'1", 180 lbs.
ML Svc: 1 year plus
Born: 11-17-59 in
Highland Park, MI

PITCHING:

Brad Havens is a starting pitcher and will be among the lefthanders the Twins are counting on to start again this season. Of his 33 games in 1982, he started in 32 of them. He is a 200-inning pitcher and led the club in strikeouts.

He has a three-quarter delivery, and the potential to be an outstanding major leaguer. He is young, and throws fairly hard. He combines his fastball, termed "sneaky," with an above average curveball and change-up. Despite his young age and relative inexperience, his off-speed stuff is impressive.

Havens' fastball is above average, and has been timed at 86 MPH. It is his primary pitch. He uses his curveball quite a bit of the time, second only to his fastball. He throws his curveball at at different speeds, thus allowing him another off-speed pitch. Havens does not throw a slider, and his curve breaks down more than sideways. His primary change-up is a straight one. When behind in the count, he is most likely to throw his fastball. He is equally effective against left and righthanders. Seldom uses the brushback, and is of average abilities in pressure situations.

Counted among Havens' strengths is that he is unnerving; he does not get excited or lose his composure. He is confident in his ability to win and will win more and more often as the Twins improve and get him more runs.

Minnesota was baseball's worst team in 1982, and of their 60 total wins, Havens himself won 10. His victories ranked second highest on the team. The Metrodome is an extremely difficult park to pitch in, especially to lefthanders. Havens would do well in New York's Yankee Stadium and Detroit's Tiger Stadium facing a lefthanded lineup.

FIELDING:

Overall, Haven rates as an above average fielder who fields bunts well. He holds runners on base well, and has an average move to first. His running speed is considered average. He has a solid presence on the mound, and is very alert.

OVERALL:

He may be in the big leagues for a long time if he can continue to develop. He was rushed into the majors by a club that needed him in a hurry. He is adapting very well.

Robinson: "Havens is one of a handful of young pitchers who, if given the chance to develop, can win. He has the poise, stuff, and pitches to be a very good pitcher. He knows what he has to do to get hitters out."

Martin: "He is above average; has excellent strikeout potential. If he stays up, he could be a key and potentially good pitcher."

1982 STATISTICS

W	L	ERA	G	GS	CG	IP	H	R	ER	BB	SO	SV
10	14	4.31	33	32	4	208	201	112	100	80	129	0

CAREER STATISTICS

W	L	ERA	G	GS	CG	IP	H	R	ER	BB	SO	SV
13	20	4.12	47	44	5	286	277	145	131	104	172	0

HITTING:

A .301 hitter in his rookie year, Kent Hrbek posted extremely impressive statistics. His idol is Ted Williams, and teammates have nicknamed him "Ted."

He is big, strong, and lefthanded. Hrbek uses an open stance against lefthanded pitchers (at the advice of Rod Carew), because it enables him to see the ball better. Against right-handers, he squares more to the plate. He hits out of a semi-crouched stance back in the box. He can and will bunt if the infield allows. He has some difficulty hitting lefthanded curveballs.

Hrbek is very strong, and swings extremely hard. He hits both high and low pitches. If throwing him breaking balls, they MUST be low. Pitchers should jam him inside on the fists. He uses the entire ball park to hit, and against righthanders, he resembles former Twins' All Star, Tony Oliva. He has superb long ball power, but considers himself a line drive hitter. For a rookie, he has demonstrated adeptness at hitting behind the runner, in the clutch, and with men in scoring position. He will hit just about anything in the middle of the plate, but he does not, however, handle off-speed pitches well.

Hrbek tailed off dramatically in home runs during the second half of last season, probably due to a nagging hand injury. He does well in Tiger Stadium and Yankee Stadium. Overall, he is an above average to excellent hitter, and had a consistent, solid start to what might be a long and successful major league career.

BASERUNNING:

He has above average speed to first, and will go hard into second to break up the double play. Hrbek is considered a smart but conservative runner. He slides feet first, and overall, his baserunning is probably the weakest part of his game.

KENT HRBEK
INF, No. 14
LR, 6'4", 215 lbs.
ML Svc: 1 year plus
Born: 5-21-60 in
Minneapolis, MN

1982 STATISTICS

AVG	G	AB	R	H	2B	3B	HR	RBI	BB	SO	SB
.301	140	532	82	160	21	4	23	92	54	80	3

CAREER STATISTICS

AVG	G	AB	R	H	2B	3B	HR	RBI	BB	SO	SB
.294	164	599	87	176	26	4	24	99	59	89	3

VS. RHP

VS. LHP

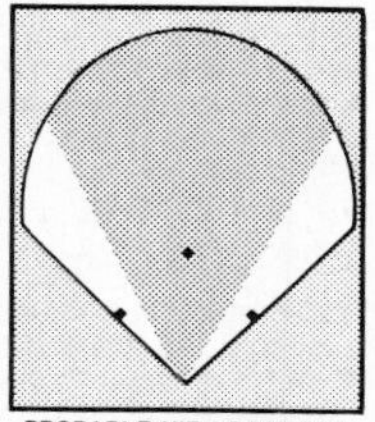
PROBABLE HIT LOCATIONS

FIELDING:

Hrbek has a strong, accurate arm and above average range. He is among the American League's best in stretching for throws in the dirt at first base. He is a talented fielder who makes all the necessary plays well, and is rated with the league's best fielders.

OVERALL:

Robinson: "Kent is an outstanding young hitter who combines power and consistency at bat. He handled all pitchers remarkably well last season."

Martin: "Outstanding rookie year both offensively and defensively. He received my vote for American League Rookie of the Year. He has power, poise, and presence."

Harwell: "He just has great potential, and a chance to be an outstanding major leaguer."

DARRELL JACKSON
LHP, No. 31
SL, 5'10", 151 lbs.
ML Svc: 4 years
Born: 4-3-56 in Los Angeles, CA

PITCHING:

Darrell Jackson is a thin, rangy lefthander who has been a starter. With the Twins, he was moved back to the bullpen due to his shoulder and arm problems. He has been effective as a long reliever, but has also pitched some outstanding games as a starter. Everything depends, of course, on his physical and mental condition.

At times, Jackson has thrown the ball nearly 90 MPH. Last year, during his arm difficulties (he spent much of his time on the disabled list), his fastball was clocked at 86 MPH. He is an overhand pitcher with a live arm when it's healthy. His problem has been inconsistency, which has puzzled himself as much as the Twins. He can be overpowering to lefthanded hitters, especially when he gets his fastball inside on the fists. Against right-handers, he needs to pitch low but is quick enough to come up if the hitter has been set up properly. Jackson has displayed a fine curveball, but that too has been inconsistent.

He stopped throwing the slider due to elbow tenderness. His straight change-up needs improvement and he seldom throws it. When behind in the count, he will most likely throw his fastball. He will not hesitate to throw the brushback pitch.

Jackson has considerable success in Yankee Stadium but struggles in Boston's Fenway Park. If his arm is sound, his moving fastball is alive, which is probably his greatest strength. A weakness is that he needs to have better command of his pitches.

FIELDING:

Jackson's move to first is rated average, but he has a tendency to become lackadaisical with runners on base. When he is concentrating, he keeps runners close. He is an average fielder.

OVERALL:

He is a question mark, trying to return to the major leagues after arm problems. If he heals, he can pitch there again.

Martin: "At one time, he had great potential and a world of stuff. But he has had personal problems; he did not fulfill expectations last year."

Harwell: "Just an average pitcher."

1982 STATISTICS

W	L	ERA	G	GS	CG	IP	H	R	ER	BB	SO	SV
0	5	6.25	13	7	0	44	51	33	31	24	16	0

CAREER STATISTICS

W	L	ERA	G	GS	CG	IP	H	R	ER	BB	SO	SV
20	27	4.39	102	60	3	410	425	219	200	186	229	1

HITTING:

Randy Johnson tries to pull most pitches, probably because of the near proximity of the Metrodome's right field fence. He stands upright at the plate, hits from a closed stance in the back of the box. Unlike many lefthanded hitters, Johnson is clearly a high ball hitter. He hits the inside fastball well. Pitchers should throw him away, using off-speed stuff. He will sometimes lunge for off-speed stuff in the dirt.

Basically, Johnson is a line drive hitter with sporadic power. He is most effective against righthanded pitchers, probably because they are virtually all he sees as a platoon player. He does not hit curveballs, off-speed or sinkers well, especially from lefthanders.

In other hitting regards, Johnson is rated average. Overall, his rating is also average. Because he does possess some power, he is regarded as a good prospect with a chance to improve. He is also a streak hitter who had observers excited when he got off to a quick and surprising start in 1982, but cooled just as quickly and finished the season disappointingly.

BASERUNNING:

Johnson is a mediocre baserunner who rarely steals. Pitchers should not be particularly concerned with him on first base. Baserunning is the weakest part of his game; he did not steal a single base all last season.

FIELDING:

Johnson rates as an average to poor fielder. Arm strength and throwing accuracy are below average, and it is clear that it is his hitting

RANDY JOHNSON
OF, No. 48
LL, 6'2", 189 lbs.
ML Svc: 1 year plus
Born: 8-15-58 in Miami, FL

1982 STATISTICS

AVG	G	AB	R	H	2B	3B	HR	RBI	BB	SO	SB
.247	89	235	26	58	10	0	10	32	30	46	0

CAREER STATISTICS

AVG	G	AB	R	H	2B	3B	HR	RBI	BB	SO	SB
.243	101	255	26	62	10	0	10	35	32	50	0

VS. RHP

VS. LHP

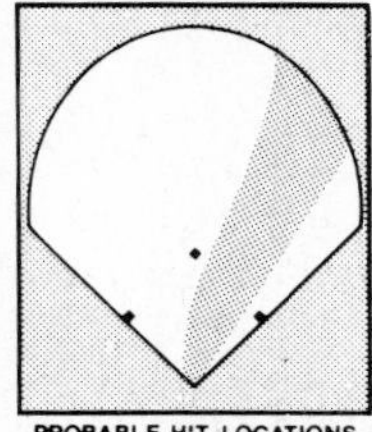
PROBABLE HIT LOCATIONS

ability that will have to keep him in the big leagues. He is no more than a platoon player, and is unimpressive.

OVERALL:

Robinson: "He will have to hit in order to help the Twins. He has some power, but is doubtful as an everyday player."

Martin: "He has not yet reached his potential and will hit more consistently with experience. He is primarily an offensive player."

HITTING:

Tim Laudner hits from an extremely open upright stance and stands low in the batter's box. He is a high ball hitter who should be pitched down and away from both left and righthanders. He tries to pull everything, and if you get the fastball up and in, he will hit it a long way. He has considerable power if he gets his pitch. He is a streak hitter, and has been most successful against lefthanded pitching.

Laudner is average at hitting in the clutch and needs improvement at hitting behind the runner. Ditto for hitting with men in scoring position, in the hit-and-run, and in bunting. He is perhaps over-matched at this time in his career. Pitchers should throw him breaking balls down and away. Also pitch him change-ups, but he will hurt you with mistakes. He hits well in Boston's Fenway Park. The pitch that he hits the best is the high fastball on the inner half of the plate. He has trouble with breaking pitches. He shows good power, and has the potential to become a good hitter.

BASERUNNING:

Laudner tried to steal twice last season and was caught both times. He needs improvement as a runner, and has poor speed to first. He does not run well at all, and has difficulty breaking up the double play. He is a conservative feet first slider, and overall, baserunning is the weakest part of his game.

FIELDING:

Laudner needs improvement at learning the opposing batters' strengths and weaknesses, although he usually calls his own pitches during the game. His arm strength, release point and accuracy are all average. He is average at blocking balls, average in fielding bunts, and again at holding runners close to the bases. He doesn't handle pitchers as well as he should, and rates mediocre to poor overall as a catcher. He may not be ready to catch in the big leagues now, but appears ready and willing to improve.

TIM LAUDNER
C, No. 15
RR, 6'3", 212 lbs.
ML Svc: 1 year plus
Born: 6-7-58 in
Mason City, IA

1982 STATISTICS

AVG	G	AB	R	H	2B	3B	HR	RBI	BB	SO	SB
.255	93	306	37	78	19	1	7	33	34	74	0

CAREER STATISTICS

AVG	G	AB	R	H	2B	3B	HR	RBI	BB	SO	SB
.247	107	349	41	85	21	1	9	38	37	91	0

VS. RHP

VS. LHP

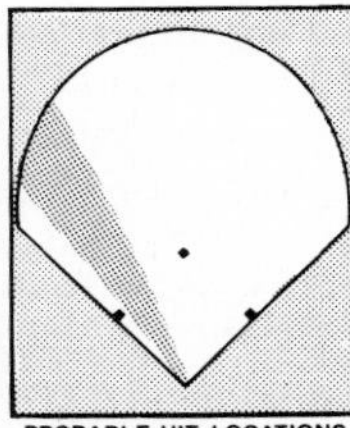
PROBABLE HIT LOCATIONS

OVERALL:

Robinson: "He is getting a chance to play at an early age and should continue to get more experience. I think that he will help the Twins in a couple of years. He has a lot of home run potential."

Martin: "He deserves a shot at being the No. 1 catcher--look for him to keep on improving. In the Metrodome, he has the chance to develop into a fine power hitter."

JEFF LITTLE
LHP, No. 45
RL, 6'6", 220 lbs.
ML Svc: 1 year plus
Born: 12-25-54 in Fremont, OH

PITCHING:

Jeff Little seems to have enough stuff to pitch in long relief. He did well in that role last season. He is a lefthanded pitcher with a three-quarter delivery, sometimes less. His weakness is control; he led the club in wild pitches last season. However, his wildness in some cases may be beneficial. He is a good strikeout pitcher with a live fastball that travels very well at 86 MPH.

He possesses a fine curveball, which he throws second most often. It is an effective pitch. His curve does not break down much, and may be more a combination of a curve and slider, also known as a "slurve." When it is thrown low and in-and-out, it is effective. Little does not throw a lot of off-speed stuff. His change-up is straight, but is not good and needs work. His primary pitch is the fastball, and he is most likely to throw it when behind in the count. He seems tougher on righthanded hitters because he gives them a lot of motion.

Hitters do not have to be especially concerned about Little brushing them back. He seems to be most concerned with throwing the ball over the plate. He appears at best, average in pressure situations. At this stage of his career, his control is what causes him the most trouble. He could also use more velocity.

FIELDING:

Little has a very good move to first base, but is slow in his delivery to home plate because of a high leg kick. He is average at fielding bunts, and overall, fields his position with average abilities.

OVERALL:

An average pitcher who lacks consistency.

Robinson: "He is a hard thrower who needs to get the ball over the plate more. I think his best bet to help the Twins will be in relief as a short or long man."

Martin: "An average pitcher with fair presence on the mound. He is more of the control type of pitcher."

1982 STATISTICS

W	L	ERA	G	GS	CG	IP	H	R	ER	BB	SO	SV
2	0	4.21	33	0	0	36	33	20	17	27	26	0

CAREER STATISTICS

W	L	ERA	G	GS	CG	IP	H	R	ER	BB	SO	SV
3	1	4.09	40	2	0	55	51	29	25	36	43	0

BOBBY MITCHELL
OF, No. 10
LL, 5'10", 170 lbs.
ML Svc: 1 year plus
Born: 4-7-55- in
Salt Lake City, UT

1982 STATISTICS

AVG	G	AB	R	H	2B	3B	HR	RBI	BB	SO	SB
.249	124	454	48	113	11	6	2	28	54	53	8

CAREER STATISTICS

AVG	G	AB	R	H	2B	3B	HR	RBI	BB	SO	SB
.247	143	465	49	115	11	6	2	28	56	57	8

VS. RHP

VS. LHP

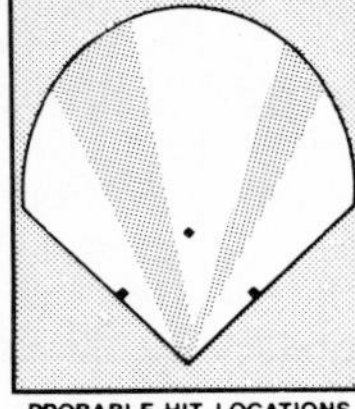
PROBABLE HIT LOCATIONS

HITTING:

Like many lefthanded swingers, Bob Mitchell is a low ball hitter. Pitchers should keep the fastball away and up on him and throw a lot of breaking balls. Mitchell hits with a closed, upright stance, and stands in the center of the box.

Against righthanders, he will hit slightly to the right of second base; against lefties, he hits slightly to the left of second. He is a line drive hitter without much power, although he is capable of hitting the ball out of the park. His tendency is to drive the ball to the alleys, and he will hit doubles and triples. He has shown that he hits better against righthanded pitching. Overall, he is rated average in the clutch. He almost has to be a leadoff hitter.

Except for his bunting, which is above average, Mitchell rates average in other hitting departments. He has yet to prove that he can hit everyday big league pitching. He needs improvement hitting at critical moments and behind the runner.

Mitchell's best power is with low fastballs thrown inside. He has not demonstrated that he can hit the change-up consistently; the same with other off-speed and breaking stuff. He can be classified as a streak hitter. Overall, Mitchell is just a very average hitter, despite his .300 average in the minors.

BASERUNNING:

Mitchell's 17 attempts (he was caught nine times) led the club in stolen base tries. He has excellent speed to first, is above average at breaking up the double play, and at stealing. He is a smart runner who will go if allowed to. He is an aggressive runner, although he was slowed somewhat due to a leg injury last season.

FIELDING:

The Twins consider Mitchell among the best center fielders in their 22 year history. His arm is above average in strength, and his throwing accuracy rates equally as high. He throws well to home plate, and has exceptional range. He can get the ball anywhere in the park, and committed only one error last season. Fielding is easily the strongest part of his game.

OVERALL:

Robinson: "He has been looked upon for most of his career as a defensive specialist and has been trying to shake that tag. He is the best center fielder that the Twins have, and has a good shot at being an everyday player."

Harwell: "I think that Mitchell would be most effective hitting first or second in the lineup, but he is a platoon type of player whose defense can't be ignored."

Martin: "Basestealing and defense are his greatest attributes, and he could be an effective leadoff man."

JACK O'CONNOR
LHP, No. 33
LL, 6'3", 203 lbs.
ML Svc: 2 years
Born: 6-2-58 in
Yucca Valley, CA

PITCHING:

O'Connor was one of the few pitchers to shut out the American League champion Brewers last season. He is a tall, young, rangy lefthanded starter who has demonstrated that he can win in the big leagues. He is expected to improve as well.

Jack O'Connor throws overhand and has a fastball that averages 87 MPH. He is primarily a fastball pitcher who became a much more determined and gutsy pitcher last season. The fastball is his best pitch, followed by an average slider and an average curveball. He needs to throw more change-ups when behind in the count; too often he goes for the fastball. His control can be erratic, but last year it was, in general, adequate and did not hurt him too often. He has a similar effectiveness against left and righthanded hitters.

In the past, O'Connor has seldom thrown the brushback pitch, but hitters can expect to see more of it this season. He is currently rated average in pressure situations, but in the latter part of the 1982 season, he began to challenge the hitters more often and found it successful. He has the stuff to do it.

He is not always consistent, and needs help after five or six innings. But when he is "on," will finish games. His six complete games tied for the staff lead last year. He has a strong arm that needs more game experience. When he is good, he has solid command of all his pitches. O'Connor is thought to be among Minnesota's starting five in 1983, and could have a standout season. He has a good moving fastball, and if he improves his control and poise, could really be impressive.

FIELDING:

O'Connor has a fair move to first base and rates average as a fielder overall. He fields bunts average and hustles to field his position. He is a good athlete.

OVERALL:

O'Connor seemed to become a tougher competitor late last season, and with better control, could be among the league's best lefties. Overall, he is rated above average.

Robinson: "It is best for him to start, which is what he has been doing since he returned from the minors. He is a hard thrower, and gained some valuable major league experience last season. I look forward to him doing better this season."

1982 STATISTICS

W	L	ERA	G	GS	CG	IP	H	R	ER	BB	SO	SV
8	9	4.29	23	19	6	126	122	63	60	57	56	0

CAREER STATISTICS

W	L	ERA	G	GS	CG	IP	H	R	ER	BB	SO	SV
11	11	4.64	51	19	6	161	168	90	83	87	72	0

PETE REDFERN
RHP, No. 17
RR, 6'2", 190 lbs.
ML Svc: 5 years
Born: 8-25-54 in
Glendale, CA

PITCHING:

Pete Redfern was a disappointment in 1982. His overall stuff is above average and he should have performed better than he did. He was counted on to be the club's top starter just one season ago, but suddenly there was an abundance of trade talk concerning him.

He is a righthanded starter who shared bullpen duty after becoming ineffective last season. He throws between overhand and three-quarter, and is thought to have overall good control, although he did average more than six walks per nine innings in 1982. Redfern can be outstanding or awful, and his inconsistency has bothered club officials, as well as himself. He has been bothered by arm problems.

He is a power pitcher whose fastball is 88 MPH, and above average. He has an over-the-top curveball that breaks sharply down when he is throwing it well; when he is not, however, it flattens out and is ineffective. Redfern's second pitch is the curveball. He also throws a slider, which is rated above average. With his stuff, it is an enigma as to why he doesn't win consistently. He allowed considerably more hits than innings pitched last seaon.

Redfern throws an average straight change-up. When he is pitching well, he will throw any of four pitches when behind in the count. When he is not pitching well, he tends to go to his fastball, which will move up and inside to righthanded hitters. His fastball to a lefthander moves well when thrown from the waist down. He has better success against righthanders than lefthanders.

Redfern seldom throws a brushback pitch, although his erratic control and good velocity prevent batters from crowding the plate. He needs improvement at pitching in pressure situations; probably needs more concentration. Perhaps Redfern's greatest weakness is that he is "not a finisher." Another criticism is that he has not learned "how" to pitch.

FIELDING:

Redfern rates highly in fielding categories; he has a quick move to first base, is quick off the mound, and fields bunts well. Overall, he is above average in fielding his position.

OVERALL:

The Twins are tiring of waiting for Redfern to produce to his potential. This will be a key season in his career.

Robinson: "He has good presence on the mound, but 1982 was not a good year for him. He has not pitched well, but also has been bothered by tendinitis. Considering his overall stuff, this guy should win. He was expected to be the mainstay of the staff."

Harwell: "He has a good body and arm and is still young enough to develop into a good pitcher."

Martin: "Possibly a reason for his not winning more is that he has been bothered from time to time by arm problems. Even so, he does have the natural stuff to win."

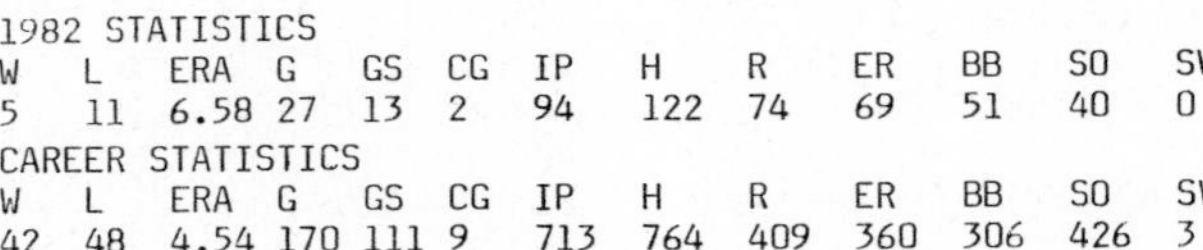

1982 STATISTICS

W	L	ERA	G	GS	CG	IP	H	R	ER	BB	SO	SV
5	11	6.58	27	13	2	94	122	74	69	51	40	0

CAREER STATISTICS

W	L	ERA	G	GS	CG	IP	H	R	ER	BB	SO	SV
42	48	4.54	170	111	9	713	764	409	360	306	426	3

FRANK VIOLA
LHP, No. 51
LL, 6'4", 195 lbs.
ML Svc: 1 year
Born: 4-19-60 in Hempstead, NY

PITCHING:

Frank Viola, a half-season out of college, is considered the best looking young pitcher on the club's staff. When he is right, he has excellent stuff.

He has starting stuff and should be used that way to be most effective. His delivery is smooth and overhand and he has a fine fastball, timed at 89 MPH. It is his primary pitch. When kept down, it sinks and tails off. When up, it is straight. He must pitch low. His fastball is termed "sneaky." Viola has an average major league curveball, which, considering he is almost fresh out of college, is impressive. The curve is his second most used pitch. He also throws a slider that is considered average. His change-up is straight, his fourth most used pitch, and is rated average. When behind in the count, Viola is most likely to go to his fastball. He seems to have the same effectiveness against righthanded hitters as lefthanders.

He is considered "average" in pressure situations. Overall, he has good stuff. He is not afraid to pitch inside, which is admirable, and he changes speeds fairly well.

Viola has a tendency to overthrow when he gets in trouble. His main weakness is a lack of experience, but he'll be getting much more of that this season. His style is a combination of power and finesse. His 2-to-1 strikeout-to-walk ratio is impressive.

FIELDING:

Viola has a good move to first base. He is average at fielding bunts and average overall. Needs more experience.

OVERALL:

Viola has the potential to become a standout lefthander; it seems only a matter of time.

Robinson: "He has great presence and poise for a young pitcher; has all the tools to be outstanding."

Harwell: "Good stuff for a young pitcher; he has a bright future."

Martin: "One of the best young lefthanders in the league. He is impressive with poise and intelligence. He should definitely be a winner."

1982 STATISTICS

W	L	ERA	G	GS	CG	IP	H	R	ER	BB	SO	SV
4	10	5.21	22	22	3	126	152	77	73	38	84	0

CAREER STATISTICS

W	L	ERA	G	GS	CG	IP	H	R	ER	BB	SO	SV
4	10	5.21	22	22	3	126	152	77	73	38	84	0

GARY WARD
OF, No. 32
RR, 6'2", 207 lbs.
ML Svc: 2 years
Born: 12-6-53 in
Los Angeles, CA

1982 STATISTICS

AVG	G	AB	R	H	2B	3B	HR	RBI	BB	SO	SB
.289	152	570	85	165	33	7	28	91	37	105	13

CAREER STATISTICS

AVG	G	AB	R	H	2B	3B	HR	RBI	BB	SO	SB
.289	260	920	140	266	46	15	32	131	71	162	18

VS. RHP

VS. LHP

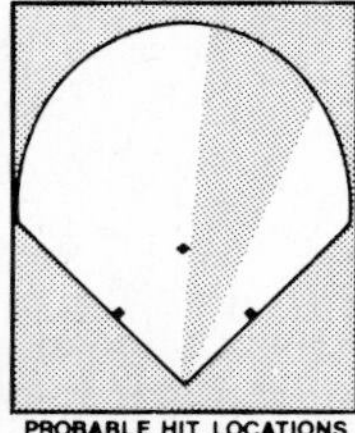
PROBABLE HIT LOCATIONS

HITTING:

Ward had a monumental second half of the 1982 season, causing many observers to feel he may have been the Twins' most valuable player. He led the club in hits, doubles, triples and home runs and was second in RBIs.

He hits from a closed, upright stance in the back of the box. He is a high ball, fastball hitter who should be pitched inside. From the middle of the plate out, he has exceptional power to right field, where his best power is. Best chances to get him out are with breaking balls and change-ups.

Ward is an opposite field hitter who also has some power to left-center field. He is strong, intense and can drive the ball. He will drive in runs in critical situations. He does not, however, allow himself to walk enough, and he is not a good bunter.

Ward also does not hit the change-up well. He was extremely consistent in 1982. He does not appear to hit well in Comiskey or Anaheim parks, but hits well in Tiger Stadium and Seattle's Kingdome due to their short power alleys.

BASERUNNING:

Ward has above average speed to first base and above average ability to break up the double play. His basestealing ability is also rated above average. He is an aggressive, smart baserunner who slides feet first. He stole 13 of 14 bases attempted.

FIELDING:

His throwing arm and accuracy rate only average, although his trememdous enthusiasm for playing the outfield increases his range to above average. He is best at coming in on balls. His strong desire to improve has aided his fielding immensely. His best position is left field.

OVERALL:

Robinson: "He has proved to the Twins that he is an everyday player. He is big and strong and has paid his dues in the minors. He might hit 30 home runs next year."

Harwell: "He is a solid, all around player who would be best hitting No. 5 or No. 6 in the lineup."

Martin: "He is a productive hitter capable of a hot streak. He may be moved to center field next year if Jim Eisenreich (forced out with nervous disorder) can't return to the lineup."

RON WASHINGTON
INF, No. 24
RR, 5'11", 160 lbs.
ML Svc: 1 year plus
Born: 4-29-52 in
New Orleans, LA

1982 STATISTICS

AVG	G	AB	R	H	2B	3B	HR	RBI	BB	SO	SB
.271	119	451	48	122	17	6	5	39	14	79	3

CAREER STATISTICS

AVG	G	AB	R	H	2B	3B	HR	RBI	BB	SO	SB
.267	157	554	60	148	20	7	5	45	18	95	8

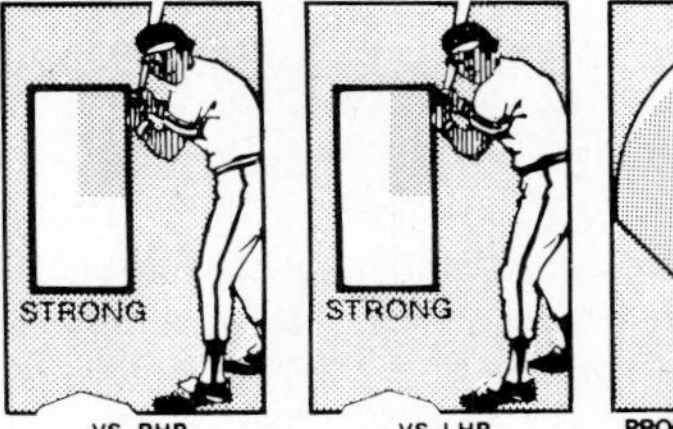

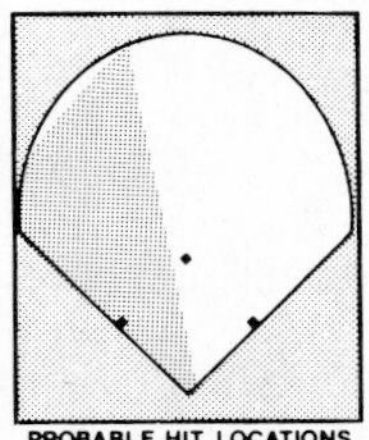

HITTING:

A solid, consistent hitter, Ron Washington bats from a closed, crouched stance in the back of the batter's box. He is a high ball hitter, and should be pitched outside, low and away by both right and lefthanders. He is a straight-away hitter who has shown occasional power, but is mostly a line drive hitter.

Perhaps Washington's strongest attribute as a hitter is his ability to advance runners. He hits behind the runner quite well. Until last season, he had spent considerable time in the minor leagues where he learned good bat control. His hit-and-run ability is above average, and he is a fine bunter.

Washington will hit off-speed pitching. He is deficient at hitting breaking balls and sinkers, and should be choosier with his pitches. He does not walk enough for a leadoff or No. 2 hitter. He played sparingly during the last month of the 1982 season, perhaps because the Twins wanted to take an everyday look at shortstop Len Faedo.

BASERUNNING:

Washington is not considered a major cause of concern to pitchers, but will steal if he is taken for granted on the basepaths. He will also take an extra base when the opportunity is there. His speed, ability to break up the double play, and stealing ability are all rated only average. He may be, however, the smartest runner on the club in terms of instincts, but his overall baserunning style is conservative.

FIELDING:

Washington's basic value to the Twins is his ability to play several positions in the infield, including catcher. He has a strong, accurate throwing arm, and an above average range. He is considered a better than average shortstop, and manager Billy Gardner likes his eager attitude.

OVERALL:

Robinson: "He has paid his dues in the minors, and has surprised a lot of people with outstanding play at shortstop. Look for him to be the team's No. 1 shortstop in 1983."

Martin: "Washington is a hustling player who has taken advantage of an opportunity to play more regularly."

AL WILLIAMS
RHP, No. 28
RR, 6'4", 184 lbs.
ML Svc: 2 years
Born: 5-7-54 in
Pearl Lagoon, NIC

PITCHING:

Al Williams is a tall, slender, strong righthander who throws with a lot of motion and relatively little experience. He has an exceptional curveball, a fine fastball, and is working to improve his change-up. He has the stuff to be a consistent winner if he develops.

Williams is a starter and one of only three Twins' pitchers who had winning records in 1982. His delivery is three-quarter. He does not seem particularly astute at pitching to hitters' weaknesses. His fastball is 86 MPH, which is above average. In some games, he will throw it 90% of the time, and in others, considerably less, depending upon the effectiveness of his breaking stuff. When the two are clicking, he can be overwhelming.

Williams gets exceptional spin on his curveball, which is probably the best pitch on the club when he is throwing it well. He will throw the curve when he is behind in the count. He also throws a hard slider. His effectiveness appears equal on right and lefthanded hitters.

When he came to the big leagues two years ago, he had some problems with hiding the ball adequately in his delivery, but seems to have improved as of late. He is a former guerilla fighter from Nicaragua and attributes his "coolness" on the mound to his personal background as a soldier. He does not get excited in pressure situations.

Perhaps Williams' greatest weakness is inconsistency. He can be dazzling one start, and just terrible the next. If he puts it together, he could be outstanding. His stuff allows him the potential to be a standout reliever, but consistency will have to improve. As with most inexperienced pitchers, he is making a transition from being a "thrower" to a "pitcher."

FIELDING:

Williams has an average move to first. He is average at fielding bunts, the same at fielding his position. Sometimes, with runners on base, he appears more concerned at getting the ball to the plate than he does with holding the runners close.

OVERALL:

Williams has an abundance of potential that could be realized any season now. More experience is vital.

Robinson: "Overall, he has pretty good stuff, but has just no consistency at all."

Harwell: "He has an excellent fastball and breaking pitch; he could be more effective in short relief."

Martin: "He is coming back gradually after two years of not being in baseball in the late 1970's, and after a trip to the minors in 1982. You have to stay with a pitcher with a good arm and heart."

1982 STATISTICS

W	L	ERA	G	GS	CG	IP	H	R	ER	BB	SO	SV
9	7	4.22	26	26	3	153	166	74	72	55	61	0

CAREER STATISTICS

W	L	ERA	G	GS	CG	IP	H	R	ER	BB	SO	SV
14	16	3.90	74	43	5	309	331	138	134	95	115	0

SAL BUTERA
C, No. 11
RR, 6'0", 189 lbs.
ML Svc: 3 years
Born: 9-25-52 in Richmond Hill, NY

HITTING, BASERUNNING, FIELDING:

Butera is a streak hitter who battles pitchers and always seems to get his bat on the ball. He is a high ball hitter who should be pitched down with everything, and inside with the fastball. He hits straightaway, mostly ground balls through the infield holes. Seldom reaches the alleys and is considerably deficient in power.

He will surprise a team by hitting in the clutch, sometimes with weak hits because he fights the pitcher to the end. He does not strike out much.

Butera did not attempt even one stolen base last season. He has poor speed to first and needs improvement in his overall baserunning.

Butera is exceptionally durable and determined to play with injuries and pain. His eagerness to play hurt is why his manager likes him so much. He is rated above average at knowing hitters' strengths and weaknesses and calls every pitch. Arm strength is average to above average, and will surprise some by throwing out the best stealers in the league. He has a quick release and throws with excellent accuracy. He blocks balls and fields bunts well. He is a thinking man's catcher and holds baserunners well. Pitchers respect his ability and are confident in his judgment.

OVERALL:

Robinson: "He is a very heady catcher who does a good job with Minnesota's young pitchers. He is strictly a back up catcher. He is a perfect example of a guy with not a whole lot of abiltiy playing in the big leagues for a number of years. He grows on you and has performed better than anyone thought he could."

JESUS VEGA
INF, No. 39
RR, 6'1", 190 lbs.
ML Svc: 1 year plus
Born: 10-14-55 in Bayamon, PR

HITTING, BASERUNNING, FIELDING:

Jesus Vega is a part-time reserve player. He is considered a streak hitter who has some power. He is a fastball hitter who primes himself for the fastball. He should be pitched low and away with fastballs by righthanders, and inside by lefthanders. Vega can hit line drives in the power alleys. He is more effective against lefthanded pitching because he has been used primarily as a platoon player.

In most other hitting regards, Vega is rated only average. He has some pull power inside against lefthanders. He does not like to walk and needs improvement in controlling his swing. He is aggressive and has a tendency to hit ground balls more against lefties than righthanders.

Vega has above average speed to first base and is rated an aggressive baserunner. In seven attempts last season, he stole six bases.

As a first baseman, Vega's arm is rated average. He also is rated average in throwing accuracy and has average range. As a fielder, he rates average to below average. He doesn't seem to concentrate on fielding. He is deficient at fielding balls not hit directly at him.

OVERALL:

Robinson: "He can do a lot of things--be a designated hitter, play first base, outfield and steal a base. If he is to stay in the big leagues, that will be his best bet."

Martin: "He has always been impressive in the minors. In the majors, he is a reserve player, with ability to hit the occasional long ball."

YANKEE STADIUM
New York Yankees

Seating Capacity: 57,545
Playing Surface: Natural Grass

Dimensions
Left Field Pole: 312 ft.
Left-Center Field: 430 ft.
Center Field: 417 ft.
Right-Center Field: 385 ft.
Right Field Pole: 310 ft.
Height of Outfield Walls:
Left Field: 8 ft.
Center Field: 7-8 ft.
Right Field: 9-10 ft.

The first time that Gary Nolan, then a pitcher with the Cincinnati Reds, saw Yankee Stadium in the 1976 World Series, he quipped, "What did they do--lay out this ballpark sideways?"

Actually, it just looks that way because of the tremendous expanses in left, right-center and out to straightaway-center. Yankee Stadium holds a unique place for players and fans because it will always be known as "The House that Ruth Built." It had a sense of majesty before it was redone during the 1974-75 seasons, with three monuments placed in deep-center field, but the reconstruction managed to keep the three tiers intact as well as the feeling that the greats of baseball once played on the very same grass that today's ballplayers perform on.

It was, and will always be, a ballpark for lefthanded hitters. The right field foul pole is only 310 feet away, and as the stands swing out towards right-center field, a lefthanded hitter with average power can easily reach the 353-foot mark in right, or the 385-foot mark in right-center. In left field, the pole is actually only 312 feet away, but the stands recoil sharply, and 25 feet away from the pole, the distance balloons to 387 feet. As the stands end and the bleachers start, a righthanded hitter stares at a sign that reads 430 feet. The latter is the left-center field alley, known as "Death Valley" by righthanded hitters.

Because of the park's dimensions, opposing teams throw nothing but lefthanded pitchers at the Yankees (with the exception of their righthanded aces), and when Dick Howser managed New York, he once surmised that some teams might even try to import lefthanders from Japan just to pitch in Yankee Stadium.

In the past few years the Yankees have drastically changed their own pitching philosophy, and now carry four lefthanded starters.

The grass is generally beautifully hued, and allowed to be high, but the infield continually presents problems to infielders. The infield dirt is lumpy and the entire infield actually slopes downward. The peculiar "hump" effect continues into the outfield, and many opposing centerfielders see only the top part of a batter's body when playing deep-center.

Because of the sense of history in Yankee Stadium, and despite the moans of the Yankee righthanded hitters, Yankee owner George Steinbrenner will not move in the fences to help the righthanded hitter as has been suggested by many.

DOYLE ALEXANDER
RHP, No. 52
RR, 6'3", 190 lbs.
ML Svc: 12 years
Born: 9-4-50 in
Cordova, AL

PITCHING:

Doyle Alexander pitches overhand, drops to three-quarters frequently, and sometimes to sidearm. He does not have an effective fastball, and if he tries to throw it past a hitter, righty or lefty, gets into trouble. His main arsenal, given the fact that he spots the fastball, consists of a curve, slider, change and sinker. He is a smart veteran, who will not use his sinker on artificial turf, where it tends to be hit into the ground and take high hops. When healthy, and in command of all his pitches, he can get batters out with any pitch, providing his control is with him. Without control, Alexander can get into trouble.

He has been a winner with the Yankees, Orioles, Rangers, Braves and Giants, but would like to completely forget 1982. He missed most of spring training after a trade, came back too soon, and when hit rather hard by the Mariners in May, punched a dugout wall and broke his right hand. The Yankee front office did not take kindly to that, but he did come back--again too soon, was hit hard, and sent for a complete physical by the brass. He was embarrassed by statements made by George Steinbrenner, to wit: "I'm afraid my infielders will get killed if he pitches."

Hitters can look for any of Alexander's pitches, but when he is effective and spots the ball, gets them out and gets many ground balls. He can also get by without his finesse-type pitches in Yankee Stadium, where long drives are mere fly ball outs.

FIELDING:

Alexander fields his position well, and has an excellent move to first base. Runners can steal on him if he throws an off-speed pitch to the plate, and they get a decent jump.

OVERALL:

Harwell: "Arm troubles have lessened his effectiveness."

Martin: "Alexander looked like an outstanding pitcher early in his career, with Baltimore, but never really made it big. He had several good years, but overall has been inconsistent. Injuries and attitude have hampered him."

Robinson: "Doyle has been around and knows how to pitch. The injury to his hand slowed him last year. I doubt very seriously if he will be with the Yankees in 1983. Average stuff with good control."

1982 STATISTICS

W	L	ERA	G	GS	CG	IP	H	R	ER	BB	SO	SV
1	7	6.08	16	11	0	66	81	52	45	14	26	0

CAREER STATISTICS

W	L	ERA	G	GS	CG	IP	H	R	ER	BB	SO	SV
108	101	3.72	336	245	55	1812	1775	834	750	607	716	3

STEVE BALBONI
INF, No. 66
RR, 6'3", 225 lbs.
ML Svc: 2 years
Born: 1-16-57 in
Brockton, MA

1982 STATISTICS

AVG	G	AB	R	H	2B	3B	HR	RBI	BB	SO	SB
.187	33	107	8	20	2	1	2	4	6	34	0

CAREER STATISTICS

AVG	G	AB	R	H	2B	3B	HR	RBI	BB	SO	SB
.192	37	114	10	22	3	2	2	6	7	38	0

VS. RHP

VS. LHP

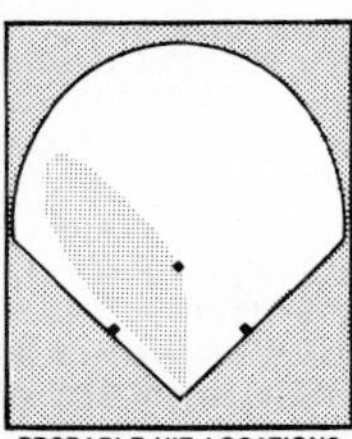
PROBABLE HIT LOCATIONS

HITTING:

Steve Balboni carries to the team an almost legendary minor league home run and RBI record, but his batting flaws while in pinstripes have also made him carry his baggage back and forth to Columbus, the Yankees' Triple A affiliate.

He has a gate-like swing, with very little wrist snap. His stance is square, upright, but he tends to look at pitches with his chin tucked under his left shoulder, leading to what amounts to vision from only his left eye while at the plate.

Pitchers feed him a steady diet of curves, low, in the dirt and on the outside part of the plate. They also get him out with fastballs on the outside corner, and fastballs up and in. A hanging slider or fastball from the knees to the belt can be embarrassing for a pitcher.

Balboni, when playing every day and free of assorted ailments, can hit pitches that normally get him out with sheer brute strength. He has broken his bat and put outfielders on warning tracks 420 feet away. He should be able to hit lefties, but in 1982, off-speed pitches and low sliders were something he could not touch. He needs a total overhaul in his swing, and must learn patience at the plate.

BASERUNNING:

He runs like a truck stuck in gear heading uphill and is absolutely no threat to steal or take an extra base.

FIELDING:

A surprise. Like many big men, Balboni has little range at first, but he is not afraid to dive or get in front of a wicked smash. He is the perfect target at first, but must improve his pickups of throws in the dirt. He does have the ability to field grounders in the hole and start a double play.

OVERALL:

Robinson: "Can only help if he hits. He has a lot of holes as a hitter and will have to cut down on strikeouts. I doubt if New York will ever give him a chance."

Martin: "Very raw at the plate, but immensely powerful. He can certainly turn the fastball around, but the question is, how often?"

DON BAYLOR
OF/DH, No. 25
RR, 6'1", 210 lbs.
ML Svc: 11 years
Born: 6-28-49 in
Austin, TX

1982 STATISTICS

AVG	G	AB	R	H	2B	3B	HR	RBI	BB	SO	SB
.263	157	608	80	160	24	1	24	93	57	69	10

CAREER STATISTICS

AVG	G	AB	R	H	2B	3B	HR	RBI	BB	SO	SB
.264	1492	5457	812	1442	241	22	213	820	534	644	259

VS. RHP

VS. LHP

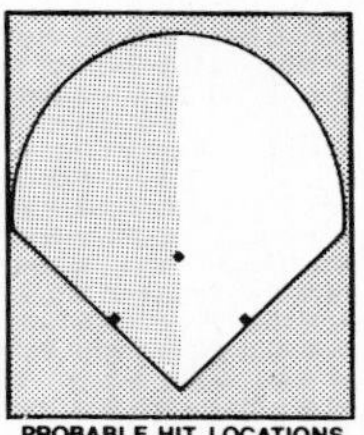
PROBABLE HIT LOCATIONS

HITTING:

Don Baylor is one of the strongest hitters in baseball, but has a tendency to overswing. He can be fooled easily. He will not lay off an inside pitch, which he more often than not pulls foul. But make a mistake, and he will usually hit the ball hard--if not out of the park, then a line drive at least.

His stance is upright and slightly closed, and he explodes with his swing. He is primarily a low ball hitter. The best way to pitch to him is high and tight, or away from the plate as he basically tries to pull everything. Because of his strength, he can still pull an outside hard one to the left side, which results in many double plays.

Baylor is a power hitter who hits more line drives than home runs. He often finds the alleys. He is a streak hitter, one who is horrendous when he is going bad, but spectacular when he is going good. He is among the best clutch hitters in baseball.

BASERUNNING:

Once he was among the fastest men in baseball, but age and injuries have slowed him somewhat. Baylor still possesses above average speed and commands the attention of opposing pitchers. He can still steal a base when needed. He is an aggressive baserunner and infielders should beware of him when attempting to turn a double play. He is among the best at breaking up double plays.

FIELDING:

In recent years, Baylor has become a full time designated hitter, against his wishes. He would like to play every day in the field, but his lack of ability prevents it. Shoulder injuries have weakened his throwing arm considerably, and even in left field where a strong arm is not essential, he is a liability. He also has problems with fly balls. He can play adequately at first base, but then so can most players.

OVERALL:

Martin: "Baylor is a solid, class person. He is a strong hitter and a game-breaker."

Robinson: "When he gets hot, no one in the league can match him."

Harwell: "He is a great offensive player, both when hitting and running."

RICK CERONE
C, No. 10
RR, 5'11", 185 lbs.
ML Svc: 8 years
Born: 5-19-54 in
Newark, NJ

1982 STATISTICS

AVG	G	AB	R	H	2B	3B	HR	RBI	BB	SO	SB
.227	89	300	29	68	10	0	5	28	19	27	0

CAREER STATISTICS

AVG	G	AB	R	H	2B	3B	HR	RBI	BB	SO	SB
.243	576	1932	203	469	93	12	32	226	130	193	2

VS. RHP

VS. LHP

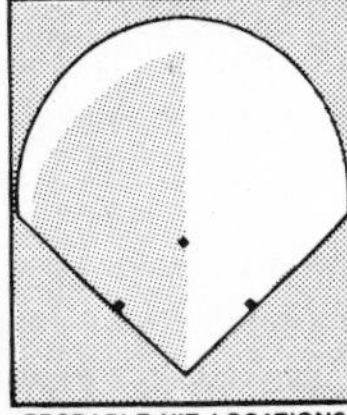
PROBABLE HIT LOCATIONS

HITTING:

Good thumbs is what Rick Cerone needs. In 1981, he broke his right thumb and lost a year. In 1982, he broke his left thumb and lost another year. Any player on a team, with the exception of a pitcher, can get by with playing after a broken thumb, but a catcher needs a thumb more than he needs shin guards.

Like most of former batting coach Charlie Lau's pupils, Cerone stands off the plate and tries to go with the pitch. He bats from a closed stance, and has been crouching a bit more. Lefthanded pitchers try to bust the slider in on his hands, and have their fastballs tail away from him. Righthanded pitchers use high, tight fastballs, low sliders, and change-ups. With good hands and bat control, Cerone can battle pitchers and generally manage to get a piece of the ball. The broken thumbs obviously affected his ability to generate the power and line drives he showed he had in the 1980 season.

BASERUNNING:

Cerone has come under criticism for mental blunders on the basepaths in the past few years. He can, however, stretch a single into a double as well as any catcher in the league, and has an aggressive style when rounding first base, often taking an extraordinarily wide turn. Cerone often lets his lack of hitting or defensive mistakes affect him when on base. He tends to be extremely defensive when criticized about basepath mistakes, indicating that he is playing all-out to win, and that an attack is better than a retreat.

FIELDING:

While both of his thumbs were in working order, Cerone proved he was one of the best defensive catchers in the league. Cat-quick when it came to fielding bunts or high chops, he had a lightning-like release when throwing out potential stealers. These qualities were honed even finer as the 1981 season got under way, but then back-to-back broken thumbs set him back. His throwing was affected, and his passed balls zoomed up to an alarming degree.

Unlike many big league catchers, Cerone is known to "catch with his thumbs," and the pounding eventually showed. In addition, Cerone was catching several new pitchers, and seemed to have trouble adjusting to the type of break on their pitches. He was also playing without a contract, adding to his problems behind the plate. For 1983, Cerone is armed with new contract, two healed thumbs, and should be able to challenge Detroit's Lance Parrish for All Star status in the league.

OVERALL:

Martin: "Better than average defensive catcher, agile behind plate. Feisty hitter who can beat you in the clutch. Works well with pitchers."

Robinson: "Cerone is a good player when healthy. Good catcher, good hitter. Playing for a better team has made him a better player."

ROGER ERICKSON
RHP, No. 35
RR, 6'3", 199 lbs.
ML Svc: 5 years
Born: 8-30-56 in Springfield, IL

PITCHING:

Roger Erickson has a sling-shot motion to the plate. He has a rapid windup and seems to straight-arm the ball, but he gets excellent velocity on both his fastball and late-breaking slider, his two main pitches. He uses a turned-over fastball against lefthanded hitters, and is at his best when he keeps that pitch on the outside and lower portion of the plate. Against righthanders, he likes to bust the fastball inside and to keep the slider low and away. He also uses his turned-over fastball against certain righties, if he is looking for a double play, or looking to set up the hitter for his rising fastball.

He is one of the few Yankee pitchers who is not afraid to throw at a batter's belly, legs or feet. He tries to keep hitters honest, and will often--when ahead in the count--buzz a fastball under a batter's chin.

FIELDING:

He is a good athlete who fields his position well, and moves quickly on bunts. He has an extremely tricky move to first base, almost a balk move. He takes his stretch, peeks at the runner, and does not take his eyes off the runner until a split-second before he releases the ball to home plate. He keeps his left leg in a plane that seems as though he will throw to first, and keeps many runners glued to first with the move. When he does throw to first, he is quick, and generally throws the ball where the first baseman will have little difficulty in tagging a sliding runner.

OVERALL:

The Yankees decided they needed a quality righty starter after they began the 1982 season, and acquired Erickson from the Minnesota Twins. Erickson, however, had trouble adjusting to the situation, a situation that saw three managers and five pitching coaches. He started off in a shaky manner, but bounced back with four straight wins.

His next problem was that the team started to fall hopelessly out of the race, and the Yankees brought up four minor leaguers to pitch.

Erickson continued to pitch, frequently in relief, but a shoulder injury in August finished him. It would appear that in 1983, he has the most legitimate chance of becoming the lone Yankee righthanded starter, pitching behind Guidry, Rawley, Righetti and Shirley.

1982 STATISTICS

W	L	ERA	G	GS	CG	IP	H	R	ER	BB	SO	SV
8	8	4.61	23	18	2	111	142	65	57	29	49	1

CAREER STATISTICS

W	L	ERA	G	GS	CG	IP	H	R	ER	BB	SO	SV
35	52	4.14	130	117	24	781	855	411	359	243	358	1

GEORGE FRAZIER
RHP, No. 43
RR, 6'5", 205 lbs.
ML Svc: 5 years
Born: 10-13-54 in
Oklahoma City, OK

PITCHING:

Only two pitchers in Yankee history have ever appeared in more games than Frazier did in 1982. Many claim the tall righthander is unlucky, and point to the 1981 World Series when a series of bloops and high chops made him the second pitcher in history to lose three games in a World Series, but Frazier realizes that as a rookie, he at least got the chance to pitch in so many important games.

He throws overhand, but adds a three-quarter and sidearm delivery at times. His fastball is better than average, but is made to look faster because of the variety of breaking balls he throws. Against righthanders, he likes to throw a big sweeping curve that drives the hitter off the plate and catches the inside corner. When he has a righty leaning back, he throws a sharp slider on the outside corner.

Against lefthanders, he keeps his fastball up and away, and tries to keep the curve and slider low and in. Because of the huge break on his ball, he is more effective against righthanded batters.

Frazier has what many believe to be a rubber arm. He has been blessed by avoiding arm and shoulder trouble, and throws virtually every day. He is usually the first Yankee on the field, and before a game will often loosen up with the bullpen catcher or ballboy. He then throws in the bullpen, and often volunteers to pitch if the bullpen is short a man or two that day. At times, he can be seen in hotels throwing a baseball against a wall, at night or in the morning.

FIELDING:

A former basketball player, Frazier's height and jumping ability are a tremendous asset to him on the mound. He can cut off high bouncers that shorter pitchers cannot, and he often runs down choppers between home and first and runs to the bag himself. He is sneaky-fast in his move to first base, but when he forgets to keep a runner close, he can be stolen on.

OVERALL:

A valuable pitcher who came into his own after several disappointing years. Frazier is never afraid to come into a game, regardless of the inning, score or batter.

Robinson: "This guy can pitch anywhere. He has gained a lot of experience over the last couple of years and his above average fastball and slider will keep him in the big leagues. Very good stuff."

1982 STATISTICS

W	L	ERA	G	GS	CG	IP	H	R	ER	BB	SO	SV
4	4	3.47	63	0	0	111	103	51	43	39	69	1

CAREER STATISTICS

W	L	ERA	G	GS	CG	IP	H	R	ER	BB	SO	SV
7	16	3.38	140	0	0	216	210	101	81	72	119	7

HITTING:

They don't call Oscar Gamble "Doc" for nothing. Doc is short for Doctor, and that's what the Yankees think Gamble is--a specialist with a Doctorate in hitting. He has more home runs the past two years, per at-bat, than any other Yankee.

He bats from a severe crouch with a wide open stance. His back foot (the left one) is almost on top of home plate, and with the exception of Steve Kemp, Gamble stands closer to the plate than any batter in baseball. The stance, and his uppercut swing, make Gamble a dead--and dangerous--long ball pull hitter. If a pitcher, righty or lefty, gets a fastball in, and down, he can turn and watch it wind up 400 feet away as Gamble trots the bases.

But that stance can also hinder Gamble, particularly against right-handers who cut and run their fastball away from him, or who throw him off-speed stuff. Lefthanders pitch him away with either hard stuff or sliders, and both lefties and righties occasionally try to throw the high hard one past Gamble. At times, they get away with it, but if it does not have the proper velocity or location, it will wind up in the bleachers.

BASERUNNING:

He has surprising speed, and utilizes it on the basepaths. He seems to be running in place when he leaves the batter's box, or starts off from first or second when he takes off on a base hit, but accelerates rapidly. His running style is half-conservative and half-aggressive, but when in the latter mood, takes every chance imaginable and climaxes them with head first slides. Gamble is a much smarter baserunner than most baseball people give him credit for, and will often check--on his own--with whomever is managing the Yankees at the time to see if they

OSCAR GAMBLE
OF/DH, No. 17
LR, 5'11", 177 lbs.
ML Svc: 14 years
Born: 12-20-49 in Ramer, AL

1982 STATISTICS

AVG	G	AB	R	H	2B	3B	HR	RBI	BB	SO	SB
.272	108	316	49	86	21	2	18	56	58	47	6

CAREER STATISTICS

AVG	G	AB	R	H	2B	3B	HR	RBI	BB	SO	SB
.270	1386	4049	593	1095	171	29	179	593	526	483	46

VS. RHP

VS. LHP

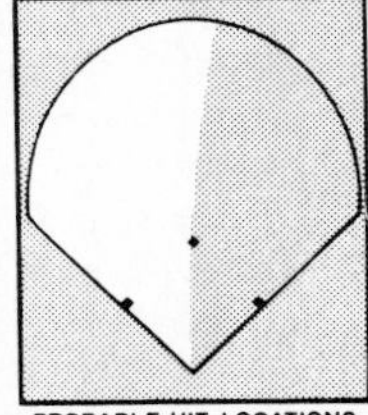
PROBABLE HIT LOCATIONS

would like him to steal. The fact that he stole 10 bases last year, more than any year since 1975, attests to that.

FIELDING:

Gamble is a 99% designated hitter who plays the field on rare occasions. When he does, and shakes the dust, he exhibits an extraordinary throwing arm, and an amazing degree of accuracy. His throwing arm can be compared favorably with Dave Winfield, Tony Armas and Dwight Evans. In the field, he does have trouble coming in on a ball, however.

OVERALL:

Martin: "Gamble is strictly a DH, and a dangerous one at that. He is a leave-your-feet type of hitter with a big swing. Will kill the mistake."

Robinson: "He is a definite home run threat in Yankee Stadium, and any place else for that matter."

RICH GOSSAGE
RHP, No. 54
RR, 6'3", 217 lbs.
ML Svc: 11 years
Born: 7-5-51 in
Colorado Springs, CO

PITCHING:

Because he was such an effective dribbler, Bob Cousy of the Boston Celtics was instrumental in having a clock put into NBA games. If Rich Gossage continues his unbelievable relief pitching, he may get the American League to shorten games from nine to seven innings. If he comes in the game in the seventh inning with his team in the lead, forget it.

He must be seen to be appreciated. With the exception of 1979 (torn ligaments in his thumb) and September of last year (shoulder problems), Gossage has been the most effective relief pitcher in baseball. Some might point to Sutter, Fingers or Quisenberry, but Gossage at his best is unhittable.

He throws from a three-quarter motion, and puts every bit of his burly body into every pitch. When he is rolling, batters have virtually no chance. They know what to expect, but it does them no good because his fastball, clocked at an average of 95 MPH, simply explodes before it reaches the plate. Gossage has absolutely no idea where the ball will go. He starts the blazer in the general direction of the middle of the plate, but it invariably winds up East, West, North or South of the plate--but in the strike zone. Because it is so explosive, batters swing at many fastballs that are out of the strike zone.

In the last two years, Gossage has been throwing a slider, and when he has thrown two bullets past a batter, and comes in with the slider, it is cruel and unusual punishment. Batters cringe, watch it break, and walk sullenly and silently back to the dugout.

FIELDING:

Gossage falls off towards first base after releasing the ball, so several batters have tried to bunt him toward the third base line. If the Yankee third baseman is deep, a bunt is an automatic hit if the batter can get his bat on the ball. Baserunners rarely run on Gossage, because the ball gets to home plate so fast. He is not particularly agile on the mound, but is not likely to hurt his team with his fielding.

OVERALL:

His main "flaw" is that Gossage needs a day or two off after pitching three-four innings in a game.

Harwell: "Great asset to Yankees because he intimidates the opposition."

Martin: "It is trite to say 'Awesome,' but that's what he is. He can (and does) win a pennant for you."

Robinson: "Gossage is there by himself. Everything a short reliever has to have, he's got. And the hitters know it. There is no guesswork when you hit against him. Just get ready for something hard."

1982 STATISTICS

W	L	ERA	G	GS	CG	IP	H	R	ER	BB	SO	SV
4	5	2.23	56	0	0	93	63	23	23	28	102	30

CAREER STATISTICS

W	L	ERA	G	GS	CG	IP	H	R	ER	BB	SO	SV
68	68	2.90	511	37	16	1149	906	413	370	494	986	184

KEN GRIFFEY
OF, No. 6
LL, 6'0", 200 lbs.
ML Svc: 10 years
Born: 4-10-50 in Donora, PA

1982 STATISTICS

AVG	G	AB	R	H	2B	3B	HR	RBI	BB	SO	SB
.277	127	484	70	134	23	2	12	54	39	58	10

CAREER STATISTICS

AVG	G	AB	R	H	2B	3B	HR	RBI	BB	SO	SB
.304	1174	4341	742	1320	224	62	72	478	461	455	160

VS. RHP

VS. LHP

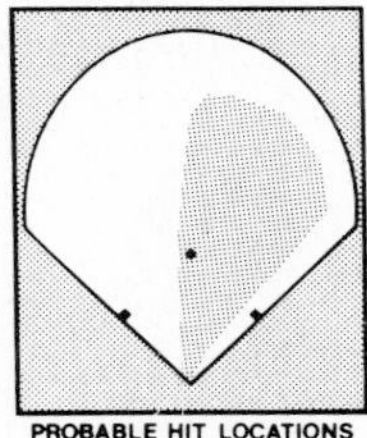
PROBABLE HIT LOCATIONS

HITTING:

Ken Griffey never stopped hitting while he was a member of the Cincinnati Reds, but he never even started hitting as a New York Yankee. His lifetime batting average of .307 (he is one of only eight men active in the AL to compile an average above .300) dipped 30 points, but a knee and thigh injury, coupled with the adjustment to a new league, was obviously no help.

Griffey has a slightly open stance, and bats from a slight crouch. When at his best, he hits the ball where it is pitched, but against righthanders tends to pull the ball a lot more. He can hit high curves by either righties or lefties, and also hits high fastballs exceptionally well. Off-speed pitches give him trouble, but Griffey can handle sharp-breaking curves thrown by righties or lefties. He does not "bail out" against lefthanders, but with bad legs in 1982, never fully had the proper weight shift to go along with his ability as a hitter.

He has trouble with pitches thrown in on his hands, but can handle any pitch out over the plate.

BASERUNNING:

Griffey shows that he has solid fundamentals on the basepaths. He knows when to take the extra base and when to stay put. With good legs, on artificial turf, Griffey was a basepath buzzer who knew he had an edge on most outfielders because of his knowledge and speed. A 1979 knee operation and recurring leg ailments have curtailed his speed, but not his baseball sense.

FIELDING:

Griffey is a better than average fielder with good lateral movement, gets a decent jump on the ball, but has recently displayed a tendency to overthrow the cutoff man. A fairly accurate thrower from right field for most of his career, Griffey seemed a bit confused in the American League and threw too high on many occasions last year. He can, however, come in on a ground single and throw on the run, and this helps his overall fielding. Poor positioning in the outfield, either by Griffey's lack of knowledge of how to play AL hitters, or by coaches' failure to move him, cost the Yankees several games.

OVERALL:

Robinson: "Griffey will be better in 1983. Has lost a step from his high-flying days in Cincinnati. Changing leagues has affected him, mostly in hitting."

Martin: "A fine player who was caught up in the 'Manhattan Madness' of 1982. He can hit, hit with power and produce. A team should put him in the outfield and leave him alone. He seemed to want out of New York, but was a standout in the National League."

RON GUIDRY
LHP, No. 49
LL, 5'11", 162 lbs.
ML Svc: 8 years
Born: 8-28-50 in Lafayette, LA

PITCHING:

Ron Guidry prides himself on his ability to use every piece on a chess board. He is close to becoming a master, and there is no ballplayer in the league who can beat him at chess.

Recently, Guidry has taken that philosophy and converted it into his pitching pattern. At his best in 1978, Guidry threw fastball, slider . . . and then slider-fastball. He was untouchable. Because he had a late start as pitcher and because he is not a big man like Seaver, Palmer, Ryan, Jenkins, Perry and the like, Guidry has realized that in order to be effective for more than a year or two, he must conserve some of his power pitches, and in 1982 he began using an overhand curve and change-up to give batters something else to think and worry about.

Like many Yankee pitchers, Guidry had to go through a season of five pitching coaches and a 40-man roster. Every time he looked up, he had a different infield. It did not particularly please him, because Guidry gets as much of a kick out of three groundballs as he does with three strikeouts. He needs a defensive team behind him, something the Yankees did not provide him with in 1982.

He tried to finesse, but frequently got into trouble, either by letting up too much, walking the eighth or ninth hitter in the lineup, or by errors. It was then he junked his curve and change and went to pure power. When he did, he was the Guidry of the past four years, the winningest lefthander in the American League. He retains his 92 MPH fastball, and slider that explodes as it reaches the plate. Lefties or righties make no difference to Guidry when he has both his power pitches, his control . . . and a defense behind him.

Incredible as he has been, and will be again, Guidry has a problem, and it usually starts when he has a batter 0-2 in the count. He will not brush a batter back, and will not come up and in. Rinky-dink hitters hang in, and Guidry usually comes outside with an 0-2 pitch. With his speed, all the batter has to do is stick out his bat, and even if the ball is a foot outside, they can bloop it to right for a damaging hit.

FIELDING:

Guidry is unbelievably quick off the mound, handles bunts and high chops as well as any pitcher in baseball, and is in reality, a fifth infielder.

OVERALL:

Harwell: "Guidry is one of baseball's best pitchers. A fine athlete."

Robinson: "Without doubt, Ron is the Yankees' best pitcher. He may have lost a little off his fastball, but he is still outstanding. Although he is not quite the finisher he used to be . . . with Gossage, who needs to be?"

1982 STATISTICS

W	L	ERA	G	GS	CG	IP	H	R	ER	BB	SO	SV
14	8	3.81	34	33	6	222	216	104	94	69	162	1

CAREER STATISTICS

W	L	ERA	G	GS	CG	IP	H	R	ER	BB	SO	SV
101	42	2.91	210	174	51	1322	1130	476	428	396	1084	4

HITTING:

White Sox batting coach Charlie Lau doesn't tinker and he doesn't tear--he teaches. Steve Kemp, already a good hitter, was better last year. He has a slightly-closed, semi-crouched stance high in the batter's box, and that separates him from most hitters. He stands as close as he can get to the pitcher. Kemp is a consistent line drive hitter who hits both righthanders and lefthanders equally well. Lefties will throw him a steady diet of breaking balls to try and get him out. If they throw him fastballs, Kemp will hit them even if they are up and in. Righthanders throw fastballs down and away, but Kemp can handle their breaking balls better than he can off a lefty.

Lau's instruction and Kemp's maturation have taught him the strike zone. He drew a White Sox team-high of 89 walks last season. He is more selective against lefthanders, drawing 65 walks. Although he would like to pull the ball more, Kemp seems to hit in both gaps. He dislikes cold weather and takes time to get going. In 1982, he did not hit his fourth homer until mid-June, and finished with 19. Ironically, only four of his home runs came in Comiskey Park--his home park--and lefthanded hitters usually have a feast there.

Because of his ability to make contact, and hit with men on base, he is suited to batting third-fourth-fifth in the lineup.

BASERUNNING:

Kemp's hard-nosed, aggressive style at bat and in the field is also flashed on the bases. He will slide head or feet first, into any base. He can break up the double play, and likes to try for third, even if the ball is hit in front of him. With average speed, he is not a threat to steal.

STEVE KEMP
OF, No. 22
LL, 6'0", 190 lbs.
ML Svc: 6 years
Born: 8-7-54 in San Angelo, TX

1982 STATISTICS

AVG	G	AB	R	H	2B	3B	HR	RBI	BB	SO	SB
.286	160	580	91	166	23	1	19	98	89	83	7

CAREER STATISTICS

AVG	G	AB	R	H	2B	3B	HR	RBI	BB	SO	SB
.285	844	3084	469	879	137	19	108	520	469	445	25

VS. RHP

VS. LHP

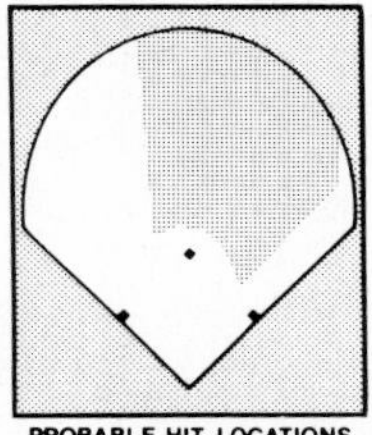
PROBABLE HIT LOCATIONS

FIELDING:

His outfield skills are rated average, probably because he does not get a good jump on balls. He is, however, likely to catch any ball he gets to. He has made progress as an outfielder, but his arm remains no better than average.

OVERALL:

Martin: "He has made strides defensively since he came up. Kemp is really an aggressive, hard-nosed hitter, and an adequate fielder."

Robinson: "The Tigers initially traded him because they thought he had lost bat speed and the ability to pull the ball. With the White Sox, he remained a tough customer, and in New York, he should provide some good power."

RUDY MAY
LHP, No. 45
LL, 6'2", 205 lbs.
ML Svc: 15 years
Born: 7-18-44 in Coffeyville, KS

PITCHING:

Despite his age, Rudy May might have the best curveball of any left-hander in the league. His advantage is that he throws it when behind in the count, to righties or lefties, and can get it over the plate. He seems to be injury-prone, but when healthy, can still buzz his 88 MPH fastball past any hitter. He has an outstanding ratio of walks to strikeouts per nine innings.

May has an excellent off-speed change, which tends to act like a screwball to righthanded batters. He does not use it very often against lefties, preferring to use his curve, slider, and "other" pitch. The latter, it is claimed, is a spitter, or scuff ball. Former Yankee manager Dick Howser said flatly that May has a spitter, but only uses it when he needs a key strikeout or important double play.

May's greatest asset, aside from his breaking ball, is his ability to go from one to four. He can start, pitch in long relief, pitch in short relief, or pitch to one particular batter. He rarely complains, and rarely knocks his teammates, manager or owner.

He did come in for a bit of criticism in 1982 when he refused to be traded to Kansas City for Hal McRae. The latter led the league in runs batted in . . . a fact not easily missed by the principal Yankee owner.

FIELDING:

May is, however, the worst fielding pitcher on the Yankees, and may be the worst in the league. He handles bunts as though they were live grenades..

OVERALL:

Like Woody Fryman of the Montreal Expos, May can be extremely valuable to a team because of his experience, willingness to work, and ability to handle himself in tough situations.

Harwell: "A talented veteran who is very versatile."

Martin: "May is still a fine pitcher, now effective out of the pen."

Robinson: "May just keeps rolling along. Has done just what the Yankees have asked of him. Pitching anywhere they need him and pitching well. I see him being used the same way in 1983. His curveball will keep him here for a while."

1982 STATISTICS

W	L	ERA	G	GS	CG	IP	H	R	ER	BB	SO	SV
6	6	2.89	41	6	0	106	109	43	34	14	85	3

CAREER STATISTICS

W	L	ERA	G	GS	CG	IP	H	R	ER	BB	SO	SV
151	151	3.43	520	360	87	2603	2292	1135	993	946	1744	12

JOHN MAYBERRY
INF, No. 28
LL, 6'3", 225 lbs.
ML Svc: 14 years
Born: 2-18-50 in Detroit, MI

1982 STATISTICS

AVG	G	AB	R	H	2B	3B	HR	RBI	BB	SO	SB
.218	86	248	27	54	7	0	10	30	35	43	0

CAREER STATISTICS

AVG	G	AB	R	H	2B	3B	HR	RBI	BB	SO	SB
.253	1620	5447	733	1379	211	19	255	879	881	810	20

VS. RHP

VS. LHP

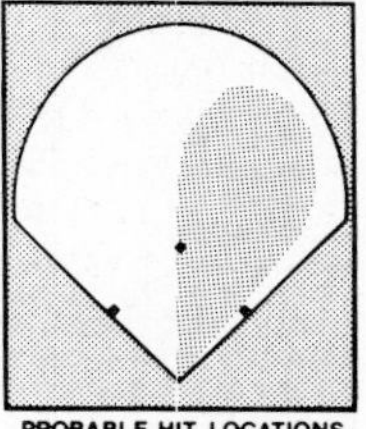
PROBABLE HIT LOCATIONS

HITTING:

John Mayberry is a big man with a big bat, a slightly closed stance and an imposing figure. 255 lifetime homers attest to that. But Mayberry seemed to have lost the zip in his bat and the desire to produce in 1982 after coming to the Yankees. Pitchers threw fastballs by him, pitches that he once clobbered. Lefties threw him off-speed pitches and curves, and Mayberry had no success with them. Righthanders broke the slider in under his hands and the fastball on the outside corner. Mayberry is a notorious low ball hitter, who can handle a high pitch if it does not have enough velocity or rotation.

BASERUNNING:

He is the slowest runner in the league, and was further hampered in 1982 by a bruised heel and extra weight. It invariably required three base hits to score him from first base, unless one of the hits cleared the fences or rolled to distant walls.

FIELDING:

Little range, average arm, but soft hands around the bag. Mayberry is better than most first basemen on throws in the dirt.

OVERALL:

Harwell: "He's not hitting as he did in the past."

Martin: "A solid performer during the good years with Kansas City, and a couple with Toronto. Mayberry was a home run threat in the middle of the lineup, and a fine defensive player. The last two years have not been good ones, and he may be running down."

Robinson: "Originally, John looked like a good trade for the Yankees, but he has not materialized. Yankee Stadium looks perfect for his swing. It will be interesting to see if he can bounce back, though it looks like he has lost a little pop in his bat."

JERRY MUMPHREY
OF, No. 22
SR, 6'2", 185 lbs.
ML Svc: 9 years
Born: 9-9-52 in
Tyler, TX

1982 STATISTICS

AVG	G	AB	R	H	2B	3B	HR	RBI	BB	SO	SB
.300	123	477	76	143	24	10	9	68	50	66	11

CAREER STATISTICS

AVG	G	AB	R	H	2B	3B	HR	RBI	BB	SO	SB
.288	885	2931	403	843	119	40	27	293	267	388	142

VS. RHP

VS. LHP

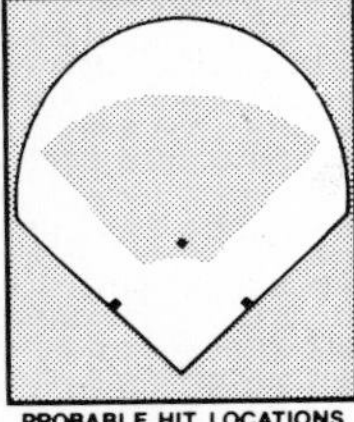
PROBABLE HIT LOCATIONS

HITTING:

Consistent, consistent, consistent--that's Jerry Mumphrey all over. He bats .300. He fields the same way. He runs the same way. He contributes to a team in the same way. He never gets too high. He never gets too low.

Mumphrey is a switch-hitter and he has virtually the same strengths and weaknesses from both sides of the plate. Because he has natural speed, he will probably--barring injuries--continue to bat at least .300. He is a stand-up hitter, stance slightly closed, and if there is one difference in his technique, it is that he can hit fastballs much better from the left side than he can from the right side.

Batting righthanded, Mumphrey has difficulty with high outside fastballs--his bat does not seem quick enough to get around on them. Batting lefthanded, he has almost the same problems, but occasionally can hit the high outside fastball a long way to the opposite field. Batting either way, Mumphrey has trouble with an off-speed pitch, particularly if he expects a fastball, on any part of the plate. His power is from the left side, and though he is weaker batting right, he can adequately handle fastballs from the middle of the plate on in. He has trouble with hard pitches thrown on the inside corner from the right side, and with low sliders and fastballs turned over from the left side. Because of his good speed, medium speed grounders are often base hits.

BASERUNNING:

Mumphrey is a better than average baserunner, although his stolen bases dropped drastically when he switched from the National League to the American League. Many observers believe that the tremendous amount of lefthanded pitchers in the American League cut down his ability to steal bases because of their good moves to first base.

FIELDING:

Like his hitting, Mumphrey is solid in the field, but has one major flaw. His range is as good as any centerfielder in the league with the exception of Dwayne Murphy or Rick Manning, but Mumphrey tends to chase long smashes in either alley while looking at the ball. He loses a step or two in tracking down balls in that manner, but his excellent speed generally bails him out. Just when you think he is in a fielding slump, he will make a diving catch or cut off a ball you think he cannot get to.

OVERALL:

Robinson: "Good player. If healthy will be even better this year. Good tools and can do a lot of things for you. Injuries slowed him down last year."

Martin: "With health, a good all around ballplayer. Gets on base, and when on, can move the bases. Excellent range in center field."

BOBBY MURCER
INF, No. 2
LR, 5'11", 160 lbs.
ML Svc: 16 years
Born: 5-20-46 in Oklahoma City, OK

1982 STATISTICS

AVG	G	AB	R	H	2B	3B	HR	RBI	BB	SO	SB
.227	65	141	12	32	6	0	7	30	12	15	2

CAREER STATISTICS

AVG	G	AB	R	H	2B	3B	HR	RBI	BB	SO	SB
.277	1899	6708	970	1858	283	45	251	1042	861	840	126

VS. RHP

VS. LHP

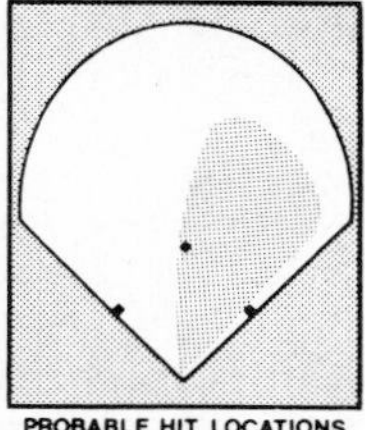
PROBABLE HIT LOCATIONS

HITTING:

Hitting is what they pay him for--period. Because Bobby Murcer does nothing else, he has become a much more disciplined hitter, knowing he might have only one pinch-hit a game, and possibly none if the opposition uses a lefty starter and a lefty reliever.

Murcer is still dangerous, particularly in Yankee Stadium, Toronto and Detroit. He will try to pull everything if the situation calls for the long ball, or hit to left field if he thinks a single or double will suffice.

He stands fairly square to the plate, slight crouch, bat held loosely off his shoulders, and tends to look for the fastball in a certain area. Regardless of his lack of playing time, Murcer is dangerous on any type of low pitch, from lefties or righties. High pitches give him trouble, unless they lose something on the way to the plate, or are hanging curves.

Depending on the situation, lefties and righties pitch him differently. With men on base, pitchers try to throw hard stuff up and in. With the bases empty, Murcer sees low sliders on the outside part of the plate from lefthanders, and fastballs up and away from righthanders. Because he is called upon to hit in key situations, he tries for the long ball more often than not, but only gets it if the pitcher makes a mistake or falls behind in the count and must throw something over the plate.

BASERUNNING:

Murcer was once one of the best, still has speed, but rarely gets the steal sign because he will come to bat late in the game. He can still go from first to third when required.

FIELDING:

He has not put on a glove in a regular game since the summer of 1980.

OVERALL:

Martin: "Bobby is in his swan song days with the Yankees. He didn't hit for average but showed he could still come off the bench and be a factor with the bat. Solid .275-.280 hitter during his career."

Robinson: "This might be his last year as a Yankee. The inactivity has hurt him, though he is still a threat with the short right field fence in Yankee Stadium. Murcer has gotten the most out of his ability."

DALE MURRAY
RHP, No. 33
RR, 6'4", 205 lbs.
ML Svc: 7 years plus
Born: 2-2-50 in
Cuero, TX

PITCHING:

In 1982, many Yankee batters could not wait to face Dale Murray. He had never been that tough to hit. But after the season, they realized that Murray had changed. He had become tougher, and the Yankees wanted him with them, rather than against them.

Murray joins a formidable bullpen. In Toronto, because of injuries and because manager Bobby Cox did not have a quality lefthanded reliever, Murray WAS the bullpen. He appeared in a club record of 56 games, all in relief. He did not lose a ballgame for the Blue Jays from May 18th through August 12th.

The husky righthander did indeed become tougher to hit. He always had a fastball that was clocked in the 88-92 MPH range, but often had trouble with location, and could not change to another out pitch. That situation was rectified when Murray developed a sinker and a forkball. Because the ball sank to an alarming degree, many batters claimed that it was a Gaylord Perry-type sinker . . . meaning a pitch that had moisture on it.

Murray throws three-quarters, and with the addition of the sinking fastball and slider, became extremely effective against both lefthanded and righthanded batters. The ball dips either in or out to righthanders, and tails away from lefthanders. In 1982, Murray allowed only three home runs, and one of them was an inside-the-park job.

In addition to showing he was effective against the Yankees, Murray pitched extremely well against the Red Sox, White Sox, Tigers and Mariners. He did, however, have trouble against the Orioles, Royals and Angels.

FIELDING:

He rates average in fielding and move to first base, but because of his experience and temperament, knows what to do with a bunt or grounder when he gets one.

OVERALL:

Murray does his job, and if he is effective, he doesn't gloat. If he is ineffective, he doesn't sulk. His disposition is what is needed for a relief pitcher, and he helped Cox and the Blue Jays climb out of the cellar for the first time in their history. If there was pressure on him, it was self-imposed, as it is with many big leaguers. Murray figures to face a different type of pressure in a place frequently called "The Bronx Zoo," but should realize he has Gossage and Frazier with him. Murray can be called on to pitch to one batter, or even give the Yankees an inning or two when Gossage is unavailable. Pitching in a bigger park like Yankee Stadium should also benefit Murray.

1982 STATISTICS

W	L	ERA	G	GS	CG	IP	H	R	ER	BB	SO	SV
8	7	3.16	56	0	0	111	115	48	39	32	60	11

CAREER STATISTICS

W	L	ERA	G	GS	CG	IP	H	R	ER	BB	SO	SV
50	44	3.74	455	1	0	772	826	372	321	302	341	59

GRAIG NETTLES
INF, No. 9
LR, 6'0", 185 lbs.
ML Svc: 16 years
Born: 8-20-44 in
San Diego, CA

1982 STATISTICS

AVG	G	AB	R	H	2B	3B	HR	RBI	BB	SO	SB
.232	122	405	47	94	11	2	18	55	51	49	1

CAREER STATISTICS

AVG	G	AB	R	H	2B	3B	HR	RBI	BB	SO	SB
.252	1406	5057	694	1273	185	17	230	759	576	674	18

VS. RHP

VS. LHP

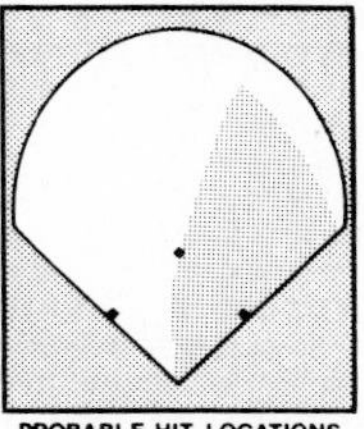
PROBABLE HIT LOCATIONS

HITTING:

Graig Nettles is one of baseball's prime examples of a streak hitter. He is a notoriously slow starter, but when he gets on one of his torrid streaks, there are no pitches that can get him out. Conversely, when he is slumping, any pitcher in the league can get him out. He stands fairly straight up in the box, square stance. On a streak, he tends to pull everything thrown at him, as indicated by the fact that he has hit more home runs than any third baseman in American League history. His favorite power pitches are high fastballs from either a lefty or righty pitcher, and hanging curves, also by either type pitcher.

When his timing is off, Nettles can be struck out by fastballs on the outside of the plate and change-ups. Hard throwing lefty pitchers also can get him out by sharp, low-breaking sliders. Although a definite pull hitter, Nettles can go to the opposite field in certain situations. In the past two years, despite injuries, Nettles has been practicing to hit to left field, particularly in ballparks where teams expect him to pull and pitch him away.

BASERUNNING:

Nettles is a slow runner who has a slow break from the batter's box, and often a slow break from first base on a hit. His lack of speed is offset by his ability to judge the strength of an outfielder's arm. He is known as a "gamer" in key situations, and can take out second basemen in double play situations, as well as taking an extra base when least expected.

FIELDING:

In 1982, Nettles had the worst fielding year of his career and yet he was still head and shoulders above every third baseman in the league with the exception of Buddy Bell. No observer or Yankee player would deny that fact, but when you have been acknowledged as the best in the business, fielding flaws are more easily discernible. Despite his sub-par year, Nettles remains a master at positioning himself, playing the hitter, knowing what pitch will be thrown to the batter, and knowing exactly where he will throw the ball if it is hit to him. He remains flawless in starting the double play. Throughout his career, he never let his hitting affect his fielding, or his fielding affect his hitting, and he is probably the one Yankee who has won more games with his glove than his bat.

OVERALL:

Robinson: "This year could be a very decisive year in his career. If he doesn't do the things he can do easily, the Yankees might make a change. They are looking at his age. Injuries have slowed him down. He is an outstanding fielder."

LOU PINIELLA
OF/DH, No. 14
RR, 6'2", 200 lbs.
ML Svc: 16 years
Born: 8-28-43 in
Tampa, FL

1982 STATISTICS

AVG	G	AB	R	H	2B	3B	HR	RBI	BB	SO	SB
.307	102	261	33	80	17	1	6	37	18	18	0

CAREER STATISTICS

AVG	G	AB	R	H	2B	3B	HR	RBI	BB	SO	SB
.290	1665	5633	624	1636	292	39	99	744	350	524	31

VS. RHP

VS. LHP

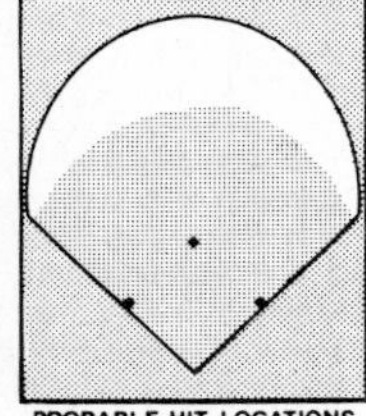

PROBABLE HIT LOCATIONS

HITTING:

If there is one ballplayer on the New York Yankees who has never disgraced himself when it comes to hitting in the clutch or with men on base, it is Lou Piniella. Virtually every major league hitter has a weakness or can be pitched to in a certain way at a certain time, but when the money is on the line or the game simply must be won, opposing teams know very well that "The Book" doesn't work with Piniella.

Piniella does not have one batting stance--he has dozens. Against some pitchers, he holds the bat further away from his body. Against others, he wraps the bat around his right shoulder and his hands are much closer to his head. He has a stance he uses when he tries for the long ball, and another when he realizes that contact is all that is needed to move a runner along. Like most veteran professional hitters, Piniella understands the mechanics of hitting and knows that the bat must be held lower as the calendar tolls the years.

Despite the myriad of stances, Piniella has learned that hitting boils down to the first step as the pitch approaches. If that first step is proper, the hands automatically propel the bat into the hitting position. If there were no mirrors in the locker room, Piniella would bring his own. He continually monitors his style this way, practicing the first step, watching his hands, and refining the art of getting his hips out of the way.

BASERUNNING:

Piniella is not fast but has the knack of going from first to third as well as any player in the league. He tends to slow down while heading for second, letting the outfielder think he will settle for second--and then speeds up while the outfielder nonchalants the ball. He generally gets to third base. He will not steal, but can in a must situation, particularly on the delayed steal if either the shortstop or second baseman take their eyes off him.

FIELDING:

In 1982, Piniella was the oldest active player in the league (not counting pitchers). He did DH, but also played both left and right field. He can catch any ball he can get to, although it may not look pretty. His arm is stronger than people give him credit for, but because it is not nearly as powerful as Dave Winfield's, he makes up for it by throwing on the dead run after charging a base hit.

OVERALL:

Robinson: "Piniella has to get more at-bats than he did last year. He did not play that much early in the year. But the tougher the situation, the better he is. This guy can hit--that's what he is, a professional hitter."

WILLIE RANDOLPH
INF, No. 30
RR, 5'11", 166 lbs.
ML Svc: 8 years
Born: 7-6-54 in
Holly Hill, SC

1982 STATISTICS

AVG	G	AB	R	H	2B	3B	HR	RBI	BB	SO	SB
.280	144	553	85	155	21	4	3	36	75	35	16

CAREER STATISTICS

AVG	G	AB	R	H	2B	3B	HR	RBI	BB	SO	SB
.271	964	3538	587	959	135	48	25	292	556	285	179

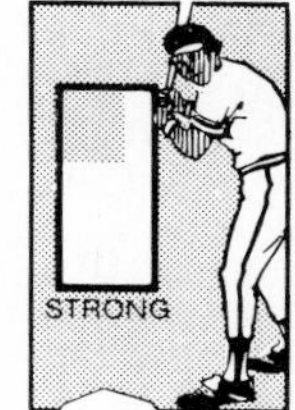

VS. RHP

VS. LHP

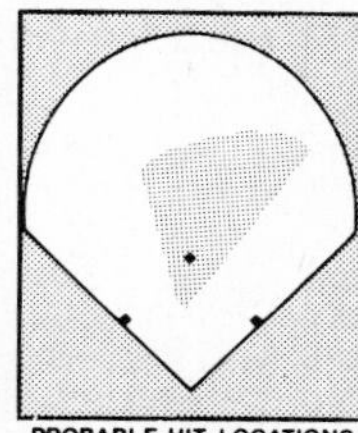
PROBABLE HIT LOCATIONS

HITTING:

Willie Randolph is the type of player who must be left alone. In 1980, then-manager Dick Howser left him alone and Randolph hit .294, his highest batting average to date. He also led the league that year in walks with 119.

Randolph prefers to bat leadoff, because he takes pride in his on-base percentage and his ability to draw walks. He can be quick-tempered, or he can be morose and moody, depending on his personal views of the team.

He bats almost straight up in the box, with a slightly closed stance, his weight evenly distributed. When he is hitting to his full potential, he uses all parts of the field, and surprisingly has more power to right-center than he does to straightaway left. With runners on base, opposing pitchers try to keep the ball in on him, because he likes to get his arms extended and hammer the ball to right or right-center. When Randolph slumps, he tends to jump at the ball, and that produces easy ground balls to short and third. When he waits on the ball, with or without runners on base, Randolph will hit his .290. He is an excellent high ball hitter.

BASERUNNING:

Randolph is an extremely aggressive baserunner, and will often run through a stop sign at third base if he feels he can score. His speed enables him to go from first to third on virtually any hit to right or center, and he gets an edge on many throws from the outfield by sliding head first. He leads the Yankees in stolen bases every year, but because the team had offensive problems in 1982, Yankee managers could not turn him loose.

FIELDING:

Randolph is considered to have the best range of any major league second baseman, with the possible exception of Frank White of the Kansas City Royals. But Randolph has no peer when it comes to turning the double play. One of his favorite ploys, with runners on first and second or first and third, is to force the runner at second, and if he knows he cannot double up the runner at first, fire to third or home, where he has caught many an unsuspecting runner. He has a better than average arm, and helps the outfielders on relays with strong throws to third or home on extra-base hits.

OVERALL:

Martin: "Randolph is a good percentage player. He will hit in the .270s, get on base, and has better than average speed. In 1982, however, he seemed to be disenchanted with the Yankee scene."

Robinson: "Willie has fallen into the same rut as most of the Yankees with a sub-par performance in every area, though he is usually the steady man. He could be among the best all around players."

SHANE RAWLEY
LHP, No. 26
LL, 6'0", 155 lbs.
ML Svc: 5 years
Born: 7-27-55 in Racine, WI

PITCHING:

After Shane Rawley had one of his four straight overpowering appearances in September of last year, then-manager Clyde King was asked if the converted reliever might be Number Two or Three man on the Yankee starting staff for 1983. King's answer was one to consider. "Why limit him," King said, "to Number Two or Three?"

That is where Rawley finds himself this year. There is no question that Rawley had three adjustments to make when traded from Seattle to New York. First, the losing atmosphere, in Seattle, to the "Win-at-all-costs" philosophy of New York. Second, the change from being a two-pitch reliever (fastball, slider) to a four-pitch starter (fastball, slider, curve, change). Third, the mental toughness required to pitch out of jams from the first inning on, throughout the game.

The adjustments came, little by little, and when Rawley blitzed the Kansas City Royals in a national TV game in September, George Brett openly admitted that no pitcher was able to handle the Royals in one single game like Rawley did.

Rawley cannot throw a straight ball. Every pitch he throws, be it slow, fast, mediocre, on his head and between his legs, moves one way or another. When Rick Cerone returned as a regular catcher, he had more than his share of passed balls because of the snake-like movement on Rawley's breaking and fast balls.

FIELDING:

Rawley needs improvement on his handling of bunts and throws to all bases. He does however, have a better than average pick-off move to first base. He was a better fielder with Seattle, because of the artificial surface there and the bunts that got to him quicker and straighter, but if Rawley is to make good on his prediction that he will give the Yankees 15-20 wins this year, he must improve his fielding.

OVERALL:

Rawley might turn out to live up to the Yankees' expectations. Like many new team members in 1982, he seemed uncomfortable when joining a team of once-proud veterans who knew they could count on their pitchers when the money was on the line. When he found out there were still championship caliber players on the team, players who despised embarrassment, he pitched like a man who wanted to win--and did.

1982 STATISTICS

W	L	ERA	G	GS	CG	IP	H	R	ER	BB	SO	SV
11	10	4.06	47	17	3	164	165	79	74	54	111	3

CAREER STATISTICS

W	L	ERA	G	GS	CG	IP	H	R	ER	BB	SO	SV
31	41	3.88	252	22	3	541	534	251	233	246	328	39

PITCHING:

The American League's Rookie of the Year in 1981, Dave Righetti found himself in the minors in June of 1982. The rest of the American League applauded the move that demoted Righetti--because they didn't have to face him. But Righetti came back, they had to face him again, and he started flirting with no-hitters, particularly against the Boston Red Sox.

The ironic part about Righetti is that most observers believe him to be a fastball pitcher. That analysis and observation is obvious, because this lefty can throw 95 MPH--with incredible fluidity and ease of motion. Others, however, believe that Righetti is essentially a breaking-ball pitcher, blessed with the ability to throw the ball through the proverbial brick wall.

There is little wasted motion when Righetti throws his fastball or slider. Batters see his graceful form, time the ball--then watch it buzz past them. If there is an over-exertion, it is after Righetti releases the ball, because he often falls off to the side of the mound, his back to the batter.

When he keeps his fastball up in the strike zone, and his slider down, Righetti is superb. When he came back from the minors, armed with the fifth Yankee pitching coach (Sammy Ellis), he frequently struck out the first three-four-five men to face him. If he had a problem, it was one bad inning, or with his control. Because the Yankees were extremely non-offensive in 1982, it only took that one bad inning to cost Righetti a game. And, to add to the irony of Righetti, when he walked more than the usual quota of batters, but maintained his stuff, he generally won. It was the bases-on-balls in close, low-scoring games that hurt him.

DAVE RIGHETTI
LHP, No. 19
LL, 6'3", 198 lbs.
ML Svc: 3 years
Born: 11-29-58 in San Jose, CA

FIELDING:

Because he has the habit of turning his body after certain pitches, more than the usual amount of ground balls sneak past Righetti up the middle. His quickness, however, enables him to field his position as well as can be expected. He is excellent on bunts down the third base line (when in position), and actually better on rollers or bunts down the first base line.

OVERALL:

Harwell: "Dave is a fine young pitcher. He will improve because of his good attitude and natural ability."

Robinson: "Unlimited potential and now it will be interesting to see if he can bounce back from up and down season. Look for him to have big year in 1983."

Martin: "Great stuff . . . superior fastball. Somebody beats him, but it's not the Red Sox."

1982 STATISTICS

W	L	ERA	G	GS	CG	IP	H	R	ER	BB	SO	SV
11	10	3.79	33	27	4	183	155	88	77	108	163	1

CAREER STATISTICS

W	L	ERA	G	GS	CG	IP	H	R	ER	BB	SO	SV
19	15	3.19	51	45	6	305	240	120	108	156	265	1

ANDRE ROBERTSON
INF, No. 55
RR, 5'10", 155 lbs.
ML Svc: 2 years
Born: 10-2-57 in Orange, TX

1982 STATISTICS

AVG	G	AB	R	H	2B	3B	HR	RBI	BB	SO	SB
.220	44	118	16	26	5	0	2	9	8	19	0

CAREER STATISTICS

AVG	G	AB	R	H	2B	3B	HR	RBI	BB	SO	SB
.220	45	119	16	26	5	0	2	9	8	19	0

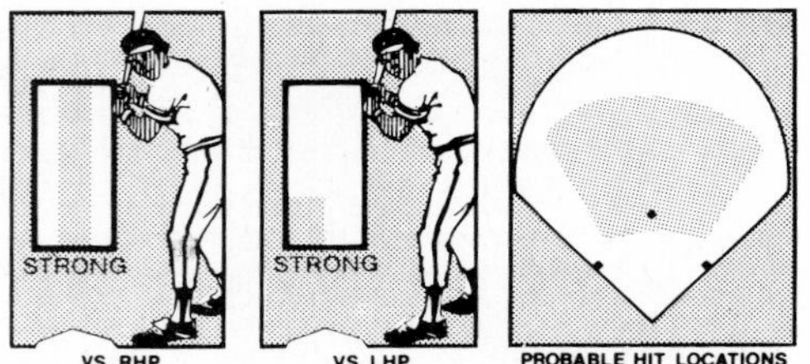

HITTING:

With Andre Robertson at the plate, if you closed your eyes and opened them quickly, you would think it was Willie Randolph at bat. Robertson, like Randolph, stands almost straight up, weight evenly distributed, with a slightly closed stance. He holds his bat over his right shoulder, and strides into pitches, toward the plate, like Randolph. Robertson was a special project of former Yankee batting coach Charlie Lau, who always stresses the importance of hitting to all fields.

Robertson will pull fastballs thrown in, and try and slap curves over the plate up the middle or to right-center. Because he has not had much playing time, his hitting mechanics are not as sound as they should be, and pitchers get him out with pitches he can normally handle. Lefties and righties try to keep the fastball up, and on the inside part of the plate. Righties also try and throw their curves low and away. Robertson, like Randolph, tends to be overly aggressive and eager at the plate, and often hits good pitches into the ground for easy outs. When he waits on the ball, he can hit to all fields, and can occasionally surprise with his power.

BASERUNNING:

He never got that much of a chance, but Robertson does have better than average speed, and knows how to run the bases. He tends to run bases "by the book," meaning that he will almost always try to go from first to third on a hit to right field, and hold at second on a hit to left or left-center.

FIELDING:

Robertson is probably the best young infielder in the American League. He has a stronger arm than any Yankee infielder, and has shown he can play both second and short. He is much more than adequate in turning the double play while playing second, and maybe even better as a shortstop. He has excellent range, and can throw with strength while off balance, in the hole, or behind the bag.

OVERALL:

If there is a crown jewel, Robertson is it. The Yankees traded away their entire farm system except Robertson. Because of his age and unlimited potential as a fielder and hitter, Robertson was asked for by every single team that wanted to trade with the Yankees. He was, like Elliot Ness, the "Untouchable." Because Graig Nettles, Roy Smalley and Willie Randolph have been beset by various ailments, Robertson will surely see more playing time this year, and is unquestionably a regular Yankee infielder of the future.

PITCHING:

Bob Shirley is a compact, quick pitcher. His fastball peaks at 90 MPH and though he is subject to control problems, at times he will use it well against a particular hitter's weakness. Shirley's best pitch, however, is a big breaking curve which can make even the best hitters look weak. Some regarded Shirley's curve as one of the best in the National League.

Strictly a three-quarter pitcher, Shirley uses a tight, economic motion when he is on. He has a slider, but he doesn't count on it. His strength is the fastball which he uses to get ahead in the count. His curve is his out pitch, particularly against lefthanded hitters, who rarely face a more difficult pitch.

He is an inexplicable sort, superb in one outing and terrible in another, completely unable to find the strike zone. When he gets into trouble, it seems to be in late innings. His ability in pressure situations seems contingent upon his control. When he has his pitches and stays ahead of the hitters, he is an ice-man.

Much of Shirley's problems with control and overall performance seem connected with the indecision with which teams approach him. After coming to the Reds in a late spring training trade last year, he spent the first half of the season pitching in long and short relief. He had been used in that capacity with other clubs, but has never seemed comfortable with that assignment.

When he was moved into the starting rotation, he seemed to solve much of his control problem and pitched effectively the remainder of the season.

BOB SHIRLEY
LHP, No. 32
RL, 5'11", 180 lbs.
ML Svc: 6 years
Born: 6-25-54 in
Oklahoma City, OK

FIELDING, HITTING, BASERUNNING:

With his compact motion, Shirley has a very good move to first and is adept at keeping runners close. His fielding is excellent. In the National League, he was a poor hitter and runner, but will not have to worry about that in the American League.

OVERALL:

Shirley is a talented pitcher, but he lacks consistency. At times, he seems to lack confidence but that could be because of his shifting status throughout his career. On most occasions, he is--despite control problems--highly effective against teams which are loaded with lefthanded hitters. He has excellent stuff but has had poor results.

McCarver: "Shirley is one of the true mysteries of our game. He has a supernatural curve with good velocity and a good fastball, but his wildness has persisted throughout his career. He is absolutely one of the toughest pitchers in the league against lefthanded hitters."

Coleman: "His rookie year, 1977, was his best. Since then, he seems to be going downhill gradually. But he can still be effective, especially against certain lefthanders."

1982 STATISTICS

W	L	ERA	G	GS	CG	IP	H	R	ER	BB	SO	SV
8	13	3.60	41	41	1	152	138	74	61	73	89	0

CAREER STATISTICS

W	L	ERA	G	GS	CG	IP	H	R	ER	BB	SO	SV
53	74	3.62	266	145	12	953	934	445	384	381	557	13

ROY SMALLEY
INF, No. 55
SR, 6'1", 182 lbs.
ML Svc: 8 years
Born: 10-25-52 in Los Angeles, CA

1982 STATISTICS

AVG	G	AB	R	H	2B	3B	HR	RBI	BB	SO	SB
.255	146	499	57	127	15	2	20	67	71	104	0

CAREER STATISTICS

AVG	G	AB	R	H	2B	3B	HR	RBI	BB	SO	SB
.259	1027	3706	495	959	152	18	94	457	512	578	18

VS. RHP

VS. LHP

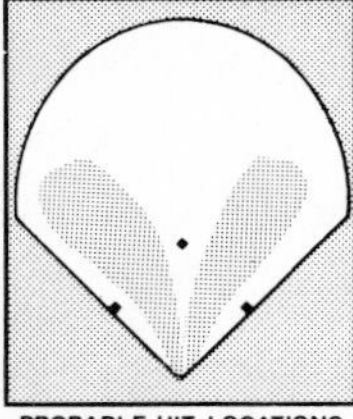
PROBABLE HIT LOCATIONS

HITTING:

Roy Smalley might be the only major leaguer in history to lead his team in homers and sacrifice bunts in one year. That, of course, occurred with the Minnesota Twins. Today, the switch-hitting shortstop third baseman is a member of the Yankees. With the Twins, he was the virtual "attack," but with the Yankees, he is just another hitter.

Smalley seemed to develop mechanical problems at the plate, but improved almost overnight when Lou Piniella was named hitting instructor. He bats straight up, square stance both ways, and always tries to pull every pitch thrown to him. Adjustments in his stance, hand position and hip movement, have now enabled him to handle pitches that gave him trouble, and he finished the 1982 season with more home runs than any Yankee shortstop in history.

Batting from either side, Smalley is plagued by fastballs busted in on the inside corner of the plate. He steps into most pitches, and therefore seems to have a slight blind spot on the inside corner. He can handle the majority of pitches from the knees to the letters, but frequently chases outside breaking balls from both righties and lefties. His homer total was considerable, because Smalley is lean. His swing, improving daily as 1982 wore on, became more a wrist-hand-arm swing, and enabled him to meet the ball with the maximum impact.

BASERUNNING:

Smalley is slow and rarely takes chances on the basepaths. The Yankees do not use him to steal, do not use him to hit-and-run and frequently hold him up at third base on singles to the outfield if he is starting from second base.

FIELDING:

A shortstop throughout his career, Smalley was moved to third base when he was traded to New York. Once Bucky Dent was traded, he moved back to short, but wound up the year alternating at both positions. Whether at short or third, Smalley displays a strong and accurate throw. He is quick, but hampered by a chronic bad back which limits his ability. At short, he has adequate range, but has trouble with grounders up the middle, because he tends to shy away from stretching too much or bending too low. He has the same problem backhanding grounders over the bag at third, but if he does field the ball, his powerful throws generally nail the runner.

OVERALL:

Robinson: "I don't care what you say, but when a player goes to New York (especially from Minnesota) there is an adjustment he has to make. Not only on the field, but off the field. It has affected Smalley's play overall. I look for him to be a better player this year."

DAVE WINFIELD
OF, No. 31
RR, 6'6", 220 lbs.
ML Svc: 10 years
Born: 1-3-51 in
St. Paul, MN

1982 STATISTICS

AVG	G	AB	R	H	2B	3B	HR	RBI	BB	SO	SB
.280	140	539	84	151	24	8	37	106	45	64	5

CAREER STATISTICS

AVG	G	AB	R	H	2B	3B	HR	RBI	BB	SO	SB
.284	1362	4924	735	1399	228	48	204	800	551	690	149

VS. RHP

VS. LHP

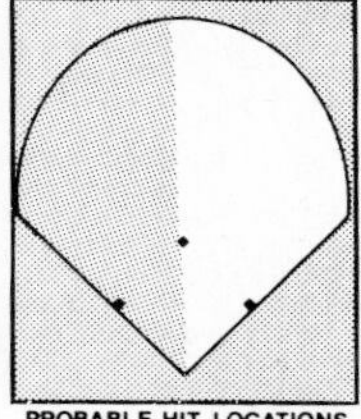
PROBABLE HIT LOCATIONS

HITTING:

Dave Winfield was never taught how to hit in the minor leagues, because he never played in the minor leagues. He still has batting flaws, so one can only muse about how good he could really be if he stopped chasing curves in the dirt and high fastballs out of the strike zone. And one can only guess how many homers he would hit if the left and left-center field fences in mammoth Yankee Stadium were really brought in.

Winfield, a huge man, has a wide stance, closed, and stands further away from home plate than any batter in the league. His flaw is that he tends to lunge at pitches and frequently does not make the contact he should. However, when he strides into a pitch from righties or lefties, he has his weight balanced and hits the ball with the sweet part of the bat, and the ball just rockets off of it.

The Dodgers exposed his penchant for chasing breaking balls in the dirt in the 1981 World Series. This was picked up by American League pitchers in 1982, but when he stopped chasing and waited, pitchers then tried to blaze the fastball past him on the inside corner because of his tendency to stride into every pitch. They had some success, but if they missed by two or three inches, a third baseman was likely to be decapitated. Winfield can hit homers to right, right-center, left, and left-center and likewise with extra base hits.

BASERUNNING:

No runner in the league can match him when he goes from first to third. In one instance, his steps--monstrous ones--were counted and it took him 10 strides to get from first to third. His incredible stride and pure speed make him a threat to steal, or to stretch any ordinary single into a double, and a double into a triple.

FIELDING:

There is none better in left field in any park in the League. Ninety-nine percent of all runners will not attempt to stretch a single into a double when he fields the ball because of his cannon-like and accurate arm. If he has one fault, it is his "arrogance" when fielding a grounder. He dares runners to try and take an extra base by cocking his arm. At times, runners take up his dare and narrowly beat his bullet throws, whereas they would have stayed put had Winfield simply picked up the ball and thrown it to the base they were headed for.

OVERALL:

Martin: "Has adjusted to the American League. Fine fielder and has learned to play Fenway Park left field wall better than any non-Red Sox player. Good to watch."

Robinson: "Yankees' best player. Doing it all and can be even better this year."

BUTCH WYNEGAR
C, No. 27
SR, 6'0", 194 lbs.
ML Svc: 7 years
Born: 3-14-56 in York, PA

1982 STATISTICS

AVG	G	AB	R	H	2B	3B	HR	RBI	BB	SO	SB
.267	87	277	36	74	12	1	4	28	50	33	0

CAREER STATISTICS

AVG	G	AB	R	H	2B	3B	HR	RBI	BB	SO	SB
.256	857	2937	352	753	120	10	40	345	398	280	8

VS. RHP

VS. LHP

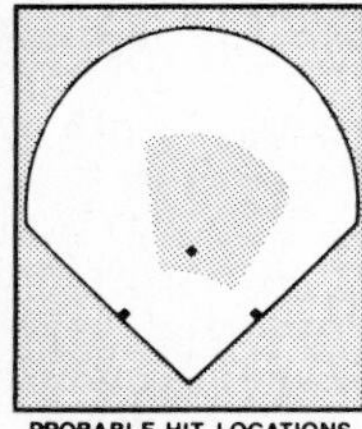
PROBABLE HIT LOCATIONS

HITTING:

Butch Wynegar would like to pull the ball, particularly in parks with short right field fences, but he winds up hitting line drives. He is a switch-hitter with a bit more power batting left, and a better hitter batting lefthanded. Righthanders try to keep the ball away from him, but Wynegar has indicated that he can pull a high, outside fastball, the pitch that seems to be the one he shouldn't handle.

Anything low, be it a fastball or breaking ball, Wynegar can hit batting lefty. As a righty, he has trouble with curves, low and away, and fastballs, up and in. He is a better off-speed hitter than some people think. His stance is square and upright, both ways.

BASERUNNING:

Wynegar might be the slowest Yankee. His drastic weight loss and debilitating effects after a viral infection in 1982 left him weaker and slower than usual, but even if he is in top shape, he is no threat to steal or play hit-and-run with. He rarely takes an extra base, and loses hits when his grounders in the hole are fielded by infielders, even if they are diving and tumbling when making the play. He is probably the Yankee most likely to be doubled up, either at bat or on base.

FIELDING:

Wynegar is considered to be the best low ball catcher in the league. He has an outstanding ability to block pitches in the dirt, and has excellent reflexes when it comes to backhanding, blocking or scooping low pitches. He calls his own game, handles pitchers well and leaves nothing to be desired when throwing out potential base-stealers. His arm and release are above average when it comes to accuracy.

His main flaw as a receiver seems to be in plays at the plate. Even before the illness, Wynegar seemed a bit averse when it came to tagging runners out. Rather than block the plate, Wynegar generally goes out for the ball, and must grab it, turn and dive for the sliding runner. On at least four occasions last year, runners that seemed to be dead ducks at the plate were able to elude his dives. He is not as quick as Cerone on slow chops or bunts, but makes up for the lack of speed with sure-handedness and accurate throws.

OVERALL:

Robinson: "He is a Number One catcher for any club. He does a great job behind the plate calling a game. Switch-hitting is a big plus for him. I also think it has taken him a year to get adjusted to New York."

Martin: "1982 was pretty well lost for him due to injury and sickness. He will hit in the .260s and get on base. He seems more comfortable in the powerful Yankee order than when he had to hit cleanup at Minnesota."

DAVE LaROCHE
LHP, No. 34
LL, 6'2", 200 lbs.
ML Svc: 13 years
Born: 5-14-48 in
Colorado Springs, CA

PITCHING AND FIELDING:

It takes forever for Dave LaRoche's blooper pitch, dubbed "La Lob" to reach home plate, and it must have seemed forever for the veteran reliever to get through the 1982 season. The Yankees called LaRoche up from Columbus (AAA) on four separate occasions.

LaRoche, hunches up when he releases the ball, and pitches from either straight overhand or three-quarters. He has lost quite a bit off his fastball, and it took him several months to shake off the pitching flaws he had acquired with the California Angels. The "La Lob" excites the fans, and surprisingly, has gotten out nine of 10 batters who try to hit it.

He continues to have better success against lefthanded batters, particularly if he keeps his curve on the outside portion of the plate. Because his curve and blooper are slower than normal, LaRoche can often throw an unexpected fastball past a hitter, be he lefty or righty.

He is not particularly quick or agile on the mound, but has a better than average move to first base.

OVERALL:

Martin: "Still can get people out, changes speed, keeps hitters off balance. A bit flaky, but all good relievers have to be a little that way--especially after his year (1982) of commuting between Columbus and New York."

Robinson: "Can do many things for a staff. In 1982 he was just like the Sporting News--comes once a week."

OAKLAND ALAMEDA COUNTY COLISEUM
Oakland A's

Seating Capacity: 50,219
Playing Surface: Natural Grass

Dimensions
Left Field Pole: 330 ft.
Left-Center Field: 375 ft.
Center Field: 400 ft.
Right-Center Field: 375 ft.
Right Field Pole: 330 ft.
Height of Outfield Wall: 10 ft.

The home of the Oakland A's is acknowledged to be one of the best pitcher's parks in the American League. When the A's were three-time World Champions in 1972, '73, and '74, pitching usually bailed them out, and when the 1981 A's won the Western Division, it was the same story.

That situation might not be the case if all the games were played in the day time, because balls travel much better in the day in Oakland. At night, however, the Bay area air seems to get so heavy that balls simply die as they reach the warning track.

The park was in almost complete disarray prior to the purchase of the club by a group headed by Roy Eisenhardt. The outfield fences had no padding, and in 1980, Ruppert Jones (then with the New York Yankees) almost died when he crashed into the center field fence trying to catch a ball. The new owners, however, have padded the fences, renovated the stadium, remodeled the clubhouses and made it a comfortable place to watch baseball games.

The Coliseum has more foul territory down the lines in left and right than any park in the league, an obvious hindrance to batters. Since Oakland teams have had excellent pitching and a superb outfield defense, they usually have an advantage in the park. In addition, long balls hit during night games, particularly in the cold nights in April, May, and September seem to be somewhat of an optical illusion. Batters hit what look like certain home runs, but then the balls appear to drop sharply--in mid-flight--and wind up in an outfielder's glove.

The Coliseum has four levels of seats from the left field foul pole to the right field foul pole, and one level from left-center to right-center. Wind is a factor, because it can easily blow in over the bleacher seats in center.

The infield grass and dirt are well manicured and produce less bad hops than in many parks. The bullpens are in foul territory down the left and right field foul lines. The dugouts are further away from either foul line than in any park in either league, and that extra foul territory enables infielders to catch fouls that would be in the stands in any other park.

DAVE BEARD
RHP, No. 33
LR, 6'5", 190 lbs.
ML Svc: 2 years
Born: 10-2-59 in Atlanta, GA

PITCHING:

Someday, Dave Beard is going to become a short reliever in the Goose Gossage mold. But at age 23, the 6'5" righthander has a lot to learn before he becomes the save man the A's expect he will eventually be. Beard's fastball arrives at the plate in the mid-90 MPH range, and it is going to become an even more effective pitch when he perfects the slider that he is adding to his game plan.

Two years ago, while pitching in Triple-A ball, Beard discovered that he was perfectly suited, from a mental standpoint, to become a short reliever. He has also been used as a starter and a long reliever, but is best suited to be a guy to go two innings at the most. Last year he was used in three roles and still had a decent season. If he had been used in just one role, he probably would have fared a lot better.

Beard throws his fastball most of the time and he has good control of it. He rarely throws a curve, but batters are seeing more and more sliders come from his direction. For a youngster, Beard has good presence on the mound. To date, he has not been one to use a brushback pitch and he is another of the A's who doesn't utilize a spitter. At present his fastball is rated above average and his slider is quickly approaching that level.

FIELDING:

Beard is rated an average fielder with an average move to first base.

OVERALL:

Beard is a young man who may reach greatness in the not too distant future. Once he masters the use of more than just a fastball, he may turn into one of the top relievers in the game of baseball. He is aggressive on the mound and likes the idea of going after any hitter he is called upon to face.

Robinson: "He's going to be a good one. He emerged as the A's No. 1 reliever at the end of the 1981 season. He's got the right makeup for a short reliever, but he is just a kid as far as pitching is concerned. His greatest weakness is the lack of experience."

Harwell: "Beard is a good reliever who is going to get a lot better when he learns to throw another pitch besides the fastball."

1982 STATISTICS

W	L	ERA	G	GS	CG	IP	H	R	ER	BB	SO	SV
10	9	3.44	54	2	0	91	85	41	35	35	73	11

CAREER STATISTICS

W	L	ERA	G	GS	CG	IP	H	R	ER	BB	SO	SV
11	11	3.38	75	2	0	120	106	52	45	46	100	15

TOM BURGMEIER
LHP, No. 16
LL, 5'11", 180 lbs.
ML Svc: 14 years
Born: 8-2-43 in
St. Paul, MN

PITCHING:

Tom Burgmeier is a lefthanded long-relief man. At 39 years old, he is in excellent physical condition, and is a reliable and crafty veteran. He relies on his above average control to spot his pitches, and he really works on a batter's weak spots. Burgmeier's fastball lacks the velocity to overpower hitters, but his ability to put it where he wants it still makes it his most effective pitch. His curve is his second best pitch and he'll often use it when he's ahead in the count, especially against lefthanders.

Burgmeier has been pitching in the majors since 1970 and he knows his job. He has good control and he seldom makes the mistake of trying to overpower hitters. Instead he uses his experience to pitch around hitters, nick the corners, and mix-up his speeds. During his career, he has had outstanding success against Cleveland, Toronto, and Texas, but the Yankees and Orioles both have a history of giving him trouble.

FIELDING:

Burgmeier is one of the best fielding pitchers in either league. He is a fine all around athlete, and is very quick and agile coming off the mound. He pounces on bunts and has an accurate arm to first. In short, Burgmeier not only knows what to do in every situation, he also has the natural ability to get it done.

OVERALL:

Burgmeier gets the most out of his ability. He's very confident on the mound and does his job of keeping the Sox close for 4 or 5 innings at a time. He's getting older, but has kept himself in shape and last season's stats (7-0; 2.29 ERA) suggest he has at least another couple of good years left.

Robinson: "The Red Sox got a lot of mileage out of Tom. I think he's a better pitcher now than he was ten years ago."

Harwell: "Tom has great poise on the mound and is a top-notch fielder."

Martin: "Tom is a durable, total professional. He's done an awful lot with average tools."

1982 STATISTICS

W	L	ERA	G	GS	CG	IP	H	R	ER	BB	SO	SV
7	0	2.29	40	0	0	102	98	30	26	22	44	2

CAREER STATISTICS

W	L	ERA	G	GS	CG	IP	H	R	ER	BB	SO	SV
70	48	3.29	679	3	0	1139	1127	482	416	344	537	95

JEFF BURROUGHS
OF, No. 3
RR, 6'0", 200 lbs.
ML Svc: 13 years
Born: 3-7-51 in
Long Beach, CA

1982 STATISTICS

AVG	G	AB	R	H	2B	3B	HR	RBI	BB	SO	SB
.277	113	285	42	79	13	2	16	48	45	61	1

CAREER STATISTICS

AVG	G	AB	R	H	2B	3B	HR	RBI	BB	SO	SB
.260	1424	4873	653	1271	205	16	222	790	732	997	16

VS. RHP

VS. LHP

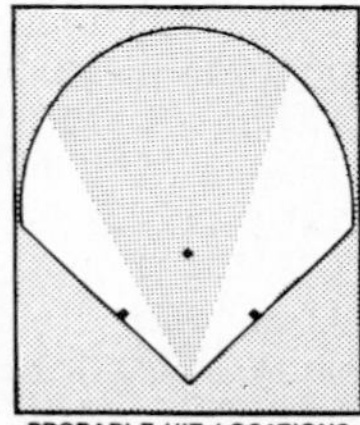
PROBABLE HIT LOCATIONS

HITTING:

The A's signed Jeff Burroughs early last season for just one reason--they needed a righthanded hitter with power. Burroughs not only fit the bill, he filled it. He is one player who enjoys the role of designated hitter and is probably still in the majors because there is a DH.

Burroughs has his eye trained to hit just about anything that comes his way on the inside half of the plate, especially if it happens to be a high fastball. Throw him a good breaking pitch away and he'll probably make out, but he is extremely patient and will wait for his pitch.

He is a power hitter who can uppercut the ball for homers that exit stadiums as long line drives. He is very effective at hitting lefthanders. He is good in the clutch and his eagle eyes help him draw a lot of walks. He is average at hitting with men in scoring position and needs work on the hit-and-run and on his bunting. He hits the ball from right-center to left-center. He is average at hitting a good curveball and just so-so at pouncing on sinkers and sliders.

Burroughs is especially at home in parks with shallow alleys like Seattle and Minnesota, and his batting eye also lights up in Fenway Park and Tiger Stadium. On the other hand, Yankee Stadium isn't his garden spot.

BASERUNNING:

Even late in his career, his overall baserunning needs work. He doesn't make waves on base. Pitchers pay him little bother. When he does slide he goes in feet first.

FIELDING:

On several occasions, when his more talented teammates were injured, Burroughs was called upon to play the outfield in 1982. He did not disgrace himself. The balls he reached he usually caught, but his lack of speed has always handicapped him on defense. In his prime he had an above average arm and could throw on target. However, of late, his ratings have dropped to average.

OVERALL:

Martin: "A decent DH bet. Will hit in the .260s (he led the A's with a .277 average last year) with double-figure home runs if he plays enough. The DH rule was made for him."

Robinson: "For Jeff, this might be his last year. He has good power, but for him to be appreciated, he has to play more and in Oakland it's all dead ends. He probably has seen his better years, but he's still a threat for the long ball."

WAYNE GROSS
INF, No. 10
LR, 6'2", 205 lbs.
ML Svc: 7 years
Born: 1-14-52 in Riverside, CA

1982 STATISTICS

AVG	G	AB	R	H	2B	3B	HR	RBI	BB	SO	SB
.251	129	386	43	97	14	0	9	41	53	49	3

CAREER STATISTICS

AVG	G	AB	R	H	2B	3B	HR	RBI	BB	SO	SB
.235	736	2225	255	523	91	8	76	270	331	326	19

VS. RHP

VS. LHP

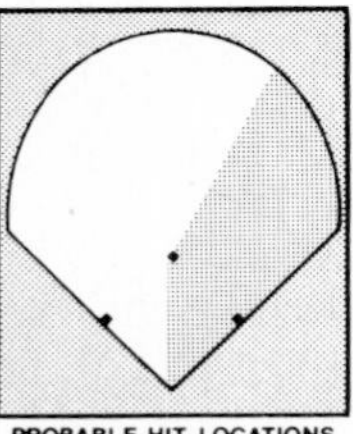
PROBABLE HIT LOCATIONS

HITTING:

Wayne Gross is a high ball hitter who tries to pull every pitch thrown his way. However, if spring lasted into September, Gross might be one of the all-time greats.

Because Gross is a pull hitter, the key to getting him out is to pitch him outside. Recently he has been strictly platooned to hit against righthanders. If they keep the ball down and away from him, they will have success. He is a line drive hitter and can hit home runs, although last year his output was limited to nine. He considers high fastballs out over the plate to inside a delicacy. He can be fooled with a change-up; and curves, sliders and sinkers also give him trouble. Rate Gross average, but able to deliver a sting if the pitcher makes a mistake.

In mid-season 1982, Gross was moved to the No. 2 spot in the order to enable leadoff hitter Rickey Henderson to have better chances to steal. Gross handled hitting second well, but is normally more suited to hitting fifth or sixth. He has an upright stance and stands low in the box.

BASERUNNING:

Gross has 19 career thefts and at least three of them have been of home plate. At 6'2", 205 lbs., he runs like a train and is thus not considered a major base stealing threat. His speed to first needs work and once he's there, pitchers aren't prone to pay him a great deal of attention. In fact, baserunning is rated the poorest part of Gross' game.

FIELDING:

There is probably no one who has worked harder at learning to play third base than Gross. At fielding pop flies he is one of the best. But because he is a self-made man at his position, he is rated just average. He is good at backhanding the ball and has pretty quick reactions for a big man. His range is sufficient, and his arm and throwing accuracy are average. He can turn the double play and has improved greatly at fielding bunts. Gross rarely plays there, but he may be the best first baseman the A's have. He likes to play first base better than he does third.

OVERALL:

Robinson: "He can make a fairly decent contribution even though he hits for a low average. The best bet is for him to be platooned."

Martin: "He is a professional who responds well to platoon treatment. He can hurt you occasionally with the long ball."

Harwell: "Gross is a long ball threat and a good team player."

PRESTON HANNA
RHP, No. 49
RR, 6'1", 185 lbs.
ML Svc: 6 years
Born: 9-10-54 in
Pensacola, FL

PITCHING:

Preston Hanna, primarily a middle reliever, joined the A's from Atlanta in July of 1982 and was used in a variety of roles--short man, middle man and as a starter when needed. Hanna was originally signed by the Braves in 1972 and spent the years between 1978 and 1981 at the major league level.

Hanna's big pitch is his fastball, which he throws most of the time in the 85-90 MPH range. He complements his heater with a hard curve and once in awhile offers a slider. His curve is actually a "knuckle curve", which can be devastating if he has his control. Hanna has good natural ability, but has been rated as an average pitcher because of inconsistency with his control. He needs specific improvement in the area of pitching to a batter's weakness.

He is equally effective against righthanded and lefthanded hitters. Unlike many of his new teammates, he does not throw a spitball. When he needs an out he will most often go to his fastball. Seldom, if ever, will he brushback a hitter. He is an average pitcher when working in pressure situations.

FIELDING:

Hanna's fielding is rated about the same as his pitching--average. He is quick, and gets off the mound well to field bunts. There is nothing special about his move to first base. He fields his position adequately, but without noticeable strength in any one particular area.

OVERALL:

Hanna's rating as an average pitcher could be upgraded if he can become more consistent. He has good poise on the mound and his fastball could be a wonder if he could learn to control it a bit more than he does now.

Harwell: "Hanna is a power pitcher with a good curve and good natural ability. But he needs to do something about his lack of control."

Robinson: "Hanna is an average pitcher with average stuff who can pitch anywhere . . . start, short or long relief. He has to rely on getting the ball to the right spot. He does not throw his hard and average stuff with all pitches."

1982 STATISTICS

W	L	ERA	G	GS	CG	IP	H	R	ER	BB	SO	SV
3	4	4.82	43	3	1	84	90	49	45	61	49	0

CAREER STATISTICS

W	L	ERA	G	GS	CG	IP	H	R	ER	BB	SO	SV
17	25	4.62	156	47	1	436	452	250	224	279	253	1

MIKE HEATH
C, No. 2
RR, 5'11", 176 lbs.
ML Svc: 5 years
Born: 2-5-56 in
Tampa, FL

1982 STATISTICS

AVG	G	AB	R	H	2B	3B	HR	RBI	BB	SO	SB
.242	101	318	43	77	18	4	3	39	27	37	9

CAREER STATISTICS

AVG	G	AB	R	H	2B	3B	HR	RBI	BB	SO	SB
.242	384	1274	121	309	46	8	15	135	77	128	15

VS. RHP

VS. LHP

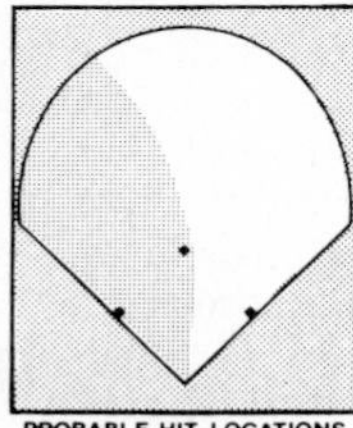
PROBABLE HIT LOCATIONS

HITTING:

Mike Heath has shown signs that he has the ability to become a much better hitter than he is. He's had four full seasons in the major leagues and has yet to break out of the .240 mold.

A line drive hitter, Heath will occasionally jerk one out of the park, as he did eight times in 1981. He is a high fastball hitter who doesn't handle much of anything else with a whole lot of success. Breaking balls and change-ups mystify him. He is a pesky type of hitter, a spoiler, but generally not considered a threat. His stance is upright, closed and he uses the middle of the box. Both righthanders and lefties would be best off pitching Heath outside. He is a high ball hitter because he tries to pull every pitch. He has about equal ability to hit lefties and righties. He is average at hitting in the clutch and hitting behind the runner. But he is good on the hit-and-run and is a fine bunter, often using that mode as a way of getting on base with a hit.

BASERUNNING:

Heath isn't the quickest human being on two feet and is thus considered a conservative runner and not much of a threat to steal.

FIELDING:

If he isn't already, Heath is heading toward the top as the finest catcher in the American League. He has an outstanding arm, knows the hitters and is not at all afraid to rattle them. He has a good release point and his throwing accuracy is excellent. He is improving each year at calling games (a weak spot in the beginning) and does call the pitches.

Pitchers on the A's staff are becoming more comfortable with him behind the plate with every passing day. He springs on bunts and is out to nail down base thiefs like a hungry puma on its prey. If he has a weakness it is his temper, but he has also improved his control of that problem. Heath is also quite capable of playing left or right field and has also been used at third base as well.

OVERALL:

Robinson: "This guy should start to exert himself soon. He is in a holding pattern with the ability to do better. If Heath does not come on with the bat this year, my thoughts are that he never will. He's a tough, everyday, take-charge guy who has to hit better if he wants the recognition. I have heard some say he is the best all around catcher in the American League, but I doubt that. If he hits . . . I might change my mind."

Martin: "Heath has made great strides in the last two years. He is busy behind the plate, keeps the ball in front of him and catches a good game."

RICKEY HENDERSON
OF, No. 35
RL, 5'10", 180 lbs.
ML Svc: 4 years
Born: 12-25-58 in
Chicago, IL

1982 STATISTICS

AVG	G	AB	R	H	2B	3B	HR	RBI	BB	SO	SB
.267	149	536	119	143	24	4	10	51	116	94	130

CAREER STATISTICS

AVG	G	AB	R	H	2B	3B	HR	RBI	BB	SO	SB
.290	504	1901	368	553	77	18	26	165	331	255	319

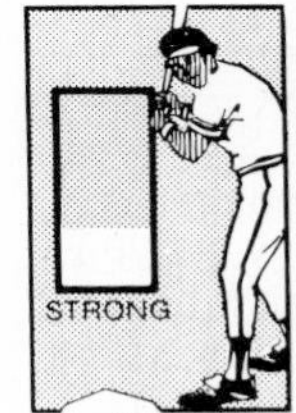

VS. RHP

VS. LHP

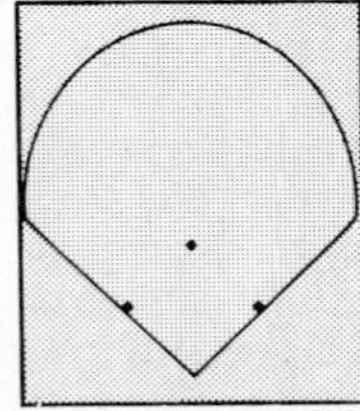
PROBABLE HIT LOCATIONS

HITTING:

Rickey Henderson bats out of a pronounced crouch, perhaps the most defined in the game. At the last second, he comes uncoiled and extends himself, which enables him to hit high pitches. He has a great eye and his stance makes it hard for pitchers to throw to him. He draws walks well and may become the greatest leadoff hitter in the history of the sport. He can hit pitches from either lefties or righties, but may be a little rougher on left-handers. He hits line drives, beats out grounders for hits with his great speed, and is showing the power hitting potential that one day may enable him to hit 20 or 25 homers in a season. He uses the entire field with his bat. Pitchers should send him a diet of curves, low and outside, change-ups or low fastballs.

Henderson is a little impatient, and making him wait can disturb him. But because of his great speed, he is never going to have a long slump. He's a good clutch hitter, can hit behind the runner and with men in scoring position. He should learn to become a better bunter to improve his offensive capabilities even more. Parks with soft surfaces, like Detroit and Milwaukee, tend to give him trouble and he is definitely not wild about hitting under domes.

BASERUNNING:

Henderson may get the green light to steal on his own this season. Who knows to what heights this new twist may lead him? He is already the most powerful force in baseball on the base-paths and as he becomes a smarter runner he will continue to improve. He has great speed, gets a good jump and is always a threat to steal. He is tremendously aggressive and drives pitchers crazy. His head first slide has become famous, but he may mix in a few feet first landings in the future to take some of the wear and tear off his body.

FIELDING:

Henderson is becoming one of the finest left fielders in the game. He has an above average arm and pinpoint throwing accuracy. He has great range and throws well to home. He can outrun the ball in either direction. He charges the ball well and the head high liners that used to give him problems no longer seem to bother him.

OVERALL:

Robinson: "Henderson might be the best player in the league. He is just a tremendous all around player in every area."

Martin: "Now that the basestealing record is his, he can concentrate on becoming more of a hitter and hit with some power and some idea. He'll channel his running into a team-aiding concept. After all, he's only 24 years old."

Harwell: "The greatest stealer. Tremendous speed. He will be even better when he learns the moves of opposing pitchers."

MATT KEOUGH
RHP, No. 27
RR, 6'2", 175 lbs.
ML Svc: 6 years
Born: 7-3-55 in
Pomona, CA

PITCHING:

Since Matt Keough became a regular in the major leagues in 1978, he has had just two winning seasons. Both were while Billy Martin was managing the A's. If anyone was sorry to see Martin fired, it was Keough, who credits Brash Billy with turning his career around. In 1980 and 1981, Keough was a combined 26-19, but fell on hard times again in 1982 and finished at 11-18, receiving a decision in all but five of his 34 starts.

Keough is mainly a breaking ball pitcher, but can also deliver a "sneaky" fastball that has been clocked in the high 80s. After a 2-17 season in 1979, he quit throwing a slider and last year developed a cut fastball. Keough is a control pitcher who must keep the ball down to be effective. Last year he had problems with his control and was the victim of 38 home runs. He also uses a screwball and sinker and has been known to offer up a spitter when he feels the need to throw one. He has a straight change, which he turns over. Keough is rated an above average pitcher in pressure situations, but when he doesn't have his control and is forced to spot the ball, he is not apt to be effective. The righthander has learned how to pitch, but has a tendency to let things upset him at times and thus can get into trouble.

FIELDING:

All aspects of Keough's defensive game are above average to excellent. He has a good move to first base, fields bunts well and knows where to position himself when the ball is in play.

OVERALL:

There are certain teams Keough should stay home against. During his career he has not fared well against Chicago, Texas or Baltimore. He seems to have his best luck against New York and Kansas City. Keough himself couldn't figure out just what went wrong last season and is hoping to get his wires connected correctly again this season.

Robinson: "Keough is a good overall pitcher who has had a lot of ups and downs since he has been at Oakland and nothing bothers him. 1982 was a long year for Keough. He has not pitched well. It looks like he has lost something off his fastball and his control has not been that good."

Martin: "Another Oakland pitcher with a lot of innings thrown and a lot of hits given up. But he competes well and can be a top pitcher."

Harwell: "Keough is a pitcher with a good variety of pitches. He has good stuff, but is inconsistent."

1982 STATISTICS

W	L	ERA	G	GS	CG	IP	H	R	ER	BB	SO	SV
11	18	5.72	34	34	10	209	233	144	133	101	75	0

CAREER STATISTICS

W	L	ERA	G	GS	CG	IP	H	R	ER	BB	SO	SV
48	72	4.07	156	151	53	1016	1013	524	460	425	482	0

BRIAN KINGMAN
RHP, No. 50
RR, 6'1", 190 lbs.
ML Svc: 4 years
Born: 7-27-54 in
Los Angeles, CA

PITCHING:

"Woe the Luck," a clever little tune by Dan Hicks and the Hot Licks, perfectly describes Brian Kingman, whose moons seem to have been lined up in the wrong orbit for eternity. Every pitcher, player and coach on the A's insists that Kingman has the best stuff on the pitching staff. One couldn't tell it by looking at the righthander's stat sheet. In 1979, Kingman's first year in the majors, he was 8-7. It has been all downhill since, including an 8-20 nightmare in 1980. That year the A's were shut out five times when Kingman was on the mound and they averaged just 2.8 runs in each of his 30 starts. Yet he managed to finish with a respectable 3.83 ERA.

Kingman's fastball, which he cuts so that it sinks, arrives at the hitter traveling in the high 80s. His curveball, which at times has an orbit that would make space shuttle pilots envious, is what he uses to get strikeouts. If he has a slider, he doesn't use it often; once in a while he'll change pace and he is not one to load up the ball.

Rate Kingman a power pitcher who could be awesome if he could learn to show his ability while actually standing on the mound. He can be equally effective against lefties or righties if his good overhand curve is working. If behind on the count, look for the heater. When Kingman gets in trouble, he has a tendency to fall apart and will give up a lot of hits. He is only average in pressure situations and must improve in that area.

FIELDING:

Kingman's move to first is average, just as is his ability to field bunts. He is an average fielding pitcher. There have been times, especially when he is in the midst of getting shelled, that he seems to forget where he should be in certain situations.

OVERALL:

The firing of manager Billy Martin may have been the best thing that ever happened to Kingman. The two never really got along, and the pitcher has said that a trade might be the best thing that could happen to his career. There is no doubt that when Kingman is at his best, he is unbeatable. But he must shake the image that he is a loser and the attitude that goes along with that image. Now that the A's have had a change of managers, Kingman might just turn himself around.

Robinson: "Kingman needs a change of scenery. He can be a much better pitcher. He's got too good an arm to go on like this. He might have the best stuff on the staff, but he has not been able to take it to the mound with him."

Martin: "He has enough stuff to be a winning pitcher, but he must stop giving up a hit an inning. He should be approaching his peak years. If healthy, he can strike people out. Kingman needs a strong winning season to bolster him."

1982 STATISTICS

W	L	ERA	G	GS	CG	IP	H	R	ER	BB	SO	SV
4	12	4.48	23	20	3	122	131	64	61	57	46	1

CAREER STATISTICS

W	L	ERA	G	GS	CG	IP	H	R	ER	BB	SO	SV
23	45	4.10	91	82	21	546	565	276	249	204	272	1

MICKEY KLUTTS
INF, No. 9
RR, 5'11", 189 lbs.
ML Svc: 4 years
Born: 9-30-54 in
Montebello, CA

1982 STATISTICS

AVG	G	AB	R	H	2B	3B	HR	RBI	BB	SO	SB
.178	55	157	10	28	8	0	0	14	9	18	0

CAREER STATISTICS

AVG	G	AB	R	H	2B	3B	HR	RBI	BB	SO	SB
.239	177	493	46	118	26	1	11	54	33	90	1

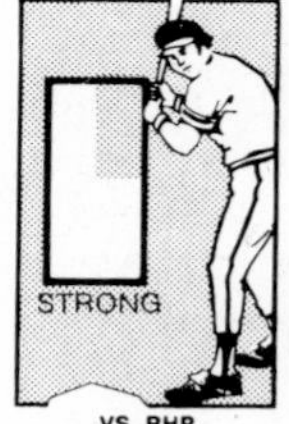

VS. RHP

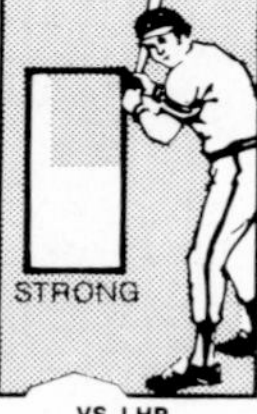

VS. LHP

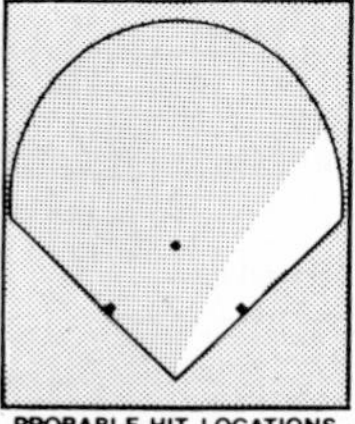
PROBABLE HIT LOCATIONS

HITTING:

One wonders what direction Mickey Klutts' career might have taken had he been able to stay healthy. He is one guy who has spent just about as much time on the disabled list as he has in the lineup and on the bench combined. If he could play one full, injury-free season, this report might have read a lot differently.

Klutts is a much stronger hitter against lefthanded pitchers and has been platooned because of it. He'll pull the ball to the left side, occasionally with power, and can reach the gap in left-center. He is a high ball hitter who should be pitched away. In spurts, he has shown that he can handle major league pitching. Change of speed pitches and fastballs running away leave him in trouble. He doesn't like anything run off the plate. High fastballs delight him. Good curves, sinkers and sliders will get him out.

Klutts' execution with a bat is average from his ability to hit in the clutch to his talent for bunting. He needs work at hitting with runners in scoring position. It is best to position Klutts low in the lineup.

BASERUNNING:

Klutts is by no means slow, but he is not rated as a good baserunner. He has above average speed to first, but has stolen just one base in his career. Pitchers aren't likely to pay him much attention. He uses a head first slide at times and is average at breaking up double plays.

FIELDING:

As a third baseman, Klutts is average at best, maybe below average. His arm, accuracy and range are all middle-of-the-road. He is neither exceptional nor horrid at fielding bunts and is so-so at turning the double play.

OVERALL:

Robinson: "No one knows. He has got more days on the disabled list than days of playing on the roster. He has some potential, but I think you have seen his best. He can help if he hits, but it looks like we will never find out because of his injury-prone career. He's not a very good third baseman."

Martin: "Klutts has never made it as big as was thought. Because he is injury-prone it's hard to get a line on him."

RICK LANGFORD
RHP, No. 22
RR, 6'0", 180 lbs.
ML Svc: 7 years
Born: 3-20-52 in
Farmville, VA

PITCHING:

Rick Langford is one guy who nearly always finishes what he starts. In 1980 he completed 28 of his 33 starts, including a streak of 22 straight complete games between May and September, a modern day major league record. The following year he finished 18 of his 24 starts, but last season fell off somewhat by completing only 15 of 31 starts in what was a dismal season all around for the veteran righthander. Many feel that Langford has become a six or seven inning pitcher, and under new manager Steve Boros, Langford may get the hook around the seventh even if he holds a lead. Why? In 237 1/3 innnings last year, Langford yielded 265 hits. He has always given up a lot of hits, but in 1982, many seemed to leap off opposing bats in late innings.

If baseball is a game of inches, Langford's game is one of centimeters. He is a finesse pitcher who is in big trouble if his sinker or slider are just a fraction off target. His fastball is just average, but it is sneaky if he gets it in the right spot. His sinker, a good one, runs away from lefthanders. Several scouts have seen evidence that Langford has a forkball, and they also suspect that he throws a spitter. His straight change is a good "off" pitch.

He appears unflappable while on the hill, very workman-like. He'll nibble a hitter to death with his breaking pitches. When behind on the count he mixes it up with fastballs and sliders. Most important in Langford's case, is that he knows how to pitch and has a fine knowledge of every hitter in the American League. However, last season he was consistently unable to get the big out when he needed it in crucial situations. To win, Langford must keep the ball low in the strike zone, but last season, he was getting his pitches up.

FIELDING:

Langford is one of the better fielding pitchers on the A's staff. His move to first base is above average. Although it is not sneaky, it is quick. He is adept at fielding bunts and always knows where to position himself while a play is in progress.

OVERALL:

If the A's can put together a decent bullpen and allow Langford to become the seven inning starter he should be, he could return to form in 1983. True, he had an off year in 1982, but so did the rest of the team. He experienced some soreness in his arm, but there is nothing so wrong with him that a few less innings on the mound won't cure.

Robinson: "Langford gives you a good day's work every time he takes the mound. He is getting a lot more out of his ability than most people do. He can pitch."

Martin: "He throws a lot of innings and keeps his team in the game. He's not a power pitcher, but he throws strikes. He just keeps throwing. He is an above average pitcher."

Harwell: "Langford is a smart pitcher who tries to keep hitters off balance with a variety of pitches."

1982 STATISTICS

W	L	ERA	G	GS	CG	IP	H	R	ER	BB	SO	SV
11	16	4.21	32	31	15	237	265	121	111	49	79	0

CAREER STATISTICS

W	L	ERA	G	GS	CG	IP	H	R	ER	BB	SO	SV
69	87	3.75	211	173	85	1347	1383	636	561	371	616	0

CARNEY LANSFORD
INF, No. 4
RR, 6'2", 195 lbs.
ML Svc: 5 years
Born: 2-7-57 in
San Jose, CA

1982 STATISTICS

AVG	G	AB	R	H	2B	3B	HR	RBI	BB	SO	SB
.301	128	482	65	145	28	4	11	63	46	48	9

CAREER STATISTICS

AVG	G	AB	R	H	2B	3B	HR	RBI	BB	SO	SB
.292	659	2590	390	757	131	17	57	326	200	351	78

VS. RHP

VS. LHP

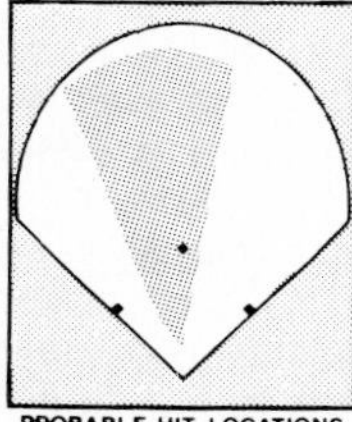
PROBABLE HIT LOCATIONS

HITTING:

Lansford was bothered by an assortment of minor injuries last year, but he is still acknowledged as a legitimate .300 hitter. He pulls the ball fairly well, which was an asset in Fenway. Lansford is a strong line drive hitter, and can consistently power the ball up the left-center alley. He's aggressive with the bat and is rated above average to excellent in clutch situations.

He has the ability to hit any pitch and to hit it hard, but he is particularly effective against anything high and on the inside half of the plate. He is considered adequate against off-speed deliveries and handles curves and sliders fairly well. Opposing pitchers generally try to work Lansford up and inside, out of the strike zone, and then throw him curves down and away. However, there is really no pitch he can't hit and no single way to get him out.

Lansford is not only aggressive but he is also consistent. He hits well with men on base and is willing to sacrifice an at-bat to move runners along. He seldom bunts and is rarely asked to. Lansford is rated above average to excellent in all offensive phases of the game.

BASERUNNING:

Lansford is just as aggressive on the basepaths as he is with his bat. He's not exceptionally fast, but his intensity and willingness to go for the extra base keep opposing pitchers and fielders on their toes. He'll slide hard to break up the double play and he knows when to try to go from first to third on a base hit.

FIELDING:

Lansford has an above average arm both in terms of strength and accuracy. His range at third is only satisfactory, but he makes a lot of good reaction plays diving to his left to plug the hole between third and short. He's aggressive charging bunts and squibblers and has quick hands when starting the 5-4-3 double play.

OVERALL:

Lansford is steady and consistently good in all phases of the game. When he's not plagued by injuries, his stats should improve significantly.

Harwell: "Lansford is tough in the clutch and generally hits with power and consistency."

Martin: "One of the top all around players in the league. He plays hard and intelligent baseball. He is a fine a third baseman as they come."

Robinson: "Carney is a top player. He can help any team when he's healthy."

DAVEY LOPES
INF, No. 15
RR, 5'9", 170 lbs.
ML Svc: 11 years
Born: 6-3-46 in
East Providence, RI

1982 STATISTICS

AVG	G	AB	R	H	2B	3B	HR	RBI	BB	SO	SB
.242	128	450	58	109	19	3	11	42	40	51	28

CAREER STATISTICS

AVG	G	AB	R	H	2B	3B	HR	RBI	BB	SO	SB
.260	1335	5040	817	1313	184	42	110	426	643	743	446

VS. RHP

VS. LHP

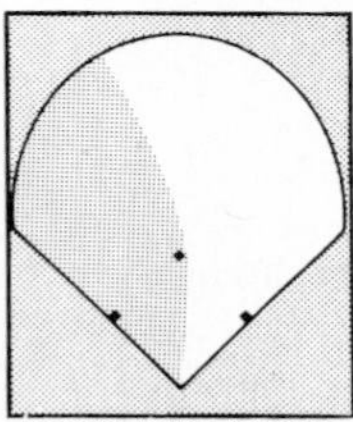
PROBABLE HIT LOCATIONS

HITTING:

All around, Davey Lopes is a strong offensive player. He is not particularly outstanding in any one particular area with his bat, but he is solid in all aspects of his hitting game, especially if the opposing pitcher is foolish enough to get a fastball up . . . letters to eyeballs.

Last year, Lopes hit just .242, almost 20 points below his lifetime average. But he still managed to help the A's in a number of ways. His stance is upright with just a hint of a crouch and he stands in the center of the box. He is usually more effective hitting against lefthanders and will go after the first pitch, especially if he is reading fastball.

He pulls to the left side, but can also cause damage straightaway. He has good power, which usually nets him home runs pulled to left. If a pitcher wants Lopes on a platter, a diet of breaking balls away, curves and sinkers should do the job nicely. Make a mistake and he'll hurt you. He is a good bunter and draws walks. He is a solid hitter with runners in scoring position. He is just average in the clutch, executing the hit-and-run and batting behind the runner. Lopes is a fair hitter now with some power for a little guy.

BASERUNNING:

Lopes is an excellent baserunner, and proof of that lies in the fact that he has the highest success rate in steal attempts of any man who ever played the game. He has excellent speed to first and once there can play havoc with the defense. He is a craftsman at reading a pitcher's moves, gets good leads and excellent jumps. He is a smart runner and pitchers pay him lots of mind. He slides feet first and is perfectly capable of breaking up a double play.

FIELDING:

Lopes has never been known to the public as a standout defensive player, yet he won a Gold Glove while with the Dodgers in 1978. He is rated an average second baseman. He has average arm strength, but is accurate with his throws. He has decent range and moves equally well from right to left. He is not afraid to turn the double play, and will occasionally come up with a defensive gem in the clutch.

OVERALL:

Martin: "Lopes was a good solid hitter for the Dodgers for nine years. He was not a particularly solid second baseman, but fits in. With the A's he was a decent player having a fair year with a bad team."

Robinson: "He is an excellent leadoff or second place hitter, but due to Rickey Henderson and Dwayne Murphy, he has to hit down in the lineup some. He has given Oakland players some guidance and leadership. He is a steadying influence."

PITCHING:

When Steve McCatty was 14-7 and finished second in the American League Cy Young Award voting in 1981, he discovered that he had learned how to pitch. He arrived at spring training in 1982 with high hopes, but those were quickly dashed when he developed arm trouble, primarily tendinitis in his right shoulder, that hampered him the entire season. He was told to rest during the off-season and is keeping his fingers crossed that he will be able to return to form this year.

It was in 1981 that manager Billy Martin gave McCatty the green light to throw the pitches he wanted to throw. The previous year, when he was 14-14, McCatty took the mound on most occasions with strict orders from the bench. He was not happy about pitching with reins on, but evidently learned from the experience. He proved that in 1981.

McCatty earns his meat and potatoes with his fastball, which ranges in speed from the mid-80s to 90s. The heater is his main pitch and he complements it with a curveball, slider and an occasional straight change. He is equally effective against lefthanded and righthanded hitters. His fastball, when in top form, has good movement and will rise and run in on hitters.

McCatty is primarily a three-quarter delivery man, but on occasion comes over the top. The curve, his second best pitch, is thrown hard and down and has helped him cut down on giving up numerous home run balls. He throws a hard slider that is rated above average. McCatty throws the slider 40% of the time, and it is short, quick and above average. McCatty is a very aggressive pitcher who throws hard all of the time. He works fast, likes to challenge the hitter, and has been known to drop a hitter in the dirt. He is one of the few Oakland pitchers who does not utilize a spitter. His main weakness is that he is given to sporadic wild spells.

STEVE McCATTY
RHP, No. 54
RR, 6'3", 205 lbs.
ML Svc: 4 years
Born: 3-20-54 in Detroit, MI

FIELDING:

All aspects of McCatty's defense are average. He is not the quickest man in baseball, but does know how to position himself in any given situation. With work, he could be a better fielder than he is at present.

OVERALL:

Nothing seems to faze McCatty on the mound . . . good times or bad. He is very aggressive and seems to truly dislike any hitter he faces. Now that he is permitted to pitch the way he wants to, he seems much more at ease with himself at his profession. A comedian of sorts off the field, he is strictly business on the mound. Now all that remains to be seen is whether or not his ailments of last season will mend.

Robinson: "McCatty struggled most of last season. He seemed to get behind and was forced to come in to hitters. He should be a better pitcher than he is."

1982 STATISTICS

W	L	ERA	G	GS	CG	IP	H	R	ER	BB	SO	SV
6	3	3.99	21	20	2	1283	124	162	57	70	66	0

CAREER STATISTICS

W	L	ERA	G	GS	CG	IPI	H	R	ER	BB	SO	SV
45	36	3.63	120	55	37	756	715	345	305	326	377	0

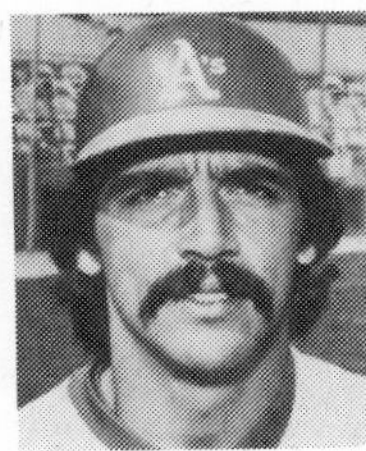

DAVE McKAY
INF, No. 39
SR, 6'0", 195 lbs.
ML Svc: 5 years
Born: 3-14-50 in
Vancouver, BC

1982 STATISTICS

AVG	G	AB	R	H	2B	3B	HR	RBI	BB	SO	SB
.198	78	212	25	42	4	1	4	17	11	35	6

CAREER STATISTICS

AVG	G	AB	R	H	2B	3B	HR	RBI	BB	SO	SB
.229	645	1928	191	441	70	15	21	170	86	337	20

VS. RHP

VS. LHP

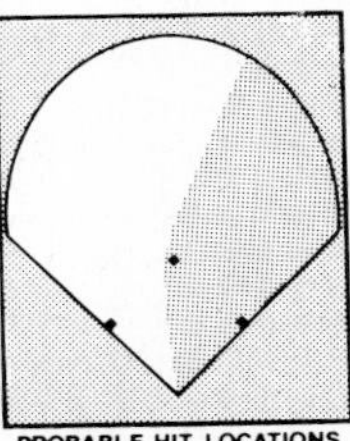
PROBABLE HIT LOCATIONS

HITTING:

Dave McKay has probably added years to his career because he is a switch-hitter, but he may return to hitting as a natural righthander in 1983 because he feels that by undergoing an off-season weight training program he can get more thump out of his bat strictly as a righthander.

Against righthanded pitching he is strictly a low ball hitter, while from the other side he prefers high pitches. Righthanded pitchers will find it easier to make an out of McKay by throwing him a lot of inside breaking balls and change-ups, while lefties should throw everything away and fastballs in particular, up. Defenses should line up for him to pull slightly as a lefthanded hitter. Righthanded, he hits pretty much straightaway. He is primarily a line drive hitter who will add an occasional grounder.

Almost all aspects of McKay's game at the plate are rated average, including his ability to hit with men in scoring position, draw walks, execute the hit-and-run, bunt, clutch-hit and hit behind the runner. Overall, McKay is not known for his hitting, but from time to time he will surprise the opposition with the big hit.

BASERUNNING:

McKay is a smart baserunner, although not overly aggressive. He has 20 stolen bases in his entire career, but had six last season. He has average speed and pitchers don't pay a lot of attention to him when he is on base. However, he is a hard-nosed player who can break up the double play. He slides feet first.

FIELDING:

McKay's real value to any team is that he plays third, shortstop, second and is learning to catch. He has a fine throwing arm and is very accurate, but last year he was kept pretty much in a utility role. He is probably strongest as a third baseman because he fields bunts well and his range at the other two infield positions is just average.

OVERALL:

Martin: "McKay is a steady, versatile player. He fits well into an infield, and when he plays regularly can provide a poor infield with some respectability. He is a good back up player and can DH."

Robinson: "I think his best bet is to play in and out of the lineup. Dave can play several positions for you and is as steady as they come. He's a hard worker and quiet."

DAN MEYER
OF, No. 7
LR, 5'11", 180 lbs.
ML Svc: 9 years
Born: 8-3-52 in Hamilton, OH

1982 STATISTICS

AVG	G	AB	R	H	2B	3B	HR	RBI	BB	SO	SB
.240	120	383	28	92	17	3	8	59	19	33	1

CAREER STATISTICS

AVG	G	AB	R	H	2B	3B	HR	RBI	BB	SO	SB
.256	1015	3531	393	905	141	30	85	442	200	264	61

VS. RHP

VS. LHP

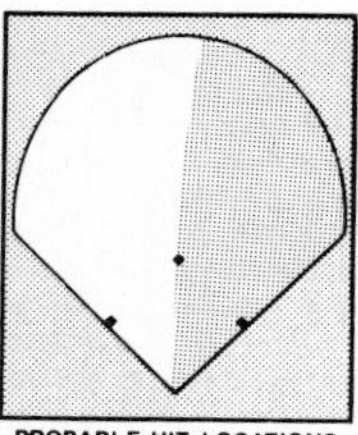
PROBABLE HIT LOCATIONS

HITTING:

There was a time when Dan Meyer was strictly a pull hitter, and he still has a tendency to do so in parks like Tiger Stadium and the Kingdome in Seattle. But lately Meyer has been able to diversify a bit more. He can take a righthander into the alley in right-center field and a lefty into the gap in left-center. He is a low ball hitter who has a slightly open, upright stance and a habit of nervously twitching his head and neck while at the plate. Martin, Robinson and Harwell were in some disagreement as to just where this lefthanded hitter should be pitched. Robinson said strictly outside, Harwell said definitely inside and Martin suggested that righthanders should throw in and lefthanders out. But they all agreed that it would be better to throw him breaking balls because he'd get rich on a diet of fastballs.

Lefthanders will have an easier time getting him out than righties, and he's quite liable to turn any fastball up into a frozen rope. Meyer doesn't handle the change-up very well. Hang anything to him and he'll head for the bank, and when he gets hot, it really doesn't matter what comes up to the plate because he is a fine streak hitter with power. He has had some difficulty moving runners along and he drew just 19 walks last season while recording 383 at-bats. Hitting is the strongest part of Meyer's game.

BASERUNNING:

Meyer is a smart runner, but then again, he doesn't run much to begin with. His style might best be described as conservative, his speed average. He nabbed only one base in 1982, his first season in Oakland. He can break up a double play, but hasn't had many opportunities.

FIELDING:

One reason Meyer may have a fairly long career is that he is able to play the outfield, third base and first base. When he was on defense last year in Oakland, he was used primarily as a first baseman. At all positions he rates average marks, but outfield is certainly not his strong suit. His arm strength and throwing accuracy are strictly middle of the pack, as is his range from his left to right. When he plays the outfield he is best at charging balls and has trouble with those hit over his head.

OVERALL:

Robinson: "Dan is right on target for his lifetime average. He's going to give you an average job in all areas. I think I would try to get him in there on an everyday basis. He'd be good at the No. 5, 6 or 7 spot in the lineup."

Martin: "He's made himself a versatile player, assuring employment in the major leagues."

DWAYNE MURPHY
OF, No. 21
LR, 6'1", 180 lbs.
ML Svc: 5 years
Born: 3-18-55 in
Merced, CA

1982 STATISTICS

AVG	G	AB	R	H	2B	3B	HR	RBI	BB	SO	SB
.239	151	543	84	130	16	1	27	94	93	122	26

CAREER STATISTICS

AVG	G	AB	R	H	2B	3B	HR	RBI	BB	SO	SB
.254	598	1946	300	494	56	10	66	267	359	403	77

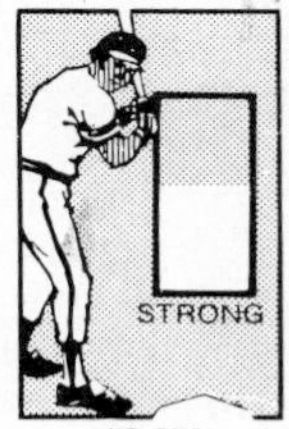

VS. RHP

VS. LHP

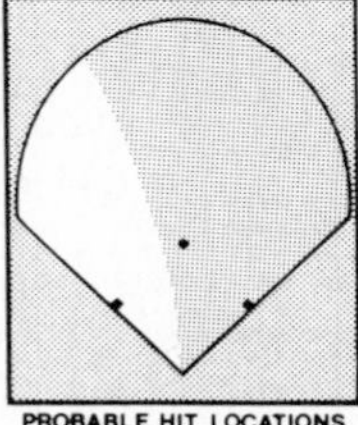
PROBABLE HIT LOCATIONS

HITTING:

As the seasons pass, Dwayne Murphy continues to become more of a power hitter, but has been held in check somewhat because he has been given the job of hitting behind thief Rickey Henderson in the No. 2 spot in the A's order. With his power, some feel it would make more sense to have him in the three spot.

Nonetheless, Murphy has become an ideal No. 2 hitter. He takes a lot of pitches and he gets a lot of fastballs to hit when he is on base. He is good at screening out the catcher and has developed into a good, two-strike hitter, although he does strike out a lot. His stance is upright and squared and he stands in the center of the box to low in the box. He is essentially a high ball hitter, but can reach down and golf a liner now and then. Southpaws can get ahead of Murphy on the count and then send breaking pitches off the plate. Righthanders should make a bad outside pitch that's well off the plate. Murphy is a lefthanded hitter who is best suited for hitting righthanders. He is a pull hitter who can drive the outside pitch to left. Murphy can handle the change-up and isn't bad with curves and other breaking pitches.

He is a good to excellent clutch hitter and he has led the A's in game-winning hits. He is above average at hitting behind the runner and with runners in scoring position. He is a fine bunter and can draw walks when he's not thinking homer. He might be best described as a player who doesn't hit for high average, but is patient with a need to get in his allotted cuts. He hits especially well in Oakland.

BASERUNNING:

Murphy is a very talented base runner who can steal. He has excellent speed to first and is aggressive. Pitchers are constantly aware of his presence. He's a real pro at breaking up double plays and smart like a fox when running. He slides feet first.

FIELDING:

He's won Gold Gloves in center field the past two seasons, and is apt to win a lot more. He is virtually without a weakness on defense. His arm is strong and his throw is accurate. He has nailed more than one runner at the plate. He plays shallow because he is an expert at getting to balls hit over his head. He is also magnificent at charging balls.

OVERALL:

Robinson: "He's a good player who is tough and durable. There are not too many things he cannot do."

Martin: "He could be one of the game's great players before he's through. He is a fine all around player who is often overlooked when 'experts' talk about outfielders. He quarterbacks one of the league's best outfields, and is a patient, intelligent hitter."

Harwell: "Great speed . . . strong arm. One of the top outfielders in the American League."

PITCHING:

In this nation given to crazes like hula hoops, disco and video games, Mike Norris has his own particular attraction. He has, it appears, become all consumed with throwing screwballs--Slow ones, fast ones, and some in between. Norris came of age in 1980 when he just missed winning the Cy Young Award with a 22-9 record accompanied by a 2.53 ERA. The following year he was 12-9, but last season, because of arm problems and a lack of self-discipline, fell off to 7-11 with a 4.76 ERA. After watching Norris in 1982, new A's pitching coach Ron Schueler wondered what happened to the pitcher's fastball. Schueler fully intends to return Norris to form this year.

The fastball should be Norris' main pitch. The screwball, curve, change-up and a rare slider should be used to complement the heat. Norris' fastball has a good tail on it, running in to righties and away from lefties. He is especially strong against righthanders when he throws them sliders and breaking balls away. His screwball is outstanding, but if that is all the hitter is looking for, the pitch isn't quite so effective. Norris' strength lies in his ability to use his entire bag of pitches to keep hitters guessing.

And, by the way, there is a very effective spitter in his repertoire. When Norris is on his game, he is a fast worker and all business. When he is not on his game he sometimes comes unglued at the seams. His control took a leave of absence last year and thus his stats paid a dear price. When he's behind on the count, look for the fastball.

FIELDING:

Anyone who watched Norris play defense in 1982 didn't see the real

MIKE NORRIS
RHP, No. 17
RR, 6'2", 172 lbs.
ML Svc: 5 years
Born: 3-19-55 in San Francisco, CA

Michael Kelvin Norris. A two-time Gold Glove winner, at times last season he appeared completely lost at his position. He has an excellent move to first base and he is well above average at fielding bunts because of his cat-like quickness. When at his best, rate him an excellent fielder with a great deal of confidence and poise.

OVERALL:

The question here is, Will the real Norris stand up in 1983? There is no doubt that he has as much ability as any pitcher in baseball. He might just be the best all around athlete on the Oakland roster. If Schueler can work a little magic, and Norris is healthy and takes charge of himself, Norris once again can be one of the choice picks of the crop.

Robinson: "Injuries slowed him down last year. He has all the pitches to be a winner again. Sometimes I think he throws too many screwballs."

Martin: "He went from a superior fastball pitcher to a breaking ball pitcher mainly because of arm problems. He is subject to emotional upsets, which hurt him. With arm rest, and a decent bullpen, he can still be a big winner."

Harwell: "Norris has excellent presence on the mound and is equally effective against lefthanders and righthanders with his screwball."

1982 STATISTICS

W	L	ERA	G	GS	CG	IP	H	R	ER	BB	SO	SV
7	11	4.76	28	28	7	166	154	103	88	84	83	0

CAREER STATISTICS

W	L	ERA	G	GS	CG	IP	H	R	ER	BB	SO	SV
53	54	4.37	171	141	50	1008	880	489	440	454	557	0

BOB OWCHINKO
LHP, No. 51
LL, 6'2", 195 lbs.
ML Svc: 6 years
Born: 1-1-55 in
San Diego, CA

PITCHING:

Bob Owchinko is another of the A's pitchers who worked to mixed reviews in 1982, but who may benefit from the fact that Billy Martin is no longer manager of the club. Like oil and water, Owchinko and Martin did not mix. Owchinko, who joined the A's at the start of the 1981 season, has been used primarily as a lefthanded short relief man. He is especially effective against lefthanded hitters. He appeared in 54 games last season, yet had only a 2-4 record with three saves as a short man. He suffered from a severe lack of consistency which might now mend with Martin's departure.

The rap on Owchinko, who mixes fastballs and curves, is that he is only average at pitching to a hitter's weakness. His motion and big breaking ball that hooks down can tie up a lefthanded batter. But too much of anything can be bad for anyone, and Owchinko tends to rely a little too heavily on his curve. Then, when he is behind on the count, he dishes up a fastball that is just average, and sometimes the hitter has a feast. And Owchinko has had a tendency to get behind hitters more often than not. He does not change speeds enough, and he leans toward throwing all his pitches hard with his three-quarters delivery. Owchinko does not possess a straight change and has not been accused of throwing spitballs.

FIELDING:

Owchinko has an above average move to first base, although he isn't prone to using it often. The rest of his defense, including the ability to field bunts, is rated average.

OVERALL:

It will be interesting to see how Owchinko handles the new field management in Oakland. It certainly doesn't figure to cause him any harm. Before joining Oakland, he was primarily a starter at San Diego and then in Cleveland. Maybe manager Steve Boros and pitching coach Ron Schueler can mold him into a reliever who is consistent.

Robinson: "Owchinko has good presence on the mound. He likes to take the mound in any situation and can pitch whenever and wherever you need him."

Martin: "He has provided more than just a little help to a mediocre bullpen. He can make tough pitches coming out of the bullpen against lefthanded hitters."

1982 STATISTICS

W	L	ERA	G	GS	CG	IP	H	R	ER	BB	SO	SV
2	4	5.21	54	0	0	102	111	60	59	52	67	3

CAREER STATISTICS

W	L	ERA	G	GS	CG	IP	H	R	ER	BB	SO	SV
33	55	4.36	222	97	10	781	827	407	378	321	424	5

JOE RUDI
OF, No. 26
RR, 6'2", 200 lbs.
ML Svc: 16 years
Born: 9-7-46 in
Modesto, CA

1982 STATISTICS

AVG	G	AB	R	H	2B	3B	HR	RBI	BB	SO	SB
.212	71	193	21	41	6	1	5	18	24	35	0

CAREER STATISTICS

AVG	G	AB	R	H	2B	3B	HR	RBI	BB	SO	SB
.264	1547	5556	684	1468	287	39	179	810	369	870	25

VS. RHP

VS. LHP

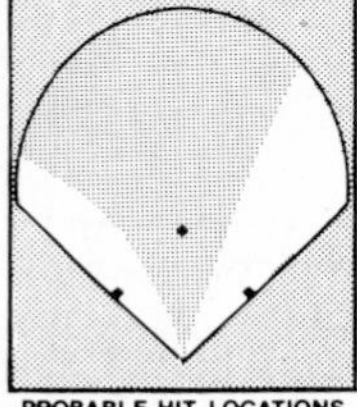
PROBABLE HIT LOCATIONS

HITTING:

Righthanded pitchers should keep in mind that Joe Rudi can be struck out with high fastballs inside and breaking balls away, while lefthanders might benefit by jamming him with hard stuff. Pitch him low from the right or left, and you can start looking for a new profession while you dream of all those line drives he delivered into the alleys.

Rudi is easy to spot at the plate. He has a pronounced closed stance, stands low in the box and upright with a slight crouch at the top of his frame. He is by no means the hitter he was in his prime, which is now history. But he still has the ability to hit in the clutch. Rudi is a smart hitter who can still hit beyond the runner, execute the hit-and-run and draw a walk. As a bunter rate him average.

There is no one pitch he can't handle if it arrives in the right spot. Breaking balls down nice and slow can usually send him back to the dugout scratching his head, while those fastballs inside also give him fits. Rudi can still handle a straight change. Until 1982, Rudi was always a fairly consistent hitter, but now that he does not play regularly, that can no longer be said of him. Last year he was not happy with his .212 average or at producing just five home runs in 71 games. His long career, which began in Oakland in 1969, is fast drawing to a close.

BASERUNNING:

Speed was never Rudi's ticket to stardom, but he is a smart baserunner just as he is a smart hitter and defensive player. He was never fast in his prime and now, at age 36, he is even slower. He has average speed to first and since he has just 25 career steals cannot be considered a base-stealing threat. He slides feet first.

FIELDING:

Rudi played some first base for the A's last year, but he will always be considered and remembered as a left fielder. His arm strength is still above average and he can still throw the ball through the hole in the eye of a needle. Some people believe that because he no longer plays regularly he has lost some of his ability to play defense. However, since he has lost any speed he once had, the fact that he spends most of his time at first base or as a designated hitter, it is probably for the best.

OVERALL:

Harwell: "Age has cut into his skill. He was once a top clutch hitter."

Robinson: "Rudi is a great guy to have on a team but this might be his last year. He has been slowed by injuries and has not played that much."

Martin: "My evaluations have to take into consideration the type of player Rudi was several years back. Now he is valuable some as a DH, but mainly as a man with class, a player who was largely self-made and a player who knows how to win."

HITTING:

Fred Stanley has not lasted over a decade in the major leagues because of his ability to hit a baseball. His .216 lifetime batting average is testimony to that. If bats provided power to light cities, Stanley would live in the dark.

He is a mediocre to average fastball hitter. Stanley is not particularly adept at handling change-ups, but a pitcher still shouldn't throw it too often. In the American League, with its designated hitter, Stanley is the perfect guy to stick in the No. 9 hole. He handles righties slightly better than he does lefties and hits straightaway. For such a Punch and Judy hitter, he lofts far too many balls into the air. His stance is closed, upright and he stands in the center of the box.

Outside pitches give Stanley fits. He is just average in the clutch, in hitting behind the runner, and needs work at hitting with men in scoring position. However, he does make contact and is thus above average when called upon to execute the hit-and-run. He can also set down a bunt. Once behind in the count, he's in trouble. It is safe to say that offense is the weakest link in Stanley's game.

BASERUNNING:

Stanley has 11 career thefts. A's third base coach Clete Boyer says that when Stanley runs it looks as if he's carrying a piano on his back. Stanley is a smart, if slow, baserunner. He is never a threat to steal and thus pitchers pay him no mind. He slides feet first and is just average at breaking up a double play.

FIELDING:

Stanley doesn't have the strongest throwing arm of any shortstop around, but he is always on the bullseye with his throws. He has good range and is above average at moving to either his right or left. He is adept at turning the double play and often will come up with a clutch defensive play. Stanley positions himself well, which might be the strong point of his defensive skill. He can also play second base.

FRED STANLEY
INF, No. 11
RR, 5'11", 167 lbs.
ML Svc: 13 years
Born: 8-13-47 in
Lake City, IA

1982 STATISTICS

AVG	G	AB	R	H	2B	3B	HR	RBI	BB	SO	SB
.193	101	228	33	44	7	0	2	17	29	32	0

CAREER STATISTICS

AVG	G	AB	R	H	2B	3B	HR	RBI	BB	SO	SB
.216	816	1650	197	356	38	5	10	120	196	243	11

VS. RHP

VS. LHP

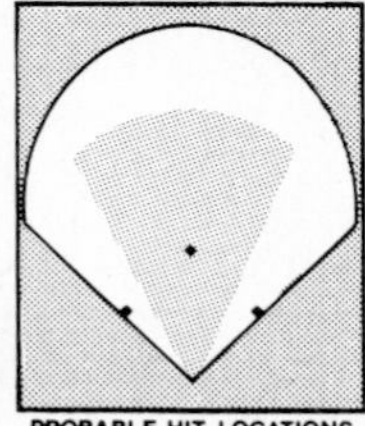
PROBABLE HIT LOCATIONS

OVERALL:

Robinson: "Stanley gives you a good job at shortstop and that's about it. He is a good reliable shortstop with average ability."

Martin: "He will give you a steady performance at shortstop and is good for a ball club. He has a sense of humor and keeps things loose. On a good club he'd be a very good back up shortstop."

Harwell: "He is a veteran. He's a good team man with limited ability."

TOM UNDERWOOD
LHP, No. 31
RL, 5'11", 177 lbs.
ML Svc: 9 years
Born: 12-22-53 in Kokomo, IN

PITCHING:

If the A's have a jack-of-all-trades on their pitching staff, it is Tom Underwood. Although Oakland acquired the lefthander to use mainly as a reliever, last year he pitched in every imaginable situation. He appeared in 56 games, more than any other pitcher on the staff, and was utilized as a starter on 10 occasions, middle relief man and late-inning stopper. His 10-6 record and 3.29 ERA gave him the best statistics on the club. Between mid-June and late August, he appeared in 25 games, recorded seven wins, two saves and did not suffer a loss. In the first 15 innings he worked last year, which covered five appearances, he did not give up a run of any kind.

When Underwood was younger his bread-and-butter pitch was his fastball, but of late he is given to throwing more and more breaking pitches, mainly curveballs. His fastball arrives at the plate in the mid to low 80s range. His curve, a good one, comes from over the top and breaks down. He also utilizes a slider and is effective against lefthanders with it when he throws it away from them. Underwood's main weakness is that his control is spotty at times and he is given to making some simply horrible bonehead mistakes.

Underwood used to have the reputation that if you could stay close to him you could get him. He's doing much better in that area now. There has never been any doubt that Underwood has a good, live arm, but he has been inconsistent. He has a change-up, but does not show it often. He isn't given to knocking hitters down and he doesn't keep a spitball in his bag of tricks. Give Underwood stars when he pitches against Seattle, Texas and Toronto and he's seen a few stars against the Sox, Red or White, and the Brewers.

FIELDING:

Underwood has a good, quick move to first base, but is given an average rating at fielding bunts. However, he is rated above average as an all around defensive player.

OVERALL:

There are times when Underwood can be brilliant, while there are other moments when he has no business being in uniform. But in 1982, there were signs that he was using his head on the mound more often than not. Now, if he can just continue the trend in 1983 and beyond.

Robinson: "Underwood has the capability to be a better pitcher. He has a live arm and has become good at starting or relieving. He can pitch anywhere."

Martin: "Still a pretty good gamer. Early in his major league career he figured to be better than he became. He had good stuff. He is versatile, and besides relieving, he can start if you need him."

Harwell: "Underwood has a good variety of pitches, but he is inconsistent."

1982 STATISTICS

W	L	ERA	G	GS	CG	IP	H	R	ER	BB	SO	SV
10	6	3.29	56	10	2	153	136	66	56	68	79	7

CAREER STATISTICS

W	L	ERA	G	GS	CG	IP	H	R	ER	BB	SO	SV
76	80	3.89	291	187	35	1370	1320	670	592	581	847	13

MITCHELL PAGE
OF, No. 6
LR, 6'2", 205 lbs.
ML Svc: 6 years
Born: 3-1-53 in
Compton, CA

HITTING, BASERUNNING, FIELDING:

Used strictly as a lefthanded designated hitter, Mitchell Page was sent down to the minors last season simply because he wasn't proving himself at the plate. Page tends to swing at a lot of bad pitches . . . it may really be that he has poor eyesight. Yet he is an excellent low ball hitter who should be pitched outside. He can also be pitched up and in. He hits line drives and can place them from left to right-center with power. He hits well with men in scoring position, but not if it's in the clutch.

His bunting needs work, and he is average at hitting behind the runner, on the hit-and-run, and in drawing walks. Low fastballs are his cup of tea, while good fastballs and curves away give him trouble. Hang a curve to him, and kiss it good-bye.

Page is an above average baserunner. He has good speed to first, can break up a double play and always keeps the pitcher on his toes.

He is an outfielder by trade, but has not played defense in the majors for some time. He is not a good outfielder. He has speed, but all other defensive phases are sub-par.

OVERALL:

Martin: "Page had a brilliant rookie season in 1977 (The Sporting News Rookie of the Year), a solid second year, but then went downhill. He is a player with potential that he has never taken advantage of. From now on, it is completely up to him."

JIMMY SEXTON
INF, No. 19
RR, 5'11", 175 lbs.
ML Svc: 5 years
Born: 12-15-51 in
Mobile, AL

HITTING, BASERUNNING, FIELDING:

Jimmy Sexton is a fastball streak hitter who should be pitched low and away, and he'll likely make out via a grounder. He is a straightaway hitter, and is not good at hitting breaking pitches and does only a fair job at hitting the change. He needs improvement at hitting with men in scoring position. However, he is a fair contact hitter with a good eye. Sexton can be effective on the hit-and-run, can bunt, and draw a walk now and then.

Sexton has good speed and the ability to run the bases. Last year, he set a single season major league record by stealing 16 times without being caught. He is smart and aggressive on the basepaths.

Sexton is average at fielding his position, which is usually shortstop, although he can also play second and third. His arm is average as is his throwing accuracy. Although not necessarily a weak fielder, Sexton won't win any Gold Gloves.

OVERALL:

Robinson: "He might be able to help a big league club doing just what he is doing now--utility. His greatest assets are his ability to steal and then his defense. He is a borderline big leaguer."

AL WOODS
OF, No. 20
LL, 6'3", 195 lbs.
ML Svc: 5 years plus
Born: 8-8-53 in
Oakland, CA

HITTING, BASERUNNING, FIELDING:

Everyone was impressed with Al Woods' swing from the time he hit a pinch-homer in his first major league at-bat in the Jays' first game. Unfortunately, he has never completely fulfilled expectations.

He used to be able to handle the curveball, and hit well against lefthanded pitching, but his role now is mostly as a platoon left fielder and pinch-hitter. He has never been noted as a clutch hitter or run producer.

Woods is a high ball hitter and righthanders should keep the ball away from him. Lefthanders can go in and down.

An Oakland native, he has always done well against the A's, and he did fairly well against Detroit and Cleveland.

An average runner at best, who is not aggressive and seldom tries to steal.

He has shown some improvement in his fielding. Has always lacked arm strength for anywhere but left field, and this is awkward for him as a lefty thrower. Limited range because of his lack of speed.

OVERALL:

Robinson: "Didn't have a good year. Looks like he is odd man out in Toronto."

Martin: "Has stayed on as a capable extra man on this team. Can be platooned."

THE KINGDOME
Seattle Mariners

Seating Capacity: 59,438
Playing Surface: Artificial (AstroTurf)

Dimensions
Left Field Pole: 316 ft.
Left-Center Field: 357 ft.
Center Field: 410 ft.
Right-Center Field: 357 ft.
Right Field Pole: 316 ft.
Height of Outfield Walls:
Left Field: 11 ft. 6 in.
Center Field: 11 ft. 6 in.
Right Field: 23 ft.

"If you can pitch in the Kingdome and not allow home runs," says Shane Rawley of the New York Yankees, "you can pitch in a phone booth and not allow home runs."

Rawley pitched for the Seattle Mariners prior to his trade to the Yankees, and was barely able to escape the fate of many pitchers who must pitch in the Kingdome. Balls rocket off the bat in the windless Dome, and before the Metrodome in Minneapolis was built last year, the Kingdome invariably had more home runs hit in it than most parks in the majors. To add to the ease with which batters hit homers, the Dome has fairly short fences. It is only 316 feet to left and right fields, and 357 feet in left and right-center. Dead center is a mere 410 feet. The fence had been a uniform 11 feet, six inches, but in right field, where the fence extends up to 23 feet, a line was painted at the 11'6" mark. Balls hit above the line were ruled homers. Last year, the line on that fence was raised to 23 feet, but the difference did not seem to matter to batters.

The Kingdome is notorious for its speakers, hoisted above the field. Balls that were not supposed to reach those speakers, did. The ground rules provide that outfielders catching balls off the speakers are entitled to an out. If the ball falls on the field, the batter can get as many bases as he wants. In 1980, Bob Watson smashed balls there on back-to-back nights, balls that were ticketed for the upper deck in left-center. Both high smashes hit two different speakers, fell to the AstroTurf, and went for a double and a triple, respectively.

The speakers have been raised, but several balls still managed to find them last year. In addition to the speakers, a basketball scoreboard hangs high over home plate, and, naturally, several high fouls have hit the board and dropped harmlessly into the catcher's mitt for outs.

When the Dome was first erected, many infielders and outfielders had difficulty picking up pop-ups and fly balls, because the top of the Dome was the same color as the baseball. The hue has been changed, but in day games, it is still difficult to pick up flies.

The Kingdome is extremely drab and dark, and presents a gloomy atmosphere for ballplayers. Since it is also the home of the Seattle Seahawks of the NFL, it appears that football, not baseball, was in the mind of the builder when it was erected.

LARRY ANDERSEN
RHP, No. 39
RR, 6'3", 180 lbs.
ML Svc: 2 years
Born: 5-6-53 in
Portland, OR

PITCHING:

Andersen was out of place in the role of a long reliever last year. He doesn't have the overpowering stuff a manager wants from a bullpen stopper, but the righthander doesn't have the assortment to let him work long spells.

He has always been a sidearmer, but began experimenting last year with a submarine style similar to Kansas City's Dan Quisenberry. It will take time and patience before a decision can be made on whether it is a wise alteration.

When he's called upon with men on base, he has done a good job of getting out of an inning, but doesn't have the ability to maintain it for more than one time through the order. With his sidearm delivery and a slider that breaks quickly, he has most of his success against righthanders.

Andersen doesn't have false confidence in his fastball. When he's in trouble, he'll go to his sinker or slider and hope for a ground ball, knowing he's not going to get a strikeout except on a rare occasion. His attitude is a big plus. He will pitch as often and as long as he is asked, and doesn't look for excuses.

FIELDING:

He has a quick move to first base, but a slow delivery to the plate that negates the impact of his move. Flirts with a fake to third and a throw to first, but doesn't go hard enough to third to catch anybody.

Is decent coming off the mound to field his position, but nothing spectacular.

OVERALL:

A journeyman pitcher who does what he's told, even if he doesn't always get the results that he would hope for. Will try anything to get the job done. Short on ability, but long on desire.

Martin: "A busy pitcher. He does okay considering he often throws a lot in the bullpen without getting into the game."

Harwell: "Has a good sinker and slider and tends to keep his pitches low, but lacks the velocity that he needs to be a solid reliever."

1982 STATISTICS

W	L	ERA	G	GS	CG	IP	H	R	ER	BB	SO	SV
0	0	5.99	40	1	0	79	101	56	53	23	32	1

CAREER STATISTICS

W	L	ERA	G	GS	CG	IP	H	R	ER	BB	SO	SV
3	4	4.64	103	1	0	184	197	107	95	56	91	6

JIM BEATTIE
RHP, No. 45
RR, 6'6", 220 lbs.
ML Svc: 4 years
Born: 7-4-54 in
Hampton, VA

PITCHING:

Jim Beattie finally began to fulfill the promising scouting reports last summer, only to once again fall victim to a career-long problem of tendinitis in his right shoulder. He missed starts several times during the season, including his final three, but went on a special conditioning program this past winter that is supposed to strengthen the shoulder area.

A healthy Beattie showed signs of being an overpowering pitcher--he won six straight in late May and June, twice striking out a career-high 10 batters. He pitched a Mariner record 19 consecutive scoreless innings, including a two-hitter against Detroit.

He combines a fastball that is consistently in the low 90s with a good sharp slider. The slider is his "out" pitch--when he's got it, he gets hitters out; when he doesn't he's out of the game. Beattie needs to develop an off-speed pitch that he has confidence in to get him through troubled times. Control problems have haunted him, but in the last year he cut down immensely on walks, showing an increased amount of confidence in his own ability.

His biggest problem is having to pitch against the New York Yankees. He seems to press hard to try and prove to the Yankees that he is better than the pitcher that owner George Steinbrenner made a whipping boy of before he was sent to Seattle.

When Beattie's going well, he comes over the top, but has a tendency to drop down and short-arm the ball when his shoulder is bothering him.

FIELDING:

Despite his size, Beattie is fairly agile--a testimony to his basketball playing days at Dartmouth. Comes off the mound well, and has a good idea of where to go with the ball once he has fielded it.

He has trouble holding runners on base. A big twist in his delivery gives an average baserunner a definite advantage in a basestealing situation. He has worked to develop a quick stride to the plate that he uses in some cases, but not every time a top runner is on first.

OVERALL:

Beattie shows signs of becoming a stopper for the Seattle staff, but to fulfill his potential, he is going to have to find a cure for his constant arm ailments.

Robinson: "So far Beattie has been an in and out starter. Needs more consistency. Has to have good control. Has had problems in finding the right delivery or point of release."

Harwell: "He was finding himself in 1982."

1982 STATISTICS

W	L	ERA	G	GS	CG	IP	H	R	ER	BB	SO	SV
8	12	3.34	28	26	6	172	149	73	64	65	140	0

CAREER STATISTICS

W	L	ERA	G	GS	CG	IP	H	R	ER	BB	SO	SV
25	44	4.06	114	99	10	630	621	317	284	273	340	1

BOBBY BROWN
OF, No. 44
SR, 6'1", 207 lbs.
ML Svc: 4 years
Born: 5-24-54 in Norfolk, VA

1982 STATISTICS

AVG	G	AB	R	H	2B	3B	HR	RBI	BB	SO	SB
.241	79	245	29	59	7	1	4	17	17	32	28

CAREER STATISTICS

AVG	G	AB	R	H	2B	3B	HR	RBI	BB	SO	SB
.247	281	797	107	197	23	7	18	73	55	147	61

VS. RHP

VS. LHP

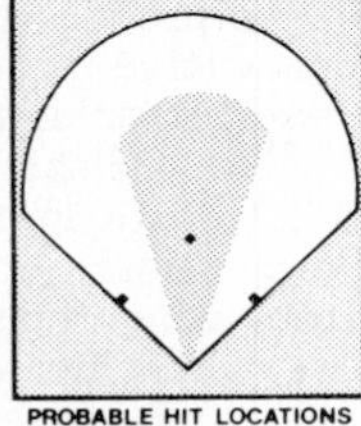
PROBABLE HIT LOCATIONS

HITTING:

Physically, Brown has all the tools to be a total offensive player. He is strong, he is fast, and he is a switch-hitter. Unfortunately, he has never put these tools to use. He makes better contact from the right side of the plate, but considers himself better batting left. A slight pull hitter, he seems content with trying to hit the ball on the ground and use his speed to get on base. Brown runs hard down the line, taking advantage of any lapses by the defense.

Brown is not afraid to lay down a bunt, but with his speed, it wouldn't hurt if he tried this trick more often. He seems best suited as a leadoff man, but needs to get on base more. With the new American League approach of a dual leadoff hitter (Nos. 1 and 9), he fits the ninth spot well.

He has trouble with breaking balls and fastballs away. He tries to pull them. If a pitcher makes a mistake and gets the ball down and in when he is hitting lefthanded, Brown will make the pitcher pay. He seems to be a better hitter against the harder throwers--six of his runs are off Cleveland's Len Barker.

BASERUNNING:

Running the bases is easily the strongest part of Bobby Brown's game. If he played every day, it is very likely that he would lead the league in stolen bases. Last season, he was successful in 28 of 34 attempts with only 245 at-bats. He has excellent acceleration, studies pitchers, and reacts well to the first move of a pitcher. When a base has to be stolen, he can do it. He is not intimidated by any pitcher. He will get the best jump possible and go for the base. When Brown does get picked off, he has the baserunning sense to keep breaking for second so as not to give an out away. Sometimes, he can get a little carried away trying to take the extra base, and tries to force things to happen.

FIELDING:

His speed helps Brown to overrun a lot of his mistakes, but even so, he is still only an average defensive player. At times, he seems to lose concentration, and as a result fails to catch balls that should be routine. He has a tendency to overrun balls in the gaps. Brown's arm is average at best, but he does throw consistently to the cutoff man, and gets rid of the ball quickly.

OVERALL:

Robinson: "Bobby Brown has been up and down in a lot of organizations. He can help a team, but not in 162 games. If you spot play him, he will give you a boost."

TERRY BULLING
C, No. 11
RR, 6'0", 195 lbs.
ML Svc: 2 years
Born: 12-15-52 in Lynwood, CA

1982 STATISTICS

AVG	G	AB	R	H	2B	3B	HR	RBI	BB	SO	SB
.221	56	154	17	34	7	0	1	8	19	16	2

CAREER STATISTICS

AVG	G	AB	R	H	2B	3B	HR	RBI	BB	SO	SB
.226	133	340	34	77	11	0	3	28	45	41	2

VS. RHP

VS. LHP

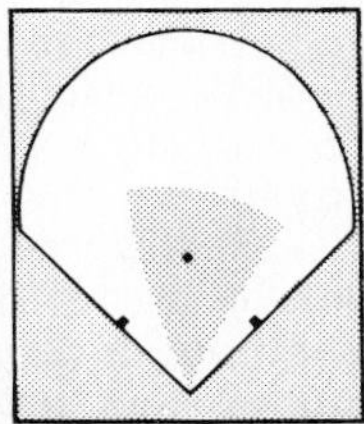
PROBABLE HIT LOCATIONS

HITTING:

Not much of a power hitter, Terry Bulling lives in the opposite field. He is at home in the No. 8 spot in the order, and is at his best doing the little things. A good hit-and-run man, he will almost always hit behind the runner--whether it's on orders or through his own efforts. He has medium-range fly ball power, but most of his hits are on the ground. Also a solid bunter, although he doesn't have anywhere near the speed it takes to turn his bunts into base hits. His power is negligible even in the Kingdome.

Bulling will inside-out the inside pitch and uses a slightly crouched stance in the middle of the box. He has trouble with breaking pitches, especially low and away. Mediocre fastballs can make him seem like a better than mediocre hitter.

He does well in short spurts but the more he plays the more trouble he seems to have at the plate. He can be overanxious, although he rarely tries to hit with the power he doesn't have. In his two full big league seasons, he has been used primarily against lefthanded pitchers. It's hard to expect much improvement; he's nearing 30 years old, which means what you see is basically what you get.

BASERUNNING:

Bulling does the best with what he has, but doesn't have much. He is not a threat to steal a base, but will barrel into the pivot man on the double play. If he gets there in time to have an impact, however, is another question.

FIELDING:

He's a favorite of pitchers because he gives a good target and works hard to call a game that fits each pitcher's strength that day. He is above average in arm strength, accuracy and release. If the pitchers give him a chance, he can throw out most baserunners. Bulling is a hustler, and not afraid of getting hurt. He does a good job of blocking balls in the dirt, and can adjust to a mix-up in signs with the pitcher.

OVERALL:

His calling in life is as a back up catcher. Won't embarrass a team at the plate, but won't impress. Does a good job behind the plate and working with pitchers. Fundamentally sound.

Martin: "At his age, you have to assume he's reached his potential. His great value to a team is his defense. He's suitable as a back up catcher."

MANNY CASTILLO
INF, No. 32
SR, 5'9", 160 lbs.
ML Svc: 1 year plus
Born: 4-1-57 in
Santo Domingo, DR

1982 STATISTICS

AVG	G	AB	R	H	2B	3B	HR	RBI	BB	SO	SB
.257	138	506	49	130	29	1	3	49	22	35	2

CAREER STATISTICS

AVG	G	AB	R	H	2B	3B	HR	RBI	BB	SO	SB
.256	145	516	50	132	29	1	3	49	22	35	2

VS. RHP

VS. LHP

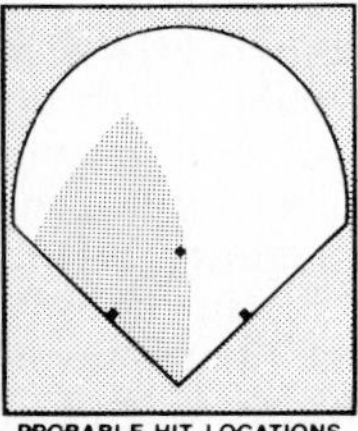
PROBABLE HIT LOCATIONS

HITTING:

With less than seven strikeouts per one hundred at-bats, the numbers would seem to say that he is a contact hitter. Castillo is actually not as disciplined as that--he will take the first strike and then start hacking. He walks less frequently than he strikes out.

Castillo is a good candidate for the No. 2 spot in the order where he can hit-and-run. He is very good at bringing in the man on third with less than two out. He says that he hits lefthanders better than righthanders, but by mid-season last year, he was platooned and only facing righthanders. He shows a lack of power, but that might improve as his confidence builds. Despite more than eight years as a pro, he is still getting his feet on the ground.

Castillo likes the ball away so that he can go to the opposite field. He has most of his trouble with breaking pitches and sinking fastballs. He is still learning the pitchers and with the contact that he does make should improve as a hitter.

BASERUNNING:

Not much of a threat. Castillo gets a lot of doubles, but this is because he often hits in the gaps. The only time he will try to steal is on a hit-and-run, or the back end of a double steal.

FIELDING:

Castillo is steady but unspectacular. He has trouble coming in on the slow roller and on bunts. Has a decent lateral move, but rarely makes a great play. His quick hands keep him from being eaten up by bad hops. He doesn't bobble the ball, gets rid of it quickly, and has a strong and accurate arm. Good at starting the double play.

In emergencies, Castillo was able to play a little at second base, but he doesn't have the quickness on his feet to become a regular there. Considering his lack of exposure at second, he does make the pivot well, but would need to work more overall to have an everyday chance.

OVERALL:

Martin: "He can get his bat on the ball, and is a pretty good No. 2 hitter. Fine defense at third base with quick reactions. Maybe he is the team's answer at third."

Robinson: "This kid can be a good player. Defense and hitting the ball around will be the things that he does the best."

BILL CAUDILL
RHP, No. 37
RR, 6'1", 175 lbs.
ML Svc: 4 years
Born: 7-13-56 in Santa Monica, CA

PITCHING:

After spending his first three years as a non entity in the Chicago Cub bullpen, Caudill finally got a chance to be the stopper for Seattle in 1982, and emerged as one of the best in the American League.

Caudill doesn't have much finesse in his style of pitching. He throws a fastball that is consistently in the 90s. He'll challenge anybody, and when his ball is up and moving, he can get anybody out. He has a durable arm, and seems to thrive on work. When he spends too much time sitting, Caudill has trouble throwing strikes, and shows a tendency to take a little off his fastball in hopes of finding control. When that happens, the pitch straightens out and Caudill gets in trouble.

He needs to come up with some type of breaking pitch he can go to on off days to make hitters aware of something besides his fastball. When he's going good, it doesn't matter whether he's working against a left-hander or righthander. Only two hitters seemed to present a consistent problem for him--Reid Nichols of Boston who had game-winning homers on back-to-back nights, and Roy Smalley of the New York Yankees.

He was especially tough against the Chicago White Sox ("It's as close as I can get to the Cubs," he said. "There's something about the mention of Chicago that gives me a little extra"), and the Oakland Athletics, a motivation that stemmed from former manager Billy Martin leaving him off the All Star team.

FIELDING:

He is a power pitcher with more than a strikeout per inning. Goes into a game with little on his mind except overpowering hitters. He doesn't hold runners on very well. Adequate in fielding his position, but he doesn't have to rely on his own defense to get out of situations--he relies instead on his fastball.

OVERALL:

The tougher the situation, the tougher Caudill gets. He likes the challenge of coming into a game with a lead and putting out a rally. Tends to get a bit too relaxed if he comes into a game down by a run or with too big of a lead to work with, a common ailment for top shortmen.

Harwell: "Outstanding short reliever. Has consistent command of an overpowering fastball."

Robinson: After a 6-18 career, last year was a great one for him. Does not try to fool hitters, just blows them away. He was unhittable."

Martin: "The kind of stud you need to seal off a game."

1982 STATISTICS

W	L	ERA	G	GS	CG	IP	H	R	ER	BB	SO	SV
12	9	2.35	70	0	0	95	65	25	25	35	111	26

CAREER STATISTICS

W	L	ERA	G	GS	CG	IP	H	R	ER	BB	SO	SV
18	27	3.52	201	24	0	384	341	169	150	166	372	27

BRYAN CLARK
LHP, No. 48
LL, 6'2", 185 lbs.
ML Svc: 2 years
Born: 7-12-56 in Madera, CA

PITCHING:

Obviously, there's something in Clark's left arm that excites scouts. There is also something in his determination that makes an impression. He spent his first six years in pro ball at the Class A level, then a year split at AA and AAA, and the majority of the last two years having finally made it to the big leagues.

He has been used in every role--long reliever, short reliever, mop up man and starter. Wants to be a starter, but mid-way last year, he began to accept his role in the middle innings.

Clark actually appears best suited for the job of relief. He has a fastball in the high 80s that moves so much it is at times difficult for catchers to handle, much less hitters to hit. His slider is his "out" pitch, and is extremely tough on lefties. He has problems, however, when he tries to throw too many off-speed pitches, especially his slow curveball because it hangs more than it breaks. Clark has a tendency to be wild, but can work to his advantage--it keeps the hitters from digging in.

Confidence has never been a negative point for Bryan Clark. At times he may have believed in himself too much. He used to have problems just sitting in the bullpen waiting to pitch. This resulted in his being sent out at the start of 1982, and he blamed it on a bad mental outlook. He's claimed that things have improved and the results would seem to back that up.

FIELDING:

Clark's fastball moves so much that it can be a problem for catchers. Has a decent move to first, but not quite as good as it will have to be if he ever develops into a short reliever. He is an outstanding athlete, which is reflected in his quickness coming off the mound to field his position.

OVERALL:

Clark's biggest improvement in the last two years has been from a mental standpoint. He used to let what he felt was unfair treatment bother him when he pitched. Last year, however, he seemed to become more determined each time he felt he was wronged. He also seemed to be able to handle the defensive breakdowns that had flustered him his rookie year.

Martin: "Needs to break through. Has a good arm. Has become more of a pitcher than he was. He still walks too many."

Harwell: "Good athlete, average stuff, excellent fielder."

1982 STATISTICS

W	L	ERA	G	GS	CG	IP	H	R	ER	BB	SO	SV
5	2	2.75	37	5	1	114	104	44	35	58	70	0

CAREER STATISTICS

W	L	ERA	G	GS	CG	IP	H	R	ER	BB	SO	SV
7	7	3.47	66	14	2	207	196	98	80	113	122	2

AL COWENS
OF, No. 16
RR, 6'2", 200 lbs.
ML Svc: 9 years
Born: 10-25-51 in Los Angeles, CA

1982 STATISTICS

AVG	G	AB	R	H	2B	3B	HR	RBI	BB	SO	SB
.270	146	560	72	151	39	8	20	78	46	81	11

CAREER STATISTICS

AVG	G	AB	R	H	2B	3B	HR	RBI	BB	SO	SB
.277	1185	4120	541	1141	187	59	72	529	306	464	100

VS. RHP

VS. LHP

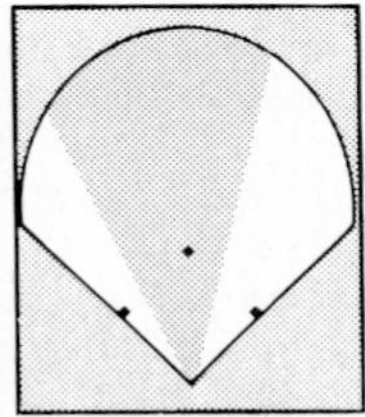
PROBABLE HIT LOCATIONS

HITTING:

Al Cowens rarely swings until he's been thrown strike one. When he is going well, he will not pull a home run foul. He likes to go up the middle with line drives, and when he's in a groove, he can hit home runs that will land in the left field stands. He will go the other way with outside pitches. Despite fears of being frightened by right-handers since being beaned by Ed Farmer in 1979, Cowens has the ability to stay in on them. Last season, he showed good power against righties, accounting for 16 of his 20 homers.

He stands deep in the box, in a semi-crouch with a closed stance--a classic pupil of the Charley Lau school of hitting.

Cowens can handle hard stuff, whether it be fastballs or breaking pitches. Has trouble with off-speed pitches. The best bet is to try and burn him inside and then go away with off-speed breaking selections. He gets himself out more often than the pitchers do. He can go into a slump by jerking his head too fast and taking his eye off the ball.

BASERUNNING:

Cowens can run better than he gets credit for. He didn't get many opportunities to show his ability with the Mariners, normally batting behind the likes of Bruce Bochte and Richie Zisk.

He is aggressive when he hits the ball, always looks for the double if he already has a single, or for a triple if he knows he's got a double. If an outfielder takes his time going after a ball, Cowens will take the extra base. Does not run into an out trying to create something that doesn't exist.

FIELDING:

Cowens is an excellent right fielder. He gets a good jump on balls both in front and behind him, and runs well enough to cut off balls in the gap. Can also fill in for the center fielder as need arises.

Cowens' arm isn't as strong as it once was, but he is very accurate. Unassuming baserunners find themselves in trouble trying to test his arm because he always keeps his throws down and hits the cutoff man.

OVERALL:

Harwell: "A good all around player."

Robinson: "The rap on him was that he couldn't hit righthanded pitching anymore. This has haunted him since Ed Farmer hit him in the face in 1979. Patience (by Mariner Manager Rene Lachemann) is paying off and suddenly he's not over the hill."

JULIO CRUZ
INF, No. 6
SR, 5'9", 160 lbs.
ML Svc: 5 years
Born: 12-2-54 in
Brooklyn, NY

1982 STATISTICS

AVG	G	AB	R	H	2B	3B	HR	RBI	BB	SO	SB
.242	154	549	83	133	22	5	8	49	57	71	46

CAREER STATISTICS

AVG	G	AB	R	H	2B	3B	HR	RBI	BB	SO	SB
.243	681	2486	378	603	76	15	15	150	310	316	257

VS. RHP

VS. LHP

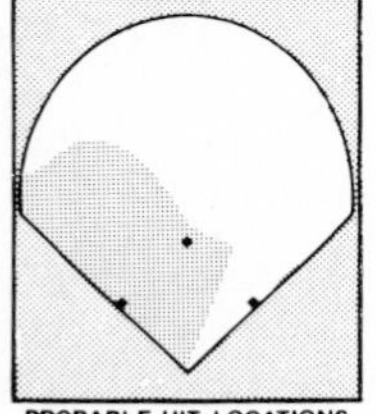
PROBABLE HIT LOCATIONS

HITTING:

A switch-hitter, Julio has yet to learn to take advantage of his speed from the left side of the plate. He is definitely a better hitter righthanded for both average and power. He had eight home runs last year, seven of them righthanded and the one lefthanded was inside-the-park. From the left side, he normally pops the ball up into left field, having been unable to learn to beat the ball into the artificial surface. He is still afraid to bunt, having only two bunt hits last year.

Most teams play their left fielders on the line against him batting left, and third basemen never have to cheat on him because of his hesitancy to bunt the ball. He will chase the fastball up out of the strike zone and has no chance against overpowering types. Most pitchers handle him by keeping pitches down and in, and getting him to chase pitches out of the strike zone. Cruz hasn't shown the patience at the plate to get the walks that would allow him to exploit his speed.

He could become an excellent leadoff hitter if he begins to put his natural abilities to use in getting on base. He's his own worst enemy during slumps, trying a new stance every day (sometimes even at bat), compounding his problems.

BASERUNNING:

Once he gets on base, Cruz becomes one of the best players around. He is an excellent basestealer, studying pitchers' moves and keeping notes, parlaying his knowledge and his speed into a better than 80% success ratio. He is extremely aggressive with right-handed pitchers on the mound, although he is hesitant at times against lefthanders with good moves. He is always on his own, a reflection of respect for his common sense on the bases.

FIELDING:

The more you watch Cruz play second base, the more inferior every other second baseman becomes. He has shortstop range and an arm that would be adequate for a shortstop, which means it is excellent for a second baseman. His biggest problem is that he doesn't always play on his feet. He is agile and at times becomes too acrobatic in making plays. Cruz is impossible to take out on the double play because of his excellent jumping ability, which allows him to wait until the last moment before having to get the relay and unload it.

OVERALL:

Robinson: "Lots of raw talent and just finding out how to use it. Should learn how to bunt better. When his head is screwed on right he can play."

TODD CRUZ
INF, No. 2
RR, 6'1", 185 lbs.
ML Svc: 3 years
Born: 11-23-55 in
Highland Park, NJ

1982 STATISTICS

AVG	G	AB	R	H	2B	3B	HR	RBI	BB	SO	SB
.230	136	492	44	113	20	2	16	57	12	96	2

CAREER STATISTICS

AVG	G	AB	R	H	2B	3B	HR	RBI	BB	SO	SB
.230	302	947	81	218	41	3	21	97	29	177	4

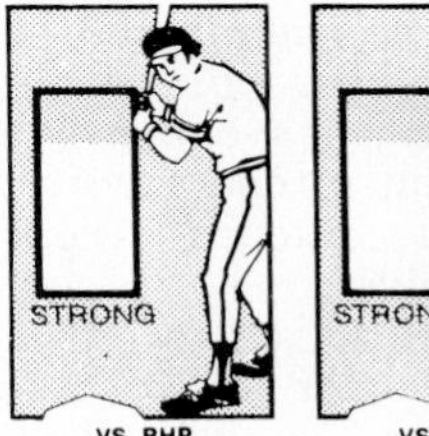

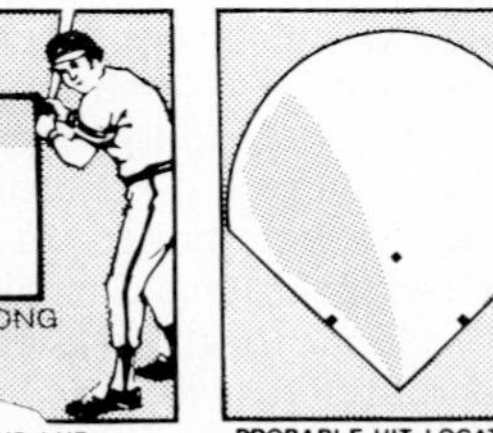

HITTING:

Given a chance to play every day in the big leagues for the first time last season, Cruz surprised a lot of folks with his power and his ability to hit in the clutch. He had 9 game winning RBIs and tied for best on the Mariners. Actually, he hit much better on the road than he did in the Kingdome where he was too concerned about the closeness of the fences.

Cruz loves the high fastball. He is definitely a free swinger who tries to pull every pitch. He chases fastballs up, way up and over his head, and breaking balls in the dirt. He goes after change-ups with a fastball swing. He must lead the league in 0-2 counts--strikes out a lot and walks infrequently.

Cruz is temperamental. Early in the season he was pinch-hit for and did not hide his anger. Once he showed his abilities in the clutch, however, he didn't have to worry about that any more. He proved to be the best bunter on the Mariners, executing the sacrifice virtually every time the sign was given. He does not, however, run well enough to include bunting in his daily offensive routine.

BASERUNNING:

Cruz is deceptively slow. Despite great range in the field, he doesn't show much on the bases. He accepts limitations and doesn't run much, but does go from first to third pretty well.

FIELDING:

If he doesn't have the strongest arm in the American League, he's second. As well as having good velocity, he has a quick release. He flicks his wrist instead of having to windup, allowing him to make off-balanced throws and get outs, especially when the runners slow up a step thinking he'll concede them a base hit.

He is the perfect artificial surface shortstop. His arm allows him to play deep. He's not afraid to dive for balls, but normally doesn't have to. Cruz has good instincts, and normally takes a step or two before the ball is hit in anticipation of what will happen. He likes to play with one hand, side-stepping balls instead of getting in front of them when he has a chance. It causes him to get more bad hops than he probably should because his body isn't in the way to knock the ball down.

OVERALL:

Martin: "Coming into his own as a major leaguer. He is a fine shortstop with a gun for an arm. Maybe the best power arm in the American League at short. He needs to hit more, and strikes out a lot."

GARY GRAY
INF, No. 29
RR, 6'0", 215 lbs.
ML Svc: 3 years
Born: 9-21-52 in New Orleans, LA

1982 STATISTICS

AVG	G	AB	R	H	2B	3B	HR	RBI	BB	SO	SB
.257	80	269	26	69	14	2	7	29	24	59	1

CAREER STATISTICS

AVG	G	AB	R	H	2B	3B	HR	RBI	BB	SO	SB
.240	211	625	65	150	23	3	24	71	34	126	5

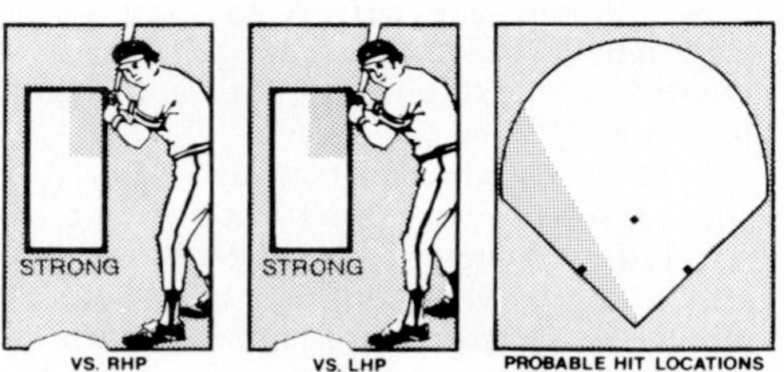

HITTING:

There is no gray area for Gary Gray. He is a streak hitter in the truest sense of the word. When he's hot, he's one of the hottest, but when he goes into a cold spell, there is a heavy breeze from his swings and a lot of pop-ups when he makes contact.

He'll tomahawk the high fastball. Some of his power is negated by the tremendous overspin he puts on a ball. When he is on a streak, he seems to handle most pitches. But normally he hits his best on fastballs up--inside or out. There is so much coil in his swing that he has a hard time making the adjustment to change-ups. Breaking pitches that truly break leave him with broken hopes. Veteran pitchers with a wide assortment of pitches create serious problems for him.

He actually shows an ability to hit righthanders much better than lefthanders and his average was nearly 60 points higher in 1982. That can be credited to the fact that the majority of lefties in the American League rely on the off-speed and breaking pitches that give Gray so much trouble.

BASERUNNING:

His corkscrew swing takes a couple of steps away from him going to first and Gray can't afford that. He's below average in the speed department, and rarely takes the extra base. If he gets a stolen base, it's only because of a breakdown on a hit-and-run, a missed sign, or a failure on the part of the opposing pitcher and/or catcher.

FIELDING:

He was tried in the outfield, but the results weren't pretty. Doesn't fail for lack of effort; he just doesn't judge fly balls very well. He is adequate at first base but doesn't make the game-saving plays. The biggest problem Gray presents is for the other infielders; he doesn't reach out and catch the ball, and his tendency to wait back on throws leads to more than a normal amount of bad hops that wind up as errors against the fielders. His footwork is inconsistent. Sometimes he will range for a ball, but other times he immediately breaks back to first base and lets ground balls roll unmolested into the outfield.

OVERALL:

Robinson: "He is a big strong righthanded hitter with a lot of holes. But he can hurt you if you get it in the wrong spot."

Harwell: "He can be a dangerous streak hitter."

HITTING:

Steve Henderson has a "slow bat." That's not necessarily bad. It allows him to adjust to the change-up and curve, but does not allow him to fight off good fastballs. He'll invariably hit them to the opposite field. Thus, the book on Henderson is fastballs inside. It's all right to mix them up and try to keep them down. The most effective pitch is inside fast to make him inside-out the ball.

He only pulls off-speed pitches, making it important for infielders to know what their pitcher is going to throw. He can be shaded straightaway or even to the right. Because of his ability to go up the middle or to right field, and to stay with sinkers and sliders, Henderson is very effective at hitting behind the runner. On a team that needs a No. 2 hitter or even a leadoff man, he is not to be a bad choice.

But he's no longer much of a threat to reach the wall. He needs to play to get in a groove. After a slow 1982 start with the Cubs, especially in the field, he seldom started. He had two exceptional games in August, including five hits in Los Angeles. However, none reached the outfield grass.

Henderson dipped to .232 last season after a lifetime .287 previous five. He was very unhappy at the end of 1982.

BASERUNNING:

This is now Henderson's strong point. He's an aggressive, effective hustler on the bases, although he still does not get a good jump in stealing. He knows how to work the bases and enjoys breaking up the double play. He has been known to slide every way, including head first.

STEVE HENDERSON
OF, No. 28
RR, 6'1", 187 lbs.
ML Svc: 6 years
Born: 11-18-52 in Houston, TX

1982 STATISTICS

AVG	G	AB	R	H	2B	3B	HR	RBI	BB	SO	SB
.233	92	257	23	60	12	4	2	29	22	64	6

CAREER STATISTICS

AVG	G	AB	R	H	2B	3B	HR	RBI	BB	SO	SB
.282	671	2344	322	660	100	40	42	613	267	461	66

VS. RHP

VS. LHP

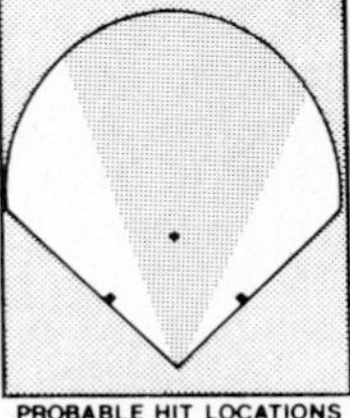
PROBABLE HIT LOCATIONS

FIELDING:

Weak. Henderson does not get a good jump on a ball, often misjudging line drives. He has never had a good arm, his ball tails and his range is not better than adequate. He is most effective coming in, but his throws on the run deceive him.

OVERALL:

Coleman: "Had some big years with the New York Mets, but has not played up to potential since. A liability on defense."

Kiner: "He has not been able to adjust to major league pitching, especially the inside fastball."

McCarver: "He seems to get a lot out of his ability. He can hit the ball with authority the other way. He goes all out, but is short on defense."

MIKE MOORE
RHP, No. 52
RR, 6'4", 205 lbs.
ML Svc: 1 year
Born: 11-26-59 in Eakly, OK

PITCHING:

The No. 1 pick in the June 1981 amateur draft, Moore was force-fed at the big league level in 1982. He wasn't an instant hit, but he wasn't a failure, either. The big righthander has an overpowering fastball that travels at 93-96 MPH. When he came out of college he also had a decent change-up and an average to above average slider. But somewhere between the draft and last year, the two of them disappeared. So did Moore's control, which was a major asset.

It is going to take some work, but the raw ability is there for Moore to live up to his No. 1 draft status. He will be a big strikeout pitcher if he gets a little movement on his fastball and a breaking pitch to complement the heater. He has his best success in the Kingdome, where hitters complain that poor lighting makes it difficult to pick up his fastball.

His biggest problem was early last season when he seemed so concerned with throwing breaking pitches when he got behind in the count. The hitters were able to gear up for his fastball, which needs more movement, and finally, Moore was ordered not to throw any more breaking pitches until he was ahead in the count. Following that, he began to have some degree of success.

FIELDING:

He has an excellent pick-off move that is deceptive because of his size. He is one of only three pitchers to actually pick Rickey Henderson off first base, and it was on a play where Henderson did not even break to second. Great athlete. Can field bunts and balls back up the middle exceptionally well.

OVERALL:

Moore has the attitude that will allow him to live up to his potential. Even during his tough times, never doubted that he belonged in the big leagues and that he could get hitters out. Never felt he was overmatched, just felt he needed to be more intelligent in his approach. Has great resiliency in his arm.

Robinson: "Gaining his experience in the big leagues. This guy has an outstanding future, but as always, the team wants to rush him."

Martin: "Moore has a chance to be an outstanding pitcher, he just needs time. He is extremely intelligent and has an outstanding fastball."

1982 STATISTICS

W	L	ERA	G	GS	CG	IP	H	R	ER	BB	SO	SV
7	14	5.36	28	27	1	144	159	91	86	79	73	0

CAREER STATISTICS

W	L	ERA	G	GS	CG	IP	H	R	ER	BB	SO	SV
7	14	5.36	28	27	1	144	159	91	86	79	73	0

GENE NELSON
RHP, No. 24
RR, 6'0", 172 lbs.
ML Svc: 2 years
Born: 12-3-60 in Tampa, FL

PITCHING:

Gene Nelson became a concern of the Mariners last summer. He wasn't living up to his potential and it was difficult to understand why. Confidence has never been a problem. He believes that he belongs in the big leagues, and has no fear of the opposition. Physically, he has no reason to have any either.

The young righthander had some arm trouble in his early minor league days, but has shown no ill effects the last couple of years. He was slowed by a virus in 1981, but seemed strong last year.

He's got an average fastball velocity-wise, but it has great movement. He has a good sharp slider. And he has one of the better change-ups around. He got himself into problems, however, by falling in love with his change-up--he once threw six straight change-ups to Kent Hrbek, the sixth of which was drilled into the right field stands for a game-winning home-run.

When he's going well he comes right at hitters, gets ahead in the count and puts them away. But too often he seems afraid to challenge a hitter, winds up getting behind in the count and having to groove a pitch that spells his doom.

If he doesn't get too stubborn to learn from his mistakes and decides to listen to the advice of his peers, these problems can be overcome.

FIELDING:

At times Nelson seems to forget about baserunners, a problem that is compounded by a poor move and a big leg whip in his delivery to the plate. He is off balance when he delivers a pitch, which makes it tough on him to field his position. If his delivery is smoothed out, this should improve.

OVERALL:

Young and full of potential. In time should be a solid starter, but still suffers from many of the afflictions of youth.

Martin: "He has the tools to be an above average pitcher with more experience."

Robinson: "Nelson has a chance to be a good starting pitcher. As the team gets better, so will he."

1982 STATISTICS

W	L	ERA	G	GS	CG	IP	H	R	ER	BB	SO	SV
6	9	4.62	22	19	2	123	133	41	38	60	71	0

CAREER STATISTICS

W	L	ERA	G	GS	CG	IP	H	R	ER	BB	SO	SV
9	10	3.28	30	26	2	162	173	65	59	83	87	0

GAYLORD PERRY
RHP, No. 36
RR, 6'4", 215 lbs.
ML Svc: 21 years
Born: 9-15-38 in Williamston, NC

PITCHING:

Once a pure power pitcher, Perry has weathered the test of time by developing into a finesse pitcher. He spots his fastball, rarely throwing it for strikes. He doesn't really need to rely on it that much.

He has a good curveball and change-up, an outstanding forkball, and has been accused of throwing the best spitter of anybody in the game. He studies hitters constantly for an extra edge, even watching the batting practice of the opposition to try and pick up a weakness he can exploit.

Age has taken away some of his stamina, but for six or seven innings he can keep his team in a game (10-2 in games which Seattle scored four or more runs last year). He can have some trouble early, but will fight back to keep the score down and give his offense a chance to get back into the game.

Perry is not afraid to remind hitters that part of the plate belongs to him, and he's not afraid to remind his teammates that they are supposed to make the routine plays. At times he lets mistakes bother him in pitching to the next batter, which makes the errors more costly.

As well as his assortment of pitches, he has a varied assortment of moves on the mound to get prepared to pitch. He wipes his forehead, tugs at his cap, hitches his pants, wipes his chest and wipes the back of his neck. All of it is part of Perry's ploy to at least make hitters think a loaded pitch is coming. He'll go so far as to journey to the batting cage during batting practice and shake hands of opponents, leaving the residue of a sticky substance to help entrench it in the minds of hitters that the baseball may have a little dab on it.

FIELDING:

He may be the oldest pitcher in the American League, but it hasn't slowed him down. He'll catch anything he can get close to, and he's not afraid to dive for a ball. His reactions are still good. He has a decent pick-off move and needs it because of his big leg kick that allows runners to get an extra step on their jump. Perry's forkball and spitter do take abnormal breaks, and if a catcher isn't alert, he'll be chasing down a wild pitch.

OVERALL:

Perry carries Hall of Fame credentials, but hasn't developed a Hall of Fame attitude. He still has a driving desire to win, and with proper support can do the job. He was a major influence on the positive mental approach of his Mariner teammates, and played a big part with the club's improved pitching.

Robinson: "Perry can still win, but certainly not the pitcher he was. Always uses a little psychology on opposing teams, making certain they don't forget about his alleged spitter."

Martin: "May be a clubhouse lawyer, may get away with murder, but he has won over 300 games. Enough said."

1982 STATISTICS

W	L	ERA	G	GS	CG	IP	H	R	ER	BB	SO	SV
10	12	4.40	32	32	6	216	245	117	106	54	116	0

CAREER STATISTICS

W	L	ERA	G	GS	CG	IP	H	R	ER	BB	SO	SV
307	251	3.05	747	660	300	5164	4724	2020	1750	1330	3452	11

DAVE REVERING
INF, No. 9
RL, 6'4", 205 lbs.
ML Svc: 5 years
Born: 2-12-53 in Roseville, CA

1982 STATISTICS

AVG	G	AB	R	H	2B	3B	HR	RBI	BB	SO	SB
.202	98	257	25	52	11	1	8	32	34	51	0

CAREER STATISTICS

AVG	G	AB	R	H	2B	3B	HR	RBI	BB	SO	SB
.265	557	1832	205	486	83	16	62	234	148	240	2

VS. RHP

VS. LHP

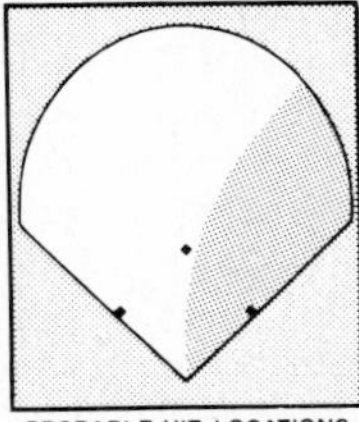
PROBABLE HIT LOCATIONS

HITTING:

In the last two years, Revering's style of hitting has completely changed. He once lived off his power in the alleys, taking the outside pitch and driving it deep to left-center. When he was playing in New York however, he saw Yankee Stadium's inviting right field porch, and quickly ruined his hitting abilities.

He squares off in the box with an upright stance, but has developed a tendency to pull his head back in an attempt to pull every pitch. He doesn't meet the ball with the authority of his earlier years. He is a low ball hitter, and his abortive attempts to pull have made him especially vulnerable to pitches on the outer part of the plate. Breaking and off-speed pitches are paramount problems. This habit of pulling his head back also keeps him from watching the ball as long as he should in order to make solid contact. If the pitch hangs, however, he does have the power to make a pitcher pay for his mistake.

Like so many power hitters, he can go on some big streaks, but to do that he has to play regularly. The problems that he has created for himself over the past two years have made teams hesitant about running him out there every day.

If Revering can manage to regain his former hitting form, he has a chance to be back in the lineup as a solid No. 4 or 5 hitter.

BASERUNNING:

He is never a threat to steal or to take the extra base. Revering could use improvement in baserunning fundamentals, but his biggest problem cannot be alleviated--he is just too slow.

FIELDING:

He gets his feet crossed up at times around first base. Revering doesn't come out to catch throws, waiting instead for them to come to him. If they take a bad bounce and go another way, he has trouble digging them out of the dirt. At times he moves well to his left and right. He came to the Mariners last season rusty from too little playing time.

OVERALL:

Harwell: "A platoon player and streak hitter. He has not lived up to his major league potential."

Robinson: "Revering has a good bat which is more effective against righthanded pitching. I doubt very seriously, though, if he can play everyday."

HITTING:

Simpson has a big looping swing which is not well suited for his type of offense. He's a line drive hitter with limited power. His big swing makes him vulnerable to overpowering fastballs. Simpson will hit a mediocre fastball down with authority. He can handle the change-up or an off-speed breaking pitch if it isn't set up well by a strong diet of hard stuff. If a pitcher isn't going to throw him strikes, Simpson is not afraid to take a walk.

He has mainly been used as a platoon player, but at times has seemed to handle lefthanders as well as righthanders. Though he seems to play well in spurts, he loses something at the plate if he plays too much.

Can leadoff, but is best suited in the lower part of the lineup--possibly ninth to give a manager the versatility of back-to-back baserunners who have speed. Simpson bunts well and can lay it down for a hit or sacrifice. Likes to hit-and-run but can be pitched to, especially with men in scoring position.

JOE SIMPSON
OF, No. 18
LL, 6'3", 190 lbs.
ML Svc: 4 years
Born: 12-31-51 in Purcell, OK

1982 STATISTICS

AVG	G	AB	R	H	2B	3B	HR	RBI	BB	SO	SB
.257	105	296	39	76	14	4	2	23	22	48	8

CAREER STATISTICS

AVG	G	AB	R	H	2B	3B	HR	RBI	BB	SO	SB
.249	516	1278	150	318	52	10	9	116	79	169	44

VS. RHP

VS. LHP

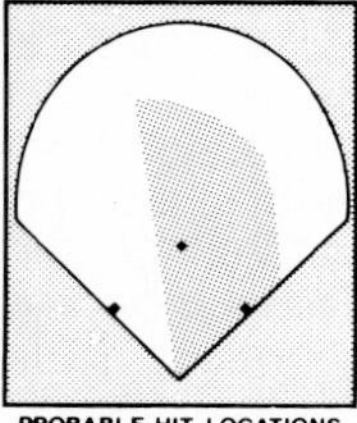
PROBABLE HIT LOCATIONS

BASERUNNING:

Simpson never has taken full advantage of his speed on the bases. He doesn't steal the number of bases he would be expected to steal with his speed. He is aggressive and always tries to force a mistake by the defense, but too often the mistakes don't come. He takes advantage of what the defense gives him. Always looks for a chance to score from second base on any type of hit--including a ground ball when a first baseman might go to sleep.

FIELDING:

Simpson can do a decent job at all three outfield positions. He is a bit too mechanical at times, and it keeps him from taking advantage of his natural abilities. He hesitates on sinking balls in front of him and this leads to bad hops on artificial surfaces. He does move well laterally and always backs up fellow outfielders. Simpson has a strong accurate arm, but takes a long time to get rid of the ball, allowing opponents to get an extra base on him.

OVERALL:

Harwell: "A good solid platoon player."

Martin: "Does a better job for the team than most people think. Will hit .250 to .260 and play anywhere in the outfield. Capable of a big play."

MIKE STANTON
RHP, No. 46
RR, 6'2", 200 lbs.
ML Svc: 4 years
Born: 9-25-52 in
St. Louis, MO

PITCHING:

After a career of hope and promise, Stanton found a home in the Seattle bullpen last summer as the righthanded set-up man for stopper Bill Caudill. He did make a start in September, but it was an emergency.

He can pitch a lot of innings, but has to be careful because if he warms up for a couple nights in a row, even if he doesn't get into a game, he isn't available for a day or two because of tenderness in his right arm.

Stanton is best suited in a short role because he has two basic pitches--a 90+ fastball and a small, quick breaking slider that eats up righthanders. He can get by with that, but if he is going to stretch out at all, he needs to come up with some type of an off-speed pitch he can rely on for a strike to keep hitters honest. Has a herky-jerky type motion that also keeps hitters off balance.

He is highly competitive, sometimes too much so. Has a tendency to have explosive reactions when he doesn't get the job done--whether it be from his own problems or those of the people in the field behind him. Has been given up on by several organizations, but never gave up on himself, and came to Seattle on a spring training tryout.

FIELDING:

Stanton's move to first is adequate, but nothing special. Doesn't lose anything when he works out of the stretch, which is important for a reliever. He follows through in a good position to field the ball back at him, and can handle the bunt without any difficulty.

OVERALL:

He's always been considered a journeyman type pitcher, but seemed to become little more than that in Seattle last year, where he was given a regular role, and was able to prepare for it.

Robinson: "Have to have a guy like this on a team. He's willing to pitch whenever you need him."

Harwell: "Strong arm. Still has potential, but also has a low boiling point."

1982 STATISTICS

W	L	ERA	G	GS	CG	IP	H	R	ER	BB	SO	SV
2	4	4.16	56	1	0	71	69	37	33	21	49	7

CAREER STATISTICS

W	L	ERA	G	GS	CG	IP	H	R	ER	BB	SO	SV
6	12	4.93	138	3	0	217	230	129	119	103	173	15

RICK SWEET
C, No. 8
LR, 6'1", 200 lbs.
ML Svc: 1 year
Born: 9-7-52 in
Longview, WA

1982 STATISTICS

AVG	G	AB	R	H	2B	3B	HR	RBI	BB	SO	SB
.256	88	258	29	66	6	1	4	24	20	24	3

CAREER STATISTICS

AVG	G	AB	R	H	2B	3B	HR	RBI	BB	SO	SB
.256	88	258	29	66	6	1	4	24	20	24	3

VS. RHP

VS. LHP

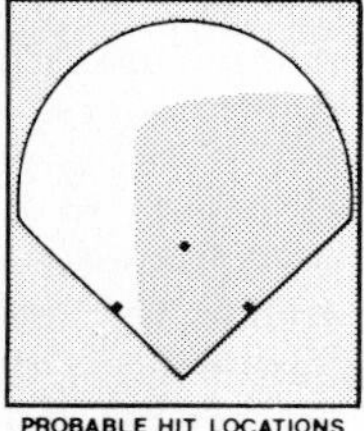
PROBABLE HIT LOCATIONS

HITTING:

Although he likes to consider himself a switch-hitter, Sweet is definitely lefthanded with a bat. He was used almost exclusively against righthanded pitchers last summer and in his few shots at southpaws (2-for-23) did nothing to change that thinking. He is considering a move to full-time status as a lefthanded hitter, which would be a good idea. Righthanded, he has a weak swing and is easily pitched to with any type of pitch. Lefthanded, he has shown signs of being a solid big league hitter. He keeps the ball in the air and grounded into only one double play in 1982. He can advance runners, especially from second to third and third to home.

Like most lefthanded hitters, Sweet handles the ball down and in pretty well. He has problems with breaking balls away, but can handle most fastballs. Not much as a pinch-hitter, a problem considering his use as a platoon player. He spends a great deal of time before a game getting himself mentally psyched, and blames the emotional letdown of sitting and waiting on the bench for his problems.

BASERUNNING:

Sweet has above average speed for a catcher, but not enough to be considered a basestealing threat. He will take the extra base, and though not a conservative runner, he doesn't take foolish chances. He has good enough speed down the first base line so that coming out of the lefthanded batter's box doesn't double him up much. Sweet gets the most out of what he has with his hustle.

FIELDING:

With less than a full season in the American League, Sweet is still learning about opposing hitters. He takes advice from the Mariner staff and other catchers and puts it to use in setting up pitch selection. He is an excellent competitor, and has long been a favorite of Gaylord Perry's behind the plate, although teammate Terry Bulling also earned Perry's respect last summer.

He is a constant conversationalist which annoys some hitters, but it is more an extension of his outgoing personality than an attempt to upset batters. With his decent arm he can throw out a base stealer if pitchers give him a chance. Not afraid to try and pick off a napping runner. He hustles all the time, catching pop-ups that some would give up on and making most bunt plays.

OVERALL:

Martin: "A latecomer, he's a journeyman-type player. He can help behind the plate and give you some defense."

ED VANDE BERG
LHP, No. 51
RL, 6'2", 175 lbs.
ML Svc: 1 year
Born: 10-26-58 in Redlands, CA

PITCHING:

In the long run, Vande Berg could wind up as a solid starting pitcher, but right now, he is a lefthanded shortman who was long on production in his rookie year.

After only a year as a reliever in the minors, he made the Mariners last season and proved to be consistent and durable. He set a major league record with 78 appearances as a rookie, and only once had to sit out with a sore arm. He has a fastball in the high 80s, but his big pitch is a wicked slider that he will throw no matter what the count is. Also has a curveball, but doesn't use it much in short relief. He never has had a change-up, but has the potential to develop one. The first time that Rick Sweet caught Vande Berg last season he didn't know that the change-up was lacking and called for it. Vande Berg threw it nonetheless and struck out Detroit's Lance Parrish.

He never seems to be fazed by tight situations. Last season he entered games with a total of 98 men on base and only 13 scored. Gets a lot of double play grounders, and can come up with a strikeout if the situation demands it. He has good control, and it would seem that he would have a definite advantage against lefthanders, but in his role as shortman wound up facing most righthanded pinch-hitters. He has a unique delivery in which he seems to throw his glove at the batter before releasing the ball.

Vande Berg gets the job done and gets an overall above average rating.

FIELDING:

When he follows through, Vande Berg is always in a position to field the ball. He comes off the mound in a hurry, and has no qualms about getting the lead runner in a sacrifice situation. Excellent move to first that is helped by the fact that he is lefthanded and has a deceptive delivery to the plate.

OVERALL:

The effects of a busy first year will be interesting on his arm. He always seems to be in command of the situation. Never gets down on himself after a bad outing, and comes back the next time throwing strikes.

Harwell: "Good young lefthander who will continue to improve."

Robinson: "You'd never know that he has only been in pro ball a short time . . . it is very difficult for a lefthanded hitter to catch up with his slider. The hitters don't get to see him that often, and that makes him tougher."

1982 STATISTICS

W	L	ERA	G	GS	CG	IP	H	R	ER	BB	SO	SV
9	4	2.37	78	0	0	76	54	21	20	32	60	5

CAREER STATISTICS

W	L	ERA	G	GS	CG	IP	H	R	ER	BB	SO	SV
9	4	2.37	78	0	0	76	54	21	20	32	60	5

HITTING:

Take a drawing out of a book on hitting, put the prescribed stance into real life, and Richie Zisk will come alive. He has a perfect stance, squared at the plate, bat cocked and weight evenly distributed.

The better the team, the better the hitter. On a club that expects to struggle offensively, Zisk tends to try and shoulder too much of the burden, knowing that as a designated hitter, his only way of helping the club to win is to drive in some runs. Sometimes, however, he tries to do too much.

Zisk can go on some pretty good hot streaks, and when he does he uses the entire playing field. He is strong enough to hit the ball out of any part of the park, especially in the Kingdome. Gets himself into some problems, however, in parks like the Dome or Fenway because he tries to pull the ball just a bit too much. He developed this problem in Texas, where the wind keeps the ball from going out to right field.

He spends hours reviewing films to pick up flaws in his hitting and looks over pitching charts to understand how opponents pitch him in certain situations. He doesn't have any problem with particular pitches, especially when he is on a streak. Fastballs in--way in--are the best way to get him out.

He does seem to have trouble with righthanders who drop down like Mark Clear of Boston or Mike Witt of California. They make life miserable for him, and when they are in the game, Zisk is better off on the bench. He likes to hit with men in scoring position, but rarely has the type of protection behind him in the lineup that forces pitchers to give him something decent to hit.

RICHIE ZISK
OF, No. 22
RR, 6'2", 212 lbs.
ML Svc: 10 years
Born: 2-6-49 in
Brooklyn, NY

1982 STATISTICS

AVG	G	AB	R	H	2B	3B	HR	RBI	BB	SO	SB
.292	131	503	61	147	28	1	21	62	49	89	2

CAREER STATISTICS

AVG	G	AB	R	H	2B	3B	HR	RBI	BB	SO	SB
.290	1363	4859	651	1408	233	26	195	756	503	849	8

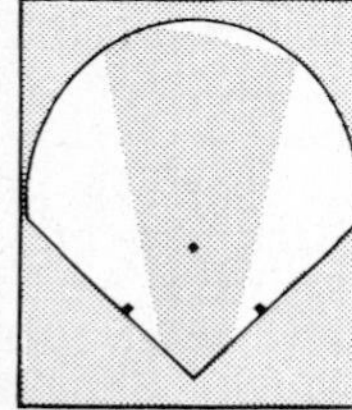

BASERUNNING:

Six knee operations have removed the speed he once had. He can pull off a delayed steal since manager Lachemann gave him the green light. He has a hard time going from first to third because of his bad legs.

FIELDING:

Zisk hasn't played in the field for two years. He is fundamentally sound, but his lack of speed is even more evident in the outfield than it is on the basepaths.

OVERALL:

Robinson: "Strictly an offensive player. Zisk is a free swinger who will strike out, but will also win big games for you with a hit. He has power, a lot of it, and is a good hitter."

DAVE EDLER
INF. No. 24
RR, 6'1", 190 lbs.
ML Svc: 1 year plus
Born: 8-5-56 in
Sioux City, IA

HITTING, BASERUNNING, FIELDING:

Edler is a line drive hitter who is not afraid to go the other way to take advantage of bouncing balls off the wall in the Kingdome. He also likes to hit holes on the right side of the infield.

Has good bat control, and is a definite threat to hit-and-run, making him a good No. 2 hitter, especially against lefthanders. Doesn't chase too many bad pitches. Still, a manager would like to see more power from him. Likes the high ball, but will go with the outside pitch to move runners over. Edler struggles with breaking pitches, especially away. Concentration seems to lessen with nobody on base.

Has better than average speed and can steal a base in the right situation. He doesn't try to force things, is not afraid to take an extra base, and watches the coaches carefully for the sign to take an extra base.

Defensive lapses were his biggest weakness in 1982. Has decent range and good hands, but his throwing is erratic. The more time he has to throw the ball, the wilder it becomes.

OVERALL:

Edler suffered a mental setback under the guidance of former manager Maury Wills and never has regained the air of confidence that made him seem special.

Robinson: "Very inexperienced. Just needs a chance to play. Seattle would like him to be their starting third baseman. 1983 will be an important one for him. If he's going to improve, it will have to come this year."

DAVE HENDERSON
OF, No. 42
RR, 6'2", 210 lbs.
ML Svc: 1 year plus
Born: 7-21-58 in
Dos Palos, CA

HITTING, BASERUNNING, FIELDING:

Though platooned most of last season, David Henderson got several chances to play regularly, and was fairly impressive. He is strong enough to hit with power to the opposite field, but is basically a dead pull hitter. He tends to hit in streaks, sometimes going with the pitch, sometimes not.

He is an impatient hitter, has trouble with off-speed and breaking pitches. The breaking pitch away was especially deadly to him, but last season he started to lay off the balls that bounced in the dirt in the lefthanded batter's box. Henderson can hit line drives with good power and is quick enough to get around on inside pitches.

Very tentative on the bases, however, which can be attributed to his inexperience. Not afraid of contact in breaking up double plays, and can get to second base pretty quickly. Can take the extra base.

He has shown only glimpses of greatness in the big leagues. Henderson has shown an ability to go back on a ball as well as anyone, and is not afraid of running into walls. Has been most consistent on balls which he has to go laterally to catch. Also has a strong and accurate arm, but seems tentative in the outfield.

OVERALL:

Martin: "Impressive young player. Has sting in his bat. Runs well. Good defensive outfielder."

PAUL SERNA
INF, No. 38
RR, 5'8", 170 lbs.
ML Svc: 1 year plus
Born: 11-16-58 in
El Centro, CA

HITTING, BASERUNNING, FIELDING:

Paul Serna doesn't present much of a strike zone, but will always help pitchers out--he is a wild swinger. Pitchers start him off with a fastball up and keep moving the pitches up the more he swings. If he begins to lay off that, they can unload breaking balls and rid themselves of him. Off-speed pitches are out of his realm of ability.

If a pitcher hangs one Serna has good enough pop to drive the ball. He tries to pull everything, which causes problems especially with pitchers beginning to work him away.

He hits in streaks, and should be a good bunter, but isn't. Serna shows a lot of anxiety at the plate, which adds to his problem of handling breaking pitches and the pitches away. He tries to be aggressive, but doesn't have the speed to do some of the things he wants to do. He is an adequate fielder, can make the routine plays, but is slow at times covering second on theft attempts and double plays. Doesn't make double play pivot well.

Limited range but does have a strong arm. Quick hands and good reactions. He will never be enough of an offensive player to get an every day shot at that spot.

OVERALL:

Serna made it to the big leagues on his hustle, which might be good enough to keep him around on a back up basis, but if he starts to relax, his days will be numbered if not counted out.

STEVE STROUGHTER
OF, No. 60
LR, 6'2", 190 lbs.
ML Svc: 1 year
Born: 3-15-52 in
Visalia, CA

HITTING, BASERUNNING, FIELDING:

Stroughter is a strong lefthanded hitter and can hit to the opposite field. He is a journeyman minor league hitter who can drive a low fastball, but doesn't see enough of them to make a living. He enjoyed his limited success against righthanders, but is easy to pitch to. Pitchers keep the ball away and feed him a steady diet of breaking pitches. He likes to go after the first pitch.

If he's going to come back to the big leagues, he's going to have to become more disciplined and accept his role as a pinch-hitter. He's going to have to mentally discipline himself for that job, which he had problems handling in 1982.

Stroughter has decent speed and keeps his head in the game. Goes hard to all the bases and will give the little extra.

It's glove work, or lack thereof, that has been his biggest stumbling block. He made a couple of spectacular plays, but doesn't get a good jump on balls. He breaks his back on balls that are in front of him, and comes in on balls hit over his head. Has an adequate arm, but won't force baserunners to keep from taking that extra base.

OVERALL:

Robinson: "A fringe big league player who finally got a chance to get into the big leagues after 10 years in the minor leagues."

ARLINGTON STADIUM
Texas Rangers

Seating Capacity: 41,284
Playing Surface: Natural Grass

Dimensions
Left Field Pole: 330 ft.
Left-Center Field: 383 ft.
Center Field: 400 ft.
Right-Center Field: 383 ft.
Right Field Pole: 330 ft.
Height of Outfield Wall: 11 ft.

Arlington Stadium is probably the only natural grass stadium that can come close to an artificial surface when it comes to holding heat. The brutal Texas sun makes it almost impossible to play day games, and the Texas Rangers schedule almost all of their games at night, even on Sunday. The intense heat tends to dry out the grass, and makes it close to the billiard table-type artificial surfaces. Water seems to have no effect on either the dirt or the grass--both are always hard.

Wind is a definite factor in this stadium. It invariably blows strongly from right to left, and lefthanded hitters must absolutely smash a ball to get it into the right field seats. Righthanded hitters, conversely, get a break, because these same wind currents propel baseballs out into left and left-center.

In 1982, the fences were actually pushed back a bit, making it an excellent pitcher's ballpark (with the exception of the strong winds that help high flies).

On days when wind presents no major factor, batters benefit from the rock-hard infield, but naturally have to supply their own power to the seats in left or right. The foul line territory is a bit wider than in many other parks, but not nearly as large as the Oakland Coliseum.

Hitters have no complaints about the background from which they hit, but the excessive heat and humidity tend to make their hands sweat more than they would like.

HITTING:

Whatever he decides to throw Buddy Bell, a pitcher must be sure he gets it right where he wants it. If he makes a mistake, there's a good chance Bell will hit it.

Bell is primarily a fastball hitter although he can be struck out with a good fastball in on the fists. Curves should be kept low and outside, but he has the ability to hit curves as well as sliders. Basically a pull hitter, Bell adjusts with two strikes and will then try to go to the opposite field. As a result he doesn't strike out often, and usually puts the ball into play. He also hits the change-up well, especially with two strikes.

Bell likes to swing at the first pitch. The best way to pitch him is to change speeds and move the ball around. One of his greatest attributes is his consistency; he rarely goes into long slumps. Bell has been one of the best clutch hitters in the league over the past several seasons although his batting average with runners in scoring position was down in 1982. While not considered a power hitter, Bell will hit about 15 homers a year and regularly hits with distance to the alleys.

BASERUNNING:

Bell has only average speed, but is an intelligent baserunner and doesn't hesitate to break up the double play. He is not much of a threat to steal, but gets a good jump when the ball is hit and cuts bases well when trying for an extra base hit.

FIELDING:

Bell has won four consecutive Gold Gloves and deserves them. He has excellent range to both his right and his left and a strong, accurate throwing arm. He is particularly adept at diving to knock down a hard hit ball then scrambling to his feet to throw the runner out.

BUDDY BELL
INF, No. 25
RR, 6'2", 185 lbs.
ML Svc: 11 years
Born: 8-27-51 in Pittsburgh, PA

1982 STATISTICS

AVG	G	AB	R	H	2B	3B	HR	RBI	BB	SO	SB
.296	148	537	62	159	27	2	13	67	70	50	5

CAREER STATISTICS

AVG	G	AB	R	H	2B	3B	HR	RBI	BB	SO	SB
.285	1523	5769	733	1642	264	37	122	701	479	496	40

VS. RHP

VS. LHP

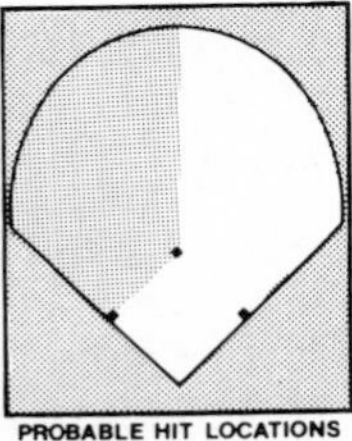
PROBABLE HIT LOCATIONS

His less-than-average 1982 may, in part, be attributed to recurring back problems and bone chips in his right knee. He underwent arthroscopic surgery the last week of the season to correct the knee.

OVERALL:

Robinson: "Might be the top player in the league. He plays every day--just write his name in the lineup. A top clutch player."

Harwell: "A premier player, on both defense and offense. Good leadership qualities."

Martin: "One of the game's best at his position, a tough, productive hitter. Very competitive. He deserves to be with a winner. He's playing up to his potential and more, but because of where he has played, just hasn't gotten the publicity he deserves."

LARRY BIITTNER
INF/OF, No. 33
LL, 6'2", 200 lbs.
ML Svc: 11 years
Born: 7-27-47 in Pocahontas, IA

1982 STATISTICS

AVG	G	AB	R	H	2B	3B	HR	RBI	BB	SO	SB
.310	97	184	18	57	9	2	2	24	17	16	1

CAREER STATISTICS

AVG	G	AB	R	H	2B	3B	HR	RBI	BB	SO	SB
.273	1151	3035	305	829	139	19	29	336	227	271	10

VS. RHP

VS. LHP

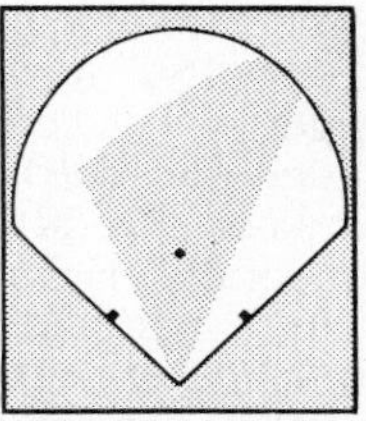
PROBABLE HIT LOCATIONS

HITTING:

Used primarily as a pinch-hitter against righthanded pitchers, Biittner is a classic, hard-nosed player who is generally tough in the clutch. He's a high ball hitter, who stays deep in the batter's box and uses a closed and upright stance. A straightaway hitter who will flare the ball into the opposite field, Biittner is strongest against right-handed pitching. He's been around long enough, however, that he is an accomplished "mistake" hitter. A pitcher's error will result in a Biittner single.

Good fastballs in and anything down will give Biittner trouble. He waits well and will drive the change-up, but good breaking balls, particularly from lefthanders, give him problems. A contact hitter, Biittner produces with runners in scoring position but he is not consistently able to hit behind the runner. He is an average bunter, but is seldom used in that role.

Biittner will go for a bad pitch now and again, especially high and away. He likes to go the other way and sometimes it will get him in trouble. On occasion, he will display some power but is usually a pattern hitter. Against lefties, he'll drop soft liners over the left side. Against righthanders, he'll hit more sharply and generally up the middle.

BASERUNNING:

Biittner is no threat on the bases. He is slow and conservative and pitchers can generally forget about him and concentrate on the batter. He is smart on the bases and seasoned, but in really tight situations, he'll be replaced by a pinch-runner.

FIELDING:

Biittner is used in the outfield and at first base. In either situation, fielding is not his strong suit. His range and arm are limited though he will get the job done. At both positions, he survives on good game sense and good knowledge of his limitations.

OVERALL:

Biittner is a good situational player, who can come off the bench cold and deliver a clutch hit or an RBI. If another's injury pushes him into a starting role, he will not hurt his team in the field, but neither will he dazzle anyone with his defense.

McCarver: "Larry is not a regular, but he is certainly a capable player in the spot he fills. He's a good contact pinch-hitter, who rarely strikes out. Always play him shallow in left."

Coleman: "He's an excellent journeyman hitter. I'd say he's one of the best pinch-hitters in the league. But the rest of his skills are limited."

Kiner: "Biittner is the only free agent the Reds have ever signed and he's proven his worth as a pinch-hitter and fill-in man at first and in the outfield."

DAN BOITANO
RHP, No. 54
RR, 6'1", 185 lbs.
ML Svc: 5 years
Born: 3-22-53 in Sacramento, CA

PITCHING:

Dan Boitano's fastball can get up to 85 MPH or even a little better and appears even faster because the Rangers' staff is overloaded with finesse pitchers.

One problem he has is that he does not change speeds well and, as a result, hitters can eventually time him. For that reason, he is most effective as a short reliever, which is how he was used mostly after being called up from the minors.

Boitano is pretty much a power pitcher who will turn the ball over occasionally, mixing in a sinker and a slider. His curve is the same as his slider and doesn't break much. He tries to keep his pitches in to most hitters, especially righthanders, and will move hitters off the plate. He usually tries to come in with the fastball when behind in the count, giving the batter a pitch to look for.

He has the ability to strike people out, retiring 28 in 30 innings pitched last year, but he also gave up more hits than innings pitched with 33. Boitano was inconsistent last year; he pitched extremely well on some occasions, and not so well on others. He also has had some control problems.

FIELDING:

Boitano has a good, quick release and short windup, and because he is a fastball pitcher, he is one of the toughest on the Rangers' staff to steal on. He has only average abilities in other facets of his fielding.

OVERALL:

Robinson: "At this point, he is the low man on a poor Texas staff. This is his fourth big league team. To me, it looks like he needs to change speeds more. Hitters can just sit on his fastball on the inside half of the plate. Nothing much to go with the fastball."

Harwell: "Poor all around ability."

Martin: "Boitano was a good acquisition for Texas. He throws the ball hard out of the bullpen, and well enough to strike people out, but is inexperienced in the American League."

1982 STATISTICS

W	L	ERA	G	GS	CG	IP	H	R	ER	BB	SO	SV
0	0	5.34	19	0	0	30	33	19	18	13	28	0

CAREER STATISTICS

W	L	ERA	G	GS	CG	IP	H	R	ER	BB	SO	SV
2	2	5.70	51	0	0	71	86	47	45	28	52	0

STEVE COMER
RHP, No. 11
SR, 6'3", 205 lbs.
ML Svc: 5 years
Born: 1-3-54 in Minneapolis, MN

PITCHING:

Steve Comer has had an up-and-down major league career. He won 17 games as a starter in 1979--no righthander won more. He developed arm problems the following year and only won two games while spending some time in the minors on a rehabilitation program. He bounced back as a successful short reliever in 1981, but fell back again in 1982 although he was healthy.

His best pitch is a change-up which he throws under all circumstances. The joke around the league is that he throws it at three speeds: slow, slower and reverse.

Comer is most effective against free swinging, fastball-hitting teams. As an example, for years he had great success against the Baltimore Orioles.

His biggest weakness is that he doesn't have a curveball to speak of, and lacks the velocity on his fastball to set up the change. When he is effective, everything is at the knees, but if he gets the ball up even a little he's in trouble.

Comer is probably most effective as a starter, although he'll have a hard time winning a spot in the Texas rotation in 1983. He has some success as a short reliever but, without a good strikeout pitch, has his limitations in that role.

His big Texas ballpark is well suited to him. He relies heavily on the fielders making the plays behind him. His delivery is almost sidearm at times with a good sinking motion on pitches when he is throwing well.

Comer has a stoic disposition. Nothing seems to rattle him on the mound.

FIELDING:

Comer sets up well after he releases the ball. What he lacks in quickness he makes up for in a good follow through and readiness to field a bunt or cover first. He has a decent move to first base, but his lack of velocity on pitches allows runners to get a good jump.

OVERALL:

Robinson: "I'm afraid his big league career might be in trouble. Comer just isn't throwing hard enough to make everything else work. He's more effective against righthanders because he drops down and runs his pitches inside to them."

Martin: "Comer is a puzzlement coming out of the bullpen if his predecessor throws hard. He has had some success in the past as a starter. His change acts like a knuckler, but isn't. When he's right, he can be equally effective against righthanders and lefthanders; neither can cope with his junk. When he throws a fastball, it's meant as a change-up."

1982 STATISTICS

W	L	ERA	G	GS	CG	IP	H	R	ER	BB	SO	SV
1	6	5.10	37	3	1	97	133	64	55	36	23	6

CAREER STATISTICS

W	L	ERA	G	GS	CG	IP	H	R	ER	BB	SO	SV
39	29	3.80	151	81	18	575	605	280	243	210	205	13

DANNY DARWIN
RHP, No. 44
RR, 6'3", 190 lbs.
ML Svc: 4 years
Born: 10-25-55 in Bonham, TX

PITCHING:

Although he has the best arm on the Rangers' staff, the Texas organization has never been able to decide whether Danny Darwin should be a starter or a reliever. He has been switched back and forth almost every year since being brought up in 1978. The plan for this season is to have him be a starter again. He was a reliever in 1982, and only pitched 89 innings.

Darwin had impressive statistics as a reliever. They are misleading because he frequently gave up a hit to the first batter he faced, which often scored runs that were charged to the previous pitcher.

He is a power pitcher who drops almost sidearm, making him especially effective against righthanded batters. His fastball approaches 90 MPH. He tries to run his fastball in on righthanders, and gets good sinking action on his pitches. He has been hurt by occasional lapses of control.

He also has a pretty good slider, but is hurt by a lack of an effective off-speed pitch. Darwin has been working on a forkball and a straight change which will make his fastball even more effective.

He usually goes with his fastball when behind in the count, but uses the slider as his out pitch.

Darwin is at a point in his career where he needs to blossom into the kind of pitcher people have expected him to be. He has a good chance to do it if he can master the change-up, and if the Rangers finally decide on a role for him and let him settle into it. He is probably better suited to being a starter. He owns the best arm on the staff, and needs to pitch more than 89 innings a year.

FIELDING:

A quick move to first and the ability to get the ball to the plate in a hurry make Darwin one of the more difficult pitchers on the Texas staff to steal against. He is rated average overall at fielding his position.

OVERALL:

Robinson: "His record was very deceiving this year--he has not been that effective. He has been lucky. Darwin has the ability to be overpowering, but in the past has been a hot-and-cold pitcher. He should be better than he's been. He lacks confidence, and does not seem to want to take charge."

Martin: "Darwin has been a quality reliever, but throws well enough to be effective as a starter. Very good poise. Throws hard, and strikes people out."

1982 STATISTICS

W	L	ERA	G	GS	CG	IP	H	R	ER	BB	SO	SV
10	8	3.44	56	1	0	89	95	38	34	37	61	7

CAREER STATISTICS

W	L	ERA	G	GS	CG	IP	H	R	ER	BB	SO	SV
37	25	3.42	154	32	8	432	369	182	164	175	329	15

BUCKY DENT
INF. No. 7
RR, 5'11", 184 lbs.
ML Svc: 10 years
Born: 11-25-51 in Savannah, GA

1982 STATISTICS

AVG	G	AB	R	H	2B	3B	HR	RBI	BB	SO	SB
.193	105	306	27	59	10	1	1	23	21	21	0

CAREER STATISTICS

AVG	G	AB	R	H	2B	3B	HR	RBI	BB	SO	SB
.248	1250	4086	413	1012	154	21	38	388	304	316	14

VS. RHP

VS. LHP

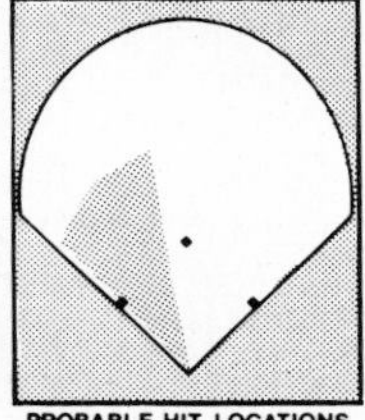
PROBABLE HIT LOCATIONS

HITTING:

Bucky Dent batted .193 for the Yankees and Texas in 1982, almost 60 points below his lifetime average. Most observers attribute that to the fact that Dent did not play regularly after the Yankees acquired shortstop Roy Smalley early in the year. Dent did play regularly after being traded to Texas in August, but his hitting was only marginally better.

Pitchers should keep fastballs up and away. He is capable of hitting fastballs down and in. Has trouble with breaking pitches away. One of the reasons Dent has trouble with outside pitches is that he tries to pull everything.

Before 1982, Dent was a pretty good contact hitter. He could hit behind the runner and handle the hit-and run. He is also a decent bunter, although he doesn't often try to bunt for a base hit. Dent lacks power. Most of his hits are line drives that clear the infield or grounders that get through the holes. He doesn't often reach the alleys. Has somewhat more success against lefthanded pitching. Can be fooled by the change-up and over-matched by excellent breaking stuff.

Dent is not to be considered an offensive player--he should hit down in the order--but has to hit better than he did in 1982 to help a team.

BASERUNNING:

Dent is a careful baserunner. That is, with only average speed he doesn't often try to steal or take an extra base unless he's sure he can make it. As a result, he isn't often thrown out doing something foolish but neither does he make opposing pitchers or fielders aware of him.

FIELDING:

Steady and dependable are the words used most often to describe Dent. He does not have great range, but makes up for it with a pretty good knowledge of how to play hitters and a fairly strong accurate arm. While he doesn't often make the spectacular play, he rarely fails to make the routine play either.

OVERALL:

Robinson: "As steady as they come. Should be a better player next year if he plays every day."

Harwell: "Steady fielder, poor hitter."

Martin: "1982 was a nightmare for him with the Smalley-Steinbrenner problem. Couldn't adjust and it ruined his year. Is a better player than his '82 statistics. Solid shortstop who knows what it is to win. His situation was handled poorly in New York and his year went down the chute. Looking forward to a fresh start in 1983."

JOHN GRUBB
OF, No. 6
LR, 6'3", 180 lbs.
ML Svc: 11 years
Born: 8-4-48 in
Richmond, VA

1982 STATISTICS

AVG	G	AB	R	H	2B	3B	HR	RBI	BB	SO	SB
.279	103	308	35	86	13	3	3	26	39	37	0

CAREER STATISTICS

AVG	G	AB	R	H	2B	3B	HR	RBI	BB	SO	SB
.280	1063	3365	448	941	171	25	67	347	435	436	26

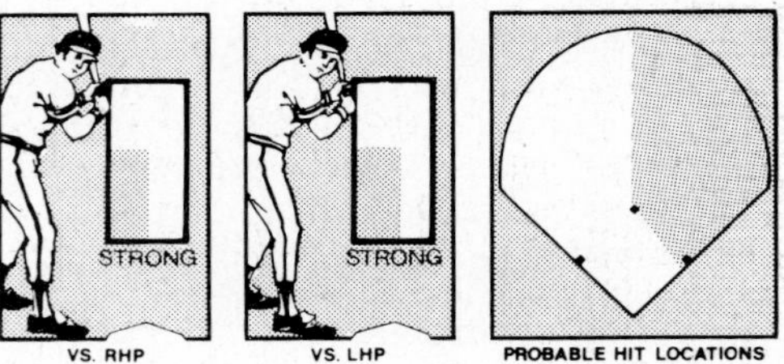

HITTING:

Strictly a platoon player most of his career, John Grubb is prone to long streaks, both hot and cold. He also has been susceptible to a string of minor but nagging injuries over the past few years.

He sits on low fastballs, especially inside. Pitchers should keep fastballs up and mix in slow breaking pitches. Grubb is a good curveball hitter against righthanded pitching. He is a line drive hitter with occasional power, and basically, a pull hitter.

He has been at his best against Boston throughout his career which isn't surprising since the Red Sox staff is traditionally loaded with righthanders.

Grubb shows an above average ability to hit in the clutch, is average at getting the bunt down and in executing the hit-and-run.

His quick bat and short stroke make it tough to sneak a pitch past him and often allow him to wait on breaking pitches without having to stand deep in the batter's box. As a hitter, he had glaring weaknesses.

BASERUNNING:

Baserunning is the weakest part of Grubb's game. He has only average speed, does a pretty good job of breaking up the double play, but is not a threat to steal. Does not make mistakes on the bases, but does not take many risks either. Grubb can't really stretch it to the extra base.

FIELDING:

Grubb is slow getting rid of the ball but he compensates for it with a strong and fairly accurate arm. He has limited range, but is able to go back on the ball well. He won't hurt a team with his glove, but doesn't make a big contribution either.

OVERALL:

Robinson: "He can stay in the big leagues for a while longer with his bat and as a platoon player. Good, quick stroke, and at his best being platooned. He has been injury prone."

Harwell: "An average performer."

Martin: "Steady, not spectacular. He has decent speed and a good glove. Will hit in the .270's consistently when platooned properly, maybe better."

RICK HONEYCUTT
LHP, No. 40
LL, 6'1", 190 lbs.
ML Svc: 5 years
Born: 6-29-54 in
Chattanooga, TN

PITCHING:

Rick Honeycutt was the Rangers' biggest pitching disappointment in 1982. After being the best Texas pitcher just a year earlier, he slumped to 5-17 with a 5.27 ERA last year. He is a sinkerball pitcher, but had trouble keeping his pitches down. He also lost his curve, which was a good second pitch. He went to the Florida Instructional League at the end of last season and reportedly recovered both his good sinker and curve.

Honeycutt does not throw hard. His fastball is in the low 80s and he'll spot it to lefthanders and turn it over for righthanders. When he's pitching well, he has good control. He doesn't get a lot of strikeouts, but prefers to induce the batter to hit the ball on the ground. As a result, he can often get the double play when he needs it. The better the infield he has behind him, the more effective he'll be.

Since being caught cutting the baseball late in the 1980 season, Honeycutt has been accused frequently of doctoring his pitches but has maintained his poise throughout. He has been a starter throughout his career, but spent some time in the bullpen last season to try to regain his stuff. The Rangers are hoping that his bad year was a combination of having his tonsils removed shortly before spring training, and the long layoff just before regular season forced by several games being snowed out.

He has shown the ability to pitch under pressure in the past, and is under pressure to regain 1981 form this year.

FIELDING:

Honeycutt has a good quick move to first, although his slow delivery allows runners to get a pretty good jump once he commits himself to throwing home. He's average to good fundamentally in covering bunts, covering first and the overall handling of the fielding aspects of his position.

OVERALL:

Robinson: "Honeycutt has to be a better pitcher than he showed last year. He needs to keep the ball down and that might have been his problem. Everything was up the times I saw him pitch last year--he looked like he was making bad pitches and lost some confidence. He has been a winner, though, and knows how to pitch. Is also pitching in a good park for him."

Harwell: "Coming off a bad year with a bad club. However, he has shown previously that he is capable of winning in the majors. The two reasons for his losing career record are Seattle and Texas, the two teams he has pitched for."

Martin: "Outstanding poise and presence on the mound. His greatest weakness is the overall pitching pattern he uses to set up opposing hitters."

1982 STATISTICS

W	L	ERA	G	GS	CG	IP	H	R	ER	BB	SO	SV
5	17	5.27	30	26	4	164	201	103	96	54	64	0

CAREER STATISTICS

W	L	ERA	G	GS	CG	IP	H	R	ER	BB	SO	SV
42	64	4.29	149	131	33	852	919	451	406	258	333	0

HITTING:

Dave Hostetler is a big swinger who hit 22 home runs in two months after being called up from the minors in late May, then didn't hit another the rest of the season.

Hostetler needs to be more selective. He can be jammed because he likes to extend his arms to get maximum power in his swings. He will swing at pitches out of the strike zone, especially when he's behind in the count. Righthanders should keep fastballs down and in and throw him a lot of slow breaking stuff. Lefthanders have had some success with sliders inside.

He tends to hit the ball straightaway, which particularly hurts him in Arlington Stadium where the wind blowing in can keep the ball in the park. He showed an ability to fight off tough pitches for base hits.

Hostetler has great power. He gets under the ball much of the time, won't wait for many walks and has trouble bunting, although he isn't often called on to sacrifice. He has shown some ability to drive in runners in scoring position. The big question mark for 1983 is whether his real level is nearer the hot first two months he had or the cold last two. He was dropped from clean-up to sixth and seventh in the order by the end of the season.

So far, he has been inconsistent in his major league career, strikes out a lot, and can miss badly on one pitch and hit the next one out of the park.

BASERUNNING:

Average speed, and average ability on the bases. Hostetler doesn't take chances, and is not a threat to steal--nothing a pitcher has to worry about when he's on first or second.

FIELDING:

He has limited range at first base, and tends to have some trouble with grounders hit sharply right at him.

DAVE HOSTETLER
INF, No. 12
RR, 6'4", 215 lbs.
ML Svc: 2 years
Born: 3-27-56 in Pasadena, CA

1982 STATISTICS

AVG	G	AB	R	H	2B	3B	HR	RBI	BB	SO	SB
.232	113	418	53	97	12	3	22	67	42	113	2

CAREER STATISTICS

AVG	G	AB	R	H	2B	3B	HR	RBI	BB	SO	SB
.236	118	424	54	100	12	3	23	68	42	115	2

VS. RHP

VS. LHP

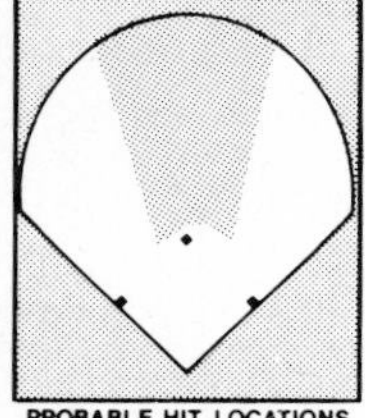
PROBABLE HIT LOCATIONS

Some thought is being given to having him play as a designated hitter next season. He is adequate at starting the first-to-second-to-first double play, but needs to improve coming in for bunts.

OVERALL:

Robinson: "A big swinger--he will swing at a few bad balls, but don't get one in his zone. He has a great attitude and may need it because Arlington Stadium is not suited to him. The wind blows in all the time, and I've seen it make grown men cry. So far, he doesn't seem to have let it bother him. He's been a pleasant surprise . . . big and strong."

Harwell: "Tremendous power. Hostetler can be a top notch home run hitter."

Martin: "Dave has raw power from a 6'4", 215 lb. frame. He can be pitched to, but will get his share of home runs. Lots of potential."

PITCHING:

Charlie Hough's career took a turn for the better when he became a full-time starter in 1982. A reliever most of his career, he got a chance to start in five games in September 1981 as an experiment when Texas was out of the race. He won four of the five to earn a spot in the rotation and was Texas' most effective starter last year.

Hough is the only pitcher in the American League to throw the knuckleball, which makes him that much more effective. He used to give in and throw a fastball or a slider when behind in the count, but now he often throws the knuckler even in those situations.

Sometimes, he has trouble when the knuckler is working too well and he can't control it. At other times, it flattens out and is hit hard.

How effective Hough will be in a game is usually evident in the first couple of innings. If the knuckler isn't working, or is uncontrollable, he will have trouble right away. If the pitch is working, he will be effective right from the start.

He's more suited to being a starter than a reliever for two reasons. First, if he is having an "off" game, he can be taken out with plenty of innings left for his team to recover. Second, it is dangerous to bring a knuckleball pitcher into the game late with the go-ahead run on third because of the possibility of the passed ball or wild pitch.

A veteran with lots of poise, Hough is equally effective against both right and lefthanded hitters. Batters know what's coming most of the time but have trouble doing anything about it.

FIELDING:

Because the knuckleball takes a long time to get to the plate, and because of the increased possibility of a passed ball or a wild pitch and the fact that the catcher often has a hard time getting a good grip on the ball to throw to second, Hough is prone to having bases stolen on him. Catcher Jim Sundberg was often handcuffed by the pitch when Hough was acquired from the Dodgers in mid-1980, but has adapted about as well as any catcher can. Hough is average in other aspects of his fielding.

CHARLIE HOUGH
RHP, No. 49
RR, 6'2", 190 lbs.
ML Svc: 11 years
Born: 1-5-48 in Honolulu, HI

OVERALL:

Robinson: "The thing about the knuckleball is that it's either going to be very good or very bad. It depends on how he's throwing rather than how the other team is hitting. If he's throwing the ball right, it doesn't matter who's at bat. The knuckler is a trick pitch, though, and when it's not working he can get belted."

Harwell: "Good control of knuckleball, but a lack of variety in his pitching repertoire can hurt him if it's not working. He proved he can pitch effectively as a starter."

Martin: "Hough had a good year with a bad team in 1982. Consistent. He learned the knuckleball when he hurt his arm in the minors and stuck with it to succeed in the majors."

1982 STATISTICS

W	L	ERA	G	GS	CG	IP	H	R	ER	BB	SO	SV
16	13	3.95	34	34	12	228	217	111	100	72	128	0

CAREER STATISTICS

W	L	ERA	G	GS	CG	IP	H	R	ER	BB	SO	SV
69	62	3.58	472	57	16	1170	973	523	465	557	780	61

LaMAR JOHNSON
INF, No. 36
RR, 6'2", 232 lbs.
ML Svc: 9 years
Born: 9-2-50 in Bessemer, AL

1982 STATISTICS

AVG	G	AB	R	H	2B	3B	HR	RBI	BB	SO	SB
.259	105	324	37	84	11	0	7	38	31	40	3

CAREER STATISTICS

AVG	G	AB	R	H	2B	3B	HR	RBI	BB	SO	SB
.287	792	2631	294	755	122	12	64	381	211	307	22

VS. RHP

VS. LHP

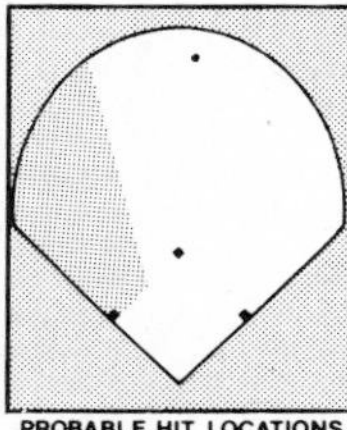
PROBABLE HIT LOCATIONS

HITTING:

Righthanded pitchers shouldn't throw LaMar Johnson sliders while lefthanders will be successful most of the time going down and in with a curveball.

His career must be considered in two parts. Before 1981, he was one of the more consistent long ball hitters in the American League while playing regularly. In the past two seasons in both Chicago and Texas, he played part-time and was not nearly as effective.

In general, Johnson has trouble hitting pitches that are down in the strike zone. He has trouble with the change-up. Because he is primarily a streak hitter, being platooned is not helpful to his hitting, although he has more success against lefthanders.

The Rangers thought that his weight might be a problem, so they wrote a clause into his contract that paid a bonus if he weighed in at less than the prescribed poundage 10 times during the season. He earned the bonus each time but this did nothing noticeable to help his production.

Johnson stands low in the box with a closed, upright stance and makes his best contact on pitches that are up and out over the plate. He has a tendency to swing at the first pitch. During his career he has usually hit well in Baltimore's Memorial Stadium and Chicago's Comiskey Park. He isn't as effective in the larger parks.

BASERUNNING:

Johnson is not a threat to steal and isn't a particularly smart runner. He has below average speed, and isn't aggressive when on base.

FIELDING:

After May of last season, Johnson spent most of his time platooning as a designated hitter. Before that he played some first base but was below average.

He lacks range, especially to his right and has trouble coming in to field the bunt. Average throwing arm and accuracy.

OVERALL:

Robinson: "Has been relegated to a second-string position and I doubt he can help anyone that way. Johnson has been a good hitter, but hasn't been playing much the last two years. For him to contribute, he has to play. Don't think he can DH or pinch-hit for you. He had been a consistent hitter up to the last two years, but it doesn't look like he has a chance to play at Texas."

Harwell: "A power hitter, but not as effective as he was. Can get hot, but has hitless streaks, too. He hits better in smaller parks because of their home run potential."

Martin: "Johnson is a hard hitter to the gaps. He had good run production in the mid-1970's with the White Sox, and has been a pretty good offensive player through his career. Not really much of a fielder anymore."

JON MATLACK
LHP, No. 32
LL, 6'3", 200 lbs.
ML Svc: 11 years
Born: 1-19-50 in
West Chester, PA

PITCHING:

Considered the ace of the Texas staff as recently as 1980, Jon Matlack has been disappointing the past couple of years. While he has the best stuff on the staff, his effectiveness hasn't been what it should be. He has excellent control, a good fastball, good curve and good slider, all with movement. He uses a palmball as a change-up. He has plenty of savvy.

Matlack pitches better in one-sided games, possibly because when the score is close he has a tendency to try to be too fine, falls behind and then has to come in with his pitches.

One of his problems has also been changing roles over the past two years. A starter at the beginning of 1981, he was sent to the bullpen as a short reliever late in the season, but had only one appearance in the last month. He was a starter, long and short reliever in 1982.

He has had some problems on the mound since his role as the Rangers' player representative during strike season of 1981, but denies that was a distraction. He admits to some mechanical adjustments that have, he says, been made.

Matlack is tougher on lefthanders than righthanders, but has had problems with consistency lately. He'll be going along well, but then one thing that goes wrong often leads to several others.

FIELDING:

Matlack takes his time delivering the ball but compensates for that with an above average move to first. His overall effectiveness fielding his position is average, although his follow through leaves him in a good position to get off the mound to field a bunt or cover first.

OVERALL:

Robinson: "Matlack still throws the ball well, but is unable to do the job when the game is on the line. He pitches well when the team is ahead or way behind. Maybe I'm expecting too much of him because he has a career .500 record. He shows good poise on the mound, and looks like he is going to get everyone out. He knows how to pitch."

Harwell: "Experience and ability to use several pitches are his greatest tools."

Martin: "Matlack was a better pitcher in the National League. He used to throw harder. His attitude is one of his weaknesses."

1982 STATISTICS

W	L	ERA	G	GS	CG	IP	H	R	ER	BB	SO	SV
7	7	3.53	33	14	1	47	158	64	58	37	78	1

CAREER STATISTICS

W	L	ERA	G	GS	CG	IP	H	R	ER	BB	SO	SV
123	122	3.14	336	309	95	2289	2186	927	798	611	1478	3

PAUL MIRABELLA
LHP, No. 34
LL, 6'2", 196 lbs.
ML Svc: 5 years
Born: 3-20-54 in Belleville, NJ

PITCHING:

Paul Mirabella was acquired from the Chicago Cubs late in spring training 1982 and made the team primarily because none of the other candidates for lefthanded short reliever had proven they could do the job. He was inconsistent through the year as he was used as both a short and long reliever. At one point he retired 17 straight batters over several appearances; at other times he had trouble getting even lefthanded batters out.

Mirabella relies primarily on an 83-84 MPH fastball, mixing in curves and sliders. He throws from three-quarter delivery, and had some control problems in 1982, in part because he often went a week or more between appearances.

He sometimes lacks poise, and hasn't developed an outstanding out pitch. He has a fairly live arm, but his main problem recently has been a lack of consistency. He seldom brushes a hitter back, preferring to work the outside corners.

FIELDING:

Mirabella has just an average move to first base, especially so for a lefthander. Average in his ability to field bunts, and average at covering first on a ground ball hit to the right side of the infield. He won't win any Gold Gloves, but is not a liability either.

OVERALL:

Robinson: "Mirabella has had a shot with three big league clubs besides Texas and could not stick. He should be able to help a big league team in some capacity. Texas wanted him to be a lefthanded short man, but he hasn't done the job. Though he had several winning years at Triple A, he has been unable to get it together in the big leagues."

Harwell: "His greatest strength is experience and overall ability."

Martin: "Not used much. He could win in minors but has trouble in the big leagues. He provides a live, but inconsistent arm for the bullpen."

1982 STATISTICS

W	L	ERA	G	GS	CG	IP	H	R	ER	BB	SO	SV
1	1	4.80	40	0	0	50	46	28	27	22	29	3

CAREER STATISTICS

W	L	ERA	G	GS	CG	IP	H	R	ER	BB	SO	SV
9	19	5.06	101	28	3	238	263	150	134	122	118	4

LARRY PARRISH
INF/OF, No. 9
RR, 6'3", 215 lbs.
ML Svc: 9 years
Born: 11-10-53 in
Winter Haven, FL

1982 STATISTICS

AVG	G	AB	R	H	2B	3B	HR	RBI	BB	SO	SB
.264	128	440	59	116	15	0	17	62	30	84	5

CAREER STATISTICS

AVG	G	AB	R	H	2B	3B	HR	RBI	BB	SO	SB
.263	1095	3851	480	1012	223	24	117	506	279	696	22

VS. RHP

VS. LHP

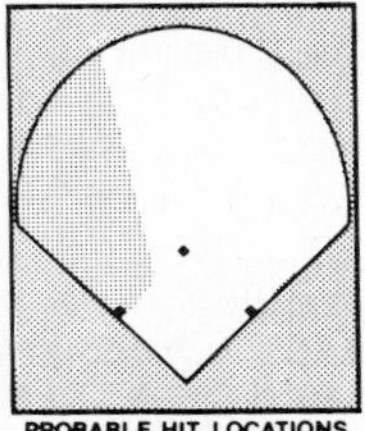
PROBABLE HIT LOCATIONS

HITTING:

Larry Parrish has plenty of holes in his swing, but is also capable of hitting his pitch a long way. He had lots of trouble with curveballs in 1982, especially in situations where he wasn't looking for it such as 3-0 or 3-1 counts. There are several explanations for this. His trade to Texas from Montreal late in spring training brought him to a league where pitchers often throw breaking stuff even when behind in the count. He had to get new contact lenses early in the year and took a while to adjust to them. And there is some suspicion that a wrist he broke two years ago still bothers him in cold weather.

Whatever the reason, he was hitting under .200 with just one home run just before the All Star break. Then he went on a tear and ended up with respectable overall numbers.

Parrish stands deep in the box, moves into a pitch and tries to pull almost everything. Fastballs, especially from righthanders, should be kept inside and low. Curves, sinkers and sliders are effective, but must be kept down. Parrish will jump on a hanging curve or any other pitch that is up in the strike zone.

Over the past few years, he has been primarily a streak hitter who has his best success against lefthanded pitching. He hits well in the clutch, but is not a good bunter. His value to a team is in his power potential.

BASERUNNING:

Parrish is an aggressive runner who does a good job of breaking up the double play. He has only average speed, however, and is not a threat to steal. He compensates for his lack of speed by being an intelligent runner who does not take unnecessary chances.

FIELDING:

Parrish has one of the strongest outfield arms in baseball and is generally accurate on throws both to third and home. He was moved to the outfield from third base, where he had played for a decade, and made an excellent transition. While he has limited range, he is surehanded on the balls he gets to.

OVERALL:

Robinson: "He has great tools and can use them. Arlington Stadium in Texas is not the best ballpark for him--the wind blows in all the time and that has discouraged previous Rangers such as Richie Zisk. He will have to whip the mental aspect of playing his home games there. It took him a half year to get over the shock of going to Texas and the American League."

Harwell: "Parrish hits the long ball, but isn't a consistent hitter for average, and not as good as he once was. He has lost both consistency and some power."

MIKE RICHARDT
INF, No. 2
RR, 6'0", 170 lbs.
ML Svc: 1 year plus
Born: 5-24-58 in
Los Angeles, CA

1982 STATISTICS

AVG	G	AB	R	H	2B	3B	HR	RBI	BB	SO	SB
.241	119	402	34	97	10	0	3	43	23	42	9

CAREER STATISTICS

AVG	G	AB	R	H	2B	3B	HR	RBI	BB	SO	SB
.239	141	473	36	113	12	0	3	51	24	49	9

VS. RHP

VS. LHP

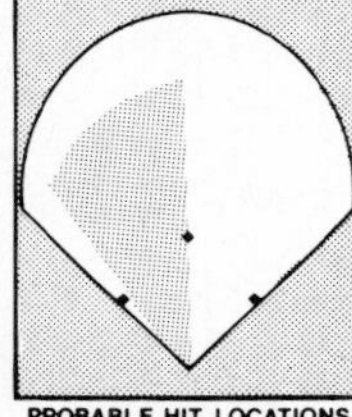
PROBABLE HIT LOCATIONS

HITTING:

Because he bats from an upright stance and usually tries to pull the ball, Mike Richardt has trouble with curveballs, particularly low and outside. Through most of his career, he has been a good fastball hitter, but he even had trouble with fastballs in 1982. This was at least partly because he was weakened most of the year by a persistent throat infection. He had his tonsils removed immediately after the season and, as a result, is expected to be stronger in 1983.

A pretty good contact hitter, Richardt lacks power but has displayed an ability to hit in the clutch. He led the Rangers in batting average with runners in scoring position last year despite his low overall average.

A rookie in 1982, Richardt will become a better hitter in the major leagues as he learns to go to right field with outside pitches. His aggressiveness at the plate can be used against him; with two strikes he tends to chase a high fastball that's out of the strike zone.

Because he has good bat control, he can help the team by hitting behind the runner, but at this point in his career, he needs to hit down in the order. He is a better hitter against lefthanded pitching than against right-handers.

BASERUNNING:

Has decent speed, but Richardt hasn't been given that much of a chance to demonstrate his baserunning ability so far. Pitchers should be aware of him on the bases. As his confidence increases, so will his ability to help the team with his running.

FIELDING:

Richardt has a reputation for being only an adequate fielder but is actually much better than that. He led American Association (minor league) second basemen in fielding percentage in 1981, and surprised the Rangers with his steadiness and range at second base in 1982.

He goes to his right slightly better than to his left and has only an average arm. His range is above average and he has a quick release and throws accurately. While not the smoothest second baseman in the league at turning the double play, he is nevertheless effective. He is a better fielder than given credit for.

OVERALL:

Robinson: "Just needs experience and is getting it now. There's no reason why he will not be around for a long time. He was a good player for a rookie and is going to be a good hitter."

Harwell: "He's improving and will make himself a good major leaguer within two years."

Martin: "Richardt gets his bat on the ball. He has some speed, is young and could develop."

MICKEY RIVERS
OF, No. 17
LL, 5'10", 162 lbs.
ML Svc: 13 years
Born: 10-30-48 in Miami, FL

1982 STATISTICS

AVG	G	AB	R	H	2B	3B	HR	RBI	BB	SO	SB
.235	19	68	6	16	1	1	1	4	0	7	0

CAREER STATISTICS

AVG	G	AB	R	H	2B	3B	HR	RBI	BB	SO	SB
.295	1269	5007	708	1478	217	70	56	446	246	427	253

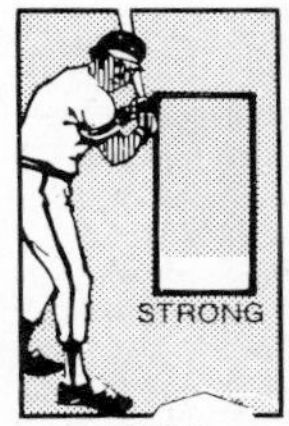

VS. RHP

VS. LHP

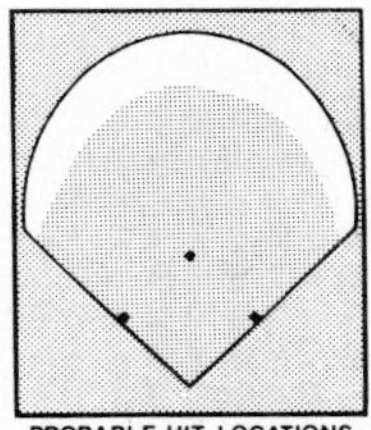
PROBABLE HIT LOCATIONS

HITTING:

Mickey Rivers is an anxious hitter. He likes to swing at the first pitch, so starting him out with a fastball in the strike zone is to be avoided. He can be made to chase slow, breaking pitches out of the strike zone, particularly when behind in the count. In general, the ball should be kept down. He can hit a righthander's curveball better than a lefthander's. He can pull, but also goes the other way frequently.

Coming off an injury-filled season during which he played only a handful of games, Rivers is a question mark. He's 34 years old and it's been two years since he's had a productive season.

He has been a leadoff hitter much of his career, but doesn't draw many walks. He can bunt, so is better suited to batting second at this point in his career. Rivers doesn't strike out often and can be effective hitting behind the runner. He likes to chop the ball into the ground and run, making him more effective on artificial turf.

Underwent arthroscopic surgery on his right knee late in spring training. He reinjured it in his first at-bat after coming back, joined the team in August and, after only a few games, badly twisted his ankle running out a ground ball and missed the rest of the season.

BASERUNNING:

Baserunning used to be one of the strongest parts of Rivers' game, but he has lost a step and is no longer aggressive on the bases. He rarely tries to steal anymore and does not help his team by breaking up the double play. He can still take an extra base on occasion, but is also frequently thrown out trying it. Rivers is prone to being picked off first.

FIELDING:

He still has the ability to outrun the ball into the alleys. Rivers' arm is below average and he does not attempt to hit the cutoff man. While he led the American League outfielders in assists in 1981, that is more a reflection of the number of runners who test him than the strength of his arm.

OVERALL:

Robinson: "Has had some big years but will have to prove himself again. 1983 is a key year in his career. At his age, I don't know if he wants it badly enough. When he makes up his mind to play, he can play. He'll have a hard time beating out George Wright in center field."

Harwell: "Not as effective as in earlier years. Has lost a step or two in speed."

Martin: "1983 a question, maybe, because he's coming off some injuries. When he was with the Yankees, he was an intimidating factor because of his speed."

BILLY SAMPLE
OF, No. 5
RR, 5'9", 175 lbs.
ML Svc: 5 years
Born: 4-2-55 in Roanoke, VA

1982 STATISTICS

AVG	G	AB	R	H	2B	3B	HR	RBI	BB	SO	SB
.261	97	360	56	94	14	2	10	29	27	35	10

CAREER STATISTICS

AVG	G	AB	R	H	2B	3B	HR	RBI	BB	SO	SB
.277	398	1134	183	314	63	4	22	111	99	102	30

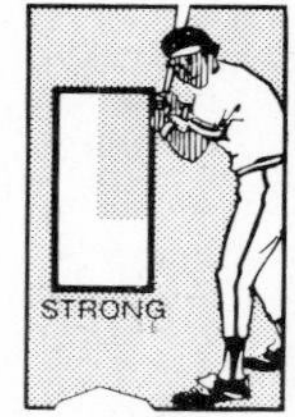

VS. RHP

VS. LHP

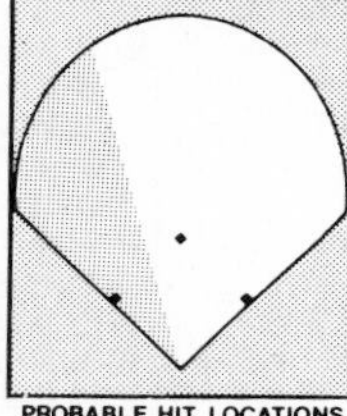
PROBABLE HIT LOCATIONS

HITTING:

Billy Sample tended to hit the ball to right-center when he first came up to the big leagues, but now tries to pull everything. In general, he is a high ball hitter who will chase a pitch up and out of the strike zone when he gets two strikes on him. He has a good concept of the strike zone, but is an aggressive hitter who doesn't get many walks.

He has not yet lived up to his potential but has also not had more than 360 at-bats in a season. Sample had been playing and hitting well in 1981 when the strike hit, and was doing the same in 1982 when he injured his wrist. Although he is not considered a power hitter, he did hit 10 homers last season.

Sample has good speed, and can bunt for a base hit. He is a good second hitter who can protect a runner and handle the hit-and-run.

He handles sinkers and sliders better than curveballs. Fastballs should be kept out and down. Breaking balls are good bets to get him out. He will jump on the fastball up and in. Sample is somewhat more effective against left-handed pitching. He is a line drive hitter who generally makes contact. He is a good wrist hitter with a quick stroke.

BASERUNNING:

Sample has excellent quickness out of the batter's box and above average speed getting to first base. The pitcher must be aware of him when he's on base. He is very aggressive at breaking up the double play. A smart runner, Sample should be encouraged to steal more bases.

FIELDING:

Sample makes up for having an average arm by throwing to the cutoff man whenever possible. He has good range and is extremely, perhaps overly, aggressive in pursuit of fly balls. Twice in the past few years, he has injured himself diving for an uncatchable ball in the late innings of a one-sided game.

His best assets are excellent range, plenty of hustle and the ability to come in on short fly balls.

OVERALL:

Robinson: "Has a lot of tools, but he has to do it soon and I think he could if he gets a chance to play every day. He will be a much better player when he plays regularly. He is a good outfielder with an average arm at best, and most teams keep running when the ball is hit to him."

Harwell: "He's coming into his own. Good hitter and a better than average fielder."

Martin: "Better than average contact hitter who can get on base. Fair outfielder. Has speed."

DAVE SCHMIDT
RHP, No. 24
RR, 6'1", 185 lbs.
ML Svc: 1 year
Born: 4-22-57 in Niles, MI

PITCHING:

Dave Schmidt was having success as a reliever early in the year, but later on, the Rangers decided to experiment with him as a starter and he hurt his arm.

He is extremely competitive. Schmidt mixes an above average fastball with a good, quick slider. In clutch situations, he also throws a palmball that some think is a spitter. Whatever it is, he uses it as his change of pace. He still depends on his fastball most of the time when he is behind in the count.

Schmidt is not an overpowering pitcher, but keeps the ball where he wants it, usually down. He has a good walks-to-strikeouts ratio, although he could be more effective with a better team in the field behind him.

His greatest asset is his ability to pitch accurately and consistently to the batter's weakness. He will come inside, and has great poise for a youngster--he seems to thrive on pressure situations. Although Schmidt did not have impressive minor league statistics, he has a chance to be a much better pitcher at the major league level.

Schmidt is generally more effective against righthanders, and can take advantage of an anxious hitter.

FIELDING:

Schmidt has an above average move to first, especially for a righthander. He has an average ability to field a bunt and in other aspects of his defensive game.

OVERALL:

Robinson: "Very inexperienced, but is now getting a chance to pitch in the big leagues. He just might be a better pitcher in the big leagues than he was in the minors when he was not too impressive. He shows good poise for a youngster, and does a good job of keeping the ball down. He has to put the ball where he wants it to be effective."

Harwell: "Has an excellent chance to be a standout pitcher. Dave is a good competitor who battles all the way. Excellent poise."

Martin: "Schmidt is a young reliever with good stuff and a solid year under his belt. He was the most effective reliever on the Texas staff after Darwin in 1982. It's told he has a good spitter."

1982 STATISTICS

W	L	ERA	G	GS	CG	IP	H	R	ER	BB	SO	SV
4	6	3.20	33	8	0	109	118	45	39	25	69	6

CAREER STATISTICS

W	L	ERA	G	GS	CG	IP	H	R	ER	BB	SO	SV
4	7	3.19	47	9	0	141	149	56	50	36	82	7

BILL STEIN
INF, No. 13
RR, 5'10", 170 lbs.
ML Svc: 9 years
Born: 1-21-47 in
Battle Creek, MI

1982 STATISTICS

AVG	G	AB	R	H	2B	3B	HR	RBI	BB	SO	SB
.239	85	184	14	44	8	0	1	16	12	23	0

CAREER STATISTICS

AVG	G	AB	R	H	2B	3B	HR	RBI	BB	SO	SB
.263	810	2457	239	647	103	16	41	263	172	358	14

VS. RHP

VS. LHP

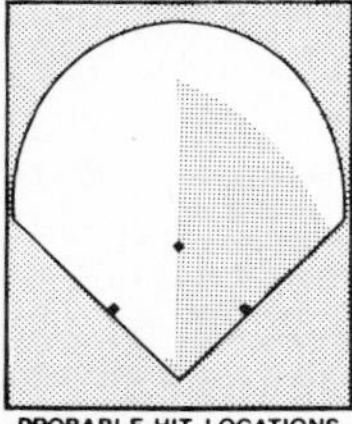
PROBABLE HIT LOCATIONS

HITTING:

Bill Stein is a very aggressive hitter who has the ability to come into the game cold and still get his swings. As a result, he has developed into one of the better pinch-hitters in the game.

Because he is so aggressive, a good out pitch would be a slow breaking ball. Fastballs should be kept down and away or right in on his fists. While not known as a power hitter, he can hit the ball out of the park if he gets a fastball up in the strike zone or a hanging curve. He hit 13 home runs at Seattle in 1977.

Stein's best attribute, though, is his ability to hit in the clutch. In 1981, for example, he got a hit in seven straight pinch-hit appearances. He can be overexposed, however, and is most effective being spotted in certain situations instead of playing every day. More effective against lefthanded pitching.

Stein tries to hit the ball through the middle and often goes to right field with an outside pitch. He is average in both bunting ability and the hit-and-run. His overall hitting ability is the strongest part of his game.

BASERUNNING:

Stein is strictly average on the bases; he doesn't hurt the team but isn't a plus, either. He is, however, an intelligent runner, realizes his limitations and doesn't take chances.

FIELDING:

He has an average arm with average range, but compensates somewhat with good accuracy on his throws. Stein is valuable because of his versatility; has played third, second and first base as well as some outfield in the past two years. He's adequate at third base, and has had somewhat less success at second. Average in his ability to come in for a bunt and turn the double play.

OVERALL:

Robinson: "Bill is a very aggressive hitter. He comes off the bench slashing and often hits the first pitch. He can stay around just on his bat. He's the DH or pinch-hit type, and is on a club where he hasn't played much in the field since Buddy Bell has been at third."

Harwell: "One of the game's best pinch-hitters. He has put in good years as an average, back up major leaguer. A good team player."

Martin: "Stein is a contact hitter who will average around .260. The 1981 strike killed his best year at the plate. He can come off the bench."

JIM SUNDBERG
C, No. 10
RR, 6'0", 195 lbs.
ML Svc: 9 years
Born: 5-18-51 in Galesburg, IL

1982 STATISTICS

AVG	G	AB	R	H	2B	3B	HR	RBI	BB	SO	SB
.251	139	470	37	118	22	5	10	47	49	57	2

CAREER STATISTICS

AVG	G	AB	R	H	2B	3B	HR	RBI	BB	SO	SB
.258	1267	4068	426	1049	175	26	52	431	481	569	18

VS. RHP

VS. LHP

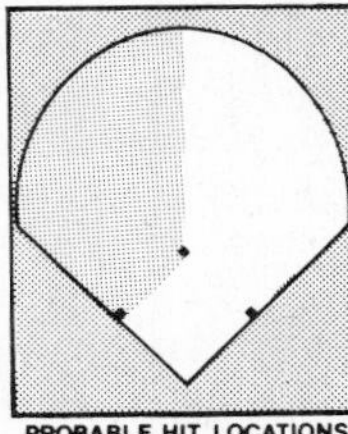
PROBABLE HIT LOCATIONS

HITTING:

Jim Sundberg has developed into a decent hitter over the past few seasons, especially considering that he's averaged almost 150 games per season behind the plate since 1974.

Because he gets so much playing time, Sundberg has developed a hitting pattern over the past few seasons. He starts out fast, tails off at midseason, and finishes strong.

He has trouble with fastballs up and in and curves down, although he is basically a low ball hitter. Sundberg is more effective against lefthanded pitching. He doesn't often try to go to right field with a pitch. He is a dependable bunter, good on the hit-and-run, and draws walks well.

Has developed some power relatively late in his career with 10 homers in each of the last two seasons. He also gets the ball into the gaps with regularity, and as an example, has 26 career triples.

A line drive hitter, Sundberg is well suited to Arlington Stadium. Overall, a solid though not spectacular hitter who can hurt you if he gets his pitch.

BASERUNNING:

Sundberg is a pretty good baserunner for a catcher. He has only average speed but plays within his limits. No threat to steal, but he runs the bases well, doesn't take unneccessary chances and keeps his head up. He makes the most of the abilities he has.

FIELDING:

Before 1982, Sundberg was the winner of six straight Gold Gloves. He combines excellent arm strength and accuracy with good mechanics. The percentage of runners thrown out trying to steal is down over the past couple of seasons, but this can be attributed in large part to a pitching staff that generally does a poor job of holding runners on base. Similarly, passed ball statistics are up dramatically in past three years because the Rangers acquired knuckleballer Charlie Hough.

Sundberg is still one of the premier defensive catchers in baseball. He has worked hard at learning hitters and calling pitches, which was not always his strongest point.

OVERALL:

Robinson: "A good everyday player. His performance seldom varies. Jim has a lot of confidence and is more relaxed now than in early years. Outstanding receiver and thrower."

Harwell: "Greatest value to the team are his defense and leadership."

Martin: "One of the game's best defensive catchers. Sundberg works well with the pitching staff, and is not afraid to throw to any base at any time. A .275 hitter since 1977."

FRANK TANANA
LHP, No. 34
LL, 6'3", 195 lbs.
ML Svc: 10 years
Born: 7-3-53 in
Detroit, MI

PITCHING:

Frank Tanana has had a decent hits-to-innings pitched ratio in the past two years, but posted won-loss records of 4-10 and 7-18. Part of the reason is that the teams he has been pitching for, Boston and Texas, haven't scored many runs while he's on the mound.

He did have a great fastball when he first came up to the majors, but after a series of arm injuries, just doesn't anymore. His fastball tops out at 80-82 MPH.

Tanana relies on guile and control. He uses the fastball to set up his big curve which he may throw 70% of the time. He uses his curve as a change-up. He has made an excellent adjustment to being a finesse pitcher, and is not afraid to come inside; in fact, he must keep his pitches in to righthanders in order to be effective. He usually has a great deal of success against lefties.

Tanana is an experienced pitcher with a good idea of what he's trying to do while he's on the mound. He has been a starter most of his career and, because of past arm problems, should remain one. A thorough professional who normally remains unruffled, he occasionally let lack of run support get to him in the second half of the 1982 season. Arlington Stadium is well suited to his pitching style with it's big outfield.

FIELDING:

Because he has a slow, looping windup, Tanana does not do a very good job of keeping runners from getting a good jump. He does, however, have a better than average move to first, fields his position well and is fundamentally sound in all aspects of fielding his position.

OVERALL:

Robinson: "Tanana has adjusted well to not having a fastball. He keeps hitters off balance and mixes his slow stuff well. He knows he can no longer overpower hitters, and goes in and out with the fastball. When he was younger he used to keep it inside all the time. He's a much better pitcher than his record indicates. Very unlucky, but knows how to pitch."

Harwell: "A smart pitcher--has lost velocity but gets by with savvy and experience. Control and experience are his greatest assets."

Martin: "A knowledgeable pitcher who had to change from power to finesse because of an arm injury. He is still at an age where he can win again. Tanana remains an above average pitcher despite two big losing seasons in a row."

1982 STATISTICS

W	L	ERA	G	GS	CG	IP	H	R	ER	BB	SO	SV
7	18	4.21	30	30	7	194	199	102	91	55	87	0

CAREER STATISTICS

W	L	ERA	G	GS	CG	IP	H	R	ER	BB	SO	SV
113	106	3.26	279	271	104	1949	1802	786	707	520	1398	0

GEORGE WRIGHT
OF, No. 26
SR, 5'11", 180 lbs.
ML Svc: 1 year
Born: 12-12-58 in Oklahoma City, OK

1982 STATISTICS

AVG	G	AB	R	H	2B	3B	HR	RBI	BB	SO	SB
.264	150	557	69	147	20	5	11	50	30	78	3

CAREER STATISTICS

AVG	G	AB	R	H	2B	3B	HR	RBI	BB	SO	SB
.264	150	557	69	147	20	5	11	50	30	78	3

VS. RHP

VS. LHP

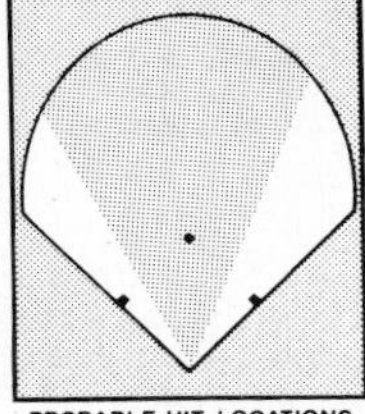
PROBABLE HIT LOCATIONS

HITTING:

Turned into a switch-hitter two years ago, George Wright had enough problems from the left side that some amount of thought was given to making him a strictly righthanded batter at midseason. However, he began to hit better lefthanded in the last few months of the season and, surprisingly, showed more power lefty than righthanded. When Wright is batting righthanded, pitchers should keep the ball down and away and throw plenty of breaking pitches. Lefthanded, a pitcher can go up and in with the fastball.

Early in the season he was tentative lefthanded; he improved as he gained confidence but still ended up with a much higher batting average righthanded.

He can be fooled with change-ups but is learning quickly as a hitter after coming to the majors directly from Double-A. Wright has occasional power, and needs to improve his discipline at the plate and cut down on strikeouts. He also needs to work on hitting behind the runner and bat control. Should improve his average in coming years by bunting his way on base.

BASERUNNING:

Wright is an aggressive baserunner with excellent speed. Although he will take the extra base and does a good job of breaking up the double play, he has not had the green light to steal and, as a result, didn't steal many bases in 1982.

He gets out of the batter's box quickly and has the ability to beat out a ground ball or a high chopper in the infield.

FIELDING:

Wright may play the shallowest center field in the American League but has such great speed that he is seldom hurt by it. Has an above average arm, although he does need to improve his accuracy.

He has excellent range and the ability to go into the gaps to run down a long fly ball. At this point in his career, defense is the strongest part of his game.

OVERALL:

Robinson: "Good looking player. I think he will be around for a long time. If he hits, it's a plus. Defensively, will be the top center fielder in the American League within a couple years. Wright was one of the few bright spots on the Texas team last season. He's a pretty good hitter for a rookie and learning fast."

Harwell: "He hasn't reached his full potential yet, but coming on strong."

Martin: "Fast young player who won a job early. Shows excellent defensive ability. Hit steadily with some power from the leadoff spot. He had a good rookie year and will get better."

JOHN PACELLA
RHP, No. 45
RR, 6'3", 195 lbs.
ML Svc: 4 years
Born: 9-15-56 in Brooklyn, NY

PITCHING:

Pacella will have to improve in nearly every area to return to the major leagues. For the Twins, he pitched in just about every situation and had little success in any. He is a righthander who should be in the bullpen; whether it be short or long relief, has yet to be determined. He pitches with a three-quarter motion and is average at best in terms of pitching consistently to batters' weaknesses. Mostly, he is a fastball pitcher, but his fastball is below average.

Pacella uses a slider second most, an average pitch for him. His curveball, used third most, is below average, the same with his straight change-up. When behind in the count, he is likely to throw the fastball. He seems more effective against righthanders. He seldom brushes back a hitter. He does not throw a spitball, and is average in pressure situations.

His greatest strength is that he has been around and might be able to help a young staff such as the Twins. But he needs more stuff, or else he might not return from the minor leagues.

FIELDING:

Pacella is average at fielding bunts, average with his move to first, and average overall.

OVERALL:

He needs to improve in a hurry.

Robinson: "His presence and poise on the mound are good, but the results haven't been. He is an average pitcher with average stuff. Best bet for him is to be used in long relief."

Harwell: "His strength is command of pitches; his weakness is lack of stuff."

DON WERNER
C, No. 20
RR, 6'1", 175 lbs.
ML Svc: 7 years
Born: 3-8-53 in Appleton, WI

HITTING, BASERUNNING, FIELDING:

Don Werner hit well early in 1982 when he was playing about once a week, but as his playing opportunities became more infrequent, his hitting suffered.

Pitchers should stick with curveballs against Werner, although he also has trouble with good fastballs. He can handle an average fastball up in the strike zone, but lacks power. Werner swings down on the ball and usually hits line drives or ground balls. He's more effective against lefthanders. He tends to hit the ball up the middle when he makes contact. Not a good bunter.

Werner lacks speed, doesn't often attempt to steal, and generally doesn't get a good enough jump to be effective in breaking up double plays.

As a catcher, Werner has above average mechanics and calls a good game. He gets good marks for release point, arm strength and accuracy. Does a good job handling pitchers, holding baserunners, and blocking pitches in the dirt. His catching ability is the strongest part of his game.

OVERALL:

Martin: "Werner is an eternal minor leaguer, but is a catcher so he can get a job. Has had a long time to make it and really hasn't. It's hard to get a line on a hitter who only bats 60 or so times a year."

EXHIBITION STADIUM
Toronto Blue Jays

Seating Capacity: 43,737
Playing Surface: Artificial (AstroTurf)

Dimensions
Left Field Pole: 330 ft.
Left-Center Field: 375 ft.
Center Field: 400 ft.
Right-Center Field: 375 ft.
Right Field Pole: 330 ft.
Height of Outfield Wall: 12 ft.

The home of the Toronto Blue Jays is completely symmetrical. The stadium is virtually wide open, with low seating areas down the left and right field foul lines. In left field, however, the stands are high and that offers some help in stopping the wind. Because of that construction, wind usually whips in over the seats behind third towards right field, helping lefthanded hitters.

It is the only ballpark in the American League East to have an artificial surface and that surface is a bit harder than other artificial turfs in either league. The surface, however, is true, offering little problem to both infielders and outfielders as far as bouncing balls are concerned. The speed of the turf, naturally, forces infielders to play deeper and outfielders to shade the alleys to prevent balls from going through.

While the park seems tailor-made for power hitters, home runs do not come that easily because of the heavy atmosphere. On mild days with a mild breeze, conversely, balls jump to both right and left fields. The problems that face the Jays, playing 81 home games in the Stadium, is that to date, they have not tailor-made their ball club to handle the nuances of artificial surface, as have the Kansas City Royals and World Champion St. Louis Cardinals. Because they are hampered by a lack of longball hitters, the Jays invariably hit less homers in their park than does the opposition.

Both bullpens are open. The Jays use the left field foul territory for theirs, and the opposition uses the right field foul territory. The mound rarely causes any problems, nor do the dugouts which are both at field level.

If any one hitter in baseball has taken advantage of the left field fence, it has been Cliff Johnson, who killed Toronto pitching while a member of the New York Yankees and Oakland A's. Johnson has recently been acquired by Toronto to help them in their power shortage.

Exhibition Stadium is a football field first of all, with the baseball facilities being built around it. It is one of the top hitter's parks in the American League. It is an excellent park for line drive hitters, but average to below average for home runs. Completely covered by Monsanto AstroTurf, it is the largest artificial playing surface in North America, and anytime a stadium has AstroTurf, hitters are going to get more hits and fielders are going to be better fielders.

Although symmetrical in its distances, the ball travels much better to right field. In fact, it's like a jet stream with the wind blowing that way most of the time. This is brought about because right field is the open part of Exhibition Stadium.

JESSE BARFIELD
OF, No. 29
RR, 6'1", 170 lbs.
ML Svc: 1 year plus
Born: 10-29-59 in
Joliet, IL

1982 STATISTICS

AVG	G	AB	R	H	2B	3B	HR	RBI	BB	SO	SB
.246	139	394	54	97	13	2	18	58	42	79	1

CAREER STATISTICS

AVG	G	AB	R	H	2B	3B	HR	RBI	BB	SO	SB
.243	164	489	61	119	16	4	20	67	46	98	5

VS. RHP

VS. LHP

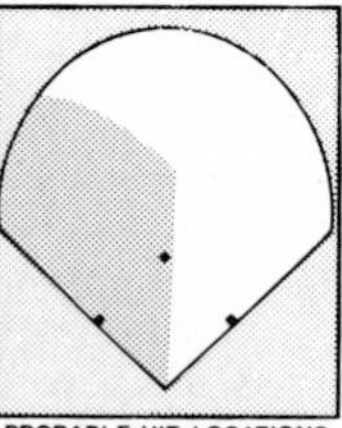
PROBABLE HIT LOCATIONS

HITTING:

Barfield is a low ball hitter with good power, especially against left-handed pitching. He used to try to pull everything and struck out a lot, but he has become a better hitter by going up the middle and to the opposite field. He handled pitches in 1982 that had given him trouble in previous years.

He maintained an average around .275 until a September slump. Barfield started out being used only against lefthanders, and hit even the good ones. He has trouble with righthanders who keep the fastball in tight, and throw breaking pitches away. But don't get the ball out over the plate, or look out.

He hits from a closed, upright stance, low in the box. He is strong and can deliver the long ball even in the big parks like Chicago. He has hit very well against Chicago, Boston, Kansas City and Texas, facing mostly lefthanders. In New York, however, the lefties gave him trouble, and he had some difficulty against California and Baltimore righthanders.

He was a good run producer, hitting in the middle of the batting order, and figures to improve all his stats with experience. Made excellent progress in his first full season, considering he had just jumped up from Double A.

BASERUNNING:

He is an average runner, but too conservative. He stole 25 bases in the minors, but did not try to steal last season. Barfield should manage to steal some bases if he becomes more aggressive.

FIELDING:

As a right fielder, he is already being compared with Boston's Dwight Evans. His arm is strong and accurate and he was second in outfield assists to Dave Winfield of the Yankees.

He plays his position like a veteran. He goes back to the wall well, makes the play in the alley, going to his right, and also towards the line, and isn't afraid to dive for the ball.

OVERALL:

Robinson: "One of the finest young talents in the league."

Martin: "He is one of the league's brightest prospects. He can hit, field and throw and has been handled intelligently."

Harwell: "A good young player who will continue to improve."

BARRY BONNELL
OF, No. 9
RR, 6'3", 200 lbs.
ML Svc: 5 years
Born: 10-27-53 in Milford, OH

1982 STATISTICS

AVG	G	AB	R	H	2B	3B	HR	RBI	BB	SO	SB
.293	140	437	59	128	26	3	6	49	32	51	14

CAREER STATISTICS

AVG	G	AB	R	H	2B	3B	HR	RBI	BB	SO	SB
.268	680	2166	259	580	97	17	37	239	164	252	48

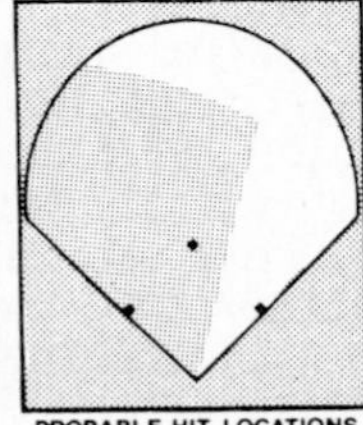

HITTING:

Bonnell is a righthanded batter with a closed stance. He stands almost upright in the box and towards the back. He hits the ball mostly to left field. He prefers the fastball and likes it up. Pitchers should keep the fastball down, and stay away with the breaking pitches.

Bonnell tends to be a streak hitter, went 5-for-5 in his first game of the season, and flirted with .400 for most of the first half. Manager Cox, who had him at Atlanta, started him only against lefthanders, then used him against all kinds of pitching because of his hot bat.

Playing regularly, Bonnell's average slowly dropped and fell below .300 in September. He has become a more aggressive hitter than ever before. He will swing at bad pitches early in the count, and has sacrificed some power for average. Bonnell saw a lot of brushback pitches in the second half of the season, and to his credit, stood fast against them (he was hit in the face in 1980 and suffered a broken cheekbone). Because he has become a less selective hitter than ever before, he does not draw many walks. Bonnell is a good bunter, and will bunt for a base hit if he catches a third baseman back. He hits well against Milwaukee, Kansas City and California. Baltimore pitchers did a number on him, and Boston and Detroit handled him well.

BASERUNNING:

He stole nine times without being thrown out in the second half and finished with a career high 14 steals in 16 attempts. He has above average speed to first. A smart runner, becoming more aggressive.

FIELDING:

An excellent outfielder, Bonnell was used last season in both left and center. Good range, and cuts off a lot of balls down the line and holds them to singles. He has an above average arm in terms of both strength and accuracy.

OVERALL:

Robinson: "Finally has shed the utility tag that has followed him around. He is playing better than at any time in his career."

Harwell: "A player who has found himself after a struggle."

Martin: "Has become a good day to day player and a better hitter."

JIM CLANCY
RHP, No. 18
RR, 6'4", 202 lbs.
ML Svc: 5 years
Born: 12-18-55 in
Chicago, IL

PITCHING:

Clancy's progress has been impeded by injuries, which wasted his 1979 season, and a good part of 1981. He was completely sound in 1982 and successfully mastered the transition from a thrower to a pitcher.

He is a fastball-slider type pitcher, with a three-quarter delivery. He also throws a forkball, and has started to work on a straight change-up. The biggest improvement last season was in his control. He threw less pitches and more strikes.

He was most effective against the California Angels and the Oakland A's. The Angels' veterans rate his slider as the best in the league. He doesn't give in to the hitters, and will throw the slider even when he is behind in the count.

He throws hard, in the 85-90 MPH range. He can get by with the fastball at times until he gets the slider going, and the slider on occasion is awesome. He is a hard worker and a good competitor, seldom misses a turn and gets a good percentage of complete games.

His ERA suffered from a couple of bad games against Milwaukee and Chicago, but overall, he pitched better than his record indicates. He rates with the best power righthanders in the league.

FIELDING:

He used to have trouble with the ball hit back through the middle, but was much improved in 1982. He is average in fielding bunts and covering first. He has improved his move to first and his release recently, and is not as vulnerable as he once was to stolen bases.

OVERALL:

Robinson: "Clancy is pitching better than ever before. Cut down on his number of pitches, and learned how to pitch. Good slider and throws it when behind sometimes. Throwing strikes, too."

Martin: "Can still be a standout in the American League. Overcame some arm trouble. Experience adds to his learning capabilities. Like Stieb, he should be kept by Toronto."

Harwell: "A well rounded starter, with two good pitches, fastball and slider."

1982 STATISTICS

W	L	ERA	G	GS	CG	IP	H	R	ER	BB	SO	SV
16	14	3.71	40	40	11	266	251	122	110	77	139	0

CAREER STATISTICS

W	L	ERA	G	GS	CG	IP	H	R	ER	BB	SO	SV
51	70	3.97	152	150	41	977	938	494	440	438	530	0

DAVE COLLINS
OF, No. 29
SL, 5'10", 175 lbs.
ML Svc: 8 years
Born: 10-20-52 in
Rapid City, SD

1982 STATISTICS

AVG	G	AB	R	H	2B	3B	HR	RBI	BB	SO	SB
.253	111	348	41	88	12	3	3	25	13	49	13

CAREER STATISTICS

AVG	G	AB	R	H	2B	3B	HR	RBI	BB	SO	SB
.274	886	2843	402	778	101	25	24	210	158	400	222

STRONG

VS. RHP

VS. LHP

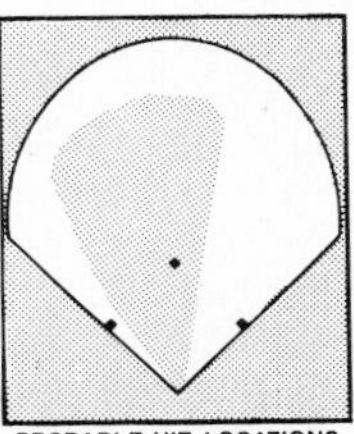

PROBABLE HIT LOCATIONS

HITTING:

Dave Collins did not hit for the cycle in 1982, but his playing career went full cycle. He came from the quiet of the mid-west to the noise of New York, the artificial surface of Cincinnati to the grass of Yankee Stadium, batting leadoff to batting eighth or not at all, and from playing every day to playing once a week.

He is a switch-hitter with more power from the left side, can hit low pitches batting lefty and high pitches batting right. Against lefthanded pitchers, he can be struck out by a steady variety of breaking balls on the outside corner and fastballs on the inside portion of the plate. Batting either way, he hits the fastball better than the breaking ball, and has trouble with off-speed pitches from either side of the plate.

BASERUNNING:

Because he was the "Odd-man-out" in the crazy quilt Yankee year of 1982, Collins saw little playing time. When he did, he used his speed as his greatest asset. He was the fastest Yankee, and at times so anxious to prove his worth, made mental mistakes on the basepaths. Collins never regained the basestealing form he flashed with the Reds because of all the lefthanded pitchers he saw. He is so fast, that there is no way he could possibly be thrown out going from first to third, scoring from second on a single, or tagging up and scoring from third on any medium-range fly ball.

He manages to beat out more than his share of bunts by simply outrunning the ball to first base.

FIELDING:

He is a switch-hitter and might also be called a switch-fielder. He played left, center and right, and was used at first base. Wherever he was used, Collins played to his fullest capabilities, never giving an inch, but was hurt by a lack of instinctive baseball sense. As an outfielder, he threw to the wrong base more often than not, and as a first baseman, was often confused after fielding a grounder with men on base. His arm, regardless of his position, is average and baserunners did not hesitate to run on him any chance they got.

OVERALL:

Martin: "Unfortunately, he didn't know where to play half the time, and wasn't turned loose on the bases. He was a good all around player in the National League."

Harwell: "Speed is his greatest asset."

Robinson: "Collins has a lot of tools and will be a better player this year. Regular grass hurt him offensively, but that should change with his trade to Toronto. It is important to find a position for him to play everyday, again, Toronto might be the answer."

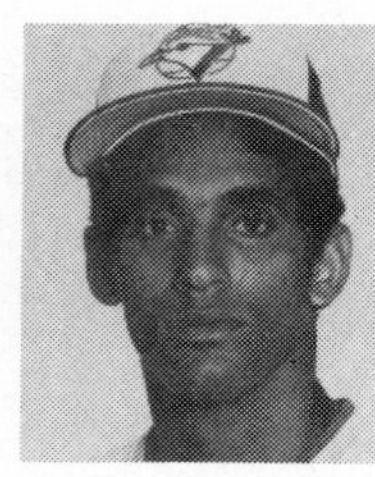

DAMASO GARCIA
INF, No. 7
RR, 6'0", 165 lbs.
ML Svc: 3 years
Born: 2-7-57 in Moca, DR

1982 STATISTICS

AVG	G	AB	R	H	2B	3B	HR	RBI	BB	SO	SB
.310	147	597	89	185	32	3	5	42	21	44	54

CAREER STATISTICS

AVG	G	AB	R	H	2B	3B	HR	RBI	BB	SO	SB
.284	380	1469	171	417	71	11	10	78	47	139	82

HITTING:

Garcia moved up closer to the plate last season so that he could handle the outside pitch better. He can hit the ball hard to the opposite field for extra bases. A righthanded hitter, he has a closed stance with a slight crouch, and leans toward the back of the box.

He is a fastball hitter, either high or low, and loves to go after the first pitch. Garcia is one of the best bad ball hitters in the league.

Pitchers who do the best job on him try to make him chase the breaking pitch out of the strike zone. He goes up to the plate to hit, and seldom takes the base on balls.

Garcia hit all of his home runs off righthanders, but his average was slightly better against the lefties. He was so consistent that he went hitless only once all season in back to back games.

He hit well against Boston, Cleveland, Detroit, Kansas City and Milwaukee. The teams that gave him the most trouble were Baltimore, California, Chicago and Seattle.

BASERUNNING:

Garcia has improved steadily and became more aggressive as the season wore on. His totals were impressive because he did not run just for the numbers. He became adept at stealing third and was 10-for-10.

FIELDING:

Above average in all phases. Garcia has a great arm and makes force plays at second that others hesitate to try. He turns the double play with the best, and is so agile that he seldom gets taken out.

He has tremendous range both ways, and will charge the ball and make the play barehanded. Also excels on pop-ups down the right field line.

OVERALL:

Robinson: "Just a good all around player who can do a lot of things for you. Makes the double play with the best of them. Has been the best player on the team when it comes to hitting, stealing, and defense."

Harwell: "A fine young player, coming into his own."

Martin: "Came out of the woodwork to become one of the best all around second basemen in the league in an era of outstanding second basemen."

JERRY GARVIN
LHP, No. 36
LL, 6'3", 195 lbs.
ML Svc: 5 years
Born: 10-21-55 in Oakland, CA

PITCHING:

Jerry Garvin is a lefthander with a high leg kick and a herky-jerky motion. For most of the season, he was the Jays' lone lefthander, and that created problems for manager Bobby Cox.

His chief role was in situations to get out a lefthanded hitter. However, he had difficulty in getting the job done and didn't get the work he needed to stay sharp. Without good control, he was in trouble. Most frequently when he came into a game, even if he got his man, the opposition would change to a righthanded hitter, and Garvin was gone.

His most effective pitch is his forkball, as long as he can get it over for strikes. His fastball always has been short on velocity, and righthanded power hitters such as Cliff Johnson have terrorized him.

His 1982 stats indicate his problems: many more hits than innings pitched, and almost one walk every other inning. Ten of the hits he gave up were home runs.

FIELDING:

Garvin has an outstanding move to first base, although the runners are cautious when he is on the mound. He fields his position well.

OVERALL:

He was pitching winter ball to get sufficient work in the hope of finding his groove again. He will be hard pressed to stick in the major leagues in 1983.

Robinson: "An average pitcher, with average stuff, who can help a team because of his ability to start or relieve."

1982 STATISTICS

W	L	ERA	G	GS	CG	IP	H	R	ER	BB	SO	SV
1	1	7.25	32	4	0	58	81	48	47	26	35	0

CAREER STATISTICS

W	L	ERA	G	GS	CG	IP	H	R	ER	BB	SO	SV
20	41	4.42	196	65	15	607	648	319	298	219	320	8

JIM GOTT
RHP, No. 38
RR, 6'4", 200 lbs.
ML Svc: 1 year
Born: 8-3-59 in
Hollywood, CA

PITCHING:

Jim Gott is a big, strong righthander with an overhand delivery and outstanding breaking pitches. He was a rookie last season who had never even pitched in Triple A.

The Jays drafted him from the St. Louis Cardinals organization for $25,000 and he turned into a real bargain.

Gott worked hard on his mechanics under pitching coach Al Widmar last season, and moved into Jays' four-man starting rotation in mid-May. He combined with Roy Lee Jackson on a one-hitter against Baltimore for his first major league win. His lone complete game was a 1-0 decision over the Detroit Tigers in 10 innings.

Gott had a problem with a recurring blister on the middle finger of his right hand, the finger he used to put pressure on the ball on his curve and slider. His fastball is around 90 MPH. His curveball has a very tight spin, and his slider is big and hard.

After struggling with his control for five minor league seasons, his progress in 1982 was impressive. He must cure a tendency to overthrow when he gets in trouble, and he needs more consistent command of his breaking pitches.

FIELDING:

Gott's inexperience showed at times. He has an above average move to first, and is average in fielding bunts and in his overall rating as a fielder.

OVERALL:

Gott pitched winter ball in Venezuela, hoping to find a cure for the blister problem and to gain some more experience.

Robinson: "He has a lot of potential which I think he will start fulfilling soon. Has all the qualities to be a good one."

Harwell: "A breaking ball pitcher who needs fine control to be more effective."

Martin: "Good stuff. Strong potential to be a consistent starter and winner."

1982 STATISTICS

W	L	ERA	G	GS	CG	IP	H	R	ER	BB	SO	SV
5	10	4.43	30	23	1	136	134	76	67	66	82	0

CAREER STATISTICS

W	L	ERA	G	GS	CG	IP	H	R	ER	BB	SO	SV
5	10	4.43	30	23	1	136	134	76	67	66	82	0

ALFREDO GRIFFIN
INF, No. 4
SR, 5'11", 165 lbs.
ML Svc: 4 years
Born: 3-6-57 in
Santo Domingo, DR

1982 STATISTICS

AVG	G	AB	R	H	2B	3B	HR	RBI	BB	SO	SB
.241	162	539	57	130	20	8	1	48	22	49	10

CAREER STATISTICS

AVG	G	AB	R	H	2B	3B	HR	RBI	BB	SO	SB
.251	602	2253	237	565	89	39	5	144	108	209	59

VS. RHP

VS. LHP

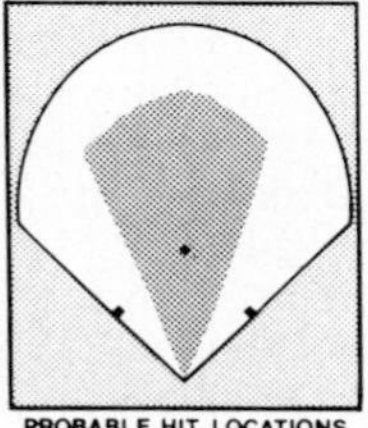
PROBABLE HIT LOCATIONS

HITTING:

A switch-hitter with no power, Griffin bats better from the left side. He has a closed stance, almost upright and chokes up on the bat. He might benefit from copying Rickey Henderson and crouching a bit to narrow his strike zone, although he is reluctant to take a base on balls.

He does not bunt as well as he should. Considering his good speed, he really ought to improve his bunt and try it more often when on grass. Griffin is a low ball hitter batting left, and a high ball hitter from the other side. He hits straightaway, and sometimes to the opposite field.

He has a tendency to chase bad pitches, and both the curve and the change-up can make him look bad. His run production was surprisingly good considering he batted ninth, and he was often lifted with men on base and the Jays trailing to make way for a better bat.

BASERUNNING:

Griffin's got speed, and just watch him fly on a triple. He has never been a good percentage basestealer, however, and gets thrown out too often. He should learn to pick his chances better, because he has what it takes to be a well above average basestealer.

FIELDING:

Griffin led the American League's shortstops in errors for three successive seasons and for half of 1982, even though he made only seven errors from mid-June until the end of last season. He was somewhat less erratic last season, and had his best defensive effort with the Jays in 1982.

Griffin has great range and gets to balls that others would not, but he makes too many throwing errors on balls where there is no play.

He prefers playing on grass to the artificial turf, and turns the double play well. He plays hurt, and doesn't miss a game.

OVERALL:

Robinson: "An awful lot of talent here. I think he might be on the verge of giving it to us. He has been erratic in the field for several years, but showed signs of putting it all together in the last half."

Martin: "Still too erratic. He may now be goaded by Toronto's prospective superstar, Tony Fernandez."

ROY LEE JACKSON
RHP, No. 25
RR, 6'2", 194 lbs.
ML Svc: 2 years plus
Born: 5-1-54 in
Opelika, AL

PITCHING:

Roy Lee Jackson is a hard thrower with a three-quarter delivery who relies mostly on his fastball and a slider that is wicked when he keeps it down.

He had some difficulties in the first half of last season and lost six decisions without a win between April and July. His confidence suffered, but pitching coach Al Widmar found a flaw in his mechanics and corrected it. He had a good second half, and a strong finish. He was especially effective at home where he had a 7-1 record. He also won five of his last seven decisions. He was the top man in the bullpen in strikeouts with 71 in 97 innings, and also had the lowest ERA.

Jackson is tough on righthanded hitters when his slider is working. 1982 was only his second season in relief after being a starter in the minor leagues. Should improve as he gets more experience.

He pitched well against California, Milwaukee, Minnesota and New York. He had trouble with Detroit and Oakland.

FIELDING:

Jackson's move to first base is only fair and needs improvement. He is average in fielding bunts, and in fielding his position in general.

OVERALL:

Harwell: "A good solid short man with above average stuff."

Robinson: "Jackson should be a better big league pitcher. He has pitched better than his record indicates. His problem is that Murray and McLaughlin get the ball before him."

Martin: "What has been expected of him and never materialized might still come about after two years as a reliever."

1982 STATISTICS

W	L	ERA	G	GS	CG	IP	H	R	ER	BB	SO	SV
8	8	3.06	48	2	0	97	77	37	33	31	71	6

CAREER STATISTICS

W	L	ERA	G	GS	CG	IP	H	R	ER	BB	SO	SV
11	19	3.72	127	16	1	283	263	130	117	102	185	13

CLIFF JOHNSON
C-INF, No. 44
RR, 6'4", 225 lbs.
ML Svc: 10 years
Born: 7-22-47 in
San Antonio, TX

1982 STATISTICS

AVG	G	AB	R	H	2B	3B	HR	RBI	BB	SO	SB
.238	73	214	19	51	10	0	7	31	26	41	1

CAREER STATISTICS

AVG	G	AB	R	H	2B	3B	HR	RBI	BB	SO	SB
.250	887	2474	346	619	113	6	130	441	359	472	9

VS. RHP

VS. LHP

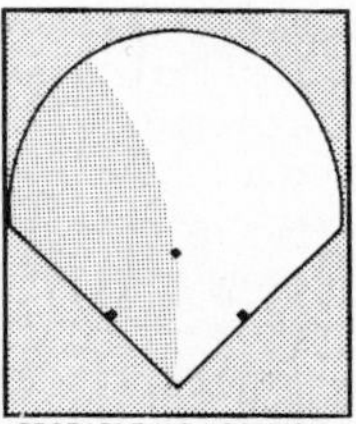
PROBABLE HIT LOCATIONS

HITTING:

When Cliff Johnson is in a groove he'll collect his share of towering drives and liners into the gaps, especially in left-center field. He is extremely tough against lefthanded pitchers.

Johnson stands low in the box with just a hint of a crouch to his upright stance. He can hit just about anything thrown his way when he is in one of his streaks, but it is safest to approach him with outside pitches in most instances. There is no doubt that he can still hit in the clutch, but he has been accused of not giving a second thought to hitting behind a runner. His eyes light up and his bat catches fire when he is at the plate with runners in scoring position. He isn't given to drawing a lot of walks and he'll never be sent up to the plate with the express purpose of delivering a bunt.

Johnson will chase a fastball up and out of the strike zone when behind on the count, and a pitcher could throw him 20 consecutive breaking pitches and Johnson would still be geared to hit the fastball. Don't hang a curve to him, and he can handle a pitch down if it is hard. Change-ups aren't his favorite and he is so-so against the sinker and slider.

BASERUNNING:

Johnson began his major league career at Houston in 1973 and since then has nine stolen bases, including the five he had with the A's in 1981. He can hardly be considered a threat to steal, and at this stage in his career, isn't about to take it up. He utilizes the feet first slide and has average ability to break up the double play. Baserunning may be the weakest part of his game.

FIELDING:

Johnson is a catcher by trade, but did not serve a stint behind the plate except in spring training in his two years with the A's. However, he did put in a few games at first base. As a catcher he was rated sub-par and needed improvement in blocking balls and fielding bunts. He is also given an average to below average grade in all aspects of the way he plays first base.

OVERALL:

Martin: "Johnson is a veteran who is still around because of his bat. He is a strong hitter for power, not average."

Robinson: "If he didn't hit, he wouldn't be much help. But he can be awesome when he gets in a streak, although it was a struggle for him last year."

Harwell: "Johnson is best used as a designated hitter at about the fourth spot in the lineup."

LUIS LEAL
RHP, No. 48
RR, 6'3", 205 lbs.
ML Svc: 2 years plus
Born: 3-21-57 in
Barquisimeto, VEN

PITCHING:

Leal is a control type of pitcher, and throws a fastball, slider, curve and change. Most likely to go with the fastball or slider when he gets into trouble.

He has made tremendous progress considering this was only his fourth year in professional baseball, and actually his first full season in the American League.

His fastball and slider are both above average. At times, he looks unbeatable. He gets hurt when he gets the ball up. Sometimes, he appears to lose his concentration. He does not brush back the hitter.

He suffers by comparison to teammates Stieb and Clancy, but lacks their experience. He still has not reached his peak.

He did his most effective pitching at home in Exhibition Stadium where he had an 8-3 record, and gave up less home runs than either Stieb or Clancy. He has always pitched well against the New York Yankees and the Boston Red Sox, and has always experienced a lot of trouble with California.

He has a tendency to go in streaks. He went eight starts without a win last June, and in August, won only one of eight starts.

FIELDING:

Average in handling bunts and fielding his position in general. Average move to first base.

OVERALL:

Robinson: "Leal is a comer. As the team gets better, he will get better. Spots the ball around. Has four pitches and can use them effectively. Good control."

Harwell: "A good arm, and will improve."

Martin: "An effective complement to the harder throwing Stieb and Clancy. His control is always an asset."

1982 STATISTICS

W	L	ERA	G	GS	CG	IP	H	R	ER	BB	SO	SV
12	15	3.93	38	38	10	249	250	113	109	79	111	0

CAREER STATISTICS

W	L	ERA	G	GS	CG	IP	H	R	ER	BB	SO	SV
22	32	3.94	80	67	14	439	449	211	192	154	208	1

JOEY McLAUGHLIN
RHP, No. 50
RR, 6'2", 205 lbs.
ML Svc: 3 years plus
Born: 7-11-56 in
Tulsa, OK

PITCHING:

McLaughlin is a power pitcher, and throws his fastball 85 MPH and up. He also has a knuckle-curve and slider. His ability to get the strikeout when needed is a big asset.

He had great success after the strike in 1981, especially with his change-up. But too much of anything is not good. He fell in love with the change and was throwing it too frequently. The hitters started looking for it, and that's bad. He was hurt by the home run ball, and had occasional lapses in control.

He got things under control in June of last year and had 5 wins and 3 saves in the rest of the month.

It was an injury-marred season for him. He had a pulled rib muscle, and developed tendinitis in his right shoulder. The Jays preferred to let him rest it, rather that give him cortisone.

McLaughlin is still young, and seems to have made the adjustment from starter to stopper, and also the shock of changing teams and leagues.

FIELDING:

Has a fair move to first base, but it could stand improvement. Average in fielding his position.

OVERALL:

Robinson: "A hard thrower who can strike people out. Think he has found his niche."

Harwell: "A strong armed reliever who can work often."

Martin: "A decent reliever with long or short capabilities."

1982 STATISTICS

W	L	ERA	G	GS	CG	IP	H	R	ER	BB	SO	SV
8	6	3.21	44	0	0	70	54	27	25	30	49	8

CAREER STATISTICS

W	L	ERA	G	GS	CG	IP	H	R	ER	BB	SO	SV
20	23	3.72	179	12	0	341	332	163	141	141	197	27

MIKE MORGAN
RHP, No. 63
RR, 6'3", 195 lbs.
ML Svc: 3 years
Born: 10-8-59 in Tulare, CA

PITCHING:

Mike Morgan has the four basic pitches--fastball, curve, slider and change. He is an overhand pitcher who releases all four from the same general location. Where the pitches will go is one of his problems, because walks have hurt him.

Morgan, due to injuries to veterans Rick Reuschel and Doyle Alexander, was given the Yankees' fifth starting spot in 1982. When Roger Erickson was also hurt, Morgan was Number Four behind Guidry, John and Righetti. The emergence of Rawley as a starter saw Morgan go to the bullpen, and the young pitcher did not take the demotion too kindly. He had a brief encounter with manager Clyde King about his status, but came out second best.

Morgan's curve is his best pitcn, and he, like many young Yankee pitchers, was taught the pitch by Pat Dobson in Nashville (AA). He is not afraid to throw it to a lefty or righty, regardless of the count or situation, but because he walked a lot of batters, started coming in with the fastball more and more in key situations. His fastball is in the 87-90 MPH range, but tends to come in straighter than it should, making it hittable. He also runs into trouble when he forgets to snap his curve, and it hangs, right in the hitter's eyes, where it eventually winds up in the power alleys for an extra base hit.

FIELDING:

Morgan is better than average on the mound and handling bunts, but has a tendency to either let a runner bother him too much--or not enough. He will rush his delivery if the runner bothers him, or, if he does not seem annoyed or disturbed by a runner, will have second base stolen on him.

OVERALL:

Martin: "Morgan is a pitcher who can get strikeouts, but is still learning the major league trade. He has been brought along very fast, maybe too fast."

Robinson: "He was the longest of the long shots to make the Yankee team in 1982. He was not even considered, but he gained a slider and curve last year and was best young pitcher in camp. Look for him to be much better this year."

1982 STATISTICS

W	L	ERA	G	GS	CG	IP	H	R	ER	BB	SO	SV
7	11	4.37	30	23	2	150	167	77	73	67	71	0

CAREER STATISTICS

W	L	ERA	G	GS	CG	IP	H	R	ER	BB	SO	SV
9	24	5.05	46	39	5	239	288	146	134	125	88	0

LLOYD MOSEBY
OF, No. 15
LR, 6'3", 200 lbs.
ML Svc: 2 years plus
Born: 11-5-59 in
Portland, AR

1982 STATISTICS

AVG	G	AB	R	H	2B	3B	HR	RBI	BB	SO	SB
.236	147	487	51	115	20	9	9	52	33	106	11

CAREER STATISTICS

AVG	G	AB	R	H	2B	3B	HR	RBI	BB	SO	SB
.233	361	1254	131	292	60	12	27	141	82	277	26

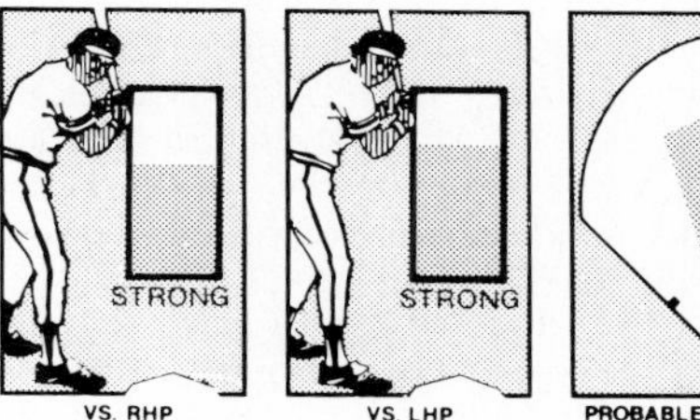

HITTING:

Lloyd Moseby is a big strong lefthanded hitter, who stands upright, with an open stance, well back in the box.

He still hasn't found his groove, but he is young and the potential is there. After leading the Venezuelan winter league in hitting, everybody was expecting this would be the year, but he never got it going.

His average was about the same against lefthanders as righthanders, and he hit six of his home runs off the lefties. He was the only lefthanded bat Bobby Cox left in against lefthanders until late in the season.

A line drive hitter, he likes the ball down. He has trouble with the fastballs on his fists, and strikes out on the fastball up and in.

An Oakland native, Moseby has always hit well against the A's, as well as Boston, California and Kansas City. Detroit and Milwaukee pitching handled him well.

BASERUNNING:

He runs well, both going to first and on extra base hits. He became more aggressive in the second half of the season, stealing successfully in seven of ten attempts.

FIELDING:

Moseby has an above average arm and range. Comes in well and blocks the ball on the artificial turf. Played shallower this year, picking off more balls coming in, but the odd one got over his head.

OVERALL:

Robinson: "Outstanding athlete with power, speed and great arm. Cannot give up on this talent. Can do everything."

Martin: "All around potential. Just about to turn the corner. If he bears down and learns, he could be special."

Harwell: "A good young player, who keeps improving."

HOSKEN POWELL
OF, No. 22
LL, 6'1", 185 lbs.
ML Svc: 4 years plus
Born: 5-14-55 in
Selma, AL

1982 STATISTICS

AVG	G	AB	R	H	2B	3B	HR	RBI	BB	SO	SB
.275	112	265	43	73	13	4	3	26	12	23	4

CAREER STATISTICS

AVG	G	AB	R	H	2B	3B	HR	RBI	BB	SO	SB
.257	554	1773	235	456	78	17	16	153	139	156	41

VS. RHP

VS. LHP

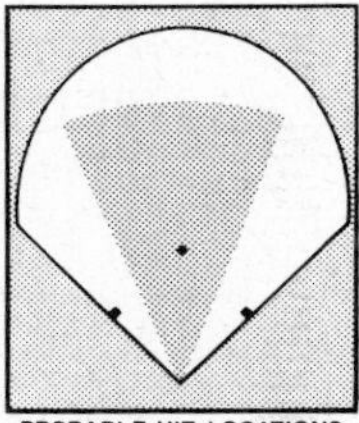
PROBABLE HIT LOCATIONS

HITTING:

A lefthanded hitter, Powell uses a closed stance and stands in the center of the box.

The Jays acquired him for a utility role, and he did surprisingly well, both playing right field, and coming off the bench to pinch-hit. He set a team record with 10 pinch-hits and was disciplined enough to get an occasional walk.

He's a fastball hitter and likes to jump on a first-pitch fastball. A line drive type hitter, he hits the ball straightaway and can occasionally pull the ball for extra bases or a home run.

He should be pitched down and on the outside half of the plate. Jam him inside with the fastball, and then go away from him with the breaking pitches. Last season Powell had trouble with pitchers who threw a lot of change-ups and with lefthanders who could throw hard sliders.

He hit well against Baltimore, Cleveland, Kansas City and New York. Boston and California were the teams that seemed to give him the most problems.

BASERUNNING:

Powell gets out of the box quickly and has above average speed going down the line to first. Once there, however, he tends to be a cautious and conservative baserunner. He'll occasionally steal a base and he'll run hard to break up a potential double play. On the other hand, he seldom challenges outfielders by going for an extra base and his moderate leads off first rarely disturb opposing pitchers.

FIELDING:

Powell has only adequate range as an outfielder and is noticeably better coming in after fly balls than he is going out after them. His arm is rated average to above average both in terms of strength and accuracy. In short, Powell is a competent major league outfielder, who the Jays are hoping can continue to improve.

OVERALL:

Currently, his value is as a utility player, part-time outfielder and pinch-hitter.

Martin: "Powell is a young line drive hitter. He's a young prospect who's getting the opportunity to improve his skills while playing in the majors."

Robinson: "Powell has some ability. Best bet is against righthanded pitching."

LEON ROBERTS

OF, No. 3
RR, 6'3", 200 lbs.
ML Svc: 9 years
Born: 1-22-51 in Vicksburg, MI

1982 STATISTICS

AVG	G	AB	R	H	2B	3B	HR	RBI	BB	SO	SB
.230	71	178	13	41	7	0	2	11	11	30	1

CAREER STATISTICS

AVG	G	AB	R	H	2B	3B	HR	RBI	BB	SO	SB
.269	788	2479	314	666	118	27	70	301	235	398	25

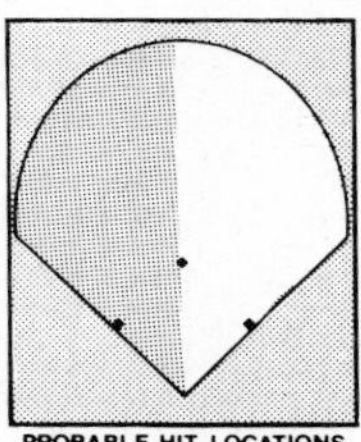

HITTING:

A big, strong righthanded hitter with an upright stance, Leon Roberts likes to spread out and stand way back in the box.

Roberts tries to pull everything and is a low fastball hitter. He can hurt you, but can also be pitched to if you get the ball in the right spot.

Roberts worked hard last season, but seemed to be tied up in his swing and couldn't pull the trigger. It wasn't until the final two weeks of the season that he hit the ball well against both Seattle and Minnesota.

Rival pitchers have their best success against Leon, throwing him a steady diet of breaking balls and occasionally crossing him up with a fastball up and in. Roberts has learned to hit the slider fairly well but still has a lot of trouble trying to make contact against change-ups.

He is used primarily as a designated hitter or left fielder against left-handed pitching. He also sees action as a late inning pinch-hitter against southpaws.

BASERUNNING:

Roberts is not a threat on the basepaths. He is slow out of the box and lacks speed down the line. Once on first, he tends to clog the basepaths for runners behind him. He is no threat to steal and too slow to break up potential double plays.

FIELDING:

His lack of speed really handicaps Roberts in the outfield, especially on artificial turf such as the surface of Toronto's Exhibition Stadium. Balls seem to pick up speed every time they bounce and this just highlights Leon's lack of swiftness. He has limited range in the outfield and an arm that is only considered average both in terms of strength and accuracy.

OVERALL:

If Roberts could get the bat going, his best spot would be as a DH and pinch-hitter.

Robinson: "Needs to get it together if he is going to be in the big leagues next year. Can only help if he hits."

Martin: "A one-way player now. Has some sting in his bat but not consistently."

DAVE STIEB
RHP, No. 37
RR, 6'1", 185 lbs.
ML Svc: 3 years plus
Born: 7-22-57 in
Santa Ana, CA

PITCHING:

In the second half of last season, Stieb was one of the best righthanded starters in the league. He has an excellent fastball in the 90 MPH range, and a good hard slider. Currently working on spotting a change-up.

Stieb uses a nice compact three-quarter delivery. He can get inside on lefthanded hitters with his slider--better than anyone in the league.

At times he experienced some difficulties in location on the slider, and this was the pitch that was hit for home runs. Stieb had a tendency last year to make his pitches too good when he was ahead in the count, instead of wasting one.

A fast worker, with good control, he led the league in innings pitched, complete games and shutouts. He was 4-0 with two shutouts against Kansas City. Also pitched well against Milwaukee by not walking even one batter.

He continually strives for excellence. He used to get upset if anybody hit the ball hard, or if there was a bad play behind him, but now he is maturing.

He has always experienced difficulty in beating Baltimore. Earl Weaver used to try to upset him by having his players step out of the box to break his rhythm.

He leads the Jays in winning and whining about wanting to be traded. He can't wait to pitch in a World Series.

FIELDING:

Stieb is a converted outfielder, so he has a feel for the ball. He is probably the best fielding pitcher in the league. He handles the ball back through the middle, is great on bunts and covering first.

He is always among the leaders in total fielding chances, and double plays.

OVERALL:

Robinson: "I believe that Stieb can be even better than he is now, which isn't indicative of the pitcher's record. Gives you his best at all times."

Martin: "Could be one of the AL standouts. Wants to be with a contender, understandably. But Toronto should try to sign him and keep him. He's a 'franchise' type pitcher."

1982 STATISTICS

W	L	ERA	G	GS	CG	IP	H	R	ER	BB	SO	SV
17	14	3.25	38	38	19	288	271	116	104	75	141	0

CAREER STATISTICS

W	L	ERA	G	GS	CG	IP	H	R	ER	BB	SO	SV
48	47	3.53	115	113	51	844	790	364	331	269	390	0

WILLIE UPSHAW
OF/INF, No. 26
LL, 6'0", 185 lbs.
ML Svc: 3 years
Born: 4-27-57 in Blanco, TX

1982 STATISTICS

AVG	G	AB	R	H	2B	3B	HR	RBI	BB	SO	SB
.267	160	580	77	155	25	7	21	75	52	90	8

CAREER STATISTICS

AVG	G	AB	R	H	2B	3B	HR	RBI	BB	SO	SB
.246	350	976	128	240	39	11	27	107	90	155	15

VS. RHP

VS. LHP

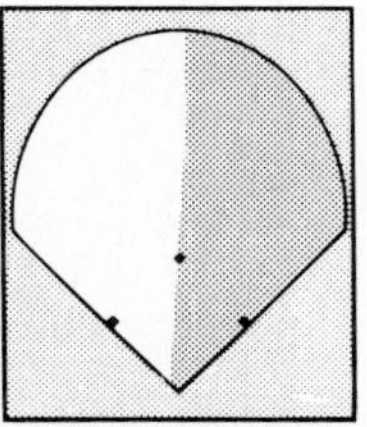
PROBABLE HIT LOCATIONS

HITTING:

Upshaw finally got a chance to play every day in the major leagues last season, and was the team leader in home runs, RBIs and game-winning RBIs.

A pull hitter with a quick bat, he batted fourth against righthanders, lower down against lefties. The Jays saw an unusually high number of lefthanders, and Upshaw batted .277 with six homers against them.

He has a closed stance, with a slight crouch, and stands in the middle of the box. He's a low ball hitter, and likes to hit just about everything on the inside part of the plate.

It's best to keep the ball away from him, and change speeds.

He was very consistent last season except for a 10 day slump in June and another in September. Both happened at a time when the whole team wasn't hitting and he didn't get much to hit.

He hit best against Cleveland, Chicago, Kansas City and Seattle. California and Oakland figured in both his slumps.

BASERUNNING:

He has good speed and was thrown out only once in eight attempts in the second half. Will likely improve on his stolen base total next season. A good baserunner and getting more aggressive.

FIELDING:

Upshaw has an average arm, but great range and good at making the force at second base. Also adept on digging the ball out of the dirt.

OVERALL:

Robinson: "Toronto was certain he could do the job when they traded Mayberry. He did not disappoint them. For his first full season of big league playing, he did a terrific job all around."

Harwell: "An emerging star. Now a solid major leaguer."

Martin: "Will get better in offensive production with more experience in the strike zone."

ERNIE WHITT
C, No. 12
LR, 6'2", 200 lbs.
ML Svc: 4 years
Born: 6-13-52 in Detroit, MI

HITTING:

Whitt was platooned last year against righthanded pitching, and used occasionally as a pinch-hitter. He hits the fastball up, and on the inside half of the plate.

He showed more power in 1982, hit for a better average, and seemed to have more confidence at the plate than ever before.

His final numbers might have been even better but he missed most of the final month with injuries.

He should be pitched away both with breaking balls and the fastball. Does not chase bad pitches, and hits fairly well with men on base. He is a good bunter, not only in sacrifice situations, but occasionally will drop one down trying for a hit.

He hit well against Baltimore, Detroit and Milwaukee and had the most trouble against California and Chicago.

He hits from a closed stance, a slight crouch, and low in the box.

1982 STATISTICS

AVG	G	AB	R	H	2B	3B	HR	RBI	BB	SO	SB
.261	105	284	28	74	14	2	11	42	26	35	3

CAREER STATISTICS

AVG	G	AB	R	H	2B	3B	HR	RBI	BB	SO	SB
.240	318	837	75	201	40	4	19	101	73	110	9

VS. RHP

VS. LHP

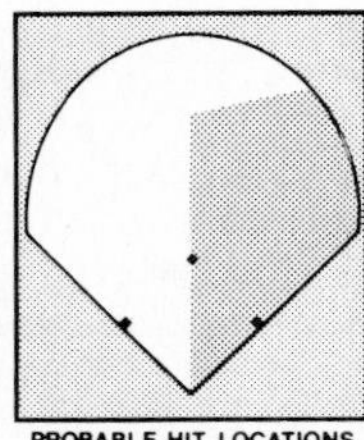
PROBABLE HIT LOCATIONS

BASERUNNING:

An average runner at the best, but he will surprise at times and steal, usually successfully, four or five times a year. A smart runner, who seldom makes mistakes on the bases.

FIELDING:

He has above average knowledge of opposing batters' strengths and weaknesses and calls his own game. He will get on his pitcher when necessary.

His arm is average, but he has a good release and his throws are usually accurate.

He blocks the low pitches well, is adept at fielding the bunt and does a good job of holding runners.

OVERALL:

Harwell: "One of the American League's most improved players. Regular work has really refined his skills."

Robinson: "Can help you if you play him against righthanded pitching. Good receiver and throwing and hitting for a much better average."

Martin: "An intelligent player, can be platooned according to the pitching."

GARTH IORG
INF, No. 12
RR, 5'11", 170 lbs.
ML Svc: 4 years
Born: 10-12-54 in Arcata, CA

HITTING, BASERUNNING, FIELDING:

Garth Iorg is a righthanded hitter with an unusual stance. He spreads his feet enough so that he can lean back with all his weight on his back foot. A spray hitter, he hits well to the opposite field, and is adept at hitting behind the runner.

Iorg was used primarily against lefthanded pitching, and batted second in the order. He goes up swinging, and seldom walks. He is aggressive, and an excellent pinch-hitter when you want to get something started. Will lay down a bunt occasionally.

He's a high ball hitter. Get him out on breaking balls and changes. Stay away from him with the fastball except to spot it up and in occasionally.

He hit well against Boston, Kansas City, Minnesota and New York. Baltimore and Cleveland pitching gave him the most trouble.

He gets out of the box well going to first, and has average speed, but seldom tries to steal a base.

He can play second, third and short, but third base is his best position. His range is limited at the other two spots.

OVERALL:

Robinson: "A tough competitor, plays within himself. He had his best year last season, and played more than ever."

Harwell: "Excellent extra player who can play several positions."

Martin: "A decent part-time player. Good off the bench."

BUCK MARTINEZ
C, No. 13
RR, 5'11", 190 lbs.
ML Svc: 11 years
Born: 11-7-48 in Redding, CA

HITTING, BASERUNNING, FIELDING:

Martinez never has hit for a high average. Last season, batting instructor Cito Gaston persuaded him to move up on the plate a bit more, and he began to handle the outside pitch better. He also hit twice as many home runs as ever before. He bats upright with a closed stance, low in the box. He is platooned, and used almost exclusively against lefthanded pitching.

Martinez has difficulty with the breaking pitch away and should be pitched on the outside half of the plate. He likes to hit the ball up, and he will hit mistakes. He his able to hit behind the runner with somewhat above average abilities.

Below average in speed, easy to double up if he gets the ball on the ground. No threat to steal.

Martinez's strength as a receiver is in handling the pitchers and calling the game. He works well with the young pitchers, and he has an excellent book on the opposing hitters.

Blocks the low pitches well and fields the bunt adequately. His arm is average in strength and accuracy.

OVERALL:

Robinson: "Good receiver and thrower. He has been in the big leagues for 11 years as a platoon catcher."

Martin: "A steady, average journeyman. A good player to have on your ball club."

RANCE MULLINIKS
INF. No. 5
LR, 6'0", 170 lbs.
ML Svc: 6 years
Born: 1-15-56 in
Tulare, CA

HITTING, BASERUNNING, FIELDING:

Mulliniks was platooned at third base last season against righthanded pitching. He is a lefthanded hitter with a closed stance in the middle of the box.

Reports on players often differ from team to team, and Rance Mulliniks is a good example of how scouting reports can differ. While most teams have Mulliniks labeled as a low ball hitter, Earl Weaver and the 1982 Orioles saw him as a high ball hitter, which is unusual for a lefthander. Baltimore pitched him good stuff and down at all times, while many other teams kept things up in the strike zone. Good scouting paid off for the Birds, Mulliniks hit only .176 against them with no RBIs.

He is a situation type hitter, who can pull the ball or go the opposite way. As a pinch-hitter, he can get a hit or take a walk to get things started.

Only average speed, but a smart baserunner. Tends to be conservative and seldom tries to steal a base.

He was obtained to be shortstop insurance. Wound up playing mostly third base where he had very little experience. He let the ball play him at first, but improved steadily.

OVERALL:

Robinson: "Hasn't hit much, but gives Toronto a good spot player for the infield, mostly at third base."

Martin: "Your garden variety platoon player. Can play in the majors, but not day to day."

THE NATIONAL LEAGUE

ATLANTA-FULTON COUNTY STADIUM
Atlanta Braves

Seating Capacity: 52,785
Playing Surface: Natural Grass

Dimensions
Left Field Pole: 330 ft.
Left-Center Field: 385 ft.
Center Field: 402 ft.
Right-Center Field: 385 ft.
Right Field Pole: 330 ft.
Height of Outfield Wall: 6 ft.

Almost everyone complains about some aspect of Atlanta-Fulton County Stadium. Fans and ballplayers alike are outspoken in their criticism of the unkempt appearance of the ballpark. One ex-player remarked that the Atlanta Stadium was the only ballpark that looked old when it was still brand new. Unfortunately, the condition of the park has gotten worse, rather than better with age.

Fielders complain about the horrible condition of both the infield and the outfield. The infield surface is particularly treacherous. There is no such thing as a routine grounder in Atlanta. The rocks and ruts undoubtedly account for many of the errors committed by Atlanta's Rafael Ramirez, an otherwise outstanding defensive ballplayer.

Outfielders are also forced to negotiate the ruts and rough spots in the playing field. The bullpens, located prominently in foul territory, present additional hazards when a fielder is chasing a foul pop. On the bright side, however, there is plenty of foul territory in Atlanta giving a hustling outfielder a lot of opportunities to change a foul ball from a strike to an out.

A pitcher's chief problem is the atmosphere. It helps make Atlanta the Number One launching pad for roundtrippers in the National League. Although the physical dimensions of the park are considered standard, the thin, light air lets the ball take off like a rifle shot. There are a lot of home runs hit in Atlanta that would have been routine outs in most other major league parks. Not only does the atmosphere favor the hitters, but the fences in right and left fields are only six feet high. Hitters understandably love to play in Atlanta and are willing to ignore most of the stadium's shortcomings.

PITCHING:

Steve Bedrosian blossomed into one of the best short relief pitchers in the National League during the 1982 season. He combines his good size with a slightly herky-jerky motion, and a powerful three-quarter to overhand delivery to intimidate opposing hitters.

Bedrosian is strictly a power pitcher. His fastball, clocked up to 95 MPH, is one of the best in the league. He combines this pitch with his better than average slider, and that's usually enough to get by for three or four innings late in a game.

He's had good success against lefthanders, but is considered devastating against righthanders. Teams like Montreal, Philadelphia, and Los Angeles, with a lot of righthanded hitters, are obvious targets for Bedrosian's work.

His 8 wins and 11 saves last season bolstered his confidence, and he showed remarkable poise and concentration on the mound, especially for such a young pitcher.

Bedrosian is a no-nonsense, two-pitch pitcher. Because he throws every pitch as hard as he can, there is some concern about the soundness of his arm. He seldom throws a change-up, and he really needs to add some off-speed pitches to his arsenal. Not only would that improve his effectiveness, but it might also help prolong his career.

STEVE BEDROSIAN
RHP, No. 32
RR, 6'3", 200 lbs.
ML Svc: 1 year plus
Born: 12-6-57 in
Methuen, MA

FIELDING, HITTING, BASERUNNING:

Bedrosian has an average move to first base, but can look awkward going after bunts or short tappers in front of the plate. Used almost always in late relief, he only came to bat twenty-six times in 1982. His only hit was a single, and that tells the tale of Bedrosian as a hitter and a baserunner.

OVERALL:

McCarver: "There are few pitchers who can blow people away for a long period of time without an off-speed pitch of some kind. If Steve could develop a third pitch, he could become consistently awesome."

Kiner: "Bedrosian has an outstanding arm and the potential to be a top flight pitcher. However, until he can develop an off-speed pitch, his progress will be hampered."

1982 STATISTICS

W	L	ERA	G	GS	CG	IP	H	R	ER	BB	SO	SV
8	6	2.42	64	3	0	137	102	39	37	57	123	11

CAREER STATISTICS

W	L	ERA	G	GS	CG	IP	H	R	ER	BB	SO	SV
9	8	2.74	79	4	0	161	117	53	49	72	132	11

BRUCE BENEDICT
C, No. 20
RR, 6'1", 185 lbs.
ML Svc: 4 years
Born: 8-18-55 in Birmingham, AL

HITTING:

Bruce Benedict waits for high fastballs. Consequently, pitchers try to work him down and away. He has trouble hitting against pitchers with good curves, sliders or sinkers. Benedict doesn't often drive the ball with a lot of power; he lacks the strength and quick bat to consistently pull the ball, and is a straightaway hitter. He has a good eye, draws walks well, and doesn't chase bad pitches.

Playing a full game behind the plate in the Atlanta heat seems to take a lot out of Benedict. He often seems to wither during his third or fourth at-bat during a game. Manager Torre most often bats him late in the lineup, and Benedict has always been willing to sacrifice an at-bat to move a runner along.

BASERUNNING:

Benedict runs the bases like a catcher. He is slow but careful, and he seldom, if ever steals. He won't try to take an extra base, and opposing pitchers are never distracted when he's on. He hustles into second, but isn't really quick enough to break up the double play.

FIELDING:

The young Atlanta pitching staff seems to trust Benedict's judgement behind the plate. He's learned the strengths and weaknesses of opposing hitters and calls a smart game. His arm is very strong and quite accurate. He is quick on his feet going after fouls and bunts dropped in front of the plate. Benedict excels in his ability to handle Niekro's knuckleball--no easy task for any backstop.

His intelligence and poise behind the plate more than compensate for any of his shortcomings with the bat.

1982 STATISTICS

AVG	G	AB	R	H	2B	3B	HR	RBI	BB	SO	SB
.246	118	386	34	95	11	1	3	44	37	41	4

CAREER STATISTICS

AVG	G	AB	R	H	2B	3B	HR	RBI	BB	SO	SB
.249	426	1296	95	323	50	3	10	129	137	122	9

VS. RHP

VS. LHP

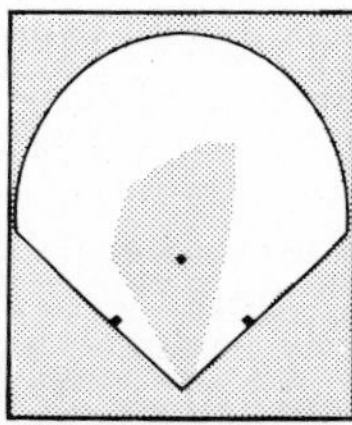
PROBABLE HIT LOCATIONS

OVERALL:

McCarver: "Benedict is a fine young catcher who wasn't given enough credit when Atlanta was going well. He's very mature and accepted the responsibilities of a starting catcher as soon as he was called up from the minors."

Kiner: "He's become an excellent defensive catcher and has an arm that's strong enough to keep baserunners honest."

Coleman: "Benedict has excellent leadership qualities and is a very unselfish player. He needs to improve his hitting."

TOMMY BOGGS
RHP, No. 40
RR, 6'2", 200 lbs.
ML Svc: 5 years
Born: 10-25-55 in Poughkeepsie, NY

PITCHING:

After a 12-9 year in 1980, and a 3-13 mark in 1981, this looked like the season that would finally tell the tale about Tom Boggs. Unfortunately, arm troubles cast a bleak shadow over his 1982 season.

Boggs is a starting pitcher, and before his injury, had the ability to throw quality pitches. His fastball, at 88 MPH, has always been a good pitch for him. His curve is less effective, because Boggs never seems to get on top of it in order to get the good rotation necessary for a sharp break. He also throws a slider, and when he was healthy, this was usually his out pitch.

Boggs has better than average control, and when he falls behind in the count, he can throw either the fastball or the slider for strikes. He never seems to adjust to a particular batter's weakness. For example, he generally works every righthander the same way; fastballs in and sliders away. He handles pressure fairly well, and can maintain his poise and concentration when things are going his way. Adversity, however, can upset Boggs and cause him to make careless mistakes.

His return to the Braves at the end of the season was promising. It now looks like 1983 will be the season of judgment for him.

FIELDING, HITTING, BASERUNNING:

Boggs has a very quick move to first and manages to keep opposing baserunners fairly honest. He's also a better than average fielder, and often helps himself defensively on the mound. Boggs has average luck with his bat and is uneventful on the basepaths.

OVERALL:

Kiner: "Boggs returned from his injury at the end of past season and pitched well enough to help the Braves win the divisional title. He'll be a good starter for them if his arm is sound."

McCarver: "Before his injury, Tommy never had the stats to support people's expectations. He had good stuff, but a below .500 career average. Sometimes an injury can make a player concentrate harder and improve his performance. Both the Braves and Tom hope those are the inadvertent results of his most recent injury."

1982 STATISTICS

W	L	ERA	G	GS	CG	IP	H	R	ER	BB	SO	SV
2	2	3.30	10	10	0	46	43	22	17	22	29	0

CAREER STATISTICS

W	L	ERA	G	GS	CG	IP	H	R	ER	BB	SO	SV
20	44	4.12	105	94	10	570	591	291	261	198	267	0

BRETT BUTLER
OF, No. 22
LL, 5'10", 160 lbs.
ML Svc: 1 year plus
Born: 6-15-57 in
Los Angeles, CA

1982 STATISTICS

AVG	G	AB	R	H	2B	3B	HR	RBI	BB	SO	SB
.217	89	240	35	52	2	0	0	7	25	35	21

CAREER STATISTICS

AVG	G	AB	R	H	2B	3B	HR	RBI	BB	SO	SB
.230	129	366	52	84	4	3	0	11	44	52	30

VS. RHP

VS. LHP

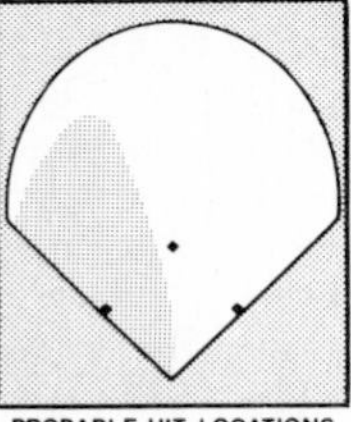
PROBABLE HIT LOCATIONS

HITTING:

If Brett Butler isn't the most marketable name in Atlanta, what is? All Butler has to do is prove he can hit major league pitching. His minor league career average is over .330, which indicates that Butler has the ability to put wood on the ball. Last season, however, he only managed to hit .217. He must develop more refined big league hitting skills to bring his major league totals closer to his minor league stats in order to have a promising future in Atlanta.

Primarily a singles hitter, Butler doesn't have a lot of power. He tries to hit it up the middle against right-handed pitchers, and goes to the opposite field against lefties. The outfield usually comes way in on Butler, because he lacks the power to drive the ball by them.

Butler has a good eye but isn't very selective at the plate. He can be jammed with hard stuff inside, and is apt to fish after low curves. Because of his lack of power, he doesn't see too many change-ups, and he still hasn't proved he can handle a major league curveball.

BASERUNNING:

Butler is fast. He stole twenty-one bases for the Braves last season and was only caught eight times. He is an aggressive runner and is always prepared to try for the extra base. Pitchers and outfielders have to be on their toes. With his speed and aggressiveness, Butler could be an important factor on the bases, but the rules still say, you can't steal first.

FIELDING:

His excellent speed gives him better than average range and allows him to run down any mistakes he might make in judging a ball. Butler's arm is strong and accurate. He moves exceptionally well laterally and is a defensive asset in the outfield.

OVERALL:

Kiner: "Butler has a fine minor league record but still isn't able to hit major league pitching. I think he'll have a tough time making the team this season."

McCarver: "Butler needs to increase his strength through weight-lifting, once a taboo in the major leagues. If he improves his hitting, he could be a future star in Atlanta."

PITCHING:

1982 was a year of transition for Rick Camp. After two previous successful seasons as an outstanding short-relief man, Camp worked his way into manager Joe Torre's starting rotation. He only completed three of his twenty-one starts, and his 11-13 won-loss record suggests that the jury is still out on his effectiveness as a starter.

Camp is basically a two-pitch pitcher. He throws a fastball at better than 85 MPH. His fastball is considered extremely heavy, and it sinks on its way to the plate. A better than average slider complements his sinker, and serves to keep batters off balance. Like most sinkerball pitchers, Camp has only a mediocre curve, and rarely, if ever, throws a change-up.

Camp's sinker forces batters to hit a lot of ground balls. Unfortunately, the infield in Atlanta isn't smooth enough to guarantee his infielders will be able to handle them cleanly. He is a bit more effective against righties than lefties, and the heaviness of his sinker not only breaks a lot of bats but makes it very hard for righthanders to pull the ball.

His years as a short relief man have given Camp added poise on the mound, and he seldom gets rattled. He walked 52 batters in 177 innings last season and had 68 strikeouts. He needs an off-speed pitch to go with his sinker and hard slider if he is to continue to improve as a starter.

RICK CAMP
RHP, No. 37
RR, 6'1", 198 lbs.
ML Svc: 5 years
Born: 6-10-53 in Trion, GA

FIELDING, HITTING, BASERUNNING:

Camp is fairly quick off the mound and fields his position adequately. In 41 at-bats he had only one hit, a double. But Torre, understandably, doesn't think of him as a potential pinch hitter. When Camp hit his double, he ran all the way to second without stopping, and that was the extent of his 1982 baserunning.

OVERALL:

Kiner: "Camp turned out to be a good fourth starter for Atlanta. He has to keep his sinkerball down to be effective."

McCarver: "Rick made that rare transition from short relief to a good starting pitcher. He has a good, natural sinker with a heavy downward movement."

Coleman: "Camp was a great reliever for two years and now starts. I think the verdict is still out about his starting abilities."

1982 STATISTICS

W	L	ERA	G	GS	CG	IP	H	R	ER	BB	SO	SV
11	13	3.65	51	21	3	177	199	84	72	52	68	5

CAREER STATISTICS

W	L	ERA	G	GS	CG	IP	H	R	ER	BB	SO	SV
34	28	3.15	277	26	3	525	560	225	184	174	228	54

CHRIS CHAMBLISS
INF, No. 10
LR, 6'1", 215 lbs.
ML Svc: 12 years
Born: 12-26-48 in
Dayton, OH

1982 STATISTICS

AVG	G	AB	R	H	2B	3B	HR	RBI	BB	SO	SB
.270	157	534	57	144	25	2	20	86	57	57	7

CAREER STATISTICS

AVG	G	AB	R	H	2B	3B	HR	RBI	BB	SO	SB
.280	1710	6442	777	1806	339	39	151	815	478	757	37

VS. RHP

VS. LHP

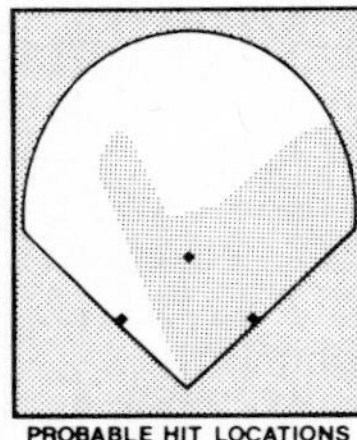
PROBABLE HIT LOCATIONS

HITTING:

Chris Chambliss is "Mr. Consistency" for the Atlanta Braves. A strong man, he faces pitchers with a closed, upright stance. He prefers the ball high and on the outside half of the plate. When pitchers oblige him, Chambliss has the strength to reach the alleys and the discipline to go to the opposite field, especially against lefthanders.

A line drive hitter, Chambliss relies almost entirely on his arm strength to power the ball. He is seldom fooled by change-ups and is considered a good curveball hitter. Pitchers have their best success against Chambliss when they can keep their fastballs on the inside corner of the plate.

His bat has slowed a bit over the years, and when he's jammed by a pitch, can't get the arm extension he needs to power the ball. Chambliss can also look bad chasing breaking balls away from the plate, but he's still considered a clutch performer who has the skills and experience to hit well with men in scoring position and to advance runners in hit-and-run situations.

BASERUNNING:

Chambliss is not a fast runner. He is a big man and hustles down the line, but his lack of speed makes him a cautious and conservative baserunner. He's too slow to steal a base or stretch a base hit.

FIELDING:

Chambliss is an above average defensive first baseman. He has quick, soft hands, and can field any ball he can reach. He anticipates the ball, and can turn the 3-6-3 double play exceptionally well for a righthanded first baseman. He handles the short hop very well. The only knock on Chambliss in the field is that his range is limited, and this is a deficiency that is not apt to improve with age.

OVERALL:

Kiner: "Chambliss does a first class job day in and day out. In my opinion, he should be less defensive at the plate and more willing to go for the long ball in Atlanta's home run type of park."

Coleman: "Chambliss provides quiet but firm leadership. He's been a definite plus for every team he's ever played for."

McCarver: "Chambliss is a leader in his actions both on and off the field. He's a class individual who is the very definition of professionalism."

KEN DAYLEY
LHP, No. 55
LL, 6'0", 178 lbs.
ML Svc: 1 year
Born: 2-25-59 in Jerome, IN

PITCHING:

Ken Dayley is a top lefthanded pitching prospect for the Braves. He throws hard and relies on his 90 MPH fastball to overpower hitters. He also has an average curveball, and a fair to good slider which he throws mostly to lefthanded batters. He'll show a hitter his change-up, but it still needs a lot of work if he's ever going to use it to get batters out. When the chips are down, most hitters are confident that Dayley will challenge them with his heater.

Dayley has some control problems and is just wild enough with his pitches to keep hitters from digging in against him. He's still young, and sometimes appears to lose his poise and confidence on the mound. Dayley needs to learn how to go after a hitter's weak spots, instead of challenging everyone with his fastball. He should also develop the control to locate his pitches more precisely.

FIELDING:

Dayley looks like a good athlete. He has a lefthander's natural advantage holding runners close to first, and he fields his position competently. He was five-for-twenty at the plate last season, and doesn't have the rusty gate swing that so often characterizes a pitcher.

OVERALL:

Coleman: "Ken needs very good control to win and should work to improve his change-up as well as his move to first base."

McCarver: "Ken struck out 162 batters at Richmond in 1980. He looms on the Braves' horizon as a fine prospect. If you get a talented lefthanded pitcher, you always do your best to develop him."

Kiner: "Ken is a good young prospect who just needs experience and better control to become a reliable major league starter."

1982 STATISTICS

W	L	ERA	G	GS	CG	IP	H	R	ER	BB	SO	SV
5	6	4.54	20	11	0	71	79	39	36	25	34	0

CAREER STATISTICS

W	L	ERA	G	GS	CG	IP	H	R	ER	BB	SO	SV
5	6	4.54	20	11	0	71	79	39	36	25	34	0

PETE FALCONE
LHP, No. 33
LL, 6'2", 185 lbs.
ML Svc: 8 years
Born: 10-1-53 in Brooklyn, NY

PITCHING:

Pete Falcone is a mystery that no one can solve. Now that he's in Atlanta, manager Joe Torre will try to figure him out for the second time. He throws hard, has far above average stuff and has no arm trouble. But he doesn't win.

It is control that is his problem. Falcone seems to have no idea where the ball is going. His fastball is inconsistent, and it flattens out sometimes. His curve, which is a knuckle curve, has a downward rotation like Burt Hooton's, and often bounces in the dirt. He began using his slider and a cut fastball more often last season, but couldn't control them either.

He relies on his fastball when he gets behind in the count, and takes something off it to improve his control. That's trouble. When Falcone is on, he'll throw the curve in any situation, but he seems to lack concentration.

Pete will throw three sensational games a year to tease his manager, but then the mystery begins, he loses control and becomes unreliable.

FIELDING, HITTING, BASERUNNING:

Though lefthanded, Falcone has only an average move to first. He is an average fielder, too. He is not a bad hitter, and in recent seasons has learned to put the bat on the ball. He has below average speed on the bases.

OVERALL:

The Mets questioned Falcone's willingness and true desire to win. It was felt that he accepted defeat as if he had no control over it.

Kiner: "His 8-10 record in 1982 was deceiving. Pete didn't win the games his team needed when it meant something."

Coleman: "He has the tools, but continues to be erratic in his pitching patterns."

McCarver: "Pete is inconsistent, but when he churns up a good one, he can be impressive. He has pitched from behind throughout his career and still is in the major leagues. That says something about his potential. He has great stuff that you hate to waste."

1982 STATISTICS

W	L	ERA	G	GS	CG	IP	H	R	ER	BB	SO	SV
8	10	3.84	40	23	3	171	159	82	73	71	101	2

CAREER STATISTICS

W	L	ERA	G	GS	CG	IP	H	R	ER	BB	SO	SV
56	79	4.11	257	186	21	1208	1168	609	551	554	751	5

TERRY FORSTER
LHP, No. 51
LL, 6'4", 210 lbs.
ML Svc: 12 years
Born: 1-14-52 in Sioux Falls, SD

PITCHING:

Forster is a power pitcher best suited for short relief, which has been his role since 1976 when he last started a game. He has an excellent slider, which is one reason for his numerous arm injuries. He comes at a hitter overhand, often jerking his pitches.

His fastball moves very well at 90 MPH, but it is the slider which he uses as an out pitch. He throws the slider about 40% of the time. He doesn't mix many pitches; rather he throws his fastball and slider and says, "Here it is, hit it." He's most effective pitching against lefthanded batters.

At one time in his career, he was the ace lefthander in the bullpen. But since his elbow troubles (two operations in less than a year) he hasn't shown the same ability to close out a game. He's a top competitor who has had difficulty throwing strikes consistently, especially since his surgery.

He's very aggressive on the mound, sometimes to the point of getting over-excited. Overall rating, average.

FIELDING, HITTING, BASERUNNING:

Forster was an excellent hitter at one time in his career and though he hasn't had a hit in four years (0-for-4), he still has a career batting average of .397 in the majors (.342 in the NL). In the field, Forster rates below average in his pick-off move and his ability to field bunts. He's not much of a baserunner.

OVERALL:

Forster has above average stuff but his troubles with injuries have kept him from being a consistent pitcher in recent years. His location with his pitches has caused him to get into trouble.

McCarver: "He has a wicked slider that can make lefthanded batters feel futile--if he can throw strikes with it. He's still young enough (31) to have some productive years yet."

Coleman: "Forster really jumps at the hitters."

1982 STATISTICS

W	L	ERA	G	GS	CG	IP	H	R	ER	BB	SO	SV
5	6	3.04	56	0	0	83	66	38	28	31	52	3

CAREER STATISTICS

W	L	ERA	G	GS	CG	IP	H	R	ER	BB	SO	SV
43	59	3.40	446	39	5	898	848	386	339	374	662	103

GENE GARBER
RHP, No. 26
RR, 5'10", 175 lbs.
ML Svc: 10 years
Born: 11-13-47 in Lancaster, PA

PITCHING:

Gene Garber appeared in 69 games last season, the most by any Atlanta pitcher. Despite his high number of appearances, his unique windup (in which he turns completely away from the hitter), and his full sidearm delivery, are still distracting to opposing batters, especially righthanders.

Of course, Garber didn't register a team-leading 2.34 ERA by relying solely on an unusual windup and delivery. He also has excellent command of three different pitches. His fastball is about 85 MPH, and consistently sinks. He gets the most out of his fastball by mixing it frequently with a straight change. By gripping the ball with his middle finger tucked beneath it, Garber is able to use a full motion without having to throw the ball hard. This is an excellent pitch for him and a difficult one for hitters to pick up. His third pitch has the rotation of a curve but slides away horizontally rather than dropping.

Garber is an aggressive competitor and he's not unwilling to brush hitters back if he thinks they are getting too comfortable at the plate. He mixes his pitches extremely well and has enough confidence in them to use any one of them in any situation. He can, however, be bothered by occasional wildness.

FIELDING, HITTING, BASERUNNING:

Garber doesn't have an exceptional move to first base, but he throws over often to keep runners close. He is one of the better fielding pitchers in the National League and is remarkably effective fielding bunts and covering his position. Garber seldom gets a chance to bat, but no doubt remembers every bounce of the two hits he garnered last season.

OVERALL:

McCarver: "Gene is a bulldog of a competitor, and was a premier reliever in 1982. His best pitch is his change-up, and hitters who sit on his off-speed pitch are vulnerable to his fastball."

Kiner: "Garber had his best year last season. He was the Braves' No. 1 stopper, and he did an excellent job."

1982 STATISTICS

W	L	ERA	G	GS	CG	IP	H	R	ER	BB	SO	SV
8	10	2.34	69	0	0	119	100	40	31	32	68	30

CAREER STATISTICS

W	L	ERA	G	GS	CG	IP	H	R	ER	BB	SO	SV
70	77	3.27	618	9	4	1050	986	449	381	311	647	149

TERRY HARPER
OF, No. 21
RR, 6'1", 195 lbs.
ML Svc: 1 year
Born: 8-19-55
in Douglasville, GA

1982 STATISTICS

AVG	G	AB	R	H	2B	3B	HR	RBI	BB	SO	SB
.287	48	150	16	43	3	0	2	16	14	28	7

CAREER STATISTICS

AVG	G	AB	R	H	2B	3B	HR	RBI	BB	SO	SB
.260	109	277	28	72	6	1	4	27	31	50	14

VS. RHP

VS. LHP

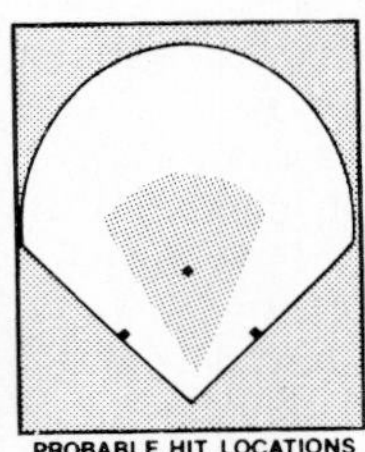
PROBABLE HIT LOCATIONS

HITTING:

Although Terry Harper saw limited action last season, he showed enough talent and potential to make people want to take a longer look this year. He hit .287 and demonstrated the ability to hit the ball with authority. He hits straightaway, but will try to pull the ball against lefthanded pitching.

Harper seemed to be more comfortable against lefthanded pitching, and hit best when the ball was outside where he had the opportunity to extend his arms. Righthanders can jam him with fastballs in on the hands. He can also look bad at times chasing curves down and away. However, he did prove that he could get around on a major league fastball, and had average success against change-ups and sliders.

Strangely enough, Harper put together better stats last season with Atlanta than he had in previous years in the minors. He definitely has major league potential, but time will tell.

BASERUNNING:

Harper has better than average speed. He's quick out of the box and hustles down the line. He runs hard to break up the potential double play, and might become an exciting basestealer. He attempted eleven steals last season and was caught four times. Experience should improve his knowledge of the pitchers' different motions. Harper learns quickly, and can exploit their weaknesses to his advantage.

FIELDING:

Harper has a rifle for an arm, and he knows how to aim it. He has better than average range in the outfield, and gets a good jump on the ball. He was originally signed as a pitcher, and his transformation into a talented outfielder speaks well of both his coaching and his own effort.

OVERALL:

McCarver: "Harper is a strong throwing outfielder who's coming into his own with the bat. His better than average speed makes him an excellent prospect for the Braves."

Kiner: "Terry has all around ability. He showed promising signs of good potential during the stretch drive in 1982."

BOB HORNER
INF, No. 5
RR, 6'1", 210 lbs.
ML Svc: 5 years
Born: 8-6-57 in Junction City, KS

1982 STATISTICS

AVG	G	AB	R	H	2B	3B	HR	RBI	BB	SO	SB
.261	140	499	85	130	24	0	32	97	66	75	3

CAREER STATISTICS

AVG	G	AB	R	H	2B	3B	HR	RBI	BB	SO	SB
.278	553	2072	324	576	80	3	138	389	171	280	8

VS. RHP — VS. LHP — PROBABLE HIT LOCATIONS

HITTING:

One of the best young home run hitters in the league, Bob Horner's hands are lightning quick when he has a bat in them. He crowds the plate when he's at bat and tends to pull the ball to left against right as well as lefthanded pitching. He has a tremendously powerful swing and seems to excel in clutch situations.

Because he crowds the plate so tightly, Horner is susceptible to being jammed with high, hard, inside fastballs. If a pitcher misses with this pitch, however, Horner can send it out of the park in a hurry, especially if the game is being played at home in Atlanta's launching pad of a stadium. Horner is also proficient against change-ups and sliders. On the negative side, a good curveball pitcher, especially a righthander, can give him problems at the plate.

Horner has developed discipline as a hitter and has a good idea of the strike zone. He enjoys coming up to the plate with men in scoring position and hits well against St. Louis, San Diego, and Houston. With his swing and his power, Horner is rarely asked to hit-and-run or to bunt. If he is, the opposing team should count their blessings.

BASERUNNING:

Horner is a slow baserunner. His big swing makes him late out of the box, and he simply doesn't move that quickly down the line. He's not a threat to stretch a base hit or to steal a base. This lack of speed makes him a conservative baserunner, and without a bat in his hands, he can be safely ignored by rival pitchers.

FIELDING:

Horner has an average arm both in terms of accuracy and strength. He also has limited range as a third baseman. He has to improve his ability to get in front of grounders, especially those hit down the line. Horner charges bunts fairly well and is not considered an outstanding defensive player. Many of his errors, however, could be attributed to the treacherous surface of the Fulton County Stadium infield.

OVERALL:

McCarver: "He's one half of the Murphy-Horner tandem which gives the Braves the best one-two home run punch since Aaron and Mathews. He's a talented hitter with lightning fast hands, and he explodes the head of the bat through the strike zone."

Kiner: "Horner has a great natural swing and his statistics would look great on a player with less natural talent. I think he should be able to hit for a higher average.

Coleman: "One of the league's best power hitters."

GLENN HUBBARD
INF, No. 17
RR, 5'8", 165 lbs.
ML Svc: 4 years
Born: 9-25-57 in
Hahn AFB, GER

1982 STATISTICS

AVG	G	AB	R	H	2B	3B	HR	RBI	BB	SO	SB
.248	145	532	75	132	25	1	9	59	59	62	4

CAREER STATISTICS

AVG	G	AB	R	H	2B	3B	HR	RBI	BB	SO	SB
.243	502	1812	218	441	75	9	29	177	178	253	17

VS. RHP

VS. LHP

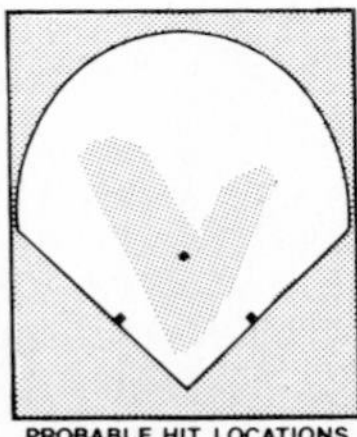
PROBABLE HIT LOCATIONS

HITTING:

Glenn Hubbard has surprising power for a man his size. He is a fastball hitter who can line the ball through the gaps against righthanded pitching, and can pull the ball a bit more against southpaws. He has a good batting eye, draws a fair share of walks, and hits well behind baserunners. Hubbard is also considered a smart hitter who's willing to do anything to help his team. This makes him especially valuable in sacrifice and hit-and-run situations.

Pitchers generally work Hubbard down and away. He sees a lot of curveballs and still hasn't proved that he can handle a major league change-up. Since he prefers the ball up, Hubbard gets a lot of sinkers. Nevertheless, he's a consistent hitter who handles the bat well and is considered an important part of the Braves' offensive machine.

BASERUNNING:

Hubbard tries to use hustle and aggressiveness to make up for his lack of speed on the bases. He'll slide hard to break up the double play, and is always a threat to try for an extra base if he thinks an outfielder is being nonchalant. Although he lacks speed and quickness, opposing pitchers are wary of him because he's so aggressive on the basepaths.

FIELDING:

Hubbard positions himself very well at second base. He studies the hitters, and often seems to find the special edge in position that compensates for his lack of quickness. He moves better toward first than he does toward the keystone sack, but is considered absolutely fearless as the pivot man in double plays. He has a strong arm, but it is his tenacity more than anything else that defines him as a defensive ballplayer.

OVERALL:

Hubbard is an intelligent ballplayer who works hard, consistently gives 100% and manages to get the utmost out of his abilities.

McCarver: "A little player with a big heart. He makes contact with the bat and never gives an inch at second base."

Coleman: "Hubbard is an underrated player. He gives all he has and is a big plus for his club."

RUFINO LINARES
OF, No. 25
RR, 6'0", 170 lbs.
ML Svc: 2 years
Born: 2-28-55 in
San Pedro de Macoris, DR

1982 STATISTICS

AVG	G	AB	R	H	2B	3B	HR	RBI	BB	SO	SB
.298	77	191	28	57	7	1	2	17	7	29	5

CAREER STATISTICS

AVG	G	AB	R	H	2B	3B	HR	RBI	BB	SO	SB
.279	155	444	55	124	16	3	7	42	16	57	13

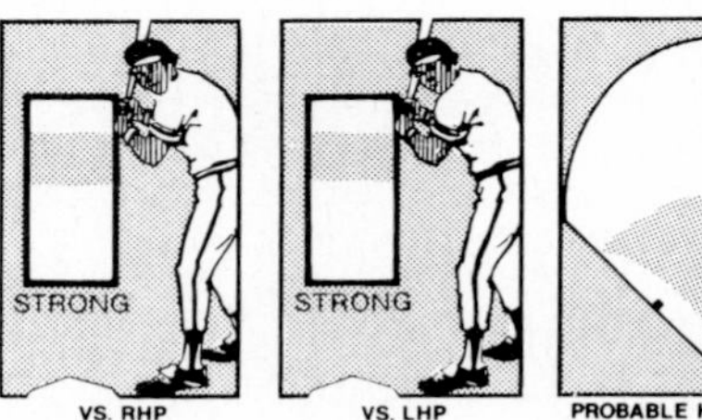

HITTING:

Rufino Linares was quoted as saying, "I can hit in any league." After successfully hitting in the minors, his .298 average in 1982 seems to justify his confidence.

Linares is a free swinging, righthanded outfielder. He uses a closed, slightly crouched stance and looks for the high fastball. He drives the ball up the gaps against righthanded pitching, but is more of an opposite field hitter against southpaws. He lacks the power to reach the alleys consistently, but has the quick hand action necessary to sting the ball, and consequently, hits a lot of line drives and sharp grounders.

Linares can be jammed with an exceptionally good fastball and can also be made to look bad chasing breaking balls away. On the other hand, he handles sinkers and sliders fairly well.

A lack of patience seems to be Linares' main problem as a hitter. He has to learn to be more selective at the plate. He drew only seven walks in almost 200 at-bats last season, and that's a good indication of how anxious he appears at the plate.

BASERUNNING:

Linares has above average speed down the line to first. Once on first, however, he tends to become hesitant and conservative. He has enough speed to steal bases, but usually takes only a moderate lead, and appears unsure about the pitcher's motion. With more experience and confidence, he could become a much more exciting and effective baserunner.

FIELDING:

Linares has an average arm, but he gets a good jump on the ball. With his speed, he has above average range. He looks much better coming in on the ball than he does tracking down fly balls hit over his head. Once again, Linares seems to have the potential to improve with experience.

OVERALL:

McCarver: "Linares' arm extension reminds me of a tapir's nose extension--it's long. And he uses his arm strength to drive the ball with amazing power."

Kiner: "At this point in his career, he seems most valuable as a pinch-hitter against lefthanded pitching."

Coleman: "Linarez hasn't evidenced the discipline necessary to be a better than average major league hitter. Not much thought seems to go into what he does at the plate."

RICK MAHLER
RHP, No. 42
RR, 6'1", 190 lbs.
ML Svc: 3 years
Born: 8-5-53 in
Austin, TX

PITCHING:

Rick Mahler was the second most frequent starter for the Braves last season. His 9-10 won-loss record and 4.21 ERA weren't exceptional, but many baseball people feel that Mahler has finally developed into a reliable starting pitcher.

Mahler has an exceptional curveball. In fact, some say he has one of the top five curves among National League righthanders. He mixes speeds on the curve well and manages to keep hitters off balance. Mahler also throws a better than average fastball, and doesn't hurt himself too often with wildness. His slider gives him a third effective pitch.

When he falls behind in the count, Mahler has confidence in all three of his pitches, and batters can't accurately anticipate one more than the others. He has a nice relaxed motion and always appears confident and poised on the mound.

One shortcoming of Mahler's is that his pitches sometimes appear to be too true; they lack movement and are always around the plate. This may help account for the high number of runs scored against Mahler last year.

FIELDING:

Rick has an average move to first base, but is better than average fielding bunts around the mound as well as in covering first base on balls hit to the right side. As a hitter, he is average for a pitcher, and is slow on the bases.

OVERALL:

McCarver: "Rick has come into his own as a very formidable starter. Inconsistency is a chief problem, but when he's throwing well, he's tough to beat."

Kiner: "Mahler became a .500 pitcher after moving into the Braves' starting rotation."

Coleman: "Under the tutelage of minor league pitching coach, Johnny Sand, Mahler has shown some fine improvement."

1982 STATISTICS

W	L	ERA	G	GS	CG	IP	H	R	ER	BB	SO	SV
9	10	4.21	39	33	5	205	213	105	96	62	105	0

CAREER STATISTICS

W	L	ERA	G	GS	CG	IP	H	R	ER	BB	SO	SV
17	16	3.86	90	47	6	343	352	163	147	116	172	2

DALE MURPHY
OF, No. 3
RR, 6'5", 215 lbs.
ML Svc: 5 years
Born: 3-12-56 in Portland, OR

1982 STATISTICS

AVG	G	AB	R	H	2B	3B	HR	RBI	BB	SO	SB
.281	162	598	113	168	23	2	36	109	93	134	23

CAREER STATISTICS

AVG	G	AB	R	H	2B	3B	HR	RBI	BB	SO	SB
.265	719	2591	381	686	97	11	128	407	283	568	63

HITTING:

Dale Murphy stands low in the box and faces pitchers with a slightly closed, upright stance. He hits with exceptional power to all fields. He doesn't have to pull the ball to jack it out of the park. Pitchers have to move the ball around against him.

Murphy often swings at bad pitches, and his strikeout total is high, but when he's hot, Murphy can hit anything and everything. He also tends to hit the ball a long way. He's considered better than average against change-ups and sliders and he waits well on curves. Pitchers have to mix their pitches continually if they hope to get by Murphy. He's devastating in clutch situations and loves to hit with men in scoring position.

The park in Atlanta is tailor-made for Murphy, but he also hits well in San Diego and New York. He's seldom asked to hit-and-run, and if he bunts, he is doing the opposing team a favor.

BASERUNNING:

Murphy has better than average speed, especially for a man his size. He runs hard and is aggressive, breaking up the double play at second. He's considered a smart baserunner, and when pitchers concentrate too hard on pitching to either Horner or Chambliss, Murphy is likely to steal a base.

FIELDING:

A first-rate defensive outfielder, Murphy has an excellent throwing arm. He has good range in the outfield and comes in on the ball extremely well. At 6'5" he's also tall enough to reach over the fence to steal homers from then-disgruntled hitters.

OVERALL:

Coleman: "Murphy is the best player I saw in the National League in 1982. He's a great player now and I think he'll improve with experience."

McCarver: "Murphy is a quiet and unassuming young man and one of the nicest baseball players you'll meet. He is an outstanding talent and a potential MVP."

Kiner: "One of baseball's newest and best talents. He has everything it takes to be a great one."

PHIL NIEKRO
RHP, No. 35
RR, 6'2", 195 lbs.
ML Svc: 18 years
Born: 4-1-39 in Blaine, OH

PITCHING:

Quite simply, Phil Niekro is one of the truly great knuckleball pitchers in the history of baseball. Although he relies almost exclusively on his knuckleball, Niekro will throw an occasional slider or a fastball when he falls behind in the count. His fastball, clocked at about 80 MPH, doesn't intimidate hitters, but it can catch them off balance after they've grown accustomed to the much slower and more frustrating knuckler.

Niekro really throws two kinds of knucklers--one moves in on hitters and one that tends to dance away. Neither left nor righthanded batters have an advantage against Niekro because the knuckleball doesn't play favorites--it torments everyone with an equal degree of unpredictability.

Niekro can beat himself when he fails to control his knuckler because he really doesn't have another pitch that's outstanding. However, he is as confident and crafty on the mound as he is talented. After more than 250 career victories, he doesn't rattle, and his presence and poise on the mound are outstanding. He excels when the pressure is greatest, and at 43 years of age, he is still the ace of the Atlanta staff.

FIELDING:

Niekro's move to first is either excellent or a balk. Since the umpires rarely call it as an illegal move, most baserunners have to stay close or risk the embarrassment of being picked off. Phil is as quick as a cat coming off the mound and pounces on squibblers and bunts with amazing quickness. He is an excellent fielder and a defensive plus when he's on the mound.

Niekro also hits with surprising power and has used his bat to help himself win quite a few ballgames over the years. As a baserunner, Niekro is careful rather than fast, and doesn't make any foolish rally-squelching mistakes.

OVERALL:

Niekro is an exceptionally quick worker on the mound. When he starts, if you're not at the park on time, you may miss half the game. He's a proven winner and a legitimate Hall of Fame candidate.

McCarver: "Niekro is a 43-year-old legend. He may be able to pitch effectively for another five years because the knuckleball doesn't seem to wear out an arm the way other pitches do."

Coleman: "Niekro is an outstanding player and person. He could easily end up in the Hall of Fame."

Kiner: "Niekro has excellent poise on the mound and a super personality. Last season, he had a year that made him a definite Cy Young candidate."

1982 STATISTICS

W	L	ERA	G	GS	CG	IP	H	R	ER	BB	SO	SV
17	4	3.61	35	35	4	234	225	106	94	73	144	0

CAREER STATISTICS

W	L	ERA	G	GS	CG	IP	H	R	ER	BB	SO	SV
257	220	3.16	705	561	224	4416	4006	1823	1551	1347	2784	30

PASCUAL PEREZ
RHP, No. 22
RR, 6'2", 186 lbs.
ML Svc: 1 year
Born: 5-17-57 in Cristobal, DR

PITCHING:

Pascual Perez started in eleven games last season though he didn't manage to complete any of them. However, he did manage to put together a 4-4 won-loss record and a 3.06 ERA. His ERA was the third lowest on the staff, behind relievers Garber and Bedrosian.

Perez uses a high leg kick that is reminiscent of Hall of Famer Juan Marichal's delivery. Perez throws a 90 MPH fastball off that motion, and gets better than average movement on it. He throws a slider, rather than a curve, and has very good success with it.

His slider really sweeps away from righthanded batters, and Perez has enough confidence in it to throw it in clutch situations. He lacks a good change-up which cuts down on his overall effectiveness.

Perez has to stay ahead in the count if he is to be a consistent winner. Without a change-up, hitters can afford the luxury of guessing fastball, and they get it more often than not. As he gains more experience, Perez should also learn the hitters better and be able to pitch more effectively to their particular weaknesses.

FIELDING, HITTING, BASERUNNING:

Perez has a quick move to first, but his high kick gives good baserunners that extra split second they're always looking for. Perez is a good all around athlete and fields his position more than adequately. He only managed three hits in 1982, but two of them were for extra bases.

OVERALL:

Kiner: "Pascual was new to the National League this season. For a slightly built player, he throws exceptionally hard and has a good slider."

McCarver: "Pascual has a chance to become a good pitcher because of his loose, natural motion. His pitches tail and dart, and he seems especially tough on righthanded batters."

1982 STATISTICS

W	L	ERA	G	GS	CG	IP	H	R	ER	BB	SO	SV
4	4	3.06	16	11	0	79	85	35	27	17	29	0

CAREER STATISTICS

W	L	ERA	G	GS	CG	IP	H	R	ER	BB	SO	SV
6	12	3.56	35	26	2	177	192	91	70	53	82	0

HITTING:

Biff Pocoroba used to be a switch-hitter, but concentrated on hitting only from the left side during the past season. He hit mostly against righthanders in 1982, and once again proved himself an outstanding low ball hitter. He pulls the ball to right, and has the power to reach the right-center field alley.

Pocoroba excels in clutch situations, and he is usually among the team leaders in pinch-hitting and game-winning hits. He rarely bunts, but has the bat control necessary to be effective in hit-and-run situations. He is patient at the plate, has a good eye, and knows how to hit behind the baserunner.

Pitchers like to keep the ball up on Pocoroba. He can hit a curve from a righthander, but has problems against good southpaws. He handles sinkers and sliders better than change-ups. When he sees enough action to keep sharp, Pocoroba is a consistently good hitter.

BASERUNNING:

Pocoroba has only average speed. He is no threat to steal, or to go for an extra base. His chief assets as a baserunner are his realization of his limitations and the discipline to play within them.

FIELDING:

A torn rotator cuff curbed what might have been an outstanding career for Pocoroba. The injury has severely limited his throwing ability, and has relegated him to spot duty as a back up catcher. When he does play, Pocoroba still calls an excellent game, and is much better than average in his ability

BIFF POCOROBA
C, No. 4
SR, 5'10", 180 lbs.
ML Svc: 8 years
Born: 7-25-53 in
Burbank, CA

1982 STATISTICS

AVG	G	AB	R	H	2B	3B	HR	RBI	BB	SO	SB
.275	56	120	5	33	7	0	2	22	13	12	0

CAREER STATISTICS

AVG	G	AB	R	H	2B	3B	HR	RBI	BB	SO	SB
.256	537	1335	120	342	65	2	19	156	168	102	6

VS. RHP

VS. LHP

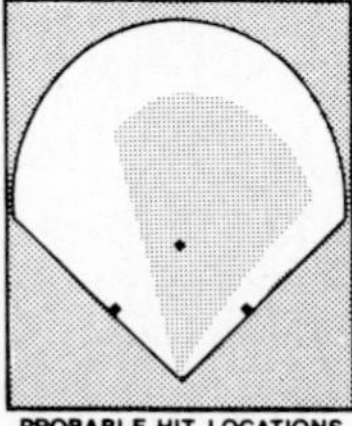
PROBABLE HIT LOCATIONS

to handle Niekro's knuckleball. Pocoroba excels at handling pitchers, and but for the injury, might have been a premier catcher in the National League.

OVERALL:

Kiner: "Due to his inability to throw like he could before his injury, Pocoroba has had to be a back up catcher and a pinch-hitter."

Coleman: "Pocoroba had a big year with his bat, but his arms still can't sustain the daily grind of playing regularly."

RAFAEL RAMIREZ
INF, No. 16
RR, 6'0", 170 lbs.
ML Svc: 2 years
Born: 2-18-59 in
San Pedro de Macoris, DR

HITTING:

In a lineup filled with power hitters like Murphy, Horner and Chambliss, a singles hitter like Ramirez is even extra valuable. He prefers the ball up in the strike zone, and has the strength to pull the ball to left against lefthanded pitching. Against righthanders, Ramirez seems content to try to push the ball into the gaps.

Despite his .278 average, Ramirez had trouble with good curveball pitchers and often seemed intimidated by hard-throwing righthanders. He showed a tendency to go after change-ups, but seemed to be lunging rather than timing his swing effectively. Ramirez also appeared to lack patience at the plate and developed a reputation for swinging at more than his share of bad pitches.

He's considered an above average bunter, and surprised everyone by hitting ten home runs last season. Ramirez seems to improve as the season progresses.

1982 STATISTICS

AVG	G	AB	R	H	2B	3B	HR	RBI	BB	SO	SB
.278	157	609	74	169	24	4	10	52	36	49	27

CAREER STATISTICS

AVG	G	AB	R	H	2B	3B	HR	RBI	BB	SO	SB
.259	302	1081	121	280	46	7	14	83	62	129	26

BASERUNNING:

Ramirez is quick out of the box, and has above average speed down the line. Once on base, he's a genuine threat to steal. He's still learning the pitchers' motions, and he doesn't always get a good jump. Ramirez stole twenty-seven bases last season, second highest on the club, but was caught fourteen times, which was a club high. He's not big enough to break up the double play at second, but he's an aggressive runner and willing to gamble for the extra base.

FIELDING:

His thirty-eight errors last season say a lot about the condition of the Atlanta infield, but they also indicate that Ramirez can be an inconsistent fielder. He has the strong arm necessary for a major league shortstop, but his throwing is erratic, especially going to first base on a 4-6-3 double play ball. His range is better than average, and he covers the gap up the middle very well.

OVERALL:

McCarver: "Rafael's defense faltered last season, but he has the reactions of a good shortstop, and he's learned to handle the bat well."

Kiner: "Ramirez provided a strong bat down the stretch, but is still not a steady, dependable fielder."

Coleman: "A good shortstop, who, along with Hubbard, gives Atlanta one of the best double play combinations in the league."

JERRY ROYSTER
INF, No. 1
RR, 6'0", 165 lbs.
ML Svc: 8 years
Born: 10-18-52 in Sacramento, CA

1982 STATISTICS

AVG	G	AB	R	H	2B	3B	HR	RBI	BB	SO	SB
.295	108	261	43	77	13	2	2	25	22	36	14

CAREER STATISTICS

AVG	G	AB	R	H	2B	3B	HR	RBI	BB	SO	SB
.252	907	2909	402	733	101	26	19	216	275	334	159

HITTING:

As a major league hitter, Jerry Royster has never fulfilled the expectations he raised when he hit .333 for Albuquerque in 1975. He is a high fastball hitter who can poke the ball through the infield or bloop it in front of an outfield defense. He lacks the power to reach the alleys consistently, but is fast enough to beat out a fair share of infield hits.

Royster likes to sit back and wait for the high inside fastball, and consequently, most pitchers choose to work him down and away. He has a lot of trouble handling a good curveball, and is largely ineffective against pitchers who throw a lot of sinkers and sliders.

Royster makes the most of his speed as a hitter and is a good bunter. He is used often in hit-and-run situations, but his difficulties hitting curves limit his effectiveness even in this role. Every once in a while, however, Royster can go on a tear. In 1982, during the period from late August to early September, he led the Braves in hitting. No one is able to figure out the why or hows of streaks like that, but Atlanta certainly welcomed it as a pleasant surprise.

BASERUNNING:

Royster has good speed. He gets a good jump off first and could probably steal 30-40 bases a year if he played regularly. He runs hard on the bases, and opposing outfielders have to stay alert or Royster will try for an extra base. He's fast and aggressive, and is often used as a pinch-runner in crucial situations.

FIELDING:

As an infielder, Royster appears most comfortable at third, but has an arm that is no better than average. He has seen action at second, short, and in the outfield as well. His range as a defensive player is not exceptional, and he makes his share of careless errors. Royster's chief value as a fielder is his versatility, and the Braves are fortunate that he has the skills to fill in adequately, if not always exceptionally, at so many different positions.

OVERALL:

Kiner: "Royster is a good utility player who can help in both the outfield and the infield."

Coleman: "Fills a valuable role for the Braves as an all around utility player."

McCarver: "Royster is valuable for his late inning defense, pinch-hitting and pinch-running."

BOB WALK
RHP, No. 43
RR, 6'3", 195 lbs.
ML Svc: 3 years
Born: 11-26-56 in
Van Nuys, CA

PITCHING:

Known to his teammates as "Twirlybird," Bob Walk has developed a reputation for forgetfulness. Once he walked up to the plate without his bat, and on another occasion he arrived on the mound without his glove. His most important memory lapse, however, has to do with the strike zone. Walk is an erratic pitcher who suffers a great deal from a lack of control.

He uses a fastball clocked at above 90 MPH, and an average slider as his second pitch. Unfortunately, he can't rely on throwing either pitch for a strike in a pressure situation. His curveball needs improvement and he rarely, if ever, throws a change-up.

The speed of his fastball, coupled with his control problems, makes Walk an especially difficult pitcher for right-handed batters. Many of them give ground against him, and if he could ever spot his pitches, he would be much more effective.

Walk works hard and isn't intimidated by anyone. He was the starting pitcher for the Phillies in the opening game of the 1980 World Series, and kept them in the game long enough to pick up credit for the win. If he's ever going to help Atlanta to the Series, Walk has to work out his control problems, improve his slider, and develop a third pitch.

FIELDING, HITTING, BASERUNNING:

Walk has an average move to first base and is considered an adequate fielder. He had six RBIs last season, but is not really a threat with the bat. On the bases, he is a cautious runner and not a threat to steal or take an extra base.

OVERALL:

Coleman: "Walk is a young, maturing righthanded pitcher. He has been bothered by arm problems, and the way he appears to overthrow the ball, he may not last long."

Kiner: "Bob has been plagued with arm troubles and needs more major league experience."

McCarver: "He could develop into a good major league pitcher if he ever learns how to consistently throw his pitches for strikes."

1982 STATISTICS

W	L	ERA	G	GS	CG	IP	H	R	ER	BB	SO	SV
11	9	4.87	32	27	3	164	179	101	89	59	84	0

CAREER STATISTICS

W	L	ERA	G	GSA	CG	IP	H	R	ER	BB	SO	SV
23	20	4.71	71	62	5	359	383	208	188	153	194	0

HITTING:

Claudell Washington shared the team leadership for game-winning hits with Dale Murphy and was a top clutch performer all season. Washington stands in the center of the box and uses a closed, upright stance. He is primarily a low ball hitter and prefers the ball on the outside half of the plate so he can get the full arm extension he needs to really drive the ball. He has the power to reach the alleys, but shows a willingness to go to left against right-handed pitching.

Most pitchers try to jam Washington with hard inside fastballs. He also sees a lot of breaking balls away, especially from southpaws. Change-ups still seems to bother Washington, and although he can handle curves from a righty, a good lefthanded curveballer can give him fits.

Over the seasons, Washington has proved that he is a consistent hitter. If he could ever solve the mystery of how to handle good lefthanded pitching, his stats might improve dramatically.

BASERUNNING:

Washington has above average speed, and he uses it to run the bases aggressively. Opposing pitchers can't afford to ignore him because when he's on base, Washington is the bravest of the Braves--the man on the team most likely to try for the theft. He led the team in stolen bases last season and has developed a reputation for sliding hard into second to break up the double play.

FIELDING:

Washington has one of the strongest arms in the National League. Not only is it strong, but it is also very accurate. His speed helps broaden his range in the outfield and enables him to catch up to any mistakes he makes judging fly balls.

CLAUDELL WASHINGTON
OF, No. 18
LL, 6'0", 190 lbs.
ML Svc: 8 years
Born: 8-31-54 in
Los Angeles, CA

1982 STATISTICS

AVG	G	AB	R	H	2B	3B	HR	RBI	BB	SO	SB
.266	150	563	94	150	24	6	16	80	50	107	33

CAREER STATISTICS

AVG	G	AB	R	H	2B	3B	HR	RBI	BB	SO	SB
.279	1059	3906	527	1088	200	45	78	487	235	724	201

VS. RHP

VS. LHP

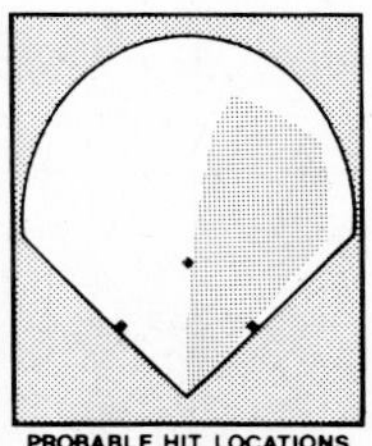
PROBABLE HIT LOCATIONS

He covers the gap in right-center extremely well, and is considered a steady and reliable defensive outfielder.

OVERALL:

Kiner: "Claudell is a fine defensive player and good on the bases. He is also one of the strongest players in the league. His one deficiency is his inability to handle lefthanded pitching."

McCarver: "Claudell has been a consistent hitter in both leagues, and in my opinion, still hasn't reached his full potential."

Coleman: "Washington is a good man to have on your club. He contributes all he can and doesn't create problems."

KEN SMITH
INF, No. 11
LR, 6'1", 195 lbs.
ML Svc: 1 year plus
Born: 2-12-58 in Youngstown, OH

HITTING:

Ken Smith is used almost exclusively as a lefthanded pinch-hitter for the Braves during the 82 season. Basically a low ball hitter, Smith showed limited power and had only one extra base hit in 41 at bats. Opposing pitchers had success at jamming Smith with high inside fastballs. In the limited action he saw, Smith looked better against sinkers and hard sliders than he did against curves and off-speed pitches.

He appears to be a pull hitter but didn't get enough at-bats in the majors for a more complete report.

Smith stole 22 bases while playing for Richmond in the Triple A League, but he wasn't on base often enough in the big leagues to characterize himself as a baserunner. Smith also saw very little action in the outfield.

OVERALL:

Smith saw limited pinch-hitting duty in 1982 and needs more playing time to be judged fairly as a major league outfielder.

BOB WATSON
INF, No. 8
RR, 6'2", 212 lbs.
ML Svc: 16 years
Born: 4-10-46 in Los Angeles, CA

HITTING:

After an excellent career with the Astros and a few seasons with with Yankees, Bob Watson returned to the National League and filled the role of a righthanded pinch-hitter for the Braves. Watson is nearing the end of his career, but he can still get around on a high outside fastball. He hit five homers and had 22 RBIs for the Braves and opposing pitchers still respect his powerful swing.

His bat has slowed a bit with the years, and Watson can now be jammed with a good, hard, inside fastball. He prefers the ball away, and is still deadly effective against off-speed pitches. He performs well in the clutch, and is a valuable veteran to have around a young team.

Watson's better days as a defensive ball player are behind him, and he doesn't play in the field anymore. When he gets on base late in a game, Torre usually sends in a pinch-runner.

OVERALL:

Coleman: "Watson is a good, aggressive player and a worthwhile man to have on your team."

Kiner: "Bob is the only man to hit for the cycle in both leagues. After an outstanding career, he's winding it up as a pinch-hitter."

McCarver: "After having had a superb career, Bob is still a longball threat and respected by opposing pitchers."

LARRY WHISENTON
OF, No. 28
LL, 6'1", 190 lbs.
ML Svc: 1 year plus
Born: 7-3-56 in
St. Louis, MO

HITTING:

Whisenton was the most frequently called upon pinch-hitter on the Atlanta team last season. He was used almost exclusively against righthanded pitching, and established himself as a dead pull hitter.

Most pitchers tried to jam him with inside fastballs to prevent him from getting the arm extension he likes. Whisenton also had problems with sharp breaking curves. When he was hitting the ball well, Whisenton would hit sharp grounders and hard line drives. He doesn't show a lot of power.

On the basepaths, he seldom took advantage of his speed, and was generally a conservative baserunner. In his limited playing time in the outfield, he showed an average arm and competent defensive ability.

OVERALL:

Coleman: "Whisenton is still an unknown soldier, who doesn't play very often."

Kiner: "He had his best year in the minors in 1981, but still couldn't put it together in 1982. He'll be hard pressed to make the club this season."

McCarver: "Whisenton was used almost exclusively as a pinch-hitter by Joe Torre, and he did a nice job."

MATT SINATRO
C, No. 14
RR, 5'9", 174 lbs.
ML Svc: 1 year plus
Born: 3-22-60 in
Hartford, CT

HITTING, BASERUNNING, FIELDING:

Matt Sinatro saw extremely limited action for the Braves in 1982. Like most young players, he looks for the fastball up and over the plate. He can handle that pitch and tries to pull it to left field. When Sinatro gets underneath the ball, however, he's more of a straightaway hitter. He doesn't have a lot of power, and still seems to have difficulties hitting major league curves and change-ups.

Sinatro has above average speed and proved to be an effective basestealer in the minors. His speed is surprising for a catcher, and he should be able to get a fair share of leg hits.

Sinatro is still in the process of learning to be an effective major league catcher. So far, he's shown only an average arm. His throws to second tend to be high, and he's still learning how to handle pitchers and how to call an intelligent game. He seems to have the tools, but needs some extra seasoning.

OVERALL:

McCarver: "Matt has good, quick reflexes behind the plate. He has a quick bat and above average speed. All of this adds up to make him a good candidate to become a solid major league catcher."

WRIGLEY FIELD

Chicago Cubs

Seating Capacity: 37,272
Playing Surface: Natural Grass

Dimensions
Left Field Pole: 355 ft.
Left-Center Field: 368 ft.
Center Field: 400 ft.
Right-Center Field: 368 ft.
Right Field Pole: 353 ft.
Height of Outfield Wall: 11 ft. 6 in.

Wrigley Field is the only park in the major leagues not to have field lights. This lone bastion of daytime baseball also boasts of vine covered outfield walls and basket-type screens on top of the walls to prevent fan interference. Despite, or perhaps because of these oddities, Wrigley Field remains a baseball fan's delight.

The infield grass is thick and lush, while the dirt portion of the infield remains rough and uneven. This strange combination of infield qualities allows infielders to play very shallow defensively. The grass slows grounders down considerably, and every time the ball bounces on the dirt, the infielders risk a bad hop.

The outfield presents its own range of peculiar features. To begin with, the angle of the sun makes Wrigley's right field one of the toughest outfield positions to play in the National League. The vine covered walls offer added leverage to outfielders reaching for high line drives, but the vines are also capable of camouflaging a ball while an opposing baserunner streaks for an extra base. The wind in Chicago is notorious, and infield flies can become home runs as easily as potential homers can be blown back into play. The foul lines run next to padded concrete walls and this deters outfielders from charging too hard after foul balls. The bullpens, with their raised mounds, are also on the field of play, and the unexpected shift in terrain has caused more than one ballplayer to stumble head first into the direction of the walls.

The mound is rated excellent by pitchers and everyone loves to hit in Wrigley. The dirt in the batter's box feels good in the player's hands and has a consistency perfect for allowing a hitter to dig a good toe-hold. Hitters also enjoy the wire mesh overhang around the outfield because it gives them a better shot at hitting a home run.

Dugouts which are very close to the field of play, glare from the sun, crazy winds, vine covered walls, and no field lights are all part of the charm of this quirky ballpark. Nevertheless, Dallas Green, the new president of the Cubs, believes that he has to draw more fans if the Cubs are to become financially able to compete with the other teams in the signing of the better free agents. One way to increase attendance would be to install lights and play baseball at night. Most baseball people agree that Green is right, but all who consider themselves traditionalists will surely lament the modernization of baseball's most unique park.

HITTING:

Bowa is closing in on 2,000 hits but has lost at least a step. At age 37, the hits won't come easy. Still, he has an uncanny way of getting on base. Call it moxie.

Moving from the Phillies after 12 years and transferring from artificial turf to grass left him struggling to get above .200 until late in the season. It was an unusual season another way. He hit better righthanded (.293 to .232). As a righty, he's a highball hitter with more pop. As a lefty, he'll pepper the hole on the right side of the diamond.

When lefthanded pitchers throw him up and away, he's in trouble. He drags the bat head which usually results in a hanging fly ball to left. Righthanded pitchers are advised to keep the ball down and away. He'll pull inside mistakes, especially fastballs.

Offense is his redeeming feature, with fastballs and change-ups being his strength. Last season with the Cubs, he was equally successful from both sides of the plate (.274 lefthanded, .264 right), but managers fear him most from left where he likes to pull. He homered on the second pitch of the season off righthander Mario Soto.

BASERUNNING:

Running has slipped as his speed has slowed, but he is good in certain situations and batterymen still respect him for his smarts. With a hound dog's nose for the plate, he's as good as there is at coming around from second base. He's adept at the hook slide. Has lost much however, from his prime years.

FIELDING:

An excellent shortstop for years, Bowa has lost "a couple of yards" according to a scout. He doesn't make the big play as often, and can't go into the hole as before, but he remains valuable afield for his positioning and leadership, which are considered exemplary. Once he got used to Wrigley Field grass and Cub pitchers, his overall defense improved.

LARRY BOWA
INF, No. 1
SR, 5'10", 155 lbs.
ML Svc: 13 years
Born: 12-8-45 in
Sacramento, CA

1982 STATISTICS

AVG	G	AB	R	H	2B	3B	HR	RBI	BB	SO	SB
.246	142	499	50	123	15	7	0	29	39	38	8

CAREER STATISTICS

AVG	G	AB	R	H	2B	3B	HR	RBI	BB	SO	SB
.263	1881	7314	866	1921	219	88	13	458	396	493	296

VS. RHP

VS. LHP

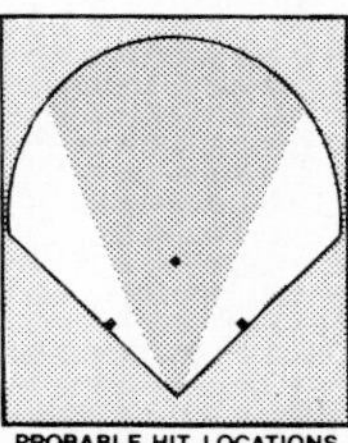
PROBABLE HIT LOCATIONS

OVERALL:

Coleman: "Not too much left. He's playing on instincts and experience. But he still can give you the big game when it counts. He'll do anything to win."

McCarver: "He blew through his potential by far surpassing what people thought he could do. He twice was cut by his high school team. He has an irascible, fiery spirit that is both his friend and enemy. Has shown people time and again not to underestimate him."

BILL BUCKNER
INF, No. 22
LL, 6'1", 185 lbs.
ML Svc: 12 years
Born: 12-14-49 in Vallejo, CA

1982 STATISTICS

AVG	G	AB	R	H	2B	3B	HR	RBI	BB	SO	SB
.306	161	657	93	201	34	5	15	105	36	26	15

CAREER STATISTICS

AVG	G	AB	R	H	2B	3B	HR	RBI	BB	SO	SB
.297	1573	6014	713	1789	318	33	103	725	282	265	137

VS. RHP

VS. LHP

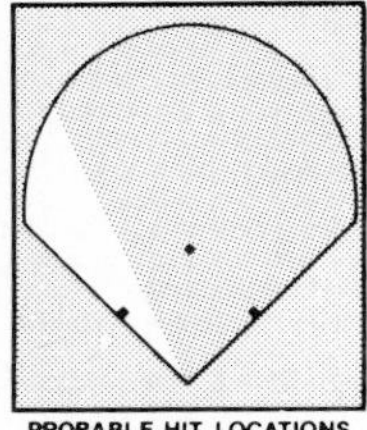
PROBABLE HIT LOCATIONS

HITTING:

There simply is no book on how to pitch this man. He'll even chase--and hit--waste pitches. If he has a fault, it's overanxiousness. He can't stand to walk any more than strike out. Thus he'll hit lazy flys on bad outside pitches and slow bounders inside.

With excellent bat control, Buckner uses every inch of the field although he hits lefthanders more straightaway. He may be baseball's best lefthanded hitter against southpaws. Against righties, no part of the field can be left unguarded. He pulls inside pitches so sharply the first baseman has little time to react. By all means do not pitch him down. Inside, maybe. Down, never. He has great command of the low pitch. The best bet is to jam him on the fists, but that too is just a gamble. Mixing speeds and locations are other possibilities.

Until the last few years, Buckner's RBI totals have not been high, mainly because few runners were on base. But he is the National League leader over the last 2 seasons, while hitting just 23 home runs.

He can hit-and-run, drag bunt, and pull when necessary. Loves to hit his old team, the Dodgers.

BASERUNNING:

A severely broken ankle eight years ago has limited his running but not stopped him. By lulling a pitcher into a false sense of security, Buckner is a master at the unexpected steal, and he'll take an extra base whenever he senses an opportunity. But he's not without faults. His exuberance sometimes leads to overaggressive outs.

FIELDING:

A practitioner of deceit, Buckner is exemplary at the quick foot. He's sometimes halfway to the dugout before the umpire completes the call. He also is strong on scooping the short-hop throw. His ankle limits his effectiveness on the bunt, but he has better-than-average range and a good, fairly accurate arm. His glove sometimes deceives him for its floppiness.

OVERALL:

Kiner: "Outstanding offensively, he had his greatest year. He's tough to strike out and will consistently get the big hit."

McCarver: "He is one quality player . . . a player you can't allow to beat you."

Coleman: "Quick to anger and hard to handle, he knows how to play and what to do."

BILL CAMPBELL
RHP, No. 39
RR, 6'3", 190 lbs.
ML Svc: 9 years
Born: 8-9-48 in
Highland Park, MI

PITCHING:

It took this excellently conditioned free agent from the Red Sox half a season to adjust to a new league, but once Bill Campbell did that and ironed out a mechanical flaw in his delivery, he closed 1982 as a major spoke in a strong Cub bullpen with a 1.79 ERA in his last 45 innings.

Because Campbell was effective in a couple of long stints, the Cubs may convert him to a starter. He is in good shape at age 34, and could make the adjustment. His last start was in 1975 with Minnesota.

With a fastball at 87 MPH he appears recovered from previous shoulder problems. He has other pitches, including a faithful screwball that is just as effective against lefthanded hitters. He can break it into the dirt when it is going good. His slider breaks more than his curve.

Twisting the ball behind his back before throwing, he has a herky-jerky delivery. Hitters must discipline themselves not to swing at his motion. He has the most trouble with teams that don't swing at balls off the plate.

Campbell is just what you would want in a short man, he is unawed by tight situations.

FIELDING, HITTING, BASERUNNING:

Campbell is by far the best fielding pitcher on the Cubs. He is quick off the mound, throws accurately to bases and holds runners well. Claiming to be a good hitter from his minor league days, he was proud of a single in seven tries in the National League. His baserunning ability is average for a pitcher.

OVERALL:

Coleman: "He still has outstanding skills when he's having his good days. He's a fine competitor."

Kiner: "He was the best at short relief until arm trouble. In my opinion, he can be used more often in tough situations. He's not as devastating as he once was, but is improving."

McCarver: "He appears to be very antsy on the mound, but is in complete command. He's pitching in a tough ballpark. He was used too much with the Twins (over 167 innings by a reliever is an AL record). Good fork ball (screwball)."

1982 STATISTICS

W	L	ERA	G	GS	CG	IP	H	R	ER	BB	SO	SV
3	6	3.69	62	0	0	100	89	44	41	40	71	8

CAREER STATISTICS

W	L	ERA	G	GS	CG	IP	H	R	ER	BB	SO	SV
63	46	3.42	470	9	2	877	829	371	333	365	633	110

JODY DAVIS
C, No. 7
RR, 6'4", 200 lbs.
ML Svc: 2 years
Born: 11-12-56 in
Gainesville, GA

1982 STATISTICS

AVG	G	AB	R	H	2B	3B	HR	RBI	BB	SO	SB
.261	130	418	41	109	20	2	12	52	36	92	0

CAREER STATISTICS

AVG	G	AB	R	H	2B	3B	HR	RBI	BB	SO	SB
.259	186	598	55	155	25	3	16	73	57	120	0

VS. RHP

VS. LHP

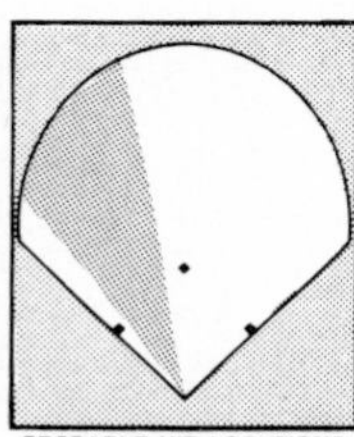
PROBABLE HIT LOCATIONS

HITTING:

The best way to pitch Jody Davis is down . . . down . . . down. There is nothing he likes better than high fastballs over the plate so he can get full extension. When he learns to hit other pitches in other locations, the Cubs feel he will hit with the best catchers in the game. With his size and more experience he should hit 20 home runs, especially in Wrigley Field. He had 12 last season.

He is a very predictable hitter who can be pitched by the book--fastballs to set up change-ups and breaking balls. He does not handle the change or curve and is just average against the slider. However, beware of mistakes, especially by lefthanded pitchers.

Davis has a unique swing. His stance is closed and upright as he stands deep in the box, but he opens up with his hips. This allows him to pull occasionally, but mostly he's an alley hitter, also conducive to Wrigley.

Like many big men, he strikes out a lot (92 in 1982). This partly is due to his inability to hit down-and-in pitches.

Although not called upon to bunt often, he's surprisingly good at it and will do so on his own for hits. The Cubs expect improvement with men on base. The best things that can be said now are that he's a battler and consistent.

BASERUNNING:

Davis is slow. He needs improvement in every category, including breaking up the double play. With his size, he should be able to intimidate. He's mostly a hook slider. He's not a dumb runner, just conservative.

FIELDING:

This is Davis' strong suit, and the Cubs are helping his development by letting him call the pitches. He is above average with his arm and mechanics. His arm is strong, accurate. Early in 1982 he needed mental reminders. From then on, he was fine. Few runners tested him or took big leads.

OVERALL:

McCarver: "The Cubs got him in the winter draft of 1979 and he was a steal. He is an excellent catcher with a deadly throwing arm. He can only get better."

Coleman: "He could develop into one of the National League's better catchers. He does everything pretty well, and has some power when he connects."

LEON DURHAM
OF, No. 10
LL, 6'2", 215 lbs.
ML Svc: 3 years
Born: 7-31-57 in
Cincinnati, OH

1982 STATISTICS

AVG	G	AB	R	H	2B	3B	HR	RBI	BB	SO	SB
.312	148	539	84	168	33	7	22	90	66	77	28

CAREER STATISTICS

AVG	G	AB	R	H	2B	3B	HR	RBI	BB	SO	SB
.295	331	1170	168	345	62	17	40	167	111	185	60

VS. RHP

VS. LHP

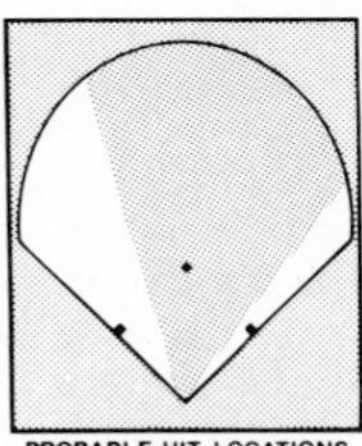
PROBABLE HIT LOCATIONS

HITTING:

A line drive hitter, Leon Durham handles low balls expertly and is almost as effective when they're at the belt. He finds the high pitch difficult. Lefthanders can get him out on curveballs, particularly when they are tight inside. He hits outside lefty pitchers with authority to left field, so shade him. Righthanders are advised to fastball him inside to tie him up. He has excellent power against them.

Durham is still growing. His pull power is yet to come. By using most of the field, he drives managers crazy. They don't know where to position their people. The only area that needs improvement is the hit-and-run. The Cubs don't ask him to bunt, but he'll do it for respect. He has the good eye and patience to some year draw 100 walks.

Durham waits well on the change-up and can hit the righthander's curve. Sliders and sinkers are no problem. He's always consistent, unusual for a young batter.

Ahead of most players offensively, even veterans, Durham is the first Cub with Triple Crown potential since Billy Williams. He is getting close to Williams' sweet swing. He has many plusses, but must avoid injuries. He's finely muscled.

BASERUNNING:

Again, Durham is advanced. He is rated above average to excellent on the bases, getting a great jump for a big man. He needs work, though, on his first step in stealing. He takes the pivot man out and is smart as well as aggressive. He'll even take a base sliding head first on occasion.

FIELDING:

A team man, Durham has had to play out of position in the majors. He's a first baseman by trade, but is serving an apprenticeship in the outfield. He's more effective in right, where he has learned to play Wrigley Field's sun. In center, he's adequate. His speed helps. There is a belief he plays too deep, thus limiting his range. His arm strength is best when he charges the ball.

OVERALL:

Kiner: "One of the promising stars of the game who has all the good points--run, hit, field and hit with power. He's not yet a great home run hitter, but should get much better as he learns to pull."

McCarver: "Great power the other way. He plays the game very hard and could lead the league in hitting some year, but plays entirely too deep in center. Better in right field until he can get to first."

WILLIE HERNANDEZ
LHP, No. 38
LL, 6'2", 180 lbs.
ML Svc: 5 years
Born: 11-14-55 in Aguada, PR

PITCHING:

Convinced that his career was temporarily derailed by former Manager and General Manager Herman Franks, Hernandez rebounded from 1-9 in 1980 and banishment to Iowa in 1981 to lead the Cubs in appearances with 75. He had a 1.70 ERA in the last two months and a string of 16 scoreless innings in late May-early June. Thus he hopes that he has dispelled forever the notion that he has lasted almost six years because he is lefthanded. He appreciates new Manager Lee Elia for keeping the faith.

He is perfectly suited to short relief. Teams adjust to him the second time around the order and so he seldom pitches beyond two innings. He throws deceptively hard. Lefthanded batters are hard put to handle him when he sidearms them. When he's on, he can move the fastball in and out. When he gets the curve over, it's effective. He shows the slider mainly to lefthanders. Hernandez is developing a screwball change.

Sometimes his Latin temperament gets in his way. He can't handle teams with righthanded power like Montreal, but is strong against the lefties in Pittsburgh. He is one of few pitchers around who thrives in Wrigley Field.

FIELDING, HITTING, BASERUNNING:

If he's not hurried, he'll make the play. He can handle bunts, could be better at holding runners. Hernandez is seldom in a game long enough to bat for himself, but thinks he could hit .200. He probably could. He's average on the bases.

OVERALL:

McCarver: "Willie has the standard equipment of fastball, slider, curve and now is benefiting by throwing a poor-man's scroogie. He just tries to turn it over. He jerks the ball on delivery. He should be given credit for fighting his way back to the major leagues."

Kiner: "He reached his highest performance level this year. He was used wisely by his manager."

Coleman: "Had some good years in the past, may have found himself in 1982. Has the potential to be a good pitcher if he continues to work at it."

1982 STATISTICS

W	L	ERA	G	GS	CG	IP	H	R	ER	BB	SO	SV
4	6	3.00	75	0	0	75	74	26	25	24	54	10

CAREER STATISTICS

W	L	ERA	G	GS	CG	IP	H	R	ER	BB	SO	SV
25	28	3.83	312	10	0	446	439	209	190	179	311	17

FERGIE JENKINS
RHP, No. 31
RR, 6'5", 210 lbs.
ML Svc: 17 years
Born: 12-13-43 in Chatham, ONT

PITCHING:

Fergie Jenkins has had a remarkable career. For mostly second division teams, he has won 59 more games than he has lost. With a two year contract that will carry him to age 40, he is certain to surpass 300 victories. What makes him so special, especially after being put on the back burner by Texas? Superb control with an exemplary slider.

Like fine wine, Jenkins is smooth, but without the mellowing of age. He has yielded a few miles on his fastball, but he cuts it to give the impression of a slider. He has a forkball that acts as a change. His curve is above average, too. He uses it primarily against lefthanded hitters. In other words, he has made a graceful transition from power pitcher to control artist.

Jenkins is toughest against an all righthanded team like the Dodgers. He consistently throws his breaking pitches down and away. He has to avoid hanging them against lefthanded batters.

FIELDING, HITTING, BASERUNNING:

Jenkins still moves well off the mound, but oh, that pick-off move. It can cost him. He makes a quick-step flip that, if he's not careful, will flair past first base and down the line. His motion is so easy that runners have an easy time getting a good jump.

Jenkins' greatest offensive thrill came in 1965 when he homered to win his debut with the Cubs. He has hit 12 since, but none lately. His power now is occasional, but he remains a threat. As an all around athlete, he can move around the bases, but not particularly fast.

OVERALL:

McCarver: "Fergie changes speeds with his pitches the way Picasso painted--innovatively. He stays away from all batters, but will come in when backed into a corner. He refuses to give in. He is, in short, poetry in motion."

Kiner: "I give him an excellent rating. He gives in to no batter. It makes no difference whom he's facing. He's one of the best in the baseball world."

Coleman: "One of the great righthanded pitchers in last 20 years. He can still beat you. May have a year or two left."

1982 STATISTICS

W	L	ERA	G	GS	CG	IP	H	R	ER	BB	SO	SV
14	15	3.15	34	34	4	217	221	92	76	68	134	0

CAREER STATISTICS

W	L	ERA	G	GS	CG	IP	H	R	ER	BB	SO	SV
278	217	3.30	631	565	266	4331	3966	1765	1589	951	3096	7

JAY JOHNSTONE
OF, No. 21
LR, 6'1", 190 lbs.
ML Svc: 17 years
Born: 11-20-45 in
Manchester, CT

1982 STATISTICS

AVG	G	AB	R	H	2B	3B	HR	RBI	BB	SO	SB
.241	119	282	40	68	14	1	10	45	45	43	0

CAREER STATISTICS

AVG	G	AB	R	H	2B	3B	HR	RBI	BB	SO	SB
.267	1593	4475	544	1195	205	36	96	504	401	588	49

VS. RHP

VS. LHP

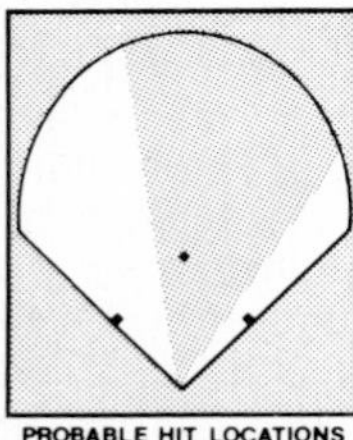

PROBABLE HIT LOCATIONS

HITTING:

Jay Johnstone is a guess hitter. He is a dead fastball batter who is greatly respected when he's on a hot streak. Rusty from four years of pinch-hitting and platooning, Johnstone had 10 home runs and 7 game-winning RBIs in less than a full year with the Cubs.

Meticulous at the plate, he likes to get ahead of pitchers, then sit on their fastball. He should be thrown strikes at the start, then teased with breaking balls. As patient as he is on most pitches, Johnstone does not wait well on the change-up, sometimes throwing his bat at it. He's strong against the slider.

Advice to pitchers: bring the ball up once in a while.

Johnstone will use all fields, but likes to pull righthanders. That's when he's best. He's strong in the clutch, making him valuable coming off the bench. He can hit behind runners but just average on the bunt.

No one works harder at hitting than this man. Manager Lee Elia once saw him hit a bucket of balls blindfolded. If he's in a slump, he'll come out early for live practice or stay late to hit off a tee. This desire has kept him in the game since 1963.

BASERUNNNING:

He's getting up in age now, and sometimes won't run grounders out full steam. But fielders should not doze off. He's fairly smart on the paths and will move up a base when he sees an opening. Otherwise, he's no threat.

FIELDING:

Johnstone is so deep into offense than you can almost hear his mind when he's on defense. As a result, he's not the most polished outfielder. But he "cheats" a good game, and once in a while will pop a good throw. He's best at coming in for shallow flies and singles, which helps him set up for throws. He surprised everyone but himself by playing Wrigley Field's wall as if he had built it. He's not a great fielder in left or right, but not bad.

OVERALL:

McCarver: "Jay will go to his grave with the ability to hit a fastball. He has worked very hard to become a good hitter. He should, and could, be a better defensive player.

Kiner: "As a pinch-hitter, he's very good. He has another asset, that of court jester. He keeps his team loose."

Coleman: "A good pro hitter who is best against righthanded pitching. One of baseball's great 'flakes.' "

KEN KRAVEC
LHP, No. 37
LL, 6'0", 180 lbs.
ML Svc: 6 years
Born: 7-29-51 in Cleveland, OH

PITCHING:

After hanging around the American League strikeout leaders, the White Sox, Kravec may have lost his fastball and sharp breaking pitches in his transfer to the National League. His curveball is flat, and all that he has left is a slider. He goes about things in reverse, setting up the fastball with the breaking ball. He appears to have a good running fastball to lefthanded hitters, but doesn't use it often enough.

His greatest asset is his experience. If he is not fine with his pitches, he is in trouble. He has a herky-jerky, over-the-top delivery. Outrighted last season to the minor leagues, Kravec may be on the last legs of a career.

FIELDING, HITTING, BASERUNNING:

An average fielder, he is not particularly adept at throwing to first. Idle with the bat in the American League, he's 0-for-8 in the National League as a hitter.

OVERALL:

McCarver: "With mostly breaking balls, he is a typical American League pitcher. He throws them any time, regardless of the count. If he threw his fastball more often, he would probably have better success."

Kiner: "After doing well with the White Sox, he is now at the crossroads of his career. He will be lucky to stay in the majors unless his fastball improves."

Coleman: "He can fill in anywhere, but is no better than the eighth or ninth man on a staff."

1982 STATISTICS

W	L	ERA	G	CS	CG	IP	H	R	ER	BB	SO	SV
1	1	6.12	13	2	0	25	27	20	17	18	20	0

CAREER STATISTICS

W	L	ERA	G	GS	CG	IP	H	R	ER	BB	SO	SV
43	56	4.49	160	128	54	859	814	476	426	404	557	1

RANDY MARTZ
RHP, No. 34
RR, 6'4", 210 lbs.
ML Svc: 2 years
Born: 5-28-56 in
Harrisburg, PA

PITCHING:

The jury is still out on the role of this country boy who grew up throwing baseballs against a corncrib. Is he a starter? Reliever? Randy Martz is young and big but seldom goes beyond six innings, before he runs out of gas.

He is a double play type pitcher. When the fastball is working, it sinks, making it nasty to hit. A herky-jerky delivery helps. He's still working on establishing a second pitch; his slider is inconsistent, and he doesn't have a curve. Coach Bill Connors is trying to teach him one. On occasion, Martz has a palmball, or slip pitch, that acts as a change. One day he has it--the next day, he doesn't.

Although Martz does not throw many pitches, he falls behind too often and has to come across. When that happens, hitters can sit on whatever he throws. He generally has control and will back hitters away. He also is well poised and not afraid of the hitter.

The Cubs want to establish his future soon. He had success as a reliever the second half of 1981's split season.

FIELDING, HITTING, BASERUNNING:

Hit the ball up the middle and Martz can't handle it. He's cumbersome. He's one of the many Cub pitchers who has trouble afield. As a hitter, he has a good eye, leading the team in walks. But he's like most pitchers when he swings--mostly air. There is room for improvement if he'll work at it. As a runner, he's slow. Strictly one base at a time.

OVERALL:

Coleman: "He has a chance to become a good pitcher. He throws a heavy ball and has a good idea, but needs to develop his skills."

McCarver: "Plagued with wildness, Randy doesn't stay ahead of hitters often enough. His fastball can create problems for righthanded hitters because it jumps at them. With more experience, he could be a good one."

Kiner: "A .500 pitcher if given enough starts. He would be a fifth man on most staffs. His breaking ball needs control to be effective. He has a good idea about his job."

1982 STATISTICS

W	L	ERA	G	GS	CG	IP	H	R	ER	BB	SO	SV
11	10	4.21	28	24	1	147	157	80	69	36	40	1

CAREER STATISTICS

W	L	ERA	G	GS	CG	IP	H	R	ER	BB	SO	SV
17	19	3.79	67	44	2	285	288	143	120	96	97	7

JERRY MORALES
OF, No. 24
RR, 5'10", 175 lbs.
ML Svc: 11 years
Born: 2-18-49 in Yabuccoa, PR

1982 STATISTICS

AVG	G	AB	R	H	2B	3B	HR	RBI	BB	SO	SB
.284	65	116	14	33	2	2	4	30	9	7	1

CAREER STATISTICS

AVG	G	AB	R	H	2B	3B	HR	RBI	BB	SO	SB
.260	1378	4441	505	1156	190	36	95	559	389	604	37

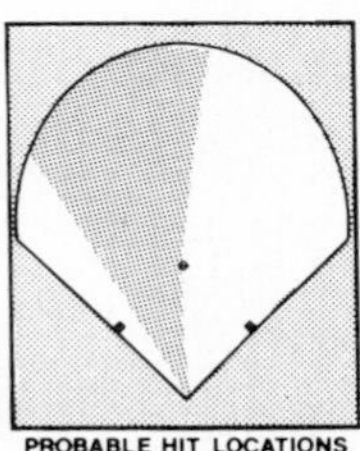

HITTING:

Jerry Morales's stance is recognizable from great distances: up, up and away. Standing almost on his tip-toes, he holds his bat head-high, his wrists at eye level. Give him a pitch around the letters or shoulders and he'll drive it to the wall or over it. Give him one down and he'll fight it. Give him a change and he'll lunge at it. But stay away from the high fastball, especially on the first pitch. He's a gap hitter, either field, but will try to pull lefthanders. They are wise to jam him.

He is to be pitched breaking balls down and change-ups. The slider is not for him. Show the fastball only as a surprise.

Morales is not the hitter he was in the mid-1970s when he drove in 173 runs in two seasons. He had three unhappy years elsewhere, then came back to "my city" (as he calls Chicago), and hit .286 and .284 as a platoon player (sixth or seventh in the lineup are good spots) and pinch-hitter. He's comfortable at these roles, and happy again at the plate.

At one time a tough out, Morales is like a Pac Man player with men in scoring position--his eyes light up as he goes for the kill. Time has taken its toll, but he's still to be feared.

BASERUNNING:

Morales is not going to get any faster, but he gets by from experience. He's one of those don't-underestimate-him kind who will take the extra base when he sees it. Otherwise, he's not a steal threat and is conservative going around.

FIELDING:

Need a reserve who can play all three spots? Morales is your man, even in center field. Somehow, he gets to the ball, often slowing up to make the catch after a long run. Despite his short stature, he gets away with playing deep. His arm isn't as strong as it used to be, and the accuracy is just average.

OVERALL:

Coleman: "Does everything fairly well, but nothing outstanding. He had some great years with Chicago because of the small park and its poor teams."

McCarver: "Jerry has had a good major league career, but it seems he went to a fourth or fifth outfielder before his time."

Kiner: "At his stage of career, he's a fill-in outfielder with good defensive ability and able to pinch-hit against lefthand pitching."

KEITH MORELAND
C/OF No. 6
RR, 6'0", 200 lbs.
ML Svc: 4 years
Born: 5-2-54 in
Dallas, TX

1982 STATISTICS

AVG	G	AB	R	H	2B	3B	HR	RBI	BB	SO	SB
.261	138	476	50	124	17	2	15	68	46	71	0

CAREER STATISTICS

AVG	G	AB	R	H	2B	3B	HR	RBI	BB	SO	SB
.275	276	881	82	242	35	4	25	142	72	103	4

VS. RHP

VS. LHP

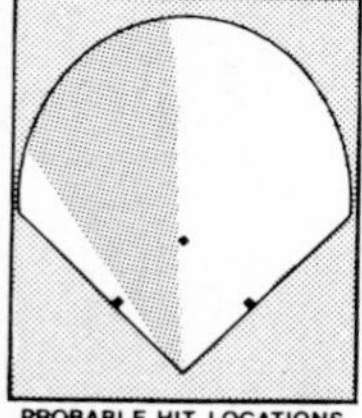
PROBABLE HIT LOCATIONS

HITTING:

Life was wonderful for Keith Moreland the first time around with his new team, the Cubs. But the second time around was miserable. By pitching away and then jamming him, opponents minimized his power while dropping 50 points off his average.

An intense hitter, Moreland put so much pressure on himself that he had to be platooned.

It doesn't matter if the pitch is up or down, Moreland can usually hit it, particularly up and over the plate for full arm extension. Opinions vary whether he should be pitched in or out. Best bet is to mix it up.

He has good power to left and left-center, but has been known to drive the right-center gap. He hits practically everything hard and is better known to drive the lefthanders, although he held up well against righties last season.

Don't signal the bunt or hit-and-run. He can hit behind runners, but prefers to swing away. Moreland is too impatient for walks.

He has trouble with breaking balls, particularly curves that either back him off the plate or sweep away. He's murder on the fastball and will hit sinkers with authority. A great spring hitter and occasionally streaky, Moreland needs consistency to have a big power season expected of him. If he's ever going to hit, now is the time.

BASERUNNING:

Slow afoot, Moreland makes up for it in hustle. An ex-football player (roverback at Texas), he enjoys breaking up the double play. Not a bad situation runner, he's considered conservative and needs improvement on technique.

FIELDING:

He's neither a good catcher nor outfielder. Determined that he was a catcher, the Cubs took spring training and a month into the season to find out that he wasn't either one. Everything he did was average or worse. Runners got good jumps and went into second standing up. At best, his arm is mediocre. His arm is better suited for the outfield, but is erratic. He has no range. Failure to practice in left field when he wasn't in the lineup further disappointed the Cubs.

OVERALL:

Coleman: "He's a fine, young hitter with excellent attitude, but should be in the American League as a designated hitter. He does not have a position. He's a good man on a team, but must play to find out if he can hit."

Kiner: "He has defensive inabilities, but has to be used somewhere in the lineup to take advantage of his bat."

DICKIE NOLES
RHP, No. 48
RR, 6'2", 190 lbs.
ML Svc: 3 years
Born: 11-19-56 in Charlotte, NC

PITCHING:

He has a reputation as a head hunter, one of the best--or depending upon the viewpoint, worst. To Noles, though, it's just intimidation. You against me. Let's have a go at it.

When Noles is going good, especially with his 90 MPH fastball, he jumps right at the hitter. He uses it to get ahead. When that happens, he turns to the curve and slider. They are effective when his control is on. But that's his problem--control. Some days he has it--some days he doesn't. When he doesn't, hitters either wait for the forced strike or wait him out. Having worked on different ways to throw the change, Noles is now working on the three-fingered style that worked for Mario Soto. Until then, his strengths are the fastfall and brushback.

Starting is his niche. He has to pitch in rotation to be effective; he's too wild for a reliever.

FIELDING, HITTING, BASERUNNING:

Noles has a nice, quick move to first base, though sometimes too quick. He has balked with it. He handles bunts adequately, but overall is not a particularly good fielder. As a hitter, he takes a big cut, both feet sometimes leaving the ground. But that's all it is--a big cut. He struck out 35 times in 56 tries with one walk. Unaccustomed as he is to being on base, he is not a good runner.

OVERALL:

Kiner: "A pitcher with a good arm and aggressive style, he had his best year with a chance to pitch."

Coleman: "A young man with a good arm, he has not learned how to pitch or how to control his emotions. To be a good pitcher, he must first win the war with himself."

McCarver: "Dickie is very excitable. He works extremely fast and seems to pitch without a lot of thought at times. If he can take charge of his emotions while maintaining his fire and spirit, he can be a big winner. You love a pitcher who really wants the ball. He does."

1982 STATISTICS

W	L	ERA	G	GS	CG	IP	H	R	ER	BB	SO	SV
10	13	4.42	31	30	2	171	180	99	84	61	85	0

CAREER STATISTICS

W	L	ERA	G	GS	CG	IP	H	R	ER	BB	SO	SV
16	23	4.14	106	55	2	400	397	211	184	164	218	6

HITTING:

A big strong righthanded hitter, he takes a squared upright stance in the middle of the box. Nordhagen is a high ball hitter, who likes the ball on the inside half of the plate, and tries to pull everything to left. He likes to dig-in in the batter's box and some pitchers are beginning to try to run him off the plate with more than his share of inside hard stuff. Most other pitchers try to keep the ball away from Wayne and work the ball on the outside corners.

When opposing pitchers oblige him, Wayne has the power to reach the alleys and in both left and right-center and is strong enough to hit the ball out of the park. Unfortunately, he still seems to be mystified by good major league curves and off-speed pitches.

His .288 lifetime average and power stats appealed to the Jays who were desperate to get the lefthanded pitchers off their backs. But Nordhagen was injured much of the past season, first with a lower back problem, then with a leg injury. He failed to hit with the power expected and had only one home run. He hit well against his former team, Chicago, and also against Baltimore and California, especially in the first half of the season. He had little success against Boston, Cleveland, and Milwaukee.

BASERUNNING:

Nordhagen does not run well. His big swing makes him slow getting out of the box and he doesn't really have the speed to accelerate down the line. He is no threat to steal and can clog the bases when there are runners behind him. Wayne is most often removed for a pinch-runner when he is in scoring position.

FIELDING:

Wayne has a gun for an arm and is rated above average in terms of accuracy as well as strength. Unfortunately, he is slow getting to the ball and has limited range as a defensive outfielder. Nordhagen's chief value is as an offensive player and his future seems most secure as a DH or pinch-hitter.

WAYNE NORDHAGEN
OF, No. 30
RR, 6'2", 195 lbs.
ML Svc: 7 years
Born: 7-4-48 in
Thief River Falls, MN

1982 STATISTICS

AVG	G	AB	R	H	2B	3B	HR	RBI	BB	SO	SB
.270	72	185	12	50	6	0	1	20	10	22	0

CAREER STATISTICS

AVG	G	AB	R	H	2B	3B	HR	RBI	BB	SO	SB
.285	480	1384	146	394	76	8	38	199	54	156	2

VS. RHP

VS. LHP

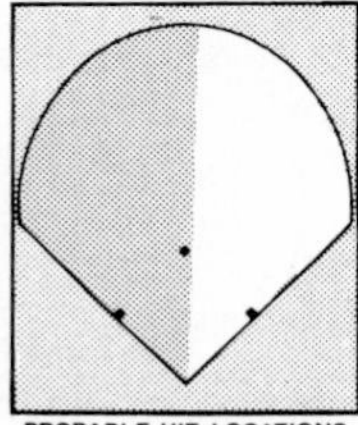
PROBABLE HIT LOCATIONS

OVERALL:

Robinson: "If he can stay healthy, Wayne might prove to be the effective righthanded DH that Toronto so desperately needs.

"Martin: "The Jays have tried Wayne in the outfield, at first, third, and even catching. He has a pretty good bat and might fill the bill as a DH."

Harwell: "Nordhagen has the power to handle big league fastballs and could do the job as a pinch-hitter or DH."

CHUCK RAINEY
RHP, No. 42
RR, 5'11", 195 lbs.
ML Svc: 3 years
Born: 7-14-54 in San Diego, CA

PITCHING:

1982 was supposed to be the year Chuck Rainey finally came into his own as a major league pitcher. Unfortunately, 1982 turned into another frustrating and disappointing year. His 7-5 record with the Boxton Red Sox included three excellent complete game shutouts, but his 5.02 ERA is really a better indication of the year he had.

Rainey lacks an outstanding fastball. This means that he has to be extremely careful with his control. He also throws a fairly good slider and an average curve. Righthanders have a lot of trouble with his slider when he can control it, but Rainey often has more trouble locating his pitches than hitters have hitting them. When he falls behind in the count, he usually throws his fastball, but at 83-85 MPH, he seldom throws it by anyone. When it sinks, it's an effective pitch; but when it doesn't drop, it can be hit and hit hard.

Chuck is unflappable on the mound and often gives the impression that he's not giving 100%. This is unfortunate because it's totally untrue. Rainey is a tough competitor. During his career he's had excellent success against Toronto and Kansas City but the Angels always manage to hit very well against him. It remains to be seen how he will fare in the National League.

FIELDING:

Rainey has a quick move to first and he keeps rival baserunners honest. His ability to field bunts and to cover his position defensively is rated average.

OVERALL:

Rainey has had problems with arm injuries. He has no single overpowering pitch but he knows where to place the ball. A year without arm problems, improved control, and increased self-confidence could help make 1983 the season Rainey finally puts it all together.

Martin: "Chuck has a placid, no windup delivery and an effective slider. He's unflappable and can throw shutouts when he has his control."

Robinson: "If he can stay healthy, this is the time he should begin to improve as a pitcher."

Harwell: "Rainey has to be extra-fine with his control to be effective."

1982 STATISTICS

W	L	ERA	G	GS	CG	IP	H	R	ER	BB	SO	SV
7	5	5.02	27	25	3	129	146	75	72	63	57	0

CAREER STATISTICS

W	L	ERA	G	GS	CG	IP	H	R	ER	BB	SO	SV
23	14	4.38	74	56	9	360	374	192	175	158	161	1

ALAN RIPLEY
RHP, No. 33
RR, 6'3", 200 lbs.
ML Svc: 4 years
Born: 10-10-52 in Norwood, MA

PITCHING:

Discovered by the Red Sox as a semi-pro player, Allen Ripley was given a big break by the Cubs, but had some bad breaks in 1982. He broke a finger, then hurt his throwing shoulder and reinjured it. Because his innings fell short of expectations, he was outrighted to Iowa so that the Cubs could protect extra players. He has had enough bright moments as a starter, however, even after a horrendous beginning in relief, to indicate that he is heading in the right direction.

Ripley has good breaking pitches that he can get over when he is behind in the count, and is confident of his change-up, especially to righthanders. He needs more confidence in his fastball. Ripley is also tough on righthanded teams, and has tied Mike Schmidt up in knots--believe it or not.

FIELDING, HITTING, BASERUNNING:

Average defensively, Ripley hangs in as a hitter. With an unorthodox swing, he takes his cuts and occasionally drives the ball. He is not a bunter, and is average on the basepaths.

OVERALL:

McCarver: "Allen uses his breaking ball like most use their fastball. He can make righthanded hitters look foolish when he drops down and throws his curveball."

Kiner: "At this point in his career, he needs a faster fastball to become a true starting pitcher."

Coleman: "He knows how to pitch and tries hard, but has a small amount of ability."

1982 STATISTICS

W	L	ERA	G	GS	CG	IP	H	R	ER	BB	SO	SV
5	7	4.26	28	19	0	122	130	61	58	38	57	0

CAREER STATISTICS

W	L	ERA	G	GS	CG	IP	H	R	ER	BB	SO	SV
23	27	4.52	101	67	4	464	521	256	233	148	229	1

RYNE SANDBERG
INF, No. 23
RR, 6'1", 175 lbs.
ML Svc: 1 year plus
Born: 9-18-59 in
Spokane, WA

1982 STATISTICS

AVG	G	AB	R	H	2B	3B	HR	RBI	BB	SO	SB
.271	156	635	103	172	33	5	7	54	36	90	32

CAREER STATISTICS

AVG	G	AB	R	H	2B	3B	HR	RBI	BB	SO	SB
.270	169	641	105	173	33	5	7	54	36	91	32

VS. RHP

VS. LHP

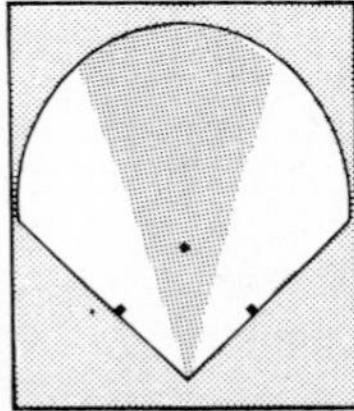
PROBABLE HIT LOCATIONS

HITTING:

Sandberg has only just begun. Barring injury, he will play for the next ten years, thanks to his ability to reach base and the expected power he'll provide as he matures. For now, he's mostly a high fastball hitter, both feet leaving the ground when the pitch is in his eyes. He lacks strength for a fairly big man, but compensates by using the middle of the field to drive into the slots. Strength will come as he gains experience.

Pitch Sandberg down with curves (he's getting better) and change-ups (he lunges after them). He stays with sliders fairly well and will get better. He is overmatched against good pitchers like Steve Carlton, but handles most of the others. For a young player, Sandberg is exceptional at hitting behind the runner. He also is strong with men in scoring position. However, he needs to work on bunting and pitch selection. He only walked 36 times, not enough for a man at the top of the order. Cutting down on his 90 strikeouts is imperative. Because of his speed, he is tough to double up--grounded into just seven double plays.

The Cubs marvelled at the way he kept his composure during his 1-for-32 start, and another slump late in the season when he was shifted from third to second base. When he wasn't streaking, he was consistent.

BASERUNNING:

Running is considered a strong part of his game. He had the second fastest time to first base by righthanded hitter in the National League. He's deceptively fast, teammate Larry Bowa likening his long effortless gait to Joe DiMaggio. He also is smart, accounting in part for 103 runs for a below average team. He picks his spots to run, thus was only caught stealing 10 times in 45 tries. Pitchers had heard that this rookie was swift, but didn't know that he was so aggressive.

FIELDING:

As a third baseman, he is graded to slightly above average with good arm and range. Shortshop Bowa helped him with positioning. Out of necessity, the Cubs may try him at second base or even outfield. Wherever, he will not be considered liability. He's a good learner.

OVERALL:

McCarver: "The Cubs would not have made the Bowa-for-Ivan DeJesus deal without Ryne. Quick feet on defense. Cubs haven't had a great third baseman since Ron Santo, but Ryne could be it."

Kiner: "His range and pivot at second need improvement but he has a chance to be a fine major leaguer overall."

LEE SMITH
RHP, No. 46
RR, 6'5", 220 lbs.
ML Svc: 2 years
Born: 12-4-57 in
Jamestown, LA

PITCHING:

Before their very eyes, hitters are seeing Lee Smith mature from a boy into a man. Part of a new wave of hard throwers in the league, he has been timed up to 97 MPH, even when he is tired. Veterans liken him in size and intimidation to Bob Gibson. Finally, and here's the bad news for hitters, he's getting the idea. He's not there yet, but gaining fast.

Forced into a starter's role in 1982 when injuries cut the Cubs thin, Smith struggled. He didn't get far into his starts. But back in the bullpen, he allowed just four runs in his last 43 innings (0.83 ERA) to close the season as one of the most awesome short relievers in the league.

To complement his overpowering fastball, which good hitters have been known to sit on, Smith has an adequate slider. His curve is improving, and he is working on a change-up, but until he can throw them consistently, he will keep throwing the heater with hopes that it stays in the strike zone. Fortunately for hitters, he is usually up-down or outside wild, staying away from the brushback.

For variety and surprise, Smith will come in sidearm. He came into his own in pressure situations by completing 29 of 30 appearances in the second half of the 1982 season.

FIELDING, HITTING, BASERUNNING:

Smith works hard on defense, but is still unpolished. He is average in handling the bunt, and needs overall improvement.

An athlete who played basketball in college, Smith goes about hitting and running diligently. He doesn't make much contact, but when he does, the ball travels. He lurches around the bases.

OVERALL:

McCarver: "A lot of clubs would love to have this flamethrower with the awesome physical presence. He just rears back and throws. When he drops down sidearm to righthanded hitters, they give. He has control problems at times, and needs an off-speed pitch."

Coleman: "Big and strong with an excellent arm, Smith needs experience. He can be outstanding if he masters a second pitch."

Kiner: "One of the up-and-coming stars in the league. He has a great fastball and is improving with the consistency of his breaking ball. He was the biggest reason for the Cubs' second-half improvement last year."

1982 STATISTICS

W	L	ERA	G	GS	CG	IP	H	R	ER	BB	SO	SV
2	5	2.69	72	5	0	117	105	38	35	37	99	17

CAREER STATISTICS

W	L	ERA	G	GS	CG	IP	H	R	ER	BB	SO	SV
7	11	2.97	130	6	0	206	183	78	68	82	166	18

SCOT THOMPSON
OF, No. 25
LL, 6'3", 175 lbs.
ML Svc: 4 years
Born: 12-7-55 in
Grove City, PA

1982 STATISTICS

AVG	G	AB	R	H	2B	3B	HR	RBI	BB	SO	SB
.365	49	74	11	27	5	1	0	7	5	4	0

CAREER STATISTICS

AVG	G	AB	R	H	2B	3B	HR	RBI	BB	SO	SB
.262	355	797	88	209	36	7	4	59	59	84	12

VS. RHP

VS. LHP

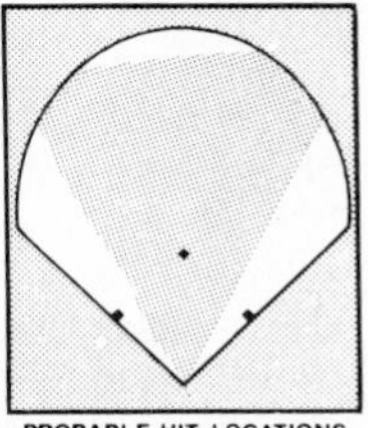
PROBABLE HIT LOCATIONS

HITTING:

A top prospect when he arrived in 1979, Scot Thompson hit .289 and finished third in National League Rookie of the Year balloting. But from a combination of injuries, coaching attempts to get him to pull, being platooned and a lack of confidence from all of these things, he hasn't been the same.

Last season may have been a turnaround for him. He brought a .344 average back from Iowa and hit .365 in limited appearances for the Cubs.

Because Thompson still can't pull for someone his size (fair power to left-center, none to right) and is limited defensively, he remains an enigma. He could use a full season, which he hasn't had in almost four years, to prove himself. With long arms, Thompson prefers pitches over the plate. Around the belt, please. With a slow bat, he often drives the left-center gap. Consequently, he should be jammed with fastballs. Throw in breaking balls too, both in and out.

He is average among major leaguers in all offensive categories. He can't handle the curve and is fair on most of the others with the occasional exception of fastballs.

BASERUNNING:

Thompson had 35 stolen bases in Triple A four years ago, only 23 total since. Perhaps because his neck was violently twisted in a 1980 double play collision in Pittsburgh, he has been timid on bases. He's no longer a theft threat and is slow to first base on grounders.

FIELDING:

This is one area where Thompson has improved. He proved once again he fears no wall by breaking a collarbone making a game-saving catch against the Phillies, crashing into Wrigley Field's bricks. Although he lacks good range for such a long-legged man, he is adept at charging the ball. He is one of many Cubs who can play first base, his natural position.

OVERALL:

Coleman: "He appeared to be a good hitter when he first came up, but has yet to develop. Still finding himself after the big buildup."

McCarver: "Scot is a mistake hitter. Good pitching can get him out. Aggressive in the outfield. Could turn into an above average player."

Kiner: "He is improving his defensive play, but should be a better hitter. His ability regressed to the point where he had to go back to the minors."

PITCHING:

The higher the kick, the better for this veteran, whose lift with the lead leg is as high as Juliet Prowse's. Dick Tidrow doesn't have her good looks, but with a nickname like "Dirt," he doesn't want them. With a glowering stare, long hair and full mustache, he promotes the villain image. It's his trademark.

His pitching trademark is a sidearm fastball that sinks, but he has to be at the top of his kicking game to be consistent with it. He also throws a curve/slider combination which is called the "slurve," and it is a very good one. Tidrow's change-up is only average,but as a short man who must be ready with his best pitches, he doesn't use the change too often anyway.

Hitters suspect Tidrow throws a spitball (not even his pitching coach knows for sure). Whatever it is, it drops dramatically.

Tidrow had some rough times over the last few years. He made the adjustment of going from the winning Yankees to a losing team, the temporary role of short man to replace Bruce Sutter, the trading of his good friend Bill Caudill, and health problems at home. But with new management last season, a better Cub bullpen with Lee Smith as short man and family woes cleared up, Tidrow proved that he has a few years left. If only he didn't have to face Mike Schmidt.

DICK TIDROW
RHP, NO. 41
RR, 6'4", 213 lbs.
ML Svc: 11 years
Born: 5-14-47 in
San Francisco, CA

FIELDING, HITTING, BASERUNNING:

Keeping runners honest never has been a strong suit. He's slow throwing to first and getting rid of the ball to plate. Perhaps this is due to altering his style. He didn't hit for years while in the American League, and so had a major league average below .100.

OVERALL:

Kiner: "With an excellent arm, he's perfectly suited for long and short relief."

Coleman: "With poise and experience, he has been a clutch performer. He's underrated. It would help him if he was with a better club."

McCarver: "Sutter said he could not have been as effective for the Cubs without Dirt. He was to the Cubs what Ron Davis was to the Yankees' Rich Gossage. He's a very respected, durable reliever."

1982 STATISTICS

W	L	ERA	G	GS	CG	IP	H	R	ER	BB	SO	SV
8	3	3.39	65	0	0	103	106	45	39	29	62	6

CAREER STATISTICS

W	L	ERA	G	GS	CG	IP	H	R	ER	BB	SO	SV
104	95	3.55	622	137	32	1742	1680	773	687	580	969	47

BUMP WILLS
INF, No. 17
SR, 5'9", 177 lbs.
ML Svc: 6 years
Born: 7-27-52 in
Washington, DC

1982 STATISTICS

AVG	G	AB	R	H	2B	3B	HR	RBI	BB	SO	SB
.272	128	419	64	114	18	4	6	38	46	76	35

CAREER STATISTICS

AVG	G	AB	R	H	2B	3B	HR	RBI	BB	SO	SB
.266	831	3030	472	807	128	24	36	302	310	441	196

VS. RHP

VS. LHP

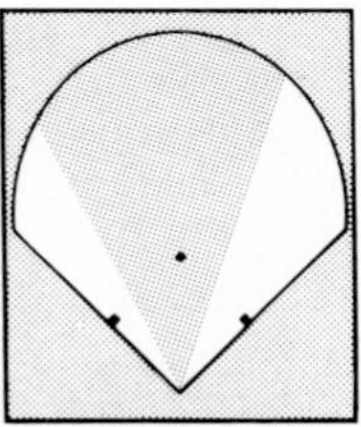
PROBABLE HIT LOCATIONS

HITTING:

Wills is a rare combination of spray and power. He's like a cobra coming out of a closed crouched stance to strike at high fastballs. He will, though, drop down for low pitches from righthanders.

The trick is to tie him up with inside breaking balls. This is especially true for righties who then should come back with an outside pitch for fly balls to left. Lefthanders might have luck by spinning their pitches on the outside.

Offense is his redeeming feature, with fastballs and change-ups being his strength. Last season with the Cubs, he was equally successful from both sides of the plate (.274 lefthanded, .264 right), but managers fear him most from left where he likes to pull. He homered on the second pitch of the season off righthander Mario Soto.

With good speed, he's best at leading off although he could be more selective. He doesn't walk enough. He also can be used eighth as a "second" leadoff man. Power for a little man is not surprising, considering the weight work. He's strongly muscled. He needs work in hitting behind the runner and is not particularly good in the clutch. He likes to swing away (76 strikeouts) and will go after bad pitches. Beware of an occasional bunt.

BASERUNNING:

Like his famous father Maury, Bump not only has all the tools, but utilizes them. He gets a good jump, has speed to score from first on a long single and is smart on the paths. Pitchers respect him at all times. He slides hard and pops up quickly. Average at breaking up the double play.

FIELDING:

Glaring deficiencies here. He's at the stage in his career where he may have to settle for designated hitting or coming off the bench. Shoulder tendinitis further hampered him in 1982, reducing his arm strength and accuracy to below average. He has fair range to his left but practically none to his right. He has to overplay that side. The ball has to come right to him. Even then it's likely to go through. He does not have good hands and is weak on the double play.

OVERALL:

Coleman: "He helps a team only by running and at the plate. Poor defensive skills at a skill position makes him a defensive liability."

McCarver: "No pun intended, but it runs in the family. He can score a lot of runs but could walk 15% more."

JUNIOR KENNEDY
INF, No. 15
RR, 6'0", 185 lbs.
ML Svc: 5 years
Born: 8-9-50 in
Gibson, OK

HITTING, BASERUNNING, FIELDING:

Kennedy is a standard, righthanded high ball hitter who hits to the other side and should be pitched low. He fights those pitches. Inside curves also are a nemesis. Play him toward the right.

He has to do the small things to be effective, and does. He can bunt, hit behind runners and draw walks. At 32 years old, Kennedy still gets around on the fastball, but has lost some pop. Any kind of breaking ball should work. He is not tough in the clutch.

His biggest thrill was a grand-slam home run with the Reds against the Cubs in 1980.

His baserunning is strictly average. He's smart going around, but limited in speed and take-out skills.

Kennedy's ability to move around is his plus. For a utility man, he does just what's needed. He's best at second base, where he has the most experience, and adequate at shortstop and third.

OVERALL:

Kiner: "Your typical good-field/no-hit infielder."

McCarver: "A steady ball player, but not spectacular. You hate to relegate a player to utility duty, but it appears that was Junior's position in his baseball career."

MIKE PROLY
RHP, No. 36
RR, 5'10", 185 lbs.
ML Svc: 5 years
Born: 12-15-50 in
Jamaica, NY

PITCHING:

A journeyman long reliever who can start in an emergency, Mike Proly relies on the sinking action of his fastball and slider. He will throw the change-up for show, but seldom throws a curve. He has two areas to work in with righthanded hitters--in with the sinker and away with the slider.

Without a great overall repertoire of pitches, he cannot afford to walk many batters. He doesn't have the kind of stuff to stop a team on a roll, but if the sinker is in shape, he can stop even hot teams. He has not had an ERA above 3.90 in five years.

He is a bulldog on the mound, and while he was pitching for the White Sox, was in two fights.

FIELDING, HITTING, BASERUNNING:

A fast delivery and quickness off the mound makes Proly a reliable defensive player. He can hit, too.

OVERALL:

McCarver: "Mike's greatest asset is his ability to throw a ground ball. He is best in natural grass parks like Wrigley Field for turning hard-hit grounders into double plays. He is not afraid of any hitter."

Kiner: "He has good poise and an above average sinker and control. Proly is able to keep the ball low in the strike zone."

GARY WOODS
OF, No. 57
RR, 6'2", 190 lbs.
ML Svc: 3 years
Born: 7-20-53 in Santa Barbara, CA

HITTING, BASERUNNING, FIELDING:

Gary Woods is your basic, average major league reserve, although he got off to such a fast start last season, the Cubs temporarily started him. He's a straightaway hitter who occasionally drives mistakes, particularly high ones, from lefthanders.

He's best against the fastball, worst against the curve. He annoys pitchers by making them throw strikes and annoys himself by taking strikes. He can hit behind the runner and is fairly tough in the clutch. Steve Carlton knows about that.

Throw him breaking pitches, down and away.

Woods is a slightly better than average runner. He is smart but doesn't always utilize his speed. It has diminished slightly. He could be more aggressive.

The arm is strong and there is accuracy, but he plays a little too deep and is limited coming in.

OVERALL:

Kiner: "Gary has not been able to handle major league pitching with any consistency."

Coleman: "One of many players who rounds out a roster. Has some power and is a dangerous pinch-hitter against lefthanders."

RIVERFRONT STADIUM
Cinncinati Reds

Seating Capacity: 52,392
Playing Surface: Artificial

Dimensions
Left Field Pole: 330 ft.
Left-Center Field: 375 ft.
Center Field: 404 ft.
Right-Center Field: 375 ft.
Right Field Pole: 330 ft.
Height of Outfield Wall: 14 ft.

Tom Seaver once commented that if he ever owned a ballpark, he would want it run just like Riverfront Stadium. The park is meticulously well cared-for and provides maximum comfort to both the fans and the players.

The artificial surface at Riverfront Stadium is kept in remarkably good shape. The park is considered to have a fast infield, but it is one that almost guarantees a good hop. This allows the infielders to play exceptionally deep, and Dave Concepcion plays so deep that he has mastered the skill of throwing the ball from short to first on one hop to cut down on the trajectory of his throw.

The bullpens are located in the field of play and are considered hazardous to both the pitchers trying to warm up and to the outfielders chasing foul balls.

The batter's box is composed of soft and pliable dirt and allows hitters to dig in comfortably and to get that much sought after feel of real dirt on their hands. There isn't a lot of foul territory behind the plate or down either line. This benefits the hitters because foul balls are most often out of play. There is no barrier between the dugouts and the field of play, but this danger is minimized because the dugouts are only a few inches lower than the level of the playing field.

The outfield is surrounded by a 14 foot fence and ranges from 330 feet down each line to 404 feet in center field. The ball carries extremely well making it another major advantage for the hitters.

JOHNNY BENCH
C/INF, No. 5
RR, 6'1", 215 lbs.
ML Svc: 16 years
Born: 12-7-47 in
Oklahoma City, OK

1982 STATISTICS

AVG	G	AB	R	H	2B	3B	HR	RBI	BB	SO	SB
.258	119	399	44	103	16	0	13	38	37	58	1

CAREER STATISTICS

AVG	G	AB	R	H	2B	3B	HR	RBI	BB	SO	SB
.268	2048	7348	1059	1969	366	22	377	1322	867	1240	68

VS. RHP

VS. LHP

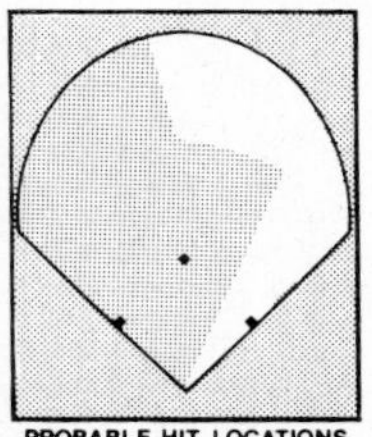
PROBABLE HIT LOCATIONS

HITTING:

Johnny Bench is now a player in the midst of a transition forced by age and injury. In past years, Bench stood deep in the box, typical of most power hitters, with a slightly closed and upright stance. His hits were "shots," whether they were extra base drives to the left-center alley or into the seats.

Today, Bench stands higher in the box and with a greater emphasis on going with the pitch. In 1981, he used the approach to compile the best average of his career. In 1982, he oscillated between these two styles and consequently, had one of his worst years. However, he remain a dangerous hitter, who can effectively handle any pitch. Pitchers must work him high and inside, and low and away. He hits Philadelphia's Steve Carlton as well as anyone can.

Bench is now more refined in his style and can wait and pick up the off-speed pitch. A late breaking curve seems to present the most difficulty for Bench. He can lay down a good bunt, hit behind the runner, and be used in any variance on the hit-and-run. Though his ability in the clutch seemed to drop last season, it is difficult to say whether it was due to an absence of other bats in the lineup, or a reduction in skills. In any case, Bench is still a hitter who must be handled with extreme care by left and righthanded pitchers.

BASERUNNING:

Bench is a slow baserunner, but he compensates for his lack of speed with aggressiveness and intelligence. He will steal a base occasionally using surprise and a knowledge of pitchers and their moves to get a good jump. On the bases, he is aware of his job and is an imposing figure from first to second in a double play situation.

FIELDING:

During his prime, Bench was probably the most coveted player in baseball. Now, he is simply a player without a position. In 1981, he played first base, where he was adequate. In 1982, he played third, where he was just better than horrible. Though he still has the great arm, he has a very limited range and shows a lack of confidence in even the most routine plays. Since he has asked the club not to catch, his best position is probably first where he seems more comfortable and is less of a liability.

OVERALL:

Coleman: "Johnny is a sure-fire Hall of Famer. He's been a credit to the game, but he has outlived his usefulness in Cincinnati and should go to the American League where he can be a designated hitter."

McCarver: "John has been such a dominant figure for the Reds for so long, it just doesn't seem possible that his ability is on the wane. Unfortunately, idealism and baseball are incompatible allies. Realism must dictate."

BRUCE BERENYI
RHP, No. 38
RR, 6'3", 215 lbs.
ML Svc: 3 years
Born: 8-21-54 in
Bryan, OH

PITCHING:

Bruce Berenyi has a terrific fastball. It's consistently clocked around 96 MPH and explodes as it approaches the plate. Catchers take a beating while Berenyi is on the mound and so do the hitters, if he is on. But that is his problem, control. Berenyi is off as much as he is on. He can be very wild and while his tendency toward wildness serves to intimidate opponents, it also reduces his effectiveness.

Besides the big fastball which he depends on about 75% of the time, Berenyi throws a slider which some believe is his best pitch. It's quick and he seems to have more control of that pitch. He also has a curve and with these three pitches, has much more success against righthanded hitters.

Because of erratic control, he walks a lot of batters. Another in the Reds' line of classic power pitchers using the standard overhand and three-quarter motions, Berenyi has not developed a change of any sort. Even his curve has a hard, quick break. Since he has the powerful fastball and slider, some believe he would be much more successful with a straight change. But control is his chief problem.

FIELDING, HITTING, BASERUNNING:

Thus far in his career, Berenyi has been a middle of the road fielder. But frankly, his performance on the mound is usually so good, or so bad, that he rarely gets a chance to show what he can do. At the plate, Berenyi is not a factor. He is big and strong, but he seldom connects on a pitch. On the bases, he's slow.

OVERALL:

Generally, Berenyi is regarded as having some of the best stuff in the National League. On one night, Berenyi can overwhelm and dominate a club with a powerful and poised performance. The next time out, maybe against the same team, he can be horrible--his poise going out the window with his control. There are times, even when he is going well, that he seems shaky and unsure of himself.

McCarver: "Bruce need only throw strikes to be effective. His fastball is very hard and heavy. His slider has a late bite which makes it very difficult to pick up. Hitters commit themselves too soon and the pitch eats them up. I look for great things from him, if his control improves."

Coleman: "When he has his control, he's a tiger. His fastball is one of the best in the league. When he loses, he usually beats himself."

Kiner: "Berenyi has as much stuff as any pitcher in the National League. When he is pitching well, you watch him and wonder how he can lose."

1982 STATISTICS

W	L	ERA	G	GS	CG	IP	H	R	ER	BB	SO	SV
9	18	3.36	34	34	4	222	208	90	83	96	157	0

CAREER STATISTICS

W	L	ERA	G	GS	CG	IP	H	R	ER	BB	SO	SV
20	26	3.73	61	60	9	376	339	171	156	196	160	0

CESAR CEDENO
INF, No. 28
RR, 6'2", 190 lbs.
ML Svc: 13 years
Born: 2-25-51 in
Santo Domingo, DR

1982 STATISTICS

AVG	G	AB	R	H	2B	3B	HR	RBI	BB	SO	SB
.289	138	492	52	142	35	1	8	57	41	41	16

CAREER STATISTICS

AVG	G	AB	R	H	2B	3B	HR	RBI	BB	SO	SB
.289	1650	6224	942	1801	378	56	171	835	575	776	503

VS. RHP

VS. LHP

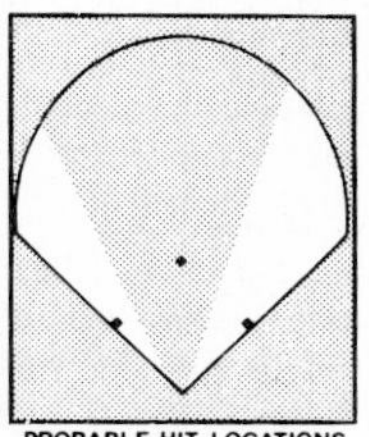
PROBABLE HIT LOCATIONS

HITTING:

Cesar Cedeno is a straightaway "sting" hitter. He hits the ball sharply and up the middle. He has better than average power to the alleys, though it seems to have decreased in the last five years. A high ball hitter who guesses well, Cedeno will pull the ball more against lefthanded pitchers. His strongest zone is the left-center alley.

Pitchers work him carefully, moving the ball around, jamming him with a quick one and hoping to catch him guessing wrong. Some will work him low. He seems equally effective against right and lefthanders, but there is a natural tendency for him to fare better against lefties. Cedeno is regarded as a quality clutch hitter, but last season some noted a failure to hit with runners in scoring position.

Though he often guesses at the plate, Cedeno has a good awareness of the strike zone and will draw his share of walks. He is disciplined at the plate, and is effective hitting behind the runner and in hit-and-run situations. He bunts well and bunts for base hits. A slow starter who tends to get hot with the weather, Cedeno has very quick hands which allow him to handle sliders and sinkers relatively well. A good change will fool him but then, only once. He's a smart hitter.

BASERUNNING:

Cedeno has slowed somewhat, and had a broken ankle in 1980. He is still above average in speed, but does not get the jump he once did. Pitchers are still aware of his speed and acknowledge him as a baserunning threat. He is smart and aggressive on the paths. Once one of the greatest parts of his game, Cedeno is now rated just above average on the basepath.

FIELDING:

Like his baserunninng ability, time and injury have taken their toll on Cedeno. Though once a classic performer in center field, he will probably open the season in right or left, making room for Eddie Milner. His arm is still good. His throws are strong and accurate and he charges the ball very well, much better than he moves back to the fence for a catch.

OVERALL:

McCarver: "As good as he has been, Cedeno hasn't lived up to the Superstar tag given him early in his career. The broken ankle in the 1980 playoffs seems to have slowed him down."

Coleman: "He used to be great. The ankle problem has cost him a tremendous amount of speed in the last two years and seems to still be bothering him. Ten years ago, I thought Cedeno was a Hall of Fame candidate. But, he never really lived up to his potential and now injuries have really taken their toll."

Kiner: "Billed as the next Willie Mays, his home run and RBI totals have been very disappointing."

DAVE CONCEPCION
INF, No. 13
RR, 6'1", 180 lbs.
ML Svc: 13 years
Born: 6-17-48 in Aragua, VEN

1982 STATISTICS

AVG	G	AB	R	H	2B	3B	HR	RBI	BB	SO	SB
.287	147	572	48	164	25	4	5	53	45	61	13

CAREER STATISTICS

AVG	G	AB	R	H	2B	3B	HR	RBI	BB	SO	SB
.273	1758	6317	749	1723	285	44	85	726	506	876	249

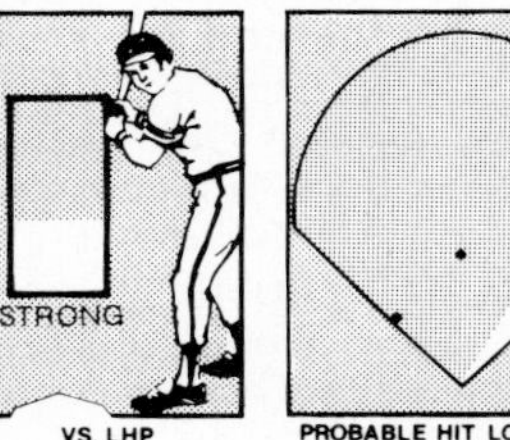

HITTING:

Dave Concepcion has the reputation of being one of the toughest outs in the league and the toughest out in the Reds' lineup. To pitchers, he is an unusually troubling hitter who is, at once, a good contact man with good power.

He will hit to all fields responding to game situations and burn opponents with power to the alleys. He uses a closed, upright stance and works from the center of the box. He's a high ball hitter and pitchers must work him low and away. Concepcion will, however, go fishing for a high hard one away. It's a risky move, though, because of his ability to go the other way, but it is not as risky as going inside where Concepcion's quickness usually wins.

He is equally effective against left and righthanded pitchers. The best bet is to get ahead of him and then go with breaking pitches. This sometimes works for righthanders, but Concepcion pulls the ball well on breaking pitches from lefties. His weak spot, and it is not significant, seems to be sinkers and sliders, down. He bunts well, but doesn't like to, and has a good eye for the strike zone. The result is a lot of balls off the sweet part of his bat. Because of his shots, Concepcion has better results in parks with an artificial surface.

BASERUNNING:

Concepcion is faster than most and is a basestealing threat. He has stolen 249 bases in his career, but in the past three seasons, his frequency in stealing bases has dropped. Pitchers must still pay attention to him. He gets a good lead. Concepcion is usually smart and aggressive on the bases.

FIELDING:

Only Ozzie Smith of the Cardinals outshines Concepcion in the field, particularly on artificial turf. He plays deep and goes to the holes well. He is excellent going to his left and better than most to his right. His arm is accurate and what he has lost in strength, he makes up with his patented one-bounce throw to first. Obviously, however, he can only use this on artificial surfaces. After 13 years in the big leagues and an operation on his throwing arm, defense is still regarded as one of the strongest parts of Concepcion's game.

OVERALL:

Concepcion is a class competitor who has improved with age. A consistent, clutch performer.

McCarver: "One of the best shortstops to ever play the game. He's a good RBI man, hits for average and is a Gold Glove fielder. He has good speed and can steal bases. There's not much left."

Coleman: "He has slowed some but he is still the most complete shortstop in the National League."

Kiner: "He is the No. 1 all around shortstop in the league."

DAN DRIESSEN
INF, No. 22
LR, 5'11", 190 lbs.
ML Svc: 10 years
Born: 7-29-51 in
Hilton Head, SC

1982 STATISTICS

AVG	G	AB	R	H	2B	3B	HR	RBI	BB	SO	SB
.269	149	516	64	139	25	1	17	57	82	62	11

CAREER STATISTICS

AVG	G	AB	R	H	2B	3B	HR	RBI	BB	SO	SB
.270	2277	4113	577	1109	210	11	114	585	566	563	144

VS. RHP

VS. LHP

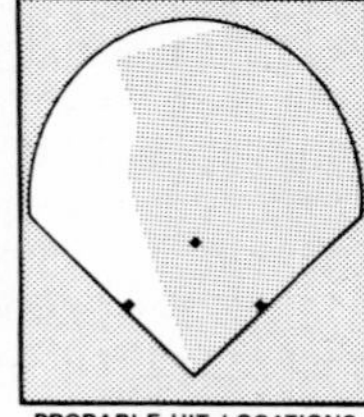
PROBABLE HIT LOCATIONS

HITTING:

Dan Driessen is a good, consistent contact hitter who can hurt a careless pitcher with power. Driessen is as relaxed at the plate as he is working at his home in the yard and will spray the park with clutch hits. Using a closed stance and a slight crouch, he keeps his head and shoulders out over the plate.

Driessen is a low ball hitter who is particularly good against lefthanded pitchers. A pitcher's safest approach to Driessen is to keep the ball away. Lefthanders must observe that rule as well as paying attention to mixing their speeds and their pitches. Driessen has an excellent eye, bunts well and, as a matter of course, hits well with runners in scoring position and equally well behind the runner.

The majority of his hits are line drives and hard grounders from center to right, but he can go to the opposite field and with power. Off-speed pitches can fool him, but not twice in the same game. His strengths are the fastball, slider and sinker, and with the kind of discipline Driessen has at the plate, a pitcher is forced to come in with one of these staples sooner or later. Driessen rarely chases bad pitches.

BASERUNNING:

Driessen has above average speed, and in previous years when the Reds had more power, was more of a threat to steal. The threat is still there and pitchers must be alert when Driessen is on. He is aggressive and smart on the bases, and comes in very hard when he slides, particularly in double play situations. His instincts on the bases are very good.

FIELDING:

Driessen is a skilled performer with great range and game awareness. He makes the tough play look easy. His arm is strong, he has good hands, and his feet are sure and quick. He will field a bunt as well as he will go deep to his right for a hard ground ball. He is an excellent defensive first baseman.

OVERALL:

There are questions about Driessen. Given his skills at the plate, some ask why he does not hit for a better average. Given his fielding skills, some ask why he has not been awarded a Gold Glove. The only answer offered is that consistency, in Driessen's case, overshadows his overall talent.

Coleman: "A solid player on offense and defense. He is productive, but he probably could be obtained in a trade for some young prospects. He doesn't fit in the Reds' youth movement."

McCarver: "Danny does everything well, but it is a real mystery why he doesn't hit 20 points higher every year. All of the elements are there: quick, strong hands, patience and a good eye. He could be, however, a little more aggressive at the plate. But the best kept secret in the baseball world is his incredible defensive ability."

RICH GALE
RHP, No. 32
RR, 6'7", 225 lbs.
ML Svc: 5 years
Born: 1-19-54 in
Littleton, NH

PITCHING:

At 6'7", Rich Gale is the tallest pitcher in the major leagues. He was a victim of poor offensive support in 1982, but in the late stages of the season he lost his consistency and was removed from the Giants' starting rotation. His status for 1983 is in a cloud. A hard-thrower, he comes straight over the top with his fastball, which has a velocity in the 90 MPH range. His second best pitch is a slider with a sharp, biting action. He seldom throws his curve, which is very readable because he strains to get on top of it. Gale's fastball is consistently up in the strike zone, which makes it tough for him in the low ball National League. Had some good years in Kansas City before the Royals sent him to San Francisco in the deal that brought them Jerry Martin. Besides control, Gale is hampered by the fact that he's basically a one-speed pitcher. And he's fidgety--he puts his infielders to sleep between pitches. But he has good, hard stuff and can overpower hitters when he gets ahead in the count early.

FIELDING, HITTING, BASERUNNING:

A poor pick-off move combined with the fact that the lanky Gale takes a long time to complete his delivery make him one of the league's most vulnerable pitchers to the stolen base. He is a good athlete--he was a basketball star at the University of New Hampshire, and fields his position well. Quite naturally for his size, he has good power at the plate--he doesn't make contact often, but he did hit a home run in Chicago last season to beat the Cubs, 2-1, in a network television game. Foot speed is not one of his long suits.

OVERALL:

McCarver: "Rich's height must be against him. He's a high ball pitcher in a league where they don't give you the letter-high strike. NL umpires work the slots between the catcher and the hitter, giving them a better view of the low strike. In the AL, the umpire stands behind the catcher, so his view of the low pitch is impaired. If Rich threw more low strikes, he could be tough."

Coleman: "Rich should be better. If he pitched quicker, he wouldn't drive everybody crazy. He's the slowest worker in the league."

Kiner: "He had a tough first year in the NL. His inability to get his pitches over in the right location proved to be his undoing. He needs to improve his control to be effective."

1982 STATISTICS

W	L	ERA	G	GS	CG	IP	H	R	ER	BB	SO	SV
7	14	4.23	33	29	2	170	193	91	80	81	102	0

CAREER STATISTICS

W	L	ERA	G	GS	CG	IP	H	R	ER	BB	SO	SV
49	47	4.34	149	133	21	837	837	453	404	396	437	1

GREG HARRIS
RHP, No. 37
SR, 6'0", 165 lbs.
ML Svc: 2 years
Born: 11-2-55 in Lynwood, CA

PITCHING:

Harris is one of those pitchers whose marginal ability places him firmly in the role of long relief and spot starter. He is a control pitcher with a very deliberate motion and three-quarter delivery. He pitches most hitters safely, away, and uses this approach exclusively against righthanders.

His fastball tops at 85 MPH, which is his biggest problem. He has a good change, but his lack of muscle on the fastball reduces the effectiveness of the change-up.

Harris relies on his breaking pitches. He will use his curve, his best pitch, as much as 35% of the time. Against righthanded hitters, it is invariably his out pitch. His slider is judged above average and when behind in the count, he will go to either of his breaking pitches. Most effective against righthanded hitters, Harris has no consistent out pitch against lefties.

FIELDING, HITTING, BASERUNNING:

For a righthanded pitcher, Harris has a very quick move to first. He fields his position well, and is especially sure in handling bunts. He is a switch-hitter and can lace the ball up the middle. On the bases, he shows the same quickness he displays in the field.

OVERALL:

There are many positive things about Harris. His curveball can be excellent, his slider effective. He has an exceptionally good attitude about the game and in pressure situations, does not rattle. However, there is no way he can make up for the lack of velocity on his fastball. He can destroy teams with heavy righthanded lineups. He has, for instance, won five games in his major league career. Four of those came against the Phillies.

McCarver: "A righthanded batter must take the inside part of the plate away from Greg and always look for the pitch away. It's the only way to have success against him. Lefthanders don't have any problem."

Coleman: "If he had movement and more velocity on his fastball, Greg Harris would be another story."

1982 STATISTICS

W	L	ERA	G	GS	CG	IP	H	R	ER	BB	SO	SV
2	6	4.83	34	10	1	91	96	56	49	37	67	1

CAREER STATISTICS

W	L	ERA	G	GS	CG	IP	H	R	ER	BB	SO	SV
5	11	4.67	50	24	1	160	161	92	83	65	121	2

BEN HAYES
RHP, No. 45
RR, 6'1", 180 lbs.
ML Svc: 1 year
Born: 8-4-57 in
Niagara Falls, NY

PITCHING:

Ben Hayes throws everything hard. Though young and relatively inexperienced, he challenges hitters with his fastball and slider. His fastball will reach 90 MPH and has a tendency to run in on righthanded hitters. The pitch has some hop to it and appears to be on top of the hitter rather quickly. His slider is quick and has a late break. The fastball-slider combination makes him particularly effective against righthanded hitters.

He has a curve but seldom uses it. It is average, at best, and he doesn't seem to have a great deal of confidence in the pitch. His motion and three-quarter delivery is somewhat jerky which adds to the deception of his fastball.

He gets into a problem once in a while because everything he throws is hard. He will offer a straight change, but very rarely. Hayes needs to come up with a good off-speed pitch to be highly effective. When he's trailing the hitter, he will always go to the fastball or slider. An alert hitter can look for it and rough him up .

FIELDING, HITTING, BASERUNNING:

Hayes reacts well in the field, particularly fielding bunts. He is a well-schooled baserunner, but only average at the plate.

OVERALL:

Hayes' jump to the major leagues was hastened by injuries to Tom Hume. But overall, he responded well in short relief situations. He challenged the hitters heads-up and was surprisingly poised for a rookie in his position.

His hard pitches will be his stock in trade, but he has to learn an off-speed pitch to make the most of his power pitches.

Reds management was pleased with Hayes' development last season but wonders how he will respond in pressure situations or a pennant race.

McCarver: "Hayes is a standard equipment pitcher and right now he doesn't appear to pose any special problems for big league hitters. He needs experience, and experience could change that."

1982 STATISTICS

W	L	ERA	G	GS	CG	IP	H	R	ER	BB	SO	SV
2	0	1.97	26	0	0	45	37	12	10	22	38	2

CAREER STATISTICS

W	L	ERA	G	GS	CG	IP	H	R	ER	BB	SO	SV
2	0	1.97	26	0	0	45	37	12	10	22	38	2

PAUL HOUSEHOLDER
OF, No. 21
SR, 6'0", 180 lbs.
ML Svc: 3 years
Born: 9-4-58 in
Columbus, OH

1982 STATISTICS

AVG	G	AB	R	H	2B	3B	HR	RBI	BB	SO	SB
.211	138	417	40	88	11	5	9	34	30	77	17

CAREER STATISTICS

AVG	G	AB	R	H	2B	3B	HR	RBI	BB	SO	SB
.222	181	531	55	118	16	6	11	50	41	106	21

VS. RHP

VS. LHP

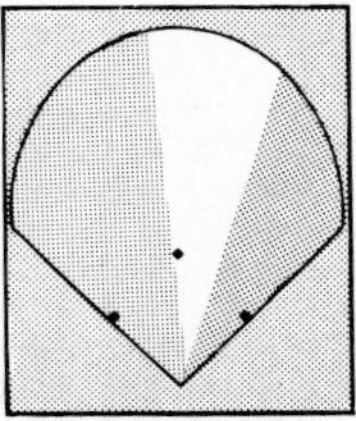
PROBABLE HIT LOCATIONS

HITTING:

"House," as he is called by his teammates, is a switch-hitter who thus far has demonstrated more skill from the right side of the plate and power from both sides. Batting right, Paul Householder is a high ball hitter against lefthanded pitchers who likes to pull and should be worked away and down. He likes the high pitch when batting left, too, but will go for a low one out over the plate. Righthanded pitchers will work him away and sometimes come back with a hard, tight pitch.

A highly touted rookie, Householder struggled in 1982, and some argued that he tried too hard to be a power hitter. When he did connect, he hit the ball sharply and with authority. Still sorting through his performance with the bat, Householder was an average hitter in clutch situations, an area in which most believe he will improve. Because he is by nature a pull hitter looking for the extra base hit, he seldom hits behind the runner and can't be depended upon in hit-and-run situations. He is a poor bunter and has not learned the strike zone which means he does not draw a lot of walks, and will bite on pitches that would be balls. He is strongest on pitches that are belt high and over the plate, but cannot hit curves. Good sinkers and sliders will generally fool Householder, but they have to be down. A good change will catch him lunging.

BASERUNNING:

Householder did not steal anywhere near the number of bases expected, mainly because he did not get on base enough. Householder has above average speed. At times, however, he does not run with intelligence--a quality that should come with experience. Nevertheless, baserunning is still one of the strongest parts of Householder's game.

FIELDING:

Householder has above average range with a good strong arm. His throws are always hard but they are not always accurate. Though his range is particularly noteworthy, he is much better coming in on the ball than going back. He seems to have particular problems going back to his right.

OVERALL:

Householder has great tools but is, at this point, only a mediocre performer. He should eventually come around, but the Reds may be over-billing him.

Kiner: "Paul got off to a slow start and never could turn it around. He still has good potential and should be given another chance."

McCarver: "Good minor league stats earned Paul the regular right field position. He probably would have been much better breaking in within a veteran outfield instead of starting with a brand new unit. Paul is undergoing a tenuous introduction to major league baseball."

TOM HUME
RHP, No. 47
RR, 6'1", 185 lbs.
ML Svc: 6 years
Born: 3-29-53 in
Cincinnati, OH

PITCHING:

Tom Hume is an outstanding short relief man. He is a power pitcher, who never veers away from his strength. He mixes his 90 MPH fastball with one of the best sinkerballs in the National League. The result is a lot of strikeouts in critical situations and a lot of ground balls which end up in double plays. He also uses a slider and curve, but it is usually when he is ahead in the count. He seems uncomfortable with his curve and if given the choice would proceed: fastball, sinker, slider.

Besides having a nice array of pitches, Hume is adept in finding a hitter's weakness and directing his attention in that area. Varying his motion from straight overhand to three-quarter, Hume is particularly effective against righthanded hitters working his fastball and sinker inside on the fists. The movement on his fastball is excellent and only increases the hitter's difficulties.

If Hume has a problem, it is that he sometimes becomes predictable in using the fastball to get ahead in the count and then immediately following with the sinker. However, the sinker is so strong that he manages to get by with it. Some think that Hume would be even more effective if he would work on his change-up which he almost never uses. He is unflappable by nature and equally removed on the mound. No matter how tight a game might be, nothing affects this man.

FIELDING, HITTING, BASERUNNING:

Hume is not fast on the basepaths, but is quick in fielding his position. Most rate him above average. While his move to first has not drawn high marks, he does evidence the same quick feet and motion. He gets into trouble with basestealers because of the sinker ball. Catchers seem to have difficulty coming up with the ball and making a quick, smooth throw to second. As a hitter, Hume doesn't show much but occasionally he will connect and send one to the wall.

OVERALL:

Hume suffered a knee injury in May of last season. Though a full recovery is expected, only time will tell.

Kiner: "In a world of flaky short relief men, Hume is a paradox. Quiet and unassuming, he gets the job done and extremely well. He is one of the tops in the trade."

McCarver: "His sinkerball, when hit, has an anvil-like heaviness. It's very tough to pull even when you know it is coming."

Coleman: "Hume is one of those guys who just goes out and comes at you with strikes. He's one of the best in the league."

1982 STATISTICS

W	L	ERA	G	GS	CG	IP	H	R	ER	BB	SO	SV
2	6	3.11	46	0	0	63	57	24	22	21	22	17

CAREER STATISTICS

W	L	ERA	G	GS	CG	IP	H	R	ER	BB	SO	SV
41	43	3.49	288	40	5	648	655	274	251	190	309	73

WAYNE KRENCHICKI
INF, No. 12
LR, 6'1", 175 lbs.
ML Svc: 4 years
Born: 9-17-54 in Trenton, NJ

1982 STATISTICS

AVG	G	AB	R	H	2B	3B	HR	RBI	BB	SO	SB
.283	94	187	19	53	6	1	2	21	13	23	5

CAREER STATISTICS

AVG	G	AB	R	H	2B	3B	HR	RBI	BB	SO	SB
.255	152	278	28	71	11	1	2	27	18	35	5

VS. RHP

VS. LHP

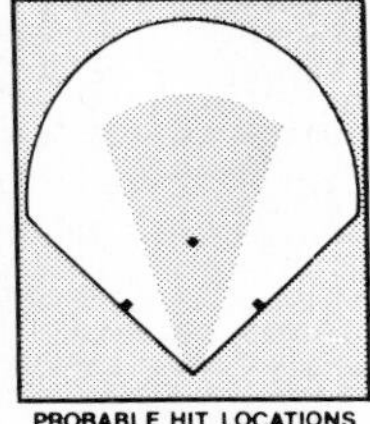
PROBABLE HIT LOCATIONS

HITTING:

Wayne Krenchicki is a line drive, straightaway hitter who last year showed that he has a keen ability to come through in the clutch. He is a high ball hitter who likes to get his arms out over the plate, He is a good fastball hitter who waits well and shows good discipline with the bat.

He is much more effective against righthanded pitchers who will work him inside and down. Lefthanders will work him outside and sometimes try to jam him. Krenchicki doesn't show a lot of power but he will reach the alleys against righthanders and displays poise in clutch situations, where he is judged above average in performance.

Though he has had limited major league experience, Krenchicki has shown that he can handle himself in hit-and-run situations and has a discerning eye for the strike zone. His greatest vulnerability at the plate is good stuff down. He cannot hit a good curve and has trouble with good sinkers and sliders. A consistent and aggressive hitter in 1982, Krenchicki's bat is now regarded as one of the strongest parts of his game.

BASERUNNING:

Krenchicki does not have great speed on the bases and is generally conservative. He is a smart runner, however, and though he does not have a lot of speed, he will challenge pitchers and take a base. They have to be aware of Krenchicki at first. His baserunning can be improved and probably will with time.

FIELDING:

Krenchicki can play third, short or second, but seems most comfortable at third and is most effective there. At third, he can be slick. He is quick and has good hands. He has a fine arm and good range, judged above average in both categories. He is best moving to his left but "picks" well to his right. Krenchicki handles the double play well and from third, will handle bunts with balance and smoothness.

OVERALL:

Krenchicki is probably the Reds' most effective player coming off the bench and could start for a lot of major league clubs.

McCarver: "Wayne has been a pleasant surprise for the Reds. With John Bench struggling in his transition to third, Wayne did a bang-up job and hit .300 for most of the year. He may, very well, have overcome the tag as a utility player."

Coleman: "His minor league record didn't indicate anything special, but he seems to have the mental toughness to become a good pinch-hitter, if nothing else. He had some awfully big hits last year and seemed to do well when the pressure was on."

RAFAEL LANDESTOY
INF, No. 7
SR, 5'9", 165 lbs.
ML Svc: 6 years
Born: 5-28-53 in Bani, DR

1982 STATISTICS

AVG	G	AB	R	H	2B	3B	HR	RBI	BB	SO	SB
.189	73	111	11	21	3	0	1	9	8	14	2

CAREER STATISTICS

AVG	G	AB	R	H	2B	3B	HR	RBI	BB	SO	SB
.244	472	1107	118	270	31	16	2	80	96	109	52

VS. RHP

VS. LHP

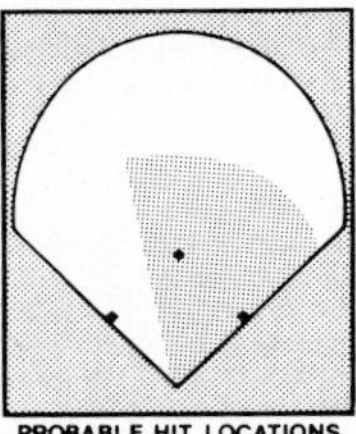
PROBABLE HIT LOCATIONS

HITTING:

Landestoy is a switch-hitter who shows more power from the right side, but is most effective lefthanded. Batting right, he is basically a straight-away hitter, and will pull the ball. He doesn't have a lot of power, but he is capable of stinging a liner into the alley. Batting left, he is more refined and more likely to go with the pitch. He'll get a lot of gap hits.

From either side, Landestoy is a high ball hitter, who likes the pitch in the middle of the plate. Righthanded pitchers can jam him but they are better off working him away and down. Lefthanders will have more success using off-speed pitches and fastballs down. Curves will get him most of the time, as will good sinkers and sliders. Landestoy is, however, the kind of hitter who thrives on mistakes and high fastballs.

He is not considered a good clutch hitter. In fact, some say he is too much of a guess hitter in pinch-hit situations. For that reason, he is judged average in hit-and-run situations and hitting behind the runner. Because he guesses at the plate, he doesn't draw many walks and is not very strong against the change. He bunts very well, but overall is rated a mediocre contact hitter.

BASERUNNING:

Landestoy is an excellent base-stealer. He has above average speed and gets an exceptionally good jump. He is a very smart and sometimes aggressive runner. He has the speed to turn turf-bounces into base hits, and will be used as a pinch-runner as often as he is used as a pinch-hitter.

FIELDING:

A good utility man, Landestoy plays short, third and second equally well. He has a strong arm and throws with above average accuracy from all three positions. His range is greatest to his left. To his right, his range is more limited. He has good body control and at second and short turns the double play well. At third, he does not appear to be nearly as comfortable but is very quick and sure-handed fielding the bunt.

OVERALL:

Coleman: "Landestoy is a good journeyman player who won't hurt you defensively. He can run, but his bat is weak . . . He can't hit well enough to play everyday."

McCarver: "Rafael hasn't been give an opportunity to play everyday. If he had more of a chance, he might surprise some people . Reputations in baseball, like being a good utility man, are tough to escape."

Kiner: "A borderline player, Landestoy is best used as a utility player. He does have good running ability."

CHARLIE LEIBRANDT
LHP, No. 44
RL, 6'4", 200 lbs.
ML Svc: 4 years
Born: 10-4-56 in Chicago, IL

PITCHING:

Charlie Leibrandt has been used in virtually every capacity--short relief, long relief and as a spot starter. If he is nothing else, he is resilient and can go to the mound often. Not blessed with good velocity or extra-special stuff, Leibrandt is an average major league pitcher who survives on heart and control. He is probably most effective as a long relief man and occasional starter.

His fastball, a pitch he uses approximately 60% of the time, tends to be too true, but on his best days it will run in on lefthanded hitters and sometimes sink. His curveball lacks good rotation which prevents a dramatic break and consequently is difficult to distinguish from a slider. He will go to a change infrequently and it is not a serious threat.

Leibrandt uses his fastball when he needs a strike, but he also consistently puts the breaking ball over the plate. Because he lacks strong stuff or an overpowering breaking ball, righthanded hitters can settle in and wait for their pitch. Righthanders also find it easy to pick up Leibrandt's pitch because of his slow and somewhat jerky motion.

His greatest moments seem to come against teams with a lot of lefthanded hitters and, oddly enough, because of his motion. He releases the ball from an upright position, appearing to jerk the pitch across his body. As a result, his ball appears to be on top of lefthanders quickly.

FIELDING, HITTING, BASERUNNING:

Leibrandt has improved his move to first, but a year ago it was completely predictable. If, at the point of rest, he dropped his chin to his chest, he was throwing home. Baserunners got an extraordinary jump on him. He has learned to disguise his move, but once in a while, he will slip into his old pattern. Tall and slender, Leibrandt is an otherwise average defensive performer. On the bases, he won't hurt his club and at the plate, he won't help it.

OVERALL:

Leibrandt is, without question, a player who gets the most of his ability. His effort can never be questioned, but he is a man who has no ace and when he suffers a lapse in control, it is in the worst possible place--high, where hitters unload on him.

McCarver: "Charlie is too true. He must be very fine with his pitches to be effective. If he has his control and can nip the corners, he can be a tough assignment."

Kiner: "Leibrandt is a pitcher who needs a lot of help from his hitters. The Reds gave him that in 1980, when he had a 10-9 season. But now that the Reds aren't able to do that, it will take a lot of improvement on Charlie's part to get above .500."

1982 STATISTICS

W	L	ERA	G	GS	CG	IP	H	R	ER	BB	SO	SV
5	7	5.10	36	11	0	107	130	68	61	48	34	2

CAREER STATISTICS

W	L	ERA	G	GS	CG	IP	H	R	ER	BB	SO	SV
16	17	4.43	82	42	6	315	360	164	155	119	106	2

BRAD LESLEY
RHP, No. 50
RR, 6'6", 220 lbs.
ML Svc: 1 year
Born: 9-11-58 in Turlock, CA

PITCHING:

Brad Lesley's nickname, "The Animal" says it all. He is an original. A big bear of a down home boy, this is the player who, when he was still rampaging through the minor leagues, looked at a reporter and confessed that he loved "throwin' strikes and breakin' a guy's bat off at the handle more than anything."

His game is strikeouts, and he does it on brute strength and with a spirit that is totally unique in major league baseball. He stalks the mound. He growls at hitters and when he gets a strikeout, he's apt to bay at the moon and water at the mouth. It's not unusual to see him run from the mound to the third baseman to retrieve a ball after a strikeout so he can get back to business. Teammates will tell you that they run away from him after a successful outing. His enthusiasm has no bounds, and a handshake with Lesley might take them right to the ground or to the trainer's room.

He is nothing but raw power, a fastball about 90 MPH, a barrel of intimidation and a healthy slider. He has no curve and Reds' pitching coach Bill Fisher is the first to say Lesley's attempt at a change is plain terrible.

His control is good, thankfully, and thus far in his career he has had equal success against right and lefthanded hitters. He comes straight over the top with his best and when he's right, he's trouble.

His only weaknesses right now seem to be inexperience and only a cursory knowledge of hitters around the league. The only questions about him concern his durability and poise. Can he stand up to a full major league season, and can "The Animal" rage when his club is really in contention, not as they were in 1982?

FIELDING, HITTING, BASERUNNING:

Lesley can be a disaster in the field. His move is average, but going after a bunt he looks bad, "like a tank with one tread shot off", according to coach Fisher. He's big and strong, but he doesn't hit and on the bases he is very, very slow.

OVERALL:

Lesley appears to have a good future ahead of him, but he needs time and it has yet to be determined whether or not he can work three or four days consecutively and still be the effective and intimidating short relief man he was late last season. One thing is for sure, he is very determined. If it is left up to him, he will make and make it big.

1982 STATISTICS

W	L	ERA	G	GS	CG	IP	H	R	ER	BB	SO	SV
0	2	2.58	28	0	0	38	27	13	11	13	29	4

CAREER STATISTICS

W	L	ERA	G	GS	CG	IP	H	R	ER	BB	SO	SV
0	2	2.58	28	0	0	38	27	13	11	13	29	4

HITTING:

Nicknamed "Diamond Head" by his teammates, Eddie Milner proved himself to be the gemstone of the Reds' rookie crop. A high ball hitter, Milner has some power to the alleys, good bat control and will bang the ball in the clutch. Primarily a straightaway line drive hitter, both left and righthanded pitchers will work him down and change speeds with success.

Milner shows an advanced ability to hit behind runners and in hit-and-run situations. He will deliver with runners in scoring position and will seldom bite on bad pitches, producing a fair amount of walks. Blessed with good natural speed, some say Milner should bunt more often. He bats well but not enough and could add some points to his average.

Milner handles the bat well, but he will have trouble with good breaking balls. When he does chase a bad pitch it is usually a strong sinker or slider. He is still adjusting to the finesse of good major league pitching and at times will be fooled by a good change-up. He will hit righthanders better and with more authority, driving the ball up the middle and into right-center. Against lefthanders, he'll slap and punch the ball to the opposite field. Milner has already proven himself a quality major league hitter and a better than average leadoff man.

BASERUNNING:

Milner has excellent speed to first and good, quick feet breaking for second. He is aggressive and smart on the paths and is always a threat to steal. Pitchers were alerted to his talents early and they don't forget him when he takes a lead. Much like his hitting, however, he is still learning and has not established himself as a consistent base thief. He does, however, show a lot of savvy for a young player. Baserunning could become the strongest part of his overall game.

EDDIE MILNER
OF, No. 57
LL, 5'11", 170 lbs.
ML Svc: 3 years
Born: 5-21-55 in Columbus, OH

1982 STATISTICS

AVG	G	AB	R	H	2B	3B	HR	RBI	BB	SO	SB
.268	113	407	61	109	23	5	4	31	41	40	18

CAREER STATISTICS

AVG	G	AB	R	H	2B	3B	HR	RBI	BB	SO	SB
.265	127	415	62	110	24	5	4	32	42	41	18

VS. RHP

VS. LHP

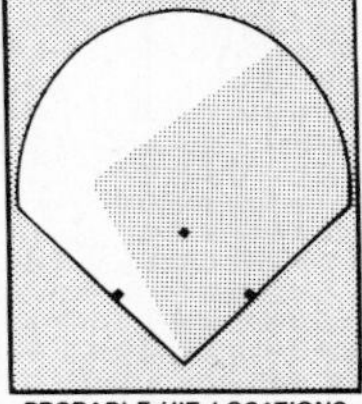
PROBABLE HIT LOCATIONS

FIELDING:

A small player, Milner has an above average arm and accuracy. He gets a great jump on the ball and is superb moving to his left and right. He is equally strong chasing the deep shot over his head, or charging the low liner. Milner has the potential to be a Gold Glove winner and will, almost certainly, displace Cesar Cedeno as the Reds' centerfielder this spring.

OVERALL:

McCarver: "Eddie has a bright future. He's the finest talent to come out of the Cincinnati system in quite awhile. He has good speed, a good arm and makes contact with occasional pop. He's a fine young player."

Coleman: "A good young, hustling player with a good attitude. The only thing he lacks is consistent power."

Kiner: "Eddie has not mastered major league pitching. He can run very well and is an outstanding defensive outfielder. He could develop into a good hitter for average, but he has no real power."

RON OESTER
INF, No. 16
SR, 6'2", 185 lbs.
ML Svc: 4 years
Born: 5-6-56 in
Cincinnati, OH

1982 STATISTICS

AVG	G	AB	R	H	2B	3B	HR	RBI	BB	SO	SB
.260	151	549	63	143	19	4	9	47	35	82	5

CAREER STATISTICS

AVG	G	AB	R	H	2B	3B	HR	RBI	BB	SO	SB
.268	368	1217	149	326	51	13	16	110	103	178	13

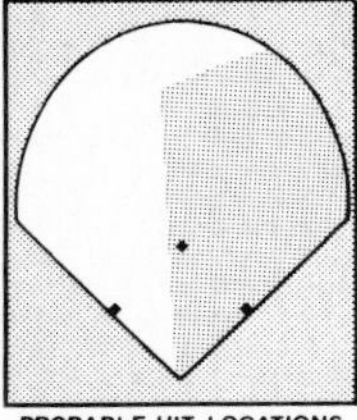

HITTING:

Ron Oester is a switch-hitter who should probably stick to the left side. From the left side he has much more power, much more grace and usually about 20 more points on his average. He is strictly a low ball hitter this way who will drive the ball sharply and with some power. As a righthanded hitter, he shows little power, goes for the high ball and has a tight, awkward swing. On either side, he can be jammed. Pitchers invariably work him inside with success.

Primarily a straightaway hitter, Oester has trouble with high fastballs as a lefthanded hitter, and breaking balls when batting righthanded. A good curve will usually get him and he only has fair success against sinkers and sliders.

He has a bad eye at the plate. He can come through in the clutch, but is much more dependable hitting behind the runner. He has average bunting ability and is average in hit-and-run situations. Oester is a streaky hitter, however, and can get hot at any time. In one of these periods, his singles will turn into doubles and he'll cause a lot of trouble for pitchers.

BASERUNNING:

Oester has above average speed, but does not get a good jump when he attempts to steal, and is caught very often. He is, however, hard-nosed on the bases and will use anything short of a hammer to break up a double play. It seems, particularly on the bases, that Oester's desire to do well overtakes good baseball sense.

FIELDING:

Oester has above average range and a good arm, good enough that the Reds tried him at third for a short time last season. He goes to his left and right equally well and can be excellent turning the double play. Though his fielding is usually one of the strongest parts of his game, he can have breakdowns. For a while last season, Oester could turn the most routine play at second into an adventure.

OVERALL:

It's possible that Oester's failings last season were a result of trying too hard and attempting to spur a flat club. He's expected to improve with experience.

McCarver: "Ron plays very hard and always hustles. He should hit for more average and probably will with more experience. He's a dedicated, intelligent player who excels on defense."

Coleman: "Oester sometimes seems to have lost some of his enthusiasm for the game. It might be because he feels he's not being handled well by management. Still, he can be a good player."

Kiner: "Oester goes hot and cold, but I look for him to be around for quite awhile."

FRANK PASTORE
RHP, No. 35
RR, 6'3", 210 lbs.
ML Svc: 4 years
Born: 8-21-57 in Alhambra, CA

PITCHING:

There is a certain way to anger Pastore and that is to tell him how much he resembles Tom Seaver on the mound. Their physical stature and motion is almost identical. Both come straight over the top getting their strength from their legs and hips. But that's where the resemblance ends. Pastore is primarily a fastball pitcher.

The fastball makes up about 90% of his repertoire and that's the pitch he uses when he trails the hitter. He doesn't, however, have Seaver's strong slider. Instead, he has a strong curveball that breaks away and down. He has a slider, but it is not fierce and he only goes to it occasionally. The curveball is often his strikeout pitch. It has a heavy rotation and is tough on hitters. Even when a batter connects with the curve, it's usually an easy out. With the curve and a rare straight change, Pastore, like most righthanders, is most effective against righthanded hitters.

He's young, but even in the past two years when injuries have plagued him, he demonstrates poise on the mound. Though he would have to be classified as a power pitcher with his 90+ MPH fastball, he spots the fastball well and is always thinking on the mound. In fact, some say he thinks too much, especially about his mechanics. That's when he gets in trouble and has a breakdown in his otherwise good control.

FIELDING, HITTING, BASERUNNING:

Pastore has a good, quick move to first and gets off the mound well to field bunts. He has quick hands and will occasionally spear a ground ball or line drive back to the mound. Pastore will not hurt his cause with a defensive blunder. He is a good hitter and takes it seriously. He'll put the ball in play and pull it into the alley, but he cannot bunt. On the bases, he'll play it smart. He may not be fleet but he won't be caught sleeping.

OVERALL:

For the past two years, Pastore has been troubled by a dislocated tendon in the middle finger of his right hand which has led to problems. It affects his control and his power. When healthy Pastore is a dedicated and competitive pitcher. He studies the craft and studies the opponent. He does not ruffle easily and does not think there is an out he cannot get. If he can correct the problem in his finger, he can be an excellent pitcher.

McCarver: "He's a talented pitcher. It's all a matter of whether he is healthy or not."

Kiner: "Even with the problem in his finger, Pastore has a good walks to innings pitched ratio. He figures to be a big winner, but he has to get the problem in his hand worked out."

1982 STATISTICS

W	L	ERA	G	GS	CG	IP	H	R	ER	BB	SO	SV
8	13	3.97	31	29	3	188	210	86	83	57	94	0

CAREER STATISTICS

W	L	ERA	G	GS	CG	IP	H	R	ER	BB	SO	SV
31	36	3.81	110	87	16	600	598	288	254	157	348	4

JOE PRICE
LHP, No. 49
RL, 6'4", 220 lbs.
ML Svc: 3 years
Born: 11-29-56 in
Inglewood, CA

PITCHING:

Joe Price is the Tom Selleck of the Reds' pitching staff, and is often accused of making dates with women during his warm-up time in the bullpen. But once in the game, it's back to the business of baseball. Price is primarily used as a short reliever. He has started, however, and club officials believe he can handle that assignment as well as the short position.

Ironically, Price is a lefthander who breaks the rule of lefthanders. He is much more effective against righthanded hitters than lefties.

His fastball is a "fooler." He will generally keep it low, but a lot of his strikeouts come on his high fastball which will come in at about 90 MPH. His control on the fastball is above average, and he'll use it with his curve against righthanded hitters. Against lefthanders, he mixes the fastball with a slider, and that is where he gets into trouble. For some reason, Price has a tendency to hang the slider to lefties.

When in trouble and behind in the count, Price will use either the curve or the fastball. But after all is said and done, he is a fastball pitcher with one very distinct characteristic. When Price is on the mound, he is the polar opposite of teammate Brad "The Animal" Lesley, who storms about the mound like an angered bull. With the bases loaded and a full count on the hitter, Price will exude the impression of a minimally interested patron at an unimpressive art show. There is not a glimmer of passion until the moment he releases the pitch, but that fastball is a "fooler" and the hitter never has time to look.

FIELDING, HITTING, BASERUNNING:

Price has a good, quick move to first, but like most tall pitchers, he is anything but graceful in fielding the position. He doesn't come off the mound well to field a bunt and when he has to, he is all arms and legs and the legs aren't moving that quickly.

As a hitter, he's poor, and on the bases he suffers from the same gait he uses in the field, a slow one.

OVERALL:

A contradictory pitcher, Price's best weapon is his fastball. He is a very poised and mature athlete, who has yet to see his best days.

McCarver: "Joe has a good moving fastball and a good curve, but he has got to work on the hanging slider."

Coleman: "You can't scare this guy."

1982 STATISTICS

W	L	ERA	G	GS	CG	IP	H	R	ER	BB	SO	SV
3	4	2.85	59	1	0	72	73	26	23	32	71	3

CAREER STATISTICS

W	L	ERA	G	GS	CG	IP	H	R	ER	BB	SO	SV
26	27	1.53	138	59	13	484	461	90	82	132	325	7

CHARLIE PULEO
RHP, No. 25
RR, 6'3", 190 lbs.
ML Svc: 1 year plus
Born: 2-7-55 in
Glen Ridge, NJ

PITCHING:

As with most Mets pitchers last season, Charlie Puleo filled several roles. He appeared most comfortable and effective as a starter, and the Reds plan to use him in that role.

Charlie is a breaking ball pitcher who has a deceptively easy motion. The ball gets to the plate faster than the hitter expects. He doesn't have the control to pitch to the batter's weaknesses. Control, in and out of the strike zone, is a problem for Puleo. If he keeps his fastball down, he can get a lot of ground balls. But he will throw it until the opposition starts killing it.

Puleo throws an occasional curve. It can be effective if he throws it out of the strike zone on a two-strike count. His best pitch, his slider, is particularly effective against right-handed hitters. His pitches tend to be too true.

Puleo gets himself in trouble because of wildness, but handles pressure situations well. He is a thinker and a good competitor.

FIELDING, HITTING, BASERUNNING:

Puleo does more to help himself than most pitchers. He is quite alert on the mound and fields his position intelligently at least, if not always well. Only three National League pitchers, all of them with more innings pitched, had more assists than Puleo, and no pitcher was involved in more double plays than he was. He foiled several sacrifice bunt attempts and turned them into double plays. Though he is a below average hitter, he is accomplished as a sacrifice bunter.

OVERALL:

Coleman: "Looks good for a first-year pitcher. He overpowered the Padres at times, but good fast-ball-hitting teams like the Dodgers and Expos probably would hurt him."

McCarver: "Charlie could be a good short reliever or a fifth starter. His greatest asset is keeping the ball in play on the ground. He has shown signs of getting guys out consistently."

1982 STATISTICS

W	L	ERA	G	GS	CG	IP	H	R	ER	BB	SO	SV
9	9	4.47	36	24	1	171	179	99	85	90	98	1

CAREER STATISTICS

W	L	ERA	G	GS	CG	IP	H	R	ER	BB	SO	SV
9	9	4.16	40	25	1	184	187	100	85	98	106	1

MARIO SOTO
RHP, No. 36
RR, 6'0", 185 lbs.
ML Svc: 6 years
Born: 7-12-56 in Bani, DR

PITCHING:

Mario Soto is quickly becoming one of the most feared starters in baseball, mentioned frequently in the same breath as Philadelphia's Steve Carlton and Fernando Valenzuela in Los Angeles. Soto lives on his fastball. That's what brought him to the big leagues, but it is not the pitch which has elevated him to such lofty status. After beginning his career as a long relief man, Soto began to develop a change. That's the pitch which has made his career. In fact, it has become his strikeout pitch and the tool he calls upon in tight situations. He also throws a slider but it takes a back seat to the set-up fastball and his money pitch, the change.

Soto hurls himself into a game and if he is criticized, it is because his emotion sometimes gets the better of his judgment and his skills. He will, as a result of his competitiveness, drive a hitter off the plate with a brushback pitch and then use the slider, particularly against righthanded hitters. But he is always working his way back to a spot for the change.

Like all of his pitches, the change comes from a three-quarter delivery and is successful because there is no variance, or tip-off, in his motion. His greatest fault seems to be his temperament. Though poised in critical game situations, Soto can be razzed to a point where he loses control of his pitches and his cool. It may not stop him from becoming a great pitcher, but it very well could.

FIELDING, HITTING, BASERUNNING:

Soto's move to first gets average to above average marks. He is very quick and pounces on bunts. He is gifted with good athletic ability and generally fields the position well. On the bases, he demonstrates good instincts and good spirit with better than average speed. As a hitter, he leaves a lot to be desired, even for a pitcher. But at times he will drop an "excuse me" single over the infield.

OVERALL:

Soto is generally regarded as having the best fastball-change combination in baseball, a mix that takes him from anonymity to the top of the game. He can, and does, dominate opponents. He seems to be particularly effective against Philadelphia, Los Angeles and Atlanta. No one questions his talent, but there are questions about whether or not Soto can learn to control his temper as well as his pitches.

McCarver: "I call his change a palmball. Without this pitch he would be a .500 pitcher, but with it, he's deadly. No lefthanded hitter is safe. He holds the ball, not with his fingers, but back in his palm with his thumb and index finger looped to the side of the ball. Deception comes with the whipping arm motion which leads a hitter to lunge at the pitch, thinking that it might be a fastball."

Coleman: "The only thing holding him back from greatness is his temper and the ball club he plays for."

1982 STATISTICS

W	L	ERA	G	GS	CG	IP	H	R	ER	BB	SO	SV
14	13	2.79	35	34	13	257	202	88	80	71	274	0

CAREER STATISTICS

W	L	ERA	G	GS	CG	IP	H	R	ER	BB	SO	SV
42	38	3.32	155	82	28	738	576	297	272	285	696	4

ALEX TREVINO
C/INF, No. 29
RR, 5'10", 165 lbs.
ML Svc: 5 years
Born: 8-26-57 in Monterrey, MX

1982 STATISTICS

AVG	G	AB	R	H	2B	3B	HR	RBI	BB	SO	SB
.251	120	355	24	89	10	3	1	33	34	34	3

CAREER STATISTICS

AVG	G	AB	R	H	2B	3B	HR	RBI	BB	SO	SB
.258	367	1078	94	278	34	6	1	100	81	123	8

VS. RHP

VS. LHP

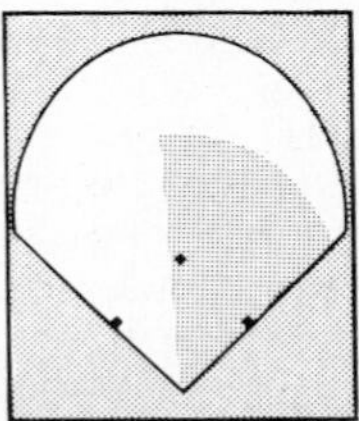
PROBABLE HIT LOCATIONS

HITTING:

Alex Trevino probably has the most unusual swing in all of baseball. Some go as far as calling it "weird." It is inside-out to the extreme. Consequently, most of his hits are tailing flares to the opposite field. In most cases, it will appear as though Trevino is slinging at the pitch, instead of swinging. Occasionally, he'll reach a pitch and drive it into the right-center alley, but it is a rarity--just as anything he hits to the right of second base. Most defenses will position themselves against Trevino as if he were a lefthanded hitter.

Trevino is a strict high ball hitter and will have trouble with anything inside or down. Left and righthanded pitchers can jam him with equal success. A singles hitter all the way, Trevino doesn't show much power. However, he does have good success against the change-up and will sometimes pull one. He has trouble with good breaking pitches, particularly a strong curve.

Because of his tendency to go to right, Trevino has good success in hitting behind the runner. He is average to below in the clutch and doesn't, thus far in his career, show a great eye at the plate. His bunting needs work as does most of his work at bat. Trevino is a "pet project" of Reds' hitting coach Ted Kluszewski.

BASERUNNING:

As catchers go, Trevino is quick on the bases. He gets down to first well and, some believe, could steal some bases. He is conservative on the bases, shows intelligence but often appears anxious.

FIELDING:

Trevino is still learning the trade, especially in the area of handling pitchers and knowing opposing hitters. He is blessed with good arm strength and an exceptionally quick release, but more often than not last season, Trevino's throws to second ended up in center field. His accuracy was horrible. He is very quick in fielding bunts, holds runners well because of his arm strength and can be excellent in blocking pitches in the dirt. His greatest weakness as a catcher is the inaccuracy of his throws.

OVERALL:

McCarver: "Alex was given a chance to play regularly after being a back up player with the Mets, but he hasn't performed as most thought he would. He has excellent actions behind the plate--he sucks up low pitches--but may not be strong enough to play 130 games a year."

Kiner: "He is a good hustling catcher with a great desire to play. He has quickness defensively, but lacks a strong bat. I think he would make a good utility man."

Coleman: "He's been a disappointment to the Reds, but he could get better. He must throw with more accuracy."

HITTING:

Duane Walker will hit and he will hit in the clutch, though his major league experience is very limited. He is basically a line drive hitter who will take the ball into the gaps. He likes the high ball, but will go down and get the low pitch, too. Pitchers have most success working him inside. Lefthanders can confuse him with sliders down.

Walker is most effective against righthanded pitching. He is troubled, however, by good breaking pitches. He doesn't hit the curve well, and struggles with sinkers and sliders. A good change will also fool him.

Walker is poised and reserved and will produce the key hit. His lack of bat control reflects his experience and makes him questionable in hit-and-run situations. He does, however, display a keen eye at the plate and draws his share of walks.

He has home run power but the pitch has to be up and down the middle of the plate. Walker is finding his way with major league pitchers but today is viewed as an average "young" hitter who should improve. He has fair home run potential and better than average RBI abilities.

BASERUNNING:

Walker has above average speed and uses it well on the bases. He will get some leg hits and will steal bases. He gets a good jump, and appears to have good instincts on the bases. At times however, he appears anxious, as if afraid of making a mistake. His baserunning is viewed as potentially very strong.

FIELDING:

Walker is a solid outfielder. He has above average range and good awareness in the field. He goes back on the ball very well which allows him to play shallow in a tight game and cut down the loop hit. His arm is average, but

DUANE WALKER
OF, No. 58
LL, 6'0", 180 lbs.
ML Svc: 2 years
Born: 3-13-57 in Pasadena, TX

1982 STATISTICS

AVG	G	AB	R	H	2B	3B	HR	RBI	BB	SO	SB
.218	86	239	26	52	10	0	5	22	27	58	9

CAREER STATISTICS

AVG	G	AB	R	H	2B	3B	HR	RBI	BB	SO	SB
.218	86	239	26	52	10	0	5	22	27	58	9

VS. RHP

VS. LHP

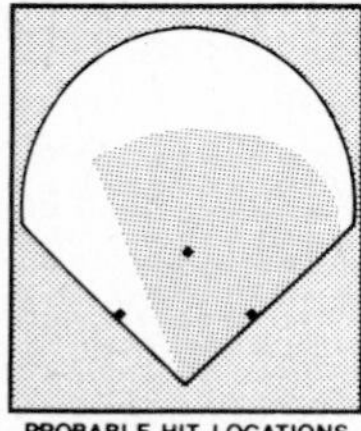
PROBABLE HIT LOCATIONS

his accuracy is very good. At this point, Walker's fielding may be the most polished part of his game.

OVERALL:

In his limited playing time, Walker has performed surprisingly well. If he sticks with this major league club, he will be used as platoon player and pinch-hitter. His is a familiar refrain --he needs time, but it doesn't look like he will get it.

Coleman: "Duane is a solid outfielder who looks like he might be a comer. Time will tell, but it looks like he has a chance to become a pretty good player."

McCarver: "Seven years of minor league experience says a lot. Nowadays, the good talents take about three years to develop . . . He has never had a regular shot, but his tools appear competent enough to make him a utility outfielder."

GERMAN BARRANCA
INF, No. 12
SR, 6'0", 170 lbs.
ML Svc: 4 years
Born: 10-19-56 in
Veracruz, MX

HITTING, FIELDING, BASERUNNING:

Batting left, Barranca goes for low pitches, will spray them up the middle, and can be jammed. Batting right, he likes the high ball. Pitchers will work him outside with success. Barranca doesn't show much power. He's a punch man who is a fair pinch-hitter. He seems vulnerable to good off-speed pitches. A good change, sinker, slider or curve will cause him trouble. He can handle most fastballs, even out of his strong zone.

He is best batting right, and can occasionally reach the left-center alley and seems to have more bat control from this side. He will hit behind the runner with above average success and is equally effective in hit-and-run situations. He has an average bunt.

Barranca seems best suited for second base. He has an average arm and range. At third, he fields the bunt well and at second he is dependable on the double play. He is an adequate defensive player, nothing flashy.

It was Barranca's ability to combine timely hits with stolen bases which brought him to the majors. He gets a good lead but is inexperienced and cautious about taking a base.

OVERALL:

McCarver: "German appears to be a good contact hitter with good speed who, if given a chance to play regularly, could surprise people."

TOM LAWLESS
INF, No. 17
RR, 6'0", 165 lbs.
ML Svc: 1 year plus
Born: 12-19-56 in
Erie, PA

HITTING, BASERUNNING, FIELDING:

Tom Lawless is a singles hitter and vulnerable to the fastball. He will spray the ball through, and just over, the middle of the infield. Against lefthanders, he is more likely to reach the left side, but will never reach the alleys. Good heat is the best way to dispose of him. He can not hit the curve, but has better success with sinkers and sliders. He is strongest against lefthanders who make the mistake of giving him something off-speed and up. Lawless has not developed a keen sense of the strike zone, but has relatively good bunting skills.

Lawless has above average speed and excellent basestealing abilities. He gets an excellent jump and shows good instincts. He is smart and aggressive and shows no fear of contact.

Lawless uses his speed well in the field. He has above average range and will move deep into the holes to make a play. Though his arm is of average strength, he throws with exceptional accuracy and has good body control in all situations. Very quick hands and turns the double play very well.

OVERALL:

Coleman: "Tom Lawless will only be a good player if he improves with the bat. He runs well and plays a decent enough second base. He's gotten to the majors mostly on desire."

DAVE VAN GORDER
C, No. 60
RR, 6'2", 205 lbs.
ML Svc: 2 years
Born: 3-27-57 in
Los Angeles, CA

HITTING, BASERUNNING, FIELDING:

Dave Van Gorder is a straightaway, contact hitter. He has a rather stiff looking swing and is most effective against high pitches out over the plate. Against righthanders, he will take the ball up the middle. Against lefthanders, Van Gorder has more success pulling the ball and shows more power. He can be jammed. He was weak last season against curves and had almost as much trouble with good sinkers and sliders. He is, however, a good mistake hitter. Van Gorder has poor bat control, hasn't learned the strike zone, doesn't draw a lot of walks and his bunting needs improvement.

Van Gorder is slow on the bases and shows signs of inexperience. He will give you his best effort, but will not become a big league success on the basis of his baserunning.

Van Gorder has a limited knowledge of opposing hitters and their strengths. Mechanically, he is solid behind the plate, blocks pitches well and fields the bunt with above average quickness. He handles pitchers well and usually calls a decent game. His arm is weak, but is generally accurate and he has a relatively quick release.

OVERALL:

McCarver: "It is very tough to tell about this young catcher. He had average minor league statistics which would indicate a struggle in the major leagues."

Coleman: "Dave looks like he has leadership capabilities. His bat is so-so and he seems comfortable behind the plate . . . It looks like it is going to take awhile."

THE ASTRODOME
Houston Astros

Seating Capacity: 45,000
Playing Surface: Artificial (AstroTurf)

Dimensions
Left Field Pole: 340 ft.
Left-Center Field: 390 ft.
Center Field: 406 ft.
Right-Center Field: 390 ft.
Right Field Pole: 340 ft.
Height of Outfield Wall: 10 ft.

When its construction was completed in 1965, the Astrodome was widely billed as the eighth wonder of the world. It was the first stadium to install an artificial surface on the playing field. It's surface was named "Astroturf," and became a necessity when they discovered that real grass couldn't grow beneath the dome. Although the artificial surface has been widely imitated, the Astrodome retains several other peculiar characteristics. For instance, there are several huge speakers which hang from the ceiling over the field of play. If a fly ball ever hits one of them, it is considered in play. A batted ball doesn't have to go over the fence to be a home run in the Astrodome. Instead, any ball which hits the fence above an orange line which runs at a height of 10 feet from foul line to foul line is considered a homer. This particular characteristic makes the umpire's job more difficult because they really have to hustle on any high fly hit to the outfield.

Then there's the dome itself. The roof was originally translucent, but players discovered that it was often impossible to locate fly balls. The roof has since been painted, but even with the darker color, it is often difficult for fielders to follow the flight of the ball especially during day games when the sun is bright.

When there is a large crowd in the Astrodome, the noise can be deafening, since the closed roof tends to prevent the sound from escaping upward. Many pitchers find fault with the slope of the mound in this park. It has a tendency to flatten out more quickly than in other parks, and this forces a pitcher to work much harder to keep his pitches down. The level plane of the mound can often cause a pitcher to alter his normal pitching motion and this can cause injuries to the arm as well as to an ERA.

On the bright side for pitchers, the Astrodome is considered by many to be the toughest park in the National League in which to hit a home run. The ball does not carry at all, and to reach the fences, a batter really has to drill a pitch. Consequently, pitchers can often survive an outing in the Astrodome even if they lack their best stuff.

Both infielders and outfielders have had to learn that a ball hit on the ground can really pick up speed on the Astroturf. This usually forces the fielders to set up deeper defensively when playing in Houston. On the positive side, fielders never have to worry about bad hops, tricky winds or a sloppy infield.

HITTING:

Late in the 1981 season, Alan Ashby made several subtle changes in his stance and swing. As a result, he began to look awkward, even raising his front foot into the air as he swung, and he became a much improved hitter. Unorthodox, yes, but effective--this switch-hitter gained power and consistency from both sides.

A high ball hitter both left and righthanded, Ashby likes to pull but will hit line drives to the opposite field lefthanded. Don't give him a belt-high fastball. Pitchers are more effective keeping the ball down, but if Ashby, a smart hitter, is expecting it, he will golf the ball for power. Ashby thrives on hitting mistakes.

Because he has been so much more effective lefthanded, Ashby abandoned switch-hitting briefly but has subsequently resumed it. He has been platooned, sitting out against the good lefthanded pitchers. He does have power righthanded, but strikes out more and doesn't approach his lefthanded consistency. Ashby is an effective clutch hitter who doesn't scare under pressure.

BASERUNNING:

Lack of speed makes Ashby a below average runner. He is basically conservative on the bases, probably a good concept because when he has gambled in the past, he has usually paid the price. On a close play, he isn't afraid of contact.

FIELDING:

Ashby's prime asset is his rapport with pitchers. A genuinely nice person, Ashby is a 24-hour-a-day catcher. Pitchers always know they can discuss their trade with him. The Houston pitching staff presents an unusually hard job for a catcher. Nolan Ryan throws over 90 MPH heat, and Joe

ALAN ASHBY
C, No. 14
SR, 6'2", 190 lbs.
ML Svc: 8 years
Born: 7-8-51 in
Long Beach, CA

1982 STATISTICS

AVG	G	AB	R	H	2B	3B	HR	RBI	BB	SO	SB
.257	100	339	40	87	14	2	12	49	27	53	2

CAREER STATISTICS

AVG	G	AB	R	H	2B	3B	HR	RBI	BB	SO	SB
.237	812	2479	230	588	108	11	42	290	264	383	6

VS. RHP

VS. LHP

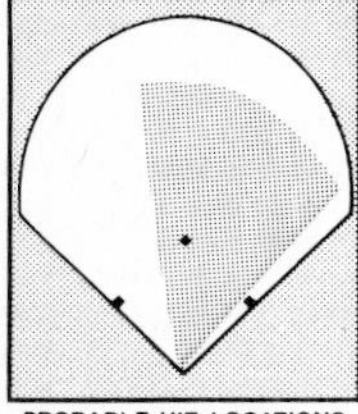
PROBABLE HIT LOCATIONS

Niekro tosses unpredictable knuckleballs. Ashby handles them all well. Houston's talented staff remains a challenge for any catcher. Until 1982, his arm was rated above average, but Ashby threw out only about 20% of enemy basestealers then. A finger injury was a big problem, and Houston pitchers didn't give him much help holding runners. Ashby has a quick release and above average arm strength.

OVERALL:

McCarver: "Few guys appear to be as naturally cut out for a position as Alan is for catching. He knows the meaning of taking total control of a game. He is effective and respected, an intelligent catcher who puts the proper emphasis on what should be done."

Coleman: "A quality major league catcher. Very smart."

DAN BOONE
LHP, No. 31
LL, 5'8", 132 lbs.
ML Svc: 2 years
Born: 1-15-54 in
Long Beach, CA

PITCHING:

At 5'8", and 132 lbs., Dan Boone is believed to be the smallest pitcher in major league history. This causes one obvious problem: He doesn't get a lot of heat on his fastball, which travels only 80-85 MPH.

Boone does have his assets. His slider and curve are effective. So is his sinker. And his fastball does have good movement in either direction. He throws a screwball, and last year he began working on a knuckleball. His change-ups frequently cause hitters to lunge at pitches. When he uses his entire repertoire and controls each pitch, he is a success. But as a short-reliever who has never started a major league game, he has had little opportunity to utilize all his pitches in the same game.

Boone's breaking pitches are similar to those of another ex-Padres pitcher, Randy Jones. But Boone doesn't have Jones' fastball and apparently does not throw hard enough to start. He is poised, intelligent and a willing learner.

Lack of consistency has been Boone's only problem to this point, and that may be explained by his huge variety of pitches and his inexperience. If his mastery and control improve, and if he keeps his pitches down, potentially he is a good short-reliever, particularly on a staff of power pitchers.

FIELDING, HITTING, BASERUNNING:

In his rookie 1981 season, Boone picked-off five runners in 63 innings, an outstanding ratio. Runners must respect his move. His poise on the mound is good. He runs well but seldom gets an opportunity to bat.

OVERALL:

Boone resembles Bobby Shantz except that he is even smaller than Shantz and is yet to gain an opportunity to pitch as a starter. A 25-10 minor league record indicates potential.

Kiner: "He has overcome the problem of being the smallest player in the majors, but he still needs more power on his pitches."

McCarver: "Dan is very smooth for a young pitcher. His effectiveness could depend on the pitcher before him. For example, if Dan followed Nolan Ryan, it would be the express train becoming the local-hop."

1982 STATISTICS

W	L	ERA	G	GS	CG	IP	H	R	ER	BB	SO	SV
1	1	4.71	20	0	0	28	28	16	15	7	12	2

CAREER STATISTICS

W	L	ERA	G	GS	CG	IP	H	R	ER	BB	SO	SV
2	0	3.46	57	0	0	91	91	39	35	28	55	4

HITTING:

Jose Cruz can turn any pitcher's fastball around and send it out of the park. Righthanders seldom get away with pitching him inside heat. Cruz also can hit even a good righthander's curve with authority. But good left-handers give him trouble with breaking pitches, and because he lunges into the ball, change-ups are often effective against him.

A strictly pull hitter for several years, Cruz still prefers to pull, especially against righthanders. But he became one of the game's best hitters when he learned to drive the outside pitch to left field--and when he is on his hottest streaks, half his hits usually are to the left side away from his power. Cruz is more disciplined against righthanders, and he will chase bad pitches, especially outside, and strike out against lefthanders.

Cruz is almost never hurt, loves to play baseball 12 months a year and enjoys hitting most, perhaps accounting for his aggressiveness. One of his nicknames in Houston is "Chop-Chop" because of his knack at beating pitches into the turf and using his speed to beat out high-chopping infield hits. He has excellent power, too, when he gets the fastball. Primarily a high ball hitter, Cruz will hit a low pitch hard, too, if he is expecting it.

BASERUNNING:

Until a knee injury and age slowed him slightly, Cruz was good for 30-40 stolen bases each season. He remains a threat, especially at key points in a game. Cruz tends to run on the first pitch and gets a good jump. He is subject to being picked-off by a smart pitcher. One strong point is that he runs hard to first base on every ground ball, and even the slightest misplay enables him to reach safely.

JOSE CRUZ
OF, No. 25
LL, 6'0", 175 lbs.
ML Svc: 11 years
Born: 8-8-47 in Arroyo, PR

1982 STATISTICS

AVG	G	AB	R	H	2B	3B	HR	RBI	BB	SO	SB
.275	155	570	62	157	27	2	9	68	60	67	21

CAREER STATISTICS

AVG	G	AB	R	H	2B	3B	HR	RBI	BB	SO	SB
.281	1587	5255	682	1475	260	61	108	694	618	644	242

VS. RHP

VS. LHP

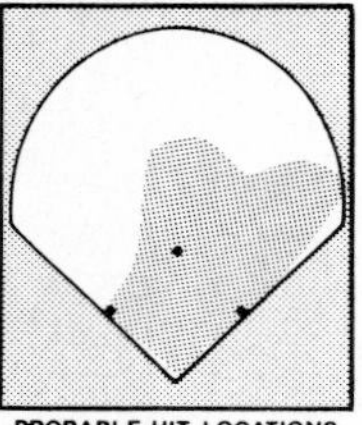
PROBABLE HIT LOCATIONS

FIELDING:

Cruz has improved noticeably as a left fielder. His speed is a chief asset. He has experienced problems in the past with ground balls, accounting for more than a few errors. His arm is strong but not always accurate. Cruz plays deep and normally charges the ball well, though on bloopers he tends toward conservatism. He has worked hard on his defense, and has played center field in an emergency.

OVERALL:

Kiner: "Cruz is one of the most unnoticed and underrated players in the National League."

McCarver: "A totally dedicated athlete who always gives 100%, Cruz has good speed and power and hits for average."

PHIL GARNER
INF, No. 3
RR, 5'10", 177 lbs.
ML Svc: 8 years
Born: 4-30-49 in
Jefferson City, TN

1982 STATISTICS

AVG	G	AB	R	H	2B	3B	HR	RBI	BB	SO	SB
.274	155	588	65	161	33	8	13	83	40	92	24

CAREER STATISTICS

AVG	G	AB	R	H	2B	3B	HR	RBI	BB	SO	SB
.263	1208	4168	507	1097	212	61	71	498	365	531	182

VS. RHP

VS. LHP

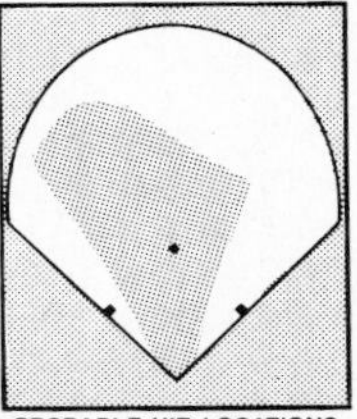
PROBABLE HIT LOCATIONS

HITTING:

For several seasons at Pittsburgh, Phil Garner was dubbed the best eighth-place hitter in baseball. At Houston, where the lineup pales in comparison with the Bucs' thunder, Garner became a clean-up batter. In his new role, he excelled as well, leading the Astros in home runs and RBIs last year. Garner likes the fast-ball high, but he will hit anything--high, low, fast, slow--and has enough strength, despite his size, to take advantage of the Astrodome alleys. Lefthanders fare best keeping the ball down; righthanders occasionally can jam Garner. He can be fooled once on a change-up, but if a pitcher tries it again he usually pays the price.

A spray hitter to all fields, Garner will pull lefthanders more. He is excellent at hitting behind runners and at his best with men in scoring position. He is smart enough to take advantage of the artificial surfaces, and he knows the strike zone well. His No. 1 hitting quality is his aggressiveness. Phil Garner will never give in to an opponent, no matter what the situation. Among the most competitive athletes, Garner thrives on pressure and is at his best when a game is on the line.

BASERUNNING:

Garner combines speed, daring and all-out hustle to remain an excellent basestealer and one who will go from first to third on a hit. He is among the game's smartest runners and also one of the best at breaking up double plays. He never hesitates to go into the dirt.

FIELDING:

As a second baseman, Garner is among the highest rated in range, arm strength, accuracy and making the double play. With his considerable experience, he positions himself well. The Astros may move him to third base, where he hasn't played regularly for several seasons and admits to being apprehensive. But, again, his sound arm and his knack for getting to every ball hit close to him should serve Garner well.

OVERALL:

Kiner: "He's known as Scrap-Iron and he lives up to that name. He is a solid all around player who will beat you any way he can."

McCarver: "Scrap-Iron plays the game as hard as anybody. He is totally dedicated to winning. Not enough superlatives are available to character-ize his performance."

Coleman: "Phil is a good player and a great competitor, a solid pro who loves the game. He is a winner."

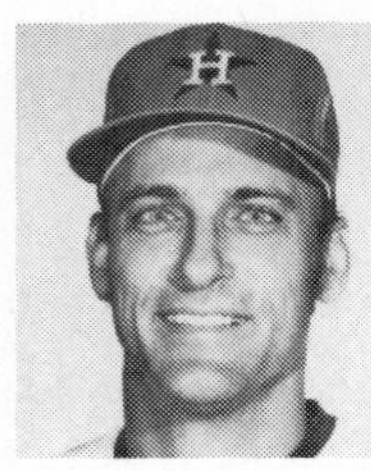

ART HOWE
INF, No. 18
RR, 6'1", 185 lbs.
ML Svc: 7 years
Born: 12-15-46 in Pittsburgh, PA

1982 STATISTICS

AVG	G	AB	R	H	2B	3B	HR	RBI	BB	SO	SB
.238	110	365	29	87	15	1	5	38	41	45	2

CAREER STATISTICS

AVG	G	AB	R	H	2B	3B	HR	RBI	BB	SO	SB
.262	798	2484	251	652	124	23	41	281	257	269	10

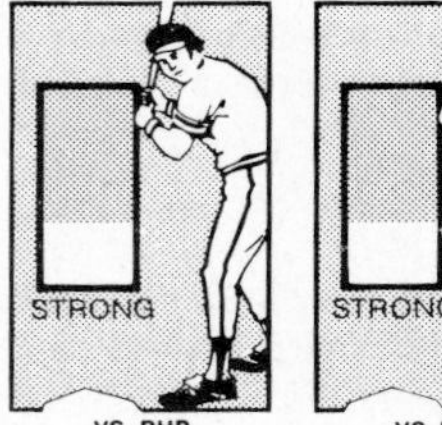

VS. RHP

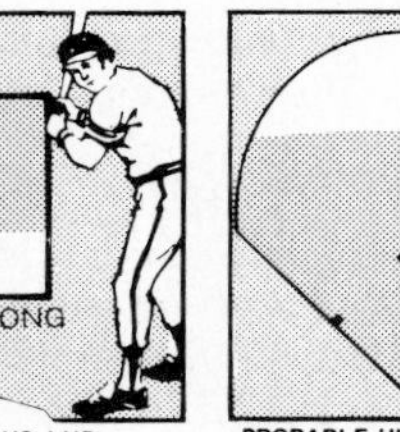

VS. LHP

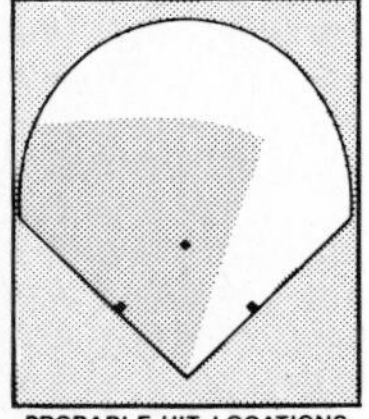
PROBABLE HIT LOCATIONS

HITTING:

Art Howe slumped from .296 in 1981 to .238 in 1982, but an assortment of injuries may have been more of a factor than any decline in ability. Howe is one of the few high ball hitters effective against a good pitcher's curve. Fastballs, curves, sliders, change-ups--Howe will hit any pitch hard if it's high. Against a lefthander with a runner on first, he'll hit the low pitch to right field well to execute the hit-and-run. Otherwise, he is primarily a pull hitter against righthanders. Some righthanders have success jamming Howe with fastballs. Lefthanders ordinarily fare better keeping the ball low and away.

He is not a pure power hitter, but Howe does have enough strength to send a ball over any fence. He is a good gap hitter. A smart, dedicated "situation" hitter, Howe will sacrifice himself to help his team. He may not always hit good pitches hard but he usually will get a piece of the ball. Howe has produced clutch hits for the Astros throughout his years in Houston. His career average undoubtedly would be higher except that Howe has endured numerous injuries and, being a competitor, usually tries to play despite pain--sometimes with declining results offensively.

BASERUNNING:

Howe does not have even average speed and isn't a threat to steal, but he will gamble and take the extra base on some hits. An especially hard slider, Howe will break up the double play if he gets close enough to second base.

FIELDING:

A starter for Houston at third base, second base and first base, Howe works hard on his defense and has been adequate or better at every position. At third, he has limited range and only average arm strength, but excellent hands and accuracy are assets. For a big man, he comes in on balls with surprising grace and with positive results--he's tough to bunt against. Overall, he is underrated as a third baseman. The good hands help him at first base. So does an intense desire to get the job done.

OVERALL:

Kiner: "Howe has good leadership ability and will make it as a manager one day. He will do anything to help his team."

Coleman: "He gives you 100% each time out. Tough to retire when his team needs a hit. A total pro."

McCarver: "A real pro who has worked hard to get where he is today. He gets the most out of his defensive ability."

BOB KNEPPER
LHP, No. 39
LL, 6'2", 200 lbs.
ML Svc: 5 years
Born: 5-25-54 in Akron, OH

PITCHING:

Inconsistency has marked Bob Knepper's career. In 1981, he was 9-5 with a 2.18 ERA for Houston. In 1982, he was 5-15 with a 4.45 ERA. Explanations for this have ranged from a lack of mental toughness, to poor pitch selection--bad preparation to bad luck.

Nobody questions Knepper's stuff. His fastball travels only at about 88 MPH but has good movement and, usually, pinpoint control. His curve is devastating to lefthanded batters. His slider is rarely used but is frequently mistaken by hitters for his fastball.

Some critics felt Knepper failed to challenge hitters early last season--he permitted almost 30 first-inning runs, far more than in any other inning. His endurance is good. When he is sharp, he has no trouble finishing.

Control of his curve often is the key to Knepper's success. Last year, his control wasn't as sharp as it had been in the past. Another problem, which Knepper can't solve, is that his teammates gave him precious little run support.

FIELDING, HITTING, BASERUNNING:

In Knepper's first week as an Astro pitcher in 1981, he helped win a game with his bat. Asked if that was typical of his offensive contribution, he said, "No, I'm actually a lousy hitter." Credit Knepper with honesty. Knepper struck out about half his at-bats last year. And in the Astros' lineup, that's costly. He is an average bunter. As a fielder, Knepper is average, too, but seldom beats himself. He has no speed on the bases.

OVERALL:

Overall, Knepper has excellent qualities for a starting pitcher--a moving fastball, a sharp-breaking curve, good control and the ability to go the distance. But at times he almost seems too relaxed. In a roller-coaster career, he hit rock bottom in 1982.

McCarver: "It's hard to believe Bob's record. A lack of run production usually puts a lot of pressure on pitchers of his ilk and, being only human, they yield. With a team that scores a lot of runs, Bob could be a consistent winner."

Coleman: "If somebody could light a fire under him, he could be a very good pitcher. He lacks mental toughness."

1982 STATISTICS

W	L	ERA	G	GS	CG	IP	H	R	ER	BB	SO	SV
5	15	4.45	33	29	4	180	193	100	89	60	108	1

CAREER STATISTICS

W	L	ERA	G	GS	CG	IP	H	R	ER	BB	SO	SV
61	70	3.56	191	184	46	1210	1199	539	479	400	667	1

ALAN KNICELY
C, No. 11
RR, 6'0", 194 lbs.
ML Svc: 1 year plus
Born: 5-19-55 in Harrisonburg, VA

1982 STATISTICS

AVG	G	AB	R	H	2B	3B	HR	RBI	BB	SO	SB
.188	59	133	10	25	2	0	2	12	14	30	0

CAREER STATISTICS

AVG	G	AB	R	H	2B	3B	HR	RBI	BB	SO	SB
.197	70	147	12	29	2	0	4	14	16	35	0

VS. RHP

VS. LHP

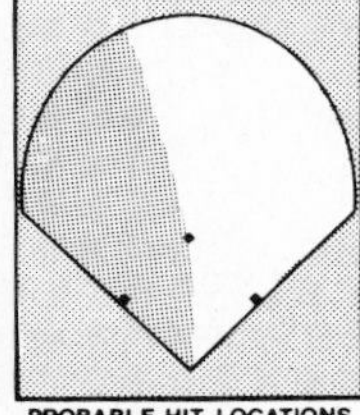
PROBABLE HIT LOCATIONS

HITTING:

Alan Knicely began his professional career as a pitcher, but his bat was so strong that he was converted into an outfielder, a third baseman and, finally, a catcher. In the minors, he had superb power credentials, and he hit for consistency, too. But with the Astros, Knicely has struggled at bat. In fairness, he has never had a chance to start regularly.

A high ball, fastball hitter, Knicely has been fooled by the smarter pitchers, and he has experienced considerable trouble with low, off-speed deliveries. He is primarily a pull hitter, but can hit mistakes out of any park--even the Astrodome--to any field. He has been more effective against lefthanded pitchers, but that may be because of such limited experience against major league righthanders.

Even though the Astros desperately need righthanded power, Knicely is in a predicament--he doesn't field well enough for the club to play him unless he hits with consistency and power. And he hasn't hit enough that the Astros have been willing to accept his defensive shortcomings. Some scouts and coaches believe all Knicely needs is time, that he eventually will adjust to big league pitching. Based on his impressive minor league credentials, he is almost certain to get that opportunity some day soon.

BASERUNNING:

Knicely hasn't been on base enough yet to judge intangibles, but on the plus side he is a hard-nosed, aggressive young man and on the minus side, he is slow afoot. He is no threat to steal and is not likely to collect many leg hits.

FIELDING:

So many position changes have made it impossible for Knicely to excel at any one spot. As a catcher, he lacks experience handling Joe Niekro's knuckleball, a big disadvantage in Houston. To his credit, when Knicely has caught Niekro, he hasn't been embarrassed. Otherwise, when Knicely did start, pitchers' performances didn't suffer. He is a willing worker and a popular man with the moundsmen. His arm is strong but undisciplined. Overall he lacks polish. As an outfielder, his arm strength atones for lack of range. But in the Astrodome, he is not an asset in the outfield. At third base he is not smooth, but the good arm helps.

OVERALL:

McCarver: "Knicely is still young enough to fulfill his potential, but the Dome is a tough hitters' park."

Coleman: "He has a quick bat. He needs work on his pitch selection and defense, but he has a chance because of the live bat."

HITTING:

Ray Knight is a model of consistency at bat. Despite lacking the power to hit home runs frequently and the speed to get infield singles, Knight is a .300 threat. With his closed, upright stance, Knight will hit line drives to left field and bloopers to right. He assaults high fastballs from lefthanded or righthanded pitchers. He adapted well to the Astrodome in his first Houston season, electing to abandon his power stroke and use the big park to his advantage. To avoid potential conflict, he used that approach on the road, too. As a result, he became more of a spray hitter, often connecting to the opposite field. Breaking balls down are the best approach against Knight for a righthanded pitcher; some lefties have had success with fastballs away. But Knight is a smart hitter who will adjust. He will pull change-ups hard. He is excellent at hitting behind the runner. An aggressive hitter, Knight seldom walks, and doesn't strike out often.

Until injuries and illness took their toll late in 1982, Knight was batting near .320. He is a "gamer" who continued to play regularly despite injuries. Nobody enjoys playing--and hitting--more than Knight. Fifth or sixth in the order may be his best spots, but he was an ideal third hitter for the punchless Astros. What he may lack in raw hitting talent, Knight makes up for in desire and by thriving under pressure.

BASERUNNING:

Knight would be a threat to win the batting title if he possessed even average speed. But he is slow, and he is at his slowest from home to first. He is not a basestealer, but his hustle, his competitiveness and his willingness to sprawl into the dirt (or into an opposing fielder) sometimes help him go from first to third or from second to home.

RAY KNIGHT
INF, No. 22
RR, 6'2", 190 lbs.
ML Svc: 6 years
Born: 12-28-52 in Albany, GA

1982 STATISTICS

AVG	G	AB	R	H	2B	3B	HR	RBI	BB	SO	SB
.294	158	609	72	179	36	6	6	70	48	58	2

CAREER STATISTICS

AVG	G	AB	R	H	2B	3B	HR	RBI	BB	SO	SB
.281	753	2332	266	656	144	19	38	280	268	268	10

VS. RHP

VS. LHP

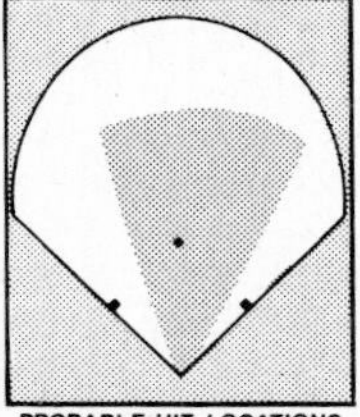
PROBABLE HIT LOCATIONS

FIELDING:

Best described as a battler at third base. Knight may not be smooth, but he gets the job done. He stops what he can reach, and quickness with his first two steps helps offset his lack of speed. Knight positions himself well at third. His arm has always been adequate, but a shoulder injury hastened a move to first base during last season. At first, Knight was admittedly uncomfortable, occasionally making the wrong play. He needs experience at first base.

OVERALL:

Coleman: "Ray Knight has made himself a major leaguer with sheer determination and hard work. There are more talented players in the minors."

McCarver: "Ray is a consummate professional, a team player who plays when he is hurt. He is very, very tough."

FRANK LaCORTE
RHP, No. 31
RR, 6'1", 180 lbs.
ML Svc: 5 years
Born: 10-13-51 in San Jose, CA

PITCHING:

In 1980 and 1981, Frank LaCorte joined Joe Sambito and Dave Smith to give Houston one of the deepest and best bullpens in baseball. In 1982, with Sambito sidelined because of elbow surgery and Smith bothered by chronic back trouble, LaCorte was called upon to be the relief ace. He failed miserably, compiling a 1-5 record, only seven saves and a 4.48 ERA.

A power pitcher, LaCorte likes to throw his 90 MPH fastball to get ahead of hitters, then curve them (especially righthanders) for the final strike. His stuff is excellent, but his problem is control. When LaCorte is behind in the count, he stays away from his breaking pitches, and as a result, hitters can hop on his heat.

Confidence seems directly related to LaCorte's success. One good performance tends to lead to another, but the reverse also is true. When he is at his best, LaCorte can intimidate right-handed hitters with his fastball-curve combination. His fastball has good movement. When he is at his worst, LaCorte is down on himself or believes "luck" is against him. In those instances, he becomes erratic, and for him, control trouble and loss of composure can be killers.

FIELDING, HITTING, BASERUNNING:

A good athlete, LaCorte has good fielding instincts, but in pressure situations has been known to rattle and throw the ball away. An asset is his quickness afield--he can make the big play to end an inning. He seldom hits, but LaCorte isn't cheated on his swings. For a pitcher, he is above average as a runner.

OVERALL:

LaCorte would be much more valuable if he threw strikes consistently. And sometimes when he does throw strikes, his pitches are too true, a trait pitchers can ill afford. He has a good enough arm to be much more of a success if he controls both his pitches and his emotions.

Coleman: "He is an average pitcher who should be way above average with his stuff. He is his own worst enemy. When things aren't going well, he loses his poise."

McCarver: "Frank can and does fit in well with a superb Houston bullpen. But he would be questionable as the only short man because of his inconsistency in throwing strikes."

1982 STATISTICS

W	L	ERA	G	GS	CG	IP	H	R	ER	BB	SO	SV
1	5	4.48	55	0	0	76	71	44	38	46	51	7

CAREER STATISTICS

W	L	ERA	G	GS	CG	IP	H	R	ER	BB	SO	SV
18	38	4.86	203	31	1	407	389	339	220	217	311	23

MIKE LaCOSS
RHP, No. 51
RR, 6'4", 190 lbs.
ML Svc: 5 years
Born: 5-30-56 in
Glendale, CA

PITCHING:

After Cincinnati released Mike LaCoss during 1982 spring training, the Astros gave him a tryout and signed the tall righthander just before opening day as a 10th pitcher. Mere insurance. Before the season ended, he was starting regularly and effectively and probably will begin 1983 in the rotation.

LaCoss' chief weapon is a good sinker, which reacts almost as a spitball would. As a result, he secures numerous ground balls, which is the main reason he looms as a good short-reliever. His fastball has only average movement, and he doesn't have good rotation on his curve. He has trouble controlling both his curve and slider. LaCoss needs a change-up to start effectively over a long period.

His only weakness as a starter in August and September was tiring late in games, and perhaps that's because he spent the first four months of the season in relief.

At 6'4", he intimidates some right-handed hitters with his size if not his fastball. He has been known to brushback hitters but that may be due more to overall control problems than anything else.

In earlier years at Cincinnati, LaCoss showed great promise. The fact that he shook off the bitter disappointment of his surprising spring release and pitched well at Houston when other Astros were struggling is a credit to LaCoss and should give him renewed confidence entering 1983.

FIELDING, HITTING, BASERUNNING:

LaCoss' size is a liability. He has a loop in his throw to first base. He is average at fielding bunts. His overall hitting and running ability is not good.

OVERALL:

Critics have accused LaCoss of an attitude problem. Some consider him "spacy" and out of synch with what is happening around him. But others say he is a true competitor when given the ball. He enjoyed some success at Cincinnati before running out of favor with management and the press there. He had no similar problems in Houston in 1982. The jury is still out on LaCoss as a starter.

McCarver: "If Mike had an off-speed pitch, he would be more formidable. He could be a good short-relief man."

Coleman: "A good looking young pitcher in 1978, he has declined badly since that time. He needs more confidence. And he needs a killer instinct. He improved last year with every successful outing."

1982 STATISTICS

W	L	ERA	G	GS	CG	IP	H	R	ER	BB	SO	SV
6	6	2.90	41	8	0	115	107	41	37	54	51	0

CAREER STATISTICS

W	L	ERA	G	GS	CG	IP	H	R	ER	BB	SO	SV
38	41	4.16	146	97	13	664	722	345	307	277	236	1

OMAR MORENO
OF, No. 18
LL, 6'3", 170 lbs.
ML Svc: 6 years
Born: 10-24-52 in
Puerto Armuelles, PAN

1982 STATISTICS

AVG	G	AB	R	H	2B	3B	HR	RBI	BB	SO	SB
.245	158	645	82	158	18	9	3	44	44	121	60

CAREER STATISTICS

AVG	G	AB	R	H	2B	3B	HR	RBI	BB	SO	SB
.255	944	3585	530	915	115	59	25	263	314	633	412

VS. RHP

VS. LHP

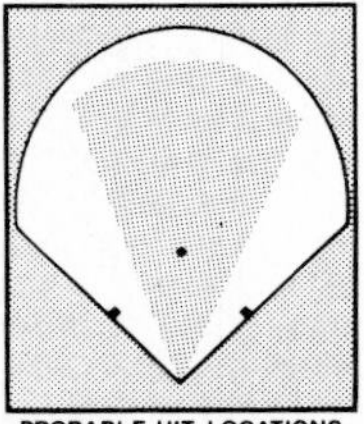
PROBABLE HIT LOCATIONS

HITTING:

After six seasons, Omar Moreno has had only one good year with the stick. This is somewhat surprising since he is one of baseball's fastest sprinters. One problem is that he is not a good bunter. If he improved in this area, he could leg out many more hits than he presently does. Another liability is strikeouts (over 100 a year), especially damaging since he is not a power hitter.

Moreno should be pitched fastballs inside. He has a tendency to lunge at breaking pitches and has great trouble against lefthanders. In 1979, he learned how to hit to the opposite field, but he did not continue his improvement. He has taken batting instruction from Harry Walker, a former Pirate manager, and Bob Skinner, a Pirates' coach. It is possible that he could be the victim of too many teachers, or it could be that he doesn't absorb what he learns about hitting.

BASERUNNING:

Moreno is one of the best baserunners in the game. He is a constant threat to steal, and to take the extra base. He occasionally runs into a streak where he is picked off base too often. It lasts for a week or 10 days, no longer. He bothers pitchers when he is on base because he takes a big lead.

FIELDING:

Perhaps Moreno isn't the best center fielder in the big leagues, but he rates right behind the best. He covers a large amount of the outfield territory. His arm is fair, and a major flaw is that he doesn't charge base hits consistently.

OVERALL:

No problems to a manager. Durable. Will play when hurt. Played 503 consecutive games before a back injury benched him. Moreno is a good competitor, but doesn't wear his competitive spirit on his shirt sleeve.

Kiner: "Moreno is an outstanding fielder with great range. He is one of the best basestealers in the league despite a very low on-base percentage. He should improve that with better batting average and walks to really reach his full potential."

Coleman: "A premiere basestealer and above average fielder. He has a lot of trouble with lefthanded pitching, and it keeps him from being a complete player."

McCarver: "Omar was sent unsuccessfully to batting coach Harry Walker a few years ago. Moreno has a loop in his swing that often causes him to hit the bottom half of the ball resulting in it going in the air. In order to utilize his speed, he has to be able to hit ground balls the other way."

JOE NIEKRO
RHP, No. 36
RR, 6'1", 190 lbs.
ML Svc: 15 years
Born: 11-7-44 in Martins Ferry, OH

PITCHING:

After toiling from 1967-1971 in the major leagues with some success using conventional pitches, Joe Niekro spent the next four seasons trekking back and forth from the majors to the minors. He was seemingly finished. Even the Atlanta Braves, whose only respected pitcher was Joe's brother, Phil, didn't have room for Joe Niekro. But courageously, Joe worked to learn Phil's specialty, the knuckleball, in the minors. In 1975, he asked the Astros for a chance. And with Houston, Joe has become one of the premier pitchers in the game.

Joe's knuckler is equal to Phil's and indeed one of the best ever thrown. But there are differences. Joe's knuckler is probably the hardest yet delivered by a pitcher. And Joe complements the pitch with a fastball, curveball and slider. He does, however, tend to "telegraph" the curve by getting on top of it too much.

Niekro uses the knuckler almost exclusively to get ahead on the count and as his out pitch. Once behind, however, he turns to his other pitches. Doubt is always in hitters' minds. And if on one particular day Niekro's slider is effective, he may use it 30-40% of the time.

As with any knuckleball pitcher, his main problem is control, especially with runners on base and the threat of steals and wild pitches or passed balls. Niekro's control has improved remarkably. On a windy day, he is almost unhittable and uncatchable. He is at his best protecting a lead.

Steady under pressure, Niekro has won almost every big game he has pitched for Houston.

FIELDING, HITTING, BASERUNNING:

Niekro seldom makes a mistake in the field, and deserves consideration for the Gold Glove. However, he is reasonably easy to steal against because of the knuckleball. His pick-off move isn't bad, and he hastens his delivery to give runners less time. Only an average hitter, he usually makes contact with men on base. He went two years at one stretch without missing a bunt attempt. He has no speed on the bases but is a smart runner.

OVERALL:

Niekro is the only Houston pitcher to win 20 games back-to-back and he barely missed winning the league ERA title in 1982. He has become one of the best pitchers in baseball.

McCarver: "Joe received a devastating blow to most egos when he was sent to the minors after several years in the majors. But instead of bad mouthing his misfortunes, he worked courageously to learn the knuckleball. He has made a steadfast impression."

Coleman: "He probably can pitch well into his 40s with his knuckleball. He worked hard for many years to become a good pitcher."

Kiner: "He is one of the best in the National League today."

1982 STATISTICS

W	L	ERA	G	GS	CG	IP	H	R	ER	BB	SO	SV
17	12	2.47	35	35	16	270	224	79	74	64	130	0

CAREER STATISTICS

W	L	ERA	G	GS	CG	IP	H	R	ER	BB	SO	SV
162	141	3.44	534	336	87	2563	2484	1095	981	829	1197	16

HITTING:

Terry Puhl gained national prominence by hitting .526 in the 1980 National League Championship Series against Philadelphia. But he hasn't showed that form since that time with any consistency. Puhl averaged .290 his first four major league seasons, but he has slumped to .251 and .262 the past two years.

Righthanded pitchers are jamming him with success; lefthanders are giving him trouble with off-speed deliveries outside. A young man who listens well, Puhl may have accepted too much advice and experimented with too many hitting approaches. He showed signs late in 1982 of his former abilities which included spray hitting to all fields, excellent bunting form and, except in the Astrodome, average power.

The speculation in Houston is that Puhl, who was signed out of Canada and never played in high school, may be able to hit twenty home runs a year as he matures. A slot hitter, he likes to go up the middle. He is an excellent fastball hitter. Puhl's expertise at drag bunting combines with his good speed to make him effective in bunting for hits.

Even in his best years, Puhl was prone to slumps and hot streaks, with the latter keeping him near .300. During the past two seasons, his slumps have been longer lasting. One theory is that Puhl will regain his touch if the Astros find a home for him in the order--he has shifted from leadoff to third frequently and has hit sixth, seventh and even eighth.

BASERUNNING:

Quick and intelligent, Puhl consistently steals 20-30 bases depending on his playing time. An aggressive runner, Puhl gets a good jump and has a good feet first slide. He studies pitchers well. Speed also helps on infield hits as Puhl gets a good jump out of the batters' box.

TERRY PUHL
OF, No. 21
LR, 6'2", 197 lbs.
ML Svc: 5 years
Born: 7-8-56 in Saskatchewan, CAN

1982 STATISTICS

AVG	G	AB	R	H	2B	3B	HR	RBI	BB	SO	SB
.262	145	507	64	133	17	9	8	50	51	49	17

CAREER STATISTICS

AVG	G	AB	R	H	2B	3B	HR	RBI	BB	SO	SB
.279	748	2806	396	782	120	33	35	227	278	273	138

VS. RHP

VS. LHP

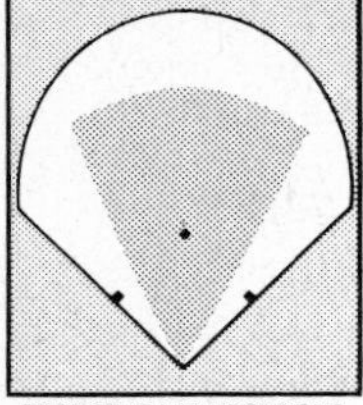
PROBABLE HIT LOCATIONS

FIELDING:

In 1979, he tied a major league record by playing 150 games without an error, primarily in right field. His arm is only average in strength, but he is accurate and doesn't make mistakes. His hands are superb. He isn't afraid to dive into the turf or collide with walls. He has been asked to play center field often but, though adequate in that role, he is better in right.

OVERALL:

McCarver: "High marks in all categories for a man who never played in high school. Extremely incredible instincts. He is a marvelous all around athlete, as fundamentally sound as there is in the game today."

Kiner: "He has good all around potential but needs to come back to previous standards. He didn't reach his potential last year."

HITTING:

A dependable part-time catcher for several years, Luis Pujols gained his first extended starting opportunity for almost a month in 1982 when Alan Ashby was sidelined because of a broken finger. And Pujols went 2-for-47 offensively during that span.

Because his bat speed is extremely slow, Pujols has trouble with good fastballs, expecially inside. Nor does he often handle a righthander's curve. He is usually platooned against lefthanded pitchers. Pujols is most effective against junkballers--like Randy Jones, Chris Welsh. If the fastball has no zip and is belt high, he has enough power to hit it out of the park. Pujols doesn't react well to surprise pitches, and strikes out often. He is primarily a pull hitter, and usually hits ground balls.

He can, however, be surprisingly dangerous in clutch situations and despite a below-.200 average, his RBI ratio is good. With time and instruction, Pujols may have enough tools to improve as a hitter. The slow bat aside, his stroke isn't bad. One problem Pujols shares with other unproven Astro hitters is that the team gets such good pitching and so little offense that almost every game is low-scoring and almost every at-bat a pressure situation. Pujols has never had a chance to relax as a hitter.

BASERUNNING:

Pujols is not a threat to steal or take an extra base, but to his credit he knows it. He doesn't make many mistakes because of his conservative approach. His speed from home to first isn't bad for a catcher--still, he is usually one step shy of an infield hit.

FIELDING:

Pujols has retained his back up job

LUIS PUJOLS
C, No. 6
RR, 6'1", 195 lbs.
ML Svc: 3 years
Born: 11-18-55 in
Santo Domingo, DR

1982 STATISTICS

AVG	G	AB	R	H	2B	3B	HR	RBI	BB	SO	SB
.199	65	176	8	35	6	2	4	15	10	41	0

CAREER STATISTICS

AVG	G	AB	R	H	2B	3B	HR	RBI	BB	SO	SB
.192	271	757	46	145	25	6	6	68	47	151	1

VS. RHP

VS. LHP

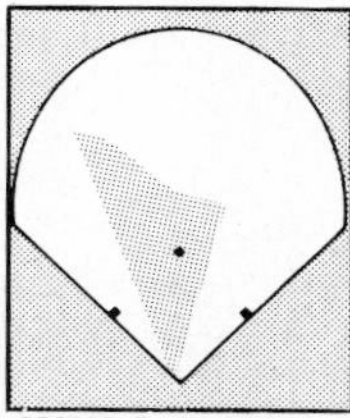
PROBABLE HIT LOCATIONS

over several challengers for quite a few years for two main reasons: his ability to handle Joe Niekro's knuckleball and his willingness to work hard. Pujols did have more trouble with Niekro's knuckler in 1982 than in the past, but Niekro admits his specialty never had so much movement. Pujols' arm speed and accuracy are average--he has a tendency to throw high. One complaint is that he makes too many trips to the mound to discuss form with pitchers.

OVERALL:

McCarver: "Luis is a good back up catcher who handles Joe Niekro's knuckleball well. He appears to have better tools than his record implies. He should be a better hitter."

Coleman: "Luis is a hard worker who could get better. His bat and lack of speed hold him back."

BERT ROBERGE
RHP, No. 42
RR, 6'4", 190 lbs.
ML Svc: 2 years
Born: 10-3-54 in Lewiston, ME

PITCHING:

Bert Roberge, a short reliever with promise, has come up with a split-finger fastball like Bruce Sutter. However, unlike Sutter, Roberge has not been able to develop full mastery of it. When this Astro righthander is controlling it, however, he can be tough on hitters because the pitch, similar to a forkball, explodes as it reaches the plate.

Without reliable control, Roberge cannot rely on the split-fingered fastball enough to throw it regularly. His regular fastball, which travels only about 85 MPH, can seem 10 MPH faster if he is mixing it well with the split-finger delivery. He will use both pitches at any time.

Because he rarely throws a curve, Roberge is equally effective against righthanders and lefthanders. He has had some good outings under pressure in an up-and-down career. He's also had some horrendous ones. Wildness remains a problem, not so much in throwing strikes but more so in not throwing the ball to specific locations in the strike zone.

Houston's fine bullpen depth and talent have hurt Roberge's chances of pitching in the big leagues.

FIELDING, HITTING, BASERUNNING:

A tall man, Roberge is only an average fielder. And because his delivery is slow and his pitches not quick, he is easy to run against on the bases. He has had almost no opportunity to hit, bunt or run the bases himself.

OVERALL:

For a pitcher with limited big league experience, Roberge has good poise and doesn't scare under pressure. One detriment is that fellow Astro Dave Smith throws a forkball similar to Roberge's and for two pitchers so alike to be on the same staff isn't good. His fastball and other conventional pitches are not solid enough to keep Roberge in the majors, but if he develops the other pitch, we've already seen what a pitcher like Sutter can mean to a team.

Kiner: "The split-finger fastball can keep him in the major leagues if he can develop better control of the pitch so he can use it more often."

McCarver: "Roberge lacks experience, but he could become a very good short reliever if given the chance. On another staff, he could be No. 1."

1982 STATISTICS

W	L	ERA	G	GS	CG	IP	H	R	ER	BB	SO	SV
1	2	4.21	22	0	0	25	29	12	12	6	18	3

CAREER STATISTICS

W	L	ERA	G	GS	CG	IP	H	R	ER	BB	SO	SV
6	2	3.78	62	0	0	81	73	34	34	33	40	7

VERN RUHLE
RHP, No. 48
RR, 6'1", 187 lbs.
ML Svc: 7 years
Born: 1-25-51 in Coleman, MI

PITCHING:

A spot starter most of his Houston career, Vern Ruhle would be a regular on most staffs. Not blessed with awesome ability, Ruhle uses intelligence, diversity, poise and control to retire batters. Indeed, his chief asset may be that there is absolutely no pattern to how he pitches an opponent except the pattern in his head.

Ruhle throws a fastball, which at 85-90 MPH has above average movement, a slider, a sinker, a change-up and, at times, a curve. He controls each pitch, and he keeps the ball down. When he is pitching to spots well, he is capable of a shutout on any day.

It is a credit to Ruhle's determination and poise that he has survived so long in Houston without ever assuming a full time starter's job. History shows that contrary to the way he has been used, Ruhle is highly effective when he pitches regularly and is mostly ineffective when he is sent to the bullpen. He is also ineffective if he goes two or three weeks without pitching, a frequent occurrence with the pitching-rich Astros.

Ruhle has a downward movement not only on his sinker but on his other pitches as well. And he cuts his fastball both directions. He makes it impossible for a hitter to pick up his rhythm.

FIELDING, HITTING, BASERUNNING:

A fast worker capable of two-hour games or less when he is dominating hitters, Ruhle slows considerably with men on base, throwing to first base constantly. He should work more quickly, even with men aboard. He is extremely intelligent; he won't make the bad play afield. He used to be a terrible hitter, but he makes contact now, and despite having no punch, can help himself at bat. He has a good eye and will draw walks. He is an average runner with good instincts for a pitcher.

OVERALL:

After compiling a 12-4 record in 1980, Ruhle experienced two consecutive losing seasons but has not pitched badly. Seemingly recovered from back trouble which hindered him for several years, Ruhle perhaps could win big as a regular starter and may get the chance this season. He throws many pitches at many speeds to many spots. He is poised and smart.

Coleman: "The lack of a great fastball is his only negative. Ruhle has an excellent ability to pitch to hitters' weaknesses. He would be a good fourth starter on any club."

Kiner: "At best he is a fifth starter and long relief man. The veteran righthander will be hard pressed to make the Astro team in 1983."

McCarver: "Composed and experienced, Vern gets a lot of mileage out of less than average ability. His keen insights into hitting enable him to fool hitters. He uses his ability as intelligently as Don Sutton."

1982 STATISTICS

W	L	ERA	G	GS	CG	IP	H	R	ER	BB	SO	SV
9	13	3.93	31	21	3	149	169	81	65	24	56	1

CAREER STATISTICS

W	L	ERA	G	GS	CG	IP	H	R	ER	BB	SO	SV
55	61	3.57	188	154	28	1033	1079	478	410	246	402	2

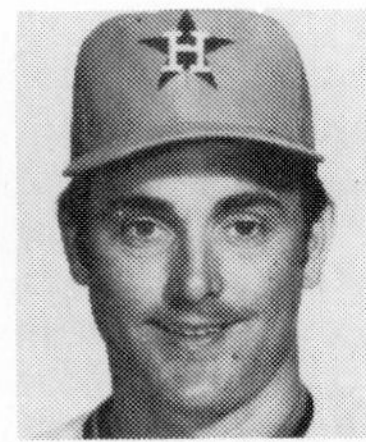

NOLAN RYAN
RHP, No. 34
RR, 6'2", 195 lbs.
ML Svc: 15 years
Born: 1-31-47 in Refugio, TX

PITCHING:

Nolan Ryan has pitched five no-hitters, more than any other pitcher in baseball history. He will set a new career strikeout record this season. His curve and fastball make him the most dominant pitcher in the game when he is at his best and when he controls both pitches. His fastball has been clocked at 100 MPH, and can still reach 97-98 MPH. At age 35, his arm remains the best in baseball.

At times, Ryan tries to be too precise and goes for the corners instead of utilizing his overpowering ability. He occasionally shows too much inconsistency, but when he is going well, he can blow anyone away.

Over the past two years, Ryan has become more of a complete pitcher. He continues to amass strikeouts, but his walk total is way down. He will throw his fastball in any situation regardless of the count, one of the few pitchers in baseball who can get away with it. When ahead, he destroys hitters with his curve. The key to his success is the curve--when he has command of it, Ryan can be unhittable. He is working on a change-up but rarely throws it. Ryan doesn't need special pitches. He terrorizes righthanded hitters, and lefties don't fare much better.

FIELDING, HITTING, BASERUNNING:

Ryan's big delivery and follow through are a handicap at holding runners. He compensates by not putting many runners on base. He has worked to get the ball to his catcher faster with men on base--98 MPH does help. Not a bad fielder, Ryan doesn't make mental errors. He takes some pride in his hitting, but is average at best. He can produce the occasional sacrifice fly. He is no gazelle on the bases.

OVERALL:

The game has produced few better arms. Ryan is capable of dominating any game on any day, depending on his control. And, if anything, he may be improving with age, rare for a power pitcher.

Coleman: "He has the best arm of any starter in baseball. On certain nights, he is unhittable."

Kiner: "When he has his control, it doesn't matter if the batter is right or lefthanded. Nolan is awesome."

McCarver: "If he ever threw a brushback, it could kill somebody. He can be superhuman when his control is sharp. Nolan is very much in control of his emotions. But his biggest priority should be not falling behind on the count. If his control is off, you can sit on the heater and, if down, hammer it. If his control is on, call in the cows."

1982 STATISTICS

W	L	ERA	G	GS	CG	IP	H	R	ER	BB	SO	SV
16	12	3.16	35	35	10	250	196	100	88	109	245	0

CAREER STATISTICS

W	L	ERA	G	GS	CG	IP	H	R	ER	BB	SO	SV
305	186	3.11	487	453	188	3325	2389	1311	1149	1921	3494	3

JOE SAMBITO
LHP, No. 35
LL, 6'1", 190 lbs.
ML Svc: 6 years
Born: 6-28-52 in Brooklyn, NY

NOTE: In June 1982, Joe Sambito underwent surgery for the removal of a bone chip and the reconstruction of a totally ruptured ligament in his throwing elbow. At this writing, there is no way of knowing if Sambito will return in 1983. Pitcher Tommy John had similar surgery performed in 1974, and returned to Major League form in 1976. Each case is individual, and the following scouting report is based on Sambito's pre-surgery form.

PITCHING:

Joe Sambito is a short relief power pitcher with excellent control. He is one of the league's quality relievers, and generally uses his own pitching strengths to beat hitters rather than their particular weaknesses. Much of his strength comes in the form of a blazing fastball. It is his best pitch, and he will throw it at anytime.

He has a good slider and uses it to jam right-handed hitters, preventing them from leaning out over the plate. When he mixes his fastball and slider, Sambito has the power and control to be highly effective for the short route. Because of his sidearm delivery, he does not have a real curveball. Good curves generally must be thrown overhand. This lack of reliable change-up keeps him from being a complete pitcher.

Sambito will use a brushback in the interest of protecting his teammates.

FIELDING, HITTING, BASERUNNING:

Sambito has an average move to first, but for a lefthander it should actually be better. He fields the ball well, backs up first and can take care of bunts.

As a short reliever, Sambito seldom has a chance to hit, and as a result, is easy to fan. His bunt is adequate, and he runs the bases with only average speed.

OVERALL:

Sambito has the guts of a burglar, is in total control and unshakeable on the mound. He also has a penchant for keeping his hair in place at all times. He is a smooth worker, and may be somewhat colorless from a fan's point of view, but not so to opposing batters who find him very tough.

Coleman: "Sambito is one of the best short relief pitchers in the business. He absolutely does not scare."

McCarver: "Sambito is the most dependable member of a very dependable bullpen. He has nerves of steel and is absolutely unflappable. Great control is the sign of a short reliever because he comes into situations where falling behind in the count would be devastating."

1982 STATISTICS

W	L	ERA	G	GS	CG	IP	H	R	ER	BB	SO	SV
0	0	0.71	9	0	0	12	7	2	1	2	7	4

CAREER STATISTICS

W	L	ERA	G	GS	CG	IP	H	R	ER	BB	SO	SV
33	32	2.37	321	5	1	487	402	152	128	139	395	72

MIKE SCOTT
RHP, No. 30
RR, 6'3", 215 lbs.
ML Svc: 3 years
Born: 4-26-55 in Santa Monica, CA

PITCHING:

Mike Scott was a dilemma with the Mets last season. They expected a 13-7 record and got just the opposite. Mike gave up an inordinate amount of hits--185--in 147 innings while losing the starting job he was given. By the end of the season, the Mets thought he was better suited for short relief. He was quite effective as a temporary replacement for Neil Allen.

Scott throws hard and can do so for nine innings, if he were only able to remain in the game. He has a very smooth three-quarter delivery, and relies on his fastball and slider. His slider is his best breaking pitch, and he resists the urging of both his manager and catcher to throw more off-speed pitches. When he did use a change-up, he had good motion on it and it was fairly effective.

He goes to his fastball when he falls behind in the count, which is not too often, and he tries to keep his pitches down. He could mix his pitches better than he does and needs to improve his location within the strike zone. Scott is slightly more effective against righthanded hitters than lefthanded hitters and has all kinds of problems against Keith Hernandez of the Cardinals.

Although Scott's stuff once was his greatest asset, he seemed to regress last season. He doesn't doctor the ball yet, but maybe he should. He also needs to improve his poise on the mound.

FIELDING, HITTING, BASERUNNING:

Mike has an exceptional pick-off move to any base and had seven pick-offs last season. He is an active fielder and covers his territory well. He is an above average hitter, and occasionally can even pull a ball in the gaps. He has average speed on the bases.

OVERALL:

The Mets became annoyed at Scott's stubborness and traded him. They felt he should have been a much better pitcher than he turned out to be. Being in a pitcher's park, the Astrodome might help him.

Coleman: "Looked like an up-and-comer for two years, but slipped badly last year."

Kiner: "He has not improved in the last two years despite good exposure."

McCarver: "Inconsistency has been Mike's tag. But he could be a good pitcher someday."

1982 STATISTICS

W	L	ERA	G	GS	CG	IP	H	R	ER	BB	SO	SV
7	13	5.14	37	22	1	147	185	100	84	60	63	3

CAREER STATISTICS

W	L	ERA	G	GS	CG	IP	H	R	ER	BB	SO	SV
14	27	4.65	84	60	3	364	414	214	188	122	151	3

HITTING:

A switch-hitter, Tony Scott is a paradox. In 1981, he hit .284 lefthanded and .218 with no power righthanded. In 1982, he hit .278 righthanded and .214 lefthanded. From either side, Scott is a "mistake" hitter who prefers the high fastball. He can be jammed with frequent success--the low, inside curve gives him the most trouble. Scott lacks the power desired in most starting center fielders and only occasionally did he show enough punch in 1982 to reach the Astrodome alleys.

His speed does enable Scott to get infield hits on grounders to the left side, but he doesn't bunt often enough, another potential asset wasted. Scott was at his worst last season in RBI situations--he didn't have enough pop in his bat even to produce sacrifice flies with regularity. He does handle the bat well, but tends to slap at sliders or sinkers or any pitch that fools him. He had been a more effective hitter in the past than in 1982, and when he is in form, Scott is a line drive hitter.

The coming season looms critical for Scott. He helped the Astros considerably with his bat late in 1981 after they traded Joaquin Andujar to St. Louis for his services. And it could be, regardless of the reasons, that 1982 was a mere fluke washout of a season for Scott, who didn't play well in any aspect of the game. Renewed confidence, and/or more punch in the Astros' order to help him, may be the answer.

BASERUNNING:

Normally highly aggressive, Scott was more conservative in 1982--but perhaps that's because he reached base less than normal. Scott gets a good jump, and combined with excellent speed, he is always a threat to steal. When he bats lefthanded, his speed running to first base gives infielders trouble on most ground balls.

TONY SCOTT
OF, No. 30
SR, 6'0", 175 lbs.
ML Svc: 7 years
Born: 9-18-51 in Cincinnati, OH

1982 STATISTICS

AVG	G	AB	R	H	2B	3B	HR	RBI	BB	SO	SB
.239	132	460	43	110	16	3	1	29	15	56	18

CAREER STATISTICS

AVG	G	AB	R	H	2B	3B	HR	RBI	BB	SO	SB
.251	841	2525	301	635	100	27	15	231	164	401	119

VS. RHP

VS. LHP

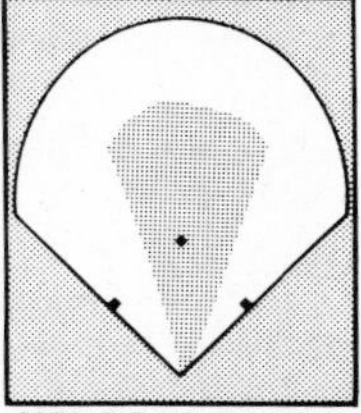
PROBABLE HIT LOCATIONS

FIELDING:

Like other aspects of his game, Scott had an off-year in center field, at least until August. Nagging injuries may have been a problem, Scott hiding some ailments because of an intense desire to play. Previously, despite playing a shallow center field, Scott ran down almost everything hit over his head or to either side. But he had trouble in the 1982 early season getting his usual good jump. His arm strength is below average and though he doesn't lack accuracy, he did tend to throw to the wrong base last year.

OVERALL:

Kiner: "An outstanding defensive outfielder who had his worst year at the plate."

Coleman: "He needs to hit better, particularly with men on base."

DAVE SMITH
RHP, No. 45
RR, 6'1", 190 lbs.
ML Svc: 3 years
Born: 1-21-55 in
San Francisco, CA

PITCHING:

Righthander Dave Smith and left-hander Joe Sambito provided awesome one-two bullpen punch in 1980 and 1981. During that time, Smith compiled a 2.28 ERA. But Smith suffered from back pain throughtout most of 1982. Though he pitched most of the season, Smith was inconsistent; his motion and delivery as well as his location and velocity were obviously affected.

When healthy, Smith is a high quality reliever because he throws a better than average major league fastball, a good slider and one of the best forkballs in baseball. And he controls each pitch well. The forkball, which dips dramatically as it reaches the plate, is his out pitch--when it is on, his strikeout total is high and he can throw ground balls for double plays.

Smith was converted from a starter and did remarkably well under pressure even as a rookie. His poise is excellent; so is his choice of pitches. He will throw all three pitches plus a curve, which is less effective because he telegraphs it in his delivery, when behind in the count.

For the first time, control was a problem for him in 1982, and at times it was a big one. And that's not very good in late-inning situations.

FIELDING, HITTING, BASERUNNING:

An above average fielder, Smith helps himself by cutting off some of the many grounders hit off his forkball. He is deliberate with runners on base, among the few Astro pitchers who is good at holding runners on base. His hitting and baserunning experience is limited.

OVERALL:

Smith was an outstanding reliever before the back trouble, and at his age should regain that distinction assuming he is healthy. He has talent, poise and a desire to win.

McCarver: "When he is throwing well and without pain, he doesn't have a weakness. He has ice water in his veins. He may be one of the top three short-relievers in the league. When healthy, he and Sambito are the best one-two combo in the league."

Coleman: "He was part of baseball's top bullpen in 1981. But the forkball didn't break as well in 1982. His back problem had to be bothering him."

1982 STATISTICS

W	L	ERA	G	GS	CG	IP	H	R	ER	BB	SO	SV
5	4	3.84	49	1	0	63	69	30	27	31	28	11

CAREER STATISTICS

W	L	ERA	G	GS	CG	IP	H	R	ER	BB	SO	SV
17	12	3.06	148	1	0	241	213	80	82	86	165	29

DICKIE THON
INF, No. 10
RR, 5'11", 150 lbs.
ML Svc: 3 years
Born: 6-20-58 in
South Bend, IN

1982 STATISTICS

AVG	G	AB	R	H	2B	3B	HR	RBI	BB	SO	SB
.276	136	496	73	137	31	10	3	36	37	48	37

CAREER STATISTICS

AVG	G	AB	R	H	2B	3B	HR	RBI	BB	SO	SB
.274	300	914	124	250	52	12	3	62	61	99	50

VS. RHP

VS. LHP

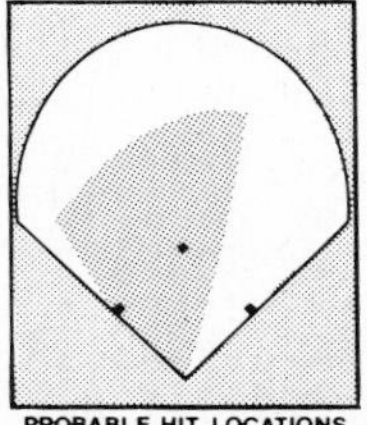
PROBABLE HIT LOCATIONS

HITTING:

Acquired before the 1981 season from California for pitcher Ken Forsch, Dickie Thon, who boasted excellent minor league hitting credentials, showed little aggressiveness that first year with Houston. Nor did he excel early in 1982. But in mid-June last year, then-manager Bill Virdon decided to put Thon in his lineup at shortstop and as the leadoff hitter. Thon responded with a 21-game hitting streak, matching the longest string in the National League all year.

Using a slightly crouched stance, Thon is a good contact hitter. He is most likely to pull the ball but is also able to hit it hard up the middle. He doesn't have home run power but does have the punch to line doubles and triples into the Astrodome alleys.

Quick hands give Thon good bat speed. A fastball hitter, Thon can be retired on good off-speed pitches but will pick on mistakes. He will bunt for hits, and should become a better bunter with more playing time. He also has a good eye, and he became more disciplined as he relaxed into his starter's role. For about two months, he had a .500 on-base percentage in his first at-bat of games. Thon did not hit well this season with teammates on base, but that is a disease which seems to be contagious in Houston. More playing time, which Thon is certain to get this year, should help him respond to RBI situations.

BASERUNNING:

On a club which traditionally has possessed good runners, Thon is among the best to come along in several seasons. He not only has good speed but is aggressive and smart. He doesn't hesitate to steal a third base. His speed helps him to get infield hits.

FIELDING:

Previously a utility man at second, third and short, Thon took over the latter at midseason from veteran Craig Reynolds and was exceptional. His range improved with experience during the year and it is now his prime defensive asset. He will make the difficult hard throw, but has been prone to err on easier tosses. Playing full-time brought more consistency. He has good hands. Thon shows signs of becoming one of the best shortstops in the league.

OVERALL:

Coleman: "Thon is the best young shortstop in the National League. If his bat improves, he'll be an All Star in a couple of years."

Kiner: "For the first time in his career, Thon got a chance to play regularly and he came through."

HITTING:

Denny Walling is a pinch-hitter and spot starter who bats almost exclusively against righthanded pitchers. A good low ball hitter, Walling hits the low inside fastball with power and has won several important games for the Astros with late home runs. Walling tries to pull most pitches, and the outside breaking ball is the best bet against him. He will hit any pitcher's mistake, even the best. Walling was the chief nemesis of Rollie Fingers when Fingers was with the Padres.

Though he seldom plays against lefthanders, Walling is a different type of hitter, more inclined to go to the opposite field and better against the high pitch. The slider gives Walling trouble, but don't throw him a sinker.

He doesn't scare under pressure, but in 1982, Walling had his worst season off the bench. He has not hit well enough over a long period to remain in the starting lineup. One detriment in Houston is that the Astros' bench the past few seasons has been filled with lefthanded hitters in Walling's mold. He has not been able to enjoy the individual acclaim that accompanies even a team-leading pinch-hitter, and after several years in such situations, a bench man is hard pressed to remain happy and effective. The answer could be more pressure opportunity for Walling in 1983. Or it could be an eventual change of scenery. If he could regain his old form, Walling potentially is a good American League designated hitter.

BASERUNNING:

Having average speed, Walling has been utilized as a pinch-runner, but only occasionally. He is not aggressive but will steal if the pitcher ignores him. Used primarily as a pinch-hitter, Walling gets few chances on the bases but he doesn't hurt his team in that area.

DENNY WALLING
OF/INF, No. 29
LR, 6'1", 185 lbs.
ML Svc: 5 years
Born: 4-17-54 in Neptune, NJ

1982 STATISTICS

AVG	G	AB	R	H	2B	3B	HR	RBI	BB	SO	SB
.205	85	146	22	30	4	1	1	14	23	19	4

CAREER STATISTICS

AVG	G	AB	R	H	2B	3B	HR	RBI	BB	SO	SB
.266	467	1022	128	272	36	14	15	141	135	188	22

VS. RHP

VS. LHP

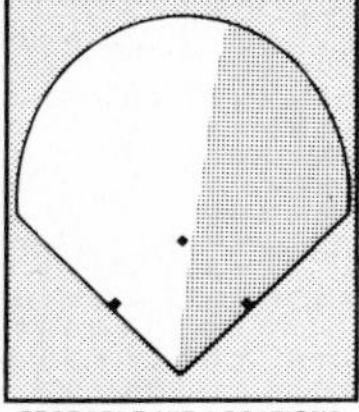
PROBABLE HIT LOCATIONS

FIELDING:

As an outfielder, Walling is handicapped in a big park by limited arm strength and limited range. But he has good hands, good hustle and will make the occasional excellent catch. As a first baseman, Walling is no liability. Again, his hands are an asset. He seldom makes the bad play, but neither is he likely to make an outstanding play.

OVERALL:

Coleman: "I thought he could play every day, but it looks like he'll be an extra man."

McCarver: "He could be a good lefthanded designated hitter in the American League."

Kiner: "The 1983 season will be crucial as far as his career in the majors is concerned."

KIKO GARCIA
INF, No. 23
RR, 5'11", 178 lbs.
ML Svc: 6 years
Born: 10-14-53 in
Walnut Creek, CA

HITTING, BASERUNNING, FIELDING:

Against righthanded pitchers, Garcia tries to hit everything up the middle. Against lefties, he tries to pull more. Garcia has limited power, but can hit a high fastball with punch. A righthanded pitcher's curve gives him trouble. So do most change-ups, though the pitcher is doing Garcia a favor by throwing him the change. He is a one-handed hitter in that one hand flies off the bat upon contact, but this isn't unusual.

A streak hitter, Garcia can get in a good groove if he plays regularly but only for a limited period. He will spray balls around more during these times. He is not apt to bunt often for hits, but is good at sacrifice bunts.

He has not been effective off the bench, striking out more than when he received rare starting opportunities.

With his experience, Garcia should be better at taking an extra base on teammates' hits, but he is a conservative runner. Rarely is he a threat to steal.

A dependable back up shortstop, Garcia gets a good jump on grounders, especially those through the middle. His arm strength and accuracy are average, and he is above average at turning the double play. He can also play third and second base.

OVERALL:

Kiner: "Since his 1979 post-season heroics, Garcia's career has gone downhill. He will have to improve in 1983."

CRAIG REYNOLDS
INF, No. 12
LR, 6'1", 175 lbs.
ML Svc: 6 years
Born: 12-27-52 in
Houston, TX

HITTING, BASERUNNING, FIELDING:

Craig Reynolds is a front-foot hitter, a lunger with a sweeping swing who has tried other approaches but always returned to his unorthodox style. Reynolds tries to pull almost exclusively. He would be more consistent as a spray hitter. Lefthanded pitchers who put curves on the outside corner retire Reynolds consistently. He will hit the high fastball, and against righthanders he will drive the ball into the right-center field alley.

For a lunger, he waits on the ball well and can handle all but the best change-ups. Reynolds has a good eye, but he isn't patient enough to walk. He has an above average bunt. His two bad years may be due to his futile effort to change batting styles, and a vertigo problem which hampered him. The dizziness remains a concern for this season.

Reynolds has above average speed and utilizes it well. He is a smart runner who studies pitchers. He has enough speed to bunt for hits.

Reynolds has only average range and average arm strength. He has a sidearm motion that doesn't help him on plays in the hole, but he is a highly consistent shortstop who gets the most of his abilities. He makes few mistakes, though grounders up the middle often elude him. He doesn't scare in making the double play and comes across the bag well.

DODGER STADIUM
Los Angeles Dodgers

Seating Capacity: 56,000
Playing Surface: Natural Grass

Dimensions
Left Field Pole: 330 ft.
Left-Center Field: 380 ft.
Center Field: 400 ft.
Right-Center Field: 380 ft.
Right Field Pole: 330 ft.
Height of Outfield Wall: 10 ft.

Dodger Stadium is considered by many fans and players to be the flagship ballpark in the National League. In the 1960s it was almost impossible to hit a home run in this park. Then the Dodger management moved home plate closer to the fences and the park developed the reputation of being a bandbox. Today, home runs are a regular occurrence in Los Angeles. Some attribute this to the shortened distance; others point to the retirement of Koufax and Drysdale.

Despite the comparative increase in home runs, Dodger Stadium is still considered a pitcher's ballpark. For example, all pitchers love the way the mound is sloped in this park. Although there is a rule that states all pitching mounds must be no higher than 10 inches, the mound here seems to taper off dramatically and batters get the impression that the pitcher is a lot closer than the standard 60 feet 6 inches when he begins his windup.

The batter's box is a sore point both literally and figuratively with hitters and baserunners. The dirt around home plate is packed down very hard and this makes it difficult for batters to dig in and almost impossible for them to grab a handful of dirt to help improve their grip on the bat. Furthermore, anyone who has tried to slide hard into home will attest to the exceptionally hard and rough surface around the plate.

The infield in Dodger Stadium is also hard and choppy. Grounders skip off the thick, plush grass onto the rough dirt and take some awful hops. In the outfield, the chief complaint centers around the fact that the light-colored stands and sea of white shirts behind the plate make it extremely difficult during day games to catch sight of the ball when the hitter makes contact. On the positive side, wind is seldom, if ever, a factor in Los Angeles, and there is a great deal of territory in both left and right to chase down foul flies and pop-ups.

The bullpens are safe and secluded, and the dugouts offer players all the comforts of home. The fans have grown accustomed to the immaculate condition of the stands and must be shocked when they attend a game in other cities.

DUSTY BAKER
OF, No. 12
RR, 6'2", 200 lbs.
ML Svc: 11 years
Born: 6-15-49 in Riverside, CA

1982 STATISTICS

AVG	G	AB	R	H	2B	3B	HR	RBI	BB	SO	SB
.300	147	570	80	171	19	1	23	88	56	62	17

CAREER STATISTICS

AVG	G	AB	R	H	2B	3B	HR	RBI	BB	SO	SB
.282	1596	5758	789	1622	265	19	206	837	573	756	124

VS. RHP

VS. LHP

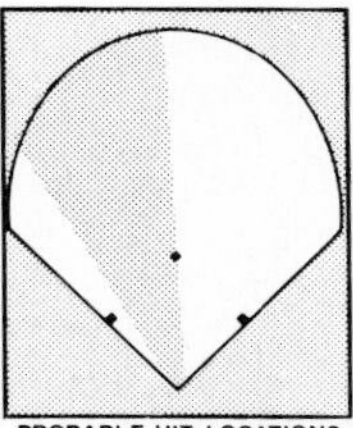
PROBABLE HIT LOCATIONS

HITTING:

A pitcher cannot pitch Baker away and get away with it. A tall, rangy man Baker likes to extend his hands. He's aggressive at the plate and doesn't like to walk. He stands upright in the box with a squared-away stance.

It's best to work Baker with breaking pitches down and in. He has power, mainly to left, but he can go deep to right-center as well. Against right-handers he'll hit long fly balls; against lefthanders, it's line drives and ground balls.

He is an excellent man at the plate in clutch situations--he says he thrives on them. He hits well with runners in scoring position. He can come through with the big hit. With 16 game winning RBIs in 1982, he ranked second on the club (to Guerrero's 18) and fifth in the National League.

Baker is consistent, always around the .300 mark. He hits in hot streaks, and when he's on one, he's virtually impossible to get out. He doesn't generally start the season strongly, but seems to finish well. He likes to think of himself as a "big game" player and has a .375 average for three NL Championship Series to prove it and though his World Series average is only .232, one year (1977) he hit .399.

BASERUNNING:

Baker has only average speed on the bases, but he is aggressive, especially at breaking up a double play. He is rated a tough slider. He will take the extra base any time it's possible. Though he stole 17 bases in 1982, he was thrown out stealing 10 times. But he'll steal when necessary.

FIELDING:

He's an above average outfielder but not a great one. He will make the play or the big throw. He has a tendency to miss the cutoff man. He can go back on a ball well, and charge it, too. He moves well laterally, and though he sometimes tends to play too deep, Baker has good range.

OVERALL:

He is one of the best clutch players in the game. His swing is not fluid but he overcomes that with strong hands. Through his own work he has made himself a pretty good outfielder.

McCarver: "Simply a great ballplayer. Dusty is the most dangerous clutch hitter for the Dodgers, and he earns his money."

Coleman: "Baker is a great hitter, and one of the toughest outs in the league."

MARK BELANGER
INF, No. 8
RR, 6'2", 170 lbs.
ML Svc: 16 years
Born: 6-8-44 in
Pittsfield, MA

HITTING:

Belanger's strength is not his hitting, as evidenced by his .231 career average. But he does handle the bat well, has an above average bunt, and is especially strong at hitting to the right side to advance a runner.

He is not a good hitter, but a smart one. That is, he knows he doesn't have power and doesn't try to hit home runs. He will try to spray the ball around, to make contact to get the ball into play.

He likes fastballs that are up in the strike zone and he has difficulty with breaking pitches. To get him out, pitchers merely need to throw him breaking pitches off the plate. Against righthanders he'll go to right field more but will pull lefthanders.

Best spot in the lineup--No. 8.

BASERUNNING:

At one time, Belanger was an excellent baserunner and basestealer. He remains a smart runner, aggressive at times. He doesn't make dumb mistakes on the bases.

FIELDING:

One of the best shortstops in his prime, he seems to simply absorb ground balls. His throwing arm is strong and accurate. He gets rid of the ball extremely well. Even in a new league after 15 years in the American League he knows how to play hitters. A very smart infielder. His range is excellent; he can go to his right well to make a play behind third and he goes behind second well, too.

1982 STATISTICS

AVG	G	AB	R	H	2B	3B	HR	RBI	BB	SO	SB
.240	54	50	6	12	1	0	0	4	5	10	1

CAREER STATISTICS

AVG	G	AB	R	H	2B	3B	HR	RBI	BB	SO	SB
.228	2016	5784	676	1316	175	33	20	389	576	839	167

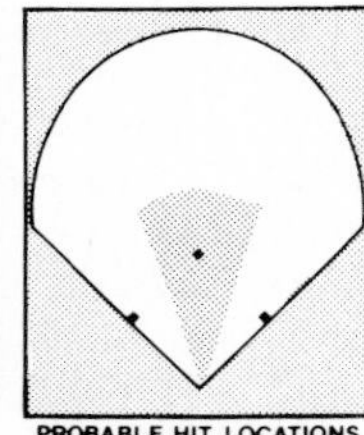

OVERALL:

In his prime, Belanger was one of the best shortstops to ever play the game. Never a strong hitter, he still manages to advance runners. At 38, he's in an excellent position--for himself as well as the club--as a back up shortstop.

Coleman: "Just keep it down and you'll get him."

McCarver: "He's a magician."

HITTING:

Pitch to Cey high and tight and low and away. Hard stuff inside gives him trouble. He likes to get his hands out over the plate, has a slightly open stance and stands in close to the plate. His short stature gives a very tight strike zone. Coupled with an excellent eye, Cey is a tough power hitter.

Cey's long ball pitch is the fastball away. Any curveball thrown him must be down. He has compact power, and is always steady and ready for a big hit. Because of this, the change-up gives him trouble. It's the pitch to get him out with.

Righthanded pitchers with good sinkers and sliders can be especially difficult for him. On the other hand, Cey spells trouble even for good fast-ballers like Mario Soto, Tom Seaver and Nolan Ryan.

Cey does not have a consistent ability to hit to the opposite field. He is a pull hitter, and he gets under a lot of pitches and flies to center.

His bunting ability is average, but he is rarely asked to bunt.

Cey's greatest strength is his power and clutch hitting ability. He gets hot with the bat and can turn a game around with one swing. He is especially dangerous because he swings only at strikes. He could be a better hitter, he's rated above average, but would sacrifice his explosive power.

He hits well at home (Dodger Stadium makes balls jump) and generally likes small parks like Chicago's Wrigley Field and Atlanta.

BASERUNNING:

Cey has average to below average speed. He takes a walking lead, but is no threat to steal more than five bases a year. He is an average slider, and could improve it a bit to be a stronger baserunner.

RON CEY
INF, No. 10
RR, 5'9", 185 lbs.
ML Svc: 10 years
Born: 2-15-48 in Tacoma, WA

1982 STATISTICS

AVG	G	AB	R	H	2B	3B	HR	RBI	BB	SO	SB
.254	150	556	62	141	23	1	24	79	57	99	3

CAREER STATISTICS

AVG	G	AB	R	H	2B	3B	HR	RBI	BB	SO	SB
.264	1481	5216	715	1378	223	18	228	842	765	838	20

VS. RHP

VS. LHP

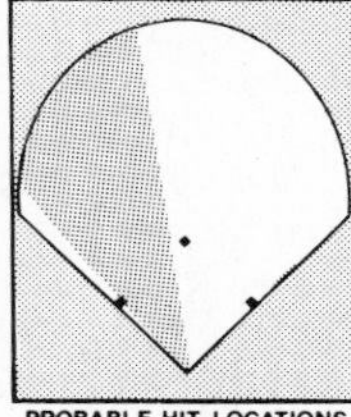
PROBABLE HIT LOCATIONS

FIELDING:

In his tenth season as a third baseman, Cey is currently rated an average to below average fielder. He does not have great range, tends to play shallow to cut down on distance, and some balls get by him that shouldn't. He moves better to his left than to his right, finding it tough to get sharp grounders hit down the line. Arm strength is average, Cey has good hands and can catch the balls he gets to.

OVERALL:

McCarver: "Cey is a classic power hitter--a winner and clutch performer, does an adequate job on defense, and a tough out in tight situations."

Coleman: "His best days are behind him, but still has an explosive bat and can carry the club for short periods when hot."

HITTING:

Guerrero is an outstanding fastball hitter. When he first appeared in the majors, he could not handle the curveball at all, but has improved immeasurably. Still, a pitcher should throw him breaking balls away. He likes the ball low and can go down after a pitch and drive it out of the park.

Guerrero hits well for average, drives in runs and hits with power.

Guerrero hits righthanders as well as lefthanders, and pulls the ball with power against either. He hits well in the clutch, producing 18 game-winning RBIs in 1982 to rank third in the league. He is very aggressive at the plate but will take a walk. He has cut down considerably on swinging at bad pitches. He started the 1982 season batting in the sixth position in the order but by May was batting No. 4 which is where he should hit.

From the opposition's standpoint, the worst thing about Guerrero is that, at 26, he's still young and still learning.

BASERUNNING:

Guerrero is not considered a basestealing threat but he does have deceptive speed and can, if necessary, steal a base. He improved his overall baserunning from early in the 1982 season when several times he was caught rounding a base too far. Early in the year consistently slid head first, a concession to the broken ankle he suffered in 1977 in the minors while sliding. As a result of his head first slides he injured his shoulder, then began sliding feet first.

FIELDING:

Guerrero rates as a decent outfielder with an above average throwing arm and above average accuracy.

PEDRO GUERRERO
OF, No. 28
RR, 5'11", 190 lbs.
ML Svc: 3 years
Born: 6-29-56 in
San Pedro de Macoris, DR

1982 STATISTICS

AVG	G	AB	R	H	2B	3B	HR	RBI	BB	SO	SB
.304	150	575	87	175	27	5	32	100	65	89	22

CAREER STATISTICS

AVG	G	AB	R	H	2B	3B	HR	RBI	BB	SO	SB
.305	353	1175	170	358	55	9	53	189	112	191	31

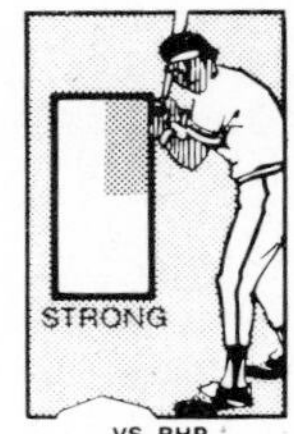

VS. RHP

VS. LHP

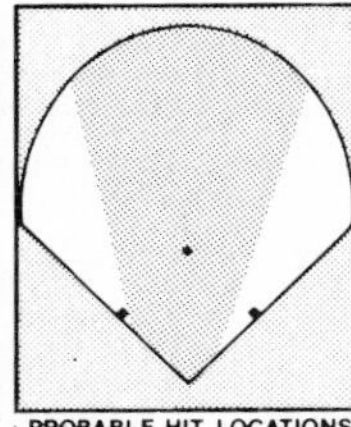
PROBABLE HIT LOCATIONS

His best suit, though, may be third base. He was an infielder in the minors, but with no spot on the Dodgers' infield when he came to the majors, he went to the outfield. He played some third base in 1981 and 1982. As an outfielder, he does not go back on a ball particularly well but does get to balls hit to his left or right.

OVERALL:

He is a dangerous hitter, especially when the game is on the line. He is a dead fastball hitter who can adjust to the breaking pitch. He is very strong.

McCarver: "Incredible upper body strength. He looks as though he's using someone else's torso. He's fearless in the clutch."

Coleman: "One of the most dangerous hitters in the league."

BURT HOOTON
RHP, No. 46
RR, 6'1", 210 lbs.
ML Svc: 11 years
Born: 2-7-50 in
Greenville, TX

PITCHING:

Hooton has become an excellent pitcher with the Dodgers, a solid starter who keeps his club in the game. He had knee surgery during the 1982 season, ending with a 4-7 record, the only time with the Dodgers he's won less than 11 games. His forte is consistency, along with a knuckle-curve which he developed himself. His fastball is better than average, 88 to 90 MPH, but he throws it only about 50% of the time. Mostly, he relies on his knuckle-curve.

Hooton's change-up is good enough to keep batters off balance. He's in complete control when he's pitching, and his poise is a huge asset.

Hooton has been a big game pitcher for the Dodgers, winning once in the NL divisional series, two games in the Championship Series and three World Series games.

Batters hit many fly balls against Hooton indicating that he's better suited pitching in parks with large dimensions. Possibly that's one reason he was only 34-44 in four-plus seasons pitching in Chicago's Wrigley Field. Overall rating, above average to excellent.

FIELDING, HITTING, BASERUNNING:

Hooton does not hold runners on base well at all and his pick-off move is below average. He is not particularly strong at fielding. He is not a good hitter (career average: .136). When running the bases, it's one base at a time.

OVERALL:

Hooton is a good clutch pitcher, a total professional. His concentration is excellent, he's very much in control when on the mound.

McCarver: "He has an excellent knuckle-curve; it has a very biting downward movement. He knows how to pitch."

1982 STATISTICS

W	L	ERA	G	GS	CG	IP	H	R	ER	BB	SO	SV
4	7	4.03	21	21	2	120	130	57	54	33	51	0

CAREER STATISTICS

W	L	ERA	G	GS	CG	IP	H	R	ER	BB	SO	SV
134	114	3.22	364	324	82	2256	2083	905	807	657	1280	3

STEVE HOWE
LHP, No. 57
LL, 6'1", 180 lbs.
ML Svc: 3 years
Born: 3-10-58 in
Pontiac, MI

PITCHING:

Howe has excellent poise for a young pitcher, and in a short time has become the Dodgers' No. 1 short man in the bullpen. He pitched only two months in the minors, but in three years in the big leagues he's accumulated 38 saves and 19 wins with a career ERA of 2.38.

He throws a good, live fastball--87-90 MPH--with a slight jerk in his delivery which gives his pitch a desirable tail to it. He comes overhand with his pitches, throwing little off-speed stuff, preferring to stay with his fastball, his "money pitch." He throws an above average slider when he wants to come inside to righthanded batters. It breaks late, making it quite effective.

Like most short relievers, Howe is most effective one time through a lineup. His strength is his fastball, which he can throw for a strike just about anytime. He is seldom hurt by a home run, giving up only six in nearly 150 innings. The only question is his durability. He tends to require more rest than most short relievers. He did have some arm trouble during the 1982 season from overwork. He started the season slowly but recovered to put together a strong season.

FIELDING, HITTING, BASERUNNING:

Howe gets off the mound in a hurry, showing his overall athletic ability. His pick-off move is better than average. He's not much of a hitter, but he seldom gets an opportunity. He's been to the plate only 19 times in three years with one hit.

OVERALL:

Howe rates as an above average relief pitcher. He is best pitching to lefthanded batters. Righthanders don't mind batting against him. Besides his fastball, his No. 1 asset is his poise.

McCarver: "It's rare you find a young pitcher with his presence--that's something you can't teach. He is fearless for the most part."

Coleman: "He's bordering on becoming excellent."

1982 STATISTICS

W	L	ERA	G	GS	CG	IP	H	R	ER	BB	SO	SV
7	5	2.08	66	0	0	99	87	27	23	17	49	13

CAREER STATISTICS

W	L	ERA	G	GS	CG	IP	H	R	ER	BB	SO	SV
19	17	2.38	166	0	0	238	221	77	63	57	120	38

KEN LANDREAUX
OF, No. 44
LR, 5'11", 164 lbs.
ML Svc: 5 years
Born: 12-22-54 in
Los Angeles, CA

1982 STATISTICS

AVG	G	AB	R	H	2B	3B	HR	RBI	BB	SO	SB
.284	129	461	71	131	23	7	7	50	39	54	31

CAREER STATISTICS

AVG	G	AB	R	H	2B	3B	HR	RBI	BB	SO	SB
.275	624	2235	299	614	101	33	41	264	165	230	75

VS. RHP

VS. LHP

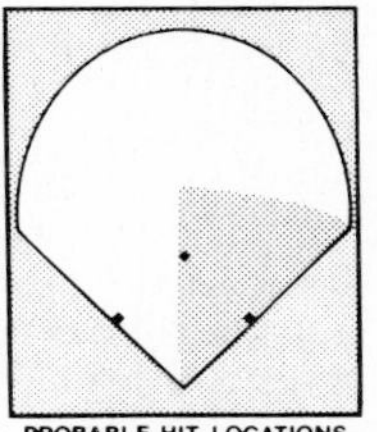
PROBABLE HIT LOCATIONS

HITTING:

Landreaux handles the bat well, is a good bunter, a man who generally makes contact. He doesn't have a lot of power, and isn't a big RBI man. But he puts the ball in play and makes a good No. 2 hitter in the lineup. He is better suited against righthanded pitching, and tends to pull the ball against righthanders and hit straightaway against lefthanders. He has a knack for putting the ball on the ground between first and second base, getting numerous base hits through that hole. He likes the ball out over the plate, away from him; he does not like to be jammed.

He prefers fastballs to breaking pitches but handles the slider and the change fairly well. Generally starts the season well but then tails off the second half. Has shown spectacular consistency at times; to wit: a 31 game hitting streak in 1980, the longest in the majors that year.

BASERUNNING:

Landreaux has good speed and rates above average on the bases. He stole 31 bases in 41 tries in 1982. He could be more aggressive though, especially in making pitchers aware of him on the bases.

FIELDING:

Landreaux has average ratings in most defensive categories and above average in range because of his speed. But he does not rate high overall as an outfielder because of his tentativeness in center field. His biggest fault is a reluctance to "take charge" in the outfield. Numerous fly balls in short center fell in for base hits last season--many in Landreaux's turf.

He doesn't have an exceptionally strong arm, but he's fairly accurate. He does catch balls he gets to, and he gets to most because of his speed. He should get to more, though, which is where his timidity comes in. Doesn't like to get close to fences or other fielders.

OVERALL:

Landreaux is a good ballplayer, but not a spectacular one. He should be better but lacks aggressiveness.

McCarver: "He needs to assert himself more."

HITTING:

If you pitch to Marshall high you're liable to get hurt. He is a young player with exceptional power to all fields. He tends to pull lefthanders more often than righthanders, and is a straightaway hitter.

A so-so fastball out over the plate, and it's trouble. He waits well on a change-up for such a young player; he might be fooled once, not twice. Breaking pitches appear to be the best to throw to Marshall as he still tries to adjust to major league pitching. He appears to be a better than average clutch hitter, but he didn't face that many tough situations in 1982. He hit five home runs but drove in only nine runs. He did not do well as a pinch-hitter (3 for 20), but did hit one pinch homer.

Though he is tall, he crouches at the plate. He tends sometimes to lunge at pitches but he is strong enough to hold up on pitches that are too far outside. He's only 23 with little more than 200 at bats in the majors, so he's still learning.

BASERUNNING:

For a big man, Marshall possesses average to above average speed. In the minors he once stole 22 bases, another time 21. In 1982, he only took two bases. Baserunning is certainly not his No. 1 strength--his nickname is "Big Foot"--but he is aggressive on the bases. He slides feet first, goes hard into second to break up a double play, and doesn't make "bonehead" base-running mistakes.

FIELDING:

It appears that Marshall's position in the big leagues will be the outfield,

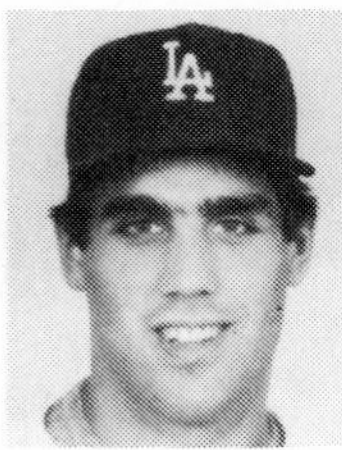

MIKE MARSHALL
INF, No. 5
RR, 6'5", 220 lbs.
ML Svc: 1 year plus
Born: 1-12-60 in Libertyville, IL

1982 STATISTICS

AVG	G	AB	R	H	2B	3B	HR	RBI	BB	SO	SB
.242	49	95	10	23	3	0	5	9	13	23	2

CAREER STATISTICS

AVG	G	AB	R	H	2B	3B	HR	RBI	BB	SO	SB
.233	63	120	12	28	6	0	5	10	14	27	2

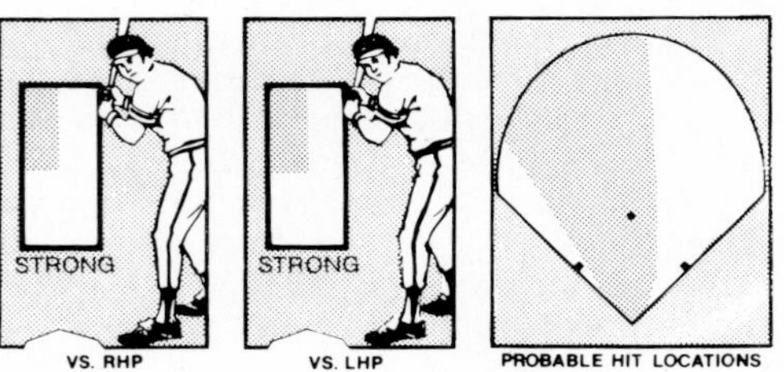

though he played first base almost exclusively in the minors. He is still learning, but has a good, strong and accurate throwing arm. With his big, loping strides he is able to cover considerable ground in the outfield. He doesn't appear to shy away when near the wall or another fielder. Overall, he rates as an average outfielder but with the potential to get better.

OVERALL:

Marshall has great potential. He figures to become a productive offensive player in the major leagues.

McCarver: "Could be a superstar. He has amazing poise for a 23 year old. It's hard to believe he was a sixth-round (draft) pick."

RICK MONDAY
OF, No. 16
LL, 6'3", 200 lbs.
ML Svc: 16 years
Born: 11-20-45 in Batesville, AR

1982 STATISTICS

AVG	G	AB	R	H	2B	3B	HR	RBI	BB	SO	SB
.257	104	210	37	54	6	4	11	42	39	51	2

CAREER STATISTICS

AVG	G	AB	R	H	2B	3B	HR	RBI	BB	SO	SB
.265	1856	5911	925	1566	239	63	234	748	887	1455	98

VS. RHP

VS. LHP

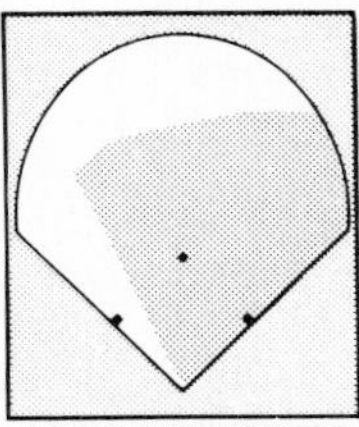
PROBABLE HIT LOCATIONS

HITTING:

Monday has become a good clutch hitter who hits line drives to all fields and is especially adept at reaching the alleys. His ability to cut down on his strikeouts has improved his hitting greatly.

Monday stands deep in the box and uses a slightly crouched stance. He is a good low ball hitter and likes the ball on the inside part of the plate. It's best to pitch him high and inside, or high and away. He is very strong with good power; he hits long, towering home runs to right field and line drive homers to left.

He rarely bats against lefthanders but righthanders who have success against Monday pitch him tight. He handles breaking pitches above average; he doesn't handle the change-up well at all.

Because he doesn't strike out anywhere near as often as he once did, he has become a good hit-and-run man. He hits behind runners well and he also bunts extremely well. He didn't fare well as a pinch-hitter in 1982 (4 for 35) but in 1981 he batted .348.

BASERUNNING:

At one time Monday was considered an excellent baserunner and basestealer. He still rates above average on the bases, though not as a basestealer (he was 2 for 3 stealing in 1982). He knows how to run the bases, and will take the extra base whenever possible. He is still aggressive on the bases, though far from reckless.

FIELDING:

Monday no longer has the strong throwing arm he had when he was younger but he is well-schooled. He hits the cutoff man regularly, he knows hitters and how to play them and he knows the parks and the type of bounce to expect. His range is adequate, compensated for by the fact that he knows where he should play. He takes charge on pop-ups hit between him and an infielder. In a spot role, he is an excellent outfielder and, though right field appears to be his best position, he can play center and left as well.

OVERALL:

Coleman: "A quality fourth outfielder and pinch-hitter. Murders the fastball about thigh-high. Has been nagged by injuries, including a tear in his Achilles heel."

McCarver: "Injuries have curtailed greatness . . . he probably could have been a more productive player."

TOM NIEDENFUER
RHP, No. 49
RR, 6'5 , 225 lbs.
ML Svc: 1 year plus
Born: 8-13-59 in
St. Louis Park, MN

PITCHING:

Niedenfuer is a power pitcher who's most effective in short relief, getting one or two outs at a critical time in the game. Should never be used for an extended period; he's best going through a lineup one time, no more. His fastball is excellent, clocked at 90-95 MPH. He rarely throws a curveball and needs to develop a change-up. His strength, naturally, is his fastball; his weakness is that the fastball is his one solid pitch.

He's still young, only 23, and has pitched professionally only two years after first being drafted on the 36th round (and not signing), then being bypassed altogether after pitching at Washington State University. Still, he has been compared with Yankees' Goose Gossage, primarily because of his size.

For someone with limited experience in the big leagues, Niedenfuer has displayed good poise. He's not afraid to move a batter off the plate. As he pitches more, he'll be even more at home in tight spots. He's shown pretty good control pitching with men on base. Overall rating, average.

FIELDING, HITTING, BASERUNNING:

Niedenfuer's pick-off move is average, at best, and he doesn't handle himself in the field that well. As a hitter, he's been to the plate only three times in the majors without a base hit.

OVERALL:

If Niedenfuer comes up with a specialty or an off-speed pitch, he could be a reliable short relief specialist. Right now, everything is based on his fastball.

McCarver: "Regardless of how hard you throw, if your location isn't great or if you don't have an effective off-speed pitch, you won't be able to deal effectively with major league hitters."

Coleman: "Can become effective because of his arm. Lack of pro experience may cause him to be a little unsure of himself."

1982 STATISTICS

W	L	ERA	G	GS	CG	IP	H	R	ER	BB	SO	SV
3	4	2.71	55	0	0	69	71	22	21	25	60	9

CAREER STATISTICS

W	L	ERA	G	GS	CG	IP	H	R	ER	BB	SO	SV
6	5	3.03	72	0	0	95	96	33	32	31	72	11

PITCHING:

Once Jerry Reuss realized his fastball, not his curveball was his No. 1 pitch he became a premier pitcher. His fastball, consistently in 93 MPH range, is the pitch he uses 80 to 85% of the time. When he was younger, though, he threw his curve much more than he does now.

He is a power pitcher who comes over the top. His size, along with a high kick, gives his fastball even more zip. At one time in his career he threw the ball up, but now when he's on, he keeps it down consistently. Because he has such good movement on his fastball, he is accused from time to time of doctoring the ball.

He seems to relish the ticklish situations, going to the fastball when he needs a strikeout.

In a sense, he was "reborn" when he was traded to Los Angeles. He somehow got lost in the shuffle in Pittsburgh and complained about being used out of the bullpen. He was used in relief for a time when he came to the Dodgers, and pitched well, too. In eight relief appearances at the start of the 1980 season he had three wins and three saves and a 1.41 ERA. Upon becoming a starter he threw six shutouts including a no-hitter in San Francisco. Overall, rates high.

JERRY REUSS
LHP, No. 41
LL, 6'5", 225 lbs.
ML Svc: 12 years
Born: 6-19-49 in
St. Louis, MO

FIELDING, HITTING, BASERUNNING:

For his size, Reuss moves off the mound well. He gets into position to field a ball hit back at him. He has a decent move to first.

As a hitter, he gets his cuts and will occasionally drive a ball to left. But he's not considered a good hitter; his career batting average is well under .200. As a baserunner, he is slow, strictly one base at a time.

OVERALL:

Reuss is a quality pitcher on a quality staff. At one time he was erratic (14-14 one year, 9-13 the next) but has since become a consistent winner. Once he harnessed his fastball he became an outstanding pitcher.

McCarver: "Reuss is a classic starter--intelligent and absolutely fearless. He is a model pitcher that any team in baseball would love to have."

1982 STATISTICS

W	L	ERA	G	GS	CG	IP	H	R	ER	BB	SO	SV
18	11	3.11	39	37	8	254	232	98	88	50	138	0

CAREER STATISTICS

W	L	ERA	G	GS	CG	IP	H	R	ER	BB	SO	SV
161	129	3.52	422	376	109	2609	2565	1158	1019	862	1444	9

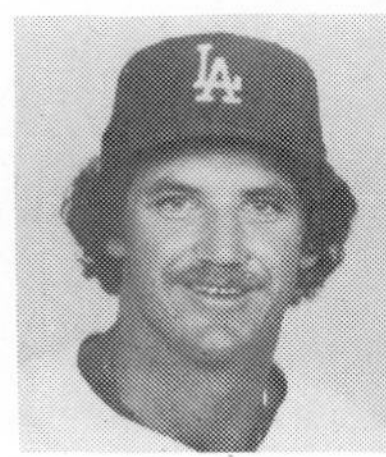

RON ROENICKE
OF, No. 40
SL, 6'0", 180 lbs.
ML Svc: 1 year plus
Born: 8-19-56 in Covina, CA

1982 STATISTICS

AVG	G	AB	R	H	2B	3B	HR	RBI	BB	SO	SB
.259	109	143	18	37	8	0	1	12	21	32	5

CAREER STATISTICS

AVG	G	AB	R	H	2B	3B	HR	RBI	BB	SO	SB
.253	131	190	24	48	8	0	1	12	27	40	6

VS. RHP

VS. LHP

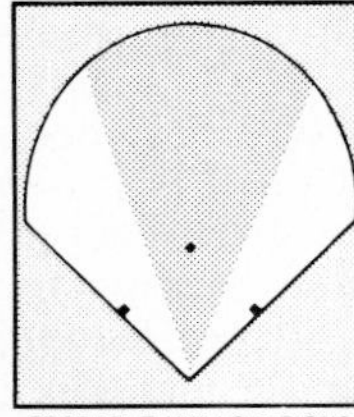
PROBABLE HIT LOCATIONS

HITTING:

Even though Roenicke maintains he is a better hitter righthanded, in his brief time in the major leagues he has shown more accomplished hitting lefthanded. Righthanded he appears to like low pitches; lefthanded high pitches away. Either way he should be pitched inside. It appears he can be jammed batting from an upright stance.

He is primarily a line drive hitter, but on occasion he's shown some power. He is not likely to hit the ball out of the park, but can reach the alleys from either side of the plate. He hits off-speed pitches extremely well, and can wait on a pitch. He has an excellent eye, and posted impressive minor league statistics.

Roenicke bunts well and gets a good number of infield hits. If he gets the bat on the ball, and doesn't hit a fly ball, he's a threat to get a base hit.

He hasn't had that much opportunity, though he has shown an ability to drive in runs in the clutch. At the start of the season he was used primarily as a pinch-hitter, a role he doesn't particularly like, but he did hit .295 in that role.

The best way to get him out is to run the ball in on him. He's a good fastball hitter.

BASERUNNING:

He has better than average speed despite the operations on both knees midway through the 1980 season. He is actually faster now than he was before he injured his knees. He is an intelligent runner and a definite threat to steal. He is very aggressive on the bases and is quite adept at breaking up a double play.

FIELDING:

Roenicke rates average in all categories but in time, should become a strong outfielder. He can get a ball from any of the three outfield positions, and is fundamentally sound. Hits the cutoff man regularly and makes the smart throw.

His greatest strength is being able to go anywhere to get a ball. He doesn't show any fear of running into fences or of balls hit between fielders.

OVERALL:

As a young player who is a switch-hitter, Roenicke has great potential. The only thing, he needs a chance to play regularly.

McCarver: "At a young age, he appears to know how to play the game."

VINCENTE ROMO
RHP, No. 38
RR, 6'1", 180 lbs.
ML Svc: 8 years
Born: 5-21-43 in
Santa Rosalia, MEX

PITCHING:

Romo throws sidearm, overhand, three-quarter--just about any pitch from any angle. His key is deception. Purchased from the Mexican League at mid-season by the Dodgers, Romo started and relieved, though his main value is as a long reliever.

His fastball is so-so, about 83-84 MPH is all, but it's made quicker by the large assortment of breaking pitches he uses. He throws a good curveball, an average slider, an occasional change-up and a screwball. He is most effective pitching to righthanded batters although he can be tough on lefthanders, too, if his screwball is working well.

Romo isn't the best at working out of tight spots, which is probably one reason he pitched so long in Mexico before getting a call to return to the majors. His strength is both his durability--reportedly, he'll be 40 in May--and his large assortment of breaking, or "junk" pitches. His weakness is his lack of a good fastball.

FIELDING, HITTING, BASERUNNING:

Romo's fielding was greatly affected in 1982 because of a knee injury that required surgery. As a veteran, he's got a decent move to first base, though nothing outstanding. As a hitter, he swings at about anything, seldom connecting.

OVERALL:

He has a 32-33 record with five major league clubs over 15 years. He's underrated because he pitched in Mexico from 1975 until the Dodgers purchased him in 1982. He's crafty, can adapt to any role and can be an asset as a spot starter or long reliever. He's not likely to go out and pitch nine innings, however.

McCarver: "Two or three catchers are needed to have fingers enough just to give the signs to this 'man for all pitches.'"

1982 STATISTICS

W	L	ERA	G	GS	CG	IP	H	R	ER	BB	SO	SV
1	2	3.03	15	6	0	35	25	12	12	14	24	1

CAREER STATISTICS

W	L	ERA	G	GS	CG	IP	H	R	ER	BB	SO	SV
32	33	3.36	335	32	4	645	569	269	241	281	416	51

BILL RUSSELL
INF, No. 18
RR, 6'0", 180 lbs.
ML Svc: 13 years
Born: 10-21-48 in
Pittsburgh, KS

1982 STATISTICS

AVG	G	AB	R	H	2B	3B	HR	RBI	BB	SO	SB
.274	153	497	64	136	20	2	3	46	63	30	10

CAREER STATISTICS

AVG	G	AB	R	H	2B	3B	HR	RBI	BB	SO	SB
.265	1780	6220	684	1647	251	54	45	547	392	580	139

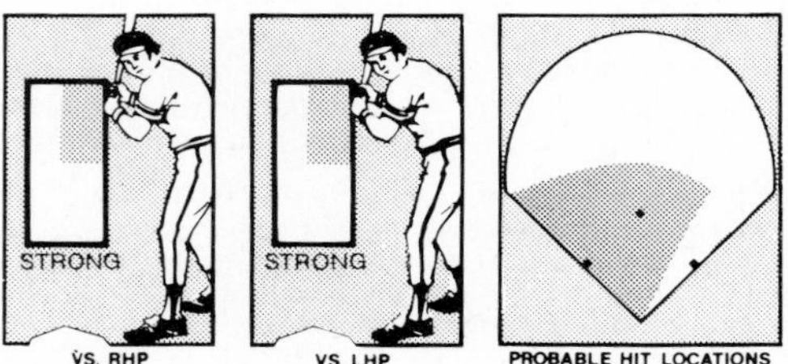

HITTING:

Russell is an excellent clutch hitter, a far better hitter with men on base, especially in scoring position. He sprays the ball well to all fields, and he can be counted upon to make contact. Russell does not strike out often, nor does he walk a lot.

Russell is a dead high ball hitter and hits as well against righthanded pitching as he does against southpaws. He doesn't hit many home runs but he does have some pop.

It is best to keep the ball down against Russell. He knows the strike zone and seldom swings at bad pitches. He crouches slightly at the plate, deep in the box, and likes the ball out over the plate. He hits line drives, and can hit behind a runner. A good, hard fastball that's down in the strike zone is the best pitch to get Russell. He handles the change-up extremely well, also breaking pitches that are up.

Russell generally hits better as the season progresses. He is a consistent hitter, though he's never hit for a high average. Russell is a good No. 8 hitter or can bat in the more demanding No. 2 position.

BASERUNNING:

Once a feared baserunner, Russell has slowed some but still rates above average. Pitchers pay attention when he's on base. He breaks up the double play well.

FIELDING:

Russell came to the Dodgers as an outfielder--one of the best in the organization, according to former manager Walter Alston--but was switched to the infield when it was thought he would not hit well enough to play center field. Actually, he has had to learn to play shortstop in the major leagues and, at times, it shows. He is not a smooth shortstop, and never will be.

Russell tends to lose his concentration on seemingly easy plays. He had difficulty throwing in 1981 after having the index finger on his right hand crushed by a pitch in September 1980. He threw considerably better last season, but is still inconsistent. He has better than average range, but because of his inconsistent throwing, his overall fielding rates average.

OVERALL:

Russell remains a good clutch hitter but is inconsistent and often erratic defensively.

McCarver: "He'd come off his deathbed to hit a high fastball. He kills the Phillies in Veteran's Stadium."

STEVE SAX
INF, No. 23
RR, 5'11", 175 lbs.
ML Svc: 1 year plus
Born: 1-29-60 in
Sacramento, CA

1982 STATISTICS

AVG	G	AB	R	H	2B	3B	HR	RBI	BB	SO	SB
.282	150	638	88	180	23	7	4	47	49	53	49

CAREER STATISTICS

AVG	G	AB	R	H	2B	3B	HR	RBI	BB	SO	SB
.281	181	757	103	213	25	7	6	56	56	67	54

VS. RHP

VS. LHP

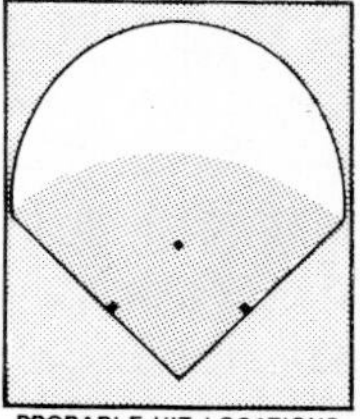
PROBABLE HIT LOCATIONS

HITTING:

Steve Sax is an aggressive, pesky kind of hitter. He battles the pitcher, he makes contact, he puts the ball in play. In a short time he has proven to be an excellent leadoff hitter. He bunts well, and he works pitchers for a base on balls. He doesn't drive in many runs, but does get on base and score. Last season he led the club with 88 runs scored.

Best to keep the ball down to Sax, or up and inside; he can drive a ball that's out over the plate. He hits well to the opposite field and sprays the ball to all fields. He hits well behind a runner and has proven himself to be a fair hitter in the clutch.

Sax hits line drives, and for a relatively small player he has some sock. He likes to hit the ball in the gap and take off running; he has good speed. He handles the change-up very well, but has trouble with breaking pitches that are down in the strike zone.

Sax is the catalyst to the Dodgers' offense; when he gets on, things tend to happen. He even runs out his bases on balls like his acknowledged idol, Pete Rose.

BASERUNNING:

Sax is an excellent baserunner and basestealer (with 49 steals, he established a Dodger rookie record in 1982). He's quick on the bases, quite aggressive, smart and still learning. He gets out of the batter's box well. If anything, he's over-aggressive (he was thrown out 19 times in 1982).

FIELDING:

Sax rates average at second base and needs to improve, especially when turning the double play. He doesn't get rid of the ball quickly enough, something that will come with experience. He sometimes rushes his throws on the double play, drawing needless errors. His range is average but he battles ground balls. He isn't afraid to dive for grounders, either behind second or when he goes to his left. He has played professionally only five years, and only one full season in the majors. He is still learning, but shows much promise.

OVERALL:

Sax is enthusiastic, aggressive and still learning. He was the 1982 National League Rookie of the Year. His only shortcoming is turning the double play.

Coleman: "A future All Star second baseman, to be sure."

McCarver: "He does all the things a good leadoff hitter should do. He can get by because of his feisty makeup and will fight you until he wins."

MIKE SCIOSCIA
C, No. 14
LR, 6'2", 220 lbs.
ML Svc: 2 years
Born: 11-27-58 in
Upper Darby, PA

1982 STATISTICS

AVG	G	AB	R	H	2B	3B	HR	RBI	BB	SO	SB
.219	129	365	31	80	11	1	5	38	44	31	2

CAREER STATISTICS

AVG	G	AB	R	H	2B	3B	HR	RBI	BB	SO	SB
.246	276	789	66	194	26	2	8	75	92	58	3

VS. RHP

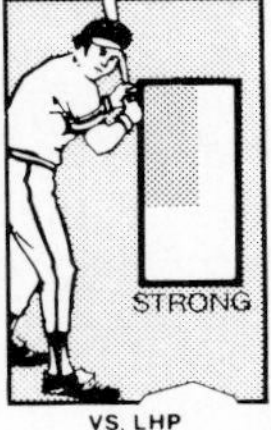

VS. LHP

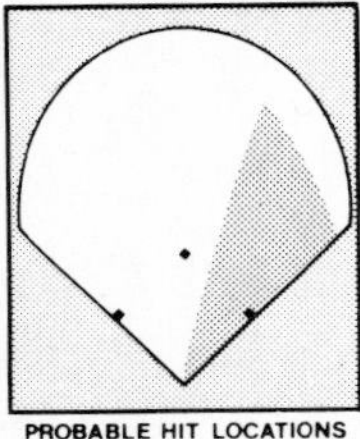
PROBABLE HIT LOCATIONS

HITTING:

Mike Scioscia should be pitched down and away. He tries to pull everything, which has been his undoing. He has worked at hitting line drives to the opposite field, and when he does that he is a much better hitter. He should hit with more power than he does, though he hits many balls that are caught at the warning track. He shows his best power going to left-center.

Scioscia doesn't strike out an inordinate amount of the time, has a fairly good eye and is able to draw a walk. He hits well on pitches that are up and over the plate. He is much more effective against righthanded pitching and rarely plays against lefthanders. Despite a low batting average, he does hit fairly well in the clutch. He's definitely a better hitter with runners in scoring position.

Scioscia recognizes his shortcomings as a hitter and is willing to work on them. He had a disappointing 1982 season, and is far from a good pure hitter. He has a "hitch" in his swing he has not been able to conquer--but he is big and strong.

BASERUNNING:

Running, whether from home to first, first to third or second to home, is definitely Scioscia's weakest part of the game. If catchers are supposed to be slow, Scioscia lives up to it. He's slow. He is, however, excellent at breaking up a double play.

FIELDING:

Scioscia's No. 1 forte behind the plate is the way he blocks it off to enemy runners. He is recognized as the best in baseball at blocking the plate. He is rated average in most other phases of catching.

He is quick to learn batters' weaknesses--and strengths--and works closely with his pitcher, calling his own pitches. For a young catcher, he displays considerable aggressiveness behind the plate.

Scioscia did not, however, progress in 1982 the way the Dodgers had hoped he would. His throwing arm is strong enough and reasonably accurate, but he still takes too long to get rid of the ball. Nonetheless, he was the first catcher to throw out Montreal's Tim Raines in 1981.

He also speaks some Spanish, enough to converse with Fernando Valenzuela who speaks no English.

OVERALL:

Coleman: "Great at blocking the plate. It's like trying to knock down a California redwood."

McCarver: "Blocks home plate as well as anyone I've seen since John Roseboro."

DAVE STEWART
RHP, No. 48
RR, 6'2", 200 lbs.
ML Svc: 2 years
Born: 2-19-57 in Oakland, CA

PITCHING:

Stewart is a power pitcher who lives up to his nickname--"Smoke." He throws a fastball clocked at 92-95 MPH. If he gets it moving, he can be devastating, especially to righthanded batters. If he gets it up, he'll give up home runs. That's been one of his failings: the home run pitch.

Stewart started 14 games in 1982, relieved in 31. His best suit is long relief, although in his first two full years in the big leagues he's done a little of everything. He became the Dodgers' No. 1 righthanded short man out of the bullpen late in the 1981 season, but lost that job when he gave up two critical homers in the National League mini-series against Houston.

So far, his lack of consistency has been a problem. When he's on, he's strong; when he's not, he's hittable. He stays with his fastball, only going to his curveball and slider when he's ahead in the count. He's working on a change-up, and when--if?--he develops it, he should be much tougher.

His strength is his fastball. His weakness is occasional wildness and a fastball that's too good; that is, one that's too straight.

FIELDING, HITTING, BASERUNNING:

Stewart is an excellent athlete who's "in" the game when he's on the mound. He bounces off the mound well to field bunts. His pick-off move to first is rated average to above average. As a hitter, he's about average for a pitcher. And as a baserunner, he has better speed than most pitchers.

OVERALL:

Stewart's fastball rates high, his control and demeanor on the mound less than average.

Coleman: "His fastball is quick but straight; he should be better than he's shown. Still has a chance to become a good pitcher with better control in the strike zone."

1982 STATISTICS

W	L	ERA	G	GS	CG	IP	H	R	ER	BB	SO	SV
9	8	3.81	45	14	0	146	137	72	62	49	80	1

CAREER STATISTICS

W	L	ERA	G	GS	CG	IP	H	R	ER	BB	SO	SV
13	11	3.49	78	14	0	191	178	85	74	63	110	7

DERREL THOMAS
OF, No. 30
SR, 6'0", 160 lbs.
ML Svc: 11 years
Born: 1-14-51 in
Los Angeles, CA

1982 STATISTICS

AVG	G	AB	R	H	2B	3B	HR	RBI	BB	SO	SB
.265	66	93	13	26	2	1	0	2	10	12	2

CAREER STATISTICS

AVG	G	AB	R	H	2B	3B	HR	RBI	BB	SO	SB
.250	1294	4116	502	1030	134	45	37	491	336	397	496

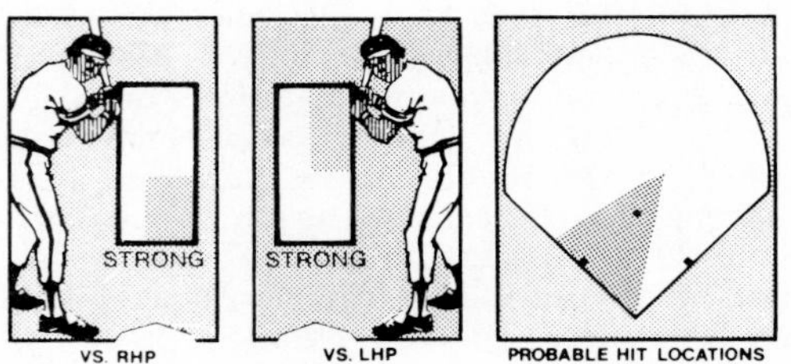

HITTING:

Thomas covers the plate quite well from both sides; he likes the ball down batting lefthanded, up when hitting righthanded. He has surprisingly good power for someone considered a singles hitter. But he is best at spraying the ball to all fields. He should be pitched inside, righthanded as well as lefthanded. He is a better hitter lefthanded, though his average in 1982 would indicate otherwise (.228 lefthanded, .344 righthanded). He generally gets the bat on the ball and is also a better than average bunter. Doesn't handle off-speed pitches especially well. As a part-time player his hitting over the years has been quite consistent.

BASERUNNING:

Running the bases has always been a strong part of Thomas' game. He is an aggressive runner, always looking to take an extra base or to come home from third on a ball that doesn't get that far from the catcher. He goes in hard on double plays; too hard, according to some second basemen and shortstops around the league. Pitchers are aware he can steal bases, though he's slowed some because of age and a broken bone in his leg suffered midway through the 1982 season. One year (1975) he stole 28 bases.

FIELDING:

As an infielder, Thomas rates average; as an outfielder better than average. He has played every position on the field except pitcher (he caught five games in 1980). As an outfielder, his best position is center field. He throws accurately, and well, from the outfield and has exceptional range, especially in center. Goes back on the ball very well.

OVERALL:

As a utility player, Thomas rates very high. He's a valuable player. But his prime value is just that, as a utility man, not as an everyday player, no matter which position he's playing.

McCarver: "He has the worth of three good players with all he can do. He is the Dodgers' best center fielder."

Coleman: "One of the best at going back."

FERNANDO VALENZUELA
LHP, No. 34
LL, 5'11", 200 lbs.
ML Svc: 2 years
Born: 11-1-60 in
Navajoa, Sonora, MX

PITCHING:

Valenzuela is a complete pitcher with excellent stuff--primarily a screwball--and finesse. He stands on the right side of the rubber, unusual for a lefthander, and looks upward with each pitch. His fastball alone is not that effective--he throws it 85-87 MPH--but because of his screwball, his fastball is seems much quicker.

He is actually more effective pitching against righthanded batters because of his screwball, which breaks away from them. He uses his curveball primarily to lefthanded batters. He has occasional wild streaks but he has the ability to control all his pitches. A batter cannot sit on any one pitch with Valenzuela.

He handles himself with incredible calm on the mound, especially in tight situations.

He can handle most any type of lineup in any park, although he had problems against San Francisco. He's 3-5 in his career against the Giants and he's lost five in a row to them. Overall rating, excellent.

FIELDING, HITTING, BASERUNNING:

Valenzuela holds runners well even with a high kick in his delivery. As a hitter, he's the best on the Dodgers' pitching staff, with 16 hits in 1981, 16 more in 1982, including a home run.

OVERALL:

Valenzuela is a smart pitcher who has learned quickly how to pitch to hitters throughout the league. He has good stuff and uncanny poise while pitching.

Coleman: "He's the most complete young pitcher to come into the game in years."

McCarver: "He is in the major leagues to stay. He has outstanding poise and presence--few pitchers have come to the majors with his calm. His screwball is excellent because most hitters swing at the illusion of a strike--he gets a lot of swinging strikes out of the strike zone."

1982 STATISTICS

W	L	ERA	G	GS	CG	IP	H	R	ER	BB	SO	SV
19	13	2.87	37	37	18	285	247	105	91	83	199	0

CAREER STATISTICS

W	L	ERA	G	GS	CG	IP	H	R	ER	BB	SO	SV
34	20	2.62	72	62	29	495	395	162	144	149	395	1

BOB WELCH
RHP, No. 35
RR, 6'3", 190 lbs.
ML Svc: 4 years
Born: 11-3-56 in Detroit, MI

PITCHING:

Welch has a good, live fastball. He challenges hitters with it and when he's up with it, he has more pop. He is strictly a starting pitcher; he was asked to relieve at one time but developed elbow problems.

He developed a curveball last season, though it is not that much of an asset. Hitters can no longer simply sit on his fastball. He is also working on a change-up which he threw last year about 5% of the time. He is a power pitcher. His fastball is timed at 93 MPH. At times he gets wild, and that is his undoing. He'll always go to his fastball when he needs to make a big pitch. It is only when he's ahead in the count that he goes to a breaking pitch. He's more effective to righthanded hitters because of the way he cuts his fastball, causing it to dart away.

Welch has extremely good poise on the mound, and even at a young age has shown remarkable ability in pressure situations. His strikeout of Reggie Jackson to end Game Two of the 1978 World Series is a prime example. He is not at all afraid to go inside to batters to move them off the plate. He has made remarkable strides since overcoming an alcohol problem following the 1979 season. In the three years since he has won 14, 9 and 16 games. Overall rating, average to above average.

FIELDING, HITTING, BASERUNNING:

He throws to first more than most righthanders and has developed a quick, deceptive pick-off move. He handles himself well fielding bunts and tappers to the mound. He throws well to all the bases and is not reluctant to try to cut down the lead runner on a sacrifice attempt.

He is not a strong hitter. When he does get on base, he doesn't make mistakes, but just doesn't have much speed.

OVERALL:

Welch has the potential to become a consistently successful pitcher in the big leagues. He has an excellent fastball, a good, live arm and exceptional poise. As he continues to develop a breaking pitch and a change-up he should only improve his stature.

Coleman: "His fastball has been eating hitters alive."

1982 STATISTICS

W	L	ERA	G	GS	CG	IP	H	R	ER	BB	SO	SV
16	11	3.36	36	36	9	235	199	94	88	81	176	0

CAREER STATISTICS

W	L	ERA	G	GS	CG	IP	H	R	ER	BB	SO	SV
51	35	3.23	139	116	19	782	704	305	281	259	535	8

STEVE YEAGER
C, No. 7
RR, 6'0", 205 lbs.
ML Svc: 10 years
Born: 11-24-48 in Huntington, WV

1982 STATISTICS

AVG	G	AB	R	H	2B	3B	HR	RBI	BB	SO	SB
.245	82	196	13	48	5	2	2	18	13	28	0

CAREER STATISTICS

AVG	G	AB	R	H	2B	3B	HR	RBI	BB	SO	SB
.232	979	2801	296	651	100	12	81	319	280	584	12

VS. RHP

VS. LHP

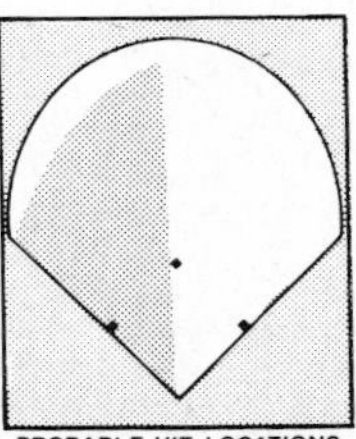
PROBABLE HIT LOCATIONS

HITTING:

Yeager is a high ball hitter who likes the ball away even though he tries to pull everything. His best pitch is a pitcher's "mistake." That's the one he hits the best.

Yeager does have power--one year he hit 16 home runs, another year 13 even though he hit only .216--and mostly his home runs come on pitches that are up in the strike zone. He seldom golfs a ball for any distance.

He is notoriously weak against a good curveball pitcher. Actually, he is weak against all so-called "superstar" pitchers. He had four years in a row in which he hit .216 or less. Yeager was platooned the last several years and is far more effective against lefthanded pitching, especially soft-throwing left-handers.

The weakest part of Yeager's game is hitting, but he is also a solid competitor and seems to play his best when something is on the line. In four World Series he has a .316 career average.

Yeager should be platooned, especially since undergoing knee surgery in 1982, combined with the fact that he's 34 years old. In the batting order, he should bat seventh or eighth.

BASERUNNING:

Yeager is generally aggressive on the bases but does not steal at all (only a dozen stolen bases in 11 years in the big leagues). He is average at breaking up a double play.

FIELDING:

Yeager is one of baseball's top defensive catchers. He knows opposing batters, their strengths and weaknesses, and calls a good game behind the plate. He has an excellent arm, is quick to release a throw and is above average in his accuracy. He will block balls well and is always in the proper position to field a bunt. He is aggressive in every phase of catching--calling the game, throwing to any base, any time. Handles pitchers well, and has their confidence.

OVERALL:

Yeager's value is in defense and in leadership. He could--and should--improve as a hitter. Has complained about being platooned.

McCarver: "He who complains about lack of playing time in one organization runs into problems elsewhere."

PAT ZACHRY
RHP, No. 40
RR, 6'5", 175 lbs.
ML Svc: 7 years
Born: 4-24-52 in Richmond, TX

PITCHING:

Pat Zachry lives by his slider and change-up. His slider is better than average and his change-up, even though he overexposes it, is one of the most effective in the league. All of his pitches are delivered three-quarters with a herky-jerky motion in which he seems to push the ball to the plate. He falls to his right which gives the impression that he is throwing more sidearm.

He pitches "backwards," using his off-speed pitches to set up his fastball, which he should throw more often. His curveball is average with fair rotation. He doesn't throw his slider hard, but keeps it away from hitters. His change-up is the palmball type and is his strikeout pitch, especially against lefthanded hitters. He tends to fall in love with it.

Zachry is crafty and resourceful, but he is hampered by his own impatience and temper. He can lose his composure because of a teammate's error or his own failure to retire a batter. He wants to pitch a perfect game badly and very nearly did last season. He is bothered more by mistakes--his and others'--than by pressure.

He seldom gives in to a hitter's strength and consequently falls behind too often. He usually is most effective early in the season and tends to break down or wear down as the season progresses.

FIELDING, HITTING, BASERUNNING:

Off the mound, Zachry is an average pitcher, adequate as a defensive player and inadequate as a batter. He doesn't run particularly well, either.

OVERALL:

Moving to the Dodgers undoubtedly will help motivate Pat. He can help a winning team, but not a loser.

McCarver: "Pat is a competent pitcher who has been injured frequently. He had a bright future after winning the National League Rookie of the Year award in 1976. He doesn't use his fastball enough, and if he did, it would make his change-up more effective. His stuff is good enough for him to be an above average pitcher, but he has been his own worst enemy."

1982 STATISTICS

W	L	ERA	G	GS	CG	IP	H	R	ER	BB	SO	SV
6	9	4.05	36	16	2	137	149	69	62	57	69	1

CAREER STATISTICS

W	L	ERA	G	GS	CG	IP	H	R	ER	BB	SO	SV
58	60	3.56	185	153	29	1020	986	462	403	412	570	1

JOSE MORALES
INF/PH, No. 17
RR, 6'0", 195 lbs.
ML Svc: 9 years
Born: 12-30-44 in St. Croix, VI

HITTING, BASERUNNING, FIELDING:

A very disciplined hitter, Morales developed into one of the game's best pinch-hitters. He goes to right field well, likes to drive low fastballs toward the alley in right-center. Strictly used as a pinch-hitter against lefthanded pitching. He hasn't got a lot of power but hits the ball hard. Since he's generally used in a situation that requires a base hit, he'll swing at bad pitches occasionally.

He hits off-speed pitches well, he waits on pitches and is especially good at hitting a change-up. Lefthanded sinkerball pitchers are especially to Morales' liking. He should be pitched inside and jammed if possible.

Simply not a baserunner. When he does get on, he's immediately lifted for a pinch-runner.

He was a catcher but doesn't play in the field at all any more.

OVERALL:

An excellent pinch-hitter, Morales once had a record 24 pinch-hits in one season and has more than 100 in his career. His bat has slowed some but still rates high as a hitter.

McCarver: "He's not up there to walk."

OLYMPIC STADIUM
Montreal Expos

Seating Capacity: 58,838
Playing Surface: Artificial

Dimensions:
Left Field Pole: 325 ft.
Left-Center Field: 375 ft.
Center Field: 404 ft.
Right-Center Field: 375 ft.
Right Field Pole: 325 ft.
Height of Outfield Wall: 12 ft.

Olympic Stadium in Montreal was originally the site of the 1976 Olympic Games. The park is rumored to have cost almost a billion dollars to construct and holds the dubious distinction of being the most expensive structure ever to house a major league baseball team.

Ironically, the artificial surface in the infield is probably the worst in the National League. The surface is marred by seams that run jaggedly from the foul lines toward the outfield. These thick seams often deflect the path of grounders and have had the more serious effect of catching the spikes of baserunners. Tim Raines, the Expos' outstanding outfielder, became a victim of these treacherous seams while rounding first on a base hit. His spikes were snagged by one of the seams and Raines was injured. Ballplayers agree that this surface must be improved quickly before one of their careers is jeopardized.

The ball makes a funny sound coming off the bat in Olympic Stadium. The acoustics make it sound as if every hit comes off a broken bat. Outfielders who react to the sound of the bat meeting the ball can often be fooled in Montreal. Aside from this peculiarity, the ball carries well--better, in fact, than you would expect in the cool moist Canadian climate.

During afternoon games the shadows that creep from home plate to the pitcher's mound make it exceptionally difficult for hitters to see the ball as it leaves the pitcher's hand. This is an important factor during any day game played in Montreal and gives the pitchers a big advantage.

Although fielders have to be careful about the seams in the infield, the artificial surface is very fast and allows them to play deeper defensively. This gives them a better angle going after grounders and a better chance to reach grounders that would ordinarily be sure base hits. There is plenty of room along the foul lines and no dugout steps to worry fielders as they chase foul pops.

The Canadian fans are a noisy, spirited group. Montreal's ultra-modern transit system whisks them to the park in comfort. The fans respond by chanting throughout the game, often in unison, and their cheers can be deafening. This unqualified fan support is a noticeable factor in most Montreal home games and may help account for the Expos' excellent overall won-lost record at home.

PITCHING:

No one on the Expos had a more frustrating year in 1982 than Ray Burris. Coming off of a good 1981 performance (9-7, 3.04 ERA), Burris was rewarded with a three-year contract at $500,000 per, and expected to be a regular in the 1982 starting rotation. But Burris went 0-3 in his first three starts, despite a league leading 1.17 ERA, because the Expos scored a total of one run for him.

With his confidence shattered and his record at 0-7, Burris volunteered for the bullpen and finally recorded his first win in relief in June against the Cardinals.

The big (6'5") righthander depends largely on a good, but not overpowering, sinking fastball (86-89 MPH) that he mixes with an effective slider. Occasionally, he will toss in a change-up to throw the batter off stride. Burris has good control but is too predictable, going mostly to the fastball when he falls behind in the count. He throws too many pitches at the same speed and in the same pattern--inside to lefties and away to righties.

Overall rating, average.

FIELDING, HITTING, BASERUNNING:

Burris is a pretty good fielding pitcher with an acceptable move to first.

RAY BURRIS
RHP, No. 48
RR, 6'5", 195 lbs.
ML Svc: 9 years
Born: 8-22-50 in
Idabel, OK

He is a fair hitter who can belt a high fastball, and is no threat on the bases.

OVERALL:

Despite good control and a durable arm, Burris became the victim of the team's lack of offensive support. If the Expos give him some runs in 1983, he should bounce back to winning form.

Coleman: "Has an identical windup to Ferguson Jenkins. Burris lost too many games for a pitcher of his caliber."

McCarver: "He can improve by changing speeds more often and not pitching in such predictable patterns. Should come in more on righthanded batters and away more on lefties. He is much better than his 1982 record."

Kiner: "Though he led the league in ERA through the early part of 1982, Burris' final 4-14 record has put his job at Montreal in jeopardy."

1982 STATISTICS

W	L	ERA	G	GS	CG	IP	H	R	ER	BB	SO	SV
4	14	4.73	37	15	2	123	143	77	65	53	55	2

CAREER STATISTICS

W	L	ERA	G	GS	CG	IP	H	R	ER	BB	SO	SV
76	97	4.19	344	217	34	1547	1671	811	721	521	749	4

GARY CARTER
C, No. 8
RR, 6'2", 215 lbs.
ML Svc: 8 years
Born: 4-8-54 in Culver City, CA

1982 STATISTICS

AVG	G	AB	R	H	2B	3B	HR	RBI	BB	SO	SB
.293	154	557	91	163	32	1	29	97	78	65	2

CAREER STATISTICS

AVG	G	AB	R	H	2B	3B	HR	RBI	BB	SO	SB
.269	1104	3881	545	1044	187	19	171	609	434	541	31

HITTING:

Once regarded as strictly a streak hitter, Gary Carter shattered that image in 1982 and helped turn Montreal's offense around.

A line drive pull hitter with devastating power, Carter attacks the ball from a slightly open stance, almost squatting on his back leg with his front leg rather straight. He is a fastball hitter with a preference for lefthanders and can pound a sinker or slider. He does have some trouble with a change-up and good curve.

Carter likes to extend his arms, so righthanders who can keep the fastball tight and down, and screwballing southpaws, have a chance against him. When he is hot, however, he will hit just about anything for distance. He is great in the clutch and rarely strands men in scoring position. He is not as effective hitting behind the runner, working the hit-and-run, or bunting.

BASERUNNING:

As is the case with most catchers, baserunning is the weakest part of Carter's game. However, he is a fierce competitor by nature, and will always hustle whether it is running up the line to first or into second to try to break up a double play. Opposing pitchers are not concerned about him stealing, however.

FIELDING:

Carter is the best catcher in the league, and the Montreal management confirmed that by signing him to a $15 million, multi-year contract at the start of 1982.

He is a great student of the game and has learned how to take advantage of opposing batters' weaknesses. When he is behind the plate, he calls the pitches and is extremely good at handling the pitching staff.

He has the arm strength and throwing accuracy to keep baserunners honest, and the quickness to turn bunts into routine outs.

OVERALL:

Carter is a great talent and team player who gives his best effort every time out. He provides the Expos with hitting, defense, and leadership.

Coleman: "He's worth every penny of his contract."

McCarver: "The best defensive catcher I ever saw was Jerry Grote; the best power hitter was Johnny Bench. Gary Carter combines the best of both."

Kiner: "Definitely the best all around catcher in the game."

HITTING:

His performance at the plate last season was Warren Cromartie's worst showing since becoming a Montreal regular in 1977. Usually a consistent .285 hitter, Cromartie spent most of 1982 below .250.

He is a low ball hitter against right and lefthanded hurlers and has a slight edge on righties. Standing high in the box in a closed, crouched stance, Cromartie pulls righthanded pitches through the hole in the right side of the infield, but he will go the other way with good power against lefties. More of a line drive hitter than a slugger, he can reach the alleys for extra bases, and owns the club record for doubles, with 46. He will occasionally park one. Cromartie will come through in the clutch and does not strand men in scoring position very often.

Cromartie goes after the hard stuff--fastball, sinker, or slider. He has more trouble with off-speed pitches, the change-up and curve. Overall rating, above average.

BASERUNNING:

Cromartie is not known for his speed on the basepaths and is rarely called on to steal. He will do his best to break up a double play with a hookslide.

FIELDING:

A former first baseman, Cromartie's ability in the outfield can vary from spectacular to so-so. He has adequate range and can catch the ball if he tracks it down. He is better at coming in on the ball than backtracking, and his peg home is considered average for accuracy and distance.

WARREN CROMARTIE
INF, No. 49
LL, 6'0", 200 lbs.
ML Svc: 6 years
Born: 9-29-53 in
Miami, FL

1982 STATISTICS

AVG	G	AB	R	H	2B	3B	HR	RBI	BB	SO	SB
.254	144	497	59	126	24	3	14	62	69	60	3

CAREER STATISTICS

AVG	G	AB	R	H	2B	3B	HR	RBI	BB	SO	SB
.280	918	3436	409	963	196	28	57	328	267	337	41

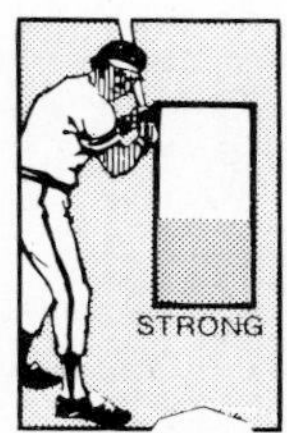

VS. RHP

VS. LHP

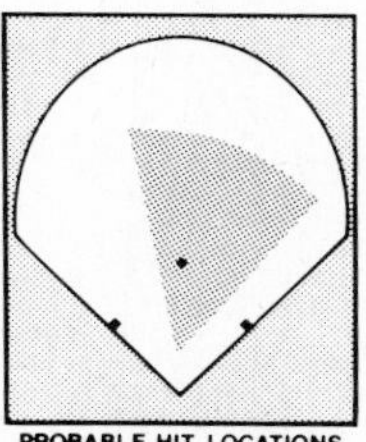
PROBABLE HIT LOCATIONS

OVERALL:

Cromartie normally adds clout to the line-up. He is a good No. 3 batter who might benefit from being platooned when a good curveball artist is on the mound.

McCarver: "Warren's bat is his greatest value to the team."

Kiner: "Cromartie is a versatile player with a strong bat who can be used in the outfield or first base. After five good years, 1982 was a disappointment. But look for him to bounce back."

ANDRE DAWSON
OF, No. 10
RR, 6'3", 192 lbs.
ML Svc: 6 years
Born: 7-10-54 in Miami, FL

1982 STATISTICS

AVG	G	AB	R	H	2B	3B	HR	RBI	BB	SO	SB
.301	148	608	107	183	37	7	23	83	34	96	39

CAREER STATISTICS

AVG	G	AB	R	H	2B	3B	HR	RBI	BB	SO	SB
.285	877	3437	521	978	177	47	133	470	209	564	184

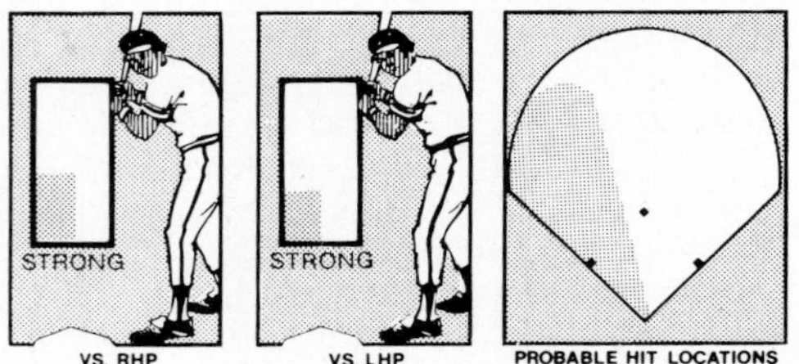

HITTING:

Batting out of a closed crouch, this All Star outfielder will hit just about anything thrown at him by either righties or lefties, though Andre Dawson especially loves soft-throwing southpaws. He is a pull hitter with power who not only reaches the alleys, but can send the ball out of sight. Despite injuries to both his knees and his left wrist in 1982, Dawson lived up to his reputation by being one of the National League's batting leaders all year.

He likes to go after low fastballs, slightly outside, and occasionally has a tendency to reach too far outside. He can handle a change-up, curve, and sinker fairly well, but a good slider from a righthander will give him some trouble. Pitchers must try to keep the ball away from the "meaty" part of the plate.

Dawson hits well in the clutch, particularly with men in scoring position. He's a good bunter, but, oddly enough, is just average when he has to hit behind the runner or execute the hit-and-run. Overall rating, above average to excellent.

BASERUNNING:

Dawson is an excellent baserunner, and is rated as one of the fastest righthanded batters from home to first. On base, he is aggressive, smart, and strong. He gets a good jump on a pitcher and makes opposing batteries respect his basestealing ability. Dawson is not timid about breaking up double plays. He likes to barrel in feet first and really bust it up.

FIELDING:

Like his batting and baserunning, Dawson's fielding also gets an excellent rating. His arm strength and throwing accuracy are among the best in the league. His speed and ability to react to flyballs the instant they are hit allow him to play a very shallow center field. From that position, he not only can snare a lot of would-be singles but also can range back to haul in just about anything that is still in the ballpark.

OVERALL:

In addition to having tremendous ability, Dawson is a very conscientious team man who gives 100% of himself all the time.

Coleman: "Andre Dawson is a superstar on and off the field."

McCarver: "One of the best, Dawson will be the MVP someday. He must learn to relax and allow his total ability to come through."

Kiner: "Dawson is one of the few players around who can do it all."

HITTING:

When the Expos acquired Doug Flynn from the Texas Rangers in early August 1982 to "solve" their second base problem, they got an unexpected bonus. Flynn not only brought them a much needed reliable glove, he developed a very hot bat.

He is a high fastball hitter who tries to pull but gets most of his hits on short flies and grounders toward the middle of the field. Sometimes he will reach the alleys. Flynn has difficulty with low, inside fastballs and most good breaking pitches, whether from a righty or lefty, but has slightly better success against lefthanders. He is a better than average bunter, but is not an effective hit-and-run batter. He is weak in the clutch and hitting behind the runner, and could help his offense by trying to draw more walks. He hits better in larger parks where the outfielders are farther apart.

Overall rating, average.

BASERUNNING:

Flynn is not fast and does not present much of a threat on the basepaths.

FIELDING:

There is little doubt about Flynn's value on defense. A superior glove man--he won the Gold Glove in 1980 and was runner-up twice. Flynn can play shortstop or the keystone, but he prefers the latter. He has very good range and is slightly better moving to his left than his right. His arm is strong and accurate. His ability to make clutch defensive plays and turn double plays has stabilized the Expos' infield.

DOUG FLYNN
INF, No. 23
RR, 5'11", 165 lbs.
ML Svc: 8 years
Born: 4-18-51 in
Lexington, KY

1982 STATISTICS

AVG	G	AB	R	H	2B	3B	HR	RBI	BB	SO	SB
.244	58	193	13	47	6	2	0	20	4	23	0

CAREER STATISTICS

AVG	G	AB	R	H	2B	3B	HR	RBI	BB	SO	SB
.240	912	2708	206	651	77	31	7	220	107	216	11

VS. RHP

VS. LHP

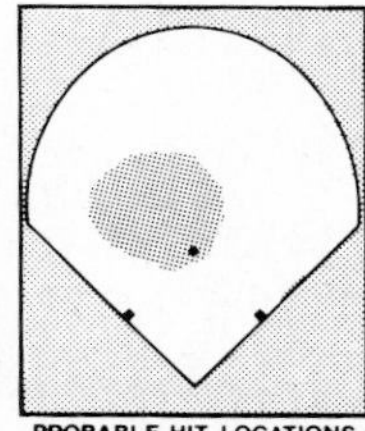
PROBABLE HIT LOCATIONS

OVERALL:

A No. 8 spot batter, Flynn swings at too many bad balls. He might contribute more to the offense if he were platooned. If the team needs defense, he should play every day.

McCarver: "Doug is a good defensive player but is a one-zone hitter (high) who has trouble with most breaking balls. If Montreal is to be a contender, Flynn must contribute more to the offense."

Robinson: "Flynn is not going to hit much. One problem at the plate is that his left side starts to lean when a pitch is thrown."

Harwell: "He is getting the most out of his ability."

TERRY FRANCONA
OF, No. 16
LL, 6'1", 190 lbs.
ML Svc: 1 year plus
Born: 4-22-59 in
Aberdeen, SD

1982 STATISTICS

AVG	G	AB	R	H	2B	3B	HR	RBI	BB	SO	SB
.321	46	131	14	42	3	0	0	9	8	11	2

CAREER STATISTICS

AVG	G	AB	R	H	2B	3B	HR	RBI	BB	SO	SB
.300	80	226	25	68	3	1	1	17	13	17	3

VS. RHP

VS. LHP

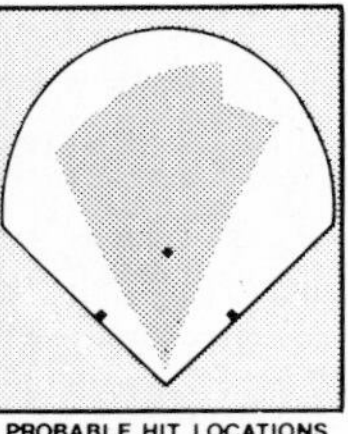
PROBABLE HIT LOCATIONS

HITTING:

Terry Francona was spotted as a "can't miss" prospect while still in college, and was named College World Series MVP and The Sporting News Player of the Year in 1980. He was quickly signed by Montreal and assigned to Memphis.

Francona used his bat to literally blast his way out of the minors in record time. He played in just under 200 games, split between Memphis and Denver, and compiled a .300+ average before being called up by the Expos to play left field during their 1981 drive. He hit .274 in 34 games.

Francona was off to a great start last season, when disaster struck. He suffered ligament and cartilage damage in June, underwent knee surgery two days later, and was lost for the season.

A slashing line drive hitter with an upright closed stance, Francona makes good contact but does not pull the ball consistently. He is a spray hitter, going more to the opposite field and straightaway. He likes anything high and has much better success against righthanders. He can be jammed inside and down. He is better at hitting a sinker or slider than a hard-breaking curve or change-up.

Francona has a good eye and rarely strikes out. He is a dependable bunter, but his effectiveness in the hit-and-run, and hitting behind the runner, needs improvement.

BASERUNNING:

Francona does not have great speed, but he can be aggressive on the basepaths and is not afraid to break up a double play, usually with a hookslide.

FIELDING:

A good defensive outfielder despite his lack of speed, Francona gets a jump on the ball and can make the play coming in or going back. His arm strength is average, but he has good throwing accuracy.

OVERALL:

Francona has great natural ability, but he might benefit from being platooned until he has had more experience against major league lefties.

Coleman: "Good bat and good baseball instincts. Has a chance to be .300 hitter as No. 2 or No. 7 batter."

McCarver: "Good looking young hitter. Could be great for a long time if he recovers completely from knee surgery."

Kiner: "A major league player with good hitting and defensive abilities plus a great desire."

WOODIE FRYMAN
LHP, No. 35
RL, 6'2", 215 lbs.
ML Svc: 16 years
Born: 4-12-40 in
Ewing, KY

PITCHING:

For a pitcher who reached the big leagues before many of his current teammates had reached puberty, Woodie Fryman still has an amazing amount of zip on the ball. He can't go too many innings now, but as a short reliever, Fryman has an extremely effective overhand delivery. Usually called in as a stopper in the middle innings, he goes to his two best pitches, a humming, sinking, 85-90 MPH fastball, and a sharp-breaking slider. He will occasionally drop in a change-up, and, very rarely, a curveball.

Fryman is much tougher on lefthanded swingers than righthanders, but he will move back any hitter who tries to crowd the plate. As for putting anything extra on the ball, he has never been accused of throwing a spitter, but he has been around long enough to know all the tricks of the trade.

Cool and durable, Fryman responds to pressure very well. His main weakness is his reliance on power, which makes him throw too many pitches at the same speed. But it is hard to criticize his technique because he posted his best W-L record in 1982 and could repeat it in 1983.

FIELDING, HITTING, BASERUNNING:

Fryman has a poor move to first for a lefthander and does not hold the runners well. Though he is not very quick, he is good at fielding bunts and other grounders because he knows how to position himself well.

At bat, he will punch at the ball and try to put it in play but is not a hitter. He does not expend his energy on the basepaths . . . very slow.

OVERALL:

At first glance, Fryman looks like he would be more at home back on the farm--until he starts to throw. He has a good strike-out record and is most effective against teams with a predominantly lefthanded lineup.

Coleman: "He puts out an honest effort every time. He's a marvel at his age. He can still get people out."

McCarver: "Woodie gives the Expos very good lefthanded short relief to go with Reardon from the right side. A power pitcher who comes right at you, he tries to jam everyone. He's most effective one time through the lineup."

Kiner: "At age 42, Fryman does an outstanding job as a spot relief man, especially against lefthanded hitters. A throwback to the 'old time' players, Fryman is always ready to pitch, despite aches, pains or weather."

1982 STATISTICS

W	L	ERA	G	GS	CG	IP	H	R	ER	BB	SO	SV
9	4	3.75	60	0	0	69	66	36	29	26	46	12

CAREER STATISTICS

W	L	ERA	G	GS	CG	IP	H	R	ER	BB	SO	SV
141	152	3.78	619	322	68	2409	2359	1129	1013	890	1586	56

BILL GULLICKSON
RHP, No. 34
RR, 6'3", 210 lbs.
ML Svc: 2 years
Born: 2-20-59 in Marshall, MN

PITCHING:

When Bill Gullickson came up to Montreal in 1980 and posted impressive stats, he appeared ready to be one of the dominant righthanders in the league. The next two seasons have been disappointments as his W-L slipped below the .500 level, although his strikeout record in 1982 was second best among the Montreal starters.

Gullickson has had a run of hard luck, getting minimal support from the Expos both at bat and in the field. In addition, he had problems with his delivery that affected his control in 1982 and took weeks to correct.

A hard-throwing sidearmer, Gullickson's best pitches are a 90 MPH fastball and a combination curve and slider that he calls a "slurve." When that curve/slider is working, it can be the best breaking ball in the league, and Gullickson will use it regardless of the count. The "slurve" will get hitters swinging at it even out of the strike zone. He throws his fastball about half the time, but it can sometimes get away from him. His wild fastball makes hitters loose, but Gullickson has some trouble keeping it away from the middle of the plate.

Though he is naturally much tougher on righthanded batters, he goes after the hitter no matter where he takes his stand. He is not afraid of pressure situations.

FIELDING, HITTING, BASERUNNING:

Gullickson is an adequate fielder, but his move to first could be improved. Hitters have found that they can run on him.

At bat, Gullickson takes his cut and gets an occasional hit. He is slow on the bases.

OVERALL:

Gullickson has the guts, presence and concentration to be a much better pitcher than his record shows. This will improve when he has better control and the team gets him some runs.

McCarver: "Bill is probably the most sought-after young pitcher in the majors. He should be a consistent, big winner."

Coleman: "Last two seasons were setbacks, but he still should be right up there."

Kiner: "Gullickson has the ability and all around stuff to be a 20 game winner. He has been a hard-luck pitcher but look for that to change in 1983."

1982 STATISTICS

W	L	ERA	G	GS	CG	IP	H	R	ER	BB	SO	SV
12	14	3.57	34	34	6	236	231	101	94	61	155	0

CAREER STATISTICS

W	L	ERA	G	GS	CG	IP	H	R	ER	BB	SO	SV
29	28	3.20	81	75	14	535	502	208	190	145	390	0

PITCHING:

Rebounding from an elbow problem that sidelined him in September 1981, and an arthroscopic examination in November of that year, Charlie Lea has kept his personal record intact--he has never had a losing season in his professional career.

Spotted as the fourth or fifth starter in 1982, and sometimes as a long reliever, Lea was almost unbeatable when he was on. In May of last year, he pitched 26 scoreless innings, winning three shutouts. (Note: Lea threw a no-hitter against the Giants on May 10, 1981.)

Lea throws most of his pitches overhand, varying that occasionally with a three-quarter delivery. He generates a lot of power through great arm extension when he throws his favorite pitch, an inside fastball that has been timed at 88-90 MPH. This can be especially effective against lefthanded batters, because it saws the bat off for most of them.

His second best pitch is a deceptively-breaking slider that he will go to against righthanders, often when he gets behind in the count. He will throw a change-up to break up the pattern. His curveball has a poor rotation and he uses it infrequently.

Lea is not afraid of pressure situations, and has the control to handle them well. With a little more work on his change-up, Lea could be extremely tough in 1983.

CHARLIE LEA
RHP, No. 53
RR, 6'4", 190 lbs.
ML Svc: 2 years plus
Born: 12-25-56 in
Orleans, FRANCE

FIELDING, HITTING, BASERUNNING:

Lea's move to first is better than average, and the same holds true for fielding his position. He is a fair hitter, but does not extend himself on the basepaths.

OVERALL:

Lea shows good poise and presence on the mound. With his record and experience, he should move up in the rotation this year.

McCarver: "Lea is a quiet competitor. His arm extension on the fastball gives him that little extra to get guys out. But I'd like to see him throw more off-speed pitches."

Coleman: "Charlie gets a lot of mileage out of his ability. If his arm stays sound, he'll be around a long time."

Kiner: "Although Lea has never had a losing season in professional ball, he must develop a curveball if he wants to become a potential 20-game winner."

1982 STATISTICS

W	L	ERA	G	GS	CG	IP	H	R	ER	BB	SO	SV
12	10	3.24	27	27	4	177	145	70	64	56	115	0

CAREER STATISTICS

W	L	ERA	G	GS	CG	IP	H	R	ER	BB	SO	SV
24	19	3.65	64	57	6	345	311	155	140	137	202	0

RANDY LERCH
LHP, No. 47
LL, 6'3", 190 lbs.
ML Svc: 6 years
Born: 10-9-54 in Sacramento, CA

PITCHING:

Lerch is a lefthander with an excellent arm and should be an above average pitcher. He isn't, more because of mental shortcomings than physical ones. His biggest problem probably has been a lack of confidence and a fear of not succeeding.

He throws an above average fastball which is his best pitch and the one he relies on most of the time. His second pitch is a curve that is only average and he sometimes throws a slider, also average. He throws a change-up at times, but has trouble getting it over the plate.

He normally throws halfway between straight overhand and three-quarters overhand and has experimented with a no-windup delivery. He tends to experiment with new deliveries and pitching strategies which may be one reason for his inconsistencies. Although his fastball is his best pitch, he has pitched games where he will throw mostly breaking balls. Lefthanders will have some trouble against him because of his deceptive motion.

Lerch is the type of pitcher who will either pitch a shutout or get knocked out in the second or third inning. He often has trouble with his control and is behind in the count a lot, usually a sure sign that a fastball is coming.

FIELDING:

Lerch has just an average move to first base. He is an average fielding pitcher but tends to throw the ball away a lot. He also will throw the ball away on a pick-off attempt.

OVERALL:

He could be a lot better but probably never will be because of his inability to cope with adversity.

Robinson: "An average pitcher with average stuff."

Martin: "Could have been better. The potential was there when he was with Philadelphia. Not consistent."

1982 STATISTICS

W	L	ERA	G	GS	CG	IP	H	R	ER	BB	SO	SV
10	7	4.45	27	24	1	131	280	79	69	59	37	0

CAREER STATISTICS

W	L	ERA	G	GS	CG	IP	H	R	ER	BB	SO	SV
52	57	4.45	186	155	18	969	1219	535	479	363	424	1

HITTING:

One of the most consistent hitters in the game today, Oliver bats from a closed, upright stance. Gifted with an uncanny sense of timing, he has the quick reflexes and strength to lay off a pitch until the last instant and still make contact with power. Oliver hits righties and lefties almost equally well, with a slight preference for righthanders. Basically a straightaway hitter, he likes to jump on high fastballs and drill them on a line between first and second. He has amazing bat control, which enables him to pull off-speed pitches into outfield slots.

A perennial .300 hitter, Oliver isn't called on to bunt very often. He is highly effective in hit-and-run situations, however, and generally delivers in the clutch. He has little trouble handling fastballs out over the plate, curveballs and change-ups. He has more of a problem with pitchers who can jam him with a fastball low and inside and then come back with a good sinker or slider.

Oliver prefers ballparks with an artificial surface, because, with his power, he gets a lot of hits on sharp grounders through the infield.

BASERUNNING:

Though he has only average speed going from the plate to first, Oliver does not have to be exceptionally fast because he gets so many clean hits. He is known as a "smart" baserunner, however, who can hurt you by taking that extra base if he sees the defense getting careless. Aggressive but not reckless, Oliver doesn't steal very often but he has above average ability to break up a double play. This takes a lot of pressure off the batters who follow him and puts it on the opposing battery who have to worry about him getting a jump on the ball.

AL OLIVER
OF, No. 0
LL, 6'1", 203 lbs.
ML Svc: 15 years
Born: 10-14-46 in Portsmouth, OH

1982 STATISTICS

AVG	G	AB	R	H	2B	3B	HR	RBI	BB	SO	SB
.331	160	617	90	204	43	2	22	109	61	59	5

CAREER STATISTICS

AVG	G	AB	R	H	2B	3B	HR	RBI	BB	SO	SB
.305	1996	7737	1062	2362	454	71	206	1163	452	652	82

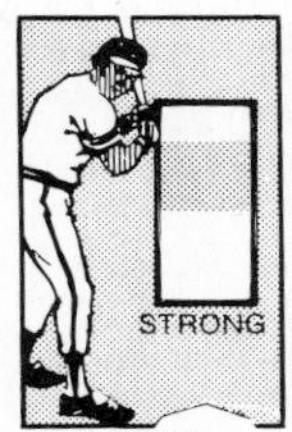

VS. RHP

VS. LHP

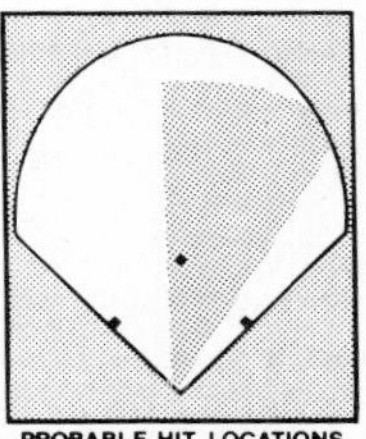
PROBABLE HIT LOCATIONS

FIELDING:

Originally an outfielder and occasionally a first baseman, Oliver was installed full-time at first when he came to the Expos from the Texas Rangers last May. His defensive play in general is rated no higher than average in any category.

OVERALL:

McCarver: "Al is a classic example of a good off-speed hitter. His bat is always back so that even if he may be fooled, he can still attack the ball."

Coleman: "You know he's going to hit it hard somewhere. A very, very tough out."

Kiner: "Oliver led the league in hitting and RBIs, which more than makes up for his fielding lapses."

DAVID PALMER
RHP, No. 46
RR, 6'1", 205 lbs.
ML Svc: 4 years
Born: 10-19-57 in Glens Falls, NY

PITCHING:

A hard-throwing righthander, David Palmer seemed doomed to have bad luck ever since joining the Expos in 1979. Brought up from Memphis at the end of the 1978 season as a reliever, he began the 1979 campaign in the bullpen but soon joined the rotation and ran off eight straight wins, seven as a starter, and finished the season with a fine 10-2 record, 2.63 ERA.

He underwent knee surgery at the end of 1979. He won his first three 1980 decisions, posted an 8-6 record with a 2.98 ERA and had surgery on his right elbow for ligament damage at the end of the year. 1981 was a complete washout, and Palmer's chances of returning ranged from slim to none.

In May 1982, after not throwing a pitch for 18 months, Palmer went six innings against Houston, gave up two hits and the Expos won 6-1. More importantly, however, Palmer pitched without pain. He hurled his first complete game in June, a three-hit, 5-2 win over the Pirates, and went on to post an excellent comeback season. At one point, his record at Olympic Stadium, carried over from 1980, was 13-0.

Pitching with a stiff-arm delivery, Palmer does not throw as hard as he once did, but his fastball still travels at 90 MPH. He uses it less frequently, relying more on control pitches like a curve and slider. He has developed a palmball that gets a lot of hitters swinging at it out of the strike zone. He mixes his pitches well and will throw any of them in any situation. He is particularly tough on righthanded batters who have a problem with his slider.

He is very poised for a young pitcher who has had so many setbacks, and responds well under pressure.

FIELDING, HITTING, BASERUNNING:

Palmer is a fine athlete and handles his position well. He has a very good pick-off move and is quick off the mound in fielding bunts. Hitting and baserunning are not his strong points.

OVERALL:

Palmer's fastball still has a lot of zip, but he seems to be laying off it and relying too much on breaking stuff to get him out of tight spots. It is great for a pitcher to have such confidence in his control, but Palmer may become less effective if batters don't have to worry about the fastball blowing past them.

Coleman: "He can be a big winner if the arm stays healthy."

McCarver: "One of a number of fine young pitchers to be developed in Montreal's farm system, Palmer made a dramatic comeback in 1982. Now, everything depends on the arm holding up."

1982 STATISTICS

W	L	ERA	G	GS	CG	IP	H	R	ER	BB	SO	SV
6	4	3.18	13	13	1	73	60	34	26	36	46	0

CAREER STATISTICS

W	L	ERA	G	GS	CG	IP	H	R	ER	BB	SO	SV
24	13	2.89	78	44	6	336	303	132	108	98	198	2

TIM RAINES
OF, No. 30
SR, 5'8", 165 lbs.
ML Svc: 2 years
Born: 9-16-59 in
Sanford, FL

1982 STATISTICS

AVG	G	AB	R	H	2B	3B	HR	RBI	BB	SO	SB
.277	156	647	90	179	32	8	4	43	75	83	78

CAREER STATISTICS

AVG	G	AB	R	H	2B	3B	HR	RBI	BB	SO	SB
.281	265	980	159	275	45	15	9	80	126	117	156

VS. RHP

VS. LHP

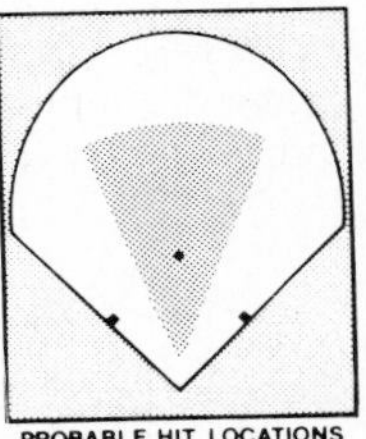
PROBABLE HIT LOCATIONS

HITTING:

Compactly built, strong and fast, Tim Raines is an ideal major league leadoff man. A switch-hitter who bats out of a closed crouch, Raines has more power as a lefthander, but his 1982 stats are higher as a righty. Although primarily a straightaway line drive hitter, he also beats out infield grounders against righthanded pitching, particularly in parks with an artificial surface where he often intentionally hits down on the ball. He can hit to the opposite field from either side of the plate and will reach the alleys, where a high percentage of his shots fall in for doubles.

Raines is a proven .300 hitter, but some of his effectiveness can be reduced by pitching him inside regardless of which side he stands on. He is murder on belt-high fastballs, can handle sinkers and sliders, but has problems with good curveballs and change-ups.

With a good eye and excellent bat control, Raines will lay off close pitches and take his walk. He also can outleg a sacrifice bunt for an infield hit when batting lefty. He can hit behind the runner and will come through in a hit-and-run situation.

BASERUNNING:

Raines is dynamite on the basepaths. A strong, smart, aggressive runner, he is extremely fast from home to first and fearless when it comes to breaking up double plays. He will probably provide the main competition for Oakland's Rickey Henderson as the leading basestealer for many years ahead.

FIELDING:

An All Star second baseman in the minors, Raines was converted into a leftfielder at Montreal. His speed gives him excellent range and the ability to move in or back with the ball. The one area that can stand improvement is his throwing. His arm strength and accuracy are rated as average. On a throw to home, he tends to lay back on the ball.

OVERALL:

His sophomore year did not live up to his record-breaking rookie year. Raines is young and still learning, with remarkable talent, incredible speed, and deceptive power.

McCarver: "A slow start in 1982 but made up ground in a hurry.

Coleman: "Have to believe something was bothering him in 1982. He didn't play with the same intensity or enthusiasm."

JEFF REARDON
RHP, No. 41
RR, 6'1", 190 lbs.
ML Svc: 3 years
Born: 10-1-55 in Dalton, MA

PITCHING:

A hard-throwing righthander, Reardon relies largely on his rising fastball to get him out of trouble. It is his favorite pitch and he uses it to challenge the batter about 70% of the time. Using an overhand delivery, it travels between 92 and 94 MPH, and is one of the best fastballs in the league. Righthanded batters usually have more difficulty hitting that pitch than lefties, but, in either case, it can leave them looking.

Reardon sometimes will change to a three-quarter delivery to righthanders. He also will throw a slider, a highly effective breaking ball, when he has it under control. He seldom uses his curveball, because it has a tendency to hang.

Reardon suffers from occasional wildness, but he does not usually intend it as a brushback. Probably his greatest weakness is a susceptibility to chronic back problems.

Just about unbeatable in the first part of 1982, Reardon is one of the main reasons the Expos were able to stay in the hunt so long last season.

FIELDING, HITTING, BASERUNNING:

Reardon's move to first is considered average, but he rates higher than average in fielding his position in general. Hitting and baserunning abilities are limited.

OVERALL:

Reardon shows a lot of poise for a young pitcher. As a short reliever, he is continuously faced with tough men-on-base situations, but his hopping fastball gives him the ability to blow any hitter away. One of the best at his job.

McCarver: "Jeff's fastball causes hitters to pop it up or foul it back. I thought he would be less effective because he doesn't have a speciality pitch and must rely on the fastball. But, even still he has been very effective."

Coleman: "Reardon is a pitcher who really goes after the hitters."

Kiner: "One of the best relief pitchers without a freak pitch. He comes at you with a fastball and a curve."

1982 STATISTICS

W	L	ERA	G	GS	CG	IP	H	R	ER	BB	SO	SV
7	4	2.06	75	0	0	109	87	28	25	36	86	26

CAREER STATISTICS

W	L	ERA	G	GS	CG	IP	H	R	ER	BB	SO	SV
19	13	2.26	197	0	0	310	243	88	78	113	246	42

STEVE ROGERS
RHP, No. 45
RR, 6'1", 175 lbs.
ML Svc: 9 years
Born: 10-26-49 in Jefferson City, MO

PITCHING:

Completing his sixth consecutive winning season with 10 or more victories in each, Steve Rogers has become one of the best righthanders in baseball. If he had not been victimized by the porous Expo defense, Rogers would have had a real shot at the 20-game winner's circle in 1982.

Don't be fooled by his jittery, head-shaking, herky-jerky actions on the mound--Rogers is one of the most controlled hurlers in the league, as opposing batters have discovered. He also has plenty of power and a breaking ball that drops like a hot rock. Roger's fastball hums at 90+ MPH, and he uses it about half the time, but especially in double play situations. He has a dependable curveball that he will go to regardless of the count, particularly against righthanders. And his slider is a great spot pitch. Occasionally, he will show the batter a change-curve just to upset his timing.

Rogers mixes his pitches well and always challenges the batter, regardless of which side of the plate the hitter is on. He is not a brushback style of pitcher and does not throw a spitter, though his sinker sometimes acts like one.

Rogers is tough in pressure situations. He is the man you want on the mound when you really need a win.

FIELDING, HITTING, BASERUNNING:

Rogers is a better than average fielder and has a very good move to first. At bat, he always tries to make contact to put the ball in play . . . and is a good bunter. He does not extend himself on the basepaths.

OVERALL:

This man is a quality pitcher who can adapt to any circumstance and any ballpark, which he proved during the 1982 campaign when he was 10-0 on the road at one point.

McCarver: "Steve certainly should be considered one of the top pitchers in baseball. He has excellent equipment plus intelligence (he has a B.S. in petroleum engineering from Tulsa University) and uses both while doing his job."

Coleman: "Is a master craftsman. Has refined the art of pitching and also become a very good competitor."

Kiner: "Rogers is the epitome of a thinking man's pitcher. He exploits a batter's patience and won't give in to the hitter when behind on the count. He is very consistent."

1982 STATISTICS

W	L	ERA	G	GS	CG	IP	H	R	ER	BB	SO	SV
19	8	2.40	35	35	14	277	245	84	74	65	179	0

CAREER STATISTICS

W	L	ERA	G	GS	CG	IP	H	R	ER	BB	SO	SV
133	254	3.04	324	322	114	2359	2139	896	798	700	1393	2

SCOTT SANDERSON
RHP, No. 21
RR, 6'5", 198 lbs.
ML Svc: 4 years
Born: 7-22-56 in
Dearborn, MI

PITCHING:

Scott Sanderson is a fireballing righthander, and at 6'5", is an intimidating figure on the mound, particularly to righthanded batters. Sanderson rears back and slings his fastball right over the top at 92-95 MPH and is deadly to righthanded batters. He does not throw to a batter's weakness, he just tries to overpower him.

In addition to his fastball, Sanderson has developed a slow curve that improves the more he throws it. He now has the confidence to throw it in tight situations. His third pitch is a slider that he shows mostly to righthanded hitters. It is hard to distinguish it from a cut fastball and is not a money pitch yet. He is working on a change-up.

Sanderson's power, occasional wildness and his willingness to throw a brushback combine to keep batters loose in the box and help his commendable strikeout record. When he can't get his curve over, however, he is in trouble because he is then limited to his one dependable pitch, the fastball.

He handles pressure situations wel because he is a tough competitor, but he has not quite gotten over the hump of knowing how to protect a lead.

FIELDING, HITTING, BASERUNNING:

Sanderson is a good athlete and can field his position well. He is very good at covering bunts, but could improve his move to first.

He likes to swing at the plate and is not an automatic out. In fact, he went to the instructional league to improve his hitting. High spot in 1982 was a grand slam he hit against the Cubs in a 10-6 win.

Sanderson puts the same high energy into baserunning that he does everything else.

OVERALL:

Sanderson is a gutsy pitcher who comes right at you and dares you to hit his best stuff. He usually is much more effective at home than on the road and must develop more consistency.

McCarver: "Needs more off-speed stuff and has been working on it. A different pitcher than when he first came up but has yet to reach anywhere near his peak."

Coleman: "At the point in his career where he should become a consistent winner--but hasn't. Another question mark on an Expo team that should be dominating--but isn't."

Kiner: "1982 was an off year in spite of his .500 record. With better control of his curve, he can do big things in the future."

1982 STATISTICS

W	L	ERA	G	GS	CG	IP	H	R	ER	BB	SO	SV
12	12	3.46	32	32	7	224	212	98	86	58	158	0

CAREER STATISTICS

W	L	ERA	G	GS	CG	IP	H	R	ER	BB	SO	SV
50	40	3.20	131	120	24	801	740	313	285	220	548	1

DAN SCHATZEDER
LHP, No. 43
LL, 6'0", 195 lbs.
ML Svc: 6 years
Born: 12-1-54 in
Elmhurst, IL

PITCHING:

Originally a successful starter when he came up with Montreal in 1977, Dan Schatzeder then spent two losing years with Detroit before returning to the Expos in June 1982, and a place in the bullpen as a long reliever. It was not a triumphant return. Despite a decent 82-85 MPH fastball, a sharp-breaking curve, a working slider, and an occasional change-up, Schatzeder's time on the mound was largely a losing effort, and his ERA ballooned.

He is tough for lefthanders to hit because he hides the ball so well that they have difficulty picking it up before it is on them. He has enough natural ability and a sufficient variety of pitches to be much better than his record, but he finds ways to beat himself. He relies too much on power, and as a result, throws too many hittable balls.

Schatzeder performs better with the bases empty. With runners on, he seems to lose his composure and become shaky.

FIELDING, HITTING, BASERUNNING:

Schatzeder fields his position well and has a good move to first.

He is better with a bat than many moundsmen and does a creditable job on the bases.

OVERALL:

It is a mystery why Schatzeder isn't a winner. He may not be able to hang on with Montreal.

Coleman: "Schatzeder could be having arm problems. He may have to come up with a trick pitch as his only chance to stick."

McCarver: "I can't understand why he isn't a consistent winner, but he's strangely ineffective. He's back for the second time with the Expos, so they obviously haven't given up on his stuff."

1982 STATISTICS

W	L	ERA	G	GS	CG	IP	H	R	ER	BB	SO	SV
1	6	5.32	39	4	0	69	84	46	41	24	33	0

CAREER STATISTICS

W	L	ERA	G	GS	CG	IP	H	R	ER	BB	SO	SV
37	40	3.82	155	86	16	661	596	300	281	251	336	1

BRYN SMITH
RHP, No. 38
RR, 6'2", 200 lbs.
ML Svc: 1 year plus
Born: 8-11-55 in
Marietta, GA

PITCHING:

Despite an impressive record as a starter in the minors, Bryn Smith has only been called on to be the No. 2 righthanded reliever, behind Jeff Reardon, since graduating to Montreal late in 1981. He has been effective in both short and long relief roles.

Smith is an excellent control pitcher who probes a batter's weakness with a very deliberate overhand, and sometimes three-quarter, delivery. His fastball--clocked at 85-87 MPH--is not overpowering but is useful in setting up his other pitches. He leans heavily on his slider rather than his curveball and will go to it in any situation. However, his real pay-off toss is a palmball, a great pitch that dips down sharply. It is so deceptive that batters will swing at it even though it frequently drops well below the strike zone. It is especially effective against righthanded hitters, although lefties also have trouble with it.

Smith has the confidence to throw any of his pitches at any time and has learned he can work his way out of pressure situations. He seldom uses a brushback pitch.

Based on the poise and potential he has shown so far, 1983 could be a turning point for Smith if he can add a little more zip to his fastball and throw it more often.

FIELDING, HITTING, BASERUNNING:

Smith gets average marks with a glove. He does, however, have a good move to first. Because he was at bat so few times in 1982, not much can be said about his hitting or baserunning.

OVERALL:

The general feeling about Smith is that he can only get better with experience.

Coleman: "The Expos' management likes him. He just hasn't had much of a chance to pitch."

McCarver: "His pitching would be rather routine if it were not for his palmball. Look for big things from Bryn."

Kiner: "After several years in the minors, Smith's palmball got him to the majors. With the exposure and experience of the 1982 season behind him, he should be a big help to the club in 1983."

1982 STATISTICS

W	L	ERA	G	GS	CG	IP	H	R	ER	BB	SO	SV
2	4	4.20	47	1	0	79	81	43	37	23	50	3

CAREER STATISTICS

W	L	ERA	G	GS	CG	IP	H	R	ER	BB	SO	SV
3	4	4.01	54	1	0	92	95	47	41	26	59	0

CHRIS SPEIER
INF, No. 4
RR, 6'1", 175 lbs.
ML Svc: 12 years
Born: 6-28-50 in
Alameda, CA

1982 STATISTICS

AVG	G	AB	R	H	2B	3B	HR	RBI	BB	SO	SB
.257	156	530	41	136	26	4	7	60	47	69	1

CAREER STATISTICS

AVG	G	AB	R	H	2B	3B	HR	RBI	BB	SO	SB
.247	1675	5806	618	1436	236	46	83	582	703	754	30

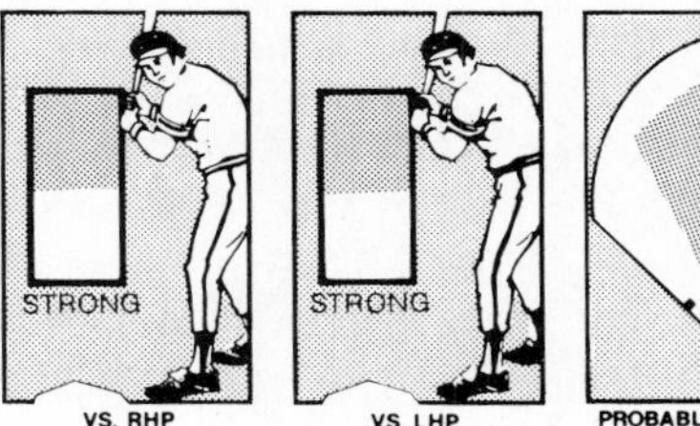

HITTING:

One of the toughest clutch hitters in the game, Chris Speier is a line drive hitter who can also lay one down, hit behind the runner, and come through on the front end of a hit-and-run play.

He lives off the high fastball from either a righty or lefty. From a slightly closed stance about midway in the box, he hits righthanders straightaway, but is more effective against southpaws whom he can pull or take to the opposite field. He does not have a lot of power but can reach the alleys and will hit one out occasionally. He has trouble with pitchers who keep the ball down and outside. He does not do well against a sharp-breaking off-speed pitch, and is bothered more by righties than lefties, especially sinkerball throwers.

A synthetic surface helps his average because many of his grounders will bounce through for hits. A good No. 7 or No. 8 stickman, Speier is in the lineup primarily for his glove and not his bat.

BASERUNNING:

Speier will steal a base now and then but has only average speed. He is fairly aggressive on the bases and will do his part in breaking up a double play. In general, however, baserunning is the weakest part of his game.

FIELDING:

Speier is a solid major league shortstop with six standout years at San Francisco before coming to Montreal in 1977. Speier can be described as the "glue" that holds the Expos' somewhat shaky infield together.

On the field, he is a step slower and ranges to his left better than his right. But his experience, sure-handedness, and knowlege of the hitters helps him compensate for that lost step. He also has very good arm strength, release, and throwing accuracy. He comes up with more than his share of clutch plays, and can start a snappy double play or be the pivotman.

OVERALL:

A tough competitor, Speier plugs up a critical hole in the Montreal defense and helps settle down the younger players. He does not have to be platooned but should be rested periodically because of a chronic back problem.

McCarver: "A good, steady, experienced shortstop, Chris is a winning ball player. He might pick up his batting average if he went to right more."

Coleman: "Whatever abilities he may lack, he makes up for with his knowlege of the game."

Kiner: "Speier is a hard-nose, every day type of shortshop."

HITTING:

Tim Wallach, Montreal's No. 1 pick in the 1979 amateur draft, hit a homer in his first professional at-bat, did it again in his first official major league appearance in 1980. He has continued to pound opposing pitchers ever since.

A high ball hitter, Wallach can hammer anything up and out over the plate against righties or lefties. He has good power to the opposite field against righthanders, but will pull more effectively against southpaws. Many of his hits are into the alleys for extra bases. He will hit in the clutch, particularly with men in scoring position, and has a good enough eye to draw walks. His bunting needs improvement.

Wallach has trouble with pitchers who can keep the ball down and inside. He doesn't like curveballs but has learned to handle most change-ups.

He hits in streaks. In one three-game stint, he hit four round-trippers and drove in 10 runs, and during a West Coast swing, he hit safely in all 10 games.

BASERUNNING:

Wallach is not a great threat on the bases and has only average speed to first.

FIELDING:

An All Star third baseman in the minors, Wallach still has a lot to learn about covering that position in the big leagues. He has average fielding ability and must show more improvement in reacting to bunts. He has a strong arm but only average throwing accuracy. That, combined with his slow release of the ball, affects his ability to start double plays.

TIM WALLACH
INF, No. 29
RR, 6'3", 220 lbs.
ML Svc: 2 years
Born: 9-14-58 in Huntington Park, CA

1982 STATISTICS

AVG	G	AB	R	H	2B	3B	HR	RBI	BB	SO	SB
.268	158	596	89	160	31	3	28	97	36	80	6

CAREER STATISTICS

AVG	G	AB	R	H	2B	3B	HR	RBI	BB	SO	SB
.259	234	819	109	212	40	4	33	112	52	122	6

VS. RHP

VS. LHP

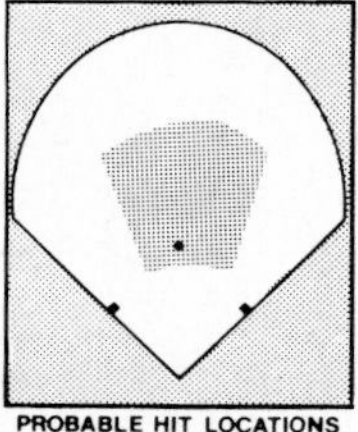
PROBABLE HIT LOCATIONS

OVERALL:

Although his greatest value to the team is presently his hitting, Wallach shows a lot of promise and determination and will improve his fielding.

McCarver: "Tim doesn't pull the ball as well as he might, but with more experience he'll start looking for more pitches to jerk."

Coleman: "When the Expos gave him the third base job, he responded as well as he could. He'll get better."

Kiner: "Wallach's first full season in the major leagues proves he's a player to watch. He had a sensational finish in 1982."

JERRY WHITE
OF, No. 18
SR, 5'11", 172 lbs.
ML Svc: 6 years
Born: 8-23-52 in
Shirley, MA

1982 STATISTICS

AVG	G	AB	R	H	2B	3B	HR	RBI	BB	SO	SB
.243	69	115	13	28	6	1	2	13	8	26	3

CAREER STATISTICS

AVG	G	AB	R	H	2B	3B	HR	RBI	BB	SO	SB
.259	581	1138	150	295	49	9	20	106	134	163	53

VS. RHP

VS. LHP

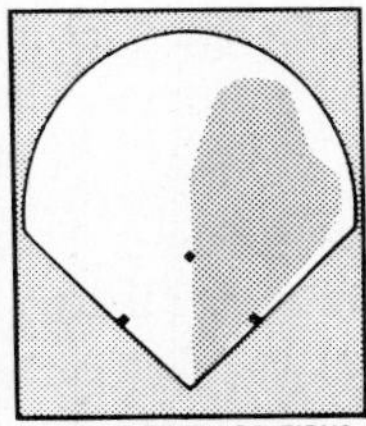
PROBABLE HIT LOCATIONS

HITTING:

Switch-hitting Jerry White, one of the most feared pinch-hitters in the game, generates surprising power from both sides of the plate.

Batting out of a slightly closed, almost upright stance, White is a line drive pull hitter who likes to punch a low fastball from a righthander and a higher speed pitch from a southpaw. Don't be fooled by his deceptively low batting average. He can reach the alleys from either side and is most dangerous in the clutch with men in scoring position.

He handles a bat extremely well and can be counted on in hit-and-run or bunt situations. White also draws more than his share of walks.

Pitchers have had some success jamming him because he likes to extend his arms. He handles a change-up better when batting righthanded and the sinker or slider when lefthanded. He has trouble with a good curve either way.

White will get extra hits in ballparks with an artificial surface because there he tries to hit down on the ball.

BASERUNNING:

White has good speed to first and is a threat on the bases, especially in a close game. He is aggressive and not afraid to take out the opposing infielder to break up a double play.

FIELDING:

White is very important to the Expos as one of the best fourth outfielders in the National League. He has good range and can move in any direction, but he is a shade better at coming in for the ball than retreating in left field. He has the arm strength and accuracy to make the long throw home.

OVERALL:

White could play regularly on a lot of clubs.

McCarver: "He handles all facets well, especially in view of his limited playing time. A devastating pinch-hitter, he can fill in with the best. He keeps himself ready by working hard but may not be durable enough to play every day."

Coleman: "Probably would like more playing time, but is extremely valuable as a fourth outfielder and pinch-hitter."

JOEL YOUNGBLOOD
OF, No. 25
RR, 5'11", 175 lbs.
ML Svc: 7 years
Born: 8-28-51 in
Houston, TX

1982 STATISTICS

AVG	G	AB	R	H	2B	3B	HR	RBI	BB	SO	SB
.240	120	292	37	70	14	0	3	29	17	58	2

CAREER STATISTICS

AVG	G	AB	R	H	2B	3B	HR	RBI	BB	SO	SB
.267	730	2071	266	553	113	19	38	226	175	322	42

VS. RHP

VS. LHP

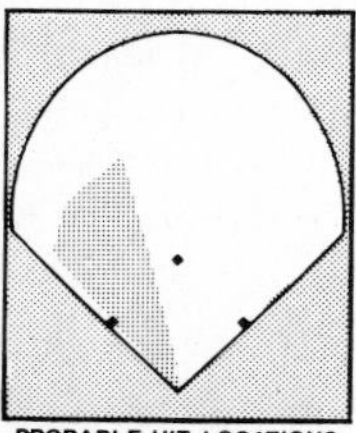
PROBABLE HIT LOCATIONS

HITTING:

Joel Youngblood has the potential to be one of the best utility men in the league. Not only can he play the infield and outfield well but he swings a solid stick, which is why the Expos acquired him from the New York Mets in August 1982.

A stand-up batter with a closed stance, he has good power and loves to pull a high fastball, regardless of who the pitcher is. Overall, he does better against lefthanders and will send line shots into the alleys when he connects. He is a good clutch hitter and dangerous with men in scoring position. He is usually dependable in hit-and-run or bunt situations. He should be pitched outside and down by righties and lefties. And because he is always looking to jump on a fastball, he can be set up with a change-up and curve. Although he is a good glove man, hitting figures to be the strongest part of his game.

BASERUNNING:

Youngblood has good speed but rates no better than average going to first or stealing bases. His best year for stolen bases was 1979, when he swiped 18. He is aggressive, however, in breaking up double plays.

FIELDING:

Youngblood is a confident fielder with very good range. He moves well with the ball and is better coming in on it than retreating. His arm strength and throwing accuracy get high marks.

OVERALL:

The Expos are waiting to see whether his big batting surge in 1981 can be repeated or if Youngblood is really just a .270+ batsman. Possibly, he should be platooned for a while and then tried as the No. 2, 6, or 7 man in the batting order.

Coleman: "A basically solid player. Why he doesn't play more often is a mystery to me."

McCarver: "Joel tries to pull too much. He has deceptive strength and could get more out of his talent by just trying to meet the ball."

Kiner: "Good man to have around, but doesn't want to accept a role as a utility player, even though that's where he would fit in well."

TIM BLACKWELL
C, No. 17
SR, 5'11", 185 lbs.
ML Svc: 7 years
Born: 8-18-52 in
San Diego, CA

HITTING, BASERUNNING, FIELDING:

Blackwell is not a good natural swinger, and uses a closed, upright stance. He has good power to right center against righthanded pitching, especially when he gets his favorite pitch, a low fastball. Lefthanders throw him a lot of inside, off-speed pitches which he tends to hit straightaway and on the ground.

Blackwell does have a good batting eye and draws more than his share of walks. He also has above average bunting ability. He can usually handle change-ups but has some difficulty with a good curve, sinker, or slider. Pitchers who know him try to set him up with tight fastballs and then get him reaching for their off-speed stuff.

Blackwell runs well for a catcher and has above average speed going to first. Once on base, he is an aggressive runner and has been known to steal when least expected.

Conscientious and intelligent, he knows opposing batters well enough so his pitchers rely on him to call the game. Good arm strength, excellent release point and throwing accuracy. He is quick and agile, blocks wild pitches and pounces on bunts.

OVERALL:

A tireless worker, Blackwell gets the most out of his abilities and would be the regular catcher on some other team.

McCarver: "Montreal did a smart thing in getting a good back up catcher for Gary Carter, the position being so vulnerable to injury. Tim fills that role as well as anyone could."

Coleman: "He's a player who loves the game and plays up to his ability."

WALLACE JOHNSON
INF, No. 1
SR, 6'0", 173 lbs.
ML Svc: 1 year
Born: 12-25-56 in
Gary, IN

HITTING, BASERUNNING, FIELDING:

Johnson is a light-hitting switcher with much more power as a lefty. He is basically a singles hitter, and as a lefty he can slap the low fastball from a righthanded pitcher to right center. On the other side of the plate, he prefers a high ball from southpaws but is not nearly as effective. Because of his speed, he can beat out a lot of slow grounders, and is also adept at bunting for a hit.

Righthanders can jam him inside, while lefties should keep the ball down and outside. He doesn't handle a change or a curve too well but has better luck with a sinker or slider.

He has great speed to first and on the bases, but he needs major league experience before he is really dangerous. He is aggressive at breaking up double plays going in either feet first or head first.

Johnson has good range but stabs at the ball instead of scooping it up. Lacks the soft hands of a solid infielder. Arm strength, throwing accuracy, and double play-making ability are rated average.

OVERALL:

Obviously needs more all around experience and could develop into a good No. 2 batter if used regularly.

Coleman: "The verdict is still out on him."

McCarver: "May be the Expos' answer to the future."

Kiner: "Needs a chance to develop by playing more, possibly back in the minors."

BRAD MILLS
INF, No. 24
LR, 6'0", 195 lbs.
ML Svc: 1 year plus
Born: 1-19-57 in
Lemon Cove, CA

HITTING, BASERUNNING, FIELDING:

Brad Mills saw limited action in 1982, and then mostly against right-handed pitching. Although not noted for his power, he is a high fastball hitter who can line his shots straight-away to the alleys. He has shown some ability to hit in the clutch, with men in scoring position. He can lay one down or wait out a walk.

Righthanders feed him a lot of change-ups and curves that break down and out. If he makes contact with a sinker or slider, he can take it to the opposite field. A .300 hitter in the minors, Mills has not been in the majors long enough to establish himself.

Mills appears to be a promising third baseman with decent hands. He has good range and moves to his left a little better than his right. His arm strength and throwing accuracy are adequate for starting double plays.

OVERALL:

Needs more playing time to gain experience and confidence.

Coleman: "Based on what I've seen, he should be playing regularly for somebody. Doesn't look like he'll get a chance in Montreal."

McCarver: "Not a lot of punch, but would make a good utility player."

Kiner: "Mills does not have big league defensive skills yet. If he makes the Expos in 1983, it will be because of his bat."

DAN NORMAN
OF, No. 44
RR, 6'2", 195 lbs.
ML Svc: 5 years
Born: 1-11-55 in
Los Angeles, CA

HITTING, BASERUNNING, FIELDING:

A one-time switch-hitter who was acquired from Wichita in 1982, Dan Norman now bats only from the left side of the plate. He is a high fastball hitter who stands off the plate in a closed crouch. He tries to pull and is more successful against lefthanders, but if he gets his pitch from a righty he can pop it to left-center. He has the power to reach the alleys.

Norman has difficulty hitting the ball on the ground the other way, which hurts his ability to hit behind the runner, start the hit-and-run, or bunt. He does not handle low, breaking pitches well . . . or anything other than a high fastball. He is used primarily as a pinch-hitter against lefthanders.

He gets down the line fairly quickly, but, otherwise, his baserunning is not notable.

Norman is considered a fair outfielder, but he lacks experience. He has an average rating in all departments.

OVERALL:

McCarver: "I don't think he has shown the ability to play every day. Pretty good pinch-hitter who has shown occasional punch."

Coleman: "A journeyman outfielder. Platoon player at best."

Kiner: "He tries hard but can't make a starting lineup in the majors. Does not have a good swing."

WILLIAM A. SHEA STADIUM
New York Mets

Seating Capacity: 55,300
Playing Surface: Natural Grass

Dimensions
Left Field Pole: 338 ft.
Left-Center Field: 371 ft.
Center Field: 410 ft.
Right-Center Field: 371 ft.
Right Field Pole: 338 ft.
Height of Outfield Wall: 8 ft.

Contrary to popular opinion, Shea Stadium is not a reserve runway for nearby LaGuardia Airport. However, the ballfield's proximity to the airport gives it its most notable characteristic--noise. Low flying jets are a constant source of distraction to the ballplayers and annoyance to the fans.

The field itself, on the other hand, is almost entirely satisfactory. The infield is a traditional blend of well-manicured grass and carefully groomed dirt. Over the years, the bumps and ruts seem to have been ironed out and infielders no longer complain about erratic bounces and hops.

The pitcher's mound has served the likes of Seaver, Koosman, Ryan, Swan and McGraw. If today's Mets staff lack the reputation of these names, the fault does not lie in the tilt of the mound or the height of the rubber. The bullpens are safely placed behind the fences in right and left fields and present no problem in terms of safety or distraction from the fans.

The batter's box is well maintained and hitters generally feel comfortable at Shea, although the constant overhead noise does tend to thwart the concentration of some players. Foul territory is another minor problem at Shea. There are no barriers around the dugouts to protect infielders who are chasing pop fouls.

The outfield is surrounded by an eight foot wall and ranges from 338 feet down the lines to 410 feet in dead center. The wind really whips around Shea, but unless it is blowing straight out, any homer hit in this park is considered a legitimate shot. Cheap roundtrippers are a rarity at Shea. The outfield grass is allowed to grow higher at Shea than in other parks, and the grass can slow a ball down considerably. Alert baserunners can often stretch a single or take an extra base if they see that the outfielder is merely going through the motions.

NEIL ALLEN
RHP, No. 13
RR, 6'2", 185 lbs.
ML Svc: 4 years
Born: 1-24-58 in Kansas City, KS

PITCHING:

Neil Allen is like the little girl with the curl. When he is good he is very, very good, and when he is bad, he is horrid. Or worse. There's very little grey area with him. Allen can be a dominant relief pitcher for three weeks and be battered in his next three appearances. Even with his inconsistency, Allen is one of the the premier relief pitchers in the National League, second, perhaps, only to Sutter.

He is a power pitcher with an extraordinary curveball. The rotation on his curve is as good as there is in the major leagues. His curve, when he gets it over, is his most effective weapon. He uses the fastball and curve almost exclusively, relying on the fastball about 60% of the time. He should develop a slow change.

He tries to get ahead with the fastball and relies on it when he is behind. But he will throw the curve when he is behind and goes for the kill. Righthanded hitters, particularly Ron Cey, and predominantly righthanded teams like the Dodgers, Expos and Phillies are especially vulnerable to his curve.

Allen usually is excellent in pressure situations, but sometimes lacks concentration when he starts an inning and single-handedly creates a tough spot for himself.

FIELDING, HITTING, BASERUNNING:

Neil's delivery is one of the quickest in the league despite his rather high kick. He also has an above average move to first base. Then-Expos coach Steve Boros didn't want Tim Raines running on Allen.

A good athlete, Allen normally fields his position well. As a relief pitcher, though, he seldom gets to bat and is nothing special when he does.

OVERALL:

Allen was bothered by illness and arm trouble last season, and the teams' poor performance in his absence proved his value to them. The Mets still consider him a potential starting pitcher.

Coleman: "One of the best relief pitchers in the game."

Kiner: "Neil has the potential to be among the top three relief pitchers, but lacks consistency in the control of his curve."

McCarver: "He has control problems early in his outings. I don't quite understand why."

1982 STATISTICS

W	L	ERA	G	GS	CG	IP	H	R	ER	BB	SO	SV
3	7	3.06	50	0	0	64	65	22	22	30	59	19

CAREER STATISTICS

W	L	ERA	G	GS	CG	IP	H	R	ER	BB	SO	SV
23	33	3.39	202	5	0	327	316	137	123	143	253	67

BOB BAILOR
OF, No. 4
RR, 5'10", 160 lbs.
ML Svc: 7 years
Born: 7-10-51 in
Connellsville, PA

1982 STATISTICS

AVG	G	AB	R	H	2B	3B	HR	RBI	BB	SO	SB
.277	110	376	44	104	14	1	0	31	20	17	20

CAREER STATISTICS

AVG	G	AB	R	H	2B	3B	HR	RBI	BB	SO	SB
.266	698	2348	287	625	92	22	8	177	156	135	68

VS. RHP

VS. LHP

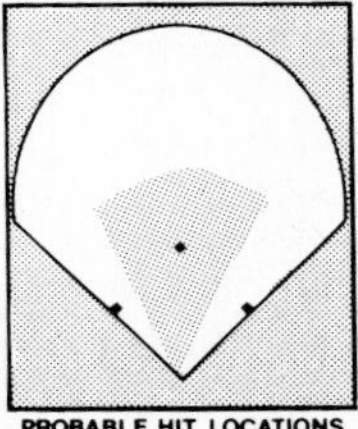
PROBABLE HIT LOCATIONS

HITTING:

Bob Bailor is a pesky hitter who usually finds a way to accomplish whatever is necessary. He lacks power, but can reach the alleys if a pitcher makes a mistake with a pitch high in the strike zone. He had batted .284 and .277 as a platoon player over the last two seasons with the Blue Jays. Within his limitations, he is a consistent offensive player.

Most of his hits are straightaway line drives. He rarely pulls a pitch, but is more apt to pull against lefthanded pitchers. Generally, Bailor is most effective against lefthanded pitchers, and particularly against Gary Lucas and Steve Carlton.

He is regarded as a better than average hitter in the clutch and is particularly adept at doing the "little" things--hitting behind the runner, bunting, and executing the hit-and-run. He is most effective when batting second in the order. If not used there, he probably should bat sixth or lower.

To be effective, a pitcher should keep the ball low. A righthanded pitcher should keep it away. Bailor can be overmatched by a better than average fastball and put off by a righthander's breaking ball. But to throw him a change-up is to do him a favor.

BASERUNNING:

Though not exceptionally fast, Bailor is a better than average baserunner because of his natural instincts and aggressiveness. Pitchers are aware of his basestealing prowess (he stole a career high 20 bases last season) and infielders know that he is willing to break up a double play.

FIELDING:

Bailor has an average arm with average accuracy. He shows better than average hands, has good range and can flat out play the game. His greatest asset to a defense is his diversity. He can play second base, third base, shortstop and all three outfield positions, though he seems most effective as a shortstop. On the double play pivot, however, he is merely adequate.

He made spectacular plays in the Mets outfield in 1981 but played only four games in the outfield last season. As an infielder, he is unafraid of baserunners; as an outfielder, he is unafraid of walls. Bailor is not a finesse player, but he gets the job done.

OVERALL:

McCarver: "Bob has done a good job as a Met. He is a competent player who isn't fancy but does his job in a smooth steady fashion."

Kiner: "He is an outstanding utility player who gives 100% effort."

Coleman: "Knows the game, has good instinct and provides leadership."

HUBIE BROOKS
INF, No. 7
RR, 6'0", 178 lbs.
ML Svc: 2 years
Born: 9-24-56 in
Los Angeles, CA

1982 STATISTICS

AVG	G	AB	R	H	2B	3B	HR	RBI	BB	SO	SB
.249	126	457	40	114	21	2	2	40	28	76	6

CAREER STATISTICS

AVG	G	AB	R	H	2B	3B	HR	RBI	BB	SO	SB
.278	248	896	82	249	44	5	7	88	56	150	16

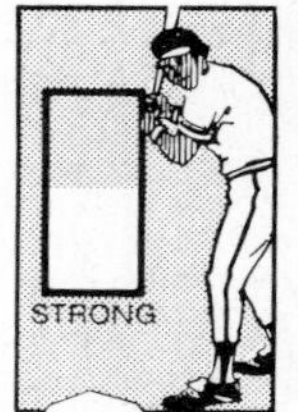

VS. RHP

VS. LHP

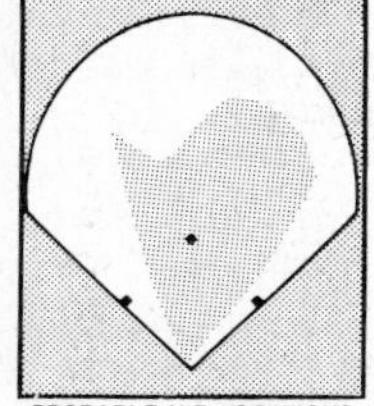
PROBABLE HIT LOCATIONS

HITTING:

Hitting is his primary function with the Mets and what Hubie Brooks does best. He is a line drive hitter who already has a .300 season to his credit but is still learning his trade. He can be helpful batting either second or sixth.

He is a high ball hitter who is susceptible to inside pitches partially because of his closed stance and because he hasn't yet learned to pull. He prefers pitches out over the plate or on the outside corner. He hits exceptionally well to the opposite field, and consequently, he is comfortable in hitting behind the runner.

Brooks shows extra base power, particularly to the right-center field alley. He is strong, but does not have a home run swing.

Though he was regarded as a tough out in clutch situations his 1981 rookie season, but Brooks did not fare so well in those situations last season when his batting average dropped 58 points. He is an average bunter and handles his bat well on the hit-and-run.

Lefthanded and righthanded pitchers should mix their pitches and keep them in on Brooks. He is likely to have more success against lefthanders.

When he is swinging well, he can foul off a number of good pitches and wait for one he can drive. Other times, he is not so patient and swings at bad pitches. He needs to work on drawing walks.

BASERUNNING:

Brooks could be a much better baserunner with more work and a more aggressive approach to his baserunning. He takes too short a lead to be effective as a basestealer, but has slightly better than average speed. His instincts on base are questionable.

FIELDING:

Hubie looked to be a fine outfielder in his 1980 tour with the Mets, but he has since moved to third base where he has had difficulty.

His strong arm is his greatest asset at third. Though he played shortstop at Arizona State, he sometimes seems unfamiliar with regular infield routines. His hands are average. His throwing is erratic, but improving. Brooks is tough, and is willing to take a ball off his chest or chin. He charges bunts well, and has the tools to be a better than average third baseman but he needs work. The Mets had toyed with the idea of moving him back to the outfield, but they are well-stocked there.

OVERALL:

McCarver: "Hubie had a banner year in 1981, but had an injury-plagued 1982 season. He is a talented hitter, but limited on defense. He plays the game hard."

Kiner: "He needs to show more power and ability to pull inside pitches."

Coleman: "It looks like the Mets finally have found a third baseman after 20 years of looking."

GEORGE FOSTER
OF, No. 15
RR, 6'1", 195 lbs.
ML Svc: 11 years
Born: 12-1-48 in Tuscaloosa, AL

HITTING:

Based on his disappointing 1982 performance, George Foster is an over-anxious hitter with occasional power who is not productive in clutch situations. Based on the preceding seasons however, he is an awesome power hitter with no glaring weakness. Overlooking 1982 for a moment, it must be said that Foster is a player who thrives on clutch situations and can beat a team with a home run over the center field wall or a single through the right side.

But one cannot overlook last season for too long. Foster definitely appeared confused and/or overanxious, frequently taking a third strike or chasing pitches that were in the dirt with two strikes. He had always been considered a streak hitter, but last year, he never streaked. He didn't even hit in the late summer as he had in the past. Still, Foster IS a feared slugger who always has the potential to reach any fence.

Foster's batting stance didn't change when he joined the Mets. He still was closed, upright and deep in the box, and preferred low pitches and took uppercut swings. He continued to handle change-ups and sliders well. He showed good plate coverage which allowed him to hit the ball to all fields. But he didn't hit it as far, as hard, or as often.

Foster had been susceptible to hard-throwing righthanded pitchers who kept the ball inside, especially Craig Swan, now a teammate. And his continued use last season of a very heavy bat sometimes prevented him from getting the bat around on other pitchers. He can, if asked to, execute the hit-and-run. He isn't and shouldn't be asked to bunt.

1983 looks good for Foster. Determined not to repeat last year's performance, he very well should return to being himself--an awesome power hitter with no glaring weakness.

1982 STATISTICS

AVG	G	AB	R	H	2B	3B	HR	RBI	BB	SO	SB
.247	151	550	64	136	23	2	13	70	50	123	1

CAREER STATISTICS

AVG	G	AB	R	H	2B	3B	HR	RBI	BB	SO	SB
.282	1458	5133	758	1448	236	40	261	944	528	1038	47

VS. RHP

VS. LHP

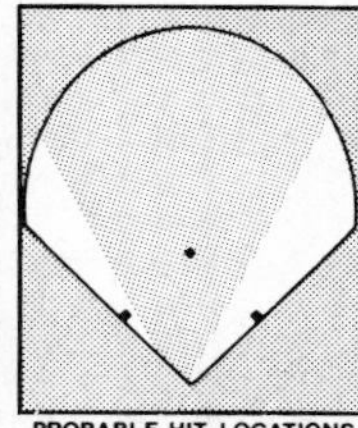
PROBABLE HIT LOCATIONS

BASERUNNING:

Foster is not paid for his base-running. And shouldn't be. He is not fast and lacks aggressiveness to the point where he often avoids sliding.

FIELDING:

He is not paid for his defense, either. His throws are neither strong nor accurate. His range is, at best, average. And he lacks aggressiveness in the field, too.

OVERALL:

McCarver: "Don't be deceived and think he's through or even relegated to mediocrity. He has awesome strength and can carry a team with his bat. Maybe the problem was he wasn't surrounded by quality players as he was in Cincinnati."

Kiner: "He has to have a sharp turnaround in 1983 or his career is in question."

RON GARDENHIRE
INF, No. 19
RR, 6'0", 175 lbs.
ML Svc: 1 year plus
Born: 10-24-57 in Butzbach, GER

1982 STATISTICS

AVG	G	AB	R	H	2B	3B	HR	RBI	BB	SO	SB
.240	141	384	29	92	17	1	3	33	23	55	5

CAREER STATISTICS

AVG	G	AB	R	H	2B	3B	HR	RBI	BB	SO	SB
.243	168	432	31	105	18	1	3	36	28	64	7

VS. RHP

VS. LHP

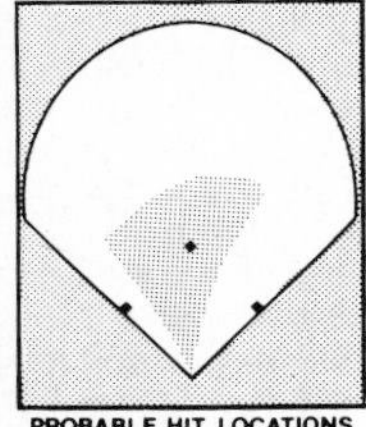
PROBABLE HIT LOCATIONS

HITTING:

Ron Gardenhire is cut from the same cloth as Bob Bailor, though he has demonstrated neither Bailor's versatility nor some of Bailor's offensive skills. He is below average in most phases of hitting except bunting and the hit-and-run. Hitting from a slightly closed stance, he is a high ball, straightaway hitter who hits mostly ground balls and short line drives. He probably will hit more to the right side as he gains experience. What little power he has is to the right-center field alley.

He is more productive against left-handers than righthanders, but not productive in clutch situations. He might benefit from regular play on an artificial surface. He is a No. 8 hitter.

Pitchers, both left and righthanded, should use curveballs that are low and on the inside part of the plate. A good fastball can overmatch him. He copes well with change-ups.

To offset these deficiencies, Gardenhire is a battler who concedes nothing at the plate. He is learning to do the little things a player of his sort must do.

BASERUNNING:

Gardenhire's hard-nosed approach is evident in his baserunning. Gardenhire runs hard to first base and has the speed and desire to disrupt potential double plays. He slides hard at every base. His prowess as a basestealer is average, but pitchers should be aware of him because he will run if they neglect him. He also takes advantage of outfielders' lapses.

FIELDING:

An above average shortstop, Gardenhire throws well and with better accuracy than most. His range is above average, particularly to his left. In his first full season, he made more than his share of clutch plays and more than his share of errors--29. These came in bunches, oddly enough when he was swinging the bat well. Some of these defensive blunders could be attributed to the uneven infield surface at Shea Stadium. He tends to field ground balls while he is in motion, and not set. He charges soft high hoppers well.

OVERALL:

Ron is the kind of player who probably will have a long major league career because he can play a key position and because he is highly motivated and works to improve his game.

Kiner: "Ron needs to become consistent defensively if he is to be an asset to his club because his hitting does not offset his fielding."

McCarver: "Ron probably won't hit for a high average, but he makes all the plays at shortstop. He's a competitor who really will battle you."

BRIAN GILES
INF, No. 23
RR, 6'1", 165 lbs.
ML Svc: 1 year plus
Born: 4-27-60 in Manhattan, KS

1982 STATISTICS

AVG	G	AB	R	H	2B	3B	HR	RBI	BB	SO	SB
.210	45	138	14	29	5	0	3	10	12	29	6

CAREER STATISTICS

AVG	G	AB	R	H	2B	3B	HR	RBI	BB	SO	SB
.097	54	145	14	29	5	0	3	10	12	32	6

VS. RHP

VS. LHP

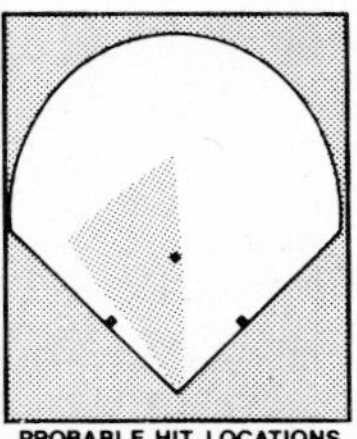
PROBABLE HIT LOCATIONS

HITTING:

Brian Giles has deceptive power. He is slightly built, but his bat moves quickly through the strike zone because of his strong wrists. He needs to move closer to the plate, however, even as much as six inches closer. Even though he moved in a bit last season when he was promoted from the minor leagues, he still stands exceptionally far from the plate and, consequently, he has trouble covering anything thrown outside.

Pitchers should, therefore, keep the ball away from him. He likes low fastballs. Though he handles the breaking ball fairly well, one from a righthanded pitcher causes him trouble because of his position in the box.

He tends to be overanxious and tries to pull pitches that he shouldn't. When he begins hitting the ball to the opposite field, Giles will be a much tougher out.

He handles the bat well enough when he is called on to bunt, hit behind the runner or execute the hit-and-run. His production in clutch situations is, at this point, average.

Giles has the potential to hit in the .270-.280 range with perhaps 10 home runs each year.

BASERUNNING:

Giles accelerates quickly and has better than average speed. He runs the bases well and will improve when he learns more of the tendencies of the opposing pitchers and outfielders. He is a threat to steal and is usually successful.

FIELDING:

No matter how much he improves his offense, Giles' defense probably will remain his strongest point. He has exceptional instincts and seems completely confident in whatever he does in the field. His grasp of the game is like that of a veteran. He has sponge hands, a good-but-not-great arm, and excellent lateral movement. His range to his left is better than to his right.

His work on the double play is far above average, and despite his slight build, Giles is able to take the kind of punishment a second baseman often receives.

OVERALL:

He could be an exceptional second baseman who will contribute to an offense if he is batting either high or low in the order. Giles appears to take everything in stride, though sometimes he appears to be too easy going, but he usually gets the job done. His greatest asset is his well-advanced grasp of the game.

HITTING:

Danny Heep was a power hitter to all fields at every minor league classification. He continues to hit to all fields, but in limited playing time with the Astros, he did not duplicate his minor league power.

Heep is a high ball hitter who likes to extend his arms. He could hit high fastballs into the spacious Astrodome alleys. He has experienced some problems with off-speed deliveries, but he seldom looks embarrassed. Heep showed more aggressiveness in the latter part of the season. Previously, he had a tendency to take too many pitches--his walk total had been good, but he was called out too often on strikes.

Even in a weak lineup, his best spot in the order is probably sixth. But if he matures, Heep eventually could become a third-place hitter. He may only need improved confidence as a hitter. A quiet, sensitive young man, he was hurt deeply in 1981 when then-Astro manager Virdon initially named him as the starting first baseman, then took the job away three weeks into the season. By May that year, Heep was back in Triple A.

BASERUNNING:

Heep has only average speed and is conservative on the bases. With his good build and intelligence, he could learn to take better advantage of what speed he does possess, especially in turning singles into doubles and doubles into triples on gap hits.

FIELDING:

As a first baseman, Heep's biggest asset is good hands. What he reaches, he catches. Good reflexes help offset a lack of speed, so his range isn't bad.

DANNY HEEP
INF, No. 24
LL, 5'11", 185 lbs.
ML Svc: 2 years
Born: 7-3-57 in
San Antonio, TX

1982 STATISTICS

AVG	G	AB	R	H	2B	3B	HR	RBI	BB	SO	SB
.237	85	198	16	47	14	1	4	22	21	31	0

CAREER STATISTICS

AVG	G	AB	R	H	2B	3B	HR	RBI	BB	SO	SB
.246	165	395	28	97	25	1	4	41	40	55	0

VS. RHP

VS. LHP

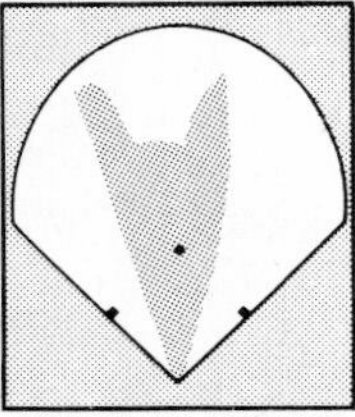
PROBABLE HIT LOCATIONS

Throwing lefthanded is an edge in making plays at second base. He has played a little in the outfield, and his arm strength and accuracy are average. He doesn't make "bonehead" plays.

OVERALL:

McCarver: "Heep has not blossomed yet as a major league hitter but it is tough for a hitter in the boring style of offensive play endemic to the Astrodome (playing for one run; bunting early in games). He does have a super stroke. Minor league stats indicate he is a natural hitter. He must be given a chance to play."

RON HODGES
C, No. 42
LR, 6'1", 185 lbs.
ML Svc: 9 years
Born: 6-22-49 in
Franklin County, VA

1982 STATISTICS

AVG	G	AB	R	H	2B	3B	HR	RBI	BB	SO	SB
.246	80	228	26	56	12	1	5	27	41	40	4

CAREER STATISTICS

AVG	G	AB	R	H	2B	3B	HR	RBI	BB	SO	SB
.238	492	1070	94	255	41	2	18	115	152	157	9

VS. RHP

VS. LHP

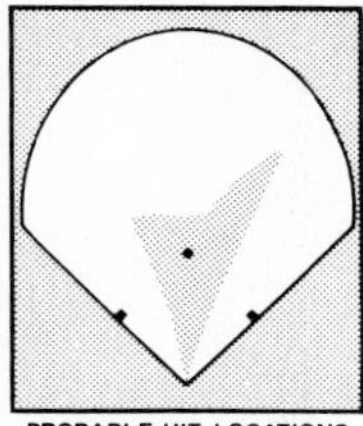
PROBABLE HIT LOCATIONS

HITTING:

After three seasons of relative inactivity, Ron Hodges was pressed into service last season and responded well with some career highs. He had five home runs, and twenty-seven runs batted in.

He is a low ball hitter who often hits line drives and ground balls to the opposite field. But he will lift a low, inside pitch and has power when he does. Hodges' best power is to right-center field. He can and should be jammed, especially with breaking balls and high fastballs. He waits well on change-ups.

Ron is best suited to be a sixth or seventh hitter who should try to hit the ball straightaway more than he does. He is far more productive against righthanded pitching and shouldn't be used against a southpaw unless the No. 1 catcher is injured, as John Stearns was last season.

His ability to hit in clutch situations and hit behind runners is average, but because he is a good contact hitter, he is a good man for the hit-and-run. Hodges can bunt well, but because he lacks the speed to beat it out to first, that skill is wasted.

BASERUNNING:

He is no threat on the bases, though he is not slow. He makes few mistakes as a baserunner.

FIELDING:

Ron is actually a better catcher than he has been given credit for. He has an above average knowledge of opposing hitters and plays his position well considering how infrequently he plays. Some Mets pitchers even preferred him over Stearns as their catcher. Hodges was Randy Jones' catcher early last season when Jones was pitching well.

Hodges' throwing arm appeared much stronger last season, even before he began to play regularly in place of Stearns. His accuracy and release were better than most, though his release might have been a little slow. He demonstrated a good ability to hold runners on first base.

OVERALL:

Hodges can come off the bench after a long layoff and perform decently. As a reserve catcher, he is playing up to his potential, but, as evidenced last season, he would be more productive if he played more. Though his duty is limited, he is a good, smart hitter when called on.

McCarver: "If you're a back up player long enough, you begin to believe you should be. This seems to have happened to Ron. But I feel he appears to have more ability than his managers believe."

Kiner: "Ron is a good organization man who keeps his mouth shut. He probably will stay in the game as a coach or manager after he retires as a player."

RANDY JONES
LHP, No. 35
RL, 6'0", 180 lbs.
ML Svc: 10 years
Born: 1-12-50 in
Fullerton, CA

PITCHING:

Randy Jones seemed to have regained his touch early last season. At one point, he had a 4-2 record and 2.74 ERA. Then his season collapsed--he finished with a 7-10 record and 4.60 ERA that prompted the Mets to release him and put his career in jeopardy.

When Jones was pitching effectively in April and May, he seemed to be the same pitcher who had 42 victories in 1975 and 1976. His control was sharp, and he kept his pitches low. He was also able to throw the slider again, a pitch he had abandoned in recent seasons. The reincarnation of his slider made opposing batters, particularly righthanded hitters, produce ground ball after ground ball.

Then suddenly, his sinker stopped sinking, he lost his control and all of his pitches were up. His downfall was blamed partially on Shea Stadium. In two seasons with the Mets, Jones had a 4-14 record at home.

For Jones to be effective he must have absolute control and keep the ball down. It's that simple. He probably would benefit from a big park with natural grass. His fastball can't overpower a hitter, the slider he threw the second half of the season didn't have much break. He rarely threw his curve. The change-up he threw so infrequently wasn't effective because most of his other pitches were off-speed.

Through all the trouble, he maintained his poise as he always had done on the mound, regardless of the situation. He never did scare easily.

FIELDING, HITTING, BASERUNNING:

Randy covers his position well, though he doesn't have a particularly good move to first. As a hitter and baserunner, he is average to below average.

OVERALL:

Coleman: "Randy went from one of the best pitchers in baseball to a mediocre pitcher after hurting his shoulder in 1976."

Kiner: "Unless he regains his pinpoint control, his career is in jeopardy."

McCarver: "Randy can't pitch high, and he's been unusually wild the last two years."

1982 STATISTICS

W	L	ERA	G	GS	CG	IP	H	R	ER	BB	SO	SV
7	10	4.60	28	20	2	107	130	68	55	51	44	0

CAREER STATISTICS

W	L	ERA	G	GS	CG	IP	H	R	ER	BB	SO	SV
100	123	3.43	305	285	73	1931	1915	875	735	503	735	2

MIKE JORGENSEN
OF, No. 22
LL, 6'0", 192 lbs.
ML Svc: 13 years
Born: 8-16-48 in Passaic, NJ

1982 STATISTICS

AVG	G	AB	R	H	2B	3B	HR	RBI	BB	SO	SB
.254	120	114	16	29	6	0	2	14	21	24	2

CAREER STATISTICS

AVG	G	AB	R	H	2B	3B	HR	RBI	BB	SO	SB
.245	1376	3113	396	762	117	11	92	387	478	527	56

VS. RHP

VS. LHP

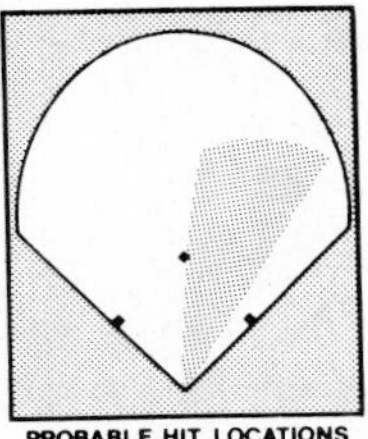
PROBABLE HIT LOCATIONS

HITTING:

Though his role has been reduced to that of a reserve, Mike Jorgensen still has the power and ability to hurt an opposing pitcher. He is an effective pinch-hitter who can get a runner in from third base when the situation calls for it.

He is a low ball hitter. Do not throw this man a sinker. A righthanded pitcher can get Jorgensen with inside pitches. A lefthander would be more effective throwing breaking balls away, though he rarely faces lefthanded pitching. He used to hang in against lefthanders, but he was beaned by Andy Hassler in 1979.

Against righthanders, he tends to hit line drives to the right side. If he hits to left, it usually is in the air. Against lefthanded pitchers, he hits the ball up the middle. He has power, and when playing with some regularity, he puts balls in the gaps. Jorgensen hits well behind the runner and is reliable in clutch situations. He makes pitchers throw strikes and is a patient hitter who handles off-speed pitches well.

BASERUNNING:

Jorgensen, like any experienced player his age, is not too fast, not too daring and not much of a threat. But he knows how and when to run and won't run his team out of an inning.

FIELDING:

Defense certainly is the strongest point of his game. Jorgensen is the ideal late-inning first base or outfield defensive replacement. If the Mets led in late innings more often, Jorgensen would play more. His range still is above average, especially to his right at first base. His hands are soft and as good as any in the National League, and he is adept at saving low throws.

In the outfield, he does a good job on balls hit over his head and can catch anything he gets to. His arm is not particularly strong in the outfield, but he positions himself well and gets rid of the ball quickly. More importantly, he knows where and when to throw.

OVERALL:

Kiner: "He doesn't hit with enough power to be a regular first baseman, but is a good man to have on a team."

Coleman: "He hasn't been the same hitter since he was beaned in Texas."

McCarver: "Mike still is young and talented enough to have some productive years."

DAVE KINGMAN
INF, No. 26
RR, 6'6", 210 lbs.
ML Svc: 11 years
Born: 12-21-48 in Pendleton, OR

1982 STATISTICS

AVG	G	AB	R	H	2B	3B	HR	RBI	BB	SO	SB
.204	149	535	80	109	9	1	37	99	59	156	4

CAREER STATISTICS

AVG	G	AB	R	H	2B	3B	HR	RBI	BB	SO	SB
.237	1392	4727	672	1120	175	24	329	878	447	1400	75

HITTING:

Dave Kingman can strike out against any pitcher--and he can hit a home run off anybody, too. Some may hit more home runs, a few occasionally may hit them further, but no one hits them higher. Kingman has a severe uppercut that frightens pilots over Shea Stadium and pitchers anywhere. But the man can be pitched to.

He is primarily a low ball hitter, and has a liberal idea of the strike zone, though it has improved over what it was five years ago. One time he will swing at a pitch six inches off the plate and miss by a foot. The next time, he swings at one seven inches off the plate and hits it 500 feet.

Pitchers should be successful throwing high fastballs and breaking balls down. A low fastball in the strike zone is an invitation for a home run. He also hits change-ups well. If he hits a pitch, he hits it hard and to the left side. He is a dead pull hitter. Maybe one of every 30 balls he hits is straightaway. One of every 250 goes to right. Teams overshift against him.

Kingman swings for home runs and nothing else. He is not asked to execute the hit-and-run and rarely hits behind the runner. He bunts more often than most sluggers, particularly when slumping and even when men are in scoring position.

His slumps are deep and prolonged, but the other side of that is he drives in runs in bunches and can carry a team. The prototype cleanup hitter. His batting average with men on base is substantially higher than his overall average. And he is even better with runners in scoring position.

He usually hits well in Wrigley Field. He always has, and continues to battle Dick Ruthven. He has major problems against Steve Carlton, Bruce Berenyi, Nolan Ryan and Don Sutton.

BASERUNNING:

He runs very well for a man his size and is a vicious slider. Second basemen beware on double play pivots. He doesn't steal much, but usually is successful. He is not aggressive.

FIELDING:

A liability no matter where he plays. Kingman has a strong throwing arm that is reasonably accurate. But he needs to improve his defense and chooses not to work at it.

OVERALL:

His offense more than compensates for his defense. He is a quiet man whom teammates sometimes resent for his unwillingness to work before a game on his poor defense.

McCarver: "The Grand Canyon's dimensions are too small for him. He has incredible strength."

Kiner: "What you see is what you get . . . lots of homers and RBIs (and a low batting average with it). 1982 was a typical Kingman year. He plays hard and often."

TERRY LEACH
RHP, No. 43
RR, 6'0", 215 lbs.
ML Svc: 1 year plus
Born: 3-13-54 in
Selma, AL

PITCHING:

Terry Leach had been considered a relief pitcher, then in his final appearance last season, he pitched a 10-inning, complete game, a one-hitter against the Phillies. Despite that performance, however, he still is regarded primarily as a short reliever.

Leach has a low sidearm--almost submarine--delivery and keeps the ball down. It makes him quite effective against righthanded hitters. He throws his fastball often and has above average control of it. He uses it when he is behind in the count. His curve is ineffective and he rarely throws it. His slider complements his sinker, and he mixes those two pitches well.

Righthanded hitters are bothered by his unusual delivery and have trouble picking up the ball. He must improve in his work against lefthanded batters to be a more complete pitcher.

He needs to change speeds more often and have more consistent command of his pitches. Leach does, however, get a lot of ground balls and maintains his cool in pressure situations.

FIELDING, HITTING, BASERUNNING:

He is quick off the mound. Leach's delivery motion makes it difficult for him to hold runners, and he tends to fall to the first base side on his follow-through which affects his fielding of bunts. He is a below average hitter even for a pitcher and he is rarely on base.

OVERALL:

Because it has natural grass, Shea Stadium is good for Terry, but apparently he always will be behind Neil Allen as a short reliever.

McCarver: "Terry can throw ground balls, but at the same time, he can also throw a lot of line drives."

Coleman: "He thrusts his fist in the air after getting an important out. Some players on opposing teams--especially Dusty Baker--aren't thrilled by that at all."

1982 STATISTICS

W	L	ERA	G	GS	CG	IP	H	R	ER	BB	SO	SV
2	1	4.17	21	1	1	45	46	22	21	18	30	3

CAREER STATISTICS

W	L	ERA	G	GS	CG	IP	H	R	ER	BB	SO	SV
3	2	3.49	42	2	1	80	72	33	31	30	46	3

ED LYNCH
RHP, No. 36
RR, 6'5", 210 lbs.
ML Svc: 2 years
Born: 2-25-56 in Brooklyn, NY

PITCHING:

Ed Lynch is making the most of the talent he has. He doesn't throw particularly hard, and his stuff is only slightly above average.

He is tall and releases the ball way out in front of him which makes his fastball more effective. He is not overpowering, and his fastball must sink for it to be effective, although he does have good control of it. He has a weak curve with poor rotation, and rarely throws it. Lynch also throws a "slurve" (a combination curve and slider), that breaks more than the average slider and is quite effective. He should throw his change-up more often.

He tries to get ahead with his fastball and relies on it when he is behind. When Lynch keeps the ball low, some lefthanded hitters have problems against him. There are also some right-handed hitters that he can intimidate and dominate because of his physical size. He is not reluctant to move a batter off the plate with tight pitches.

Lynch hasn't yet learned how to exploit the hitters' weaknessess, and his questionable ability in pressure situations is what keeps him from being a short reliever. He works indecisively at times, and is best suited to be a starter or long reliever.

FIELDING, HITTING, BASERUNNING:

A former college basketball player, Ed is a good athlete and a better than average fielder. He has improved his ability to hold runners on base. He is a poor hitter who was hitless in 32 at-bats last season, although he is a faster than average runner for a pitcher.

OVERALL:

McCarver: "Lynch could be a sleeper to be picked up in a trade. His record and stuff are incompatible. He should have a better career record and could have one if used in short relief or as a starter."

Coleman: "If he comes up with a consistent out pitch--maybe something tricky--he has a chance. He seems to be a pretty decent competitor and has the type of rubber arm that can be used often."

1982 STATISTICS

W	L	ERA	G	GS	CG	IP	H	R	ER	BB	SO	SV
4	8	3.55	43	12	0	139	145	57	55	40	51	2

CAREER STATISTICS

W	L	ERA	G	GS	CG	IP	H	R	ER	BB	SO	SV
9	14	3.48	65	29	0	238	248	101	92	66	87	2

JESSE OROSCO
LHP, No. 47
RL, 6'2", 174 lbs.
ML Svc: 1 year plus
Born: 4-21-57 in
Santa Barbara, CA

PITCHING:

At this stage, Jesse Orosco is quite similar to Pete Falcone five years ago--so much potential but no results yet. The Mets are convinced that will change.

He has an outstanding arm and can blow hitters away in short outings, but he doesn't yet know how to pitch. The Mets expect Jesse to improve his skills under the tutelage of Tom Seaver.

About 60% of Orosco's pitches are fastballs. He just rears back and throws. His fastball is clocked consistently in the 90 MPH range and runs in on lefthanded hitters. He throws a curveball occasionally, but he chokes it and it doesn't have good rotation. His curve sometimes acts like a slider. He uses it more often than his curve, and although it moves well, he can't control it. Orosco needs to develop a straight change to make him more effective.

He should be harder on lefthanded hitters, and in most cases, he is, but his fastball isn't enough for exceptional lefthanded hitters like Al Oliver.

Orosco needs more game experience to learn about both his job and the hitters' weaknesses. He must also become more poised on the mound. He was more effective in the second half of last season, but before that, he was unreliable in close games.

FIELDING, HITTING, BASERUNNING:

His move to first base is better than average as is his instinct as a fielder. Orosco is also a better than average runner with average speed.

OVERALL:

McCarver: "He's got to be tough against lefty hitters. I bail out in the broadcast booth. His talent has yet to surface, but I'll take my chances on a positive prognosis for Jesse. He has a good arm that isn't often found."

Coleman: "A lot of clubs want him in a trade. He's got great stuff and eventually should be a very good pitcher. He needs experience and more confidence."

1982 STATISTICS

W	L	ERA	G	GS	CG	IP	H	R	ER	BB	SO	SV
4	10	2.72	54	2	0	109	92	37	33	40	89	4

CAREER STATISTICS

W	L	ERA	G	GS	CG	IP	H	R	ER	BB	SO	SV
5	13	3.07	80	4	0	161	138	61	55	68	129	5

HITTING:

Gary Rajsich is a mirror image of teammate Dave Kingman in some ways. Opposing teams used an overshift against him the first time they faced him. He is a dead pull hitter with above average power, but for a young hitter to pull so much is not a good sign. Unlike Kingman, he has worked hard to learn to hit the ball the other way.

He plays almost exclusively against righthanded pitchers and likes low pitches from them. When Rajsich sees a lefthander, he looks for a high pitch to drive. Because of his tendency to pull, he should be pitched outside, but he can be effectively crowded with fastballs. He has trouble with off-speed pitches, particularly the change-up. He may overcome that shortcoming if and when he plays more regularly. But he can handle a slider well. He has holes in his strike zone that can be exploited.

He has a short, compact swing that usually delivers line drives when he makes contact. He is not reliable in hit-and-run situations, but almost can't help but hit behind a runner.

He batted as a pinch-hitter 35 times with two hits for a .057 average. He tends to strike out frequently as a pinch-hitter. Remove these statistics, however, and he batted .315. He looked good in the spring and then late in the season when he played more regularly. Long periods of inactivity will hurt him.

BASERUNNING:

Rajsich is an aggressive and, despite his inexperience, intelligent runner who has pretty good speed. He will break up a double play if he can get to the base and always looks to take an extra base.

FIELDING:

Rajsich saw little defensive action in his first full season. He is not a gifted outfielder, but neither is he a liability. His throwing arm is strong, he has average accuracy and his range is a shade better than average. He is not adverse to running into walls, getting his uniform dirty or working to improve his defense.

GARY RAJSICH
OF, No. 21
LL, 6'2", 205 lbs.
ML Svc: 1 year
Born: 10-28-54 in Youngstown, OH

1982 STATISTICS

AVG	G	AB	R	H	2B	3B	HR	RBI	BB	SO	SB
.259	80	162	17	42	8	3	2	12	17	40	1

CAREER STATISTICS

AVG	G	AB	R	H	2B	3B	HR	RBI	BB	SO	SB
.259	80	162	17	42	8	3	2	12	17	40	1

VS. RHP

VS. LHP

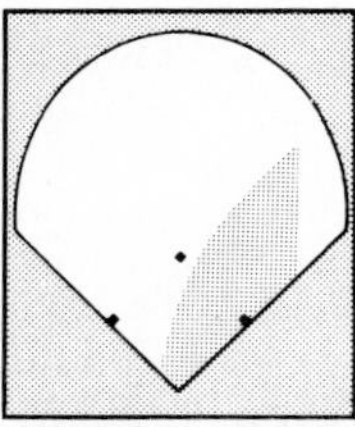
PROBABLE HIT LOCATIONS

OVERALL:

The Mets, in need of a lefthanded hitting regular, had intended to give Rajsich a chance to be part of the right field platoon. But the presence of Danny Heep may change that.

McCarver: "He had good minor league production, but he hasn't played enough in the big leagues to judge him."

Coleman: "He should do better based on his minor league record."

Kiner: "When he got the chance to play, he did well."

TOM SEAVER
RHP, No. 41
RR, 6'1", 210 lbs.
ML Svc: 16 years
Born: 11-17-44 in Fresno, CA

PITCHING:

Tom Seaver has been a prototype for other major league pitchers. In Seaver's prime, he was a premier power pitcher who combined a 95 MPH fastball with pinpoint accuracy and a hard, dependable slider--all of this delivered with a classic overhand motion. In those years, Seaver delivered his best and challenged hitters to do anything about it. But there was another Seaver even in those days, which became increasingly apparent as time forced concessions on the well-known Seaver style.

He is an intelligent pitcher and it is that quality which most characterizes the Seaver of 1983. His fastball has slowed to the mid-80 MPH range, but it is still his staple, and in most critical situations, is the pitch a hitter sees. His slider is still solid and is used often, particularly against righthanded hitters, with whom Seaver has always enjoyed his greatest success. His curve, which was never rated highly, is seen more often these days, but is not regarded as a powerful weapon.

In the last five years, Seaver has made two primary changes. On occasion, the classic overhand motion is shed for a three-quarter delivery. He will also dish up an occasional straight change, but this is a foil, nothing more, in the Seaver scheme. He has not added an extra or junk pitch, but continues, through careful study of his opponents, to force hitters to go for his pitch or a bad pitch. It is never as fast as it was, but it is more often than not precisely where he wants it. His skill is now in an artistic mix of pitches. The essence of the young Seaver remains.

FIELDING:

Seaver is an average fielder but better than average in getting off the mound to field a bunt. He is always in control during the game and will rarely hesitate in making a play. His motion from the stretch involves a high leg kick which many baserunners find an invitation to steal, particularly since his move is neither quick or deceiving.

Seaver has always taken batting practice seriously and consequently is a "battler" at the plate. As pitchers go, he is better than most, providing a timely hit here and there. He is a slow runner, but doesn't make mistakes.

OVERALL:

Seaver had a bad year last season, but it was largely viewed as a result of injury and illness. Seaver is a certain Hall of Famer and an odds-on choice to bounce back this season."

McCarver: "Seaver is a Picasso on the mound, who paints corners instead of pictures. His transition from a power pitcher to a pitcher who works hitters has been successful and complete."

Kiner: "Seaver is a stylist on the mound, a thinker. He will certainly come back."

1982 STATISTICS

W	L	ERA	G	GS	CG	IP	H	R	ER	BB	SO	SV
5	13	5.50	21	21	0	111	136	75	68	44	62	0

CAREER STATISTICS

W	L	ERA	G	GS	CG	IP	H	R	ER	BB	SO	SV
264	156	2.69	525	519	208	3899	3151	1276	1163	1118	3137	1

RUSTY STAUB
INF, No. 10
LR, 6'2", 215 lbs.
ML Svc: 19 years
Born: 4-1-44 in
New Orleans, LA

1982 STATISTICS

AVG	G	AB	R	H	2B	3B	HR	RBI	BB	SO	SB
.242	112	219	11	53	9	0	3	27	24	10	0

CAREER STATISTICS

AVG	G	AB	R	H	2B	3B	HR	RBI	BB	SO	SB
.279	2715	9488	1180	2651	486	47	287	1412	1227	865	47

VS. RHP

VS. LHP

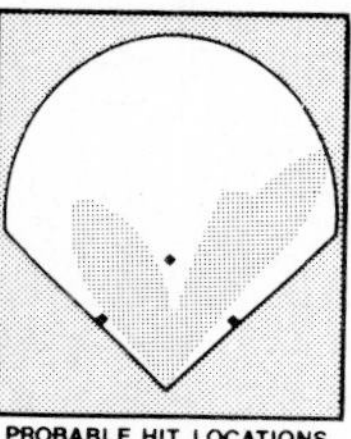
PROBABLE HIT LOCATIONS

HITTING:

Rusty Staub is a professional hitter. He has made adjustments through his career and remains a formidable adversary for any pitcher. He is also a guess hitter who frequently guesses right. Though he hits to left field more often now than he did when he played regularly, he still has power to right field and, given the proper circumstances, he can go deep.

Staub prefers pitches low. Right-handed pitchers can keep it low against him if they keep it away, too. Staub will try to hit their pitches to left. A lefthander can get away with inside pitches if they tail in. He usually hits the ball up the middle against left-handers.

No one particular pitch always gives him trouble, but he is less apt to hit a low inside breaking ball.

Because of his fine bat control and ability to make contact, Staub remains a respected and feared hitter in clutch situations. He can hit the ball where it has to be hit. He is an above average hitter with runners in scoring position or when a runner needs to be advanced. He has a good idea of the strike zone. He knows how to draw a walk, but usually he is used in situations where a hit is needed.

He remains consistent despite the fact that his playing time has been reduced greatly.

BASERUNNING:

It was once said, "Staub scored all the way from first on the home run." He is one of the slowest runners in the game, and an automatic double play if he hits the ball on the ground. He is almost always removed for a pinch-runner.

FIELDING:

At one time, Staub was a slow but very efficient outfielder with an exceptional arm. He is still a smart outfielder with good hands, but some of the strength is gone from his arm, and his lack of speed makes him a liability. His range at first base is not good and he appears awkward there, but he can be adequate.

OVERALL:

The Mets would benefit greatly from the use of the designated hitter. Staub still is a productive hitter with the ability to drive in critical runs.

Coleman: "Rusty is runnning out the string in what probably will be his last year."

Kiner: "Rusty is one of the best students of hitting in the game and probably would make an ideal designated hitter or batting coach."

McCarver: "No one knows more about 'how' to hit than Rusty. A real student of the art, he belongs in the American League as a designated hitter."

JOHN STEARNS
C, No. 12
RR, 6'0", 185 lbs.
ML Svc: 8 years
Born: 8-21-51 in
Denver, CO

1982 STATISTICS

AVG	G	AB	R	H	2B	3B	HR	RBI	BB	SO	SB
.293	98	352	46	103	25	3	4	28	30	35	17

CAREER STATISTICS

AVG	G	AB	R	H	2B	3B	HR	RBI	BB	SO	SB
.260	798	2664	326	693	151	10	46	311	319	292	90

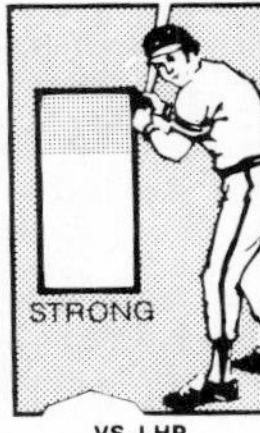

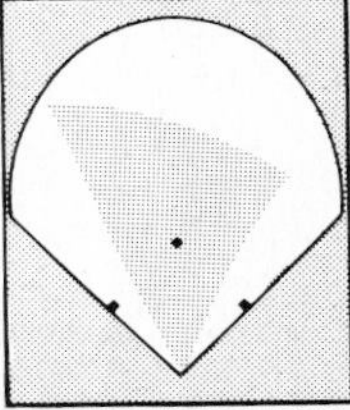

HITTING:

John Stearns is yet to become the hitter he was expected to be, though he has improved gradually throughout his major league career. He is a capable hitter who has not shown the power he did as a collegian.

Stearns is a high ball hitter who is strong but doesn't have a home run swing. He tends to hit the top half of the ball and thus has no lift. He can reach either power alley with a well-stung line drive. He is more effective against lefthanded pitching. He sits on the ball from the middle of the plate when facing a lefthander and hits it hard and usually straightaway. Lefthanders must keep the ball low against him. Curves trouble him, but he can handle sliders and change-ups well.

Stearns can pull righthanded pitching, but has become quite efficient hitting the ball to right field and is a tougher out when he goes that way. Righthanders are most effective when they jam him. He tends to pull their inside pitches foul.

Prior to last season, Stearns would choke the bat in critical situations, but in 1982, he became more relaxed and benefited from it. He also began to demonstrate more home run power before an injury caused him to miss most of the second half of the season. He is accomplished with the bat in other areas--hitting behind the runner, hit-and-run and bunting. He is a constant threat to bunt, even with a runner on third base. He is most effective as a No. 2 hitter.

BASERUNNING:

John is a good baserunner by any standard and an extraordinary one compared to other catchers. He is fast and runs hard and aggressively. He takes delight in upending a second baseman. A constant threat to steal, Stearns established the National League record for stolen bases by a catcher with 25 in 1978.

FIELDING:

Stearns still is learning and improving as a catcher. He has overcome his primary fielding problem, pop-ups, and he has improved the mental part of his game as well. He seems to base some of the pitches he calls for, however, on how he himself hits, a big mistake.

As a defensive player, he is more than adequate. He is quick to field bunts and does a good job blocking pitches in the dirt. His throwing improved last season and his release is quick. He savors blocking the plate and looks forward to the contact. He also plays both third and first base adequately.

OVERALL:

He is highly motivated, always trying to hit a six-run home run. His game is more well rounded than most catchers.

McCarver: "John needs to refine his skills behind the plate. To his credit, he is a gamer, a good hitter and good baserunner."

HITTING:

As a minor league hitter, Darryl Strawberry was powerful and productive and had few flaws. He swings easily, but the ball jumps off his bat. He has enough power to hit balls out to right and left-center field. He can, and does, hit the ball to all fields, but as he matures, he probably will pull more.

He likes the ball low and out over the plate where he can take best advantage of the power in his long arms. Off-speed pitches will pose problems for him until he adjusts to the major leagues. He walked frequently in the Double A league--100 times in 129 games last season--but also strikes out too often--145 times. Strawberry should become a solid No. 3 or 4 hitter.

BASERUNNING:

Darryl has exceptional speed, and was the fastest player in the Mets' minor league organization last season. He knows how to use his speed, and stole 45 bases last season. He is a threat to steal virtually anytime that he is on base.

FIELDING:

He has better than average range, and a powerful arm, though his throwing accuracy is weak. He has good instincts and appears to know how to play the game. With the increased playing time in the majors that he is expected to get, Strawberry has the potential to develop into a better than average outfielder.

DARRYL STRAWBERRY
OF, No. 18
LL, 6'6", 190 lbs.
Born: 3-12-62 in
Los Angeles, CA

VS. RHP

VS. LHP

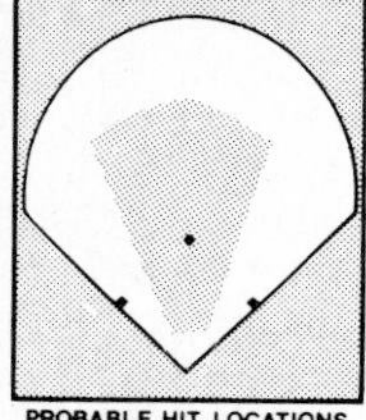
PROBABLE HIT LOCATIONS

OVERALL:

Thus far, on the minor league level, Darryl Strawberry has proven that he is capable in the five key areas. He can hit, hit with power, run, throw and catch. He appears to have the potential to be above average in four of those areas--all except throwing. He has also demonstrated an ability to hit well in clutch situations, and rises to the occasion. Strawberry has star potential.

PITCHING:

Craig Swan seemed to complete his comeback last season. Because of a rotator cuff problem, he had pitched only 142 innings in two years. Last season, he worked 166 innings in relief and as a starter and pitched his first two complete games since 1980. His record was good for a last place team--four victories over .500. Even after his shoulder problems, Craig remains a very qualified starting pitcher, quite capable of shutting down any team.

Swan still throws hard, though not as hard as he once did. He depends on his fastball, slider and his location. His fastball often is too high. He has better control of the slider since the injury. He rarely uses his curve, because it doesn't have good rotation and Swan will normally use a change-up just to throw the hitters off. When he has his change-up mechanics working properly, however, he uses it often and effectively.

He still has the unusual follow-through--with left leg stiff--he developed before the injury. But he no longer jumps after delivering a pitch.

He throws a fastball and, occasionally, a slider when he gets behind in the count. And he must stay ahead of hitters to be effective. Right-handed hitters are more vulnerable to his breaking pitches.

CRAIG SWAN
RHP, No. 27
RR, 6'3", 215 lbs.
ML Svc: 8 years
Born: 11-30-50 in Van Nuys, CA

FIELDING, HITTING, BASERUNNING:

Craig is not particularly agile and as a result, is not a good overall fielder. Despite the fact that he falls toward first base on his follow through, he does play bunts well. He has had seasons where he has hit well, but is generally regarded as a typically poor hitter. He runs awkwardly and not very fast.

OVERALL:

Swan has been bothered by injury and illness through most of his career.

McCarver: "Craig used to be able to really blow, but then the rotator cuff was damaged, and some thought he wouldn't come back from that. But as is often the case after a serious injury, he is 'pitching' more now than just 'throwing.' To his everlasting credit, he approached his problem intelligently and is still a quality pitcher."

1982 STATISTICS

W	L	ERA	G	GS	CG	IP	H	R	ER	BB	SO	SV
11	7	3.35	37	21	2	166	165	70	62	37	67	1

CAREER STATISTICS

W	L	ERA	G	GS	CG	IP	H	R	ER	BB	SO	SV
56	63	3.49	192	166	25	1114	1061	489	432	319	618	1

MIKE TORREZ
RHP, No. 21
RR, 6'5", 210 lbs.
ML Svc: 14 years
Born: 8-28-46 in
Topeka, KS

PITCHING:

Mike Torrez has a well-deserved reputation as a work horse, and has traditionally led whatever club he played for in starts-per-season. Last year however, Torrez had more than his share of problems trying to finish what he started. He is a power pitcher, but instead of challenging hitters, he tends to nibble at the corners. He has good velocity on his fastball, but often chooses to rely on an average curve or slider in tough situations. Torrez has never developed a good change of pace, and control problems still plague him.

Torrez often finds himself behind in the count, and that puts him in a lot of tough situations. He gets behind by trying to be too fine with his breaking stuff, and he too often ignores his better-than-average fastball. The Red Sox were disappointed with his 9-9 record in 1982, and Mike became the object of a lot of verbal abuse. His troubles with control, especially early in the game, coupled with his apparent loss of composure on the mound caused Sox manager Houk to yank Torrez early and often. In fact Torrez only went the distance once in 31 starts last year.

Last season, however, was not a typical year for Mike. During his career he's completed almost 35% of his starts. Torrez was a 20-game winner with Baltimore in 1975, and interestingly enough George Bamberger was his pitching coach at the time.

FIELDING:

Torrez has an adequate move to first for a righthanded pitcher. His fielding is only average, and he still is rated weak in his ability to handle bunts effectively.

OVERALL:

Torrez had a .500 season but he should have done better. He seemed visibly upset both at his treatment by the fans and by Houk's quick hook. However, Mike is still a reliable professional who always gives his best shot. A new team and a new league might help Torrez forget some of his Boston blues.

Martin: "Torrez is best when he challenges hitters with his fastball. He's at his worst when he tries to be cute and gets behind in the count."

Harwell: "Mike can be relied on to give you 5 or 6 good innings. I think his best pitch is his slider."

Robinson: "Torrez was hot and cold in 1982. He gets in trouble with his lack of control. He should use the fastball more and go after the hitter."

1982 STATISTICS

W	L	ERA	G	GS	CG	IP	H	R	ER	BB	SO	SV
9	9	5.23	31	31	1	175	196	107	102	74	84	0

CAREER STATISTICS

W	L	ERA	G	GS	CG	IP	H	R	ER	BB	SO	SV
174	138	3.90	444	416	112	2781	2752	1349	1204	1237	1292	0

HITTING:

A once-formidable hitter, Ellis Valentine has lost some of his clout. He now is a mediocre hitter who can hurt a team occasionally. He used to be a big RBI man, a candidate to bat number three, four or five. Now he's just average and best suited for batting sixth. He can be pitched to.

Some of his trouble can be traced to the pronounced hitch in his swing and his being hit in the face with a pitch in 1980. He still was bailing out at times last season.

Valentine is a high ball hitter who prefers the ball on the inside half of the plate. Pitchers should throw him curveballs low and away and then come inside hard with a fastball. He is more effective against lefthanded pitching because he is vulerable to breaking balls. He is mostly a straightaway hitter who can pull if he chooses to.

He can handle a change-up or a slider, but a good curve will cause him problems. He has the power to reach the alleys, but doesn't do it as often as he should considering his size. He is average in his execution of the hit-and-run and hitting behind the runner. He draws walks fairly well, but he is no longer anywhere near as good as he used to be.

BASERUNNING:

Valentine's baserunning is nothing special. He has gained weight in his legs and consequently has lost some of his speed. He runs the bases conservatively and is not much of a threat to steal.

FIELDING:

Among National League outfielders, Ellis has one of the strongest and most accurate arms. He does like to show it off though, and sometimes will make a long, perfect but unsuccessful throw to third base that allows a runner to

ELLIS VALENTINE
OF, No. 17
RR, 6'4", 218 lbs.
ML Svc: 7 years
Born: 7-30-54 in
Helena, AR

1982 STATISTICS

AVG	G	AB	R	H	2B	3B	HR	RBI	BB	SO	SB
.288	111	337	33	97	14	1	8	48	5	38	1

CAREER STATISTICS

AVG	G	AB	R	H	2B	3B	HR	RBI	BB	SO	SB
.283	797	2857	345	808	158	13	108	427	160	406	57

VS. RHP

VS. LHP

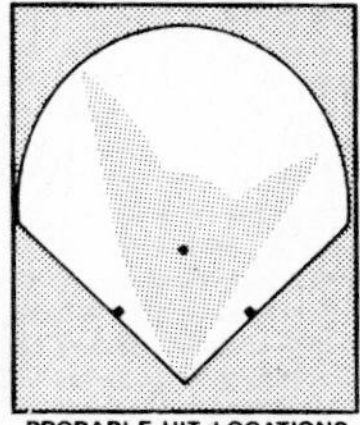
PROBABLE HIT LOCATIONS

advance to second. On the other hand, his throws home are something to behold. His range in the outfield is about average. He is more effective coming in on balls than going back.

OVERALL:

The Mets had serious doubts about Valentine's desire to play so they made no effort to re-sign him and allowed him to leave for free agency.

McCarver: "One wonders about a talent like Ellis. There are those with far less talent doing much better. Is it motivation? Desire? I can't answer that."

Kiner: "He was not happy in Montreal or in New York. But he still has strong potential for stardom."

Coleman: "He was a great ballplayer at one time, but now he is just decent."

TOM VERYZER
INF, No. 11
RR, 6'1", 185 lbs.
ML Svc: 9 years
Born: 2-11-53 in
Port Jefferson, NY

1982 STATISTICS

AVG	G	AB	R	H	2B	3B	HR	RBI	BB	SO	SB
.333	40	54	6	18	2	0	0	4	3	4	1

CAREER STATISTICS

AVG	G	AB	R	H	2B	3B	HR	RBI	BB	SO	SB
.244	893	2686	240	655	80	12	13	224	137	305	9

VS. RHP

VS. LHP

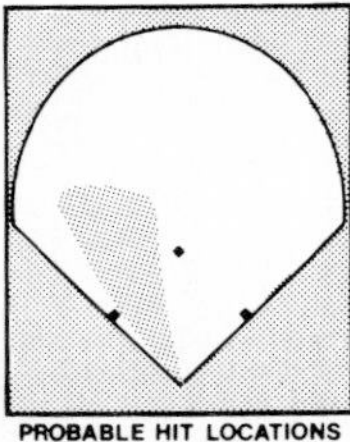
PROBABLE HIT LOCATIONS

HITTING:

Tom Veryzer has more power than the average middle infielder. He has batted higher than .270 twice in the last five years, but is a career .250 hitter. He is a high ball hitter who should be pitched away and down. He tries to pull, but is mostly a straightaway hitter against righthanded pitchers.

Most of his hits are ground balls and short line drives, but he has more than occasional power and can reach the alleys more often than most shortstops and second basemen. He will hit almost anything high in the strike zone. He handles change-ups, sliders and sinkers fairly well, but has trouble with curves.

He provides average production in clutch situations and needs to improve his hitting with men in scoring position and his ability to draw walks. He handles the bat about average in hit-and-run and bunting situations and is best suited to bat second, seventh or eighth.

BASERUNNING:

Tom had average speed last year before he broke a bone in his left leg. He is a smart baserunner, but not much of a threat to steal or take an extra base.

FIELDING:

Veryzer played shortstop exclusively throughout his professional career until last season when manager George Bamberger used him at second base as well. He had developed into an adequate second baseman who could turn the double play fairly well before the leg injury.

He has an average arm with better than average accuracy for a shortstop. His range is sufficient, but not out of the ordinary in any way.

OVERALL:

McCarver: "Tom had weight problems several years ago and when he solved them, injuries seemed to beckon him. He has been injured so much the last couple of years, it's hard to tell if he still can play effectively."

Kiner: "He's a good utility man when he's not hurt."

MOOKIE WILSON
OF, No. 1
SR, 5'10", 170 lbs.
ML Svc: 2 years
Born: 2-9-56 in Bamberg, SC

1982 STATISTICS

AVG	G	AB	R	H	2B	3B	HR	RBI	BB	SO	SB
.279	159	639	90	178	25	9	5	55	32	102	58

CAREER STATISTICS

AVG	G	AB	R	H	2B	3B	HR	RBI	BB	SO	SB
.273	278	1072	155	293	38	20	8	73	64	180	89

VS. RHP

VS. LHP

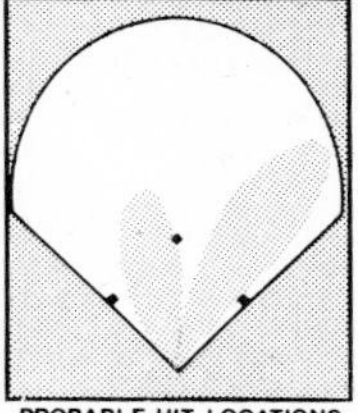
PROBABLE HIT LOCATIONS

HITTING:

Mookie Wilson is the Mets' only switch-hitting regular. He is a natural righthanded hitter. He has more power batting righthanded, but is a more effective hitter batting lefthanded because he is closer to first base.

As a lefthanded hitter, he prefers low pitches and tries to hit the ball on the ground and up the middle. He can pull though, and his power may surprise some pitchers. He should be pitched inside with breaking balls.

As a righthanded hitter, he has a stiffer swing and is a straightaway hitter. He is more likely to hit fly balls as a righthanded hitter. He prefers high fastballs and should be pitched inside and down. His speed makes him a natural leadoff hitter, but he doesn't bunt well or walk enough for a player in that spot. He also strikes out far too often for leadoff. Wilson must learn to bunt more effectively to get on base to take full advantage of his speed.

He can deliver extra base hits in clutch situations and does well with runners in scoring position.

He hits sliders and sinkers better than curves and waits well on change-ups. He can be overmatched by some fastballs particularly Nolan Ryan's and Lee Smith's.

BASERUNNING:

Mookie is exceptionally fast and he runs hard all the time. His speed to first base is excellent and he is above average in breaking up double plays. He is one of the league's most effective basestealers. He commands a pitcher's constant attention and is willing to run no matter how often a pitcher throws to the base. He uses head first and feet first slides.

FIELDING:

His speed makes him an exceptional centerfielder. He has no trouble going back, coming in or going into the gaps. He makes few mistakes--he does, however, have trouble picking up the ball in day games--but he can outrun almost any mistake. His arm has improved greatly in two seasons and now is above average for a center fielder. He charges well and gets rid of the ball very quickly.

OVERALL:

Kiner: "Mookie needs to improve his on-base percentage to reach his maximum potential. He has become an excellent defensive player."

McCarver: "There is a bright future in store for Mookie. He is the best all around player on the Mets, a very competent switch-hitter and always is alertly in the game."

Coleman: "He should learn to drag bunt."

BRUCE BOCHY
C, No. 59
RR, 6'4", 210 lbs.
ML Svc: 4 years
Born: 4-16-55 in
Landes de Boussac, FR

HITTING, BASERUNNING, FIELDING:

Bruce Bochy is big and strong, but his strength does not translate to power with the bat. He is not a contact hitter either, so his offense is inadequate, and prevents him from being more suitable as a starting or even platoon catcher. He appears hesitant at the plate. His bat is not quick. He doesn't seem to swing hard enough, and is particularly susceptible to curveballs.

Bruce is a typical No. 3 catcher on the bases--slow and no threat to steal or take an extra base.

Bochy's greatest asset as a catcher is his handling of pitchers. Though he plays infrequently, he has a good rapport with the pitchers. He knows what they can do. He sets a good target, and pitchers seem to enjoy pitching to him. Bochy is adequate in the physical aspects of his position. He moves well enough and blocks low pitches well, and his arm is slightly better than average.

OVERALL:

Bochy can be a competent catcher in a limited role. If he were to hit with either more power or more consistency, he could become a platoon catcher.

CARLOS DIAZ
LHP, No. 36
RL, 6'0", 170 lbs.
ML Svc: 1 year
Born: 1-7-58 in
Honolulu, HI

PITCHING:

Carlos Diaz is a lefthander and is used exclusively in short relief. He throws a better than average fastball and usually manages to keep it down. His curve has good rotation, and he also throws a fairly good slider. Despite his ability to throw good breaking pitches, Diaz will most often resort to his fastball in a tight situation. He doesn't try to finesse hitters, concentrating instead on trying to overpower them. He needs experience and better control if he's going to succeed as a major league reliever.

OVERALL:

Kiner: "Carlos had a below average rookie year and needs to show considerable improvement to stay on a major league roster."

McCarver: "Nicknamed 'The Mad Hawaiian,' Carlos seems to have picked up some of Al Hrabosky's mannerisms. He could develop into a good reliever."

SCOTT HOLMAN
RHP, No. 28
RR, 6'0", 190 lbs.
ML Svc: 1 year
Born: 9-18-58 in
Santa Paula, CA

PITCHING:

This is a year of decision for Scott Holman who once was considered the Mets' brightest pitching prospect. He appears to have come back completely from the arm problems that interrupted his progress in 1980 and 1981. He seems ready to move into the Mets' rotation and become a reliable starting pitcher.

Scott Holman's greatest assets are his control of his curve, the movement on his fastball and his ability to keep the ball low. His fastball is average, but it moves so much that Scott can throw it for a strike on a 3-0 count and not make it too good. He can throw his curve when he is behind in the count and have total confidence in it. His change-up is a very good one. Scott appears to have good poise on the mound and to be very competitive.

FIELDING, HITTING, BASERUNNING:

Scott is average to above average in other phases of his game, and he is willing to work to improve his fielding and hitting.

OVERALL:

If this young pitcher doesn't take a place in the Mets' rotation and perform well, the club will be very surprised. The Mets brought him back slowly from his arm problems and expect him to be successful this season.

RICK OWNBEY
RHP, No. 65
RR, 6'3", 170 lbs.
ML Svc: 1 year
Born: 10-20-57 in
Corona, CA

PITCHING:

Rick Ownbey needs to improve his control and learn how to close out a team when he is close to a victory. The physical equipment appears to be in place. He has a live arm that throws a better than average fastball, but a problem with it seems to be that it doesn't move enough.

His curveball is average, but his forkball has an exceptional break. He must learn to control it more and keep it out of the dirt. The lack of control Ownbey demonstrated last season after being promoted doesn't appear to be a chronic problem, however. To his credit, he did show poise when his wildness got him in trouble.

It appeared that Rick was over-throwing and trying to do more than he was capable of after he was promoted in 1982. When he learns to pitch within himself, his control will improve.

FIELDING, HITTING, BASERUNNING:

Rick is a gifted athlete who is quick off the mound and capable with the bat. He has a good pick-off move and is an above average hitter for a pitcher.

OVERALL:

Ownbey needs experience and more of a killer instinct to become a solid frontline starting pitcher.

JORGE ORTA
OF, No. 31
LR, 5'10", 175 lbs.
ML Svc: 10 years
Born: 11-26-50 in
Mazatlan, MX

HITTING, BASERUNNING, FIELDING:

Orta did not adapt well to strictly pinch-hitting last season and hit only .150. He does his best hitting when playing regularly.

He generally makes contact, strikes out infrequently, and is best when hitting line drives. He handles the low pitch extremely well and likes to pull the ball. He must be pitched inside with fastballs, up and away with breaking pitches. He's a good contact hitter, and better suited to a park with artificial turf because of the many ground balls he hits. As his playing time and his at-bats decreased, so did his batting average. As a regular, he has shown he hits well; as a pinch-hitter, he has problems.

Orta is quite conservative on the bases, though once during the 1982 season he was called out at second and a double play was allowed because of an overzealous slide in an attempt to break it up.

He is not a good outfielder which keeps him from playing as a regular. His range and his throwing arm are rated below average.

OVERALL:

As a good hitter with defensive limitations, Orta probably belongs in the American League as a designated hitter. And he is a good hitter.

McCarver: "He is a classic low ball hitter; he can just flat out handle a pitch around the knees."

VETERANS STADIUM
Philadelphia Phillies

Seating Capacity: 65,454
Playing Surface: Artificial

Dimensions
Left Field Pole: 330 ft.
Left-Center Field: 375 ft.
Center Field: 408 ft.
Right-Center Field: 375 ft.
Right Field Pole: 330 ft.
Height of Outfield Wall: 12 ft.

Philadelphia's Veterans Stadium has a relatively new artificial playing surface. This new surface is much softer than the concrete-like substance it replaced and is much easier on the ballplayers' legs. For some reason, however, during the summer months, this surface tends to get unbearably hot and players have been seen soaking their feet in buckets of ice-water between innings. The dirt cutouts around the bases also create problems for infielders—especially when a ground ball takes a wicked hop after hitting the lip of one of these cutout areas.

There are dugout steps which always present a hazard to catchers and infielders chasing foul balls, but in Philadelphia there is also a lip in front of the dugouts and this adds to the difficulties of chasing a foul pop. Veterans Stadium has one final ground hazard that worries infielders, especially the first basemen. The warmup mound for Philadelphia's starting pitcher is in front of the Phillies' dugout. This added obstacle is only on the first base side, however, because pitchers for the visiting team warm up in a bullpen which is off the field of play.

Hitters generally enjoy batting in this park. The lights are well placed and ballplayers say they can pick up the flight of the ball very well at night. The dirt in the batter's box can get too hard during the summer months but is generally rated as good. Finally, the ball travels exceptionally well in Philadelphia. Hits seem to jump off the bat in this park better than any place else in the league except at Riverfront Stadium in Cincinnati.

The only other peculiarity of this field is that the stands jut out along the foul lines and make it difficult for outfielders to judge and play the ball off the walls. This architectural oddity has helped turn a lot of doubles into triples at Veterans Stadium.

PORFI ALTAMIRANO
RHP, No. 57
RR, 6'0", 175 lbs.
ML Svc: 1 year
Born: 5-17-52 in Esteli, NIC

PITCHING:

A late comer to professional baseball, Porfi Altamirano was the "sleeper" in the Phillies' bullpen last season. The 30-year-old rookie was used with great success in short relief, and occasionally longer.

Essentially a control pitcher, Altamirano has deceptive speed because of his whip-like delivery that he throws with a sidearm to three-quarter arm motion. He depends on his 85-88 MPH fastball about half the time and mixes it with good breaking stuff. His curve makes righthanded batters look bad, particularly when thrown sidearm, because it either freezes them or has them reaching.

The righthander from Nicaragua has a good sinker, an effective slider that is his second best pitch, and an average straight change. He showed great presence on the mound for a first-year man and responded well in pressure situations.

Altamirano missed most of August with a sore hand but still finished the season with one of the best W-L records on the staff. He should be even better in 1983.

FIELDING, HITTING, BASERUNNING:

Altamirano has a better than average move to first. He has cat-like reflexes and fields his position well.

He only had four turns at the plate in 1982, with one hit, so his hitting and baserunning cannot be rated.

OVERALL:

With his poise and potential, all Altamirano needs to be a great stopper for Philadelphia is more major league experience.

McCarver: "A colorful guy with an unorthodox delivery. He's unshakable on the mound and could be a key factor for the Phillies in the future."

Kiner: "Although he is breaking into the majors at a relatively 'old' age, Altamirano has the ability to develop into a top flight relief man."

1982 STATISTICS

W	L	ERA	G	GS	CG	IP	H	R	ER	BB	SO	SV
5	1	4.15	29	0	0	39	41	19	18	14	26	2

CAREER STATISTICS

W	L	ERA	G	GS	CG	IP	H	R	ER	BB	SO	SV
5	1	4.15	29	0	0	39	41	19	18	14	26	2

MARTY BYSTROM
RHP, No. 50
RR, 6'5", 200 lbs.
ML Svc: 2 years
Born: 7-26-58 in
Coral Gables, FL

PITCHING:

Few rookies have had a more impressive entry into the major leagues than Marty Bystrom when he was brought up by Philadelphia in September 1980. The strong young righthander posted a phenomenal 5-0 record, won National League pitcher of the month honors and helped the Phillies make it to the league championship and the World Series.

Since then, Bystrom has been plagued by shoulder problems. They caused him to miss the second half of 1981 and start the 1982 season on the disabled list.

When healthy, Bystrom throws a good mix of pitches from a three-quarter arm delivery. He has a fine moving fastball that has been clocked up to 90 MPH, and he goes to it about half the time. He has a good curveball and will often use it when he gets behind in the count, which is unusual for a young pitcher. And when his control is on, Bystrom will come in with a sweeping slider, regardless of the count. His fourth pitch is a straight change that also depends on his control.

Bystrom keeps the batters loose, and holds up well under pressure. He has a good variety of pitches and the potential to become a top-notch pitcher providing he can overcome his shoulder ailments.

FIELDING, HITTING, BASERUNNING:

Bystrom shows a good move to first but takes too long to deliver the ball. He is quick off the hill for a big man and rates well at fielding.

His hitting and baserunning are not his strong points.

OVERALL:

Coleman: "He helped the Phils in 1980 and can do it again if the arm problems disappear."

McCarver: "In 1980, Marty came up for a cup of coffee and stayed for dinner. He established himself, and it's now a matter of healing his ailing shoulder."

1982 STATISTICS

W	L	ERA	G	GS	CG	IP	H	R	ER	BB	SO	SV
5	6	4.85	19	16	1	89	93	53	48	35	50	0

CAREER STATISTICS

W	L	ERA	G	GS	CG	IP	H	R	ER	BB	SO	SV
14	9	3.72	34	30	3	179	174	80	74	60	95	0

STEVE CARLTON
LHP, No. 32
LL, 6'5", 218 lbs.
ML Svc: 17 years
Born: 12-22-44 in Miami, FL

PITCHING:

Steve Carlton, the 1982 winner of an unprecedented fourth Cy Young Award, is one of the most valuable starting pitchers in baseball. He is a power, control and breaking ball pitcher all wrapped into one package. His perfect overhand delivery combined with his indestructible concentration have made him one of baseball's most enduring and successful southpaws.

Carlton throws a 93 MPH fastball. He has excellent control with it, and uses it about half of the time. He occasionally drops his hand on delivery, however, and his fastball flattens out losing some of its effectiveness. He throws his curveball with above average control and it sails along with a great downward motion. Carlton used to throw it more often than he does now, but the addition of a devastating slider to his arsenal has lessened his need to throw the curveball as often.

Carlton's key pitch these days is one of the best sliders ever to be tossed from a mound. In reality, he does not throw the slider for strikes as often as hitters think, but the appearance of it as a strike is due to Carlton's excellent control of it. Though his slider is tough from both sides of the plate, lefthanders have particular trouble with it. He is currently working on a straight change, and at this point has average control of it. Hitters may start to see more of it in 1983.

At age 38, he continues to be in top notch physical form. He is heavily involved in martial arts training, and it keeps his reflexes quick and his concentration intense. He cannot be distracted when he is on the mound. Though he sometimes gets off to a slow start in a game, he finds his groove quickly and can be unstoppable. In all likelihood, Carlton will have three or four more seasons of excellent pitching.

FIELDING, HITTING, BASERUNNING:

Carlton works very fast. He has an excellent move to first, is close to a balk everytime, but is consistently accurate. Carlton is thought to be a better fielder than he is. He does not cover first well at all, and has considerable trouble fielding bunts to his left. More hitters should try to push balls between him and first to get on base.

He is one of the best hitting pitchers in the game and has kept himself in many games with his bat. He is a smart baserunner but is slow and appears awkward at times.

OVERALL:

McCarver: "Steve is a picture of perfection with his classic delivery and incredible mechanics. He has superhuman strength and endurance--truly a rare physical specimen. He is the league's top lefthanded strikeout pitcher ever, and he never misses a start."

Coleman: "If Carlton gets off to a slow start, the hitters must get him early or forget it. He is the National League's best pitcher. If you had only one game to win, he would have to start."

1982 STATISTICS

W	L	ERA	G	GS	CG	IP	H	R	ER	BB	SO	SV
23	11	3.10	38	38	19	295	253	114	102	86	286	0

CAREER STATISTICS

W	L	ERA	G	GS	CG	IP	H	R	ER	BB	SO	SV
285	184	3.00	587	569	242	4273	3716	1616	1426	1440	3434	1

LARRY CHRISTENSON
RHP, No. 38
RR, 6'4", 213 lbs.
ML Svc: 8 years
Born: 11-10-53 in
Everett, WA

PITCHING:

Eight year veteran Larry Christenson has overcome arm, groin and back injuries and is still the hardest throwing on the Philly staff. The 6'4" righthander fires an overhand 90+ MPH fastball which he mixes with a big breaking curve, a very effective change-up or slip pitch, and an improved slider. He now has enough confidence in the slider to use it when he gets behind in the count . . . and as a strikeout pitch. One indication of his increased effectiveness last season was the large number of checked swings by opposing batters--a sure sign that they (particularly righthanded hitters) had trouble picking him up.

Christenson could be even tougher in 1983 if he can get more movement on his fastball. It now comes in very hard, but very straight. He should also ease up a little on his curve, which he throws too hard, causing it to lose some of its downward action. Christenson might also help himself by tossing an occasional brushback to keep the hitters loose. If he stays healthy, he has the power and poise on the mound to be a big winner.

FIELDING, HITTING, BASERUNNING:

Defensively, Christenson has a little trouble fielding his position because his back condition makes bending a problem. He does have a very good move to first however, and can keep runners close and prevent them from getting a jump on him.

Christenson is a strong hitter. He and Rick Wise now share the career record for Philadelphia pitchers with 11 home runs. On the bases, however, he rates no better than average.

OVERALL:

His ERA shows that he has the ability to be a consistent winner, but his teammates did not score a lot of runs for him in 1982.

McCarver: "Christenson rarely gets rocked. Teams have a tough time mounting big innings against him, so he almost always keeps the Phillies in the ballgame. Could be excellent someday."

Kiner: "When healthy, he is a top flight starter who can help his cause with his hitting ability."

Coleman: "Should be better. The arm strength is there, but he has been injured for half of his career."

1982 STATISTICS

W	L	ERA	G	GS	CG	IP	H	R	ER	BB	SO	SV
9	10	3.47	33	33	3	223	212	95	86	53	145	0

CAREER STATISTICS

W	L	ERA	G	GS	CG	IP	H	R	ER	BB	SO	SV
81	67	3.78	234	211	27	1355	1359	623	570	378	737	4

IVAN DeJESUS
INF, No. 18
RR, 5'11", 175 lbs.
ML Svc: 7 years
Born: 1-9-53 in
Santurce, PR

1982 STATISTICS

AVG	G	AB	R	H	2B	3B	HR	RBI	BB	SO	SB
.239	161	539	53	128	21	5	3	59	54	70	14

CAREER STATISTICS

AVG	G	AB	R	H	2B	3B	HR	RBI	BB	SO	SB
.254	987	3570	482	908	140	38	17	236	364	488	169

VS. RHP

VS. LHP

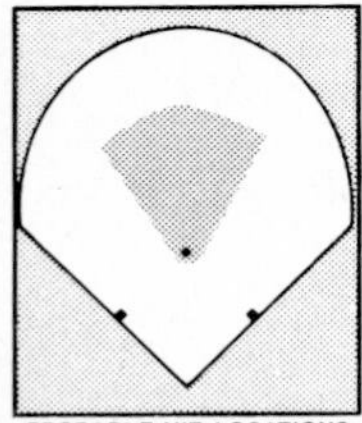
PROBABLE HIT LOCATIONS

HITTING:

DeJesus is a consistent singles hitter. He makes decent contact with the ball, but lacks the power it takes to be anything but an average hitter.

He is a high ball hitter who has trouble against lefthanded pitching. Against righthanders, he hits tight up the middle and pulls the ball just a bit more against lefties. When he hits into right rield, it's usually fairly short and in the air.

Pitchers can get DeJesus out by keeping the ball down. He likes them high and can hit high nothing pitches and ones that hang. He can hit an average change-up, but a pitcher shouldn't throw him too many or he will be doing him a favor. Cannot hit a curveball well, but can get some mileage out of a bad sinker or slider.

DeJesus is an average clutch hitter whose best position in the lineup would be as the No. 7 or 8 hitter or possibly 1. He is rated average in hitting behind the runner, in drawing walks, with men in scoring position and in the hit-and-run. Overall, DeJesus is an average to below average hitter.

BASERUNNING:

DeJesus is quick and gets out of the box well and off to first with above average speed. He gets a good jump on the bases, although he has slowed down a step in the past two seasons. As the No. 8 batter, his speed can't be utilized as much as it should. He is aggressive and smart on the basepaths. He can and will steal if the battery isn't looking. A good feet first and hookslide further combine to make him an above average baserunner.

FIELDING:

DeJesus is a superb shortstop whose agility and footwork make him a standout. He has excellent strength and accuracy. Moves very well to his left, and above average going right. His quickness gives him great range, and he can turn an exciting double play.

His reflexes are quick, he is strong and able to make the crucial defensive plays. Overall, DeJesus is a premier shortstop whose bat is the only part of his game that prevents him from being a fine all around player.

OVERALL:

McCarver: "Ivan is a marvelously endowed shortstop whose build is more like a trapeze artist. His incredible footwork and durability aid and abet a cannon hanging from his right shoulder."

Coleman: "DeJesus really seems to have benefitted from his trade to Philadelphia. He is a better overall player on the Vet's artificial surface than he was at Wrigley Field."

BOB DERNIER
OF, No. 22
RR, 6'0", 160 lbs.
ML Svc: 1 year plus
Born: 1-5-57 in
Kansas City, MO

1982 STATISTICS

AVG	G	AB	R	H	2B	3B	HR	RBI	BB	SO	SB
.249	122	370	56	92	10	2	4	21	36	69	42

CAREER STATISTICS

AVG	G	AB	R	H	2B	3B	HR	RBI	BB	SO	SB
.260	142	381	61	99	10	2	4	22	37	69	47

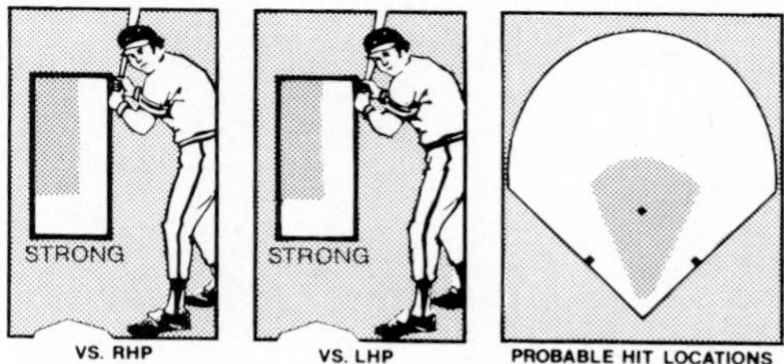

HITTING:

Basically a straightaway hitter, Dernier stands far off the plate and has a tendency to lunge at outside pitches. This takes some power away from his natural stroke and can throw him slightly off stride if he does make contact. He likes to hit outside fastballs, and he will often chase pitches that are wide and out of the strike zone.

He has not yet developed the eye to time off-speed deliveries consistently. Consequently, he can be fooled by pitchers with good curveballs, change-ups and particularly sliders from righthanders.

His acceleration going from home to first enables Dernier to beat out infield hits that would be routine outs for most other batters. This is especially true where the field has artificial turf like Philadelphia. He is a good bunter and is always a threat to lay one down for a hit. He can also go to the opposite field and has unusual pop for a player with such a lean build.

Dernier is an intelligent young player who has been showing a lot of promise in pressure situations. With more instruction and experience, his overall hitting will undoubtedly improve and make him even more dangerous at the plate.

BASERUNNING:

Dernier has the ability to become one of the game's leading all time basestealers. He gets down the line better than any righthanded batter in the league now. His incredible speed and tough as nails willingness to slide head first make him a formidable threat every time he gets on base. Opposing batteries try to keep him tight to the bag, with mixed success. The one area where he needs some improvement is learning to judge how big a lead he should take off first. That should come with experience . . . then watch him fly.

FIELDING:

An overall excellent fielder, Dernier's speed gives him tremendous range in the outfield. He can move to his left or right equally well. Though his arm strength is rated as average, his throwing accuracy doesn't suffer because he has the instinctive ability to get set up quickly to throw after the catch.

OVERALL:

McCarver: "Dernier is one of a handful of talented rookies. His mind will be his ally. Durability, because of his compactness, will also be his hallmark."

BO DIAZ
C, No. 6
RR, 5'11", 190 lbs.
ML Svc: 4 years
Born: 3-23-53 in
Cua, VEN

1982 STATISTICS

AVG	G	AB	R	H	2B	3B	HR	RBI	BB	SO	SB
.288	144	525	69	151	29	1	18	85	36	87	3

CAREER STATISTICS

AVG	G	AB	R	H	2B	3B	HR	RBI	BB	SO	SB
.270	344	1074	121	290	65	3	30	167	62	74	6

VS. RHP

VS. LHP

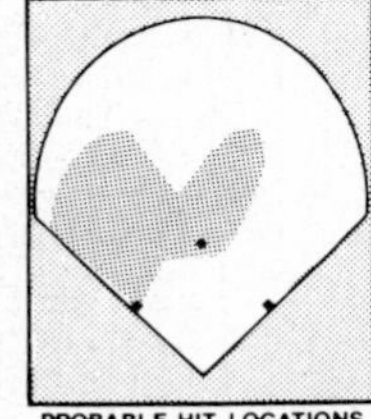
PROBABLE HIT LOCATIONS

HITTING:

Diaz stands low in the box and puts most of his weight on his back leg, allowing him to meet the ball with greater impact. Has shown decent home run potential, but it is expected that his specialty will become hard line drives.

Diaz is a pull hitter against lefthanders. Against righthanders, he is a true gap hitter showing good power to the alleys, especially right-center. He is a high ball hitter, and can hit anything on the inside part of the plate. Righthanders should pitch Diaz outside breaking balls, and if they have good ones, sliders down and away. Lefthanders with good control can send him low outside fastballs.

His abilities in the clutch are excellent, his good eye enables him to draw walks when his team needs them. Bunting ability is average. He gained a tremendous amount of confidence last season, is rated above average as a hitter and has very promising future potential.

BASERUNNING:

He is slow and conservative on the basepaths, uses a feet first slide and has trouble breaking up the double play. Overall, his baserunning must improve to complete his otherwise fine offensive skills.

FIELDING:

In 1982, Diaz became the regular Philadelphia catcher. Though he called for some incorrect pitching from time to time, he's earned the respect of his pitchers and will probably do a better job this season.

Diaz has a fine arm and can throw runners out with good consistency. Arm strength, release point and accuracy are all rated above average to excellent. He needs a little improvement at blocking balls; he occasionally comes up on balls in the dirt. Very good at fielding the bunt. Overall, he is rated average to above average, and should continue to improve.

OVERALL:

Coleman: "Diaz has become a vital force with Philadelphia. He has shown good determination with improving his hitting and it looks as though it's paying off."

Kiner: "Diaz is the best hit-and-run man in the league. His hitting is made for the power spot. It's interesting that he was traded for his defensive abilities, and then provided Philadelphia with strong power hitting."

ED FARMER
RHP, No. 46
RR, 6'6", 212 lbs.
ML Svc: 7 years
Born: 10-18-49 in
Evergreen Park, IL

PITCHING:

Long-striding Ed Farmer has a 90 MPH fastball, a wicked curve . . . and trouble finding the plate. His third pitch is a very ordinary slider, which he uses only occasionally.

Originally a starter when signed by Cleveland in the 1967 free agent draft, Farmer is now primarily a short reliever, though he may still be asked to start in a pinch. An imposing figure at 6'6", Farmer has always thrown hard but lacks control and records almost as many bases-on-balls as strikeouts. Even during his best year, 1980, when he saved 30 games for the White Sox, he recorded more walks than strikeouts.

This righthander would be awesome if he could get his curveball over without sacrificing the break. Now, he predictably relies on his fastball when he's behind in the count, and the batters know it. He seemed to lack confidence in 1982 and would frequently walk behind the mound to compose himself.

Because of his difficulty in controlling his big-breaking curve, Farmer has developed a reputation as a head hunter, and hitters, especially right-handers, are alert for an inadvertent brushback.

FIELDING, HITTING, BASERUNNING:

Farmer does not have a particularly good move to first but is somewhat better at fielding his position overall. He is not a hitting pitcher, and is rarely on the bases.

OVERALL:

Coleman: "A great reliever with the White Sox a couple of years ago, but he can't find the groove with Philadelphia."

Kiner: "Farmer has bounced around with average success because of his inability to get pitches over with consistency. He has an outstanding curve."

McCarver: "Farmer's stuff has never been questioned; it's his consistency in throwing strikes. He's a manager's dilemma: he is more effective if he gets a lot of work, but he can't get work until he's more effective."

1982 STATISTICS

W	L	ERA	G	GS	CG	IP	H	R	ER	BB	SO	SV
2	6	4.86	47	4	0	76	66	44	41	50	58	6

CAREER STATISTICS

W	L	ERA	G	GS	CG	IP	H	R	ER	BB	SO	SV
30	37	4.21	354	27	0	587	561	316	275	324	372	75

GREG GROSS
OF, No. 23
LL, 5'11", 175 lbs.
ML Svc: 9 years
Born: 8-1-52 in
York, PA

1982 STATISTICS

AVG	G	AB	R	H	2B	3B	HR	RBI	BB	SO	SB
.299	119	134	14	40	4	0	0	10	19	8	4

CAREER STATISTICS

AVG	G	AB	R	H	2B	3B	HR	RBI	BB	SO	SB
.292	1109	2687	347	785	94	39	6	220	701	182	34

VS. RHP

VS. LHP

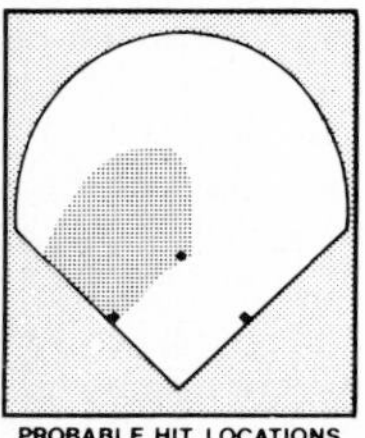
PROBABLE HIT LOCATIONS

HITTING:

Gross is a sound fundamentalist with a picture-perfect stroke. He uses a closed upright stance and stands high in the box. He bats lefthanded and hits everything to the opposite field. He has very little power (only 6 homers in 9 years), and his most frequent hits are line drives and grounders between second and third. Only occasionally hits deep into the outfield.

Gross is a good fastball hitter and likes them belt high and over the plate. He waits well on the change-up, and can hit the sinker or slider decently. Gross can be jammed, makes outside contact with the ball and can be struck out on off-speed stuff down and fastballs in.

He is a good pinch-hitter who does well in the clutch, but his inability to pull the ball into right field makes him a poor bet to hit behind the runner. Gross has a good eye, draws walks well and can give you a good bunt. His infield-type of hitting is well suited to artificial parks. Overall, his hitting is the strongest part of his game, always consistent, and rated above average.

BASERUNNING:

Gross lacks real swiftness, getting down to first and around the bases with average speed. Not a basestealer, he'll try to steal three or four bases a year and may make it once or twice. He is a smart runner who knows his own limitations. He began to be a bit more aggressive on the bases in 1982, but the lack of natural speed will prevent him from being more than average.

FIELDING:

Gross makes a good 4th outfielder for his club. His attention to the fundamentals of the game are clearly visible when he is in the field. Though his arm strength is rated average to above average, he always hits the cut-off man and has excellent accuracy. His throw to home will be on the money if he has the ball in shallow outfield. He tends to play a bit too deep in center field, but comes in on the ball well, but again, lack of speed or above average arm strength prevents him from being an everyday player.

OVERALL:

McCarver: "Greg credits Gary Sutherland (ex-Major Leaguer) with his concentration on fundamental play. What he lacks in talent, he makes up for with intelligence, hard work and application. His off-season workout program has strengthened him as well."

Kiner: "One of the National League's best pinch-hitters."

HITTING:

Last season was only Hayes' third professional season. At the plate, he had his share of rookie troubles, especially with the change-up and off-speed breaking pitches. He looks for the fastball, especially early in the count.

Righthanders usually pitched Hayes inside, and he had a difficult time with those offerings. Most of the time, he saw hard stuff inside early in the count and then change-ups away when he had two strikes.

Hayes has a closed stance with a slight crouch. He stands near the front of the box and likes to pull the ball. He has above average power and don't be surprised if he hits 25 homers a year in the near future. He has good speed, but seldom bunts. He is a low ball hitter. Righthanders should keep the ball in on him and lefties should give him breaking stuff on the outside corner. As a rookie, he murdered Baltimore and Minnesota pitching.

BASERUNNING:

Hayes has very good speed that gives him more than his share of infield hits. On the bases, he gets a fair lead. He is very aggressive. He will try to steal at almost every opportunity. A skinny 6'5", he has a long stride and seems to glide over the ground. Once he gains experience, he could steal 40-50 bases a season. He does a good job of going from first to third on a base hit.

FIELDING:

The Indians originally signed Hayes as a first baseman, although they played him at third in the minors. When he actually played for Cleveland, they made him into an outfielder. Therefore, not only did he have to cope with the usual problems facing a rookie, he had

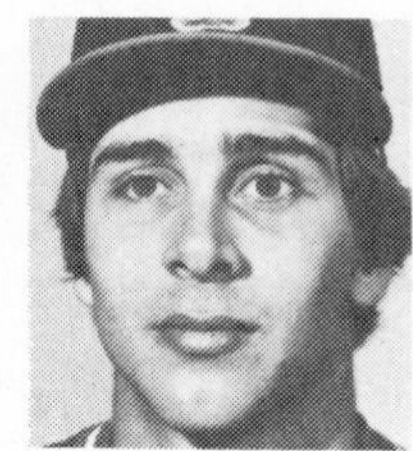

VON HAYES
OF, No. 8
LR, 6'5", 190 lbs.
ML Svc: 1 year
Born: 8-31-58 in Stockton, CA

1982 STATISTICS

AVG	G	AB	R	H	2B	3B	HR	RBI	BB	SO	SB
.250	150	527	65	132	25	3	14	82	42	63	32

CAREER STATISTICS

AVG	G	AB	R	H	2B	3B	HR	RBI	BB	SO	SB
.252	193	636	86	160	33	5	15	99	56	73	40

VS. RHP

VS. LHP

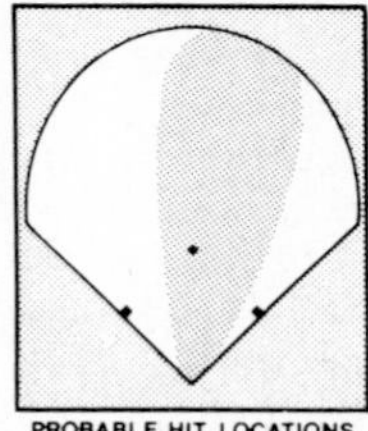
PROBABLE HIT LOCATIONS

to learn a new position on the big league level.

Now in Philadelphia, he should remain in the outfield, where he has adapted quite well. He has an above average arm, but he still throws like an infielder. He needs to get more of his body into his throws and then he will have a very good arm.

OVERALL:

Robinson: "One of the finest rookies in the league. He has not hit for as high an average as predicted, but surpassed expectations in home runs and RBI production. He is going to be an outstanding player for a long time. He is learning to play the outfield. He has a lot of natural ability and a great attitude."

Harwell: "A bright young player who will be a star."

AL HOLLAND
LHP, No. 19
RL, 5'11", 210 lbs.
ML Svc: 3 years
Born: 8-16-52 in
Roanoke, VA

PITCHING:

Holland had been perhaps the most sought-after member of the Giants' pitching staff. He is a classic example of a late-inning reliever. He comes in to throw the ball past hitters for one trip through the lineup, and that's all he is asked to do. Lack of a good off-speed pitch can get him into trouble beyond that. He has a passable curve and slider, but he uses them basically, to set up his fastball. His fastball is consistently in the 90 MPH range and up.

A squat, powerfully built man nicknamed "Capone" by teammates, he puts all his strength into his delivery. He subscribes to the theory of challenging the hitters and is absolutely fearless on the mound. Although he is a lefthander, it makes little difference whether he is facing lefthanded or righthanded hitters because he relies so little on breaking pitches. The ball is on top of the hitter before he knows it, and Holland is not above brushing back hitters he feels are standing too close to the plate.

Al was tried as a starter at the beginning of the last season, but doesn't have enough pitches for that role. He also discovered he became too restless between starts. A great competitor and a manager's dream, he seems to want the ball every day. He put together an amazing streak near the end of the 1982 season--17 2/3 consecutive hitless innings. Overall rating, excellent.

FIELDING, HITTING, BASERUNNING:

Holland has just an average move to first base, but he fields his position well. His aggressiveness shows up in his defense--he'll never pass up a decent chance to get the lead runner on an attempted sacrifice. Not much of a hitter, but a decent bunter. He's slow, but on base so rarely it hardly matters.

OVERALL:

Coleman: "When he comes in, a hitter knows he's going to be challenged. He has a great fastball."

McCarver: "Very cocky and sure of himself, Al is one of the best left-handed short men around. For sheer power for three innings, there are few in his class."

1982 STATISTICS

W	L	ERA	G	GS	CG	IP	H	R	ER	BB	SO	SV
7	3	3.33	58	7	0	129	115	56	48	40	97	5

CAREER STATISTICS

W	L	ERA	G	GS	CG	IP	H	R	ER	BB	SO	SV
19	11	2.61	164	10	0	321	280	110	93	123	247	19

GARRY MADDOX
OF, No. 31
RR, 6'3", 185 lbs.
ML Svc: 10 years
Born: 9-1-49 in Cincinnati, OH

1982 STATISTICS

AVG	G	AB	R	H	2B	3B	HR	RBI	BB	SO	SB
.284	119	412	39	117	27	2	8	61	12	32	7

CAREER STATISTICS

AVG	G	AB	R	H	2B	3B	HR	RBI	BB	SO	SB
.287	1464	5541	698	1590	304	59	104	679	278	694	234

VS. RHP

VS. LHP

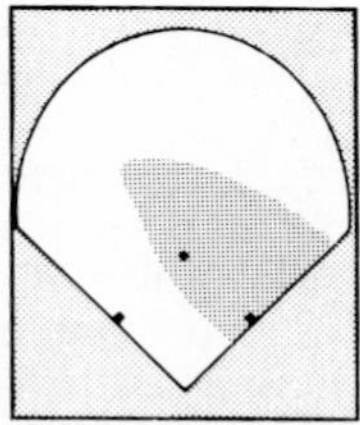
PROBABLE HIT LOCATIONS

HITTING:

Maddox is a low ball hitter with occasional power. Most of his hits are straightaway and opposite field line drives and grounders. Maddox will, however, pull the curveball and do some damage with it. He swings at a lot of first ball fastballs, and will chase bad pitches. He tends to be an erratic undisciplined hitter.

Maddox should be pitched with high inside fastballs. He hits the change-up well, but has difficulty with sinkers or sliders thrown in on him, often swinging wildly at them. Pitchers should not show him the same pitch twice in a row.

He does not have the patience at the plate consistently to stay ahead of the count. Average in his abilities in the clutch, with men in scoring position, in the hit-and-run and bunting.

When Maddox is swinging well, he is still a valued bat in the lineup and is a good No. 6 or 7 hitter. The lack of discipline at the plate however, will ultimately contribute to his more selective use by his club.

BASERUNNING:

Maddox used to be a better basestealer and overall runner than he is today. His speed to first is still above average, but he must get a better jump to pick up more stolen bases. He tends to hookslide into second on the double play and is a bit too conservative. Although he is a fast runner, he makes more baserunning errors than he should, and is overall average.

FIELDING:

Maddox plays center field very shallow and moves back well on the ball. His speed gives him excellent fielding range and he can track a fly ball exceptionally well. His arm strength is average, and he does not charge the ball enough, sometimes enabling the baserunners to get farther than they should. Throwing accuracy and strength are rated average. Overall, Maddox's fielding is the strongest part of his game.

OVERALL:

McCarver: "A quality player for the last decade, Garry received strong competition from Bob Dernier in '82 and went on the DL twice with hamstring pulls. He's a very conscientious player, perhaps hampered by the inflexibility of his no-trade contract clause."

Kiner: "An outstanding defensive center fielder, but he doesn't reach the full potential of his offensive abilities. His knowledge of the strike zone could be improved."

GARY MATTHEWS
OF, No. 34
RR, 6'3" 190 lbs.
ML Svc: 10 years
Born: 7-5-50 in
San Fernando, CA

1982 STATISTICS

AVG	G	AB	R	H	2B	3B	HR	RBI	BB	SO	SB
.281	162	616	89	173	31	1	19	83	66	87	21

CAREER STATISTICS

AVG	G	AB	R	H	2B	3B	HR	RBI	BB	SO	SB
.288	1445	5381	809	1548	248	46	173	737	630	791	148

VS. RHP

VS. LHP

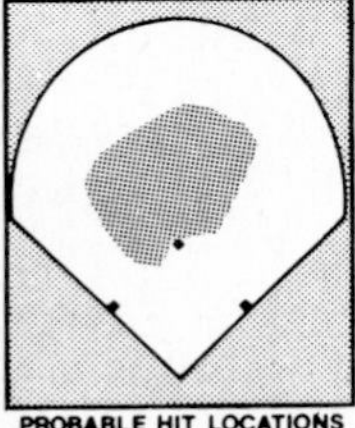
PROBABLE HIT LOCATIONS

HITTING:

Gary Matthews is an aggressive money hitter whose competitive spirit and crouched stance right on top of the plate dares pitchers to throw him tight.

He is a high ball hitter and should be pitched inside by righthanders. He hits mostly straightaway with good consistent power especially to right-center. More effective against righthanders. Against lefthanders, he pulls the ball just a bit more and should be pitched outside. He can be jammed and will chase high fastballs up and out of the strike zone with two strikes on him. It's possible to fool Matthews once in a while with a good change-up, but it would be dangerous to try it too often. He can hit a good pitcher's curveball, and if he sees a thigh-high sinker or slider, he'll send it sailing.

Matthews is a good solid No. 3 man in the lineup with excellent clutch hitting abilities. He hits well behind the runner, is a good contact man in the hit-and-run, and has an average bunt.

Overall rating, above average.

BASERUNNING:

Matthews gets out of the box well and down to first with above average speed. He's fast and has a tenacious feet first and hookslide that has broken up many double plays. Though he is rated above average at stealing, his speed and aggressiveness should enable him to be even better.

FIELDING:

Matthews' playing weakness is his defense. Though he is very aggressive in left field, he has an average fielder's range and sometimes battles with the ball. His arm strength and throwing accuracy are average to above average, his speed and aggressiveness compensate somewhat for his lack of real good hands. He appears shaky going back for long flies and is better coming in. He has an average to above average throw to home. Often replaced in late innings because of his average defensive abilities.

OVERALL:

McCarver: "Pete Rose says Gary reminds him of himself--one hell of a compliment. Gary has an irrepressible human spirit, concerns himself with his team and his burning desire to win."

Coleman: "Gary Matthews is a throwback to another era. He plays hard everyday, is a tough out, and pitchers better throw him only their best stuff."

Kiner: "Matthews is an all-out type of player with good power and good desire. His stolen base percentage of above 80% is excellent."

TUG McGRAW
LHP, No. 45
RL, 6'0", 186 lbs.
ML Svc: 15 years
Born: 8-30-44 in Martinez, CA

PITCHING:

Tug McGraw has been one of the league's quality short relievers over an unusually long time. He uses a picture perfect overhand delivery and comes straight over the top. Arm surgery in the Fall of 1981 may catch up to McGraw this season. Though he showed positive signs of recovery in 1982, a question remains if his arm can take the continued strain.

McGraw is both a breaking ball and control pitcher. He uses his fastball more often than many hitters think. Though it is generally thrown at 87-89 MPH, to the hitter it appears about 200 MPH as they look for his breaking pitch. His slider is a fine complement to his fastball and he uses it often with above average control. His screwball may very well be the best in the game. Righthanders find it nearly impossible to get a piece of. His curveball has a great downward rotation, and he uses it about 20% of the time with average control. McGraw's screwball makes him more effective against righthanders.

His four pitches are all extremely effective and his longevity on the mound may be because he is likely to throw any pitch at any time regardless of the count. He throws a brushback pitch from time to time.

He has excellent poise on the mound, and thrives on pressure situations. However, McGraw must be able to maintain his consistency and confidence after the 1981 surgery in order to continue his outstanding career.

FIELDING, HITTING, BASERUNNING:

McGraw is a fine athlete with quick reflexes. His move to first is rated average to above average. He watches the runners closely and they respect his accuracy. He fields his position well, is rated above average in fielding bunts, covering first, and can make fine plays from the mound.

He gets very little chance to hit, but he doesn't have a bad swing. Average baserunning speed.

OVERALL:

McGraw gets an excellent rating. The fans love his carefree and enthusiastic attitude. After a big third out, he bangs his glove jubilantly on his hip as he walks off the field in an expression of glee.

McCarver: "Tug is as charismatic as one can possibly be, and he backs that up with a quality durable arm. A question remains, however, as to whether he has fully recovered from off-season surgery."

Coleman: "McGraw has the consistent ability to slam the door on the opposition late in the game. When his arm is sound, he ranks right up there with Rollie Fingers as one of the best."

Kiner: "Tug has had a colorful career as an outstanding short relief man. Could be over the hill, but he'll be the last to quit. 'You Gotta Believe'."

1982 STATISTICS

W	L	ERA	G	GS	CG	IP	H	R	ER	BB	SO	SV
3	3	4.31	34	0	0	39	50	19	19	12	25	5

CAREER STATISTICS

W	L	ERA	G	GS	CG	IP	H	R	ER	BB	SO	SV
92	91	3.10	765	38	5	1421	1224	556	490	553	1053	179

LARRY MILBOURNE
INF, No. 17
SR, 6'0", 165 lbs.
ML Svc: 9 years
Born: 2-14-51 in
Port Norris, NJ

1982 STATISTICS

AVG	G	AB	R	H	2B	3B	HR	RBI	BB	SO	SB
.257	125	416	40	107	13	5	2	26	20	32	3

CAREER STATISTICS

AVG	G	AB	R	H	2B	3B	HR	RBI	BB	SO	SB
.256	838	2101	260	537	62	22	10	156	112	143	38

VS. RHP

VS. LHP

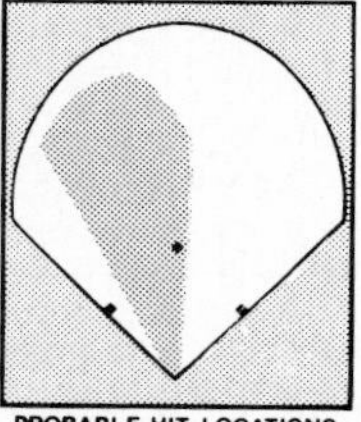
PROBABLE HIT LOCATIONS

HITTING:

Milbourne made a name for himself when he took over for an injured Bucky Dent in the middle of 1981 and was the Yankee starting shortstop. He hit over .300 for New York that season. In 1982, he was traded by the Yankees to Minnesota early in the season. He was unhappy with the Twins and pouted. On the field, this showed up in a lack of hustle.

Cleveland traded for Milbourne in July 1982 and he was installed as the starting second baseman. He was a .280 hitter with the Tribe. He played more in 1982 than in any other big league season.

A switch-hitter, Milbourne is a high ball hitter who likes inside pitches. To get him out, throw him low and away with everything. He has excellent bat control and seldom strikes out. He has little power and usually hits the ball to the opposite field. He is a quality hit-and-run man and an effective bunter, especially when bunting for a hit. He has trouble with sinkers and low sliders.

Overall, he is an average big league hitter.

BASERUNNING:

An above average runner, Milbourne steals few bases. He does not get a very good lead and he isn't aggressive on the bases. He moves well from home to first base, especially when batting lefthanded. In this area, he does not make the most of his ability.

FIELDING:

Milbourne has dependable hands and an average pivot at second base. His range is limited. In 1981, he was a reliable shortstop for the Yankees. When he played that position for the Indians, he make seven errors in 15 starts and had serious trouble turning the double play.

OVERALL:

Probably one of the best utility infielders in the game, Milbourne looks better when he is used sparingly than when he is an everyday player. He can step into the lineup for a couple weeks and turn in a commendable performance.

Robinson: "Milbourne can do a lot of things for you. He might have finally shed his tag as a utility player after all these years, although I like him best as a super-sub. Making the plays at second is his most important job. If he hits, it's a plus."

Martin: "Has some tools and speed, but he also has had some attitude problems at times."

SID MONGE
LHP, No. 21
SL, 6'2", 195 lbs.
ML Svc: 7 years
Born: 4-11-51 in
Agua Prieta, MX

PITCHING:

Sid Monge is an effective lefthanded short and middle relief pitcher. His previous experience had been in the American League with Cleveland and California. His 1982 season with Philadelphia got off to a shaky start, but as he began to learn the National League hitters and produce some key strikeouts, he became an important member of the bullpen.

He has a little bit of a jerk in his three-quarter delivery and is considered a control pitcher. He throws an 87 MPH fastball with above average control and he uses it a little over half the time. Its effectiveness is good; some hitters get locked into waiting for a breaking ball and instead get his heater. His curveball is his weakest pitch. He has average control and will only occasionally throw it. Monge's slider is his breaking ball. It has a good break and he'll use it often as it is his best pitch to lefthanded hitters. Monge also throws an above average screwball which is very good now and looks like it will get better. When he's throwing the scroogie well, he can be especially dangerous to righthanded hitters.

His overall effectiveness, however, is against lefthanded hitters; he can drop down and throw sidearm once in a while, changing his break, and his fastballs can just tie up a hitter and keep him from swinging.

When Monge is behind in the count, righthanders are likely to see the screwball, lefthanders are likely to see either the fastball or slider. Monge has excellent and consistent control over all of his pitches and his finesse is his greatest strength. His stamina is somewhat suspect. Overall rating, above average.

FIELDING, HITTING, BASERUNNING:

Monge has an average move to first, is slow to field bunts and cover first, and gets an overall average rating as a fielder.

He is not a good hitter, a slow baserunner, and is rated overall below average.

OVERALL:

Coleman: "Monge is still getting better. With more stamina, I really think he could become a starter. He has fine control and can take care of some good hitters."

Kiner: "His greatest strength is his hard screwball. Yet, even with his good stats, I find him unimpressive."

1982 STATISTICS

W	L	ERA	G	GS	CG	IP	H	R	ER	BB	SO	SV
7	1	3.75	47	0	0	72	70	35	30	22	43	2

CAREER STATISTICS

W	L	ERA	G	GS	CG	IP	H	R	ER	BB	SO	SV
36	36	3.49	342	17	4	631	566	278	245	288	405	49

JOE MORGAN
INF, NO. 8
LR, 5'7", 160 lbs.
ML Svc: 18 years
Born: 9-19-43 in
Bonham, TX

1982 STATISTICS

AVG	G	AB	R	H	2B	3B	HR	RBI	BB	SO	SB
.289	134	463	68	134	19	4	14	61	85	60	24

CAREER STATISTICS

AVG	G	AB	R	H	2B	3B	HR	RBI	BB	SO	SB
.274	2410	8508	1528	2335	408	95	246	1031	1710	920	663

VS. RHP

VS. LHP

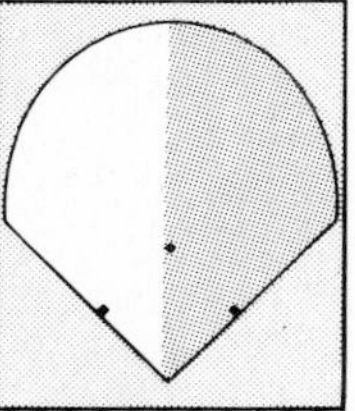
PROBABLE HIT LOCATIONS

HITTING:

Morgan is a two-time National League MVP and last season, at age 38, he regained his old form and put together a fine year. There are few things Joe can't do with a bat. He is a "guess" hitter but a good one; he still has good reflexes and can still hit the ball out of the park.

Morgan is a high ball hitter, and pitchers should generally keep the ball away from him because he will try to pull everything and can't drive the ball the other way, into left. When he has slumped or had trouble making contact, Joe will sacrifice power and just try to meet the ball and hit it up the middle. He almost never swings at a pitch out of the strike zone and last season became the league's all-time career leader in walks. He's also a fine bunter, rises to the occasion with men in scoring position and is an excellent hit-and-run man. The best bet is to keep the ball down, change speeds on Joe and try to outguess him, which isn't easy.

BASERUNNING:

Morgan still has very good speed and knows how to use it. He's one of the smartest baserunners in the game, knows just when to go for a base and when not to. He can decoy an outfielder into throwing to the wrong base. He has stolen as many as 67 bases in a season, and although he no longer is up to that, he's almost a lock to steal successfully when one run would make a difference--as witness his 24-for-28 record in 1982. He is a master at getting to know a pitcher's move, and gets a great lead.

FIELDING:

Morgan never has had a strong arm but he was and is one of the best in the game at the double play relay because of his quick and accurate release. His range now is only average, but he goes to his left very well and can make the throw to second falling away.

OVERALL:

Coleman: "Joe has gotten as much out of his ability as any player in the game."

Kiner: "Morgan lost about 15 pounds and came up with a comeback season. After losing the weight, Joe was able to do things the way he used to."

McCarver: "Joe is a consummate professional. Always referred to as 'Little Joe,' he becomes a foot taller with a bat in his hand. He has rebounded after a couple of off years. He could be a big league manager someday."

RON REED
RHP, No. 42
RR, 6'6", 225 lbs.
ML Svc: 15 years
Born: 11-2-42 in
LaPorte, IN

PITCHING:

Short relief specialist Ron Reed is coming off his best overall season since joining the Phillies bullpen in 1976. He led the staff in ERA, saves, and most consecutive scoreless innings.

Primarily a power thrower, Reed challenges hitters with a fastball that he delivers either overhand or from a three-quarter position at speeds ranging from 88 to 93 MPH. Actually, he has two kinds of fastball--one that he cuts and that acts like a slider, and one that sinks. His next best pitch is a slider that looks so much like his cut fastball that it is hard to tell them apart. He does not have much of a curve, and goes to a change-up infrequently. He is working on a forkball, but that still needs improvement.

Part of the 6'6" Reed's success is due to his ability to throw hard; part is because of the arm and leg action in his delivery which makes the pitch hard for hitters to pick up. His motion is particularly intimidating to righthanders and makes them very wary about getting too set in the box.

Reed is tough under pressure, as a short reliever must be. If he has one major fault, it is throwing too many pitches at the same speed.

FIELDING, HITTING, BASERUNNING:

Reed fields his position reasonably well, but his move to first can be improved. Good baserunners can get the jump on him.

He can make contact at the plate and is a better than average hitter for a pitcher. He is not too swift on the bases, however.

OVERALL:

Reed a is superbly conditioned 40 year old who is durable and has great presence on the mound. He was a good starting pitcher years ago, and is still good in the clutch.

Kiner: "A quality short relief man, he has the ability to be consistent. His size and motion make him especially tough on righthanded hitters."

Coleman: "Good competitor who still throws hard. There is always a place in the bullpen for a pitcher like him."

McCarver: "Reed is much better in relief than as a starter because he relies so heavily on his heater."

1982 STATISTICS

W	L	ERA	G	GS	CG	IP	H	R	ER	BB	SO	SV
5	5	2.66	57	2	0	98	85	30	29	24	57	14

CAREER STATISTICS

W	L	ERA	G	GS	CG	IP	H	R	ER	BB	SO	SV
137	133	3.46	639	236	55	2311	2218	1013	891	585	1351	83

BILL ROBINSON
OF, No. 28
RR, 6'3", 197 lbs.
ML Svc: 13 years
Born: 6-26-43 in
McKeesport, PA

1982 STATISTICS

AVG	G	AB	R	H	2B	3B	HR	RBI	BB	SO	SB
.250	66	140	14	35	9	0	7	31	12	34	1

CAREER STATISTICS

AVG	G	AB	R	H	2B	3B	HR	RBI	BB	SO	SB
.253	1462	4357	536	1106	229	29	166	639	262	816	71

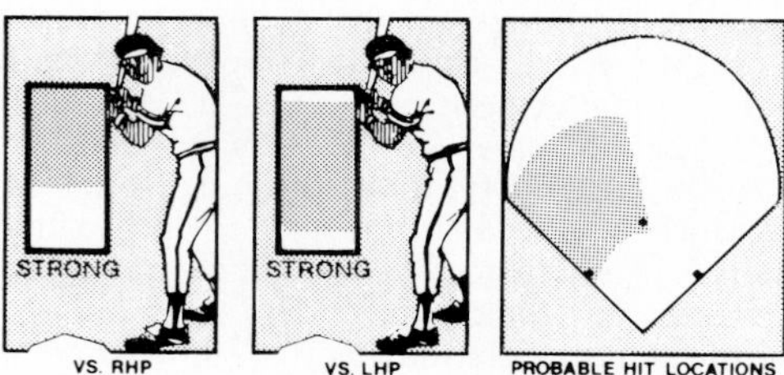

VS. RHP   VS. LHP   PROBABLE HIT LOCATIONS

HITTING:

Bill Robinson has had a long career in baseball, and returned to Philadelphia in June 1982 after spending seven years in Pittsburgh. At 40 years old, he can still get hot with the bat and probably has another productive year or two left. Robinson's best use is as a pinch hitter and outfield replacement.

Robinson is a high ball hitter and hits breaking balls very well. He should be pitched down and outside, and can be jammed. He is a pull hitter and has good power. Most of his hits are strong line drives often reaching the alleys. Good low pitches will get Robinson out, but hanging stuff or mistakes up and over the plate may get shot into left field. He waits well on the change-up, pitchers should use it carefully. Sinkers or sliders must be thrown way down in the strike zone to get him. Though he is best with high pitches, he has deceptively good strength against low pitches from lefthanders, and can hit southpaws better than righthanders.

Robinson hits well in tight situations. Average abilities in hitting behind the runner, but very good with men in scoring position. He has a good eye and doesn't swing at too many bad pitches. Above average bunt. Although Robinson's hitting has slowed somewhat in the past few years, he continues to handle the bat well, and in his present position as pinch-hitter is rated above average.

BASERUNNING:

Robinson is an overall average runner. He is smart and doesn't take too many chances. Aggressive in his attempts to break up double plays and has a good feet first slide.

FIELDING:

In earlier career years, Robinson was used in the outfield and at first and third. His best defensive use is as a replacement in the outfield. His arm strength and accuracy are average. He does not have good range, comes in better on balls than he does going back, but will make the plays he gets to. Overall, average fielder.

OVERALL:

McCarver: "Bill is a winner and is used to it. He doesn't frighten very easily, provides leadership to the team and has been in many pennant races. That's why the Phillies brought him back.

Coleman: "He was a late bloomer and is still productive against lefthanded pitchers. Bill is also an outstanding citizen."

HITTING:

Batting either left or right, Rose hits straightaway and to the opposite field. The only time he'll try to pull is when he's batting left and a man is on first. He does not hit for power; his hits are generally solid line drives and hard grounders. From either side, the defense can generally give him the right field line.

He is a high ball hitter, but also likes low ones from righthanders. He has a bit more trouble going to the opposite field batting right. He has more power and is considered more effective batting left. There is no one way to pitch Rose. Though lefthanders' sinkers and good off-speed stuff occasionally frustrate him, he has an excellent eye and doesn't chase bad ptiches. He can draw walks as easily as he hits. A great leadoff or No. 2 hitter, he is rated excellent in the clutch and with men in scoring position. Also excellent at hitting behind the runner and is a good contact man in the hit-and-run. Rose is an above average bunter, but he has lost some running speed making it tougher for him to bunt for a hit.

BASERUNNING:

Rose is one of the smartest baserunners in the game. He can lull a pitcher to sleep and steal a big base. He has only average speed, but if he can reach second on a double play attempt, he'll send the fielder flying. Rose's patented headfirst slide and his aggressive, intelligent baserunning make him an exciting and effective runner.

FIELDING:

At first, Rose is one of the most aggressive at fielding bunts. He takes excessive pride in defense. His arm strength and accuracy are rated average to above average. He does, however, have limited range in moving either to his left or right. Above average in turning the double play and is excellent in putting everything together to make the clutch defensive plays.

PETE ROSE
INF, No. 14
SR, 5'11", 203 lbs.
ML Svc: 20 years
Born: 4-14-41 in
Cincinnati, OH

1982 STATISTICS

AVG	G	AB	R	H	2B	3B	HR	RBI	BB	SO	SB
.271	162	634	80	172	25	4	3	54	66	32	8

CAREER STATISTICS

AVG	G	AB	R	H	2B	3B	HR	RBI	BB	SO	SB
.308	3099	12544	1995	3869	697	126	158	1164	1358	1022	179

VS. RHP

VS. LHP

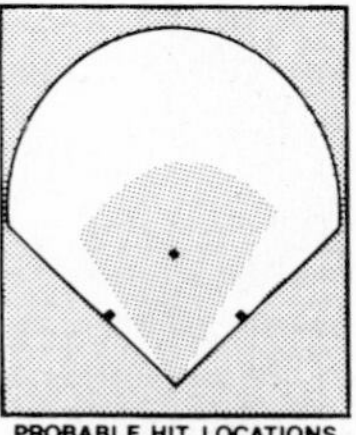
PROBABLE HIT LOCATIONS

OVERALL:

McCarver: "If a scout went out to sign Pete Rose, he wouldn't sign him on the basis of his talent--can't run, hit for power, has limited range, average throwing--but he can beat you with EVERYTHING. He knows exactly what he has done and can do."

Coleman: "Pete Rose is living proof of the old adage 'If you want to do something badly enough, it can be done.' Pete's a self-made player who deserves every accolade he's received."

Kiner: "Rose is a Hall of Fame player who puts more into the game of baseball than he takes out."

DICK RUTHVEN
RHP, No. 44
RR, 6'3" 190 lbs.
ML Svc: 9 years
Born: 3-27-51 in Sacramento, CA

PITCHING:

Dick Ruthven is an intense competitor who lives or dies by his breaking ball. A control pitcher with a very good rotation on his curve, Ruthven is tough to beat when he is hitting his spots. When his control is off, as it was in the early part of 1982, he is a picture of pure frustration on the mound.

A methodical worker with a high, deliberate kick, this righthander uses an overhand delivery for all of his pitches. They include an 84-87 MPH fastball that should be used more often, an occasional slider and an infrequent straight change. He has also developed a palmball, but does not show it too often. When he gets behind in the count, Ruthven relies on off-speed pitches and can throw any one of them over the plate. He is particularly effective against righthanded hitters.

Ruthven's biggest problems are his inability to relax on the mound and a tendency to be too fine too early in the count. He would be better off getting ahead of the batter and then going for spots, especially early in the game when his control might be shaky.

FIELDING, HITTING, BASERUNNING:

Ruthven fields his position well and is quick at covering bunts. His main problem on defense is his high kick--it gives baserunners a chance to get a good jump.

When he makes contact with the bat, Ruthven hits almost everything to right field. For a pitcher, he is a pretty good baserunner.

OVERALL:

Ruthven is an above average pitcher who could be even better if he stopped fighting with himself and relaxed more.

McCarver: "Dick is a very intelligent man who ponders the cerebral part of pitching maybe a little too much. He can be exceedingly confident or exceedingly down on himself, depending on his last start. However, he certainly is a fine addition to any staff."

Kiner: "His curveball is above average, and he needs it to win. He has had a couple of elbow operations, but if his arm stays healthy, he's a winner."

1982 STATISTICS

W	L	ERA	G	GS	CG	IP	H	R	ER	BB	SO	SV
11	11	3.79	33	31	8	204	189	99	86	59	115	0

CAREER STATISTICS

W	L	ERA	G	GS	CG	IP	H	R	ER	BB	SO	SV
100	98	4.02	274	263	66	1701	1684	841	760	645	962	1

MIKE SCHMIDT
INF, No. 20
RR, 6'2", 203 lbs.
ML Svc: 10 years
Born: 9-27-49 in
Dayton, OH

1982 STATISTICS

AVG	G	AB	R	H	2B	3B	HR	RBI	BB	SO	SB
.280	148	514	108	144	26	3	35	87	107	131	14

CAREER STATISTICS

AVG	G	AB	R	H	2B	3B	HR	RBI	BB	SO	SB
.265	1485	5129	964	1360	253	44	349	965	958	1279	155

VS. RHP

VS. LHP

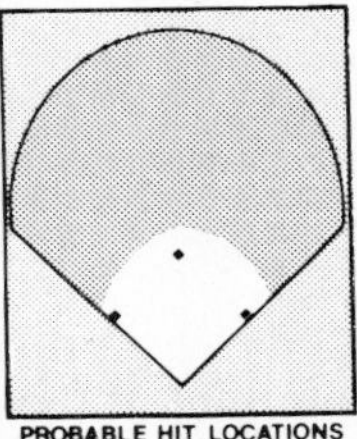
PROBABLE HIT LOCATIONS

HITTING:

Mike Schmidt is one of the most prolific power hitters in the game today. He stands low in the box and far away from the plate, giving him more time to pick his pitch. It also enables him to hit all fields.

A pitcher must not make a mistake pitching to Schmidt. Good sweeping curves from righthanders are the best to get Schmidt out with. He can hit both high and low fastballs, but especially loves the low ones. A pitcher with very good stuff can pitch him high and inside, but otherwise it should be outside and right there. Schmidt has an excellent eye and is very selective. He'll hammer sinkers or sliders that are thrown in his zone.

Schmidt wants to hit behind the runner all the time and because of his power, never should. He is excellent in the clutch; the best in the league for three years. Schmidt likes to use the bunt as an element of surprise. His home runs tend to come in streaks, but those streaks can last as long as ten or twenty games.

BASERUNNING:

Average speed to first, Schmidt is a strong runner who knows just when to go and who to steal against. Aggressive on the basepaths. He's rated above average in stealing, will steal over ten bases a year--all at just the right time. He takes a walking lead, and keeps the pitchers on their toes. He uses an effective feet first slide, and is very good in breaking up the double play.

FIELDING:

Schmidt is the best third baseman in the league. He plays his position very deep, has exceptional arm strength and well above average accuracy. He positions himself very well and has great range. Mike rarely misses a barehand pickup and can easily fire to first or second while on the run, off balance, or standing on his head. A drag bunt laid down when he's playing deep may be the best way for a hitter to get on base. Schmidt has great hands and an unbelievable move to his left, able to reach far, wide, and high for everything hit his way.

OVERALL:

McCarver: "There are not enough good things to say about Mike. He is the best player in the game today--period. Mike is also extremely intelligent and articulate. His analysis of things may be too good, however, and he sometimes analyses plays during the course of the game. You really have to reach to say anything bad about Mike."

Kiner: "In my opinion, Schmidt is the best player in the National League. He is an outstanding defensive player and power hitter."

Coleman: "He is the most feared hitter in the league, and along with Gary Carter, the most complete player in the National League as well."

OZZIE VIRGIL
C, No. 11
RR, 6'1", 195 lbs.
ML Svc: 1 year plus
Born: 12-7-56 in
Mayaguez, PR

HITTING:

Virgil is used as a pinch-hitter against lefthanded pitching, and has good power with a lot of pop in his swing.

Virgil is a good looking natural hitter who needs more playing time to prove himself. He likes to jump on pitches that are high and inside and has had some good powerful line drives and grounders. He is a pull hitter, and when he does send one the opposite way into right field, it will be in the air for an easy out.

Pitchers should keep the ball down. High mistakes are what Virgil likes to see. He does not handle the change-up well, and at this point, is hitting sinkers and sliders with a fair amount of success. As a pinch-hitter, Virgil has shown above average abilities in clutch situations and with men in scoring position. He does not hit well behind the runner, jumps a bit too fast at high pitches to draw walks, and has an average to below average bunt.

1982 STATISTICS

AVG	G	AB	R	H	2B	3B	HR	RBI	BB	SO	SB
.238	49	101	11	24	6	0	3	8	10	26	0

CAREER STATISTICS

AVG	G	AB	R	H	2B	3B	HR	RBI	BB	SO	SB
.223	56	112	12	25	7	0	3	8	10	9	0

VS. RHP

VS. LHP

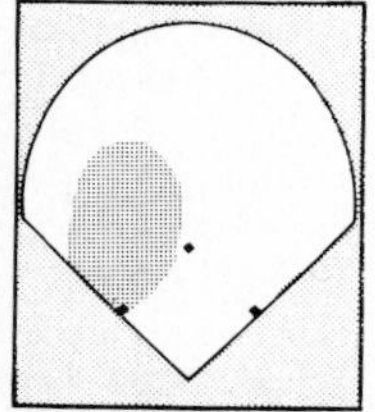
PROBABLE HIT LOCATIONS

BASERUNNING:

Virgil does not get to first quickly enough to beat out Major League arms, or into second to break up double plays. He is conservative on the basepaths, and overall, his baserunning must improve if he is to have a stronger chance of additional playing time.

FIELDING:

As back up catcher to Bo Diaz, Virgil saw little playing time. Although his outings did show him to be a better catcher than was originally thought, he still needs much improvement. He has a deceptively strong arm but takes a long time getting rid of the ball. His accuracy is off at times. He is rated average at blocking balls in the dirt, but is getting better. Also average at fielding the bunt and handling pitchers. Must improve his accuracy and release point in order to hold the baserunners with consistency. Virgil is in the early stages of a career and is showing some improvement.

OVERALL:

McCarver: "Ozzie is a 'hitter that catches' as opposed to a 'catcher that hits.' He must work and work on his defense. If he is willing to work hard and shows the capacity to learn quickly, he may be a fine catcher."

Coleman: "Virgil is a fine looking young hitter, though some people feel he is a lazy catcher who needs to work harder."

LUIS AGUAYO
INF, No. 16
RR, 5'9", 173 lbs.
ML Svc: 2 years
Born: 3-13-59 in
Vega Baja, PR

HITTING, BASERUNNING, FIELDING:

Aguayo is a singles hitter with only occasional pop in his bat. He is a high ball hitter and should be pitched down and inside. He handles the high fastball well, but has had trouble with change-ups and low sinkers and sliders. Against righthanded pitching he goes straightaway, but pulls lefties a bit more. He is showing some decent clutch hitting ability and can hit behind the runner. He does not draw walks well, but makes a good contact man in the hit-and-run. Average to above average bunt. Overall, hitting is rated average.

Aguayo is conservative, but runs well. He can get into second to break up the double play, and if given more opportunity could be an above average basestealer.

His arm strength is above average enabling him to take over as a late-innings defensive replacement at third, short or second. He has only average range but an accurate arm. He does not appear to have the kind of swiftness and outstanding talent that will make him an everyday player. Overall, average fielder.

OVERALL:

Kiner: "Has had little exposure, but looks like a fine defensive player. It's tough when you play back-up to such a fine second baseman like Manny Trillo."

JOHN DENNY
RHP, No. 40
RR, 6'3", 190 lbs.
ML Svc: 8 years
Born: 11-8-52 in
Prescott, AZ

PITCHING:

John Denny, an experienced starter in both leagues, came back to the senior circuit when the Phillies aquired him from Cleveland to help with their 1982 September stretch drive.

Formerly a power pitcher, Denny is now a breaking ball specialist with an outstanding curve that he throws from a three-quarter delivery. He still has an 85 MPH fastball that he mixes with the curve and sometimes turns it into a sinker. He also tosses a slider and a change-up, but they are not his money pitches.

When his control is on, Denny's righthanded slants are tough on the hitters, especially righthanded ones who go fishing for his curve. Denny has the ability and intelligence to exploit a batter's weakness and the experience to hang tough in pressure situations.

Denny came to the Phillies too late in the season to contribute much, but watch him in 1983 when he can start in the regular rotation.

FIELDING, HITTING, BASERUNNING:

Denny is an adequate fielder with a good move to first.

He had no batting average with Cleveland, and did not appear often enough with the Phillies to rate his ability at bat or on the bases.

OVERALL:

Kiner: "Good solid pitcher. If he gets his curve over, he is hard to beat."

Harwell: "Denny is injury prone. When healthy, he is an above average starter."

BOB MOLINARO
OF, No. 25
RL, 6'0", 180 lbs.
ML Svc: 6 years
Born: 5-21-50 in Newark, NJ

HITTING, BASERUNNING, FIELDING:

A lefthanded pull hitter, Molinaro bats out of a crouched stance and has a habit of adjusting his feet a lot before taking a swing. He is used primarily against righthanders and likes to go after low fastballs and anything down and inside that he can yank to right field. He has trouble with breaking balls, particularly good curveballs and high hard ones.

As would be expected of a pinch-hitter, Molinaro handles a bat fairly well, hits in the clutch, can execute the hit-and-run, and is a better-than-average bunter. He has a good idea of the strike zone and has the discipline to wait for a walk.

Although he was an adept base-stealer in the minors (he stole 50 with Iowa in 1979), Molinaro has not been a threat in the majors. He is rated average in all baserunning categories.

Because he is used solely as a pinch-hitter, Molinaro has no rating as an outfielder.

OVERALL:

Kiner: "A marginal player. He has been a good pinch-hitter and might hang on in the majors as that."

Coleman: "An extra man on the roster. Not top major league talent."

McCarver: "As a pinch-hitter, his most dominant trait is the way he moves his feet so much. Generally, not a good hitter's trait."

DAVE ROBERTS
INF, No. 10
LL, 6'3", 192 lbs.
ML Svc: 14 years
Born: 9-11-44 in Gallipolis, OH

HITTING, BASERUNNING, FIELDING:

More of singles hitter than a slugger, Roberts crouches at the plate and holds his bat very low. Because of his stance and his liking for high balls, the righthander often hits the bottom half of the ball and pops up a lot. He is basically a straightaway hitter but may pull lefthanded deliveries a little and occasionally reaches the alleys.

Roberts has trouble hitting pitchers who can keep the ball outside and down, and pitchers with good curveballs. He is better at handling a sinker or slider, especially if it hangs up a little. Roberts has been described as a "mis-take" hitter who does well when the pitcher's control is off.

Roberts has average speed to first and on the bases. He is not likely to steal, but he will try to break up a double play, going in either feet first or head first.

A versatile infielder, and sometime catcher, Roberts' greatest value to a team is his defensive ability. He can and has played every infield position except pitcher. He has a good, accurate arm and can move to his right or left. He can handle bunts and turn double plays. He is often used as a late-inning defensive substitute.

OVERALL:

McCarver: "Roberts enjoyed some rather fruitful years with the Padres. It's hard to say when the slide began, but he isn't the player people thought he was destined to be."

Coleman: "He's a player with limited skills. His value now is his versatility."

THREE RIVERS STADIUM
Pittsburgh Pirates

Seating Capacity: 54,449
Playing Surface: Artificial (Tartan Turf)

Dimensions:
Left Field Pole: 335 ft.
Left-Center Field: 375 ft.
Center Field: 400 ft.
Right-Center Field: 375 ft.
Right Field Pole: 335 ft.
Height of Outfield Wall: 10 ft.

Three Rivers Stadium, the home of the Pittsburgh Pirates, has a unique artificial playing surface--Tartan Turf. It seems softer to the touch than other artificial playing surfaces but doesn't appear to be cushioned as well. This makes playing in Pittsburgh rough on a player's legs because of the lack of resiliency in the carpet. Like the other artificial surfaces throughout the league, however, the Tartan Turf adds to the speed of ground balls and can become especially treacherous in wet weather.

The dirt in the batter's box at Three Rivers is soft and easy to dig into, thus insuring that the players who form the famous "Lumber Company" are always comfortable when hitting at home. However, despite the composition of the batter's box, the fence, 10 feet high and stretching from 335 feet in the corners to 400 feet in center, insures that any homer hit at Three Rivers is a legitimate shot. As a matter of fact, this stadium is considered by many to be the fairest park in the league to both hitters and pitchers.

The dugouts are on field level and present no problems to anyone trying to catch a foul pop-up. The bullpens are separated from the field of play by an eight foot high cyclone fence. The cinder warning track in the outfield is a mixed blessing. It warns the fielder that he is nearing the wall but the sudden shift in surfaces can cause a player to lose his footing.

The only real complaint lodged against Three Rivers is about the slope of the pitching mound. Several pitchers have indicated that they seem to be going uphill when they finish their motion. This makes it harder for them to keep their pitches down and easier for the hitters to hit their pitches out.

ROSS BAUMGARTEN
LHP, No. 34
LL, 6'1", 180 lbs.
ML Svc: 5 years
Born: 5-27-55 in Highland Park, IL

PITCHING:

Ross Baumgarten went the entire 1982 season without a win. He broke two fingers on his pitching hand in April and was on the disabled list for two months. He is what is known as a junk-baller.

He throws at two speeds--slow and slower. His fastball is his change-up and is only about 80 MPH. He throws a slow breaking curve quite a lot, and his slider is really a cut fastball. He throws a straight change about 5% of the time.

Baumgarten is a little more effective against lefthanders, but not much. It's hard to find a particularly strong point for this pitcher because his lack of a major league fastball is a glaring deficiency.

Baumgarten claims that inactivity has hampered his control. He isn't the type who can relieve often because he says he can't adjust to throwing four times a week. He has good poise on the mound and maybe some season he will be able to put it together. Four years ago he was considered an outstanding young pitcher with the Chicago White Sox, but at this point, his future is bleak.

FIELDING, HITTING, BASERUNNING:

He is a fair fielder. His move to first base is adequate. Baumgarten isn't a good hitting pitcher, and is overall, well below average. He has no speed on the bases and just can't help himself in the areas of running and hitting.

OVERALL:

Baumgarten seems to have developed a negative approach after failing to win for more than 12 months with two different clubs. He might benefit from a new start with a club that will give him a chance in the rotation.

Kiner: "Unless there is a vast turnaround, this year could be his last."

McCarver: "As a lot of American League pitchers find out, there are more good hitters in the National League."

Coleman: "He had a very poor showing, perhaps there are arm problems."

1982 STATISTICS

W	L	ERA	G	GS	CG	IP	H	R	ER	BB	SO	SV
0	5	6.55	12	10	0	44	60	33	32	27	17	0

CAREER STATISTICS

W	L	ERA	G	GS	CG	IP	H	R	ER	BB	SO	SV
22	36	3.99	90	84	10	496	492	246	220	211	222	0

DALE BERRA
INF, No. 4
RR, 6'0", 190 lbs.
ML Svc: 4 years
Born: 12-13-56 in Ridgewood, NJ

HITTING:

Dale Berra was probably the most improved hitter in the National League in 1982. He was hitting .181 in early June and then turned it around. His biggest problem is that he takes too many pitches. Often, he finds himself behind with an 0-2 count just because he is looking for a certain pitch. He is a good low ball hitter, but has trouble with fastballs high and tight.

Some scouts have made the mistake of reporting that Berra is a high ball hitter. This report has changed drastically especially after last summer when Berra batted over .300 for three months and clobbered the low pitch consistently. Occasionally he will try to bunt for a base hit and has had fair success. He is just fair at moving up runners with his bunts.

BASERUNNING:

Berra rates below average, but not because of lack of speed, because his speed is average. He just doesn't have good instincts on the bases, and as a result, he makes mistakes. He doesn't take extra bases as often as he should. If a pitcher doesn't keep him close to the bag, however, he will steal.

FIELDING:

Without a question, Berra was the most unpredictable fielder in the league last season. Any scout who saw him play shortstop in April and May had every right to believe he would never make it. He made an astonishing turnaround and developed into a better than average fielder during the season. He still has a lot to learn about the shortstop position having played mostly at third base where he was an exceptional fielder.

1982 STATISTICS

AVG	G	AB	R	H	2B	3B	HR	RBI	BB	SO	SB
.263	156	529	64	139	25	5	10	61	33	83	6

CAREER STATISTICS

AVG	G	AB	R	H	2B	3B	HR	RBI	BB	SO	SB
.238	447	1304	133	310	53	7	27	151	91	214	22

VS. RHP

VS. LHP

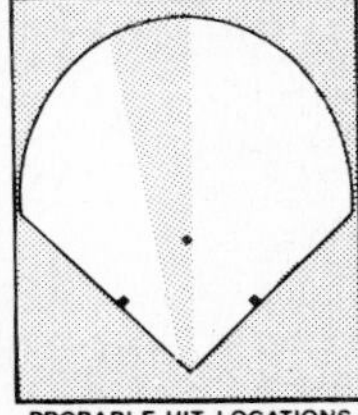
PROBABLE HIT LOCATIONS

OVERALL:

Eager to improve. Plays hurt and rarely makes a big thing about injuries. Living in shadow of his Hall of Fame father may not have helped him early in his career. Now he is on his own which is the way he wanted it all the time.

McCarver: "Dale credits manager Chuck Tanner and Bob Skinner for staying with him. He has proved his critics wrong and plays better than most thought he could."

Coleman: "He has finally put it all together and has become a fine major league infielder. He still has a lot to learn, but is definitely going in the right direction."

Kiner: "Berra offsets his defensive lapses with his power and hitting and is steadily improving as a shortstop."

NOTE: Jim Bibby was inactive during the 1982 season following surgery on his rotator cuff last April. As a rotator cuff injury is a very serious one for pitchers, Bibby's future is in doubt. Before his injury, Bibby was one of the most powerful righthanders in the National League. What follows is a report on his pre-surgery form.

JIM BIBBY
RHP, No. 26
RR, 6'5", 250 lbs.
ML Svc: 10 years
Born: 10-29-44 in
Franklington, NC

PITCHING:

Bibby has a very good fastball, and in recent years also developed a good breaking pitch. He works both sides of the plate well. Bibby is quite capable of overpowering even the big home run hitters. He is especially effective through seven innings, but then often loses some zip from his fastball. When that happens, he's out, because he is almost exclusively a fastball pitcher.

He has a weak curveball which he hardly ever uses because of its poor rotation. He throws a hard slider which sometimes appears to be his fastball. Control is above average, and Bibby will toss the brushback to keep the hitters off guard.

FIELDING, HITTING, BASERUNNING:

Bibby is a below average fielder, and is slow in fielding bunts. Also slow covering the first base bag. He does not have a good move over to first, making him an easy victim of basestealers. He is a fair baserunner, and a decent hitter who may hit one home run a year.

OVERALL:

Bibby is a pitcher with a successful past but a clouded future. Even if he recovers from his April 1982 surgery, he may not be able to become a regular starter until May or June of 1983.

McCarver: "It would be a shame if that torn rotator cuff ended Jim's career. He is an intense competitor and was starting to become very impressive in Pittsburgh."

1982 STATISTICS

Did not play in 1982

CAREER STATISTICS

W	L	ERA	G	GS	CG	IP	H	R	ER	BB	SO	SV
106	89	3.61	303	227	56	1628	1454	732	653	662	1029	8

JOHN CANDELARIA
LHP, No. 45
SL, 6'7", 232 lbs.
ML Svc: 8 years
Born: 11-6-53 in
New York, NY

PITCHING:

John Candelaria could be regarded as baseball's mystery pitcher. He can be very good or very bad. He has an overpowering fastball and a good breaking pitch. His control is well above average. There are games when he simply overpowers hitters, and then . . . there are games when it seems he hasn't got any zip on his fastball and his breaking pitch is flat.

Candelaria is big and strong. His sidearm/three-quarter delivery puts a lot of strain on his arm. He is a power pitcher, and he seems to deliver the ball in a sort of "sling-shot style" with his foot hitting the ground before his arm comes around. He throws a 90 MPH fastball and likes to work it on the outside corner. His curveball gets occasional but very effective use--it is big and hard and very tough on left-handed hitters. He changes speeds off his curve somewhat infrequently and uses it to throw the hitters offstride. When behind in the count, he'll send the fastball to righthanders and the curveball to lefties. He is much more effective against lefthanded hitters, because of his delivery and physical size.

Injuries have hampered what could have been a marvelous career. In 1981, Candelaria suffered nerve damage in his left bicep, and his arm problems may be the reason why he can run hot and cold from one game to the next. He also injured his back as a youngster and says that he pitches in pain all the time.

"The Mad Hatter" as he is nicknamed, says he isn't strong enough to pitch nine innings regularly and his incomplete game record through the years bears him out. Occasionally, he is used in relief and he is a standout when he pitches two innings or less.

FIELDING:

Candelaria fields bunts very well. Often he is slow covering the bag on grounders to the right side. He is an above average hitter and a good bunter. Last year, he batted from both sides of the plate, but does not follow the traditional switch-hitting philosophy, sometimes batting left against lefthanded pitchers. He has some power from the right side.

OVERALL:

John gives a false impression to many people that he is the no-care type athlete. Untrue. Candelaria is a tough competitor, but a free spirit as well. Chuck Tanner calls him "my money pitcher."

Kiner: "When healthy, he is as good as any pitcher in the National League."

Coleman: "Candelaria has a great arm and keeps his cool. I might question his lack of desire to be really great . . . I don't think he wants it badly enough."

McCarver: "John has one of the best winning percentages in baseball. Because Chuck Tanner isn't overly impressed with complete games, even when Candelaria is healthy, it's tough for him to finish one off. If he stays injury-free he will be more than a formidable force."

1982 STATISTICS

W	L	ERA	G	GS	CG	IP	H	R	ER	BB	SO	SV
12	7	2.94	31	30	1	175	166	62	57	37	133	1

CAREER STATISTICS

W	L	ERA	G	GS	CG	IP	H	R	ER	BB	SO	SV
95	61	3.13	218	211	40	1417	1311	547	493	334	805	4

RICHIE HEBNER
INF, No. 2
LR, 6'1", 195 lbs.
ML Svc: 14 years
Born: 11-26-47 in Boston, MA

1982 STATISTICS

AVG	G	AB	R	H	2B	3B	HR	RBI	BB	SO	SB
.241	93	249	31	60	8	0	10	30	30	24	5

CAREER STATISTICS

AVG	G	AB	R	H	2B	3B	HR	RBI	BB	SO	SB
.275	1723	5781	810	1588	260	56	193	94	603	683	29

VS. RHP

VS. LHP

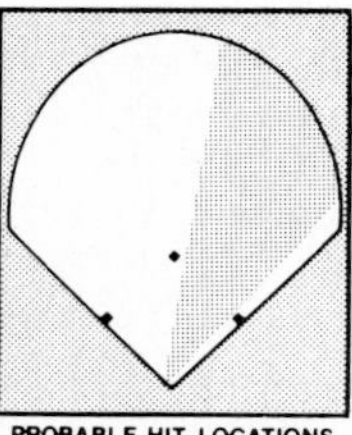
PROBABLE HIT LOCATIONS

HITTING:

If you give Richie Hebner a low fastball in any situation, he will hit it. He was a notorious low ball hitter in his previous stints with the Pirates, as well as with the Mets, and continued the low ball tendency while he was with the Tigers. He bats from a closed, crouched stance deep in the box. Regardless of the speed of the pitch, Hebner can get around on fastballs on the inside part of the plate, but has trouble (particularly against New York's Rich Gossage) with rising fastballs out over the plate or towards the outside corner. He is a dead pull hitter who tries to pull most pitches thrown to him, and would probably be more effective if he went with the pitch. Playing, however in the friendly confines of Tiger Stadium, Hebner often tried to reach the right field seats with pitches he simply could not handle.

He is better than average in clutch situations because he does not "bail out" against curveballing lefthanded pitchers.

Lefthanded pitchers should try and keep their curves low and away, and their fastballs up. Righthanders can use low sliders in on his hands, and fastballs that tail away from him. Despite having overall success with Hebner, pitchers will often find that they cannot get him out with any one particular pitch consistently. Hebner is a streak hitter, and when hot, seems to be able to get a piece of almost anything.

BASERUNNING:

Hebner does not have good speed and is less than average at going from first to third, stretching base hits, or breaking up double plays. Unlike some of the more aggressive players, when Hebner drills a long ball into the right-center field gap, he will tend to watch it, rather than run all-out from home plate, and he usually winds up with a double instead of a triple. He is no threat to steal.

FIELDING:

Hebner has played third and first, but at both spots, he has limited range. He is probably better suited to playing first base because his arm is not as good as it should be for that position. He was acquired by the Pirates who need a veteran pinch-hitter, and he will most likely serve in that role in 1983.

OVERALL:

Hebner can hit when needed, and it is that ability which will allow him to stay in baseball with certain teams in certain situations.

Harwell: "He is living up to his potential as a big leaguer. He is a veteran who can still hit."

LEE LACY
OF, No. 17
RR, 6'1", 175 lbs.
ML Svc: 10 years
Born: 4-10-48 in
Longview, TX

1982 STATISTICS

AVG	G	AB	R	H	2B	3B	HR	RBI	BB	SO	SB
.312	121	359	66	112	16	3	5	31	32	57	40

CAREER STATISTICS

AVG	G	AB	R	H	2B	3B	HR	RBI	BB	SO	SB
.281	936	2546	363	716	116	29	48	252	210	345	116

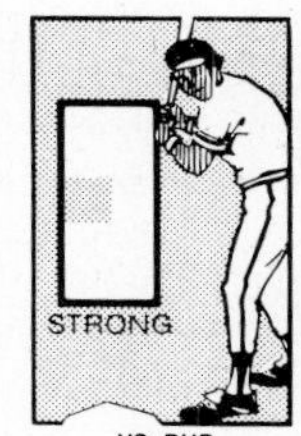

VS. RHP

VS. LHP

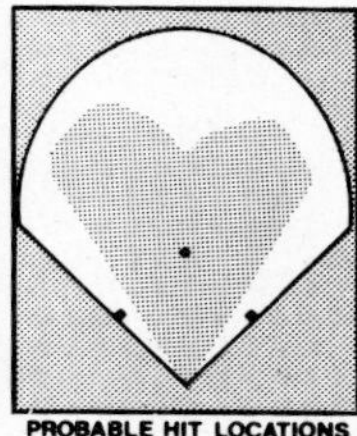
PROBABLE HIT LOCATIONS

HITTING:

Lee Lacy is regarded as a good hitter who does not accrue RBIs. Platooned most of his career, he is exceptionally talented against southpaws. He is blessed with good speed, and legs out many high choppers on artificial turf. Lacy can be a streaky hitter, but when the roller coaster ride is over, he is a .280+ hitter.

In 1982, he became more consistent and as a result, showed more offensive strengths than he showed as a platoon player. Opposing teams can expect line drives and occasional power from Lacy. They can also do well pitching him inside. Lacy is a spray hitter, but in recent seasons, has pulled the ball more.

BASERUNNING:

Lacy has emerged as one of the game's best baserunners. He gets down the line well and always has. In recent seasons, he has become a basestealing threat and he is a daring runner on the bases. He takes the extra base consistently.

FIELDING:

In the past, Lacy was tabbed a below average fielder. Maybe years ago that was correct, but he has become at least an average fielder and his speed has helped him become above average at times. His position? Pure versatility. He can play all 3 outfield positions and third base. His arm is above average, but not always accurate.

OVERALL:

Big plus to ball club. There aren't many non-regulars in the big leagues who can do all the jobs that Lacy can do. Unhappy when he is not playing which is a natural reaction.

McCarver: "Lee Lacy may be the best utility player in the game. He has a ton of ability and plays hard. It's truly amazing that his play is consistent while his playing time is not."

Kiner: "He is an outstanding pinch-hitter against lefthanders and though he should be platooned, is above average in all ways."

BILL MADLOCK
INF, No. 5
RR, 5'11", 190 lbs.
ML Svc: 9 years
Born: 1-12-51 in Memphis, TN

1982 STATISTICS

AVG	G	AB	R	H	2B	3B	HR	RBI	BB	SO	SB
.319	154	568	92	181	33	3	19	95	48	39	18

CAREER STATISTICS

AVG	G	AB	R	H	2B	3B	HR	RBI	BB	SO	SB
.316	1210	4439	646	1404	249	33	108	575	417	311	151

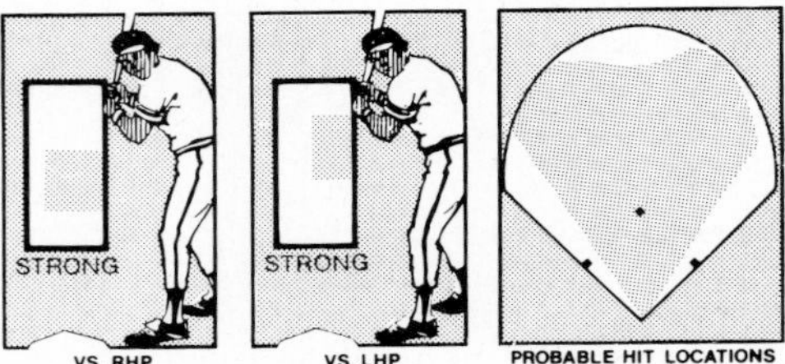

HITTING:

Bill Madlock has been described by many baseball scouts as a "pure" hitter. He is a consistent .300-plus hitter who likes the ball up, but there really isn't one type of pitch that he can't handle. Equally tough against right and lefthanded pitching, he hits to all fields and has power enough to hit 15 or more home runs each year. He is always high up in production of two-base hits.

Madlock seems to get better in the second half of the season and many people believe that it's because he gets to know the new pitchers in the league better.

He is a good hit-and-run man and will surprise a team and bunt for a hit. Madlock is a tough hitter with two out and runners in scoring position. Prefers to bat third in lineup--that's the spot he batted in when he won 3 National League batting championships.

BASERUNNING:

His speed is deceptive. Madlock doesn't appear to have good speed running to first base, but he has above average speed on the bases. He can steal and can take the extra base. He is a very knowledgeable baserunner.

FIELDING:

Not a Gold Glove third baseman, but Madlock is still well above average. His arm is not strong, but it is very accurate. He charges bunts well, has good range, especially to his left. Madlock can also play first base when necessary.

OVERALL:

Madlock was named team captain for 1983, replacing Willie Stargell. He is well respected by his teammates and by manager Chuck Tanner for whom Madlock handles the overall defense.

Coleman: "Madlock is one of the game's best offensive players. He can run and hit with the best of them. He is certainly the 'Captain' of his team."

Kiner: "Bill has become a leader with his consistent defensive play and excellent hitting. He is a real threat to add on to his 3 batting titles. I consider him one of the top 5 hitters in the game."

McCarver: "His short compact stroke is a study in excellence. Reminds me of Dusty Baker as far as compactness of his swing. There is no consistent way of getting him out. Bill is smart as a fox in the box."

LEE MAZZILLI
OF, No. 24
SR, 6'1", 180 lbs.
ML Svc: 7 years
Born: 3-25-55 in Brooklyn, NY

1982 STATISTICS

AVG	G	AB	R	H	2B	3B	HR	RBI	BB	SO	SB
.251	95	323	43	81	10	0	10	34	43	41	13

CAREER STATISTICS

AVG	G	AB	R	H	2B	3B	HR	RBI	BB	SO	SB
.267	831	2978	392	795	143	21	71	337	419	424	152

VS. RHP

VS. LHP

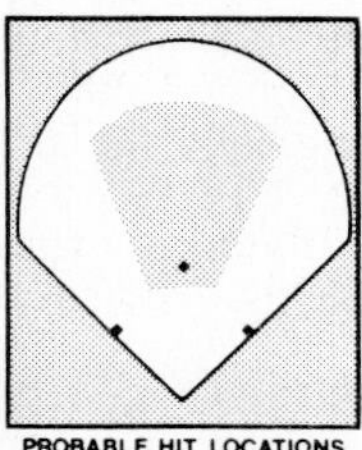
PROBABLE HIT LOCATIONS

HITTING:

Lee Mazzilli is switching leagues and teams as frequently as he switch-hits at the plate. In either league and from either side of the plate, Mazzilli bats straight up, feet parallel to the plate. He is a better hitter, with more power, batting lefthanded. When he does bat lefty, pitchers can get him out by using fastballs up and away and sliders down and in. He has trouble with off-speed pitches, but when he does not try for the long ball, can time a change-up and drop it somewhere for a hit. Batting righthanded, he is pitched low and away. Either way, he hits the fastball up and over the plate.

He is a straightaway hitter, but occasionally shows signs of power from either side of the plate, and that power can be down either foul line or in the alleys.

BASERUNNING:

Mazzilli has good speed and good baseball instincts. He knows when and how to steal, and when and how to slide (feet first). He knows when to gamble on the basepaths, and when to try and score. He gets a good jump when stealing and when leaving any base on a hit to the outfield. He can beat out drag bunts, batting lefty, because he still retains enough speed to outrun a first baseman or pitcher to the bag.

FIELDING:

Mazzilli was at home in center field with the Mets, unhappy when moved to right with the Mets, completely out of sorts in left field with the Rangers, and somewhat confused at first base with the Yankees. 1982 is a year he wants to forget, because virtually all of his skills were tarnished, primarily because of playing for three teams, and because of ruptured tendons in his hand and other injuries. His speed gives him the necessary range to play center field, but his throwing arm, somewhat suspect, left him vulnerable while with Texas last year.

OVERALL:

Robinson: "He was the on the disabled list for a while in Texas, and never seemed happy there anyway. His situation may improve now that he's back in the National League, but it remains to be seen if he can make it back to the status he had with the Mets."

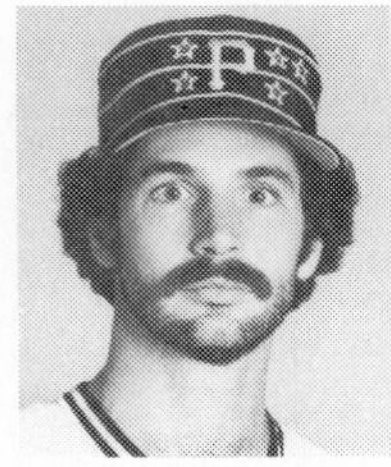

LARRY McWILLIAMS
LHP, No. 49
LL, 6'5", 175 lbs.
ML Svc: 1 year
Born: 2-10-54 in Wichita, KS

PITCHING:

McWilliams' biggest asset is his ability to both start and relieve. He discarded a full windup delivery in 1981, and after Atlanta traded him to Pittsburgh in May 1982, he developed into an effective pitcher. His quick no-windup motion is deceiving and makes his fastball appear faster. It is actually only about 86-88 MPH. He changes speeds well, and has good control. He throws a good forkball; it is the pitch that initially kept him in the majors. He mixes his pitches very well. His slider dives out of the strike zone to righthanded hitters.

His ability to hit the corners last season has made him an improved pitcher. McWilliams is not overpowering, but fools batters with his style. He is intent on not wasting time on the mound. Larry is very tough on lefthanded hitters, and can pitch often.

FIELDING, HITTING, BASERUNNING:

He gets a good rating in every category. He fields his position well. McWilliams can hold runners close to the bag. He makes contact with the bat, and is an excellent bunter. He can bunt for a hit and advance the runners. His baserunning is well above average for a pitcher.

OVERALL:

McWilliams' failure in the Atlanta organization has not dampened his confidence. He could be the type of pitcher who will develop into a big winner later in his career. The change of scenery from Atlanta to Pittsburgh was something that McWilliams seemed to need and the Pirates figure to benefit.

Coleman: "Larry is a decent pitcher who can do well against lefthanded hitting teams. The forkball is his best pitch."

McCarver: "His no-windup delivery does not allow a hitter to get ready, and that's good for him because hitters like a pitcher that has a comfortable rhythm, and Larry does not."

Kiner: "McWilliams has had flashes of brilliance, but has lacked consistency. He has done a good job for Pittsburgh, and last season, combined with reliever Gene Garber to stop Pete Rose's 44-game hitting streak."

1982 STATISTICS

W	L	ERA	G	GS	CG	IP	H	R	ER	BB	SO	SV
8	8	3.84	46	20	2	160	158	79	68	44	118	1

CAREER STATISTICS

W	L	ERA	G	GS	CG	IP	H	R	ER	BB	SO	SV
31	28	4.15	110	83	12	527	530	268	243	148	292	1

JIM MORRISON
INF, No. 2
RR, 5'11", 178 lbs.
ML Svc: 5 years
Born: 9-23-52 in
Pensacola, FL

1982 STATISTICS

AVG	G	AB	R	H	2B	3B	HR	RBI	BB	SO	SB
.279	44	86	10	24	4	1	4	15	5	14	2

CAREER STATISTICS

AVG	G	AB	R	H	2B	3B	HR	RBI	BB	SO	SB
.261	421	1335	156	349	67	3	46	152	77	187	26

VS. RHP

VS. LHP

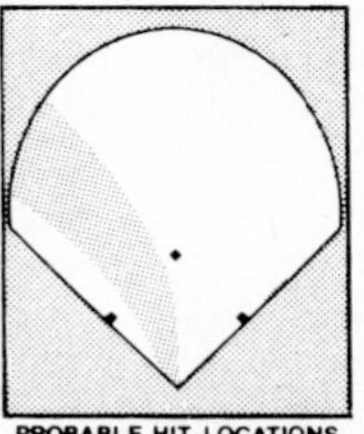
PROBABLE HIT LOCATIONS

HITTING:

Jim Morrison is a pull hitter with some power. Off-speed pitches give him trouble. He is a good hitter coming off the bench. Morrison isn't the type to become overanxious--he makes the pitcher throw strikes. His biggest asset is that he is an improving player. He was not much of a hitter with Philadelphia several years ago, but developed with the Chicago White Sox. His role with the Pirates is mainly as a back up infielder, and he has enough smarts to stay sharp as a hitter by working hard in pre-game practice. Morrison is an excellent bunter, and can move up the runners.

BASERUNNING:

Morrison has only fair speed and he is no threat to steal a base. He is a smart baserunner, however, and won't be caught off a base or caught making the mistake of foolishly trying for the extra base.

FIELDING:

Morrison plays several positions, but is not above average at any one of them. His best position is probably third base. He has played first and second base, and Manager Chuck Tanner used him in left field in 1982. His arm is erratic, and he will probably only see action as a back up infielder.

OVERALL:

A good extra man on a club, Morrison knows his job and is a non-complainer. He has a good knowledge of the game and is valuable as a late-inning pinch-hitter.

McCarver: "He appears awkward in the field sometimes, though he seems to try hard enough. I don't think he was trained properly on the basepaths."

Coleman: "Morrison can fill the bill for a few weeks; a team needs that."

PAUL MOSKAU
RHP, No. 41
RR, 6'2", 205 lbs.
ML Svc: 6 years
Born: 12-20-53 in St. Joseph, MO

PITCHING:

After an exceptionally rapid rise through the Cincinnati farm system, Paul Moskau spent almost three years toiling for the Reds. He joined the Pirates last season but injuries plagued him and he spent much of his time on the disabled list.

Moskau relies almost entirely on his above average fastball. Clocked up to 90 MPH, the fastball is not only Moskau's bread-and-butter pitch, it is almost his complete menu. His curve is only average and he seldom has success throwing either a slider or a change. This is unfortunate because it gives hitters the luxury of simply sitting back and waiting for the inevitable fastball. What's worse is the fact that Moskau has a tendency to serve his fastball high--right where hitters relish it most.

Occasionally Paul Moskau can overpower a team when his control is extra fine and his fastball has that extra bit of zip. As hitters learn to wait him out, however, he loses his effectiveness. When he falls behind in the count, he's never been able to rely on anything but his fastball. Obviously, a one-pitch pitcher can have a lot of trouble in the majors, especially when that pitch is a high fastball that has to be a strike. Moskau seems to realize this and he tends to lose his poise on the mound and to visibly lack confidence.

FIELDING, HITTING, BASERUNNING:

Moskau's move to first is very quick and he can catch opposing baserunners napping. He's also quick off the mound fielding bunts and he covers his position more than adequately. Paul's a good athelete and a better than average hitter for a pitcher. He has average ability as a bunter and runs the bases with average speed.

OVERALL:

Moskau has a major league fastball but has to develop another pitch if he is to become an effective major league performer.

McCarver: "Paul's inability to get his breaking pitches over the plate allows rival hitters to sit and wait for his fastball."

Coleman: "Moskau looked like a good young pitcher three years ago but he seems to have gone backwards rather than improved since then."

1982 STATISTICS

W	L	ERA	G	GS	CG	IP	H	R	ER	BB	SO	SV
1	3	4.37	13	5	0	35	43	21	17	8	15	0

CAREER STATISTICS

W	L	ERA	G	GS	CG	IP	H	R	ER	BB	SO	SV
29	25	4.08	140	84	7	602	606	290	273	229	358	5

HITTING:

Steve Nicosia has developed into a good opposite field hitter. He has problems with timing when he's hitting because he doesn't play very often as the No. 2 catcher. He is a good bunter, moving runners up a base, but is no threat to bunt for a base hit because he lacks speed. Pitchers will try to throw him breaking balls away and fastballs inside.

He hits well against class pitchers and has a better than .300 average against Steve Carlton. Starts mostly against lefthanded pitchers, but is capable of producing big hits against righthanders. Still young enough to become a No. 1 catcher, and capable of being a consistent .275 plus hitter.

BASERUNNING:

Nicosia recognizes his limitations on the bases and is rarely is thrown out trying for extra base. He is a hard driving runner who is capable and eager to break up double plays. No threat to steal a base.

FIELDING:

Nicosia's arm is above average, and his reflexes behind the plate are above average as well. He does a fine job handling pitchers whose control is poor. He digs balls out of the dirt, comes out of his crouch quickly, and has a quick release which helps him cut down basestealers. Manager Chuck Tanner says Nicosia is an excellent handler of pitchers. He noted that as a rookie in 1979, Nicosia started four World Series games against Baltimore.

STEVE NICOSIA
C, No. 16
RR, 5'10", 185 lbs.
ML Svc: 4 years
Born: 8-6-55 in Paterson, NJ

1982 STATISTICS

AVG	G	AB	R	H	2B	3B	HR	RBI	BB	SO	SB
.280	39	100	6	28	3	0	1	7	11	13	0

CAREER STATISTICS

AVG	G	AB	R	H	2B	3B	HR	RBI	BB	SO	SB
.250	226	641	65	160	37	1	8	60	67	56	3

VS. RHP

VS. LHP

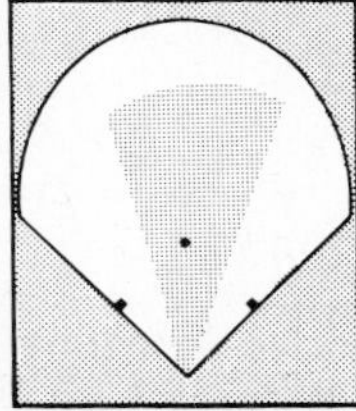
PROBABLE HIT LOCATIONS

OVERALL:

Good team man. No trouble to manager although Nicosia is on record that he wants to become a No. 1 catcher--with some big league team. Will be in big leagues a long time because there are few, if any, second-string catchers better than he is.

McCarver: "He does a nice job, and if given the chance, could probably surprise a lot of people."

Coleman: "He's a lunging-type of hitter, not above average in any department."

DAVE PARKER
OF, No. 39
LR, 6'5", 230 lbs.
ML Svc: 9 years
Born: 6-9-51 in
Jackson, MS

1982 STATISTICS

AVG	G	AB	R	H	2B	3B	HR	RBI	BB	SO	SB
.270	73	244	41	66	19	3	6	29	22	45	7

CAREER STATISTICS

AVG	G	AB	R	H	2B	3B	HR	RBI	BB	SO	SB
.310	1157	4296	660	1325	267	58	154	689	318	688	111

VS. RHP

VS. LHP

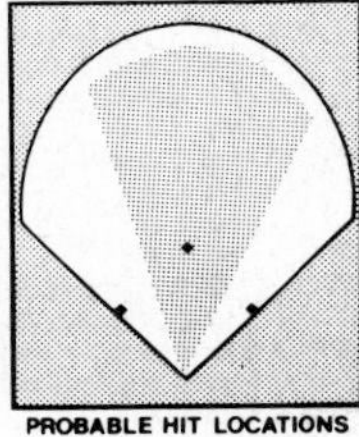
PROBABLE HIT LOCATIONS

HITTING:

There is little question that Parker is one of the best hitters in baseball--that is, when he is healthy. His problems in recent seasons have been physical. He hasn't had an injury-free season since 1978 when he won his second batting title. Reporting on a healthy Parker is easy. He is a good fastball hitter and he has line drive power to all fields. He likes the ball away and has had problems with fastballs up. Off-speed pitches he handles exceptionally well.

Dave Parker will be 31 years old in June and has a history of weight problems. Being so tall, his extra poundage seems to prevent him from getting around on fastballs. Not one to accept instruction from coaches, he prefers to swing his own way out of a slump. He is difficult to pinpoint as a hitter because of various injuries that have limited his ability. Once a great hitter, he's now an average hitter, capable of returning to a peak when he won two National League batting titles.

BASERUNNING:

Well above average in all phases. Gets away from the plate quickly. Takes the extra base. Can steal bases with consistency. Effective at breaking up double plays because he is big and strong. His slides are hard, but clean.

FIELDING:

Fair would be the best way to describe Parker's defense. Once again, we're talking of the Parker who has been injured in recent seasons. When he is healthy, he is a good fielder with a strong, but not always accurate, arm. Seems to have problems with stadium lights at night games.

OVERALL:

There are two Dave Parkers. The healthy one is a near superstar. The aching one has become a slightly above average player. He insists he hasn't lost his desire which could mean he will return to near peak form in 1983.

Coleman: "One of the best--a superstar. Injuries have hobbled him but when he is in top form with his weight under control, he is a great player with great desire."

Kiner: "Even with his league leadership in hitting, I don't really think that Parker has reached his full potential as a home run hitter. Top star."

TONY PENA
C, No. 6
RR, 6'0", 175 lbs.
ML Svc: 2 years
Born: 11-20-57 in
Montecristi, DR

1982 STATISTICS

AVG	G	AB	R	H	2B	3B	HR	RBI	BB	SO	SB
.296	138	497	53	147	28	4	11	63	17	57	2

CAREER STATISTICS

AVG	G	AB	R	H	2B	3B	HR	RBI	BB	SO	SB
.301	212	728	70	219	38	6	13	81	25	84	3

VS. RHP

VS. LHP

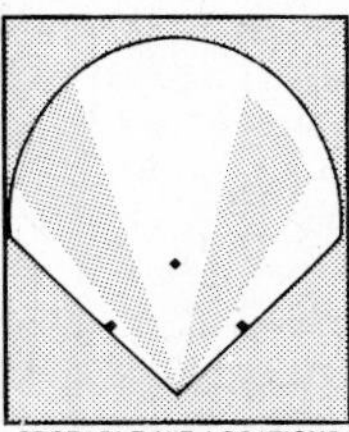
PROBABLE HIT LOCATIONS

HITTING:

Tony Pena is one of the best young hitters in the game. When he is hot, he can handle almost any type of pitch. He has been nicknamed "Boom Boom" because he occasionally tries to hit the ball off the face of the earth. He is an aggressive hitter, and has a tendency to hit in streaks. When he slumps, he chases bad breaking pitches. He likes fastballs out over the plate. Pena sometimes has problems with good fastballs, especially inside and low. He has good power to left and left-center fields.

Pena is very efficient at going with the pitch. He hits the ball hard to the opposite field, but doesn't have home run power in that area. Pena is the type who will learn quickly and improve in all facets of the hitting game. In two full seasons, he is only a shade under Gary Carter as a hitter and he figures to hit over .290 with consistency.

Pena is also an excellent hitter with two out and runners on base.

BASERUNNING:

His speed is slightly above average, and it won't get any better because he is a catcher. He doesn't take a big lead off first base and is not a threat to steal any base. However, he is capable of taking extra bases, going from first to third on singles and stretching singles into doubles.

FIELDING:

Pena rates well above average in almost all areas. He has a strong arm, and an extremely quick release. He can throw from one knee better that many can on two feet. He handles pitches in the dirt very well because he sits lower than any other catcher. Pena is also a good handler of pitchers despite his limited experience. He is very durable, and doesn't allow bruises on his fingers and hands to keep him out of the lineup.

He is an extremely daring thrower, and will attempt pick-offs at any base during any inning of the ball game. He is a young catcher who is still learning, and though he called a few sub-par games last season, is expected to do better in 1983.

OVERALL:

The nearly unanimous decision is that Pena has unlimited potential. His enthusiam is always at a high level. He is a tough competitor, and loves the challenge of facing the best pitchers in the game, and his attitude is first-class in all areas.

Kiner: "Pena could become the National League's top catcher in a very short time."

Coleman: "He has a great arm and release but is somewhat scatter-armed at times--he just needs to continue his progress to become one of the game's better players."

McCarver: "Tony is one of the finest young prospects as a catcher that I have seen. He attacks the ball when he is both throwing and hitting. He is quick as a cat, and really sucks up low balls. Excellent potential."

JOHNNY RAY
INF, No. 3
SR, 5'11", 170 lbs.
ML Svc: 1 year plus
Born: 3-1-57 in
Chouteau, OK

1982 STATISTICS

AVG	G	AB	R	H	2B	3B	HR	RBI	BB	SO	SB
.281	162	647	79	182	30	7	7	63	36	34	16

CAREER STATISTICS

AVG	G	AB	R	H	2B	3B	HR	RBI	BB	SO	SB
.276	193	749	89	207	71	7	7	69	42	43	16

VS. RHP

VS. LHP

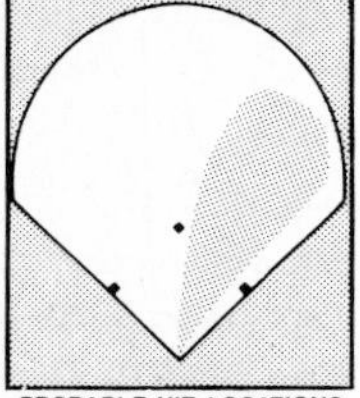
PROBABLE HIT LOCATIONS

HITTING:

Johnny Ray is a switch-hitter but he hits much better from the left side of the plate. He is an excellent contact hitter and had one of the best strikeout per at-bat ratios in big leagues in 1982. From the left side, he has some good power. Ray has little power batting right. He doesn't have any major weaknesses as a hitter, and can handle the low inside pitch, the low outside pitch, and the pitches that are up in the strike zone. He uses the entire field as a hitter.

Although he doesn't hit very well righthanded, he is nonetheless a tough out against any pitcher in clutch situations. He had two big game-winning hits while batting righthanded last season. He has adjusted to batting in the No. 2 spot in the order, and has learned to take more pitches than he would have if he were batting lower in the order. Ray is also a good bunter and can advance the runners.

BASERUNNING:

Ray is an excellent example of a player who utilizes average speed. He gets out of the batter's box quickly. He gets a good jump from first base on steal attempts. Ray has excellent instincts and is rarely thrown out trying to take an extra base.

FIELDING:

Defense was not supposed to be Johnny Ray's strength before the 1982 season. He improved steadily in the field, however, and increased his range as well. He has good hands and is better defensively when playing on artificial turf. His arm, once considered by many to be quite weak, is now rated average.

OVERALL:

Ray has a good baseball mind for such a youngster. He is a good student of the game, and can be taught to improve because he is eager to. This is a very important rookie quality. His future is bright, and he showed himself to be very durable last season by playing in all of his team's games. The last National League rookie to play in every game was Richie Allen with the 1964 Phillies.

Coleman: "So far, Ray is a quality player who had a good first year. He needs some defensive improvements to refine his game."

Kiner: "He has just outstanding potential at second base, needs a little improvement both as a defensive player, and as a righthanded hitter to become an everyday top-flight player."

McCarver: "I am really glad to see a talented guy like Johnny Ray finally get a chance to play in the major leagues. He can only improve, and should be around for a long time."

RICK RHODEN
RHP, No. 29
RR, 6'3", 195 lbs.
ML Svc: 8 years
Born: 5-16-53 in Boynton Beach, FL

PITCHING:

Rick Rhoden is a starting pitcher--period. He is not the type who can relieve and is a good competitor. His fastball is by far his best pitch, and it can bang by a batter at around 90 MPH. Rhoden spots it well and keeps it inside on lefthanded hitters. He will throw an occasional curveball, but really does not have good rotation on it. His slider is his second best pitch, and he has an average change-up. Rhoden does not have as good a motion as he should with his change. He needs a reliable off-speed pitch badly.

When he is behind in the count, the hitter should look for the fastball--he throws it very often. So often in fact, that it is widely believed that he does something to the ball, either scuffs or wets it up.

In 1982, Rhoden had problems with the location of his pitches. He didn't walk an abundance of hitters, but he was behind in the count too often, and it cost him when he had to pitch in a hole. Rhoden can pitch every fifth day--sometimes on the fourth--and always give a creditable account of himself.

When his breaking pitches are effective, he gets a lot of ground ball outs. He is more effective to right-handed hitters--lefthanders find his delivery too readable. He tends to tire in late innings, but could become stronger in future seasons as he recovers more completely from his 1979 shoulder surgery.

FIELDING, HITTING, BASERUNNING:

Rhoden is a good fielder and one of the very best hitting pitchers in the league. He has home run power. On the bases, he is very slow. As a youngster, he was a victim of osteomyelitis which affected his left knee, and as a result, one leg is now shorter than the other. His handicap does not affect him, however, in covering the first base bag or on grounders hit to the right side of the mound.

OVERALL:

He is a tough competitor. Rhoden needs exceptionally good defense behind him because he makes the hitters hit balls on the ground so often. He is capable of winning 16 games a season. Since his shoulder operation, he has come back and pitched regularly, if not always successfully, indicating that he is now healthy.

Kiner: "Rhoden has a professional approach to pitching. Because his fastball sinks, he gets few fly balls. Has an outstanding record in April."

McCarver: "Incredible courage--so many guys would have given up a long time ago. Nonetheless, he's got to have a better breaking ball. If these big league hitters can sit on the fastball all the time, they'll hit you hard and often. It's awfully tough just to blow them away consistently."

1982 STATISTICS

W	L	ERA	G	GS	CG	IP	H	R	ER	BB	SO	SV
11	14	4.14	35	35	6	231	239	115	106	70	128	0

CAREER STATISTICS

W	L	ERA	G	GS	CG	IP	H	R	ER	BB	SO	SV
69	48	3.66	195	167	33	1169	1171	526	476	368	601	0

DON ROBINSON
RHP, No. 43
RR, 6'4", 231 lbs.
ML Svc: 5 years
Born: 6-8-57 in Ashland, KY

PITCHING:

Don Robinson is basically a starting pitcher, but when he relieved in a few games last season, he was pretty effective. He is a power pitcher with good stamina. Robinson doesn't lose much off his fastball in the late innings. His curveball breaks quickly, and is above average, though his control has been erratic. Sometimes, his curveball will land in the dirt, and because of this, very attentive baserunners can steal on him.

He has pitched several games in which he has given up less than four walks, but occasional wildness has also given him games where he has walked more than six batters.

Robinson has had three shoulder operations and the last one was in October 1981. He made a big comeback in 1982 and showed that he hadn't lost any velocity on his fastball. His 92 MPH fastball is the hardest-thrown on the Pirate's staff.

He jerks the ball a bit in his delivery, but this is tough to pick up. He is the type that will challenge the long ball hitters late in the game, and doesn't let a loss affect his performance the next time out.

FIELDING, HITTING, BASERUNNING:

Robinson is one of the best hitting pitchers in the National League. He has good power and makes solid contact. He fields his position well, has quick feet and holds runners close to the bases. He is a good baserunner, but his speed is slightly below average. He is the type who can help himself in all areas of the game.

OVERALL:

Robinson is an outstanding competitor. His manager, Chuck Tanner, seems to stick with him longer in late innings than any other Pirate starter. He is a non-complainer--to a fault. He rarely tells the club trainer or Tanner when he is aching physically. Potential to be a big winner.

Kiner: "When healthy, he is one of the top pitchers in the game. He's got a power curveball and can also help himself with his bat."

McCarver: "Don has to steer clear of further body damage in order to be the consistent winner I think that he can be. It's tough for Pirate starters to win 20 games for Tanner because he so often goes to his bullpen."

1982 STATISTICS

W	L	ERA	G	GS	CG	IP	H	R	ER	BB	SO	SV
15	13	4.28	38	30	6	227	213	123	108	103	165	0

CAREER STATISTICS

W	L	ERA	G	GS	CG	IP	H	R	ER	BB	SO	SV
44	40	3.99	537	113	22	814	800	396	361	280	516	4

ENRIQUE ROMO
RHP, No. 15
RR, 5'11", 185 lbs.
ML Svc: 6 years
Born: 7-15-47 in
Santa Rosalia, MX

PITCHING:

Enrique Romo has been utilized as both a long reliever and a late inning man, having greater success in the former role. He has a deceptive motion which fools hitters, and is capable of throwing the ball from many angles. His most effective pitch is the screwball, although on some occasions his fastball comes to life enough to make his breaking pitches even more effective.

Romo has a temper which occasionally gets him into trouble. If he feels that umpires are giving him bad calls, he can lose his effectiveness. He pitches equally well against both right and lefthanded hitters and is very durable. He will use a brushback pitch when it serves a purpose. Inconsistency is his biggest drawback.

FIELDING, HITTING, BASERUNNING:

Romo may be the most underrated pitcher in the National League in all 3 categories. He is an excellent fielder. He will charge bunts, covers first base well and has all-around quickness. In his role as a middle-inning reliever, he doesn't get to bat much, but he is one of the better hitters and baserunners in the league.

OVERALL:

His value to the Pirates often is overlooked because middle-inning relievers rarely get a chance to excel. He won nine games in 1982 which shows he can get the job done when he is right. His moody temperament often works against him.

McCarver: "Enrique really jumps at the hitter. He was one of the reasons the Pirates were World Champs in 1979. His confidence is probably at a low ebb right now. He is an effective reliever and could probably help a pennant contender in September."

Kiner: "Romo has got to be one of the slowest working pitchers in the history of baselball. He's so hard to play behind because he throws so many pitches to each batter, working them up to 3-2 and 2-2. His wild delivery--he just throws from everywhere-- and his screwball are his strongest assets."

1982 STATISTICS

W	L	ERA	G	GS	CG	IP	H	R	ER	BB	SO	SV
9	3	4.36	45	0	0	87	81	43	42	36	58	1

CAREER STATISTICS

W	L	ERA	G	GS	CG	IP	H	R	ER	BB	SO	SV
44	33	3.45	350	3	0	603	548	259	231	203	436	52

MANNY SARMIENTO
RHP, No. 38
RR, 5'11", 170 bls.
ML Svc: 4 years
Born: 2-2-56 in Cagua, VEN

PITCHING:

Whether it's starting, long relief or short relief, Manny Sarmiento is a versatile pitcher. He was effective in all three roles last season. Two recent developments have made Sarmiento an improved pitcher. A newly acquired forkball and 30 extra pounds of meat (he brought his weight up from 165 to 195). He has an above average fastball and a late breaking slider to round out his assortment of pitches. The latter is a difficult pitch to reach and the former is masked nicely by his herky-jerky motion with flash. More effective against righthanded batters, he is an eager worker and a team man. He seems to have benefitted from the minors after being jettisoned by Seattle a few years ago.

FIELDING, HITTING, BASERUNNING:

Sarmiento is an above average fielder. He is especially good at fielding bunts and covering the first base bag on grounders hit to the right side of the mound. As a hitter, he makes contact but has no power. A good baserunner with above average speed.

OVERALL:

Sarmiento has a good temperament which is important because of his role in manager Chuck Tanner's plans. He says he never had confidence when he pitched with Cincinnati, but he sure has it now.

Kiner: "Sarmiento's career has had high and low spots with signs of good ability . . . but there has been no consistency. He is a Pirate reclamation project."

Coleman: "When he was in the minors, he learned a new pitch--a hard forkball or split-fingered fastball. He has the chance to be a decent pitcher."

McCarver: "When I faced both pitchers, Mario Soto and Manny Sarmiento, it was Sarmiento who impressed me more. I couldn't believe that Cincinnati would release him. Since a basic element of hitting is establishing a rhythm at the plate, Sarmiento's breaking slider is especially tough to pick up and hit with proficiency."

1982 STATISTICS

W	L	ERA	G	GS	CG	IP	H	R	ER	BB	SO	SV
9	4	3.39	35	17	4	165	153	69	62	46	81	1

CAREER STATISTICS

W	L	ERA	G	GS	CG	IP	H	R	ER	BB	SO	SV
23	17	3.58	176	22	4	430	387	189	171	136	234	8

ROD SCURRY
LHP, No. 19
LL, 6'2", 180 lbs.
ML Svc: 3 years
Born: 3-17-56 in
Sacramento, CA

PITCHING:

For sheer pitching equipment--the fastball and curve--Rod Scurry rates with the best in baseball. He developed into an outstanding short relief man in 1982. He wasn't only effective against lefthanded batters; he handled the righthanded hitters as well. Occasionally, he'd turn in a poor performance, but he always showed the ability to rebound.

As a starter early in the 1981 season, Scurry didn't seem to concentrate on every hitter. His stuff is more effective over a short period of time. He responded positively to his role as a late innings man. He has an awesome curveball, it is hard and has a big break. Occasionally, he'll let up on it, and then it tends to flatten out. If he develops an effective change-up, he'll be a more effective hurler. When he's behind in the count, the hitter will see the fastball, but Scurry is always experimenting with doing different things with his curve.

FIELDING, HITTING, BASERUNNING:

Scurry's fielding is average. He covers the first base bag very well, but doesn't always keep runners close to the base. His high kick motion gives runners an extra chance to steal, but he needs it because it makes his pitching effective. As a hitter, he has a smooth swing and can hit "mistakes."

OVERALL:

If Scurry picks up where he left off last season, he will soon rank among the top relievers in the big leagues. He needs to become more consistent with his control. Occasionally, he has trouble throwing strikes with consistency. When his control is good, he is almost unhittable.

Coleman: "Scurry has a great arm and seems to be gaining more confidence. He can get a strikeout when you need it."

Kiner: "He has a wicked curve and the control to use it on any pitch. He combines with Tekulve to give Pittsburgh an outstanding lefty-righty relief duo."

McCarver: "Rod will go far as his control will carry him. Sometimes he experiments a bit too much with it--changing speeds instead of throwing the hard, quality curve. Scurry is young and strong and has little chance of burn-out."

1982 STATISTICS

W	L	ERA	G	GS	CG	IP	H	R	ER	BB	SO	SV
4	5	1.74	76	0	0	104	79	26	20	64	95	14

CAREER STATISTICS

W	L	ERA	G	GS	CG	IP	H	R	ER	BB	SO	SV
8	12	2.50	123	7	0	216	176	71	60	121	188	21

JIMMY SMITH
INF, No. 11
RR, 6'3", 185 lbs.
ML Svc: 1 year
Born: 9-8-54 in
Santa Monica, CA

1982 STATISTICS

AVG	G	AB	R	H	2B	3B	HR	RBI	BB	SO	SB
.238	42	42	5	10	2	1	0	4	5	7	0

CAREER STATISTICS

AVG	G	AB	R	H	2B	3B	HR	RBI	BB	SO	SB
.238	42	42	5	10	2	1	0	4	5	7	0

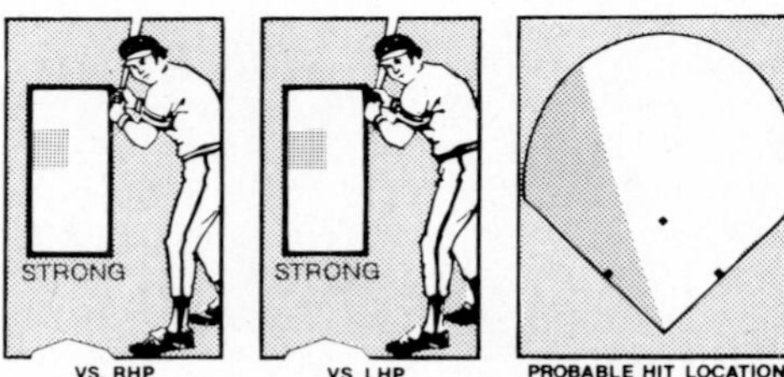

HITTING:

Jimmy Smith seems to be the personification of that familiar baseball label, "Good field, No hit." After more than six seasons in the minors, he finally got his chance to play in the majors last season. Since he had never hit that well in the minors, his lack of success with the bat shouldn't have surprised that many people.

Smith can usually make contact with a high outside fastball and he can also get around on a hanging curve. Everything else seems to give him trouble. Righthanded pitchers can take the bat out of his hands with a combination of good inside fastballs and curves away. Southpaws who can keep the ball down also have no trouble with Smith.

Jimmy bunts fairly well and can be used in sacrifice situations. All in all, however, his lack of ability with the bat severely limits his value to a major league club.

BASERUNNING:

Smith is not exceptionally fast out of the box, nor does he have outstanding speed on the basepaths. The few times he was on base this season, he failed to display good baserunning instincts. He consistently neglected to get a good jump and was doubled off base too often in 1982. At best he's an average baserunner and no threat to steal or try for an extra base.

FIELDING:

Smith is rated an above average fielder. His arm is strong enough for him to make the plays from deep in the hole at short. He also has better than average range as a shortstop and is considered to be a bit better going to his left than his right. He has good hands and can turn the double play both at short and at second. He's played occasionally at third and has filled in adequately, although he's definitely most comfortable at shortstop.

OVERALL:

Jimmy's chief value is as a defensive utility player. His lack of hitting ability is a major liability and has hindered his career even in the minors.

Coleman: "Smith won the Silver Glove award as the best fielding shortstop in the minors. He needs a chance to play more in order to find out whether or not he can help a big league ballclub."

KENT TEKULVE
RHP, No. 27
RR, 6'4", 175 lbs.
ML Svc: 8 years
Born: 3-5-47 in
Cincinnati, OH

PITCHING:

Kent Tekulve is one of the most durable late-inning relief pitchers in the game. His tall and pencil-like stature makes him appear fragile, but opposing hitters will tell you that's not true. He relieves in 80+ games a year. He throws sidearm and submarine style and on rare occasions throws from three-quarters.

Tekulve is a sinker-slider pitcher, and his best pitch is the fastball that sinks. It is his bread-and-butter pitch. He rarely throws sliders in key situations. Tekulve has a tendency to ignore a baserunner with two out, giving the runner a chance to steal a base. He is particularly effective against righthanded batters. During the 1982 season, in particular, he had problems with lefthanders and was constantly behind, them issuing twice as many walks to lefthanded batters than to righthanders. He doesn't allow one or two bad relief performances to get him down. The brushback pitch is not his style.

FIELDING, HITTING, BASERUNNING:

His fielding is adequate, hitting is atrocious and he gets on base so rarely it is difficult to rate his baserunning ability.

OVERALL:

Tekulve thrives on pressure situations. He rarely has any physical ailments and he is at his best when he is used about four times a week. His control suffers when he doesn't pitch for four or five days. He is not a strikeout reliever, but gets many ground ball outs.

McCarver: "An effective sinker-slider pitcher is not as much in vogue today as it once was. Today the special pitch is 'in.' Teke is an exception to that. He has incredible control for a guy with stuff so good."

Kiner: "He has the ideal approach to a tough job. With his odd delivery, he can make his fastball sink at all times. He makes the majority of batters hit the ball on the ground."

1982 STATISTICS

W	L	ERA	G	GS	CG	IP	H	R	ER	BB	SO	SV
12	8	2.87	85	0	0	129	113	47	41	46	66	20

CAREER STATISTICS

W	L	ERA	G	GS	CG	IP	H	R	ER	BB	SO	SV
60	47	2.75	571	0	0	827	729	292	253	293	460	127

GENE TENACE
C, No. 18
RR, 6'0", 190 lbs.
ML Svc: 13 years
Born: 10-10-46 in Russelton, PA

HITTING:

From his closed stance, Gene Tenace looks for pitches up in the strike zone that he can pull. He is basically a guess hitter, but is dangerous when he gets a fastball. Tenace is used almost exclusively these days against lefthanded pitchers, who should try to pitch him down and change speeds. Tenace has trouble with curveballs from righthanders.

He has an extremely good eye and draws a lot of walks per times at-bat, but sometimes he is too selective and unaggressive and takes a lot of borderline pitches he should be swinging at. But a pitcher should not make a mistake--he is one of the best mistake shooters in the league.

1982 STATISTICS

AVG	G	AB	R	H	2B	3B	HR	RBI	BB	SO	SB
.258	66	124	18	32	9	0	7	18	36	31	1

CAREER STATISTICS

AVG	G	AB	R	H	2B	3B	HR	RBI	BB	SO	SB
.242	1502	4328	644	1049	174	20	201	668	972	981	36

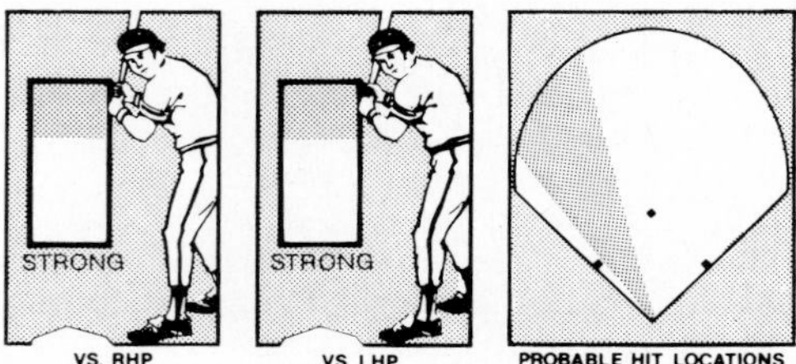

BASERUNNING:

Tenace has average to slightly below average speed for a catcher, but is an intelligent runner and a tough man at breaking up the double play. He is not, however, a basestealing threat.

FIELDING:

Tenace makes up for an average arm with his knowledge of opposing hitters' strengths and weaknesses. Pitchers respect that knowledge and rarely shake him off. He gets the ball away quickly on steal attempts, and moves out fast on bunts. Basically, though, he has been used as a back up catcher, whose best position is probably first base.

OVERALL:

McCarver: "A hard-nosed pro who may manage one of these big league clubs someday. He serves his role as a back up first baseman and part-time catcher well. He can be a team leader. Gene could be a more aggresive hitter, but is certainly formidable in the role he plays.

Coleman: "Tenace is a home run threat--especially against lefthanders."

JASON THOMPSON
INF, No. 30
LL, 6'3", 210 lbs.
ML Svc: 7 years
Born: 7-6-54 in Hollywood, CA

1982 STATISTICS

AVG	G	AB	R	H	2B	3B	HR	RBI	BB	SO	SB
.284	156	550	87	156	32	0	31	101	101	107	1

CAREER STATISTICS

AVG	G	AB	R	H	2B	3B	HR	RBI	BB	SO	SB
.266	959	3289	461	874	141	10	161	567	528	591	7

VS. RHP

VS. LHP

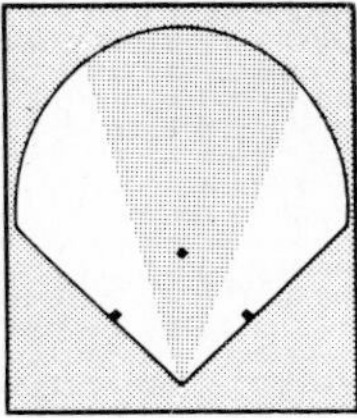
PROBABLE HIT LOCATIONS

HITTING:

Jason Thompson is a bona-fide long ball hitter who has power to all fields. Possessed with an excellent knowledge of the strike zone, Thompson receives 100 or more free passes per season. He strikes out frequently, but don't expect to fool him with the same sequencing on his next at-bat. Pitch him up and in; righthanders can try low inside curveballs with a little prayer. He relishes the low fastball but can be fooled by change-ups. He has a unique loop in his swing and appears to push the ball through the strike zone. Because he shortens his swing against lefthanders, his home run power is reduced, hitting only one against southpaws in 1982. A lifetime .266 hitter, Thompson is capable of .285 and higher.

Some have misunderstood Thompson's low key approach to hitting, confusing it with indifference. While rarely showing anger after striking out or complaining to umpires, he is a very competitive player. He hits well in all parks except Candlestick in San Francisco.

BASERUNNING:

Thompson has below average speed, but is a 100% player who will run as fast as he can from base to base.

FIELDING:

Thompson's fielding is at best, average. Although he has underrated hands, he has little range in the field and rarely charges bunts with the intent of a forceout of the baserunner. Average in digging throws out of the dirt. Thompson had difficulty with his foot movements around the bag, and Pirate first base coach Al Monchak helped him out a great deal with that. Arm strength and accuracy are only average.

OVERALL:

Last season, Thompson became the eighth player in baseball history to hit 30 or more home runs in each league. He may soon hit 40 homers in a season. He is a good team man who keeps a low profile, and has developed a winning attitude in Pittsburgh.

Kiner: "Thompson is an outstanding ball player who would fit in well on any team. He has proven himself to be one of the top players in the league."

McCarver: "The Pirates were glad they got stuck with Jason after a trade deal was foiled by the Commissioner. He has turned out to be a consistent power hitter for the Buccos."

Coleman: "I think that Thompson would be better in the American League as he is not a good defensive player."

DICK DAVIS
OF, No. 28
RR, 6'3", 195 lbs.
ML Svc: 6 years
Born: 9-25-53 in
Long Beach, CA

HITTING, BASERUNNING, FIELDING:

Dick Davis is strictly a platoon type of player at best. He can handle low inside fastballs better than most hitters, but has difficulty with breaking pitches. When he has two strikes against him, he tends to swing at bad pitches. He rarely makes good contact on a change-up. Davis is at his best swinging against lefthanded pitchers, but can't adjust to his role as a sub and isn't a good pinch-hitter.

Davis gets an excellent rating in speed, but a below average rating in overall baserunning. He doesn't take a big lead off the base and doesn't get a good enough jump. If he ever concentrated on his baserunning, he would improve because he certainly has enough speed.

He is only an average fielder. His arm isn't accurate, and he doesn't get a good jump on balls coming his way. His best outfield position is in left field. Davis will occasionally misjudge a fly ball or line drive, but sometimes his speed in the field will make up for these mistakes.

OVERALL:

Davis may benefit from a full season with a club that is not in contention. He is the no-trouble type in the clubhouse, though he was dissatisfied after riding the bench in both Milwaukee and Philadelphia.

McCarver: "Dick thinks that he should play more often, but he has rarely been given the chance. He is, however, a tough out against left-handers."

Coleman: "Davis is just an average player with few quality skills."

MIKE EASLER
OF, No. 24
LR, 6'1", 196 lbs.
ML Svc: 5 years
Born: 11-29-50 in
Cleveland, OH

HITTING, BASERUNNING, FIELDING:

Mike Easler is a good fastball hitter who likes the ball off the plate. However, he can be jammed in tight with a fastball that moves. His biggest problem is southpaws--they give him fits. As a result, Easler is ususally platooned against righthanders. Destroying the New York Mets has been his favorite pastime of late. Easler has home run power to right and right-center. As an RBI man it's either feast or famine for Easler. He drives in runs in bunches, then goes for weeks with less than 6 RBIs.

Easler's speed is below average. He is no threat as a basestealer. He slides hard and has a knack of breaking up double plays.

His lack of defense kept him in minor leagues for 10 years and for one season--in 1980--his defense in left field improved. In 1982, his fielding was below average and his arm, which has never been strong, seemed to become weaker. Easler has one plus--he rarely misses the cutoff man.

OVERALL:

His asset to a contending team would be as a sub-outfielder and pinch-hitter. Hard worker. He makes the most of what talent he has. He seems to press when he gets a chance to play every day. Good attitude.

Coleman: "Easler is a quality hitter, but a very weak fielder."

McCarver: "He's make the most of his chance to play.

RANDY NIEMANN
LHP, No. 23
LL, 6'4", 200 lbs.
ML Svc: 1 year
Born: 11-15-55 in Fortuna, CA

PITCHING:

Randy Niemann is used mainly in long relief. He seems to be lacking in big league equipment. His fastball and breaking pitches are only fair. Niemann nibbles at the plate instead of challenging hitters. He throws a forkball, and although it is only average, it can be considered his greatest strength. He had arm surgery in 1981 and his physical condition remains questionable. He is a marginal pitcher in all respects. He doesn't have great stuff, and doesn't seem to have much of a major league future.

FIELDING, HITTING, BASERUNNING:

Defensively, Niemann is fair. He has rarely batted in big leagues so it is difficult to judge him as a hitter. In pre-game practices, he has shown power, hitting many balls out of the park. Baserunning unknown, but he is definitely not a speedster.

OVERALL:

Niemann doesn't give the club any trouble. He is very quiet, but has the desire to make it in the big leagues. Maybe he needs a chance with a non-contending club. If he gets a chance to pitch, he may surprise some people.

McCarver: "Randy is a bit short-suited--does not have a wealth of ability, but can churn up a good game now and then."

Coleman: "His forkball has helped him improve, but he is a long reliever or spotstarter at best."

BUSCH MEMORIAL STADIUM
St. Louis Cardinals

Seating Capacity: 50,222
Playing Surface: Artificial

Dimensions
Left Field: 330 ft.
Left-Center Field: 386 ft.
Center Field: 414 ft.
Right-Center Field: 386 ft.
Right Field: 330 ft.
Height of Outfield Wall: 10 ft. 6 in.

Home of the 1982 World Champions, Busch Memorial Stadium is in need of repair. The artificial surface has become thin and is even worn out in spots. This gives infielders the impression that they're playing on concrete, and routine ground balls often race through the infield for surprise base hits. Unfortunately for other National League teams, this kind of surface was ideal for Whitey Herzog's run-and-gun offense, and may not be improved until Whitey feels forced to change the character of his team.

While Busch Stadium may favor contact hitters and those who slap at the ball, it is definitely considered a tough park by those who hit the ball in the air. The ball simply does not carry well in St. Louis. Even though the power alleys are a reasonable 386 feet from the plate, the ball has to be hit exceptionally well to clear the fence.

The mound in St. Louis draws frequent complaints from pitchers. The slope is not considered steep enough and pitchers are often uncomfortable trying to adjust their delivery to compensate for this. As if to even things up, the dirt in the batter's box often gets very hot and hard. This makes it difficult for batters to dig in and to find that extra bit of leverage.

The lights are considered excellent in Busch Stadium and many batters feel they can see the ball better during night games in St. Louis than in any other National League park. There is ample room to chase fouls down both foul lines, but infielders have to be cautious of the dugout steps. The bullpens are in the field of play in St. Louis but they rarely seem to cause any problems.

With the exception of the complaints about the mound, Busch Memorial Stadium is definitely considered a pitcher's ballpark. Unless the ball is hit directly down the line, it simply won't carry well in St. Louis. Over a full season this peculiar atmospheric condition serves to erase a lot of pitching mistakes. The park is ideally suited for a speedy team of contact hitters, and this is exactly the kind of team Whitey Herzog has put together.

JOAQUIN ANDUJAR
RHP, No. 47
SR, 5'11", 180 lbs.
ML Svc: 7 years
Born: 12-21-52 in
San Pedro de Macoris, DR

PITCHING:

Joaquin Andujar, the top starting pitcher on last year's World Champions, will deliver the ball from almost anywhere--sidearm, three-quarter and overhand--and that accounts in large part for his effectiveness. Armed with a fastball clocked at 90 MPH, Andujar is basically a power pitcher. He does not show a change-up much although he was beginning to work on an off-speed pitch toward the end of last season.

Troubled by control problems early in his career, Andujar has his walks under two per game now. His slider is a hard, quick-breaking pitch and his curveball is most effective when he drops down to righthanded hitters. It can be a devastating pitch if he keeps it down. He probably throws his fastball 65% of the time, primarily to lefthanders, and that is his main pitch when he falls behind in the count.

Andujar's pitching pattern is as erratic or unpredictable as his personality. Righthanded batters are surprised and even confused when he goes sidearm on them, although he almost always seems to throw his sidearm breaking pitch with two strikes. He will brush hitters back, sometimes when it isn't even necessary. He is not known for doctoring pitches although one observer said, "I wouldn't put it past him."

His greatest strengths are his good stuff and the way he jumps at the hitter in his delivery. Occasionally, he will lose his temper on the mound and that will hamper his effectiveness but he has harnessed that to a large degree.

FIELDING, HITTING, BASERUNNING:

Andujar is exceedingly quick to bounce off the mound to field bunts or to cover a base. His move to first is excellent, and he has been known to throw some of his best fastballs on pick-off tries. His fielding is enhanced by the fact that he lands with his body square toward home plate rather than off balance.

At the plate, Andujar does not walk much. He had 44 strikeouts and no walks last year. He's a free-swinging switch-hitter who employs an unusual philosophy of whom he bats righthanded against. Basically, he bats righthanded when he is bunting or trying to hit a home run, and lefthanded when he is trying to make better contact. His baserunning is above average because of his speed although he doesn't get on base that often.

OVERALL:

Andujar has established himself as one of the top righthanders in baseball and not only against Montreal, against who he is 11-1 lifetime.

Coleman: "He is a pitcher with excellent stuff, but sometimes he's his own worst enemy."

Kiner: "He's a hot dog, but he has a lot of ability."

McCarver: "Andujar is sometimes erratic, always flashy and dramatic and more often than not, effective. Joaquin is on a club made for him because of his good defense and the big dimensions of the ballpark."

1982 STATISTICS

W	L	ERA	G	GS	CG	IP	H	R	ER	BB	SO	SV
15	10	2.47	38	37	9	265	237	85	73	50	137	0

CAREER STATISTICS

W	L	ERA	G	GS	CG	IP	H	R	ER	BB	SO	SV
63	59	3.37	228	148	33	1102	1022	470	412	401	509	7

DOUG BAIR
RHP, No. 40
RR, 6'0", 180 lbs.
ML Svc: 6 years
Born: 8-22-49 in Defiance, OH

PITCHING:

Doug Bair is an over-the-top power pitcher who doesn't mess much with the curveball. He pitches from a straight-up stance, not bending his back as much as is traditional, but his extra zip on the fastball (88 to 90 MPH) allows him to get away with that. His curveball doesn't have good rotation but he does have a good slider if he can keep it from going over the middle of the plate. He throws a change but it isn't very deceptive.

Bair will throw mostly the fastball or slider when he is behind in the count. He is somewhat more effective against righthanded batters than lefthanders. Bair is not the "stopper" reliever he once was with Cincinnati, but he has a live arm, is durable and is a perfect foil for Bruce Sutter. Sometimes he can be wild and high in the strike zone and he has trouble pitching to spots.

FIELDING, HITTING, BASERUNNING:

Baserunners can go on Bair because he takes a long time to get rid of the ball to the plate. He is not much of a hitter or baserunner, but then relievers rarely get a chance to bat. He did, however, hit a three-run homer two seasons ago.

OVERALL:

Bair is on top of the relief pitchers' cycle. Many short relievers lack consistency because they burn out if they're used too much, but Bair's arm has returned close to its former strength.

Coleman: "Bair has a good fastball but sometimes it's straight and down the middle of the plate. He's not the reliever he once was, but he's still a good man to have on the staff."

McCarver: "Doug throws hard and has a good slider, but he would be better off if he had some kind of off-speed pitch."

1982 STATISTICS

W	L	ERA	G	GS	CG	IP	H	R	ER	BB	SO	SV
5	3	2.55	63	0	0	91	69	27	26	36	68	8

CAREER STATISTICS

W	L	ERA	G	GS	CG	IP	H	R	ER	BB	SO	SV
34	30	5.25	343	0	0	514	477	216	300	245	409	67

BOB FORSCH
RHP, No. 31
RR, 6'4", 200 lbs.
ML Svc: 8 years
Born: 1-13-50 in
Sacramento, CA

PITCHING:

Forsch has been the anchor of the Cardinals' rotation for several years and is considered one of the top control pitchers in the league. He is not overpowering at 86 MPH, but his fastball has good movement and tails away from lefthanded hitters. He throws almost strictly from the three-quarters motion and he jerks the ball at the last instant to increase its movement.

His fastball is the pitch he uses most often although he would just as soon throw his slider when he falls behind the hitters. His fastball is much more effective than many that are thrown harder than his because of its movement. Forsch's curveball can be a big breaking one and he uses it as a change of speeds pitch. He is a mild-mannered man, but is not adverse to putting a righthanded batter on his rear end if the situation warrants.

Forsch absolutely will not give in to hitters though he is smart enough to know which ones he has to pitch around. He works a lineup as well as anybody and can get any of his three pitches over the plate with regularity. Occasionally his fastball will be too true and lefthanders will take advantage of him.

FIELDING, HITTING, BASERUNNING:

One of the top athletes on his team, Forsch is an adept fielder--he signed as a third baseman--and he is better at holding runners on after adopting Jim Kaat's straightlegged style of keeping them close. Forsch helps himself at bat and has the power to drive the ball out of the park. While not fast, he is an intelligent baserunner.

OVERALL:

Forsch applies his intelligence to make the most of his ability.

McCarver: "Bob can overpower you but his modus operandi is keeping the hitters totally at his command."

1982 STATISTICS

W	L	ERA	G	GS	CG	IP	H	R	ER	BB	SO	SV
15	9	3.48	36	34	6	233	238	95	90	54	69	1

CAREER STATISTICS

W	L	ERA	G	GS	CG	IP	H	R	ER	BB	SO	SV
108	83	3.50	275	266	51	1766	1705	792	688	509	721	1

DAVID GREEN
OF, No. 27
RR, 6'3", 165 lbs.
ML Svc: 1 year plus
Born: 12-4-60 in
Managua, NIC

HITTING:

Green is in the mold of George Hendrick--tall, lean, and has a great arm. He hits something like Hendrick, too, from a closed stance. Righthanders can pitch him down and away, but can jam him. Lefthanders are better off staying away, too. Through hard work, Green has learned to hit the ball the other way against righthanders. Against lefthanders, he is more dangerous right now, with the ability to hit the ball with authority to all fields. The ball can jump off his bat with the classic pop and eventually he will be a 15 to 20 home run man when he gets the chance to play regularly.

Though he was used sparingly, Green was one of the best clutch hitters on the World Champions last year. He can hit behind the runner and can drive the ball with regularity into the power alleys. His hand action is quick and his batting eye is good for one so young; he's only 23 years old. If the ball is out over the plate, he will destroy it. Good curveballs will give him trouble. He is best hitting third or sixth in the lineup to utilize his speed.

BASERUNNING:

Green is one of the fastest players in baseball. He eats up ground in huge chunks with his loping gait. His base-stealing is not what it will eventually be because he does not generate enough early speed and he does not know what he should about pitchers and catchers yet.

1982 STATISTICS

AVG	G	AB	R	H	2B	3B	HR	RBI	BB	SO	SB
.283	76	166	21	47	7	1	2	23	8	29	11

CAREER STATISTICS

AVG	G	AB	R	H	2B	3B	HR	RBI	BB	SO	SB
.260	97	200	27	52	8	1	2	25	14	34	11

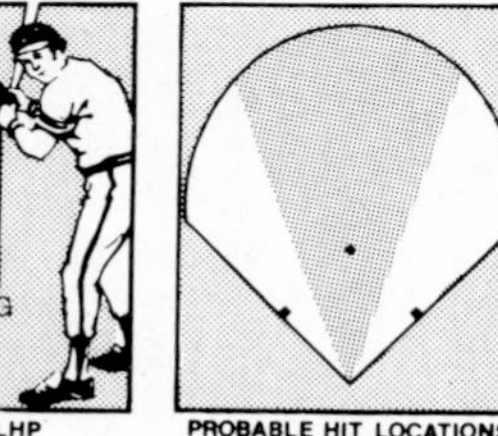

FIELDING:

Green's arm and accuracy are well above average although he needs work on his release. His range is startling. He closes gaps incredibly quickly both to his right and to his left.

OVERALL:

McCarver: "A bright future lies ahead for David. He can do everything well--hit, hit for power, throw, and run. He covers center field like a graceful swan."

GEORGE HENDRICK
OF, No. 25
RR, 6'3", 195 lbs.
ML Svc: 11 years
Born: 10-18-49 in Los Angeles, CA

HITTING:

George Hendrick is considered one of the game's great cripple hitters, that is, one who jumps all over a pitcher's mistakes. Hendrick begins his swing from an extremely closed stance--it looks as if his knees are inverted--from as far back in the batter's box as possible. But his arm extension gives him perhaps the best plate coverage in the National League. Most observers say that Hendrick should be pitched inside, way inside, and low. Otherwise, his incredible hand action will produce a rocket shot. Hendrick hits as many balls hard as any player in baseball.

Hendrick is most effective when he pulls the ball although when he's fooled by a pitch, he can still hit effectively to right field. He is considered one of the league's best clutch hitters, having 104 RBIs last season. You won't see him take many pitches or bunt. He probably would be even more effective in a hitters' park like Wrigley Field rather than in spacious Busch Stadium. He exerts strong, though silent, leadership.

BASERUNNING:

Hendrick's running is a source of controversy among experts. Some feel that he doesn't put out and others feel that he does "when he smells a hit."

Hendrick actually has average or above average speed but doesn't like to steal bases and takes one of the game's shortest leadoffs.

FIELDING:

Don't let his easy throwing motion or casual style deceive you. Hendrick is a well above average outfielder. He is one of the best at coming in on a ball and plays what one expert says is a "swan-like" right field.

1982 STATISTICS

AVG	G	AB	R	H	2B	3B	HR	RBI	BB	SO	SB
.282	136	515	65	145	20	5	19	104	37	90	3

CAREER STATISTICS

AVG	G	AB	R	H	2B	3B	HR	RBI	BB	SO	SB
.280	1463	5290	712	1479	242	22	214	823	415	743	54

VS. RHP

VS. LHP

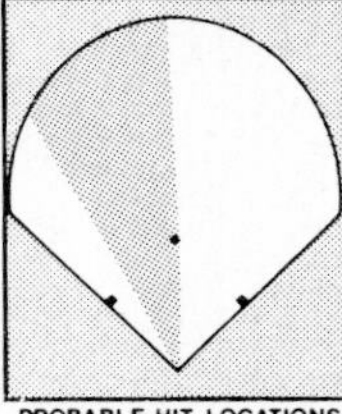
PROBABLE HIT LOCATIONS

OVERALL:

McCarver: "George is the best-kept secret class act in the major leagues, and with that swing of his, it looks like he has two sets of arms.

Bad labels in baseball seem to stick with you longer than in most businesses. To be different shouldn't imply that you are wrong. It was in George's case until traded to an organization which, ironically, has a tradition for staid conformism. Under Whitey Herzog's relaxed, yet serious direction, Hendrick is made to feel at home and his production has soared, making his acquisition for Eric Rasmussen the greatest heist since the Great Train Robbery in Britain."

Coleman: "One of the rare talents in the game, but he doesn't always apply himself. Should have been a great all around player. Instead, he's a dangerous hitter who doesn't help a team much with his legs or defense."

KEITH HERNANDEZ
INF, No. 37
LL, 6'0", 185 lbs.
ML Svc: 8 years
Born: 10-20-53 in
San Francisco, CA

1982 STATISTICS

AVG	G	AB	R	H	2B	3B	HR	RBI	BB	SO	SB
.299	160	579	79	173	33	6	7	94	100	67	19

CAREER STATISTICS

AVG	G	AB	R	H	2B	3B	HR	RBI	BB	SO	SB
.275	1110	3858	628	1061	250	46	78	569	561	506	80

VS. RHP

VS. LHP

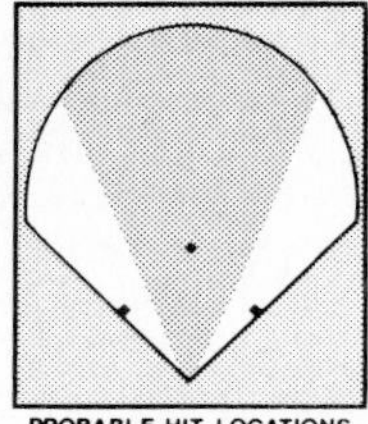
PROBABLE HIT LOCATIONS

HITTING:

Keith Hernandez is one of those rare types of lefthanded hitters who may hit lefthanded pitching as well, if not better, than righthanders. He glides into everything at the plate and his swing is one of the smoothest around. They call him a "wall-to-wall" hitter, although he has a tendency to go the other way more against lefthanders.

If there would be a pattern to pitching him, it would be to throw no pattern at all. Move the ball around, and don't throw him the same pitch more than once. A tailing fastball on the hands from lefthanders gives him the most trouble. Hernandez likes the pitch up and away and extending his arms, he can hit the pitch solidly to left field. Then again, he hits the low balls, too. He almost always can handle even the best pitchers' breaking balls. Even Steve Carlton has trouble with him, especially if he throws the ball thigh-high.

Hernandez is one of baseball's best clutch hitters, as witness his 94 RBIs on only seven home runs last year. He also has one of the best eyes in baseball, and is always among the league leaders in walks.

BASERUNNING:

Hernandez is a sneaky runner, picking his spots to run, but he hardly ever is thrown out. He gets a walking lead and then takes off when you least expect it, though his speed is only average.

FIELDING:

Five consecutive Gold Gloves tell this story. His arm at first base is one of the best around, and in fact, he takes the relay throws from the right field corner. His soft hands enable him to suck up any kind of throw like an octopus. His range is unsurpassed, and the best play he makes defensively is charging the bunt and firing to second for the forceout.

OVERALL:

McCarver: "There are no departments of the game in which Keith does not excel."

Coleman: "One of the top five consistent hitters in the league."

TOM HERR
INF, No. 28
SR, 6'0", 175 lbs.
ML Svc: 3 years
Born: 4-4-56 in
Lancaster, PA

1982 STATISTICS

AVG	G	AB	R	H	2B	3B	HR	RBI	BB	SO	SB
.266	135	493	83	131	19	4	0	36	57	56	25

CAREER STATISTICS

AVG	G	AB	R	H	2B	3B	HR	RBI	BB	SO	SB
.262	328	1136	166	298	45	18	0	98	114	109	58

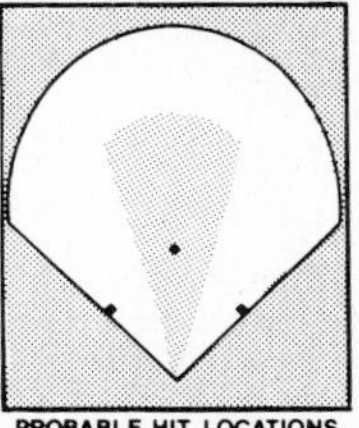

HITTING:

A switch-hitter, Tom Herr probably is more effective batting from the left side and he is notably effective at hitting the high pitch away from him. Herr has never hit a home run in the major leagues and must guard against trying to do too much at bat. He has been in the .260s the last two years but eventually, with better discipline, he may be a .280 hitter. Basically, he is a spray hitter who performs best when he is batting leadoff. He has come a long way as a hitter and throws in the odd bunt to keep the defense honest. Uses his above average speed to leg out grounders.

Herr can be pitched to down and away with breaking balls. He probably is better lefthanded because he moves the ball around although he can be fooled by a righthander's breaking stuff. He tends to try to top-hand the ball more when he hits righthanded and tries for too much power. Herr is a fairly effective clutch hitter from his leadoff spot and can handle the bat on the hit-and-run. Once, two seasons ago, he knocked in eight runs in a three-game series while batting eighth.

BASERUNNING:

Baserunning is one of the best parts of Herr's game. He is capable of stealing 30 or more bases with a high percentage of success. Herr has above average speed and baserunning intelligence and should be more of a threat this year than he was in 1982, when he was plagued by a succession of leg injuries. Even when hurt, though, Herr was still aggressive on the bases.

FIELDING:

Herr has made only 14 errors total in the last two seasons and has improved greatly on the double play. He and shortstop Ozzie Smith are one of the league's best double play combinations. He has played in the shadow of Manny Trillo for two years and is probably underrated but his range, arm and accuracy are all above average. He is equally adept at going to his left or right for balls and almost never errs on a routine play. He has improved every year.

OVERALL:

McCarver: "Bigger than most people think, Tom is a fine second baseman but he should hit for a higher average. If he stays within himself and doesn't try to do too much with the bat, he could lift his batting average 20 points."

Kiner: "Herr fits perfectly into the Cardinals' plan of defense and speed."

HITTING:

Lefthanded-hitting Dane Iorg is one of the National League's top pinch-hitters, especially against righthanded pitching. Cardinals' manager Whitey Herzog uses him regularly against teams which have good righthanded pitchers, such as Montreal, and Iorg has hit almost .450 against the Expos in the last three seasons. Iorg has little home run power although he can plug the alleys, notably to the opposite field. He is not a pull hitter. Lefthanded pitchers, whom he rarely faces, can give him trouble but no one should give him a fastball up and over the plate.

Basically, Iorg should be given a steady diet of breaking balls away or tight fastballs. He has been a .300 hitter in virtually every league in which he has played and is adept at moving along or driving in baserunners because he strikes out infrequently.

Iorg is not regarded particularly as a good bunter but in the situations in which he is employed, a bunt is not what is needed. "The best thing about him," said Herzog, "is that he can hit the tough righthanders."

If he is platooned and allowed to pinch-hit often enough to stay sharp, he's a good bet to hit .300. Could stand to be more aggressive in pulling the ball.

BASERUNNING:

If Iorg tries to steal, a sign has been missed. His speed is only average, though he is an intelligent runner who is aware of his liabilities. He is aggressive when trying to break up double plays.

FIELDING:

Iorg has only an average arm, although he normally is very good at throwing to the right base. He is sure-handed, catching everything he can get to. His best position probably is first base, but with Keith Hernandez playing 160 games a year, there is little opportunity for him to play there.

DANE IORG
OF, No. 19
LR, 6'0", 180 lbs.
ML Svc: 5 years
Born: 5-11-50 in Eureka, CA

1982 STATISTICS

AVG	G	AB	R	H	2B	3B	HR	RBI	BB	SO	SB
.294	102	238	17	70	14	1	0	34	23	23	0

CAREER STATISTICS

AVG	G	AB	R	H	2B	3B	HR	RBI	BB	SO	SB
.297	438	1032	96	307	65	6	6	140	72	111	4

VS. RHP

VS. LHP

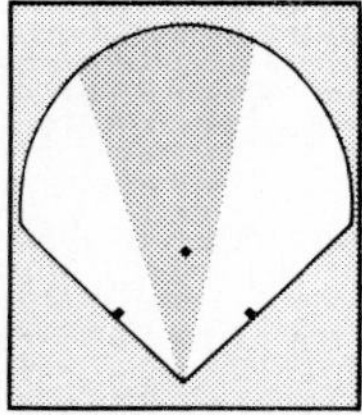
PROBABLE HIT LOCATIONS

OVERALL:

Coleman: "Iorg has been the League's best pinch-hitter over the past three to four years. Managers hate to face him with the game on the line."

McCarver: "A solid .300 hitter when used properly and Whitey Herzog does just that with Cardinals."

JIM KAAT
LHP, No. 36
LL, 6'5", 195 lbs.
ML Svc: 21 years
Born: 11-7-38 in
Zeeland, MI

PITCHING:

Jim Kaat is basically used to retire one or two lefthanded batters in a relief role, although he still has the durability to be a starting pitcher or long reliever. Remarkably, he is entering his 25th season of major league pitching.

His herky-jerky motion still is unnerving to a hitter and he constantly has tried to adjust his pitching to stay a step ahead of the hitters. Last year, he first tried to revive his quick-pitch delivery that had been successful in the American League and then he began to go to a more sidearm motion. He alternates between three-quarter and sidearm now and can throw any pitch from either motion.

His strong suit is control, although sometimes he is too true early in the count. He still has a respectable fastball of about 87 MPH. He doesn't throw his curveball much anymore although he throws the slider quite a bit. However, it doesn't have the classic slider spin and it has little movement. Kaat's strength has always been his fastball, even at age 44, and he has stuck with his strengths, considering the hitter merely an impediment in reaching the catcher. Lefthanded hitters still can be intimidated by his fastball, especially when it is thrown sidearm. His sinking fastball to lefthanders is a biting one that is heavy and hard. His poise in pressure situations is unparalelled. He has been in every kind of situation.

FIELDING, HITTING, BASERUNNING:

Kaat is a 16-time Gold Glove winner and still is extremely agile. His move to first isn't really outstanding, but he steps off the rubber a lot and then delivers quickly to the plate. His reactions are considered incredible for a man of any age. Kaat always has taken pride in his hitting and can hurt you. As a baserunner, he is slow but smart.

OVERALL:

Coleman: "A true professional. A credit to the game."

McCarver: "His career has been marked by honesty, aggressiveness, hard work and an infectious love for the game. Kitty will try everything he can think of to get you out--quick pitch, double-pump, triple-pump, brushbacks. He is a glorious warhorse who has stood the tests of time."

1982 STATISTICS

W	L	ERA	G	GS	CG	IP	H	R	ER	BB	SO	SV
5	3	4.08	62	2	0	75	79	40	34	23	35	2

CAREER STATISTICS

W	L	ERA	G	GS	CG	IP	H	R	ER	BB	SO	SV
283	237	3.45	874	625	180	4493	4572	2019	1723	1073	2442	18

JEFF KEENER
RHP, No. 44
LR, 6'1", 170 lbs.
ML Svc: 1 year
Born: 1-14-59 in
Albion, IL

PITCHING:

Keener is a Kent Tekulve-type pitcher, with almost an underarm delivery. He has a good sinker and slider and is as effective against righthanded hitters as he is against lefthanders. He doesn't change speed much but his sinker and slider serve the same purpose. Keener also has no curveball, but he can be deadly against righthanded hitters if he can keep his sinker and slider away from them.

One problem Keener has is that all of his pitches are the same speed and batters can time him if he stays in long enough. It would appear that his future will be one as a short reliever who should be replaced before he goes through a lineup the second time.

FIELDING, HITTING, BASERUNNING:

A sinkerballer rarely has a good move to first and Keener is no exception. As for his hitting and baserunning, no one in the National League has any idea. Keener didn't bat at all last season.

OVERALL:

Keener showed some moxie when pressed into tight situations. He might be strictly a specialist against right-handed hitters.

McCarver: "Jeff has a super slider that has all the characteristics of a big out pitch. His sinker also will serve him well because of the Cardinals' outstanding defense. Someday, he could become a premier short reliever."

1982 STATISTICS

W	L	ERA	G	GS	CG	IP	H	R	ER	BB	SO	SV
1	1	1.61	19	0	0	22	19	8	4	19	25	0

CAREER STATISTICS

W	L	ERA	G	GS	CG	IP	H	R	ER	BB	SO	SV
1	1	1.61	19	0	0	22	19	8	4	19	25	0

JEFF LAHTI
RHP, No. 32
RR, 6'0", 180 lbs.
ML Svc: 1 year
Born: 10-8-56 in
Oregon City, OR

PITCHING:

At present, Jeff Lahti is best used as a long or short reliever rather than a starter. Whitey Herzog gave the youngster one start last year and Lahti worried himself to death over it. He was gone by the fifth inning. Lahti's forte is a hopping fastball and his motion, in which he literally leaps at the hitter, there is little finesse involved.

The Lahti fastball is in the 90 MPH range. His curveball doesn't have good rotation and he uses it only rarely. However, he does have a late-breaking, effective slider. A change-up would help Lahti but he really doesn't have one as yet. He would be well to remember that body movement should not be speeded up when throwing the change. Deception is in the arm movement, not the body.

Lahti must stay ahead to be effective because his off-speed stuff isn't that advanced. He can be nasty to righthanded hitters, notably if he can keep his fastball and slider on the outside. He was placed in some pressure situations by Herzog last year and handled them well.

FIELDING, HITTING, BASERUNNING:

Lahti's pick-off move is average but he is quick at fielding bunts and covering his position, in general. His hitting is poor to non-existent, meaning that he hasn't run the bases very much either.

OVERALL:

Lahti is raw but has all the characteristics of a successful pitcher in the future.

McCarver: "Jeff's fastball appears to get on top of the hitters in a hurry, which is a good sign."

1982 STATISTICS

W	L	ERA	G	GS	CG	IP	H	R	ER	BB	SO	SV
5	4	3.81	33	1	0	56	53	27	24	21	22	0

CAREER STATISTICS

W	L	ERA	G	GS	CG	IP	H	R	ER	BB	SO	SV
5	4	3.81	33	1	0	56	53	27	24	21	22	0

PITCHING:

Dave LaPoint normally is a starter, but Whitey Herzog spots him against lefthanded-hitting teams. He also uses him in the bullpen, both in short and long relief. His stuff is not overwhelming although he does have an outstanding off-speed pitch for a youngster. The pitch has been variously referred to as a screwball, palmball or even change-up, but it is a pitch he is not afraid to throw to righthanded hitters and a pitch he will go to when behind in the count.

LaPoint will pitch mostly from the three-quarter position although he will drop to sidearm sometimes. Despite his good off-speed pitch, LaPoint will throw fastballs most often. His curveball is not a good one because it doesn't have good rotation although his slider is better than average.

He gets quite a few strikeouts against righthanders with his screwball/palmball and has the ability to throw the breaking ball over the plate when he is behind in the count. LaPoint was put into some difficult situations in the pennant race and showed savvy. He has a problem sometimes in that he might be too true with his fastball--that is, throwing it for strikes when a screwball out of the strike zone would suffice. He also will have to concentrate on keeping his weight down.

DAVE LaPOINT
LHP, No. 39
LL, 6'3", 205 lbs.
ML Svc: 1 year plus
Born: 7-29-59 in
Glens Falls, NY

FIELDING, HITTING, BASERUNNING:

LaPoint gets rid of the ball quickly to first base. Otherwise, his fielding skills are marginal. At bat, he gets his swings and advances runners reasonably well, but he is not a good average hitter. He is a slow runner on the bases, when he gets on.

OVERALL:

He has the ability to be a 15-game winner with regular work.

McCarver: "Any pitcher, particularly a lefthander, who throws fairly hard and has a pitch like the screwball, has a good start toward getting hitters out. Illusions serve their purpose in that most strikeouts come on balls out of the strike zone."

Coleman: "He could lose a few pounds and be more effective."

1982 STATISTICS

W	L	ERA	G	GS	CG	IP	H	R	ER	BB	SO	SV
9	3	3.42	42	21	0	152	170	63	58	52	81	0

CAREER STATISTICS

W	L	ERA	G	GS	CG	IP	H	R	ER	BB	SO	SV
11	3	3.69	50	26	0	178	199	82	73	67	90	1

WILLIE McGEE
OF, No. 51
SR, 6'0", 160 lbs.
ML Svc: 1 year
Born: 11-2-58 in
San Francisco, CA

1982 STATISTICS

AVG	G	AB	R	H	2B	3B	HR	RBI	BB	SO	SB
.296	123	422	43	125	12	8	4	56	12	58	24

CAREER STATISTICS

AVG	G	AB	R	H	2B	3B	HR	RBI	BB	SO	SB
.296	123	422	43	125	12	8	4	56	12	58	24

VS. RHP

VS. LHP

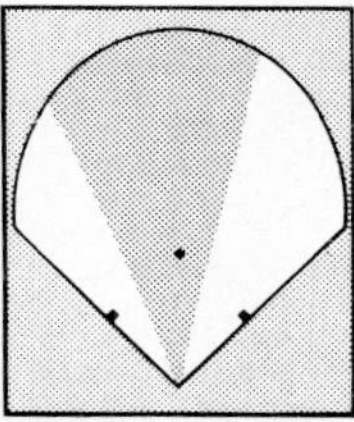
PROBABLE HIT LOCATIONS

HITTING:

A switch-hitter who jumped from Double A to the majors last year--with a month's stop in Triple A--Willie McGee probably has more pop righthanded but is a better average hitter lefthanded. Late in the season he was platooned against some lefthanded pitchers. McGee has deceptively quick hands but has little patience at the plate and often cuts and slashes at pitches out of the strike zone, especially high pitches. Pitchers can jam him effectively but must keep it down. Batting righthanded, he sprays the ball to all fields. He tends to pull a bit more hitting lefthanded.

McGee can reach the power alleys occasionally, but his best work in Busch Stadium will be done by chopping down on the field and using his blinding speed to first. He was timed in 3.7 seconds batting lefthanded which is the fastest in the league. He is a deceptive clutch hitter. Though he had just four home runs, he knocked in 56 runs even though he was not with the Cardinals all season. He will see a steady diet of off-speed pitches out of the strike zone or hard stuff in, but if a mistake is made, his quick hands will enable him to drive a ball into the gap. He does well against the sinker or slider, usually slapping it to the opposite field.

BASERUNNING:

In short, he is a blur, but McGee must work hard on getting a good jump from first base on steal attempts. A 24-base stealer last year, he is programmed as one who could steal 50 bases. He improved from the early part of the season last year. In his first 16 steal attempts, he was thrown out eight times. Then he was 16 for 20 the rest of the year.

FIELDING:

McGee's range is the equal of any in the League, and he covered more ground late in the season when he gained enough confidence to run veteran outfielders off balls. He can come in or break back with equal facility and his arm, while average, is better than it looks because of his accuracy and his quick release.

OVERALL:

McCarver: "Willie is a clone of Lonnie Smith. His smooth easy gait is his trademark. He appears to have a stiff swing, but his wrists come through the strike zone with obvious authority."

STEVE MURA
RHP, No. 38
RR, 6'2", 188 lbs.
ML Svc: 4 years
Born: 2-12-55 in
New Orleans, LA

PITCHING:

Steve Mura was one of the few pure "downers" among curveball pitchers today, throwing his pitch from a direct overhand motion. He was used both as a starter and reliever last year although he is most effective as a starter. He has too many control problems to be anything but a starter.

Mura's fastball is not outstanding but appears to be faster than it is because most hitters are looking for his big breaking curve. He throws his curveball maybe 25% of the time and mixes in an occasional slider giving the hitter another breaking ball to look for. He also changes off his breaking ball. However, when he is behind, he is most apt to come in with his fastball. Righthanded batters are vulnerable on low and away breaking balls.

He is considered to have one of the best "arms" in the league because he has three pitches. But sometimes his confidence is lacking and he fights himself and his coaches too much. He has matured, though, since he left the stifling losing atmosphere that he encountered in San Diego.

FIELDING, HITTING, BASERUNNING:

Mura is an above average fielder but a well below average hitter. Despite this, he drove in eight runs two seasons ago. His baserunning rarely is a factor in games.

OVERALL:

Mura was a better pitcher with a better team and showed more poise than he had before.

Coleman: "He always had a good arm and now he's gaining the confidence and maturity to go with it."

McCarver: "Not many pitchers can boast the type of curveball Steve has, since most curves are thrown on at least a somewhat horizontal plane. His fastball would be ordinary were it not for his curve, but it appears to be much faster with the curve. He is smart and very aware of these weapons."

1982 STATISTICS

W	L	ERA	G	GS	CG	IP	H	R	ER	BB	SO	SV
12	11	4.05	35	30	7	184	196	89	83	80	84	0

CAREER STATISTICS

W	L	ERA	G	GS	CG	IP	H	R	ER	BB	SO	SV
29	38	3.97	138	82	12	573	573	275	253	258	327	4

KEN OBERKFELL
INF, No. 10
LR, 6'1", 185 lbs.
ML Svc: 5 years
Born: 5-4-56 in Highland, IL

1982 STATISTICS

AVG	G	AB	R	H	2B	3B	HR	RBI	BB	SO	SB
.289	137	470	55	136	22	5	2	34	40	31	11

CAREER STATISTICS

AVG	G	AB	R	H	2B	3B	HR	RBI	BB	SO	SB
.290	509	1696	216	492	81	22	8	161	188	121	32

VS. RHP

VS. LHP

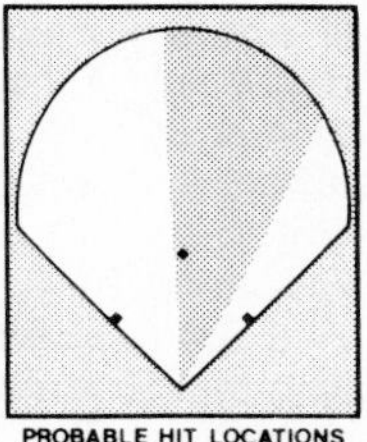

PROBABLE HIT LOCATIONS

HITTING:

Ken Oberkfell is a good line drive, high ball hitter who learned to pull the ball more by opening up his stance, especially against lefthanded pitchers. Predominantly a fastball hitter, Oberkfell should be jammed by righthanders and dished up breaking balls low and away by lefthanders.

Oberkfell can hit with authority to the opposite field but like a lot of lefthanders, he occasionally hits the bottom half of the ball against southpaws, causing numerous warning-track fly balls. A player who rarely strikes out, Oberkfell takes advantage of his big home ballpark, Busch Stadium, by hitting drives into the gap.

Has improved considerably in his ability to hit lefthanders although he is platooned against such formidable opponents as Steve Carlton and John Candelaria. Oberkfell is patient at the plate, is a good bunter and does a reasonable job of advancing runners when he bats second although when he hit sixth and seventh, he didn't drive in runs as he was expected to. Has shown himself to be a consistent .290 to .300 hitter although he has had injury problems (knee in 1980, broken thumb in 1982).

BASERUNNING:

An above average baserunner, Oberkfell is a player who can steal 20 bases a year. He compensates for his lack of blazing speed by picking his spots to run and pitchers have to watch him carefully.

FIELDING:

The league's top percentage fielder at third base last year, Oberkfell has successfully negotiated the difficult switch from second base to third. Possessor of an accurate arm, Oberkfell also excels at fielding balls hit to his left and he will make the big play that can take a pitcher out of a jam.

OVERALL:

McCarver: "A smart heads-up player who gets a lot out of his ability. Goes about his job with a respectable thoroughness. Offense has suffered a bit since being moved to third from second because of his defensive concerns."

Coleman: "With hard work, Oberkfell has made himself a steady major league player."

DARRELL PORTER
C, No. 15
LR, 6'0", 193 lbs.
ML Svc: 10 years
Born: 1-17-52 in
Joplin, MO

HITTING:

Darrell Porter is a dead pull hitter, one of the few effective open stance hitters in baseball. His crouch enables him to hit low balls better than high balls and he loves the ball from the middle of the plate on in. Lefthanded pitchers can jam him although they are better off staying away. Porter's plate coverage is good so it is advisable to try to make him swing at pitches out of the strike zone entirely. He will try to pull everything against both righthanded and lefthanded pitchers. Porter hangs in against lefthanded pitchers but is more effective against righthanders.

Porter is able to hit behind the runner with his natural pull stroke, and is about an average hitter in the clutch. His good eye enables him to draw a lot of walks and he will jump all over a pitcher's mistake. Off-speed stuff can be a problem for Porter and if he bites, you have him. His below regular season averages in the last two years make one wonder if he has as quick a bat as in the past. But then his post season and MVP World Series performance last year indicated he was still the Porter that manager Whitey Herzog saw in 1979.

BASERUNNING:

Porter runs reasonably well for a catcher and is fearless at breaking up double plays. He will not steal a base unless it absolutely is given to him. He will surprise you, though, with his ability to go from first to third on singles.

FIELDING:

After recovering from a torn rotator cuff suffered in 1981, Porter has built his arm strength to a respectable level and has developed a quicker release. However, he occasionally tends to push the ball, leading with his elbow. His handling of the not-highly-regarded Cardinal pitching staff drew high marks from teammates and opponents alike. His mechanics are excellent behind the plate and he is tough to knock off his feet in home plate collisions.

1982 STATISTICS

AVG	G	AB	R	H	2B	3B	HR	RBI	BB	SO	SB
.231	120	373	46	86	18	5	12	48	66	66	1

CAREER STATISTICS

AVG	G	AB	R	H	2B	3B	HR	RBI	BB	SO	SB
.248	1273	4149	582	1030	176	100	133	606	684	710	261

VS. RHP

VS. LHP

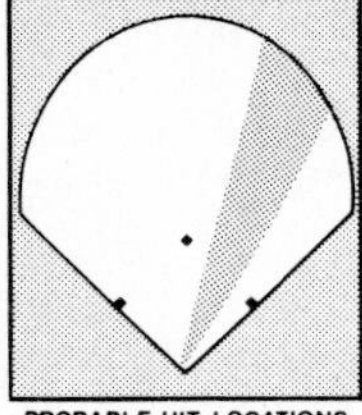
PROBABLE HIT LOCATIONS

OVERALL:

McCarver: "In appraising a catcher's ability with the bat, one must keep in mind that catching winners overshadows all else as a catcher. Darrell is a winner. He could hit for a higher average but Whitey Herzog got him because he is a winner."

Coleman: "Darrell Porter is a quality catcher who handles a game very well."

MIKE RAMSEY
INF, No. 5
SR, 6'1", 170 lbs.
ML Svc: 3 years
Born: 3-29-54 in Roanoke, VA

1982 STATISTICS

AVG	G	AB	R	H	2B	3B	HR	RBI	BB	SO	SB
.230	112	256	18	59	8	2	1	21	22	34	6

CAREER STATISTICS

AVG	G	AB	R	H	2B	3B	HR	RBI	BB	SO	SB
.245	230	511	52	125	19	3	1	38	33	68	10

VS. RHP

VS. LHP

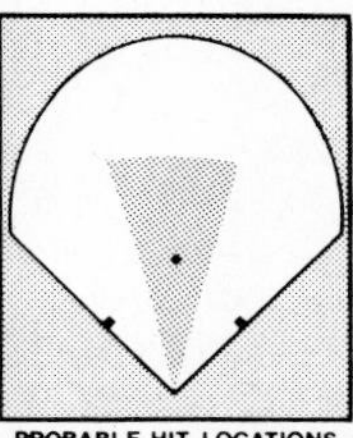
PROBABLE HIT LOCATIONS

HITTING:

Mike Ramsey, the Cardinals' super-sub, is yet another St. Louis switch-hitter. He has more power hitting righthanded, his natural side, but is a more effective hitter lefthanded. Ramsey is a crouch hitter without much power--he has only one home run lifetime--and handles the low breaking ball well when batting lefthanded. Hitting righthanded, he is a better high ball hitter although he doesn't hit the ball effectively to right field. Pitchers should jam him with fastballs and throw breaking balls away, especially righthanders. Though he plays only sporadically, Ramsey is an effective clutch hitter and hits behind the runner reasonably well. He is a good hit-and-run man and bunter.

BASERUNNING:

Ramsey has above average speed and must be watched carefully. He gets an excellent jump off first base, is a smart baserunner and is aggressive at breaking up double plays. He will slide either head first or feet first.

FIELDING:

Perhaps the strongest facet of Ramsey's game, because he can play three positions with nearly equal ability although his best position is second base. His arm is above average, except when he's throwing from the shortstop hole. His range to his left is good particularly when he is playing third base. Showed his toughness by playing 14 consecutive errorless games at shortstop in September when incumbent Ozzie Smith was hurt. He turns the double play rather well, and changes bunts well when playing third base.

OVERALL:

McCarver: "If given the opportunity I think Mike could be a regular second baseman. He is an extremely valuable man on a contender because he plays three positions well, hits for an average and runs well."

Coleman: "Ramsey is a good back up infielder who has made himself a good player."

LONNIE SMITH
OF, No. 27
RR, 5'9", 170 lbs.
ML Svc: 3 years
Born: 12-22-55 in Chicago, IL

1982 STATISTICS

AVG	G	AB	R	H	2B	3B	HR	RBI	BB	SO	SB
.307	156	592	120	182	35	8	8	69	64	74	68

CAREER STATISTICS

AVG	G	AB	R	H	2B	3B	HR	RBI	BB	SO	SB
.314	352	1100	239	345	65	15	13	103	113	146	128

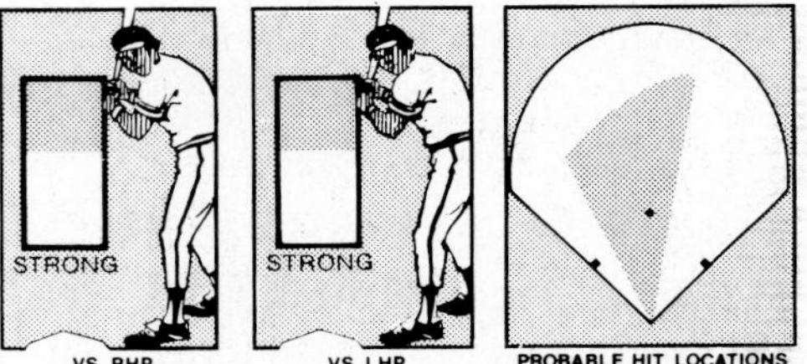

HITTING:

Given an everyday job for the first time in his career, Lonnie Smith became one of the most feared and consistent offensive players in the league. He spent only a week under .300 and his great speed and basestealing ability enabled him to ignite many big innings for the Cardinals. He is the type of hitter for which there is no particular style of pitching, other than to move it around and vary speeds. He often is hit by a pitch because he stands close to the plate and dives into the ball.

Basically a straightaway hitter, Smith will try to pull the ball more against lefthanders and he has good extra base, if not home run power. He drove in 69 runs while batting mostly first and second, giving an indication of his ability to hit with runners on base. His speed enables him to take advantage of the artificial turf where he plays his home games.

BASERUNNING:

Smith will be even better when he learns to improve his jump. He also has trouble occasionally getting out of the batter's box. His tendency to fall has earned him the nickname "Skates," but there are few baserunners or base-stealers more aggressive than he in breaking up a double play. He goes into second like a bullet.

FIELDING:

Smith is a better fielder than he has been given credit for. Yes, he does fall down once in a while and his arm is sometimes erratic, but he can outrun a lot of mistakes. Once had a very strong arm before he hurt it in his early years in the minor leagues.

OVERALL:

McCarver: "Lonnie had the bad rap of looking bad while catching balls in the outfield. Occasionally, he did, but more often than not, he came up with the catch. Any flaw on defense can be excused since he has remarkable offensive stats and potential, power, speed, and contact. One of the toughest dudes around. You simply cannot hurt the man."

Kiner: "Great at setting up an inning."

Coleman: "One of the top players in the league."

OZZIE SMITH
INF, No. 1
SL, 5'10", 150 lbs.
ML Svc: 5 years
Born: 12-26-54 in Mobile, AL

1982 STATISTICS

AVG	G	AB	R	H	2B	3B	HR	RBI	BB	SO	SB
.248	140	488	58	121	24	1	2	43	68	32	25

CAREER STATISTICS

AVG	G	AB	R	H	2B	3B	HR	RBI	BB	SO	SB
.234	723	2724	324	637	88	20	3	172	264	198	172

VS. RHP

VS. LHP

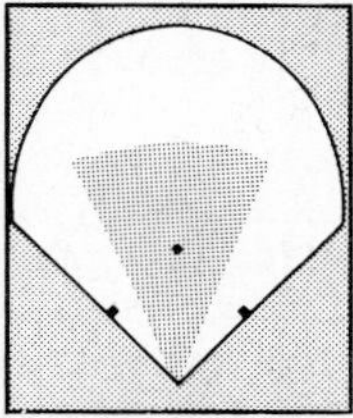
PROBABLE HIT LOCATIONS

HITTING:

They don't pay this fielding magician to hit although he gradually is becoming more effective. Ozzie Smith probably has more power hitting righthanded--both of his home runs last year were hit from that side. Blessed with a good eye, Smith draws his share of walks and is usually one of the 10 or 20 toughest hitters in the league to strike out. Smith is mostly a high ball hitter and the best way to pitch him is hard stuff inside. The outfield should play shallow at all times although this 150-pounder can occasionally jerk a pitch when batting righthanded.

Smith probably is more effective against righthanded pitching, particularly on artificial turf where he can use his great speed to beat out hits. He is improving in his ability to move runners along, although his bunting ability has been consummate for several years. He gets the most out of what he has offensively and he can nail the off-speed fastballs which are up in the strike zone and the low fastball when he is batting lefthanded.

BASERUNNING:

Smith has excellent speed and is capable of stealing bases at an 80% clip when he is healthy. He had the best percentage on the Cardinal team last year despite being hampered with a bad knee and then a bruised thigh. He moves almost as if he were on a hydrofoil and he must be observed carefully by pitchers.

FIELDING:

People say Smith might be the best shortstop ever. The only rap that could possibly be used against him is that his arm is just average but his lightning-quick release time and accuracy more than make up for that. Smith can throw out any hitter in the league by one step from virtually any spot on the field.

His acrobatic ability--he did backflips before the seventh game of the World Series last year--enables him to make plays that no one else active can make. He routinely dives for grounders but is on his feet in an instant, making one wonder if he ever had dived at all. His range is excellent in all directions--north, east and west--and he is never touched at second base on a double-play ball pivot because of his ballet-like grace. They call him "The Wiz."

OVERALL:

Kiner: "He compares with all the greats defensively."

McCarver: "I've never seen anyone quite like him. He easily could have made it in the circus. The man has Elgin Baylor-type body control. He's a winner who finally is on a club where he can prove that image."

JOHN STUPER
RHP, No. 48
RR, 6'2", 200 lbs.
ML Svc: 1 year
Born: 5-9-57 in
Butler, PA

PITCHING:

John Stuper was both a reliever and starter in the minor leagues but he mostly started for the Cardinals and was impressive in post-season play. He primarily is a fastball pitcher although he has a sharp-breaking slider, which he throws almost as hard as his 88 MPH fastball. He also can cut his fastball and, if he keeps the ball down, he can be very effective. Thus far, Stuper does not employ the curveball very often. A change-up would help him. There are times when he has trouble getting anything but his fastball over the plate. If he is to be more successful he will have to have something else to turn to when he is behind on the count.

Stuper, a righthander, is better against righthanded hitters because his pitch, which looks as if it will be away, tails back over the plate. A highly intelligent man, Stuper displayed poise beyond his years and received invaluable experience in the pennant drive, playoffs and World Series. He must, though, develop better control to be an even bigger winner.

FIELDING, HITTING, BASERUNNING:

Stuper's move to first is extremely quick and he is more than adequate at fielding batted balls and covering a bag. He has a slow bat and he is not a dangerous baserunner either.

OVERALL:

Stuper could use an off-speed pitch to offset his fastball.

McCarver: "John can overthrow on occasion. He has a chance to be a consistent winner because of his strength, durability, good moving fastball and late-breaking slider."

1982 STATISTICS

W	L	ERA	G	GS	CG	IP	H	R	ER	BB	SO	SV
9	7	3.36	23	21	2	136	137	55	51	55	53	0

CAREER STATISTICS

W	L	ERA	G	GS	CG	IP	H	R	ER	BB	SO	SV
9	7	3.36	23	21	2	136	137	55	51	55	53	0

PITCHING:

The best. Those two words say everything necessary to say about Bruce Sutter. He figured in an astonishing 50 of the 99 wins the Cardinals had last season--saving 39 and winning 11, counting post-season games.

The reason why Sutter is regarded as the top relief pitcher in baseball is his devastating split-fingered fastball, which starts out so invitingly in the strike zone and then dive-bombs into the dirt as a helpless hitter swings where he thought it was. Sutter runs to the mound very confidently all the time and then capitalizes on this aura of superiority. He pitches out of the stretch even with nobody on base because he has better torque on his delivery. Sutter will throw a fastball as a diversion although last year he discovered that more hitters were laying off first-pitch split-fingered balls so he increased his fastball use to as much as 20% in some games.

There is no curveball in the Sutter arsenal and no more than an occasional slider, if that. When he gets behind, you know what's coming but can you hit it? The only way to combat Sutter is try to get ahead in the count and make him throw a regular fastball. He is equally effective against lefthanded or righthanded batters because his ball breaks down, not across. It used to be that his arm got tired in August, but Whitey Herzog has an almost unfailing rule of using him only in the eighth or ninth inning and only if the Cardinals are tied or ahead.

BRUCE SUTTER
RHP, No. 42
RR, 6'2", 190 lbs.
ML Svc: 7 years
Born: 1-8-53 in
Lancaster, PA

FIELDING, HITTING, BASERUNNING:

Sutter has only an average move to first but makes up for it with a quick release to the plate, giving his catcher a chance to throw out runners. He was troubled by knee and groin injuries last season and wasn't able to cover first or play bunts as he should have. He is not paid for his hitting and shouldn't be.

OVERALL:

Sutter is the most consistent reliever in the league and he has yet to have a bad year in seven.

McCarver: "Bruce's split-fingered fastball is the best of its kind ever thrown. Bruce needs a dependable back up or long reliever as a carrier needs escorts and he has that in Doug Bair."

1982 STATISTICS

W	L	ERA	G	GS	CG	IP	H	R	ER	BB	SO	SV
9	8	2.90	70	0	0	102	88	38	33	34	61	36

CAREER STATISTICS

W	L	ERA	G	GS	CG	IP	H	R	ER	BB	SO	SV
44	43	2.52	418	0	0	676	523	218	189	207	612	220

STEVE BRAUN
INF/OF, No. 26
LR, 5'10", 180 lbs.
ML Svc: 1 year
Born: 5-8-48 in Trenton, NJ

HITTING, BASERUNNING, FIELDING:

Steve Braun is a professional pinch-hitter, and good clubs such as the Cardinals can afford to carry such a specialist. Whitey Herzog almost never plays Braun and almost never has him hit against lefthanded pitching. But, used against righthanders, Braun had a pinch-hitting average of .293. This veteran can deal most easily with a high pitch. He has good power to right-center, but occasionally will hit to left field. His abilities to hit behind the runner and in the clutch are rated average, but he does have the ability to help his on-base percentage with a keen batting eye. Braun traditionally reaches base about 40% of the time because of his ability to draw walks. He doesn't miss many good pitches.

Off-speed stuff will give Braun the most trouble and change-ups also can bother him, especially when he hasn't played a lot. Everything should be kept down.

Braun is not a basestealing threat and has only average speed. He often is run for when he reaches base as a pinch-hitter.

He can play third base, as he did on Opening Day last year, but his best position is left field. He was bothered by a bad arm last year and didn't play much after April.

OVERALL:

Coleman: "His bat carries him. His other skills are marginal."

JULIO GONZALES
INF, No. 14
RR, 5'11", 165 lbs.
ML Svc: 6 years
Born: 12-25-53 in Caguas, PR

HITTING, BASERUNNING, FIELDING:

Julio Gonzalez is a high ball hitter from his closed stance. He has considerable trouble with the low pitch. He'll pull the ball on the ground against both righthanded and lefthanded pitching. He has little power but his ability to hit in the clutch and move the runners is good for a player who rarely gets to bat. He is used almost exclusively against lefthanded pitchers or as a pinch-hitter, but is above average at the hit-and-run, the bunt and at drawing the base on balls. Pitchers should not do him any favors by throwing change ups. When he plays, which is infrequently, he should bat seventh or eighth.

Gonzalez is a good basestealer although his speed is only average. He makes up for his lack of speed by getting a good jump and pitchers must look over at him.

Like Mike Ramsey, the Cardinals' other utility man, Gonzalez can play three positions effectively, with his best position being second base. He makes all the routine plays and has a strong, accurate arm. His range is good, especially to his left. Gonzalez can make the double play and at third, gets a good jump on bunts.

OVERALL:

McCarver: "Julio could play as a platoon player on some clubs. There are some players who are made for the utility role. His stamina is questionable, but he is certainly a good fill-in."

TITO LANDRUM
OF, No. 21
RR, 5'11", 175 lbs.
ML Svc: 2 years
Born: 10-25-54 in Joplin, MO

HITTING, BASERUNNING, FIELDING:

If he's able to get his arms out, Landrum can be an effective hitter, especially with high fastballs. But he can be handled with hard stuff inside and a lot of breaking balls away. Landrum basically is a pull hitter, trying to drive the ball on the ground, and has little power. He mostly is used against lefthanded pitching or as a late-inning defensive replacement.

He is not a patient hitter, drawing few walks, and hasn't shown a particular adeptness for hitting in the clutch or hitting behind the runners. He does swing at quite a few bad balls, a normal sign for a player who gets few chances to impress.

Landrum has above average speed but should be a better basestealer than he is. He gets a poor jump for one who runs well. It would also help if he got on base more often.

His forte probably is as a defensive player, where he has good range and quickness, notably at coming in on a ball. He does, however, take some time in getting the ball away sometimes.

OVERALL:

Landrum generally is acknowledged to have good tools but it is believed he doesn't use them to his full advantage.

Coleman: "He's a good player but he has to hit more to really help a club."

Kiner: "He'll be hard-pressed to make the club in 1983."

JACK MURPHY STADIUM
San Diego Padres

Seating Capacity: 51,362
Playing Surface: Natural Grass

Dimensions
Left Field Pole: 330 ft.
Left-Center Field: 370 ft.
Center Field: 410 ft.
Right-Center Field: 370 ft.
Right Field Pole: 330 ft.
Height of Outfield Wall: 17 ft.

San Diego's Jack Murphy Stadium is one of the two or three toughest parks in the National League in which to hit a home run. The outfield fence stretches from 330 feet down each line to 410 feet in dead center. Not only is the fence distant, but, at 17 feet, it is also the tallest wall in the league. When you add the fact that the ball doesn't carry well at all in San Diego, you can begin to realize that a round tripper in Jack Murphy Stadium is a shot to be proud of.

The infield in this park is a delight for fielders. The rich natural turf slows down grounders, giving infielders enough time to get in front of most of them. The field is also well groomed and this guarantees the fielders their fair share of true hops. Visiting infielders, especially those used to playing on the faster, artificial surfaces, sometimes forget to charge grounders and this has led to some embarrassing errors. There is one additional problem for infielders in San Diego; that is the low placement of the lights. This occasionally causes them to lose sight of high choppers in the glare and is not a problem usually encountered in other stadia.

The dugouts are on field level and present no problems. The bullpens, however, are on the field of play--in the corners--and can influence the way an outfielder must play a fly ball.

The condition of both the pitcher's mound and the batter's box are excellent in San Diego. The height and slope of the mound are good for most pitchers and batters enjoy being able to dig a comfortable foothold in the loose soft dirt around the plate.

One final pitfall must be mentioned about this park. The stands jut out near the foul lines about 30 feet from the outfield wall. This odd angle hasn't caused any injuries yet, but a number of players have had near misses after diving for a ball in the outfield.

HITTING:

Kurt Bevacqua performs better under pressure than when nothing is on the line. It is a quality that has made him one of the game's most respected righthanded pinch-hitters.

He is a high fastball hitter. Opponents play him straightaway or slightly to pull. No real home run threat, he hits mostly line drives or grounders because he gets on top of the ball. He is strong enough to reach the fences in left-center and right-center and has become a better hitter since learning to hit to the opposite field.

Bevacqua sometimes chases fastballs that are above the strike zone. Righthanders can give him trouble with good fastballs in on the hands and breaking balls low and outside. He is particularly effective against lefthanders, even the likes of Steve Carlton or Fernando Valenzuela, and is more apt to pull the ball against southpaws.

Lacking speed, Bevacqua gets few infield hits. He will take a walk, but has the strikeout ratio of a power hitter because of an occasional tendency to overswing. However, he rises to the occasion with runners in scoring position, can hit and run and is an average bunter. Pitchers must keep the ball down on him and change speeds. He hits any pitch that is up in the strike zone and can guess the pitch, but not the location.

Being a line drive hitter, Bevacqua hits better in ballparks with big outfields or on synthetic turf, where sharp grounders have a better chance of going through.

BASERUNNING:

Bevacqua is a slightly below average runner and is conservative on the basepaths, but will steal an occasional base and is aggressive in breaking up the double play.

KURT BEVACQUA
INF, No. 7
RR, 6'2", 195 lbs.
ML Svc: 11 years
Born: 1-23-47 in
Miami Beach, FL

1982 STATISTICS

AVG	G	AB	R	H	2B	3B	HR	RBI	BB	SO	SB
.252	64	123	15	31	9	0	0	24	17	22	2

CAREER STATISTICS

AVG	G	AB	R	H	2B	3B	HR	RBI	BB	SO	SB
.236	766	1743	173	412	74	11	21	217	164	260	12

VS. RHP

VS. LHP

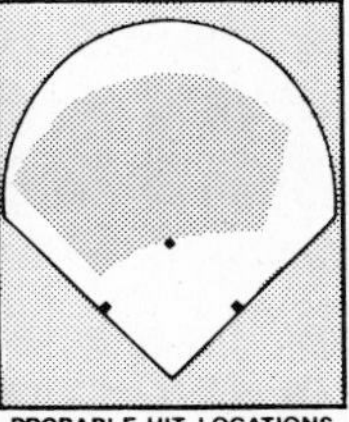
PROBABLE HIT LOCATIONS

FIELDING:

He has an average arm and accuracy, but Bevacqua lacks range in the field. He does his best filling in at first base, but also has had experience at second, third and in left field.

OVERALL:

An experienced, knowledgeable hitter whose chief value is his ability to come off the bench and hit in clutch situations or fill in occasionally at one of four different positions. Has leadership ability, as well.

Coleman: "Bevacqua is one of the best pinch-hitters in the game. He likes the challenge and rises to the occasion. Keeps things lively in the clubhouse."

McCarver: "He is a good utility infielder, and is more than competent against lefthanded pitchers."

JUAN BONILLA
INF, No. 3
RR, 5'9", 170 lbs.
ML Svc: 1 year plus
Born: 2-12-56 in Santurce, PR

1982 STATISTICS

AVG	G	AB	R	H	2B	3B	HR	RBI	BB	SO	SB
.280	45	182	21	51	6	2	0	8	11	15	0

CAREER STATISTICS

AVG	G	AB	R	H	2B	3B	HR	RBI	BB	SO	SB
.287	144	551	51	158	19	4	1	33	36	38	4

HITTING:

Although he is not a home run hitter, Juan Bonilla grips the end of the bat, strides into every pitch, and swings from his heels. His aggressive style makes him susceptible to getting hit by inside fastballs and increases the risk that he'll be beaned by a pitch. Nonetheless, Bonilla remains fearless at the plate.

He crouches in a closed stance in the back of the batter's box and makes sharp, remarkably consistent contact with fastballs that are up in the strike zone. Against lefthanders, he hits line drives and hard grounders up the middle and to right field. He can pull the ball against lefthanders or when righthanders throw him high breaking pitches.

Bonilla's style makes him vulnerable to off-speed pitches or to fastballs that are inside or down. He also will chase the high fastball that is out of the strike zone. Because of his willingness to hit the ball to the opposite field, Bonilla is about as effective against righthanders as lefthanders. He occasionally reaches the alleys, is above average at hitting in the clutch, and is excellent at hitting behind the runner on hit-and-run plays. He is an above average bunter who does not strike out often but is extremely difficult to walk. He normally bats second or eighth in the lineup.

Because he hits the ball sharply, Bonilla fares better on hard, synthetic surfaces and in parks with big outfield dimensions. He is a consistent hitter, and that is the strongest part of his game.

BASERUNNING:

Bonilla has slightly below average speed going to first base and is hardly any threat at all to steal a base. He is a conservative baserunner.

FIELDING:

Bonilla is below average in range and in going to his right for ground balls, but has good hands and rates as average in arm strength and accuracy. He is slightly below average in turning the double play, but above average at making clutch plays. He frequently dives for balls, turning them into outs.

OVERALL:

A courageous player with leadership qualities, Bonilla made a late season comeback after missing four months with a compound fracture of his left wrist, an injury he suffered in a first base collision. At second base, he placed second to Philadelphia's Manny Trillo in a vote of the National League players in 1981.

Coleman: "Bonilla is a pretty good offensive player with good hands on balls he can get to."

FLOYD CHIFFER
RHP, No. 39
RR, 6'2", 180 lbs.
ML Svc: 1 year
Born: 4-20-56 in
Long Island City, NY

PITCHING:

Used primarily in short relief during his last three seasons in minors, Floyd Chiffer also served in long relief as a San Diego rookie and did better than expected in both roles.

A righthander with a three-quarter delivery and a strong, supple arm, Chiffer has an 88 MPH fastball, a hard slider and a forkball that he is inclined to use as his out pitch. When behind in the count, as he is too often, he generally comes in with either the fastball, with which he attempts to jam righthanded batters, or the slider. His pattern is to try to get ahead in the count with his fastball, setting up the forkball or slider.

Chiffer had problems with his control and hung too many breaking pitches, allowing one home run for every nine innings he pitched. However he has good poise on the mound and more desire than confidence, a quality that should improve after he has had more experience at the major league level and becomes better acquainted with the hitters.

He should become much more effective if he can develop a curve or a better change-up, but the real key to his future lies in whether he can develop better control than he had in 1982, when he walked an average of 3.9 batters per nine innings.

Perhaps more than most of the young San Diego pitchers, Chiffer will miss the counsel of veteran bullpen coach Clyde McCullough, a wise and effective tutor with a gift of communicating with inexperienced hurlers, who passed away last season.

FIELDING, HITTING, BASERUNNING:

Chiffer is hitless in his first eight at-bats as a big leaguer and needs to work on his bunting, but shows the ability to make contact. He fielded his position reasonably well. Has fairly good move to first base and, from the stretch, unloads ball to plate quicker than most Padre pitchers. Average baserunner.

OVERALL:

He has the arm for further improvement and should learn to make fewer mistakes with his breaking balls. His progress will depend largely on whether he can improve his control.

Coleman: "Chiffer needs more experience to exploit a fine assortment of pitches. Should get better, depending on his control."

McCarver: "Outstanding stuff, knows the 'how' in pitching at a very young age. Hitters are inclined to swing at his forkballs that are out of the strike zone. Righthanders are vulnerable to his fastballs in, his sliders away and his forkballs down. He can get you out in three areas, but gets behind in the count too much. He should be heard from for a long time."

1982 STATISTICS

W	L	ERA	G	GS	CG	IP	H	R	ER	BB	SO	SV
4	3	2.95	51	0	0	79	73	33	26	34	48	4

CAREER STATISTICS

W	L	ERA	G	GS	CG	IP	H	R	ER	BB	SO	SV
4	3	2.95	51	0	0	79	73	33	26	34	48	4

LUIS DeLEON
RHP, No. 55
RR, 6'1", 153 lbs.
ML Svc: 1 year plus
Born: 8-19-58 in Ponce, PR

PITCHING:

Luis DeLeon was generally considered the National League's most effective rookie relief pitcher last season. He mixed an above average fastball--88 MPH--with a hard sinker and a sweeping slider that was particularly effective against righthanded hitters. He displayed exceptional control, and walked only 16 batters, nine of them intentionally, in 102 innings, and permitted only 93 baserunners (77 via hits).

He is especially effective against predominantly righthanded-hitting teams such as the Braves, Dodgers, Phillies and Expos. DeLeon has a tendency to hang his slider, gave up ten home runs, and had problems with lefthanded hitters because of his sidearm delivery and his lack of a change-up that would keep power hitters offstride.

Because of a loose, supple arm and a natural pitching delivery, DeLeon is able to pitch often. He isn't afraid to throw strikes and is enthusiastic about his work. He developed into the Padres' No. 1 reliever in the second half of the season after Eric Show and Dave Dravecky were promoted to the starting rotation.

His fastball has enough velocity and movement that enables DeLeon to pitch inside to hitters, particularly righthanders, and set them up for sliders on the outside corner.

FIELDING, HITTING, BASERUNNING:

DeLeon is a good athlete with above average fielding and baserunning skills. He has a fairly good move to first base, but is slow delivering the ball to the plate, an area in which he needs to show improvement. Needs a lot of work on his hitting and batting. He is easy to strike out.

OVERALL:

DeLeon has extreme poise, guts and determination. He has two excellent pitches, the fastball and slider, and delivers them with exceptional control. He needs a third pitch, a change-up, screwball, forkball or curve, to become a premier reliever over an extended period of time. He had two brief periods of arm trouble in 1982 because of the overuse of his slider.

Coleman: "One of the best young control pitchers to come along in years. DeLeon is never afraid, and has an excellent attitude."

Kiner: "Had an excellent first year in majors, and became the No. 1 man in the bullpen down the stretch."

McCarver: "Luis started off about third or fourth in effectiveness in that awesome San Diego bullpen. However, he may be their No. 1 man now. A biting, moving fastball and sweeping slider that can freeze righthanded batters are his trademarks. Very poised and relaxed in his delivery."

1982 STATISTICS

W	L	ERA	G	GS	CG	IP	H	R	ER	BB	SO	SV
9	5	2.03	61	0	0	102	77	25	23	16	60	15

CAREER STATISTICS

W	L	ERA	G	GS	CG	IP	H	R	ER	BB	SO	SV
9	6	2.07	71	0	0	117	88	29	27	19	68	15

DAVE DRAVECKY
LHP, No. 43
RL, 6'1", 195 lbs.
ML Svc: 1 year
Born: 2-14-56 in
Youngstown, OH

PITCHING:

Dave Dravecky had most of his minor league success as a starter, but didn't move into the San Diego rotation until he had proven himself in middle and short relief. He was regarded primarily as a control and breaking ball type pitcher until mid-1982 when slight alterations in his three-quarter delivery improved his fastball and moved it into the average to above average category at 85-88 MPH.

Blessed with a fluid motion, Dravecky throws a running, sinking fastball about 65% of the time and mixes it with what is rated to be an average slider. He seldom throws a change-up and is more apt to challenge hitters with his fastball than his slider when he's behind in the count.

Critics believe Dravecky must change speeds more often if he is to continue to progress in the big leagues. However, he keeps the ball down pretty consistently, and has above average control. He can get a batter to hit the balls on the ground in double play situations, and has a high ratio of strikeouts-to-walks. He is slightly better against lefthanders because he can go away from them with low sliders. He has above average poise, especially in pressure situations.

Because of his sinking fastballs, Dravecky seems more effective in ballparks with grass infields that make it more difficult for ground balls to find holes. He pitches best against left-handed hitting teams such as Pittsburgh, San Francisco and St. Louis.

FIELDING, HITTING, BASERUNNING:

Dravecky is a good athlete. He has a fairly good move to first base; it is one that is improving. He is average to slightly above at fielding his position, and should work to improve that skill because he makes so many batters hit the ball on the ground and up the middle. He seldom strikes out and is almost impossible to walk. He is a fair bunter, but an overall weak hitter. He has average speed as a runner but is no threat to steal.

OVERALL:

Dravecky has a bright future because he has exceptional poise and control for a rookie lefthander. He is ambitious, has a loose, supple arm and can either start or relieve. He has the confidence that comes with winning 43 of his first 67 professional decisions.

Coleman: "Dravecky jumped from Class AA to big leagues in one season. He's getting better and has a chance to be outstanding in a few years if he continues to develop."

Kiner: "He made a big jump in spite of lacking a blazing fastball. Dravecky bears watching."

1982 STATISTICS

W	L	ERA	G	GS	CG	IP	H	R	ER	BB	SO	SV
5	3	2.57	31	10	0	105	86	37	30	33	59	2

CAREER STATISTICS

W	L	ERA	G	GS	CG	IP	H	R	ER	BB	SO	SV
5	3	2.57	31	10	0	105	86	37	30	33	59	2

HITTING:

Tim Flannery is a straightaway hitter who lacks speed and power, but has become a useful hitter by making good contact with the bat and developing a good eye for the strike zone.

Primarily a high fastball hitter, Flannery prefers the ball out over the plate, but changed somewhat as a hitter in 1982 when he improved at pulling the inside pitch. The change forced right fielders to stop playing him so far off the line and opened up the alley in right-center for extra base hits in the future. Learning to pull the ball has improved Flannery's ability to execute hit-and-run plays.

Normally, however, Flannery hits line drives and ground balls either up the middle or to the opposite field against righthanded pitchers. He often goes the other way against lefthanders whom he seldom pulls. He hits for a better average against righthanders and does well against their off-speed stuff. Lefties should pitch him inside with fastballs and go away from him with curves. Righthanders should crowd him with fastballs.

Flannery is good at driving in runs from third with fly balls, bunts fairly well and can execute the hit-and-run. As an eighth place hitter, his best spot, he doesn't walk much or strike out very often.

BASERUNNING:

Handicapped by lack of speed, Flannery is no threat to steal but can break up a double play. Rated smart, but conservative, as a baserunner.

FIELDING:

He improved his ability to turn the double play in 1982 after taking over for injured regular second baseman Juan Bonilla in May. His arm strength and range are rated slightly below average, and his throwing accuracy is above average. He goes better to his left than to his right. Flannery often dives for balls and has the knack of making clutch defensive plays.

TIM FLANNERY
INF, No. 6
LR, 5'11", 170 lbs.
ML Svc: 3 years
Born: 9-29-57 in
Tulsa, OK

1982 STATISTICS

AVG	G	AB	R	H	2B	3B	HR	RBI	BB	SO	SB
.264	122	379	40	100	11	7	0	30	30	32	1

CAREER STATISTICS

AVG	G	AB	R	H	2B	3B	HR	RBI	BB	SO	SB
.245	276	803	61	197	27	9	0	65	54	71	4

VS. RHP

VS. LHP

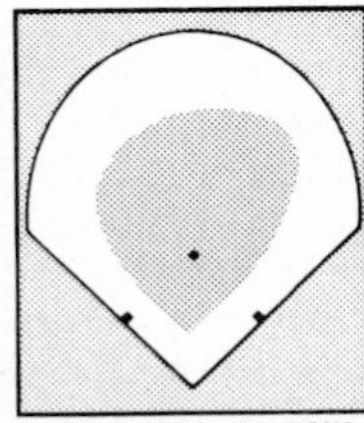
PROBABLE HIT LOCATIONS

OVERALL:

A singles hitter who makes contact, Flannery is a fierce competitor and team man who strives to offset his lack of speed and power.

Coleman: "He gets the most out of what he has to give, and is a winning type of player. Above average pinch-hitter and is a better player than his skills indicate. Will do anything to win."

Kiner: "A utility type player with a limited range; a pinch-hitter with no power. A good back up at second, short or third."

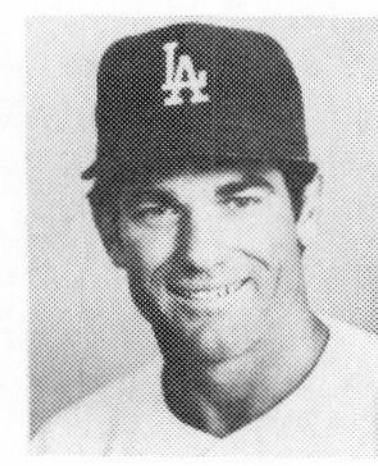

STEVE GARVEY
INF, No. 6
RR, 5'10", 190 lbs.
ML Svc: 12 years
Born: 12-22-48 in
Tampa, FL

1982 STATISTICS

AVG	G	AB	R	H	2B	3B	HR	RBI	BB	SO	SB
.282	162	625	66	176	35	1	16	86	20	86	5

CAREER STATISTICS

AVG	G	AB	R	H	2B	3B	HR	RBI	BB	SO	SB
.301	1727	6543	852	1968	333	35	211	992	367	751	77

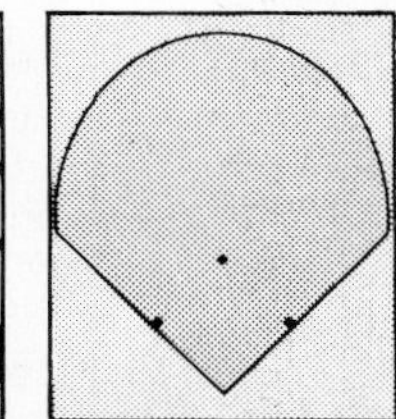

HITTING:

To get Garvey out, a righthander should keep the ball inside, a lefthander outside--and neither necessarily needs to throw a strike. By his own admission, Garvey will go after anything he thinks he can hit. And he's up there to swing the bat, not to walk. He walked only 20 times (10 times intentionally) in 1982.

He'll chase an outside pitch and look bad, but he can come right back and hit the ball out on the next pitch. He will take full advantage of a pitcher's mistake.

Garvey drives pitches that are up, though not necessarily in the strike zone. He's so strong that he fights off pitches on his wrist and he waits well on the change-up. He's a good breaking ball hitter, so it's best to throw fastballs away--far away.

He hits well behind runners on a hit-and-run play, and he also bunts extremely well. Third basemen realize this, but because of Garvey's extreme power they cannot risk playing him shallow.

Earlier in his career he was content to get base hits, going more for average than home runs. But in 1976, when he began to believe he was a good power hitter, too, he hit 33 homers. It was the Los Angeles Dodgers' record, and 20 more than he hit the year before.

Overall, Garvey is an exceptionally consistent hitter with good power who seems to get stronger as the season goes on.

BASERUNNING:

As a basestealer, he runs better than one might expect (he stole 19 bases in 1976). He likes to take a walking lead and if the pitcher doesn't stop him, he's a good bet to steal. He goes hard into second when breaking up a double play, generally with a football-style rolling slide.

FIELDING:

When Garvey is catching the ball, he's excellent. He fields ground balls well and he's especially strong at digging at low throws, undoubtedly saving his infielders numerous errors. But when he's throwing the ball it's another story. All teams, when sacrificing, bunt towards Garvey at first. Seldom does he even attempt to get the lead runner on a sacrifice. He has won four Gold Gloves for his glove, not his arm.

OVERALL:

Garvey has shown remarkable durability over the years (he takes a streak of 1,107 consecutive games into the 1983 season) as well as a steady bat. He has been a very productive hitter.

McCarver: "His achilles heel is his arm."

HITTING:

Tony Gwynn is a straightaway hitter who has a slightly closed stance with a slight crouch, and bats from the center of the box. He is primarily a fastball hitter who can handle that pitch upstairs or down. He also hits hanging breaking balls, but has some problems with low breaking stuff and fastballs inside, particularly from lefthanders. He has trouble waiting on off-speed stuff, but is learning not to be overanxious as he gathers more experience.

Considering his lack of professional playing time, Gwynn is well disciplined and has a pretty good eye at the plate. He will take a walk and makes good contact. He hits better against right-handers. He is a below average home run threat, but hits frequent line drives up the alleys into left-center and right-center. He has the speed to beat out ground balls in the holes and will occasionally drag bunt for a base hit. Gwynn's batting style makes him more effective on synthetic turf and in ballparks with big outfield gaps. He hits the ball where it is pitched. He does not often pull the ball, but can and could bat second in the lineup because of his ability to bunt and to handle the bat in the hit-and-run. He is average to slightly above average at hitting with men in scoring position, at bunting, and on the hit-and-run.

BASERUNNING:

Gwynn has above average speed going to first base, and at this point is slightly above average as a basestealing threat and at breaking up the double play. He is a heady baserunner, but needs to become more aggressive on the basepaths.

FIELDING:

One of Gwynn's few real drawbacks is his slightly below average throwing arm. His accuracy is about average,

TONY GWYNN
OF, No. 53
LL, 5'11", 185 lbs.
ML Svc: 1 year
Born: 5-9-60 in
Los Angeles, CA

1982 STATISTICS

AVG	G	AB	R	H	2B	3B	HR	RBI	BB	SO	SB
.289	54	190	33	55	12	2	1	17	14	16	8

CAREER STATISTICS

AVG	G	AB	R	H	2B	3B	HR	RBI	BB	SO	SB
.289	54	190	33	55	12	2	1	17	14	16	8

VS. RHP

VS. LHP

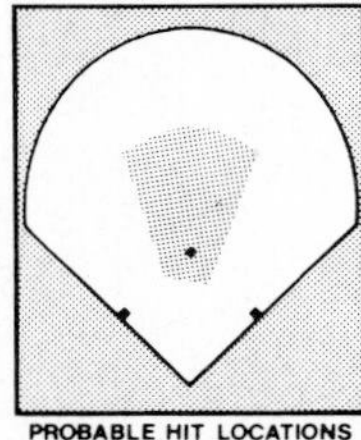
PROBABLE HIT LOCATIONS

though he sometimes misses the cutoff man, allowing runners to take an extra base. He has above average to excellent range in left field or center. He goes well to either side, and is also good at charging the ball.

OVERALL:

Gwynn is an above average hitter, fielder and baserunner who does everything well except throw and hit with power. An intelligent, dedicated player.

Coleman: "Should become an excellent hitter because he does everything else well. He is fundamentally sound with great understanding of the game."

Kiner: "Gwynn should develop into an outstanding player. He made it to majors after only one year in minors."

McCarver: "Gwynn has shown great promise and has a bright future. He shows great instincts in the outfield."

RUPPERT JONES
OF, No. 22
LL, 5'10", 175 lbs.
ML Svc: 6 years
Born: 3-12-55 in
Dallas, TX

1982 STATISTICS

AVG	G	AB	R	H	2B	3B	HR	RBI	BB	SO	SB
.283	116	424	69	120	20	2	12	61	62	90	18

CAREER STATISTICS

AVG	G	AB	R	H	2B	3B	HR	RBI	BB	SO	SB
.255	783	2891	411	737	145	27	77	349	337	505	111

HITTING:

Ruppert Jones is a straightaway hitter with power up the alleys into left-center and right-center. Operating low in the batter's box, he has a slightly closed stance, hits from a moderate crouch and has a good eye for balls and strikes.

Well disciplined at the plate, Jones will take a walk and has a good on-base percentage, but is relatively easy to strike out. He is primarily a high fastball hitter who prefers the ball out over the plate, where he can get full arm extension. He has problems with good fastballs over the inside corner of plate, with curveballs down and in from righthanders, and curves away from lefthanders.

Jones has the speed to beat out ground balls in the holes, is content to make contact against lefthanders, and has good power going to the opposite (left) field. He is an occasional threat to bunt for a base hit, but is inconsistent when asked to bunt the runner to second.

Long considered a streak hitter, Jones had a remarkably consistent first half in 1982, but tailed off badly after suffering a foot injury in late July. He has a history of injuries and illnesses. Plays aggressively and with flair when he is healthy. He has leadership qualities, but seemed to lose interest after his late season injury and batting problems, which began when he struck out eight times in a row.

BASERUNNING:

Jones has above average speed going to first base and the quickness to steal 20-30 bases a year. He is a smart, aggressive baserunner with above average skills at breaking up the double play.

VS. RHP

VS. LHP

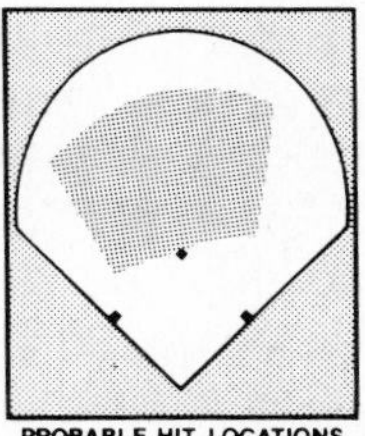
PROBABLE HIT LOCATIONS

FIELDING:

Defensively, Jones gets a good jump on balls hit to center field, has above average range and is good at going back or coming in on balls. He has only average arm strength, but is fairly accurate with his throws.

OVERALL:

Jones is maturing as a hitter, has some power, drives in runs and can bat anywhere from third through fifth in the order.

Coleman: "Jones is an all around good player, the Padres' best until he got hurt. Does everything well."

Kiner: "Jones can hit 20 homers and 30 doubles a year. He has been a very erratic hitter in the past, but came through with an above average season in 1982."

TERRY KENNEDY
C, No. 16
LR, 6'4", 220 lbs.
ML Svc: 4 years
Born: 6-4-56 in
Euclid, OH

1982 STATISTICS

AVG	G	AB	R	H	2B	3B	HR	RBI	BB	SO	SB
.295	153	562	75	166	42	1	21	97	26	91	1

CAREER STATISTICS

AVG	G	AB	R	H	2B	3B	HR	RBI	BB	SO	SB
.286	381	1330	146	380	85	5	29	191	86	201	1

VS. RHP

VS. LHP

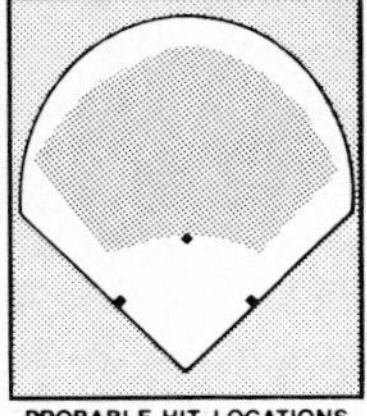
PROBABLE HIT LOCATIONS

HITTING:

Terry Kennedy underwent a remarkable transformation at the plate in 1982, when he learned to pull the ball and developed into a power hitter. Primarily a gap hitter, he was second in the league in doubles. After a bad start, he became remarkably consistent. He was among the National League leaders in RBIs while hitting sixth most of the year, and developed a reputation for delivering key hits in game-winning situations.

Kennedy is an aggressive hitter who is reluctant to accept a base on balls. He strikes out a lot, though he has a good knowledge of the strike zone. He readily goes to the opposite field, particularly against lefthanders with good breaking stuff and depending upon the score and situation in the game.

Although he does not have an overly quick bat, Kennedy has improved his swing speed and can pull a good righthander's fastball if he is looking for it, and he waits well enough to jerk a righthander's curve. Against lefthanders, he is more inclined to hit the ball up the middle or to left field and does it well. He likes the ball out over the plate and up in the strike zone. Is susceptible to good fastballs inside.

BASERUNNING:

Kennedy is big even for a catcher, and lacks the speed to beat out topped rollers or ground balls in the hole and is not a threat to steal bases.

FIELDING:

Because of his size, Kennedy's slow footwork also slows down his release time on throws and detracts from his strong arm and above average accuracy. His pitchers, however, are largely responsible for his low percentage of runners caught stealing. He has improved at handling pitchers and at blocking pitches in the dirt.

OVERALL:

One of the game's most productive hitters, Kennedy is hard working and is developing leadership qualities. He may eventually shift to first base because of his size, and could be a future great.

Kiner: "Kennedy has become an outstanding hitter who will challenge Gary Carter for top-hitting catcher honors."

McCarver: "Kennedy is an above average catcher who should get better. He must watch his weight, and his size is not in his favor. He has good power, but does his best in big parks that are suited for gap hitters. His bat speed will improve as his strength increases."

Coleman: "One of the better hitters around, and should continue to improve."

JOE LEFEBVRE
OF, No. 18
LR, 5'10", 175 lbs.
ML Svc: 3 years
Born: 2-22-56 in Concord, NH

1982 STATISTICS

AVG	G	AB	R	H	2B	3B	HR	RBI	BB	SO	SB
.238	102	239	25	57	9	0	4	21	18	50	0

CAREER STATISTICS

AVG	G	AB	R	H	2B	3B	HR	RBI	BB	SO	SB
.243	262	635	82	154	13	5	20	73	80	113	6

VS. RHP

VS. LHP

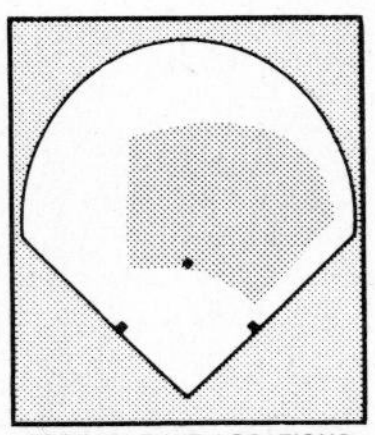
PROBABLE HIT LOCATIONS

HITTING:

Joe Lefebvre is a pull hitter with above average power who has been slow to develop after three impressive minor league seasons. He is a high fastball hitter who likes the ball out over the plate so he can get full arm extension. He often gets jammed with inside fastballs, a problem that sometimes leaves him with painful hand bruises.

Lefebvre is much more effective against righthanders, and does not pull as often against southpaws. He has trouble with curveballs and pitches that are out of the strike zone because he is prone to become overanxious at the plate and is not a disciplined, patient hitter. He seldom draws a walk and strikes out often because there are several types of pitches that he doesn't handle well and he often swings at bad balls. He has the power to reach the alleys, but hasn't done it often enough to nail down a regular job in right field or at third base.

Lefebvre is below average as a clutch hitter, at hitting with runners in scoring position, at bunting and at executing the hit-and-run. He has an average ability to hit behind the runner, and is regarded as purely a streak hitter who goes into prolonged slumps that are intensified by his overanxiousness to succeed.

BASERUNNING:

Lefebvre has slightly below average speed running to first base and has stolen only six bases in two seasons. He can break up a double play if he gets there on time, and is conservative on the basepaths.

FIELDING:

One of Lefebvre's biggest assets is a rifle arm. Because of it, he is ideally suited to right field, where he makes up for his lack of speed by getting a good jump on the ball and charging balls hit in front of him. He is inexperienced at third base, but has good hands and is not afraid to get in front of the ball. He can bobble grounders but still get outs because his arm is both powerful and accurate. He does, however, need improvement on handling bunts and slow-hit grounders and on positioning himself for each hitter.

OVERALL:

Lefebvre could become a destructive hitter against righthanders if he learns to relax at the plate and become more selective. Overly ambitious, he tends to fight himself when things aren't going well and becomes his own worst enemy.

Coleman: "Lefebvre has many fine tools but is much too intense and must learn the strike zone."

HITTING:

Sixto Lezcano is an experienced power hitter who crouches noticeably in a closed stance, positioning himself from the center to the back of the batter's box. Although he will pull certain pitches, he is a straightaway hitter because he frequently drives the ball up the alleys in right-center and left-center and can hit the ball over the fence in right field.

Primarily a fastball hitter, Lezcano can jump on hanging breaking balls and handles all sorts of pitching. He has a history of hitting better against right-handers, and can handle the fastball either up or down if it is out over the plate. Pitchers must pitch him fastballs in or breaking balls low and away.

Lezcano was remarkably consistent last season, despite injury problems that have persisted throughout his career. He crowds the plate and is prone to being hit on the hands and wrists by pitchers trying to jam him with fastballs or attempting to move him back.

He has a good eye for balls and strikes and walks often. He is an aggressive hitter, who will rise to the occasion with men in scoring position and can drive in important runs. Has surprising strength for someone his size, and did much in 1982 to disprove his reputation as one who uses his injuries as an excuse.

BASERUNNING:

Lezcano has had foot problems in the past, and is rated as an average to slightly below average runner. He is a smart baserunner, average at breaking up the double play and below average as a basestealing threat.

FIELDING:

Fielding is one of Lezcano's strongest points. He is a right fielder who has above average arm strength and accuracy, gets a good jump on the ball, and is adept at going back on the ball or coming in.

SIXTO LEZCANO
OF, No. 14
RR, 5'10", 175 lbs.
ML Svc: 8 years
Born: 11-28-53 in Arecibo, PR

1982 STATISTICS

AVG	G	AB	R	H	2B	3B	HR	RBI	BB	SO	SB
.289	138	470	73	136	26	6	16	84	78	69	2

CAREER STATISTICS

AVG	G	AB	R	H	2B	3B	HR	RBI	BB	SO	SB
.277	995	3406	459	942	164	30	123	486	451	634	36

VS. RHP

VS. LHP

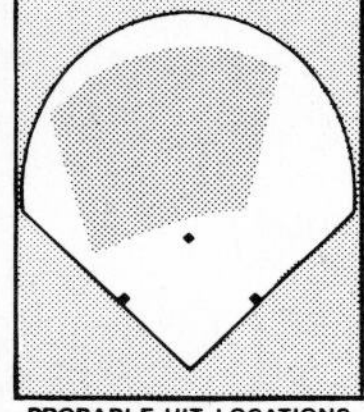
PROBABLE HIT LOCATIONS

OVERALL:

Coleman: "Lezcano is a quality major league player who has lived up to his full potential. Does everything but run real well. Tough in the clutch when you need a hit or a walk and has a good eye."

Kiner: "Lezcano recovered from an off-year and solved National League pitching. His absence with injuries the last three weeks of the season hurt the Padres' chances of winning the Western Division championship."

McCarver: "An excellent hitter who makes good contact for someone with power. A great talent who does things quite smoothly."

PITCHING:

Tim Lollar was baseball's most improved pitcher in 1982 because he learned to throw strikes with his 90 MPH fastball and hard slider, developed confidence in his change-up and was permitted to start on a regular basis for the first time in his five seasons as a professional.

A power pitcher with an overhand delivery, Lollar learned to work both corners of the plate and became adept at jamming hitters, particularly righthanders. He is also effective against lefthanders, going away from them with his hard slider.

He throws a live fastball 65% of time, the slider about 30%. He is not afraid to challenge hitters, and will throw the slider when behind in the count if he has control of it that day. Can beat anybody when he's right.

He won 10 of his first 12 decisions, two of them shutouts, but hit a rut in mid-season after developing Reynaud's Phenomenon, a circulatory problem that causes a numbness in the first two fingers of his pitching hand.

A free spirit both on and off the field, Lollar shows unusual poise for his age, but sometimes seems to lose his concentration. He gets hurt when he forgets to stay on top of his slider and hangs it, as he did on many of the 20 home runs he allowed.

He does not have a consistently outstanding slider, but compensates with his ability to move the ball around and change speeds. He has pitched only 540 innings professionally, his early progress having been slowed by an indecision over whether he had greater potential as a power-hitting outfielder.

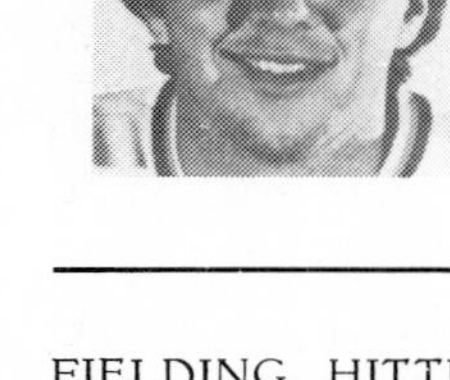

TIM LOLLAR
LHP, No. 48
LL, 6'3", 195 lbs.
ML Svc: 2 years
Born: 3-17-56 in Poplar Bluff, MO

FIELDING, HITTING, BASERUNNING:

An All-American as a designated hitter at Arkansas, Lollar has outstanding power at the plate (3 homers in 1982) and was even used as a pinch-hitter, but has problems with breaking balls and changes of speed. He is an average fielder and needs an improved move to first. Average to below average runner.

OVERALL:

Lollar has merely scratched the surface of his pitching potential. He has the strength, intelligence and desire to improve with experience if he can avoid a worsening of his circulatory problem.

McCarver: "Lollar has blossomed into one of the quality starters in the National League. He handles pressure situations well for his age and is a talented hitter with a great stroke. Can beat any team when he is on."

Coleman: "Lollar loses his control sometimes, but he has an outstanding fastball, an excellent slider at times, and he'll challenge the hitters. He has a chance to be great if he stays healthy and doesn't let his free spirit rule him."

1982 STATISTICS

W	L	ERA	G	GS	CG	IP	H	R	ER	BB	SO	SV
16	9	3.13	34	34	4	232	192	82	81	87	150	0

CAREER STATISTICS

W	L	ERA	G	GS	CG	IP	H	R	ER	BB	SO	SV
19	17	3.83	72	46	4	341	312	152	145	158	201	3

GARY LUCAS
LHP, No. 25
LL, 6'5", 200 lbs.
ML Svc: 3 years
Born: 11-8-54 in Riverside, CA

PITCHING:

A scout can rate a player's running, throwing, hitting and fielding ability without knowing what's going on in the mind and heart of someone struggling the way Gary Lucas did in 1982.

A sinker-slider control pitcher with a deceptive three-quarter sidearm delivery, this lefthanded short relief specialist fell short with the Padres' first real title contender after pitching effectively for two years with last place San Diego teams. Lucas' problems may have been compounded in mid-season when manager Dick Williams suggested publicly that Lucas, his most experienced reliever, might not be equal to the pressure of competing for high stakes. Williams vowed never again to use Lucas in clutch situations, a promise he could not keep, and there were clubhouse whispers that the Padres might have won their division except for Lucas' failures.

Lucas allowed fewer hits than innings pitched and had an average of only 2.03 unintentional walks per nine innings. However, his 16 saves were outweighed by 10 losses and his inability to hold late-inning leads on a number of other occasions.

When he's right, Lucas throws strikes at the knees or below. He can go away from lefthanded hitters with his slider or use it to jam righthand hitters looking for a pitch outside. It was part of his problem in 1982 that hitters stopped swinging at sinkers that were out of the strike zone, causing him to fall behind in the count and forcing him to come up with 85 MPH fastballs. Normally more effective against lefthanded batters, Lucas had trouble with both when the chips were on the line.

FIELDING, HITTING, BASERUNNING:

A below average baserunner, Lucas also went hitless, struck out more than half the time and needs work on his bunting. Holds men on base well and is difficult to run on.

OVERALL:

Coleman: "Lucas must keep the ball low to all hitters to be effective. He's a hard worker and an excellent man on a team but he needs to mature in pressure situations and isn't aggressive enough."

Kiner: "Lucas lacked command of his pitches in 1982, batters quit swinging at balls out of the strike zone and he went right down the drain."

McCarver: "Lucas can get the ground ball with his sinker when he's behind in the count or in a jam. He makes lefthanded hitters give in when he drops down and throws sidearm. When his control is right, he can make righthanded hitters give up on the slider he throws on the outside corner."

1982 STATISTICS

W	L	ERA	G	GS	CG	IP	H	R	ER	BB	SO	SV
1	10	3.24	65	0	0	97	89	42	35	29	64	16

CAREER STATISTICS

W	L	ERA	G	GS	CG	IP	H	R	ER	BB	SO	SV
13	25	2.91	168	18	0	337	305	127	109	108	202	32

JOHN MONTEFUSCO
RHP, No. 27
RR, 6'1", 192 lbs.
ML Svc: 8 years
Born: 5-25-50 in
Long Branch, NJ

PITCHING:

A free agent dropped by Atlanta, John Montefusco made a fine comeback as a starting pitcher after he stopped popping off, got himself back in shape and regained his control. Cortisone shots cured his early season hip problem and Montefusco kept the Padres close in most of the games he started. A lack of endurance usually keeps him from lasting more than six or seven innings.

Montefusco uses a herky-jerky three-quarter delivery and throws a 88-90 MPH fastball about 60% of the time. His out pitch against righthanded hitters is his hard slider, a sweeping-type of pitch that is very effective. He will throw the fastball or slider when he's behind in the count, depending on which pitch is working the best on that particular day.

He is a veteran who remains more of a power pitcher and thrower than one with finesse. John sometimes loses composure and control when he thinks that the home plate umpire isn't giving him the corners. He has problems with lefthanded hitters and would be much more successful if he could develop a better third pitch--an effective change-up, curve or forkball.

He isn't afraid to challenge hitters, but does not keep the ball down consistently and gives up too many home runs (one every 11 innings in 1982). He also gives up long fly balls and is best suited to the bigger ballparks in San Diego, Houston and St. Louis. He has the most success against predominantly righthanded hitting teams. He is dependent upon good relief support.

Montefusco decided in 1982 that he has never been in top-flight shape physically and has begun a conditioning program.

FIELDING, HITTING, BASERUNNING:

Montefusco is poor at holding runners on base, which is a serious flaw in the late innings of close games. Below average baserunning speed, he has deteriorated as a hitter and strikes out more than half the time. An average bunter.

OVERALL:

A keen competitor, Montefusco profited by being placed on a one-year $100,000 contract with incentive bonus clauses that kept his nose to the grindstone. He has matured after a history of problems with managers.

Kiner: "Montefusco lost his overpowering fastball, but can still pitch .500 because of his control and experience. He mixes up his pitches now and can throw to spots."

Coleman: "Takes charge on the mound. With Montefusco, it's simply a matter of whether he has good stuff the day he pitches. A good man in big games; he doesn't scare."

McCarver: "John concerns himself with his own strengths, rather than the hitter's weakness. Gets ahead with fastballs, rarely throws breaking balls if he's behind in the count. An above average pitcher."

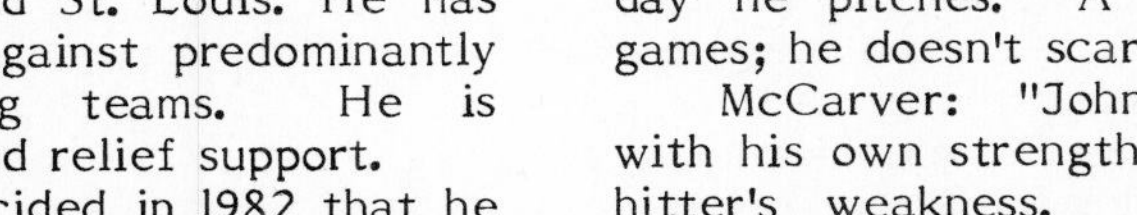

1982 STATISTICS

W	L	ERA	G	GS	CG	IP	H	R	ER	BB	SO	SV
10	11	4.00	32	32	1	184	177	93	82	41	83	0

CAREER STATISTICS

W	L	ERA	G	GS	CG	IP	H	R	ER	BB	SO	SV
71	76	3.54	243	216	31	1443	1395	639	568	451	986	1

JOE PITTMAN
INF, No. 8
RR, 6'1", 180 lbs.
ML Svc: 1 year plus
Born: 1-1-54 in
Houston, TX

HITTING:

A singles hitter with speed, Joe Pittman is primarily a high fastball hitter who hits the ball straightaway. He has the speed to first base to beat out slow rollers or balls hit in the hole. He also bunts well, but lacks the power to drive the ball up the alleys with any degree of consistency.

Pittman hits mostly short line drives and ground balls to the shortstop or second base, encouraging outfielders to shorten up and shade him toward center. He hits lefthanders better than righthanders and is vulnerable to breaking pitches from righthanders. It's best to pitch him outside and keep the ball down.

Accustomed to batting at the top of the order, or near the bottom, Pittman has shown a below average ability to drive in runs. He does not walk often, and is prone to striking out against righthanded breaking ball pitchers. He bunts well and is average at executing the hit-and-run.

Because he often hits the ball on the ground Pittman hits for a higher average in synthetic turf parks. However, natural turf improves his chances of bunting for base hits.

BASERUNNING:

Baserunning is one of the things that Pittman does best. Possessed with above average speed, he has the ability to steal 20 or more bases if he played regularly. He is a smart, aggressive runner who can take the extra base and help a team as a pinch-runner in critical, late-inning situations.

FIELDING:

A second baseman by trade, Pittman has the range and arm to also fill in at third base or shortstop. His arm strength, accuracy and range are

1982 STATISTICS

AVG	G	AB	R	H	2B	3B	HR	RBI	BB	SO	SB
.250	70	128	16	32	3	0	0	7	9	15	8

CAREER STATISTICS

AVG	G	AB	R	H	2B	3B	HR	RBI	BB	SO	SB
.261	112	268	27	70	7	2	0	14	20	31	12

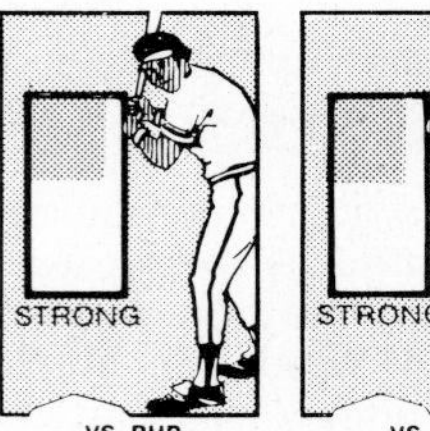

VS. RHP

VS. LHP

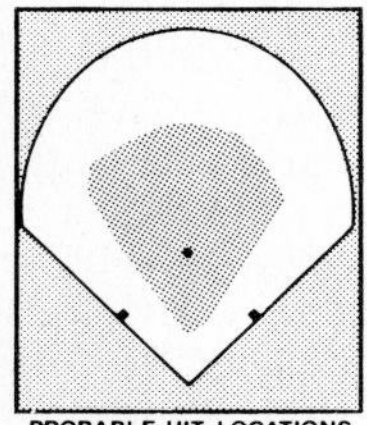
PROBABLE HIT LOCATIONS

all rated average, as is his ability to turn the double play, field bunts and make clutch defensive plays.

OVERALL:

Pittman is a journeyman utility infielder who makes up for his lack of power with his baserunning and his ability to fill in well in the middle of the infield.

Coleman: "Does a lot of things fairly well, but is not an everyday player. Accepts his role and is cool under fire."

McCarver: "Joe should be a better player, he really hasn't been given a chance. His tools in all areas are at least average."

Kiner: "Borderline player who needs to improve both offensively and defensively."

GENE RICHARDS
OF, No. 17
LL, 6'0", 175 lbs.
ML Svc: 6 years
Born: 9-29-53 in Monticello, SC

1982 STATISTICS

AVG	G	AB	R	H	2B	3B	HR	RBI	BB	SO	SB
.286	132	521	63	149	13	8	3	28	36	52	30

CAREER STATISTICS

AVG	G	AB	R	H	2B	3B	HR	RBI	BB	SO	SB
.292	844	3181	447	930	112	60	23	229	321	391	228

VS. RHP

VS. LHP

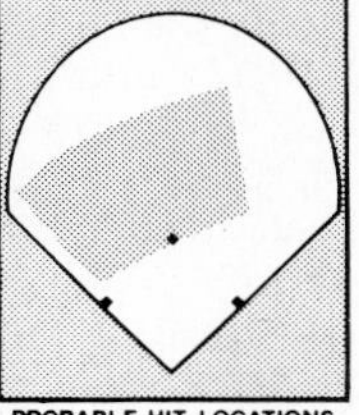
PROBABLE HIT LOCATIONS

HITTING:

Gene Richards chokes up on the bat about six inches, and is an ideal leadoff batter because of his speed. He gets off to slow starts at the plate and does better during the second half of the season.

Primarily a fastball hitter who prefers the ball up, Richards can drive the low fastball when he's in a groove. He tends to be a streak hitter whose slumps are puzzling because of his short stroke and his emphasis on making contact. He has little power, and is more likely to hit the ball to the opposite field or up the middle than to pull it. He frequently drives the ball up the alleys in left-center and right-center.

Richards has below average ability to drive in runners in scoring position and to hit behind the runner because he does not often pull the ball. He will bunt for a base hit, but doesn't bunt as often as he should. He is a line drive and ground ball hitter who benefits from synthetic turf fields and parks with big dimensions, such as St. Louis, Houston and San Diego.

Richards does much better against righthanded pitchers. He does not hit the breaking ball well, especially against lefthanders, and often gives up on inside fastballs that he takes for strikes. He is a better hitter leading off because he sees more fastballs in that spot than he did when he batted third in 1980. He will take a walk, but should do it more often.

BASERUNNING:

He is a fleet runner, but was slowed a bit after arthroscopic knee surgery in April 1982. He is an accomplished basestealer who slides hard into the bag, feet first. He lacks keen instincts on the bases, and has to be urged to be more aggressive on the basepaths.

FIELDING:

Richards has improved his arm strength and throwing accuracy, and is now average to slightly above. He is an uncertain fielder and loses balls in the lights and sun. He comes in well on some balls, but generally has problems going back.

OVERALL:

He is a better than average hitter and baserunner, below average at fielding and driving in runs. A moody player lacking leadership qualities.

McCarver: "Richards is a good contact hitter, has excellent speed, and should be a better defensive player because of his speed."

Coleman: "Is not a good fielder, but is doing his best with the ability he has. His greatest value is getting on base and stealing."

LUIS SALAZAR
INF, No. 4
RR, 6'0", 185 lbs.
ML Svc: 2 years
Born: 5-19-56 in Barcelona, VEN

1982 STATISTICS

AVG	G	AB	R	H	2B	3B	HR	RBI	BB	SO	SB
.242	145	524	55	127	15	5	8	62	23	80	32

CAREER STATISTICS

AVG	G	AB	R	H	2B	3B	HR	RBI	BB	SO	SB
.279	298	1093	120	305	38	18	12	125	48	177	54

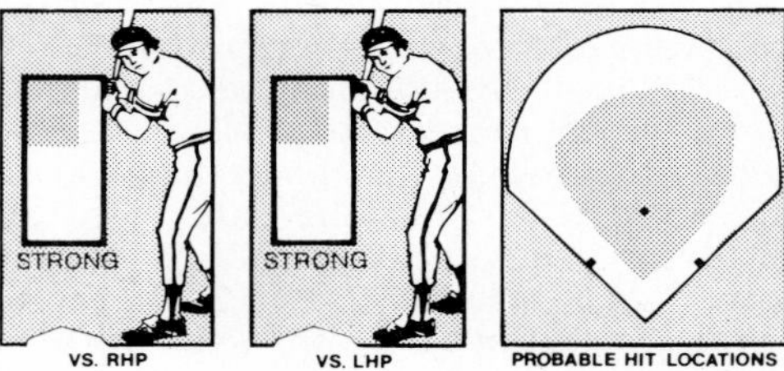

HITTING:

Luis Salazar generally hits the ball up the middle and to right field, but must be classified as a spray hitter because he will sharply pull off-speed pitches.

Basically a line drive hitter, he has the speed to beat out slow rollers and ground balls in the holes. He has moderate home run power and the ability to drive the ball up the alleys, hitting slicing liners into the right field corner or pulling the ball over the bag at third. He also bunts occasionally to take advantage of his good speed.

Salazar is a high fastball hitter who likes the ball out over the plate. He tends to uppercut the ball, collapses his left arm in the swing and frequently overswings. He can be burned with fastballs inside and will chase bad breaking balls away. He is undisciplined at the plate, will seldom take a walk and has a history of slow starts and strong second half finishes.

He is average at hitting in the clutch or with runners in scoring position. Salazar likes to hit to right field, but is not dependable on the hit-and-run because he often does not make contact. He strikes out every six or seven times at bat and normally hits for a higher average against right-handers. He seems to have problems hitting in cold weather, but heats up with the bat when the temperature rises.

Salazar performs with enthusiasm, but seems to need a more analytical approach to hitting to become more patient and selective at the plate. He now swings at too many bad pitches.

BASERUNNING:

Salazar has above average speed going to first base, is adept at taking the extra base, gets a good lead off the base and is an above average basestealing threat. He is an aggressive baserunner with a feet first slide.

FIELDING:

He has an outstanding throwing arm, average accuracy and above average range going to his left. A converted outfielder still making adjustments at third base, Salazar is erratic in fielding ground balls and handling either bunts or topped rollers.

OVERALL:

Coleman: "Luis takes at least 20 points off his average by swinging at bad pitches. He has tools to be a great player, but still makes careless mistakes and must analyze the game better. Good man on a ball club."

Kiner: "He failed to live up to his potential in his first full season in the majors. His defense at third base was off and returning him to the outfield might be worth consideration."

ERIC SHOW
RHP, No. 44
RR, 6'1", 185 lbs.
ML Svc: 1 year plus
Born: 5-19-56 in Riverside, CA

PITCHING:

Eric Show was one of the National League's most impressive rookie pitchers in 1982 because he established himself as a short reliever in the first half of the season, and as a starter in the second half.

For half a season, Show was a power pitcher, mixing high velocity fastballs (89-90 MPH) with a hard slider. In short relief, he exasperated manager Dick Williams with his habit of walking the leadoff batter in the late innings of close games. Once he was promoted to the starting rotation, Show partly corrected his bad habit of trying to overthrow the ball. Concentrating on throwing strikes and getting ahead of the hitters, he developed a sinking fastball that sunk so much he was sometimes falsely accused of throwing a spitter.

Show will develop into an outstanding pitcher once he harnesses his penchant for strikeouts, learns to stay ahead of the hitters and develops an off-speed pitch be it a change-up, forkball, or slow curve to go with his hard stuff.

FIELDING, HITTING, BASERUNNING:

Show is rated an average fielder for a pitcher, but should strive for improvement in this area because of the number of grounders that are hit back through the box when he throws his sinker. He is rated above average in holding runners on base and has a fairly quick delivery to the plate. He needs lots of work on his hitting and bunting.

OVERALL:

Show has been a consistent winner in his five seasons as a professional and has the tools to become a 20-game winner. He averaged only three walks and seven hits per nine innings in 1982 and had two shutouts in 14 starts, but needs to develop an off-speed pitch and must learn to become more relaxed and composed in pressure situations.

Unlike the average player, Show has a wide range of off-field interests. A physics major in college, he studies politics, religion, philosophy, is a whiz on the jazz guitar and has the intelligence to master the art of pitching.

McCarver: "Show has two areas of the plate in which he can get you out--inside and outside. He is a two-pitch pitcher, but so was Bob Gibson."

Coleman: "Show has excellent potential. He must learn to get ahead of the hitters, and he should continue to improve. He is a good student of the game. He is most effective against righthanded hitters, but can handle any hitter when he has his best fastball."

Kiner: "Eric was very productive as a rookie, he merited consideration for Rookie of the Year."

1982 STATISTICS

W	L	ERA	G	GS	CG	IP	H	R	ER	BB	SO	SV
10	6	2.64	47	14	2	150	117	49	44	48	88	3

CAREER STATISTICS

W	L	ERA	G	GS	CG	IP	H	R	ER	BB	SO	SV
11	9	2.71	62	14	2	173	134	58	52	57	110	6

ELIAS SOSA
RHP, No. 36
RR, 6'2", 205 lbs.
ML Svc: 11 years
Born: 6-10-50 in
La Vega, DR

PITCHING:

Sosa is a journeyman righthanded reliever who caught on with Detroit at the end of spring training last year. The Tigers were his seventh stop in an 11-year major league career.

A power pitcher, Sosa still relies on his 88-90 MPH fastball. He uses it most of the time but also goes with the slider, which rates slightly above average as well. He has a curve but doesn't use it very much. Sosa does have a forkball, or palmball, which he'll use occasionally as an extra pitch, but when he's behind in the count, look for the fastball. He'll just try to blow the hitter away.

He is more effective against righthanders since he faces them most of the time. That's been his job as a reliever--to get righthanders out.

Sosa was hampered last season by a lack of knowledge of the American League hitters, since he pitched virtually his entire career in the National League. He still has good poise and presence on the mound and will challenge hitters. He's starting to lose more and more of those challenges, though, to the home run.

FIELDING:

Sosa's move to first base is good for a righthander. It is quick and rates average to slightly above. He still fields bunts well and rates average at fielding his position overall.

OVERALL:

Sosa appeared in 38 games for Detroit, the second highest on the team. In 1983, however, his future is not secure. He still has an ability to get hitters out for an inning or two, though not as consistently as he once did.

Robinson: "A veteran who still knows how to pitch. Did not do a bad job in 1982."

Martin: "Sosa is a hard-throwing righthander who I think will be better in 1983 after getting a year to know the American League. Above average stuff and well suited for short relief."

1982 STATISTICS

W	L	ERA	G	GS	CG	IP	H	R	ER	BB	SO	SV
3	3	4.43	38	0	0	61	64	31	30	18	24	9

CAREER STATISTICS

W	L	ERA	G	GS	CG	IP	H	R	ER	BB	SO	SV
58	47	3.23	560	2	0	846	801	347	304	317	493	87

GARRY TEMPLETON
INF, No. 1
SR, 5'11", 170 lbs.
ML Svc: 6 years
Born: 3-24-56 in Lockey, TX

1982 STATISTICS

AVG	G	AB	R	H	2B	3B	HR	RBI	BB	SO	SB
.247	141	563	76	139	25	8	6	64	26	82	27

CAREER STATISTICS

AVG	G	AB	R	H	2B	3B	HR	RBI	BB	SO	SB
.296	854	3553	519	1050	150	77	31	345	120	461	265

HITTING:

Garry Templeton is a switch-hitter who is blessed with above average speed. He often merely slaps at the ball lefthanded, usually hitting grounders to the left side or short line drives to left or left-center. However, he has the ability to line the ball up the alleys in left-center and right-center when facing righthanded pitchers. Templeton rarely pulls the ball from the left side, and outfielders tend to play him like a righthanded pull hitter.

Templeton has a slightly higher lifetime average from the right side of the plate and slightly more power from that side. He experienced the worst year of his career in 1982 when he switched from an AstroTurf home field to grass. He made many ground ball outs in San Diego that would have been hits in St. Louis. He was further slowed by injuries to both knees and missed the last three weeks with a lower back sprain but, batting third, led National League shortstops in run production with 64 RBI, and 76 runs scored.

An undisciplined first ball, fastball hitter, Templeton swings at too many bad pitches, especially high fastballs. He averages a walk per week, strikes out too much and last season, often failed to drive in runners from third with less than two out. A low ball hitter from left side, can be jammed with sliders. He pulls the ball righthanded, and likes pitches up and out over the plate from that side. Above average bunter and average hitting behind the runner.

BASERUNNING:

Templeton stole 27 bases even with knee problems, and could steal 50 if healthy. His condition could improve with an exercise program.

FIELDING:

Templeton is judged to have the greatest range among National League shortstops, going either to his left or right. He has a strong, erratic arm. He makes most difficult plays but tends to bobble easy chances, and his arm can be inconsistent. He is best at going back on shallow pop-ups in the outfield.

VS. RHP

VS. LHP

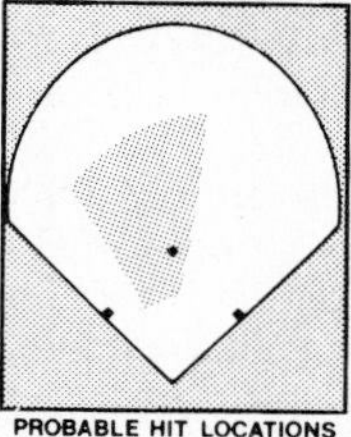
PROBABLE HIT LOCATIONS

OVERALL:

He has outstanding ability and could lead the league in hitting if he becomes more selective at the plate.

McCarver: "He turns the double play like a magician, and makes spectacular plays routinely. Garry is not even close to peaking. He goes to his left and right better than anyone I've seen, and can be almost as good as he wants to be. He could turn out to be the best player in the game."

Kiner: "Has unlimited potential, but demonstrated little of it in 1982."

CHRIS WELSH
LHP, No. 26
LL, 6'2", 185 lbs.
ML Svc: 2 years
Born: 4-15-55 in Wilmington, DE

PITCHING:

Because he has a below average major league fastball, only 75-78 MPH, Chris Welsh is the kind of pitcher who has to live by his wits. When he has complete command of his fastball, screwball and slider, Welsh keeps the ball down consistently and, over nine innings, can be expected to retire as many as 18 to 20 batters on ground balls.

He has an unorthodox, herky-jerky three-quarter pitching delivery that is particularly effective against power hitters with big swings. Like pitchers Tommy John and Randy Jones who have similar stuff and pitching styles, Welsh tends to have problems with contact hitters who are patient and willing to go up the middle with him or to the opposite field.

Because he tries to make batters hit the ball on the ground, Welsh is more effective on grass and can't win without good infield support. His best pitch, the screwball, makes him more effective against righthanded hitters, though he can handle lefthanders when he stays on top of his slider and can spot it low on the outside corner.

He gets hurt often when he gets his pitches up in the strike zone and when his breaking balls are flat. His fastball, though lacking velocity, tends to run away from righthanded batters and in on lefthanders. Welsh was injured in spring training, fracturing his foot, and missed the first three weeks of the season. He was generally inconsistent and was switched to spotstarting and long relief in mid-season.

FIELDING, HITTING, BASERUNNING:

Welsh began to develop into a first-rate hitter (.262 average, 11 RBI) in 1982. He is adept at picking runners off first base and second but, from stretch, is slow in delivering ball to plate. He is an average baserunner.

OVERALL:

Welsh had problems with his delivery after winning five of his first six decisions last season. He falls behind on too many hitters and needs better control. He has a bad habit of looking straight down at the ground when delivering the ball.

Coleman: "Motion is Welsh's key asset because he doesn't have much stuff. He can't survive if his control is off, and must be letter perfect on every pitch."

McCarver: "Fair stuff but he finds it difficult to throw to spots. He seems fairly poised but is handicapped by a flat breaking ball and he may be trying to be too true."

Kiner: "Welsh uses his fastball to set up his screwball which he uses as his out pitch. He seems more effective against righthanded hitters because of his screwball."

1982 STATISTICS

W	L	ERA	G	GS	CG	IP	H	R	ER	BB	SO	SV
8	8	4.91	28	20	3	139	146	88	76	63	48	0

CAREER STATISTICS

W	L	ERA	G	GS	CG	IP	H	R	ER	BB	SO	SV
14	15	4.38	50	39	7	263	268	143	128	104	99	0

ED WHITSON
RHP, No. 32
RR, 6'3", 200 lbs.
ML Svc: 5 years
Born: 5-19-55 in Jefferson City, TN

PITCHING:

Whitson had two seasons with the Indians. For most of 1982, he was used out of the bullpen, primarily in middle relief. He was very inconsistent in that role. In August, injuries opened a spot in the starting rotation for him and he was one of the better pitchers around during the last two months of the year.

There is nothing tricky about Whitson's delivery. He has a compact windup and he throws three-quarter. He gets a lot of his body into his pitches. He is a power pitcher. His fastball is 88-90 MPH and especially tough when he keeps it low because it will sink. His slider can be vicious and righthanded hitters often swing at it as it breaks out of the strike zone. His curveball is average. He has a palmball that serves as his change-up, but he seldom uses it.

Usually, Whitson has good control, although he will have an occasional period when he has trouble getting anything over. This often happened to him when he pitched in relief.

Once he became a starter, Whitson was very effective against Milwaukee and Boston. Even though his fastball is his most reliable pitch, he beat these teams with his curve and slider. He has the ability to keep power hitters off stride.

Whitson may have the arm to pitch out of the bullpen, but it is a question if he has the makeup to handle the job. He did not like relief while in Cleveland, and openly complained about it. He will be a happier player if he remains a starter in San Diego.

FIELDING:

Whitson often forgets there are runners on base, which makes him very prone to the stolen base. He gets into a pattern where he will look to first only once and then throw to the plate. Good baserunners pick up on this tendency and take advantage of it. He needs to make more throws to first base.

He handles ground balls pretty well and usually covers first base when the situation calls for it.

OVERALL:

Whitson has the ability to be a very fine major league pitcher. In the past, he has had low earned run averages, but losing records. He is best suited as a starter. He does have a tendency to tire in the last few innings of a game.

Robinson: "Since becoming a starter, Whitson has been outstanding. The Indians liked him so much they traded John Denny to Philadelphia for him in September 1982. Overall, he has good stuff and now in San Diego, I believe he will develop into a top notch pitcher."

Martin: "Whitson is durable and had a fine year in the American League. He was a good starter in the NL, a fine reliever and starter with Cleveland, and will be welcomed back to the National League."

1982 STATISTICS

W	L	ERA	G	GS	CG	IP	H	R	ER	BB	SO	SV
4	2	3.26	40	9	1	107	91	43	39	58	61	2

CAREER STATISTICS

W	L	ERA	G	GS	CG	IP	H	R	ER	BB	SO	SV
34	41	3.55	181	91	11	690	671	312	272	282	383	7

ALAN WIGGINS
OF, No. 2
SR, 6'2", 165 lbs.
ML Svc: 1 year plus
Born: 2-17-58 in
Los Angeles, CA

1982 STATISTICS

AVG	G	AB	R	H	2B	3B	HR	RBI	BB	SO	SB
.256	72	254	40	65	3	3	1	15	13	19	33

CAREER STATISTICS

AVG	G	AB	R	H	2B	3B	HR	RBI	BB	SO	SB
.261	87	268	44	70	3	3	1	15	14	19	35

VS. RHP

VS. LHP

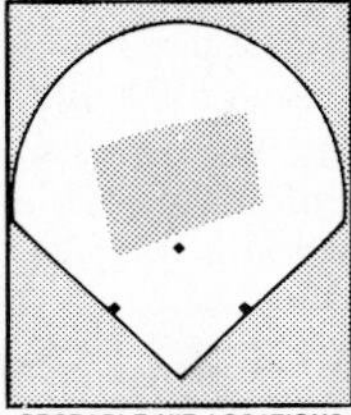
PROBABLE HIT LOCATIONS

HITTING:

Alan Wiggins has outstanding speed, but little power. A switch-hitter, he hits better from the right side. Righthanded, he can drive the ball up the alleys in left-center and right-center.

Lefthanded, Wiggins is a constant threat to beat out grounders not hit directly at infielders. He bunts more from the left side because of his speed and its shorter distance to first base. From the left side, he often hits soft liners over the shortstop, making it mandatory for a left fielder to play shallow and slightly shade the foul line. Wiggins is a high ball hitter righthanded, and a low ball hitter lefthanded. Righthanders should try to pitch him fastballs inside; lefthanders should pitch him outside and keep the ball down. He hits mostly to the opposite fields and likes off-speed pitching, but has a problem with hard stuff.

Wiggins is best suited as a leadoff batter because of his speed and baserunning ability, but must improve his ability to get on base. He has a fairly good eye, but doesn't walk nearly as much as he should. Wiggins is a below average hitter with runners in scoring position. Batting lefthanded, is below average on the hit-and-run because of the problems he has pulling the ball. He is an above average bunter and infielders must shorten up when he's at bat.

BASERUNNING:

A superior baserunner, Wiggins has excellent speed to first base, gets big leads and good jumps, is expert at sliding feet first and is good at breaking up double plays.

FIELDING:

Wiggins has exceptional range defensively and excels at going to the left field line to turn extra base hits into singles. He charges the ball well, goes back well, has average arm strength and slightly above average accuracy. He gets rid of the ball quickly. Outstanding left fielder.

OVERALL:

Coleman: "Wiggins can do everything but hit. He must find a way to get on base more often."

McCarver: "Tom Lasorda said Alan is the fastest man that he has ever seen and I agree. He generates full steam after only a couple of steps. Could be a superstar some day."

Kiner: "Wiggins hasn't lived up to his full potential because of personal problems and should be platooned at this stage. He will have to hit and steal to offset what I consider his poor throwing."

DAVE EDWARDS
OF, No. 24
RR, 6'0", 177 lbs.
ML Svc: 4 years
Born: 2-24-54 in
Los Angeles, CA

HITTING, BASERUNNING, FIELDING:

Dave Edwards' hitting skills seem to have been eroded by his role as a part-time player and pinch-hitter during the last four seasons. Released by San Diego at the end of the 1982 campaign, he is a straightaway type hitter who crouches in a square stance in the back of the box. He is primarily a high fastball hitter who has problems with breaking balls. He hits lefthanders better than righthanders, reaches the alleys occasionally and has the capability of hitting 8-10 home runs a season.

Edwards is above average in his speed going to first base and in his ability to break up the double play. He is not, however, as good a baserunner as he should be and is not much of a threat to steal.

He has the above average range to play center field and the arm strength to play in right. Edwards has average throwing accuracy and is good at going back on a ball or coming in for one. His defensive ability is his biggest asset.

OVERALL:

Edwards has been hurt by not getting to play more often and has a tendency to press when he is in the lineup. He seldom walks, is ineffective as a pinch-hitter, has never made enough contact to hit for a high average. Hitting makes him a fringe player.

STEVE SWISHER
C, No. 9
RR, 6'2", 205 lbs.
ML Svc: 9 years
Born: 8-9-51 in
Parkersburg, WV

HITTING, BASERUNNING, FIELDING:

Steve Swisher is basically a high fastball hitter who has problems with breaking balls. He hits straightaway, and should be played slightly to pull. He hits better against lefthanders because he has had few opportunities to face righthanders as a back up catcher for the last five seasons. He has a little power, but seldom reaches the alleys, and is a weak hitter who strikes out too much.

Swisher is a below average runner and is no threat to steal a base (none in the last four seasons).

Defensive ability is the thing that kept Swisher in the big leagues for nine seasons. He has always been regarded as a good handler of pitchers, but has lost much of the arm strength and accuracy he once had and was not chosen by any team in the re-entry draft after ending his San Diego contract and becoming a free agent at the end of the 1982 season.

OVERALL:

Coleman: "Steve is a veteran catcher who has come to the end of the line. He might try managing in the minor leagues. He knows much about the game, but physically can't play well anymore."

McCarver: "A back up catcher who simply lacks punch offensively."

CANDLESTICK PARK
San Francisco Giants

Seating Capacity: 58,000
Playing Surface: Natural Grass

Dimensions
Left Field Pole: 330 ft.
Left-Center Field: 365 ft.
Center Field: 400 ft.
Right-Center Field: 375 ft.
Right Field Pole: 335 ft.
Height of Outfield Wall: 9 ft.

In no other park in the National League is the wind as dominant a force as it is in San Francisco. Ironically, before a day game, the wind seldom interferes with pre-game warm-ups or batting practice. Once the game begins, however, usually about 1:30 p.m., the wind is strong enough to play havoc with fly balls, blow dirt in the eyes of batters, and cause unusual problems just trying to throw the baseball.

Since the wind most often blows from left to right, righthanded power hitters generally dislike hitting in Candlestick. Lefthanded home run hitters can't wait to hit when the wind is blowing out, but suffer like everyone else when the strong gusts are blowing in.

Apart from the hardships caused by Mother Nature, infielders also complain about the texture of the infield at Candlestick. The red clay infield is attractive to look at but it is also hard and choppy, making ground balls more difficult to field cleanly. The batter's box is also composed of this hard clay-like dirt and hitters often have problems digging out a comfortable foothold.

The pitcher's mound, however, is excellent and seldom draws a complaint. The dugouts are on field level and there is more than ample room for catchers and infielders to chase foul balls without having to worry about steps or fences.

Candlestick would be a perfectly adequate ball park if it had just been constructed somewhere else--where the wind and the sun and the cold evenings weren't such distracting elements.

JIM BARR
RHP, No. 23
RR, 6'3", 205 lbs.
ML Svc: 11 years
Born: 1-10-48 in
Foster City, CA

PITCHING:

A long reliever and spot starter, Jim Barr's main asset is his pinpoint control, administered with a smooth, three-quarter delivery. He goes mainly with a fastball, with a velocity in the high 80s. Barr consistently tries to keep it away from the hitter's strength. He also throws a slider frequently, keeping it away from the hitter, and an off-speed curve, his third pitch.

If he is confronted by a number of lefthanded batters, you'll see Barr flash a straight change that he tries to "turn over" against then with fair success. He is naturally more effective against righties most of the time. Barr has an excellent, low-key temperment and does not rattle in tight spots. Some hitters in the National League think he might use a 'foreign substance' on some of his pitches, but their complaints have yet to reach the din stage. An old pro from the old school, he's not averse to an occasional brushback pitch.

FIELDING HITTING, BASERUNNING:

Barr has a good, quick pick-off move to first base and is a fine fielding pitcher. He also can help himself at the plate, as witness his .250 average in 1982. And he runs the bases hard (he is a good athlete) and intelligently enough to even be used as a pinch-runner on occasion. He can bunt when called on to do so, and makes contact--he struck out only six times in 34 total plate appearances in 1982.

OVERALL:

McCarver: "Barr tries to throw every pitch away from the hitter. He'd rather bite off the head of a rattle-snake than come in. He's a dartthrower who relies on control but tries to throw to spots too often for his own good. He's very intelligent, has complete confidence on the mound. He is a great competitor who is good enough not to be relegated just to long relief."

Coleman: "Barr is a veteran who has been around. He lacks overpowering stuff, but he had the tenacity to fight his way back from the minors when his career appeared to be over. He's a good addition to any staff. He can start or relieve and won't scare off."

1982 STATISTICS

W	L	ERA	G	GS	CG	IP	H	R	ER	BB	SO	SV
4	3	3.29	53	9	1	128	123	54	47	20	36	2

CAREER STATISTICS

W	L	ERA	G	GS	CG	IP	H	R	ER	BB	SO	SV
96	109	3.54	401	252	64	1972	2064	861	775	449	694	10

DAVE BERGMAN
INF, No. 16
LL, 6'2", 180 lbs.
ML Svc: 4 years
Born: 6-6-53 in
Evanston, IL

1982 STATISTICS

AVG	G	AB	R	H	2B	3B	HR	RBI	BB	SO	SB
.273	100	121	22	33	3	1	4	14	18	11	3

CAREER STATISTICS

AVG	G	AB	R	H	2B	3B	HR	RBI	BB	SO	SB
.245	388	576	71	141	22	3	9	46	88	78	8

HITTING:

Bergman is a pretty good contact hitter who hits the ball pretty much straightaway and usually does not strike out--only 11 times in 140 total appearances in 1982. He is a low ball hitter who can be jammed. He has fair extra-base power and when he gets a chance to play for any length of time, can send the ball through the alleys, especially left center, with authority. Besides jamming him, you can get him out with off-speed pitches, which is true of most players who are not regulars. He isn't fast enough to bunt his way on base often, but he is a fine bunter when a sacrifice is in order. Bergman rarely faces lefthanded pitchers and has trouble with good breaking stuff from lefthanders. Throw him high fastballs, breaking stuff and off-speed pitches. He murders low fastballs.

VS. RHP

VS. LHP

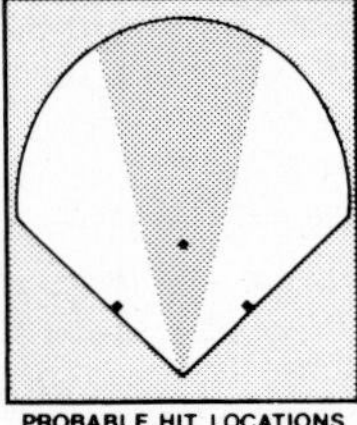
PROBABLE HIT LOCATIONS

BASERUNNING:

Bergman has only average speed on the bases, but his ability to play the game shows up here as well as elsewhere. He rarely makes a base-running mistake, even though he does not pose a threat to steal.

FIELDING:

Bergman has been tried in the outfield and found wanting, but if you stick to first base with him, you won't go wrong. He's the best defensive first baseman on the Giants and one of the better ones in the National League, and is frequently used as a late-inning defensive replacement by manager Frank Robinson. He has good hands and is able to take advantage in starting double plays, in spite of the fact that he is a lefthanded thrower.

OVERALL:

Bergman is a valuable major league commodity who has accepted the fact that he has been classified as a role player and has filled those roles well. He can give you a bunt or a sacrifice fly, pinch-hit against righthanders, do a good job at first base and fill in effectively when a regular is injured.

Coleman: "Dave could develop into a solid hitter. Lack of power and being a lefthanded thrower limit him to positions that require more power."

McCarver: "Dave is a pretty good, well traveled pinch-hitter and part-time player."

FRED BREINING
RHP, No. 48
RR, 6'4", 185 lbs.
ML Svc: 3 years
Born: 11-15-55 in
Pacifica, CA

PITCHING:

Breining came out of the Giants' bullpen, where he had been just another in an impressive collection of relievers, and became the club's most effective starter for the last month of the 1982 season. He played a major role in San Francisco's surprising stretch drive. Manager Frank Robinson has Breining mentally penciled in as a rotation starter for 1983.

The tall righthander undoubtedly will continue to rely primarily on his effective forkball, bolstered by a fastball that approaches 90 MPH, and will try to develop at least one more pitch, most likely a slider. Breining hides his pitches well and has a deceptive delivery. He'll often try to get ahead with the fastball, then force the hitters to swing at the forkball. He has excellent control and, when he's right, induces lots of ground balls. Falling behind the hitters probably is his main problem but it's the exception rather than the rule with him.

FIELDING, HITTING, BASERUNNING:

One of three Giants pitchers in 1982 to bat over .200, Breining will make contact as often as not, although when he does connect it's never for power. His five sacrifice bunts in 1982 ranked him second on the pitching staff.

In the field, his pick-off move to first base is only average and, because of his lanky frame, he can be run on. Otherwise, he fields his position adequately. He is a decent baserunner for a pitcher.

OVERALL:

Before the decision to make Breining a starter, it was felt by some clubs that he could be plucked from the Giants' talent-rich bullpen and turned into a No. 1 short reliever, since he often was used in situations where the club was far behind. That no longer is the case, of course--Breining has shown his potential as a starter and the Giants hope to capitalize on it.

McCarver: "He has a funky delivery, hides his pitches very well, has pretty good presence and poise on the mound. If he stays ahead of the hitters, can use his forkball effectively."

1982 STATISTICS

W	L	ERA	G	GS	CG	IP	H	R	ER	BB	SO	SV
11	6	3.08	54	9	2	143	146	61	49	52	98	0

CAREER STATISTICS

W	L	ERA	G	GS	CG	IP	H	R	ER	BB	SO	SV
16	8	2.96	104	10	2	228	250	93	75	94	138	1

BOB BRENLY
C, No. 15
RR, 6'2", 200 lbs.
ML Svc: 1 year plus
Born: 2-25-54 in
Coshocton, OH

1982 STATISTICS

AVG	G	AB	R	H	2B	3B	HR	RBI	BB	SO	SB
.283	65	180	26	51	4	1	4	15	18	26	6

CAREER STATISTICS

AVG	G	AB	R	H	2B	3B	HR	RBI	BB	SO	SB
.293	84	225	31	66	6	2	5	19	24	30	6

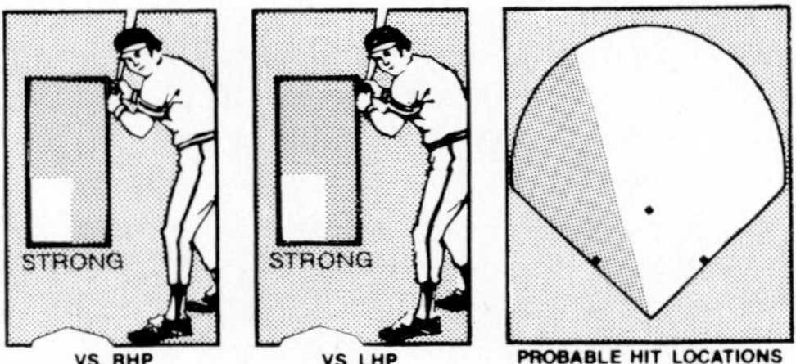

HITTING:

Brenly is basically a pull hitter who handles the bat well and with some pop. He's a high ball hitter who stands fairly square in the batter's box and away from the plate, so he should be pitched down and away. A strong hitter, he broke Mike Schmidt's Ohio University home run record, but he was hampered last season by a broken collarbone (in spring training) and a rib injury, which probably held his power numbers down all year.

If he has shown a major drawback thus far, it would be a tendency to try to pull too much. Thus he needs to improve his ability to hit behind the baserunner. A late-bloomer, Brenly was a consistent minor league hitter but never got a real chance until the 1981 major league strike, when Giants manager Frank Robinson got a chance to watch him play at Phoenix and was impressed enough to promote him as soon as the strike ended. The early "book" on Brenly was to feed him a steady diet of breaking pitches, but he has worked hard to shed the label of being strictly a fastball hitter. Very aggressive at the plate--sometimes too much so for his own good.

BASERUNNING:

Brenly runs well for a catcher, although he's hardly a major threat to steal a base. But he has been used as a pinch-runner for Milt May, his slow-footed fellow catcher, in the late innings of a close game, thereby saving Robinson from having to use up an extra body for that purpose.

FIELDING:

One of Brenly's strongest assets is his aggressiveness behind the plate. He handles himself well and gets the most out of his talent. He has an extremely quick release on his throw to second base, making up for what has looked to be only average throwing velocity. Threw more effectively near the end of last season, when the effects of a rib injury worked off.

OVERALL:

McCarver: "Appears to know what he's doing behind the plate. Contact hitter who has good hand action with the bat."

Coleman: "A strong young hitter. Has a lot of the same mannerisms of a young Mike Ivie at the plate. Will develop as a good hitter."

Kiner: "Brenly has an average arm but makes up for this by a quick release. He has some good power, and could develop into a fine catcher."

JACK CLARK
OF, No. 22
RR, 6'3", 205 lbs.
ML Svc: 6 years
Born: 11-10-55 in New Brighton, PA

1982 STATISTICS

AVG	G	AB	R	H	2B	3B	HR	RBI	BB	SO	SB
.274	157	563	90	154	30	3	27	103	90	91	6

CAREER STATISTICS

AVG	G	AB	R	H	2B	3B	HR	RBI	BB	SO	SB
.276	852	3036	482	837	163	29	132	485	380	458	54

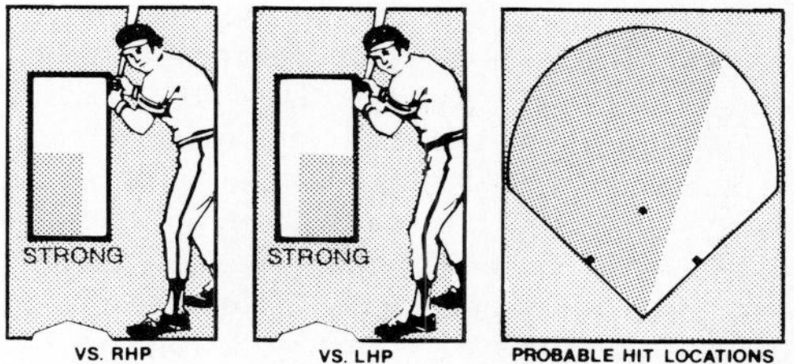

HITTING:

Clark was dragging a .194 average behind him in late May of last year but then came to life and became one of the hottest hitters in the National League, putting together his first 100-plus RBI season. Much sought after by other clubs, whose parks would be conducive to better numbers than windy Candlestick Park, Clark is one of the NL's most feared hitters and can carry the Giants when he's going well.

He's a low ball hitter with a lightning like bat. Against righthanders, he has good power to all fields and should be jammed with hard stuff or thrown breaking pitches away. Against lefthanders, he tends to pull more and should be thrown hard stuff away. Clark is a fine clutch hitter who is consistently among the league leaders in game-winning RBIs. He has developed a good knowledge of the strike zone and resists the temptation to swing at bad pitches even when he's being pitched around. The ball just explodes off his bat.

BASERUNNING:

Jack has shown considerable improvement in this area, which was a real weakness for him. He had lacked alertness on the bases and still doesn't take full advantage of his pretty fair speed. He is not a threat to steal, but he has become more aggressive in going for the extra base, and he has cut down on his genuine mistakes.

FIELDING:

Clark has all the tools to be an excellent right fielder. He has good speed and charges the ball well, but he doesn't work on his throwing enough to take full advantage of his excellent arm strength, and he also could work on getting a better jump on the ball. He has a smooth, gliding stride going after a ball and makes it look easy.

OVERALL:

McCarver: "Jack is as good as he wants to be--a marvelous talent who makes things look easy at times but, as with most gifted athletes, appears to lay back at times. He has occasional run-ins with management. He could be a dominant player in the National League for the next decade if he pushes."

Kiner: "Day in and day out, Clark is one of the best players in the game. He's a top clutch hitter and has an outstanding arm."

Coleman: "A tough clutch hitter who can kill you when he's hot. No telling what he could do if he didn't have to play 81 games at Candlestick Park. He sometimes has an attitude problem."

CHILI DAVIS
OF, No. 30
SR, 6'3", 195 lbs.
ML Svc: 1 years plus
Born: 1-17-60 in
Kingston, JAM

1982 STATISTICS

AVG	G	AB	R	H	2B	3B	HR	RBI	BB	SO	SB
.261	154	641	86	167	27	6	19	76	45	115	24

CAREER STATISTICS

AVG	G	AB	R	H	2B	3B	HR	RBI	BB	SO	SB
.258	162	656	87	169	27	6	19	76	46	117	26

VS. RHP

VS. LHP

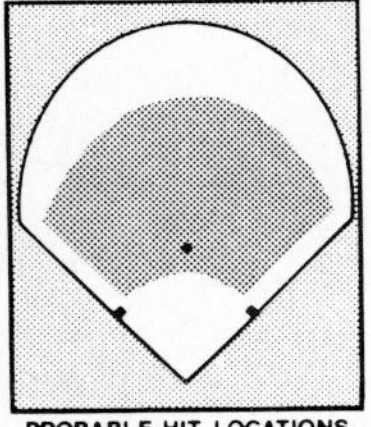
PROBABLE HIT LOCATIONS

HITTING:

Davis is a switch-hitter with more power from the left side. Batting left, Davis is a low ball hitter, has a slower bat from this side and can be jammed. Pitches should be high and inside. Batting right, Davis likes high pitches. His bat is quicker going right, and pitches should be kept down and away from him.

As a rookie in 1982, Davis was showing signs of developing into a fine hitter, but smart veteran pitchers could out-think him and hard throwing pitchers gave him trouble. He can spray the ball, but often goes straight-away. Davis is a good fastball hitter, and had a little difficulty with off-speed curves and change-ups. Davis hits well behind the runner and with men in scoring position, showing excellent RBI potential. Has an above average bunt and could learn to take more advantage of it for additional base hits. He has a good personal make-up, and is rapidly improving his hitting to becoming an extremely valuable bat in the lineup.

Overall, Davis is rated an average to above average hitter.

BASERUNNING:

Davis is an above average to excellent baserunner, whose speed to first is better when he hits from the left side. His extra speed and power batting left combine to make him a good base hit threat. He could use some improvement in his basestealing techniques; he tends to get thrown out more often than he should for someone so fast. His sliding ability shows excellent development, and he has good raw talent on the bases.

FIELDING:

Candlestick Park's windy conditions make it a very tough park to gauge outfield balls, but in center field Davis is able to do the job. He has an above average fielder's range and his speed helps him to cover a tremendous amount of ground in any field in the league. His arm strength is rated average, but very accurate. Davis moves equally well to both his left and right, and has been able to handle the shifts both coming in and going back for the ball. At this point, he is rated above average.

OVERALL:

Coleman, McCarver and Kiner: "Davis has all the earmarks of becoming a big star in the National League, but time will tell."

DARRELL EVANS
INF, No. 41
LR, 6'2", 205 lbs.
ML Svc: 12 years
Born: 5-26-47 in Pasadena, CA

1982 STATISTICS

AVG	G	AB	R	H	2B	3B	HR	RBI	BB	SO	SB
.256	141	465	64	119	20	4	16	61	77	64	5

CAREER STATISTICS

AVG	G	AB	R	H	2B	3B	HR	RBI	BB	SO	SB
.251	1711	5825	862	1462	222	31	232	838	1043	850	80

VS. RHP

VS. LHP

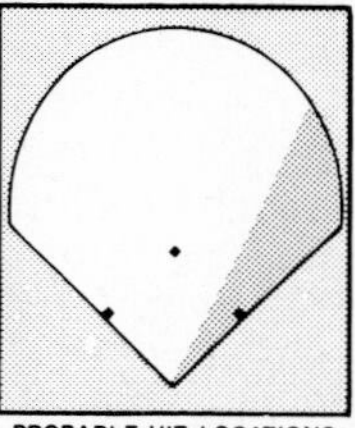
PROBABLE HIT LOCATIONS

HITTING:

Evans is a pull hitting, power hitting lefthanded batter with an excellent knowledge of the strike zone. He stands back in the batter's box and is one of the comparatively few hitters who have realized success with an open stance. Evans murders pitches that are up and in. He also hits lefthanders better than the average lefty hitter because he's difficult to jam.

Evans almost never swings at a pitch out of the strike zone and has consistently been among the National League leaders in bases on balls. At times, in fact, he has been accused of being too selective for his own (or his team's) good, especially in situations where a hit and not another baserunner was called for. He has been a consistent run producer over the years but should have hit for higher average, with his quick bat. Darrell hit 41 home runs back in 1973 when he was with the Braves and played half the season in the cozy Atlanta ballpark, and when he was traded to San Francisco, which is a much more difficult home run park, he refused to adjust his approach to hitting. Thus he has been victimized by a lot of fly balls that died on the warning track.

BASERUNNING:

Evans has lost a step since his younger days, of course, but he can still steal a base when he wants to. Basically conservative on the bases, he is an intelligent runner with good instincts.

FIELDING:

Evans was used at third and first base last season. At third, where he has spent most of his career, he has had erratic streaks but in general has earned ranking among the National League's better ones, and has a strong, accurate arm. At first base he has been excellent--very steady.

OVERALL:

McCarver: "Evans would be a much better hitter if he tried to go up the middle more. You can't teach an old player (Evans is 36) new tricks, but any player who tries to hit the ball up the middle or the other way can improve himself, regardless of age. Almost no strictly-pull hitters in the NL hit for any kind of high average and Darrell is no exception."

Kiner: "This veteran third baseman has been around for 12 years now and he had another typical season--good defense, good power and a batting average (.256) near his lifetime level (.251)."

Coleman: "Darrell is a quality major league hitter with good power. His defense leaves quite a bit to be desired."

ATLEE HAMMAKER
LHP, No. 17
LL, 6'2", 195 lbs.
ML Svc: 1 year plus
Born: 1-24-58 in Carmel, CA

PITCHING:

As a starter, Hammaker had an impressive rookie season. He demonstrated excellent control, which seems to be unusual in a lefthander, and a good, live arm. His three-quarter style of delivery causes his fastball to tail away from righthanded hitters. That and 90 MPH velocity make it his best pitch and he'll throw it more than half the time.

He also has an above average slider (his second-best pitch) and a curve, but lack of tight spin gives his breaking pitches a tendency to flatten out. He has a straight change that is inconsistent but can be effective at times and could become a formidable part of his repertoire with more work. His control is good enough and he has enough confidence in it to throw breaking pitches when he gets behind in the count, which doesn't happen too often.

He is more effective against lefthanded hitters because his fastball runs in on them and he can also drop down and sidearm them on occasion. His biggest weakness probably is that although he has the ability to throw strikes, sometimes he puts them in a part of the strike zone that is a hitter's strength. Turning point in his season came on June 24 in Houston when he went the distance to beat Joe Niekro 4-3 in 10 innings, giving him a tremendous amount of confidence.

FIELDING, HITTING, BASERUNNING:

Hitting is so far removed from Hammaker's list of strong points that it became a standing joke last season. Listed as a switch-hitter, he often batted lefthanded against lefthanded pitchers. Not that it mattered. His average was .068. And on those rare occasions when he did get on base, he demonstrated his slowness afoot. He also needs work on his defense and his move to first base is not as effective as a lefthander's move should be.

OVERALL:

Hammaker seems to have an excellent temperament for the game. He rarely appears flustered and has pitched his way out of several tight situations. He has plenty of time to deal with his weaknesses.

Coleman: "He changes speeds very well and is especially tough on lefthanded hitters. He should throw more straight change-ups to righthanders because he's got a good one."

McCarver: "His tailing fastball is his ally. His flat breaking ball could and should improve. He probably will be better than a .500 pitcher."

Kiner: "Hammaker had a remarkable season last year. He had near perfect control and command of his pitches. He certainly appears to be a bright star of the future."

1982 STATISTICS

W	L	ERA	G	GS	CG	IP	H	R	ER	BB	SO	SV
12	8	4.11	29	27	4	175	189	86	80	28	102	0

CAREER STATISTICS

W	L	ERA	G	GS	CG	IP	H	R	ER	BB	SO	SV
13	11	4.37	39	33	4	214	233	110	104	40	113	0

PITCHING:

Krukow has a very compact delivery, somewhere between overhand and three-quarter in style, and is considered a control and breaking ball pitcher. Krukow's control can be erratic, and this lack of true consistency is his greatest weakness. His best pitch is his curveball. When he is on with it, the pitch has an excellent rotation and is very tough to hit. Krukow can, however, be wild with his curve early in the count. He uses his curveball as needed--a bit less than half the time with average to above average control. Krukow has a decent slider with average control, he uses it less often than the fastball or curve, and mostly to righthanded hitters. He does have a straight change, it needs improvement, but he rarely uses it.

Krukow's deadly breaking balls make him more effective against righthanded hitters. If he gets behind in the count, he is most likely to throw his fastball, but righthanders have a good chance of seeing either his curve or slider. Krukow is a hard competitor and frequently sends a brushback pitch that will put righthanded hitters into the dirt. He has a lot of guts and will challenge anyone.

Krukow is a quality starter with an intimidating presence on the mound. He is showing signs of continued improvement and is able to throw his breaking ball in for a strike when behind in the count. His greatest weakness, however remains his lack of consistency. Overall rating, above average.

MIKE KRUKOW
RHP, No. 39
RR, 6'4" 205 lbs.
ML Svc: 5 years
Born: 1-21-52 in
Long Beach, CA

FIELDING, HITTING, BASERUNNING:

Krukow has an above average move to first and is very quick. He has an unusual way of coming into his set delivery, by holding his arms at his chest instead of his waist. Krukow is a good athlete who is rated above average in fielding bunts and covering first.

He is a good fastball hitter with a strong bat for a pitcher. Average baserunning.

OVERALL:

McCarver: "Mike is a consummate competitor and battles you all the way. He was very glad to get away from the Cubs and go to a contender. Some of his breaking balls are in the dirt, however, and he throws a lot of wild pitches."

Coleman: "Krukow has a chance to become an excellent pitcher but needs more consistency. He has a mean streak that keeps hitters from digging in."

Kiner: "A good solid starter with a good curveball. I find him to be an ideal man in the starting rotation."

1982 STATISTICS

W	L	ERA	G	GS	CG	IP	H	R	ER	BB	SO	SV
13	11	3.12	33	33	7	208	211	87	72	82	138	0

CAREER STATISTICS

W	L	ERA	G	GS	CG	IP	H	R	ER	BB	SO	SV
58	61	3.96	183	173	16	1036	1055	518	456	414	676	0

BILL LASKEY
RHP, No. 45
RR, 6'5", 190 lbs.
ML Svc: 1 year
Born: 12-20-57 in Toledo, OH

PITCHING:

Laskey was a strong candidate for National League Rookie of the Year until he hit a slump the last month of the season, probably because he'd gotten more work than he was used to. He was the Giants' No. 1 starter for most of the 1982 season and was among the League's ERA leaders for much of it and is being counted on to regain that form in 1983.

Laskey is a strong competitor who seems to thrive on jams when he can reach back and pitch his way out. He has outstanding control for a rookie, challenges the hitters, has a good live fastball in the 90 MPH range and has a deceptive herky-jerky delivery that makes it look even faster. That fastball is his best pitch, but he has an excellent slider as well that "freezes" righthanded hitters, and a curve that gives the hitters something else to think about even if it's only an average one.

He radiates confidence and his style--throwing strikes, challenging the hitters--makes him the kind of pitcher teammates enjoy playing behind because he doesn't give them a chance to get bored. He can pitch inside to lefthanded hitters better than most righthanders can because of his knack for working the corners, so it doesn't bother him to face a lefty-laden lineup.

FIELDING, HITTING, BASERUNNING:

Laskey's move to first base, like that of almost any tall young righthander, is average at best. But he is at least adequate defensively and won't often beat himself in the field. He is a halfway decent hitter who makes contact almost as often as not. His baserunning speed and ability are so-so.

OVERALL:

McCarver: "Few young pitchers have his presence on the mound. He has the guts of a burglar and good stuff, including a running, exploding fastball, and he can only get better. His height and his short-arm delivery make him appear to jump at the hitters, which makes it tough on righthanded hitters especially because it throws off their timing."

Coleman: "Laskey is an excellent competitor. Great poise for a rookie. The Giants' best starter."

Kiner: "Although he doesn't throw hard and has almost no curveball, his consistency with his fastball, slider and straight change has made him a good starter."

1982 STATISTICS

W	L	ERA	G	GS	CG	IP	H	R	ER	BB	SO	SV
13	12	3.14	32	31	7	189	186	74	66	43	88	0

CAREER STATISTICS

W	L	ERA	G	GS	CG	IP	H	R	ER	BB	SO	SV
13	12	3.14	32	31	7	189	186	74	66	43	88	0

GARY LAVELLE
LHP, No. 46
SL, 6'1", 200 lbs.
ML Svc: 8 years
Born: 1-3-49 in
Scranton, PA

PITCHING:

A lefthanded power pitcher with a distinctive high, winding leg kick reminiscent of Warren Spahn, Lavelle has been one of the most consistent short relievers in the National League for the last eight years.

He has a 90 MPH fastball that is his "out" pitch, tailing away from righthanded hitters. He also throws an effective curve, using a sweeping motion, and an occasional change-up that is made effective by his hard stuff. He can get righthanded hitters out, but he is devastating against lefthanders, who must contend with a "heavy" fastball that tails in on them, and a curveball that "freezes" them. When Lavelle gets into trouble, it's usually when he falls behind the hitters. But when he's right, which is most of the time, he is an excellent pressure pitcher who can overpower hitters.

He put together a streak of 114 innings, between August 1976 and July 1977, when he did not allow a home run. He pitched two scoreless innings in the 1977 All Star Game, striking out Reggie Jackson and Carl Yastrzemski.

An intelligent, quiet leader who is active in the Fellowship of Christian Athletes, Gary served for a while as the Giants' player representative. Overall rating, above average.

FIELDING, HITTING, BASERUNNING:

Lavelle's high, exaggerated kick makes him extremely difficult to "read" for would-be base thieves, some of whom have charged that he has a "balk move" to first base. A righthander with that kind of kick would be stolen on with abandon, but runners are not able to get enough of a lead to run on Lavelle.

He is also a good fielder who doesn't beat himself defensively. Don't look for him to contribute much with the bat or to be any kind of threat on the bases.

OVERALL:

McCarver: "Lavelle is very stable on the mound, a poised veteran with excellent, often 'nasty' stuff. His fastball moves like a spitter, and with his curveball he has two outstanding pitches. I'm surprised he isn't used more often by manager Frank Robinson, but the Giants have a truly outstanding bullpen and the fact that Gary isn't used more often proves it."

Coleman: "He should be even better than he is. He still has good stuff, but he gets himself in trouble with erratic control."

1982 STATISTICS

W	L	ERA	G	GS	CG	IP	H	R	ER	BB	SO	SV
10	7	2.67	68	0	0	104	97	35	31	29	76	8

CAREER STATISTICS

W	L	ERA	G	GS	CG	IP	H	R	ER	BB	SO	SV
61	59	2.85	514	3	0	792	745	292	251	321	557	95

HITTING:

LeMaster seems to alternate between decent and poor seasons at the plate, and 1982 was a poor one. For someone who obviously is not a power hitter, he tries to pull the ball too much. Pitch him down and you shouldn't have too much trouble with him. LeMaster strikes out too often for someone who doesn't walk enough, and tends to swing at the pitcher's pitch rather than the one he wants. He also tends to lunge, and has problems with breaking and off-speed pitches, especially from righthanders.

Johnnie experimented with switch-hitting and worked with Harry Walker before the 1981 season. He abandoned the idea, but he went on to have a good year and the process seemed to help him concentrate more. Maybe he should do it every winter--with concentration he could rid himself of some of his bad habits. He has a decent stroke.

BASERUNNING:

LeMaster has above average speed but does not use it to full advantage. He was caught stealing only four times in 17 attempts in 1982. He's a smart runner who gets a good jump, but he lacks aggressiveness.

FIELDING:

Defense is the strongest part of LeMaster's game. He has a strong, accurate arm and goes into the hole about as well as any shortstop in the business. He has a very quick release and can throw the ball well when he's off balance. He turns the double play extremely well.

JOHNNIE LeMASTER
INF, No. 10
RR, 6'2", 180 lbs.
ML Svc: 6 years
Born: 6-19-54 in
Portsmouth, OH

1982 STATISTICS

AVG	G	AB	R	H	2B	3B	HR	RBI	BB	SO	SB
.216	130	436	34	94	14	1	2	30	31	78	13

CAREER STATISTICS

AVG	G	AB	R	H	2B	3B	HR	RBI	BB	SO	SB
.225	601	2088	185	469	80	16	11	158	159	344	37

OVERALL:

The consensus is that if LeMaster could just maintain an average in the .250 range, he would be regarded in the upper echelon of shortstops because of his defensive ability.

McCarver: "When you speak of shortstops, you must speak first of defense. That's why Johnnie is in the major leagues. He's an underrated shortstop because he doesn't hit for high average."

Coleman: "LeMaster is the second best defensive shortstop in the National League, behind Ozzie Smith."

Kiner: "He needs to improve at bat to become a positive element in the Giants' attack."

JEFF LEONARD
OF, NO. 26
RR, 6'4", 200 lbs.
ML Svc: 4 years
Born: 9-22-55 in Philadelphia, PA

1982 STATISTICS

AVG	G	AB	R	H	2B	3B	HR	RBI	BB	SO	SB
.259	80	278	32	72	16	1	9	49	19	65	18

CAREER STATISTICS

AVG	G	AB	R	H	2B	3B	HR	RBI	BB	SO	SB
.269	365	1086	132	292	52	16	16	151	105	210	50

HITTING:

Leonard is one of the best clutch hitters the Giants have. It is this quality that prompted manager Frank Robinson to stay with him even when he wasn't going well and to pronounce him the leading off-season candidate for left field in 1983.

Leonard wound up batting a modest .259 last year, and his 65 strikeouts in only 304 total plate appearances attest to the fact that he can look bad in the batter's box. But Leonard knocked in 49 runs with only 72 hits, an excellent ratio, and probably would have had a really big year had a wrist injury not sidelined him for nearly three months. With runners in scoring position, Leonard batted .330, so he obviously thrives on pressure.

He is a high ball hitter who can go to all fields with some power, and he should be jammed or pitched down. He'll frequently line the ball up the alley in right-center. He's a good "mistake" hitter. He can be fooled by good, slow breaking stuff, but if you throw him hard stuff, make sure to keep it down or in.

BASERUNNING:

Leonard has good speed and uses it to advantage. He has had eight seasons in pro ball in which he stole 18 bases or more. He took 18 last season again, and obviously would have stolen a lot more had the injury not put him on the shelf.

FIELDING:

Leonard's defense needs some work. He had been shifted from one field to another so much that Robinson figured a permanent home in left field would help. Leonard has trouble with the outfield lights and the windy conditions in Candlestick. He has decent range and is better at coming in on the ball, but is overall an average fielder.

OVERALL:

This former Houston Astro never has lived up to his full potential, but if he can stay healthy, he should get the chance in 1983.

Kiner: "Leonard has had great success at the Triple A level, but he hasn't been able to put it all together in the majors. In 1979 with Houston, he hit .290, but he hasn't had a complete season since."

Coleman: "Has to hit with some punch to be effective."

RENIE MARTIN
RHP, No. 39
RR, 6'4", 190 lbs.
ML Svc: 4 years
Born: 8-30-55 in
Dover, DE

PITCHING:

Renie was a starter most of 1982 but he became inconsistent in the latter stages of the season. The feeling was that he might be more effective as a long reliever and spot starter, which was his most successful role in Kansas City before the Giants picked him up in the Vida Blue trade.

Employing a stiff-arm style of delivery, Martin relies on control to be effective. He has a good but not great fastball (in the 80s), but he backs it up with a slider. The slider is his best pitch and one he will throw at any time. He also has a decent curve that lacks the biting spin needed to be outstanding. He uses his lanky frame to his best advantage, so the hard stuff is on top of hitters in a hurry. He comes right at hitters and stays ahead in the count, so he generally is able to make them hit his pitch.

He's more effective against right-handed hitters because he uses his fastball in and slider away to keep them from protecting both sides of the plate. On the other hand, his pitches sometimes tend to straighten out and come in too fat, and that's when he gets into trouble. Overall rating, average.

FIELDING, HITTING, BASERUNNING:

Martin has a good move to first base and holds the runners close to the bag. A good athlete, he fields his position well and helps himself at the plate.

Despite the fact that he did not bat for five previous professional seasons, because of the AL's designated hitter rule, he stepped into the National League and teed off for a .265 average. He was even called upon by Giants manager Frank Robinson to pinch-hit on one occasion. He is, however, nothing special as a baserunner.

OVERALL:

McCarver: "Martin is very much in control on the mound and appears to be a winner. With his stiff-arm delivery, it's surprising he hasn't had more arm trouble. He's a good fifth starter who will never be spectacular, but will always keep his team in games. He'll usually give up an average of 3½ runs per nine innings. He's a good athlete, which is unusual, because pitchers, being such specialists, tend not to be."

Coleman: "Martin has one of the best curveballs in the league. He needs to spot his fastball better."

1982 STATISTICS

W	L	ERA	G	GS	CG	IP	H	R	ER	BB	SO	SV
7	10	4.65	29	25	1	141	148	91	73	64	63	0

CAREER STATISTICS

W	L	ERA	G	GS	CG	IP	H	R	ER	BB	SO	SV
21	28	4.30	115	45	3	375	368	420	179	177	181	11

MILT MAY
C, No. 7
LR, 6'0", 192 lbs.
ML Svc: 12 years
Born: 8-1-50 in
Gary, IN

1982 STATISTICS

AVG	G	AB	R	H	2B	3B	HR	RBI	BB	SO	SB
.263	114	395	29	104	19	0	9	39	28	38	0

CAREER STATISTICS

AVG	G	AB	R	H	2B	3B	HR	RBI	BB	SO	SB
.266	1069	3399	291	905	138	11	70	415	273	312	2

VS. RHP

VS. LHP

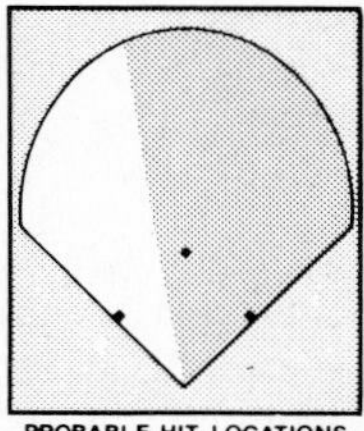
PROBABLE HIT LOCATIONS

HITTING:

Although Milt May is a lefthanded hitter he has earned a reputation as one who hangs in well against lefthanded pitchers. A "pure" line drive hitter, he'll go with the pitch, generally slapping the ball away from him for soft liners to left and center, otherwise hitting hard liners or grounders to the right side.

He has hit more for average and less for power since becoming a Giant and having to play in a park that discourages the long ball. He generally makes contact and has proved to be a fine hit-and-run man. He is a high ball hitter, handles off-speed pitches well and should be pitched down and away. He stands upright in the middle of the batter's box and employs a closed stance.

Milt has a good idea of the strike zone and rarely swings at bad pitches. Despite his lack of foot speed, he does not hit into many double plays. He is one of the Giants the opposing team least likes to see at bat in a clutch situation. He is a consistent major league hitter who, if he did run better, probably would be around .300 every year. He is intelligent, thinks like a catcher at the plate and rarely is embarrassed. He has a smooth and picturesque swing.

BASERUNNING:

May is probably the slowest base-runner on the Giants roster and, in the late innings of a close game, will more than likely leave for a pinch-runner if he gets on base. He knows his limitations and never takes unnecessary risks on the bases. This is the weakest part of his game.

FIELDING:

May calls an excellent game, has an excellent knowledge of the hitters and exerts a quiet leadership during a game which was especially helpful to the Giants' young pitching staff last season. His arm is strong and true, but he has been hampered on throws to second base by a slow release. He does the "little things" well, like blocking pitches in the dirt and fielding bunts.

OVERALL:

McCarver: "Milt handles pitchers very well and calls an excellent game. He has a slow bat, but starts his swing early, sweeping his bat through the strike zone. He has made the most out of his ability."

Kiner: "May has an average arm and is a good back up catcher with a lot of experience. He can pinch-hit as a double duty man."

GREG MINTON
RHP, No. 38
SR, 6'2", 190 lbs.
ML Svc: 5 years
Born: 7-29-51 in
Lubbock, TX

PITCHING:

Minton is one of the best short relievers in the business. He's a power pitcher (consistently around 90 MPH) and comes right at the hitters. His bread-and-butter pitch isn't simply a fastball--it's a sinker that, when it's on, "falls off the table" and is virtually impossible to hit in the air.

He seems to be more effective with runners on base or pitching out of trouble. He'll fall behind in the count, and when he comes in at the start of an inning he'll frequently allow a baserunner or two. But he gets the job done, as his record attests. A practical joker with an off-the-wall sense of humor (his nickname is "Moon Man"), he's all businesss on the field. Strictly a late-inning man, Minton backs his vaunted sinker with an excellent slider and rarely throws anything else. But then, he doesn't really need anything else. Even when the hitter expects the sinker, there's little he can do with it but hit it on the ground and hope it finds a hole, which is why it doesn't hurt Minton as much as some pitchers to fall behind in the count.

Greg owns the longest streak on record of consecutive innings without allowing a home run (269 1/3) and it's no accident, although he admits he survived a few instances in the streak when he got the ball up. That doesn't happen often. Only when it does is he in serious trouble. Overall rating, excellent.

FIELDING, HITTING, BASERUNNING:

Minton is a more than adequate fielder, although his move to first base is just average. A switch-hitter, he usually gets a piece of the ball on those rare occasions when he does come to the plate. He isn't much of a baserunner.

OVERALL:

McCarver: "Minton has no peer in handling pressure situations. His sinker acts like a spitter and is equally effective against hitters from either side of the plate. It's virtually impossible to lift with any consistency. He's a pillar of strength on the mound."

Coleman: "One of the best relievers in the National League, Minton throws the 'heaviest' ball in the league. His great slider makes him slightly more effective against righthanded hitters."

1982 STATISTICS

W	L	ERA	G	GS	CG	IP	H	R	ER	BB	SO	SV
10	4	1.83	78	0	0	123	108	29	25	42	58	30

CAREER STATISTICS

W	L	ERA	G	GS	CG	IP	H	R	ER	BB	SO	SV
24	24	2.81	274	6	0	451	419	164	141	174	186	74

TOM O'MALLEY
INF, No. 39
LR, 6'0", 180 lbs.
ML Svc: 1 year
Born: 12-25-60 in Orange, NJ

HITTING:

O'Malley was batting .229 last June when teammate Joe Morgan suggested he switch from a closed stance to one that was basically square. The 21 year old wound up batting .275 and looks ready to be the Giants' third baseman from the start this year. O'Malley was promoted from Triple A early last season and never went back down, so he had almost no experience at that level and apparently didn't need any more than he got. He makes fairly consistent contact and hits the ball with some authority, though not the home run type. A high ball hitter who likes to extend his arms, he should be jammed with hard stuff or fed breaking balls away. He'll hit the ball to all fields--in fact, he sliced a ball over left field in Shea Stadium in his second big league game. Just a youngster, he'll get stronger and his power will improve. He looks comfortable in clutch situations. He needs to learn the strike zone better. That, too, will come.

1982 STATISTICS

AVG	G	AB	R	H	2B	3B	HR	RBI	BB	SO	SB
.275	92	291	26	80	12	4	2	27	33	39	0

CAREER STATISTICS

AVG	G	AB	R	H	2B	3B	HR	RBI	BB	SO	SB
.275	92	291	26	80	12	4	2	27	33	39	0

VS. RHP

VS. LHP

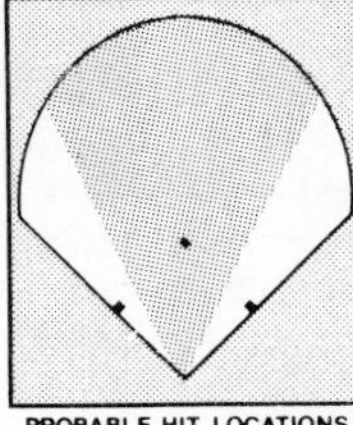
PROBABLE HIT LOCATIONS

BASERUNNING:

This is the weakest part of O'Malley's game. He does not have good speed and will have to develop his baserunning instincts in order to avoid being a liability on the basepaths. In any event, he'll never be a major threat to steal.

FIELDING:

O'Malley displayed good range, above average arm strength, and has outstanding accuracy. He doesn't rattle in tough situations and is very smooth. He goes to his left extremely well and better than average to his right. He handles bunts well. In general, he tends to play shallow.

OVERALL:

McCarver: "For his age, O'Malley is a very poised young man who handles himself marvelously. He's a mature young hitter with a good stroke who can only get better at the plate. He's very much in control at third base, too. His power output should increase, because you get stronger as you get older. He has great hands and a strong arm."

Coleman: "O'Malley does a lot of things well for a youngster and could blossom in time. Right now he does a number of things fairly well but no one thing outstandingly well."

CHAMP SUMMERS
OF, No. 6
LR, 6'2", 205 lbs.
ML Svc: 9 years
Born: 6-15-48 in
Bremerton, WA

HITTING:

Summers is primarily a pinch-hitting specialist in the National League where there is no designated hitter, and his .323 average in that role indicates how effective he was in 1982. He has the perfect approach, to come off the bench swinging the bat and swinging it hard.

He's a typical strong low ball hitter and a dead pull hitter, so it's a good idea to keep the ball away from him. Lefthanders should throw him breaking balls. Righthanders, if they have good stuff, also have the option of jamming him. He usually hits the bottom half of the ball and hits it into the air or on a line. Summers is a "mistake" hitter who is quite capable of hitting the ball out of the park. He's a fine clutch hitter who should be fed breaking pitches and fastballs away. He'll murder a low fastball. He rarely bats against left-handed pitchers.

1982 STATISTICS

AVG	G	AB	R	H	2B	3B	HR	RBI	BB	SO	SB
.248	70	125	15	31	5	0	4	19	16	17	0

CAREER STATISTICS

AVG	G	AB	R	H	2B	3B	HR	RBI	BB	SO	SB
.260	622	1295	191	337	60	4	53	203	177	221	15

VS. RHP

VS. LHP

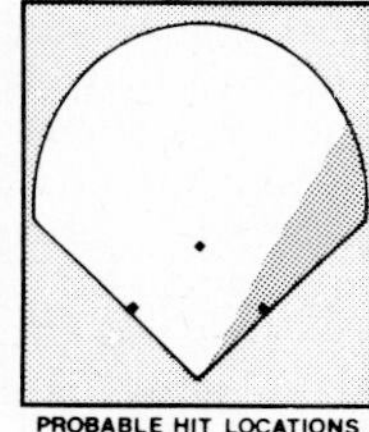
PROBABLE HIT LOCATIONS

BASERUNNING:

Summers does not earn his living on the bases. He does not have good speed, thus is not aggressive on the bases and usually is lifted for a pinch-runner when he gets aboard in the late innings of a tight game. He has 15 steals in 6 full seasons and parts of 3 others.

FIELDING:

Defense, too, has been a shortcoming for Champ. Not the most graceful of outfielders, he had problems with Candlestick Park's elements in left field on those rare occasions when he played defense, although he can go to his right fairly well. His arm is average at best.

OVERALL:

McCarver: "Summers was a much better player in the American League, where he could be used as a DH. Hitting really is his only real plus. He is very strong and can hit your mistakes a long way."

Kiner: "Champ has gotten a lot of mileage out of baseball since his first at-bat in the major leagues when he pinch-hit for Reggie Jackson (then with Oakland). He is an average fielder but has been a good pinch-hitter and is continuing that role with the Giants."

Coleman: "A solid hitter, but defense and lack of speed prevent him from playing every day."

MIKE VAIL
OF, No. 23
RR, 6'0", 185 lbs.
ML Svc: 8 years
Born: 11-10-51 in
San Francisco, CA

1982 STATISTICS

AVG	G	AB	R	H	2B	3B	HR	RBI	BB	SO	SB
.254	78	189	9	48	10	1	4	29	6	33	0

CAREER STATISTICS

AVG	G	AB	R	H	2B	3B	HR	RBI	BB	SO	SB
.283	597	1509	139	427	68	11	33	210	72	293	3

VS. RHP

VS. LHP

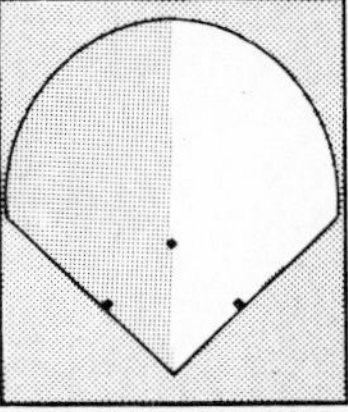
PROBABLE HIT LOCATIONS

HITTING:

Mike Vail goes to the plate as if his life, not livelihood, depends upon his performance with the bat. He is determined and fierce and will never be seen taking a controlled or half-hearted swing. He stays well off the plate, stands in the middle of the box and has a slight crouch about his stance. He is a high ball hitter and has a tendency to go after the first pitch.

Righthanded pitchers have success with Vail by working him down and away with breaking balls. Lefthanders will use the same method and can also use their fastball down and in. A pull hitter who likes to get his arms out over the plate, Vail will drive the ball to the left-center alley with power and take the ball out of the park, if he gets his pitch. More often, however, he'll send sharp liners over the shortstop.

Vail can hit in the clutch, but not with regularity. At times, his desire to hit the ball hard results in a strikeout and runners stranded. He does not hit behind runners well because of his tendency to pull and his anxiousness at the plate makes him vulnerable to the change-up, unless it floats high. He has trouble with curves and sharp sinkers and sliders. But he can go on a tear--all his weaknesses disappearing--and rip the cover off the ball. Primarily used as a pinch-hitter, Vail will not draw a lot of walks (in fact, he seems to view them with particular disdain), and is not highly reliable in the hit-and-run or bunting situations. Vail is there to swing the bat and he goes about it like an angered boxer.

BASERUNNING:

Vail will give you the same determined approach on the bases that he displays at the plate, but, again, his anxiousness creates problems. He runs hard, but not fast. He is aggressive, but not smart, and he'll get caught taking chances. Often, he's pulled for pinch-runners. This is the weakest part of his game.

FIELDING:

Again, determined but reckless. When Vail draws an outfield assignment, he shows average range and speed. His arm is adequate. He will make a fly ball an adventure. If he has to go back on the ball, it is a suspense story. All of this said, Vail has improved in the outfield. A few years ago, he was horrible. If he was stronger in the field, he would probably play more.

OVERALL:

Vail is a pinch-hitter and platoon player. A good hitter at times, the rest of his skills are marginal. He will never be a regular.

McCarver: "Mike is a good pinch-hitter and utility outfielder. But, if he is not hitting, there is nothing that will keep him in the lineup."

Coleman: "Vail started his career with a 23-game hit streak. That's been the highlight of his career."

Kiner: "He's a good fastball hitter, but he seems short in every other category."

JIM WOHLFORD
OF, No. 1
RR, 5'11", 175 lbs.
ML Svc: 10 years
Born: 2-28-51 in
Visalia, CA

1982 STATISTICS

AVG	G	AB	R	H	2B	3B	HR	RBI	BB	SO	SB
.256	97	250	37	64	12	1	2	25	30	36	8

CAREER STATISTICS

AVG	G	AB	R	H	2B	3B	HR	RBI	BB	SO	SB
.259	902	2476	305	641	95	28	13	236	197	308	86

VS. RHP

VS. LHP

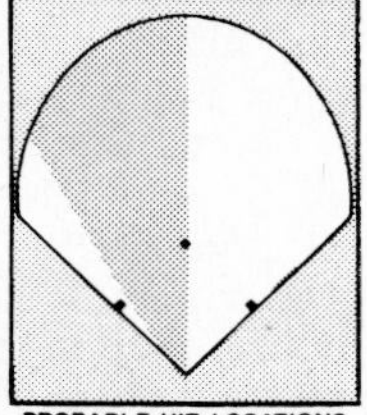
PROBABLE HIT LOCATIONS

HITTING:

Wohlford played everyday for quite a while early last season and had his average up to .363 in late May before he began to taper off. He is probably best suited to what he has done most of his career--play part-time. One reason for this is that he is too intense for full-season, full-time duty.

He won't hit much for power, but otherwise Wohlford is a pretty effective hitter: a line drive specialist who generally makes contact. He likes the ball high and out over the plate. Right-handers should pitch him up and in, lefthanders low and away. His favorite slot is left-center field, although he pulls lefthanders a bit more. If you have a good breaking ball, use it as your "out" pitch against him even though he waits on the ball fairly well. He's a pretty good hit-and-run man.

BASERUNNING:

Wohlford averaged nearly 17 stolen bases a season during the four years when he was more or less a regular in the American League. Since then, he has not stolen more than eight per season. He has deceptive speed on the bases, appearing to glide without lifting his feet very high. He probably should be more aggressive.

FIELDING:

A former infielder, Wohlford is sure-handed in left field and comes in for the ball very well. His throwing arm is only average.

OVERALL:

Wohlford is the type of player every club needs--unspectacular, but with no major weakness aside from the fact that he doesn't hit many home runs. He is a decent hitter with decent baserunning speed and decent defensive skills.

McCarver: "Jim is a pretty good fourth outfielder and a good pinch-hitter against lefthanders. He's a line drive hitter with fair speed, and he fits into the Giants' plans well."

Coleman: "Wohlford was a better player in the American League. He has been somewhat disappointing after signing with the Giants as a free agent."

Kiner: "Jim's main value is as a pinch-hitter and utility player."

DUANE KUIPER
INF, No. 18
LR, 6'0", 175 lbs.
ML Svc: 8 years
Born: 6-19-50 in Racine, WI

HITTING, BASERUNNING, FIELDING:

Kuiper is a contact hitter, but is a tough out. He is good judge of the strike zone. He stands high in the batter's box and likes to extend his hands and punch the ball up the middle. He should be pitched low and away. A good clutch hitter, and the outfield should play shallow.

A knee injury in 1980 left him without good foot speed, so he isn't able to capitalize on his bunting ability to get base hits, only to sacrifice. A good fastball hitter who also can time the change-up pretty well, Kuiper has most trouble with curveballs. He's a smart runner, but he has been forced to be conservative on the bases because of his bad knee.

The knee injury has also cut down Kuiper's range, but he has great hands and an accurate arm. He's particularly adept at going to his left for a ball, spinning and throwing to second base for a fielder's choice or double play. He's smart and knows where to play the hitters.

OVERALL:

Coleman: "Kuiper is a good on-base pinch-hitter and spot player at second base. He's a contact hitter with no power. His baserunning and fielding skills have suffered since his knee injury."

McCarver: "He hasn't much strength and perhaps could build that up with a good weight program."

Kiner: "Although he has hit but one home run in more than 3,000 at-bats, he's a fine fielder and a singles hitter who seldom strikes out."

GUY SULARZ
INF, No. 21
RR, 5'11", 165 lbs.
ML Svc: 1 year plus
Born: 11-7-55 in Minneapolis, MN

HITTING, BASERUNNING, FIELDING:

Guy Sularz doesn't figure to use his bat to hold onto a big league job. He usually hits "mistakes" when he does hit. He's a high ball hitter who should be pitched inside. He can be jammed, and in any case he should be pitched down if you pitch him away. A spray hitter without much punch. Pitchers with a decent assortment of pitches have a big advantage over him.

Baserunning is one of Sularz's strong points. He has a history of stealing bases in the minor leagues, including 124 thefts at Phoenix in 1981 when he was, of course, playing regularly. Has good speed and is an aggressive baserunner, and the Giants have used him often as a pinch-runner.

Sularz has played all the infield positions and has acquitted himself well. Best position probably is third base, and his worst probably is shortstop, although the problems he has had at short are due as much to inexperience there as to anything else. He has good, soft hands and quick reflexes.

OVERALL:

McCarver: "Sularz hasn't really been given much of a chance. He seems to be most adept at pinch-running and playing late-inning defense, with an occasional role as a pinch-hitter. But the fact that Guy spent 4 years in Triple A ball and is 27 appears to categorize him as a utility player. Baseball is unfair sometimes with its 'labeling' policies."

MAX VENABLE
OF, No. 49
LR, 5'10", 185 lbs.
ML Svc: 2 years
Born: 6-6-57 in
Phoenix, AZ

HITTING, BASERUNNING, FIELDING:

Max Venable is a line drive pull hitter. He is deadly against pitches down and in. He has good speed and makes contact, and stays with breaking pitches pretty well. Likes to hit with men on base--one season in the minors he drove in 101 runs while batting leadoff.

He undoubtedly would have walked and bunted his way on base more often had he not been in situations where he had to (or felt he had to) swing the bat most of the time.

Venable's speed on the bases is one of his chief assets. He was successful on 9 out of 12 stolen base attempts in 1982, is a good athlete and has strong legs. He has become more aggressive on the basepaths under Frank Robinson's managing.

Often used as a late-inning defensive replacement, Venable has excellent range and a strong, accurate throwing arm. He is capable of the spectacular play, and his speed allows him to make up for any errors in judgment. If he were able to play every day, he might become one of the league's better defensive outfielders.

OVERALL:

Kiner: "Runs well, not much power, average bat, good defense. Max needs to play, which is why he has been shuttled between Triple A and the major leagues."

McCarver: "The Giants appear to have picked up a bargain when they drafted Venable from the Dodger organization in 1978. He has good speed, and lefthanded hitters hit better in Candlestick Park because the wind blows out toward right field."

PLAYER INDEX

A

Aguayo, Luis	NL, Phi
Aikens, Willie	AL, KC
Alexander, Doyle	AL, NY
Allen, Neil	NL, NY
Allenson, Gary	AL, Bost
Almon, Bill	AL, Chi
Altamirano, Porfi	NL, Phi
Andersen, Larry	AL, Sea
Anderson, Bud	AL, Cleve
Andujar, Joaquin	NL, St.L
Aponte, Luis	AL, Bost
Armas, Tony	AL, Bost
Armstrong, Mike	AL, KC
Ashby, Alan	NL, Hou
Augustine, Jerry	AL, Milw
Ayala, Benny	AL, Balt

B

Bailor, Bob	NL, NY
Baines, Harold	AL, Chi
Bair, Doug	NL, St.L
Baker, Dusty	NL, LA
Balboni, Steve	AL, NY
Bando, Chris	AL, Cleve
Bannister, Alan	AL, Cleve
Bannister, Floyd	AL, Chi
Barfield, Jesse	AL, Tor
Barker, Len	AL, Cleve
Barnes, Richard	AL, Chi
Barojas, Salome	AL, Chi
Barr, Jim	NL, SF
Barranca, German	NL, Cinn
Baumgarten,Ross	NL, Pitt
Baylor, Don	AL, NY
Beard, Dave	AL, Oak
Beattie, Jim	AL, Sea
Bedrosian, Steve	NL, Atl
Belanger, Mark	NL, LA
Bell, Buddy	AL, Tex
Bench, John	NL, Cinn
Benedict, Bruce	NL, Atl
Beniquez, Juan	AL, Cal
Berenyi, Bruce	NL, Cinn
Bergman, Dave	NL, SF
Bernard, Dwight	AL, Milw
Bernazard, Tony	AL, Chi
Berra, Dale	NL, Pitt
Bevacqua, Kurt	NL, SD
Bibby, Jim	NL, Pitt
Biitner, Larry	AL, Tex
Bird, Doug	AL, Bost
Black, Bud	AL, KC
Blackwell, Tim	NL, Mont
Blue, Vida	AL, KC
Blyleven, Bert	AL, Cleve
Bochy, Bruce	NL, NY
Boitano, Dan	AL, Tex
Boggs, Tom	NL, Atl
Boggs, Wade	AL, Bost
Bonilla, Juan	NL, SD
Bonnell, Barry	AL, Tor
Bonner, Bob	AL, Balt
Boone, Bob	AL, Cal
Boone, Dan	NL, Hou
Boris, Paul	AL, Minn
Bowa, Larry	NL, Chi
Braun, Steve	NL, St.L
Breining, Fred	NL, SF
Brenly, Bob	NL, SF
Brennan, Tom	AL, Cleve
Brett, George	AL, KC
Brookens, Tom	AL, Det
Brooks, Hubie	NL, NY
Brouhard, Mark	AL, Milw
Brown, Bobby	AL, Sea
Brunansky, Tom	AL, Minn
Buckner, Bill	NL, Chi
Bulling, Terry	AL, Sea
Bumbry, Al	AL, Balt
Burgmeier, Tom	AL, Oak
Burleson, Rick	AL, Cal
Burns, Britt	AL, Chi
Burris, Ray	NL, Mont
Burroughs, Jeff	AL, Oak
Butera, Sal	AL, Minn
Butler, Brett	NL, Atl
Bystrom, Marty	NL, Phi

C

Cabell, Enos	AL, Det
Caldwell, Mike	AL, Milw
Camp, Rick	NL, Atl
Campbell, Bill	NL, Chi
Candelaria, John	NL, Pitt
Carew, Rod	AL, Cal
Carlton, Steve	NL, Phi
Carter, Gary	NL, Mont
Castillo, Bobby	AL, Minn
Castillo, Carmello	AL, Cleve
Castillo, Manny	AL, Sea
Castino, John	AL, Minn
Castro, Bill	AL, KC
Caudill, Bill	AL, Sea
Cedeno, Cesar	NL, Cinn
Cerone, Rick	AL, NY
Cey, Ron	NL, LA
Chambliss, Chris	NL, Atl
Chiffer, Floyd	NL, SD
Christenson, Larry	NL, Phi
Clancy, Jim	AL, Tor
Clark, Bobby	AL, Cal
Clark, Bryan	AL, Sea
Clark, Jack	NL, SF
Clear, Mark	AL, Bost
Collins, Dave	AL, Tor
Comer, Steve	AL, Tex
Concepcion, Dave	NL, Cinn
Concepcion, Onix	AL, KC
Cooper, Cecil	AL, Milw
Corbett, Doug	AL, Cal
Cowens, Al	AL, Sea

Craig, Rod AL, Cleve
Cromartie, Warren NL, Mont
Crowley, Terry AL, Balt
Cruz, Jose NL, Hou
Cruz, Julio AL, Sea
Cruz, Todd AL, Sea
Curtis, John AL, Cal

D

Darwin, Danny AL, Tex
Dauer, Rich AL, Balt
Davis, Chili NL, SF
Davis, Dick NL, Pitt
Davis, Jody NL, Chi
Davis, Ron AL, Minn
Davis, Storm AL, Balt
Dawson, Andre NL, Mont
Dayley, Ken NL, Atl
DeCinces, Doug AL, Cal
DeJesus, Ivan NL, Phi
DeLeon, Luis NL, SD
Dempsey, Rick AL, Balt
Denny, John NL, Phi
Dent, Bucky AL, Tex
Dernier, Bob NL, Phi
Diaz, Bo NL, Phi
Diaz, Carlos NL, NY
Dilone, Miguel AL, Cleve
Dotson, Rich AL, Chi
Downing, Brian AL, Cal
Dravecky, Dave NL, SD
Driessen, Dan NL, Cinn
Durham, Leon NL, Chi
Dwyer, Jim AL, Balt
Dybzinski, Jerry AL, Cleve

E

Easler, Mike NL, Pitt
Easterly, Jamie AL, Milw
Eckersley, Dennis AL, Bost
Edler, Dave AL, Sea
Edwards, Dave NL, SD
Edwards, Marshall AL, Milw
Eichelberger, Juan AL, Cleve
Engle, Dave AL, Minn
Erickson, Roger AL, NY
Evans, Darrell NL, SF
Evans, Dwight AL, Bost

F

Faedo, Lenny AL, Minn
Fahey, Bill AL, Det
Falcone, Pete NL, Atl
Farmer, Ed NL, Phi
Felton, Terry AL, Minn
Fergusen, Joe AL, Cal
Fingers, Rollie AL, Milw
Fischlin, Mike AL, Cleve
Fisk, Carlton AL, Chi
Flanagan, Mike AL, Balt
Flannery, Tim NL, SD
Flynn, Doug NL, Mont
Foley, Marv AL, Chi
Foli, Tim AL, Cal
Ford, Dan AL, Balt
Forsch, Bob NL, St.L
Forsch, Ken AL, Cal
Forster, Terry NL, Atl
Foster, George NL, NY
Francona, Terry NL, Mont
Frazier, George AL, NY
Fryman, Woodie NL, Mont

G

Gaetti, Gary AL, Minn
Gale, Rich NL, Cinn
Gamble, Oscar AL, NY
Gantner, Jim AL, Milw
Garber, Gene NL, Atl
Garcia, Damaso AL, Tor
Garcia, Kiko NL, Hou
Gardenhire, Ron NL, NY
Garner, Phil NL, Hou
Garvey, Steve NL, SD
Garvin, Jerry AL, Tor
Gedman, Rich AL, Bost
Geronimo, Cesar AL, KC
Gibson, Kirk AL, Det
Giles, Brian NL, NY
Glynn, Ed AL, Cleve
Goltz, Doug AL, Cal
Gonzalez, Julio NL, St.L
Gossage, Rich AL, NY
Gott, Jim AL, Tor
Gray, Gary AL, Sea
Green, David NL, St.L
Grich, Bobby AL, Cal
Griffen, Alfredo AL, Tor
Griffey, Ken AL, NY
Grimsley, Ross AL, Balt
Gross, Greg NL, Phi
Gross, Wayne AL, Oak
Grubb, John AL, Tex
Guerrero, Pedro NL, LA
Guidry, Ron AL, NY
Gullickson, Bill NL, Mont
Gura, Larry AL, KC
Gwynn, Tony NL, SD

H

Haas, Moose AL, Milw
Hairston, Jerry AL, Chi
Hammaker, Atlee NL, SF
Hanna, Preston AL, Oak
Hargrove, Mike AL, Cleve
Harper, Terry NL, Atl
Harrah, Toby AL, Cleve
Harris, Greg NL, Cinn

Hassey, Ron	AL, Cleve
Hassler, Andy	AL, Cal
Hatcher, Mickey	AL, Minn
Havens, Brad	AL, Minn
Hayes, Ben	NL, Cinn
Hayes, Von	NL, Phi
Heath, Mike	AL, Oak
Hebner, Richie	NL, Pitt
Heep, Danny	NL, NY
Henderson, Dave	AL, Sea
Henderson, Rickey	AL, Oak
Henderson, Steve	AL, Sea
Hendrick, George	NL, St.L
Hernandez, Keith	NL, St.L
Hernandez, Willie	NL, Chi
Herndon, Larry	AL, Det
Herr, Tom	NL, St.L
Hickey, Kevin	AL, Chi
Hill, Marc	AL, Chi
Hodges, Ron	NL, NY
Hoffman, Glenn	AL, Bost
Holland, Al	NL, Phila
Holman, Scot	NL, NY
Honeycutt, Rick	AL, Tex
Hood, Don	AL, KC
Hooton, Burt	NL, LA
Horner, Bob	NL, Atl
Hostetler, Dave	AL, Tex
Hough, Charlie	AL, Tex
Householder, Paul	NL, Cinn
Howe, Art	NL, Hou
Howe, Steve	NL, LA
Howell, Roy	AL, Milw
Hoyt, LaMarr	AL, Chi
Hrbek, Kent	AL, Minn
Hubbard, Glen	NL, Atl
Hume, Tom	NL, Cinn
Hurst, Bruce	AL, Bost

I

Iorg, Dane	NL, St.L
Iorg, Garth	AL, Tor
Ivie, Mike	AL, Det

J

Jackson, Darrell	AL, Minn
Jackson, Reggie	AL, Cal
Jackson, Ron	AL, Cal
Jackson, Roy Lee	AL, Tor
Jenkins, Fergie	NL, Chi
John, Tommy	AL, Cal
Johnson, Cliff	AL, Tor
Johnson, LaMar	AL, Tex
Johnson, Randy	AL, Minn
Johnson, Wallace	NL, Mont
Johnstone, Jay	NL, Chi
Jones, Lynn	AL, Det
Jones, Randy	NL, NY
Jones, Ruppert	NL, SD
Jorgensen, Mike	NL, NY

K

Kaat, Jim	NL, St.L
Keener, Jeff	NL, St.L
Kelleher, Mick	AL, Cal
Kemp, Steve	AL, NY
Kennedy, Junior	NL, Chi
Kennedy, Terry	NL, SD
Keough, Matt	AL, Oak
Kern, Jim	AL, Chi
Kingman, Brian	AL, Oak
Kingman, Dave	NL, NY
Kison, Bruce	AL, Cal
Klutts, Mickey	AL, Oak
Knepper, Bob	NL, Hou
Knicely, Alan	NL, Hou
Knight, Ray	NL, Hou
Koosman, Jerry	AL, Chi
Kravec, Ken	NL, Chi
Krenchicki, Wayne	NL, Cinn
Krukow, Mike	NL, SF
Kuiper, Duane	NL, SF

L

LaCorte, Frank	NL, Hou
LaCoss, Mike	NL, Hou
Lacy, Lee	NL, Pitt
Lahti, Jeff	NL, St.L
Lamp, Dennis	AL, Chi
Landestoy, Rafael	NL, Cinn
Landreaux, Ken	NL, LA
Landrum, Tito	NL, St.L
Langford, Rick	AL, Oak
Lansford, Carney	AL, Oak
LaPoint, Dave	NL, St.L
LaRoche, Dave	AL, NY
Laskey, Bill	NL, SF
Laudner, Tim	AL, Minn
Lavelle, Gary	NL, SF
Law, Rudy	AL, Chi
Law, Vance	AL, Chi
Lawless, Tom	NL, Cinn
Lea, Charlie	NL, Mont
Leach, Rick	AL, Det
Leach, Terry	NL, NY
Leal, Luis	AL, Tor
Lefebvre, Joe	NL, SD
LeFlore, Ron	AL, Chi
Leibrandt, Charlie	NL, Cinn
LeMaster, Johnnie	NL, SF
Lemon, Chet	AL, Det
Leonard, Dennis	AL, KC
Leonard, Jeff	NL, SF
Lerch, Randy	NL, Mont
Lesley, Brad	NL, Cinn
Lezcano, Sixto	NL, SD
Linares, Rufino	NL, Atl
Little, Jeff	AL, Minn
Lollar, Tim	NL, SD
Lopes, Davey	AL, Oak
Lowenstein, John	AL, Balt

Lucas, Gary NL, SD
Luzinski, Greg AL, Chi
Lyle, Sparky AL, Chi
Lynch, Ed NL, NY
Lynn, Fred AL, Cal

M

Maddox, Garry NL, Phi
Madlock, Bill NL, Pitt
Mahler, Mickey AL, Cal
Mahler, Rick NL, Atl
Manning, Rick AL, Cleve
Marshall, Mike NL, LA
Martin, Jerry AL, KC
Martin, Renie NL, SF
Martinez, Buck AL, Tor
Martinez, Dennis AL, Balt
Martinez, Tippy AL, Balt
Martz, Randy NL, Chi
Matlack, Jon AL, Tex
Matthews, Gary NL, Phi
May, Milt NL, SF
May, Rudy AL, NY
Mayberry, John AL, NY
Mazzilli, Lee NL, Pitt
McBride, Bake AL, Cleve
McCatty, Steve AL, Oak
McClure, Bob AL, Milw
McGee, Willie NL, St.L
McGraw, Tug NL, Phi
McGregor, Scott AL, Balt
McKay, Dave AL, Oak
McLaughlin, Joey AL, Tor
McRae, Hal AL, KC
McWilliams, Larry NL, Pitt
Meyer, Dan AL, Oak
Milbourne, Larry NL, Phi
Miller, Rick AL, Bost
Mills, Brad NL, Mont
Milner, Eddie NL, Cinn
Minton, Greg NL, SF
Mirabella, Paul AL, Tex
Mitchell, Bobby AL, Minn
Molinaro, Bobby NL, Phi
Molitor, Paul AL, Milw
Money, Don AL, Milw
Monday, Rick NL, LA
Monge, Sid NL, Phi
Montefusco, John NL, SD
Moore, Charlie AL, Milw
Moore, Mike AL, Sea
Morales, Jerry NL, Chi
Morales, Jose NL, LA
Moreland, Keith NL, Chi
Moreno, Omar NL, Hou
Morgan, Joe NL, Phi
Morgan, Mike AL, Tor
Morris, Jack AL, Det
Morrison, Jim NL, Pitt
Moseby, Lloyd AL, Tor
Moskau, Paul NL, Pitt
Mullnicks, Rance AL, Tor
Mumphrey, Jerry AL, NY
Mura, Steve NL, St.L
Murcer, Bobby AL, NY
Murphy, Dale NL, Atl
Murphy, Dwayne AL, Oak
Murray, Dale AL, NY
Murray, Eddie AL, Balt

N

Nahorodny, Bill AL, Cleve
Nelson, Gene AL, Sea
Nettles, Graig AL, NY
Newman, Jeff AL, Bost
Nichols, Reid AL, Bost
Nicosia, Steve NL, Pitt
Niedenfuer, Tom NL, LA
Niemann, Randy NL, Pitt
Niekro, Joe NL, Hou
Niekro, Phil NL, Atl
Nolan, Joe AL, Balt
Noles, Dickie NL, Chi
Nordhagen, Wayne NL, Chi
Norman, Dan NL, Mont
Norris, Mike AL, Oak

O

Oberkfell, Ken NL, St.L
O'Connor, Jack AL, Minn
Oester, Ron NL, Cinn
Oglivie, Ben AL, Milw
Ojeda, Bob AL, Bost
Oliver, Al NL, Mont
O'Malley, Tom NL, SF
Orosco, Jesse NL, NY
Orta, Jorge NL, NY
Otis, Amos AL, KC
Owchinko, Bob AL, Oak
Ownbey, Rick NL, NY

P

Pacella, John AL, Tex
Paciorek, Tom AL, Chi
Page, Mitchell AL, Oak
Palmer, David NL, Mont
Palmer, Jim AL, Balt
Parker, Dave NL, Pitt
Parrish, Lance AL, Det
Parrish, Larry AL, Tex
Pashnik, Larry AL, Det
Pastore, Frank NL, Cinn
Pena, Tony NL, Pitt
Perconte, Jack AL, Cleve
Perez, Pascual NL, Atl
Perkins, Broderick AL, Cleve
Perry, Gaylord AL, Sea
Petry, Dan AL, Det

Picciolo, Rob AL, Milw
Piniella, Lou AL, NY
Pittman, Joe NL, SD
Pocoroba, Biff NL, Atl
Porter, Darrell NL, St.L
Powell, Hosken AL, Tor
Price, Joe NL, Cinn
Proly, Mike NL, Chi
Pryor, Greg AL, KC
Puhl, Terry NL, Hou
Pujols, Luis NL, Hou
Puleo, Charlie NL, Cinn

Q

Quirk, Jamie AL, KC
Quisenberry, Dan AL, KC

R

Raines, Tim NL, Mont
Rainey, Chuck NL, Chi
Rajsich, Gary NL, NY
Ramirez, Rafael NL, Atl
Ramsey, Mike NL, St.L
Randolph, Willie AL, NY
Rawley, Shane AL, NY
Ray, Johnnie NL, Pitt
Rayford, Floyd AL, Balt
Reardon, Jeff NL, Mont
Redfern, Pete AL, Minn
Reed, Ron NL, Phi
Remy, Jerry AL, Bost
Renko, Steve AL, Cal
Reuss, Jerry NL, LA
Revering, Dave AL, Sea
Reynolds, Craig NL, Hou
Rhoden, Rick NL, Pitt
Rice, Jim AL, Bost
Richards, Gene NL, SD
Richardt, Mike AL, Tex
Righetti, Dave AL, NY
Ripken, Cal, Jr. AL, Balt
Ripley, Allen NL, Chi
Rivers, Mickey AL, Tex
Roberge, Bert NL, Hou
Roberts, Dave NL, Phi
Roberts, Leon AL, Tor
Robertson, Andre AL, NY
Robinson, Bill NL, Phi
Robinson, Don NL, Pitt
Rodriguez, Aurelio AL, Chi
Roenicke, Gary AL, Balt
Roenicke, Ron NL, LA
Rogers, Steve NL, Mont
Romero, Ed AL, Milw
Romo, Enrique NL, Pitt
Romo, Vincente NL, LA
Rose, Pete NL, Phi
Royster, Jerry NL, Atl
Rozema, Dave AL, Det
Rucker, Dave AL, Det
Rudi, Joe AL, Oak
Ruhle, Vern NL, Hou
Russell, Bill NL, LA
Ruthven, Dick NL, Phi
Ryan, Nolan NL, Hou

S

Sakata, Lenn AL, Balt
Salazar, Luis NL, SD
Sambito, Joe NL, Hou
Sample, Billy AL, Tex
Sanchez, Luis AL, Cal
Sandberg, Ryne NL, Chi
Sanderson, Scott NL, Mont
Sarmiento, Manny NL, Pitt
Saucier, Kevin AL, Det
Sax, Steve NL, LA
Schatzeder, Dan NL, Mont
Schmidt, Dave AL, Tex
Schmidt, Mike NL, Phi
Scioscia, Mike NL, LA
Scott, Mike NL, Hou
Scott, Tony NL, Hou
Scurry, Rod NL, Pitt
Seaver, Tom NL, NY
Serna, Paul AL, Sea
Sexton, Jimmy AL, Oak
Shirley, Bob AL, NY
Show, Eric NL, SD
Simmons, Ted AL, Milw
Simpson, Joe AL, Sea
Sinatro, Matt NL, Atl
Singleton, Ken AL, Balt
Slaton, Jim AL, Milw
Smalley, Roy AL, NY
Smith, Bryn NL, Mont
Smith, Dave NL, Hou
Smith, Jim NL, Pitt
Smith, Ken NL, Atl
Smith, Lee NL, Chi
Smith, Lonnie NL, St.L
Smith, Ozzie NL, St.L
Sorensen, Lary AL, Cleve
Sosa, Elias NL, SD
Soto, Mario NL, Cinn
Speier, Chris NL, Mont
Spillner, Dan AL, Cleve
Splittorff, Paul AL, KC
Squires, Mike AL, Chi
Stanley, Bob AL, Bost
Stanley, Fred AL, Oak
Stanton, Mike AL, Sea
Stapleton, Dave AL, Bost
Staub, Rusty NL, NY
Stearns, John NL, NY
Stein, Bill AL, Tex
Stewart, Dave NL, LA
Stewart, Sammy AL, Balt
Stieb, Dave AL, Tor

Stoddard, Tim AL, Balt
Strawberry, Daryl NL, NY
Stroughter, Steve AL, Sea
Stuper, John NL, St.L
Sularz, Guy NL, SF
Summers, Champ NL, SF
Sundberg, Jim AL, Tex
Sutcliffe, Rick AL, Cleve
Sutter, Bruce NL, St.L
Sutton, Don AL, Milw
Swan, Craig NL, NY
Sweet, Rick AL, Sea
Swisher, Steve NL, SD

T

Tananna, Frank AL, Tex
Tekulve, Kent NL, Pitt
Templeton, Garry NL, SD
Tenace, Gene NL, Pitt
Thomas, Derrell NL, LA
Thomas, Gorman AL, Milw
Thompson, Jason NL, Pitt
Thompson, Scot NL, Chi
Thon, Dickie NL, Hou
Thornton, Andre AL, Cleve
Tidrow, Dick NL, Chi
Tobik, Dave AL, Det
Torrez, Mike NL, NY
Trammell, Alan AL, Det
Trevino, Alex NL, Cinn
Trillo, Manny AL, Cleve
Trout, Steve AL, Chi
Tudor, John AL, Bost
Turner, Jerry AL, Det

U

Ujdur, Jerry AL, Det
Underwood, Pat AL, Det
Underwood, Tom AL, Oak
Upshaw, Willie AL, Tor

V

Vail, Mike NL, SF
Valdez, Julio AL, Bost
Valentine, Ellis NL, NY
Valenzuela, Fernando NL, LA
VandeBerg, Ed AL, Sea
Van Gorder, Dave NL, Cinn
Vega, Jesus AL, Minn
Venable, Max NL, SF
Veryzer, Tom NL, NY
Viola, Frank AL, Minn
Virgil, Ozzie NL, Phi
Vuckovich, Pete AL, Milw
Vukovich, George AL, Cleve

W

Waits, Rick AL, Cleve
Walk, Bob NL, Atl
Walker, Duane NL, Cinn
Wallach, Tim NL, Mont
Walling, Denny NL, Hou
Ward, Gary AL, Minn
Washington, Claudell NL, Atl
Washington, Ron AL, Minn
Washington, U.L. AL, KC
Wathan, John AL, KC
Watson, Bob NL, Atl
Welch, Bob NL, LA
Welsh, Chris NL, SD
Werner, Don AL, Tex
Werth, Dennis AL, KC
Whisenton, Larry NL, Atl
Whitaker, Lou AL, Det
White, Frank AL, KC
White, Jerry NL, Mont
Whitson, Ed NL, SD
Whitt, Ernie AL, Tor
Wiggins, Alan NL, SD
Wilcox, Milt AL, Det
Wilfong, Rob AL, Cal
Williams, Al AL, Minn
Wills, Bump NL, Chi
Wilson, Glenn AL, Det
Wilson, Mookie NL, NY
Wilson, Willie AL, KC
Winfield, Dave AL, NY
Witt, Mike AL, Cal
Wockenfuss, John AL, Det
Wohlford, Jim NL, SF
Woods, Al AL, Oak
Woods, Gary NL, Chi
Wright, George AL, Tex
Wynegar, Butch AL, NY

Y

Yaeger, Steve NL, LA
Yastrzemski, Carl AL, Bost
Yost, Ned AL, Milw
Youngblood, Joel NL, Mont
Yount, Robin AL, Milw

Z

Zachry, Pat NL, LA
Zahn, Geoff AL, Cal
Zisk, Richie AL, Sea